HARRY C. TREXLER LIBRARY

Gift of

Dr. and Mrs. Bernard
Frank

American Jewish Year Book

American Jewish Year Book 1991

VOLUME 91

Prepared by THE AMERICAN JEWISH COMMITTEE

Editor
DAVID SINGER
Executive Editor
RUTH R. SELDIN

THE AMERICAN JEWISH COMMITTEE
NEW YORK
THE JEWISH PUBLICATION SOCIETY
PHILADELPHIA

COPYRIGHT © 1991 BY THE AMERICAN JEWISH COMMITTEE
AND THE JEWISH PUBLICATION SOCIETY
All rights reserved. No part of this book may be reproduced in any form without permission in writing from the publisher, except by a reviewer who may quote brief passages in a review to be printed in a magazine or newspaper.

ISBN 0-8276-0402-5

Library of Congress Catalogue Number: 99-4040

PRINTED IN THE UNITED STATES OF AMERICA
BY THE HADDON CRAFTSMEN, INC., SCRANTON, PA.

Preface

This year's volume highlights recent trends in American Jewish intellectual and cultural life. In "Jewish Theology in North America: Notes on Two Decades," Arnold Eisen explicates and appraises the ideas of a number of key contemporary religious thinkers. "American Jewish Fiction Turns Inward, 1960–1990," by Sylvia Barack Fishman, explores the phenomenon of a significant group of American Jewish writers creating fiction that is explicitly Jewish—some of it "unabashedly religious in its sensibility"—and that appeals to a wider audience than anyone might have predicted. Finally, in "American Jewish Museums: Trends and Issues," Ruth R. Seldin describes the astonishing growth and spread of Jewish museums in the United States, analyzing the reasons for their flourishing as well as the problems and issues confronting them.

Regular articles on Jewish life in the United States are "Intergroup Relations," by Earl Raab and Douglas Kahn; "Jewish Communal Affairs," by Lawrence Grossman; and "The United States, Israel, and the Middle East," by Kenneth Jacobson.

Events in Israel are covered extensively by Ralph Mandel. The Israel section also includes a separate article on "Israeli Culture," by Micha Z. Odenheimer, a survey of recent trends in literature and the arts. This year's updates on Jewish life around the world include reports on Austria and France as well as other countries of Europe, the USSR, and Canada.

Updated estimates are provided for Jewish population in the United States (by Barry Kosmin and Jeffrey Scheckner, of the North American Jewish Data Bank) and in the world (by U.O. Schmelz and Sergio DellaPergola, of the Hebrew University of Jerusalem's Institute of Contemporary Jewry). Both articles discuss preliminary results of the 1990 U.S. National Jewish Population Survey, which will be reported on more fully in next year's volume.

Carefully compiled directories of national Jewish organizations, periodicals, and federations and welfare funds, as well as religious calendars and obituaries, round out the 1991 AMERICAN JEWISH YEAR BOOK. (Longtime users of the directory of national organizations will find a few changes in that section, notably, separate categories for "Schools, Institutions" and "Religious, Educational Organizations.")

We gratefully acknowledge the assistance of Terry Smith, Elliot Linzer, and many colleagues at the American Jewish Committee, especially Michele Anish and Cyma M. Horowitz of the Blaustein Library.

THE EDITORS

Contributors

HENRIETTE BOAS: Dutch correspondent, Jewish Telegraphic Agency and Israeli newspapers; Amsterdam, Holland.

Y. MICHAL BODEMANN: associate professor, sociology, University of Toronto, Canada; visiting professor, Humboldt University, Berlin, Germany.

SERGIO DELLAPERGOLA: chairman, Institute of Contemporary Jewry, and director, Division of Jewish Demography and Statistics, Hebrew University of Jerusalem, Israel.

SIMONETTA DELLA SETA: researcher in modern Jewish history, Hebrew University of Jerusalem, Israel; Israel correspondent, Italian daily *Il Giornale*.

ARNOLD EISEN: associate professor, religious studies, and Aaron-Roland Fellow, Stanford University.

SYLVIA BARACK FISHMAN: senior research associate, Cohen Center for Modern Jewish Studies, Brandeis University; teaching associate, Brown University program in Judaic studies.

MURRAY FRIEDMAN: Middle Atlantic States director, American Jewish Committee; director, Center for American Jewish History, Temple University.

LLOYD P. GARTNER: Spiegel Family Foundation Professor of European Jewish History, Tel Aviv University, Israel.

ZVI GITELMAN: professor, political science, and Preston Tisch Professor of Judaic Studies, University of Michigan.

MURRAY GORDON: writer and consultant on European affairs; author of a forthcoming book on the Jews of Eastern Europe.

LAWRENCE GROSSMAN: director of publications, American Jewish Committee.

NELLY HANSSON: researcher, political science and sociology; adviser to the president, Representative Council of French Jewish Institutions (CRIF), Paris, France.

KENNETH JACOBSON: director, international affairs, Anti-Defamation League of B'nai B'rith.

DOUGLAS KAHN: executive director, Jewish Community Relations Council, San Francisco.

LIONEL E. KOCHAN: visiting lecturer, Oxford Center for Post-Graduate Hebrew Studies, England.

MIRIAM L. KOCHAN: writer, translator, Oxford, England.

BARRY A. KOSMIN: director, North American Jewish Data Bank, City University of New York Graduate Center.

RALPH MANDEL: journalist, translator, Jerusalem, Israel.

MICHA Z. ODENHEIMER: journalist, Jerusalem, Israel.

ROBIN OSTOW: Canada Research Fellow in sociology, McMaster University, Hamilton, Ontario, Canada.

EARL RAAB: director, Nathan Perlmutter Institute for Jewish Advocacy, Brandeis University.

JEFFREY SCHECKNER: administrator, North American Jewish Data Bank, City University of New York Graduate Center.

U.O. SCHMELZ: professor emeritus, Jewish demography, Institute of Contemporary Jewry, Hebrew University of Jerusalem, Israel.

RUTH R. SELDIN: executive editor, AMERICAN JEWISH YEAR BOOK.

MASSIMO TORREFRANCA: researcher in musicology, Hebrew University of Jerusalem, Israel; translator.

HAROLD M. WALLER: associate professor, political science, McGill University, Montreal, Canada; director, Canadian Center for Jewish Community Studies.

Contents

PREFACE v
CONTRIBUTORS vii

SPECIAL ARTICLES

Jewish Theology in North America: Notes on Two Decades	*Arnold Eisen*	3
American Jewish Fiction Turns Inward, 1960–1990	*Sylvia Barack Fishman*	35
American Jewish Museums: Trends and Issues	*Ruth R. Seldin*	71

UNITED STATES

CIVIC AND POLITICAL

Intergroup Relations	*Earl Raab and Douglas Kahn*	121
The United States, Israel, and the Middle East	*Kenneth Jacobson*	140

COMMUNAL

Jewish Communal Affairs	*Lawrence Grossman*	177

DEMOGRAPHIC

Jewish Population in the United
States, 1990 — Barry A. Kosmin
and Jeffrey Scheckner 204

OTHER COUNTRIES

CANADA — Harold M. Waller 227

WESTERN EUROPE
Great Britain — Lionel and Miriam Kochan 245
France — Nelly Hansson 260
The Netherlands — Henriette Boas 277
Italy — Simonetta Della Seta and Massimo Torrefranca 289

CENTRAL EUROPE
Federal Republic of Germany — Y. Michal Bodemann 302
German Democratic Republic — Robin Ostow 316
Austria — Murray Gordon 324

EASTERN EUROPE
Soviet Union — Zvi Gitelman 337
Eastern European Countries — Zvi Gitelman 347

ISRAEL
Israel — Ralph Mandel 353
Israeli Culture — Micha Z. Odenheimer 424

WORLD JEWISH POPULATION, 1989 — U.O. Schmelz and Sergio DellaPergola 441

DIRECTORIES, LISTS, AND OBITUARIES

NATIONAL JEWISH ORGANIZATIONS
United States 469
Canada 518

JEWISH FEDERATIONS, WELFARE FUNDS,
COMMUNITY COUNCILS
United States 521
Canada 532

JEWISH PERIODICALS
United States 534
Canada 543

OBITUARIES
Salo W. Baron (1895–1989)   *Lloyd P. Gartner*   544
John Slawson (1896–1989)   *Murray Friedman*   555

OBITUARIES: UNITED STATES 559

SUMMARY JEWISH CALENDAR,
5751–5755 (Sept. 1990–Aug. 1995) 572

CONDENSED MONTHLY CALENDAR,
5750–5753 (1990–1993) 574

SELECTED ARTICLES OF INTEREST IN RECENT VOLUMES
OF THE AMERICAN JEWISH YEAR BOOK 606

INDEX 609

Special Articles

Jewish Theology in North America: Notes on Two Decades

by ARNOLD EISEN

IF THERE IS ONE POINT OF AGREEMENT among students and practitioners of Jewish theology in North America, it is that not much creative work has been forthcoming over the last two decades. Eugene Borowitz, reflecting on "the Form of a Jewish Theology" at the start of the period under review here, wondered whether systematic Jewish thought could even be attempted in our time. "Holism" was essential, he argued, but it was perhaps unavailable.[1] Neil Gillman, for that very reason, titled his book, issued in 1990, *Sacred Fragments: Recovering Theology for the Modern Jew*. Fragments were all we had at this point in the history of Judaism, he maintained. As a result, theology could not simply be written, it had to be "recovered."[2] This sentiment is widespread. Few would disagree with Emil Fackenheim's pointed lament in 1982 that "in the realm of purely theoretical Jewish thought, and despite claims in this or that quarter to having 'gone beyond' Buber and Rosenzweig, the main characteristic of more recent Jewish thought is, by comparison, its low level. . . . The consequence is that the pioneering work then accomplished still waits for adequate successors."[3]

Our first task in this overview of the Jewish theology produced in America since Lou Silberman's *Year Book* survey in 1969,[4] then, will be to join practitioners of the craft in wondering why their number and productivity have remained so limited. To be sure, there has been a prodigious amount of Jewish religious reflection in America. Homilies, topical essays, halakhic opinions, guides for laymen, ideological statements, and prayerbook revisions abound.[5] But the theological forms known to us from past eras in the

---

[1]Eugene Borowitz, "The Problem of the Form of a Jewish Theology," *Hebrew Union College Annual*, vols. 40–41, 1969–70, p. 391.

[2]Neil Gillman, *Sacred Fragments: Recovering Theology for the Modern Jew* (Philadelphia, 1990), pp. xv-xxvii. For a brief review of Gillman's work, and of others which figure in the present essay, see David Ellenson, "The Continued Renewal of North American Jewish Theology: Some Recent Works," *Journal of Reform Judaism*, Winter 1991, pp. 1–16.

[3]Emil Fackenheim, *To Mend the World: Foundations of Future Jewish Thought* (New York, 1982), p. 7.

[4]Lou H. Silberman, "Concerning Jewish Theology: Some Notes on a Decade," AJYB 1969, vol. 70, pp. 37–58.

[5]For accounts of this outpouring in recent years, see Jack Wertheimer, "Recent Trends in

history of Judaism have largely been absent in the United States, particularly in recent decades. Understanding why that is so provides invaluable insight into the theological literature that has been produced—and tells us a great deal about the religious community that has produced it.

Our second task will be an interpretive sketch of the existing literature, focusing on the major figures and trends. Two issues clearly occupy center stage: the attempt to refine the "covenant theology" characteristic of much 20th-century Jewish thought;[6] and the confrontation with the Holocaust that, as Silberman predicted, has received far more attention in the period than any other subject. This review completed, there will be an opportunity to consider the trends emerging in the 1990s and to reflect on what they portend for the decades to come. The outlook is not entirely bleak, but no responsible observer could possibly call it bright.

Theology and Its Practitioners

A word of definition is in order at the outset. As used here, the term "theology" refers to thought (1) of a relatively systematic character that (2) is informed by serious philosophical competence and (3) evinces real grounding in Jewish history and tradition. Most articles published in most Jewish journals by most scholars and rabbis in the past two decades are beyond the purview of this essay because they tend, in the nature of the case, to be occasional pieces, often homiletic, generally topical, and aimed at a fairly wide readership. Theology, by contrast, is an elitist pursuit directed at a limited audience, even if its impact on the mass of believers is far from inconsequential. In America today—by far the most egalitarian society in which Jews have lived—concern with theology is perhaps rarer than ever before.

Several thinkers, seeking to understand why this is the case, have pointed to the Christian connotations of "theology."[7] Most normative Jewish thought, after all, has shunned the question of God's nature, believing it

---

American Judaism," AJYB 1989, vol. 89, pp. 63–162; and Arnold Eisen, "American Judaism: Changing Patterns in Denominational Self-Definition," *Studies in Contemporary Jewry,* vol. 8, 1991 (forthcoming). For more general overviews of American Jewish thought in recent decades, see Arnold Eisen, *The Chosen People in America* (Bloomington, 1983); and Robert G. Goldy, *The Emergence of Jewish Theology in America* (Bloomington, 1990).

[6]See Arnold Eisen, "Covenant," in *Contemporary Jewish Religious Thought,* ed. Arthur A. Cohen and Paul Mendes-Flohr (New York, 1987), pp. 107–112. An accessible account of how the idea of covenant figures in seminal modern thinkers is Eugene Borowitz, *Choices in Modern Jewish Thought: A Partisan Guide* (New York, 1983).

[7]Cf. the definition of theology as "the study of God and the relation between God and the universe." *Webster's New World Dictionary of the American Language,* College Edition (Cleveland, 1958), p. 1511.

inaccessible to human understanding. All but the kabbalists have preferred to examine God's interaction with and intentions for Israel and the world. Modern Jewish thinkers, for somewhat different reasons, have paid relatively little attention to God's role as creator, and only slightly more to the divine activity of redemption.[8] The focus has instead been on revelation—what God wants Jews to do, and how we know what God wants.[9]

There is also a widespread sense that the term "theology" bespeaks a systematic form rarely adopted in Judaism, even when—as with biblical and rabbinic thought—one finds a wide range of issues addressed in more or less coherent fashion. If "theology" means form rather than content, Jews have rarely engaged in the enterprise, preferring other genres such as commentary, legal code, or responsa, or—in the modern period—the essay. Still, the form is amply represented in the history of Judaism, and the presence of systematic presentations of content in every period is striking. Jews have engaged in theology in the past, and indeed they continue to do so. The question is why it has not been more evident on the American Jewish scene in recent decades.

WHY NO THEOLOGY?

One is tempted to ascribe the lacuna to an alleged American proclivity toward praxis rather than theory.[10] American Protestantism, after all, has also not generated the outpouring of theology produced in Germany. But neither has Protestant theology been utterly absent here. From the Puritan divines through Jonathan Edwards to Horace Bushnell to Paul Tillich and the Niebuhrs, America has developed a rich theological library.[11] One gets closer to the mark with the observation that this library has not grown significantly in the past 20 years, anymore than American Judaism has found successors to Abraham Heschel and Joseph Soloveitchik. The suspicion arises that something in the social and intellectual context of America in this half-century, rather than America per se, has militated against the

---

[8] The principal exception to this generalization is Franz Rosenzweig's *The Star of Redemption,* tr. William Hallo (Boston, 1985)—but even Rosenzweig has far more to say about revelation and redemption than creation.

[9] Cf. Gillman, *Sacred Fragments,* p. xx, and Michael Wyschogrod, *The Body of Faith: Judaism as Corporeal Election* (New York, 1983), p. xiii.

[10] The argument is made, for example, by Robert Gordis, long an intellectual leader of the Conservative movement, who writes that "in its pragmatic approach and its distrust of abstract theory, [Conservative Judaism] is characteristically American in spirit." See Robert Gordis, *Conservative Judaism: An American Philosophy* (New York, 1945), p. 11.

[11] For two surveys of these developments, see Sidney Ahlstrom, *A Religious History of the American People* (New Haven, 1972), particularly chs. 18–19, 37–38, 55–56; and William G. McLoughlin and Robert N. Bellah, eds., *Religion in America* (Boston, 1968).

creation of theology. Three possible components of that something come immediately to mind.

First, theology is inherently particularistic.[12] It primarily concerns a single faith community and its unique relationship to God. Theology arises when belief and practice are challenged from outside, the challenge being so serious, and internalized to such a degree, that it cannot be ignored. It proceeds by elaborating upon the distinctiveness of the inside path, and usually involves reaffirmation of the insiders' special claim to truth. American Jews, seeking integration in America denied them elsewhere, have tended to emphasize what could readily be projected outwards. They have sought to be a part rather than apart, and so have downplayed or reinterpreted key theological ideas, such as chosenness, which might have proven offensive to others. In this they have not been alone.[13] In short, pluralism and egalitarianism have exacted their toll in terms of the articulation of difference. One cannot imagine a Rosenzweig writing in America that Judaism is the fire which burns at the core of the Star of Redemption, Christianity its rays; that we stand at the goal, while they are ever on the way.[14] At most one finds a Soloveitchik averring that no individual and no community is in a position to judge the God-relationship of any other. We regard our faith as true; about the others, within certain bounds of acceptability, we cannot judge.[15] More than this probably cannot be said in America. Yet, saying less is generally not productive of theology.

A second factor militating against Jewish theology on these shores has been the lack of Jews qualified to practice the discipline or to appreciate its products. Note the apparent prerequisites for the craft: (1) firm grounding in Jewish sources of various periods—halakhic and aggadic, philosophical and mystical, from the Bible to the present (meaning, increasingly, competence in the secondary literature devoted to the texts and their contexts); (2) serious acquaintance with modern philosophy (Kant, Hegel, and Heidegger seem basic, if we accept as normative the knowledge base assumed by the 20th-century Jewish corpus from Cohen to Fackenheim); and (3) some sense of how Christian thinkers in the modern period have responded to very similar challenges (recall Heschel's use of Barth or Soloveitchik's of Kierkegaard). As we approach century's end, some understanding of social and literary theory has probably also become essential. This combination of talents is indeed a formidable demand.

---

[12]Here I expand upon the analysis in Arnold Eisen, "Theology, Sociology, Ideology," *Modern Judaism*, vol. 2, 1982, pp. 98–102.

[13]See John Murray Cuddihy, *No Offense: Civil Religion and Protestant Taste* (New York, 1978); and Arthur Hertzberg, "America Is Different," in Arthur Hertzberg, Martin E. Marty, and Joseph N. Moody, *The Outbursts That Await Us* (New York, 1963), pp. 121–81; and Arthur Hertzberg, *The Jews in America* (New York, 1989), pp. 350–88.

[14]Rosenzweig, *Star of Redemption*, pp. 298–379.

[15]Joseph Soloveitchik, "Confrontation," *Tradition*, Winter 1964, pp. 18–23.

Even if a given individual possesses it, however, he or she may well lack a fourth apparent prerequisite for the production of theology—a faith community on which to meditate. Theology in Judaism has meant both Halakhah—"life lived," as Jacob Neusner has put it—and Aggadah—life reflected upon.[16] If American Jews have rarely done theology, it is perhaps because they by and large lack both Halakhah and Aggadah in this sense. Outside of Orthodoxy there is no defined faith community within which a distinct life is lived, and which may be reflected upon. Christian thinkers, too, suffer from the absence of such communities, but the problem is if anything more troubling for Jews, precisely because Jewish theology has tended not to inquire into the nature of God but rather to probe the way Jews are meant to behave, collectively, in God's presence. Without a visible community in which covenantal commitments are enacted, the meaning of the covenant becomes more difficult to articulate.

Theologians also suffer from an acute shortage of potential readers. Previous generations of theologians wrote either for each other (a problem today, when the number of active practitioners is so small) or for congregational rabbis (probably still the primary consumers of Jewish theology) or for colleagues at the university (who today are less and less inclined to take religious belief seriously) or for educated lay people (the number of whom has declined precipitously of late). Judaism is a leisure-time activity for most American Jews, and even the most committed religiously are far less concerned with systematic belief or observance than with appropriating selected elements of the tradition in their lives. They are better served by the sort of occasional (or introductory) literature produced in abundance than they would be by systematic work which they could not read and could not easily apply. The seminaries, meanwhile—and most theologians and potential theologians are still employed by them—often focus on denominational needs: new editions of the *siddur*, revised statements of principles, reflection on the altered status of Halakhah, and so on. In this realm American Judaism has been absolutely prolific, never more so than in the past two decades.[17] Explanations of what differentiates the several move-

---

[16]Jacob Neusner, "The Tasks of Theology in Judaism: A Humanistic Program," *Journal of Religion*, vol. 59, no. 1, Jan. 1979, pp. 71–82.

[17]That is not to say, of course, that American Jews have not engaged in religious reflection of very high quality. They have. But this reflection has taken shape within genres—essays, legal responsa, homilies, and historical research—which demand analyses of a different sort. For one such analysis, see Eisen, "American Judaism" (cited in note 5). *Tradition* (published by the organization of modern Orthodox rabbis) often features sophisticated legal responsa and philosophical reflection on the nature and validity of Jewish law, while *Conservative Judaism* and the *Journal of Reform Judaism* tend to favor aggadic essays, debates on topical issues such as feminism or homosexuality, and analyses of Judaism in terms of disciplines such as anthropology and literary criticism. The Conservative movement has also given rise to impressive reflection on the nature (and legitimate revision) of Halakhah. See, for example, Elliot Dorff and Arthur Rosett, *A Living Tree: The Roots and Growth of Jewish Law* (Albany, 1988); Joel

ments are a far cry from theology, particularly when, as is often the case, they bear all the marks of authorship by committee.

The final obstacle in the path of Jewish theology in the United States is the doubly problematic character of contemporary Jewish belief. Van Harvey, writing about American Protestant theology at the same time that Silberman did his survey, gave eloquent expression to the dilemmas of what he called "the alienated theologian." Harvey described a Christian thinker "concerned with the articulation of the faith of the Christian community" but "himself as much a doubter as a believer." The doubt had been evident in Protestant thought throughout the modern period, Harvey argued, but it had emerged with particular force in the 1960s, posing "fundamental questions for the church concerning the future of theology itself."[18] In this respect Jews have perhaps had a certain advantage. The Protestant, losing faith, may well leave the Church. The Jew may nonetheless retain a primordial commitment to the Jewish people. Still, the parallel with Christianity is rather exact. Modern Judaism is beleaguered by the same forces as modern Christianity (and often influenced by the latter in its modes of defense);[19] it is also under siege of late from a new source of doubt, which has come to be known in theological shorthand as "Auschwitz." Religious *ideology*—partial in character, relying more heavily on images than concepts—can perhaps survive the twin doubts posed by modernity and the Holocaust far better than theology, which in the nature of the case must strive for system.

Still, some Jews continue to require theology. Hence the literature which we are about to survey. Borowitz, while all too aware of the dilemmas just recounted, has concluded that "it is difficult to see how one can escape the holistic question altogether."[20] Fackenheim, writing eloquently on the im-

---

Roth, *The Halakhic Process: A Systemic Analysis* (New York, 1986); and David Novak, *Law and Theology in Judaism* (New York, 1974). For a comparable work by a leading modern Orthodox thinker, see Eliezer Berkovits, *Not in Heaven: The Nature and Function of Halakha* (New York, 1983). I would call attention, finally, to Simon Greenberg's collection of essays, *A Jewish Philosophy and Pattern of Life* (New York, 1981), which—along with two volumes published previously, *Foundations of a Faith* (1967) and *The Ethical in the Jewish and American Heritage* (1977)—constitutes the most sustained attempt by an American rabbi since Mordecai Kaplan to provide a philosophy of Jewish living in America. Efforts such as these are probably far more influential on American Jewish belief and observance than the theological works analyzed in the present essay—but they will not be treated here, for reasons which I hope I have made clear.

[18] Van A. Harvey, "The Alienated Theologian," *McCormick Quarterly,* vol. 23, May 1970, pp. 234–65.

[19] On this issue, see Arnold Eisen, "Secularization, 'Spirit,' and the Strategies of Modern Jewish Faith," in *Jewish Spirituality: From the Sixteenth-Century Revival to the Present,* ed. Arthur Green (New York, 1987), pp. 283–316; and Peter Berger, *The Heretical Imperative* (Garden City, 1980).

[20] Borowitz, "Problem of Form," p. 391.

possibility of "systems" in our time, has nonetheless sought—relatively systematically—to lay the "foundations of future Jewish thought."[21] Gillman has given us "fragments" artfully combined into a fairly systematic whole.[22] All, in short, have proclaimed that a "new Jewish theology" is imperative, and have reached for syntheses which have eluded their grasp and that of their generation as a whole. We turn now to their imperfect, but nonetheless substantial, achievement.

Covenant: The Commanding Presence

A sizable portion of American Jewish theological literature of the last two decades has been focused on redefinition of the covenant relationship binding the Jewish people with God. In this respect American Jewish thinkers have carried on the line of inquiry that has preoccupied their predecessors throughout the modern period. The attractions of the covenant model for modern thinkers, and its pitfalls, are equally apparent. On the one hand, Jews seek ultimate purpose for their identity, ultimate authority for their observances, and personal relation to their Creator, and the covenant promises all three. On the other hand, the "suzerainty" paradigm of covenant (in which the sovereign binds his vassals to a set of obligations that he defines, in return promising his protection) has run afoul of the Kantian concern with autonomy and the related reluctance by many modern Jews to bear any "yoke of obligation" imposed by their religion. Commandments from on high, according to liberal thinkers, compromise human dignity and insult human reason. In short, the authority of the King of Kings has not emerged unscathed from the assault on all earthly monarchies.

The "parity treaty" model of covenant (which stipulates reciprocal obligations) has proven somewhat more attractive to modern Jews because it stresses mutuality of obligation and emphasizes partnership and relation rather than subordination and command. But the modern period has seen a lessening of personal religious experience among Jews, and a falling away from religious observance. Moreover, even before the Holocaust, Jews displayed an increasing disinclination to view history as the arena in which God rewards or punishes them for covenantal fidelity or betrayal. The fabric of the putative partnership has, as it were, frayed at both ends, and even been torn right down the middle. Jewish thinkers have found themselves drawn more and more to a theological concept which—given what they do and do not believe about revelation, commandment, and the historicity of the biblical narrative—has become less and less theologically defensible.

American Jewish theologians in recent decades have had to wrestle with

---

[21] Fackenheim, *To Mend the World*, ch. 1.
[22] Gillman, *Sacred Fragments*.

all these problems, plus others. Thus, they have come to recognize that Jewish religious knowledge, practice, and experience can no longer be assumed. The leading thinkers of the previous generation (e.g., Heschel and Soloveitchik) grew up in European settings of traditional practice and belief. Neither the current generation of thinkers nor their readers can call upon such experience. Much of the effort by current thinkers, in fact—one thinks especially of Borowitz's *New Jewish Theology in the Making* (1968), *How Can a Jew Speak of Faith Today* (1969), and *The Mask Jews Wear* (1973)—has been devoted to the question of whether American Jews can be brought to any degree of Jewishly authentic faith or observance. Borowitz, more than any other contemporary theologian, has been intimately involved with lay believers, through his work in the Reform movement.[23] It is telling that he has consistently articulated the alienation of the theologian from his or her fellow Jews most clearly, even as he has relied more heavily than any other thinker on the concept of Israel's covenant with God. Giving meaning to the covenant in the American setting is never without pathos.

EUGENE BOROWITZ

Borowitz's systematic exposition of *Liberal Judaism* (1984), addressed explicitly to the lay audience, is a case in point. The title conveys fidelity to the German liberal tradition rather than to the far more radical bent of American Reform. The organization of the book follows the traditional triad of Israel, God, and Torah. Borowitz is uncompromising in his insistence that God is real and is involved with our world. God's age-old covenant with Israel is still binding. In fact, a good Jew is defined as one who has "a living relationship with God as part of the people of Israel and therefore lives a life of Torah." Prescribed duties—both ethical and ritual—flow from this relationship. So does involvement in the life of the Jewish people as a whole and with the State of Israel: "The Covenant, being a collective endeavor, can best be lived as part of a self-governing Jewish community on the Land of Israel. A good Jew will seriously consider the possibility of *aliyah*. . . ."[24]

Borowitz knows, however, that the vast majority of Reform readers will not give that option serious consideration, any more than they will assume their covenantal duties in more than rudimentary fashion. What is more, he himself cannot accept the Torah (written or oral) as divine revelation,

---

[23]He is, for example, the author of the movement's most recent statement of principles and of an accompanying text of explanation. See Eugene Borowitz, *Reform Judaism Today* (New York, 1978). Lawrence Hoffman calls Borowitz the principal theological influence upon the new Reform *siddur*, *Gates of Prayer* (New York, 1975). See Lawrence Hoffman, ed., *Gates of Understanding* (New York, 1977), p. 6.

[24]Eugene Borowitz, *Liberal Judaism* (New York, 1984), pp. 129–36.

and is unwilling to compromise his commitment to the autonomy of each individual believer. The author emphasizes that he makes "no special claims to 'authority,' " hoping only to persuade. He can suggest appropriate behavior but he cannot guide, let alone command. If each Jew decides how to live the covenant out of the depth of knowledge and in terms of his/her own deepest commitment, Borowitz avers, "whatever we choose from the past or create for the present should rest upon us with the full force of commandment."[25]

One notes that ethics remains the heart of *mitzvah* in Borowitz's liberal Judaism, although ritual is highlighted to a degree still unusual in American Reform. But the force of both sets of obligations is not clear. Halakhah is rejected on principle, and normative communities—in practice nonexistent—would be objectionable if they did exist because of their infringement on individual autonomy. What authority remains? Borowitz seems to rely (as did Kant and Buber, in differing ways) on an inborn sense of duty or conscience that summons each and every human being. He relies, too, on his Jewish readers' unwillingness to sever the ties linking them to their parents, grandparents, and the Jewish past more generally, however much they might strain these ties to the breaking point. Conservative colleagues wrestling with the same issues—and appealing to "*mitzvah*" and "tradition" rather than "covenant" and "ethics"—find themselves in a similar sociological situation, with similar theological results.[26]

IRVING GREENBERG

One sees these same dynamics at work in the notion of "the voluntary covenant" developed by Orthodox thinker Irving Greenberg. Once more the appeal of the idea is clear: just as the rabbis had reassumed and reinterpreted the covenant with God following the destruction of the Temple, so today's Jews must undertake the more radical reinterpretation and reassumption of covenantal responsibilities mandated by the more radical destruction accomplished by the Nazis. Prophecy was gone even by the rabbis' day. Their focus on study of God's word shifted the weight of the Jewish role from passive reception of commands given on high to active partnership, often initiated from below. In another favored rabbinic metaphor, Jews enjoyed a marriage bond with God and carried it on with full devotion.[27] The word "voluntary" is crucial to Greenberg. It emphasizes that the initiative—now, more than ever—is on the human side rather than on

---

[25]Ibid., p. 125.
[26]On the Conservative dilemmas, see Eisen, "American Judaism," as well as the classic treatment by Marshall Sklare in *Conservative Judaism: An American Religious Movement* (New York, 1972).
[27]Irving Greenberg, *The Voluntary Covenant* (New York, 1982).

God's. It suggests that *we* will be faithful, *we* will uphold the covenant, even if God in the Holocaust did not—precisely the reverse of what the prophets said to Israel in the wake of Jerusalem's fall in 586 B.C.E. Issues of heteronomy and sovereignty fall away. Activism, freedom, the rescue of dignity from degradation are pronounced. "By every right, Jews should have questioned or rejected the covenant" after Auschwitz, Greenberg writes. Instead,

> the bulk of Jews, observant and non-observant alike, acted to recreate the greatest Biblical symbol validating the covenant, the State of Israel. . . . [I]n the ultimate test of the Jews' faithfulness to the covenant, the Jewish people, regardless of ritual observance level, responded with a reacceptance of the covenant, out of free will and love. For some, it was love of God; for others, love of the covenant and the goal; for others, love of the people or of the memories of the covenantal way. In truth, it hardly matters because the three are inseparable in walking the covenantal way.[28]

Greenberg builds daringly on Soloveitchik's idea of the twofold covenant of fate and destiny, the former involuntary and symbolized by Pharoah (or Hitler), the latter involving free acceptance of the yoke of the commandments, and symbolized by Sinai. The "voluntary covenant" also extends Soloveitchik's teaching that the Jewish people, committing itself to the covenant of destiny at Sinai, "had committed their very being . . . the covenant turned out to be a covenant of being, not doing."[29] In Greenberg's reading, the commitment to "being" after the Holocaust is virtually equivalent to the "doing" of commandments. One wonders, however, whether he means it to include existence a hair's breadth away from assimilation. Is it really true that "it does not matter," that any Jewish commitment inevitably carries with it all the others? Greenberg exaggerates, I believe, to make the important points that in our generation any and all Jewish commitment is remarkable, and that such commitment often takes the form of caring for the Jewish people (Israel, Ethiopian Jews, Operation Exodus) rather than *shul*-going or observance of the commandments. But a price is paid for this exaggeration: the concept of covenant is strained to the breaking point.

MICHAEL WYSCHOGROD

In *The Body of Faith* (1983), Orthodox thinker Michael Wyschogrod challenges the reigning theological paradigm of voluntarism and its accommodation to the realities of American Judaism. Where Jewish thought since Mendelssohn has stressed human adequacy and brought religion before reason's stern bar of judgment, Wyschogrod pictures a humanity largely in

---

[28]Ibid., pp. 16–28.
[29]Ibid., p. 17.

the dark, its reason blocked at every crucial turn. Only a few shafts of light guide our way—and Torah is the brightest.[30] Where most modern Jewish thinkers, particularly in America, have apologized for the idea of Jewish chosenness, universalizing it to include all righteous Gentiles and interpreting it to stress fulfillment of covenantal obligation, Wyschogrod writes that "the election of the people of Israel as the people of God constitutes the sanctification of a natural family." God did not choose according to a spiritual criterion. "He chose the seed of Abraham, Isaac and Jacob. . . . The election of Israel is therefore a corporeal election."[31] Finally, where thinkers such as Borowitz have affirmed autonomy, Wyschogrod argues that "the ethical is not autonomous in Judaism. It is rooted in the being and command of God, without which no obligation is conceivable."[32]

Most recent Jewish thought in America has skirted the issue of God, preferring when it does speak of God to employ the rationalist discourse of "spirit" or "intelligence." Wyschogrod (with brilliant use of both the Bible and Heidegger) argues the necessity of a personal God whom he calls by His personal name—"Hashem," literally, "The Name." The argument, briefly,[33] is that Heidegger was correct in claiming that beyond Being there can be only Non-Being. Identification of God with being, in the manner of Spinoza, cannot avoid the threat posed to the meaning of all human endeavor by the encompassing power of non-being. Only a God beyond both being and non-being can satisfy our demand for ultimate meaning and ultimate grounding. Only Hashem can conquer death and create life: "On the one side there is being and thought, the enterprise of Heidegger. On the other side is Hashem and faith, the enterprise of Judaism. And then there is man, who attempts to understand himself in the setting provided by these concepts and in light of the tensions generated by them." Where rational language must fall silent in its search for description of the Lord of Being, unable to transcend the limits of our world, "the power of Hashem acts through the language of revelation," the Bible, and gives us the power of speech. "Hope conquers the despair of silence," Wyschogrod asserts.[34]

Wyschogrod's argument is Jewishly and philosophically learned, captivating in its break with the conventional givens of American Jewish theology—and, of course, not without serious problems. For one, the magnificent interpretive freedom derived from Wyschogrod's refusal to demythologize the Bible's descriptions of God depends on the belief that the text is somehow divine. That belief is never argued in the book, let alone justi-

---
[30] Wyschogrod, *Body of Faith,* ch. 1.
[31] Ibid., p. xv.
[32] Ibid.
[33] Ibid., chs. 4–5.
[34] Ibid., pp. 144, 172.

fied. Unless Moses really did write the text in accord with divine instruction, it is hard to see how we can resist reason's demand for reinterpretation of the text's descriptions of God.

Second, and no less important, the conviction that Israel's is a "corporeal election" transmitted from generation to generation by the organs of generation rather than a "spiritual election" dependent upon observance of the covenant raises obvious empirical and moral dilemmas. Are Jews really one race? Are non-Jews so utterly beyond the covenant? Wyschogrod observes: "What, now, of those not elected? Those not elected cannot be expected not to be hurt by not being of the seed of Abraham, whom God loves above all others. The Bible depicts clearly the suffering of Esau. . . . The consolation of the gentiles is the knowledge that God also stands in relationship with them in the recognition and affirmation of their uniqueness."[35] Wyschogrod has preferred the minority view of election in Judaism—associated with Yehudah Halevi, the Maharal of Prague, and the Kabbalah—over the predominant stream represented by Maimonides and Mendelssohn. It is as if he wants to shout to the Jews described (and accommodated) by Borowitz: You are bound, like it or not, to an eternal covenant. Its mark is imprinted on your flesh. You cannot escape it. There is no meaning to your life—or being itself—outside the reach of Hashem. Embrace your destiny! Any other option—all the options preferred by reason and recommended on grounds of social acceptability—means suicide.

DAVID HARTMAN

The polar opposite to Wyschogrod's book in virtually every respect except the shared centrality of covenant is David Hartman's *A Living Covenant: The Innovative Spirit in Traditional Judaism* (1985). Hartman, now an Israeli, writes that his attempt to articulate a "covenantal anthropology" stressing human freedom and adequacy grew out of his experience of American pluralism, his graduate work among the Jesuits at Fordham, and his conviction that secularism can be the framework for meaningful life and rigorous ethical commitment. It also emerged from the reality of Israeli society—a feature that separates him from all the other theologians considered in the present article.[36] Hartman has "Halakhah" and "Aggadah" in the sense discussed earlier: a communal reality in which to live and on which to reflect. That reality has affected his thinking decisively.

One should note, before considering his views, that the subject of Is-

---

[35]Ibid., p. 64.
[36]David Hartman, *A Living Covenant: The Innovative Spirit in Traditional Judaism* (New York, 1985), p. 12.

rael is virtually absent from American Jewish theology.[37] That is not to say that the state does not matter, and matter deeply, to American Jews, including the theologians. Israel's existence, however, has had no major impact on Jewish religious life here. Some synagogues celebrate Israel Independence Day, and many recite a prayer for the state; sermons, now as before, are full of Israel's troubles and achievements. But Israel has not seriously altered religious observance and is not a topic for American Jewish thought except (as we will see below) in the context of the Holocaust. The sacredness of space—a prominent theme in current Israeli thought—is an alien notion to American thinkers content with Heschel's dictum that Judaism sanctifies time and not space. The possibility that our time is witnessing the first footsteps of the Messiah—as some in Israel forcefully contend—tends to frighten American Jewish thinkers rather than to receive serious consideration.

Hartman sets out to counter both the excessive zealotry of the Israeli messianists and the ethereal quality of much Diaspora thought with a call to collective covenantal responsibility. Sinai, not Exodus, is his paradigmatic event, and Sinai is interpreted as a divine "invitation" to partnership and intimacy rather than as an act of dictatorial command. Hartman's favored metaphor, in fact, is neither the suzerainty covenant nor the parity treaty but the marriage vow. God and Israel need each other. Only their partnership can bring *mitzvot* into the world. The covenant, far from precluding human initiative, creativity, and freedom, presumes it at every turn. Tradition does not merely allow innovation, it demands it. God counts on Israel's participation in the building of His kingdom. Jews freely accept this invitation because they love God and appreciate the meaningfulness of the life shaped by God's commandments.[38]

Hartman's thrust is twofold. First, he is carrying forward a theological agenda begun in our era by Soloveitchik and the Israeli thinker Yeshayahu Leibowitz, both of them inspired by Hartman's principal teacher: Maimonides. The stress falls on human activism, the centrality of human reason, the role of human initiative and creativity, the dignity of halakhic observance—all this in contrast to Christian (and classical Reform Jewish) depictions of the Halakhah as rote behavior under a burdensome yoke. Hartman rejects Soloveitchik's call for a degree of submissiveness and resignation in the face of divine decrees. Covenantal activism, he writes, enabled the rabbis (and enables us) to counter and contain the experience of life's tragedy and

---

[37]On this matter, see Arnold Eisen, *Galut: Modern Jewish Reflection on Homelessness and Homecoming* (Bloomington, 1986), pp. 156–74.
[38]Hartman, *Living Covenant,* pp. 1–8, 22–59.

terror.[39] Similarly, Hartman adopts Leibowitz's call for halakhic creativity while rejecting his restriction of the covenant to halakhic observance. The total human being is required, Hartman writes—precisely as he or she is required in a marriage.[40] Nothing less will do. Eloquently and with characteristic passion, Hartman argues the case for human adequacy, human reason, and Jewish openness to the wider world.

This points to the second task undertaken in the book: the attempt to redirect the religious understanding of Israeli society. On the one hand, Hartman seeks to break down the dichotomy between *dati* (religious) and *lo dati* (secular), not by the creation of a middle ground but by the encouragement of mutual respect. Secular readers are brought to see a halakhic life which insists upon innovation and open-mindedness. Religious readers are challenged in their assumption that faith and it alone can provide a foundation for ethics or a life of ultimate meaning. Hartman offers *a* covenant, not *the* covenant. He urges his readers, religious and secular alike, to see their shared history not as Exodus, i.e., divine manipulation, but as Sinai: an opportunity to actualize the covenant in an entire community. Borowitz, in the American context, can speak of ethics and ritual; Orthodox colleagues in America can call for greater halakhic observance; Hartman, as an Israeli, can discuss a Jewish society and culture. A thinker who does "not wish to divide my world into two separate realms, one of which is characterized by autonomous action based upon human understanding of the divine norm and the other by anticipation of and dependence upon divine intervention" requires an arena in which human beings can "unite the two realms and exercise autonomous action."[41] Israel is that realm.

One wonders whether the split between *dati* and *lo dati* can be overcome in this manner, even on the level of theory. If God really is present in our world, how ignore that presence with impunity? If God really did command Israel at Sinai, how can disobedience to His commands be taken as morally neutral? And if both these claims are in fact delusions, their consequences pernicious, how could one possibly remain placid or indifferent? Hartman's generosity, like his equanimity, seems difficult to maintain. He purchases them by robbing both secularism and faith of potent energies, and not a little profundity.

There is a related problem with Hartman's model that seems even more intractable. As we have seen, he rejects the division of his world into one realm "characterized by autonomous action based upon human understanding of the divine norm" and a second realm in which human beings await, in dependence, the "divine intervention." Hartman rather "prefers

---

[39]Ibid., chs. 3–4.
[40]Ibid., ch. 5.
[41]Ibid., pp. 232–33. See also p. 148.

to see God's will . . . as channeled exclusively through the efforts of the Jewish community to achieve the aims of the Torah given at Sinai."[42] But what happens when the awesome realities of God's presence intrude uninvited upon personal and collective life? What are we to do with the human failure and self-destructiveness which so often preclude fulfillment of covenantal responsibility? The effort to keep fear and trembling outside the bounds of covenant may be futile; moreover, it may rob the life of *mitzvah* of much pathos and passion. Hartman's model of covenant is adequate to some portion of human and Jewish experience, but not to the rest, in which darkness is pervasive and human adequacy far from unquestioned.

Each model of covenant proposed in the past two decades has the disadvantages of its own virtues. All attest to the difficulties which modernity has cast up before traditional belief. No less, they demonstrate the continuing resiliency of the covenant idea, despite and because of the fact that most Jews no longer feel bound by its traditional stipulations, the commandments. It seems likely that autonomy will remain precious to Jewish believers, and commandment fundamental. Covenant will therefore continue to feature prominently in Jewish theology, even as it continues to risk degeneration into cant—a traditional trope deprived of all traditional content. Like the bodily wounding which most symbolizes it, covenant will hold Jews, in large part, through the power of their own ambivalence.

God's Saving Presence—and Its Absence

American Jewish theology concerning the Holocaust falls broadly into two categories. Either the Holocaust was a unique event in human history which makes all the difference in the world to Jewish reflection—or it was not, and does not. The former claim can likewise be of two sorts: that of Richard Rubenstein, who holds that "after Auschwitz" the God of history, the God of the covenant, can no longer be affirmed, that Jewish existence is an absurd given, no more and no less meaningful than the existence of any other group of mortals in a senseless universe;[43] or one can hold, with Irving Greenberg, Emil Fackenheim, and Arthur Cohen,[44] that theological business as usual cannot continue, that existing models have been ruptured, that a "caesura" has opened in human thought and history dividing before

---

[42]Ibid., pp. 232–33.

[43]Richard Rubenstein, *After Auschwitz: Radical Theology and Contemporary Judaism* (Indianapolis, 1966).

[44]Irving Greenberg, "Cloud of Smoke, Pillar of Fire: Judaism, Christianity, and Modernity After the Holocaust," in *Auschwitz: Beginning of a New Era?* ed. Eva Fleischner (New York, 1977), pp. 7–55; Emil Fackenheim, *God's Presence in History* (New York, 1970) and *To Mend the World*; Arthur A. Cohen, *The Tremendum: A Theological Interpretation of the Holocaust* (New York, 1981).

from after Auschwitz—but that Judaism can and must go on, somehow. This latter version of the claim that the Holocaust makes all the difference borders so closely on the claim that it does not make all the difference as to make the two, to my mind at least, virtually indistinguishable. The two views are separated by a process of thought rather than its end-point; or, rather, one group insists on making the process explicit and devising new language to describe it, while the other regards the process as highly traditional and, therefore, not worthy of extended discussion. Eliezer Berkovits argues that the Holocaust is not unique, places it against the background of millennial persecution, cites the bewilderment of Job and the anger of Psalm 44—and claims that nothing has changed.[45] Fackenheim, Greenberg, and Cohen argue that everything has changed and devote many pages to explaining how, but end, like Berkovits, with the affirmation that Jewish life, Jewish obligation, the study of Torah, the service of God, must continue.

Not surprisingly, then, theological concentration on the subject has diminished of late. The point, after all, is *"To Mend the World"* (Fackenheim), not just to document its rupture; to "build a bridge over the abyss" (Cohen), not just to face up to *"The Tremendum."* As Rosenzweig, the crucial mentor of both Cohen and Fackenheim, put it at the close of *The Star of Redemption:* "into life."[46]

RICHARD RUBENSTEIN

Rubenstein, in an eloquent critique of Cohen's book, summarized his own point of view most concisely. "The Holocaust renders faith in either the God of classical theism or the God of classical covenant theology exceedingly difficult," if not impossible. "Judaism makes the fundamental claim that God is uniquely concerned with the history and destiny of Israel," meaning that "the classical and logically inescapable mode of interpreting a monumental national catastrophe such as the Holocaust is that of divine punishment of a sinful people." This view of the Holocaust, Rubenstein writes, is unacceptable. Covenantal affirmation is thus precluded, and Jewish movements which strive to get around the problem are all of them unsatisfactory. Reconstructionism, proposing what Rubenstein calls "ethnic religion," fails to offer "a compelling rationale for maintaining Jewish religious identity." Zionism fails to attract most Diaspora Jews. All attempts to detach Judaism from belief in the Lord of History inevitably involve departure from the "Jewish religious mainstream." In short, Jews

---

[45]Eliezer Berkovits, *Faith After the Holocaust* (New York, 1973) and *With God in Hell* (New York, 1979).
[46]Rosenzweig, *Star of Redemption,* p. 424.

must choose between a God who is absent from history, "functionally irrelevant," or regard Hitler as "the instrument of an all-powerful and righteous God of history. I wish there were a credible way out of the dilemma. In the thirty years that I have spent reflecting on the Holocaust, I have yet to find it."[47]

One should note that for Rubenstein the Holocaust is not unique—far from it; its importance lies in the quandaries that it makes unavoidable in our time. In fact, Rubenstein argues, terms such as "the tremendum" are attempts to "mystify a phenomenon that can be fully comprehended in terms of the normal categories of history, social science, demography, political theory, and economics."[48] Rubenstein does not move from the Holocaust to an altered theology, therefore. He leaves God behind altogether and focuses the inquiry on the human decisions which led one group of people to persecute and then murder another. In this respect, ironically, Rubenstein is closer to Berkovits—who likewise denies the Holocaust's uniqueness, and likewise places the blame squarely on human evil rather than divine indifference—than to the theologians for whom, as for him, the Holocaust mandates a radical response.

EMIL FACKENHEIM

Fackenheim is perhaps the best example of the latter. His earliest essays, collected in *Quest for Past and Future* (1968) and *Encounters Between Judaism and Modern Philosophy* (1973), sought to establish that the tenets of traditional faith, revelation first of all, were still philosophically respectable options. One expected, on the basis of these works, that he would proceed to a species of covenant theology more traditional than Borowitz's but, unlike Hartman's, non-halakhic. (It has in fact recently appeared, in popular form: *What Is Judaism?* [1987]). Instead, there came a break—presaging the claim that such a break is inevitable in contemporary Jewish faith as such. *God's Presence in History* (1970) laid the groundwork for Fackenheim's new direction by setting forth the two categories of "root experiences": historical events in which Jewish faith originated and "epoch-making events" that make a "new claim upon Jewish faith," testing it in light of historical experience. Exodus and Sinai are examples—probably the only ones—of the former; the destruction of the Temples, the Maccabean revolt, the expulsion from Spain, and now the Holocaust, are examples of the latter. Jewish faith had to remain open to the incursions of history if

---

[47]Richard Rubenstein, "Naming the Unnameable; Thinking the Unthinkable (A Review Essay of Arthur Cohen's *The Tremendum*)," *Journal of Reform Judaism*, vol. 31, Spring 1984, pp. 43–49.
[48]Ibid., pp. 51–54.

it were to remain vital, alive, true. Yet what faith could emerge from Auschwitz?[49]

In this book Fackenheim had only one reply: the "614th commandment." Jews were forbidden to hand Hitler posthumous victories. For secular Jews to abandon their people, or religious Jews their faith, would be to aid and abet the Nazis. Secular Israelis knew well what Fackenheim wished to teach: that "after the death camps, we are left only one supreme value: existence."[50] Fackenheim carried this lesson forward—particularly regarding the importance of the Jewish state—in *The Jewish Return into History* (1978). His most coherent statement, however—and his finest work of theology to date—came in *To Mend the World* (1982). The book is striking on two counts. First, it perceptively situates itself in the history of modern Jewish theology, so as to lay the "foundations for future Jewish Thought." Recognizing that one cannot do everything, Fackenheim focuses on key thinkers (Spinoza, Buber, and Rosenzweig) and confronts them with philosophical (Hegel, Heidegger) and historical (modernity, Holocaust, Israel) challenges. As Fackenheim puts it, "It is clearly necessary for Jewish thought (and not for it alone) to go to school with life."[51] Theology had to catch up with what history had wrought, and item number one in the curriculum was of course the Holocaust.

The second striking feature of the book is indeed Fackenheim's treatment of the Holocaust. Unrelentingly, and always thoughtfully, Fackenheim looks at the awful face of the facts and in that context asks "the central question of our whole inquiry . . . how Jewish (and also Christian and philosophical) thought can both expose itself to the Holocaust and survive." The ability to survive should not, he insists, be taken for granted. Fackenheim concedes that his previous, Kantian, confidence that "we can do what we ought to do" was a lapse into "unconscious glibness."[52]

Some 200 pages later, after situating Rosenzweig opposite Spinoza and Hegel, after confronting the challenge of Heidegger's philosophy and the conundrum of his support for the Nazis, and (less satisfactorily) after a highly judgmental survey of "Unauthentic Thought After the Holocaust," Fackenheim arrives at the effort of repair or *tikkun*. Resistance to Auschwitz, repair of Auschwitz, is possible now because it occurred then. German philosophers in the name of their philosophical convictions opposed the Nazis, on pain of death. Christian martyrs opposed Hitler in the name of Christianity. Jews defied him in Warsaw and elsewhere—and out of the ashes of the Holocaust created the single most important *tikkun* in the

---
[49]Fackenheim, *God's Presence,* pp. 3–31.
[50]Ibid., pp. 79–98.
[51]Fackenheim, *To Mend the World,* p. 15.
[52]Ibid., pp. 24, 200.

world today, the State of Israel. "The Tikkun which for the post-Holocaust Jew is a moral necessity is a possibility because during the Holocaust itself a Jewish Tikkun was already actual. This simple but enormous, nay, world-historical truth is the rock on which rests any authentic Jewish future, and any authentic future Jewish identity." Israel, the Jews' emergence from powerlessness, "has been and continues to be a moral achievement of world-historical import."[53]

The principal problem with the work, as Cohen noted in a review, is that the depiction of rupture is so convincing that the promise of repair lacks all credibility. The book, he wrote, "utterly collapses" this side of the Holocaust.[54] It is not so much that one can do what one ought to do, as that one ends up doing what one must do, what one knew all along one would do. *Tikkun* must be possible or there is no foundation of future Jewish thought, and Rubenstein's answer to Auschwitz is decisive. Fackenheim had to cross the abyss—or violate the 614th commandment. The question was never whether, but only how, he could cross. But if that is the case, if the circle of covenant must remain unbroken, how is Fackenheim different from Berkovits?

It seems that in *To Mend the World* Fackenheim has backed off somewhat from earlier unequivocal claims about the Holocaust's uniqueness. After devoting a page to a brief statement of five arguments for that uniqueness—"a complex subject that will require much space in the present work"—Fackenheim writes that "all this is by no means to deny the existence of other catastrophes equally unprecedented, and endowed with unique characteristics of their own."[55] Still, Fackenheim does not proceed from the repair of one rupture to the depiction and repair of the others. Auschwitz matters in a way Hiroshima does not because Fackenheim believes in the Hegelian notion that some peoples and events are of "world-historical" significance while others are not. In the Holocaust fully one-third of the people most associated with the God of the Bible were destroyed by the people most associated in the modern period with the project of philosophy, the crowning achievement of the human spirit.[56] That claim, outside the Hegelian framework, is difficult to defend. Even inside it, however, Cohen's charge that the rupture cannot be so speedily repaired requires an answer which Fackenheim does not provide.

---

[53]Ibid., pp. 300–304.
[54]Arthur A. Cohen, "On Emil Fackenheim's *To Mend the World:* A Review Essay," *Modern Judaism,* vol. 3, May 1983, pp. 231–35.
[55]Fackenheim, *To Mend the World,* pp. 12–13.
[56]I owe this insight to Michael Morgan—but bear full responsibility for its formulation.

IRVING GREENBERG

Greenberg's argument, very similar to Fackenheim's, is best expressed in an essay entitled "Cloud of Smoke, Pillar of Fire: Judaism, Christianity and Modernity After the Holocaust" (1977). He convincingly lays out the damage done to traditional notions of covenant and redemption, argues that "the Holocaust challenges the claims of all the standards that compete for modern man's loyalties" and allows no "simple, clear or definitive solutions," and then propounds one definitive principle. "No statement, theological or otherwise, should be made that would not be credible in the presence of the burning children." Greenberg proposes a "dialectical faith" which holds fast to the disbelief in divine redemption occasioned by Auschwitz but is also open to "moments when the reality of the Exodus is reenacted and present." The Holocaust challenges prevailing secular conceptions no less than it does religious faith; it teaches us to recognize the dangers of powerlessness as well as of power. "The cloud of smoke of the bodies by day and the pillar of fire of the crematoria by night"—powerful relocations to Auschwitz of the biblical marks of God's presence in the wilderness—"may yet guide humanity to a goal and a day when human beings are attached to each other; and have so much shared each other's pain, and have so purified and criticized themselves, that never again will a Holocaust be possible."[57] In the meantime, Greenberg counsels return to *The Jewish Way* (1988) entailed by the covenant—apparently finding it not only credible but necessary in the face of "burning children."

ARTHUR COHEN

Cohen's premise is more radical; he assumes, in effect, that nothing whatsoever is credible by that criterion. The question must be refocused, moved from religious observance to the classical ground of theology: the nature of God.

> My interest—first, last and always—is about the God who created the world, not the God who provided the occasion for religion. What Jews do about their religious life . . . of the conferred and optional requirements of living as Jews I can hardly speak. . . . I might almost assert as a first principle of any modern Jewish theology that it should begin by thinking without Jews in mind.

Cohen finds it necessary to undertake this effort—to engage in theology despite the fact that "there is virtually no modern Jewish theology"— because the Holocaust marked a novum, "the election of the Chosen People to be the first people in human history to be systematically an-

---

[57]Greenberg, "Cloud of Smoke." The quotation is found on p. 55.

nihilated. . . . Such a theological novum entails theological response."[58]
Cohen's response is as follows.[59] One must not deny either God's presence in the world or the reality of evil. God must be seen as related to every aspect of creation. God confronts us then, first of all, not as Father or King but (borrowing Rudolph Otto's classic term) as the Tremendum—a Power both awesome and mysterious. We cannot return after Auschwitz to the classic categories of Western philosophical theism. There has been a rupture, a "caesura." To repair or at least cross it, Cohen turns from the rabbis to the Kabbalah, which penetrated Western philosophy, reaching Rosenzweig and then Cohen, through the person of Schelling. "The human affect," Schelling taught,

> is toward the overflowing, the loving in God; his containment, however, the abyss of his nature, is as crucial as is his abundance and plenitude. These are the fundamental antitheses of the divine essence . . . the quiet God is as indispensable as the revealing God, the abyss as much as the plenitude, the constrained, self-contained, deep divinity as the plenteous and generous.[60]

God had made room in the divine plenitude for human beings endowed with freedom and speech. The space in which we abide, in which God gives us leave to abide, is therefore full to overflowing with our "enduring strife and tension, enlarged and made threatening by our finitude," enhanced and made more dangerous by our freedom.[61]

Cohen is not seeking language adequate to God's nature. We do not have it, he believes, for reasons that his theology helps to clarify. He seeks only to be adequate to the caesura, and this he may well have achieved—at the cost of belief in the covenant as traditionally (that is, nonmystically) understood. Like the rabbis, and without explanation, Cohen affirms the unique connection between the being of the Jewish people and the being of God. There can be no explanation of that connection, he avers. We will understand the nature of "Jewish being, Jewish history, and the meaning of God's self-narration" only "when it is done and past or else completed in the last minute of redemption."[62] As Rosenzweig put it, "not yet"; the meaning is present, but not yet apparent. "Redemption" is, significantly, the final word of the book. The covenant may be broken theologically, but its observance continues despite and because of the caesura.

---

[58] Arthur A. Cohen, "On Theological Method: A Response on Behalf of *The Tremendum,*" *Journal of Reform Judaism,* vol. 31, Spring 1984, pp. 56–63.
[59] Cohen, *The Tremendum.* See especially chs. 3–4.
[60] Ibid., p. 90.
[61] Ibid., pp. 92–94.
[62] Ibid., p. 110.

Silberman, concluding his survey of American Jewish theology two decades ago, wrote that confrontation with *hurban* (destruction) was the inescapable task of Jewish theology. Jewish thought could ignore Auschwitz only at its own peril.[63] Two decades later one can say that the task of confronting Auschwitz has probably been undertaken as thoroughly as possible at this juncture, and that the refusal to make the move of repair linking Cohen, Fackenheim, and Greenberg to Berkovits is to present no less a peril than the other to future Jewish thought. Survival, the 614th commandment, demands an answer to the question: survival for what, in what faith, with what obligation? Survival, if it is to be continuous with the Jewish past, entails some relationship to the 613 commandments which, according to the 614th, Jews are forbidden to abandon. The next generation of Jewish thinkers, while not entirely ignoring the Holocaust, will likely move on to efforts—dialectical or otherwise—to make sense of Jewish life, the previous generation having focused, perhaps necessarily, on the threat posed to Judaism by unprecedented Jewish death. That effort, in fact, is already under way, informed by recent currents in American society and undertaken by a new generation of theologians. We turn now to two of its most noteworthy exemplars.

Experience, Tradition, Community

It is doubtful that either of the two themes that have preoccupied American Jewish theology for the past 20 years will continue to hold center stage in the next 20. A new generation of theologians is now at work, and it has announced its intention (as did the previous generation) to reorient theological discourse rather substantially. Two reasons for that reorientation have already been noted: the problems besetting covenant theology in the absence of either a satisfactory notion of revelation or a community intent on covenantal observance; and the need—articulated even by those for whom the Holocaust has been central—to move from (or through) confrontation with the "rupture" or "caesura" of Auschwitz to *tikkun:* renewed Jewish commitment. The question becomes what sort of commitment, grounded in what authority, inside what sort of community? The answers emerging from a variety of quarters come in terms which have not loomed large in recent decades but which have a venerable theological history in Judaism as in other faiths: experience, tradition, and community. I will illustrate this emerging trend with the work of two thinkers who will, I expect, assume increasing importance as the decade unfolds.

---

[63]Silberman, "Jewish Theology," p. 58.

ARTHUR GREEN

The first is Arthur Green, president of the Reconstructionist Rabbinical College and as such the intellectual leader of Reconstructionism. Green is trying to take his movement, and American Judaism as a whole, in a new theological direction centered on the renewed religious experience of the individual believer. Green's approach was adumbrated in a 1976 address before Conservative rabbis[64] and further elaborated (albeit implicitly) in his masterly biography of Nachman of Bratslav, *Tormented Master* (1979). It has received its fullest expression to date in a programmatic essay entitled "Rethinking Theology: Language, Experience and Reality" (1988), the subtitle of which offers a précis of Green's argument.

First, the matter of religious language. Green begins with "one of the great tragedies of Judaism in modern times"—the widespread perception that Judaism is "empty of, or even opposed to, the depths of individual religious experience." In fact, Green argues, Kabbalah and Hassidism have bequeathed "a rich vocabulary . . . for discussion of religious states"; the problem is that that vocabulary (as we have seen in the present essay) rarely figures in contemporary Jewish discourse. Green aims to reintroduce it, thereby helping to create "a religious language that will speak both profoundly and honestly to Jews in our time."[65] Honesty, to Green, demands that Jews admit their distance from traditional symbols and beliefs. We are necessarily both insiders and outsiders to our inheritance. Profundity connotes the effort to penetrate to the wellspring of faith deep inside every human being. We should, like Hassidism, seek "spiritual wakefulness and awareness . . . cultivation of the inner life." Judaism does not so much demand leaps of faith as intensity of vision. The path does not lie in more adequate theories of revelation, but more penetrating searchings of the soul.[66]

The key, in other words, is experience. All human beings know transcendence at some moments of their lives. Religion exists to "make constant, or at least regular, [the] level of insight that has already existed in moments of spontaneous flash," and to design ways of life appropriate to the illuminations that transcendence provides.[67] Like his teacher Abraham Heschel (albeit in language more attuned to the counterculture of the 1960s), Green begins with wonder, awe, transcendence—"we praise before we prove," as Heschel put it—and only then moves to God, whom Heschel regarded as

---

[64]Arthur Green, "The Role of Jewish Mysticism in a Contemporary Theology of Judaism," *Conservative Judaism*, Summer 1976, pp. 10–23.
[65]Arthur Green, "Rethinking Theology: Language, Experience and Reality," *The Reconstructionist*, Sept. 1988, pp. 8–9.
[66]Ibid., pp. 9–10.
[67]Ibid.

the only satisfactory "answer" to the "questions" made imperative by our wonder. Green's understanding of God, however, diverges from Heschel considerably and—ironically enough, given the Hassidic language in which it is couched—brings Green remarkably close to the teaching of Mordecai Kaplan. "YHWH is, in short, all of being, but so unified and concentrated as to become Being." God is "the universe . . . so utterly transformed by integration and unity as to appear to us as indeed 'other,' a mirror of the universe's self that becomes Universal Self." God is "none 'other' than we ourselves and the world in which we live, transformed as part of the transcendent vision."[68] Kaplan, I think, could have assented to all of these formulations, and certainly to Green's caveat that "the figure of God imaged by most religion is a human projection."[69]

Where the two thinkers would differ, perhaps, is on Green's belief that human beings need to pray to God, that psychology should not be employed to explain away "supernaturalism" but rather to underline its importance as a mode of expression. In his words, " 'God' is in that sense a symbol, a human creation that we need to use in order to illuminate for ourselves, however inadequately, some tiny portion of the infinite mystery." And, besides, "our imagination, we should always remember, is itself a figment of divinity."[70]

It is clear from the quotations just cited that Green's God is far from the real personal God encountered by Heschel or Buber. Green's notion of *mitzvot* must therefore be different as well; the idea of divine covenant is utterly inapplicable. *Mitzvot* enter Green's Judaism from two directions. "The religious life is a life lived in constant striving for this awareness [of relation to the transcendent] and in response to the demands made by it." And we turn to Judaism for the pattern of that striving and response, "not because it is the superior religion, and certainly not because it is God's single will, but because it is our own . . . our spiritual home." Green prefers the "tradition in its most whole and authentic form" because "traditions work best when they are least diluted. . . . Serious Judaism means serious engagement with *mitzvot*."[71]

This statement of the Jewish religious situation is, I would suggest, remarkable in more ways than one—not least in its adaptation of Kaplan to the very different cultural milieu of the 1990s. "Such a religious viewpoint" is indeed, as Green claims, "that of mystic and naturalist at once."[72]

---

[68]Ibid., pp. 10–11. For Heschel's view, see particularly *Man Is Not Alone* (New York, 1951), chs. 1–9; for Kaplan's, see *The Meaning of God in Modern Jewish Religion* (New York, 1962) and Eisen, *Chosen People in America,* ch. 4.
[69]Green, "Rethinking Theology," p. 11.
[70]Ibid., p. 12.
[71]Ibid., pp. 10, 13.

Moreover, Green may well articulate the assumptions of a large number of contemporary American Jews (particularly intellectuals), just as Kaplan did for the generation of the 1930s. Note that the vision starts and ends with self: the experience of transcendence, the search for God leading "through our deepest and most pained emotional selves,"[73] the turn to tradition because it fulfills that quest in a "whole" and "authentic" form. This is not to accuse Green of narcissism. Quite the opposite. He has simply worked with, and for, the prevailing reality of Jewish life which Kaplan urged upon his readers over half a century ago: namely, that Judaism will either be a palpable source of meaning, enriching life in tangible ways, or Jews will not choose to accord it a central place in their lives. Moreover, like Kaplan, Green has sought to encourage that move to Judaism by couching it in language which does not challenge prevailing conceptions of reality and by deemphasizing claims of guilt or obligation. *Mitzvot* deepen life, heighten awareness, proffer the authenticity available only (or most readily) in one's natural "spiritual home"—and necessitate community. One discovers the self, and so God, when one joins with other searchers who share one's language, one's "spiritual home," one's life. "Our 'liberal' views should not serve as a cloak for cavalier desertion or disdain of our traditions," Green writes.[74] The force of that "should not" bears attention: not because God has willed it, nor even because our ancestors have covenanted with God in a way which binds us, but because what we seek in and for ourselves is achievable through no other route than "serious engagement with *mitzvot.*"

JUDITH PLASKOW

A similar appeal to experience, grounded still more powerfully in the life of a particular community of Jews, underlies Judith Plaskow's groundbreaking effort to formulate a feminist Jewish theology. If the history of Judaism written to date largely ignores the role played by women; if the tradition's classical texts were written by and for men, according little space to female characters and evincing little interest in female consciousness; if the founding moment of the Jewish people, the covenant at Sinai described in Exodus 19, excluded women entirely (the injunction "do not go near a woman" seems to indicate that "Moses addresses the community only as men")—then, asks Plaskow, where is a woman to find entrée to this tradition? How is she to appropriate it, carry it forward? Jewish women can either "choose to accept our absence from Sinai, in which case we allow the male text to define us and our relationship to the tradition," or they can

---
[72]Ibid., p. 11.
[73]Ibid., p. 12.
[74]Ibid., p. 13.

"stand on the ground of our experience, on the certainty of our membership in our own people."[75]

Note that the authority invoked to correct and supplement the "partial record of the 'God wrestling' of part of the Jewish people"—Plaskow's understanding of Torah[76]—is experience: Plaskow's, her community's, and that of the readers to whom she appeals. Accepting that authority, one can "begin the journey toward the creation of a feminist Judaism." All interpretation relies upon experience to some degree, of course. One reads the text into and out of the world as one has come to know it. One adapts tradition to reality and reality to tradition. In Plaskow's work, however, the role of experience is necessarily greater—because of the perceived lack of female consciousness and presence in the tradition that she wishes to adapt.

Plaskow's book *Standing Again at Sinai* (1990) draws upon efforts by Jewish feminists over the past two decades to create new midrash, design new rituals, and explore areas of Jewish history previously untouched, weaving them into the first systematic effort at feminist Jewish theology. After a quite sophisticated methodological introduction, Plaskow proceeds to take up each of the three topics in the classic triad—Torah, Israel, and God, adding a fourth discussion (sexuality), which is apparently central to feminist theology but which seems far less accomplished than the others. We shall focus here on several points which seem to presage the emergence of a new orientation for American Jewish theology.

First, already noted, the appeal to experience—here, in the feminist context, an experience neither purely personal nor purely human but rather gender-specific and communal. Plaskow is sophisticated enough methodologically to avoid the trap of appeal to a putative feminine mind or sensibility unified in itself and easily distinct from the masculine. She relies instead on the reasonable claim that women's experiences, however diverse they may be, have found little expression in Judaism thus far. The few women present in classical texts are either condemned outright or given short shrift; this has given rise in recent decades to a widespread feminist experience of exclusion from the tradition, suspicion of it, disenchantment with it. Plaskow also can point, however, to powerful experiences of transcendence—her own and those of others—which have engendered deep connection to the tradition. The community of feminists in which those experiences occurred becomes, for Plaskow, a point of reference in deciding the direction of feminist Judaism; it becomes, in a word, her authority.

> To say that this community is my central source of authority is not to deny the range of ideas or disagreements within it, or the other communities of which I am part. It is simply to say that I have been formed in important ways by Jewish

---

[75]Judith Plaskow, "Standing Again at Sinai: Jewish Memory from a Feminist Perspective," *Tikkun*, vol. 1, no. 2, 1986, p. 28.
[76]Ibid., p. 29.

feminism; without it I could not see the things that I see. It is to say that my most important experiences of God have come through this community, and that it has given me the language with which to express them. To name this community my authority is to call it the primary community to which I am accountable.[77]

Buber said that one carries forward that part of the tradition which speaks to one with "inner power." Kaplan stressed the role of the Jewish people in constantly redefining Judaism in accord with their highest ideals. Plaskow is less subjective than Buber, less universal than Kaplan, but like them she has dispensed with the need for revealed authority, in the belief that it is nowhere to be found. Community is all one has. It is, in fact, all one needs. "The experience of God in community is both the measure of the adequacy of traditional language and the norm in terms of which new images must be fashioned."[78]

Plaskow realizes that "to locate authority in particular communities of interpreters is admittedly to make a circular appeal."[79] Group X of Jews defines Torah as it does, on the grounds that—Group X has experienced it this way. Yet this circularity "has always been the case. . . . When the rabbis said that rabbinic modes of interpretation were given at Sinai, they were claiming authority for their own community—just as other groups had before them, just as feminists do today."[80] This claim of similarity to the rabbis, the second to which I wish to draw attention, features prominently throughout the book. It links Plaskow's work to a principal current both in recent Jewish theology and in philosophy more generally, namely: the argument that quests for objective authority will always be futile; that there is no ultimate foundation for any worldview or ethical system; that the most one can hope for is a community committed to certain norms and the view of reality that undergirds them; that one must define and fashion tradition as one goes. Time and again Plaskow argues that no other authority than one's community is available—and never was.

Hence her use of the rabbis as a role model, horrified as they might have been by the comparison. They too, after all, "expanded Scripture to make it relevant to their own times," they too "brought to the Bible their own questions and found answers that showed the eternal relevance of biblical truth."[81] The issue of revelation, which has so bedeviled Jewish theology in the modern period, is sidestepped entirely here. One need not ask what is true, but only what authentically carries on the tradition. One leaves the answer to the decision of Jewish communities.

The thrust here, as one would expect in a feminist theology, is radically

---

[77]Judith Plaskow, *Standing Again at Sinai: Judaism from a Feminist Perspective* (San Francisco, 1990), pp. 19–21.
[78]Ibid., p. 122.
[79]Ibid., p. 21.
[80]Ibid.
[81]Ibid., pp. 35, 53.

egalitarian. Plaskow expresses even more discomfort with the idea of the chosen people than Kaplan had, and no inclination whatever to sneak the doctrine in with euphemisms such as mission or vocation. Plaskow utterly rejects "Judaism's long history of conceptualizing difference in terms of hierarchical separations,"[82] and her suspicion of hierarchy extends not only horizontally (Israel's relation to the nations) but vertically (its relation to God). She rejects the "image of God as dominating Other," criticizing a "relationship [that] is never balanced," in which "the intimacy of the 'you' addressed to a listening other is overshadowed by the image of the lord and king of the universe who is absolute ruler on a cosmic plane." Plaskow goes so far as to claim that "such images of God's dominance give rise to the terrible irony that the symbols Jews have used to talk about God as ultimate good have helped generate and justify the evils from which we hope God will save us." She prefers feminine or gender-neutral images of bountiful nature, of community, of "God as lover and friend."[83] The chapter on God concludes as follows: "In speaking of the moving, changing ground and source, our companion and our lover, we name toward the God known in community that cherishes diversity within and without, even as that diversity has its warrant in the God of myriad names."[84]

It would appear that more than feminist antagonism to "patriarchalism" is at work here. Plaskow is carrying forward the democratization of "God talk" evident throughout the modern period, never more so than in America in recent decades. The redefinitions of covenant surveyed earlier represent an attempt to reconcile traditional belief in the "master of the universe" with the growing self-importance of humanity in the age of science. Soloveitchik, in his famous essay "The Lonely Man of Faith" (1965), correctly saw the Adam I of majesty and honor standing in tension with the Adam II of covenantal relationship;[85] Borowitz only testified further to the tension with his reinterpretation of the covenant so as to make ample room for autonomy, and Hartman provided still more evidence with his reconception of the covenant as an egalitarian marriage bond (not at all like the marriage bonds pictured in, say, Hosea!). Recent Jewish theology, in short, seems content to imagine God as all of Being (Green), and is eager to reconnect alienated modern selves with that Being within and without them. But there is growing evidence of a disinclination to accept a God who has mastery over individual or collective life, who stands over against us as a real, personal deity demanding obedience—and having the right to it, because God is God, and we are not. Only Wyschogrod in the 1980s ventured the

---

[82]Ibid., p. 96.
[83]Ibid., pp. 128–69.
[84]Ibid., p. 169.
[85]Joseph Soloveitchik, "The Lonely Man of Faith," *Tradition,* Summer 1965, pp. 5–67.

claim. One suspects that it will find few exponents in the 1990s, barring an Orthodox successor to the theological mantle of Soloveitchik.

Conclusion

There is reason to believe that Jewish theologians in the coming decades—whatever their denominational affiliation—will be more likely to engage in a combination of the strategies evinced by Green and Plaskow. They will probably move away from personalist conceptions of God in favor of neo-mystical formulations that ring true to contemporary experience of the transcendent. Cohen's turn to Kabbalah is a case in point. Efforts to demonstrate God's presence in history will continue unavailing; convincing answers to why "bad things happen to good people"[86] now, as ever, will continue unavailable. Revelation will not be easily reconceived. The authority for covenant, more and more, will probably be the experience of meaning which the covenant provides. "Voluntarism" and "creativity" will be paramount concerns. Authority will reside within the subcommunity of Jews with which one identifies, rather than in any given, objective set of norms binding the Jewish people, ever and always, as a whole.[87]

If the experience of personal transcendence within such subcommunities is powerful enough to resist dismissal as illusion, higher authority than this may well prove unnecessary, at least in the short run. Jews will likely continue in their present tendency of seeking tradition rather than faith—"sacred fragments" of meaning rather than entire systems of truth. If theologians find meaning in engagement with texts no matter whether they are divinely authored or even inspired, and find transcendence in rituals no matter how literal their status as divine commandment, they are unlikely to devote serious effort to proving the authority of text or ritual. It will be enough to demonstrate their profundity, their groundedness in what Gillman would call Jewish myth, their centrality to what Green would call Jews' spiritual home, their place in the lived experience of a community such as Plaskow's. It will be enough to postulate some reality underlying the various images we have of God, some link between the life we lead as Jews and the nature of ultimate reality. More than this may not be required, and so it will not be forthcoming.

The extent of this tendency should not be exaggerated. Theologians may reject Green's theology as they did Kaplan's, preferring to work with more traditional terms even if they cannot assent to them entirely. They may

---

[86]Harold S. Kushner, *When Bad Things Happen to Good People* (New York, 1983).
[87]For a Conservative statement of this position, see Elliot Dorff, *Conservative Judaism: Our Ancestors to Our Descendants* (New York, 1977), and "Towards a Legal Theory of Conservative Judaism," *Conservative Judaism,* Summer 1973, pp. 76–77.

prove suspicious of the appeal to experience, particularly when religious experience among the highly rationalist, upper-middle-class American Jewish community is if anything even rarer than belief. There is no doubt, however, that appeal to "tradition" (rather than, say, "ethics" or "Halakhah") is now widespread, from moderate Reform on the "left" to modern Orthodoxy on the "right," and no doubt either that the entrance of women into the center of Jewish religious activity—ordained as rabbis, fashioning new rituals, composing new liturgy, and now writing new theology—presages a major shift in the character of American Jewish thought. Given the waning of focus on the Holocaust and the problems besetting covenant theology, the sheer energy underlying feminist theology and the existence of a substantial readership for that theology mean that its role in American Jewish theology as a whole will only increase in coming decades, and will probably increase dramatically.

If in conclusion we were to pose for the next two decades the question that Borowitz asked 20 years ago—the "problem of the form of a Jewish theology"—the answer would seem to be that American thinkers are likely to follow the example of Irving Greenberg's *The Jewish Way* or the acclaimed collection of essays *Back to the Sources* (1986), edited by Barry Holtz. They are likely, that is, to prefer exposition of the meaning to be found in the cycle of the Jewish year over systematic statement of the truth or essence of Judaism; they will turn to modern midrash, examples of how to read traditional texts, with no reading claiming exclusive truth or correctness, rather than to interpretations that claim to give the authoritative account of "Judaism for the modern Jew." The advantage of the former approaches is apparent. One circumvents the problems of revelation that no theologian in the modern period has yet managed to solve, at the same time as one provides what readers, lay and theologically sophisticated, both seem to want. One does not argue for Jewish commitment, at least openly, but rather presumes it—and then suggests content for that commitment. The work of theology takes its place alongside literary criticism, anthropology, psychology, and so forth, much as Rashi greets us on a page of *Mikra'ot Gedolot* alongside Ramban and Ibn Ezra.[88]

The project of going "beyond Buber and Rosenzweig," then, may well lead American Jewish thinkers to explicit embrace—without apology—of the fragmentary forms which their immediate predecessors had seemed to

---

[88]These features of the "market" for Jewish thought in America probably account for the prevalence of introductory volumes such as Emil Fackenheim's *What Is Judaism?* (New York, 1988), Borowitz's *Choices in Modern Jewish Thought,* or even Gillman's *Sacred Fragments*—which concludes with a chapter entitled "Doing Your Own Theology." That is possible for the average reader, of course, only given an understanding of the enterprise radically at variance with the one assumed in the present essay.

adopt of necessity: responsa and commentary, essay and homily; fragments of Halakhah—Jewish "life lived," and of Aggadah—Jewish life reflected upon. They will offer *divrei torah,* words of Torah, along with designs for communities in which these words can be heard. And they will hope, somehow, that it will be enough to carry Jews forward to a time when acts of faith once again come more wholly and more easily.

American Jewish Fiction Turns Inward, 1960-1990

by SYLVIA BARACK FISHMAN

OVER THE PAST 25 YEARS a remarkable literary trend has occurred within the fiction of a significant group of contemporary American Jewish writers. These writers have produced a new, inward-turning genre of contemporary American Jewish fiction which explores the individual Jew's connection to the Jewish people, to Jewish religion, culture, and tradition, and to the chain of Jewish history. Although sometimes witty, this body of work wrestles with weighty spiritual matters: Jewish conceptions of faith and redemption in a post-Holocaust world; the conflict between free will and predestination in the light of Jewish belief and Jewish history; and the notion of the Jewish people as an *am segulah*, a chosen nation.

The new genre of American Jewish fiction has been unabashedly religious in its sensibility; in the words of Cynthia Ozick, one of its main practitioners, it is "liturgical in nature" and "centrally Jewish in its concerns."[1] It thus differs dramatically from the Jewish fiction of the previous quarter century, which had flourished largely by regarding Jews as a species of court jesters or existential heroes—as insightful outsiders who have special value to the Gentile world. Rather than depicting Jews primarily in terms of their universal interest or utility, the new body of fiction treats Jews, Jewish values, and idiosyncratic Jewish topics as intrinsically compelling. In addition, much in the new American Jewish fiction has moved beyond solipsistic preoccupations to an involvement in communal concerns, and has found new vitality in exploring the interaction between the two. For many contemporary American Jewish writers, the exploration of Judaism is more than a personal quest for spiritual identity—it provides an opportunity to investigate the confrontation between individual freedom and group continuity.

Fiction that focuses on Jewish spirituality has not developed in a vacuum, either in terms of the Jewish or the general literary environments. Rather, it draws upon the increased interest in religion among American intellectu-

---

[1] Cynthia Ozick, "Toward a New Yiddish," in *Art and Ardor: Essays* (New York, 1983), pp. 174-75.

als in general. As Philip Zaleski suggests, "Not so long ago religion seemed to many intellectuals like a beached leviathan gasping for air, impaled by the glittering harpoon of science. Today, graying baby boomers pack the church pews and meditation halls, and fundamentalists prosper from Teheran to Texas."[2] Moreover, American Jewish fiction that focuses on Jewish spirituality is one aspect of a larger, extensive trend toward Judaic subject matter among American Jewish writers. There has been a dramatic increase in fiction, memoirs, essays, and poetry which explore themes in Jewish history, culture, and tradition. Much of this literature has been distinguished by a knowledgeable fascination with the internal details of intensely Jewish experience now and in the past.

Jewishly literate fiction can be found today at every brow level; it has attracted a broader reading audience than anyone might have predicted. The past two to three decades have seen the "birth of an authentically Jewish American writer, growing out of and appealing to American-born generations, and enjoying great popularity," testifies Bonny Fetterman, senior editor and director of Judaica at Schocken Books. Fetterman notes that the vigorous sales of books on Jewish topics encourage publishers to acquire and publish ever more numerous volumes of American Jewish literature, as well as to reissue Jewish and Hebrew classics long out of print or unavailable to American audiences.[3] In fiction ranging from highly serious to middlebrow to frankly pulp, aspects of Jewish life which earlier in the century might have seemed to be inaccessible esoterica have been transformed into fascinating exotica instead.

The exploration of intensely Jewish subject matter is now evident both in the works of relatively new authors and in the return to internally Jewish concerns by some established authors. Thus, to touch on a few highlights of change, Elie Wiesel and Chaim Potok pioneered the extensive exploration of Jewish spirituality in American fiction; Arthur Cohen, Cynthia Ozick, and others developed and intensified the treatment of these issues; and Philip Roth responded to a transformed cultural landscape by producing *The Counterlife* (1987). After the notoriety that greeted Roth's early work, leaving him putatively traumatized by adverse reaction from a Jewish reading public uncomfortable with the intimate exploration of Jewish themes and environments, Roth virtually abandoned extensive treatment of overtly Jewish themes for three decades. *The Counterlife* brilliantly examines the paths that Jewish life can take today, from aggressive assimilation

---

[2]Philip Zaleski, "The Priest, the Rabbi, and the Best of Intentions," review of Andrew M. Greeley and Jacob Neusner, *The Bible and Us: A Priest and a Rabbi Read Scripture Together* (New York, 1990), in the *New York Times Book Review*, Sept. 2, 1990, p. 9.

[3]Bonny Fetterman, senior editor and director of Judaica at Schocken, personal communication, Aug. 1, 1990.

to Jewish renewal, from conspicuously complacent suburban America to militantly pious West Bank Israel, and ends by affirming positive Jewish connections. This extraordinary inside look at contemporary American Jewish challenges and options—the most thoughtfully Jewish book he has written since "Eli the Fanatic" and "The Defender of the Faith" appeared in the *Goodbye, Columbus* collection (1959)—is significant not only in terms of Roth's own career but also as a response to the Jewish spiritualist phenomenon in contemporary American fiction.

The spiritualist genre of Jewish fiction is best seen as the dense innermost section of a forest, with diverse flora supported by common nurturing elements and by each other as well. This mutually supportive Jewish spiritual fiction is surrounded by larger but less intensive circles of fiction focusing on diverse Jewish themes, with outer circles which grow progressively less interactive and coherently Jewish. In the outermost areas are numerous pieces of American Jewish fiction written by authors such as Norman Mailer, Erica Jong, and many younger writers, which exhibit only marginal interest in Judaism and Jewish culture.

A marginally Jewish literature might well have been expected in contemporary America because it reflects certain strong trends away from distinctive Jewish attitudes and behaviors, trends often linked under the term "assimilation." Particularistic Jewish themes in contemporary American Jewish literature, in contrast, might be considered to run counter to expectations. Indeed, American Jewish fiction of the past quarter century has often seemed polarized—as has much of American Jewish life—between literature which explores Jewish subject areas, characters, and environments and that which is essentially indifferent to them.

This essay examines recent fiction which draws on Jewish sources and/or deals with Jewish themes. Special attention is devoted to stories and novels that focus on Jewish religious or spiritual issues. Thus, the essay begins with a brief documentation of the broad scope of renewed interest in Jewish topics on the American Jewish literary scene, a phenomenon that is expressed through new works of American fiction, through translations of Jewish fiction originally written in Hebrew, Yiddish, and European languages, and through reissues of earlier Jewish classics.[4] The essay then proceeds to its main focus, an analysis of spiritual American Jewish fiction, through a close look at several significant works by authors such as Chaim Potok, Elie Wiesel, Arthur Cohen, Cynthia Ozick, Hugh Nissenson, Allen Hoffman, Jay Neugeboren, and Rebecca Goldstein. The essay indicates the thematic interrelationships between these works and some earlier pieces of American Jewish fiction and notes the impact which these themes have had

---

[4]Complete citations are provided for books closely analyzed or quoted. Only publication dates are provided for other books mentioned.

on some established Jewish writers as well. Finally, the essay explores possible reasons for the receptivity of reading audiences to particularistic Jewish fiction and suggests potential directions of such literature in the near future.

THE VARIETIES OF JEWISH EXPRESSION

Particularistic Jewish fiction is now a commonplace on the literary scene. The new literature has, perhaps paradoxically, included a wide range of topics: an attraction to historical periods and religious environments which are more idiosyncratically Jewish than those of contemporary suburban America, especially Orthodox, biblical, Jewish-socialist, or other identifiably Jewish societies; an intense and continuing interest in the human and historical implications of the Holocaust; a proliferation of literature by and about Jewish women; an increased availability of, and readership for, Jewish literature which had previously been inaccessible or unappealing to American Jewish audiences, such as out-of-print books from the immigration period and Hebrew, Yiddish, and European Jewish literature in translation; and, not least, books which focus on or are set in contemporary or historical Israel.

One has only to look backward to the fiction of the celebrities of American Jewish fiction in the 1940s, 1950s, and early 1960s to see the change. During the middle years of the 20th century, American Jewish literature was characterized by a universalistic orientation which defined the Jew through his/her relationship with Gentile Diaspora existence. As Ted Solotaroff perceptively notes, a quarter century ago, American Jewish writing won critical prominence because it brought to the American reading public the perspective of marginality, which "had the implication of standing apart, as the American-Jewish writer was perceived to do with respect to both sides of the hyphen." The American Jewish writer was acclaimed, Solotaroff posits, precisely because he was "an outsider in both the American and Jewish communities" and thus "was enabled to see what more accustomed eyes would miss."[5]

Thus, the Jewish character of the extremely popular Jewish-authored American fiction of the 1950s and 1960s had usually been other-directed: the Jew was presented as an obligatory outsider coping with American society, and/or Jewishness was presented as a theatrical species of ethnic comedy, full of streetwise Jewish humor and peppered with pungent Yiddishisms. This literary stance was probably influenced by the fact that

---

[5]Ted Solotaroff, "American-Jewish Writers, on the Edge Once More," *New York Times Book Review*, Dec. 18, 1988, pp. 1, 31, 33; p. 33.

until the late 1960s most American Jews assumed assimilation was the irresistible trend of the future, and much of the most celebrated (and notorious) American Jewish fiction focused on the process of assimilation. Philip Roth's Alexander Portnoy articulated the assimilatory hunger of his generation: "O America! America! It may have been gold in the streets to my grandparents, it may have been a chicken in every pot to my father and mother, but to me, a child whose earliest memories are of Ann Rutherford and Alice Faye, America is a shikse nestling under your arm whispering love love love love love!" (*Portnoy's Complaint*, 1967).

Orthodoxy in New Jewish Fiction

In contrast, one of the most striking features of contemporary American Jewish fiction is how often it speaks from the inside of the Jewish experience. One aspect of this insider's vision is the depiction of a bewildering array of diverse Orthodox societies and characters. This is a trend that differs markedly from American Jewish literature of the past, where Orthodox characters tended to be cranky old men or force-feeding mothers and aunts. Orthodox Jewish characters and settings now enjoy an unprecedented and variegated focus in new American Jewish fiction.[6] In addition to the authors and works which will be examined more closely later in this essay, Curt Leviant's most recent book, *The Man Who Thought He Was Messiah* (1990), reimagines and retells the life story of Rabbi Nachman of Bratslav in a narrative suffused with both spirituality and sensuality. The prolific Isaac Bashevis Singer's novella *The Penitent* (1983) is a tour de force, rejecting what the protagonist characterizes as the nihilistic libertinism and empty materialism of current Western society and championing every legal and spiritual aspect of right-wing Orthodoxy. Daphne Merkin's novel *Enchantment* (1986) is set in the little-publicized world of upper-class Orthodox German Jews on New York's West Side. Nessa Rapoport's first novel, *Preparing for the Sabbath* (1981), portrays a young woman struggling with the conflicting demands of youthful passion and spirituality, Orthodoxy and secularism, in both American and Israeli settings. Both the title of Allegra Goodman's first collection of short stories, *Total Immersion* (1989), and the themes, imagery, and subject matter of many of the stories reflect her childhood in an Orthodox family in Hawaii. Steve Stern, in *Lazar Malkin Enters Heaven: Stories* (1986), creates a mythical Jewish neighbor-

---

[6]For discussions of Orthodoxy in contemporary publishing, see Thomas Friedman, "Back to Orthodoxy: The New Ethnic and Ethnics in American Jewish Literature," *Contemporary Jewry* 10, no. 1, Spring 1989, pp. 67–77; Joseph Lowin, "Herman Wouk and the Liturgical Novel," *Jewish Book Annual* 44, 1986–1987, pp. 43–54; and B. Barry Levy, "The Orthodox Publishing Explosion in Perspective," *Jewish Book Annual* 44, 1986–1987, pp. 6–17.

hood in the South, the land of Pinch, which is inhabited by a band of emaciated, cabbalistic yeshivah boys. Savagely humorous depictions of the idiosyncrasies and foibles of Orthodox environments are found in the pages of Tova Reich's *Mara: A Novel* (1978), which knowingly depicts wealthy contemporary Orthodox New Yorkers, and *The Master of the Return* (1988), which satirizes the spiritual searchings of a motley collection of *ba'alei teshuvah*, born-again Jews, who have gathered under the aegis of the Bratzlaver Hassidim in Israel.

The recent focus on Orthodox Judaism is a reflection of the intense interest which Orthodox societies have evoked among some contemporary American Jews. Examples of both this interest and the reasons why it has grown are found in Anne Roiphe's popular *Lovingkindness* (1987), a tale of an ultra-assimilated, intermarried, and widowed feminist whose daughter becomes a devoutly Orthodox Jew, much to her mother's initial astonishment and distress. The novel illustrates the turn toward Jewish topics both within fiction and within the author's life so directly that it can be viewed as a fable for our times. Born into a casually Jewish New York family on Christmas day in 1935, Roiphe has undergone a dramatic reversal in her professional relationship with Jewish topics. She established her reputation by writing witty books which articulated the conflicts implicit in the feminine mystique; one of the best known was *Up the Sandbox* (1972), a humorous exposé of the angst in a young mother's restricted life. She also wrote, and continues to write, articles promoting feminist causes, such as abortion rights and equal-responsibility parenting. However, an article that Roiphe authored on being an assimilated Jew at Christmastime aroused so much furor and reader response that Roiphe found herself reevaluating her own relationship with Judaism. Discovering that her knowledge base was woefully inadequate, Roiphe began to study Jewish texts in earnest. She soon began to write both about her own voyage of discovery and also about Jews, both knowledgeable and assimilated, in American Jewish environments; one product of her voyage of self-discovery is her nonfiction book *Generation Without Memory: A Jewish Journey in Christian America* (1981).

Lovingkindness, a fictional exploration of Roiphe's recent Jewish interests, accurately reflects a sociological reality: acculturated American Jewish parents sometimes say they might feel more comfortable having their child marry an Episcopalian than a Hassidic Jew; the characters in Roiphe's novel do both. Annie, the protagonist, holds vehement beliefs in individual freedom and secular Western humanism, which are tantamount to fanatical religious convictions. Those convictions are challenged when her daughter, Andrea, after passing through a series of drugs and experimental life-styles, becomes a docile and obedient daughter of Israel in an ultra-Orthodox community in Jerusalem. Andrea's defection to Orthodox Judaism is, in

Annie's eyes, virtually an apostasy into an alien culture. However, Annie subsequently searches her soul and recognizes that assimilation was her own agenda, not necessarily an objectively superior path. In addition, Annie is moved by the genuine warmth, stability, and generous sense of community which she finds among Orthodox Jews. When given the opportunity to tear her daughter away from Orthodoxy, she chooses to side with the administrators of the yeshivah and to support her daughter's new life.

This fascination with Orthodox settings extends to mystery novels and to popular fiction as well. For example, Faye Kellerman's homicide-detective hero meets the widow of a kollel yeshivah student in *The Ritual Bath* (1987); their relationship continues, with the detective serendipitously discovering in a sequel, *Sacred and Profane* (1987), that he has Jewish origins and is thus an appropriate romantic interest for the Orthodox widow. Even the jacket blurb for the latter novel says much about the mainstreaming of Orthodoxy in American Jewish fiction: "Juxtaposing orthodox Judaism against a brutal and brilliantly drawn homicide investigation. . . . The central character of Peter Decker, cop burnout and would-be-orthodox Jew, is unforgettable." Indeed, naming books aimed at a broad trade audience with titles such as "total immersion" and "the ritual bath," which refer to the laws of family purity and the mikveh, would have been almost unthinkable 25 years ago.

Naomi Ragen's *Jepthe's Daughter* (1989) brings a beautiful young Orthodox woman from the affluent American Jewish world to the extremism of a cloistered Jerusalem neighborhood in a disastrous marriage to a rigid and unpleasant Hassidic Jew; she escapes the nightmare by falling in love with a seemingly Gentile gentleman who turns out to have had a Jewish mother. The protagonist of Rhoda Lerman's *God's Ear* (1989) is first a Hassidic rabbi, then an affluent insurance salesman, and finally once again a rabbi and spiritualist in unlikely Kansas. Herman Wouk, whose prolific and popular fictional output had previously seldom made reference to his personal adherence to traditional Judaism, produced protagonist I. David Goodkind, an Orthodox Jewish presidential speechwriter and adviser, in *Inside, Outside: A Novel* (1985).

Historical Novels

Like Orthodox culture, settings that are placed in earlier, more unambiguously Jewish societies from the Bible onward also provide opportunities to explore issues of Jewish identity. In particular, a fascination with the more recent Jewish past and with definitively Jewish environments, such as the *shtetl* or Jewishly intense Eastern European urban areas—often in combination with or leading up to modern American Jewish life—is evident in many different types of American Jewish literature, ranging from difficult and critically acclaimed fiction to easily accessible popular narratives. Many authors turn backward to explore the transformation of Jewish life in American Jewish immigrant societies and then trace the progress of that transformation forward through contemporary times. Some of Harold Brodkey's award-winning, experimental fiction follows this trajectory, as do several of Gloria Goldreich's best-selling popular historical sagas. Romances especially have mined the exotic settings offered by biblical, Eastern European, Sephardic, and Orthodox worlds, often in combination with American Jewish settings. In scores of popular romances by authors such as Cynthia Freeman, Belva Plain, Julie Ellis, and Iris Rainer Dart, landmarks of Jewish history previously relegated to textbooks have become plot devices in the pages of glossy-covered novels.

American Hybrids

A major focus of American Jewish fiction continues to be the interface between Jewish values and mores and contemporary American life-styles and demographics. One paradigm of such transitions is found when a gay man's lover and his former wife both show up at his son's bar mitzvah in Marian Thurm's short-story collection *These Things Happen* (1988). Another area of changing American Jewish demographics is explored in Linda Bayer's *The Blessing and the Curse* (1988) and in Julie Salamon's *White Lies* (1987), which depict the special pressures which infertility and adoption create for Jews. Indeed, Jewish peoplehood, in all its permutations, continues to attract much literary attention. Johanna Kaplan's fiction richly and often humorously captures the flavor of urban Jewish middle-class life; in Kaplan's work (*Other People's Lives*, 1975; *O My America*, 1980), conflict between Jewish-radical ideals, the more traditional historical Jewish heritage, and classical American dreams is played out alongside the conflict between several generations of American Jews. Roberta Silman also depicts the volatile relationships between Eastern European Jews and their assimilated offspring in books such as *Somebody Else's Child* (1976), *Blood Relations* (1977), and *Boundaries* (1979).

Fiction about Sephardic Jewish Americans is beginning to appear more frequently as well: Sally Benforado's stories tell of a Turkish Sephardic community descended from Spanish Jewry, some of whom find their way to the United States; stories by other new Sephardic-Jewish American authors such as Gloria Kirschheimer and Ruth Setton, each portraying a warmly human and humorous, idiosyncratic world, have been appearing in diverse journals and magazines.

Jewish socialism, another historically important element in shaping

American Jewish life, has appealed to some authors as an authentic voice of the Jewish psyche, and many authors have set their works in the urban, socialist environments of the American Jewish past. Among the best of these books, Grace Paley's short-story collections (*Enormous Changes*, 1974; *Later the Same Day*, 1985) depict a divorced daughter of two Jewish socialists as she develops her own calling to social activism and as she visits her parents in the Children of Judea retirement home. Vivian Gornick's memoir, *Fierce Attachments* (1987), vividly portrays the Jewish socialist Bronx and its colorful denizens. The historical role of socialism in American Jewish life is explored more prosaically in the novels of Meredith Tax.

Holocaust

Among the most striking of all the preoccupations of contemporary American Jewish fiction has been its obsession with the Holocaust and the lost communities of Eastern Europe. Sometimes the connection is indirect. Dozens of novels have been published over the past three decades which bring a 20th-century sensibility to persecutions, massacres, and expulsions in earlier Jewish history. Among the more notable authors dealing with subjects such as Jewish life during a variety of historical persecutions are Joanne Greenberg (*The King's Persons*, 1963, 1985) and Roberta Kalechofsky (*Bodmin, 1349: An Epic Novel of Christians and Jews in the Plague Years*, 1988). More often, Holocaust themes are explored directly in recent fiction. Elie Wiesel himself once trembled at the notion that one might transform the unutterable suffering of the victims of the Holocaust into art, and consoled himself only with the knowledge that it was his sacred duty to bear witness to the enormity of what had occurred. However, judging by the proliferation of both serious and popular fiction dealing with the Holocaust today, this anxiety no longer seems to deter many authors.

During the past 25 years, scores of Holocaust-related novels, both autobiographical and fictional, and memoirs have been published in the United States. The Holocaust motif in American Jewish literature runs the gamut from simply told personal tales to philosophical explorations of the meaning of evil to lightly fictionalized historical chronicles to cinematic soap operas in which scenes of agonized suffering are interspersed with graphically depicted sexual activity. The expansion of Holocaust-related American Jewish fiction has also given rise to an accompanying critical literature, much of which has been published by university presses, additional testimony to the critical status which Jewish literature continues to enjoy.[7]

---

[7]For example, a thorough and sensitive exploration of treatments of the Holocaust in American Jewish literature can be found in S. Lillian Kremer, *Witness Through the Imagination: Jewish American Holocaust Literature* (Detroit, 1989); see also Dorothy Bilik, *Immigrant*

Holocaust themes, along with other motifs of Jewish history, tradition, culture, and ethnicity, have been thoroughly mainstreamed, even among the most cosmopolitan of American Jewish writers. Significantly, most major contemporary American Jewish writers have at least one work which focuses on the Holocaust. Among Saul Bellow's most powerful works, *Mr. Sammler's Planet* (1970), which won a National Book Award in 1971, depicts a fastidious elderly Polish Holocaust survivor living in Manhattan during the heyday of the youth culture, who finds himself shocked and sickened by the barbarism of life in New York. In Bellow's recent novella *The Bellarosa Connection* (1989), the story's most impressive character is obsessed with facilitating the meeting between her husband and Billy Rose, who saved her husband and other Jews from the Holocaust by secret ministrations. Bernard Malamud deals with Holocaust themes obliquely but powerfully in *The Fixer* (1966), a reworking of the Yakov Beilis blood-libel case in Russia. Malamud's last novel, *God's Grace* (1982), draws more overtly than his previous work on Jewish materials and is informed by a Holocaust-related motif. Significantly, in his earlier novel *The Assistant* (1957), Malamud's protagonist has little interest in Jewish literature, liturgy, or ritual, and states that to be a Jew means "to do what is right, to be honest, to be good" and to "suffer" for other people. In *God's Grace*, however, the protagonist is a descendant of a rabbinic genealogy and has himself studied for the rabbinate; in his postnuclear Holocaust argument with God, he utilizes Jewish sources in theology, liturgy, and rabbinic literature. Norma Rosen's *Touching Evil* (1969) and Susan Fromberg Schaeffer's *Anya* (1974) are each stirring depictions of the Holocaust and its impact. Seymour Epstein's *A Special Destiny* (1986) sensitively portrays the friendship between a young German-Jewish refugee who becomes a successful playwright and the son of an unhappy Bronx Jewish family who is obsessed by the Holocaust.

Some American Holocaust literature has been controversial because of the ambiguous nature of its Jewish characters. For example, Leslie Epstein's *King of the Jews: A Novel* (1979) stirred up feelings of betrayal among some Jews with its focus on Jewish collaboration; his more recent *Goldkorn Tales* (1984) tells stories about an atheistic Holocaust survivor who contrasts his love of civilization's delights with the decline of New York City life. Jerome Badanes's *The Final Opus of Leon Solomon* (1989) presents a complicated man—survivor of Auschwitz, thief of Judaica documents from the New

---

Survivors: Post-Holocaust Consciousness in Recent Jewish-American Fiction (Middleton, Conn., 1981); Sidra Ezrahi, *By Words Alone: The Holocaust in Literature* (Chicago, 1980); Alvin Rosenfeld, *A Double Dying: Reflections on Holocaust Literature* (Bloomington, 1980); and David Roskies, *Against the Apocalypse: Responses to Catastrophe in Modern Jewish Culture* (Cambridge, 1984).

York Public Library, and suitor of a black radio personality; both witness and obsessive personality, Solomon is far from the stereotypically heroic survivor. (Badanes earlier gained recognition as the author of the 1981 award-winning documentary *Image Before My Eyes*, an homage to the rich Jewish life of prewar Poland.) Popular American novels have also drawn on Holocaust-related subject matter. Indeed, it often seems that the use of the Holocaust as a plot device has become *de rigueur* in American Jewish fiction.

Israel

Israel, both as a separate subject and in combination with other aspects of Jewish history, including the Holocaust, continues to figure prominently in American Jewish fiction, albeit no longer through the romantic glow it had enjoyed earlier in Leon Uris's *Exodus* (1958). Ted Solotaroff cogently notes that "the survival of Israel has been the paramount concern of organized Jewish life and probably the paramount source of Jewish identity" during the past quarter of a century.[8] American Jewish fiction dealing with Israel, which has increased in recent years, can be divided into three basic types: serious explorations of Israeli life, society, and history; popular fiction, including romances and mysteries, which make use of Israel as an exotic and appealing locale; and works which, rather than portraying Israeli life as an entity unto itself, present the Jewish state in its relationship to American Jewish life, as an alternative or as a source of revitalization.

Many of the motifs in Mark Helprin's *Refiner's Fire*,[9] for example, are emblematic of the wellsprings of Jewish renewal which American Jewish writers find in Israeli history and settings. Helprin gathers the most unlikely and seemingly dejudaized characters from a wide variety of settings and shows how their lives are given shape and meaning through their encounters with the land and people of Israel. In the novel, a Virginia gentleman goes first to New York in an attempt to give his life more Jewish content and consults a rabbi "whose advice consisted of coldly instructing him to purify his pots and pans by boiling water in them and dropping a hot brick." However, it is not until he bravely volunteers to serve as captain for a ship bearing illegal Holocaust survivor victims past hostile British marines into Palestine that "Paul Levy became a Jew." Helprin portrays Israel as being suffused with deep Jewish meaning, so that a gravely wounded soldier, an orphan who has been presumed doomed more than once in his life, looks out at trucks driving along the road and feels "that even the light and

---

[8]Solotaroff, "American-Jewish Writers."
[9]Mark Helprin, *Refiner's Fire: The Life and Adventures of Marshall Pearl, a Foundling* (New York, 1977).

motion of a truck blasting down the sea road were at every moment linked to an artful and all-powerful God." For Helprin and other American Jewish authors, ideas such as the ingathering of Jewish exiles and divine ordering of the life of the individual and the people seem to thrive on Israeli soil.

On a less edifying plane, note must be taken as well of the extraordinary proliferation of thrillers, mysteries, and political fantasies set in Israel. Paul Breines terms this "the Rambowitz syndrome," and comments that he knows of "roughly fifty" novels which "are linked by their idealized representation of Jewish warriors, tough guys, gangsters, Mossad agents, and Jews of all ages and sexes who fight back against their tormentors. . . . In their tough Jewish fantasies we meet muscular, manly Jews who have left behind their historic neuroses and nearsightedness in favor of fighting and fucking. We might . . . call them the first normal Jews in all of modern literature."[10]

Feminism

If Israel, the Holocaust, and intensely Jewish societies are some of the specifically Jewish themes and settings most utilized in contemporary American Jewish literature, feminist exploration is one of the most significant new generic movements.[11] In fact, feminism is often linked with Israel, the Holocaust, and Jewish societies in American Jewish fiction. Most commonly, however, feminist issues within Jewish and American culture have been explored in familiar American Jewish settings. The protagonists of American Jewish feminist literature, which includes a number of accomplished and promising writers, must struggle with a multiplicity of identities: they are Jewish, they are Americans, they are women, they are daughters and wives and lovers and mothers, they are moderns, they are heirs to an ancient tradition—not necessarily in order of importance. Among the most significant fiction dealing with Jewish feminist issues is that written by Cynthia Ozick, Grace Paley, Tillie Olsen, Alix Kates Shulman, Francine Prose, Vivian Gornick, Rebecca Goldstein, Anne Roiphe, Marian Thurm, Lynn Sharon Shwartz, and Marge Piercy. Jewish mythic exploration of feminist issues can be found in the fiction of E. M. Broner and Kim Chernin.

It is a mark of how pervasive all these trends are that even some writers who previously seemed remote from Jewish life subsequently wrote on more particularistic Jewish themes—notably Joseph Heller (*God Knows*, 1984),

---

[10]Paul Breines, "The Rambowitz Syndrome," *Tikkun*, Nov./Dec. 1990, pp. 17–18.
[11]For a fuller exploration of Jewish feminist literature, see Sylvia Barack Fishman, *Every Life a Song: Changing Portrayals of Women in American Jewish Fiction* (Hanover, N. H., forthcoming, Fall 1991).

Stanley Elkin (*The Rabbi of Lud*, 1987), and E.L. Doctorow (*The Book of Daniel*, 1971; *World's Fair*, 1985). However, the Jewish consciousness of these skilled writers is expressed primarily in a depiction of attenuated Jewish ethnicity. Even Philip Roth, who probably knows and understands the hearts of a large segment of American Jewry better than any other living writer, and whose novel *The Counterlife* does explore aspects of Jewish spirituality, primarily composes variations on psychological or sociological realities. Fundamentally, therefore, the Jewish interests of these writers differ profoundly from the central and earnest Jewish spirituality of the authors who are the true subject of this essay.

THE SPIRITUAL QUEST

Within the works of the spiritual genre of recent American Jewish writers, characters are not merely or even necessarily religiously observant themselves, but they are embarked upon spiritual or religious quests, either as individuals or as part of a group. The environments in which they live range from those that are densely Jewish to those that are openly hostile to Judaism, but the characters search within these environments for sources of faith and redemption as articulated by richly diverse strands of Jewish tradition and as informed by a post-Holocaust awareness of the absolute existence of evil.

Within Jewish spiritualist fiction, several important motifs emerge repeatedly. First, and perhaps most surprisingly, supernatural agents of redemption, messiahs and/or golems, figure in the works of many, including Elie Wiesel, Chaim Potok, Arthur A. Cohen, Cynthia Ozick, Allen Hoffman, Curt Leviant, Hugh Nissenson, and Rebecca Goldstein. Second, orphans—symbolic of a people who have become, in Paul Cowan's poignant phrase, "orphans in history," due to persecution and assimilation—are protagonists in the works of Wiesel, Cohen, Ozick, Nissenson, Jay Neugeboren, Mark Helprin, and others. In addition, fiction by Potok, Neugeboren, Roth, and others focuses on the divergent spiritual paths taken by two brothers, with the subsequent death of one brother and the survival—and guilt feelings—of his sibling. The dead-brother motif illustrates the continuing relevance of the divine injunction to "choose life" in the midst of the bewildering and momentous choices open to Jews today. In Potok and Neugeboren the introduction of Levirate marriage also speaks to issues of Jewish continuity. In addition, the "accident"—the sometimes half-intentional, sometimes random, sometimes externally imposed occurrence which profoundly affects individual Jews and Jewish societies, emerges as a major and spiritually symbolic plot element in the fiction of authors as different as Wiesel,

Potok, and Neugeboren. Moreover, many books testify to the amazing survival of the spark of Jewish spirituality, *dos pintele yid*, in the hearts of Jews who might seem externally lost to Jewish life, as Jews scattered across the Diaspora or lodged in the heart of Israel continue to reimagine themselves, to reinvent themselves, and to ask, "What is a Jew?"

The authors who focus on Jewish spirituality often seem to share a symbolic language, a loosely connected system of themes and metaphors. In some cases, this linked symbolic language appears to be consciously allusive, with authors commenting on and developing issues broached by their colleagues. In other cases, shared symbolism seems to grow out of shared concerns rather than out of deliberate commentary. It is not the purpose of this essay to delineate the precise literary kinship between each of the works under discussion, but rather to define and document the overarching Jewish spiritualist concerns that distinguish them individually and as a group. However, the fact that such a kinship exists is significant and notable, because it indicates the richness of this most intensive incarnation of contemporary particularistic American Jewish fiction.

Chaim Potok

Spiritually focused American Jewish fiction emerged as a recognizable phenomenon in the 1960s with the memoirs and stories of Elie Wiesel, which gripped the moral imagination of American Jews, and the fiction of Chaim Potok, which rapidly gained a rather surprising widespread popularity. Potok's fiction flew in the face of conventional wisdom, which in the 1950s and 1960s assumed that traditional Jewish life-styles would be washed away in the rising tides of assimilation. Much of Potok's literary career has been devoted to a sympathetic depiction of traditional Judaism in its various shades and forms, from Hassidism to "modern" Orthodoxy to the careful liberalizations of Conservative Judaism. In each of half a dozen novels, Potok tackles a major aspect of contemporary American Jewish life; each protagonist struggles to reach a compromise solution which creatively blends the demands of Jewish survival, on the one hand, and intellectual integrity, on the other.

In two popular early novels, *The Chosen* (1967) and the subsequent *The Promise* (1969), Potok creates a duo of likable young heroes, one the scion of a Hassidic dynasty, one the son of an Orthodox liberal, a passionately Jewish intellectual. The plot line of *The Chosen*, which blends such appealing elements as baseball and parent-child relationships with the intricacies of American ultra-Orthodoxy, made the latter world accessible to readers largely ignorant of its existence. The two books also exposed the American Jewish reading audience to traditional Jewish life-styles which, far from being monolithic, offer different types of spiritual answers to different kinds of people. Indeed, Potok's novels repeatedly demonstrate that moving away from the most stringent forms of Orthodoxy does not necessarily imply abandoning a commitment to Jewish ritual, culture, and peoplehood.

Perhaps one of Potok's most powerful and interesting works is *In the Beginning*,[12] a novel whose rich literary antecedents enhance its depth and literary nuance. The novel's young protagonist, David Lurie, is a sensitive child growing up and maturing among pious yet politically active Jews in an ethnically diverse, lower-middle-class Bronx neighborhood in the 1920s, 1930s, and 1940s. David's personality and life situation both recall and contrast with those of Henry Roth's young protagonist, David Schearl, in a ground-breaking novel of the Jewish immigration experience, *Call It Sleep* (1935), which was republished and lionized in literary circles in the 1960s. Indeed, both the resemblances and the differences between the two novels are instructive. Like David Schearl, David Lurie is precocious and innately spiritual; like Schearl, Lurie's father displays violent (albeit not sociopathological) tendencies which had a more natural outlet in the farms and fields of Eastern Europe than in the teeming streets of New York City, and his mother has a romantic past which somehow impinges on his identity; like Schearl, Lurie often shrinks from confrontations with both Jewish and anti-Semitic non-Jewish bullies in the mean streets surrounding his apartment house; like Schearl, Lurie finds solace and relative safety in a sickbed and "sleep."

However, whereas Schearl's world could offer him little sustenance aside from maternal love, having sheered off from the supporting matrix of Jewish communal and religious life, in Lurie's world it is religion which gives life substance, structure, and strength. As such, Potok's novel is a telling exemplar of religiosity and spirituality in contemporary American Jewish fiction: in both books, immigration brings pain and dislocation; however, in Potok's novel the religious fervor and communal concerns of the parents repeatedly draw them out of their own pain, discipline and stabilize their personal lives, and allow them to rebuild family and community.

Through the eyes of the at first very young and later the growing David, *In the Beginning* explores answers to the biblical question "What does God require of man?" David's father, Max, once a young activist who fought in the Polish army against the enemies of the Jews, works all of his life in an attempt to live up to the responsibilities which he has assumed. When his brilliant younger brother is murdered, he marries his former sister-in-law and names their eldest son David after his dead brother, in fulfillment of the biblical Levirate law. When their European friends pool their funds to

---

[12]Chaim Potok, *In the Beginning* (New York, 1975).

send the Luries to the United States, Max works tirelessly in his new land until he has brought every contributor over to join him. When the stock market crashes, erasing the funds which he had invested for their communal self-aid group, the Am Kedoshim society, Max ruins his physical and emotional health in the attempt to pay each person back. He faces the Holocaust with an activism undertaken by few (and mostly immigrant) American Jews, with unfortunately little to show for his energies in the end. Seeing the helplessness and vulnerability of even those people who, like his parents and their friends, do active battle with fate, David dreams of a "Golem," a powerful creature who might come to save the Jews from their non-Jewish enemies.

Learning from both his father's example and teaching, David comes to think of duty as a form of spirituality and communication with God. He learns that it is the "job" of man to bring God into each of the places in which he resides; to sing praises to God no matter what befalls him, just as the grasshopper sings the most intensely just before he dies; to help other Jews around the world, especially those who are in danger or enslaved; to befriend widows, the vulnerable, and the lonely; perhaps to "pay back" the enemies of the Jews with vengeance; and to live up to promises which are made to other people, even when they are expensive or difficult.

David struggles until he emerges into his own unique life-affirming mission. He finds his calling in a typically Potokian activity: the rebuilding of Jewish life through an honest but loving scholarly exploration of biblical texts. He has been told since childhood that all beginnings are difficult and painstaking, and that he must be patient. However, he learns that beginnings, however difficult, are humanity's only weapon against death. Out of pain, struggle, and chaos, the Jew defeats the deathly accidents of history by imposing order, by rebuilding, and by naming the new world he creates.

Potok's protagonists continue their attempts, in differing settings, to synthesize the best of traditional Jewish values and behaviors with the best of secular Western humanism. In *My Name Is Asher Lev* (1972), for example, Potok highlights the conflict between the callings of art and Judaism, each of which essentially demands that "Thou shalt have no other gods before me." A conflict that had immense historical and sociological impact on American Jewish life in the first half of the 20th century is examined in *Davita's Harp* (1985), which deals with the tension between the universal ideals of socialism and the particularistic prescriptions of Judaism: how can one be simultaneously a member of a chosen people and a citizen of a classless and religion-free world?

Elie Wiesel

Potok's popular yet serious novels were a major initiating force in the exploration of Jewish spiritual themes. Immense strength was continually added to the critical appeal of such fiction by the moral weight of more than a score of memoirs, short stories, novels, and essays in over three decades of writing by Elie Wiesel. Although he writes in French, Wiesel is surely the dean of American Jewish Holocaust writing. A 1986 Nobel Prize winner, Wiesel achieved international prominence as the voice of the Holocaust survivor. He has devoted his life to bearing witness to the horrors of the Holocaust, "to wrench the victims from oblivion. To help the dead vanquish death." While only one of his earlier books, *Night*,[13] deals directly with his experiences at Auschwitz, all of his works are ineradicably informed by those years.

Wiesel can never forget—and he never lets the reader forget—that the Holocaust has profound spiritual implications for contemporary Jews. Indeed, one recurring motif in Wiesel's work is the agonizing conflict between the prophetic ideals of justice and mercy, on one hand, and the physical and emotional strength needed for Jewish survival in an evil world, on the other. Having witnessed the utter indifference of much of the world to the near destruction of the Jewish people, Wiesel comes down firmly on the side of Jewish survival. However, he is ever cognizant of the spiritual price that survival exacts. Ultimately, one may say that Wiesel's anguished argument is at least as much with God as with humankind, for having created a world in which even caring and kindly people are forced sometimes to kill innocent creatures.

In *Dawn* (1961), Elisha, the protagonist, is a young man who has survived the Holocaust and joined Jewish soldiers in then Palestine who are fighting to free the land from the hold of the British. Gad, a colleague who indoctrinates new soldiers, insists that only bloodshed will convince the English to leave. He reminds Elisha that the world—which will condemn such bloodshed—repeatedly stands silent when Jews are slaughtered. "The commandment Thou shalt not kill was given from the summit of one of the mountains here in Palestine, and we were the only ones to obey it. But that's over; we must be like everyone else. Murder will be not our profession but our duty." A masked stranger tells Elisha that they now have an "eleventh commandment: Hate your enemy." Thanks to this stranger, Elisha says, "I became part of a Messianic world.... Why has a man no right to commit murder? Because in so doing he takes upon himself the function of God.... Well, I said to myself, if in order to change the course of our history we have to

---

[13]Elie Wiesel, *The Night Trilogy: Night, Dawn, The Accident* (New York, 1985); original English publication dates are: *Night*, 1960; *Dawn*, 1961; *The Accident*, 1961.

become God, we shall become Him." When Elisha is assigned the role of executing John Dawson, a British soldier who is innocent of any specific crime but whose death will teach the British a symbolic lesson, he declares that "the victim" and "the executioner" each "is playing a role which has been imposed upon him. . . . The tragic thing is the imposition."

From the vantage point of *Dawn*, Jews must redeem the world and deliver the Messiah by learning how to defend themselves with force. Wiesel's bottom line is that Judaism forbids turning the other cheek in life-threatening situations, because it is tantamount to suicide. Judaism requires that one kill in self-defense a pursuing agent of death; however, in the modern world, the distinction between a pursuing killer and the civilization supporting that killer is sometimes difficult to draw. In reacting to the necessity for Jewish violence, Wiesel's protagonist demands, "Don't judge me. Judge God," because God "created the universe and made justice to stem from injustice. He brought it about that a people should attain happiness through tears, that the freedom of a nation, like that of a man, should be built upon a pile, a foundation of dead bodies. . . ." Wiesel's protagonist comes to the startling conclusion that Jews must learn "the art of hate" in order to guarantee their physical survival. "Otherwise," he argues, "our future will only be an extension of the past, and the Messiah will wait indefinitely for his deliverance."

Wiesel's writing is powerful, however, not only because of the moral authority which it draws from his Holocaust experiences, but also because it is steeped in the vibrant, rich spectrum of Jewish history and tradition. The sights, sounds, and preoccupations of the streets and yeshivahs of his native Transylvania are woven through all of his fiction and nonfiction. In *A Jew Today*,[14] for example, Wiesel provides a glowing depiction of a Sabbath day in Sighet, a day that was not only restorative in the modern sense, not only punctilious in terms of Jewish ritual, but which was a living testimony to the humanitarian morality of Jewish law:

> . . . with the advent of Shabbat, the town changed into a kingdom whose madmen and beggars became the princes of Shabbat. I shall never forget Shabbat in my town. When I shall have forgotten everything else, my memory will still retain the atmosphere of holiday, of serenity pervading even the poorest houses: the white tablecloth, the candles, the meticulously combed little girls, the men on their way to synagogue. When my town shall fade into the abyss of time, I will continue to remember the light and the warmth it radiated on Shabbat. The exalting prayers, the wordless songs of the Hasidim, the fire and radiance of their Masters. On that day of days, past and future suffering and anguish faded into the distance. Appeased man called on the divine presence to express his gratitude. The jealousies and grudges, the petty rancors between neighbors could wait. As could the debts and worries, the dangers. Everything could wait. As it enveloped

---

[14]Elie Wiesel, "Words and Memories," *A Jew Today* (New York, 1979), pp. 8–9.

the universe, the Shabbat conferred on it a dimension of peace, an aura of love. Those who were hungry came and ate; and those who felt abandoned seized the outstretched hand; and those who were alone, and those who were sad, and strangers, the refugees, the wanderers, as they left the synagogue were invited to share the meal in any home; and the grieving were urged to contain their tears and come draw on the collective joy of Shabbat. The difference between us and the others? the others, how I pitied them. They did not even know what they were missing; they were unmoved by the beauty, the eternal splendor of Shabbat.

It is no wonder that Wiesel recalls, "Like God, I looked at the world and found it good, fertile, full of meaning." Readers find in his works, especially in his novels, such as *The Town Beyond the Wall* (1964), *The Gates of the Forest* (1966), and *A Beggar in Jerusalem* (1970), a mystical conviction of the profound spirituality of the universe and the unavoidable special destiny of the Jewish people. *Souls on Fire* (1972) retells and reinterprets the lives of the Hassidic masters; *The Testament* (1981) depicts the martyrdom of Russia's greatest Jewish poets at the hands of Stalin, as symbolized by the life and death of poet Paltiel Kossover. These works are suffused not only with the bereavement of the Holocaust but with a piercing, almost unbearable awareness of the spiritual riches of the world which the Nazis destroyed.

Hugh Nissenson

The moral dilemmas which Wiesel explores have particular resonance for post-Holocaust Jewish communities. A Jewishly conscious generation of American Jewish writers has looked to a wide variety of contemporary and ancient Jewish source materials in their literary confrontation with human and natural evils. One such writer is Hugh Nissenson, who has reported on the Eichmann trial in Israel (*Commentary*, July 1961), the progress and aftermath of the 1967 Six Day War in Israel (*Notes from the Frontier*, 1968), the impact of the Yom Kippur War (*Present Tense*, Autumn 1974), and the trial of Klaus Barbie in Lyons in 1987 (*The Elephant and My Jewish Problem*, 1988), among other events.

Like Wiesel, Nissenson writes about the bitter irony that the morality of survival often necessitates actions which may seem immoral. In "The Crazy Old Man,"[15] a story which in some ways recalls Wiesel's *Dawn*, two Sabras (native Israelis), are trying to torture information out of a terrified young Arab boy. An older and thoroughly professional Arab lieutenant watches the brutal interrogation without flinching. Suddenly, a seemingly unbalanced elderly Orthodox man who lives across the hall interrupts the interrogation and demands in Yiddish that the Israelis release their prisoners, quoting to them from Isaiah, "No lion shall be there, nor any ravenous

---

[15]Hugh Nissenson, "The Crazy Old Man," in *In the Reign of Peace* (New York, 1968).

beast shall go up thereon, it will not be found there; but the redeemed shall walk there." Ignoring the old man, the Sabras prepare to shoot the boy. The old man grabs the gun and, when the lieutenant tries to escape in the confusion, shocks everyone in the room by shooting the lieutenant: "The first round hit him in the chest, throwing him on his back. The old man walked over to him and emptied the rest of the magazine into his forehead, holding the gun a yard from his face." The boy screams out the necessary information so fast that they can scarcely write it down. Clearly, killing the lieutenant rather than the boy was a tactically superior move, but why was the religious old man willing to perform such a cold-blooded execution himself? Later, the protagonist realizes the motivation—seeing that the killing is unavoidable and longing for the coming of the Messiah, the old man acts as a kind of *shabbos goy* to preserve the purity of the land of Israel and its native-born inhabitants.

The twin upheavals of modern intellectual and social movements and the emigration to the United States, which worked in tandem to subvert the spiritually coherent world of Eastern European Orthodox Judaism, are explored in bleak and bitter detail in Nissenson's novel *My Own Ground*.[16] Schlifka, a vicious, sadistic pimp on the Lower East Side of New York, reveals the concepts which he learned and loved when he was a youngster in an Old World Gemara *heder* and knew *Maseches Shabbes* by heart by the time he was 11. After rewarding his 15-year-old assistant with a prostitute for betraying Hannele, a rabbi's impoverished daughter, Schlifka shares his belief that "for guys like us there are better things. Higher things. . . . Spiritual things." All of the characters in Nissenson's tragic little book—criminals, idealistic socialists, pious old men, and young people caught in the wake of forces larger than themselves—end badly in the wreckage of Eastern European Jewish civilization. As Hannele's father discards lifelong convictions by performing a ritual cleansing of his daughter's suicidal corpse, he instructs onlookers in Yiddish, "Israel speaks to God: When will you redeem us? And he answers: When you have sunk to the lowest level, at that time I will redeem you." A socialist friend of Hannele's, also a lapsed Jew, explains, "He believes we can force the End and bring the Messiah." And the old man continues, "You might live to see the rest: all the sparks restored, the Exile ended, death swallowed up. The Temple, you know, will be rebuilt, and the divine lovers will embrace again in the Holy of Holies, face to face. The King and His bride, who is also called the Shekinah, the Matronit, and Earth." However, as is crucial in Nissenson's fiction, not only is each of these characters ravaged by history, each one of them, in some imperfect way, retains *dos pintele yid*, some spiritual remnant, some tiny spark of the lost Jewish world.

---

[16]Hugh Nissenson, *My Own Ground* (New York, 1976).

Arthur Cohen

Such spiritual struggles are the novelistic flesh and blood of the late Arthur A. Cohen, a major figure on the Jewish literary scene, primarily through the searching intellectualism of his nonfiction books on Jewish philosophy and thinkers. Cohen's versatile works are often driven by the desire to make Jewish sense out of history. He argues that he is not alone in his enterprise, since his "quest" is much demanded by the times. In the introduction to his reader on Jewish thinking in the aftermath of the Holocaust,[17] Cohen comments that "the return of the third generation of American Jews to the Synagogue is motivated by an uninstructed quest for life meaning and the conviction that the Synagogue possesses or should possess a body of insight and instruction." This "quest" is fueled, according to Cohen, by the fact that "the reasons for escape have disappeared," while "a renascent pride . . . founded upon ethnocentrism, or the admiration of a powerful and militant Israel redivivus, or the brandishing of the sword of guilt and anger over a culpable non-Jewish world" has emerged. That pride, in turn, grows out of the knowledge that during the Holocaust "human beings died because they were thought to represent an alien meaning, because they, in fact, did represent a believed meaning, and because they transmitted the value of that meaning." Cohen dedicates his anthology—as he often does his fiction—to the search for these particularistically Jewish meanings.

The protagonists of Cohen's novels are each chosen by providence for a special and specially Jewish role in the world. Some of them respond by fulfilling their Jewish destiny and redeeming the spark of Jewishness within their souls, and some try to escape it. In an early novel, *The Carpenter Years*,[18] both the protagonist, a Jewish apostate, and the rabbi in his largely Gentile community, tire of the burden of chosenness. The rabbi's inner thoughts articulate what he experiences as the relentless responsibilities incumbent upon a serious participant in the nation of priests: "It was as if he had been appointed to come out from New York to be himself a Sabbath for the Jews. . . . He was tired of being something apart: a utensil of God."

The theme of Jewish chosenness is explored most fully in Cohen's complexly layered *In the Days of Simon Stern*,[19] which weaves together messianic strands from diverse periods of Jewish history and varying religions, cultures, and literary forms into a fable with strong political implications. The novel presents Jews as chosen by a repeatedly hostile and genocidal world

---

[17]Arthur A. Cohen, *Arguments and Doctrines: A Reader of Jewish Thinking in the Aftermath of the Holocaust* (Philadelphia, 1970), pp. xvi-xvii.
[18]Arthur A. Cohen, *The Carpenter Years* (New York, 1967).
[19]Arthur A. Cohen, *In the Days of Simon Stern* (New York, 1972).

and chosen as well by their own special culture, life-style, and values. Simon Stern is a Messiah, within the context of the novel, because he labors to physically redeem a group of Holocaust survivors despite the graphically detailed apathy and obstruction of Allied leaders and official agencies. One narrator, Nathan Gaza, reflects on his "Messiah," Simon Stern, and on the nature of the messianic redeemers and their capacity to suffer. Cohen's terms recall both Wiesel's *Dawn* and Nissenson's *In the Reign of Peace*: "Why should one be able to bear suffering? Why should one be able to tolerate the suffering of others? There can be no reason other than the fact of having given suffering to another. Not willingly but involuntarily. The hardest guilt to bear is for the crime one could not have chosen to commit.... That I live and another perish."

Stern and his colleagues labor to build a utopian walled city of refuge, modeled on the historic rabbinic colony in B'nei B'rak, for the cherished remnant saved from the concentration camps. Their purpose is betrayed by a false survivor who attempts to turn their peaceable society into a heavily armed, nihilistic machine for vengeance. However, Stern and the aristocratic Dr. Klay warn the group that reasonableness and "tenacity of will" are the truly Jewish attributes, and that "beyond madness there is still judgement." Although Stern's walled city is destroyed through his own heedlessness, his society endures, for, in this novel's final analysis, endurance through commitment to justice and mercy is the most Jewish attribute of all.

Cohen depicts the persistence of *dos pintele yid*, the spark of Jewishness, in a variety of settings, even in the rocky soil of Communist Russia. Yuri, the Russian Jewish protagonist of *A Hero in His Time*,[20] is traumatized as a young boy watching both Ukrainian Whites and Ukrainian Reds serially executing innocent old Jews as "Jew hoarders." He understands that even Gentiles who hate each other share a mutual hatred of Jews. Yuri learns to survive the brutal Communist system by evading any taint of specialness, by behaving in such a nondescript fashion that he is perceived as being safe. He comments frequently that "anyone who tries to do something to moderate the magisterium of the official view was courageous but misguided, and therefore a fool." However, despite the fact that Yuri has been baptized and that he claims to be a "real atheist," he acknowledges to himself that his parents were "Jew believers," that "they locked up a secret name" inside him, and that he believes unwaveringly in his own personal deity, whom he calls "my Lord, my Adonay, my Elohim, my El Shaddai." To Yuri, these names "mean love and father and spirit and creator and good person," and he utters the names of his personal deity "twice or three times a day." He

---

[20]Arthur A. Cohen, *A Hero in His Time* (New York, 1976).

finds himself secretly but irresistibly drawn to Jews who exhibit artistic and personal courage and discovers that he himself has a religious passion for justice. Finally, when Yuri can choose either to escape to freedom or to become a useful pawn in the Communist system, he rejects the relative safety of both options; instead, he bravely betrays the system and goes back to meet his fate, loyal to his destiny as a poet and a Jew.

Cynthia Ozick

Similar concerns are shared by the brilliant doyen of contemporary American Jewish fiction, Cynthia Ozick. One of the most influential Jewish authors writing today, Ozick's interests are emblematic of the new American Jewish literature at its highest level. She draws on classic Jewish source materials, ranging from biblical and rabbinic texts to Yiddish writers to contemporary fiction. Ozick openly and articulately espouses the creation of "liturgical" spiritual American Jewish literature; she feels that an English rich with Judaic materials must replace the role that Yiddish occupied in Ashkenazi Jewish cultures in expressing the inner heart as well as the external rhythms and concerns of Jewish life.[21] She uses not only all aspects of her own contemporary Jewish reading, thinking, and experience in her writing, but also her broad knowledge of Jewish texts.

If Ozick has one signature preoccupation, it is the conflict between the Jewish intellectual, spiritual, and cultural tradition, on one hand, and the Hellenistic sweep of artistic creativity and secular Western humanism, on the other. The conflict between art and Torah is no mere intellectual game for Ozick; she expresses it in numerous stories and novels as a deep, ongoing, even a mortal struggle. In "The Pagan Rabbi,"[22] for example, she takes to its logical extreme the talmudic prohibition against delight in nature because it may detract from Torah study or serve as a temptation to paganism. The pagan rabbi is a young Orthodox father of many children who eventually abandons his beautiful and pious wife—and loses his life—in an attempt to cohabit with a wood nymph. Too late he discovers that to separate from his Jewish soul is tantamount to death; at the very moment that he is erotically ravished by his mossy beloved, his soul appears as the archetypical wandering Jew, a ragged, bearded old man lugging a tractate of the Mishnah down a dusty road:

> Incredible flowers! Of every color! And noble shrubs like mounds of green moss! And the cricket crackling in the field. He passes indifferent through the beauty of the field. His nostrils sniff his book as if flowers lay on the clotted page, but

---

[21]Cynthia Ozick "Toward a New Yiddish," pp. 174–75.
[22]Cynthia Ozick, "The Pagan Rabbi," in *The Pagan Rabbi: And Other Stories* (New York, 1983).

the flowers lick his feet. His feet are bandaged, his notched toenails gore the path. His prayer shawl droops on his studious back. He reads the Law and breathes the dust and doesn't see the flowers and won't heed the cricket spitting in the field.

Disgusted with his weary and studious soul, the odorous wood nymph—a *belle dame sans merci*—abandons the pagan rabbi. His soul also tells him he will abandon him because he has been faithless:

> "If you had not contrived to be rid of me, I would have stayed with you till the end. . . . In your grave beside you I would have sung you David's songs, I would have moaned Solomon's voice to your last grain of bone. But you expelled me, your ribs exile me from their fate, and I will walk here alone always, in my garden"—he scratched on his page—"with my precious birds"—he scratched at the letters—"and my darling trees"—he scratched at the tall side column of commentary. . . . "The sound of the Law," he said, "is more beautiful than the crickets. The smell of the Law is more radiant than the moss. The taste of the law exceeds clear water."

In the end, the pagan rabbi hangs himself, and the story's narrator symbolically flushes three green houseplants down the toilet.

Ozick's familiarity with intensive Jewish environments suffuses much of her fiction. She is a knowledgeable observer and sometime critic of contemporary Jewish life. As a result, her fiction has the kind of dense Jewish texture that is more typical of the Yiddish writers. The disappearing world of American Yiddish writers is itself evoked in the bittersweet story "Envy; or, Yiddish in America,"[23] in which literary fame seems to depend on the acquisition of a competent translator. While this and some other fictions are set in New York, Ozick's focus in her novels and short stories frequently departs from the typical Eastern European Jewish immigrant/urban milieu. She often deals with the uniqueness of Jewish life and history and the doomed attempts of individual Jews to flee their common destiny with the Jewish people. In the story "A Mercenary,"[24] for example, a Holocaust survivor who attempts to drown his Jewish identity in the black African nationalist struggle unwittingly circles back to the frequent historical fate of Jews; perceived as a middleman, a hybrid and therefore a quisling, he may meet his doom at the hands of the black official he helped the most.

Jewish suffering and the incapacity of most Gentiles to truly enter into Jewish history are explored in "Levitation."[25] The story is told from the viewpoint of Lucy, the converted daughter of a minister married to a Jew. Lucy is putatively a sympathetic fellow traveler, but she loses patience with what she sees as the Jews' obsession with the Holocaust and other "historical atrocities" committed against them; Lucy comes to the conclusion that

---

[23]Cynthia Ozick, "Envy; or, Yiddish in America," in *Levitation: Five Fictions* (New York, 1982); first published in *Commentary*, Nov. 1969.
[24]Cynthia Ozick, "A Mercenary," in *Bloodshed and Three Novellas* (New York, 1976).
[25]Cynthia Ozick, "Levitation," in *Levitation: Five Fictions*.

Jews are "intense all the time . . . the grocers among them were as intense as any novelist." Such suffering is only interesting and real to her if she thinks of Jews dying, like Jesus, to redeem the world. Thus, Lucy decides that "every Jew was Jesus." As Lucy's husband and his friends continue to talk so incessantly that they float to the ceiling, she sees her Gentile friends as "compassionate knights," gallant and gracious and well-behaved.

Lucy's uncomprehending attitude toward, and eventual boredom with, Jewish suffering serves as a critique of universalist attitudes such as those found in Bernard Malamud's 1957 novel *The Assistant*. Malamud's protagonist, Morris Bober, is indeed a grocer who is as intense as the novelist who created him. Morris and his family suffer long and deeply. Frank Alpine, his Italian grocery assistant and disciple, puzzles over the Jewish capacity for suffering: " 'What do you suffer for, Morris?' Frank asks. 'I suffer for you,' Morris said calmly." Morris informs Frank that Jews suffer in order to teach other human beings how to relate empathetically with each other. However, Ozick's Lucy illustrates the naiveté of such a hope. After picturing Jews suffering like Christ, after picturing the martyred Jews of history "as if hundreds and hundreds of crucifixions were all happening at once," after visualizing "a hillside with multitudes of crosses" —Lucy decides that "she is bored by the shootings and the gas and the camps . . . they are as tiresome as prayer." The world causes and tolerates Jewish suffering and is finally bored by it and resentful of hearing about it, Ozick shows us in "Levitation." In Ozick's eyes, it is wrong to try to explain Jewish suffering as a Christological activity; Jews do not suffer in order to redeem the world, they suffer because the world inflicts suffering upon them and then looks away.

Ozick examines the real impact of Jewish suffering on the lives of Jews in her recent works *The Scarf*[26] and *The Messiah of Stockholm*.[27] Her novella *The Scarf* illustrates the devastation of one individual life. The protagonist, Rosa Lublin, watches her beloved little daughter brutally murdered in a concentration camp—but refuses to accept her death. She constructs an entire existence for the girl, whom she imagines to be "a tigress" of strength and beauty. Ozick portrays survivors as idiosyncratic, flawed human beings, rather than as bland symbols, and at the same time makes their pain and confusion palpable.

Ozick explores the lasting destruction which the Holocaust inflicted upon the lives of survivors and indeed upon entire societies. She argues that the riches of Eastern European Jewish intellectualism have been lost despite the rescue of a few pieces of literature. Lars Andemening, the orphaned protag-

---

[26]Cynthia Ozick, *The Scarf* (New York, 1989; a prior version of the story was originally published as "Rosa," in the *New Yorker*, Mar. 21, 1983).
[27]Cynthia Ozick, *The Messiah of Stockholm* (New York, 1987).

onist of *The Messiah of Stockholm*, imagines that he is a kind of Messiah, that he is "Europe's savior," because "he wanted to salvage every scrap of paper all over Europe . . . in all those shadowy places where there had been all those shootings—in the streets, in the forests." But Lars eventually realizes that the shootings and the chimneys that consumed millions of individual Jews consumed their culture as well. Even if he could "save" Bruno Schultz's lost manuscript, "The Messiah," he cannot save Schultz, his colleagues, and his culture.

In *The Messiah of Stockholm* Ozick addresses the paradox that there is no higher, human life without imagination, and yet "there's more to the world than just imagination." Achieving the higher life is ostensibly the goal of Midwestern parochial-school principal Joseph Brill, protagonist of the novel *The Cannibal Galaxy*.[28] Like Lars Andemening, Brill aims for intellectual glory while neglecting human beings and eventually fails them both. "To the stars, ad astra," Brill proclaims, as he devises and implements goals and methods for an all-day school with a dual-curriculum, Jewish and secular, educational program. Ozick's sharp pen provides a scathing critique of Jewish suburban pretensions and mediocrity in this novel, skewering smug Jewish physicians who spend Sundays wearing shorts and beepers, self-serving pedagogues who cheat their students by not taking them seriously as cherished, individual, developing human beings, and school administrators who hope to ride into excellence vicariously on the reputations of their most talented students.

In addition to the obvious Jewish themes of the story—the Holocaust experiences of the principal and his family, the works of Jewish synthesizer Edmund Phlegg which obsess Brill, the dual educational curriculum which he devises—the novel is rich with Jewish allusions. The novel's heroine, Hester Lilt, whose philosophical specialty focuses on the secular field of linguistic logic, delivers a brilliant university lecture in which she interweaves stories about Rabbis Akiva, Gamliel, Elazar, and Joshua with the natural sciences. Using midrashic methods and materials, Ozick's celebrated secular philosopher passionately articulates Jewish distinctiveness and the Jewish triumph over those who would have destroyed them and the Torah down through the ages. Hester's name itself recalls the Hebrew word *hester*, "hidden," as God's face was "hidden" from the Jews during the Holocaust; the biblical heroine Esther, who saved the Persian Jews from annihilation; and also Hester, the isolated adulteress of Hawthorne's *Scarlet Letter*, who lives with her little daughter as a social pariah. Lilt is a melody but also Lilith, the demonic independent woman first given to Adam and then removed to make way for the more pliant Eve. Such wordplay, involv-

---

[28]Cynthia Ozick, *The Cannibal Galaxy* (New York, 1984).

ing the full, 2500-year sweep of Jewish literature and tradition, is one of Ozick's trademarks.

Allen Hoffman

Among other fictions depicting intense, idiosyncratic Jewish themes and environments, one which stands out for its Jewish spirituality as well as its high literary quality is the title story—really a novella—of Allen Hoffman's *Kagan's Superfecta*.[29] "Kagan's Superfecta" takes place in an environment which many might perceive as antithetical to spirituality, a corrupt urban environment in which the protagonist, Moe Kagan, is both an Orthodox Jew, a *kohen*—descendant of the priestly tribe—and a compulsive gambler living on New York's upper West Side. The richly diverse, contradictory, Runyonesque urban world through which Kagan moves is almost exclusively a world of men, as thoroughly known to him as the inside of an old shoe. Fran, his well-meaning but uncomprehending Connecticut-born wife, is an alien in this milieu. In this unholy and imperfect universe, special sections of the synagogue service are auctioned off to the highest bidder, and unpleasant, power-hungry men chant the most sacred passages. However, there is more to Kagan's world than meets the average eye. Kagan sees visions and is accompanied by his own personal angel, Ozzie.

"Kagan's Superfecta" takes the protagonist on a bizarre, picaresque adventure played out on the streets and in familiar buildings within a few-block radius of Kagan's apartment. Early in the story, Kagan lolls in the steamy water of the mikveh (ritual bath) before Yom Kippur, surrounded by the white "submerging and resurfacing" bodies of other men, momentarily losing his anxiety to "the harmony of this purifying pool." Once seated in the men's section of his synagogue, however, he is tormented by visions of his superfecta, the numerical combination which he is sure will win a horse race held on the holiest day of the Jewish year: "The wiggly Hebrew print kept turning into horses before his eyes and the page numbers distracted him to the point of madness. How do they expect a person to pray with numbers on every page?" Struggling to resist the temptation to place a bet and trying to immerse himself in holiness, Kagan notices for the first time that in the Torah portion, "the High Priest drew lots" on two goats—which means that "gambling decides the most important event of Yom Kippur!" Kagan's head aches; shall he violate the sanctity of Yom Kippur to win a huge amount of money, a sure thing, which would change his and Fran's whole life for the better? Hoffman sums up the conflict between man's sacred and profane impulses in prose which manages to be simultaneously hilarious and visionary.

---

[29] Allen Hoffman, *Kagan's Superfecta* (New York, 1981).

Confused by frenetic, vivid hallucinations, Moe Kagan struggles to understand the terms of the world he lives in and to redeem his own soul. He stands at the very threshhold of heaven's closing gates during the *ne'illah* service, blessing the congregation with the other *kohanim* (priests), *tallit* over his head. Kagan prays for his wife, for the imperfect men around him, even for his own evil impulse in the person of the angel Ozzie—Azazel. Even one's evil impulses, Kagan comes to understand, can be disciplined to serve good purposes. He sees at last that each man gambles on his own soul, each Jew through his own actions and thoughts can choose God, life, and peace even at the last moment, at the very brink of disaster. Kagan realizes that "The Lord is the Mikveh of Israel. Through his unity, His oneness, we can be redeemed."

Hoffman is fascinated by the opportunities for holiness which lie directly beneath the surface of everyday life. His narrative voice is pungent with the inflections and reference points of observant, urban, contemporary Jews. Each of his stories might legitimately carry the aphorism which occurs early in "Beggar Moon":[30] "So this is a story about Jews. But it is much more than just a story about Jews; it is a Jewish story." The protagonist, a synagogue regular, gets involved with Bluma, an urban character, a talkative beggar-lady in red knee socks; he does not mean to get involved with her, but after he gives her a few rather generous handouts, she simply adopts him as her own. Moved by the soul-stirring sounds of the shofar during Elul and the High Holidays, he does not have the callousness to get rid of her. Bluma protects him from phony beggars, and she even insists on giving him used clothing for his family. Needless to say, his wife is appalled when she hears things moving in Bluma's hand-me-down bags and sees some rather impressive cockroaches emerging.

The relationship continues, with Bluma always refusing to accept any favor which she cannot in some way reciprocate or which will make her feel helpless or inadequate. Bluma becomes fused in the narrator's mind with both the moon, doomed always to be the lesser and subservient of the luminaries, and with the position of the Jews in what is fundamentally and irrevocably, until the coming of the Messiah, "a Goyishe world." Bluma grows crazier and crazier, until even her friend cannot help her. Grieving for her, not resigned to her fate, he has no choice but to wait hopefully, alert to any sign that the world—or Bluma—may be waking to some fundamental change.

---

[30]Allen Hoffman, "Beggar Moon," in *Kagan's Superfecta*.

Jay Neugeboren

One of the great spiritual conundrums from the Bible onward, the conflict between predestination versus free will, is explored in Jay Neugeboren's *The Stolen Jew*,[31] played out in the murky arena of family life. The story of the novel is seen through the eyes of Nathan Malkin, a 64-year-old author and wealthy businessman whose brother Nachman dies on the first page of the novel. Returning from Israel to New York to join his family for *shiva*, the period of mourning, Nathan reviews the life that he and Nachman shared, in painful detail. The family in which the Malkin brothers grew up epitomizes the wreckage of Jewish values on the rocky soil of American materialism.

One vignette which Nathan recalls is an especially effective symbol for the loss of an entire belief system. Nathan's father, a gentle, scholarly man but poor provider, who loved his large library of Jewish books, entrusted Nathan, the older child, who identifies strongly with his father's values, with the task of taking these *sefarim* outside before Passover each year to dust and air them. One year, however, the mother, an ambitious, domineering woman who derives joy from degrading her husband, sets her sweet, gentle, innocent younger son, Nachman, to do Nathan's task. Nathan pleads with her to let him take the books inside, because dark rain clouds threaten certain disaster to his father's library, but his mother sadistically prevents him from saving the books. As the rain pours down on the pages, turning them to pulp, the father returns home from work to witness his wife's triumphant glee at his irrevocable loss. Nathan is bitter, furious, tearfully empathetic, and little Nachman bewildered. The parents fling insults at each other and the two children huddle under the bed; Nathan retreats into the one task he can accomplish, to comfort his younger sibling, to be his brother's keeper.

Witnessing her repeated assaults on his father's dignity, Nathan hardens his heart against his mother; in response, she flaunts her favoritism, lavishing Nachman with affection and taunting Nathan with his putatively hard, cold nature. So malicious is her need to undermine her husband that she even subverts his attempt to provide Nachman, who is a musical prodigy, with violin lessons. Thus, Nachman's destiny is stolen from him; partially as a result, he matures into a sensitive but troubled adult who drifts in and out of mental institutions. He is his mother's favorite, but he emulates his father's tragically passive persona.

At the other end of the equation, Nathan writes no more books after his brilliant first novel, because he feels he must earn money to acquire for Nachman the professional help he needs. Nathan goes into business, suc-

---

[31]Jay Neugeboren, *The Stolen Jew* (New York, 1981).

ceeds brilliantly, helps his parents and his brother—and abandons his craft; his destiny also has been stolen from him. Determined that he will never be treated as his father has been treated, he emulates his mother's ambition and callousness. Nachman is "chosen" to be Abel/Jacob, the mother's favorite, the gentle dweller of the tents, and Nathan is left with the role of Esau, forced into a rough-and-tumble life of necessity.

However, Nathan's mother too is cheated of her dreams: like many Jewish women described in immigrant fiction, she takes on American values more rapidly and completely than her husband. Trapped in a lower-middle-class milieu with a husband who cannot or will not achieve the successful American life-style she longs for, Nathan's mother lashes out in frustration. She derides her husband's love for Jewish scholarship, Nathan recalls, and "even on Shabbos she would yell at him that he should go out and try to find an extra job, that she didn't have enought money to feed us, that Nachman and I would become sick and weak like him. It was terrible. . . . She would cry out to us. Oh you should have seen him! He was so handsome and strong! But in America, look at him." In this richly complex dance of betrayal, all are guilty and all are bereaved. All are stolen Jews.

In a novel within the novel—Nathan's one critical and popular success—Neugeboren examines the role of the Diaspora in exacerbating a different kind of theft, the theft of Jewish integrity, unity, and *ahavat yisrael*, love for other Jews, in the setting of 19th-century Russia. The story centers on the conscription of Jewish boys into the czar's army, specifically, the practice of rich parents buying substitutes for their sons—or even the kidnapping of poor boys by the Kehillah, an organization of Jewish communal leaders which served as a liaison between the czars and the Jewish masses. A father who has condemned these practices—citing Maimonides: "Not a single Jewish soul shall be delivered"—is later cruelly forced to choose between seeing his own son, a musical prodigy, drafted, or hypocritically allowing his son to be replaced by a poor, brilliant Talmud student. He chooses to save his own child, rather than to follow Maimonides' dictum of communal unity and self-sacrifice. The years of army service understandably strip the Talmud scholar of both his innately gentle nature and his scholarship; his spiritual birthright is stolen from him by an "accident," an external selection process. Thus, Malkin's fiction has a strong symbolic relationship with the "real" characters. And just as the characters in a novel are "free" to behave as they wish—although the novelist decides what they will in fact do—human beings are free to determine their own destiny—and yet freedom is a delusion. The frontispiece to Nathan Malkin's novel *The Stolen Jew* quotes from *Pirkay Avos*, "The Sayings of the Fathers": "Everything is foreseen, yet freedom of choice is granted. . . ."

Rebecca Goldstein

Another interesting new author in the spiritualist mode is Rebecca Goldstein, whose short stories and novels are grounded in a thorough familiarity with traditional Jewish life. Her work explores topics as different as the difficulties experienced by children of Holocaust survivors and the difficulties experienced by urban New York Jews in preppy suburban Princeton. Goldstein's story "The Legacy of Raizel Kaidish"[32] depicts the daughter of Holocaust survivors whose childhood is subsumed by her father's sadness and the "quite blue fury" of her mother's total "goodness"—a goodness later revealed to be flawed indeed.

Goldstein's protagonist in *The Mind-Body Problem*[33] is a "beautiful, brainy" young woman, Renee Feuer, who grew up in a strictly Orthodox home. After leaving home for college and then graduate school, Renee moves incrementally away from her training. She does her undergraduate work at Barnard, where she discovers modern Orthodoxy, sexuality, and totally secularized Jews, and is working on a Ph.D. in philosophy at Princeton during the action of the novel. The scope of her religious antecedents allows her to experience particularly poignant varieties of knowledgeable spiritual ambivalence. Although Renee is no longer religiously observant, she is repeatedly drawn to the richness of Orthodox life, both as she remembers it from her parental home and as she observes it in the home of her brother and sister-in-law, a pious young couple living among others of their kind in Lakewood, New Jersey.

One of the pleasures of Goldstein's novel is that religious environments are depicted unself-consciously and with a balanced awareness of both their strengths and weaknesses. One aspect of Orthodoxy which troubles Renee has to do with the position of women within Orthodox societies, especially when life circumstances put women into marginal positions. Both Renee's sister-in-law, Tzippy, and her childhood girlfriend, Fruma, have experienced negative attitudes toward women because of their infertility problems; in societies which assume that divine providence has reasons for everything, even physical problems can acquire moral significance. And yet, despite living in a world in which their women friends, rather than their husbands, must coach them through labor, because their husbands will not be bothered with the *weibszachen* of natural childbirth after infertility problems are solved, Tzippy and Fruma enjoy religious depth, meaningfulness, and serenity which Renee envies. Goldstein captures Tzippy's spirituality, which extends into her daily actions, in a tender vignette:

---

[32]Rebecca Goldstein, "The Legacy of Raizel Kaidish—A Story," *New Traditions*, Spring 1985.
[33]Rebecca Goldstein, *The Mind-Body Problem* (New York, 1983).

All at once I was crying, and Tzippy silently joined in. She had only known my father in the last year of his life, but a strong and special closeness had developed almost immediately between them. It was she who had shown my numbed family the way when he lay dying in the final days. We had already distanced ourselves from the man lying there, smelling of death and wearing the face of martyrdom. That wasn't my father suffering; my father had already gone. But little Tzippy had shown us who that person was, had walked into the room and straight over to him, kissing him, holding him, talking to him as she always had. How he had smiled at her with that wasted face.

Renee ascribes much of her own attachment to the spiritual aspects of Judaism to her beloved father, a genuinely sweet-natured, "scandalously underpaid" cantor whom she describes as "passionately religious" and "supremely content" with his lot:

His pure, sweet song was like a picture of his soul. Snatches of chazzanes would escape from him all day long, pieces of the internal singing that must have been almost constant with him. He had loved his work in all its aspects: chanting the prayers on behalf of the community, comforting the sick and the sad, instructing the boys in preparation for their bar mitzvahs. His teaching powers were legendary. He was sent all the unteachable boys from around Westchester County—the retarded, the disturbed, the hyperactive. Each yielded to his softness and managed to be bar mitzvahed. . . . And he maintained his sweet outlook throughout his final terrible illness. One of the more illustrious members of his congregation said to me, as we watched my father limping in great pain up to his place on the bimah shortly before his death, "There's not a man I envy more."

When Renee abandons religious ritual for the study of philosophy, there is more than a little religious intensity and spiritual searching in her choice. She marries a mathematical genius, and once again her choice is related to a search for definitive spiritual answers. Much to her surprise, she finds that her scholarly, Jewishly ignorant husband is as sexist—perhaps more so—as her ultra-Orthodox brother. Her college best friend, Ava, has divested herself not only of feminine dress and feminine wiles but also of any gentleness, supportiveness, or sweetness, such as those retained and deepened by Tzippy and Fruma. Renee takes a lover, a thoroughly assimilated German Jew, who gives her a splendid time in bed but shocks her by his disinterest in taking her on as a soulmate for life.

Renee finds herself increasingly disoriented and spiritually hungry. Moved by a rereading of I. B. Singer's "Short Friday" to prepare an authentic Sabbath meal, Renee prepares traditional foods: challah, chollent, gefilte fish. Her classmate Ava sees her behavior as atavistic and mocks her unmercifully; her husband and her lover are so ignorant that they do not even have any conception of the significance of their luncheon cuisine. Chilled by the intolerance and apathy of her Jewish companions, Renee notes that she "had never felt quite so separate":

I stared out at the winter-stripped elms and remembered Shabbos at home. I could hear my father's singing, the sweet warm tenor rising up in his love. Beside it, the secular chatter of the Jewish goyim I had surrounded myself with, circumcised by doctors and not knowing what it is to yearn for the coming of the Messiah, sounded insignificant and despicable. But I had despised the religiosity of my past. How could I expect anyone to share my outlook, contradictory as it is?

CONCLUSION

The quandary experienced by Rebecca Goldstein's protagonist is paradigmatic of realities affecting the lives of American Jews. American Jewish life during the past two decades has undergone a simultaneous attenuation and intensification among different segments of the population. Anyone who currently teaches in a Judaic studies department on a college campus can testify that today's young adults—third-, fourth-, and fifth-generation American Jews who are increasingly the plurality in American Jewish communities—carry little in the way of Jewish cultural baggage. At the same time, they are far less hostile to traditional Judaism than many of their parents or grandparents may have been. They express feelings of empowerment and comfort in an open culture which they take for granted, and many of them also express a yearning for greater knowledge of their spiritual and cultural roots.

The current openness to Jewish exploration was preceded by two decades of intense ethnic awareness in the intellectual and emotional lives of select sectors of American Jewry. Unlike second-generation American Jews in prior periods of American Jewish life, third- and fourth-generation Jews in the late 1960s, 1970s, and 1980s felt little need to "prove" their patriotism, their sophistication, or their modernity by jettisoning their Jewishness. During this period, groups of young American Jews interested in creative interaction with Jewish tradition formed *havurot* in which to worship and study together. Jewish studies departments proliferated on college campuses across the country. Books and films on earlier periods of American Jewish history were extensively reissued and enjoyed broad new audiences.

Both the authors and the reading audiences of American Jewish literature were profoundly affected by events in Israel, especially after the 1967 Six Day War, which marked a watershed in American Jewish involvement with Israel. That war awakened in American Jewry a terrified recollection of the Holocaust, while the reunification of Jerusalem and apparent strength of the Israeli state created widespread feelings of Jewish pride and confidence.

Moreover, Jews who once fled from the sights, sounds, and social pressures of the urban ghetto are now anxious to read literature which recaptures for them scenes and experiences from their childhood and youth. In addition, rising tides of international anti-Semitism, revisionist attempts to deny the Holocaust, and the twin challenges of intermarriage and assimilation have led many self-proclaimed Jewish secularists to take a more sympathetic view of traditional Jewish life and thought.

The combination of a cultural acceptance of ethnic particularism, increased Jewish awareness and pride, and diminution of hostility to explicitly Jewish concerns has contributed to the growth of a wide reading audience for an American Jewish literature which differs in kind from the American Jewish literature of the 1940s, 1950s, and early 1960s. Contemporary American Jewish literature, reflecting the realities of American Jewish life itself, inhabits a world that is by its nature "contradictory." But unlike the situation in the past, today's American Jewish writers draw freely on Jewish tradition and culture, as they strive to regain the richness and warmth of Jewish tradition, while retaining the broad-ranging opportunities of American culture and society. They are unafraid to confront their own spirituality, and more and more they are finding that it is a specifically Jewish spirituality. They quest for meaningful Jewish concepts of faith and redemption. They long for a messianic age; they long for a sense of community; and yet they also long for the kind of personal fulfillment which seems to run counter to communal survival and spiritual goals. Few protagonists in American Jewish fiction succeed in achieving a total integration of the secular and Jewish worlds. More often, they simply struggle with their own counterlives. Their writing has attracted a broad audience among American Jews; the pieces of the worlds they juggle effectively evoke the yearning of American Jews toward often contradictory impulses of individual freedom and dynamic continuity with the Jewish past.

Ironically, there has been considerable critical speculation that American Jewish writing may have passed its peak. The late Lothar Kahn, for example, wrote, "If there was, indeed, an American-Jewish literary Renaissance it probably commenced in the mid-fifties and extended for some fifteen to twenty years into the late sixties and early seventies. Since then Jewish literature has enjoyed a diminished critical vogue and its popularity has also lessened considerably."[34] Similar opinions have been voiced by Louis Harap and others.[35] This essay has argued that a rebirth and revitalization of

---

[34]Lothar Kahn, "American Jewish Literature After Bellow, Malamud and Roth," *Jewish Book Annual* 45, 1987–1988, pp. 5–18, p. 5.

[35]For discussions of this issue in general and in relationship to particular authors, see Louis Harap, *In the Mainstream . . . 1950s–1980s* (New York, 1987), who calls the 1950s the "Jewish Decade" and labels Saul Bellow, Bernard Malamud, Philip Roth, and Norman Mailer as the quintessential American Jewish novelists; cited in Leslie Field, "The Jewish Presence in American Literature—Once Over Lightly," *Judaica Book News*, Fall/Winter 1988, pp. 21–24, p. 22. See also Ruth Wisse, "American Jewish Writing, Act II," *Commentary*, June 1976, pp. 40–45; Joseph Lowin, "Cynthia Ozick's Mimesis," *Jewish Book Annual* 42, 1983–1984, pp. 79–90; Thomas Friedman, "Back to Orthodoxy: The New Ethic and Ethnics in American

American Jewish literature has taken place and is still in the process of developing, at the very moment in time when others have predicted its demise. The new Jewish fiction is qualitatively different from works which preceded it and is, in fact, more intrinsically and particularistically Jewish than most American fiction of the 1950s and 1960s. Moreover, this essay has demonstrated that spiritual or religious Jewish themes have flourished in a literary environment which is both more Jewish and more receptive to spirituality than at any previous time in American Jewish literary history.

It does seem likely that, as Cynthia Ozick has indicated, ethnic or sociological Jewish writing is past its prime, if for no other reason than that the ethnicity of American Jews is fast being blended into oblivion. When sociologists are pessimistic, they document the vastly diminished distinctiveness of American Jews; when they wish to be optimistic, they speak of the "transformation" of American Jewish life and culture. In either case, whether viewed through positive or negative lenses, the inescapable fact is that the particular ethnic distinctiveness which used to make American Jews feel and appear Jewish, even when they had abandoned their ties to Jewish ritual and organized Jewish life, is rapidly disappearing with each succeeding American generation.

With the passage of the *angst* of the assimilatory struggle, and lacking the bite of that dynamic so brilliantly articulated by the American Jewish literary coterie in the middle years of the 20th century, descriptions of acculturation become insipid and cease to be an engaging topic for fictional exploration. Religious and spiritual exploration, however, have emerged in American Jewish fiction as they have in American Jewish life, as gripping, often painful, and productive themes. There is every reason to believe that, at least in the near future, we will continue to witness in American Jewish fiction portrayals of the psyche of the American Jew fired to white heat, refined, redefined, and reforged on the anvils of the literary artists who articulate the spiritual struggles of their age.

Jewish Literature," *Contemporary Jewry* 10, no. 1, 1989, pp. 67–77; and Solotaroff, "American Jewish Writers."

American Jewish Museums: Trends and Issues

by RUTH R. SELDIN

MUSEUMS DEVOTED TO JEWISH content have been multiplying rapidly in the United States, becoming a significant feature of the cultural landscape. While the spotlight of publicity has been focused on the national Holocaust museum rising on the Mall in Washington, D.C., and on similar institutions in New York, Los Angeles, and points in between, these museums are in fact part of a larger phenomenon of Jewish museum growth that has been taking place, largely unheralded, since the end of World War II.

In 1950 there were only two major Jewish museums in the United States and several small synagogue-linked galleries of Judaica. At the beginning of 1991, the Council of American Jewish Museums (CAJM; itself established in 1977) numbered 35 members and associates.[1] There were, in addition, an estimated dozen or more museums or galleries not affiliated with CAJM, among them the Seattle Jewish Museum and the Regional Museum of the Southern Jewish Experience in Jackson, Mississippi. There were also at least 19 self-described Holocaust museums, including the Simon Wiesenthal Center's Museum of Tolerance in Los Angeles and the national Holocaust Memorial Museum in Washington, D.C.

These museums vary widely in the size and nature of their collections, in their housing and exhibition space, in financial resources and staffing. They also vary in their program emphases, some being "general," i.e., featuring art, history, and culture, while others are more specialized, including the historical-society museums and the Holocaust museums. All Jewish museums are alike, however, in their basic function of collecting, preserving, and exhibiting the material culture of the Jewish people, "in order to further public knowledge and appreciation of Jewish culture."[2]

Note: In addition to the published sources cited in footnotes, the information in this article is based on annual reports, newsletters, and other publications furnished by museums. The author is grateful to the following individuals who agreed to be interviewed or otherwise provided assistance: David Altshuler, Margo Bloom, Phyllis Cook, David Eden, Morris Fred, Seymour Fromer, Marian Gribetz, Sylvia Herskowitz, Joanne Marks Kauvar, Reva Kirschberg, Norman Kleeblatt, Sara Lee, Joy Ungerleider Mayerson, Joan Rosenbaum, Anne Scher, Judith Siegel, Richard Siegel, Linda Steinberg, Jay Weinstein, Marjorie Wyler.
[1]See full listing of council members and associates at the end of this article.
[2]Yeshiva University Museum brochure.

Summarizing developments of the past quarter century, Tom Freudenheim, assistant secretary of the Smithsonian Institution, told the 1990 annual conference of the Council of American Jewish Museums that, in the 1960s, when he was a young art historian starting off on his career, employed as assistant curator of Judaica at the Jewish Museum in New York, there was no Jewish museum "field," no cadre of American-trained professionals in Judaica, no grants from the National Endowments (which were created in the mid-'60s), no accreditation by the American Association of Museums—in short, no sense that Jewish museums could compete in the larger museum world, or even a sense that ethnic pride was a valid basis for operating a museum. By the end of the 1980s, all this had changed, and Jewish museums had become respected members of the general museum world.[3]

Along with the increase in their numbers and their rise in professional standing, Jewish museums have been changing their image. Once regarded primarily as repositories for ritual objects and antiquities, with a sprinkling of art on biblical and other explicit Jewish themes, today's Jewish museums are as likely to display a Hanukkah menorah fashioned from industrial parts as a brass or silver antique model, an abstract sculpture or videotape as a portrait of a bearded rabbi. Exhibits cover a seemingly limitless range of subjects relating to Jews, Judaism, and the Jewish experience, worldwide and throughout history. In addition, where programs for the public once consisted of the occasional gallery talk, today's Jewish museums offer lecture series and symposia, films, puppet shows, concerts, and parent-child "interactive" workshops, as well as extensive programs for schools that reach thousands of children, a high proportion of them non-Jewish.

Behind this transformation in image lies a growing assertiveness on the part of museums about their role—or as they term it, their "mission." In an age marked simultaneously by curiosity about things Jewish and great ignorance of them, the museum is uniquely positioned to make Jewish culture available to the widest possible audience. A recognizably Jewish institution, it is neither religious nor secular and thus transcends the ideologies, sects, and dogmas that otherwise divide and segregate Jews into factional ghettos. At the same time, as a general cultural institution, the Jewish museum offers a socially sanctioned place where nonidentifying Jews as well as non-Jews can safely sample Jewish culture.

Growth and change have inevitably given rise to new problems and challenges. The area of funding is one. Paradoxically, while Jewish museums have won increasing recognition and financing from the National Endowments for the Arts and Humanities, state and municipal arts agen-

---

[3]Remarks delivered at annual meeting of the Council of American Jewish Museums, Philadelphia, Jan. 1990.

cies, and private foundations, Jewish communal bodies accord them low funding priority. Another problem is that of heightened competition—particularly with the mushrooming of Holocaust institutions—for acquisition of objects, funding, and audience. At the same time, Jewish museums compete not only with each other but with a host of general cultural institutions, which places them under pressure to mount the kinds of crowd-drawing exhibitions and programs that will, it is hoped, attract new interest and support.

As Jewish museums have become more visible, reaching ever wider audiences, they have also come in for criticism. They have been accused, on the one hand, of being boring, of failing to touch viewers emotionally,[4] and, on the other, of paying too much attention to popular taste and not enough to strictly Jewish educational purposes.[5] Part of the problem may be that the museums tend to be scattershot in their activity, failing to articulate a clear definition of their identity and purpose, and being less effective as a result.

This article begins by exploring the factors contributing to the current flourishing of Jewish museums, followed by a discussion of the concept of a Jewish museum and the ongoing debate over its character and direction. It then presents an overview of the museums and their activities, examining the major issues they face and their prospects for the future.

THE GROWTH OF JEWISH MUSEUMS

The proliferation of Jewish museums over the last few decades represents a remarkable confluence of a number of trends—in society at large, in the broader museum world, and in American Jewish life.

There is, first, the emergence of the visual arts as an integral part of the middle-class life-style, thanks to increased wealth, leisure, and education, both formal and informal, the latter often by way of the television screen. This is expressed in ownership of art, visits to museums and galleries, participation in art classes, and the like. The spectacular growth of the auction art market in the 1980s, which was eagerly covered by the media, served to further heighten interest in the arts.

The rising attendance figures at museums are one indicator of public interest: from 200 million in 1965 to 391 million in 1984 to 500 million in 1987.[6] The proliferation of new museums is another. The 1965 directory of

---

[4]Wendy Leibowitz, "Why Are Jewish Museums So Boring?" *Moment,* Oct. 1989, pp. 10–13.
[5]Byron Sherwin, "Temples of Muses, Temples of Moses, or Galleries of Learning? Critical Problems of Jewish Museum Education," lecture delivered at 1989 annual meeting of the Council of American Jewish Museums, Chicago, Jan. 1989.
[6]American Association of Museums, cited in John Naisbitt and Patricia Aburdene, *Megatrends 2000* (New York, 1990), p. 69.

the Association of American Museums contained 4,956 entries (a thousand more than in 1950); by 1990, the number had climbed to more than 6,700. (The directory includes all types of museums, of widely varying sizes and content—art, history, scientific, natural history, etc., as well as historic sites, monuments, zoos, and botanical gardens.) One feature of the museum boom is its spread and decentralization across the country, with new museums opening and existing ones adding substantial new wings. Nor is the phenomenon limited to the United States. Europe has experienced a museum-building boom, particularly West Germany. Since 1980, eight new museums have opened in Frankfurt alone (including the Museum of Jewish History in 1989).[7]

Museum popularity has been boosted by, among other causes, new approaches in the presentation and marketing of works of art. "Beginning with the astonishing success of 'Treasures of Tutankhamen' in 1978, museums have been gripped by the 'blockbuster syndrome'—organizing exhibitions of opulent treasures or beloved masterpieces that attract stadium-size crowds."[8] The process of attracting new audiences to the museum has served to transform the nature of the institution from one inspiring awe and associated with high, largely European, culture, to a more open, informal, social gathering place. This trend has been expressed in the attention given to the public and commercial spaces: expansion of selling areas into large gift and book stores, the transformation of cafeterias into chic restaurants, and the building of auditoriums for public events. Perennially hard-pressed museums have even taken to renting out galleries, at exorbitant fees, for social events. While some critics deplore turning a museum into a "social gathering place and cultural department store," the same critics acknowledge that "the growing alliance between art museums and commerce ... can also help to make their existence possible."[9]

Yet another trend of recent years has been the spread of children's museums offering imaginative exhibits that provide for various forms of "interaction" between the viewer and the objects or technology on display. The success of these museums has not only helped to stimulate interest in museums generally but has raised audience expectations of what a museum experience should be.

The Jewish world has not been immune to any of these developments. Jews have played "a central role" in the American art world. Neither art history nor art criticism "would have much to show without its Jews." The commerce of art also "revolves heavily around Jews... and the role of Jews supporting cultural institutions in this country (including museums) has

---

[7]Ibid., pp. 62, 70–71.
[8]William Wilson, "Museum Mania Grips the Globe," *Los Angeles Times*, May 23, 1986.
[9]Ellen Posner, "The Museum Bazaar," *Atlantic*, Aug. 1988, pp. 67, 68.

been a phenomenon almost as remarkable as the generosity of Jews to Jewish philanthropic causes."[10] Although Jewish museum advocates claim that Jewish support of the general arts has not been accompanied by equivalent support for the Jewish arts, Jewish artists and Jewish museums have found benefactors, among them private collectors whose collections of Judaica or fine art form the basis of more than one of the new museums. The two oldest Jewish museums embarked on programs of expansion in the '70s and '80s—vastly increasing their collections, budgets, staffs, and audiences and undertaking major renovation or building plans with the aim of moving to greatly enlarged quarters in the early 1990s. Since the late 1950s, as will be described below, new museums and galleries have been sprouting at a steady pace.

While the impetus to create new Jewish museums, or to expand existing ones, has clearly been influenced by the popularity of museums of all sorts in American culture, it has been especially affected by the new respectability accorded specifically ethnic institutions, as evidenced by the spread of African-American, Hispanic-American, and similar museums in recent years. Neither factor alone, however, would be enough to explain the Jewish museum phenomenon. Critical to the process was the coincidental but simultaneous surge of interest among Jews in their own heritage and culture.

This development is part of what Charles Silberman has called "a major renewal of Jewish religious and cultural life" in the United States, reflecting a general openness to Jewish literature, music, and other forms of cultural expression on the part of third- and fourth-generation American Jews who are not in flight from their Jewish past—as were their second-generation parents—but who, on the contrary, are trying to recapture it.[11] Included in the younger cohorts are growing numbers of third-generation Jews with yeshivah or day-school education who not only have embraced Judaism but have the financial means to acquire art and support Jewish cultural activity.

While Silberman may be overstating the extent of participation in the renewal, there is ample evidence of a Jewish cultural flowering in the '70s and '80s, one that produced a stream of Jewish books and periodicals, the proliferation of Jewish-studies courses in universities acccompanied by an expanding Jewish scholarship, and the creation of Jewish theater and musical groups, as well as the spread of Jewish museums and galleries. Silberman and other students of Jewish life point to the establishment of Israel, which increased Jewish pride and identification, as one of the streams feeding this development. Another was interest in the Holocaust, which was slow to

---

[10]Tom Freudenheim, "The (Jewish) Jewish Museum," *Moment,* Nov. 1976, p. 52.
[11]Charles E. Silberman, *A Certain People: American Jews and Their Lives Today* (New York, 1985), p. 226.

start but by the 1960s had become intense. The awareness of the Holocaust coupled with the shock and exhilaration of the 1967 Six Day War made American Jews painfully aware of Israel's—and perhaps their own—vulnerability and sharpened the focus on issues of Jewish survival. For many, this was translated into a new curiosity about their Jewish heritage.

David Altshuler, director of A Living Memorial to the Holocaust—Jewish Heritage Museum, sees the 1980s surge in Holocaust memorializing as growing out of a potent combination of factors: the imminent demise of the last Holocaust survivors and with them their firsthand memories; the spread of revisionist history, which denies or distorts the record of the destruction of the Jews; the awakening of the children of the survivors, with a compelling need to transmit their personal histories to the world.

Several other developments relating specifically to art have contributed to the upsurge of interest in museums. In the last two decades, American Jewish artists, partaking in the new interest in Jewish heritage and identity, began to create works on Jewish themes. Growing familiarity with Israel exposed American Jews not only to the handicrafts—of varying quality—brought home by tourists but also to serious Israeli art and artists, a number of whom, like Agam and Arikha, by the 1970s had achieved international reputations and were displayed in general art museums and galleries. On the home front, a body of Jewish synagogue and ceremonial art was developing, the result of the postwar surge of suburban synagogue building that created a demand for modern ritual objects and decorations—Torah appurtenances, wall hangings, menorahs, ark doors—which induced a small number of Jewishly inclined architects and artists to begin to work in this area. Yet another current was the birth of a Jewish crafts movement in the 1960s, the child of the counterculture movement's stress on handicrafts and do-it-yourself ideology. Professional artists as well as amateurs began to develop skills in calligraphy, ceramics, needlework, weaving, woodcarving, and metalsmithing—using them to create ceremonial objects for home and public worship as well as decorative objects with Jewish motifs.

Another factor was the growing awareness of the losses and destruction of Jewish ceremonial art that had occurred during World War II and a resulting sense of urgency about rescuing and preserving what remained. The related growth of a market in ceremonial and other forms of Jewish art led to the opening of a Judaica department at Sotheby's in 1980, followed by the entry of other major auction houses into the field, their activities in turn stimulating further attention.

The director of the Jewish Museum in New York, Joan Rosenbaum, believes that interest in Jewish museums is growing because "people want to learn about their history and background." She sees Jews today as "less self-conscious" about being Jewish and regarding their Jewishness as "an option" to be explored in various contexts.

That leaves open the question of what the particular context of a museum has to offer for an exploration of Jewish identity. Sara Lee, dean of Hebrew Union College's School of Education in Los Angeles, considers museums special because they are "neutral territory," places where people can satisfy their curiosity about Jewishness without having to make any kind of organizational or ideological or even psychological commitment.

Other commentators emphasize the uniqueness of the museum as a purveyor of Jewish culture because of its focus on "the object." One Jewish educator with extensive museum experience explains that Jewish objects and works of art are "powerful communicators of values and ideas" whose "appeal is direct and concrete" and "forges a connection between the creator and the viewer, and between viewers in this era and those in previous eras. Although this connection is difficult to articulate in words, it is one which everyone has experienced at some time or another."[12]

To scholar Jacob Neusner, "the museum, with its tactile display, with its amazing capacity to teach not didactically, to inform in an interesting way" has "extraordinary power." In his view, "Museums all over the world find themselves overwhelmed by crowds, because people in the age of television seek direct encounter, and because in museums they find it. The single most powerful instrument of mass education, beyond television, is the museum. . . ."[13]

All these factors, then—the growth of a body of Jewish art, the existence of a pool of wealthy collectors willing to purchase and donate such works, education, artistic sophistication, emotions aroused by the Holocaust and events in Israel, curiosity about Jewishness and Jewish identity—combined with the general popularity of museums in American culture and the special qualities of the museum experience—have contributed to the growing prominence of Jewish museums. To these one could add the emergence of a cadre of professionals—art historians and curators as well as Jewish educators—eager to use the museum as a vehicle for educating as wide an audience as possible about Jewish culture.

WHAT IS A JEWISH MUSEUM?

The basic concept of a Jewish museum as an institution devoted to the collection, preservation, and presentation of art and objects associated with the Jewish people and heritage has been essentially unchanged since the first Jewish museums came into existence a century ago. However, this broad definition leaves considerable room for interpretation and differing ap-

---

[12]Isa Aron, "The Burgeoning World of Jewish Art," *Pedagogic Reporter*, Jan. 1985, p. 5.
[13]Jacob Neusner, *American Jewry and the Arts: We Are Jews by Reason of Imagination*, National Foundation for Jewish Culture, 1987, p. 10.

proaches. What qualifies something to be labeled "Jewish," particularly in the realm of fine art? Should a Jewish museum be limited to showing Jewish art, however that is defined, or should it be universal in its approach? What aspects of Jewishness should the museum emphasize—the religious, the secular, ancient Israel, modern Israel, the Holocaust, or American Jewish life? Finally, and underlying the previous questions, what is the museum's purpose, what "message" does it wish to impart and to whom? To the extent that there is a debate over the nature and direction of Jewish museums, it centers on these questions.

It was apparently easier to answer these questions in the 1890s and the first decades of this century, when the first Jewish museums came into being in Vienna, Prague, Warsaw, Frankfurt, and other cities. That was during the age of imperialism, a period in which palatial museums were built to house precious objects amassed throughout the world.[14] A small number of Jews—scholars, art dealers, well-to-do connoisseurs—were inspired to collect the art and artifacts of their own people and to ensure their preservation for future generations. Lending support to this activity were two contemporary developments. One was the movement known as *Wissenschaft des Judentums,* which legitimated the application of scientific methods to the study of Judaism in all its aspects. The second was the growing recognition that, contrary to the common perception that Judaism was hostile to art, the Jews in fact possessed a rich legacy of artistic treasures in the form of ceremonial objects, synagogue architecture and appurtenances, illuminated manuscripts, and the antiquities being excavated in Palestine. The showing of the J. Strauss collection, including magnificent silverwork from Italian synagogues, at the 1878 World Exhibition in Paris, helped to disseminate this new awareness and appreciation. That collection was acquired by Baron de Rothschild for the French state Cluny Museum in Paris.

Even as the existence of this body of Jewish art works gained recognition, it was also implicitly understood that a Jewish museum would be something other than an art museum, that because, through much of its history, Judaism had emphasized the written word over the visual image (among other reasons), there simply was no body of painting and sculpture and other "fine art" such as Christians had produced. It was understood, therefore, that, as an early advocate of Jewish museums, a non-Jewish art historian, Heinrich Frauberger, put it, a Jewish museum would have to "combine the points of view of the historical museum, the art museum, and a museum of ethnography." Frauberger also articulated the goals and program followed by the early Jewish museums: "To collect in photographs,

---

[14]For a fairly detailed history of the Jewish museums in the United States and Europe, see Alice M. Greenwald, "Jewish Museums—In the United States," *Encyclopedia Judaica Yearbook 1988/89,* pp. 167–81.

drawings, or originals the artistic remnants of the past and the works of the present created by Jews or for Jewish rituals. To utilize the collection correctly for artistic and scientific purposes."[15]

The first two important Jewish museums in this country—the Jewish Museum in New York, founded in 1904 at the Jewish Theological Seminary, and the museum of the Hebrew Union College in Cincinnati (now the Skirball Museum in Los Angeles), officially founded in 1913—essentially followed this model for many decades, even to being staffed by European émigrés. Their emphasis was on collection, cataloging, and scholarly research, and their collections consisted largely of synagogue and ceremonial art.

So long as the art and artifacts being exhibited in Jewish museums were explicitly Jewish in content or association, there was no question of suitability. Questions began to arise chiefly in relation to "modern art"—the art of the last century—a field in which Jews were becoming increasingly active, but producing works that could only rarely be defined as Jewish. Was Marc Chagall's "Calvary," for example, to be considered Jewish art, along with the same artist's bearded "Praying Jew"? In other words, was subject matter the chief criterion—in which case art on Jewish themes by non-Jews would be admissible—or was the accident of an artist's birth sufficient to make his creations Jewish? Jews took pride in the contributions to general culture made by the growing list of prominent Jewish artists—in Europe, Chagall, Soutine, Mané-Katz, Lipchitz, Modigliani; in America, the Soyers, Shahn, Levine, Newman, Rothko; in Israel, Rubin, Ticho, Ardon, Agam. Regardless of what they painted, should these artists not display their work in Jewish museums?

The Question of "Jewish Art"

A full or even adequate treatment of the subject of Jewish art is beyond the scope of the present article. However, since Jewish museums must establish criteria for determining what to acquire for their collections and what to exhibit, a few observations are in order.[16]

There is in fact no agreement among those concerned with the subject on what constitutes "Jewish art," or even that such an entity exists. According to one leading authority, "The style and, frequently, even the subject matter of the art of the Jews have always been rooted in and adapted from

---

[15]Cited in Avram Kampf, "The Jewish Museum: An Institution Adrift," *Judaism,* Summer 1968, p. 283.

[16]A highly regarded survey of Jews and modern art is provided in Avram Kampf, *Jewish Experience in the Art of the Twentieth Century* (S. Hadley, Mass., 1984). See also Cecil Roth, *Jewish Art,* rev. ed. (Greenwich, Conn., 1971), p. 19.

the dominant contemporary non-Jewish society."[17] Still, until the 19th century, this art was intrinsic to the Jewish community that produced it, reflecting "the collective Jewish thought, feeling, and symbolism of that community." In the process of Emancipation, however, the Jewish artist severed his ties to the community and its "collective beliefs and symbols" and "employed his art to reflect his national—or international—or personal outlook."[18]

Even as it is generally agreed, in the words of art critic Harold Rosenberg, that there is "no Jewish art in the sense of a Jewish style in painting and sculpture," and that Jewish art is "an ambiguous situation," it is also understood that certain categories of works can legitimately be labeled "Jewish." These include: any art by Jewish artists, regardless of subject matter; art depicting Jews or containing Jewish subject matter (including the Bible); synagogue and ceremonial art; folk art and handicrafts using Jewish iconography; and "metaphysical" Jewish art, such as works incorporating Hebrew letters and mystical references or motifs.[19]

The first category, that of works by Jewish artists, is legitimated on the ground that even if Jewish artists insist that they create as artists and not as Jews, it is understood that "they have not been working as non-Jews either." Says Rosenberg: "Their art has been the closest expression of themselves as they are, including the fact that they are Jews, each in his individual degree."[20] Another writer puts it even more strongly: "In a century where Jews have been subjected to the threat of extermination, it is hard to imagine that any Jew, no matter how politically radical or opposed to religious dogma, does not bear within him the memory of Jewish religion and tradition."[21]

A few writers have gone beyond this personal or ethnic definition to suggest that modern art itself is peculiarly Jewish, that because it takes radical liberties with realistic images, it can be seen as respecting the biblical interdiction against making human images. "[A]lmost all 20th-century art made by Jewish artists of the first rank suggests that there are risks involved in making figurative imagery. The more original the art, the more the power of the Second Commandment can be felt. As a result, avant-garde art made by Jews suggests a striking paradox. The more fearless and iconoclastic the art seems, the more it can be seen to respect Jewish law."[22]

---

[17]Joseph Gutmann, "Jewish Art: Fact or Fiction?" *CCAR Journal,* Apr. 1964, p. 51.
[18]Ibid.
[19]Harold Rosenberg, "Is There a Jewish Art?" *Commentary,* July 1966, pp. 57–59.
[20]Ibid., p. 60.
[21]Michael Brenson, "Jewish Artists Wrestle with Tradition," a review of the Jewish Museum show "The Circle of Montparnasse: Jewish Artists in Paris 1905–1945," *New York Times,* Nov. 17, 1985.
[22]Ibid.

Other writers assert a natural connection between Jews and modern art because both grapple with the issue of identity. Rosenberg suggests that the Jewish artist feels the modern problem of identity "in an especially deep and immediate way." The work "inspired by the will to identity," he concluded, "has constituted a new art by Jews which, though not a Jewish art, is a profound Jewish expression, at the same time that it is loaded with meaning for all people of this era."[23]

A similar thought was expressed by critic Heinz Politzer: "The modern Jewish artist finds himself utterly alone with himself and his work. Thus he has become the prototype of the modern artist, or one might say, the modern artist has become a Jew. For modern man, if he has been awake in this period, has suffered the fate of the Jew in foreboding and anxiety, if not in reality. . . ."[24]

Based on these varying interpretations and understandings of what constitutes Jewish art, Jewish museums have considerable latitude in their activities. They are undoubtedly helped by the fact that abstract and avant-garde art in general have gained wide acceptance, and that there is much greater public sophistication about art. In the end, of course, it is the individual curators and those they work with who define what is suitable for showing in their particular institutions. One might generalize and say that for Jewish museums esthetic merit is a necessary criterion for selecting a work of art, but it is not the sole one. Some Jewish component—however that is defined—is required.

Art Museum vs. Jewish Museum

In the 1960s, the most protracted and vocal debate ever to take place in the Jewish museum world erupted over the question of the place of art in a Jewish museum. The battleground was the Jewish Museum in New York, regarded as the flagship of Jewish museums by virtue of its size, age, and professional standing. By virtue of these same qualities it has also served as a testing ground and bellwether for trends in the field. (The perhaps disproportionate focus of this article on the Jewish Museum reflects its legitimate prominence and also the fact that it has been most written about, having received considerable attention from writers and critics, in the general and the Jewish press.)

The decade of the '50s saw a critical change take place in the art world, the rise to dominance of avant-garde, abstract, "imageless" art. Dr. Stephen Kayser, the German-born and -educated curator of the Jewish Museum

---

[23]Rosenberg, "Is There a Jewish Art?" p. 60.
[24]Heinz Politzer, "The Opportunity of the Jewish Museum: How Best to Encourage Art," *Commentary*, June 1949, p. 592.

from 1947 to 1961, who combined a serious interest in Jewish matters with training as an art historian, was not uninterested in these developments. With the help of art critic and Columbia professor Meyer Schapiro, in 1957 he mounted a show titled "New York School: Second Generation" that included such young—non-Jewish—artists as Jasper Johns and Robert Rauschenberg. When Kayser left the museum in the early sixties, along with the existing board, his successors and the museum's new board, which included a number of wealthy collectors, saw an opportunity to put the Jewish museum on the art world map. At the time, the more established museums were not able to react quickly to the frenetic developments then taking place in the studios of young artists downtown, and "the Jewish," as it came to be known, moved to fill this gap. With the board now led by wealthy art patrons Albert and Vera List (who donated an annex to the museum that opened in 1963), and with the administration of the Jewish Theological Seminary—the museum's sponsor—largely paralyzed by an attitude of ambivalence toward the museum, there followed close to a decade in which the Jewish aspect of the museum was downgraded and the museum made a name for itself with shows of pop and op art, Dada, and hard-edged abstractions.

The director appointed to succeed Kayser in 1962, Alan Solomon, a talented professional but a man who apparently lacked a knowledge of and interest in Jewish art, advanced the argument that Jewish sponsorship of avant-garde art was in line with the general support by Jews of progressive causes and of significant cultural activities, and that by such support, Jews demonstrated their universalism.[25] Sam Hunter, another highly regarded museum professional who succeeded Solomon in the mid-'60s, not only saw no conflict in the Jewish Museum featuring modern art, he saw it as an extension of the Jewish drive since the Enlightenment of seeking "full intellectual participation in Western culture."[26]

While these developments sent museum attendance soaring, they aroused fury and debate in the Jewish world. Leading the attack against the modern-art shows was Trude Weiss-Rosmarin, who believed the museum had "an obligation to the Jewish community," which looked "to the Jewish Museum for guidance and instruction in 'Jewish art,' that is to say, Jewish *ritual* art." She attributed the museum's new path to indifference on the part of Seminary faculty, who "are not overly happy" but who "know well that Jewish art is not sufficiently important to fuss over," and who were therefore willing to appease "contributors who are arty and would want to be ac-

---

[25]Kampf, "The Jewish Museum," pp. 291–92.
[26]Sam Hunter, "The Jewish Museum: What Is It, Why Is It, and What Next," *New York Times,* Aug. 8, 1965.

cepted by the Beautiful People of the Museum of Modern Art but can't quite make it."[27]

Supporting the museum's stance were Jewish art historians and critics like Alfred Werner who did not "believe that our Jewish Museum must be 'all Jewish,' any more than that *Commentary* need stick only to 'Jewish' topics." Still, even the broad-minded Werner noted that "a Jewish Museum without discernible Jewish content and Jewish identification is a misnomer."[28]

Arthur A. Cohen, a scholar-writer who was equally at home with professors of Jewish studies and avant-garde artists, and who curated an exhibition on "The Hebrew Bible in Christian, Jewish and Muslim Art" for the museum in 1963, had no problem with modern art in a Jewish museum, seeing "the obligation of the humanist focus of Jewish tradition to endorse and support, without prejudice, the plastic articulation of the human spirit."[29] When, a few years later, the Seminary announced that, due to "exigent financial need," the museum would discontinue its program of exhibiting contemporary art, Cohen took the museum to task in a lengthy article in the *New York Times*.[30] After praising the museum for its "pioneering" involvement in the art of the '60s, he condemned it for abandoning its "active support of the creative arts whatever their unrelatedness to Jewish interests, narrowly defined." He also pointed out that if the museum "wants to be effectively Jewish, or effectively anything, it still has to spend considerable money" if it is to "make its program of Jewish exhibitions meaningful and dramatic."

Art historian Avram Kampf, who in the mid-1970s would curate a major exhibition of modern art at the Jewish Museum, "The Jewish Experience in the Art of the 20th Century," subscribed to Cohen's view. He maintained that for the museum "to have followed its own specialized interests [in various aspects of Judaica] would not necessarily have meant abandoning the mainstream of contemporary art and life. On the contrary, a well-planned, carefully balanced program would have required keeping it open to the contemporary art world and at the same time broadening its own specialized field of interest."[31]

Jewish content was hardly lacking, it must be noted, even in this period of skewed priorities. Two shows that garnered large audiences and considerable press attention (though agreed to with much hesitation on the part of

---

[27] Trude Weiss-Rosmarin, editorial, *Jewish Spectator*, Oct. 1966, pp. 31–32.
[28] Alfred Werner, letter, *Congress Bi-Weekly*, Dec. 18, 1967, pp. 21–22.
[29] *Congress Bi-Weekly*, Nov. 20, 1967, pp. 7–8.
[30] Feb. 7, 1971.
[31] Kampf, "The Jewish Museum," pp. 289–90.

the board) were "The Lower East Side" (1966), a pioneering multimedia exhibition, and "Masada," a dramatic presentation of archaeological finds, in 1967. In addition, the museum had maintained, since 1956, the Tobe Pascher Workshop, the only one of its kind, devoted exclusively to the creation and production of modern Jewish ceremonial art.

The debate over the place of modern art in the Jewish Museum was resolved programatically, if not in substance, in the early 1970s. By that time the New York art scene had changed, the new art was being shown everywhere, and "the Jewish" no longer had a special role to play. Also, in the early '70s a self-study committee appointed by the JTS to determine the museum's future concluded that, especially in light of its budget difficulties, it should henceforth emphasize its commitment to the Jewish community. Addressing that committee, Prof. Abraham Joshua Heschel (generally regarded as one of the Seminary faculty's more knowledgeable and sympathetic advocates of the museum) saw a great future for the museum as "an inspiration to people all over America. It could be an instrument for saving our youth. It could show the beauty and meaning of Jewish life. People would come to understand that the Jewish Museum makes a real contribution to their existence."[32]

The decade of the 1970s, specifically from 1973 on, under director Joy Ungerleider, saw the museum return to an emphasis on "programs which explore the richness and diversity of Jewish life, culture, and history."[33] This approach was continued in the 1980s, under director Joan Rosenbaum, though there was apparent both a widening of subject matter and a subtle shift in emphasis. In a 1989 interview with the *New York Times,* director Rosenbaum indicated that she did not feel the museum should, on the one hand, "duplicate the Whitney or the Modern," nor, on the other, should it limit itself to showing just Jewish artists—"they should exhibit everywhere." Contemporary shows would continue to be important, she said, but her chief interest was in the context of art, the culture in which it is produced. "Because we're a museum about culture, not just history or art," she said, "we have the possibility of taking a very broad view. We can consider the political, art historical and societal aspects all at once. By looking at everything, you make Jewish culture more interesting to a wide audience."[34]

Several exhibitions mounted in the '80s reflected this line of thought (see "Exhibitions," below). That such an approach is not without risks, however, was noted in at least one critical response to an exhibition shown early in 1990 at the Jewish Museum, "War, Resistance and Politics: Dusseldorf

---

[32]Minutes of Museum Study Committee, Apr. 19, 1971, mimeo.
[33]Jewish Museum press release.
[34]Grace Glueck, "The Jewish Museum Reaches Out," *New York Times,* Apr. 4, 1989.

Artists 1910–1945" (organized by the Stadtmuseum Dusseldorf). *New York Times* critic Michael Brenson found it "problematic," not because the majority of the artists represented were not Jews, but because the show had "no clear sense of whether this is cultural history, an art exhibition or a show about German artists and Jews. . . . At the end of the show, there is a sense that the Dusseldorf avant-garde, which is promoted as the subject of the show, was only interesting to the museum insofar as it produced artists whose progressive politics helped them appreciate the nightmare of the Jews. . . . The exhibition underlines a fundamental conflict within the museum. Can it be both a far-ranging cultural and historical institution of real artistic scope and an institution in which only a special culture and history are served?"[35]

In fairness to the Jewish Museum, it should be noted that even as it has been willing to take risks in putting on controversial or difficult shows, it has also not neglected its basic mandate. In the same spring 1990 season, the museum opened an ethnographic exhibition—one brought over from the Israel Museum in Jerusalem—that was unequivocally "Jewish." "In the Court of the Sultan: Sephardi Jews of the Ottoman Empire" displayed several hundred artifacts in appropriate settings to depict the life of Jews in a particular period and part of the world. Not surprisingly, the show evoked no controversy and only positive notices.

It seems likely that the issue of universalism vs. particularism will continue to be problematic for Jewish museums, precisely because it reflects the tensions and confusion inherent in modern Jewish life. The continuing challenge will be to strike just the right balance, to do justice to both aspects.

Purpose

Behind the debates over what type of art to show and how to balance Jewish and general content lies the more fundamental question of the museum's basic goal or mission. Should it seek to appeal to as wide an audience as possible, with as broad a range of subject matter as possible, or should it focus its efforts more narrowly? In the 1960s, Avram Kampf criticized the Jewish Museum and its sponsor, the Jewish Theological Seminary, for failure to exert leadership within its own justifiable domain: by providing guidance on synagogue art and architecture, by carrying out a serious program of research and publications on its own collection, by encouraging students to engage in scholarship on Jewish art, by encouraging artists who wanted to draw on Jewish sources for their work.[36] In the 1970s, Tom Freudenheim deplored the continuing failure of the Seminary

---

[35] Michael Brenson, *New York Times,* Mar. 23, 1990.
[36] Kampf, "The Jewish Museum," pp. 289–90.

and the museum to encourage scholarly study and publication on its collections.[37]

At the time of the modern-art crisis, A.J. Heschel proposed an openly didactic role for the museum, urging it to seek "ways of teaching Jewish values in a visual manner."[38] A similar position was articulated more recently by Byron Sherwin, vice-president for academic affairs of Chicago's Spertus College. In an impassioned address to the 1989 annual meeting of the Conference of American Jewish Museums, Sherwin rejected the view that the museum is for entertainment, or passive "voyeuristic" pleasure, and proposed that its aim should be the "transmission of the constitutive values of the Jewish people. . . . The notion of art for art's sake, the separation of aesthetics from ethics, is outside the pale of the Jewish vocabulary."

Sherwin also criticized efforts to emulate the major art museums and called for resisting pressures from boards to do so. In the belief that Jewish museums have "a crucial role to play as learning resource centers," particularly for the unaffiliated, he said that the challenge for museums is to translate Jewish value-concepts into a visual medium . . . to translate "our auditory, literary tradition into a didactic, visual, participatory means of presentation." As for the museum's potential audience, Sherwin contended that "our subject matter and the manner in which we present it must define who our audiences are, rather than the converse. . . ." A museum can appeal to diverse constituencies by mounting exhibits with "multileveled and multivalent appeal . . . interpreted differently to a variety of different audiences . . . with the learning tools needed to interpret it. . . ."[39]

Not all museum professionals subscribe to Sherwin's view, and those who are sympathetic to it point to difficulties of implementation—the fact that it is simply easier to teach about history and culture than "values" in the museum setting, using art and objects. In examining museum activity, it becomes clear that decisions about emphasis and focus are as much a reflection of real-world constraints as of ideology: the availability of works of art or objects relevant to a particular subject; the means to purchase art or objects or even to foot the bills of a loan exhibition—shipping, insurance, installation, and the like. In the nature of things, a museum's character also reflects the influence of its major supporters and the pressure to attract donors in a highly competitive situation.

It is the case, too, that Jewish museum professionals tend not to be Jewish scholars or rabbis or teachers but art historians or anthropologists, who may or may not be religiously observant or Jewishly knowledgeable and who have a strong commitment to the museums as general cultural institu-

---

[37]Freudenheim, "The Jewish (Jewish) Museum," p. 51.
[38]"A Future for the Jewish Museum," Apr. 19, 1971, mimeo.
[39]Byron L. Sherwin, "Temples of Muses," pp. 18–19, 22–23, 27–28, 29–30.

tions as well as Jewish ones. In general, the people associated with Jewish museums (lay as well as professional) do not see themselves as parochial, but as serving the broader community, making a contribution to the cultural life of the community as a whole and, at the same time, serving a public-relations function for Jews and Judaism. Not insignificantly, it is on the basis of its broad cultural role that the museum can attract essential funding from non-Jewish sources.

On some level, Jewish museums in 1990 were still grappling with the questions raised in the 1960s. After the Jewish Museum decided to concentrate on its Jewish program, Tom Freudenheim, at the time director of the Baltimore Museum of Art, could claim that "the recent shift in the Museum's position is still not all that clear, because there remains a very evident inability to decide what wants emphasis in its presentation: art, Judaica, history, ethnology, archaeology (not that these are mutually exclusive)."[40] Some 25 years later, writing in response to an article in *Moment* magazine provocatively titled "Why Are Jewish Museums So Boring?"[41] Freudenheim maintained that "a major problem facing the Jewish museums is that they are probably not certain what kind of museum they are trying to be."[42]

Perhaps Freudenheim is chasing an illusory goal. Jewish museums mirror the conceptions of their times about the nature of Jewishness—conceptions that are far more complex in the late 20th century than they were a century earlier. Sociologist Samuel Heilman has noted that "the meaning of being Jewish continues to undergo transformations—a fact that will undoubtedly make nearly impossible any sort of static and universally agreed upon definition."[43] This means that museums will vary in their goals, programs, and emphases. Freudenheim himself noted that "one generally agreed-upon mission would [not] serve all Jewish museums. Each has an array of different factors to consider, and each would presumably have a different series of goals."[44]

In reality, this is precisely what has been happening. New York's Jewish Museum, for a variety of cogent reasons, feels that it must compete on a high artistic level in order merely to be visible. The Skirball Museum in Los Angeles and the National Museum of American Jewish History in Philadelphia are emphasizing American Jewish history and life. Uri Herscher, Hebrew Union College executive vice-president, explained that the Skirball shares with other museums a basic premise, "that we have a very rich

---

[40]Freudenheim, "The (Jewish) Jewish Museum," p. 29.
[41]By Wendy Leibowitz, Oct. 1989, pp. 10–13.
[42]Tom Freudenheim, "Thank You, Wendy Leibowitz," *Moment,* Oct. 1989, p. 15.
[43]"Being a Jew: The Problem of Definition," *Congress Monthly,* Mar./Apr. 1990, p. 10.
[44]Freudenheim, "Thank You, Wendy Leibowitz," p. 15.

heritage that needs to be transmitted to the total community—the people in the street beyond the Jewish community," but his point of departure—his shaping conception—differs: "In the last 50 years, Jews have had emphasized in their lives two vivid events: the Holocaust and the birth of the State of Israel. The glorious story of American Jewish life has essentially been left untold. I think it's time to emphasize a story which has been essentially positive and joyful."[45] Contrast this with the position of museums "devoted to celebrating the vitality and creativity of 20th-century European Jewish civilization . . . and the crucial lessons of the Holocaust which strove to consume it."[46]

Clearly there are different impetuses at work: to "convert" Jews—particularly the most distant—to their heritage; to educate non-Jews about Jews; to inspire the already committed; to preserve the past, but not for its own sake. The early Jewish museum was bent on preserving the Jewish material heritage. Today's museum has added to this mission the task of preserving Jews, of bringing them face to face with multiple facets of Jewish life that will somehow arouse feelings of identification. Thus, while the contemporary Jewish museum has not, at least officially, abandoned any of the traditional museum activities, there has been a definite shift in emphasis and a resulting fluidity and flexibility in the way it approaches its task.

OVERVIEW OF MUSEUMS

In 1950, as noted earlier, only two major Jewish museums were in existence in the United States—the Jewish Museum in New York and the Hebrew Union College Museum in Cincinnati (reorganized in 1972 as the Skirball Museum in Los Angeles). The first new institution of the postwar years was the B'nai B'rith Klutznick Museum, established in Washington, D.C., in 1957, first as an Exhibit Hall and renamed a museum in 1976. The decade of the 1960s saw the founding of the Judah L. Magnes Museum in Oakland (later Berkeley), California, and the Spertus Museum of Judaica in Chicago, Illinois; the decade of the '70s, the opening of Yeshiva University Museum in New York and the National Museum of American Jewish History in Philadelphia; the decade of the '80s, the creation of the San Francisco Jewish Community Museum and the Regional Museum of the Southern Jewish Experience in Jackson, Miss. The decade of the '90s is slated to witness the opening of A Living Memorial to the Holocaust–Jewish Heritage Museum in New York, the Holocaust Museum in Wash-

---

[45]Amy Stevens, "Cultural Center to Tell Story of Jews in America," *Los Angeles Times,* June 23, 1988.
[46]*A Living Memorial to the Holocaust–Museum of Jewish Heritage,* pamphlet, p. 2.

ington, D.C., and undoubtedly others as yet unidentified at the time of this writing.

Smaller museums or galleries, usually associated with synagogues, are scattered all over the country. Three of the oldest and most highly regarded are in New York City: Temple Emanu-El, Central Synagogue, and Park Avenue Synagogue. Others of note are in Richmond, Philadelphia, Buffalo, Denver, and Lawrence, Long Island, to cite but a few. There is a respected museum on the premises of the Hebrew Home for the Aged in Riverdale, N.Y., and several art galleries in Jewish community centers. The first museum devoted specifically to the Holocaust opened in 1963 (the Martyrs Memorial and Museum of the Holocaust in Los Angeles) and was virtually alone until the mid-1970s, when there began an eruption of Holocaust commemoration projects, many of them presenting visual exhibits as part of their activities.[47]

Although no exact count is possible, at the beginning of 1990, there were in the United States at least 60 institutions under Jewish auspices presenting exhibitions of Jewish materials. In addition, one could mention the general and university museums that have collections of Judaica or Bible-related archaeology—such as those at Harvard or the University of Pennsylvania— or whose subject matter relates to Jews. An example of the latter is the Lower East Side Tenement Museum in New York, which opened in 1988 as a project of the nonprofit Lower East Side Historical Conservancy. In its exhibits, Jews figure prominently but not exclusively. While all these institutions are deserving of inclusion, the present study is limited primarily to the members of the Council of American Jewish Museums (CAJM).

It is, of course, somewhat misleading to lump all the museums together as a group. The differences between them are considerable. The genre includes, at one end of the spectrum, the Jewish Museum of New York, which occupies its own six-story building, has a staff of over 40 full-time employees (plus part-timers), and a budget of over $4 million a year, and whose true peers, in many respects, are the general art or history museums of similar size. At the other end of the spectrum are galleries whose facilities consist of no more than a few display cases in a synagogue lobby, one or two part-time staffers, and budgets of a few thousand dollars.

Still, all the museums meet established criteria, have common purposes, engage in similar activities, and confront the same types of problems. It was

---

[47]The subject of Holocaust-linked institutions warrants a separate study. The 1988 *Directory of Holocaust Institutions,* published by the U.S. Holocaust Memorial Council (Washington, D.C., 1988), lists 98 such bodies, among them 19 museums, 48 resource centers, 34 archival facilities, 12 memorials, 26 research institutes, and 5 libraries, noting that many institutions fit into more than one category and not all are exclusively Holocaust-related. For a description of some of the leading Holocaust projects and a discussion of various controversies surrounding them, see Judith Miller, *One, by One, by One: Facing the Holocaust* (New York, 1990).

for this reason that CAJM was organized, in 1977, with these stated goals: "to facilitate communication between institutions through bi-annual meetings and occasional publications . . . ; maintain professional standards and a code of ethics for Jewish museum programs, operations, and personnel; strengthen advocacy for Jewish museums by promoting their work as major Jewish cultural resources; and coordinate cooperative projects."[48] CAJM is administered by the National Foundation for Jewish Culture, whose headquarters are in New York City. The foundation itself was created by the Council of Jewish Federations and is supported by federations and by independent fund raising.

Apart from differences in age, size, sponsorship, and physical facilities, the museums all have distinct institutional personalities. These reflect their origins and history, their physical and social settings, the emphases they place on different activities, and perhaps most significantly, the influence of the personalities who have shaped them.[49]

Some museums began their existence with a collection; some with an idea around which relevant objects were acquired. In both instances, the origins are themselves chapters of social history that shed light on the interests, mores, and concerns of American Jews in different periods.

The Jewish Museum and the Skirball were "unplanned" museums, that is, their parent institutions found themselves recipients of valuable objects donated by important supporters. These collections, which were placed in the libraries of the respective schools, in the care of the library directors, attracted additional gifts over the years. As the collections became larger, separate museum facilities were established. The Spertus Museum originated with the collection of Maurice Spertus, and became part of Chicago's College of Jewish Studies, subsequently renamed the Spertus College of Judaica.

At its founding, the B'nai B'rith Klutznick Museum (originally Exhibit Hall) sought to reflect "the philosophy and program of its parent organization," and was "devoted to telling the story of American Jewry's contribution to society." For its inaugural exhibition, it borrowed such items as the original correspondence between the president of Newport, Rhode Island's Touro Synagogue and George Washington and the first Hebrew book published in North America, in 1735. Eventually it acquired its own fine collection. The Magnes Museum in Berkeley grew out of the mission of one man—its director, Seymour Fromer—and a group of dedicated supporters, to preserve the heritage and history of the Jews of the West. Both museums eventually acquired or built up collections of their own and branched out into other areas of interest besides their original ones.

---

[48]National Foundation for Jewish Culture, CAJM Directory, preface.
[49]See Greenwald, "Jewish Museums—United States," for individual museum profiles.

Yeshiva University Museum was instituted as part of a master plan for university expansion, under the leadership of then president Samuel Belkin. With the backing of art patrons Ludwig and Erica Jesselson and under the guidance of art historians Karl Katz and Rachel Wischnitzer, the museum originally consisted of a permanent exhibition of specially commissioned synagogue models with accompanying slide and film presentations on the synagogue and Jewish history. Beginning with director Sylvia Herskowitz in 1975–76, the museum's concept changed to one of loan exhibitions arranged by guest curators. Soon the museum began to build up its own collection, based on earlier gifts to the university and augmented by new ones, and to offer a varied program of changing exhibitions. The National Museum of American Jewish History, which opened in the year of the Bicentennial, identifies itself as a history, not an art, museum, though art works are included in its collections and exhibitions. The museum was initiated by members of Philadelphia's historic Mikveh Israel Congregation, which erected a building on Independence Mall to house both the museum and the synagogue.

The Mizel Museum in Denver, the Plotkin Museum in Phoenix, and the Fenster Museum in Tulsa were the creations of determined individuals who saw a need in their communities and had the drive and persistence to bring their dreams to fruition.

Among the factors that help to shape an institution's character and success, some are purely matters of geography or environment. The Jewish museums in Los Angeles, Chicago, and New York have potentially large audiences, but must work hard to draw them in: local Jews are widely spread out and may have to travel a considerable distance; tourists have limited time and a wide range of attractions to choose from. By contrast, in smaller cities, Jewish museums may be among the chief cultural draws listed for tourists.

Within a city itself, location is a significant factor. In New York, the Jewish Museum occupies its own free-standing edifice, a handsome and distinctive structure in an affluent neighborhood, the portion of upper Fifth Avenue known as "museum mile." As a result, the museum is viewed as one of many cultural attractions in New York, one that can be included easily in a tourist's itinerary. The planned Living Memorial to the Holocaust–Museum of Jewish Heritage will be in one of New York's prime tourist areas, Battery Park, overlooking New York harbor and the Statue of Liberty. The National Museum of American Jewish History, too, is situated in a high-traffic tourist area in Philadelphia, near the Liberty Bell. Yeshiva University Museum, by contrast, has had to overcome the handicap of its physical location in the racially mixed and relatively inaccessible upper Manhattan neighborhood of Washington Heights. Because the location undoubtedly discourages casual, drop-in visitors, the museum staff has concentrated efforts on attracting organized group visits, by adults and children alike, most of whom reach the campus in chartered buses.

Similarly, the Skirball Museum had been located in an "undesirable" neighborhood of Los Angeles; this was scheduled to change, however, with the move, in the early 1990s, to a new home in the Hebrew Union College Skirball Cultural Center, a $40-million complex on a 15-acre site, designed by noted architect Moshe Safdie, located midway between the Westside and San Fernando Valley—and adjacent to the new J. Paul Getty museum. Here the Skirball would be closer to the centers of Jewish population in Los Angeles as well as in a more desirable and accessible location for attracting visitors at large.

Of the seven charter, or founding, members of CAJM, the Magnes Museum in Berkeley and the National Museum of American Jewish History in Philadelphia are organized as independent, nonprofit institutions. One, B'nai B'rith Klutznick, is sponsored by a national organization, and four are under the auspices of institutions of higher Jewish learning: the Jewish Museum, New York (Jewish Theological Seminary); Yeshiva University Museum, New York (Yeshiva University); Skirball Museum, Los Angeles, with branches in Cincinnati and New York (Hebrew Union College); and Spertus Museum, Chicago (Spertus College of Judaica). Two museums recently elevated to general membership status in the council are synagogue-sponsored: the Fenster Museum of Jewish Art, Tulsa; and the Temple Museum of Religious Art, Cleveland. Among the associate members of the council, 2 are branches of the Skirball; 2 are historical-society galleries; 1 is a Holocaust memorial and museum combined; 2 are galleries situated in Jewish community centers; 1 is a gallery located in a home for senior citizens; and 15 are connected with synagogues (some are community museums simply located on synagogue premises).

Collections

The collections in Jewish museums consist primarily of works of art and Judaica. The latter has been defined as creations that "serve a purpose connected with Judaism as a way of life,"[50] or as "anything used by Jews for a religious purpose or having definite Jewish associations."[51] Generally, Judaica is understood to be art and objects created for ritual and ceremonial

---

[50]Stephen S. Kayser, ed., *Jewish Ceremonial Art* (Philadelphia, 1955), introd., pp. 9–18. This definition "excludes creations by Jewish artists which are detached from Jewish objectives, but includes works which serve a Jewish purpose even though their makers were not Jewish: a situation quite common in western Europe before the Emancipation." Ibid.

[51]Jay Weinstein, *A Collector's Guide to Judaica* (London, 1985), p. 7.

purposes, in the synagogue and the home, but it includes ethnographic materials as well. The body of works includes objects made of silver and other metals, wood, textiles, glass, and ceramics. Objects range from Torah ornaments to arks and ark curtains to Sabbath tableware to circumcision and burial implements, clothing, amulets, and furniture.

Of the major collections that began to be assembled in the 1850s in Europe, a number remained on that continent; others eventually found their way to Palestine (later Israel) and America.[52] That of German businessman Salli Kirschstein was purchased for the Hebrew Union College in 1925. The collection of a Turkish antiquities and rug dealer, Ephraim Benguiat (according to Roth "uneven," but including "some fine pieces"),[53] was exhibited at the World Columbia Exposition in Chicago in 1892–93, was subsequently placed with the Smithsonian Institute in Washington, D.C., and was acquired in 1925 for the Jewish Theological Seminary by its then president, Cyrus Adler. That formed the nucleus of the Jewish Museum's collection until it was vastly augmented by another collector, Harry G. Friedman, whose donations, beginning in 1941, ultimately totaled more than 5,000 objects, amounting to about 50 percent of the museum's holdings. The medal collection of Samuel Friedenberg was another important addition to the museum's holdings.

Smaller museums, too, have been created on the basis of significant gifts of Judaica. The collection of Judge Irving L. Lehman (called "small but exquisite" by Roth) was given to Congregation Emanu-El in New York City;[54] and Cecil Roth's own collection, particularly notable for illuminated *ketubot*, was donated to Beth Tzedec Congregation in Toronto and forms the basis of a substantial museum there.

The Klutznick Museum received the Joseph B. and Olyn Horwitz collection of antique ceremonial art and the Kanof collection of contemporary ritual objects created by noted silversmiths Ludwig Wolpert and Moshe Zabari. The museum at the Hebrew Home for the Aged in Riverdale, New York, was initiated with the gift of Ralph and Leuba Baum of a collection of over 800 ceremonial objects and rare textiles.

Over the centuries, much Judaica of value was lost or destroyed as a result of pogroms, expulsions, and migrations. In the last century, experts believe that, through lack of suitable outlets, or through lack of interest or ignorance of the value of objects, much Judaica was melted down or simply discarded (Friedman's collection for the Jewish Museum, for example, was

---

[52]See Cecil Roth, "Ceremonial Objects," *Encyclopedia Judaica*, vol. 5, p. 288ff.; specifically on collectors, pp. 310–11.
[53]Roth, ibid., p. 311.
[54]Partially cataloged in Cissy Grossman, *A Temple Treasury: The Judaica Collection of Congregation Emanu-El of the City of New York* (New York, 1989).

acquired primarily by combing through secondhand stores in search of cast-off objects). In recent decades, people have become more aware of the significance of family possessions and have come to appreciate them for both their historical and possible monetary worth.

The collections in American Jewish museums are also linked to the fate of the Jews of Europe in the 1930s and 1940s. In 1939, for example, the Jewish community of Danzig sent its collection of Jewish folk art to the Jewish Museum for temporary safekeeping, not knowing that the "loan" would turn out to be permanent. Although considerable Judaica was destroyed during the Holocaust, more than originally thought survived. There was, for example, the Jewish Museum of Prague, where the Nazis stockpiled the confiscated treasures of Czech Jewry, unknowingly creating what is now one of the world's largest and finest Judaica collections in the world.[55] In 1947, world Jewish organizations formed the Jewish Cultural Reconstruction (JCR), to allocate property confiscated by the Nazis and recovered by the U.S. military government in Germany. Where possible, property was restored to original owners. Unidentifiable or unclaimed items were distributed to appropriate homes. Some 4,000 ritual objects were given to the Bezalel Museum (now the Israel Museum) in Jerusalem and smaller assemblages to Yeshiva University, Hebrew Union College, and other institutions in the United States.

The market in Judaica is an active one, with dealers, private collectors, and museum curators always on the lookout for undiscovered treasures. The entry of the major auction houses into the Judaica field in the early '80s served to raise interest and the level of knowledge about the value of the items. At the same time, growing affluence and the trend to viewing art objects as good financial investments have stimulated activity. The supply of Judaica from the 19th and 20th centuries is regarded as plentiful, while objects from the 18th and 17th centuries are rare and from earlier periods rarer still, a fact that has inspired a small industry in fakes and forgeries. All museums are interested in augmenting their collections of older Judaica; at the same time, they have also begun to collect contemporary Judaica of high quality, which they believe will become the "precious legacy" for future generations. (See "Exhibitions," below.)

Next in importance to ceremonial objects in Jewish museum collections is fine art—paintings, sculpture, and graphics—with the emphasis on works by Jewish artists, certainly including those from Israel. As discussed in the section "What Is a Jewish Museum?" the determination of what is suitable for a Jewish museum is always problematic and very much subject to

---

[55]An exhibition of several hundred items from the museum was organized by the Smithsonian Institution Traveling Exhibition Service in 1983. See David Altshuler, ed., *The Precious Legacy: Judaic Treasures from the Czechoslovak State Collections* (New York, 1983).

individual curatorial taste. Archaeological artifacts from the Middle East are another interest of Jewish museums, though only the Skirball and the Jewish Museum have significant collections in this area. Because the subject of "life in Bible times" is a popular one in museum education programs (see "Education and Public Programs," below), even smaller museums seek to acquire or borrow small collections of biblical antiquities. Art and memorabilia relating to the Holocaust are also sought after by the general Jewish museums, with a number offering educational programs on the Holocaust. Other collecting interests are folk art; photographs; coins and medals; manuscripts and rare books; historical documents; and, increasingly in recent years, items of ethnographic interest, such as clothing and jewelry, household objects, letters, posters and programs, stamps and coins, newspapers and magazines—anything illustrative of the material culture of Jews in a particular time and place.

The newest area of collecting interest is objects relating to the experience of Jews in America. Traditionally, this has been the purview of historical societies, though their focus has been on documents and archives. Museums have come to recognize the need to preserve a much broader variety of memorabilia and artifacts and even speak of adding to their staffs professional ethnographers and anthropologists who are trained in the collection and use of such material.

The HUC Skirball Museum launched "Project Americana" in the mid-'80s, "an intensive collecting effort, . . . to acquire . . . objects of Jewish history and celebration, memorabilia from everyday life, folk art and fine art. Included are items made and used in America and those few cherished things new immigrants were able to bring to the United States." With the help of "a nation-wide network of volunteers," the project had, by early 1990, netted some 1,000 objects, ranging from "Russian samovars to wedding gowns, tools and advertising signs of artisans and tradesmen, mementos of a variety of communal organizations, architectural elements from former synagogues, folk art, paintings and sculpture."[56]

Two other museums that have mounted nationwide campaigns for collectible objects relating to American Jewish life are A Living Memorial to the Holocaust–Jewish Heritage Museum in New York and the National Museum of American Jewish History in Philadelphia. This has led to complaints from local historical societies and other museums that may have been less aggressive in their efforts and fear losing out on objects of local significance. David Altshuler, director of the Jewish Heritage Museum, maintains that while competition undoubtedly exists, there are more than enough objects to go around and that the mere act of "beating the bushes"

---

[56]"Skirball Museum Description," mimeo, n.d.

elicits new material. Relying almost entirely on donations and long-term loans, that museum managed to collect some 5,000 artifacts in the space of two years.

Altshuler's reassurances notwithstanding, most experts agree that the proliferation of museums has inevitably increased competition for desirable art and objects in all subject areas. Moreover, Jewish museums are not alone in their desire for Jewish collectibles. They face competition as well from general art museums, local history societies, and private collectors.

Museum professionals are divided over possible solutions to the problem of competition. Some believe museums should specialize rather than attempt to be encyclopedic and thus avoid overlapping with sister institutions; others are inclined to accept the judgment of "free market" forces; still others urge cooperation and collaboration, with museums joining forces, for example, to purchase expensive works of art which can then be shared. Yet another proposal envisions museums compiling and sharing inventories of their collections for increased loan exhibition purposes, thereby reducing the pressure to collect, itself made more costly because of storage and preservation requirements. One consequence of present trends may well be the creation of more museums like the San Francisco Jewish Community Museum, which focuses on exhibitions and does not seek to build up its own permanent collections.

All this comes in a period when acquisition of art has become more difficult for economic reasons. As art critic Robert Hughes explained it, "American museums have in fact been hit with a double whammy: art inflation and a punitive rewriting, in 1986, of the U.S. tax laws, which destroyed most incentives for the rich to give art away. Tax exemption through donations was the basis on which American museums grew, and now it is all gone, with predictably catastrophic results for the future."[57] To deal with this new situation, curators have to put enormous time into wooing potential donors, often settling for long-term loans rather than outright gifts. Another strategy is "deaccessioning," a controversial process in which works regarded as less valuable or not in line with a museum's areas of specialization are sold and the proceeds used to acquire more desirable items.

Other issues for museums in relation to collections are improving the preservation of collections and the development of a standardized, computerized catalog of Judaica. Committees of the Council of American Jewish Museums are at work on both areas.

---

[57] *Time,* Nov. 27, 1989, pp. 60–61.

Exhibitions

Exhibitions are the heart of museum activity—the way in which works of art, ceremonial objects, artifacts from daily life, printed materials, and media are arranged and presented so as to convey a meaningful story or message, however concrete or abstract that may be.

Typically, museums offer between two and six changing exhibitions in the course of a year. A museum may create an exhibition from scratch, utilizing materials in its own collection and/or borrowed items, or it may show a loan exhibition originating with other museums or free-lance exhibition arrangers. The cost of originating an exhibit can be at least partially recouped through lending it to other museums. Conversely, the borrower museum can offer its audience changing exhibitions at less cost and effort by bringing in shows created elsewhere, and can "personalize" them through adding relevant objects from its own collection and through the related public programs it offers. The sources for traveling exhibitions include not only the American Jewish museums but the major museums in Israel as well as general museums, the Smithsonian Institution, and private exhibition organizers. With all this, museum professionals see a need for the development of more traveling exhibitions on Jewish themes, particularly those suitable for smaller exhibition spaces.

The choice of subjects itself reflects a museum's particular interests and what it perceives will appeal to a substantial audience. The calendar for just one year's schedule in one museum illustrates the remarkable range of subject matter that can be found. The Spertus Museum, Chicago, offered the following in the period September 1989 to September 1990: "Vaults of Memory: Jewish and Christian Imagery in the Catacombs of Rome" (198 color photographs provided by the International Catacomb Society augmented by artifacts from the museum's collection and loaned objects); "The Role and Activities of Jewish Immigrant Self-Help Societies in Chicago" (organized by the Chicago Jewish Historical Society, utilizing photographs, documents, and artifacts); "Agam in Chicago: The First 25 Years, 1953–1978" (49 works by Israeli artist Yaacov Agam from local collections); "Heritage and Mission: Jewish Vienna 1295–1935" (photopanels; cosponsored by the City of Vienna and Vienna's Jewish Welcome Service); "The Legacy of Bezalel" and "Recent Bezalel Graduates" (works by early and contemporary students of Jerusalem's famed art school; many from the collection of the Mizel Museum); "Unknown Secrets: Art and the Rosenberg Era" (60 works of art, historical and contemporary, relating to the Rosenberg espionage trial; organized by the Rosenberg Era Art Project); "Jew," a video installation by Pier Marton featuring taped interviews with young Jews born in Europe and now living in America; "Witness to History: The Jewish Poster 1770–1985" (50 posters created in Europe, the United States, and Israel, organized by the Magnes Museum).

In light of the broad and flexible way in which Jewish museums have come to define themselves, it is not surprising that the subjects of exhibitions are so varied. At the same time, certain themes and even the same exhibitions appear in the calendars of more than one institution. This reflects the timeliness of certain topics (the anniversary of the French Revolution, or the anniversary of the expulsion of the Jews from Spain are examples) but also certain practical exigencies, such as availability of desired materials and costs. Generally, in planning a schedule of exhibitions, an attempt is made to achieve a balance of Judaica, fine arts, ethnography, and cultural or historical subjects, as well as to include material appealing to various segments of its audience (Israel and Holocaust, for example).

Categories frequently overlap, however, particularly as the subjects selected are of a broad cultural nature. Shows like "Ashkenaz: The German Jewish Heritage" (Yeshiva University Museum, 1986–87) and "Gardens and Ghettos: The Art of Jewish Life in Italy" (Jewish Museum, 1989–90) incorporated fine art, ceremonial objects, manuscripts and books, folk art, photographs, furnishings, and artifacts from daily life—as well as music and videos—to depict the history and lives of those communities.[58] Both exhibitions were considered ground-breaking and drew high critical praise as well as large audiences.

Joan Rosenbaum, director of the Jewish Museum in New York, sees this eclectic approach—the combining of art and cultural artifacts in what she calls "contextual exhibitions"—as the hallmark of the Jewish museum. The focus of an exhibition has to be "the objects," she maintains, since that is what distinguishes museums from other cultural enterprises, but the objects must be presented in such a way as to engage the viewer's interest and emotions, which means providing a broader context for the objects.[59]

An examination of the exhibition schedules of Jewish museums in the late 1980s reveals a high interest in ethnographic/cultural exhibits, i.e., the life of particular Jewish communities, though most are more modest in scope than the two already mentioned. Some smaller exhibitions that traveled to cities other than where they originated were "Memories of Alsace: Folk Art and Jewish Tradition" (organized by the Jewish Museum, 1989); "The Jews of Kaifeng: Chinese Jews on the Banks of the Yellow River" (organized by Beth Hatefutsoth, Israel, 1989, and circulated by the National Foundation for Jewish Culture); and "Embellished Lives: Customs and Costumes of the Jewish Communities of Turkey" (organized by the Magnes Museum, 1989).

---

[58]A highly acclaimed exhibition of this sort, which was organized by the Smithsonian Institution Traveling Exhibition Service in 1983, was "The Precious Legacy: Judaic Treasures from the Czechoslovak State Collections." Largely because of space considerations, the Jewish Museum in New York was the only Jewish museum able to present the exhibition. It was shown in a number of other cities in general museums.
[59]Glueck, "The Jewish Museum Reaches Out."

"My Beloved Is Mine: Jewish Sephardic and Oriental Wedding Traditions" was shown at the Mizel Museum in Denver in early 1990—using artifacts on loan from the Magnes Museum in Berkeley. In the same period, the Jewish Museum opened "The Jews of the Ottoman Empire," which originated with the Israel Museum in Jerusalem.

Cultural/historical exhibitions based on photographs—often with accompanying artifacts—are frequently shown, often originated by organizations or independent exhibition arrangers. They are especially sought by smaller museums because they usually require less exhibition space and smaller costs for transportation, insurance, and security arrangements than exhibits of art and artifacts. One recent and much praised example in this category was "A Century of Ambivalence: The Jews of Russia and the Soviet Union, 1881 to the Present" (Jewish Museum, 1988), which took three years to prepare and included among its more than 400 photographs many brought over by recent émigrés from the USSR.

Cultural themes are also popular. The Klutznick Museum's "Hooray for Yiddish Theater in America!" (1985), which included over 250 artifacts (posters, photographs, costumes, and similar memorabilia), was enormously successful and still being circulated in 1989. "A People in Print: Jewish Journalism in America" (1988–1989), a joint venture of the Jewish Museum–New York and the National Museum of American Jewish History, Philadelphia, included over 300 drawings, periodicals, and related artifacts and two video presentations. The Jewish Museum's "Golem: Danger, Deliverance and Art" (1988) utilized paintings, prints, drawings, sculpture, video, and film to document the history of the Golem concept and legend and its use in theater, opera, and dance.

In keeping with its special interest in history and issue-oriented topics, the Jewish Museum mounted an extremely ambitious, nontraditional exhibition in "The Dreyfus Affair: Art, Truth and Justice" (1987), which went beyond merely documenting the story of Alfred Dreyfus's trial for treason and the public turmoil surrounding it but sought to explore the deeper issues raised by the affair, especially the debate among leading intellectuals and artists of the day. The exhibition drew on the voluminous materials produced during that period, using some 500 drawings, photographs, engravings, cartoons, posters, newspapers, illustrated magazines, and films. An indication of the serious attention paid to the exhibition was the publication in the *New York Times* of three separate articles on it: a "pre-story" by Elie Wiesel and two lengthy and laudatory reviews by art critics John Gross and John Russell.[60]

On a much smaller scale, but similar in seeking to depict a historic event

---

[60]Elie Wiesel, "When Hatred Seized a Nation," Sept. 6, 1987; John Gross, "In France's Dreyfus Affair, The Artists, Too, Asked 'Which Side Are You On?'" Sept. 20, 1987; John Russell, "Art: 'Dreyfus Affair' at the Jewish Museum," Sept. 25, 1987.

in its broader cultural context, was Yeshiva University Museum's "Medieval Justice: The Trial of the Jews of Trent" (1989). The exhibition was built around a 15th-century manuscript describing a famous ritual-libel case in the Tirol region, and used an array of medieval art works to illuminate the historical, political, economic, and social forces of the period.

American Jewish history is of perennial interest. Some recent exhibitions were: "Jewish Life in Northern California: Pacific Pioneers" (Magnes, Berkeley, 1988); "Pioneering Jews of Colorado" (Mizel, Denver, 1988); "Mordecai Manual Noah: The First American Jew" (Yeshiva, New York, 1988); and "Solomon Nunes Carvalho: Painter, Photographer and Prophet in 19th-Century America" (Jewish Historical Society of Maryland, in collaboration with the National Museum of American Jewish History and the Magnes Museum, 1989).

While the larger museums, with their greater resources and bigger professional staffs, have the edge in conceiving and implementing large-scale or complex exhibitions, they have no monopoly on imagination or resourcefulness. There was, for example, the exhibition mounted by Congregation Beth Ahabah Museum and Archives Trust in Richmond, Virginia, "Let Them Build Me a Sanctuary" (1989), to commemorate the bicentennial of the two founding, later merged, congregations that support the museum. Models were commissioned of the various buildings occupied over the years by the congregations; these were displayed with ritual objects and prayer books used in different periods, with explanations of changes in philosophy and practice that had taken place over the years. The Mizel Museum in Denver created "It Shall Be a Crown Upon Your Head: Headwear Symbolism in Judaism, Christianity, and Islam" (1986–87), using loan items from other Jewish museums, the Smithsonian, and local Christian and Muslim clergy. Cleveland's Temple Museum of Religious Art presented "The Loom and the Cloth" (1988), bringing together 200 antique works of fabric—ceremonial and costume—from more than 25 museums and private collections around the world—considered a remarkable feat for a museum of its size.

A significant general trend in Jewish museums is the development of the permanent "core" exhibition, one that provides visitors with a basic orientation to Judaism and Jewish history, alongside the temporary changing exhibits on various topics. The new emphasis on such exhibits stems from the recognition that visitors to many Jewish museums may well emerge from the experience as unenlightened about basic Jewish matters as when they entered. It may also reflect the makeup of today's museum audience: fewer Jewishly knowledgeable Jews and more non-Jews.

The National Museum of American Jewish History in Philadelphia opened its core exhibition, which covers the period from the arrival of the first Jews in North America to the present, early in 1990. The plans for the

Jewish Museum–New York's expanded quarters, to open in 1992, call for devoting half the gallery space to the permanent exhibit, which will incorporate many more items from the museum's holdings than were ever previously displayed, as well as radio and TV materials and access by means of computers to additional information. The exhibit will create "a total environment rather than just be a show of art and artifacts," museum director Rosenbaum told an interviewer.[61] In Los Angeles, the new Skirball Museum, too, will devote half its space to the core exhibit, which will emphasize three areas: the beliefs and practices of Judaism; American Jewish life; and the creative spirit—Jewish contributions to the arts and other areas. The museum is to feature interactive, interpretive exhibits, that is, "the objects will be presented in environments that provide a context for understanding the lives of the people who made or used them."[62]

In the area of Jewish ceremonial art, two trends are discernible. One is a growing emphasis on the contemporary, with museums seeking to contribute to the esthetic enhancement of Jewish life by encouraging artists to create, and the public to acquire, new ceremonial art. There is some tension here, however, because works that are salable do not necessarily meet museum standards of artistic quality. Therefore, to avoid serving merely as venues for "crafts shows"—or even to give that impression—museums may stage juried or invitational exhibitions, in which the exhibited items are not for sale until the exhibition closes; at the same time, a wider assortment of more "commercial" objects may be offered for sale in the museum gift shop. In their role of catalyst, museum curators may seek out gifted metalsmiths, ceramicists, and other artists (non-Jewish as well as Jewish) and commission specific works, when necessary providing guidance on ritual requirements. The B'nai B'rith Klutznick Museum in Washington, the National Museum of American Jewish History in Philadelphia, the Magnes Museum in Berkeley, and the Fred Wolf Gallery of the Philadelphia JCC Klein Branch have been particularly active in this area. A few museums have experimented with artist-in-residence programs, but have ultimately been forced to give them up for lack of space. The most extensive and long-lasting such effort was the Tobe Pascher Workshop at the Jewish Museum–New York, established for the leading Jewish metalsmith Ludwig Wolpert, which functioned from 1956 until the late 1980s.

The second trend is that of participatory exhibitions. The Skirball Museum pioneered the Purim mask exhibition—inviting both prominent artists and local Jewish schoolchildren to create masks of the chief characters in

---

[61]Joan Shepard, "Jewish Museum Plans Historic Exhibit," *New York Daily News,* June 20, 1985.
[62]Grace Cohen Grossman, "The Great American Judaica Treasure Hunt," *Reform Judaism,* Spring 1987, p. 13.

the Purim story, which were exhibited in the galleries. The San Francisco Jewish Community Museum, which had earlier sponsored a *sukkah* design contest for artists, undertook a similar Purim mask project. In addition, it originated "Hanukkah: Family Celebrations in Art," in which six families created distinctive Hanukkah settings, ranging from the whimsical (a giant dreidel) to the traditional (a replica of a *shtetl* room).

In the area of fine art, exhibits often focus on one artist or a group of artists, but there has also been an effort to organize shows around a theme. The Jewish Museum's "The Circle of Montparnasse: Jewish Artists in Paris 1905–1945" (1985) explored the experience of émigré Jewish artists—"the first generation of Jews to become professional visual artists in the West."[63] "Tradition and Revolution: The Jewish Renaissance in Russian Avant-Garde Art, 1912–1928," which originated with the Israel Museum and traveled to several American Jewish museums, documented a short-lived movement in which Jewish artists sought to blend traditional folk imagery with avant-garde trends afoot in Russia at the time of the revolution. The exhibition featured more than 140 original works by Marc Chagall, El Lissitzky, Issachar Ryback, Nathan Altman, and other artists, many of whom became leading figures in 20th-century art. The Klutznick Museum's "Continuing Witness: Contemporary Images by Sons and Daughters of Holocaust Survivors" (1989) featured paintings, sculpture, photographs, and prints by a dozen artists. And the Jewish Museum organized "In the Shadow of Conflict: Israeli Art, 1980–1989" (1989), the varied responses of 18 Israeli artists to the political and social situation in Israel.

Contemporary art remains problematic but is a central interest of most museum professionals and many museum supporters. Since the audience for Jewish museums includes people interested in more conventional, less challenging art as well as admirers of modern art, curators and directors are hard-pressed to satisfy all tastes and must engage in a delicate balancing act. They see their first obligation as assuring high quality in the art they exhibit, regardless of content. At the same time, they are equally obligated to demonstrate a Jewish justification for what they show.

It would obviously be impossible within the scope of this article to detail the artists whose works have been exhibited in Jewish museums, but here, too, a few examples offer an indication of the range and variety. In the spring of 1989, the Skirball Museum exhibited some recent gifts of 20th-century art: "The Scroll," by Los Angeles artist Ruth Weisberg, a 94-foot drawing with color wash, wrapped around the gallery, in which the artist depicted significant life-cycle events from her own experience as an American Jewish woman, incorporating scriptural and rabbinic motifs; works by

---

[63]Kenneth E. Silver, curator, in his introduction to the exhibition catalog.

six Israeli artists who work in various styles; 15 paintings by Max Band, a "School of Paris" artist who fled Nazi Europe and settled in Southern California; and "Black Forest VII," by Los Angeles artist Susan Moss, painted in memory of her grandparents who died in the Holocaust. In an exhibit considered groundbreaking, "Lights/Orot," at Yeshiva University Museum (1988), artists from MIT's Center for Advanced Visual Studies used electronic media to explore the Jewish concept of light in ritual; in 1989-90, the same museum's calendar included a show of paintings by Janet Shafner, "Modern Interpretations of Biblical Themes"; "Paintings for the Book of Psalms," by Raphael Abecassis; "A Graphic Midrash," by Alice Zlotnick; "Photographic Constructions" by Alan Rutberg; and "Photographs of the Jewish Cemetery in Venice," by Driscoll Devins and Arrigo Mamone. In an effort to make contemporary art more accessible, Spertus Museum—which has a permanent gallery for changing exhibitions of contemporary art—tries to present an accompanying videotape of the artist discussing his work generally and its Jewish significance.

Smaller institutions, too, are interested in contemporary art. Two examples are the Starr Gallery of the Jewish Community Center in Newton, Mass., which commissions works related to Hanukkah for an annual show, and the Philadelphia Museum of Judaica at Congregation Rodeph Shalom, which, in a gallery 14 by 45 feet in size, offers three exhibitions a year and prides itself on seeking out and showing promising new artists.

What lies ahead in the exhibition field is undoubtedly more emphasis on the cultures of recent Jewish immigrants to the United States, those from the USSR, Iran, South Africa, Israel, and Eastern Europe, as well as the folklore and anthropology of contemporary American Jewish life. Curators will be seeking out neglected Jewish artists of the past and will continue to encourage contemporary art on Jewish themes.[64]

TECHNIQUES

In the way it exhibits art, objects, and artifacts, the museum tells its story—and there are many ways to do it. The traditional static displays of objects in glass cases, with short accompanying explanatory labels, may be judged boring by all but the avid enthusiast. By contrast, the use of multimedia—recorded sound, audiovisuals, computer displays, and the like—may be regarded as distracting and inauthentic by the purist.

The approach to exhibition in museums generally has been changing dramatically, in an effort to make museums more interesting, to reach a wider public, and to communicate their subject more effectively. This devel-

---

[64]Nancy Berman, director, HUC Skirball Museum, in remarks to 1990 conference, Council of American Jewish Museums, Jan. 1990.

opment has given new prominence to exhibition designers and to museum educators, who are taking a greater role in creating and shaping exhibitions.[65] "Multi-experiential" activities, in imitation of such popular public attractions as Walt Disney World—are one element, one that is not necessarily favored by more traditional museum professionals. Another element is simply displaying fewer objects but presenting them in a contextual setting and with more explanations, perhaps using computers or videotapes.

In a way, the American Jewish museums have come relatively late to this approach. The Museum of the Diaspora–Beth Hatefutsoth, in Tel Aviv, which opened in 1978, showed how captivating Jewish history and culture could be when depicted in imaginative displays (though strictly speaking, Beth Hatefutsoth is not a museum, because it displays replicas, not real objects). And the Frankfurt (West Germany) Jewish Museum, which opened in 1988, "uses interactive 'theater-like installations' in its presentation of [Judaica]. Four exhibits present life-size tableaus corresponding to four 'stations in the life of the individual Jew,' namely, *brit milah* (circumcision), *bar mitzvah,* wedding ceremony and *chevra kadisha* (burial society)."[66]

Quite clearly, it is easier for museums just starting to follow the new methods. The new Skirball Museum plans to present objects "in environments that provide a context for understanding the lives of the people who made or used them,"[67] presumably not unlike what is described for Frankfurt. New York's Living Memorial to the Holocaust–Jewish Heritage Museum will offer a sophisticated interactive computer encyclopedia and a variety of multimedia displays.

Education and Public Programs

The growing emphasis by museums on their role as educational and cultural centers has led to increased emphasis on public programs of all sorts—programs that appeal to the general public and thus are often funded by local and state arts and cultural commissions. Programs geared specifically to schoolchildren are the largest component in this sphere but others are gaining in prominence—tailored for adult audiences, for children (not in school groups), and for families. The latter category includes programs for preschool children accompanied by one or more adults as well as activities for family groups with younger and older children. The rationale for such programs, as expressed by Jewish Museum education director Judith

---

[65]See William H. Honan, "Say Goodbye to the Stuffed Elephants," *New York Times Magazine,* Jan. 14, 1990, pp. 35–38.
[66]"Is Germany's New Jewish Museum Boring?" *Moment,* Oct. 1989, p.15.
[67]Grossman, "Great American Judaica Treasure Hunt," p. 13.

Siegel, is that with "fewer and fewer 'Jewish neighborhoods' with visible, tangible Jewish culture," with large numbers of Jews unschooled or with only minimal Jewish education, the Jewish museums can help to fill the "experiential gap," using, not texts and literature, but the arts and related activities.[68]

One sign of the seriousness being accorded to the education function is the growing willingness to include education professionals on the museum exhibition committee, helping to decide what will be exhibited, the exhibition design, scheduling, and so on—no longer brought in after the fact, but viewed as an integral part of the process.

Museum educators start off with the art and artifacts in the museum—whether in the permanent collection or a temporary exhibition—and use them as catalysts or springboards for exploring the wider historical and cultural contexts from which they come. The "Golem" exhibition at the Jewish Museum, for example, was accompanied by ten public programs, offered over the course of several months: a dramatic reading of an Israeli play in which an enactment of the Golem legend takes place in a concentration camp; a panel of noted writers discussing "Golems in Contemporary Literature"; a lecture on "Jewish Mysticism and the Golem"; a concert featuring two world premieres of works on the theme of the Golem; showings of two films based on the Golem legend; and a series of talks by artists whose works were featured in the exhibition.

When the Skirball Museum presented "Memories of Alsace," it arranged three related programs: a lecture on the history of the Jews of Alsace; an "Alsace Family Festival," including music, folk dancing, crafts, gallery games, and food; and a slide-illustrated symposium exploring the merger of French folk traditions with Jewish ritual. Mizel Museum offered three programs in conjunction with the exhibit "My Beloved Is Mine: Jewish Sephardic and Oriental Wedding Traditions": one, personal reminiscences by Sephardic and Oriental members of Denver's Jewish community; a lecture by a Yeshiva University professor on "Ashkenazic and Sephardic Jewry: One People, Diverse Traditions"; and a lecture on "Women's Traditions in the Sephardic and Oriental Worlds: Greece, Turkey & Morocco."

SCHOOL PROGRAMS

To provide the necessary interpretive functions, museums have built up staffs of professional educators and cadres of volunteer docents. To illustrate the growth that has taken place: the education staff of New York's

---

[68] Judith C. Siegel, "Education: Its New Place in American Museums. The Jewish Museum: A Case Study," lecture delivered at the annual meeting of the Council of American Jewish Museums, Jan. 16–17, 1989.

Jewish Museum increased from three full-timers in 1979 to seven or eight a decade later, plus part-time teachers. In 1989–90, with over 25,000 children a year attending its programs, the museum had pretty much reached the limits of the numbers it could accommodate.

Jewish museums have been remarkably successful in creating programs that are responsive to state curriculum needs and selling them to local schools—public, private, and parochial schools—ironically, somewhat more successfully than to Jewish schools. In many instances, the number of non-Jewish students visiting the museums far exceeds that of Jewish students. (At New York's Jewish Museum, the proportions are 70 percent and 30 percent; at Chicago's Spertus Museum, over half are non-Jews; at Los Angeles's Skirball Museum, the numbers are evenly divided.) Several factors are responsible for this situation. One is the museum's view of itself as a general cultural institution that makes Jewish life and culture accessible to a wide public. Another is the fact that there simply are, in a given city, more non-Jewish schoolchildren available. Another factor is logistical: Jewish schools may be at too great a distance; the crammed schedule of the day school and the short (and inconvenient) hours of the supplementary school, as well as the costs involved, make trips of any kind difficult. Against this, public schools seek out enrichment programs, respond eagerly to programs that supplement the curriculum and are effective with students, and are willing to make the trip and pay the necessary fees. There is, too, the very practical consideration that general funding sources, such as city and state arts commissions, look favorably on ethnic institutions that offer programs to the general public.

Yet another contributing factor is the often poor or nonexistent relationship that exists between the museum staff and the Jewish education establishment in a given locale, the latter often failing to recognize the educational potential of the museum. As a result, Jewish museum staffs have expended far more effort in working with state and local education authorities to develop "curriculum-based" programs of interest to the public schools than in cultivating the Jewish schools. This anomalous situation is frustrating to Jewish museum professionals themselves, who have begun to address the problem, at least in their professional meetings and in some practical steps.

Typically, classes are held in the mornings, weekdays and Sundays, before the museum opens to the general public. The programs utilize creative writing, art workshops, games and puzzles, and other activities in addition to viewing objects in the galleries.

Archaeology is the subject with the widest appeal, particularly for public schools, because it meshes easily with the curriculum, especially in social studies, e.g., life in ancient times, desert life, ancient Greece and Rome, the history of the alphabet, and so on. School programs can be built around permanent or temporary exhibits, varying the objects that are studied. Two examples from the 1989–90 school program guide of New York's Jewish Museum are "The Currency Connection" (grades 3–4), in which coins are used to learn about the social, economic, and political aspects of ancient societies, and "Through the City Gates" (grades 5–6), in which students learn about urban design, occupations, and consumer goods in ancient times by examining artifacts.

Skirball Museum's M.U.S.E. (Museum Utilization for Student Education) program offers, for grades 5–7, one or two classroom sessions and a two-hour museum visit in which students take part in "a simulated 'dig' for replicas of ancient artifacts and a museum hunt for the real artifacts they resemble."

The Spertus Museum's Artifact Center, which opened in 1989, is a complete facility devoted to archaeology and the ancient Middle East. The center includes a 30-foot "tell," or archaeological mound, where "artifacts" are discovered; a marketplace, with stalls of artisans and merchants; an Israelite house equipped with suitable props, where preschoolers and kindergarteners can engage in imaginative play; and a workshop where visitors take part in crafts, dramatics, and other creative activities.

The Holocaust is another popular topic for programs. The Jewish Museum offers, for grades 7–12, "Learning About the Holocaust Through Art," which uses works on current display supplemented by video and slide presentations. In 1989–90, students could view "Gardens and Ghettos: The Art of Jewish Life in Italy" to "witness the devastating destruction of Italian Jewry, and come to an understanding of the possible consequences of stereotyping, racial prejudice and hatred."

"Cultural Diversity and Pluralism" is another broad rubric for educational programs of interest to the public schools. These center on Jewish holidays—Hanukkah being especially popular, on Jewish ethnography, or on a general cultural topic with universal application or implications. The Skirball Museum M.U.S.E. program offers two "interactive classroom kits and museum experiences" in this area: (1) "Multi-Cultural Celebrations" for grades 4–6 provides a "classroom session, in which students explore hatboxes containing objects from and information on five celebrations in five different cultures," followed by "a 2½-hour Museum visit in which students learn about some Jewish celebrations and the objects which make them special. This visit also includes "a crafts project and a Museum hunt," followed by "an optional follow-up in the classroom: creating your own cultural museum." For grades 6–9, a program of 5–8 sessions on "Immigration and Family History" provides materials for students to learn about a German-Jewish family and a Polish-Jewish family and to research their own family histories.

American Jewish history also offers material for intercultural learning.

At the Mizel Museum, Denver, students visiting the exhibit on "Pioneering Jews of Colorado" were shown around by guides in period costume portraying prominent historical figures. Children were later given an opportunity to dress up in costume and act out the characters.

The area of Judaica is also covered in education programs. In conjunction with its exhibit "Serendipity—Treasures from the Yeshiva University Museum Collection," children visiting that museum carried out a variety of "gallery searches": name the animals used as symbols on Jewish ceremonial objects; find all the objects in the exhibition that include columns as a decorative motif; draw objects in the exhibition that have crowns; find "what's missing" in drawings of various objects. At Mizel Museum, Denver, in connection with an exhibit on Torah ornaments, children took part in a "Scribe's Workshop," where they learned hand lettering and made Torah breastplates and wimples.

Publications are an important aspect of public education. Recent years have seen a proliferation of exhibition catalogs, often containing scholarly essays and extensive illustration. Well-produced catalogs add considerably to the understanding of the background and context of an exhibition, as well as being available long after the exhibition itself has been dismantled.[69]

Funding

From the Jewish communal perspective, it would certainly seem desirable to determine how much money is actually being spent on Jewish museums and where the funds come from. However, as of the beginning of 1991, no systematic data were available on the financing of these institutions. In the absence of official documentation, some data were obtained informally for the seven "charter" members of the Council of American Jewish Museums, generally regarded as the major Jewish museums in the country.

It is well known—as well as the subject of some controversy—that vast sums of money are being invested in the creation of Holocaust museums: close to $150 million for the Washington Holocaust Memorial Museum; $50 million for the Museum of Tolerance of the Simon Wiesenthal Center in Los Angeles, and $100 million for A Living Memorial to the Holocaust–Jewish Heritage Museum in New York, not to mention the numerous smaller institutions in this category.

Among the general Jewish museums, both Hebrew Union College's Skirball Museum, in Los Angeles, and New York's Jewish Museum were in the midst of $50-million capital campaigns. The former was for a new building

---

[69]For a discussion of this subject and an extensive bibliography, see Tom L. Freudenheim, "Books on Art and the Jewish Tradition: 1980–1990," in *Jewish Book Annual* 48, 1990–1991 (New York, 1990).

in a new location; the latter, for renovation of the existing structure and an addition that would double the museum's available exhibition space, as well as to establish an endowment fund. (For the two-year duration of construction, the museum set up temporary shop in the building of the New-York Historical Society, where it would continue to offer exhibitions and programs.) All these capital programs were being funded by intensive fundraising campaigns carried out among both Jews and non-Jews, with many notable gifts from the latter category.

Capital campaigns are dramatic in scope but they are time-limited. An attempt was made to determine the amount of money expended on a continuing basis from the recent operating budgets of the seven major museums. While all seven museums willingly provided recent budget figures, it became clear that any direct comparison is not valid and may even be misleading. One reason is the use of different accounting methods; another is the extremely complicated relationships that exist between the sponsored museums and their parent bodies. Nevertheless, having offered these qualifications, the figures supplied by the museums provide a crude but legitimate barometer of the sums of money involved: Jewish Museum, New York (1988–89), $4 million; National Museum of American Jewish History (1989–90), $1.4 million; Yeshiva University Museum, New York (1989–90), $1.065 million; Skirball Museum, Los Angeles (1989–90), $786,000; Spertus Museum, Chicago (1989–90), $780,000; Magnes Museum, Berkeley (1989–90), $579,000; B'nai B'rith Klutznick Museum, Washington (1990–91), $400,000. According to Morris Fred, director of the Spertus Museum and chairman of the Council of American Jewish Museums, these figures can be expected to rise in the early '90s, not only due to normal increases but because a number of museums have undertaken costly installations of permanent core exhibitions.

To meet their annual budgets, Jewish museums put together a basket of funds from a variety of sources. Two generalizations can be made about this: one, the "mix" of funding sources is different for each institution; and two, for a given institution, the funding mix varies from year to year. For example, the proportion of government grants may be higher in a particular year, in consequence of a generous NEH grant, but lower the next year when smaller, or no, grants are received—and so on in each category of funding.

The more fortunate museums are those under institutional auspices, since at least a portion of their budgets is guaranteed. Among the sponsored institutions, four receive a substantial proportion of their support (40–50 percent) from their parent agencies: Yeshiva (Yeshiva University); Skirball (Hebrew Union College); Spertus (Spertus College of Judaica); and Klutznick (B'nai B'rith). (This support is in addition to actual housing, which is not included in the budget, though general maintenance costs are included.)

The Jewish Museum receives what amounts to token monetary support—less than 3 percent—from its sponsor, the Jewish Theological Seminary, but is housed "free" in the Seminary-owned museum edifice and is provided with certain administrative and consultative services.[70]

Some museums have major individual benefactors or foundations that provide endowments or continuing support. The Spertus Museum, Magnes Museum, Klutznick Museum, and Yeshiva University Museum have endowment funds that cover somewhere between 15 and 20 percent of their budgets.

All museums, even those with sponsors and/or endowments, must look to outside sources for some portion of their support. These include: individual donors (gifts, memberships, fund-raising events); corporations; foundations; government agencies; and Jewish federations. Program and admission fees and sales from museum shops also provide income, the latter, in some instances, a not insignificant amount.

Overall, Jewish communal funds in the form of allocations from federations account for only a small portion of museum funding. Among the major institutions, the Magnes Museum receives the most in direct federation support—over 11 percent of its budget, from the San Francisco and Bay Area federations and smaller area federations. The new museum in that area, the San Francisco Jewish Community Museum (1984), is unique in having been founded by a local federation; it began with an endowment of $1.75 million that the federation helped to raise and is housed in the federation building. (Among smaller museums, the Mizel Museum in Denver receives a federation allocation amounting to roughly 15 percent of its $100–120,000 budget.) Direct allocations are only one form of federation support. The Spertus Museum is an indirect recipient of federation funding, through the Chicago federation's support of the Spertus College of Judaica. Similarly, indirect support is given when a gallery of Jewish art is housed in a federation-supported Jewish community center. Federations also make special project grants (e.g., for a particular exhibit), and they make allocations to the National Foundation for Jewish Culture, which administers the Council of American Jewish Museums (annual budget of approximately $30,000 in direct costs).[71]

---

[70]Unlike the other institutional museums, the Jewish Museum is not located at the site of the parent institution, nor has it ever been an integral part of its teaching or research programs. Although JTS representatives sit on the museum board and faculty members serve as advisors, the museum carries out its own fund raising and in recent years has gained increasing autonomy in its management.

[71]In 1988, some 112 out of 179 Jewish community federations made allocations to the National Foundation for Jewish Culture, which in turn allocated funds to other cultural agencies, including: American Jewish Historical Society, YIVO Institute for Jewish Research, Histadruth Ivrith of America, Jewish Publication Society, and Leo Baeck Institute.

One reason for limited federation funding is the reluctance to support institutions that are under denominational auspices. Another is the perception that most museums have parent bodies caring for them and thus need less support. Primarily, though, it is widely accepted that in the competition for "the Jewish dollar," human-service needs should be given priority over art and culture. At a conference on "Art and Identity in the American Jewish Community,"[72] Phyllis Cook, executive director of the Jewish Community Endowment Fund of the San Francisco Jewish Community Federation, suggested that the community must be educated "to see the human-service aspect of arts and culture" and that "funding culture becomes a matter, not of altruism, but of self-interest."

In seeking support from individuals, Jewish museums confront an otherwise positive phenomenon, namely, the growing number of Jews serving on boards of art museums and other "high culture" institutions. An illustration of the change in this area is New York's most prestigious WASP bastion, the Metropolitan Museum of Art, which had a few Jews on its board since early in the century (e.g., Solomon Guggenheim, Benjamin Altman, Robert Lehman), but they reportedly felt "isolated and vulnerable." In the 1970s and 1980s, less out of "any devotion to ethnic egalitarianism than of a cold-eyed obeisance to economic realities," the number of Jews increased dramatically, so that by the mid-1980s, "roughly one-fifth of the Met's board was Jewish."[73]

What effect the gravitation of wealthy Jewish patrons of the arts toward the most prestigious institutions has on Jewish museums is not entirely clear. Some maintain that it has reduced the pool of prospective supporters; others that the supply of well-to-do Jews who have an interest in the arts is probably greater at present than at any previous period and that there is enough to go around. Some museum advocates believe that the new situation is actually more promising for the development of a truly committed leadership, of donors who want—in the words of Jewish Museum benefactor Albert A. List—"to link their interest in art and their bond with Judaism." He and his wife, List said, at the dedication of the Jewish Museum's List Wing in 1963, believed that their involvement with the museum "might in some way help us to articulate our understanding of art as essentially spiritual."[74]

The swelling number of foundations, in particular Jewish family founda-

---

[72]Jan. 18–19, 1987, cosponsored by the National Foundation for Jewish Culture, the Council of Jewish Federations, the Council of American Jewish Museums, Jewish Federation Council of Greater Los Angeles (Commission on the Arts, Council on Jewish Life), and the Hebrew Union College Skirball Museum.

[73]Robert C. Christopher, *Crashing the Gates: The De-Wasping of America's Power Elite* (New York, 1989), pp. 216–17.

[74]Feb. 17, 1963; typescript, JTS files.

tions, and the rise in support for the arts by corporations have made these bodies important targets of fund raising. Government, too, has assumed increasing importance in museum financing, with funds coming from arts agencies at all levels. The Institute of Museum Services, a federal agency, offers general operating and program support, with a special interest in such areas as preservation of collections. The National Endowment for the Humanities and the National Endowment for the Arts are considered major patrons, funding exhibitions and a variety of museum activities. State and local arts agencies underwrite specific projects, such as after-school art classes, lectures, and film series.

CONCLUSION

The burgeoning of Jewish museums is one of the success stories of American Jewish life. The museums testify to the integration of American Jews into the fabric of American culture, even as they assert a separate and proud Jewish identity. Within the variegated mosaic that is the American Jewish community, the exhibition galleries of a Jewish museum are probably the only place where one can see Hassidic and Orthodox Jews, Conservative, Reform, Reconstructionist, and "just Jews," Ashkenazim and Sephardim, liberals and conservatives, recent arrivals and longtime Americans mingling freely, viewing and appreciating art and objects that transcend differences in belief and life-style. At the same time, as many Jews become more distant from their roots and heritage—growing numbers of them becoming, through intermarriage, part of extensive family networks of non-Jews—museums serve as a neutral, socially acceptable meetingplace in which people of all backgrounds can be exposed to the richness and variety of the Jewish heritage. At their best, museums offer the means to discover or rediscover aspects of the Jewish experience that "create that interaction between visitor and object that sparks a sense of connectedness and understanding."[75]

Not that everyone is satisfied with the way Jewish museums are functioning. As noted above, they have been criticized for not taking their Jewish mission seriously enough, for failing to develop scholarship in Jewish art, for not teaching Jewish values, for failing to define their purpose adequately.

At the same time, they have been faulted for being boring, or for presenting only the gloomy side of the Jewish experience. Responding to the latter charges, Tom Freudenheim—who is widely respected for his professional attainments in the broader museum world and for his devotion to the cause

---

[75]Siegel, "Education: Its New Place in American Museums."

of Jewish museums—says that "most museums *are* boring," not just Jewish ones, and that he has seen "exceptionally engaging material in [Jewish] museums, and lots of boring things elsewhere." He agrees, though, that "there is a great deal more creative work to be done in Jewish museums," if they are to attract more visitors and make their message more engaging. What is needed, he maintains, is "far greater levels of financial support from the American Jewish community . . . and encouragement for museum personnel and for people wanting to enter the field as their life's work . . . for creative ideas . . . and experimentation."[76]

One step aimed at correcting some of the existing shortcomings was the establishment in 1988 of a joint program of the Jewish Theological Seminary and the Jewish Museum, the Mannekin Institute, which offers graduate courses in Jewish art and internships at the Jewish Museum and JTS Library. Although the institute does not confer degrees, the decision to offer specialized training for graduate students enrolled in other institutions clearly underscores both the growing interest in the field and the need to upgrade professional preparation.

The problems of self-definition and constant need to attract an audience are serious but not daunting. The people working in Jewish museums are capable, committed individuals who will struggle through to solutions. The one dark cloud hanging over the future of Jewish museums is the financial one—especially in a period of economic uncertainty—for only with adequate support can they ensure their survival and fulfill their promise.

---

[76]Freudenheim, "Thank You, Wendy Leibowitz," p. 19.

COUNCIL OF AMERICAN JEWISH MUSEUMS
(as of March 1991)

Charter Members

B'nai B'rith Klutznick Museum
1640 Rhode Island Avenue NW
Washington, DC 20036
(202) 857-6583
Mr. Michael Neiditch, Acting Director

Hebrew Union College–
  Skirball Museum
3077 University Mall
Los Angeles, CA 90007
(213) 749-3424
Ms. Nancy Berman, Director

The Jewish Museum
1865 Broadway
New York, NY 10023
(212) 399-3344
Ms. Joan Rosenbaum, Director

Judah L. Magnes Museum
2911 Russell Street
Berkeley, CA 94705
(415) 849-2710
Mr. Seymour Fromer, Director

National Museum of American
  Jewish History
55 North Fifth Street
Philadelphia, PA 19106
(215) 923-3811
Ms. Margo Bloom, Director

Spertus Museum of Judaica
618 South Michigan Avenue
Chicago, IL 60605
(312) 922-9012
Dr. Morris Fred, Director

Yeshiva University Museum
2520 Amsterdam Avenue
New York, NY 10033
(212) 960-5390
Ms. Sylvia Herskowitz, Director

General Members

Fenster (Gershon and Rebecca)
  Museum of Jewish Art
1223 East 17th Place
Tulsa, OK 74120
(918) 582-3732

Mizel Museum of Judaica
560 South Monaco Parkway
Denver, CO 80224
(303) 333-4156
Dr. Stanley M. Wagner, Director

Temple Museum of Religious Art
University Circle at Silver Park
Cleveland, OH 44106
(216) 791-7755
Ms. Claudia Fechter, Director

Associate Members

A Living Memorial to the Holocaust–
  Museum of Jewish Heritage
342 Madison Avenue, Suite 706
New York, NY 10173
(212) 687-9141
Dr. David Altshuler, Director

American Jewish Historical Society
2 Thornton Road
Waltham, MA 02154
(617) 891-8110
Mr. Bernard Wax, Director

Benjamin & Dr. Edgar R. Cofeld
  Judaic Museum of Temple Beth Zion
805 Delaware Avenue
Buffalo, NY 14209-2095
(716) 886-7150
Mr. Mortimer Spiller, Director

Beth Tzedec Museum
1700 Bathurst Street
Toronto, Ontario M5P 3K3
Canada
(416) 781-3511
Ms. Judith Cardozo, Curator

Central Synagogue
123 East 55th Street
New York, NY 10022
(212) 838-5122
Ms. Cissy Grossman, Curator

Cleveland College of Jewish Studies
26500 Shaker Boulevard
Beachwood, OH 44122-7197
(216) 464-4050
Ms. Leah Kaplan-Samuels,
  Program Director

Congregation Beth Ahabah
  Museum & Archives Trust
109 West Franklin Street
Richmond, VA 23233
(804) 353-2668
Ms. Cynthia Krumbein, Director

Elizabeth S. Fine Museum of the Con-
  gregation Emanu-El
Arguello Blvd. & Lake Street
San Francisco, CA 94118
(415) 751-2535
Ms. JoAnne Levy
Chairman, Museum Committee

Fred Wolf, Jr. Gallery
JCC of Greater Philadelphia
Jamison Ave. & Red Lion Rd.
Philadelphia, PA 19116
(215) 698-7300
Ms. Phyllis E. Gerson Apparies,
  Director

Judaica Museum: Hebrew Home for
  the Aged at Riverdale
5961 Palisade Avenue
Bronx, NY 10471
(212) 548-1006
Ms. Karen S. Franklin, Director

Hebrew Union College–JIR
Skirball Museum Cincinnati Branch
3101 Clifton Avenue
Cincinnati, OH 45220-2488
(513) 221-1875
Ms. Marilyn F. Reichert, Director

Hebrew Union College–JIR
Joseph Gallery
One West 4th Street
New York, NY 10012-1186
(212) 674-5300
Ms. Linda Robinson, Director
of College & Community Relations

The Jewish Community Museum
121 Steuart Street
San Francisco, CA 94105
(415) 543-8880
Ms. Linda Steinberg, Director

Jewish Historical Society of Maryland, Inc.
The Jewish Heritage Center
15 Lloyd Street
Baltimore, MD 21202
(301) 732-6400
Mr. Bernard Fishman, Director

Jewish War Veterans
National Museum, Archives and Library
1811 R Street, NW
Washington, DC 20009
(202) 265-6280
Ms. Leslie M. Freudenheim, Curator

Joseph Baron Museum
Cong. Emanu-El B'ne Jeshurun
2419 E. Kenwood Blvd.
P.O. Box 11698
Milwaukee, WI 53211
(414) 964-4100
Ms. Annette Hirsh,
Chair, Museum Committee

Kanner Heritage Museum
3560 Bathurst Street
North York, Ontario M6A 2E1
(416) 789-5131
Ms. Pat Dickinson, Coordinator

May Museum of Judaica
Temple Israel
140 Central Avenue
Lawrence, NY 11559
(516) 239-1140
Ms. Fredda Harris, Cochairman

Museum of the Congregation
Emanu-El of the City of New York
One East 65th Street
New York, NY 10021-6596
(212) 744-1400
Ms. Reva Kirschberg, Director

Park Avenue Synagogue
50 East 87th Street
New York, NY 10028
(212) 369-2600
Ms. Ita Aber, Curator

Philadelphia Museum of Judaica
at Congregation Rodeph Shalom
615 North Broad Street
Philadelphia, PA 19123
(215) 627-6747
Ms. Joan C. Sall, Curator
Mailing Address:
112 Wetherill Road
Cheltenham, PA 19012
(215) 635-1322

Plotkin Judaica Museum
 of Greater Phoenix
3310 N. Tenth Avenue
Phoenix, AZ 85013
Mrs. Sylvia Plotkin, Director

Rabbi Frank F. Rosenthal Memorial
 Museum-Temple Anshe Shalom
20820 Western Avenue
Olympia Fields, IL 60461
(708) 748-6010
Mr. Jeffery N. Mina
Chairperson of Museum Committee

Starr Gallery
Leventhal-Sidman Jewish Community
 Center
333 Nahanton Street
Newton Centre, MA 02159
(617) 965-7410 x 168
Ms. Diane Palley, Gallery Director

Temple Judea Museum
 of Keneseth Israel
York Road & Township Line
Elkins Park, PA 19117
(215) 887-8700
Ms. Judith B. Maslin, Director

Review of the Year

UNITED STATES

Civic and Political

Intergroup Relations

OBJECTIVE INDICES OF ANTI-SEMITISM in America remained relatively low in 1989, but anti-Semitism, in one form or another, in one place or another, weighed heavily in the communal concerns of American Jewry. Extremism on the Right was a source of uneasiness, as were various episodes of tension between the United States and Israel. Catholic-Jewish relations were marked by ups and downs; the most serious instance of the latter was the controversy around the Carmelite convent at Auschwitz, which reached a dramatic climax this year.

Anti-Semitism and Extremism

A continuing increase in the number of anti-Semitic incidents was reported by the Anti-Defamation League's annual audit for 1989, with more episodes of brutality than in the past and more serious violent crimes—arson, bombing, and cemetery desecration. The overall number of incidents, 1,432, was the highest ever reported in the audit's 11-year history. This figure included 845 episodes of desecration and vandalism and 587 acts of harassment, threat, and assault against Jewish individuals, their property, and institutions. The report underscored signs of growing neo-Nazi "skinhead" involvement and the troubling rise of incidents on the college campus—the latter up by a third over 1988.

Two especially violent episodes occurred in Brooklyn. In July an elderly Holocaust survivor was stabbed to death after he confronted a neighbor he suspected of painting a swastika and death's head on his door; in October two Jewish 19-year-old Brooklyn College students were severely beaten as they left a Hillel House party. Since the attack was accompanied by anti-Semitic epithets, the police labeled it a bias incident. The next day, three Brooklyn teenagers were arrested and charged with felonious assault and civil-rights violations.

Several incidents of firebombing took place during the year. The building of the San Diego *Jewish Times* was firebombed in April and again in August. The building, empty at the time of the attacks, had previously been defaced by swastikas, and anti-Semitic phone threats had been received by the newspaper. Jews and Jewish institutions in San Francisco, California; Columbus, Ohio; and Marblehead and

Wellesley, Massachusetts, were among other targets of vandalism and harassment during the year.

Several well-publicized incidents of anti-Semitic, or alleged anti-Semitic, expression occurred this year. *New York* magazine drama critic John Simon drew fire (in April) for comparing actor Mandy Patinkin's appearance in a production of *The Winter's Tale* to "a caricature in the notorious Nazi publication *Der Stuermer*" and for referring to a black actress in stereotypical terms. Though Simon's use of vicious and offensive language is virtually a hallmark of his writing, he was accused of racism and anti-Semitism by theater colleagues and Jewish agencies.

On a more serious plane, the State University of New York began proceedings in June to dismiss a tenured faculty member at the Binghamton campus because of alleged anti-Semitic slurs. According to two Jewish students, Assoc. Prof. Sid Thomas of the philosophy department had engaged in a long classroom tirade against Jews for, among other things, always "crying" about the Holocaust, and helping to bring George Bush into office. He said that "the Jews deserve to get it in the nose."

A black member of the popular rap music group Public Enemy was reportedly fired by the group in June, although rehired in August, after telling the *Washington Times* that "the Jews were wicked . . . [and] have a history of killing black men." Known as "Professor" Griff, the rap singer said that "the Jews have a grip on America" and were responsible for "the majority of wickedness that goes on across the globe." Griff, like the other members of Public Enemy, belonged to Louis Farrakhan's Nation of Islam, and said that he had obtained his knowledge of Jewish history from the Nation of Islam's historical research department.

Griff's remarks not only touched on black-Jewish relations but raised the question of how much of the anti-Semitic activity in the country was the product of organized groups.

SKINHEAD GROUPS

Indeed, much of the overt anti-Semitic activity during the year was associated with racist "skinhead" groups. In June the ADL issued a 32-page report entitled *Skinheads Target the Schools*. It reported that this loose network of racist and anti-Semitic organizations now had some 3,000 members in 31 states, up from the 2,000 in 21 states that had been reported the previous October. The report also indicated that these groups had become more militant, adding handguns, shotguns, and even semiautomatic weapons to their usual arsenal of knives, bats, chains, and steel-toed boots.

At the beginning of the year, Christopher Cook, a 19-year-old leader of a skinhead group called the Up Starts, was arrested for involvement in the vandalism of an Orthodox synagogue, Kesher Israel, in Harrisburg, Pennsylvania. Anti-Semitic graffiti and swastikas had been spray-painted on the synagogue building, causing a thousand dollars' worth of damage. Cook had only recently started a Harrisburg branch of the Up Starts, a California-based white supremacist skinhead group. He was charged under the state's new Ethnic Intimidation Act, under whose provisions the desecration of churches and synagogues, as well as other venerated objects and institutions, was subject to felony penalties, regardless of the monetary amount of the damage involved. In announcing the arrest, the Harrisburg Police Bureau noted that most of the other skinhead groups in that area were not racist or anti-Semitic and had denounced Cook's actions.

The leaders of a group identified as a "neo-Nazi skinhead ring" were arrested by New Jersey police in August, after a spurt of anti-Semitic activity around the Middlesex County area. Swastikas and graffiti such as "Six million, why not," "No kikes," and "Niggers out" had been painted on the Rutgers University Hillel building, around a New Brunswick high school, and other buildings in the vicinity.

Police reported that one of the three men, identified as 18-year-old James Donato, was "the only one who looked like a Skinhead. He was wearing punk Nazi boots and his head was shaved. The other two looked pretty much like the boy next door." The Middlesex prosecutor described murals that were found on the walls of the warehouse that served as the group's clubhouse, and even on the walls of Donato's home: "It was incredible. The walls show a progression of the type of activities these neo-Nazis were involved in since 1986. It shows how they started as a heavy metal group, and got into Satanism, sadomasochism and eventually neo-Nazi ideology." The prosecutor, Alan Rockoff, said that the group, consisting of a dozen to two dozen members, was "not highly organized or dangerous," but he was concerned about the neo-Nazi and Ku Klux Klan pamphlets that he found.

A federal case began this year in Dallas, involving 17 men charged with violating U.S. civil-rights statutes by defacing a synagogue, a Jewish center, and a mosque and attacking blacks and Hispanics, in 1988. They were all identified as members of a gang called the Confederate Hammer Skins, which had an estimated 40 to 45 members, with another 60 sometimes becoming involved with their activity. During the grand jury investigation, which began in March, 12 of the accused entered guilty pleas and became witnesses for the government. Five men—the gang's leaders—were indicted in September. One of the five, Daniel Alvis Wood, had already been convicted and sentenced on state charges the previous January. When Wood, a 20-year-old with a Hitler mustache, was sentenced to the maximum by the state judge, he gave the "Heil Hitler" salute.

Other extremist groups were not as prominent in activity as they had been in recent years, thanks to a vigorous period of prosecution by federal authorities. Lyndon LaRouche, Jr., 66-year-old leader of a right-wing group espousing anti-Semitism and various conspiracy theories, a three-time presidential candidate, was sentenced in January to 15 years in prison for tax evasion and fraud. Six codefendants were imprisoned with him. Howard Pursey, a leader of the Church of Jesus Christ Christian–Aryan Nations, which had already been weakened by federal prosecution, surfaced in Canada in March, claiming refugee status.

In public rallies called by organized bigots during the year, predominantly by skinheads, the bigots were typically outnumbered by protesters. Tom Metzger, California leader of the White Aryan Resistance, prepared for thousands of bigots to assemble in March on a farm in Napa, California, leased under false pretenses from a Jewish refugee from Nazi Germany. Fewer than 200 of his followers showed up, most of them with hair cut short and swastika jackets. By contrast, 500 protesters picketed the rally, watched by some 200 policemen. In April, when fewer than a hundred skinheads and white supremacists gathered in Coeur D'Alene, Idaho, to celebrate the hundredth anniversary of Hitler's birth, over a thousand protesters were present. Most of the protesters at both the California and Idaho rallies were not Jewish. Jewish agencies generally were of the view that neither small gathering of bigots would have received media attention without the presence of the protesters.

DAVID DUKE

One apparent success story for bigotry concerned David Duke, aged 39, former grand wizard of the Knights of the Ku Klux Klan and president of the National Association for the Advancement of White People (NAAWP), who won a seat in the Louisiana state legislature, representing the virtually all-white 81st district of Metairie, a suburb of New Orleans. He won the February election by a margin of fewer than 250 votes in a district of 21,000 voters. He ran as a Republican, although the national Republican party, President George Bush, and former president Ronald Reagan all denounced and repudiated him.

Duke notably avoided any anti-Semitic or racial statements in his campaign, concentrating on issues of taxes, welfare reform, and affirmative action. However, he remained the head of the NAAWP, whose publication, the *NAAWP Letter*, carried articles customarily attacking blacks, Jews, Zionism, and Israel. A month after his election, Duke spoke at the Chicago convention of the neo-Nazi Populist party, on whose slate he had run for president in 1988. Irwin Suall, fact-finding director for the ADL, said about Duke that "he continues to represent the racist and anti-Semitic underworld, and his appearance of respectability and mainstream politics is pure deception."

Duke announced in December that he would run for the U.S. Senate as a Republican against incumbent Democrat J. Bennett Johnston. According to a Jewish Telegraphic Agency report (December 7, 1989), Elizabeth Rickey, a member of the Louisiana State Republican Central Committee, visited his state legislative office and found that she could order racist and anti-Semitic material through Duke's mail-order business, Americana Book. She joined in the formation of a bipartisan, nondenominational coalition to fight Duke's bid for the U.S. Senate.

EVALUATING ANTI-SEMITISM

Despite these various manifestations of hostility evidenced toward Jews, the annual survey conducted for the American Jewish Committee by the Roper Organization found no increase in anti-Jewish attitudes among the American people. In answer to the key question touching on anti-Semitic attitudes, only 8 percent of the respondents thought that Jews had too much power in the United States, a smaller percentage than believed that Arab interests, blacks, Orientals, or the Catholic Church had too much power.

Also, mainstream American life offered no evidence of any upturn in anti-Semitic behavior. There were no notable reports of economic discrimination; the annual *Forbes Magazine* report on wealthy Americans included the same disproportionate number of Jews as in recent years; a disproportionate number of Jewish students and faculty continued to appear in the top universities (the "quota" restrictions that were an issue at the University of California focused on Asians, not Jews); and, while critical comments on Israel seemed to increase in the mainstream political arena (see below), overt anti-Semitic references were carefully avoided.

These facts, viewed in conjunction with the skinhead-type anti-Semitic episodes of the year, suggested that there might be substantially no more active anti-Semites among the American population at large than there had been, but that the fringe anti-Semitic and racist groups, notably the youthful skinhead-type groups, were becoming more militant and violent in their activities. Supporting that proposition was the fact that those fringe gangs and their activities were vigorously condemned in all authoritative quarters of society. Typically, after a synagogue and a Jewish community center had been defaced in Marblehead, Massachusetts, in July, a mass rally of condemnation was organized by clergy of all denominations and a spectrum of community leaders, including top school and police officials, joining with black and Jewish leaders.

Law enforcement agencies, legislators, and other public officials were uniformly active in efforts to stem skinhead-like activities. In November Attorney General Richard Thornburgh announced that the Justice Department had opened a record 41 investigations into racial and anti-Semitic violence, involving 62 defendants. He pledged "to use the full weight of criminal law against hate groups and all those who would deny the civil rights and civil liberties of all Americans." That "criminal law" included the 1988 federal Religious Violence Act, which imposed criminal penalties for damage to religious property and for the obstruction of persons in the free exercise of religious beliefs. More than 30 state legislatures had already passed hate-crimes legislation of one kind or another.

Effects of Israel-Related Events

In the ADL's annual audit of anti-Semitism for 1988, 117 anti-Semitic acts of vandalism were specifically linked by identified perpetrators to the *intifada*, the uprising in Israel's occupied territories. In 1989, although there was a sharp decline in this specific type of incident, other forms of Israel-related bigotry directed toward Jews, or tensions over Israel-related differences between Jews and others, were clearly evident. It was often difficult to make a distinction between outright bigotry and "mere" intergroup tensions, but both affected the Jewish sense of security.

Much of this ambiguous kind of tension occurred on college campuses around the country. At the University of Michigan, editorials in the student-run newspaper, the *Michigan Daily*, suggested that the Israeli intelligence service was behind the fatal bombing of Pan American flight 103 at the end of the previous year. Another editorial charged that the emigration of Ethiopian Jews to Israel was "a ruse . . . to provide more occupiers of Palestinian land." Jewish students organized a demonstration in front of the newspaper office. Dr. Amnon Rosenthal, chairman of the university's board of publications, said that these editorials were anti-Semitic because they contained "harassment and intimidation that are a form of racism." But the Ann Arbor chapter of the American-Arab Anti-Discrimination League argued that "people make a fundamental mistake in that they confuse Zionism with Judaism." The Jewish editor of the *Michigan Daily*, Adam Schrager, said that the newspaper would maintain its pro-Palestinian stance, but would make greater effort to distinguish between Zionism and Judaism, and between Zionism and the policies of a particular Israeli administration.

However, given the relationship between American Jews and pro-Israel feelings, the distinction between attacks on Jews and on Israel often remained difficult to make in practice.

At the same time that the State University of New York began proceedings to dismiss Prof. Sid Thomas because of his anti-Semitic remarks in class (see above), similar proceedings were instituted against Khalil Semaan, a tenured professor of classical and Near Eastern studies at the same Binghamton campus. The university charged that Semaan "intentionally misquoted several sources in such a way as to misrepresent the original statements." This charge related to Israeli-Arab issues; it also reflected the fact that he had had several disputes with Jewish faculty members and students over his charges of "Zionist brainwashing" by instructors.

Hard-core anti-Semites were, of course, more likely to be anti-Israel because they were anti-Jewish than the other way around. But the more potentially ominous Jewish security issue was the possibility of backlash against American Jews because of unpopular political activity on behalf of Israel. Such a backlash would presumably depend on the relative standing of Israel itself among Americans and the popularity of American government acts in support of Israel.

In the annual poll commissioned by the American Jewish Committee, released in June, the Roper Organization found that the sympathy of the American public for the Israeli cause, which had dropped considerably following the outbreak of the *intifada* at the end of 1987, appeared to have leveled off—and still was substantially higher than sympathy for the Arab cause. In 1986, 53 percent of the respondents said they sympathized with the Israeli cause, as against 36 percent in 1989. In 1989,

13 percent said they sympathized with the Arab cause, only a few percentage points above 1986. In short, it was not that the American public was much more sympathetic to the Arabs, but they were much less sympathetic to Israel. Some observers interpreted this as a sign of growing indifference.

This downward trend was compatible with the conventional theory that the American public's feelings of sympathy toward Israel were heavily if not exclusively shaped by the signals transmitted by the U.S. government. During the year, those signals were mixed. Among positive signals, the U.S. vetoed three different UN Security Council resolutions condemning Israel for its handling of the *intifada*—in February, June, and November—although the other 14 members of the Security Council voted for all three resolutions. The State Department also warned in May that the United States would withhold funds from any UN body that gave the PLO full membership. And for its part, Congress passed, and President Bush signed, in November, the 1990 foreign aid bill, which included $3 billion in all-grant to Israel.

On the other side of the ledger, the negative signals from the nation's capital were more frequent than they had been in the recent past, especially from the administration. (See "The United States, Israel, and the Middle East," elsewhere in this volume.) In January the State Department strongly criticized Israel's deportation of 15 Palestinians from the West Bank and Gaza. In the same month, U.S. representatives continued meeting with the PLO, which drew publicized denunciations from both the Conference of Presidents of Major Jewish Organizations and the Jewish Students' Network. In February the annual international human-rights report of the State Department harshly criticized Israel's handling of the *intifada* and charged Israel with "a substantial increase in human rights violations."

In May Secretary of State James Baker made a partly critical and controversial speech to the American Israel Public Affairs Committee (AIPAC) in which he urged that Israelis give up their dream of a "Greater Israel." In August Senate Republican leader Robert Dole chided Israel on the Senate floor for the "irresponsible" act of seizing a Shi'ite leader, Sheikh Abdul Karim Obeid, from his home in southern Lebanon. And there was some initial criticism of this Israeli action by the White House, after it was rumored that U.S. Marine Lt. Col. William Higgins, a prisoner of Shi'ites in Lebanon, had been hanged in retaliation for the Israeli abduction of Sheikh Obeid.

Adding to this atmosphere of increasing official criticism of Israel were the efforts of anti-Israel forces in this country to dramatize a growing tension between the two allies. A full-page advertisement placed in major American newspapers in January by the National Association of Arab Americans was headlined "Who Is Not Complying with the U.S. Position on the Middle East?" and purported to show that the PLO was more in agreement with U.S. policies than Israel.

In the same month, the American-Arab Anti-Discrimination Committee—joined by George Ball, former under secretary of state, former congressman Paul Findley, and others—filed legal charges with the Federal Election Commission against AIPAC, 27 pro-Israel political action committees, and 26 of their officers. The main charge was that AIPAC illegally coordinated the PACs' contributions to political campaigns. AIPAC officials were confident that the charges, being without substance, would be rejected; however, the brunt of the effort was to highlight the strenuous lobbying activities of the American Jewish community on behalf of Israel, which, in other propaganda campaigns, was being cast as a poor ally of the United States.

The ultimate direction of these efforts was to place the loyalty of American Jews in question, such disloyalty being the foundation stone of most anti-Semitic belief systems. In fact, the 1989 Roper survey found that there had been no rise in the belief of Americans that "most American Jews are more loyal to Israel than to the United States." However, a substantial 21 percent of all Americans did subscribe to that proposition, and another 36 percent did not choose to offer an opinion one way or another. The potential danger in these figures lay in a hypothetical backlash that might follow any seriously growing tensions between the United States and Israel.

Soviet Jewry

The new liberal emigration policy of the Soviet government created new problems and led to some policy differences between American Jews and their government. Until this year, Soviet Jews left the USSR on Israeli visas and were flown to Vienna, where they decided to go on to Israel or else "dropped out" and applied for visas to other countries. Many of those in the latter group were sent to Rome to apply for refugee status in the United States. As the number of Soviet Jewish émigrés swelled—to an unprecedented 71,000 in fiscal 1989—the administration began to reject an increasing number of refugee applicants. The government contended that given the improvements under President Mikhail Gorbachev, it was no longer valid for all Soviet Jews to claim a "well-founded fear of persecution."

Administration officials indicated that those denied refugee status could enter the United States under public-interest parole status, but doing so would deny them a variety of benefits. Growing numbers now congregated in way-stations, particularly in Ladispoli, outside of Rome, where they publicly criticized the U.S. government for rejecting their refugee status. In August, according to Mark Talisman, Washington representative of the Council of Jewish Federations, 22 percent of Soviet Jewish families in Rome seeking refugee status were refused it.

In September, when President George Bush's coordinator for refugee affairs, Jewel Lafontant, said that Jews denied refugee status by the United States "can always return to Russia in these days of *glasnost*," protest from the Jewish community was swift; so were reassurances by Deputy Secretary of State Lawrence Eagleburger who called her remarks "insensitive." Attorney General Dick Thornburgh, in response to criticism of the government's immigration policies, issued a directive ordering Immigration and Naturalization personnel in Rome to "immediately reevaluate" cases in which refugee status had not been granted.

The Bush administration, seeking a more comprehensive plan to deal with the huge numbers of applicants, drafted and subsequently implemented a plan to limit the number of Soviet Jewish refugee slots to 40,000 per year, roughly equaling the number who had first-degree or closest relatives in the United States. The plan called for an end to the processing in Rome, which would save money for both the U.S. government and U.S. Jewish philanthropies and would also stop the practice of Soviet Jews leaving on Israeli visas but dropping out in Europe (which the Israelis objected to). Beginning October 1, Soviet citizens seeking to enter the United States would have to apply for refugee status at the U.S. embassy in Moscow.

Most American Jewish groups which had fought for the principle of "freedom of choice" (Israel or the United States) felt that while the plan had problems—among them the length of time it would take to process refugee applications and the closer scrutiny of refugee applicants—it was basically fair. According to David Harris, Washington representative of the American Jewish Committee, American Jewish groups recognized that because of the "sheer numbers" of Jews permitted to emigrate, limitations were inevitable. He also noted that, unlike other refugee groups, such as the Cambodians, Soviet Jews had the alternative of Israel to go to.

With the overall improvement in conditions for Soviet Jews, traditional forms of advocacy, i.e., rallies and demonstrations, declined. Most Jewish communities agreed to a moratorium as long as conditions for Soviet Jews continued to improve. Thus, for the second straight year, the Coalition to Free Soviet Jewry voted to cancel "Solidarity Sunday" in May because of "an increase in emigration, the release of political prisoners and progress in human rights," according to Rabbi Haskel Lookstein, the coalition's chairman. Advocacy in the form of meetings between Jewish organizations and Soviet officials grew. In addition, only muted concern was expressed about the U.S. decision to participate in an international human-rights conference in Moscow in 1991.

Amidst the positive developments, increasing attention was paid to growing popular anti-Semitic expression in the USSR. Concern focused in particular on the apparent growth of nationalist organizations with anti-Semitic platforms, such as Pamyat; anti-Jewish vandalism; threats and even reports of individual cases of violence that were aimed at intimidating the Jewish community.

The Carmelite Affair

This year, American Jews became more actively involved in the controversy that had occupied European Jews for several years over the existence of a Carmelite convent on the site of the former concentration camp at Auschwitz, in Poland. European Jewry, which had learned of the convent's existence in 1985, had protested it vigorously, seeing it as a denial of Auschwitz's special significance to Jews, for whom it was the primary symbol of Jewish losses in the Holocaust. Two meetings on the subject were held between European Jewish representatives and members of the Roman Catholic hierarchy in July 1986 and February 1987; the latter produced an agreement for creating a center for "information, education, meeting and prayer" outside the Auschwitz-Birkenau camps, to be completed by February 22, 1989. It was understood, although not explicitly spelled out, that the nuns would be housed in the new facility. The written agreement on the new center emphasized that it would focus on the Jewish tragedy, the Shoah, and also on the suffering and martyrdom of the Polish and other peoples during World War II and that it would be a place for dialogue and encounter.

In February, when it was evident that ground had not even been broken for the center, American Jewish groups complained that the Polish Roman Catholic Church was not living up to the terms of the agreement. A conference between representatives of the Vatican Commission on Catholic-Jewish Relations and representatives of Jewish organizations—already postponed once to February 23, 1989, because of uncertainty over the convent's relocation—was now canceled.

Catholic authorities blamed technical difficulties for the delay in relocating the Carmelite convent. However, the addition of a 23-foot cross on the grounds of the convent—after the agreement was signed—added fuel to the controversy. Demonstrations were held at the site of the convent and throughout the world. In May, with the issue unresolved, the Anti-Defamation League of B'nai B'rith canceled a scheduled audience with the pope. One protest, in particular, led to considerable Jewish-Catholic tension and ultimately helped force a resolution of the issue. On July 14, a group of seven New York Jewish activists, led by Rabbi Avraham Weiss, climbed over the fence surrounding the convent and sought to speak with the nuns. They were beaten and dragged away by workingmen.

In the aftermath, Cardinal Franciszek Macharski, archbishop of Krakow, whose diocese encompassed the convent—announced that the promised relocation had been indefinitely postponed. He based the decision on "a violent campaign of accusations and defamation, and offensive—not only verbal—aggression, which echoed up to Auschwitz" and went on to say that the campaign was the work of "certain Western Jewish circles." Jewish groups responded strongly, insisting that the original agreement be honored. Three Roman Catholic cardinals, including Cardinal Albert Decourtray of Lyons, who had signed the original agreement, criticized Macharski's decision. Decourtray, who was joined by Cardinal Jean-Marie Lustiger, archbishop of Paris, and Cardinal Godfried Danneels, head of the Catholic Church in Belgium, stated that the original agreement "is mandatory and binding on those who signed it. Its decisions cannot be re-examined."

The controversy reached its climax when Cardinal Jozef Glemp, Roman Catholic primate of Poland, called the protests "an offense to all Poles and a threat to Polish sovereignty" and charged that Jews controlled the international news media and were directing a media attack against Poland. In referring to the July 14 protest, he spoke of Jews who "launched attacks on the convent at Oswiecim. In fact, it did not happen that the sisters were killed or the convent destroyed, because they were apprehended. . . ." Responding to the implied accusation of violent intent, one of the protesters, Glenn Richter, said that "to deny that our action, witnessed by a dozen reputable foreign journalists and hundreds of Polish citizens, was anything but peaceful in intent is incomprehensible." Rabbi Avraham Weiss retained noted attorney Alan Dershowitz to investigate what legal steps could be taken against Glemp for his remarks. In November Weiss filed suit in a Polish court charging that Glemp had slandered him. Glemp's remarks also led the Anti-Defamation League of B'nai B'rith and the World Jewish Congress, among other Jewish organizations, to boycott a church-organized ecumenical prayer service held at Auschwitz as part of Poland's ceremonies marking the 50th anniversary of Germany's invasion.

Roman Catholic cardinals John O'Connor of New York and Bernard Law of Boston and Archbishop Roger Mahoney of Los Angeles, disturbed by the escalation of events, made strong pleas for the agreement to be honored quickly. In the wake of the controversy, Glemp was forced to cancel a September trip to the United States, which would have taken him to Chicago, Cleveland, Milwaukee, and Detroit, cities in which he would have faced certain protests. Confronted by all this opposition, Glemp began to adopt a more conciliatory tone. He may have been influenced by the involvement of a West German Jewish businessman, Zygmunt Nissenbaum, who met with Glemp in mid-September and reportedly offered to help pay to relocate the convent.

A significant breakthrough occurred on September 19 when the Vatican, which previously had announced it would not get involved in the controversy, finally endorsed publicly the 1987 accord calling for the relocation of the convent. A statement issued by Cardinal Johannes Willebrands, president of the Vatican Commission for Religious Relations with the Jews, indicated as well that the Vatican was prepared to help pay for an interfaith center: "The Holy See is convinced that such a center would contribute in a significant manner to the development of good relations between Christians and Jews. In order to support the realization of this important but costly project, the Holy See is prepared to make its own financial contribution."

A day later, following informal meetings in London with Sir Sigmund Sternberg, chairman of the International Council of Christians and Jews, and other Jewish leaders, Glemp retreated from his former position. In a letter to Sir Sigmund, he wrote that the accord "shoud be implemented. . . . It is essential not only to move the convent outside the perimeter of the site, but also to set up the new cultural center. This will help us to continue the dialogue which is so dear to us. . . . The best solution to the dispute involving the Carmelite convent at Auschwitz would be for work to start as soon as possible." This development was praised by American Jewish organizations. The World Jewish Congress recommended "that the freeze be lifted in the formal dialogue with the Vatican that was instituted in February at the time of the failure to carry out the Geneva agreement on removal of the convent at Auschwitz."

Other Holocaust-Related Events

A controversy ensued early in the year when Education Secretary Lauro Cavazos refused to fund a Holocaust education program for high schools prepared by the educational group "Facing History and Ourselves." The program had reportedly been rejected partly because of pressure from right-wing groups, which said it was not balanced, that it did not adequately include the Nazi point of view. Phyllis Schlafly, conservative author and activist, criticized the program as constituting "psychological manipulation" of students. However, it was strongly endorsed by Rep. Ted Weiss (D., N.Y.) and 65 other members of Congress. In September, Cavazos reversed his decision and announced that the program would be funded.

The trial of John Demjanjuk in Jerusalem became a back-page story following the guilty verdict and death sentence handed down in April of 1988. The one development this year was the decision of Israel's High Court of Justice, in February, to postpone a hearing on his appeal until November. An American congressman, Rep. James Traficant, Jr. (D., Ohio), accused the Office of Special Investigation of discarding documents requested by Demjanjuk; the OSI denied the charge. The memos in dispute dealt with whether Demjanjuk was identified by former Nazi prison guard Otto Horn after looking at Demjanjuk's photographs for the first time, as he had testified, or only after looking at those photographs for the second time.

The OSI continued to process other cases. Neal Sher, director of the office, stated that there were nearly 600 individuals under investigation. In March it was revealed that a former Nazi collaborator, George Theodorovich, who had been living in Troy, New York, fled to Paraguay in December 1988. He had been stripped of his American citizenship and ordered deported because he had persecuted Jews in Lvov, in the Ukraine. In April the OSI began deportation proceedings against Anton Baumann of West Allis, Wisconsin, who was alleged to have been a member of the Nazi Death's Head Battalion guard at Stutthof and Buchenwald concentration camps. In August proceedings began against Anton Tittjung of Greenfield, Wisconsin, who allegedly served as a guard at the Gross Raming subcamp of Mauthausen concentration camp. In October, Bruno Karl Blach, an alleged Nazi war criminal living in Los Angeles, was arrested by the Justice Department following an extradition request by West Germany. He was accused of "having killed three persons in Austria en route from Wiener Neudorf to Mauthausen . . . in a cruel manner and acting from base motives." Finally, in December, Jakob Frank Denzinger of Akron, Ohio, was stripped of his citizenship for having concealed his membership in the Death's Head Battalion of the Nazi *Waffen*-SS. It was believed that he had fled to West Germany.

Austrian president Kurt Waldheim appeared less frequently in the news in 1989, although in December a CIA document came to light indicating that the intelligence agency had known about Waldheim's past as a German army intelligence officer since its establishment in 1946. The document was obtained by the World Jewish Congress.

Finally, a Las Vegas casino owner, Ralph Engelstad, was fined $1.5 million by the Nevada Gaming Commission for harming the image of Las Vegas as a result of his birthday celebrations for Adolf Hitler and his collection of Nazi memorabilia.

Interreligious Matters

In early September the American Jewish Committee announced that it would withdraw from the International Jewish Committee for Interreligious Consultations (IJCIC), the organization that officially represented world Jewry in its discussions with the Vatican. Rabbi James Rudin, AJC's director of interreligious affairs, had been serving as IJCIC's chairman. The move came about at the time of the Auschwitz controversy, but was primarily motivated by long-standing differences over approaches to Jewish-Christian relations, chiefly with the World Jewish Congress and the Synagogue Council of America. Meanwhile, the American Jewish Committee announced that an alternative organization would be formed by the Committee, the Anti-Defamation League of B'nai B'rith—which had withdrawn from IJCIC three years earlier—and the American Jewish Congress, which had never been a member of IJCIC.

An important development of this year was a statement on the Middle East by the National Conference of Catholic Bishops. The lengthy statement, which was prepared following a period of consultations between Catholic leaders and representatives of various communities, including the Jewish and Arab, was ratified in November. Generally, the organized Jewish community praised the statement's language with respect to Israel's need for security, continued American support, and the need for the Arab states to "enter into full diplomatic relations with Israel," while expressing concern about its language calling for the establishment of a "Palestinian homeland with its sovereign status recognized by Israel."

In other Catholic-Jewish news, a mini-controversy erupted over remarks made by Pope John Paul II at a weekly public audience that were interpreted to deny God's covenant with the Jews. In his discourse on August 2, the pope said that "we consider the coming of the Holy Spirit at Pentecost as the fulfillment of the new and everlasting covenant between God and humanity." He added that, under the Sinai covenant, God would continue to view Israel "as his special people" as long as they remained faithful to God's law. "But the history of the Old Testament shows many instances of Israel's infidelity to God. Hence God sent the prophets as his messengers to call the people to conversion, to warn them of their hardness of heart and to foretell a new covenant still to come."

When the Anti-Defamation League expressed deep concern about the implications of the remarks, Vatican officials responded by saying that they had been misinterpreted. Dr. Eugene Fisher, secretary for Catholic-Jewish relations of the National Conference of Catholic Bishops, said the pope was "affirming positives about Christianity" and had not "even taken up the question of God's continuing relationship with the Jewish people." However, following two more weeks in which similar homilies were delivered by the pope, the American Jewish Committee's Rudin said that "the time has come for a high-level clarification from the Catholic leadership," adding that the pope's remarks could be interpreted as doubting "the validity, the authenticity, and the legitimacy of Judaism."

Amidst the various Catholic-Jewish controversies of 1989, there were also some bright spots. In February the Vatican released a strong statement on racism entitled "The Church Confronting Racism—For a More Fraternal Society," which included the statement: "Anti-Zionism, which consists of opposition to the policies of the State of Israel, sometimes serves as a cover for the anti-Semitism which nurtures and provokes it." The Vatican's statement also held that "never in history was there a form of racism more serious than Nazism, whose homicidal madness above all, and to an unheard of degree, struck the Jews, but also other peoples." The report was generally well received by Jewish groups.

In the summer, 21 Polish Catholic priests and one Polish Orthodox theologian came to the United States to take courses in Judaism at the Spertus College of Judaica in Chicago for six weeks. Father Waldemar Crotowski, one of the participants, said, "Our purpose is to see Judaism with the eyes of its believers—Judaism as living Judaism."

In other interreligious news, the New York Supreme Court dismissed a lawsuit brought by the Jews for Jesus against the New York Jewish Community Relations Council, alleging that the JCRC sought to interfere with its programs. The court stated that the Jewish community had a right to fight missionary activities as an exercise of free speech.

Church-State Issues

In the arena of church-state separation, menorahs and child care were perhaps the biggest stories of the year. In February the Supreme Court heard arguments in its first case involving the display of a Jewish religious symbol (menorah) on public property. The case (*ACLU v. County of Allegheny and City of Pittsburgh*) involved separate public displays of a Christmas nativity scene and a Hanukkah menorah— the latter owned by a Chabad-Lubavitch organization—on government property in Pittsburgh.

The plaintiffs, the American Civil Liberties Union and the Anti-Defamation League, asked the Supreme Court to uphold a 1988 U.S. Court of Appeals decision barring such public displays. The American Jewish Committee, the American Jewish Congress, and the National Jewish Community Relations Advisory Council filed friend-of-the-court briefs in support of the plaintiffs. The plaintiffs argued that the placement of a menorah on the steps of the Pittsburgh City–County Building and a crèche in the Allegheny County Courthouse violated the establishment clause of the First Amendment. Samuel Rabinove, legal director of the American Jewish Committee, said, "The constitutional separation of religion and government means the government should not become involved with religions unless there is a religious need that cannot otherwise be met. . . . There is no religious need to place sacred symbols of any faith in government buildings."

A divided court ruled in July that the nativity scene was unconstitutional (5 to 4), but upheld the menorah (6 to 3). The majority opinions appeared to stress the importance of context: the crèche, standing alone, gave the impression that the county endorsed its religious message; the menorah, which stood next to a Christmas tree, was in a seasonal holiday display that had secular connotations.

In related cases, in May the U.S. Court of Appeals for the Eighth Circuit upheld a lower-court ruling allowing the state to regulate the placement of a Hanukkah menorah on the grounds of the Iowa state capitol. Lubavitch of Iowa had requested permission to erect its 20-foot menorah for the duration of the eight-day festival; state officials insisted that it be removed following each night of public candle lighting. In August a California appellate court upheld the right of the Chabad-Lubavitch movement to place a menorah at Los Angeles's City Hall, upholding lower-court decisions that the display had a valid secular purpose and did not represent excessive entanglement of church and state. Unlike in the other cases, the menorah—a 19th-century candelabrum—was there purely as a display item, set near a Christmas tree, and was not used in conjunction with any ceremonies.

On federal child-care legislation, the organized Jewish community continued to support the goals while remaining concerned about church-state difficulties. In June the Senate passed a child-care bill that included provisions allowing funds to go to day-care programs run by sectarian institutions. While Agudath Israel and Torah Umesorah–National Society for Hebrew Day Schools supported the Senate bill, the American Jewish Committee, the American Jewish Congress, and numerous other Jewish organizations opposed that particular provision. Among other provisions opposed was one that permitted sectarian day-care centers to give preference to hiring workers with compatible religious views and one that allowed preference in admission to children of parents with a "pre-existing relationship" to the facility.

The dilemma felt by many Jewish organizations was expressed by Rabbi David Saperstein, Washington representative of the Union of American Hebrew Congregations: "Do you support this bill now because of the need for child care and then take your chances by challenging the church-state violations in court, or do you oppose it now and risk not getting a child-care bill this year?" By year's end, the bill remained stalled in a House-Senate conference committee.

In April a large number of Jewish groups, including such diverse organizations as Agudath Israel and the American Jewish Congress, filed legal briefs urging the Supreme Court to strike down a Missouri law that, in effect, banned all abortions. The briefs argued that by finding that human life begins at conception, the Missouri statute established a religious viewpoint as law, which law was a violation of the establishment clause of the First Amendment. Of concern to the Aguda—which, unlike most of the other groups, did not support a pro-choice position—was the possibility that halakhically mandated abortions would not be allowed.

In September the Supreme Court agreed to hear a Nebraska case intended to test the 1984 Equal Access Act. The American Jewish Congress was serving as counsel to lawyers for an Omaha school board in *Board of Education v. Mergens*. The court would decide whether an Omaha public school had to give official recognition to a student Bible-study club that sought to meet on school grounds, against the wishes of the school board. The American Jewish Committee and the Anti-Defamation League filed friend-of-the-court briefs to support the school-board position.

In religious accommodation cases, the Attorney General of New York filed suit in January to collect more than a $1-million fine from two Brooklyn firms accused of selling nonkosher meat in a kosher establishment. It was the largest kosher fraud case in the state's history. The Cook County Circuit Court in Illinois ruled in March that a Jewish man was required to grant his wife a *get* (Jewish religious divorce decree) as well as a secular divorce, because they had signed a *ketubah* (a religious marriage certificate) at their wedding ceremony, stipulating that dissolution of the marriage would be according to Jewish law. The client had argued that because he was not Orthodox he should not be bound.

The question of Sabbath observance continued to pose legal challenges. In March the U.S. Supreme Court ruled that an employee could not be denied unemployment benefits because he refused to work on the Sabbath, even though he did not belong to an organized church or denomination. The decision in *Frazee v. the Illinois Department of Employment Security* reversed an appellate decision to deny benefits to a man who would not work on Sunday. Later in the year, Rep. Stephen Solarz (D., N.Y.) introduced the Religious Accommodation Amendment of 1989, requiring an employer, whenever possible, to allow an employee to accommodate his religious needs—including observance of the Sabbath and religious holidays. In September the American Jewish Congress accused the MCI telecommunications corporation of discriminating against a Sabbath observer and filed a complaint with the Equal Employment Opportunity Commission. Shari Shapiro of New York had been offered a position, but the offer was withdrawn after MCI discovered she was a Sabbath observer.

In March the Supreme Court agreed to hear an Oregon case involving the use of illegal drugs in religious ritual. The American Jewish Congress filed a brief supporting an Oregon supreme court ruling that American Indians who use peyote in religious ceremonies were constitutionally protected. Agudath Israel of America filed a friend-of-the-court brief in a "right-to-die" case (*Cruzan v. Harmon*), that was heard by the Supreme Court in December. Aguda supported the State of Missouri's right to keep alive a comatose patient over the wishes of the patient and the objections of the family.

In July several members of Congress, including Rep. David Obey (D., Wis.) and Rep. Lee Hamilton (D., Ind.), held up the $35-million American Schools and Hospitals Abroad program, run by the State Department's Agency for International Development, on grounds that three Israeli recipients were in violation of the guidelines prohibiting use of funds for religious purposes. The three controversial projects, all under Orthodox auspices, which were to receive a total of $8.4 million, were Sha'alvim Teachers College, Machon Alte Institute, and Or Hachayim Girls College. The three were questioned because they allegedly provided only religious training, and one of the programs was reported to have placed teachers in West Bank settlements. Two noncontroversial Israeli grant recipients were the Hadassah Medical Center and the Israel Arts and Science Academy for gifted students. Critics of ASHA charged that it had become "an international pork barrel" for pet projects of key pro-Israel legislators and their supporters.

In July the New York State legislature passed a bill, which the governor signed, permitting the Hassidic village of Kiryas Joel (about 50 miles north of Manhattan) to organize its own school district. The school district was intended solely to provide publicly funded special education for severely disabled children, who, the Hassidim contended, would feel uncomfortable in a public-school setting. The remainder of the village's children would continue to attend private schools organized by the Satmar movement. Among groups protesting the measure were the American Jewish Congress and the Anti-Defamation League. They suggested that the measure might be unconstitutional; that at best it was an inappropriate use of public funds and a bad precedent, one that would foster divisiveness.

Finally, in October Sen. Jesse Helms (R., N.C.) introduced legislation to create a "religious issues oversight board" for penal institutions, to rule on grievances from prisoners who felt that they were being denied the opportunity to express their "legitimate religious needs."

Political Affairs

In this electoral off-year, general Jewish political concerns centered primarily around American support of Israel. For Jews, this was a feeling-out period with the Bush administration, which was generally perceived to be less friendly to Israel than the previous Reagan administration. In August Lee Atwater, chairman of the Republican National Committee, addressed himself to this apparent apprehension during a visit to Israel. "After a couple of years," he said, "the people of Israel are going to know that George Bush is their friend. Maybe a couple of times they will be irritated because that's what happens among friends from time to time."

Vice-President Dan Quayle established himself as a strong voice for Israel. In his first appearance after the election before a major Jewish group, the national executive committee of the ADL, in February, he affirmed America's lasting commitment to Israel's security and his deep suspicion of the PLO.

In the Democratic camp, despite increasing pressure from Arab-American groups, the Democratic congressional delegation remained firm in its support of Israel. Friends of Israel were cheered when Democrats in the House of Representatives elected Richard Gephart of Missouri and William Gray III of Pennsylvania as their new majority leader and majority whip, respectively. Both candidates had been favored by Jewish groups over their competitors, who were seen as having weaker records on Israel.

Although Israel was a focal point of concern, the most controversial area of

Jewish political involvement was that of black-Jewish relations in general and the issue of Jesse Jackson in particular.

Chicago's Jewish community had been instrumental in electing the city's first black mayor, Harold Washington, in 1983. But in February of this year the Jews were credited with playing an important role in helping make Chicago the first city to unseat a sitting black mayor with a white challenger. Richard Daley, son of the late political boss, received more than 83 percent of the Jewish vote in the Democratic primary, according to exit polls, helping him to defeat Acting Mayor Eugene Sawyer, who succeeded Washington, who died in November 1987.

The background to this turnabout in Jewish electoral behavior was the Cokely affair. Steve Cokely, a follower of Louis Farrakhan, had been an aide to Mayor Sawyer in 1988 when he publicly delivered anti-Semitic remarks, including the charge that Jewish doctors were injecting black babies with the AIDS virus. A week passed before Sawyer fired Cokely, thereby arousing the ire of large numbers of Jews. (See AJYB 1990, p. 223.) Daley went on to win the mayoralty race in April against both the Republican candidate and a black candidate, Timothy Evans, running on an independent Harold Washington party ticket. In this election, Evans won 92 percent of the black vote, while Daley won 90 percent of the general white vote and 79 percent of the Jewish vote.

New York City's mayoral race found the Jewish community more divided than it had ever been and threatened to harm black-Jewish relations not only locally but nationally as well. David Dinkins, a black candidate, was a veteran city politician with a strong record of support for Jewish causes. He received about one-third of the 270,000 Jewish votes in his Democratic party primary race against the incumbent Jewish mayor, Edward Koch, who had become increasingly controversial, especially in the area of race relations. Dinkins won the primary with 51 percent of the vote, to Koch's 42 percent. It was reported that Dinkins's managers had expected only about 20 percent of the Jewish vote, in which case Dinkins would have lost to Koch.

In November Dinkins beat his Republican opponent, Rudolph Giuliani (who had defeated Ronald S. Lauder in the primary), to become New York's first black mayor, but by a narrow margin: 51 percent of the vote to his opponent's 48 percent. Although about 40 percent of Jewish voters, as against 30 percent of the overall white population, cast their ballots for Dinkins, this represented a significant defection to the Republican side from the predominantly Democratic Jewish electorate. Dinkins's friendship with Jesse Jackson undoubtedly hurt him, though it was believed by analysts to be less important than last-minute revelations of improprieties in his personal finances and general questions about his capabilities. However, given the strident anti-Jackson campaign mounted by militant Jewish supporters of Giuliani—denounced by mainstream Jewish leaders—black and Jewish leaders were pleased with the size of the Jewish vote, which actually provided the necessary margin of victory. In his victory speech, Dinkins said, "I want to say a special word about the Jewish community, because tonight that community is again a light unto the nations."

In Florida, a congressional race precipitated some Jewish-Hispanic or Jewish-Cuban tension. One run-off candidate for the seat vacated by the death of longtime Democratic representative Claude Pepper was Ileana Ros-Lehtinen, a Republican Cuban-American. Her Democratic opponent, Gerald Richman, who was Jewish, used as his original campaign slogan "This is an American seat," although later he changed it to "a seat for all the people." Ros-Lehtinen accused Richman of bigotry and issued a brochure saying, "We want Richman to understand . . . we, too, are Americans [even though] we weren't born in Brooklyn." The Fair Campaign Practice Committee of Dade County criticized both Richman's campaign theme and his opponent's brochure. When Ros-Lehtinen won the election, it was hailed as a turning point in the ethnic balance of power in the Miami area as well as a significant Republican victory. All parties talked about "healing" Cuban-Jewish wounds.

Although the stormy relations between Jesse Jackson and the Jews largely subsided in this off-election year, he continued to be a special focus of concern within the Jewish community. Invited to speak to an American Jewish Committee awards dinner in May, Jackson called for reconciliation, citing the common sacrifices of Jews and blacks in the civil-rights struggle. "Tonight we are called to reason," he said, "to shift from racial and religious backgrounds to economic common ground and higher ground." But in August, when Jackson called Israel's capture of Sheikh Abdul Karim Obeid "an act of terror," he was strongly criticized by most Jewish groups. Seymour Reich, president of B'nai B'rith International and chairman of the Conference of Presidents of Major American Jewish Organizations, remarked, "Mr. Jackson has shown that he continually chooses to fault the State of Israel. Unless he retracts his most recent ill-advised remarks, he will once again burn his bridges with the Jewish community."

During the New York mayoral campaign in November, Albert Vorspan, a senior vice-president of the Union of American Hebrew Congregations, said: "We do not have to support Jesse Jackson out of some misconceived Jewish guilt. I could not vote for him. But it is sick to let him become the lens through which Jews see and judge all blacks."

New York City's new mayor, David Dinkins, and L. Douglas Wilder, elected in November as governor of Virginia, the first black governor in America's history, were seen by many Jewish observers as moderate alternatives who might challenge Jesse Jackson's domination of the black political scene.

EARL RAAB
DOUGLAS KAHN

The United States, Israel, and the Middle East

THE YEAR 1989 WAS SEEN BY many observers as the start of a new era in Middle East politics, one in which three events or trends were highlighted: the closing of the Reagan presidency, growing tension in U.S.-Israeli relations, and the emergence of a serious Israeli-initiated peace proposal. The closeness and warmth in relations that had characterized the Ronald Reagan–George Shultz years showed signs of evaporating under the tenure of President George Bush and Secretary of State James A. Baker. While it was difficult to point to specific substantive differences between the two administrations, a number of comments from Washington raised hackles in Israel and led to questioning of the Bush administration's depth of commitment to the relationship. Particularly disturbing to Israel were comments by Secretary of State Baker on the inevitability of an Israeli-PLO dialogue and on the need for Israel to give up its dream of a "Greater Israel." At the same time, many of the fundamentals of the relationship—strategic cooperation, U.S. aid, and the willingness of the United States to stand up for Israeli approaches to the peace process, rather than those advocated by the international community—remained intact.

The Peace Process

As the year began, the region was still feeling the impact of the U.S. decision (December 1988) to begin official contacts with the PLO. Indeed, the decision by George Shultz, recognized by Israel as a close friend during his six years as secretary of state, was seen as an effort to make life easier for the new Bush administration, which would have had a far more difficult time taking such a radical step on its own at the very outset of its tenure. The unanswered question was whether this last-minute step by the Reagan-Shultz team would help move the stalled peace process along, as many in the Arab world contended, or whether it would prove a further obstacle to peacemaking, as many in Israel predicted.

Early in January there were reports that the new unity government in Israel might be willing to reassess its opposition to any role for an international conference. On January 10, Prime Minister Yitzhak Shamir told a visiting European Parliament delegation in Jerusalem that "negotiations can be launched under the auspices of the great powers or the UN, providing they refrain from any involvement in the substance of the talks." Shamir's comments were part of Israel's response to a European Community (EC) Mideast plan, announced on January 2, calling for movement through an international conference, for talks with the PLO, for the Palestinians' right to self-determination, and for Palestinian acceptance of Israel's basic rights. The following day, Foreign Minister Moshe Arens of Israel, in his first news conference with foreign reporters, expressed disapproval of the EC plan, indicating that the Europeans were making peace moves without consulting Israel, and that Israel was willing to suffer isolation in the world for its own security.

Shamir's comments to the Europeans, while appearing to move him closer to views expressed in the past by Shultz and Labor leader Shimon Peres, were seen by U.S. officials—following clarification by Shamir—as merely an attempt to ease mounting international pressure for Israel to enter negotiations with the PLO. According to these unnamed U.S. officials, Shamir appeared to be hoping to maintain his insistence that any negotiations should be with King Hussein of Jordan rather than with the PLO, by showing some outward flexibility on the venue and ground rules for talks.

Citing the election of new governments in the United States and Israel as providing the right conditions, on January 20, on Israeli television, Yitzhak Rabin, Israel's defense minister, offered his own proposals for moving things forward. His plan called for elections by the residents of the territories, following several months of calm, to choose Palestinian representatives who would negotiate self-rule for an interim period, which would lead to a confederation with Israel or Jordan. Rabin indicated that he was "willing to discuss with the inhabitants of the territories a neutral element to supervise elections, but not the United Nations," and suggested that "we will consider favorably the release of those leaders who are prepared to accept this path."

Rabin's plan did not have government backing, but he indicated that the government would have to draft a peace proposal in the near future and he would submit his ideas to the cabinet. The plan was quickly condemned by Palestinian leaders in the occupied territories and abroad as an attempt to bypass the PLO and prevent the establishment of a PLO state. Meanwhile, Arens told *Time* magazine that "at this stage of the game the ball's in our court," that the "government has got to enunciate its position," and that he hoped "the U.S. would support an Israeli initiative."

On January 29, Faisal Husseini, regarded as the senior PLO figure in the West Bank, was freed from prison; he indicated that Rabin's plan could form a basis for negotiations between Palestinians and Israel: "I believe the PLO will agree if it will be a real democratic and free election under the supervision of the United Nations or another international supervision and no preconditions about what will happen afterwards."

On February 1, Shamir presented his own scenario for negotiations. He told reporters of a two-stage peace process that would include "first an interim condition and this will include full autonomy, and in the second stage, direct negotiations without preconditions between Israel, Palestinian Arabs and Arab countries." He indicated that he was "deeply convinced that the moment we will get to this stage and negotiations will start, positive results will come." Shamir also said that he was prepared to withdraw Israeli troops from some of the West Bank and Gaza's population centers after the residents agreed on autonomy as a first stage. The PLO quickly rejected Shamir's statement, calling on him "to stop digging into his old stock and bringing out these goods which are out of date."

Shamir's comments were widely seen as a response to mounting international pressure to come up with a new peace initiative as a consequence of the *intifada* and Yasir Arafat's diplomatic moves. Indeed, Shamir's remarks earlier in the month on a possible international conference, Rabin's plan, and Shamir's effort to refresh Camp David were depicted as Israel's varied efforts to regain the diplomatic offensive following Arafat's December successes.

In meetings with Israeli ambassador to Washington Moshe Arad and Egyptian ambassador to Washington Abdel Raouf El Reedy on February 8, Secretary of State Baker indicated that the Bush administration wanted to take a careful step-by-step approach to reviving the Middle East peace process and would not take any policy initiatives until after meetings in the spring in Washington with Shamir and Egyptian president Hosni Mubarak. This approach stood in contrast to positions of European and Arab governments calling on the administration to make a bold, early foray into Mideast diplomacy in light of the PLO moves. The administration reportedly wanted to hear what Shamir would bring with him as an alternative proposal to international calls for including the PLO in the process and moves toward an independent Palestinian state.

The administration further sought to reassure Israel when Vice-President Dan Quayle told a meeting of the Anti-Defamation League on February 10, in Palm Beach, that the United States remained deeply suspicious of Yasir Arafat: "Those who believe that American policy is about to undergo a basic shift because we have begun to talk with the PLO are completely mistaken. We need to see real evidence of concrete actions by the PLO—actions for peace, and against terrorism—before changing our fundamental attitude to the PLO." He added, however, that the "status quo" in the territories was "clearly unacceptable," and that "Israelis understand this as well as anyone."

The Bush administration's stress on a go-slow approach was evident again on the occasion of Secretary Baker's 14-country tour of NATO members in February. In the Hague, on February 16, Baker heard Dutch foreign minister Hans van der Broek call for a U.S. Mideast peace mission as early as possible. Van der Broek was reported to have made his recommendation on the basis of a recently completed fact-finding mission for the EC by the foreign ministers of Spain, France, and Greece. Baker's aides reported that the secretary cautioned the Europeans "to be careful on how they proceeded," because "one has to till the ground carefully. If you push the level of discussions too high too soon and create too much international attention at the wrong level, you may well preempt the possibility of real movement." Rather than trying to get Israeli leaders to meet with Arafat at an international conference immediately, which had no chance of success, the administration was believed to favor some kind of negotiating process that would begin with Israelis talking to Palestinian leaders from the territories who were not identified with the PLO.

Meanwhile, the Soviet Union, following withdrawal of its troops from Afghanistan, sought to enhance its Middle East role through an 11-day tour of the region by Foreign Minister Eduard A. Shevardnadze beginning on February 17. A Soviet Foreign Ministry official indicated at the outset of the trip that "an auspicious moment has come to intensify efforts to create conditions for the holding of a Middle East peace conference. It would be unpardonable to pass it up."

Among the highlights of the Shevardnadze mission were the first visit ever by a Soviet foreign minister to Jordan, the first in 14 years to Egypt, and a meeting in Cairo with Israeli foreign minister Arens on February 22. The Arens-Shevardnadze meeting lasted two-and-a-half hours. Both parties said the talks were constructive but differences remained unresolved. Arens indicated that he and the Soviet foreign minister had expressed opposing views on the PLO—Arens calling the PLO "the major obstacle to peace in the area at this time," the Soviet calling for Israeli contact with the PLO; and on how to convene peace talks—Arens advocating direct negotiations, citing the success with Egypt, Shevardnadze reiterating the Soviet plan for an international conference under the auspices of the five permanent members of the UN Security Council.

Later that evening, Shevardnadze met with Arafat; afterward he reaffirmed Soviet support for full PLO participation in all phases of a peace initiative and made another plea for the Soviet approach: "I think it will take some time for Israel to recognize the changes in the region. We need a common effort to bring them to the understanding that the international peace conference will bring guarantees for the security of Israel, and that country needs that."

On February 23, in a major foreign-policy address in Cairo, Shevardnadze presented his government's approaches to the Arab-Israeli conflict. He warned that "time in the Middle East is working for war, not peace." He called for an end to superpower rivalry to achieve a "historic compromise." He cautioned Israel that by continuing to impede Palestinian self-determination, "Israel is not strengthening but rather undermining both its security as a state and the legitimacy of its own self-determination." But he also said, "We should rule out any attempt to isolate Israel" and noted that Moscow's plans for peace called for on-site monitoring of Arab and Israeli military installations, the banning of nuclear and chemical weapons from the region, and "verification and cooperative measures" to rid the area of terrorism.

On the very same day, President Bush, in Tokyo for the funeral of Emperor Hirohito, met with King Hussein of Jordan and President Mubarak of Egypt. Secretary Baker, briefing reporters following the meetings, reiterated the administration's cautious approach in the face of urging by the king and Mubarak for an international peace conference: "We are concerned that if we act too precipitously we might pre-empt promising possibilities that could surface if we adopted a more reasoned and measured approach." But Baker focused as well on the fact that there was a new "dynamic now in the region," including the U.S. dialogue with the PLO, which could lead to direct peace talks.

King Hussein, who had been openly critical of former president Reagan's reluctance to become more personally involved in the region's problems, told reporters after seeing Bush that he expected to be more pleased with the new administration.

Back in the United States, the president met with American Jewish leaders on March 1. According to reports, he said that he would not apply pressure on Shamir when he visited Washington in April, but made clear that he expected Shamir to arrive with some "new ideas" on how to advance the peace process. Seymour Reich, chairman of the Conference of Presidents of Major American Jewish Organizations, said following the meeting that Jewish leadership had no complaints about U.S. policy, which he described as "very consistent."

On March 13, Arens, in Washington for his first visit as foreign minister, met with Bush and Baker. Each side presented its perspective on how to move forward. According to reports, Baker told Arens that the administration expected Prime Minister Shamir to bring with him in April specific proposals for improving the atmosphere in the territories, as well as general ideas about how Israel saw the "final status" of the West Bank and the Gaza Strip. Baker reportedly described a two-tier peace process: Israelis and Palestinians should take immediate steps to reduce tensions between them in Israel and the territories, e.g., Israel reducing its troop presence in certain sectors of the West Bank in return for Palestinian promises not to engage in violent demonstrations in those areas; at the same time there would begin a general discussion of a "final settlement" for resolving Israel's security concerns and the Palestinians' quest for self-determination. On his part, Arens was reported to have told Baker that while his government would try to ease tensions in the territories, it would not negotiate with the PLO but would seek talks with King Hussein.

The following day, in an address before the Washington Near East Policy Institute, Arens expounded further on his government's approach. He opposed talking about visions for a final settlement: "I think that if the parties to the conflict, rather than concentrating on getting the negotiations going, begin to throw out their ideas as to what the final conclusion should be, they will simply subvert the process." He indicated that Israeli policy was to look for negotiating partners other than the PLO, with Jordan as the target. But he also recognized that because of Jordan's unwillingness to represent the residents of the territories, Israel would "have to address" the residents as well: "If we can fault ourselves for anything these past 20 years, I suppose it would be for not engaging them in a dialogue."

On the same day, Baker, in testimony to a House Appropriations subcommittee, suggested that Israel might eventually have to negotiate directly with the PLO: "It is an element of our policy to promote direct negotiations which can be meaningful between Israelis and Palestinians. Now, if you can't have direct negotiations that are meaningful, that do not involve negotiations with the PLO, we would then have to see negotiations between Israelis and representatives of the PLO. It may be that you can have meaningful negotiations that do not involve the PLO." Later in the day, Arens was asked about Baker's comments about the possibility of eventual Israeli talks with the PLO, and he said that Baker "did not say anything like that to me," but added that "if we are going to make an effort to identify interlocutors from the population in the territories, it's not helpful to say that if this doesn't work out, we're now going to the PLO."

Several days later (March 21), in testimony before a House subcommittee on international operations, Baker reiterated his comments about the PLO but also called on the PLO to agree to talks between residents of the territories and Israel. Despite rumors that the secretary might use the hearing to back off from his statement of a week earlier about the possibility of an Israeli-PLO dialogue, he indicated that he would not rule out such talks: "It would be wrong for us to categorically, absolutely, totally and completely rule out, under any and all circumstances, any dialogue that might lead to peace."

Late in March, the Israeli press was reporting that Shamir and his aides had prepared a document for his trip to Washington offering a new proposal to move the process forward. According to *Ha'aretz* of March 27, the proposal would include elections for representation of residents of the territories leading to discussions on autonomy. It was reported that the plan was being discussed by the four main cabinet officials—Shamir, Arens, Peres, and Rabin—and not with the entire cabinet, to avoid damaging leaks.

MUBARAK-SHAMIR VISITS

The first week in April brought the Bush administration's most serious attention to the Middle East to date. The month began with a proposal by Shamir to Mubarak that their separate visits in Washington scheduled later that week be turned into a three-way meeting with Bush. The Egyptians refused, according to an Egyptian official, because "all the Israelis are offering now are rehashed formulas that have been tried and failed before." The official added: "If Mr. Shamir will really come up with some meaningful new ideas, Egypt will respond. Shamir wants appearances without substance, and we will not give that."

On April 3, after meeting with Mubarak, Bush provided reporters with an outline of his thinking on the Middle East, the first time he had done so as president. He indicated in blunt language that the United States wanted "the end of the occupation" and suggested that "a properly structured international conference could play a useful role at an appropriate time." He said that Egypt and the United States "share a sense of urgency to move forward a comprehensive settlement through direct negotiations" and he called for "creativity" to look again at old problems and to devise imaginative ways of solving them. Mubarak, for his part, indicated agreement with Bush on most issues, and spoke of "direct negotiations between Israel and all Arab parties within the framework of an international peace conference." It was also reported that Mubarak had told Bush privately that Palestinians would never agree to elections in the territories held under Israeli supervision.

The following day, however, after talks with Baker, Mubarak seemed to be more willing to keep an open mind on what Shamir would bring to Washington. He indicated that he would withhold judgment on a reported election proposal and also publicly endorsed the Bush administration's cautious approach toward reviving the peace process, saying he agreed that "a good atmosphere" should be created first before negotiations could begin.

THE SHAMIR INITIATIVE

On April 5 and 6, Shamir met with Baker and Bush and officially presented a peace initiative. As the Israeli prime minister outlined to reporters following his meeting with the president, the proposal consisted of four points. First, it called for making the peace between Israel and Egypt, based on the Camp David accords, a cornerstone for expanding peace in the region. Second, it called on the United States and Egypt to make clear to Arab governments that they must abandon their hostility and belligerency toward Israel. Third, it proposed a multinational effort to solve the Arab refugee problem. And fourth, it proposed free and democratic elections among the Palestinian Arabs of Judea, Samaria, and Gaza. Shamir indicated that the purpose of those elections would be to produce a delegation "to negotiate an interim period of self-governing administration." Shamir's initiative immediately became the focus of diplomatic attention, remaining so, with variations, for the rest of the year.

The administration's reaction was positive. Bush gave cautious support for the election plan, indicating that Washington considered such elections "not the end of the road" but the beginning of a process that would lead ultimately to resolution of the territorial dispute and the Arab-Israeli conflict. Meanwhile, Baker characterized Shamir's ideas as "very encouraging" proposals that might "help move the peace process forward."

On April 8, the president indicated to reporters that the Mubarak and Shamir visits "have moved things forward a little bit." He added that "I can't say I'm elated, but in the Middle East, a little step can prove to be fruitful." And he noted that "the climate is better than it's been in a while." In his comments, the president emphasized that the proposed autonomy period would be a steppingstone toward a final settlement that should follow a land-for-peace formula. He explained his use of the term "the end of the occupation" during Mubarak's visit: "I do not feel that the provisions of 242 and 338 have been fulfilled. And I wanted to be clear to all the parties in the Middle East that that is my view."

On April 7, in Brazzaville, Congo, Yasir Arafat dismissed Shamir's proposal, saying it "was, as usual, inappropriate." The first reaction of Palestinian leaders in the territories reflected Arafat's. Some dismissed the Shamir plan outright. "We can accept elections only after there is no occupation of the territories," said Hanan Mikhail-Ashrawi, professor of English at Bir Zeit University. Hana Siniora, West Bank newspaper editor, said: "Elections today are not part of how to start the process." While rejection was the order of the day, questions about specifics of the plan's implementation were raised in the media. Would anti-Israel polemics be allowed in campaigning by Palestinians? Who would draft the election laws? Would residents of East Jerusalem be allowed to vote? Where would the army be during the election campaign? What would be the level of PLO involvement, even in directing the campaign from outside?

On April 12, the State Department dismissed the PLO's initial rejection of Shamir's plan: "It is not unusual in a process for different parties to stake out more extreme positions, especially at the beginning of the process." Margaret Tutwiler, State Department spokeswoman, added that Shamir's idea had "potential," indicating that "there are a lot of questions to explore, and we plan to do so in the days and weeks ahead."

Two days later, Palestinians from the West Bank offered a counterproposal to the Shamir plan. The plan, suggested as an effort to narrow the gap between Israel and the PLO, called for an Israeli withdrawal from population centers in the territories, then elections to pick representatives to the Palestine National Council, followed by negotiations for a two-year interim period, leading to an international conference where Israel and the PLO would negotiate the final status of the territories. It seemed, however, that the plan would go nowhere without Yasir Arafat's approval, not to mention certain Israeli opposition.

Meanwhile, Shamir, back in Israel, was experiencing a backlash among some of his Likud supporters. In the cabinet, on April 16, Deputy Prime Minister David Levy said he was worried that "those responsible for the *intifada* will be elected, with Israel's permission. This is a path of no return." And Planning and Economy Minister Yitzhak Modai, also of Likud, expressed concern about the future of Jewish settlements in the territories and about whether Palestinian residents of East Jerusalem would be included in the elections. Labor leaders Peres and Rabin backed the plan, pointing out that the party had promoted the idea of elections as part of its campaign platform in the fall of 1988.

Reaction to the plan, which had come to dominate the diplomatic landscape, continued apace. On April 16, Arafat indicated that elections were acceptable only if they were supervised by the UN after Israel withdrew from the territory it had captured in the 1967 war. The next day, Shamir told reporters he would not withdraw troops to pave the way for elections in the territories: "There is no room for any talk about changes in the disposition of the Israeli Defense Forces. Their deployment is necessary to maintain order. Order is also necessary to hold elections." Shamir also indicated that he opposed the participation of 140,000 East Jerusalem Arabs and thought there was "no need for observers or supervision of any kind."

On April 19 and 20, King Hussein spent two days in Washington in meetings with Bush and Baker, and on departure he gave a qualified endorsement of Shamir's proposal: "I believe that the idea of elections might be worth looking at within the context of a whole process that hopefully will come together to get us from where we are now to a final settlement. Otherwise the idea is out of context." An administration spokesman indicated that the king had been convinced to give partial support because the United States made clear that "when we talk about elections, we are talking about an idea that is directly linked to a final settlement and not an end in itself."

On the same day, the PLO formally rejected the proposal in a meeting with U.S. representative Robert Pelletreau, saying that elections under occupation would legitimize the Israeli presence and distract from the PLO's campaign for an international conference. On April 26, 83 West Bank and Gaza activists followed Arafat's lead by signing a document that rejected Shamir's plan, calling it "nothing more than a maneuver for the media, to save Israel from its international isolation." It called on Israel to talk with the PLO and to attend an international conference. It stated that the Palestinians' goal was "to establish an independent Palestinian state with Jerusalem as its capital under the leadership of the PLO." As for elections, the document said, "Palestinians chose their representatives decades ago and have reiterated their choice through the uprising."

The administration continued to downplay the significance of these rejectionist trends, calling them inevitable "background noise" that accompanied any Middle East initiative. These protestations would continue for months, officials asserted, but both sides would eventually conclude that elections were the only realistic option for beginning a dialogue that could lead to a comprehensive settlement. Concerning Israel's seriousness of purpose, administration officials seemed confident that the *intifada* and the U.S.-PLO dialogue were powerful inducements for Israel to take its own election idea seriously.

As the days passed, each of the parties—the Israelis, the Palestinians, the Americans—continued to weigh the Shamir plan. Early in May, Baker sent a letter to Arens pressing Israel for specifics on the plan. The letter reportedly asked the Israeli government to address the issue of participation in elections of Arab residents of East Jerusalem, to make provision for international supervision of the balloting, and to make a "significant link" between an interim stage of autonomy and a final stage of permanent solution of the conflict.

On May 14, the Israel cabinet, by a vote of 20–6, formally approved the Shamir proposal, but only by choosing to avoid the most difficult questions posed by Washington about how the elections would be carried out: the right of residents of East Jerusalem to vote, international supervision, the possibility of elections while the *intifada* continued, and whether Israel would make any commitment about the territories' ultimate status. Defense Minister Rabin expressed pleasure at the vote: "After many years of different stages in the national unity Government, there is a unity Government peace initiative that I believe will be received widely and with great support by the Israeli people." Among those voting against the agreement were Ezer Weizman, who argued that Israel should negotiate directly with the PLO, and Ariel Sharon and Yitzhak Modai, who asserted that the plan would lead to a Palestinian state.

Meanwhile, the United States sent a delegation of State Department officials to the Middle East to sound out the parties. The delegation, including Dennis Ross, the director of policy planning, invited 15 Palestinian leaders to meet with it in Jerusalem to discuss the plan. However, only four showed up, the others apparently trying to tell the Americans that only the PLO was authorized to speak on their behalf. Later, the prime minister reportedly told the visiting delegation that Israel had not lost hope of launching a dialogue with the "large majority" of Palestinians in the territories, which Shamir termed the "moderate majority." And he indicated that the proposed elections constituted the best method of bringing about such a dialogue. Arens, for his part, told the delegation that all four parts of Israel's proposal must be pursued, arguing that progress on the wider peace front or on any settlement of the refugees would improve the atmosphere around elections as well.

The State Department team next met in Cairo with Egypt's leaders. Egyptian officials said that the Israeli proposal was "the only thing on the table" and would not be rejected out of hand. However, they urged Ross to press Israel to broaden the election proposal as "part of the wider package" of guarantees and concessions to the PLO. At the same time, the Executive Committee of the PLO held a two-day meeting in Tunis, at the end of which a statement was issued dismissing the plan: "The Israeli Government's plan shows that in essence the call for elections is a farce, a means to deceive world public opinion."

BAKER PROVOKES CONTROVERSY

As discussions continued on how to move forward, Secretary Baker delivered a major address before the American Israel Public Affairs Committee (AIPAC), on May 22, in which he said that it was time for Israel to "lay aside once and for all the unrealistic vision of a Greater Israel" and "reach out to Palestinians as neighbors who deserve political rights." He also called for a "constructive Palestinian and broader Arab response" to Israel's proposal, and for the Palestinians to amend the PLO charter.

Shamir, in London, reacted with anger to the Baker speech, rejecting as "useless" the suggestion that Israel give up the Greater Israel idea and Jewish settlements in the West Bank. An Israeli official traveling with Shamir indicated that Baker's comment on settlements "at this stage of the diplomatic game—which is very complicated—is a big surprise." On the other hand, PLO spokesman Ahmed Abdul Rahman reacted favorably, saying that "it was a big step forward for Mr. Baker to say these things to the Israelis and the AIPAC organization." In a May 23 news conference, when asked about Shamir's comments, Baker stood by his remarks: "If you look at the speech in its entirety, you see that it was very balanced." Meanwhile, Rabin in Washington echoed Shamir's critique, if in less blunt language: "The problem today is to start the political process and the only way to do that is to leave open the ultimate solution. We have to work in phases and at this phase the less we deal with the principles of a permanent solution the better."

This was seen to be at the heart of the difference between Washington's and Jerusalem's approaches. Israeli leaders, divided on what the final status should be, were agreed that not talking about it was a way to progress; Washington insisted that only by talking about it could Palestinians be convinced to take up Shamir's proposal.

The administration continued its efforts to get the parties together. Bush and Baker communicated with Arab leaders on the occasion of an Arab summit meeting in Casablanca, May 23–25. The day before the summit opened, Baker called on the Arab world to abandon the economic boycott of Israel, stop challenging Israel's place in international organizations, and repudiate the "odious" line that Zionism is racism. On "Meet the Press" on May 29, Baker said that the United States was actively pressing the PLO in Tunis to give "the green light" to Palestinians in the territories to accept the election plan. Baker praised the proposal warmly, while acknowledging that Washington and Jerusalem still differed over various aspects of it.

Meanwhile, Congress sought to lend a helping hand to Israel. During the first week of June, Senators Rudy Boschwitz and Frank Lautenberg circulated a letter that was signed by 95 senators, calling on Baker to be "fully supportive, both in fact and appearance," of Shamir's election proposal.

On June 11–12, Egyptian minister of state for foreign affairs Boutros Ghali visited Jerusalem, the first time a senior Egyptian official had done so since the beginning of the *intifada*. Ghali reportedly offered to be an "active postman" between Israel and the PLO. Shamir's spokesman, Avi Pazner, quoted the prime minister as saying: "Israel is not interested in negotiations with the PLO, but if Egypt is prepared to encourage local Palestinians to take part in the elections and the negotiating process, that would be extremely helpful." Simultaneously, Mubarak was meeting Arafat in Cairo, and in his public comments the PLO leader sought to avoid the label of rejectionist. "We have not rejected the idea of elections, but we have specific questions on the subject. Can there be democracy without self-determination?"

On June 18, Arafat announced that in the U.S.-PLO meeting of June 8, the PLO had proposed that prominent Palestinian Americans participate in negotiations with Israel concerning elections. Mentioned as possible candidates by Arafat were Edward Said, professor of English and comparative literature at Columbia University, and Ibrahim Abu Lughod, professor of political science at Northwestern University.

THE PLAN FALTERS

In Israel, Shamir faced increasing pressure from within his own party. When Sharon, Levy, and Modai, the plan's leading opponents, forced Likud's 2,600-member Central Committee to convene, in order to consider riders to Shamir's election initiative, Sharon made his purpose clear beforehand: "I will try and bring about a decision which would erase the entire program because it's the most dangerous of all the plans the Government has ever formulated in the last 40 years." On July 5, in a bargaining session that delayed the opening of the convention, Shamir agreed to be bound by the Sharon-Levy-Modai conditions for conducting negotiations with the Palestinians. These were that: the Arab residents of East Jerusalem could not run for office or vote in the elections; no elections would take place unless the Palestinian uprising ended; Israel would not give up any territory and no Palestinian state would ever be established; and Jewish settlement would continue in the territories. Shamir's acceptance meant that while the actual plan had not been amended, he risked losing a no-confidence vote from his party should he not stick to the agreement.

Reaction by the Labor party and the United States to the Likud decision was mixed. Peres said that the plan had "suffered a very tough hit," though he indicated no decision about whether Labor would stay in the government. U.S. officials, reportedly angry over the Likud steps, avoided public criticism and tried to distinguish between the government proposal and the Likud decision, saying that the United States was continuing its effort "in support of the Israeli *government* proposal." On July 6, PLO official Bassam Abu Sharif said that Likud's pledge never to return the territories made it impossible for the PLO to consider such elections and "canceled everything." Abu Sharif added that the PLO understood from its talks with U.S. officials that the administration was committed to ending Israel's occupation and that by its steps "Likud is telling President Bush to go to hell."

American reaction intensified several days later. Baker, on a flight from Brunei to Oman before going on to Poland, told reporters that "if things totally bog down, if you can't make progress with the election proposal, then we would have to look a little bit more closely at the prospects for an international conference." Baker's sudden raising of the international-conference theme was interpreted as sending Israel a message: if Israel weighed down the election idea with heavy conditions which stymied the plan, the United States would have no choice but to go in other directions.

On July 9, Arafat said in Tunis that the PLO would not consider the elections plan because of the new conditions. He strongly criticized the U.S. role, saying that the Likud was encouraged to harden its stance by "unconditional" American support and that the U.S.-PLO dialogue had accomplished little.

In Warsaw on July 10, Baker in a news conference raised the level of dissatisfaction. He indicated that he intended to send a special envoy to Israel "to determine the extent to which the Israeli government is still committed to their elections proposal in the aftermath of the Likud party convention." He added that the conditions "give rise, at least in our minds, to a question about the seriousness of purpose."

As the days passed, talk increased that Labor might withdraw from the government. Reports circulated that U.S. officials were urging Labor to remain in the government as the likeliest way to aid the peace process. Seymour Reich, chairman of the Presidents Conference, told the press on July 12 that he had told Israeli leaders that it was "important for the unity Government to stay together." On July 14, the administration abruptly dropped the plan to send a special envoy to Israel. The about-face was explained as a consequence of assurances that Likud and Labor were nearing agreement to preserve the election plan and avert a breakup of the coalition government. Also cited was U.S. reluctance to provide ammunition to opponents of the plan, eager to charge U.S. interference.

The Israeli government coalition crisis formally ended on July 23, some three weeks after it began, when the cabinet voted 24–4 to endorse Shamir's plan as originally proposed. The vote did not force Shamir specifically to renounce the four conditions of Likud, thus leaving him with the room to negotiate with the conditions in mind while arguing that the government as a whole was not bound by them.

With the national unity government intact, attention shifted to the Palestinian side. On July 26, reports appeared in the Israeli press describing a specific list of conditions under which the PLO might allow the election plan to go forward. The terms, which were reported to have been passed on to Israel through the Soviets, included the following: the residents of East Jerusalem should be allowed to take part; election candidates should be assured freedom of speech and given immunity from prosecution; the Israeli army should be withdrawn from population centers to predetermined areas on the day of voting; and before elections, Israel should agree in principle that it was willing to give up territory.

The following day, the *New York Times* reported that it was told by Khalid al-Hassan, a senior adviser to Arafat, that the Palestinians "accept elections as part of a process," but that the "starting point for any solution is an Israeli decision to withdraw eventually from the occupied territories." On the same day, an Arafat interview in *Al Ahram,* an Egyptian daily, carried tougher themes. Arafat said elections could happen only if Israel committed itself to withdrawing all its troops from the territories within 27 months after the vote. He also called for return of Palestinian refugees and said Israel must agree on a date for Palestinian independence. On August 3, Arafat continued his negative reaction to the elections proposal. Addressing Fatah's fifth General Congress in Tunis, Arafat said the plan was merely aimed at "perpetuating the Israeli occupation of the occupied territories."

Two tracks dominated U.S. activity by mid-August. First, the administration stepped up efforts to persuade the PLO to agree to the plan. On August 14, Ambassador Pelletreau, meeting for the fourth time with the PLO representative in Tunis, Yasir Abed Rabbo, pressed the plan; an American official afterward said that the meeting "was disappointing." The PLO rejected the plan in the strongest terms to date, Abed Rabbo saying that peace could come only through an Israeli withdrawal and self-determination for the Palestinian people.

At the same time, reports circulated that the United States was backing Egypt in its efforts to circulate a ten-point working paper giving conditions under which elections in the territories would be acceptable to Cairo. The ten-point program was first conveyed by President Mubarak to Israeli officials by a delegation of U.S. congressmen in July.

EGYPT'S TEN-POINT PLAN

By September, frustration with the lack of progress was mounting. Rabin, who had first proposed elections, acknowledged that things were not going well: "I cannot deny that the peace initiative and efforts to bring a political solution between Israel and the Palestinians have lost momentum." Peres offered criticism of the Palestinians from whom in the beginning "we heard a half yes, and now nearly a complete no." Shamir, however, criticized the pessimistic assessments, saying that "we knew this would be a lengthy process" and too little time had passed to evaluate it.

The different approaches of Labor and Likud to the plan were becoming sharper and more open. Labor leaders were seen as focusing on the elections as a means of creating a Palestinian representation with which Israel could negotiate, with the implicit acquiescence of the PLO. Likud appeared determined to structure the elections in such a way that the Palestinian delegation would be independent from the PLO. Consequently, Labor tolerated the U.S. dialogue with the PLO, in the hope that Washington would persuade the PLO to give Palestinians a "green light"; Likud staunchly opposed the talks on the grounds that they only discouraged local Palestinians from breaking with the PLO.

Similarly, Labor reacted more positively to Cairo's ten-point program. The program described a series of conditions under which the elections might be held, including withdrawal of the Israeli army from the territories before election day, a moratorium on new Jewish settlements, and a prior commitment by Israel to the principle of exchanging territory for peace. Labor pointed to the proposals as a possible basis for restarting the election initiative with Egyptian assistance. Likud refused to respond to the Egyptian points, arguing that Israel must first receive an assurance from Palestinians and Arab states that they were willing to join in the proposed peace initiative before engaging in negotiations. Finally, Labor leaders hinted that they could accept some outside representatives in the Palestinian delegation, which Likud staunchly opposed.

On September 11, Peres made clear his differences with Shamir, suggesting that the Cairo points could be the basis for talks: "If the Palestinian delegation will come equipped with these ten points as their position, we should probably come equipped with our position and we can start the preparations for negotiations." Meanwhile, a PLO official told the *Washington Post* on September 13 that the Mubarak platform was unacceptable because it focused on the Israeli election proposal rather than the PLO's agenda for statehood.

The United States responded cautiously in public to Mubarak's plan, the State Department saying on September 12 that the administration would welcome the initiative "to the extent that the ten points can be helpful" in launching an Israeli-Palestinian dialogue. Reports indicated that, behind the scenes, U.S. support for the program was stronger.

On September 15, Egyptian ambassador to Israel Mohammed Bassiouny officially submitted the ten-point plan to Israel. Since Shamir's own initiative called for an Egyptian role, his government had little choice but to respond. The next day, Israel agreed to send Rabin to Cairo to discuss the proposal. The development was seen by some as the first significant sign of movement since the Shamir initiative was introduced; at the same time, it was clear that the Israeli cabinet remained divided on the Cairo plan, and the PLO was seen as undecided as well. Meanwhile, Cairo indicated that talks about its plan could be held as early as October, if Israel agreed.

On September 18, Rabin and Mubarak met in Cairo. No major agreements were reached. Mubarak, speaking to reporters, indicated flexibility: "The Egyptian ten points are not the Ten Commandments. This is not the permanent solution. All I want is the two sides to sit down for a dialogue and agree on elections and afterward address the problem. Our only aim now is the dialogue." Mubarak spoke of a dialogue "mainly with the Palestinians from the territories," but added "we should not neglect those from outside." Rabin indicated that the Israeli government had "certain problems that we have to discuss among ourselves, like the composition" of a Palestinian delegation.

In the next few days the pace of diplomacy picked up. On September 20, Mubarak made an appeal on Israeli television for Israel to join in discussions with Palestinians, claiming that in meetings with Arafat the PLO leader had approved Cairo's proposal. The following day, Shamir rejected Mubarak's appeal on the grounds that the Egyptian was trying to lure Israel into talks with the PLO.

Talk of a fundamental split within the Israeli unity government increased in light of the growing interest in the Mubarak program. Trying to avoid the appearance of taking sides in the internal Israeli dispute, President Bush, in New York for the UN General Assembly meeting, met on September 25 with Peres in the afternoon and Arens in the evening. Peres, after his meeting, said that he had urged the president to get more aggressively involved in Middle East diplomacy, noting that "no peace settlement has ever been achieved without an active American involvement." Peres also described the Egyptian plan as possibly "the most important single opportunity in a long time." It was reported that Bush emphasized in his talk with Peres the importance of Labor and Likud working together to promote Israel's election plan to the Palestinians. Arens reported that he had called on Bush to try to persuade Mubarak to meet with Shamir. Arens told the press that "if Mubarak were to sit down with Shamir and talk directly about the specific object of how we can set the stage so we can hold free and fair elections amongst the Palestinian population, there's a good chance we will reach that objective."

On September 26, however, Shamir indicated that the Egyptian proposal was unacceptable to Israel. Two days later, Secretary Baker, trying to break the deadlock, met in Washington with Arens and Egyptian foreign minister Ahmad Esmat Abdel-Meguid. Meeting with reporters afterward, Baker focused on the positive. He said that "there may be some potential for progress" in beginning negotiations over the election proposal. He stressed that the United States did not see the Mubarak points "as a competing proposal" with Shamir's initiative, hoping thereby to overcome Shamir's objection and to have the Israeli cabinet support the plan in its vote the following week. Baker described the three-way talks that had taken place that day as taking a look at the "general concept of the Israeli election proposal and how we can take practical steps to make that work."

On October 2, after meeting with Bush for an hour in the White House, Mubarak said that the Israeli government would make "a grave mistake" if it rejected the Egyptian plan. Secretary Baker, speaking to the press before the Mubarak-Bush meeting, strongly affirmed American support for the Egyptian initiative, saying the proposal offered a serious prospect for moving toward peace. Baker reiterated that the ten points "do not represent a competing proposal" to Israel's initiative, but they represented "a means of getting a dialogue established." At the same time, the administration urged Mubarak to agree to meet with Shamir to help break the stalemate. Baker also warned that if the Israeli cabinet rejected the Egyptian proposal, the United States would have to "go back to the drawing board" in search for ways to create an Israeli-Palestinian dialogue.

Meanwhile, comments by Arens on October 2 to Israeli journalists were seen as possibly reflecting a new flexibility toward the Egyptian plan. Arens was quoted as saying that an Egyptian-sponsored meeting could take place, but "the only issue on the agenda at such a meeting should be the elections." Likud continued to oppose any PLO role or any substantive discussions on the final status.

However, on October 6, after nine hours of debate stretched out over two days, the Israeli cabinet rejected Egypt's proposal. The vote was 6–6, divided strictly along party lines—Likud against, Labor for. The tie meant defeat: Likud leaders indicated that their negative votes rested on opposition to the "outside" Palestinians included in the Egyptian plan and the fact that it provided for discussing formulas for a final peace settlement in preliminary talks. Labor party officials criticized the decision, warning that it could lead to a government crisis. Peres charged Likud with deliberately trying to block any move toward settling the conflict. In response, Shamir indicated that the government would consider a suggestion by Baker that the United States, Israel, and Egypt conduct three-way consultations on the composition of an eventual Palestinian negotiating delegation.

The administration tried to play down the significance of the cabinet vote. Words such as "temporary setback" were cited and the State Department said that Secretary Baker had talked by phone that day with both Arens and Abdel-Meguid in an effort to bridge differences. U.S. officials sought to explain Baker's suggestion to Arens of September 27 that the United States, Egypt, and Israel might get together and exchange ideas on which Palestinians could come to a dialogue and on what basis the parties would meet. It was pointed out that this was not a "plan" but simply a vehicle to move forward.

On "Meet the Press" on October 8, Baker said, "I don't think the vote means things are dead in the water at all." He indicated that the parties were "going to continue to work to see if we can put this together." Two days later, the State Department indicated that Baker was seeking to organize a meeting in Washington between Arens and Abdel-Meguid. The invitation was seen as a last-ditch effort by Washington to give Israel another opportunity to pursue its own initiative, with the implication that if Israel refused, it would demonstrate that it had never been serious.

BAKER'S FIVE POINTS

On October 10, it was reported that Baker had submitted to the Israeli and Egyptian governments five points to help get around the impasse. State Department spokeswoman Margaret Tutwiler, trying to make clear there was no American plan, claimed that these points had not been put down in a letter but were rather oral communications. The points, though not publicly released, were said to include assertions that the main purpose of the peace process was the establishment of an Israeli-Palestinian dialogue; that Egypt's participation in the proposed three-way talks would not be seen as a substitute for the Palestinians, with whom Egypt would consult; that the Israeli election plan would be the basis for talks; that Israel would have to approve the composition of any eventual Palestinian delegation; and that a three-way meeting in Washington could be arranged as a way to advance the process. It was reported that Likud leaders objected to Baker's conception because they believed it implied a list would be drawn up by Egypt with the PLO and because there seemed room for the substantive discussions that Israel opposed.

Meanwhile, on October 16, the PLO's 108-member Central Council, meeting in Baghdad, issued a declaration urging "firm confrontation against the American policy," though not issuing a formal rejection of the Baker points. The next day, Shamir told a Likud party gathering that Israel would "stand firm and not give in, even if we face a clash." He asserted that the Bush administration was "trying to get Israel out of Judea, Samaria and Gaza and into negotiations with the PLO." The two reactions of opposition to the Baker plan led to widespread speculation that it would die.

The following day, in an interview reported in the *New York Times,* Shamir indicated that the peace initiative was still alive, describing how he intended to draw Palestinians into negotiations: "The populace will come to understand from the bitter experience of the *intifada* violence that this struggle will lead nowhere, and that everything the PLO stands for will produce only disasters. They will eventually grow disappointed both with the *intifada* and with the PLO and then conclude that they must negotiate with us on the basis of our initiative. I hope that will not take long."

The administration reacted critically to Shamir's comments. Spokeswoman Tutwiler indicated on October 18 that recent statements by Shamir were "unhelpful, and we're disappointed." Her words were seen as an unmistakable rebuke to Shamir, considering the carefully worded language normally used. Baker said in an interview on the same day that if the parties did not get more serious about fundamental compromises for peace, he would have "no alternative but to disengage."

Shamir responded with a conciliatory letter to Baker, calling on Washington to continue its Middle East peace efforts. At the same time, he reiterated his position that a PLO role would "have to lead to a Palestinian state," and indicated that his government was "determined to prevent such a development at all costs."

The weeks of maneuvering among the parties—the Mubarak ten points, the Baker five points—seemed about to yield to progress when Arens sent Baker a telegram on October 24 indicating that Israel would accept Baker's proposal "in principle" but had "reservations" about two important points. On the same day, Shamir said in Israel that his government would "agree to this plan after the changes we suggested are accepted." The reservations were reported to be related to Israel's desire for an American guarantee that the PLO would not be involved, directly or indirectly through Egypt, in shaping the Palestinian list; and assurances that any discussions with Palestinians would not get into matters relating to a final settlement. Arens's letter was seen as an effort by Israel to avoid responsibility for any breakdown in the process.

The continuing impasse highlighted a fundamental difference in approach between the United States and Israel. Israel saw U.S. actions reflecting a conviction that talks between Israel and the Palestinians could not be arranged without at least the tacit consent—and indirect involvement—of the PLO. Likud, on the other hand, saw the election proposal not merely as a means to circumvent direct talks with the PLO, but as an instrument to destroy its claim to represent the Palestinians. Because of U.S. unwillingness to accept Israel's strategy, the Likud-led government was seeking to advance its reservations in a way that would give Israel the power to control the process unilaterally.

On November 1, Baker phoned Arens to discuss revisions in his five-point framework. According to reports, Baker offered slight revisions in response to Israel's two reservations, deleting a section referring to "consultations" between Egypt and unspecified "Palestinians," and adding a phrase making clear that the Israeli-Palestinian talks would concern only elections and "the negotiating process."

Four days later, the Israeli government's inner cabinet passed a resolution—nine to three—that the Baker framework be approved "on the assumption" that Israel's long-standing objections be addressed by written "assurances" from Washington. Those "assurances" would indicate that the PLO would not have any direct or indirect role in the dialogue, that Palestinians taking part would be residents of the territories, and that no issue could be discussed other than the elections. Arens lauded the vote as "an important step," but many wondered how the inner cabinet resolution differed from Arens's letter to Baker, which had been turned down a week earlier. Meanwhile, Sharon, Levy, and Modai voted against the plan, Levy calling the vote "a turning point, and perhaps each of us will have to take account." The cabinet vote was seen as an effort by Shamir to induce the United States to accept conditions that effectively redefined Baker's original proposal, which would bar movement toward a PLO state or put the Palestinians in the position of rejecting elections.

On a flight returning from Australia on November 8, Baker praised the cabinet vote as "a very positive step," but then indicated that the Israeli conditions were the same that he had refused to accept before the cabinet vote, leaving little doubt that he still opposed the demands.

Through all these goings on, the Israeli media were gripped by reports that Shamir was scheduled to make a private visit to the United States beginning on November 14, but had received no invitation to see the president. On November 8, at a news conference, when asked about a meeting with the prime minister, Bush merely said, "I'm certainly willing to consider it." The Israeli media gave front-page headlines to the Bush response so close to the Shamir visit, which was widely interpreted as linked to U.S. irritation over Israel's position on the peace process. The speculation ended, however, the following day, when the White House announced that the president would meet with Shamir on November 15.

Before leaving for Washington, Shamir told reporters from the *Washington Post* and the *Los Angeles Times* that he would seek "mutual understanding" with the president, but acknowledged "clear differences" over how to advance the process. Elucidating, he said that one issue was that of the PLO, which was "not so important" to the United States because it negotiates with the PLO, but Israel was "not willing to negotiate with the PLO" because it would "express our readiness to negotiate about the Palestinian state." Shamir also pointed out that "all over the world you see movement toward more peace, more détente and more democracy," but "unfortunately in this part of the world, in the Middle East, in the Arab part of this world, you don't see it. We have not had any movement toward more peace, more acceptance of the Israeli reality. It's something discouraging."

On November 15, Shamir met with Bush and Baker in Washington and was reportedly told by the secretary that the United States could not give Israel the sort of airtight assurances it was seeking without undermining the entire peace process. Shamir emerged from the White House saying that there was "no more tension." Reports focused on the lack of a sense of urgency surrounding the talks, reflecting the fact that Egypt, acting on behalf of the Palestinians, had not responded to Baker's five points, as well as the administration's preoccupation with the dramatic events in Eastern Europe.

On his return to Israel on November 24, Shamir claimed he had made progress and said Bush and Baker had assured him "in a clear and unambiguous way that the U.S. would not ask Israel to negotiate with the PLO." Peres disagreed, saying Shamir's talks in Washington, Paris, and Rome "did not change anything" and threatened that his Labor party would resign "if the Likud continues to be obstinate."

Meanwhile, the PLO rejected efforts to put it in the background. PLO officials in Tunis told the press early in December that on December 1 the organization had told both the U.S. ambassador in Tunis and Egyptian officials in Cairo that it would accept an Israeli-Palestinian dialogue in Cairo only if it named the Palestinian delegation.

On December 6, the State Department announced that Egypt had agreed, with some conditions, to Baker's plan to prepare a dialogue between Israeli and Palestinian representatives. Spokeswoman Tutwiler indicated that the Egyptian reply "is exactly as the Israeli reply was," described as a "yes, but." At the same time, State issued an official version of Baker's five points, which had already appeared in different forms in the Arab and Israeli press:

> That because Egypt and Israel have been working hard on the peace process, there is agreement that an Israeli delegation should conduct a dialogue with a Palestinian delegation in Cairo.
>
> That Egypt cannot substitute itself for the Palestinians and will consult with Palestinians on all aspects of that dialogue. Egypt will also consult with Israel and the United States.
>
> That Israel will attend the dialogue only after a satisfactory list of Palestinians has been worked out.
>
> That the Government of Israel will come to the dialogue on the basis of the Israeli Government's May 14 election initiative. The Palestinians will come to the dialogue prepared to discuss elections and the negotiating process in accordance with Israel's initiative and would be free to raise issues that related to their opinions on how to make elections and the negotiating process succeed.
>
> That the foreign ministers of Israel, Egypt and the United States meet in Washington within two weeks.

In Jerusalem, Rabin hailed the Egyptian move as a great step forward, adding that he saw little chance that divisions within Israel's coalition government would hamper progress toward ending the conflict. The Israeli government cautiously welcomed Egypt's qualified acceptance but was reported to be concerned over the role of the PLO in any form.

As the year moved toward a close, with Washington talking of a meeting of the foreign ministers of Israel and Egypt with Baker in Washington in January 1990, Arafat met with Mubarak in Cairo to discuss the next steps. Meanwhile, in an interview on December 26, Shamir said that he preferred friendship to enmity with the Palestinians and pledged to press his elections proposal despite opposition within his own party and from many Palestinians. Shamir said the proposed foreign ministers' meeting would "certainly" take place in Washington in the second half of January. He indicated that "we want to have a meeting with some Palestinian people to talk" about how to organize the elections. Shamir said that Israel's readiness to attend the Washington meetings and hold elections in the territories showed a commitment to peace.

As the year ended, it remained unclear whether real progress had been achieved or whether each side was merely trying to win American approval by appearing to be forthcoming.

U.S.-PLO Relations

From the beginning of the Bush administration, the new element in U.S.-Israeli relations was the dialogue between the United States and the PLO. An inheritance from the last days of the Reagan-Shultz years—an ironic one at that because of the consistently pro-Israel policies of that team—it came to dominate the thinking of both Israel and the United States during 1989.

From the outset, Israel opposed the U.S. decision to deal with the PLO, citing not only the potential threat this posed to Israel, but the negative impact it would have on the peace process as well. Throughout the year, Israel sought to demonstrate that, in fact, the PLO had not changed and that the new U.S. policy was misguided.

The Bush administration was sensitive to Israeli concerns, but not to the point of discontinuing the dialogue. Instead, it sought acceptance by the PLO of an inconspicuous role, while accepting the idea that PLO approval was necessary to get Palestinians in the territories to come forward. The inherent tensions were evident early on, and they continued to surface throughout the year.

The first test of the "new" PLO came in the first days of the year. Late in December 1988, Elias Freij, mayor of Bethlehem, issued a call for a one-year truce between Israel and the Palestinians in the territories. His proposal involved a willingness by Palestinians to stop violent attacks, provided Israel released some 2,000 detainees and halted measures such as expulsions, house demolitions, and administrative detention.

On January 2, in a statement broadcast on Radio Monte Carlo, Arafat gave his response: "Any Palestinian leader who proposes an end to the *intifada* exposes himself to the bullets of his own people and endangers his life. The PLO will know how to deal with him." Freij got the message. He immediately withdrew the truce proposal. On January 3, Israeli foreign minister Moshe Arens said that Arafat's statement demonstrated Israel's contention that Arafat was a terrorist, and that the U.S. decision to open a dialogue was a mistake: "We are convinced that establishing contacts or, worse yet, extending recognition to the PLO cannot possibly promote peace in the Middle East. It is bound to encourage extremism and further acts of violence."

Meanwhile, the Knesset approved a resolution on January 4 supporting talks with Palestinians who accepted Israel and renounced terrorism, but ruling out negotiations with the PLO. The Left in Israel, however, dissented from this view, as four leftist members of the Knesset announced their intention to attend a conference in Paris in January at which PLO leaders were expected to be present. (The meeting took place in Paris on January 12.) On the same day, another group of left-wing Israelis and prominent Palestinians announced that Israeli legislators and PLO representatives would meet in New York for an "academic" conference.

An Israeli source told the *Washington Post* early in February that Arafat's Fatah faction had set up a clandestine "army" in early January inside Israel and the territories to carry out terrorist activities. This was seen as an effort to get around the ban on terrorism imposed on the PLO as a condition for its dialogue with the United States. In fact, there had been reports that cross-border attacks on Israel from Lebanon by Fatah had been curtailed.

On February 5, however, nine armed men were stopped in southern Lebanon from entering Israel; the large amount of arms the men were carrying and the direction in which they were heading indicated they were planning a terrorist attack inside Israel. A PLO representative in Tunis immediately endorsed the abortive raid, saying it was not terrorism because it was "a military mission" aimed at Israeli soldiers. Foreign Minister Arens, on the same day, lashed out at the United States and other Western nations, saying that the raid proved the PLO had not really renounced terrorism and that Israel was "aghast to see the world's great leaders lining up to pay homage." At the same time, the Israeli embassy in Washington formally appealed to the State Department to end its dialogue with the PLO.

In Iceland, on February 11, Baker said that the U.S. government had warned the PLO that recent Palestinian guerrilla actions "present us with great difficulty," but added that no decision had been made "at this time" to break off the two-month-old U.S.-PLO dialogue.

Meanwhile, pressure on Israel grew to enter negotiations with the PLO. On February 23, Shevardnadze said Soviet-Israeli relations could not advance until Israel attended an international conference with the PLO. French president François Mitterrand urged a visiting Yitzhak Shamir to talk to the PLO. And the Japanese Foreign Ministry announced that Prime Minister Noburu Takeshita had the same message for Israel.

Arafat continued his offensive on February 23, when he held a press conference in Cairo with 15 Israeli journalists and made a plea for direct talks with Israeli leaders. However, another abortive terrorist attempt from Lebanon and the killing of an Israeli soldier in Nablus on the same day generated Israeli disbelief.

On February 28, the United States stepped up its pressure on the PLO. State Department spokesman Charles Redman said, "Attacks against Israeli civilian or military targets inside or outside of Israel are contrary to the peaceful objective of the dialogue." And Redman reported that Pelletreau had told the PLO in Tunis that Washington could not condone recent actions, and that "the PLO cannot escape responsibility for the actions of its constituent elements." The PLO answered back, a member of the Executive Committee saying in Tunis, on March 1, that the organization "is not prepared to go on with meetings of this kind unless they bring results, unless they are soon translated into a formal meeting and dialogue."

But the United States continued to attempt to define the terms for continuing the dialogue. Issuing its sharpest rebuke to the PLO, on March 3 the State Department questioned Arafat's ability to control radical Palestinian factions. He said that if the PLO "cannot or will not exercise such control, it raises questions concerning the commitment undertaken in the name of the PLO—indeed, questions about the PLO's ability to carry out its commitments." The same day, Arafat said in Jordan that the PLO's guerrilla forces would continue to mount raids against Israel's northern border, even though the administration had warned that such operations could jeopardize the newly established U.S.-PLO dialogue.

The next milestone in the shaky U.S.-PLO relationship was Secretary Baker's testimony on March 14 before a House Appropriations subcommittee in which he said that the United States might someday conclude that Middle East peace required Israel to abandon its reluctance to negotiate with the PLO. The next day he repeated his view before a Senate body, saying, "We ought not to rule out categorically, absolutely, and unequivocally" PLO-Israeli talks. The following day, Arens called Baker to complain that his position "was not helpful" because it would only encourage local Palestinians to spurn any Israeli overtures and divert them to the PLO in Tunis.

On March 21, Baker offered further clarification in testimony before the House Foreign Affairs subcommittee on international operations, which was widely interpreted as an effort to reassure Shamir, who was scheduled to visit on April 6. The secretary indicated that the administration did not favor establishment of an independent Palestinian state, and that his remarks the previous week did not contain "an inevitable conclusion" that Israel must negotiate with the PLO. And he noted that while there are "some differences" between the United States and Israel, "I don't think that we should equate differences with the conclusion" that the United States would seek to force Israel to deal with the PLO.

The following day, after what was described as the first substantive discussion between the administration and the PLO, Ambassador Pelletreau indicated that he had called on the PLO to take "practical steps to reduce tensions and improve the political environment" for "direct negotiations between Palestinians and Israelis." The PLO delegation's chief, Yasir Abed Rabbo, rejected the plea, saying the uprising would continue "until Israel evacuates our homeland." On the subject of terrorism, Pelletreau said he had reiterated the administration's "very strong views on terrorism and violence," but there was no indication that the United States had decided to consider PLO guerrilla raids against military positions on Israel's northern border as terrorism. The PLO response was seen as a rebuff to Baker, who had sought a reduction in tensions to bring about direct negotiations between Israelis and Palestinians. Abed Rabbo said that an international conference should be the only forum for negotiations. On March 23, in Tunis, Arafat expressed optimism on the talks with the United States, reflecting that there was "a mutual respect and intention to lead this dialogue to success by both the American and Palestinian sides."

Meanwhile, an Israeli poll conducted late in March revealed mixed attitudes toward the PLO. On the one hand, an overwhelming majority of Israeli Jews opposed peace negotiations with the PLO at that time; only 7 percent of those polled believed that the PLO had done enough to prove that it was interested in peace with Israel. On the other hand, more than half said they would favor talks later if the PLO were to moderate its behavior. The survey was seen as particularly instructive because, while it indicated a hardheadedness among the Israeli people concerning alleged PLO change, it reflected as well a certain potential flexibility in Israeli attitudes for the future, contrary to the stated position of the Israeli government on the subject.

U.S.-Israeli differences surfaced again in comments made in April. Shamir, in a speech to the American Society of Newspaper Editors on April 13, said that Arafat and his aides had repeatedly made clear that the PLO "intended not to coexist with Israel, but to achieve in stages what the Arab states had tried a number of times and failed to achieve all at once: the destruction of Israel." Baker, on April 14, again in Senate testimony, said that certain PLO statements were not helpful, but that the administration was satisfied that to that point "the PLO is committed to what it has told us: that is, that it recognizes Israel's right to exist and has repudiated terrorism in all its forms."

In late June, word spread that the administration had secretly expanded its contacts with the PLO, meeting in Tunis with the PLO's second-highest official, Salah Khalaf. On June 29, Israeli ambassador Moshe Arad expressed Israel's "anger" and "disappointment" to the administration over these new contacts. Khalaf was a founder and leader of the Black September terrorist organization that carried out the massacre of Israeli athletes at the Munich Olympic games in 1972 and that was implicated in the 1973 killing of American ambassador to the Sudan Clio A. Noel, Jr. At the same time, members of Congress entered the fray. Sen. Connie Mack (R., Fla.) said in a letter to Baker, made public, that it was "incomprehensible to me that the administration would escalate its contacts with the PLO without any consultation with Congress or any improvement in PLO behavior." The letter further called for suspension of U.S. contacts with the PLO until Congress had a chance to review U.S. policy. Three members of the House—Mel Levine (D., Calif.), James Scheuer (D., N.Y.), and Benjamin Gilman (R., N.Y.)—held a news conference to express dissatisfaction with the expanding U.S.-PLO relationship. Levine said the Pelletreau-Khalaf dialogue was an example of "the PLO tail wagging the U.S. dog." The State Department, in turn, defended its decision to elevate its dialogue with the PLO, saying that the move was part of its overall effort to convince the PLO to approve an Israeli election proposal. However, reports, unconfirmed, soon surfaced that the United States had quietly discontinued contacts with Khalaf, so as to keep the focus on Israel's election proposal.

The split between Israel and the U.S. administration concerning the PLO appeared to grow in July. As stories circulated that the Bush administration had offered to upgrade contacts with the PLO if the organization reacted favorably to the election plan, Israel stepped up efforts to persuade Washington to break off the dialogue. Arens said in Jerusalem on July 17 that it would be impossible to hold free elections in the territories while the U.S.-PLO talks continued, because any Palestinian who sought to run independently of the PLO "would probably be dead in 24 hours." And Israeli officials made public a previously classified report by Israeli security forces asserting that the mainstream Fatah faction of the PLO, headed by Arafat, had been responsible for ten bombings as well as other attacks on civilian targets in Israel since Arafat's renunciation of terrorism in December 1988. The report said that while cross-border attacks by Fatah had ceased, cells based in the West Bank had launched at least 70 other attacks in the past six months. The ten incidents of Fatah violence inside Israel, cited in the report, included five bomb explosions, two attempted bombings, two attempted firebombings of Israeli vehicles, and a grenade attack on an Israeli civilian bus, in which the grenade did not explode.

In reaction to the news that the United States was talking with Salah Khalaf, a number of senators sponsored legislation intended to put sharp new restrictions on U.S.-PLO discussions. It was introduced by Sen. Jesse Helms of North Carolina. Helms's amendment would not have allowed the United States to negotiate with any PLO representative unless the president first certified to Congress that the Palestinian had not taken part or conspired in terrorist activity that resulted in "the death, injury or kidnapping of an American citizen." On July 19, the president expressed strong opposition to the congressional move. According to White House spokesman Marlin Fitzwater, Bush told a meeting of congressmen that he was opposed to the legislation because "at this point in the peace process, fragile as it may be, these kinds of limitations would not be helpful." Instead, the administration sought a compromise that reportedly would have the effect of barring talks with PLO figures like Khalaf, but not with PLO leaders whose involvement in violent attacks was less clear.

The following day the administration, in alliance with bipartisan Senate leadership, easily defeated the Helms amendment, the Senate voting 75–23 against it. A far less restrictive amendment, which the administration had worked out with the leadership, was then passed, 97–1, which barred contacts with the PLO only if the president knew that a participant had been involved in terrorism and informed Congress of the fact. Helms, the only senator to vote no, contended that the alternative was a "fig leaf to permit the State Department to continue to do what they've been doing." On July 22, Helms's concerns seemed to be confirmed by reports from unnamed State Department officials that the legislation did not bar future meetings with PLO officials, even Khalaf. One official, to buttress the view that it was important to talk with high-ranking PLO leaders, said that Pelletreau, in two June meetings with Khalaf in Tunis, had produced "the best response that we've had" to U.S. pressure on the PLO regarding the Israeli plan.

On August 3, Fatah began a five-day congress in Tunis; it ended by issuing a "political program" that proposed to "intensify and escalate armed action" against Israel. On August 10, the administration criticized the PLO for the Fatah declaration and warned that such militant attitudes undermined the quest for a negotiated settlement. The State Department stated that Fatah's "derogatory rhetoric on Israel, its tone of confrontation and violence and its preference for unrealistic principles and solutions instead of practical ideas for peace are unhelpful," and raised questions about the group's "commitment to accommodation, understanding and peace." Among Fatah's objectives as stated in its program were the guarantee of a "right to repatriation" for all Palestinians wishing to return to the territory they view as their homeland and the establishment of a committee to "oppose the Zionist immigration to our homeland."

The next day, Fatah rejected the U.S. criticism of its program as indicative of U.S. bias in favor of Israel. This reaction was seen as part of the PLO's internal struggle, with Arafat under pressure at the Fatah congress from military commanders and guerrilla fighters who believed the leadership had made too many concessions to Israel and the United States without getting anything in return.

The struggle between the Israeli government and the administration regarding the U.S.-PLO dialogue continued until the end of the year without any new policy developments. A study by the Foreign Broadcast Information Service (FBIS), reported in September, seemed to buttress the position of the administration. Studying PLO statements to the Arab world and abroad since the December 1988 change, it rejected Israel's contention that the PLO put out contradictory views to Arab and Western audiences. It concluded that comments have "for the most part been consistent, regardless of the media in which they appear."

Israel, for its part, continued to disseminate information that put into question the PLO's commitment. Thus, for example, Yosef Ben Aharon, chief of staff of the prime minister's office, asserted on October 23 to the *New York Times* that Israel had counted 100 attacks —79 against Israelis and 21 against Palestinians—by Fatah operatives since Arafat renounced terrorism in December 1988. Ben Aharon indicated that these terrorist activities "arouse our suspicions" and made Israel unwilling to participate in Egyptian or American peace proposals that gave the PLO a role, even deep in the background.

The year ended with the dialogue intact, Israel still urging the United States to reconsider, and the PLO vacillating between satisfaction that the dialogue was "positive," although it had produced nothing concrete (Khalaf) and criticism that one year later the United States was "doing its best to find an alternative to the PLO" in the peace efforts (Nayef Hawatmeh).

Terrorism

During the Shultz years in the State Department, Israel's handling of terrorism had become a key element in the deepening of relations between the two countries. Shultz saw terrorism as a major problem facing the democratic world and regarded Israeli policies—finding ways to counter the terrorists while holding on to democratic values—as a model for the United States and the West.

The first year of the Bush administration brought the first major challenge to the new president in dealing with a hostage situation. It quickly became clear that in this area, as in others, the Bush team was less willing to view Israel as a positive element and less willing to be sensitive to the difficult choices facing Israel in dealing with terrorists.

The episode began on July 28, when Israeli commandos abducted Sheikh Abdul Karim Obeid, a leader of the Shi'ite fundamentalist Hezballah (Party of God), from his home in southern Lebanon and brought him to Israel. The Israeli Defense Forces said that the sheikh had been "arrested" as a "preacher, inciter," and at times "a planner of attacks against Israel." Obeid was believed to have been involved in the kidnapping of Lt. Col. William R. Higgins of the U.S. Marines, who was captured near Tyre, Lebanon, in February 1988, while serving with the UN Truce Supervision Organization. Israel described the sheikh as the principal person "responsible for Hezballah activities in southern Lebanon." There was also immediate speculation that the sheikh might be used in a hostage trade for three Israeli soldiers who had been held in southern Lebanon since 1986, apparently by the Party of God or its affiliates.

Upon learning of the Israeli action, President Bush said, "I don't think kidnapping and violence help the cause of peace." He indicated that the freeing of Colonel Higgins was "very much on my mind" but added that he did not know if the kidnapping "would benefit the Higgins case or not." Immediately, a senior Party of God official dismissed the possibility of a trade and said Israel would "bear severe and dangerous consequences for the kidnapping."

Criticism of Israel came from other sources as well. Secretary-General Javier Pérez de Cuéllar of the UN called the Israeli raid a "violation of Lebanese sovereignty" and demanded that Israel return the sheikh. Egypt accused Israel of state terrorism. Israel dismissed the criticism, saying that people would understand "that this act was taken against one of the leaders of one of the most fanatical groups in Lebanon." The episode escalated in seriousness the following day when Hezballah warned that it would hang Colonel Higgins on Monday, August 1, unless Israel freed the sheikh. The White House responded by issuing a statement warning that the United States would hold the kidnappers of American hostages "fully responsible for their safety." State Department spokeswoman Tutwiler, in Paris with Baker, called the threat to kill Higgins "outrageous and uncivilized" and "an affront to the entire international civilized community."

On July 31, the Organization of the Oppressed on Earth, a group linked to the Party of God, announced that it had hanged Higgins; it distributed a graphic videotape showing a figure identified as the American twisting at the end of a rope. Five hours later a second group, the Revolutionary Justice Organization, threatened to kill Joseph James Cicippio, former acting comptroller of the American University of Beirut, who had been kidnapped on September 12, 1986. The message from the group to *An Nahar,* a Beirut newspaper, said: "The organization announces its quick resolve to execute the death sentence against the American-Israeli spy Joseph Cicippio if the struggling sheikh is not released by 6 P.M. Tuesday. Then the deadline will be set for the execution, which will be broadcast on all the screens in the world."

The dual messages provoked strong reactions and much speculation. Immediately, questions arose concerning the time that the videotape was shot. There were reports on several occasions that Higgins had died some time earlier—perhaps after the USS *Vincennes* shot down an Iranian jetliner on July 3, 1988; or of maltreatment after a failed escape attempt. Sen. David Boren (D., Okla.), chairman of the Senate Select Committee on Intelligence, indicated that the United States had "no way of knowing when he was killed," but it was "very, very likely that he has been executed."

Abruptly cutting short a cross-country trip, President Bush said that the American people had been "shocked right to the core" by the reported hanging of Higgins. He also issued an "urgent call to all parties who hold hostages in the Middle East to release them forthwith, as a humanitarian gesture to begin to reverse the cycle of violence in that region," which was read as aimed at Israel as well as Muslim fundamentalist factions in Beirut.

Although members of Congress generally expressed outrage and frustration at the reports of the hanging, Sen. Robert Dole, Republican minority leader, was critical of Israel's seizure of Sheikh Obeid. He urged the president to seek "some understanding with the Israelis about future conduct that would endanger the lives of Americans." And he continued his criticism on the Senate floor, saying, "We can't continually apologize for Israeli actions in this country when it endangers the lives of Americans in some far-off country. Perhaps a little more responsibility on the part of the Israelis one of these days would be refreshing." Lee Hamilton, Democratic congressman from Indiana and chairman of the Middle East subcommittee of the Foreign Affairs Committee, criticized Israel's lack of consultation before kidnapping Sheikh Obeid: "We like to see Israel bring us in. If we are going to be in on the crash landing, we would like to be in on the takeoff as well."

Other legislators were critical of Dole. Rep. Charles Schumer (D., N.Y.) charged that Dole was "making night day" and "making black white" and said that "Israel does not share any blame." And Sen. Alphonse D'Amato (R., N.Y.) said U.S. policy should be "more like that of Israel and the Soviet Union" in retaliating against terrorism.

Further complicating matters were comments made by Yitzhak Rabin soon after the release by the Islamic fundamentalists of the videotape. He indicated in Jerusalem that Israel had decided to seize Obeid as part of an effort to free three captive Israelis in Lebanon and had acted without consulting Washington. Now Israel offered to release Obeid and all other Shi'ite prisoners in exchange for all Western hostages as well as Israelis, because the other captives "are also threatened in the wake of Israeli action." Rabin also noted that Israel differed with the U.S. policy of not negotiating with terrorists holding hostages. He indicated that Israel preferred rescue attempts, in the manner of Entebbe in 1976, but in the case of Israeli soldiers held in Lebanon, "we are also prepared for negotiations to bring them home." Therefore, he said, the decision to offer an exchange of Shi'ite prisoners for Western hostages "is ours and ours alone." Concern mounted in Israel that the country would be blamed by Americans for Higgins's death at a time when Israel's image was already suffering because of the *intifada*.

On August 1, the kidnappers of Cicippio announced that they were postponing his killing for two days, but that the new deadline was firm if Israel did not free Obeid. Israel repeated its offer of a prisoner exchange but said it would not release the cleric for, in the words of Arens, "If we free this criminal we will only encourage additional terrorist activities."

Meanwhile, Senator Dole, trying to clarify his remarks, said that he did not directly blame Israel for the death of Higgins. However, he reiterated that Israel had "struck out alone, freelancing, apparently in the interest of gaining leverage to win the release of some of its citizens held hostage," without regard for the effect on innocent citizens of other countries. And White House spokesman Marlin Fitzwater added fuel to the fire when he said that "many people" in the administration shared the disappointment with Israel expressed by Dole.

On August 2, the *New York Times* reported that the CIA had told the White House that Higgins had probably been killed before July 5, thus lessening the focus on Israel's holding the sheikh. The president indicated that the administration was "leaving no stone unturned" to free U.S. hostages but expressed frustration at the lack of hard information.

The crisis eased the next day when the group holding Cicippio, the Revolutionary Justice Organization, announced in Lebanon that it was "freezing" a threat to kill him. This development, together with comments by Iranian president Hojatolislam Rafsanjani the following day, offering the United States help in resolving the hostage crisis, were seen as responses by Iran to U.S. diplomatic efforts, which reportedly offered an improvement in relations if progress were made with regard to the hostages.

On August 4, Shamir expressed guarded optimism about the possibility of negotiating an exchange with Shi'ite Muslim groups in Lebanon, telling reporters that "we hope we will get some proposals" through the Red Cross "and it will be the end of the crisis." This hope for an opening stemmed from the Revolutionary Justice Organization's statement surrounding the postponement of the threatened execution of Cicippio, in which it said that Israel must release Obeid, as well as the Shi'ites and *"intifada* strugglers."

The media noted that Israel would face a serious dilemma if Hezballah agreed to release either the Western hostages or the three Israeli soldiers but not both groups. It was considered unlikely that Israel would agree to either proposition, since it would find itself in great difficulty either with its own public or with the Americans. When asked whether Israel was seeking the release of all hostages and not only its own soldiers, Shamir replied, "Well, if it will happen, we will be very happy." On August 6, Rabin told a U.S. television network that no proposal excluding the three Israelis would be acceptable.

For several days stories were reported about Iranian and pro-Iranian groups rebuffing overtures from the United States and Israel, thus lowering the hopes raised days before, and of an offer to free Cicippio if Israel released Obeid and 450 Arab prisoners. Notably absent was any offer to free the three Israeli prisoners. Israel refused to comment. An administration official told the *New York Times* that while the United States was pleased that the Shi'ites were no longer talking about deadlines for executing Cicippio but about ways to arrange his release, the goal was "ending the whole episode of the hostages." Toward that end, the unnamed official added, the administration would not publicly analyze and weigh each new offer, but would instead pursue a policy of "trying to devalue the hostages." Meanwhile, Secretary Baker, in Mexico, said that the United States was "consulting very, very closely" with Israel, but was "not suggesting to Israel what they should or should not do."

While this latest threat to U.S.-Israel relations had diminished, Israel's initial hopes that the abduction of Sheik Obeid might lead to a quick and dramatic resolution of the hostage problem had been smashed. As Shamir adviser Avi Pazner put it on August 7, the array of threats, offers, refusals, and wildly conflicting statements coming from a variety of Shi'ite Muslim groups in Lebanon indicated that a solution "was going to take a long time." And Marlin Fitzwater echoed these sentiments the next day, indicating that "none of us expect a quick solution."

On August 9, Shamir called Bush. In the ten-minute conversation, the Israeli prime minister reportedly praised the president for his handling of the hostage situation and said Israel would work for the release of all hostages. Shamir reportedly reiterated that Israel would free Obeid only in exchange for the three Israeli soldiers and "all the hostages." The president, to counter reports that the administration was trying to "devalue" the issue, told reporters that he had a hard time pretending the hostages were not a national preoccupation. "No American is going to be content until these people are free. And I would not be doing my job if I didn't approach it in that manner."

As the days passed, it became clear that while the crisis over terrorist threats to kill American hostages had evaporated, with it had gone any hope of immediate movement on the hostage matter. As commentators noted, too little was still known about the Shi'ite terrorists, and the prospective roles and attitudes of Iran and Syria were still uncertain.

As for American-Israeli relations, the crisis had heightened the sense on each side that the other wasn't listening to its needs. For the United States, Israel's decision to seize Sheikh Obeid without consultation and the apparent disregard of the implications for American hostages, spoke volumes. To Israel, U.S. willingness to equate, even indirectly, Israel's taking Obeid with Shi'ite holding of hostages and the lack of understanding for Israel's concerns about its soldiers, also spoke volumes. While the crisis soon passed, the differences emphasized some of the new tensions in the relationship.

The Intifada

The decision by Yasir Arafat in December 1988 to utter the "magic" words about Israel that led the United States to start talking to the PLO was widely attributed to the impact of the *intifada* on that organization. Seeing the residents of the territories taking their destiny into their own hands, the PLO leadership found itself under increasing pressure to prove its value anew to the increasingly assertive population of the territories.

Once the U.S.-PLO dialogue began, it seemed to give a shot in the arm to the *intifada*, which at the end of 1988 had shown signs of losing its vitality and sense of purpose. As January came in, there was a strong revival of confidence and euphoria among the residents, reflected in a new willingness to challenge Israeli forces. The violence grew and with it tougher Israeli reactions, new orders by Defense Minister Rabin allowing soldiers, under certain circumstances, to shoot plastic bullets at any Palestinian observed throwing a stone, erecting a roadblock, or burning a tire, and new criticism of Rabin's tactics.

Caught between his need to protect Israel against violence and the realization that no Israeli tactics could bring an end to the uprising, Rabin looked anew to the political arena. On January 30, Rabin indicated that he no longer demanded an end to the Palestinian uprising as a condition for peace talks with residents of the territories. Searching for ways to induce Palestinians to accept political proposals, he told his party's parliamentary faction that he was "ready to speak now, to reach agreement on the process." He said that when such an agreement was achieved, "the calm will begin because, in my opinion if they want free elections, they cannot be held in an atmosphere of violence, not only between Arabs and Jews, but between Arabs and Arabs."

Early in February, the State Department issued its annual report on human-rights practices around the world. It said that Israel's response to the uprising "led to a substantial increase in human rights violations" in the territories during 1988, and that Israeli troops had caused "many avoidable deaths and injuries," that "soldiers frequently used gunfire in situations that did not present mortal danger to troops." At the same time, the survey noted that it was possible to report on conditions in the territories "by virtue of Israel's open and democratic society."

Israel reacted bitterly to the report. On February 7, Deputy Foreign Minister Benjamin Netanyahu indicated that there was no merit to the criticism, saying that Israeli troops "maintain as best they can, apart from a few exceptions, the standards of proper conduct that no country in the world could maintain." The next day, Shamir said that Israel was "sorry about any loss of life, but there's no chance to put an end to violence without taking forceful means." The cabinet issued a statement noting that the army would continue to act as it had "to insure the peace and security of all the residents and travelers" in the territories, "and will act intensively to prevent any disturbances of law and order." And the Foreign Ministry, in a long cable to Israeli diplomats, pointed out that the State Department "did not, unfortunately, give full consideration to the actions of local extremist elements and the major dilemmas which these cause for Israel."

Soon after the report appeared, the PLO introduced a resolution at the UN deploring Israel's treatment of Palestinians in the territories. It did so against the urging of Arab and European countries, which called for the PLO to give the Bush administration more time to develop a policy. On February 17, the United States vetoed the measure on the ground that it lacked balance. America's deputy representative to the UN stated that the United States had "made clear to the Government of Israel our opposition to certain Israeli practices," but said the resolution "does not take into sufficient account the context in which they occur or the excesses of the other side."

On April 5, Israel freed about 250 Arab prisoners arrested for participating in the uprising. It was widely noted that the release coincided with Shamir's critical visit to Washington, and that Washington had been asking Israel to make such a move to promote movement toward peace. Israel denied that the move was a response to U.S. requests, however, describing it as a gesture on the eve of the Muslim holiday Ramadan. Several days later, in Chicago, Shamir once again defended his government's handling of the *intifada*. He said that quelling the uprising "doesn't depend on the Israeli government," but the moment the violence would "stop or be reduced, then the tension will disappear."

By early May, a new phenomenon of the uprising began to receive attention: this was the killing of Palestinians by Palestinians for alleged "collaboration" with the Israeli authorities. Israeli officials made a connection between this violence and Shamir's elections proposal of April, Foreign Minister Arens telling U.S. ambassador to Israel William Brown that this could be an effort to prevent the emergence of candidates to participate in the elections.

As the weeks passed, it was widely noted that Israel was pursuing two different approaches to the Palestinians in the territories at the same time. One was Shamir's elections proposal, which was seen as a response to international clamor for concessions. The other was the imposition of harsher restrictions on Palestinian movements, for example, requiring all Gazans to obtain permits to travel to Israel to work, which was seen as an effort to cope with rising anger among Israeli Jews over Arab attacks inside Israel.

June brought another UN Security Council resolution condemning Israel's policies in the territories and with it, on June 9, a second veto by the Bush administration. Thomas Pickering, American representative to the UN, said that the resolution was "unbalanced" in its condemnation of Israel, "without any reference to any of the serious acts of violence by the other side."

The issue of deportations—which in 1988 had led to U.S. support of a Security Council resolution criticizing Israel—surfaced again late in June. On June 29, Israel deported eight Palestinians to Lebanon, accusing them of leading the uprising or being active in various arms of the PLO. The State Department denounced the expulsions, saying they were "harmful at any time and particularly right now when we are seeking international and Palestinian support for Israel's election proposals." On July 6 and again on August 30, the Security Council passed resolutions criticizing Israeli deportations. On both occasions, the United States abstained.

Another aspect of the *intifada* that had generated U.S. criticism from the beginning was the closing by Israel of schools in the West Bank. On July 12, Israel announced that the schools would reopen "gradually in the near future." Israeli radio reported that before classes resumed, Israeli officials would meet with Palestinian educators and students to "explain policy" and seek guarantees against disturbances. The move was seen as a gesture to the United States, since Secretary of State Baker had indicated in his policy address to AIPAC in May that reopening of schools was a step sought by the administration. It was also seen as an effort to keep the door open to West Bank Palestinians whom the government hoped to engage in negotiations on the elections proposal.

The UN General Assembly joined in the international criticism of Israel's conduct against the *intifada* on October 6. Only the United States and Israel voted against a resolution introduced by the Arab countries on behalf of the PLO. It called on Israel to halt violations of Palestinian human rights and asked UN secretary-general Javier Pérez de Cuéllar to report on the situation in the territories as soon as possible. It also asked the Security Council to consider "with urgency" measures to "provide international protection to the Palestinian civilians" in the occupied territories. The United States called the resolution "one-sided" and said it served only to "deepen divisions, harden positions and poison the atmosphere."

In November the issue of Israel's treatment of Palestinians received attention from an unusual source, the organized American Jewish community. At a news conference in Jerusalem on November 23, Seymour Reich, chairman of the Conference of Presidents of Major American Jewish Organizations, warned Israel that it must deal with charges of human-rights abuses which, he said, were the subject of great discussion in Congress and throughout the country. Reich added that he believed U.S. support for Israel was undiminished, despite some differences between the governments.

December 9 marked the second anniversary of the uprising. It was widely commented that, unlike the first year, which had brought new attention to the Palestinians and the U.S.-PLO dialogue, the second year saw no significant achievements. A kind of permanent state of war had developed, accepted as a fact of life by both Israelis and Palestinians.

U.S.-Israeli Bilateral Relations

Israel and the United States continued to benefit in 1989 from the deepening strategic and economic ties generated during the Reagan-Shultz years, despite some misgivings among Israel supporters about the different personalities in power in Washington. The one element that threatened to change the relationship was the dramatic developments taking place in the Soviet Union and Eastern Europe.

At the heart of the strategic relationship established in the '80s were two perceptions held in Washington: one, that Israel was a strategic asset in the ongoing struggle between the Americans and the Soviets, and two, that the United States could maintain close relations with Israel without weakening its position in the Arab world. As events developed in 1989, with the cold war winding down, questions were being raised about the long-term value of maintaining strategic relations, particularly if the Bush administration was more concerned about the impact of those relations on the Arab world than the Reagan team had been.

As for Israel's role in helping to maintain regional stability in the Middle East, a key question was whether the administration would obtain cooperation of Arab partners as well, which would result in a surge of U.S. arms sales to the Arabs. If such cooperation were not obtained, Israel's place would probably remain preeminent or even grow. U.S. security interests, in this view, would begin to depend increasingly on a Mediterranean naval presence, and non-European sites would be sought for the possible redeployment and storage of U.S. equipment withdrawn from Western Europe. During 1989, however, no major changes were evident in this regard. Israeli-U.S. strategic cooperation remained intact.

Early in the year, Israel Aircraft Industries announced that it had signed an agreement with Lockheed Corporation to work together on the Israeli-designed Arrow missile. The Arrow was designed to intercept incoming tactical ballistic missiles and would be tested as a possible component of the U.S. "Star Wars" antimissile program. The Defense Department had awarded Israel Aircraft a $158-million contract in July 1988 to develop the Arrow, with 20 percent of the funding provided by the Israeli Defense Ministry. It was projected that the first demonstration test of the missile would take place some time in 1990. On March 1, the administration stated its resolve to continue the process, when Deputy Assistant Secretary of Defense Edward Gnehm told the House Foreign Affairs subcommittee on the Middle East that Defense's "cooperative programs with the Israeli military reflect the U.S. commitment to Israel," and that they "will be continued and built upon in the coming years."

Meanwhile, the various U.S.-Israeli strategic and political committees established during the Shultz years continued to meet. The Joint Political–Military Group met twice, in Israel and Omaha, Nebraska, and it was reported that major progress took place in the key areas of equipment prepositioning, joint exercises, and intelligence cooperation. Particularly significant was an agreement reached in October for the United States to stockpile $100-million worth of military supplies in Israel, available both for future U.S. use or by Israel during crisis situations.

The Joint Economic Development Group, chaired on the American side by Undersecretary of State for Economic Affairs Robert McCormack, met as well. Trade volume between the two countries reached a high, following Israel's elimination, in January, of tariffs on many U.S. products, which put the United States on an equal competitive footing in this respect with the European Community.

U.S. military activity in Israel picked up during the year. In the spring, U.S. Marine Corps exercises took place in Israel, growing from the small units of the previous year to battalion-size training maneuvers. There was as well a continued increase in the number of port visits by U.S. Navy ships to Haifa for repairs and shore leave.

Meanwhile, the U.S. aid package to Israel was maintained at $3 billion in grants, with congressional support for the bill even higher than in past years. In efforts to maintain Israel's qualitative military edge, the foreign-aid bill mandated presidential reports on the Middle East arms balance and prohibited the transfer of such weapons as the Stinger missile to certain Persian Gulf countries. On the other hand, the United States did conclude a $3.1-billion sale of advanced M-1A2 tanks to Saudi Arabia, with talk abounding of a multimillion-dollar sale of new fighter aircraft to the Saudis in 1990 or 1991.

Soviet Jewry

By year's end, 62,000 Soviet Jews had emigrated to Israel, reflecting a liberalized Soviet emigration policy and concerns among Soviet Jews of emerging popular anti-Semitism and economic chaos. The prospect of hundreds of thousands of Soviet Jews going to Israel in future years inevitably raised the subject of potential U.S. financial assistance to an increasingly burdened State of Israel.

The *New York Times* reported on October 1 that a week earlier Israeli finance minister Shimon Peres had asked Washington for $400 million in loan guarantees to finance the construction of housing for Soviet Jewish arrivals. Such guarantees, under a U.S. program to finance housing projects in developing countries, would allow Israel to borrow money from commercial banks at low interest rates. Israeli officials indicated that without the loan guarantees it could not afford to borrow the money from commercial banks, because the "most favorable conditions we could expect would make the program unfeasible."

Politics immediately intruded on the issue. When Peres, in Washington, met with members of the House Appropriations subcommittee responsible for foreign aid to discuss the matter, he acknowledged that the current Israeli government would probably build some of the housing on the West Bank. Other Israeli officials indicated that inevitably, some of the Soviet immigrants would want to live in the West Bank, and the notion that the government would bar them was difficult to imagine. The following day, Marlin Fitzwater, speaking on behalf of the administration, said that the Americans "want to be helpful in any way we can," but added that "we remain opposed to settlements in the West Bank, and also opposed to the use of U.S. aid for that purpose." Secretary Baker said that although the administration opposed additional settlements, "we are very sympathetic" to Israel's desire to accept Soviet Jews and to provide adequate housing for them.

Objections also were raised in Congress about how Israel would use such guarantees. Sen. Patrick J. Leahy (D., Vt.), chairman of the Appropriations subcommittee responsible for foreign aid, said that "Israel has a legitimate concern on housing for immigrants" from the Soviet Union, but added that we "will not use American foreign aid for settlements in the West Bank." An unnamed American aid official suggested that even if Israel agreed to use loan guarantees to finance construction within Israel's pre-1967 borders, that could free other funds to build housing in the West Bank.

The brouhaha over this issue was at least in part a product of the alarm expressed by Arab representatives at the possibility that significant numbers of Soviet Jews would settle in the territories. Clovis Maksoud, the Arab League representative to the UN, called such a migration a "creeping annexation" of the territories that would undermine prospects for peace.

Israel–South Africa Relations

Toward year's end, another long-standing issue with potential to disrupt U.S.-Israeli amity surfaced once again, that of Israel's relations with South Africa. On October 25, NBC reported that Israel and South Africa had test-fired a nuclear missile on July 5 that flew 900 miles from a site in South Africa to the Prince Edward Islands in the Indian Ocean, and that Israel had provided expertise in return for South African enriched uranium. Prime Minister Shamir immediately issued a blanket denial of such cooperation; the Israeli Defense Ministry said merely that "the defense establishment strictly abides by the inner Cabinet decision of March 18, 1987, whereby no new contracts will be signed between Israel and South Africa in the defense realm." Although the ministry declined to discuss continuing work on contracts that existed before 1987, it did say that there was "no truth to the report carried by the NBC network in the United States on so-called relations with South Africa in the nuclear realm."

On October 26, the White House announced that it was "looking into the facts and issues" raised by the report, but "we don't have any conclusions at this point." On October 28, President Bush, in Costa Rica, said that if there was Israeli-South African collaboration on a nuclear missile, such an arrangement would "complicate" relations with Israel. The president said that the transfer of such technology is "taboo" and "we're not going to have that." A day earlier, however, the State Department had said that the United States had "no indication" that Israel had transferred any U.S. missile technology to South Africa, but refused to comment on reports that the two had collaborated to develop and test an intermediate-range missile. Several days later, before leaving for Australia, Secretary of State Baker said that news reports of Israel's military cooperation with South Africa had been "overblown," adding that they would not undermine U.S.-Israeli relations.

On November 11, the *Jerusalem Post* reported that the CIA had told congressmen and senators behind closed doors that Israel had indeed cooperated extensively with South Africa on ballistic missiles, but could not confirm that Israel was directly involved with South Africa in the area of nuclear weapons. According to the report, Washington had no evidence that Israel had transferred any American military technology or military equipment to South Africa in violation of Israel's commitment to the United States.

Several days later, on November 16, when Shamir was in Washington for his controversial meeting with Bush, he met with congressional leaders to discuss Israeli-South African relations. The group consisted of black and Jewish members of Congress. Shamir reportedly emphasized during the meeting that Israel was merely honoring pre-1987 contracts with South Africa.

On November 20, 11 influential members of the House Foreign Affairs Committee, including some of Israel's best friends, issued a public appeal to Shamir to suspend all remaining Israeli military ties with South Africa immediately. The two-page statement was signed by Dante Fascell (D., Fla.), Lee Hamilton (D., Ind.), four Jewish members—Larry Smith (D., Fla.), Stephen Solarz (D., N.Y.), Mel Levine (D., Calif.), and Howard Wolpe (D., Mich.)—and black members Ron Dellums (D., Calif.), Bill Gray (D., Pa.), Charles Rangel (D., N.Y.), and Alan Wheat (D., Miss.). The statement referred to Shamir's denial of any nuclear cooperation with, or transfer of any U.S. military technology to, South Africa, and said that those denials had been "substantiated by the State Department." But the congressmen made clear that they wanted Israel to terminate its pre-1987 military contracts with South Africa as well. The statement urged the United States to consider new ways to help Israel make up any security-related shortfalls resulting from the complete termination of military ties with South Africa. In releasing the statement, the congressmen said that Shamir had "pledged to review the situation and welcomed the initiation of a dialogue that will seek to address the remaining concerns."

KENNETH JACOBSON

Communal

Jewish Communal Affairs

American Jewry and the Middle East

SECRETARY OF STATE GEORGE SHULTZ'S decision in December 1988 to open talks with the PLO, followed by the replacement of the Reagan administration with that of George Bush, set the stage for dramatic conflicts within the American Jewish community over Israel's policies toward the Palestinians. American Jewry appeared relatively united on Middle East issues at the outset of 1989. Most American Jewish organizations had reacted calmly to the establishment of official U.S.-PLO relations, and in January 1989 they were virtually unanimous in opposing suggestions that Yasir Arafat be granted a visa to enter the United States. Even Jewish leaders who had pressed for the change in American policy toward the PLO did not believe that Arafat should be allowed into the country.

But this consensus evaporated on February 9, when the Conference of Presidents of Major Jewish Organizations concluded three days of talks with Israeli leaders in Jerusalem with a call to the U.S. State Department to reassess its relations with the PLO, in light of a clash between PLO members and Israeli soldiers in southern Lebanon. Conference president Seymour Reich said that unless Arafat repudiated "this latest terrorist attempt" he would urge James Baker, the new secretary of state, to cut off the dialogue with the PLO. But four member organizations of the Presidents Conference—the Labor Zionist Alliance, the Federation of Reconstructionist Congregations and Havurot, Workmen's Circle, and Women's American ORT—claimed that they had not been consulted, and dissociated themselves from Reich's statement.

At the same time, a controversial State Department report alleging Israeli human-rights abuses in the West Bank and Gaza became the occasion for some American Jewish leaders to voice their exasperation with Israeli policy. "The rejectionist stand in which Israel has been cast doesn't sit well with the American people," commented American Jewish Committee president Theodore Ellenoff, who suggested that Israel talk to the PLO "at the proper time." And Laurence Goldmuntz, president of the Jewish Institute for National Security Affairs, pointed out to the Israelis that "the underdog, in the perception of Americans, is the Palestinians. You are blowing up homes. This has got to stop."

The perception of a rift between influential American Jews and Israel grew. The National Jewish Community Relations Advisory Council (NJCRAC), made up of 11 national Jewish organizations and over 100 local community relations councils, held its annual plenum in February. In discussions of a proposed statement on the Middle East, former American Jewish Congress president Theodore Mann proposed an amendment expressing "deep concern over the profound consequences of a continuation of the status quo in the territories." It barely failed of passage, losing 157 to 151, and Mann was assured that it would be reconsidered by NJCRAC's Middle East Task Force at a later time.

On February 28, the *New York Times* published an op-ed column by Menachem Rosensaft, the president of the Labor Zionist Alliance, one of five American Jews who had met with Arafat in December in Stockholm. Prime Minister Yitzhak Shamir was scheduled to visit the United States for talks with government officials in the spring, and Rosensaft stated flatly that as long as Shamir and his Likud party controlled Israeli foreign policy, Israel would not move toward peace. He charged that a majority of Israelis rejected their government's hard-line stance, noting that the Likud-led government had been elected "before Yasir Arafat's dramatic recognition of Israel." Seymour Reich immediately chastised Rosensaft for "undermining the prime minister of Israel."

In early March, an American Jewish initiative to help Israel clarify its policy options ended in some embarrassment. The American Jewish Congress and the Anti-Defamation League of B'nai B'rith cosponsored a study—conducted for them by the Jaffee Center for Strategic Studies of Tel Aviv University—analyzing the strengths and weaknesses of various proposed solutions to the Palestinian problem. A set of recommendations separate from the analysis suggested the inevitability of Israeli-Palestinian negotiations, a view welcomed by opposition leader Shimon Peres but condemned by Prime Minister Shamir. The Anti-Defamation League immediately disavowed the recommendations, expressing "distress" over the AJCongress's failure to emphasize sufficiently that the two groups had commissioned only the analysis, not the conclusions.

Just a few days later the American Jewish Committee released the results of a poll it had sponsored, entitled *Ties and Tensions: An Update; The 1989 Survey of American Jewish Attitudes Toward Israel and Israelis,* by Steven M. Cohen. While showing that Jewish support for Israel had not declined, the data did provide cause for concern: 35 percent of the sample said they were "morally outraged" by some Israeli policies, and 54 percent claimed that during the *intifada* they had felt that "Israelis were acting wrongly." And while 90 percent still considered the PLO a terrorist organization, 58 percent believed that Israel should negotiate with it if it recognized Israel and renounced terrorism.

American Jewish disenchantment with Israeli actions was taken seriously by the Israeli government. Visiting New York in March, Deputy Prime Minister David

Levy surprised the Conference of Presidents of Major Jewish Organizations by telling its members that, while he was sure of support from the American administration, he was less certain that American Jewry was still behind Israel. Speaking to the same audience a week later, Israeli foreign minister Moshe Arens expanded on this theme. Arens evoked a historical parallel freighted with emotional impact: "During the Holocaust, it is agreed that the American Jewish leadership did not do everything it could have done or should have done. Let that be an object lesson that we never again fail to live up to our responsibilities." Saying he "couldn't understand why any Jew, any self-respecting person" could possibly meet with the PLO, Arens claimed that the erosion of American Jewish sympathy for Israel was more dangerous than the rocks of Palestinian rioters.

SHAMIR'S SOLIDARITY CONFERENCE

To mobilize the backing of world Jewry for his anticipated talks with the American administration, Prime Minister Shamir scheduled a Conference on Jewish Solidarity with Israel to be held in Jerusalem, March 20–22. It later emerged that the idea was first conceived by Rabbi Marvin Hier, dean of the Simon Wiesenthal Center. In announcing this event, Israel's ambassador to the United States stressed that, while Israel insisted on framing its own policies, it would seriously consider the views expressed by Diaspora Jews at the conference. But other Israeli officials described the planned conference as a "celebration" of Israel-Diaspora unity, noting that Israel had already taken into account American Jewish concerns by shelving proposed "Who is a Jew?" legislation. "There has been a sense of sagging morale," explained member of the Knesset Ehud Olmert, a conference organizer. "We want to say to the Jewish world: Be proud of Israel—with all its problems. Don't hide. Stand up and support us."

American Jewish leaders reacted with some ambivalence. Unlike the case in Great Britain, no notable Jews declared a boycott of the conference. Yet even some American Jewish organizations that participated—such as AJCongress and the Union of American Hebrew Congregations (UAHC)—worried that it might be used to rubber-stamp the hard-line Likud policy position on the Palestinians. On March 12, the *New York Times* carried an ad in support of the conference signed by 53 Jewish organizations and 11 past chairmen of the Presidents Conference, but that support was expressed in the vague generality of a "commitment to Israel's security, its independence, its economic vitality, and the well-being of its citizenry."

The Jerusalem conference—attended by about 1,200 Diaspora Jews—managed to satisfy both those critical of Israeli actions and those eager to express solidarity with Israel. Since the participants were free to say whatever they wanted, dissenters from the Likud line came away feeling that they had been heard. Alexander Schindler, president of the UAHC and a vocal opponent of Shamir's policies, declared himself "pleasantly surprised by the relative openness of the conference." There was, he said, "sharp and open debate, and it was very well handled." Yet the overall outcome was a renewed sense of Jewish unity. A "Declaration on Jewish Solidarity" was adopted, supporting "the democratically elected Government of National Unity in its efforts to achieve peace and security with its neighbors." "I think it is written well enough to satisfy all those who came here, who have divergent points of view," commented Ernest Michel, executive director of New York UJA-Federation.

Only on the far left of the American Jewish community was there any criticism of the conference's work. *Tikkun* editor Michael Lerner called the event "a grave disservice to the Jewish people and to Israel." Lerner felt that the American Jewish participants should have made clear to Shamir that their community rejected his stance.

Buoyed by the success of the conference, Shamir arrived in the United States on April 4. Attempts to maintain in New York the show of unity that had been achieved at the Jerusalem conference failed, however. The Zionist Organization of America mustered 200 Jews at 6:30 in the morning to welcome the prime minister at Kennedy Airport, and B'nai B'rith International took a full-page ad in the *New York Times* stating that "our strength as a community lies not in our sameness, but in our diversity—and our unity." But a meeting with Shamir at Town Hall was boycotted by the Americans for a Progressive Israel because participation would, its president said, "misrepresent us as expressing support for Shamir's policies." Anti-Shamir Jewish groups that had considered picketing outside Town Hall decided against it only when they learned that Arab groups would be demonstrating there. And 180 Jews signed a *Tikkun*-sponsored ad in the *New York Times* that stated, "No, Mr. Shamir, don't think that American Jews support your policies toward the Palestinians."

SHAMIR'S PEACE INITIATIVE

To the surprise of many American Jews, Shamir proposed to the American administration a plan for Palestinian elections that would lead eventually to local self-rule, and Secretary of State Baker showed some interest. (See "The United States, Israel, and the Middle East," in this volume.) After Shamir briefed the Presidents Conference on his talks in Washington, American Jewish leaders were deeply gratified. Even Shamir's old antagonist Menachem Rosensaft acknowledged that "it is absolutely a different tone, a different approach from his speeches and his attitude during his previous visit last year. He sounded much more moderate and held open the possibility of an eventual compromise."

Speaking to reporters at a National Press Club breakfast on May 9, Seymour Reich praised Shamir. Asserting that the great majority of American Jews backed the new Israeli proposal for West Bank elections, Reich explained that previous misunderstandings between American Jews and Israel had been due to Israel's inability to speak with one voice. "It is now clear," he said, "that Shamir speaks for the government of Israel."

Reich was overly optimistic. When Foreign Minister Moshe Arens came to the United States to work out details of the plan, Henry Siegman, executive director of AJCongress, wanted to know how Israel's new willingness to conduct elections in the territories squared with its refusal to talk to the PLO—whose supporters could very well win those elections. And when Secretary of State Baker urged Israelis to give up "the unrealistic vision of a Greater Israel" in a well-publicized speech to the annual policy conference of the American Israel Public Affairs Committee (AIPAC), on May 22, it became clear that the Shamir initiative was no guarantee of smooth Israeli-American relations.

To complicate matters further, Israel's minister of industry and trade, Ariel Sharon, traveled to the United States in June to organize opposition against the Shamir plan on the ground that it gave away too much; elections, he charged, would lead to a Palestinian state. After receiving a standing ovation at a dinner for an organization dedicated to buying up Arab properties in Jerusalem and settling Jews in them, Sharon confronted a much more skeptical audience at a meeting of the Presidents Conference. Having put such an emotional investment in the moderate-sounding Shamir plan, the conference was in no mood for Sharon's criticisms. Asserting the importance from a public-relations standpoint of Israel's agreement to back elections in the territories, Phil Baum, associate executive director of AJ-Congress, told Sharon that "it would be deplorable if this accord were somehow to be lost."

Any lingering hopes that the Shamir initiative would put relations between Israel and the United States—and those between American and Israeli Jews—back on track were soon dashed. In June, Israel's ambassador to Washington publicly chastised American Jewry for not doing enough to rally American support for the Shamir plan. In early July, Israeli and American Jewish leaders expressed outrage at reports that the American envoy in Tunis had held talks with Abu Iyad, a PLO figure involved in the Munich massacre of Jewish Olympic athletes in 1972. Then, on July 5, Shamir's Likud party forced him to accept amendments to his peace plan that were championed by Ariel Sharon: Arab residents of East Jerusalem would not vote in the proposed elections; the *intifada* would have to cease before the elections; absolutely no negotiations with the PLO; no Palestinian state west of the Jordan; and more Jewish settlements in the territories.

Caught by surprise, American Jewish spokesmen reacted cautiously, but their dismay was evident. Seymour Reich, speaking for the Presidents Conference, claimed that the amendments signified no change in the Israeli position, and ADL national director Abraham Foxman described Shamir's acquiescence to them as merely "a creative political maneuver." But officials of the AJCommittee and AJ-Congress warned that the new conditions might harm the Israeli plan's chances of success; the Committee's executive vice-president, Ira Silverman, sent a letter to Shamir asking him to "reassure the other parties in the government that you will pursue the peace plan without prior constraints."

American Jews previously distrustful of the Likud were now more openly hostile.

Menachem Rosensaft urged the Israeli Labor party to leave the coalition government to protest the new peace conditions—a step that Seymour Reich opposed on the ground that it would mean new elections and the subsequent political chaos likely to arise from the inability of any party to muster a majority. Jerome Segal, a professor at the University of Maryland, announced the formation of the Jewish Peace Lobby, whose announced purpose was to serve as an alternative to the allegedly hard-line AIPAC. Claiming the endorsement of 125 rabbis and "several dozen prominent American Jews," and advocating the creation of a demilitarized Palestinian state, the new group was discounted as too pro-PLO even by many anti-Shamir American Jewish activists.

OTHER ISRAEL-RELATED MATTERS

With the Israeli government now divided over the Likud peace plan—divided, indeed, over what that plan even meant—and with the PLO showing no interest in it, other aspects of the Middle East situation came to the fore. Early in July, Sen. Jesse Helms (R., N.C.) offered an amendment to a bill funding the State Department that would forbid the United States from having any contacts with PLO officials who had been associated with terrorist acts. AJCongress and the UAHC broke ranks with the other Jewish organizations and opposed the measure, agreeing with the administration that it would hamper the peace process. Commented Henry Siegman of the Congress, "If we wish the PLO leadership to play a constructive role by permitting the elections to go forward, then the very last thing we should be saying to the PLO is that, no matter what they do and no matter how constructive a role they play, we will never raise the level of our dialogue with them." The two Jewish groups opposed to the Helms amendment helped work out compromise language that barred contact only with those PLO members known to have participated directly in terrorism against an American citizen. The substitute passed easily.

A new threat to American-Israeli relations emerged on July 31, when Shi'ite Muslims in Lebanon announced that they had killed an American marine officer who had worked with the UN peacekeeping force and whom they had kidnapped in 1988. The Shi'ites declared that this act was in retaliation for the Israeli kidnapping of Sheikh Abdul Karim Obeid, whom the Israelis had taken from his home in Lebanon a few days before for questioning about his role in terrorist activities. President Bush seemed to blame both sides equally when he urged all parties involved to release their hostages. On the floor of the U.S. Senate, minority leader Robert Dole of Kansas stated flatly that the Israelis were responsible for the death of the marine. "When it endangers the lives of Americans in some foreign country," he said, "perhaps a little more restraint on the part of the Israelis one of these days would be refreshing." According to newspaper reports, Dole's sentiments were shared by other lawmakers who preferred anonymity. And public-opinion polls taken immediately after the incident showed a sharp drop in the percentage of Americans who considered Israel a reliable ally of the United States.

Organized American Jewry mobilized to defend Israel by emphasizing that the Jewish state and the United States were on the same side in the struggle against international terrorism, and that acrimony between the two nations played into the hands of the terrorists. It was reported in the press—but officially denied by those involved—that a telephone call from Prime Minister Shamir to President Bush to discuss coordination of hostage policy between Israel and the United States was actually orchestrated by American Jewish leaders eager to portray the two countries as partners against terrorism. AJCongress placed a full-page ad in the major national newspapers calling on Americans not "to strike out at our closest ally, beleaguered Israel, for seeking to do that which we wish we would do ourselves." Although Jewish leaders were somewhat reassured when Senator Dole subsequently softened his harsh remarks about Israel, Henry Siegman was surely correct in noting that much of the anger at the Jewish state over this episode had less to do with Israel's abduction of the sheikh than with a perceived reluctance by that country to make peace with the Palestinians.

In August Jewish groups once again began to anticipate the possibility of Yasir Arafat applying for an American visa so that he might address the UN in the fall. In meetings with State Department officials and with presidential chief of staff John Sununu, Jewish leaders stressed that even though the United States now conducted a dialogue with the PLO, Arafat's credentials as a terrorist should be sufficient to bar him from the country. While leaving its options open on the question of a visa, the administration did gratify American Jewry by announcing that any chance of the United States rejoining UNESCO would be dashed if that organization granted the PLO membership.

During the summer, American Jewry had another reason to worry about the enhancement of the PLO's image. The Public Broadcasting Service announced that it would make available to its affiliates for airing on September 6 "Days of Rage: The Young Palestinians," a television documentary. Jewish leaders condemned the show as pro-Palestinian propaganda but were fearful of taking any step that could be construed as interference with the freedom of speech. The Presidents Conference distributed information about "Days of Rage," while many local Jewish organizations sought to convince PBS affiliates in their communities not to run it.

Hoping to meet Jewish objections, the network decided to provide additional "wrap-around" programming that would place the documentary in a broader perspective: a segment before "Days of Rage" would probe the feelings of Israelis about the *intifada,* and a panel discussion afterward would elicit the views of spokesmen of differing perspectives, including Presidents Conference chairman Reich.

Just a week before the scheduled date of the show, Jewish organizations—seizing upon evidence that the documentary was partially funded by an Arab foundation—sought to have it withdrawn on the ground that financing of a project by an organization with a vested interest in it violated PBS guidelines. But rather than cancel "Days of Rage," the network ran a statement both before and after the show stating that there were allegations of improper funding that could not be verified. As it turned out, despite all the publicity, "Days of Rage" received only average ratings.

SHAMIR VISIT TO UNITED STATES

Meanwhile, the United States was attempting to bring Israeli and Palestinian representatives together in Cairo for talks based on the Shamir plan for local elections in the territories. With these efforts going nowhere, Shamir prepared for another visit to the United States in November, to meet once again with high government officials and to address the General Assembly of the Council of Jewish Federations. American Jewish leaders, both pro- and anti-Shamir, sought ways to influence the political climate in the United States.

The Presidents Conference prepared an ad to run in the *Washington Post* on the day of Shamir's arrival in the capital, but several organizations within the conference found the text too supportive of Likud positions and insisted on less specific language. Unable to meet the *Post*'s deadline, the conference ran a more general ad in the *New York Times,* simply wishing Shamir well in his negotiations. On that same day the *Times* also published another ad, sponsored by B'nai B'rith International, that virtually endorsed Shamir's views. B'nai B'rith's president was none other than Seymour Reich, who was also chairman of the Presidents Conference.

To keep the Israeli prime minister from again claiming that American Jewry stood solidly behind him, 42 Jewish leaders sent him a letter warning: "Please do not mistake courtesy for consensus, or applause for endorsement of all the policies you pursue." Specifically, the letter claimed that while "some" rejected giving up land for peace, "most American Jews" did not—a clear hint that, on this point, American Jewry and Shamir were at odds. The letter was signed by two men who had chaired the Presidents Conference, three past chairmen of NJCRAC, a number of local federation activists, and prominent figures in Reform and Conservative Judaism. Theodore Mann, a former Presidents Conference chairman who helped draft the letter, emphasized to reporters that the signatories were mainstream leaders, noting, "these are not in any way fringe people."

While in the United States, Shamir made clear his disdain for such criticism. Complaining repeatedly that the world media distorted news from the Middle East so as to cast Israel in the worst possible light, he spent much of his time visiting with pro-Likud American Jews and speaking before audiences he knew were sympathetic to him, while avoiding groups—such as the Jewish Federation Council of Los Angeles—that he suspected were hostile. Buoyed by an enthusiastic reception by 1,000 Brooklyn Jews, Shamir told Israeli reporters, "The American Jewish masses support the national unity government and, I might add, the position of the prime minister. I have more and more proof of this every day." He described the dissenters as "a voluble minority." Seymour Reich agreed, claiming that "the overwhelming majority" of American Jews backed Israel's policies.

"TIKKUN" CONFERENCE

Reich's position came under heavy attack at a November conference in San Francisco, sponsored by *Tikkun* magazine. The conference title was "Israeli Meshuggas and American Response: What Should American Jews Do in Response to the Current Policies of the Israeli Government?" *Tikkun* editor Michael Lerner said, "We are attempting to reclaim Judaism from the organized community." He argued not only that Israeli actions were immoral, but that they would ultimately erode "any credible basis for long-term support for Israel." Professor David Biale of the Graduate Theological Union in Berkeley charged that he and other critics of Israeli policies were the victims of a "witch hunt" carried out by the mainstream Jewish organizations. Thus, the situation in Israel was "a cancer that has metastasized to our shores," possibly pointing to the "progressive disintegration of the American Jewish community."

In December Seymour Reich participated in a public forum with Michael Lerner. Lerner charged that the Presidents Conference and other "establishment" organizations were not telling the truth when they alleged that most American Jews supported Israel's present course. And since Jewish leaders refused to tell Shamir that his policies were "destructive politically or morally abhorrent," Israel stood to lose the support of more and more American Jews.

Reich responded that the Presidents Conference made no claim to speak for all American Jews, but did "speak in the name of the broadest coalition of the world's largest Jewish community." While recognizing the legitimacy of diverse Jewish viewpoints, Reich pointed out that "any perception of American Jewish disaffection with Israel" could create a climate of opinion conducive to cuts in American aid to the Jewish state.

The vexing questions of who spoke for American Jewry on Israel and what were the appropriate limits on the expression of dissent from Israeli policies were no nearer solution at year's end than they were at its beginning.

Soviet Jewry

In December 1988, 3,652 Jews left the Soviet Union, the largest monthly total in nine years. The estimated figure for all of 1988—slightly over 19,000—was more than double the number of émigrés in 1987.

More good news followed. The Soviet Union signed an international human-rights agreement that affirmed religious freedom and the right to emigrate. With the acquiescence of Soviet authorities, the World Jewish Congress (WJC) established a branch in Moscow. The Solomon Mikhoels Center—the first government-sanctioned Jewish cultural center—opened in the same city, a cooperative venture of the WJC, the Executive Council of Australian Jewry, and the Moscow Jewish Musical Theater, in whose building the center was housed. Soviet jamming of radio broadcasts from Israel on Jewish culture ended. With the coming of spring, Moscow dropped restrictions on the baking of matzah and the importation of wine for Passover. In April, 12 long-time refuseniks—one had waited 15 years—were allowed to leave the USSR for Israel. And in May, for the first time in its history, the National Conference on Soviet Jewry (NCSJ) was allowed to send an official delegation into the Soviet Union to discuss emigration issues.

Many Soviet Jewry activists in the United States felt that the new reality called for a reappraisal of the Jackson-Vanik Amendment that linked the granting of most-favored-nation trading status to liberalized emigration policies. In June the NCSJ called for a waiver of Jackson-Vanik, though it insisted that this be conditioned on a continued high level of Jewish emigration, codification of the emigration laws, movement toward the resolution of cases of long-term refuseniks, and a halt to the practice of using alleged access to state secrets as grounds for refusing visas. Subsequently, AJCongress went further, announcing support for a one-year unconditional waiver, and NJCRAC's Joint Program Plan also urged President Bush to waive Jackson-Vanik for a limited time period. For the second straight year, the traditional Solidarity Sunday rally for Soviet Jewry was canceled. Rabbi Haskel Lookstein, chairman of the Coalition to Free Soviet Jews, explained that "new and innovative programs and a flexible approach are essential in light of Gorbachev's policies of *glasnost* and *perestroika.*"

CONFLICT OVER DESTINATION AND FUNDING

If the problem of getting Jews out of the Soviet Union seemed to be on its way to a solution, the unresolved questions of where the Soviet Jewish emigrants would go and how their resettlement would be financed sparked conflict. These two issues were interconnected. Most American Jews believed that the refugees should settle wherever they wished, and that those choosing the United States had a right to the financial help of the Jewish community. But Israelis—along with a number of like-minded American Zionists—tended to feel that the Soviet emigration—made possible, of course, by Israeli visas—should flow to the Jewish state, and viewed any aid for Jews going elsewhere as a deterrent to Soviet Jewish *aliyah.*

In January officials of the Jewish Agency met in New York to discuss Soviet Jewish emigration. The funding question was of great concern to those representing the American Jewish federations. Since about 90 percent of the immigrants were then coming to the United States, and it was assumed that the influx would increase substantially, the American Jewish community would have to come up with millions of dollars to pay for resettlement. Where would the money come from?

One possibility was to divert some of the funds that ordinarily would go via the

United Jewish Appeal to Israel. This approach was naturally unacceptable to the Israelis. Another proposed solution was to run a "separate line campaign," that is a fund-raising drive for domestic immigrant resettlement separate from the regular UJA-Federation appeal. This idea too did not go over well with the Israelis on the Jewish Agency Executive, who feared that those contributing to the special drive might lower their contributions to the regular appeal. Simcha Dinitz, chairman of the Jewish Agency Executive, suggested instead that the Americans dip into their capital funds and investments. At a news conference on January 12, Dinitz made clear his opinion of financial aid for the resettlement of Soviet Jews in America, saying, "The Jewish Agency was not established in order to assist the absorption of Jews in Milwaukee, Chicago, or Detroit." He announced plans to improve housing services for new immigrants in Israel so that more of them would go there than to the United States.

While the Jewish Agency reached no consensus on how American Jewry would finance resettlement costs in the United States, a few days after the meeting, the Jewish Community Federation of San Francisco announced a drive to raise $2.7 million for immigrant resettlement separate from its regular $20-million campaign. On January 31, the board of the Council of Jewish Federations adopted a resolution urging the UJA to "give serious attention" to doing this on a national level, and on February 2, heeding this call, the UJA executive committee announced its decision to run such a separate campaign under the name "Passage to Freedom." Two Jewish federations in large cities where many Soviet Jews were settling responded quickly to the UJA announcement: New York UJA-Federation launched a $25-million "Passage to Freedom" campaign, and its Los Angeles counterpart requested its biggest donors to increase their contributions, with the extra funds earmarked for the resettlement of Soviet Jews.

By late March, many details of the special campaign had been worked out, though certain ambiguities and conflicts remained. A sum of $75 million was set as the national goal of "Passage to Freedom." Local federations would conduct the campaigns in their communities and hand the money over to national UJA. While there was no way to compel a federation to participate, virtually all were expected to do so. Half of the funds raised would go toward the resettlement of Soviet Jews in the United States, and the other half would be directed abroad—to resettlement in Israel and to such organizations as the American Jewish Joint Distribution Committee and the Hebrew Immigrant Aid Society that provided services to the immigrants in Europe. Quotas for how much each community would raise were based on its previous year's contribution to the general campaign. The allocation of funds was a thorny issue since the seven large Jewish communities where the great majority of the immigrants were settling felt that they deserved the lion's share. A committee was set up to work out allocations.

By far the most controversial aspect of "Passage to Freedom" was the perception by many Israelis that the campaign constituted a further inducement to Jews leaving the Soviet Union on Israeli passports to "drop out" in Europe and settle in the West.

Despite the fact that a portion of the money raised for overseas aid would go toward immigrant absorption in Israel, on March 7, a number of Israeli lawmakers from several political parties denounced "Passage to Freedom" on the floor of the Knesset. They charged that the campaign deceitfully used the name of Israel and the cause of Zionism to promote Soviet Jewish settlement outside Israel. And the World Zionist Executive went so far as to call for closing down all services for Soviet Jewish émigrés in Ladispoli, Italy, since the 7,000 Jews there refused to go to Israel.

Stanley Horowitz, president of the UJA, expressed sympathy for the Israeli position, noting that "the overwhelming consensus of American Jewish organizations would wish that all Soviet Jews would go to the State of Israel." But, he asked, "what is an appropriate response—once the determination is made—to those who will not go to Israel?" His answer was unequivocal: "The American Jewish community is dedicated to the idea of responding to fellow Jews."

This tension between Israeli and American Jewish views was sharpened by the fact that American Jewry was not simply "responding" to Soviet Jewish immigrants, but actively seeking to bring more of them into the United States. On the basis of a new policy adopted in September 1988, the American Immigration and Naturalization Service implemented a strict definition of "refugee" that led to denial of this status to an increasing number of Soviet Jews. In January and then again in March, representatives from HIAS, the Council of Jewish Federations, the American Jewish Committee, and the National Conference on Soviet Jewry met with government officials in the hope of having the restrictions eased. When these efforts failed, the Jewish groups announced support for congressional legislation that would increase the number of refugees allowed into the country and appropriate federal funds toward their resettlement.

Angered at American Jewish aggressiveness in facilitating the immigration of Soviet Jews to the United States, Simcha Dinitz flew to New York on April 9 to confront American Jewish leaders. He expressed particular bitterness at how little money Israel would get out of "Passage to Freedom"—just 25 percent, he claimed, once the agencies assisting the immigrants in Europe received their share of the portion set aside for overseas aid. Dinitz claimed that this stinginess toward Israel reflected "the ambitions of a few Jewish professionals," not the masses of American Jewry, and insisted that Israel receive a full 50 percent of all monies raised.

At a meeting in Washington, leaders of the Jewish Agency, the UJA, and the Council of Jewish Federations conferred with Dinitz and came up with a compromise. The New York Association for New Americans (NYANA), whose funding was previously put under the category of overseas aid, would be recategorized as a domestic philanthropy, thus freeing more of the overseas money for Israel. The Jewish Agency then announced "unqualified support" for "Passage to Freedom."

Although every American Jewish community participated in the campaign, the autonomy of local federations complicated the effort. The San Francisco community was once again the first to demonstrate its independence, rejecting the guideline that all funds collected be sent to the UJA. Citing the large number of Soviet Jews settling in San Francisco, the executive director of its federation declared that all income from "Passage to Freedom" would go first for local needs; only if something were left over would any money go to national UJA. (Indeed, by the summer it was clear that the special campaign would not raise enough to finance the resettlement of immigrants in the city, and the federation had to freeze allocations to local Jewish agencies and halt funding to Lubavitch institutions.) A few smaller federations took a somewhat less defiant stand, holding back a certain proportion of receipts for local needs and sending the rest to UJA.

At the end of October, the UJA announced that it had received pledges of $38 million—a little over half of the $75 million that "Passage to Freedom" had been expected to produce—and that the great bulk of it was from "big givers." It asked Jewish communities to conduct "phone-athons" to raise the rest. Although by year's end only $50.1 million had been pledged—of which $33 million had been collected—the UJA nevertheless considered it a triumph that "Passage to Freedom" had not hurt contributions to the regular campaign.

FOCUS SHIFTS TO ISRAEL

Even while organized American Jewry strained to absorb the cost of Soviet Jewish resettlement, events were taking place that would force a shift of philanthropic focus from the United States to Israel. American Jewish agencies that felt overwhelmed by the financial burden of resettling immigrants in their communities gradually became more receptive to the Israeli argument that the Soviet Jews should be channeled to Israel. This change of heart—noticed first by Simcha Dinitz in May—was put into words by the Anti-Defamation League in a statement issued at the end of June. While reaffirming the principle that immigrants should be free to choose their destinations, the ADL declared that "the American Jewish community's first concern must be to assist those Soviet Jews wishing to settle in Israel." During the summer, delegations of American Jews active in the Joint Distribution Committee and the UJA visited Ladispoli, Italy, to survey the condition of the Soviet Jews living there and to convince them to settle in Israel.

A key factor inducing American Jewry to stress Israel as the appropriate destination for Soviet Jews was the clear determination of the American government to clamp down drastically on the flow of refugees into the United States. Richard Schifter, assistant secretary of state for human rights and humanitarian affairs, warned in the pages of *Moment* magazine (June 1989) that "in the near future the numbers of Soviet emigrants seeking to enter the United States may significantly exceed the numbers we are prepared to take as refugees." The *New York Times* of September 4 quoted confidential government documents indicating that only Soviet Jews with immediate relatives in the country would be granted refugee status. Just 35 percent of those requesting such status would qualify under this plan.

The news did not take American Jews by surprise; "the handwriting has been on the wall for a number of months," said David Harris, the American Jewish Committee's Washington Representative. And Jewish leaders declared frankly that, in light of the financial burden of resettling the Soviet Jews in the United States, they would not fight the new arrangement. Ten days later, the U.S. government announced that all Soviet citizens seeking to enter the country as refugees would be processed in Moscow, and that the transit facilities for them in Italy would be closed down. American Jewish organizations expressed their satisfaction, since it would save them the millions of dollars spent for the Italian facilities while also making it much more difficult for emigrants with Israeli visas to "drop out" in Europe and come to the United States.

On October 11, the UJA and the Council of Jewish Federations announced a new fund-raising appeal in 1990 for the resettlement of Soviet Jews that would reflect the changed situation by allocating much more of the money raised to Israel. Also in early October, responding to the fact that fewer immigrants would be arriving in America, representatives of 25 Jewish organizations met in New York to discuss a new focus for their Soviet Jewry activity: strengthening Jewish education and culture in the Soviet Union.

As 1989 drew to a close, the National Conference on Soviet Jewry announced that 71,196 Jews had left the USSR during the year, the highest annual total since record keeping began in 1968. And there was another noteworthy statistic: while over the first 11 months of the year the proportion of Soviet Jewish emigrants settling in Israel never went above 20 percent, the figure for December was 41 percent.

Jews and Liberalism

Writing in the *New Republic* (May 22, 1989), Ruth Wisse remarked on the resurgence of Jewish liberalism. This was not simply a matter of Jews supporting liberal policies and candidates, a tradition that had been amply demonstrated once more by the overwhelming Jewish backing for Michael Dukakis and the Democrats in the 1988 election. Wisse had something else in mind: "Not only do Jews continue to express their commitment to social equality and left-wing causes far beyond their proportion in the American population and contrary to the sociological pattern of their economic group, but they have begun to return to these positions *as Jews.*"

While Wisse's evaluation of this development as deplorable was surely a minority view, the public pronouncements of American Jewish leaders in 1989 confirmed her description of the facts. At the annual meeting of the American Jewish Committee in May, executive vice-president Ira Silverman warned against any shift in the pattern of American Jewish liberalism. Despite what he called "a strong rightward tide of American public opinion and governmental policies," Silverman urged American Jews to "defy the undertow and stay rooted to the liberalism which will help ensure American pluralism and social fairness, good for us and for all Americans."

Addressing the annual meeting of NJCRAC, the umbrella group that coordinates the policies of local Jewish community relations councils and the national Jewish organizations, chairman Michael Pelavin left no doubt about his liberal commitments. He asked, "If we do not fight against the injustices affecting others, will they fight the injustices affecting us?" Pelavin cited separation of church and state, civil rights, the plight of blacks in South Africa, the rights of children, the problems of the elderly, and the survival of American cities and farms as appropriate domestic priorities for American Jewry.

NJCRAC's Joint Program Plan, described as a policy blueprint for its constituent organizations reflecting a consensus of their views, spelled out in detail this agenda. In addition to policy statements on Israel and Soviet Jewry, the plan declared NJCRAC's support for abortion rights, raising the national minimum wage, increasing the supply of low-cost housing, better facilities for the elderly, passage of a federal child-care bill, and a drive to introduce universal health care.

ABORTION RIGHTS

Of all the items addressed in the Joint Program Plan, it was abortion rights that ignited the greatest enthusiasm among large numbers of Jews—apart from the Orthodox community. Proportionately twice as many Jews as non-Jews—according to recent surveys—backed the right to unrestricted abortion, and the prospect that one more Supreme Court appointment could tilt the balance in favor of restriction gave a sense of urgency to the pro-choice campaign in 1989.

The urgency focused specifically on a Missouri law denying public funds and facilities for abortion or abortion counseling, and declaring that human life begins at conception. The question of whether this law was constitutional had reached the Supreme Court in the case of *Webster v. Reproductive Health Services*. Jewish organizations presented a united front against the law, though for different reasons. The nondenominational Jewish agencies were motivated by their concern for women's freedom of reproductive choice, and feared that the Court might use this case to strike down the *Roe v. Wade* precedent that had affirmed that freedom. The stringently Orthodox Agudath Israel organization—which opposed unrestricted abortions and the *Roe v. Wade* principle—feared nevertheless that a blanket ban on abortions could conflict with Jewish law, which mandates abortion when the mother's life is in danger. Curiously, the Union of Orthodox Jewish Congregations signed on to the legal brief of the non-Orthodox organizations, apparently because it included reference to the sanctity of life in Jewish tradition. Under attack from others in the Orthodox community, the Union then claimed that last-minute changes in the text of the brief created the unwarranted impression that it backed unrestricted abortion. The Supreme Court was notified that the organization's name had been appended by mistake.

Jews were prominently represented among the 300,000 men and women who marched for abortion rights in Washington, D.C., on April 9. Many Jewish organizations sent busloads of their members to participate: the American Jewish Congress alone was able to mobilize 200 people, and the Jewish Theological Seminary was represented by 42 rabbinical and cantorial students. Jewish leaders at the march insisted that their militance was rooted in Jewish sources and concerns. "Read the Talmud, the Jewish book of law," said Lenore Feldman, president of the National Council of Jewish Women. "In Judaism, the mother's rights always come first." Many Jews were particularly incensed at the claim of the pro-life forces that legalized abortion was comparable to the Nazi Holocaust.

In early July, the Supreme Court, by a 5–4 vote, upheld the controversial Missouri law—without, however, overturning *Roe v. Wade*. The only Jewish body to express pleasure at the result was Agudath Israel, whose spokesman said that any step away from *Roe v. Wade* was a "positive development."

Non-Orthodox Jewish organizations expressed disappointment. "We believe the Court erred," said Sholom Comay, president of the American Jewish Committee. Officials of the AJCongress and B'nai B'rith International had similar reactions. The national bodies of Reform Judaism issued a joint statement that termed the decision "a deplorable attack on the religious freedom of all Americans," and pledged to fight "any attempts by state legislatures to ban or otherwise limit the right of free choice in abortion." The social justice committee of the Rabbinical Assembly (Conservative) also defended unrestricted abortion as a "fundamental right of religious freedom." Jewish women's organizations were particularly vociferous in opposition to the Court's ruling. "In many states," argued Lenore Feldman of the National Council of Jewish Women, "this decision will turn the clock back to the days before 1973 and will open the door for states to abandon women's right to choose."

In September, 14 Jewish organizations announced their participation in a national coalition to reverse the effects of the *Webster* decision. Of the 14, 7 were women's organizations: B'nai B'rith Women, Hadassah, NA'AMAT (the women's Labor Zionist body), the National Council of Jewish Women, the National Federation of Temple Sisterhoods, Women's American ORT, and the Women's League for Conservative Judaism. The participation of Hadassah was noteworthy, since this venerable women's Zionist organization had previously not taken a stand on the issue. The involvement of the Women's League for Conservative Judaism was somewhat tempered by its suggestion that, in light of Jewish tradition, women should not casually utilize the freedom to abort as a birth-control device.

On November 12, the pro-choice coalition held a rally in Washington, D.C., that drew an estimated 150,000. Jews were prominent as participants and speakers. "Jewish Tradition: Women's Lives Are Also Sacred," read one banner. "Hadassah Is Pro-choice," said another. Ann Lewis, a leading figure in the national Democratic party, stressed the important role of Jewish leadership in the movement: it "lends a voice of morality and values to the discourse," she said.

CHILD CARE

If the abortion issue provided the liberal non-Orthodox Jewish community with a relatively simple choice of right against wrong, the question of federally funded child care presented liberal Jews with a dilemma. Much of the child care in the United States—perhaps one-third—was provided by religious bodies, yet separation of church and state was as much part of the liberal agenda as federal responsibility to improve child care. Could a child-care bill be passed that would not constitute government aid to religion? Political liberals—and most Jews—hoped so. "We simply do not believe that child care should come at the expense of safeguarding the separation of church and state," said Hyla Lipsky, president of B'nai B'rith Women. Some Jewish organizations proposed that sectarian institutions be funded only for their nonsectarian programs. But the administration and its supporters on Capitol Hill opposed any such distinctions.

As Congress debated different kinds of child-care legislation in 1989, it became clear that the church-state problem was not the only hurdle that proponents had to overcome. President Bush and his congressional supporters wanted to provide federal tax credits for child-care expenses, while liberals preferred outright grants. It seemed likely that any bill authorizing grants would face a presidential veto no matter how it dealt with sectarian institutions.

By November, both houses of Congress had approved bills that included funding for the child-care programs of sectarian institutions. On November 16, the AJCommittee, AJCongress, Anti-Defamation League, B'nai B'rith Women, National Council of Jewish Women, and Union of American Hebrew Congregations joined with 14 non-Jewish organizations in a letter to House members arguing that federal aid for sectarian programs was both "unsound public policy" and "constitutionally suspect." The Jewish groups also argued against a provision in the Senate bill which would let a sectarian child-care facility receiving government money give preference in admissions and in hiring to children and workers of its own religion.

Once again, Agudath Israel swam against the tide of the Jewish community. While agreeing that direct federal payments to religious institutions raised constitutional problems, it asserted that grants to parents that would then be used to buy the sectarian child care did not. As for preferential admissions and hiring, Agudah's legal counsel maintained that religious institutions "must be permitted to maintain policies consistent with their religious identity and beliefs." Agudath Israel had a somewhat strange bedfellow on this issue, the Council of Reform Hebrew Day Schools, which, eager to apply for federal aid, noted that a refusal of funds for sectarian child care "impinges on the right of people to practice their religion."

The year ended with no child-care legislation passed. And the non-Orthodox Jewish organizations had to face up to their liberal dilemma: they dearly wanted government aid for child care, but it was clearer than ever that Congress and the president would agree to it—if at all—only if sectarian institutions were included among its beneficiaries.

Denominational Trends

The year 1989 witnessed considerable ferment within the Jewish religious denominations. Each of the branches—albeit in different ways—struggled to reconcile the drive for self-assertion, the pull of tradition, and the desirability of Jewish unity.

REFORM JUDAISM

In February Prof. Gerald Showstack of Brandeis University released a study of Reform Judaism entitled "Suburban Communities: The Jewishness of American Reform Jews." Seeking to dispel the common stereotype that those who affiliate with Reform are seeking a minimal Judaism, Showstack found that when Reform Jews are actually asked to evaluate their religious involvement, they explain it as a positive commitment to Jewish living.

There were also signs that this positive commitment translated itself—at least for some Reform Jews—into greater adherence to ritual. In its June 26 edition, the *New York Times* ran an article about the annual convention of the Central Conference of American Rabbis (CCAR) under the headline "Reform Jews Turn Back to Tradition." Asked about the surprising fact that many of the rabbis at the conference wore prayer shawls and skullcaps at Friday night services—practices rejected by classical Reform—Rabbi Samuel Karff, the organization's new president, said: "This is a different time, and just as our predecessors were influenced by their time, we are influenced by ours." A number of the congregational rabbis present spoke of a renewal of interest among their congregants in such practices as ritual circumcision, the traditional wedding ceremony, more Hebrew in the services, and bar/bat mitzvahs. Yet these Reform rabbis were well aware of the gap separating them from halakhic Jews: Reform still emphasized issues of social justice much more than the traditional denominations and also insisted on the right of the individual Jew to choose which rituals to observe and how to perform them.

Meanwhile, two rabbinical leaders of Reform who addressed the conference had very different evaluations of the swing to traditionalism. Favoring it, and even seeking its intensification, was outgoing CCAR president Rabbi Eugene Lipman. While asserting that he remained a religious and political liberal, Lipman urged his colleagues to retreat from some of the more radical and controversial Reform innovations of the recent past. He called for voluntary limits on the autonomy of rabbis, more careful scrutiny of candidates for conversion, an end to rabbinic officiation at mixed marriages, a grappling with the implications of the increasing number of non-Jewish spouses of members in Reform synagogues, and "live Zionism" that did not put political pressure on Israel.

Rabbi Alexander Schindler, president of the Union of American Hebrew Congregations—the lay body of Reform Judaism—adamantly disagreed. "Our forebears did not forge Reform Judaism to have us trade it in for a tinsel imitation of Orthodoxy," he declared. Pleading with the Reform rabbinate not to romanticize

Orthodox Judaism, Schindler pointed to Israel, where an entrenched Orthodoxy, he said, had produced "stale repression, fossilized tradition and ethical corruption."

Lipman may have expressed the increasingly traditional leanings of many rabbis and congregations, but the public posture of the Reform movement in 1989 reflected Schindler's perspective. This was especially so in regard to Israel: the unexpectedly good showing of the Reform slate in the 1988 elections to the World Zionist Congress made the movement much bolder in speaking out about Israeli issues in 1989.

Reform figures launched a barrage of attacks on the Israeli religious establishment. In April Rabbi Charles Kroloff completed his term as president of the Association of Reform Zionists of America (ARZA) with a call to fight "the extremism of the ultra-Orthodox who would transform the Jewish state into a medieval fiefdom." In July ARZA accused the Israeli Ministry of Religions of suppressing the results of a ministry survey of the religious preferences of a sample of 602 Israelis. According to ARZA, just 12 percent of the respondents said they were Orthodox, 9 percent claimed to be Reform, 3 percent identified as Conservative, and the rest either had no affiliation or did not respond. Rabbi Eric Yoffie, ARZA's executive director, claimed that the small 3-percent gap between Orthodoxy and Reform proved that "those Orthodox who dominate the Religious Affairs Ministry and wield so much clout do not necessarily speak for the religious sensibilities of the vast majority of Israeli Jews." And in December ARZA charged Israeli authorities with discrimination for letting Lubavitch Hassidim hand out literature at Ben-Gurion Airport while denying the Reform movement the same privilege.

Dr. Alfred Gottschalk—president of the Hebrew Union College, which trains Reform rabbis—also spoke out against the religious status quo in Israel. Gottschalk told a National Press Club breakfast in April that, although the Reform movement supported efforts to pass human-rights legislation in Israel, he opposed a suggested human-rights bill that would exclude marriage and divorce from its purview, leaving them in the hands of the rabbinate. "As a political compromise, it is understandable," he said, but "as a compromise of principle, it is incomprehensible." Gottschalk indicated that he would be happy with nothing less than an end to the Orthodox establishment and full recognition and equal funding for all streams of Judaism in the Jewish state.

It was the issue of whether to recognize gay rabbis that cast the most serious doubt on the notion that Reform was returning to tradition. On the last day of the annual CCAR conference in June, a special committee appointed three years earlier to study the issue presented its report. Admitting that it could reach no agreement on whether homosexual activity was under an individual's control or not, the committee as a whole neither supported nor rejected the acceptance of gays and lesbians in the rabbinate. It also hesitated to legitimate homosexual marriage, fearing that such a move would exacerbate tensions between Reform and the other movements.

Individual members of the committee spoke their minds at the conference. Rabbi

Yoel Kahn, spiritual leader of a 425-member synagogue in San Francisco that described itself as conducting "a special outreach to gays and lesbians," argued that modern science had disproven the old notion that homosexuality was a "sin or mental illness," and suggested that gay rabbis would provide useful role models since they embodied "different ways to fulfill Jewish covenantal responsibility." Prof. Eugene Borowitz of Hebrew Union College—perhaps the movement's most eminent theologian—granted that homosexuals merited equal rights, but noted that "to be a rabbi is not a Jewish right but a title of Jewish honor" that should be reserved for those who "set an example of Jewish ideals." His colleague Prof. Leonard Kravitz noted the lack of any precedent in Jewish sources for legitimating homosexuality. "Sometimes Reform Judaism has to say no, even when the modern world says yes," he insisted.

The lack of a consensus led to passage of a resolution that called on rabbis and congregations to consider the issue for a period of one year. "This is not a time for parliamentary resolutions," said committee chairman Rabbi Selig Salkowitz, "but for a sensitive and considered study, for discussion of the sources and their implications for the Reform movement as a Jewish religious community in the United States and its influence on world Jewry." But Leonard Kravitz suggested that the battle was already over. Since Hebrew Union College had decided that homosexuality would no longer be considered grounds to reject applicants for the rabbinical program, he asserted, their acceptance as rabbis by the CCAR was inevitable. HUC president Alfred Gottschalk disputed this, saying, "We do not admit homosexuals. We don't admit heterosexuals. We try to admit individuals on the basis of a total profile."

RECONSTRUCTIONISM

The Reconstructionist movement—the newest and by far the smallest denomination—also demonstrated ambivalent tendencies during 1989. On the one hand it sought to assert its own independent identity, while on the other it seemed, like Reform, to hark back to elements of the tradition. In their public statements, Reconstructionist rabbinic and lay leaders urged the movement to sharpen its identity so as to appeal to the broad masses of American Jewry. Rabbi Sandy Sasso, president of the Reconstructionist Rabbinical Association, declared that "the time has come for us to define ourselves and our course so that American Jews can understand who we are and what is our vision." And Roger Price, president of the Federation of the Reconstructionist Congregations and Havurot, suggested that "the Judaism we present must be based on positive values—a Judaism worth choosing freely, because it is simply too good to pass up."

The publication of *Kol Haneshama,* a long-awaited Reconstructionist prayer book for Friday evening services, gave some indication of how the movement hoped to develop a distinctive identity. "Reconstructionist Jews Turn to the Supernatural," read the headline in the *New York Times* (Jan. 19, 1989). Compared with the previous prayer book composed in 1945 by the movement's founder, Mordecai Kaplan, the new publication contained a mix of traditional and mystical materials that reflected the eclipse of faith in rationalism that characterized the movement's origins. Absent in the 1945 prayer book but reintroduced in 1989, for example, were references to the miracle of splitting the Red Sea, the doctrine of divine reward and punishment, and even the original *aleynu* prayer, which asserts that Jews are God's chosen people—a claim that was anathema to Kaplan.

Yet there was much about this prayer book that was distinctly untraditional. The feminist impact was unmistakable: all references to God in the male gender were eliminated, and the names of the biblical matriarchs appeared along with those of the patriarchs. Also, the wording and translation of many of the prayers were clearly influenced by such contemporary concerns as environmentalism, "New Age" mysticism, the impact of the Holocaust, and the threat of nuclear war. And even where traditional passages were reintroduced, they were followed by alternative readings that were in the spirit of Kaplan's rationalism.

If the new prayer book was any indication, Reconstructionism was determined to forge a path that was neither traditional nor radical, but a synthesis of the two. "It's the coming together of the mystical and the spiritual with the intellectually honest and rigid," explained Arthur Green, president of the Reconstructionist Rabbinical College.

CONSERVATIVE JUDAISM

For Conservative Judaism, which adheres to traditional Jewish law while at the same time reinterpreting it to meet new conditions, the tension between tradition and innovation took yet a third form. In a speech at the Rabbinical Assembly convention in March, Chancellor Ismar Schorsch of the Jewish Theological Seminary—which trains Conservative rabbis—bitterly attacked what he considered the preoccupation of many Jews with the historical memory of anti-Semitism. Referring to the hard-line position taken by many Orthodox Jews on the questions of Palestinian rights and the future of the West Bank and Gaza, Schorsch complained that if Jews "see a Nazi behind every critic and an anti-Semite behind every tree," this concern with the past "may yet well sink us, may leave us unequipped to handle the novelty and the opportunity of the present and the future." In place of history, Schorsch—himself a German-born professor of Jewish history—urged emphasis on Judaism's teachings about nature. In the same spirit as the new Reconstructionist prayer book, he pointed out that Judaism "is a rich environmental religion" and warned that "we in our arrogance over progress and the achievement of history have done a disservice to our religious sensibility."

Conservative antipathy toward Orthodoxy surfaced repeatedly during 1989. In May the Jewish Theological Seminary made a point of choosing the first Israeli woman ordained as a Conservative rabbi to deliver the commencement address; her theme was the difference between the "religious compulsion" practiced by Israeli "fundamentalists" and the more humane approach of "we tolerant Jews." The question of whether a Conservative *mohel* (ritual circumciser) would be allowed to practice in Israel became a matter of contention during the summer. When Rabbi Andrew Sacks, a graduate of the Jewish Theological Seminary, was denied permission to perform circumcisions at the Hadassah hospitals in Israel, Mercaz—the Conservative Zionist organization—joined with its Reform counterpart, ARZA, in denouncing Hadassah for alleged discrimination.

On the American scene, the Conservative movement made a sweeping decision to reduce its dependence on the Orthodox community for ritual services. At its annual convention, in March, the Rabbinical Assembly resolved that Conservative congregations would build their own mikvehs (ritual baths), because in all too many communities Orthodox rabbis did not allow existing mikvehs to be used for Conservative conversions. The RA also announced an expansion of its program to train its own experts in *gittin* (religious divorce procedures) and the establishment of a Conservative *bet din* (religious court) to deal with divorces. And in November JTS and the Rabbinical Assembly jointly sponsored "Brit Kodesh: A Sacred Covenant," a six-day intensive training session for *mohalim* (ritual circumcisers), all of them medical doctors. Upon completion of the program, participants received certificates stating that they were qualified to perform ritual circumcisions. While the immediate impetus for training these *mohalim* was the occasional refusal of Orthodox practitioners to circumcise the offspring of Conservative converts, Conservative authorities explained that this too was part of the overall effort to assert the movement's self-sufficiency and autonomy.

Conservative Judaism showed increased independence as well through a highly publicized initiative in the USSR. Unwilling to allow Orthodoxy to be the only form of Judaism taught to Soviet Jews in the era of *glasnost,* the Conservative movement sent a delegation to the Soviet Union in June—armed with Conservative prayer books, the movement's statement of principles adopted in 1988, and other literature—to expose the Jews there to the movement.

As in 1988, the Conservative branch's Cantors Assembly was the one arm of the movement that was most tied to tradition and resistant to change. Although JTS had started granting cantor's certificates to qualified women in 1987, the Cantors Assembly for the second straight year refused to admit women to its ranks. At its convention in May, the vote was 108 to 82 in favor of admittance, a better showing than in 1988, but still 19 votes shy of the two-thirds needed to change the organization's bylaws. The women affected by the decision, declaring that they were "saddened and disappointed," nevertheless expressed confidence that they would win out eventually. But Solomon Mendelson, the outgoing president of the Cantors Assembly, said that "the issue of admitting women cantors to membership is a sensitive and emotional one that poses complex questions of tradition, religious authority, the status of women in the synagogue, and many other factors."

Ironically, while the leaders of Conservative Judaism were open to innovation on many matters of policy, they also saw a need for an infusion of more traditionalism in the training of rabbis and the functioning of synagogues. Finding that many JTS students who had become interested in Judaism and decided on a rabbinic career while in college did not possess sufficient knowledge of Judaism, the Seminary upgraded its admissions requirements for September 1989 so that applicants would have to demonstrate greater ability to master Jewish texts, more facility in the Hebrew language, and wider exposure to all aspects of Jewish life. And in November, at the biennial convention of the United Synagogue of America, JTS chancellor Schorsch urged Conservative synagogues to reintroduce traditional practices that had previously been disregarded—such as informal study sessions and the placement of the *bimah* (lectern) in the middle of the room—so that services would be more participatory and less like stage performances.

ORTHODOXY

Internecine conflict between the moderate Orthodox—associated primarily with Yeshiva University and the Rabbinical Council of America (RCA)—and those with a more stringent approach to Orthodoxy continued in 1989. The key issue of debate remained how the Orthodox should relate to non-Orthodox expressions of Judaism.

An incident at the Rabbinical Council of America's midwinter conference in January indicated just how bitter the internal Orthodox debate could become. At a panel session on amending the Israeli Law of Return to exclude those who were converted by non-Orthodox rabbis—a change desired by the more extreme Orthodox—Rabbi Walter Wurzburger, a past president of the organization, suggested that the issue was more symbolic than substantive, caused an erosion of support for Israel, and should not be pressed. Suddenly, two intruders shouted at the rabbi in Yiddish, "Heretic!" and urged that he and the other panel members be excommunicated. "It's a sad day," commented Wurzburger, "when an alternative method or opinion triggers such a reaction."

At its national convention in June, the RCA sharply criticized the more extreme Orthodox for allegedly fragmentizing Orthodox education. Claiming that it was modern Orthodoxy that had pioneered the Jewish day-school movement that provides intensive Jewish education along with high-level secular education, convention chairman Rabbi Zevulun Lieberman complained that other Orthodox factions "create their own miniature institutions to serve their own purposes rather than seek the total communal good for Torah education." Rabbi Norman Lamm, president of Yeshiva University, urged his fellow moderates to be more assertive in pressing their understanding of Orthodoxy. "Moderation," he said, "requires thinking and courage . . . not ideological wimpishness."

But Lamm had to face heavy criticism even within his own institution. The August 18 issue of the *New York Jewish Week* carried a long article headlined

"Yeshiva U.'s Lamm: A Rabbi Under Siege." Based on interviews with Lamm, other administrators, faculty, students, and recent alumni, the piece gave the impression that much of the Talmud faculty rejected Yeshiva's traditional ideal of a synthesis between Torah and secular knowledge and was influencing the student body against the moderate or "centrist" vision that Lamm projected.

While subsequent letters to the newspaper demonstrated that the extent of the opposition to Lamm had been exaggerated, the article's basic thrust was accurate. If proof were needed, it came in November when 11 Talmud professors at Yeshiva University issued a letter opposing the idea of an interdenominational rabbinic panel that would deal with conversions and so solve the "Who is a Jew?" problem. "A *beth din* [rabbinical court]," they wrote, "which includes even one member who is not an Orthodox Jew . . . is without halakhic authority." The plan for such a body had been promoted by leading figures within the RCA, with at least the tacit support of Lamm. Senior Talmud professor Rabbi Aaron Soloveitchik compared cooperation with non-Orthodox bodies to the biblical sin of the golden calf, declaring that such a step would "mislead many of the innocent, ignorant Jewish masses to worship the idol of Reform and Reconstructionist Judaism."

Israel-Related Religious Issues

Two emotionally charged issues—both related to Israel—exacerbated relations between the branches of American Judaism during 1989. One was the seemingly endless controversy over "Who is a Jew?" for the purposes of the Law of Return. The other was a relatively new matter, one involving Jewish feminists but that had wider implications—the "women of the Wall."

WHO IS A JEW?

The Israeli elections of 1988 resulted in increased Orthodox representation in the Knesset while depriving each of the major political blocs of a majority. This raised the realistic possibility that either Labor or Likud might agree to Orthodox demands on "Who is a Jew?" in order to form a coalition government. Such a step, which would make those converted to Judaism by non-Orthodox rabbis ineligible for Israeli citizenship under the Law of Return, aroused the anger of many American Jews. While the eventual formation of a Labor-Likud coalition made such a possibility far less likely, the issue did not fade away.

At a conference in Jerusalem at the beginning of 1989 on "Who is a Jew?" two distinguished American Jewish intellectuals explained why the issue—which to many Israelis was merely a political bargaining chip—meant so much to the American Jewish community. Prof. Seymour Martin Lipset of Stanford University claimed that non-Orthodox Jews in the United States were angry because they believed that Israeli Orthodoxy viewed them as "Karaites," akin to non-Jews. Leonard Fein, the former editor of *Moment* magazine, had another explanation:

American Jewish fury over this question was a "surrogate" for disappointment with Israel on a host of other matters.

Whatever the reason for the issue's prominence, in February, 27 national Jewish organizations that had worked to shelve any change in the Law of Return in 1988 announced the formation of a Coalition for Jewish Unity to seek religious pluralism in Israel. Participants included all the nondenominational national agencies, the non-Orthodox Zionist organizations, and the Conservative, Reform, and Reconstructionist rabbinical and lay bodies. American Orthodoxy reacted critically. Rabbi Max Schreier, the president of the Rabbinical Council of America, charged that while this coalition supposedly pursued unity, in fact it fomented disunity because it was "aimed in a detrimental way at an important segment of the Jewish people, Orthodox Jewry."

Even while participating in the organization of the Coalition, the American Jewish Committee sent a delegation to Israel to meet with leaders of *haredi* Orthodoxy there—important figures in the Degel Hatorah, Agudah, and Shas parties, and the Belzer Rebbe. The Committee's purpose was to initiate a dialogue that might lead to mutual understanding and better relations. In a statement after the trip, AJC president Theodore Ellenoff reported that the talks had been fruitful and would be broadened in the future.

On July 24, the Israeli High Court of Justice issued two landmark rulings having to do with religious pluralism, one ordering the Interior Ministry to register non-Orthodox converts as Jews, and the other reaffirming the sole right of Orthodox rabbis to perform Jewish marriages in Israel. Predictably, non-Orthodox groups in the United States praised the decision on converts while expressing dissatisfaction with the ruling on marriage officiation; Orthodox organizations had an exactly opposite reaction.

The decision recognizing non-Orthodox conversions drew public attention to secret negotiations—encouraged by Israeli prime minister Shamir—that had been going on for months between representatives of the various American movements seeking an end to the controversy through a joint procedure for conversion that would be acceptable to all. While the negotiators focused on the narrow issue of developing a procedure for those converts seeking to move to Israel, there was hope that once such a mechanism was in place it could set the stage for a broader agreement. In September the Orthodox negotiator, Rabbi Louis Bernstein of the moderate Rabbinical Council of America, told a reporter, "I can only tell you that we're working on it, that we've met in Jerusalem and in the United States, and that there's a sincere commitment to resolve the problem by all sides."

But publicity endangered the plan. The *Algemeiner Journal,* a New York Yiddish-language weekly closely connected to the Lubavitch movement, launched a campaign against any kind of joint action between the Orthodox and the other movements on the ground that it would legitimate heterodoxy. Within Orthodoxy, pressure rose on the moderates to disavow the project. As the year ended, prospects for an agreement dimmed.

THE WOMEN OF THE WALL

On March 20—the Fast of Esther in the Jewish liturgical calendar—a group of about 60 Jewish women, both Orthodox and non-Orthodox, attempted to conduct their own prayer services at the Western Wall in Jerusalem, the *kotel*. According to traditional practice, Jewish women either pray along with a *minyan* (quorum) of men, or else pray as individuals: a women's prayer group, rare enough in the United States, was a novelty in Israel. The women had come to the Wall a few times before this, beginning in December 1988 in connection with the First International Jewish Feminist Conference, and had experienced verbal harassment. This time, an enraged band of Orthodox Jews began cursing and hurling chairs at the women, and police had to use tear gas to disperse them. What made this incident particularly noteworthy was that the women, after consultation with the rabbi in charge of the Wall, had agreed not to wear prayer shawls and not to read from a Torah scroll. Thus what the women tried to do, while highly unconventional, contravened no explicit Jewish law.

American Jewish organizations were appalled by the violence. The nondenominational agencies viewed the event as one more example of Israeli Orthodox intolerance of other points of view. For the American Jewish Congress, the stakes were nothing less than the "fundamental principles of equality and religious freedom," while the American Jewish Committee felt that the incident "underscores the ongoing need to promote a strong measure of religious respect from the ultra-right."

Orthodox response was more ambivalent. To be sure, no one condoned what was done to the women. The Rabbinical Council of America's executive vice-president, Rabbi Binyamin Walfish, said that those at the Wall who disliked what the women did had a right to protest, but "there is a proper way to protest. Let them carry signs, but to throw chairs is disgraceful." Agreeing with Walfish, Rabbi Alan Yuter nevertheless charged that the Orthodox women who participated in the services at the Wall were wrong for allying themselves with other women who were not committed to traditional Jewish law, and for improperly offending the sensibilities of those Orthodox Jews who considered a women's prayer group at Judaism's holiest site a sacrilege.

The violence at the Wall became a rallying point for North American Jewish feminists. On April 24, Jewish women in New York, Philadelphia, Baltimore, Boston, Seattle, Teaneck, Toronto, and Montreal demonstrated their solidarity with the "women of the Wall" by conducting special prayer services. The participants at the New York service included not only women involved in Jewish religious life, but also such feminist celebrities as politician Bella Abzug and author Phyllis Chesler. The interdenominational aspirations of the movement were underlined by Rabbi Helene Ferris of the Stephen Wise Free Synagogue, who declared, "We are all Orthodox in that we all have the same true opinion concerning the rights of all Jewish women to pray to their God without fear for their safety; we are Conservative as we strive to preserve the teachings of our tradition; Reconstructionist in our understanding that our religion will survive only if it exists for us and not the other way around; and we are Reform Jews as we strive to change our male-oriented tradition to a more egalitarian one."

On May 25, the Israeli High Court of Justice issued an interim order allowing the "women of the Wall" to conduct group services without a Torah and without prayer shawls, items that they could, however, use at other sites near the *kotel.* Despite the court order, the women, attempting to conduct services each Friday and on the first day of each Hebrew month (New Moon), continued to suffer harrassment. In a particularly ugly clash on August 2, security guards hired by the Ministry of Religious Affairs dragged the women away from the Wall one by one, as ultra-Orthodox women threw water and mud at them.

In October American Jews sympathetic to the efforts of the women formed an "International Committee for Women at the Kotel" to raise money for a Torah scroll to be sent to them. But even the dedication of that scroll became the subject of conflict. The event was scheduled for November 27 at the Laromme Hotel in Jerusalem, and a 30-member delegation of women from the AJCongress traveled there to present the Torah. At the last moment the Jerusalem Religious Council announced that if the ceremony took place at the hotel, its *kashrut* license would be revoked. When the hotel succumbed to the pressure, the women held the dedication elsewhere. AJCongress's executive director, Henry Siegman, found it "sad that the rabbinate in Israel should not hesitate to resort to such ugly tactics to deny Jews the privilege of dedicating a Torah scroll." On the evening after the dedication, the women and their supporters—roughly 100 people in all—marched through the streets of Jerusalem with the Torah.

The New Moon (*rosh hodesh*) service they held the next morning at the Wall proceeded without incident. But the struggle over their rights at the Wall—which was clearly a symbol of a much larger conflict over the role of women in Jewish religious life—was likely to continue.

LAWRENCE GROSSMAN

Jewish Population in the United States, 1990

THE JEWISH POPULATION OF the United States in 1990 was estimated to be 5,981,000, which represents a slight increase from the figure reported in 1989. This estimate is for the resident Jewish population of the country, including that both in private households and in institutional settings. Non-Jewish family members have been excluded from this total. As in past years, this estimate is based on local reporting, using various procedures. (See below for a brief discussion of the 1990 National Jewish Population Survey.)

While the Jewish federations are the chief reporting bodies, their service areas vary in size and may represent several towns, one county, or an aggregate of several counties. In some cases we have subdivided federation areas to reflect the more natural geographic boundaries. Some estimates, from areas without federations, have been provided by local rabbis and other informed Jewish community leaders. In still other cases, the figures that have been updated are from past estimates provided by United Jewish Appeal field representatives.

The state and regional totals shown in Appendix tables 1 and 2 are derived by summing the individual estimates shown in table 3 and then making three adjustments. First, communities of less than 100 are added. Second, duplicated counts within states are eliminated. Third, communities whose populations reside in two or more states (e.g., Kansas City and Washington, D.C.) are distributed accordingly.

The reader should be aware that population estimating is not an exact science and that collection procedures can result in annual fluctuations in community or state totals. In most cases where a figure differs from that shown last year, the increase or decrease did not come about in one year but occurred over a period of time and has just now been substantiated. Similarly, the results of a completed local demographic study often change the previously reported Jewish population figure. This should be understood as either an updated calculation of gradual demographic change or a correction of a faulty older estimate.

In determining Jewish population, communities count both affiliated and nonaffiliated residents. In most cases, counts are made by households, with that number multiplied by the average number of self-defined Jewish persons per household. Most communities also include those born and raised as Jews but who at present consider themselves of no religion. As stated above, non-Jews living in Jewish households, primarily the non-Jewish spouses and any non-Jewish children, are not included in the 1990 estimates presented in the appendix below.

Local Population Changes

The community reporting the largest documented numeric gain—based on a recent survey—is Detroit, Michigan, whose new estimate of 94,000 represents an increase of more than 20,000 persons over last year's figure. The last enumeration of Detroit's Jewish population was completed in 1963, at which time a figure of 85,000 Jews was reported. During the intervening years there was an assumption of decline. While the 1989-90 study showed this to be true for the inner city, in reality a modest growth had occurred for the larger metropolitan area. Additionally, the new study encompassed a larger geographic area than the earlier one.

The community reporting the next largest gain was Middlesex County, New Jersey, whose Jewish population estimate increased by 18,000 (to 58,000), based on a recently completed demographic study. In addition to the sprawling suburban communities of Edison, Old Bridge, East Brunswick, and Monroe, several large adult and retirement villages have been developed in recent years in the county's southern portion, attracting Jews from other areas. The county increase also reflects the growth in recent years of Orthodox communities in Highland Park and East Brunswick. Two other suburban areas of New Jersey, Princeton and Somerset County, report more modest gains.

Two western communities, Orange County, California, and Seattle, Washington, report population increases of 10,000 each, with the latter's increase documented in a demographic study completed in 1990.

The South and the Sunbelt accounted for most other communities reporting significant Jewish population increases. These include Atlanta, Georgia; Tucson, Arizona; Las Vegas, Nevada; San Antonio, Texas; and Ft. Myers, Daytona Beach, Palm Beach County, and Sarasota, Florida. Several new Jewish communities in Arizona and Colorado are listed this year for the first time, among them Cochise County and Lake Havesu, Arizona, and Evergreen and Telluride, Colorado.

The influx of about 68,000 Soviet Jews to the United States since 1988 will be reflected over the next few years when communities are able to either reevaluate their lists or conduct population studies. While the introduction of the immigrants to some places may be offset by deaths or general Jewish outmigration, one community, Baltimore, is reporting a Jewish population increase of over 1,000 in 1989 due to both the Soviet influx and a growing Orthodox population.

This year's largest decline, that of over 20,000 in Miami-Dade County, Florida, is the result of actual ongoing demographic change in recent years. The primary features of this change are an aging population, an increase in the numbers of non-Jewish immigrants settling in Jewish areas, and a preference by Jewish newcomers to Florida to locate further up the coast in Broward and Palm Beach counties.

More moderate declines have occurred in some of the older medium- and small-sized cities in the Northeast and Midwest, part of a long-term trend in these regions. The affected communities include Hartford, Connecticut; Buffalo, New York; Champaign-Urbana, Illinois; Trenton, New Jersey; Milwaukee, Wisconsin; Leominster, Massachusetts; and Flint, Michigan.

Communities in other parts of the country reporting modest losses include Albuquerque, New Mexico; Newport News, Virginia; Chattanooga, Tennessee; and Salt Lake City, Utah. The population changes for several communities in New Hampshire merely reflect adjustments to catchment-area boundaries.

CJF 1990 National Jewish Population Survey

The 1990 National Jewish Population Survey, sponsored by the Council of Jewish Federations—the first such survey since 1971—was completed in the summer of 1990. It was based on a screening of over 125,000 randomly selected households across the United States, with a follow-up survey of those who met the screening criteria. A first report of the findings was issued by CJF in spring 1991. (Next year's edition of the *American Jewish Year Book* will include a major article on the survey.)

The new study takes into account the growing difficulty in defining the boundaries of the Jewish population, due in large part to the lack of consensus on who is to be included in a count of Jews. The approach of the 1990 survey is to define a number of different populations of Jews, based on various criteria. Preliminary analysis of the data showed a core U.S. Jewish population of 5.5 million Jews defined by birth or religion. Another 625,000 persons identified themselves as Jews by ethnic background or preference, though they were currently practicing another religion. In addition, some 700,000 children currently practicing another religion could be identified as Jews by ethnic background or parentage (The study further identified a category consisting of some 1.4 million born-non-Jews who are part of households with at least one Jewish member.)

Comparing the two methods of counting the Jewish population: the present estimate of 5.9 million derived by aggregating local community estimates lies between the survey totals of a core Jewish population of 5.5 million and an ethnic Jewish population of 6.1–6.8 million.

BARRY A. KOSMIN
JEFFREY SCHECKNER

APPENDIX

TABLE 1. JEWISH POPULATION IN THE UNITED STATES, 1990

State	Estimated Jewish Population	Total Population*	Estimated Jewish Percent of Total
Alabama	9,300	4,102,000	0.2
Alaska	2,400	524,000	0.5
Arizona	71,500	3,489,000	2.1
Arkansas	2,000	2,345,000	0.1
California	919,500	28,314,000	3.2
Colorado	50,000	3,301,000	1.5
Connecticut	113,200	3,233,000	3.5
Delaware	9,500	660,000	1.4
District of Columbia	25,400	617,000	4.2
Florida	567,000	12,335,000	4.6
Georgia	72,500	6,342,000	1.1
Hawaii	7,000	1,098,000	0.6
Idaho	450	1,003,000	0.1
Illinois	257,400	11,614,000	2.2
Indiana	18,300	5,556,000	0.3
Iowa	6,350	2,834,000	0.2
Kansas	14,000	2,495,000	0.6
Kentucky	11,800	3,727,000	0.3
Louisiana	15,700	4,408,000	0.4
Maine	8,400	1,205,000	0.7
Maryland	211,000	4,622,000	4.6
Massachusetts	276,000	5,889,000	4.7
Michigan	107,300	9,240,000	1.2
Minnesota	30,500	4,307,000	0.7
Mississippi	1,900	2,620,000	0.1
Missouri	61,600	5,141,000	1.2
Montana	450	805,000	0.1
Nebraska	7,400	1,602,000	0.5
Nevada	20,500	1,054,000	1.9
New Hampshire	7,000	1,085,000	0.6
New Jersey	430,000	7,721,000	5.6
New Mexico	6,400	1,507,000	0.4
New York	1,843,000	17,909,000	10.3

State	Estimated Jewish Population	Total Population*	Estimated Jewish Percent of Total
North Carolina	16,300	6,489,000	0.3
North Dakota	750	667,000	0.1
Ohio	130,800	10,855,000	1.2
Oklahoma	5,300	3,242,000	0.2
Oregon	12,500	2,767,000	0.5
Pennsylvania	330,500	12,001,000	2.8
Rhode Island	16,100	993,000	1.6
South Carolina	9,300	3,470,000	0.3
South Dakota	350	713,000	0.1
Tennessee	19,400	4,895,000	0.4
Texas	109,000	16,841,000	0.6
Utah	3,100	1,690,000	0.2
Vermont	4,800	557,000	0.9
Virginia	67,600	6,015,000	1.1
Washington	32,800	4,648,000	0.7
West Virginia	2,400	1,876,000	0.1
Wisconsin	34,700	4,855,000	0.7
Wyoming	450	479,000	0.1
U.S. TOTAL	**5,981,000	245,807,000	2.4

N.B. Details may not add to totals because of rounding.
*Resident population, July 1, 1988. (*Source*: U.S. Bureau of the Census, *Current Population Reports*, series P-25, no. 1044.)
**Exclusive of Puerto Rico and the Virgin Islands which previously reported Jewish populations of 1,500 and 350, respectively.

TABLE 2. DISTRIBUTION OF U.S. JEWISH POPULATION BY REGIONS, 1990

Region	Total Population	Percent Distribution	Jewish Population	Percent Distribution
Northeast	50,595,000	20.6	3,029,500	50.6
New England	12,963,000	5.3	425,500	7.1
Middle Atlantic	37,631,000	15.2	2,604,000	43.6
North Central	59,878,000	24.4	669,450	11.2
East North Central	42,119,000	17.1	548,500	9.2
West North Central	17,759,000	7.2	120,950	2.0
South	84,655,000	34.4	1,155,400	19.3
South Atlantic	42,426,000	17.3	981,000	16.4
East South Central	15,344,000	6.2	42,400	0.7
West South Central	26,885,000	10.9	132,000	2.2
West	50,679,000	20.6	1,127,050	18.8
Mountain	13,328,000	5.4	152,850	2.6
Pacific	37,351,000	15.2	974,200	16.3
TOTALS	245,807,000	100.0	5,981,000	100.0

N.B. Details may not add to totals because of rounding.

TABLE 3. COMMUNITIES WITH JEWISH POPULATIONS OF 100 OR MORE, 1990 (ESTIMATED)

State and City	Jewish Population	State and City	Jewish Population	State and City	Jewish Population
ALABAMA		**Little Rock	1,300	Ontario (incl. in	
*Birmingham	5,100	Pine Bluff	100	Pomona Valley)	
Decatur (incl. in				Orange County	95,000
Florence total)		**CALIFORNIA**		Palmdale (incl. in	
*Dothan	150	Antelope Valley	700	Antelope Valley)	
Florence	150	Bakersfield-Kern		Palm Springs[N]	9,600
Huntsville	750	County	1,400	Palo Alto (incl. in	
**Mobile	1,100	Berkeley (incl. in		South Peninsula	
**Montgomery	1,300	Contra Costa County		under S.F. Bay Area)	
Selma	100	under S.F. Bay Area)		Pasadena (also incl.	
Sheffield (incl. in		*Chico	500	in L.A. Metro Area	
Florence total)		Corona (incl. in		total)	2,000
Tuscaloosa	300	Riverside total)		Petaluma (incl. in	
Tuscumbia (incl. in		***El Centro	125	Sonoma County	
Florence total)		*Eureka	500	under S.F. Bay Area)	
		Fairfield	800	Pomona Valley[N]	6,750
ALASKA		Fontana (incl. in		*Redding	145
**Anchorage	2,000	San Bernardino total)		Riverside	1,620
***Fairbanks	210	*Fresno	2,000	Sacramento[N]	12,500
Juneau	100	Lancaster (incl. in		Salinas	500
Ketchikan (incl. in		Antelope Valley)		San Bernardino area	2,800
Juneau total)		Long Beach (also		*San Diego	70,000
		incl. in Los Angeles		San Francisco Bay	
ARIZONA		total)[N]	13,500	Area[N]	196,000
Cochise County	250	Los Angeles Metro		San Francisco	45,500
*Flagstaff	250	Area	501,000	N. Peninsula	22,000
Lake Havesu City	100	Merced	170	S. Peninsula	19,500
*Phoenix	50,000	*Modesto	450	San Jose	32,000
Prescott	150	Monterey Peninsula	1,500	Alameda County	30,500
*Tucson	20,000	Murietta Hot Springs	400	Contra Costa County	21,000
Yuma	100	*Napa	450	Marin County	17,000
ARKANSAS		Oakland (incl. in		Sonoma County	8,500
Fayetteville	120	Alameda County			
**Ft. Smith	160	under S.F. Bay Area)			
Hot Springs	200				

[N]See Notes below. *Includes entire county. **Includes all of 2 counties. ***Figure not updated.

JEWISH POPULATION IN THE UNITED STATES / 211

State and City	Jewish Population
*San Jose (listed under S.F. Bay Area)	
*San Luis Obispo	1,500
*Santa Barbara	3,800
*Santa Cruz	1,200
Santa Maria	300
Santa Monica (also incl. in Los Angeles total)	8,000
Santa Rosa (incl. in Sonoma County under S.F. Bay Area)	
Sonoma County (listed under S.F. Bay Area)	
*Stockton	1,600
Sun City	200
Tulare & Kings counties	500
***Vallejo	400
*Ventura County	8,000

COLORADO

Aspen	250
Boulder (incl. in Denver total)	
Colorado Springs	1,500
Denver[N]	45,000
Evergreen	100
*Ft. Collins	1,000
Grand Junction	250
Greeley (incl. in Ft. Collins total)	
Loveland (incl. in Ft. Collins total)	
Pueblo	250
Telluride	100
Vail	100

CONNECTICUT

Bridgeport[N]	18,000
Bristol	200
Cheshire (incl. in Meriden total)	
Colchester	575
Danbury[N]	3,500
Danielson	100
Darien (incl. in Stamford total)	
Greenwich	3,800
Hartford[N]	26,000
Hebron (incl. in Colchester total)	
Lebanon (incl. in Colchester total)	
Lower Middlesex County[N]	1,475
Manchester (incl. in Hartford total)	
Meriden[N]	3,000
Middletown	1,300
New Britain (incl. in Hartford total)	
New Haven[N]	28,000
New London[N]	4,000
New Milford	400
Newtown (incl. in Danbury total)	
Norwalk[N]	9,500
Norwich (also incl. in New London total)	1,800
Putnam	100
Rockville (incl. in Hartford total)	
Shelton (incl. in Valley area)	
Southington (incl. in Meriden total)	
Stamford/New Canaan	11,100
Storrs (incl. in Willimantic total)	
Torrington	560
Valley area[N]	550
Wallingford (also incl. in Meriden total)	500
Waterbury[N]	2,700
Westport (incl. in Norwalk total)	
Willimantic area	700

DELAWARE

Dover[N]	650
Wilmington (incl. rest of state)	9,500

DISTRICT OF COLUMBIA

Greater Washington	165,000

FLORIDA

Boca Raton-Delray Beach (listed under Southeast Fla.)	
Brevard County	3,000
*Crystal River	100
**Daytona Beach	2,500
Ft. Lauderdale (listed under Southeast Fla.)	
Ft. Myers (incl. in Lee County)	
Fort Pierce	500
Gainesville	1,200
Hollywood (listed under Southeast Fla.)	
**Jacksonville	7,300
Key West	170
*Lakeland	800
Lee County	4,000
*Miami-Dade County (listed under Southeast Fla.)	
Naples	750
***Ocala	100
Orlando[N]	18,000
Palm Beach County (listed under Southeast Fla.)	
**Pasco County	1,000

State and City	Jewish Population
**Pensacola	775
*Port Charlotte-Punta Gorda	400
*St. Petersburg-Clearwater	9,500
**Sarasota	9,750
Southeast Florida	489,800
Dade County	201,800
Hollywood[N]	60,000
Ft. Lauderdale[N]	116,000
Boca Raton-Delray Beach	52,000
Palm Beach County (excl. Boca Raton-Delray Beach)	60,000
Stuart-Port St.Lucie	3,000
Tallahassee	1,500
*Tampa	12,500
Venice (incl. in Sarasota total)	
*Vero Beach	300
Winter Haven (incl. in Lakeland total)	
GEORGIA	
Albany	400
Athens	300
Atlanta Metro Area	65,000
Augusta[N]	1,400
Brunswick	100
**Columbus	1,000
**Dalton	225
Fitzgerald-Cordele	125
Macon	900
*Savannah	2,750
**Valdosta	110

State and City	Jewish Population
HAWAII	
Hilo	280
Honolulu (includes all of Oahu)	6,400
Kuaii	100
Maui	210
IDAHO	
**Boise	220
Lewiston	100
Moscow (incl. in Lewiston total)	
ILLINOIS	
Aurora area	500
Bloomington-Normal	170
Carbondale (also incl. in S. Ill. total)	100
*Champaign-Urbana	1,700
Chicago Metro Area[N]	248,000
**Danville	130
*Decatur	210
*DeKalb	200
East St. Louis (incl. in S. Ill.)	
Elgin[N]	600
Freeport (incl. in Rockford total)	
Galesburg	100
*Joliet	850
Kankakee	200
*Peoria	950
Quad Cities[N]	1,250
**Quincy	125
Rock Island (incl. in Quad Cities)	
Rockford[N]	1,000
Southern Illinois[N]	825
*Springfield	1,000
Waukegan	500

State and City	Jewish Population
INDIANA	
Bloomington	1,000
Elkart (incl. in South Bend total)	
Evansville	520
Ft. Wayne	1,100
**Gary-Northwest Indiana	2,300
**Indianapolis	10,000
**Lafayette	500
Marion	100
*Michigan City	280
Muncie	160
South Bend[N]	1,800
*Terre Haute	325
IOWA	
Ames (also incl. in Des Moines total)	200
Cedar Rapids	430
Council Bluffs (also incl. in Omaha, Neb. total)	150
Davenport (incl. in Quad Cities, Ill.)	
*Des Moines	2,800
*Iowa City	1,200
**Sioux City	630
*Waterloo	235
KANSAS	
Kansas City (incl. in Kansas City, Mo.)	
Lawrence	175
Manhattan	100
*Topeka	500
Wichita[N]	1,000
KENTUCKY	
Covington/Newport (incl. in Cincinnati, Ohio total)	
Lexington[N]	2,000
*Louisville	9,200

State and City	Jewish Population	State and City	Jewish Population	State and City	Jewish Population
Paducah (incl. in S. Ill.)		**Salisbury	400	Leominster (also incl. in Worcester County total)	500
		Silver Spring (incl. in Montgomery County)		Lowell Area	2,000
LOUISIANA				Lynn-North Shore area[N]	25,000
Alexandria	350	MASSACHUSETTS			
Baton Rouge[N]	1,200	Amherst	750	*Martha's Vineyard	260
Lafayette (incl. in S. Central La.)		Andover[N]	3,000	New Bedford[N]	3,000
		Athol area (also incl. in Worcester County total)	300	Newburyport	280
Lake Charles	300			Newton (also incl. in Boston total)	34,000
Monroe	525	Attleboro	200	North Adams (incl. in N. Berkshire County)	
**New Orleans	12,000	Beverly (incl. in Lynn total)			
*Shreveport	1,000	Boston Metro Region[N]	228,000	North Berkshire County	750
South Central La.[N]	250	Brockton[N]	8,000	Northampton	700
Tallulah (incl. in Vicksburg, Miss. total)		Brookline (also incl. in Boston total)	26,000	Peabody (incl. in Lynn total)	
				Pittsfield-Berkshire County	3,100
MAINE		Cape Cod-Barnstable County	2,900	Plymouth	500
Augusta	500	Clinton (incl. in Worcester County)		Provincetown (incl. in Cape Cod)	
Bangor	1,250			Salem (incl. in Lynn total)	
Biddeford-Saco (incl. in S. Maine)		Fall River	1,780	Southbridge (also incl. in Worcester County total)	105
Brunswick-Bath (incl. in S. Maine)		Falmouth (incl. in Cape Cod)			
		Fitchburg (also incl. in Worcester County total)	300	Springfield[N]	11,000
Lewiston-Auburn	500			Taunton area	1,200
Portland	3,900	Framingham (incl. in Boston total)		Webster (also incl. in Worcester County total)	125
Rockland	110				
Southern Maine (incl. Portland)[N]	5,500	Gardner (incl. in Athol total)		Worcester area[N]	10,100
Waterville	300	Gloucester (also incl. in Lynn total)	450	*Worcester County	13,700
MARYLAND		Great Barrington (incl. in Pittsfield total)			
*Annapolis	2,000			MICHIGAN	
**Baltimore	94,500	*Greenfield	900	*Ann Arbor	4,500
Cumberland	265	Haverhill	1,500	Battle Creek	180
***Easton Park area[N]	100	Holyoke	550	Bay City	280
*Frederick	600	*Hyannis (incl. in Cape Cod)		Benton Harbor	500
*Hagerstown	300			**Detroit Metro Area	94,000
*Harford County	1,000	Lawrence (incl. in Andover total)			
Howard County	7,200				
Montgomery and Prince Georges counties	104,500				
Ocean City	100				

State and City	Jewish Population
*Flint	1,825
*Grand Rapids	1,500
**Jackson	325
*Kalamazoo	1,000
*Lansing	2,100
*Marquette County	150
Midland	200
Mt. Clemens (incl. in Detroit total)	
Mt. Pleasant[N]	120
*Muskegon	235
*Saginaw	200

MINNESOTA
**Duluth	500
*Minneapolis	22,000
Rochester	400
**St. Paul	7,500
Winona (incl. in LaCrosse, Wis. total)	

MISSISSIPPI
Biloxi-Gulfport	150
Clarksdale	100
**Cleveland	120
**Greenville	480
**Hattiesburg	120
**Jackson	700
**Vicksburg	105

MISSOURI
Columbia	350
Hannibal (incl. in Quincy, Ill. total)	
Joplin	100
Kansas City Metro Area	19,100
*St. Joseph	265
**St. Louis	53,500
Springfield	285

MONTANA
*Billings	200
Butte	110
Helena (incl. in Butte total)	

NEBRASKA
Grand Island-Hastings (incl. in Lincoln total)	
Lincoln	1,000
Omaha[N]	6,500

NEVADA
Carson City (incl. in Reno total)	
*Las Vegas	19,000
**Reno	1,400

NEW HAMPSHIRE
Bethlehem	100
Claremont	150
Concord	450
Dover area	600
Exeter (incl. in Portsmouth total)	
Franconia (incl. in Bethlehem total)	
Hanover-Lebanon	360
*Keene	150
**Laconia	270
Littleton (incl. in Bethlehem total)	
Manchester area	2,500
Nashua area	1,000
Portsmouth area	950
Rochester (incl. in Dover total)	
Salem (also incl. in Andover, Mass. total)	150

NEW JERSEY
Asbury Park (incl. in Monmouth County)	
*Atlantic City (incl. Atlantic County)	15,800
Bayonne (listed under Hudson County)	
Bergen County (also incl. in Northeastern N.J. total)	85,000
***Bridgeton	325
Bridgewater (incl. in Somerset County)	
Camden (incl. in Cherry Hill total)	
Cherry Hill[N]	28,000
Edison (incl. in Middlesex County)	
Elizabeth (incl. in Union County)	
Englewood (incl. in Bergen County)	
Essex County[N] (also incl. in Northeastern N.J. total)	76,200
North Essex	15,600
East Essex	10,800
South Essex	20,300
Livingston	12,600
West Orange-Orange	16,900
Flemington	900
Freehold (incl. in Monmouth County)	
Gloucester (incl. in Cherry Hill total)	
Hoboken (listed under Hudson County)	
Hudson County (also incl. in Northeastern N.J. total)	13,950
Bayonne	2,500
Jersey City	5,700
Hoboken	750
North Hudson County[N]	5,000
Jersey City (listed under Hudson County)	

JEWISH POPULATION IN THE UNITED STATES / 215

State and City	Jewish Population
Lakewood (incl. in Ocean County)	
Livingston (incl. in Essex County)	
Middlesex County[N] (also incl. in Northeastern N.J. total)	58,000
Millville	135
Monmouth County (also incl. in Northeastern N.J. total)	33,600
Morris County (also incl. in Northeastern N.J. total)	33,500
Morristown (incl. in Morris County)	
Mt. Holly (incl. in Cherry Hill total)	
Newark (incl. in Essex County)	
New Brunswick (incl. in Middlesex County)	
Northeastern N.J.[N]	370,300
Ocean County (also incl. in Northeastern N.J. total)	9,500
Passaic County (also incl. in Northeastern N.J. total)	18,700
Passaic-Clifton (also incl. in Passaic County total)	8,000
Paterson (incl. in Passaic County)	
Perth Amboy (incl. in Middlesex County)	
Phillipsburg (incl. in Easton, Pa. total)	
Plainfield (incl. in Union County)	

State and City	Jewish Population
Princeton	3,000
Salem	100
Somerset County (also incl. in Northeastern N.J. total)	7,750
Somerville (incl. in Somerset County)	
Sussex County (also incl. in Northeastern N.J. total)	4,100
Toms River (incl. in Ocean County)	
Trenton[N]	6,000
Union County (also incl. in Northeastern N.J. total)	30,000
Vineland[N]	2,500
Warren County	400
Wayne (incl. in Passaic County)	
Wildwood	425
Willingboro (incl. in Cherry Hill total)	

NEW MEXICO
*Albuquerque	4,400
Las Cruces	525
Los Alamos	250
Santa Fe	900

NEW YORK
*Albany	12,000
Amenia (incl. in Dutchess County)	
Amsterdam	450
*Auburn	175
Beacon (incl. in Dutchess County)	
*Binghamton (incl. all Broome County)	3,000
Brewster (incl. in Putnam County)	
*Buffalo	18,125

State and City	Jewish Population
Canandaigua (incl. in Geneva total)	
Catskill	200
Corning (incl. in Elmira total)	
*Cortland	200
Dunkirk	120
Ellenville	1,600
Elmira[N]	1,100
Fleischmanns	115
Fredonia (incl. in Dunkirk total)	
Geneva	300
Glens Falls[N]	800
*Gloversville	420
*Herkimer	180
Highland Falls (incl. in Orange County)	
Hudson	470
*Ithaca	1,250
Jamestown	100
Kingston[N]	4,500
Lake George (incl. in Glens Falls total)	
Liberty (also incl. in Sullivan County total)	2,100
***Massena	140
Middletown (incl. in Orange County)	
Monroe (incl. in Orange County)	
Monticello (also incl. in Sullivan County total)	2,400
Newark (incl. in Geneva total)	
Newburgh (incl. in Orange County)	
New Paltz (incl. in Kingston total)	
New York Metro Area[N]	1,671,000
Bronx	85,000

State and City	Jewish Population	State and City	Jewish Population	State and City	Jewish Population
Brooklyn	418,900	**NORTH CAROLINA**		Hamilton (incl. in Butler County)	
Manhattan	274,300	Asheville[N]	1,350	*Lima	365
Queens	321,200	**Chapel Hill-Durham	2,900	Lorain	600
Staten Island	31,000	Charlotte[N]	4,000	Mansfield	250
Nassau County	311,700	Elizabethtown (incl. in Wilmington total)		Marietta (incl. in Parkersburg, W.Va. total)	
Suffolk County	106,200	*Fayetteville area	300	Marion	110
Westchester County	122,600	Gastonia	240	Middletown (incl. in Butler County)	
Niagara Falls	400	Goldsboro	120	**Newark	105
Olean	120	*Greensboro	2,700	New Philadelphia (incl. in Canton total)	
**Oneonta	250	Greenville	300	Norwalk (incl. in Sandusky total)	
Orange County	10,000	Hendersonville	135	Oberlin (incl. in Elyria total)	
Pawling	105	**Hickory	100	Oxford (incl. in Butler County)	
Plattsburg	260	High Point (incl. in Greensboro total)		**Sandusky	130
Port Jervis (also incl. in Orange County total)	560	Jacksonville (incl. in Wilmington total)		Springfield	250
Potsdam	250	Raleigh	2,775	*Steubenville	175
*Poughkeepsie	6,500	Whiteville (incl. in Wilmington total)		Toledo[N]	6,300
Putnam County	1,000	Wilmington area	500	Warren (also incl. in Youngstown total)	400
**Rochester	23,000	Winston-Salem	440	Wooster	125
Rockland County	60,000	**NORTH DAKOTA**		Youngstown[N]	4,000
Rome	205	Fargo	500	*Zanesville	120
Saratoga Springs	500	Grand Forks	150		
**Schenectady	5,200	**OHIO**		**OKLAHOMA**	
South Fallsburg (also incl. in Sullivan County total)	1,100	**Akron	6,000	Norman (also incl. in Oklahoma City total)	350
Sullivan County	7,425	Athens	100	**Oklahoma City	2,300
Syracuse[N]	9,000	Bowling Green (also incl. in Toledo total)	120	*Tulsa	2,750
Troy Area	800	Butler County	900		
Utica[N]	1,900	**Canton	2,400	**OREGON**	
Walden (incl. in Orange County)		Cincinnati[N]	23,000	*Corvallis	150
Watertown	170	**Cleveland[N]	65,000	Eugene	2,300
Woodstock (incl. in Kingston total)		* Columbus	15,200		
		**Dayton	6,000		
		East Liverpool	200		
		Elyria	250		
		Fremont (incl. in Sandusky total)			

JEWISH POPULATION IN THE UNITED STATES / 217

State and City	Jewish Population
**Medford	500
Portland	9,000
**Salem	250

PENNSYLVANIA
Allentown	6,000
*Altoona	480
Ambridge[N]	350
Beaver Falls (incl. in Upper Beaver County)	
Bethlehem	810
**Bradford	110
Bucks County (lower portion)[N]	14,500
*Butler	285
**Chambersburg	470
Chester (incl. in Phila. total)	
Chester County (also incl. in Phila. total)	4,000
Coatesville (incl. in Chester County)	
Easton area	1,200
*Erie	800
Farrell (incl. in Sharon total)	
Greensburg (also incl. in Pittsburgh total)	425
**Harrisburg	6,500
Hazleton area	410
Honesdale (incl. in Wayne County)	
Jeanette (incl. in Greensburg total)	
**Johnstown	430
Lancaster	2,100
*Lebanon	400
Lewisburg (incl. in Sunbury total)	
Lock Haven (incl. in Williamsport total)	
McKeesport (incl. in Pittsburgh total)	
New Castle	200
Norristown (incl. in Philadelphia total)	
**Oil City	145
Oxford-Kennett Square (incl. in Chester County)	
Philadelphia area[N]	250,000
Phoenixville (incl. in Chester County)	
Pike County	300
Pittsburgh[N]	45,000
Pottstown	700
Pottsville	250
*Reading	2,800
*Scranton	3,150
Shamokin (incl. in Sunbury total)	
Sharon (also incl. in Youngstown, Ohio total)	260
State College	550
*Stroudsburg	400
Sunbury[N]	160
Tamaqua (incl. in Hazleton total)	
Uniontown area	290
Upper Beaver County	200
**Washington (also incl. in Pittsburgh total)	250
Wayne County	500
Waynesburg (incl. in Washington total)	
West Chester (also incl. in Chester County)	300
Wilkes-Barre[N]	3,500
**Williamsport	415
York	1,500

RHODE ISLAND
Cranston (incl. in Providence total)	
Kingston (incl. in Washington County)	
Newport-Middletown	700
Providence area	14,200
Washington County	1,200
Westerly (incl. in Washington County)	

SOUTH CAROLINA
*Charleston	4,500
**Columbia	2,000
Florence area	210
Georgetown (incl. in Myrtle Beach total)	
Greenville	800
Kingstree (incl. in Sumter total)	
**Myrtle Beach	425
***Orangeburg County	105
Rock Hill (incl. in Charlotte total)	
*Spartanburg	320
Sumter[N]	175

SOUTH DAKOTA
Sioux Falls	135

TENNESSEE
Bristol (incl. in Johnson City total)	
Chattanooga	1,700
Jackson	100
Johnson City	210
Kingsport (incl. in Johnson City total)	
Knoxville	1,350
Memphis	10,000

State and City	Jewish Population	State and City	Jewish Population	State and City	Jewish Population
Nashville	5,560	UTAH		Radford (incl. in	
Oak Ridge	200	Ogden	150	Blacksburg total)	
		*Salt Lake City	2,800	Richmond[N]	8,000
TEXAS				Roanoke	1,050
Amarillo[N]	190	VERMONT		Staunton[N]	375
*Austin	5,000	Bennington	100	Williamsburg (incl. in	
Bay City (incl. in		Brattleboro	150	Newport News total)	
Wharton total)		**Burlington	3,000	Winchester[N]	145
Baytown	300	Montpelier-Barre	500		
Beaumont	800	Newport (incl. in		WASHINGTON	
*Brownsville	325	St. Johnsbury total)		Bellingham	300
College Station-Bryan		Rutland	550	Ellensburg (incl. in	
	400	**St. Johnsbury	100	Yakima total)	
*Corpus Christi	1,400			Longview-Kelso (incl.	
**Dallas	34,000	VIRGINIA		in Portland total)	
El Paso	4,900	Alexandria (incl.		Olympia	300
*Ft. Worth	5,000	Falls Church,		Port Angeles	100
Galveston	800	Arlington and Fairfax		Pullman (incl. in	
Harlingen (incl. in		counties)	35,100	Moscow, Idaho total)	
Brownsville total)		Arlington (incl. in		*Seattle[N]	29,300
**Houston[N]	42,000	Alexandria total)		Spokane	800
Kilgore (incl. in		Blacksburg	300	*Tacoma	1,100
Longview total)		Charlottesville	950	Tri Cities[N]	180
Lared	200	Chesapeake (incl. in		Vancouver (incl. in	
Longview	200	Portsmouth total)		Portland total)	
*Lubbock	225	Colonial Heights (incl.		**Yakima	100
Lufkin (incl. in		in Petersburg total)			
Longview total)		Danville	100	WEST VIRGINIA	
Marshall (incl. in		Fredericksburg	140	Bluefield-Princeton	250
Longview total)		Hampton (incl. in		*Charleston	1,025
*McAllen	475	Newport News)		Clarksburg	115
Midland-Odessa	150	Harrisonburg (incl. in		Fairmont (incl. in	
Paris (incl. in		Staunton total)		Clarksburg total)	
Sherman-Denison		Lynchburg area	275	Huntington[N]	275
total)		**Martinsville	130	Morgantown	150
Port Arthur	100	Newport News-		**Parkersburg	100
San Angelo	100	Hampton[N]	2,000	**Wheeling	300
*San Antonio	10,000	Norfolk-Virginia Beach			
Sherman-Denison	125		18,000	WISCONSIN	
Tyler	450	Petersburg area	550	Appleton	250
Waco[N]	450	Portsmouth-Suffolk		Beloit	120
**Wharton	130	(also incl. in Norfolk		Green Bay	260
Wichita Falls	260	total)	1,900	*Kenosha	200
				LaCrosse	150

JEWISH POPULATION IN THE UNITED STATES / 219

State and City	Jewish Population	State and City	Jewish Population	State and City	Jewish Population
*Madison	4,500	Superior (also incl. in Duluth, Minn. total)	100	WYOMING	
Manitowoc	100			Casper	100
Milwaukee[N]	28,000			Cheyenne	230
Oshkosh	150	Waukesha (incl. in Milwaukee total)		Laramie (incl. in Cheyenne total)	
*Racine	375				
Sheboygan	160	Wausau[N]	240		

Notes

CALIFORNIA

Long Beach—includes in L.A. County, Long Beach, Signal Hill, Cerritos, Lakewood, Rosmoor, and Hawaiian Gardens. Also includes in Orange County, Los Alamitos, Cypress, Seal Beach, and Huntington Harbor.

Palm Springs—includes Palm Springs, Desert Hot Springs, Cathedral City, Palm Desert, and Rancho Mirage.

Pomona Valley—includes Alta Loma, Chino, Claremont, Cucamonga, La Verne, Montclair, Ontario, Pomona, San Dimas, and Upland. Portion also included in Los Angeles total.

Sacramento—includes Yolo, Placer, El Dorado, and Sacramento counties.

San Francisco Bay Area—North Peninsula includes northern San Mateo County. South Peninsula includes southern San Mateo County and towns of Palo Alto and Los Altos in Santa Clara County. San Jose includes remainder of Santa Clara County.

COLORADO

Denver—includes Adams, Arapahoe, Boulder, Denver, and Jefferson counties.

CONNECTICUT

Bridgeport—includes Monroe, Easton, Trumbull, Fairfield, Bridgeport, Shelton, Stratford, and part of Milford.

Danbury—includes Danbury, Bethel, New Fairfield, Brookfield, Sherman, Newtown, Redding, Ridgefield and part of Wilton; also includes Brewster and Goldens Bridge in New York.

Hartford—includes most of Hartford County and Vernon, Rockville, Ellington, and Tolland in Tolland County.

Lower Middlesex County—includes Branford, Guilford, Madison, Clinton, Westbrook, Old Saybrook. Portion of this area also included in New London and New Haven totals.

Meriden—includes Meriden, Southington, Cheshire, and Wallingford. Portion also included in New Haven total.

New Haven—includes New Haven, East Haven, Guilford, Branford, Madison, North Haven, Hamden, West Haven, Milford, Orange, Woodbridge, Bethany, Derby, Ansonia, and Cheshire.

New London—includes central and southern New London County. Also includes part of Lower Middlesex County and part of Windham County.

Norwalk—includes Norwalk, Weston, Westport, East Norwalk, Darien, Wilton, part of Georgetown and part of New Canaan.

Valley area—includes Ansonia, Derby, Shelton, Oxford, Seymour, and Beacon Falls. Portion also included in Bridgeport and New Haven totals.

Waterbury—includes Middlebury, Southbury, Naugatuck, Watertown, Waterbury, Oakville and Woodbury.

DELAWARE
Dover—includes most of central and southern Delaware.

DISTRICT OF COLUMBIA
Greater Washington—includes Montgomery and Prince Georges counties in Maryland; Arlington County, Fairfax County, Falls Church, and Alexandria in Virginia.

FLORIDA
Ft. Lauderdale—includes Ft. Lauderdale, Pompano Beach, Deerfield Beach, Tamarac, Margate, and other towns in northern Broward County.

Hollywood—includes Hollywood, Hallandale, Dania, Davie, Pembroke, and other towns in southern Broward County.

Orlando—includes all of Orange and Seminole counties and part of Lake County.

GEORGIA
Augusta—includes Burke, Columbia, and Richmond counties and part of Aiken County, South Carolina.

ILLINOIS
Chicago—includes all of Cook and DuPage counties and Southern Lake County. For a total of Jewish population of the Chicago Metropolitan Region, please include Northwest Indiana, Joliet, Aurora, Elgin, and Waukegan totals.

Elgin—includes Northern Kane County, Southern McHenry County, and western edge of Cook County.

Quad Cities—includes Rock Island, Moline (Ill.); Davenport and Bettendorf (Iowa).

Rockford—includes Winnebago, Boone, and Stephenson counties.

Southern Illinois—includes lower portion of Illinois below Carlinville, adjacent western portion of Kentucky, and adjacent portion of Southeastern Missouri.

INDIANA
South Bend—includes St. Joseph and Elkhart counties and part of Berrien County, Mich.

KANSAS
Wichita—includes Sedgwick County and towns of Salina, Dodge City, Great Bend, Liberal, Russel, and Hays.

KENTUCKY
Lexington—includes Fayette, Bourbon, Scott, Clark, Woodford, Madison, Pulaski, and Jessamin counties.

LOUISIANA
Baton Rouge—includes E. Baton Rouge, Ascencion, Livingston, St. Landry, Iberville, Pt. Coupee, and W. Baton Rouge parishes.
South Central—includes Abbeville, Lafayette, New Iberia, Crowley, Opelousus, Houma, Morgan City, Thibadoux, and Franklin.

MAINE
Southern Maine—includes York, Cumberland, and Sagadahoc counties.

MARYLAND
Easton Park Area—includes towns in Caroline, Kent, Queen Annes, and Talbot counties.

MASSACHUSETTS
Andover—includes Andover, N. Andover, Boxford, Lawrence, Methuen, Tewksbury, Dracut, and town of Salem, New Hampshire.
Boston Metropolitan Region—includes all towns south and west of Boston within approximately 30 miles, and all towns north of Boston within approximately 20 miles. All towns formerly part of Framingham area are now included in Boston total.
Brockton—includes Avon, Brockton, Easton, Bridgewater, Whitman, and West Bridgewater. Also included in Boston total.
Lynn—includes Lynn, Saugus, Nahant, Swampscott, Lynnfield, Peabody, Salem, Marblehead, Beverly, Danvers, Middleton, Wenham, Topsfield, Hamilton, Manchester, Ipswich, Essex, Gloucester, and Rockport. Also included in Boston total.
New Bedford—includes New Bedford, Dartmouth, Fairhaven, and Mattapoisett.
Springfield—includes Springfield, Longmeadow, E. Longmeadow, Hampden, Wilbraham, Agwam, and West Springfield.
Worcester—includes Worcester, Northborough, Westborough, Shrewsbury, Boylston, West Boylston, Holden, Paxton, Leicester, Auburn, Millbury, and Grafton. Also included in the Worcester County total.

MICHIGAN
Mt. Pleasant—includes towns in Isabella, Mecosta, Gladwin, and Gratiot counties.

NEBRASKA
Omaha—includes Douglas and Sarpy counties. Also includes Pottawatomie County, Iowa.

NEW HAMPSHIRE
Laconia—includes Laconia, Plymouth, Meredith, Conway, and Franklin.

NEW JERSEY
Cherry Hill—includes Camden, Burlington, and Gloucester counties.
Essex County—East Essex includes Belleville, Bloomfield, East Orange, Irvington, Newark and Nutley in Essex County, and Kearney in Hudson County. North Essex includes Caldwell, Cedar Grove, Essex Fells, Fairfield, Glen Ridge, Montclair, North Caldwell, Roseland, Verona and West Caldwell. South Essex includes Maplewood, Millburn, Short Hills, and South Orange in Essex County, and Springfield in Union County.
Middlesex County—includes in Somerset County, Kendall Park, Somerset, and Franklin; in Mercer County, Hightstown; and all of Middlesex County.
Northeastern N.J.—includes Bergen, Essex, Hudson, Middlesex, Morris, Passaic, Somerset, Union, Hunterdon, Sussex, Monmouth, and Ocean counties.
North Hudson County—includes Guttenberg, Hudson Heights, North Bergen, North Hudson, Secaucus, Union City, Weehawken, West New York, and Woodcliff.
Somerset County—includes most of Somerset County and a portion of Hunterdon County.
Trenton—includes most of Mercer County.
Union County—includes all of Union County except Springfield. Also includes a few towns in adjacent areas of Somerset and Middlesex counties.
Vineland—includes most of Cumberland County and towns in neighboring counties adjacent to Vineland.

NEW YORK
Elmira—includes Chemung, Tioga, and Schuyler counties. Also includes Tioga and Bradford counties in Pennsylvania.
Glens Falls—includes Warren and Washington counties, lower Essex County, and upper Saratoga County.
Kingston—includes eastern half of Ulster County.
New York Metropolitan Area—includes the five boroughs of New York City, Westchester, Nassau, and Suffolk counties. For a total Jewish population of the New York Metropolitan Region, please include Fairfield County, Connecticut; Rockland, Putnam, and Orange counties, New York; and Northeastern New Jersey.
Syracuse—includes Onondaga County, Western Madison County, and most of Oswego County.
Utica—includes southeastern third of Oneida County.

NORTH CAROLINA
Asheville—includes Buncombe, Haywood, and Madison counties.
Charlotte—includes Mecklenberg County. Also includes Lancaster and York counties in South Carolina.

OHIO
Cincinnati—includes Hamilton and Butler counties. Also includes Boone, Campbell, and Kenton counties in Kentucky.

Cleveland—for a total Jewish population of the Cleveland Metropolitan Region, please include Elyria, Lorain and Akron totals.
Toledo—includes Fulton, Lucas, and Wood counties. Also includes Monroe and Lenawee counties, Michigan.
Youngstown—includes Mahoning and Trumbull counties. Also includes Mercer County, Pennsylvania.

PENNSYLVANIA

Ambridge—includes lower Beaver County and adjacent areas of Allegheny County. Also included in Pittsburgh total.
Bucks County (lower portion)—includes Bensalem Township, Bristol, Langhorne, Levittown, New Hope, Newtown, Penndel, Warrington, Yardley, Richboro, Feasterville, Middletown, Southampton, and Holland. Also included in Philadelphia total.
Philadelphia—includes Philadelphia City, Montgomery County, Delaware County, Chester County, and Bucks County. For a total Jewish population of the Philadelphia Metropolitan Region, please include the Cherry Hill, Salem, and Trenton areas of New Jersey, and the Wilmington area of Delaware.
Pittsburgh—includes all of Allegheny County and adjacent portions of Washington, Westmoreland, and Beaver counties.
Sunbury—includes Shamokin, Lewisburg, Milton, Selinsgrove, and Sunbury.
Wilkes-Barre—includes all of Lucerne County except southern portion, which is included in Hazleton totals.

SOUTH CAROLINA

Sumter—includes towns in Sumter, Lee, Clarendon, and Williamsburg counties.

TEXAS

Amarillo—includes Canyon, Childress, Borger, Dumas, Memphis, Pampa, Vega, and Hereford in Texas, and Portales, New Mexico.
Houston—includes Harris, Montgomery, and Ft. Bend counties, and parts of Brazoria and Galveston counties.
Waco—includes Mclellan, Coryell, Bell, Falls, Hamilton, and Hill counties.

VIRGINIA

Newport News—includes Newport News, Hampton, Williamsburg, James City, York County, and Poquosson County.
Richmond—includes Richmond City, Henrico County, and Chesterfield County.
Staunton—includes towns in Augusta, Page, Shenendoah, Rockingham, Bath, and Highland counties.
Winchester—includes towns in Winchester, Frederick, Clark, and Warren counties, Virginia; and Hardy and Jefferson counties, West Virginia.

WASHINGTON
 Seattle—includes King County and adjacent portions of Snohomish and Kitsap counties.
 Tri Cities—includes Pasco, Richland, and Kennewick.

WEST VIRGINIA
 Huntington—includes nearby towns in Ohio and Kentucky.

WISCONSIN
 Milwaukee—includes Milwaukee County, Eastern Waukesha County, and Southern Ozaukee County.
 Wasau—includes Stevens Point, Marshfield, Antigo, and Rhinelander.

Review of the Year

OTHER COUNTRIES

Canada

National Affairs

As 1989 BEGAN, CANADA appeared to be making slow but steady economic and political progress. The reelected government of Prime Minister Brian Mulroney looked forward to the implementation of the free-trade agreement with the United States, proposed a value-added tax for the country in order to increase revenues and improve economic performance, and anticipated a happy conclusion to the Meech Lake constitutional initiative. By the end of the year, although the situation appeared to be stable, beneath the surface there was growing concern about the continuing objections of three provinces to the Meech Lake accord. Without the unanimous approval of the provinces, the accord, which promised a way to get Quebec to adhere to the constitution, was scheduled to die in late June 1990.

Quebec saw Meech Lake as satisfying its "minimal" demands, especially by legitimating its character as a "distinct society" with a special vocation to protect and promote the French language and culture, even if that meant subordinating individual rights to collective needs. Underlying its position was the implicit threat that if Meech Lake were not approved, more radical demands, possibly for some form of sovereignty, might emanate from that predominantly French-speaking province.

The political imbroglio over Meech Lake discomfited the Jewish community, especially in Montreal, which was home to some 30 percent of the country's Jews. Montreal's Jews, particularly the majority who are English-speaking, were adamantly against the idea of an independent Quebec and fierce partisans of a united Canada. Jews in other parts of the country were also concerned about the prospects of dislocation for such a significant portion of the countrywide community. Many Jews across the country also sided with opponents of Meech Lake who argued that the deal was bad for Canada because it gave too much power to the provinces at the expense of the federal government.

In the period leading up to the September provincial election in Quebec, several Jews were instrumental in forming the Equality party, with Montrealer Robert Libman, a young architect, as leader. The impetus for the establishment of the new party was the Quebec government's move (by use of the "notwithstanding" clause of the constitution) to override a 1988 Supreme Court decision applying the right of free expression to the language of commercial signs—thus making mandatory the exclusive use of French on signs. Libman recruited about 20 candidates to run in constituencies with large Anglophone populations. Few of the candidates were Jewish, but the president of the party and many contributors were. Thus the party came to be seen in the eyes of many French Québécois as a Jewish party and a party that was disliked because it opposed the broad consensus of French opinion. The combination contributed to the exacerbation of French-Jewish relations.

Libman himself ran in the heavily Jewish district of D'Arcy McGee, where his opponent was Gary Waxman, the candidate of Premier Robert Bourassa's Liberal party. Waxman clearly had the support of the high-profile Jewish communal organizations, while Libman ran a sort of populist campaign designed to appeal to average voters who were concerned about the infringement of their rights. Despite his elite backing and his argument that the Jewish voters of D'Arcy McGee needed to be represented in the highest councils of the government by a member of the governing party, Waxman encountered considerable hostility, including loud booing at one meeting, and ultimately lost to Libman. The Equality party won three other seats as well.

In Vancouver, British Columbia, Michael Levy ran unsuccessfully in March for the legislature on the Social Credit ticket. He would have been the first Jewish "Socred" legislator. This was noteworthy because the governing Social Credit party had been traditionally inhospitable toward Jews and was known for its overtly Christian orientation. In October Levy attended the Socred convention and attempted to force a debate on the party constitution's reference to "Christian principles." When he was roundly booed and jeered by the delegates, he stormed out of the convention (and subsequently resigned from the party). The *Toronto Star* reported that anti-Semitic jokes had been common at the convention, including one told publicly by Premier William Vander Zalm. Vander Zalm and another minister later apologized for their jokes. F. David Radler, president of the Canadian company that purchased the *Jerusalem Post* and a Socred supporter, criticized Levy's timing in raising the Christian-principles issue and opined that the party was not anti-Semitic.

Three Jews ran in the Alberta election in March. Liberal Sheldon Chumir of Calgary was reelected to a seat in the opposition. British Columbia MP Dave Barrett, a former premier, contested the leadership of the federal New Democratic party unsuccessfully.

In Toronto, the National Council of Jewish Women (NCJW), Toronto section, found itself the center of an unwanted storm of adverse publicity because of dubious financial practices by Patricia Starr, president of the organization's charitable foundation. Starr, a prominent Liberal and community fund-raiser, stepped down as president amid allegations that her foundation had made political contributions of at least $85,000 to all three Ontario political parties. There was speculation that criminal charges might be brought in the case. In the meantime, a judicial inquiry was set up to look into relations between Starr, certain elected officials, and the land developer Tridel Corporation. In addition, the NCJW expelled Starr and two other directors of the foundation for violation of an internal by-law, and the president of the Toronto section resigned. NCJW national president Gloria Strom dissolved the foundation and declared that "these three women are not emblematic of our organization." At year's end a court was deciding whether the judicial inquiry could proceed or should be quashed, as requested by Starr and Tridel.

Relations with Israel

The highlight of the year was the state visit of President Chaim Herzog at the end of June, which came at a sensitive time in Canada-Israel relations. Many members of Parliament were unhappy with Israel's response to the uprising of the Palestinians in the occupied territories, and media criticism of Israel was growing. The Israeli president addressed a joint session of Parliament in Ottawa, met with government officials, including the governor-general, and visited the Jewish communities in Ottawa, Toronto, and Montreal. Although the position of president is above politics, Herzog spoke out vigorously in defense of Israel's handling of the *intifada* and its foreign-policy positions. In his speech to the MPs, he attacked the hypocrisy evident in much of the criticism of Israel and was particularly negative toward the media. Characterizing Israel's struggle with the Palestinians as one for existence, he said, "The choice is between maintaining law and order ... or allowing the situation to deteriorate into a new edition of Beirut or Teheran." Herzog lauded the Israeli army for exercising restraint in the face of great provocation. He also praised Mulroney as "a tried and trusted friend."

Prime Minister Mulroney spoke to Parliament in Herzog's presence. He urged Israel to be moderate and reasonable in its actions, while vowing Canadian support for Israel coupled with a "profound conviction that human rights must be respected." At a private meeting, Secretary of State for External Affairs Joe Clark pressed harder on the question of Israel's actions in the territories in relation to the Geneva Convention and reports by human-rights organizations. At another meeting, Liberal leader John Turner emphasized his party's view that the Palestinians should have a homeland on the West Bank and Gaza Strip. He praised the Israeli proposal for Palestinian elections and the PLO move to an apparently more moderate position.

Herzog was fulsome in his praise for Canada after the visit. He described Mulroney as "one of the most sincere friends of Israel" and Turner as a "tried friend." He also detected a "basic undercurrent of great friendship" throughout his visit, which helped to make it a tremendous success.

POINTS OF CONTENTION

Despite the enthusiasm of President Herzog, there were many points of contention between the two countries during the year. Additional tension was injected into the relationship because Canada began a two-year term on the United Nations Security Council in January, which made its foreign-policy positions all the more significant.

Early in the year there were rumors that Canada was about to upgrade its relations with the PLO. Up to that point, formal contacts had been limited to middle-level bureaucrats, excluding higher officials, such as ambassadors, and External Affairs Minister Clark indicated that Canada felt isolated as one of the few countries that did not deal with the PLO at a higher level. Thus, it was not surprising that Clark announced in April the removal of restrictions on top-level contacts, but he went even further by endorsing the concept of Palestinian self-determination. The Israeli government expressed deep disappointment and denounced the move as "counterproductive for peace." Most of the Jewish community was also firm in its opposition, the Canada-Israel Committee (CIC) labeling the move a "deeply disturbing departure" and Canadian Jewish Congress (CJC) president Dorothy Reitman accusing Canada of joining "the herd" of Western countries who supported the PLO. Virtually alone, Canadian Friends of Peace Now welcomed the move.

The initiative was seen as the culmination of an effort within the Department of External Affairs, aided by changing public attitudes caused by the *intifada*. Although the CIC and CJC characterized recognition of the Palestinian right to self-determination as a fundamental shift in Canadian policy, Clark claimed that Canada did not necessarily support the idea of an independent Palestinian state and certainly did not recognize the state declared by PLO chairman Yasir Arafat in Geneva in late 1988. Arab partisans, however, lauded the decision, claiming that indeed Canada had endorsed a Palestinian state. For his part, Clark tried to limit the damage with supporters of Israel by stressing Canada's support for Israel and her security, claiming that the new policy would actually help Israel find peace. In contrast, Eliahu Ben-Elissar, chairman of the Knesset's Foreign Affairs and Defense Committee, who was visiting in Canada at the time of the announcement, termed the change an unfriendly act toward Israel. Some Jewish leaders saw the move as prompted by a desire to be more in step with the European countries while Canada was serving on the Security Council. But former Canadian UN ambassador Stephen Lewis called the change "absolutely necessary. . . . It brings us back into the international picture. We had excluded ourselves by our intransigence on dealing with the PLO."

Canada's higher profile in the UN led to careful scrutiny of its votes by the Jewish community. Early in the year Canada generally voted against or abstained on resolutions hostile to Israel. However, it did support a Security Council resolution, vetoed by the United States, that strongly deplored Israeli policies and practices, particularly shooting to maintain order. And at the end of August it joined in a condemnation of the Israeli deportation of five Palestinian activists, which was adopted 14–0 with the United States abstaining. A similar resolution was adopted by the same vote in July. The CIC termed the government's "repeated endorsements of such resolutions . . . shocking and unacceptable." The CIC also criticized the double standard by which Canada was prepared to condemn Israel while the UN ignored even more serious threats in the Middle East. In November Canada was again one of 14 countries supporting a resolution—vetoed by the United States— that condemned Israeli actions in the occupied territories and called for the return of confiscated property. Despite explanations that the vote was prompted by dissatisfaction with Israel's human-rights policies, the CIC was sharply critical of what it called Canada's "slide away from Israel" by voting for a "one-sided and grossly unfair" resolution.

Canada's standing in the eyes of supporters of Israel was redeemed somewhat by its vigorous opposition to a move to elevate the PLO's status to that of an observer state. Nevertheless, the Israeli Foreign Ministry was concerned about the perceived deterioration of bilateral relations. In general, the year saw increasing disillusionment within the Jewish community's mainstream over the evolution of government policy, despite the efforts of officials, including UN ambassador Yves Fortier, to soft-pedal the changes.

OTHER ISRAEL-RELATED MATTERS

The fact that two Canadians died as victims of a terrorist bus incident on the Tel Aviv–Jerusalem highway in July seemed to have little lasting impact. Dr. Shelley Halpenny, a Vancouver dentist who had come to Israel to watch her father compete in the Maccabiah, and Fern Rykiss, a Winnipeg teenager visiting Israel on a summer program, were killed when a terrorist diverted the bus and sent it crashing into a deep ravine.

Israel encountered considerable criticism from Canadian religious groups during the year. The Canadian Council of Churches submitted a brief to the Department of External Affairs in February that accused Israel of "massive" violations of international human-rights agreements. The council recognized "the *intifada* to be a legitimate struggle of the Palestinian people under Israeli occupation to free themselves from the yoke of oppression." A similar statement issued by Canada's Catholic bishops took Israel to task for "violently repressing the popular movement which animates the *intifada.*" Both statements were attacked by CJC and other Jewish organizations for being one-sided and biased and for distorting reality. In October the Canadian Council of Churches issued a statement on the Middle East that called for Palestinian self-determination and reiterated the theme of Israeli violations of Palestinian human rights.

In other Israel-related matters, Canada-Israel trade continued to grow at a rapid pace; a Canadian company, Hollinger, purchased the *Jerusalem Post* and installed its president, F. David Radler of Vancouver, as chairman of the board; and a new Israeli embassy was opened in Ottawa. In November a conference involving Palestinian representatives and academics, along with Jews and Israelis who generally supported a Palestinian state, called for direct talks between Israel and the PLO. One of the four sponsors of the conference was Canadian Friends of Peace Now. The conference was picketed by Jewish protesters who opposed its underlying premises.

Anti-Semitism

The case of Malcolm Ross, a New Brunswick public-school teacher who had expressed anti-Semitic views in various publications, continued to wend its way through a complex legal and political process. The issue of Ross's fitness to teach arose in response to a complaint by a Moncton parent that Ross had interjected anti-Semitism into the classroom, but the local school board investigated and found no evidence to support the charge. A proposed human-rights inquiry was initially quashed by a court, but various legal moves ultimately cleared the way for one to begin. In the meantime, Ross appeared on a cable television show in Moncton and challenged the veracity of historical accounts of the Holocaust. That incident angered the school board and threatened to lead to new legal actions as the year ended.

York University historian Irving Abella spoke out on several occasions on the growing acceptance of anti-Semitism. In a February speech in Toronto, Abella charged that Israel-bashing was serving as a means to legitimize anti-Semitism. "The poison of anti-Semitism has been decanted from the old Czarist bottle and put into a new one," he asserted. He condemned as dishonest the media's use of the Holocaust image, comparing the Israelis to the Nazis. In particular he called attention to the increase in racist attitudes within Canada, citing a recent poll in which some 6 percent of Canadians admitted to being anti-Semitic, while another 20 to 25 percent displayed varying degrees of anti-Jewish prejudice.

Convicted anti-Semite Ernst Zundel appealed his conviction on charges of spreading false news by publishing Holocaust-denial material. Arguing in the Ontario Court of Appeal, defense attorney Douglas Christie contended that the trial judge had erred by accepting as fact that the Holocaust had occurred.

In another legal battle, the Supreme Court heard appeals of two cases in which the constitutionality of the country's anti-hate law was at issue. One case involved James Keegstra, whose conviction had been overturned by the Alberta Court of Appeal. The other concerned the convictions of two white supremacists in Ontario, Donald Andrews and Robert Smith of the Nationalist party. Their conviction was upheld by the Ontario Court of Appeal, necessitating a Supreme Court decision to resolve the conflicting rulings of the two appeals courts.

During the year there was a rash of anti-Semitic incidents in different parts of the country. The most publicized was the defacing of a major Toronto synagogue, in June, with swastikas and anti-Semitic slogans. A male skinhead and his female associate were charged with the crime. In July a synagogue in Saskatoon was defaced, and there was a similar incident in a Vancouver suburb in August. At about the same time, a Vancouver church official received an anti-Semitic pamphlet in the mail. In September the Shaar Hashomayim cemetery in Montreal was vandalized and 53 tombstones were desecrated.

In a tenaciously fought quasi-judicial battle at Montreal's Concordia University, Jewish students ultimately failed in their attempt to have the university discipline Palestinian students who had put up an anti-Semitic display, ostensibly as a political statement. The Jewish students contended that the display was not an exercise of free expression but rather represented the promotion of hatred. A special appeals committee of the board of governors declined to overturn a lower ruling in favor of the Concordia Collective for Palestinian Human Rights.

Evidence of neo-Nazism met with stiff resistance. A July hate rally of neo-Nazis and skinheads in Minden, Ontario, was met by a counter-rally in the same town, spearheaded by war veterans, Holocaust survivors, and B'nai Brith members, who were joined in their protest by some local citizens. A similar hate rally, scheduled for August in Sherbrooke, Quebec, was aborted after B'nai Brith officials alerted the owner of the property on which the rally was to be held to the true nature of the event.

Nazi War Criminals

There were several proceedings under way involving alleged war criminals. The main war-crimes case was that of Imre Finta, who immigrated to Canada from Hungary after World War II. He was charged under the new war-crimes legislation with aiding the Nazis in their deportation of Jews to concentration camps. The specific allegations included forcible confinement, kidnapping, manslaughter, and robbery, involving 8,617 Jews in Szeged, Hungary. Pretrial legal maneuvers occupied most of the year, with the trial itself beginning in November. As a police captain, Finta was involved in cramming Jews into freight cars so that they could be transported to the death camps in 1944, according to one witness.

Jacob Luitjens, a former botany professor at the University of British Columbia, was accused of being a Nazi collaborator in Holland and was subjected to a denaturalization hearing. The government contended that his citizenship should be lifted because he had failed to disclose, when immigrating to Canada, his membership in Dutch Nazi support groups.

In December Michael Pawlowski of Renfrew, Ontario, was charged with eight counts of war crimes and crimes against humanity for his part in the killing of nearly 500 Jews and Poles in the summer of 1942 in Byelorussia.

The pace of government action on war criminals was criticized in some Jewish quarters. B'nai Brith blamed the slow course of prosecutions on government foot-dragging, and Irwin Cotler attacked the government's alleged inaction. But William Hobson, head of the war-crimes unit in the Department of Justice, defended the government's conduct, especially in comparison to other countries and in light of the difficulties in putting together cases that would stand up in court. Moreover, it was noted, Canada had became a party to an international agreement for the sharing of information that would aid in the apprehension and prosecution of war criminals. The other countries involved were Britain, Australia, and the Soviet Union. Meanwhile, the Simon Wiesenthal Center provided Hobson with a list of 21 Lithuanian immigrants who were allegedly members of a notorious murder squad, the 12th Lithuanian Police Battalion.

JEWISH COMMUNITY

Demography

In a controversial article,[1] University of Toronto sociologist Robert Brym asserted that the core of Canada's Jewish community was shrinking, even though the nominal Jewish population appeared to be on the increase. He attributed the increase to a "rediscovery of suppressed identity" on the part of assimilated Jews, but discounted its long-term significance. He claimed that in fact the high-identity ethnic group (those identifying themselves by ethnicity rather than religion on the census) had been dropping at a 1.4-percent annual rate since 1971. In his view this portended a dangerous future for the community, which, he suggested, should reach out and make itself more attractive to its peripheral members.

Charles Shahar of the Montreal federation, Allied Jewish Community Services (AJCS), completed a demographic study of Montreal Jewry based on the 1986 mid-decade census. He found an ethnic Jewish population (there was no religion question in 1986) of 96,470. This was higher than what many people had expected, but it was well below the peak of about 115,000 reached during the 1970s, before the Parti Québécois took power. Between the census of 1981 and that of 1986, the population of the key 15–34 age group declined by 3.1 percent, largely due to emigration, and immigration dropped by more than a third. Moreover, the proportion of senior citizens remained high, about double that of the general population. Thus, the community faced serious problems of providing services for the growing senior population and the prospect of a declining financial base in the younger groups.

Shahar's report also provided data relevant to the long-standing debate over the number of Sephardic Jews in Montreal. For years the Moroccan Jews who dominated the organizations representing Sephardic Jews had claimed that they were undercounted and thus denied an adequate voice in community decision making. On the basis of the census data, Shahar found that the population of Francophone

---

[1]"The Rise and Decline of Canadian Jewry? A Socio-Demographic Profile," in *Canadian Jewry Today: Who's Who in Canadian Jewry* (Downsview, Ont., 1989).

Jews—who comprised some 80 percent of the Sephardic community—was not nearly as large as spokespersons for that community often claimed. He showed about 10,000 Jews with French mother tongue, while nearly 60,000 listed English, and the rest listed another language. Some of those in the "other" category were undoubtedly non-French-speaking Sephardim (such as Iraqis), but Shahar's analysis gave reason to question the claims made by some of 25,000–30,000 Sephardic Jews in Montreal. The fact that virtually all Ashkenazi Jews in Montreal use English as their primary language, while most Sephardi Jews are French-speaking, created a persistent problem in community relations. During the year, the Communauté Sépharade du Québec announced plans to conduct its own census with a federal government grant. It was hoped that this count would clear up some of the ambiguity resulting from conflicting interpretations of the official census.

The Ontario Region of the CJC sponsored a study entitled "Assimilation, Intermarriage and Jewish Identity in Ontario." Based on 1984 data, the study estimated that about one-quarter of Jews who married did so outside the faith. Nevertheless, as York University sociologist Stuart Schoenfeld (the study's author) pointed out, Jews were less likely to intermarry than other religious groups and more likely "to maintain their cultural traditions and social distinctiveness." At the same time, he found Jews to be currently less involved in Jewish life than at other periods in Jewish history. Schoenfeld noted that unaffiliated Jews were more likely to intermarry than affiliated Jews, that Jews in central Canada (Ontario and Quebec) were less likely to intermarry than Jews in the other provinces, and that divorced Jews were more likely to intermarry than other Jews. The report called for a number of policy initiatives to stem the tide of intermarriage.

In February Statistics Canada released data from the 1986 census that showed incomes for 76 different ethnic groups. At $47,000, Jewish men had the highest average income in the study. B'nai Brith Canada attacked the release of such information, claiming that it would "only invoke tensions [and] jealousies between ethnocultural communities."

Communal Affairs

There was considerable focus this year on the formal structure of community organizations. Changes in the community and in its relationship to the external world that had occurred over a period of many years necessitated a reexamination of some key assumptions about the various bodies representing Canadian Jewry.

RESTRUCTURING OF CJC

Some of the most important changes involved the Canadian Jewish Congress, which was finding it increasingly difficult to remain independent of the federations because of its need to obtain funds from them. At the same time, Congress was criticized for occasionally overspending its budget and for getting involved in too many causes, such as abortion, the environment, and arms control, which did not represent strictly Jewish concerns. This dissatisfaction led to the establishment of a task force headed by Carleton University economics professor Harvey Lithwick. The report by that body, issued after two years of study, was quite critical of CJC, asserting that CJC's structure had been weakened, its mandate confused, and its legitimacy undermined. It called for greater CJC accountability to the National Budgeting Conference (NBC), the budgeting arm of the federations. In particular, CJC was admonished to stick to issues on which there was a clear Jewish interest and position. Furthermore, the report called for CJC to limit itself to genuinely national matters, leaving local issues to the federations rather than to Congress regions. Thus CJC would become "the key national programming arm of the federations and hence of NBC." It would engage in national advocacy and national planning, but would be responding to the priorities set by the federations rather than by an independent CJC constituency, as had been the case in the past.

The CJC held its triennial plenary assembly in Montreal in May. In addition to electing the relatively youthful Toronto team of Les Scheininger and Moshe Ronen as president and chairman of the national executive, respectively, the assembly deferred discussion of a restructuring plan that would have increased federation involvement but was not as broad as the Lithwick report.

In November both CJC and NBC negotiators agreed on the report's recommendations, which then had to be approved by the respective organizations. However, the national executive of Congress expressed a number of reservations at its December meeting. Among these were fears that the changes would lead to a takeover of Congress by the federations, apprehension that the needs of the small communities, especially those outside of Ontario and Quebec, would be overlooked in the new structure, and concern that some aspects of current CJC programming would be terminated. As the year ended, the CJC executive was studying the report and deciding what to do.

OTHER ORGANIZATIONS

Congress was not the only national organization whose future was in limbo. The Canada-Israel Committee (CIC), a partnership of CJC, B'nai Brith, the Canadian Zionist Federation (CZF), and the federations, was also being reevaluated. The motivation for the establishment of a five-member review committee headed by Toronto lawyer Donald Carr was the increasing willingness of the constituent organizations to embark on their own initiatives, instead of going through CIC, at a time when many saw a need for the community to represent Israel with a unified voice. The pressures associated with the *intifada* exacerbated an already tense situation. One of the issues before the committee was whether CIC should have the exclusive responsibility for public advocacy; another was whether it had sufficient human and material resources to carry out that task.

The Canadian Zionist Federation, one of the community's main national bodies, faced serious organizational and financial problems. It had been operating for a prolonged period without a top executive, partly because of a resource squeeze resulting from a sharp drop in support by the World Zionist Organization and a substantial accumulated deficit. The organization consolidated its staff and physical resources in order to cope with the new problems.

Financial problems were not limited to the CZF. The United Israel Appeal (UIA), which shared in the central community fund-raising campaigns on behalf of Israel, was unhappy that its share of the money collected had been declining in recent years, dropping below half by 1988. Part of the reason for this was a squeeze on total collections, which meant that UIA had to compete with local needs for increasingly scarce resources.

ISRAEL

Community positions on Israel continued to be a source of division, especially in light of the media attention focused on Israel because of the *intifada*. Some 80 Canadian Jews participated in Prime Minister Yitzhak Shamir's Solidarity Conference in Jerusalem in March, several in prominent roles. However, some Canadian Jews dissented from the dominant community position that opposed negotiating with the PLO and the establishment of a Palestinian state. The most notable dissenter was Milton Harris, former president of CJC, who asserted that community groups did not necessarily represent all Canadian Jews. He told the annual meeting of Canadian Friends of Peace Now in Toronto in September that many Jews were alienated from the mainline organizations and from leaders who supported Israel's policies without question. Harris expressed his belief that peace could not be achieved without the establishment of a Palestinian state. At the meeting, Peace Now president Mel Shipman called for a national poll of Canadian Jewish opinion on Israel-related issues in order to determine whether Harris was right about the existing community leadership being out of touch with the grass roots.

Similar issues were debated at a Montreal meeting in March between Prof. Frederick Krantz of the Canadian Institute for Jewish Research and Dr. Frank Guttman of Canadian Friends of Peace Now. Krantz argued that publicizing dissent beyond the community undermined Israel's political situation, while Guttman countered that dissent existed and could not be covered up. A further clash occurred at a Montreal meeting in October, where Stephen Cohen and Henry Weinberg debated issues related to various Middle East peace plans, especially the implications of the "land for peace" concept.

Education

Jewish education appeared to be flourishing in Toronto, despite the continuing failure to obtain government funding, but was running into some serious problems in Montreal. Toronto's Jewish day schools reported an increase in enrollments, with 9,039 children attending 12 day elementary schools and 7 day high schools. An additional 6,049 attended supplementary schools. The total of 15,088 compared to 10,892 pupils 11 years earlier. Approximately half of the Jewish children at any time were enrolled in Jewish education; however, the high dropout rate in the higher grades continued to be a matter of concern.

In Montreal, the United Talmud Torahs (UTT) system of day schools, once the largest on the continent, encountered a number of significant problems. The most prominent was the inability to find a location to build a new school in the suburb of Cote St. Luc to replace leased premises that were no longer available. On two occasions UTT bought an option or land itself, but was unable to obtain the necessary zoning clearance from the authorities in the predominantly Jewish town. Ultimately it was decided that the school would close in 1990 and would not be replaced. The elimination of this key feeder school threatened the viability of one of UTT's two Herzliah High Schools. UTT also closed a school in the suburb of Chomedey, leaving itself with a sharply reduced base. Ultimately the 93-year-old UTT, faced with crippling financial problems, agreed to submit to a joint management committee in which AJCS, the federation, would be the dominant partner. The committee's mandate was simple: "to ensure the continued viability" of the system. Toward the end of the year, plans were announced for a renovation of UTT's Snowdon campus. It was hoped that new physical facilities would help to stem the enrollment decline in the Herzliah High School located there.

The Joseph Wolinsky Collegiate Institute, a Jewish high school in Winnipeg, suffered serious fire damage in June. The school was rebuilt and reopened in the fall.

Community Relations

Several community-relations issues had to do with schools. As already noted, Ontario's Jews were still unsuccessful in obtaining government funding for their day schools. However, a small victory was achieved when the North York board of education agreed to fund "heritage language classes" in Hebrew—30 minutes per day—in Jewish private day schools. In Calgary, the Calgary Jewish Academy signed an agreement with the Catholic school board that allowed the school to receive government funding through the board. The aid was expected to amount to about $400,000 per year for the five-year period of the agreement, which essentially continued an arrangement that had been in existence since 1984 but with a longer time frame. The other day school in Calgary, Akiva Academy, received government aid through a different method.

Another innovative method of financing Jewish education was proposed by Jewish parents and the Laurenval school board in the Montreal suburb of Laval in the wake of the closing of the UTT school in Chomedey. Faced with an absence of Jewish schools, the Laval Jewish Community Council proposed that Jewish education, supervised independently by a Jewish body, be offered within the context of a Protestant school. The plan was going ahead, despite reservations among some Jewish educators that the new model, if successful, might undermine the existing day-school structure in Montreal, especially since fees were expected to be lower at the new school. The Jewish Education Council agreed to help with planning the Jewish component of the curriculum.

In Toronto a proposed Beth Jacob school in North York ran into opposition over land-use issues. Eventually the $10-million project, to be built by the Reichmanns' Olympia & York company, was approved by the North York board of education for a site formerly occupied by a public school that had been closed.

Prayer in the public school continued to pose problems for Canada's Jews. For example, Lincoln County, Ontario, persisted in using Christian prayers and Bible readings, despite a Court of Appeal decision that banned them. By contrast, the Ottawa board of education dropped daily recitation of the Lord's Prayer and substituted the singing of the national anthem and a minute of silence. Recitation of the Lord's Prayer at Metro Toronto and Toronto City Council meetings was also discontinued, after which Jewish councillors who had backed the move were subjected to harassing hate mail and telephone calls. The government of Manitoba, the only remaining province that required daily prayer in the public schools, was defending the practice against civil-libertarian efforts to abolish it. In Montreal, the efforts of Norman Spatz resulted in a decision to remove crosses from the walls of municipal courtrooms.

Jews were busy during the year building bridges to other ethnic groups. In the wake of a number of incidents that soured relationships between Jews and French Québécois, in September about 50 people from the two groups spent a day together in dialogue. Issues such as the language question and the attitude of the majority Francophones toward minority groups dominated the discussion, which was held in Montreal. Participants were business people, academics, professionals, clergy, community workers, and representatives of the arts. The discussions were characterized by an unusual degree of frankness and a willingness to grapple with difficult matters. Plans were made to continue the dialogue and perhaps to publicize the results.

Jews and Italians in Montreal joined to protest a November interview by the president of the Quebec Chamber of Commerce, in which he was sharply critical of groups that did not integrate into the Quebec mainstream and expressed the hope that Quebec would remain "white and Francophone." The Quebec Region of CJC and the National Congress of Italian Canadians protested the words and the underlying sentiment as a "divisive and disturbing message to send to Quebecers and potential immigrants." Also in Montreal, and Toronto as well, the newly formed Polish-Jewish Heritage Foundation initiated a regular dialogue between members of the two groups.

In legal developments of interest to the Jewish community, the federal government proposed amendments to the Divorce Act that would bar the granting of a civil divorce in a situation where one spouse was preventing the conferral of a *get,* a Jewish religious divorce document. (This tactic was often used as a bargaining chip, especially by men, in order to obtain a better settlement.) At least 233 such cases were documented between 1982 and 1985. The amendments, which were welcomed by Jewish groups, were expected to be enacted in 1990.

Montreal's YM-YWHA won a major victory in Quebec Superior Court, gaining exemption from property and school taxes that constituted a serious threat to its financial integrity. A back tax bill of $2.5 million was at stake, in addition to future obligations. The judge found that the Y was available for public use and therefore was tax-exempt. The city of Montreal decided to appeal, while Cote St. Luc and Laval, two municipalities with Y branches, agreed to accept the decision.

Soviet Jewry

Canadian Jews were active in a number of ways in behalf of Soviet Jewry. Politically they continued to press the federal government to intervene with the Soviet Union. A delegation from a major Toronto synagogue, Beth Tzedec, met with External Affairs Secretary Joe Clark in September to push for a freer Soviet emigration policy and more rapid decision making on emigration requests. They also met with Soviet embassy officials while in Ottawa.

In order to meet the increasing financial demands of Jewish emigration, the National Budgeting Conference provided funds to help support refugees in transit who were waiting to come to Canada. The appropriation replaced ad hoc budgeting arrangements. Officials of the Jewish Immigrant Aid Services (JIAS) estimated that the cost of supporting a person in transit in Italy was $3,600, while the first year in Canada for a family of four cost $17,000. The total cost to JIAS for settling Soviet Jews in 1989 was estimated to be about $2 million beyond the normal budget.

In 1988, some 350 Soviet Jews settled in Canada. Most Soviet Jews were attracted to Toronto, but a surprising number went to Edmonton, where Soviet Jews were estimated to comprise about 700 of the community's 4,500 Jews. About 40 to 45 additional families were expected in 1989.

Prof. Yakov Rabkin of the Université de Montréal was working with Jews who remained in the Soviet Union. He was instrumental, along with Israeli talmudist Rabbi Adin Steinsaltz, in establishing a program of advanced Jewish studies in Moscow, which opened in February and represented the first genuine yeshivah and university-level courses in Judaica offered since 1917.

Religion

A dispute over access to a mikveh in Toronto led to the construction of a new facility. When the Sheppard Avenue ritual bath was declared unavailable for conversion purposes in 1988, non-Orthodox rabbis believed that the move was aimed at them, because other mikvehs were available for Orthodox conversions. As a result, the Toronto Board of Rabbis decided to build a new one, which was named the Toronto Community Mikvah.

In Montreal, the Quebec Region of the Rabbinical Council of Canada created a commission and Beth Din (rabbinical court) to oversee and certify all conversions directed by Orthodox members of the council. Whereas previously witnesses were not all rabbis, conversions would henceforth have to be witnessed by three Orthodox rabbis. The impetus for the change came from the Chief Rabbinate in Israel, which sought to insure uniformity of documentation of converts who might settle in Israel. In Ontario, conversions were not carried out by individual Orthodox rabbis but by the Beth Din of the Vaad Harabonim (Rabbinical Council) of Toronto.

The Montreal community expanded its *eruv,* previously limited to only parts of the metropolitan area, to include virtually all areas where Jews lived. (An *eruv* is an unobtrusive boundary marker around an area that permits observant Jews within its limits to carry objects on the Sabbath.) The move required the cooperation of Mayor Jean Doré and the city council, which agreed to it in November. The new *eruv,* which was expected to be one of the largest on the continent when it went into operation in 1990, would be maintained by the Vaad Ha'ir, an Orthodox communal body. Montreal city councillor Saulie Zajdel played a major role in convincing the municipal authorities to cooperate.

The Harry Crowe Memorial Lectures at York University in Toronto in October were devoted to "The Current Religious Debate: Exclusiveness or Inclusiveness." Rabbi Dow Marmur's (Reform) call for a joint unity Beth Din of both Orthodox and non-Orthodox rabbis was supported by Rabbis Reuven Bulka (Orthodox) and Benjamin Friedberg (Conservative) but opposed by Rabbi Immanuel Schochet (Orthodox). Marmur's motivation was to try to counter tension among the different movements. A similar theme was voiced at the Toronto convention of the United Synagogue of America in November. That organization decided to launch a campaign for a unified conversion policy at the local community level in order to deal with what was described as the most urgent problem facing Jewry.

In April Canadian Jewish women organized prayer services to demonstrate their solidarity with the women who prayed at the Western Wall in Jerusalem and were objects of harassment and violence. In Toronto, some 70 women prayed together and then marched to the Israeli consulate to protest the treatment of the Jerusalem women. The Toronto women, from six different synagogues, were joined in their march by several men. A similar number of women participated in a prayer service at a Montreal synagogue.

The Grand Rebbe of the Belzer Hassidim, Rabbi Isachar Dov Rokach, visited his followers in the Montreal suburb of Outremont in June, where he officiated at the ground-breaking ceremony for a new school. One Outremont city councillor protested that a parade by the Belzer Hassidim on St. Jean Baptiste Day, Quebec's national holiday, was an affront to Quebecers, but he was sharply criticized by several fellow councillors. The parade, with some 5,000 people participating, took place late Saturday night and lasted until the early hours of Sunday morning. A letter to the editor of a Montreal newspaper argued that a unilingual Hebrew banner on Durocher Street, welcoming the Rebbe, constituted a "profound insult to our nation" and a "degradation of the city of Outremont by foreigners."

Culture

The Marc Chagall exhibit at the Montreal Museum of Fine Arts, which opened in late 1988, attracted over 250,000 visitors before it closed in February. It was the first major Canadian exhibition of Chagall's work.

Montreal architect Phyllis Lambert helped to design and finance the Canadian Center for Architecture, which opened its doors in Montreal in May. The objective of the project was to further the development of the study and art of architecture and to demonstrate its relevance to human values. (Lambert is the daughter of the late Samuel Bronfman and the sister of Edgar and Charles.)

The Saidye Bronfman Center, the cultural focus of Montreal's Jewish community for over two decades, built an annex financed by the Bronfman family. The annex housed six fine-arts studios and administrative offices.

The University of Toronto established a center for Jewish studies, to be financed through a $1-million campaign. The acting chairman was Prof. Arthur Kruger. Queen's University in Kingston, Ontario, received an endowed chair in Jewish studies, only the second such chair in the country.

David Rome, archivist and historian of Canadian Jewry, was honored for nearly five decades of work. CJC's National Archives chairman Irving Abella presented him with a plaque at a September ceremony in recognition of a lifetime of accomplishment, including a lengthy publication list on many aspects of Canadian Jewish life. Abella observed that "no one has done more to keep alive and vibrant the study of Jewish life than David Rome," whom he described as a "national treasure."

Three Canadian cantors, David Bagley and Louis Danto of Toronto and Yaacov Motzen of Montreal, participated in two different concert tours of the Soviet Union and Eastern European countries, to introduce the Jews there to modern cantorial music. Serge Ouaknine's play *Marianne—Intérieur Nuit,* which opened in Montreal in May, commemorated the bicentennial of the French Revolution but also dealt with revolutions in general. The play ends in Auschwitz because, as Ouaknine put it, "the French Revolution was the beginning of the automatization of death." *The Courting of Sally Schwartz,* by another Montrealer, Aviva Ravel, opened in December. It depicts a romantic relationship between an American and an Israeli.

Half the Kingdom, a National Film Board production directed by Francine Zuckerman and Roushell Goldstein, is a documentary about the role of women in Judaism. It profiles seven women, three of them Canadian: Toronto columnist Michelle Landsberg, Ottawa religious studies professor Naomi Goldenberg, and Montreal feminist scholar and activist Norma Baumel Joseph. The film premiered in Halifax in November and had openings in Toronto and several other cities in

December. Morley Markson's film *Growing Up in America* opened and won a prize at the Chicago Film Festival.

Publications

University of Toronto historian Michael Marrus edited *The Nazi Holocaust,* a 15-volume work containing some 300 scholarly articles on the subject.

The 18th-century false messiah Jacob Frank is the subject of Rabbi W. Gunther Plaut's historical novel *The Man Who Would Be Messiah.* Naim Kattan, the Iraqi-born writer now living in Ottawa, published a novel, *La Fortune du Passager* ("The Traveler's Fortune"), on the theme of changing cultures without losing one's identity.

Canada's foreign policy on the Middle East is analyzed in *The Domestic Battleground: Canada and the Middle East Conflict,* edited by David Taras and David H. Goldberg. In general, the contributions show the difficulties encountered by pro-Israel forces in attempting to influence Canadian policy.

Wild Gooseberries: The Selected Letters of Irving Layton, edited by Francis Mansbridge, contains a number of outspoken pieces by the controversial poet, dating back to 1939.

New works of fiction include: *Solomon Gursky Was Here* by Mordecai Richler; *Winter Tulips* by Joseph Kertes; *A Gift of Sky* by Linda Ghan; and *Ritual Slaughter* by Sharon Drache. New nonfiction works include: *The Garden and the Gun: A Journey Through Israel* by Erna Paris; *When Freedoms Collide* by A. Alan Borovoy; *Whence They Came: Deportation from Canada* by Barbara Roberts; *Jesus and the Judaism of His Time* by Irving Zeitlin; *Walking Toward Elijah* by Rabbi Dow Marmur; *Rites of Spring: The Great War and the Birth of the Modern Age* by Modris Eksteins; *What You Thought You Knew About Judaism* by Rabbi Reuven Bulka; *This Is New York, Honey* by Michelle Landsberg; *Some People, Some Time Ago* by Mitchell Wagner; and *Third Solitudes: Canadian Jewish Authors* by Michael Greenstein.

Personalia

Sidney Altman shared the Nobel Prize in Chemistry. Gerry Weiner was given a new cabinet post: secretary of state. Justice Bonnie Helper became the first woman appointed to the Manitoba Court of Appeal, that province's highest court. Morris Fish was appointed to Quebec's top tribunal, the Court of Appeal, while former Quebec justice minister Herbert Marx joined Quebec Superior Court. Gerald Berger was appointed to the new Free Trade Review Board. Euninie Cohen was elected a vice-president of the Progressive Conservative party. Prof. Marsha Hainen became president of the University of Winnipeg. Rose Sheinin was appointed vice-rector (academic) at Concordia University. Dr. Morrie Gelfand was awarded the Order of Canada. Steve Goldman became the coach of the Ottawa Rough Riders.

Within the community: Joann Smith was elected president of Women's Canadian ORT; Ian Kagedan was appointed governmental affairs director of B'nai Brith Canada; Karen Mock became national director of the League for Human Rights of B'nai Brith Canada; Patricia Rucker was appointed editor of the *Canadian Jewish News;* Morris Zilka was appointed executive vice-president of the Jewish National Fund of Canada; Dr. Eli Rabin was elected president of Ottawa's Vaad Hair; Eric Slavens and Goldie Hershon were chosen as chairpersons of CJC's Ontario and Quebec Regions, respectively; Lionel Goldman was elected president of the Montreal YM-YWHA; Sidney Indig was appointed director of the Edmonton Jewish Federation; Rabbi Bernard Baskin retired after 40 years in the pulpit of Temple Anshe Shalom in Hamilton; and Dr. Elaine R. S. Cohen was appointed director of educational services at UTT in Montreal.

The J.I. Segal Awards for literary or educational accomplishments were presented to Yiddish literature professor Ruth Wisse, for *A Little Love in Big Manhattan,* and to Raizel Fishman Candib and Batia Bettman, Jewish educators. The book awards of the Toronto Jewish Congress Cultural Council were presented to Michael Marrus for *The Holocaust in History* and to Szloma Renglich for *When Paupers Dance.* Garth Drabinsky became the first Canadian to win the B'nai B'rith International Distinguished Achievement Award. Dr. Victor Goldbloom was awarded the Samuel Bronfman Medal by AJCS, for his work in behalf of the community. Prof. Arthur Lermer received the Rosenfeld Foundation for Yiddish Culture Award for the promotion of Yiddish language and culture. Seymour Levitan won the Robert Payne Award for his editing and translation of Rachel Korn's poems in *Paper Roses.*

Among leading Jews who died in 1989 were the following: longtime journalist Charles Lazarus, in January, aged 71; Rabbi Joseph Rodal, bookseller and former principal of the Rabbinical College of Canada, in February, aged 75; labor lawyer and community leader Louis Orenstein, in March, aged 76; Arnold Finkler, partisan leader, Holocaust survivor, and philanthropist, in April; former journalist Anne Lerner Notkin, in April, aged 86; immigration lawyer Eli Michael Berger, in May, aged 77; Leon Weinstein, supermarket executive and community leader, in May, aged 81; Rabbi Samuel Sachs, who served Goel Tzedec Synagogue in Toronto from 1927 to 1946, in May, aged 96; Joseph Berman, community leader, in May, aged 90; television broadcaster Phyllis Switzer, in July, aged 57; noted theatrical director John Hirsch, in August, aged 59; Sholem Goodman, educator and principal, in August, aged 86; sculptor Alice Winant, in August, aged 60; Kitchener leader Rabbi Phyvle Rosensweig, in November, aged 58; engineer and business executive Abbey Sankoff, in November, aged 80; Ruth Frankel, first woman Companion of the Order of Canada, in November, aged 86; Mattie Rotenberg, pioneer physicist and Toronto day-school founder, in December, aged 92; and Ralph Hyman, former editor of the *Canadian Jewish News,* in December, aged 83.

HAROLD M. WALLER

Western Europe

Great Britain

National Affairs

On May 3, 1989, Margaret Thatcher celebrated the completion of ten years as prime minister. The anniversary brought no relief, however, from the problems, primarily economic, facing the country in general and the Conservative government in particular. In February the annual rate of inflation rose to 7.5 percent and in June to 8.3 percent, the highest in seven years. When, in August, the monthly trade deficit reached £2.06 billion, the second largest on record, there was no alternative for the government but to raise base lending rates to 15 percent, the highest in eight years. In October Chancellor of the Exchequer Nigel Lawson resigned unexpectedly. Although he gave as his reason his long-running disagreement with Sir Alan Walters, the prime minister's economic adviser, it was clear that Lawson and the prime minister were also at odds over the question of British entry into the European Monetary System. A badly handled reshuffle of senior government posts in July had earlier added to Mrs. Thatcher's embarrassment.

The repercussions were felt in the political sphere. In the June elections for the European Parliament, Labor took 45 of the 78 British seats; and in December, 60 Tory MPs failed to vote for the prime minister in the first Tory leadership contest in 14 years. Mrs. Thatcher's opponent was Sir Anthony Meyer.

The principal beneficiaries of economic difficulties and Tory disarray were Neil Kinnock and the Labor party. The center parties virtually collapsed as Labor enjoyed a period of resurgence. Over the year as a whole, polls showed Labor leading the Tories by between 5 and 10 points and ending the year with a lead of 7 points. This was not only a negative reflection of the government's problems but a tribute to Labor's decision—finally approved in June—to drop such unpopular policies as unilateral disarmament, renationalization, and high taxation. Labor began to talk the more acceptable language of free markets, improved public services (including the National Health Service), and private property.

Relations with Israel

Throughout the year the government strove to convince Israeli leaders that Britain's policy was unchanged. Its aim, Foreign Minister Sir Geoffrey Howe told the *Jewish Chronicle* in January, was to secure the establishment within secure and recognized borders of the State of Israel in conditions of peace and security, while recognizing the right of the Palestinian people to self-determination. These objectives, he said, could only be secured by negotiations in circumstances free from violence.

Although Britain seemed prepared to take a back seat in these negotiations—the United States and not Britain was the main third party in Arab-Israeli negotiations, Prime Minister Thatcher emphasized in January—it was anxious to play a constructive role in promoting peace talks under U.S. leadership. Both Thatcher and Minister of State at the Foreign Office William Waldegrave urged Israel to take advantage of the new opportunities opened up by the Palestine Liberation Organization's alleged preparedness to talk and recognition of Israel's right to exist. Thatcher repeated this call during London visits by Israeli foreign minister Moshe Arens in February and Prime Minister Yitzhak Shamir in May, and again when she was in Morocco in March. Waldegrave, in Israel in February and March, emphasized that "the proliferation of weapons within the region and the inexorable demographic changes are powerful reasons why the problem will only become more intractable if the opportunity is missed."

Egyptian involvement in the peace process was explored when Thatcher met Egypt's foreign minister, Dr. Esmat Abdel-Meguid, in London in June, and when Waldegrave told Parliament in October that the government fully supported Egyptian efforts to seek clarification of Shamir's election proposals and to promote talks in Cairo between the Israeli government and Palestinians from inside and outside the occupied territories. In November Waldegrave had talks in Cairo with Egyptian president Hosni Mubarak and other leaders about the stalled peace process.

"It remains our policy that a confederation or some kind of confederate state is the right outcome," Waldegrave told the House of Commons in January, and Thatcher repeated throughout the year that Britain did not support demands for an independent Palestinian state. Although no visit to Britain by PLO leader Yasir Arafat was seriously mooted, government officials on several occasions held talks with PLO representatives. The PLO had met the criteria for Britain to hold discussions with them, Waldegrave told Jewish communal leaders protesting his meeting with Arafat in Tunis in January, when he also provoked a strong Israeli reaction by seeming to equate the former terrorist activities of some Israeli leaders with those of the PLO. Waldegrave also met with Bassam Abu Sharif, Arafat's political adviser, in London in January, and angered the Israeli embassy in London by his apparent acceptance of Abu Sharif's denial of Arafat's threat to "give ten bullets in the chest" to anyone who tried to stop the *intifada*. Abu Sharif had talks at the Foreign Office in April and in July met with Foreign Minister Howe. The Foreign

Office explained that the purpose of this first meeting between a cabinet minister and a PLO official, condemned by Israel's London embassy, was to encourage the PLO to stick to its moderate policy. The meeting was just a "short call" and did not represent an upgrading of relations between Britain and the PLO. In October senior Foreign Office official David Gore-Booth met with Arafat in Tunis.

Britain made no secret of its views on Israeli policy. In March Tim Eggar, undersecretary of state at the Foreign Office, described Israel's continuing military presence in southern Lebanon as "provocative, destabilizing and against Israel's long-term interests." In May the Foreign Office condemned Israel's handling of rioting Gaza crowds when four Arabs were killed and over 140 injured. The human cost of the tactics pursued by Israeli armed forces was "intolerable," a Foreign Office statement said. In June Britain voted in favor of a United Nations Security Council resolution condemning Israeli policies in the occupied territories. In August the Foreign Office condemned the seizure by Israeli commandos of Sheikh Abdel Karim Obeid, key figure in Hezballah terrorism in south Lebanon, but made it clear that it did not hold Israel responsible for Hezballah's retaliatory killing of U.S. Lt. Col. William Higgins.

In May the British government rejected Israel's request to buy gas masks as protection against chemical warfare, as such equipment was on the list of items banned under the British arms embargo imposed on Israel because of the invasion of Lebanon.

The Labor party's new Middle East policy—published by its national executive in May and approved by the party conference in October—called for the Palestinians to be free from Israeli occupation but stressed that built-in guarantees for Israel's security were essential. It showed a "marked improvement" on earlier Labor party pronouncements, said Peter Gruneberger, director of Labor and Trade Union Friends of Israel. The new policy recognized the PLO as the "internationally recognized representative of the Palestine people," called for a peace conference involving Israel, the PLO, and Israel's Arab neighbors to be convened by the UN Security Council, and urged Israel to talk to the PLO on the basis of Arafat's assurances. Although the document said "Jerusalem must never again be obscenely divided," Labor's October conference passed a resolution calling for a Palestinian state and the internationalization of Jerusalem.

Labor continued to find fault with Israeli policy in the territories. In February Manchester city council's ruling Labor group vetoed an official visit to Israel by its lord mayor "at this time." In June over 80 Labor MPs signed a motion calling on the government to introduce limited sanctions against Israel "to prevent an escalation of brutality in the occupied territories and to encourage the Israeli government to enter meaningful negotiations." In July the Labor-controlled Nottingham city council canceled a reception in honor of Israeli ambassador Yoav Biran in protest of Israel's treatment of the Arabs on the West Bank.

The leadership of the Conservative Friends of Israel (CFI) was divided on Middle East policy. In January Michael Latham, CFI's parliamentary group vice-president and chairman of the all-party British-Israel parliamentary group, said Israel would have to get used to the new reality of an internationally respectable PLO or become "totally isolated." But CFI director Michael Fidler wrote to the prime minister and foreign secretary urging them to avoid meeting Arafat, who "was and still is the leader of an international terrorist movement." Robert Rhodes James, CFI's new parliamentary group chairman, warmly welcomed British initiative in beginning a real dialogue with the PLO, after it had renounced terrorism and accepted Israel's right to independent existence. He was, he said, saddened by the Israeli government's negative response. In April he told a Zionist Federation (ZF) meeting that "the overwhelming majority of CFI strongly supports the growing number in Israel itself which favors the opening of negotiations with PLO." Both Latham and Rhodes James criticized Israel's kidnapping of Sheikh Obeid in August. "My concern as a British MP," said Latham, "is not just with Israel's prisoners but also with British hostages in Lebanon" whose position may have been made more difficult. With a membership of more than 200 MPs, including the prime minister and some cabinet ministers, CFI was one of the largest lobbying groups in the House of Commons.

A Conservative Friends of Palestine group was launched at a meeting addressed by the PLO's London representative, Faisal Oweida, at the party conference in Blackpool in October.

In June a new Social and Liberal Democrats Friends of Israel was formed.

Nazi War Criminals

The War Crimes Inquiry set up in February 1988 to investigate alleged Nazi war criminals living in Britain recommended in July that the law be changed to allow prosecution of people who were currently British citizens or living in the United Kingdom for war crimes committed in Germany or German-occupied territory during World War II. The 109-page Hetherington-Chalmer Report said sufficient evidence already existed against at least three individuals to warrant criminal prosecution. Of almost 300 names submitted to the inquiry, 75 needed further investigation and another 46 persons had to be traced. Because of the age and frailty of the witnesses, the report recommended use of live TV hook-ups to question those residing outside the United Kingdom. Commenting on the report, Home Secretary Douglas Hurd said, "We are impressed by the force of the argument that led the inquiry to its clear conclusion that legislation was required."

The Jewish community launched a major lobbying campaign prior to the introduction of a bill in the House of Commons to enable prosecution of war criminals. A war-crimes campaign rally was held in Manchester in October. The Union of Jewish Students (UJS) sent an information kit to every college in the country and lobbied more than 150 MPs at the House of Commons. The parliamentary All-Party War Crimes Group held a rally in London and organized a conference attended by Nazi hunters from Canada, Australia, and the United States, some 40 MPs, lawyers, historians, and Holocaust survivors and chaired by Merlyn Rees, former Labor home secretary. Simon Wiesenthal and Chief Rabbi Lord Jakobovits appeared on national television to urge passage of the bill, and a public meeting held at Friends' House, London, heard Tory MP Rupert Allason warn that Britain would stand alone with Syria as a haven for Nazi war criminals if the law was not changed.

In December the bill obtained a convincing majority in the House of Commons (348 votes to 123); in the Upper House, however—despite a moving appeal by Chief Rabbi Jakobovits—a clear majority voted against the legislation. At the end of the year it was expected that a cabinet committee, headed by Prime Minister Thatcher, would meet to consider further action.

In July lawyers for alleged war criminal Antanas Gecas prevented Scottish Television from showing a documentary film, *Crimes of War,* on the grounds that it would be prejudicial to Parliament's consideration of the war-crimes report. The program alleged that Gecas, aged 71, who lived in Edinburgh, was involved in the mass slaughter of Jews in his native Lithuania in 1941.

In October a Ministry of Defense Inquiry concluded that Austrian president Kurt Waldheim was not responsible for the murder of British servicemen that occurred when he was a Nazi intelligence officer in Greece. It also rejected charges that Britain had covered up to protect Waldheim after 1945.

Anti-Semitism and Anti-Zionism

Fewer anti-Semitic incidents were reported in the first three months of 1989 than in the same period in 1988, according to the Board of Deputies of British Jews. In the London borough of Barnet, where an estimated 20 percent of the population was Jewish, 14 out of a total of 80 cases of racial attack and discrimination were directed explicitly against Jews, according to the local Community Relations Council's annual report. "Given the number of Jews in the area," said a Board of Deputies spokesman, "the number is not significant." No marked increase was reported in the number of racial incidents in the London borough of Hackney, where 20 Jews were victims of racial harassment in 1988 and where Scotland Yard launched a London-wide information campaign against racial harassment in January.

The Holocaust memorial in London's Hyde Park was desecrated on two consecutive weekends in August, coinciding with neo-Nazi demonstrations in North London.

A controversial meeting of Euro-Ring, an underground network of European neo-Nazis, took place in Birmingham in May, after a Board of Deputies request that neo-Nazis be denied entry to Britain was refused. By contrast, in May Camden Council canceled a scheduled concert at Camden Center, Central London, sponsored by extreme right-wing groups.

Organized anti-Israel activity took various forms this year, but was most evident on the campus. In May some 150 Muslims marched through Manchester in an anti-Israel protest. In February the deputy PLO representative in London, Karma

Nabulsi, called for a boycott of Israeli goods; in November organizations supporting the Palestinians launched a "Boycott Israeli goods and holidays" movement.

Though the annual National Union of Students (NUS) conference in Blackpool in March was described as one of the most hostile to Israel in recent memory, NUS's president banned a leaflet distributed by the General Union of Palestinian Students that accused Israel of seeking the genocide of the Palestinians in the 1982 Lebanon invasion. An NUS antiracism conference in November also condemned as anti-Semitism a ban on Jewish Society participation in a London School of Economics (LSE) antiracism event on the grounds that Zionism was racist. The LSE student union later passed a motion condemning both left- and right-wing anti-Semitism.

The Sunderland Polytechnic student union defeated a motion equating Zionism with racism but passed an amendment recommending a policy of mutual recognition of Palestinian and Israeli rights. A policy of mutual recognition was also adopted by Manchester University students after the defeat of a motion condemning Israel's response to the *intifada,* proposed by Students for Palestine.

The University of Manchester's Institute for Science and Technology (UMIST) was a center of conflict this year. In May Muslim fundamentalists disrupted Jewish students' Israel Independence Day celebrations. In October UMIST's student union barred the Islamic Cultural Society for a month, after the group distributed anti-Semitic literature at the Freshers' Fair. When the union tried to reduce tension between Muslim and Jewish students by issuing a code of conduct treating both groups as equals, the UMIST Jewish Society rejected the code, claiming that Jews were victims and should not be viewed in the same light as their aggressors. In December Islamic activists failed in an attempt to have the Israeli flag and Israeli produce banned from the campus, and an anti-Israel motion at the student union was defeated.

JEWISH COMMUNITY

Demography

The Jewish population of Great Britain was estimated at 330,000.

The total number of synagogue marriages rose in 1988 for the first time in six years, according to the Board of Deputies Community Research Unit. At 1,104, it was 5.2 percent above the 1987 figure of 1,049. Within the total, the number of Progressive marriages declined (from 246 in 1987 to 228 in 1988), the largest drop occurring in the Liberal sector (from 62 to 46), while there were increases throughout the Orthodox community. Of the 702 marriages in the Central Orthodox group in 1988 (659 in 1987), 10 percent of the individuals involved had been married before.

The statistics suggested that two-thirds of young single Jews of marriageable age were not marrying in a synagogue, the research unit reported, a fact that raised concern for the community's future.

Burials and cremations under Jewish auspices fell to 4,420 in 1988 from 4,486 in 1987.

Birth statistics, based on *brit milah* (circumcision) data, showed a rise to 3,532 in 1987 from annual averages of 3,332 in 1982–86 and 3,299 in 1977–81.

British Jewry and Israel

Britain's Jewish community was "agonizingly split" over the *intifada,* the peace process, and talks with the PLO, said "shadow" foreign secretary Gerald Kaufman, whose meetings with PLO leaders, including Yasir Arafat, were condemned by some sectors of the community. Kaufman was talking to a meeting of the left-wing Zionist organization Mapam, also addressed by West Bank activist Faisal Husseini in London in March. In January the right-wing National Zionist Council passed a resolution condemning British policy vis-à-vis the PLO, while the Zionist Labor movement Poale Zion called on Israel to test the PLO's sincerity about participation in the peace process. In February British Friends of Peace Now organized the first public meeting in Britain between a Knesset member (Ran Cohen of the left-wing Citizens' Rights Movement) and PLO's London representative, Faisal Oweida.

Only 50 or so of the 130 British Jews invited to Prime Minister Yitzhak Shamir's Solidarity with Israel conference in Jerusalem in March chose to attend. It was thought that some, at least, boycotted the conference to prevent Shamir from using it to claim Diaspora support for his policies. (The critics included philosopher Sir Isaiah Berlin and MPs Greville Janner and Ivan Lawrence.) Shamir visited London in May and was greeted with a supportive reception by British Jewry at London's Guildhall, organized by various Zionist groups and the Joint Israel Appeal (JIA). During that visit there were also critical letters from Jews in the *Guardian* newspaper and a pro-Palestinian demonstration at Downing Street in which members of the Jewish Socialist Group took part.

Divided sympathies on the Board of Deputies came to a head in September, after June Jacobs, foreign affairs committee chairwoman, met PLO official Bassam Abu Sharif. In response to calls for Mrs. Jacobs's resignation, President Lionel Kopelowitz said that "while there is certainly room for differing points of view on points of detail, there must be basic agreement on fundamental issues." In November Mrs. Jacobs agreed not to confer with PLO members while she remained a committee head.

In November Lord Goodman, president of the Institute of Jewish Affairs, shared a platform with Hani al-Hassan, Yasir Arafat's chief political adviser, at a meeting that was organized by the independent Radical Society, chaired by Evelyn de Rothschild, and attended by William Waldegrave and Faisal Oweida. The Radical Society announced plans for a second meeting that would allow the Israel government's point of view to be aired.

Communal Activities

The Jewish Welfare Board (JWB) was attempting to meet the needs resulting from government cutbacks, such as providing care for Alzheimer's-disease patients discharged when large long-term mental hospitals, especially around London, were closed. In April JWB announced the purchase of a site in Hendon, North-West London, for a £400,000-center to provide services for people suffering from mental illness and for their families.

The combined family-center approach, already operating in Redbridge and Edgware, was extended to Hackney, where over 5,000 elderly Jews lived in difficult inner-city conditions. In January JWB, the Jewish Blind Society, Ravenswood Foundation, and Norwood Child Care formed the Hackney Jewish Family Service, with a staff of 26 social workers and specialists. In April Norwood and Ravenswood announced plans to build a center in Hendon to give respite to families in crisis, thus providing a new dimension to the services offered by children's agencies.

In December Norwood received official approval from the secretary of state for health to start the Norwood Jewish Adoption Society, the first of its kind in Britain, in April 1990. It would have legal authority to deal with all aspects of the adoption of Jewish children and to ensure that all Jewish children available for adoption remained within the community.

Soviet Jewry

Organizations working in behalf of Soviet Jewry responded differently to the radical changes taking place in Eastern Europe this year. For example, not all groups welcomed the February visit to Britain by the Shalom Jewish Theater group of Moscow, primarily because it was under the auspices of Vanessa Redgrave Productions and backed by the Soviet Anti-Zionist Committee. Responding to critics of the visit, Neil Bradman, National Council for Soviet Jewry chairman, who attended the only official Jewish reception for the company, which was hosted by the Institute of Jewish Affairs, said: "It is important that those involved in the campaign attend such meetings so that they can fully appreciate the complexity of the situation."

When the Bolshoi Ballet visited Britain in the summer, cochairwoman Margaret Rigal of the Women's Campaign for Soviet Jewry (35s) thought it "appalling" that the Ben Gurion University Foundation should use a ballet performance as a fund-raising event. "We are still working for refuseniks who want to leave the Soviet Union," Rigal said. "While that continues, we deplore any semi-official acknowledgement of such companies as the Bolshoi Ballet which is closely associated with the Soviet regime." Opposing her view, Bradman noted that "when Soviet artists and organizations are performing in Israel, I can not see why Jewish organizations in the diaspora should not support the Bolshoi." The 35s demonstrated outside the London Coliseum at the controversial performance in July, which raised over £40,000.

Differences over policy emerged again in August when the chief rabbi's Rosh Hashanah message upset some Soviet Jewry activists by suggesting that there was too much concentration on demanding emigration rights for Soviet Jews and not enough on improving the religious and cultural life of those wanting to stay in the Soviet Union. In October John Fenner, incoming chairman of the National Council, said that a "complete refocusing" of the movement for Russian Jewry was needed to meet the dramatic political changes in the Soviet Union.

Conventional protest methods were still employed, however. Prior to President Mikhail Gorbachev's two-day official visit to Britain in April, the National Council lobbied William Waldegrave, Neil Kinnock, and Norman Willis, Trade Union Congress general secretary. Leading members of British WIZO petitioned Prime Minister Thatcher to press Gorbachev to allow all Jewish mothers, wives, and families to go to Israel. Members of the West London Synagogue and the Student and Academic Campaign for Soviet Jewry (SACSJ) mounted a vigil outside the Soviet embassy following Gorbachev's arrival, while a daylong refusenik celebrity roll call took place at the entrance to Downing Street, where he had talks. The All-Party Parliamentary Committee for the Release of Soviet Jewry placed an advertisement in the *Times* criticizing the Soviet Union for its abuse of human rights. In their meetings, Thatcher told Gorbachev that, though Britain was pleased that the Soviet Union was granting permission to many refuseniks to leave the Soviet Union, further measures were needed to satisfy public opinion.

Neil Bradman was invited to be the first nongovernmental representative on the British government delegation to the June Human Rights conference in Paris, at which members of SACSJ lobbied delegates. SACSJ also committed itself to a two-year program to pressure Gorbachev on human rights, prior to the planned 1991 human-rights conference in Moscow.

Religion

The process of choosing a successor to Chief Rabbi Jakobovits when he reached the retirement age of 70 in February 1991 began in January 1989. The Chief Rabbinate conference, representing all sections of the community, established a 36-member committee to consider methods of selecting and appointing the chief rabbi, his duties and salary, the funding of his office, and the relationship of the Chief Rabbinate to its congregations. The committee comprised 15 United Synagogue (US) representatives, 5 from the Federation of Synagogues, 12 from the provinces, 1 from overseas, the chairman of Jews' College, and the president of the National Shechita Council, and was headed by US president Sidney Frosh. In April it appointed a 10-member subcommittee, whose first task was to concentrate on the terms, duties, and funding of the office. As the year drew to a close, Rabbi Dr. Jonathan Sacks emerged as the favorite in the search for a new chief rabbi.

A statement by the Union of Liberal and Progressive Synagogues (ULPS) in December said that the chief rabbi had no authority to speak for its members. Rosita Rosenberg, ULPS director, said the statement was issued at a time when Lord

Jakobovits's successor was being chosen to make clear that "our relationship to the office of the Chief Rabbi is not dependent on the person who fills it."

The US membership numbered some 110,000 people—about half of London Jewry and one-third of all British Jews. Members complained in April when synagogue membership fees were increased—in some congregations to over £400. For financial reasons, the US closed its Israel office, which had been opened on a six-month experimental basis as a drop-in center for US members visiting Israel.

The average age of the officers of the traditional Orthodox, right-of-center Federation of Synagogues fell from 76 to 54 when its 80-year-old president, Morris Lederman, resigned after 36 years in office and after elections in March swept out the old guard. Accountant Arnold Cohen (aged 52) was elected president, unopposed. Cohen told the *Jewish Chronicle* that the new officers would be investigating possibilities of creating new congregations, but that there would definitely be no merger with the United Synagogue. Meanwhile, some London Federation synagogues in aging and declining communities reported falling membership: at Clapton, founded 70 years ago, membership had declined from 900 at its peak to less than 400; Leytonstone and Wanstead had a total membership of 100 families, compared with 250 in the 1960s. In March, members of Shepherds Bush and Fulham Synagogue voted to close their 76-year-old institution.

The two representative bodies of British Sephardim, the Sephardi Federation of Great Britain and the British Sephardi Council, agreed in April to work together for a year as the Confederation of British Sephardim before considering a final merger. The two bodies were formed in 1986 after a dispute with the World Sephardi Federation. The three London synagogues of the Spanish and Portuguese Jews' Congregation—Bevis Marks, Lauderdale Road, and Wembley—had a combined membership of some 1,500.

The Campaign for the Protection of Shechita opposed the government's proposed new animal-slaughter legislation, describing the main change introduced—that animals had to be slaughtered in an upright pen instead of the present revolving one—as "halachically unacceptable." Dayan Yaacov Lichtenstein, head of the Federation Beth Din, and some rabbis of the Union of Orthodox Hebrew Congregations joined the protest, but the majority of British rabbinic authorities saw no objection to the new regulation. In July Chief Rabbi Jakobovits wrote to Agriculture Minister John MacGregor on behalf of all sectors of the Orthodox community expressing satisfaction that the proposals safeguarded the basic elements of kosher slaughter, but noting some anxiety about the wording of the regulations.

In September the United Synagogue formed its own slaughtering operation and withdrew from the projected London Shechita Authority (LSA), scheduled to replace the London Board for Shechita. The move followed a dispute between the US and the lay board of management formed to run the LSA and comprising representatives of the US, the Federation, the Spanish and Portuguese Jews' Congregation, and the independent Western Synagogue. Its withdrawal, the US claimed, was based on the management committee's refusal to guarantee that it "would carry out all the instructions of the rabbinical board concerning the performance and supervision of shechita." US officials denied Federation claims that the dispute was precipitated when the management committee rejected rabbinic orders to appoint Rabbi Osher Ehrentreu as the LSA's rabbinic coordinator.

In January a £1-million appeal was launched to furnish and decorate the new Liberal Jewish Synagogue in London's St. John's Wood, which would include a day-care center and nursery facilities. The synagogue and a block of flats were being built on the site of the old demolished synagogue building and were due to be completed in autumn 1990.

A new organization, Bamah (Forum), was formed in January by members of Progressive, Orthodox, Sephardi, and Masorti synagogues to promote inter-Jewish dialogue.

Education

In January the United Synagogue proposed an expenditure of £2.16 million on educational activities in 1989, from a total budget of £2.69 million. The US was disappointed by the results of a new arrangement made with the Joint Israel Appeal whereby one-third of all proceeds from the Kol Nidre appeal in US synagogues would go to education. The 1989 appeal raised less than hoped for: a total of £630,000 . Of the 1988 total, £500,000 went to Israel, £123,000 to British education.

Plans to open Immanuel College, the new Jewish secondary school in Bushey, Hertfordshire, in September 1990, appeared to be in jeopardy when the Jewish Educational Development Trust (JEDT) had difficulty raising the necessary funds. The crisis was precipitated in August by the surprise resignation from various communal posts of businessman Stanley Kalms, chairman of JEDT and Jews' College, and driving force behind the new school. Kalms explained that he had been active in communal leadership long enough, but it was rumored that he was unhappy over the inadequate fund-raising support for the school. JEDT trustees planned to meet in the new year to decide the future of the school, named after Chief Rabbi Immanuel, Lord Jakobovits.

Shortages of teachers of Jewish studies and Hebrew caused the Institute of Jewish Education at Jews' College to start a recruitment drive in January. In July the US raised salaries of Jewish studies teachers at its Jewish Free School, which employed 16 teachers for its 1,400 pupils. In February the US council voted for a major restructuring of its part-time religion classes, described by critics as "sterile, archaic and fundamentally wasteful." Plans included absorbing smaller synagogue classes into area centers, phasing out examinations, and making the curriculum more practical than academic.

Chief Rabbi Jakobovits reported in July that Jews' College had completed the most successful year in its 132-year history, with a record student intake of around 100, including part-time students. By December 129 students were enrolled, and a new one-year course leading to a certificate in higher Jewish studies had been started. This was in response to suggestions at a "Traditional Alternatives" conference sponsored by the college in May to examine Orthodoxy and the future of the Jewish people.

In June Leo Baeck College, the Progressive movement's rabbinical training institute, was certified by the Council for National Academic Awards to give degrees in Jewish studies.

A report sponsored by the Jerusalem-based International Center for the University Teaching of Jewish Civilization and released at the annual conference in Cambridge in July of the British Association for Jewish Studies contrasted lack of Jewish support for Jewish studies at British universities with Muslim encouragement of Arabic studies. The report came shortly after the failure of a plan to set up a £1.25-million foundation to support Jewish studies chairs, launched by the Center's British committee in December. Jewish studies had to rely increasingly on outside sponsorship, the report said, because of government higher education cuts. One result of the lack of funding was that young scholars had little prospect of permanent employment in Britain.

Despite the difficulties, a new lectureship in modern Jewish history was created in University College, London's Hebrew and Jewish studies department, and a two-year research fellowship in Yiddish was offered at Queen Mary College, London, where a degree course in Yiddish began in September. The college already had a center for East London studies.

At the instigation of Joint Israel Appeal chairman Trevor Chinn, the professional heads of six organizations formed a working group to review educational needs and advise how money from Israel allocated to Diaspora education could best be spent in Britain. Organizations represented were JEDT, the US board of religious education, the progressive Center for Jewish Education, the Zionist Federation's educational trust, and the British offices of the World Zionist Organization's Torah and Youth and Hechalutz departments.

In February it was announced that a major Holocaust resource center would be established at Yakar, the educational institute in Hendon, North London.

Community Relations

Chief Rabbi Jakobovits wrote to the *Times* in March condemning the publication of Salman Rushdie's *The Satanic Verses*. Both Rushdie and the Ayatollah Khomeini, who called for the writer to be killed, had "abused freedom of speech," he wrote, suggesting that Britain should bar publication of "anything likely to inflame, through obscene defamation, the feelings or beliefs of any section of society, or liable to provoke public disorder and violence."

Publications

This year's H.H. Wingate Literary Awards for excellence in books of Jewish interest went to Anthony Read and David Fisher for *Kristallnacht* (nonfiction) and to Aharon Appelfeld for *For Every Sin* (fiction).

Books on general Jewish history published this year included *The Jewish Heritage* by Dan Cohn-Sherbok; *Heroes of Israel: Profiles of Jewish Courage* by Chaim Herzog; and *Jewish History: Essays in Honor of Chimen Abramsky,* edited by Ada Rapaport-Albert and Steven J. Zipperstein.

New works on Anglo-Jewish history included *The Royal Navy and Anglo-Jewry, 1740–1820* by Geoffrey L. Green; *The Club: The Jews of Modern Britain* by Stephen Brook; *The Jews of England: A Portrait of Anglo-Jewry Through Original Sources and Illustrations* by Jonathan Romain; *The Social Politics of Anglo-Jewry, 1880–1920* by Eugene C. Black; and *Jewish Historical Studies: Transactions of the Jewish Historical Society of England,* vol. 29, 1982–1986. Memories of London's East End were contained in *Born to Sing* by Alexander Hartog; *East Endings* by Harry Blacker; and *Echoes of the East End,* edited by Venetia Murray. Two anthologies of note were *Gown and Talith,* edited by William Frankel and Harvey Miller, commemorating the 50th anniversary of the founding of the Cambridge University Jewish Society; and *A Jewish Childhood,* edited by Antony Kamm and A. Norman Jeffares.

Three books on Austrian Jewry were published this year: *Vienna and Its Jews: The Tragedy of Success, 1880s–1980s* by George E. Berkley; *Vienna and the Jews, 1867–1938* by Steven Beller; and *The Jews in the Age of Franz Joseph* by Robert S. Wistrich.

Among new works relating to the Holocaust were *Out of the Ashes: The Impact of American Jews on Post-Holocaust European Jewry* by Yehuda Bauer; *The Holocaust in History* by Michael Marrus; *The Altruistic Personality: Rescuers of Jews in Nazi Europe* by Samuel P. Oliner and Pearl M. Oliner; and personal reminiscences: *I Shall Live* by Henry Orenstein; *I Light a Candle* by Gena Turgel; *Berlin Days, 1946–1947* by George Clare; and *Alicia: Memoirs of a Survivor* by Alicia Appleman-Jurman. Martin Gilbert's *The Second World War* could also be mentioned in this category.

Newly published studies of anti-Semitism included *Traditions of Intolerance,* edited by Tony Kushner and Kenneth Lunn; *The Persistence of Prejudice: Antisemitism in British Society During the Second World War* by Tony Kushner; and *The Rise of Political Antisemitism in Germany and Austria* by Peter Pulzer.

New biographical and autobiographical works were *Justice Not Vengeance* by Simon Wiesenthal; *When Time Ran Out* by Frederic Zeller; *An English Jew: The Life and Writings of Claude Montefiore,* selected, edited, and introduced by Edward Kessler; *Arlosoroff* by Shlomo Avineri; *Scenes from a Stepney Youth* by Charles Poulsen; *Golda Meir: The Romantic Years* by Ralph G. Martin; *The Two Zions: Reminiscences of Jerusalem and Ethiopia* by Edward Ullendorff; and *Battlefields and Playgrounds,* an autobiographical novel set in Hungary during the Holocaust, by Janos Nyiri.

Books on Israel and the Middle East were *A Peace to End All Peace: Creating the Modern Middle East, 1914–1922* by David Fromkin; *Jabotinsky and the Revisionist Movement, 1925–1948* by Yaacov Shavit; *A History of Israel* by Rinna Samuel—one of many histories published to coincide with Israel's 40th anniversary; *A History of Israel's Military Elite* by Samuel M. Katz; *Suez 1956: The Crisis and Its Consequences,* edited by William Roger Louis and Roger Owen; *British Army and Jewish Insurgency in Palestine, 1945–1947* by David A. Charters; *The Closed Circle: An Interpretation of the Arabs* by David Pryce-Jones; and *The Invisible Bomb: The Nuclear Arms Race in the Middle East* by Frank Barnaby.

Works in various areas of Judaica were *Blue Horizons,* a collection of Lionel Blue's reflections; *Vocalised Talmudic Manuscripts in the Cambridge Genizah Collections* by Shelomo Morag; *The Grammar of Modern Hebrew* by Lewis Glinert; and *Tradition and the Biological Revolution* by Daniel B. Sinclair.

Among new works of fiction were *Who Ever Heard of an Irish Jew? and Other Stories* by David Marcus; *White Snake* by Leon Whiteson; *Swann Song* and *Divide and Rule* by Elizabeth Russell Taylor; *All You Need* by Elaine Feinstein; *For Every Sin* by Aharon Appelfeld; *Lewis Percy* by Anita Brookner; *Out of the Ashes* by Maisie Mosco, the fourth volume in her *Almonds and Raisins* series; *Dictionary of the Khazars: A Lexicon Novel in 100,000 Words* by Milorad Pavic; and *Cosmetic Effects* by Clive Sinclair. A noteworthy new work of literary criticism was *Joyce and the Jews* by Ira B. Nadel.

Poetry of the year included *A Century of Yiddish Poetry,* selected, translated, and edited by Aaron Kramer; *White Coat, Purple Coat: Collected Poems, 1948–1988* by Dannie Abse; and *Ripples,* poems by the late Moshe Davis.

Books on Jewish subjects for younger readers were *Examining Religions: Judaism* by Arye Forta; *The Hasidic Story Book* by Harry M. Rabinowicz; and *The Young Reader's Encyclopaedia of Jewish History,* edited by Ilana Shamir and Shlomo Shavit.

New works on Jews in distant lands were *India's Bene Israel: A Comprehensive Inquiry and Source Book* by Shirley Berry Isenberg; and *Indian Jews and the Indian Freedom Struggle,* a treatise by Percy Gourgey. An overall picture was contained in *The Jewish Communities of the World: A Contemporary Guide,* edited by Antony Lerman.

Personalia

Sir Eric Sharp, chairman and chief executive of Cable and Wireless, was created a life peer. Knighthoods went to Jack Zunz, founder and formerly cochairman of Ove Arup, the structural engineering company; Trevor Chinn, for his work as vice-chairman of the Wishing Well Appeal for Great Ormond Street Hospital for Sick Children, London; and Prof. Eric Ash, rector of the Imperial College of

Science, Technology and Medicine, London University.

In August the chief rabbi was awarded the Jerusalem Prize for his "exceptional contribution to Jewish education."

Among British Jews who died in 1989 were Beryl, Lady Stone, philanthropist and activist in Israeli and domestic educational causes, in London, in January, aged 80; Louis Jacob, atomic scientist, in Glasgow, in January, aged 84; Hilde Himmelweit, professor of social psychology at the London School of Economics, 1964–83, in March, aged 72; Meir Raphael Springer, leading figure in the World Aguda movement, in March, aged 79; Sholom Schnitzer, the Csaba Rav, an eminent talmudist, in March, aged 68; Joseph Frankel, professor of politics, Southampton University, in March, aged 75; Henry Myer, distinguished World War I soldier and leading communal figure, in April, aged 96; Jakub Kaletzky, concert pianist, in April; David Morris, pediatrician, in April, aged 73; Jacob Weinberg, rabbi of the Edinburgh Hebrew Congregation, in Edinburgh, in May, aged 89; Lydia Pasternak Slater, translator of her brother Boris Pasternak's poetry, in Oxford, in May, aged 87; Lydia Sherwood, actress, in May, aged 85; David Jones, Variety Club of Great Britain public relations officer, in May; Rudi Rome, society band leader, in May, aged 77; Maurice Lew, emeritus rabbi of the West End Great Synagogue, London, in June, aged 78, on board ship; Richard Ferdinand, Lord Kahn, distinguished Cambridge University economist, in Cambridge, in June, aged 83; Harry Ariel, Yiddish actor, in July, aged 74; Dora, Baroness Gaitskell, widow of Labor party leader Hugh Gaitskell, in July, aged 88; Boruch Moshe Cymerman, Aguda leader and educator, in July, aged 78; Lola Hahn-Warburg, who played a leading role in the rescue of Jewish children from Nazi Germany, in July, aged 78; Stanley Waldman, Master of the Supreme Court, in July, aged 65; Benny Caplan, former British featherweight boxing champion, in July, aged 77; Robert Barer, microbiologist, in July, aged 72; Julian Layton, stockbroker and champion of Jewish refugees from Nazi Germany, in August, aged 84; Saul Reizin, *Jewish Chronicle* journalist, in September, aged 77; Michael Fidler, president of the Board of Deputies 1967–73, Conservative MP, and founder and director of the Conservative Friends of Israel, in September, aged 73; Walter Stanton, headmaster of the Hasmonean School, in October, aged 74; Isaac Shasta, president of the Conjoint Board of Elders of the Manchester Congregations of Spanish and Portuguese Jews, in October, aged 78; Isaac Nathan Fabricant, rabbi of the Brighton and Hove Hebrew Congregation for over 50 years, in October, aged 83; Rabbi Dr. Alex Spitzer, for many years director of the Union of Orthodox Hebrew Congregations, in November, aged 92; Anne Frankel, journalist, in November, aged 43; Harry Livermore, Lord Mayor of Liverpool 1958–59, in December, aged 81; Myer Domnitz, Jewish educator, in December, aged 80; Samuel Pelten, Yiddishist, in December, aged 87.

LIONEL & MIRIAM KOCHAN

France

THE PERIOD UNDER REVIEW, 1988–1989, was an eventful one for France generally and for the Jews of France. From January 1988 to June 1989 there was a succession of elections—presidential, legislative, local, municipal, and European Parliament (not to mention a referendum on New Caledonia). The problems posed by the far Right, the Middle East, and the treatment of immigrants to France continued as focuses of national concern. An issue of special urgency for Jews, the Carmelite convent at Auschwitz, attracted national interest, as did the visit to Paris in May 1989 of PLO chief Yasir Arafat at the government's invitation. Last but not least, 1989 was the 200th anniversary of the French Revolution, a celebration in which the Jewish community took its own part.

National Affairs

The period of "cohabitation" between a Socialist president and a prime minister belonging to the Right ended with the victory of Socialist François Mitterrand (54 percent in the second round against 46 percent for Gaullist Jacques Chirac) in the presidential election (April 24 and May 8, 1988), and that of the Socialists (275 out of 575 seats in the National Assembly) in the legislative election that followed (June 5 and 12). On May 10, 1988, a new government was formed, headed by Michel Rocard and composed mainly of Socialists. A noteworthy feature of the elections was the success of National Front (NF) leader Jean-Marie Le Pen in the first round of the presidential election (14.4 percent), the highest the far Right had ever obtained in such an election; on the other hand, with 6.76 percent, the Communist party had its lowest vote ever.

The National Front failed to translate its presidential success into seats in the National Assembly: the reintroduction of a majority uninominal constituency system allowed it, with a global percentage of 9.65 percent, only one representative. However, the NF could still be satisfied with its results in the local and municipal elections. In the latter, the fact that it succeeded in winning seats on many city councils, occasionally proving itself indispensable for building anti-Socialist majorities, showed the party's capacity to advance in large parts of the country among an increasingly diversified population of voters. By-elections in the course of 1989 confirmed that trend: in December 1989, the NF candidates won 61.3 percent in Dreux and 47.18 percent in Marseilles (second round of legislative by-elections) and 50.81 percent in Salon de Provence (second round of a local by-election).

As in previous years, the Right was ambivalent in its dealings with the National Front. Before the presidential election, Jacques Chirac, leader of the Rally for the

Republic (RPR), expressed his intention "to understand all the French without any exception" but stressed his "uncompromising rejection" of racism. At the same time, Charles Pasqua, the director of his campaign and a prominent member of his party, said in an interview that "in the main, the National Front had the same concerns, the same values" as the Right. The situation changed in September 1988 after Le Pen's "joke" (see below), when RPR decided to "condemn any electoral alliance with the NF, on both the local and national level," and in December 1989 after the by-elections, when several leaders of the Right called for a "republican front" against the far Right.

The Right and Anti-Semitism

Before the presidential election, Claude Labbé, an important member of Jacques Chirac's party, declared that "Le Pen is neither a racist nor a Nazi," and that the real problem "is Simone Veil. The more she talks, the more anti-Semitism she creates." (Veil, a former French minister of health and former president of the European Parliament, always rated in the polls as one of France's most popular politicians, was a frequent target of the far Right. A Jew and a survivor of the camps who spoke out frequently against racism and intolerance, she was depicted by far Rightists as a symbol of "Jewish" liberalism. After she introduced the law legalizing abortion, she was accused of causing a "Holocaust of French babies.")

Remarks made by Jean-Marie Le Pen and his supporters were prominently featured in the media. One year after he declared that the gas chambers were a subject of debate among historians and "a point of detail in the history of WWII," Le Pen caused a new scandal on September 2, 1988, when, playing on the name of the civil service minister, Michel Durafour, he called him "Durafour-crématoire" (*four* = oven; *four crématoire* = crematorium, specifically that employed by the Nazis). That so-called joke provoked intense reactions, even inside the NF, and several prominent party members (including the only member of the National Assembly elected in June) decided to quit. One of the former leaders of the NF, Dr. François Bachelot, declared then that "the new line of the NF was openly founded on racism and anti-Semitism." A civil suit was brought against Le Pen three days later, but the process was delayed because of Le Pen's immunity as a member of the European Parliament (his immunity was finally lifted by a vote of that body on December 11, 1989).

In August 1989, in an interview in the far-Right fundamentalist Catholic daily *Présent,* Le Pen denounced "those international bodies that are against the national spirit," among them "the Jewish international." Although this occurred in the middle of the summer vacation period—typically a time of public indifference to news—the new anti-Jewish attack evoked an uproar. Its effect was heightened when Claude Autant-Lara (an 88-year-old film producer, elected in June 1989 to the European Parliament on the NF list) declared in an interview published by the monthly *Globe* that Simone Veil "played on our heartstrings ["played the mandolin," in the French idiom] with that [the deportation of the Jews]," adding: "But she came back, did she not? And she is feeling very good. . . . So, when one talks to me about genocide, I say, in any case, they missed old mother Veil!" The fact that Autant-Lara was also prosecuted did not stop Le Pen. In December, in a TV debate, he asked Minister of Planning Lionel Stoléru, a Jew: "Is it true that you have dual citizenship?" (meaning French and Israeli), adding: "You are a French minister. We have the right to know who you are." The political effect of these utterances was not entirely clear. On the one hand, the NF was becoming more and more isolated on the political scene and suffered the loss of some of its most active personalities; on the other hand, its identity as a party became sharper and, as the results of by-elections showed, the scandal had limited effects on the voters.

The wide publicity given to the NF somewhat blurred other phenomena, such as the increasing number of vandalism acts against synagogues and graveyards. Already in June 1988, the yearly conclave of French rabbis expressed its concern over this problem. Such attacks occurred intermittently in 1989, the identity and motivation of the perpetrators being seldom determined. (In March two skinheads were arrested for the desecration of a Jewish graveyard in the small city of Eleu-dit-Leauwette, in northern France.)

Middle Eastern Policy

Although the *intifada* took up increasing space in media reports on the Middle East, Middle Eastern policy was actually dominated in 1988–89 by three issues: the French hostages and relations with Iran; the situation in Lebanon; and the Palestinian question. The release of the last three French hostages held in Lebanon by pro-Iranian factions, just before the second round of the presidential election, allowed a definite improvement in relations with Iran (e.g., renewal of diplomatic links in June 1988; visit of Minister of Foreign Affairs Roland Dumas to Teheran in February 1989). Temporary setbacks were caused by Iranian calls to murder author Salman Rushdie and the Iranian demands to release Anis Naccache (a pro-Iranian Lebanese terrorist sentenced to life by a French court for the attempted murder, in Paris, of former Iranian prime minister Shapur Bakhtiar), on the basis of alleged promises made by Jacques Chirac prior to the release of the French hostages. As for Lebanon, France expressed its traditional involvement in that country by condemning Israel for its raids in southern Lebanon (for instance in May 1988), and by trying to intervene with humanitarian means when the interfactional wars were especially bitter, in the spring of 1989.

Relations with Israel

In 1988, according to the Israelis, relations with France showed a decided improvement. In July, Israeli ambassador Ovadia Soffer praised the "balanced and careful position" of France, which "created a climate of confidence between France and Israel without damaging the good relations France maintains with the Arab countries." That climate was not harmed even after Foreign Affairs Minister Roland Dumas met with Yasir Arafat in Strasbourg in September, where the PLO leader had been invited by the European Parliament. Ambassador Soffer described the visit of Israeli president Chaim Herzog to Paris (October 17–21) as "the crowning of good French-Israeli relations."

Warm feelings began to cool, however, toward the end of the year. France did not recognize the Palestinian state declared in November 1988 in Algiers, but in December it granted the PLO representation in Paris the diplomatic status of a "general delegation." France also supported the idea of an international conference—opposed by the Israelis—a message that was conveyed by Roland Dumas on his visit to Israel in January 1989, along with doubts about the chances of the peace plan put forward by Israeli premier Yitzhak Shamir based on elections in the occupied territories. President Mitterrand urged Shamir—on his visit to Paris in February 1989—to "take into account the reality as it is today." One month later, Mitterrand announced his intention to receive Yasir Arafat in the French capital. With the notable exception of the Jewish community, this decision met, if not with general support, at least with a good deal of understanding. Former president Valéry Giscard d'Estaing only regretted the "official character" of the visit; Simone Veil, who would have liked "very precise promises" from Arafat, still felt that "the important thing is to make peace progress"; the Socialist chairman of the National Assembly, Laurent Fabius, said that "talking with somebody does not mean that you adopt his positions."

According to an opinion poll published on May 2, the first day of Arafat's visit in Paris, 51 percent of the French felt it was "quite normal" for Arafat to be invited officially, 31 percent were against the visit, and 18 percent had no opinion; 48 percent believed that the visit would have a positive effect on a future Israeli-Palestinian dialogue. While opponents of the visit stressed Arafat's failure to repudiate past terrorist actions and the fact that the PLO covenant calling for the destruction of Israel had not been amended, most commentators focused on analyzing the implications of Arafat's declaration on TV that the covenant was *"caduque"* (obsolete).

Immigration and Related Issues

Although the return of the Socialists to the government put an end to proposed new restrictive legislation on the acquisition of French citizenship, the question of immigration still polarized French attitudes. A dramatic and revealing episode took place in the last months of 1989 when the principal of a secondary school in Creil (an outlying suburb of Paris) decided to bar three Muslim teenage girls from school as long as they wore the "Islamic scarf," the *chador*, within the school confines. The problem occupied headlines for several weeks, stimulating debate on tolerance, the rise of fundamentalism, the meaning of secularity in public schools, the role of schooling in the integration of second-generation immigrants, and so on. The picture was further complicated by revelations that in some schools a few Muslim girls would not attend classes in natural sciences, art, or physical education, because they were "against religion," and that Jewish children refused to attend lessons on Saturdays.

These issues posed a challenge to the traditional secular French view that religion was a purely private matter that should not be expressed in school. Minister of Education Lionel Jospin tried to find a middle way, encouraging dialogue and reminding schools that they were to serve as a tool for integration, not for exclusion. The Council of State finally decided that wearing religious garb or symbols in school did not harm secularity but that disseminating religious propaganda or refusing to attend certain classes should be prohibited.

The issue clearly had ramifications for the Jewish community. The Representative Council of Jewish Organizations (CRIF) supported "discussion between families, children, and teachers" in a secular school, to ensure that "schools show tolerance and respect for the various faiths," but reminded parents of the option of private religious schools for those who could not accept the rules of secular schools. Rabbi Alain Goldmann, Paris chief rabbi, declared that "those who refuse Moslem children the right to wear the *chador* or Jewish children the right to wear the *kippah* in school are intolerant," adding: "Today, it is no more the religious who show intolerance, as is often said, but the secularists."

Although the practical problem was partly solved by the end of the year, when the minister of education issued regulations in accord with the position of the Council of State, the public debate went on. It revealed a significant change in the general mood: after two decades in which "difference" was highly praised, priority was now given to integration through adherence to the common values of the French democratic and secular society. Although the Jewish community was often cited as an example of successful integration, Jewish leaders emphasized that integration had a price—the full acceptance of the common values of the national collectivity.

Nazi War Criminals

On May 24, 1989, Paul Touvier, the head of the Milice (the French fascist militia) in Lyons in 1943–44, was arrested in Nice, where he had been hiding in a monastery run by arch-conservative, dissident Catholics. Sentenced to death in absentia in 1945 and 1947, Touvier had enjoyed considerable protection in certain Catholic circles, enabling him to survive in hiding until the sentences expired in 1967. Pardoned in 1971 by President Georges Pompidou, Touvier was charged again in 1973 with "crimes against humanity," for which there was no statute of limitations. The specific crimes were the murder of Victor Basch (aged 81, former president of the Human Rights League) and his wife (aged 82), on January 11, 1944, in a suburb of Lyons; the execution of seven Jewish hostages in the Lyons area on June 28, 1944, as reprisals for the murder of Philippe Henriot, the Vichy minister of information; the arrest of the caretaker of a synagogue in Lyons and his wife (the couple was later sent to Auschwitz); and the arrest on April 24, 1944, in Montmélian (Savoie) of a group of 57 Spanish refugees and partisans, of whom only 9 came back from the camps.

Despite the arrest of Touvier, it remained difficult to bring to judgment persons involved in World War II crimes against humanity. On July 2, 1989, Jean Leguay, one of the heads of the Vichy police in the occupied zone between May 1942 and January 1944 (therefore involved in the mass arrest of Jews in July 1942), died before he could be brought to trial. He had been under indictment since 1979. In September, Serge Klarsfeld lodged a complaint of crimes against humanity against René Bousquet (aged 80 in 1989), secretary-general of the Vichy police from April 1942 to September 1943. According to Klarsfeld, the reopening of his file, which had been closed in 1949, was called for by the discovery of new evidence. This included instructions sent by Bousquet in the summer of 1942, adding new categories of Jews to be arrested from among those that had so far been spared: children under 18 and parents of very young children.

JEWISH COMMUNITY

Demography

There were no major changes in the estimated Jewish population of France, which remained, according to most sources, 550,000–600,000, mainly found in the urban areas of Paris and its suburbs (around 350,000), Marseilles and the south coast (60,000), Lyons (25,000), Strasbourg (15,000), Toulouse (12,000), Grenoble (7,000), and Bordeaux (5,000).

In June 1988, a synagogue was inaugurated on the island of Guadeloupe, French West Indies, for a community of around 3,000 souls, 95 percent of them Sephardim, which had started to develop in the mid-1970s. Composed mainly of merchants (one-third), civil servants, and members of the liberal professions, the community had its kosher meat sent by plane from Paris.

A celebration marking the departure of the 50,000th French immigrant to Israel was held at the beginning of 1989, organized by Radio Shalom, a Jewish radio station. According to figures published in *L'Arche* (January 1989), the average number of immigrants per year in the '80s was around 1,000. The average age of French immigrants to Israel in 1987 was 29; 40 percent were academics; 8 percent defined themselves as very observant, 33 percent as observant, 36 percent as nonobservant, and 23 percent as secular; 60 percent said they had no relationship with the organized Jewish community.

The main results of a large survey of French Jews were made public at the end of 1988. The study was carried out in the framework of the Fonds Social Juif Unifié

(FSJU, the United Jewish Philanthropic Fund), at the request of the French Coordination Committee for Jewish Education (an ad hoc body of communitywide representatives) and sponsored by the American Jewish Joint Distribution Committee and the commission for Jewish education of the Jewish Agency. Carried out under the supervision of a a scientific committee of French and Israeli sociologists, the survey covered a sample of over a thousand Jewish family heads selected according to several criteria: Jewish name, self-identification as a "Jew" or an "Israelite," age over 16, living in one of the 17 districts chosen for the size of their Jewish population.

The survey produced a number of interesting findings about the French Jewish community. Whereas 85 percent of the sample declared that all or most of their friends were Jews, the link to institutional Judaism appeared to be rather weak. Only three organizations were spontaneously cited by more than 25 percent of the sample: the FSJU, the organization concerned with culture and social welfare; the United Jewish Appeal, which raises money for Israel; and the Consistory, the central religious body. Thirty-five percent indicated that they had no contact at all with the organized community; 13 percent very seldom (not more than once a year); 16 percent occasionally (2–3 times a year); 13 percent often (4–5 times a year); 22 percent very often (once a month or more). A rough typology showed four concentric circles: the nucleus of the "regulars" (22 percent); the wider circle of those (30 percent) having some contact with organized communal life; the circle of the "distants" (33 percent), who had no contact with institutions but still lived in a primarily Jewish social network; and the circle of "those who turned away" (15 percent), who were cut off from all Jewish contact.

As far as religious practice is concerned, 36 percent said they were not observant at all, while 14 percent declared that they observed all the *mitzvot*. Israel and the support of Israel seemed to be a crucial factor in identification: 75 percent had gone to Israel at least once; 90 percent believed that every Jew should feel solidarity with Israel; 23 percent labeled themselves "convinced Zionists" (though 41 percent of this group did not agree that every Jew should actuallly live in Israel), 46 percent, "Zionist sympathizers," and 30 percent, "not Zionists." Education appeared to be the main avenue of contact with the organized community: 64 percent of families with children of school age had had them enrolled at one time or another in some Jewish educational framework (school, Talmud Torah, youth movement, vacation center).

The survey confirmed the postwar psychological change that had occurred in French Jewry in the direction of greater positive identification: only 5 percent of the sample labeled themselves "Israelites" (a name once considered by assimilationists as less "offensive" than the negatively connoted "Jew"). The fact that 17 percent of the sample described themselves as neither Ashkenazi nor Sephardi was interpreted as a sign of the emergence of a new, distinctive French Jewry. The fairly high socioeconomic level of the community was also illustrated by the survey: 76 percent belonged to the upper class or upper middle class (merchants, manufacturers, executives, or professionals) and 45 percent had completed higher education.

Community Relations

In the political sphere, community leaders continued to warn against the progress of the National Front and to press for freedom for Soviet Jewry and Syrian Jewry. Through the Representative Council of Jewish Organizations (CRIF), the Jewish community expressed its concern about the NF after the first round of the presidential election. It issued statements warning against any compromise "with those who oppose the values" of democracy (April 26, 1988) and called on opinion makers in business, politics, and universities to fight the far Right (end of May 1988).

In the period under review, attention concentrated heavily on the developing relations between Europe and France and the PLO. Before Yasir Arafat's appearance at the European Parliament in September 1988—an act termed by CRIF president Théo Klein as "political stupidity" and "moral hypocrisy"—CRIF focused its campaign on the problem of terrorism. Telegrams were sent to the ministers of interior and justice warning of the possible presence of international terrorists among those accompanying Arafat, and the demonstration that took place in Strasbourg on the day of the visit (September 13) paid homage to all victims of terror. CRIF's position was that "as long as the PLO has not adopted a clear stand putting an end to the option of terrorism and opening itself toward recognizing the legitimacy of the State of Israel, all those European initiatives . . . can have only negative effects." The positions stated by the PLO in Algiers during the meeting of the Palestine National Council in November 1988 did not basically change the official position of French Jewry. Chief Rabbi Joseph Sitruk said that he "hoped that the Palestinian decision was not mere theater," adding that "only the Israelis can draw the political implications" of the PLO move.

The prospect of a visit by Arafat to Paris, announced at the end of March 1989, was almost unanimously denounced by most Jewish organizations. One of the few exceptions, the Cercle Bernard Lazare, a small but influential group of Jewish intellectuals close to the Israeli Mapam party, charged that official Jewish reactions "were seldom based on political analysis." In April CRIF held a number of special meetings; on April 3, it officially expressed its disapproval of the initiative. In a letter to the French president, Théo Klein asserted that "we would probably accept the significance of your decision if we were assured that before the meeting you would obtain recognition of the legitimate rights of the Jewish people in the land of Eretz-Israel (Palestine), the disavowal of the UN resolution equating Zionism with racism, the end of violence, and the possibility of holding free elections in the territories that had been occupied until 1967 by Jordan and Egypt." In a parallel letter, Klein urged the Jewish community "to express ourselves in the quiet and dignified way befitting a free community."

Still, in April a second message was sent to Mitterrand, signed jointly by Théo Klein, David de Rothschild (FSJU), Roger Pinto (European Sephardi Federation), Joseph Sitruk (chief rabbi of France), Ady Steg (Alliance Israélite Universelle), Jean-Paul Elkann (Central Consistory), and Jacques Orfus (Federation of Zionist

Organizations in France), expressing their "indignation" and calling for a debate in Parliament so that "each citizen in this country knows the motives of your announced initiative and that political leaders... can express themselves and take their share of responsibility."

On May 1, one day before Arafat's coming, quiet demonstrations took place at sites that had been targets of terrorist attacks: Rue des Rosiers, Rue de Rennes, and the Point Show shopping gallery in Champs Elysées. A bigger demonstration was held on May 2 in Rue Copernic; the demonstration, which was supposed to be silent and dignified, got somewhat out of control, and Théo Klein had some difficulty in being heard. Demonstrations also took place in Strasbourg, Lyons, Marseilles, and Toulouse.

Communal Affairs

The second (and statutory last) term of CRIF president Théo Klein came to an end in May 1989 under the difficult circumstance of Yasir Arafat's visit to Paris. A strong and original personality, Klein was depicted as follows by the magazine *Actualité Juive*: "Often controversial but always respected and even admired by his fiercest opponents, Théo Klein has given his function a scope it did not have before." Klein himself described the "responsibility of the president of CRIF" as "double, in the sense that he has the duty both to address the outside world in the name of the community, but also to talk to the community." "Being the president of CRIF," he added, "means being able to meet a challenge every day and, if possible, remaining at peace with one's conscience."

Four candidates vied for the votes of the CRIF General Assembly. Henri Hajdenberg, president of the Renouveau Juif (an association that had been loudly critical of the Jewish establishment at the end of the 1970s), wished "to give the necessary impulse to the new dynamic and influential generation," at a time when the main strength of CRIF lay in "the reputation of its president with the administration, the media and public opinion, Jewish and non-Jewish alike," in short, its ability to influence public opinion. Jean Kahn, vice-president of CRIF, president of the Jewish community of Strasbourg, and president of the Commission on European Institutions of the European Jewish Congress, presented himself as "the successor to President Klein," emphasizing his loyalties: "loyalty to Israel, loyalty to the Jewish mission of justice and defense of human rights, loyalty to French Jewry inside a reconstituted Europe." Edouard Knoll, the president of the Jewish National Fund in France, underlined "CRIF's limited success in its relations with the Jewish population" and called for a new pattern of broader representation of French Jewry. Hubert Dayan, president of the AMIF (Association of Jewish Physicians in France), did not present any explicit program.

The elected candidate was Jean Kahn, who won in the second round, 84–22, over his main challenger, Henri Hajdenberg. Kahn, aged 60, was a former lawyer who had taken over the family textile business and had been the president of the Strasbourg community since 1972. At his first press conference, the newly elected president confirmed his intention to maintain CRIF's character as a "body for political representation" and not let it be transformed into "a militant structure." He warned against "irresponsible minorities," stressing the fact that the Jews "are a part of French society from which we do not want to exclude ourselves." One month later, the executive of CRIF appointed as vice-presidents Nicole Goldmann (vice-president of FSJU), Jacques Kupfer (president of French Herut and representative in CRIF of the Federation of Zionist Organizations), and Roger Pinto (president of Siona), while former vice-president Henry Bulawko was made honorary vice-president.

Toward the end of the year, elections took place in the Paris Consistory (Consistoire), the body concerned with Jewish religious affairs. The two lists that competed for the 14 seats to be filled (out of 26) represented, perhaps for the first time in the history of the venerable institution, two fairly different approaches to its functioning. The first list, led by lawyer Albert Benatar and supported by Consistory president Emile Touati, defined that body's purpose "inside the French national community" as "allowing as many Jews as possible to practice the *mitzvot,*" and stressing the Consistory's role as "a religious association" that should not deal with "politics, social action or anything else." The second list, led by Benny Cohen, called for more activism, for "a living Consistory, a dynamic Consistory, a Consistory where it would not be difficult to find somebody willing to talk [in public]." Out of 29,800 electors, 3,268 (less than 11 percent) took part in the vote. Benny Cohen's list won all the seats to be filled, making its leader virtually the new president of the Paris Consistory.

ISRAEL

Parallel with its political activity on matters affecting Israel, the community found various means to demonstrate solidarity with the Jewish state. In addition to public celebrations for Israel's 40th anniversary, a CRIF delegation visited Israel (May 1–6, 1988) in what was, according to Klein, "a trip to the heart of the problem and not a simple solidarity visit." A mass meeting was organized in October 1988 for the visit of Israeli president Chaim Herzog to Paris, and a reception in February 1989 for the visit of Prime Minister Yitzhak Shamir. In March the CRIF leadership decided, after a lengthy debate, to take part in the international "Solidarity Conference" of Diaspora Jews convened in Jerusalem for the purpose of expressing "support for the Israeli democracy in its search for security and for ways to peace with the Palestinians and the neighbouring Arab states."

INTERNAL DEBATES

A certain confusion could be felt in 1988, mostly among intellectuals outside the organized community, about Israel's handling of the *intifada* and the increasing dominance of the religious parties in Israeli life. Divisive as these issues were, however, more serious rifts appeared in 1989, not over the Middle East but over the self-definition of the community itself, the vision of its future, and the nature of relations between its various components. A major survey published in January 1989 in *L'Express* depicted a Jewish community wavering between "total assimilation" and the "reassertion of its identity." The writer could well have added, "wavering between acceptance and rejection of Western modernity." The national debate aroused by the *chador* school controversy over the rights of religious-ethnic communities versus general secular norms also became an internal Jewish issue. When Chief Rabbi Sitruk declared that he "could understand that one might be bothered by a *chador* or a *kippah*" but that an order to remove them would be "harsh intolerance," writer Alain Finkielkraut replied angrily that "we ought to be living in a time when the Jews are the model for Islam [in France], a model of integration; instead, the extremist and fanatic Islam is for some Jews a model for their own tribalization." Philosopher Shmuel Trigano counterattacked: "If Alain Finkielkraut has lately declared himself a secularist and an atheist, if he feels that the structure of the Jewish community is archaic and tribal, he should not demand or expect anything from the rabbinate."

As illustrated by this exchange, the end of the decade of the '80s saw French Jewry at a crossroads between two approaches—that of traditional religious observance and that of the old French secular Judaism—and split between two poles of thought: universalism and exclusiveness, openness and particularism, each position viewing the consequences of modernity for Judaism in a different light. In a community large enough to harbor any number of approaches, but in which organized life was too limited for them not to meet in the communal framework, clashes were unavoidable. Moreover, each position tended to feel excluded by the others and to convey its frustration through the national press as well as through the Jewish media, thus involving French society at large in the "Jewish wars."

Jewish-Christian Relations

Although relations between the Jewish community and the French Catholic episcopate remained basically cordial—the French rabbinate, for example, joining Church protests against Martin Scorsese's movie *The Last Temptation of Christ*—one could sense a definite deterioration. In 1988 Jews were dismayed by the meeting of Pope John Paul II with Austrian president Kurt Waldheim during the pope's visit to Austria, especially by his silence on the subject of Jewish fate in the Holocaust at a stop at the Mauthausen concentration camp. On the pope's visit to Strasbourg in October 1988, he met with representatives of the local Jewish community: René Weil, president of the Consistory of the Bas Rhin; René Gutman, chief rabbi of the Bas Rhin; and Jean Kahn, president of the Strasbourg community. They attempted to raise questions on such issues as the uniqueness of the Shoah and the Vatican's recognition of the State of Israel, but failed to engage the pope in serious dialogue.

In 1989, despite the strong support of the French bishops for carrying out the agreement reached in Geneva in February 1987 by Catholic and Jewish representatives to move the Carmelite convent at Auschwitz, the controversy over the matter poisoned the atmosphere. In February, Théo Klein, chairman of the Jewish delegation to Geneva, issued an initial protest over the delay in fulfilling the terms of the agreement. The dispute became more heated in July, when it became clear that the agreement was not being respected, and in August, when Polish cardinal Jozef Glemp denounced an alleged Jewish anti-Polish campaign through the allegedly Jewish-controlled media. In the French media, which showed an enormous interest in the issue, the opinions expressed showed the difficulty non-Jews had in understanding the Jewish point of view. Several people, among them well-known intellectuals, said that the nuns "did no harm" in praying for all the victims of Nazism and wondered about the Jewish attitude of exclusiveness toward the Holocaust. On a TV program, Jean Kahn, the newly elected president of CRIF, declared that the Jews "do not want the Shoah to be Christianized." He was answered by a Catholic priest who maintained that "other nations can claim the same distress and the Jews seem to deny that." Hostility decreased in mid-September when the Vatican issued a statement calling for the agreements to be fulfilled. In an interview on French TV on September 10 (as quoted in *Jour J*), Elie Wiesel summarized in a rather pessimistic way the effect of the controversy in France: "If they [the nuns] stay, we shall have lost; if they go, we shall also have lost: imagine the Carmelites leaving Auschwitz in front of all the TVs in the world, expelled by the Jews."

Memorializing the Holocaust

The question of keeping alive the memory of the Shoah continued to be of concern. Efforts were made to increase the awareness of non-Jewish youth: CRIF and the World Jewish Congress sent secondary schoolchildren (140 in 1988, 150 in 1989) to the site of the concentration camp at Auschwitz for what was called a "study day and not a pilgrimage"; the France Plus organization sent a group of young second-generation North African immigrants for a similar excursion. Scholarly research was encouraged by the creation of private foundations, among them the Memory of Auschwitz Foundation and the Buchman Foundation. The latter, founded by a survivor of the Holocaust to perpetuate the memory of his wife and daughter who perished in the camps, awarded its 1988 prize to the historian Joseph Billig, author of numerous works on the Holocaust and on the persecution of the Jews in France under the Vichy regime; its 1989 prize went to young historian Anne Grynberg, for her doctoral thesis on "Jewish Internees in Camps in Southern France, 1939–42," and to the American scholar William G. Glicksman, for the totality of his works. On the 50th anniversary of *Kristallnacht,* a converted train coach was inaugurated as a museum in Drancy, the city near Paris from which 80,000 Jews were deported.

Several symposiums devoted to the Holocaust were held in this period. Some followed a conventional approach, such as one sponsored by B'nai Brith in Marseilles (May '88): "How Can We Transmit the Memory of the Shoah?"; and one arranged by the Jewish students union (Union des Etudiants Juifs de France, UEJF; March '89): "From the Generation of Memory to the Generation of Recollection." A more controversial program was that organized by Shmuel Trigano on behalf of the Alliance (November '88): "Thinking Auschwitz," which aimed at "opening a new age of reflection on the Shoah in a perspective both philosophical and theological" and at "questioning Auschwitz as a means of identification for the Jews." The fact that the organizers questioned what they felt was the "institutionalization" of the Shoah (libraries, university chairs, etc.) was sharply denounced by some survivors; one of them, Henry Bulawko, termed it "blasphemous and dishonest."

Culture

Jour J, a new daily newspaper based mainly on news-agency dispatches, was launched on March 21, 1988, with the purpose of filling the gap created 15 months earlier by the discontinuation of the Jewish Telegraphic Agency's daily bulletin in French. A one-man enterprise initiated by a Jewish journalist who invested his own capital, *Jour J* received only limited financial support from the community (FSJU provided free access to its technical services and invested some funds). Although the need for such a publication was widely acknowledged, there were questions about its financial viability. It probably suffered, too, from the success of the Jewish broadcast media; a May 1988 survey found that in the Paris area, Jewish radio programs were listened to daily, on average, by some 19,000 people. In the national Jewish survey cited above, 60 percent of the sample said they listened to Jewish radio: 30 percent regularly, 30 percent occasionally. According to David Saada, director of FSJU, Jewish radio was "very clearly the first medium in the community."

On the other hand, a more specifically targeted newspaper, the monthly *Actualité Juive*, clearly aimed at the "masses" and distributed in places frequented by observant Jews (e.g., kosher butchers), was able, with 2,700 subscribers and a total run of 20,000 copies, to increase its frequency to twice a month (end of October 1988). The purpose of *Motus*, a new "bimonthly of Jewish expression," launched at the end of 1989, was slightly different: it meant to feature Jewish cultural life, to show that "the community was not closed in on itself" and "had views on the political and cultural phenomena affecting society." At the end of March 1989, the Consistory started its own new publication, *La lettre du Grand Rabbin de France*, intended for community administrators and rabbis.

Cultural life, which remained active, featured an impressive number of symposiums, some of them organized by Jewish institutions together with non-Jewish bodies. One such was on "the symbiosis of the French and Jewish cultures" (January '88), which took place in the City Hall of Paris and was sponsored by the Secretary General of the Council of Europe. Others were more directly linked to current issues, like the one organized in October '88 by the Jewish students union (UEJF), France Plus (a non-Jewish organization active in the integration of immigrants, mostly North Africans), and the monthly *Passages,* on "What Kind of Dialogue Between Arabs and Jews in Tomorrow's France?"

The Jewish community played its own part in the celebration of the 200th anniversary of the French Revolution. The first event took place at the Rachi Center (a major academic-cultural facility in Paris) in November '88, with a symposium on "Revolution, Political Power and Human Rights." In June '89 the yearly meeting of the Alliance Israélite Universelle was devoted to "The AIU and the 1789 Heritage." In October the Alliance opened a big exhibition on "Jews and Citizens," composed of documents from various museums and libraries in France and abroad. A film made by two academics, Lilly Scheer and Pierre Sorlin, *The Jews in France and the Revolution,* was shown on several different occasions.

The 1988 colloquium of French-speaking Jewish intellectuals was devoted to "The Question of the State." The 1989 colloquium on the *"Quant-à-soi"* (reserved behavior; keeping one's distance) examined the relationship between the individual and the community and between the community and the larger collectivity (nation, state). It was a subject that aroused strong feeling, and some of the sessions took place in an unusually agitated atmosphere.

The new building for the library of the Alliance Israélite Universelle was inaugurated in September 1989. Financed by the city of Paris and private donors, the new building permitted better access to the documents and more comfortable conditions for people using the library, the largest Judaica and Hebraica library in Europe (100,000 books, 20,000 periodicals, 4,000 fragments from the Cairo Genizah, and 900 manuscripts, 450 of them in Hebrew).

Publications

Works of nonfiction published in 1988–89 tended to focus on two main themes: World War II and the Holocaust, and the French Revolution and problems of emancipation. Representative of the first category were the following: Gilles and Jean-Robert Ragache's book *La vie quotidienne des écrivains et des artistes sous l'Occupation* ("The daily life of writers and artists during the occupation"); Claude Bochurberg and Jacqueline Baldran's work on *Brasillach et la célébration du mépris* ("Brasillach and the celebration of contempt"), on the anti-Semitic, collaborationist journalist and writer who was sentenced to death and executed in 1945 and who was revived as a kind of romantic figure in the '70s and early '80s; Carole Sandrel's memoir *Le Secret* ("The secret"), the story of a Jewish child who spent the war in hiding; the *Chronique du procès Barbie; pour servir la mémoire* ("Chronicle of the Barbie trial; for the sake of memory"), a collection of the main texts, documents, and evidence produced at the trial, with prefaces by Cardinal Albert Decourtray and Marek Halter; *La mémoire vaine* ("Vain memory"), a short essay by Alain Finkielkraut in which the author questions the excessive media coverage of the trial and devotes an important chapter to defining the concept of crimes against humanity; Stéphane Courtois, Denis Peschansky, and Adam Raisky's research on Jews and foreigners in the French Resistance, *Le sang de l'étranger* ("The blood of the foreigner"), the first book on the subject totally based on archival documentary sources; *La politique nazie d'extermination* ("The Nazi policy of extermination"), proceedings of a symposium held at the Sorbonne in December 1987, edited by François Bédarida, with contributions by Saul Friedländer, Yehuda Bauer, Christopher Browning, Eberhard Jäckel, Michael R. Marrus, Pierre Vidal-Naquet, Léon Poliakov, and Georges Wellers. To these publications, orginally written in French, one should add the long-awaited translation into French of Raul Hilberg's *The Destruction of the European Jews.*

The anniversary of the revolution inspired a number of publications, among them a reissue of Abbé Grégoire's famous 1787 *Essai sur la régénération physique, morale et politique des juifs* ("Essay on the physical, moral, and political regeneration of the Jews"); the narrative history of Patrick Girard on *La révolution française et les Juifs* ("The French Revolution and the Jews"); Robert Badinter's *Libres et égaux* ("Free and equal"), on the emancipation; the translation from Hebrew of Michael Graetz's *Les Juifs en France au 19ème siècle, de la Révolution française à l'Alliance Israélite Universelle* ("The Jews in France in the 19th century, from the French Revolution to the AIU"), based on vast research in documentary sources. There were also two new books on the 19th-century Jewish politician Adolphe Crémieux, minister of justice in 1848 and in 1870, best known for the decree granting French citizenship to Algerian Jews: a biography by Daniel Amson, *Adolphe Crémieux, l'oublié de la gloire* ("Adolphe Crémieux, forgotten by glory"), which was awarded the Bernard Lecache antiracist prize of LICRA (the League Against Racism and Anti-Semitism); and Carol Iancu's *Bleichröder et Crémieux, le combat pour l'émancipation des Juifs de Roumanie* ("Bleichröder and Crémieux, the fight for the emancipation of Romanian Jews").

On the subjects of anti-Semitism, the extreme Right, and racism, new books worthy of note were: *L'antisémitisme* by Yves Chevalier, based on a doctoral dissertation in sociology, an attempt to formulate a global theory of anti-Semitism, relating it to the scapegoat mechanism; *L'extrême droite en France, de Maurras à Le Pen* ("The far Right in France, from Maurras to Le Pen") by Ariane Chebel d'Appollonia; *Les langues du Paradis* ("The languages of paradise") by Maurice Olender, a study of the concepts of "Aryan" and "Semite" in the newly born social sciences in the 19th century; *Moscou, troisième Rome* ("Moscow, third Rome") by Léon Poliakov, on the Russian mystical idea of Russia as the new center for Christianity after the fall of Rome and Byzantium.

New works of history and sociology included Doris Bensimon and Joëlle Allouche-Benayoun's *Juifs d'Algérie, hier et aujourd'hui* ("Jews of Algeria, yesterday and today"), based on oral histories of Jews in France, collected as part of a study of acculturation processes; Doris Bensimon's *Les Juifs en France et leurs relations avec Israël (1945–1988)* ("The Jews of France and their relations with Israel"), a sociodemographic study of the Jewish community, giving an account of Jewish-Christian and Jewish-Muslim relations; Moïse Abinum's *Les lumières de Sarajevo, histoire d'une famille juive d'Europe Centrale* ("The lights of Sarajevo, a history of a Jewish family in Central Europe"), on the descendants of Avram Abinum, first rabbi of the Travnik community in the 17th century; and Renée David's *Femmes juives* ("Jewish women"), a collection of biographies of Golda Meir, Simone Veil, Rosa Luxembourg, and others. In *Vidal et les siens* ("Vidal and his family"), sociologist Edgar Morin presents an objective, scholarly account of the wanderings of his father and others of his family from Saloniki to France at the beginning of the century, at the same time managing to provide a rich portrait of the Judeo-Spanish communities in Greece and France. A photo album on *The Jews of Tunisia* contained texts written by 14 authors.

On Middle East issues, Jean-Jacques Servan-Schreiber published an essay, *Le choix des Juifs* ("The choice of the Jews"), in which he concludes, based on a long stay in Israel, that the future of the country lies in the high-tech development of the Negev. Théo Klein, the president of CRIF, was coauthor, with Hamadi Essid, the representative of the Arab League in Paris, of a book giving their parallel views on the Middle East, *Deux vérités en face* ("Two truths in confrontation"). Problems in Jewish-Christian relations were the impetus for Raphaël Draï's polemical *Lettre ouverte au cardinal Lustiger sur l'autre révisionnisme* ("Open letter to Cardinal Lustiger on the other historical revisionism"), describing the deteriorating climate between Jews and Christians and the feeling among certain Jews that the Church did not really accept the legitimacy of Judaism.

Personalia

Among Jews honored in 1988–89, the following were made knights in the Legion of Honor: Marie-Claire Mendès-France, the widow of former prime minister Pierre Mendès-France, and president of the Mendès-France International Center for Peace in the Middle East; author Marek Halter; historian of anti-Semitism Léon Poliakov; and Stella Rozan, president of the International Council of Jewish Women. Colette Kessler, vice-president of the Jewish-Christian Friendship Association and an active member of the French Jewish Liberal (Reform) movement, was made a knight in the National Order of Merit. Former chief rabbi René Samuel Sirat; Louis Cohn, retired director of the teaching service of FSJU; and Edgard Guedj, retired deputy director of FSJU, received the Vermeil Medal of the city of Paris.

Among prominent Jews who died in 1988 were Isaac Pougatch, aged 91, one of the most engaging figures in the Jewish community and a pillar of Jewish education in postwar France; Ita-Rosa Hallaunbrenner, aged 88, one of the main witnesses in the Barbie trial, three of whose five children were caught in Izieu (April 6, 1944) and gassed in Auschwitz, as was her husband, Jacob, who was arrested by the Lyons Gestapo; Paul Lazarus, aged 78, president of the Jewish community of Metz; Chaim Sloves, aged 83, born in Bialystock, one of the great names of 20th-century Yiddish literature; Fortunée Benguigui, aged 84, another witness at the Barbie trial, who lost three children in Izieu and who died at the very moment it was announced that she had been awarded the Legion of Honor.

In 1988 the Jewish community mourned one of its most prominent intellectuals, a man whose influence continued for decades, even after he had moved to Israel. André Néher, born October 22, 1914, in Obernai (Alsace), died on October 23, 1988, in Jerusalem, where he had lived since 1969. A graduate of the rabbinical school in Montreux, Switzerland, Néher studied German literature and wrote his doctoral dissertation (1947) on the prophet Amos; he founded the chair of Jewish studies at the University of Strasbourg. Among his 23 published works, which were translated into many languages, were *L'essence du prophétisme* ("The essence of prophecy," 1955); *Moïse et la vocation juive* ("Moses and the Jewish vocation," 1956); *Le puits de l'exil; la théologie dialectique du Maharal de Prague* ("The well of exile: the dialectic theology of the Maharal of Prague," 1966); *L'exil de la parole: du silence dans la Bible au silence d'Auschwitz* ("The exile of the word; from the silence of the Bible to the silence of Auschwitz," 1970); and *Faust et le Maharal of Prague* (1987). A member of the central committee of the Alliance Israélite Universelle, Néher was president of the French section of the World Jewish Congress from 1965 to 1969.

Several leading Jews died in 1989. Sam Hoffenberg, aged 76, a member of the executive of CRIF, secretary-general of the Memorial to the Unknown Jewish Martyr, president of Brith Ivrith Olamith and French B'nai Brith, represented the International Council of B'nai Brith in UNESCO for 18 years; a survivor of the Warsaw ghetto, he had been able to complete, a few weeks before he died and with the help of historian Patrick Girard, a book on the last Jews in Warsaw, *Le camp de Poniatowa*. The painter Benn (Bension Rabinovitch), aged 83, was born in Bialystock and lived in Paris since 1930; his works, inspired by the Bible, had been displayed in exhibitions all over the world; in 1988, Benn was awarded the Honor Prize of the Academy of Sciences, Literature and Arts of the city of Lyons, and a museum devoted to his work was opened in Pont-Saint-Esprit. Bernhard Blumenkranz, aged 76, was a distinguished historian, author of *History of the Jews in France* (1972), president of the French Commission on Jewish Archives, and vice-president of the Cercle Bernard Lazare.

NELLY HANSSON

The Netherlands

National Affairs

THE COALITION GOVERNMENT OF Christian Democrats (CDA) and Liberals (VVD), headed by Rudolf Lubbers (CDA), which had been expected to remain in office until the quadrennial parliamentary elections of 1990, was prematurely dissolved on May 2, 1989. The immediate cause was a dispute over the income-tax deduction for travel between home and place of work. However, deeper causes contributed to the breakup, such as the VVD's sense that it was dominated by the CDA (it held six posts against the CDA's ten) and disunity within the VVD over various issues, including the party's future course, whether more to the right or more to the left, or keeping to a middle course.

New parliamentary elections for the 150-member Second Chamber of Parliament were held as soon as possible after the summer holiday, on September 6, and after a brief election campaign in which the CDA and Labor (PvdA) emerged as the two main contenders. Although public-opinion polls had predicted a close race, the CDA retained all its 54 seats, whereas the PvdA lost 3, dropping from 52 to 49. The VVD dropped from 27 to 22, as had been expected, since many VVD supporters blamed the party for causing an unnecessary cabinet crisis. Of the other parties, the center-left D'66 got 12 seats, or 3 more than it had held previously. The Green Left—a combination of three extreme-left small parties, the PPR, the PSP, and the Communists—retained its 6 seats, and other parties got 1 or 2 seats, including the extreme right Centrum party, which won a seat again.

A new coalition was formed with the PvdA, and on November 7 a new cabinet was sworn in, with Lubbers as premier and minister of general affairs, Wim Kok (PvdA) as vice-premier and minister of finance, and Hans van den Broek (CDA) again, for the third time, as foreign minister. Though Kok had promised to appoint at least four women cabinet ministers, there were in fact only two. Of the fourteen cabinet ministers, two had a Jewish father (but not a Jewish mother), viz., Prof. Ernst Hirsch Ballin (Justice) and Hedy D'Ancona (Welfare and Culture). The new under secretary for education, Jacques Wallage, had two Jewish parents.

In the elections for the 25 members of the Dutch delegation to the European Parliament—which aroused little interest—the Socialists and the Green Left both made slight gains.

President George Bush of the United States and Mrs. Barbara Bush spent 25 hours in the Netherlands on July 17–18, in the first official visit of a U.S. president to the Netherlands. His visit, which followed a ten-day trip to Poland, Hungary, and France, was limited to the cities of The Hague—where he was received by Premier

Lubbers and Foreign Minister Van den Broek—and the nearby town of Leyden. It was from Leyden that the Pilgrim Fathers, from one of whom Bush is said to descend, departed for the Western Hemisphere in 1620, after a nine-year stay in the Netherlands. The visit was meant to stress the good relations between the United States and the Netherlands.

The economy prospered in 1989. Exports increased. Inflation increased by only 1.5 percent, and the national income rose by 3 percent. Some 100,000 new jobs were created. Still, unemployment remained at around 400,000, and was particularly high among the so-called *allochthones,* immigrants mainly from Turkey, Morocco, and Surinam, who now numbered about 750,000. The integration of these *allochthones*—in particular the children and youths among them, who numbered some 70 percent of the total—cost the government $500 million annually and resulted in many problems. Of the *allochthones* born in the Netherlands, about 80 percent left elementary school prematurely; there were, as well, immigrant youths who arrived in the Netherlands past elementary school age. In order to enhance employment opportunities, some municipalities gave preferential treatment to *allochtones* in positions for which their skills were adequate.

The first Muslim elementary schools opened this year in Holland, one in Rotterdam and one in Eindhoven, where Muslim children, in addition to the regular curriculum, were taught the Koran. A new mosque, with room for 850 worshipers, was opened in Eindhoven. The largest in the Netherlands, the mosque was mainly for Turks, who had collected the necessary money among themselves and their compatriots in nearby Belgium and West Germany.

Holocaust-Related Issues

The emotion-laden matter of the possible release of the last two war criminals remaining in prison in Holland, both Germans—Ferdinand H. Aus der Fünten and Franz Fischer—came to an end on January 27, when the two were freed but immediately taken to the West German frontier and expelled. Known as the "Two of Breda," they had been held in a prison in that town for over 40 years. Minister of Justice Frits Korthals Altes took the initiative in a letter to the Second Chamber of Parliament dated January 24, in which he stated that the continued imprisonment of these two men, then aged 79 and 87, respectively, was senseless and inhuman. He had support for his position, he indicated, from 19 prominent Dutchmen, many of them lawyers, who had sent him a private letter expressing this view. In order to avoid arousing public passions, a parliamentary debate was hastily scheduled for Thursday night, January 26, if necessary to be continued on Friday morning the 27th. In the debate, nearly all parties were divided among themselves, usually with two spokesmen, one in favor of the release and one against. Eventually it was decided, by a vote of 85 to 55, to release and expel the prisoners. A few hours later, the two men were taken to the West German border and there handed over to West German police. Both, in fact, died not long afterward, Aus der Fünten on April 7 and Franz Fischer on September 21.

Their deaths brought to an end an issue that had occupied the Dutch public for over 40 years. During 1942–1944, both men had occupied key positions in the deportation of tens of thousands of Jews, Aus der Fünten in Amsterdam and Fischer in The Hague. The original Four of Breda—as they then were, with the addition of Willy Lages and Joseph Kotälla—had been sentenced to death by postwar special tribunals. In 1951, with the courts unable to reach a decision on their requests for mercy, it was decided that it would be more humane to change the sentences to life imprisonment. All other war criminals jailed in the Netherlands, both Dutch and German, except the 40 who had been sentenced to death in the first postwar years and been executed, had long been released, the very last around 1960. But attempts to release these four always met with fierce opposition, from both Jewish and wartime resistance circles, to whom the four men had come to symbolize the very essence of Nazi evil.

In 1966, however, Willy Lages, who was said to be mortally ill, was released by then Minister of Justice Ivo Samkalden—who was, incidentally, of Jewish origin—and allowed to spend his last months or years in his native village in West Germany. In 1972, then Minister of Justice—later Premier—Andries van Agt wanted to free the remaining three, but backed down in the face of opposition in Parliament and the public. In 1979 Joseph Kotälla, who had been partly paralyzed for a long time, died in prison. In 1987 the remaining two wrote a letter in which they expressed regret for what they had done, without asking for mercy.

Among the aforementioned 19 persons who wrote to the justice minister, some had been prominent in resistance organizations; two were eminent lawyers of Jewish origin. In the broader public, some who had been strongly against the release in 1972 now supported it, such as (non-Jewish) psychiatrist Johan Bastiaans, who argued that healing the wounds of the past was now more important than the fear of adding to survivor trauma. All Jewish organizations continued their opposition to the release, based on Jewish sensitivities. The reason why the release came when it did was probably because the 19 letter-signers, or at least their nucleus, had announced that they would make the letter public—which would again have led to public turmoil.

As it happened, on January 23, representatives of the Jewish Social Welfare Foundation (JMW) and of organizations dealing with non-Jewish war victims were invited to see the minister of welfare, Elco Brinkman, who informed them that the government intended to release the Two of Breda. He further indicated that the government would reimburse these organizations for additional expenditures arising from increased applications for help by war victims emotionally affected by the release. (Subsequently, the Ministry of Welfare and Culture made a special grant of some $750,000 annually for three years for expanded counseling services.) On January 24, the minister of justice, in the presence of the premier and at his request, received representatives of the Ashkenazi, Sephardi, and Liberal Jewish communities, as well as of the Netherlands Zionist Organization and the Center for Information and Documentation on Israel (CIDI), to inform them of the cabinet decision. The Jewish representatives protested, but to no avail. For at least a fortnight after the release, public debate on the matter continued in the press, on radio, and TV, with emphasis on the suffering the release caused to victims of Nazism.

There were developments in the cases of two Dutch war criminals, Jan Olij and Abraham Kipp, who had been sentenced to life imprisonment *in absentia* in the postwar years, primarily for handing over numerous Jews to the Germans. Olij was discovered to be living in Argentina, but that country, after lengthy diplomatic negotiation, refused to extradite Olij, on the grounds that he was now an Argentinian national and that the crimes he was convicted of did not exist in Argentina's statute books. Kipp was found to have died several years earlier in Switzerland.

Relations with Israel

The Netherlands continued to deny diplomatic status to the representative of the Palestine Liberation Organization (PLO) in The Hague, who was the director of the PLO Information Office there. But the new incumbent in this position, Afif Safieh, a Christian Arab born in East Jerusalem, used every opportunity to enhance the importance of his position and of the PLO in the country.

Foreign Minister Hans van den Broek had been invited by the PLO in November 1988 to visit PLO headquarters in Tunisia. After the statement by PLO head Yasir Arafat in Geneva in December of that year, recognizing the State of Israel's existence and renouncing terrorism, Van den Broek thought the time had come for a cautious approach to the PLO. Rather than going himself, however, he sent a three-member delegation to Tunisia, on January 8, consisting of the director-general of political affairs in his ministry, the director of the Middle East Division, and the Netherlands ambassador in Tunisia. Although they had been promised a meeting with Arafat, he never appeared, and the delegation met only senior PLO representatives. After waiting for Arafat for nearly three days, the delegation returned home late on the 10th. It was later learned that Arafat, newly named president of the "State of Palestine," had not thought the level of the Dutch delegation high enough. Reporting to Parliament on this visit on January 13, Van den Broek stated that for the time being he would not seek to establish contact with the PLO.

Also in January, a six-member delegation of the Netherlands Federation of Trade Unions (FNV) visited Israel and the occupied areas. They asked the Histadrut to urge the Israeli government to give full rights to the Palestinian trade unions; on their return they criticized the Histadrut for failing to recognize the Palestinian trade unions fully.

From January 31 to February 2, a symposium on "The Israeli-Palestinian Problem in European Perspective" took place in The Hague. It had been organized by an ad hoc organization, the Middle East Dialogue Project, which was believed to be PLO-inspired. A 17-member PLO delegation participated, headed by Bassam

Abu Sharif, one of Arafat's main political advisers, as well as a number of left-wing Israelis, such as Me'ir Pa'il and Ran Cohen, as well as Abba Eban. The latter had been strongly advised by the Israeli government not to take part, but did so all the same. Dutch foreign minister Van den Broek had been asked to open the symposium, which he did, at least partly in deference to Eban, and then left immediately, but not before Bassam Abu Sharif shook hands with him, an act recorded by several press photographers.

From September 5 to 15, a delegation of the Netherlands Council of Churches visited Israel and the occupied areas, at the request of the Middle East Council of Churches (MECC) and the Latin Patriarch of Jerusalem, Michael Sabbah, to express solidarity with Palestinian Christians and with the Palestinians in general and to study their situation. On its return, the delegation, headed by council chairman Prof. Dirk C. Mulder, reported that the human rights of the Palestinians were being systematically violated by Israel. It also expressed support for the two-state solution and said it was Israel's turn to recognize the right of the Palestinians to a state of their own, now that the PLO had recognized the right of existence of the State of Israel. Its report got ample coverage in the Dutch news media.

Considerable commotion was caused by a solidarity meeting with the Palestinians organized by PLO representative Afif Safieh in The Hague on November 23, to mark the second anniversary of the outbreak of the *intifada* and the first anniversary of the proclamation of the Palestinian state. As speakers he had invited representatives of most political parties as well as the chairman of the Netherlands Council of Churches, Dirk Mulder. The Liberals (VVD) rejected the invitation outright; representatives of the other parties did so only after considerable pressure. Mulder kept his promise to appear; however, he explained to the audience that his group felt solidarity both with Israel and with the Palestinians. Still, OJEC, the Consultative Council of Jews and Christians, which had insisted strongly that Professor Mulder refrain from speaking, suspended relations with the Council of Churches.

On December 19, a closed meeting took place in Amsterdam of 30 persons of Jewish origin who had been individually invited to discuss the Palestinian problem. The meeting was organized by the Dutch branch of the International Center for Peace in the Middle East (ICPME) in Tel Aviv. A press communiqué afterward stated that the overwhelming majority of those present were in favor of a dialogue with the PLO.

On December 8, in Amsterdam, a small group of women of the Dutch branch of the Israeli "Women in Black," at the request of the latter, held the first of their monthly one-hour demonstrations calling for Israeli withdrawal from the occupied territories. In Israel, the mass peace demonstration around the walls of Jerusalem's Old City on December 30 was attended by representatives of Dutch peace organizations, such as Pax Christi and the IKV (Inter-Church Peace Council).

In September the Netherlands minister for development aid gave a sum of $600,000 for a period of four years to the Palestine Red Crescent for the training of nursing personnel in Cairo.

The import of fruit from the Gaza Strip to the European Common Market, on which the European Community had so strongly insisted, even threatening Israel with sanctions if it did not agree to permit shipments, was largely a failure. After the first shipment arrived in Rotterdam in December 1988, with much fanfare, only a small part of the scheduled 16,000 tons actually reached the continent, and even of this much remained unsold. The failure resulted in mutual accusations of deceit and incompetence by the Gaza fruit growers and the Dutch importer. Prospects for the 1989–90 season were not bright either.

JEWISH COMMUNITY

Demography

Although no reliable figures were available, the number of Jews living in the Netherlands was estimated at about 25,000, the large majority of whom were unaffiliated with the organized Jewish community. The Netherlands Ashkenazi community (Nederlands Israelietisch Kerkgenootschap, NIK) gave its present membership as 5,800, down several thousand from the previous year's figure. The drop resulted from a different method of calculating membership by the Ashkenazi community of Amsterdam (NIHS). The latter had hitherto counted as members all Jews of Ashkenazi origin living in the city who had not explicitly renounced their membership, even though they had not been active or involved for years. Eliminating this latter element, the number of members of the Ashkenazi community of Amsterdam and the surrounding area was reduced from 4,800 to 3,000. The Hague area had 400 members; the Rotterdam area, 360; the three together, 3,760, or 65 percent of the country total. There were, in addition, 9 middle-sized communities, ranging in size from 225 members (Bussum, east of Amsterdam) to 85 members (Groningen), totaling 1,125 members, and 21 small communities, each with fewer than 75 members, totaling 930 persons. The whole of the province of Limburg was now officially one community, and the two neighboring communities of Doetinchem and Terborg, east of Arnhem, merged to form one, De Achterhoek.

The Portuguese (Sephardi) Jewish community had some 600 members and one congregation, in Amsterdam.

The Liberal Jewish community had some 2,400 members, in six congregations, of which only those in Amsterdam and The Hague had full-time rabbis and could hold regular weekly services. Two part-time rabbis also served Liberal congregations.

Communal Affairs

For the first time in its 175-year history the NIK appointed a rabbi for itself, in the person of Dutch-born Raphael Evers, aged 38, who, in addition to having received ordination (*semikhah*) in Jerusalem, held M.A. degrees in psychology and law. Since 1981 he had been director of studies at the Netherlands Ashkenazi Rabbinical and Teachers Seminary, a position he continued to hold. The board of the NIK felt the need to have a rabbi represent it as such, as well as in contacts with the news media. Previously, rabbis in the Netherlands served only local districts, to which they were appointed by the District Councils of the NIK. The tasks of Rabbi Evers were carefully defined so as to avoid conflict with the local rabbis.

On February 12, Rabbi Lody van de Kamp, formerly rabbi of the Ashkenazi congregation of The Hague, and Rabbi Frank Lewis, formerly of London, were officially installed as communal rabbis of Amsterdam. Together with Isaac Vorst, who had already been a pastoral member of the rabbinate for many years, the Amsterdam Ashkenazi rabbinate was once again up to its traditional complement of three.

In Rotterdam, Rabbi Hans Rodriques Pereira was appointed as "central figure," primarily for pastoral work, in a part-time position.

The Sephardi community (PIG) celebrated the 350th anniversary of the União, the amalgamation of the three formerly separate Sephardi congregations in Amsterdam, on April 7–8, with a special synagogue service and a luncheon for members only. The famous Sephardi Synagogue in Amsterdam, over 300 years old, was in need of extensive restoration, which the congregation itself was unable to pay for, though the government and the Amsterdam municipality promised to pay part of the costs. A "Friends of the PIG" foundation was established, with a board consisting of both Jews and non-Jews. During his official visit to the Netherlands (October 2–4), the president of Portugal, Mario Soares, visited the synagogue and also the adjoining Sephardi Etz Hayim Library.

The Jewish community of Utrecht, with some 200 members (against 1,800 in 1940), celebrated its 200th anniversary this year. Among other activities, it published a reprint of the history of the Utrecht Jewish community written by the late Utrecht Jewish historian Jacques Zwarts, who perished in 1943, with the addition of more recent data.

The Jewish women's group Deborah celebrated its tenth anniversary with a weekend in the country, March 3–5. The newly created Deborah ring was presented, for the first time, to Bloeme Evers (née Emden), the group's inspiring chairwoman almost from the beginning.

Membership in the Netherlands Zionist Organization (NZB), which had been steadily declining, was down to about 1,200, the large majority of whom were members on paper only. Moreover, the group's financial situation caused serious concern; the subsidy of the World Zionist Organization was drastically cut, and due to overspending during previous years there was a budget deficit. Most of the local branches had practically no activities.

Sar-El, a newly established group to recruit volunteers—both Jews and non-Jews—for temporary work in Israel, for instance in hospitals, met with enthusiastic response.

The Netherlands Circle for Jewish Genealogy—established in 1987—had almost 300 members, both Jews and non-Jews, in Holland and abroad. In addition to holding monthly meetings and publishing a quarterly, *Misjpoge,* on March 13 it held a highly successful conference in the center of the country at which members could exchange information.

The cornerstone was laid for a new Jewish old-age home in Amsterdam's southern suburb of Buitenveldert, where a large number of Jews lived. It would replace the present Beth Shalom home in the western outskirts of Amsterdam, which was not conveniently situated for the city's Jewish population.

The Jewish Maimonides Lyceum in Amsterdam celebrated its 60th anniversary on March 12 with an evening program attended by some 700 former pupils.

Community Relations

The Council of State on April 18 rejected the demand by the Netherlands Society for the Protection of Animals that kosher slaughter for export no longer be permitted. The number of animals slaughtered for export—to Switzerland and to Israel—far exceeded that slaughtered for local consumption. The animal protection group did not appeal.

The cost of providing protection for Jewish buildings was a matter of continuing concern. In a memorandum to the Second Chamber of Parliament in November, the cabinet wrote that although the protection of buildings was primarily the responsibility of those directly concerned, an exception could be made for buildings of Jewish institutions in view of the continuous real danger to them and the financial efforts already made by the Jewish community for their own security needs.

Jewish-Christian Relations

The issue of the convent at the site of the Auschwitz concentration camp continued to arouse strong feeling in the Dutch Jewish community. When Holland's highest Roman Catholic official, Adrian Cardinal Simonis, told an interviewer in August that attitudes of certain fanatical Jews were inflammatory and did not help matters, Dutch Jewish representatives canceled a scheduled meeting with him, one which they had requested, largely to discuss other matters. In 1986 the same Cardinal Simonis—who later apologized for his words—had written to Cardinal Macharski of Krakow expressing support for Jewish sensibilities in the Auschwitz matter. A temporary storm was also caused by the bishop of Haarlem, Msgr. Herman Bomers, who told the Dutch-Jewish weekly *Nieuw Israelitisch Weekblad,* among other things, that, as a Christian, his ultimate hope was that the Jews would recognize Jesus as the messiah. Some weeks later, he too publicly apologized for his words.

The Netherlands Episcopate contributed $50,000 to the Polish bishops toward the construction of a center for prayer and contemplation at a site near, but not at,

Auschwitz. The Netherlands Roman Catholic Council for Israel issued a statement criticizing the convent at Auschwitz for obscuring the fact that the vast majority of persons killed there were Jews. Another voice critical of the convent was that of OJEC, the Consultative Council of Jews and Christians, which also protested the "selective indignation" expressed by a delegation of the Netherlands Council of Churches that visited Israel early in September and criticized Israel's treatment of the Palestinians but not Palestinian violence.

The so-called Houses of Learning, established under the auspices of the OJEC, where Jews and Christians together studied Bible and Judaism, continued to flourish all over the country, though nearly all the participants were non-Jewish.

Culture and Education

A facsimile edition of the Amsterdam Large *Mahzor,* written around 1240 in or near Cologne, was presented to the chairman of the Amsterdam Ashkenazi community, which owned the original volume, during the International Conference of Jewish Museums held in Amsterdam August 29–September 1. The original prayer compilation, which was presented to the congregation in 1669 by the famous Amsterdam printer Uri Phoebus Halevi, was now on permanent loan to the Jewish Historical Museum in Amsterdam. The facsimile edition, printed by Messrs. Brill in Leyden, included an introduction by Prof. Albert van der Heide of Leyden and shorter essays by other scholars. Its publication was subsidized by the Netherlands Foundation for Scientific Research.

With the teaching of Hebrew in government secondary schools threatened by a reorganization plan, teachers of Hebrew—both Jewish and non-Jewish—met on September 13 to discuss ways and means to guarantee its continuation, if only for two hours a week in the highest grades. In 1970 Hebrew was taught at 70 secondary schools in Holland; in 1989 the number had dropped to 8. In most cases instruction was of biblical Hebrew and was offered primarily for future Christian theology students.

The Anne Frank House, which had some 600,000 visitors in 1989, mostly tourists, applied for permission to build an extension. Neighbors objected to the planned addition, but no final decision had been taken by the Amsterdam municipality at year's end.

An exhibition on anti-Semitism was opened on May 25 in the Anne Frank House by Elie Wiesel, who had been invited to come from the United States for the occasion. On October 11, the Anne Frank Medal was presented to the Netherlands Auschwitz Committee for its efforts to combat anti-Semitism.

Two main temporary exhibitions were shown this year at the Jewish Historical Museum in Amsterdam, one on Russian-Jewish avant-garde artists between 1912 and 1928, originated by the Israel Museum in Jerusalem, and one on Russian-Jewish history between 1880 and 1985, originated by the Jewish Museum in New York.

Some personnel changes occurred this year in chairs of Jewish studies in Dutch institutions. Yehuda Ashkenazy retired as a teacher of Rabbinics at the Roman Catholic Theological Academies of Amsterdam and Utrecht; he had occupied the Amsterdam post for 20 years. Born in Czechoslovakia and a survivor of Auschwitz, he reached Holland in the 1960s. Known as a teacher who aroused enthusiasm for his subject, he was honored with a jubilee volume on his departure. Ashkenazy remained director of the B. Folkertsma Foundation for Jewish Studies in Hilversum. The two posts he left vacant had not been filled by the end of the year, in part because the new requirement that women be given preference in academic appointments resulted in a protracted search process.

Rena Fuks (née Mansfeld) was given a three-year appointment to a special chair in Jewish studies at the University of Amsterdam established jointly by the Foundation for Jewish Studies and the Jewish Social Welfare Foundation (JMW). Funds for the post came from unclaimed legacies assigned by the government to the JMW. Mrs. Fuks, who received her Ph.D. at the University of Amsterdam on May 11, with a thesis on the history of the Sephardic Jews in Amsterdam in the 17th and 18th centuries, had been lecturing on Jewish history and Yiddish for several years. (She was, incidentally, the wife of Leo Fuks, the retired librarian of the Bibliotheca Rosenthaliana.)

Ido Abram was appointed to a part-time position as professor of Shoah education at the University of Amsterdam in a special chair established by the Folkertsma Foundation and the Foundation for Educational Research at the university. Abram would continue to serve as director of the Pedagogical Study Center in Amsterdam.

Memorials, Restorations, and Commemorative Events

The restoration of some unused or only partly used synagogue buildings, carried out largely at non-Jewish local initiative, continued this year. In Zwolle, the capital of the province of Overijssel, the large synagogue dating from 1899, of which only part was currently being used as a synagogue, was reopened in September in an official ceremony. The adjoining street was renamed for Samuel J. Hirsch, the last chief rabbi of Zwolle, who passed away in 1941. In Boertange, in the extreme northeast, and in Meerssen, in the extreme southeast, near Maastricht, small synagogues that had ceased being used by 1940 were restored as cultural monuments.

Monuments in memory of local Jews who perished during World War II were unveiled this year in Dordrecht, in the town hall; in Vierlingsbeek, in the Jewish cemetery; in Gulpen, in the southeast of Limburg; in Gorinchem, at the site of the demolished synagogue; in Leyden, at the site of the former Jewish orphanage from which all the children were deported on March 17, 1943; in Amsterdam, at the site of the former Jewish Boys' Orphanage Megadle Jethomim, from which some 100 children were deported on March 5, 1943. The Amsterdam building was demolished some years ago, and its site was now incorporated in the modern Music Theater. The monument was erected at the initiative of a group of surviving orphans. A monument was also unveiled at the site of the former Jewish Work Village Wieringermeer, in the north of North Holland province, where from 1933 to 1941 young Jewish refugees from Germany were trained in trades and agriculture to facilitate their emigration overseas.

In Brunssum, in the south of the province of Limburg, a reunion took place on May 7 of over 700 Jews, now scattered all over the world, who had been hidden there as small children by non-Jewish foster parents during the years 1943–45. The children were taken to the village by members of the resistance group NV, many of them having been removed from the Jewish day nursery that stood opposite the Hollandse Schouwburg in Amsterdam, which in 1942–43 served as a collection center for Jews who had just been rounded up by the Nazis, prior to their transfer to Westerbork. About 1,000 children were saved in this way.

One of those who helped to smuggle the children out of the Hollandse Schouwburg was Walter Susskind, a young German Jew who was later deported to his death. In his honor, the Walter Susskind Memorial Fund was established, in Boston, for the artistic education of underprivileged children, as part of the Young at Arts Project(s) of the Wang Center in Boston. The establishment of the fund, which was initiated by Maurice and Netty Vandepoll, originally of Amsterdam and now living in Boston, was marked by a gala dinner on November 4. Among the guests were the governor of Massachusetts, Michael Dukakis, and the present mayor of Amsterdam, Ed van Thijn, himself a Jew.

A very different ceremony took place on October 17 and 18 in Bytom (formerly Beuthen) and the adjacent Szczecin in Upper Silesia, now part of Poland. A monument was unveiled to the 109 Dutch Jews who, as part of the so-called Kosel group of forced laborers, perished in this place between August 28 and December 12, 1942. Relatives and friends of the deceased attended the ceremony as guests of the Netherlands War Graves Foundation.

An exhibition was shown in May, in Apeldoorn, on the history of the "Apeldoornsche Bosch," the large central Jewish psychiatric hospital in the center of the Netherlands, dating from 1909, from which all 1,200 patients and some 50 staff members were deported January 22, 1943.

Publications

New books about Dutch Jewry included *De verdwenen Buurt. Drie eeuwen centrum Joods Den Haag* ("On the Former Jewish Quarter of The Hague") by I.B. van Creveld; *Joods Nederland* ("A Guide Through Jewish Monuments in the Netherlands") by J. Stoutenbeek and P. Vigeveno; *Antisemitisme in Nederland 1945–1948* by Dienke Hondius; and *Zonder Jas de straat op* ("Without a Coat into the Street"), a novel about second-generation Jews by Helene Weyel. The Balans publishing company, which had published the diaries of Etty Hillesum in 1983, this year published a volume containing 24 essays written in reaction to the diaries.

In addition, Dutch translations appeared this year of works by such authors as Chaim Potok, Saul Bellow, Bernard Malamud, Primo Levi, Philip Roth, Amos Oz,

Yehuda Amichai, A.B. Yehoshua, David Grossman, and Yoram Binur, and by the philosopher Emanuel Levinas and the "liberation theologian" Marc H. Ellis.

Personalia

David Goudsmit, who retired at age 80 from his position as librarian of the Sephardi Etz Hayim Library and who had been a Jewish teacher for many years, was honored at a reception on September 3 by the Netherlands Ashkenazi community. The same month, the Dutch-Jewish author Siegfried E. van Praag, who had been living in Brussels for some 50 years, was honored at a reception in Amsterdam on his 90th birthday. Prof. Hans Bloemendal celebrated his 40th year as cantor of the main Amsterdam synagogue. He had many records of cantoral music to his credit.

The Dutch Visser-Neerlandia Prize for important contributions to the spread of the Dutch language was given to a Belgian, Louis Davids, of Antwerp, who had been chief editor for many years of the *Belgisch-Israelietisch Weekblad.* The weekly was published in Dutch for its Flemish-speaking readers (written Flemish being identical with Dutch).

The film *Leedvermaak* by Frans Weiss, based on the play of the same name by Judith Herzberg, received three Golden Calf awards at the Ninth Netherlands Film Festival in September.

Among leading Dutch Jews who died in 1989 were Abel J. Herzberg, aged 95, author, lawyer, and Zionist, recipient of many Dutch literary prizes, who was regarded by many non-Jews as the leading representative of Dutch Jewry; Dr. Maurits Goudeket, aged 76, a founder member of the postwar Liberal Jewish community, which he headed for many years, a former chairman of the Netherlands Jewish Social Welfare Foundation (JMW), and active in many other Jewish organizations; Joost Glaser, aged 73, a retired officer in the Dutch army in the Dutch East Indies who, after his return to Holland, was a director of JMW, a member of the executive of the NIK, and active in B'nai Brith and in the OJEC; and Louis Alvarez Vega, aged 84, for many years secretary of the Sephardi community of Amsterdam and keeper of the Sephardi cemetery in Ouderkerk.

HENRIETTE BOAS

Italy

National Affairs

THE ITALIAN POLITICAL SCENE in 1989 was still dominated by conflict between the two main partners in the coalition government, the Christian Democrats (DC) and the Socialists (PSI). Ciriaco De Mita, prime minister as well as secretary of the Christian Democratic party, was regarded by leading members of his own party as the person chiefly responsible for the tensions. De Mita also came under fire from the press for his role in the illegal distribution of funds for the reconstruction of Irpinia, an area devastated by an earthquake in 1980. In March De Mita was removed from his position as secretary of the party and replaced by Arnaldo Forlani, who was on friendlier terms with the Socialists. In May De Mita resigned from the leadership of the government, and Christian Democrat Giulio Andreotti, the former minister for foreign affairs, was chosen as prime minister. The new coalition government he led was similar to the former one but characterized by much better relations among the partners. The Socialist Gianni De Michelis became Italy's new foreign affairs minister.

A scandal involving the Atlanta, Georgia, branch of the Banca Nazionale del Lavoro (BNL, the largest bank in Italy) unfolded before the public in the course of 1989. It came to be known as "Iraq-gate." The U.S. Federal Bureau of Investigation discovered that since 1987, the director of BNL's Atlanta branch, Christopher Drogoul, had issued letters of credit as financial guarantees for the export to Iraq of arms and other strategic items produced by Italian companies. Such export was forbidden both by the European Community (EC) and the Italian government. The credit guaranteed by the Atlanta branch of the BNL amounted to a record $3.3 million, a sum almost as large as the authorized capital of the bank.

The results of the FBI investigation were partially disclosed by the Italian press in September, along with charges that the director of a secondary branch of a publicly owned bank could not have guaranteed such large sums unless top figures in the BNL authorized his decisions, or were at least made aware of them. As a result of the scandal, Nerio Nesi, general director of the BNL, resigned. At the end of September the Iraqi ambassador to Italy, Mohammed Said al-Sahaf, threatened to suspend all payments of sums owed by his country to Italy unless the latter continued to grant credits and loans to Iraq. The press dropped the matter after a few weeks, but it raised important questions about Iraqi connections in Italy that remained unanswered.

Relations with Israel

Italy's official position regarding Israel and the Middle East did not change in 1989. Both in bilateral relations and in EC forums, Italy was highly critical of Israeli policy and quite sympathetic to the PLO. At the same time, there were some positive developments in the cultural and economic fields.

In the winter the Italian government launched an aid program of about $75 million for the Arabs of the occupied territories of Israel. The humanitarian project, the largest ever adopted by any European government, focused on providing medical equipment and personnel and developing hospitals in the West Bank and Gaza Strip.

A matter that threatened to raise tensions between Italy and Israel emerged in January, when Judge Carlo Mastelloni of Venice indicted Zvi Zamir, former head of Israeli intelligence, as being directly responsible for the sabotage of an Italian Air Force plane that crashed near Venice in November 1973, killing five Italian intelligence officers on board. The aircraft had been used a few months earlier to fly five Palestinian terrorists, freed by the Italian government, from Rome to Malta. The release of the terrorists was said to be part of a general agreement between Italian intelligence and some Arab terror organizations. From the start, Italian authorities maintained that the crash was an accident and not an act of sabotage. However, persons in the intelligence community with close ties to Libya and the Arab countries leaked rumors to the press and hinted in interviews that Israel was responsible. Their campaign was backed and supported by the Neo-Fascist party (MSI). After the indictment of Zamir, no further developments in the case occurred this year.

Prime Minister De Mita and Foreign Affairs Minister Andreotti arrived in Israel for a three-day official visit on April 23. They met with President Chaim Herzog, Prime Minister Yitzhak Shamir, Foreign Minister Moshe Arens, Deputy Prime Minister and Minister of Finance Shimon Peres, and members of the Italian Jewish community in Israel. De Mita and Andreotti expressed cautious support for Shamir's recently announced peace plan based on free elections in the territories, but insisted that Israel come to terms with the fact that the PLO was considered by the Palestinians as their legitimate representative. They even encouraged local Palestinian leaders from the territories to accept the Israeli initiative as a first step toward serious negotiations. Israeli officials expressed satisfaction with the visit, hoping that De Mita's and Andreotti's cautious if skeptical interest in Shamir's proposals would help Israel gain the support of the EC for its peace initiative.

Israeli prime minister Shamir briefly visited Italy on November 23, where he met with Italian president Francesco Cossiga, Prime Minister Andreotti, Foreign Affairs Minister De Michelis, President of the Senate Giovanni Spadolini, and other political leaders. The meetings focused on Shamir's peace plan, which Italian leaders seemed to find moderately interesting but viewed with reservations.

The already high interest of the Italian public in the Israeli-Arab conflict was heightened by the participation of some 1,200 Italians in the massive peace demonstration held in Jerusalem on December 30. The initiative for the human chain around Jerusalem's Old City walls was taken jointly by a Christian pacifist organization based in Assisi and some Israeli groups, chief among them Peace Now. The demonstration, which was intended to encourage Israeli-Palestinian dialogue, was attended by Israelis, Palestinians, Europeans, and people from all religious denominations and faiths. When the demonstration was about to end, the Israeli police attacked a group of Palestinians who were shouting pro-PLO slogans, using water cannons and plastic bullets to disperse them. Several Italians were beaten by the police, and a young Italian woman, Marisa Mannu, who was watching the scene from the window of an East Jerusalem hotel, was injured and lost her right eye as a result of glass shattered by a police water cannon. Severe criticism was expressed by the Italian press and political bodies about the behavior of the Israeli police.

Despite their political differences, cultural relations between the two countries remained strong. Significantly, Prime Minister De Mita and Foreign Affairs Minister Andreotti began their official visit to Israel in April by meeting with Rabbi Adin Steinsaltz, the renowned Talmud scholar and founder of a Moscow yeshivah. Rabbi Steinsaltz presented Andreotti with an ancient Torah crown to symbolize the fact that the Italian foreign minister had achieved "a crown even higher than those of the priesthood, royalty and Torah learning, the crown of a good name, for he helped the Jewish people to restore Torah in the USSR." Andreotti actually did play an important role in the advancement of Steinsaltz's projects in the USSR, his personal interest leading to the deep involvement of Italian institutions such as the C.N.R. (National Council for Research) and the Istituto dell'Enciclopedia Italiana, which agreed to finance the translation of the Talmud into Russian.

Italian industrialist and investor Carlo De Benedetti, owner of Olivetti and other important firms, visited Israel in July, at the invitation of Finance Minister Shimon Peres, who hoped to attract Italian investment. De Benedetti, who seemed to be particularly interested in Israeli projects in the field of communications, such as the Amos satellite, declared that he had not come to give advice and had no immediate investment plans; he also said that his interest in Israel was purely economic. He saw potential in a combination of Israeli brain power and Italian marketing capacity, but warned that the country's economic potential would soon be wasted unless Israel solved its problems with the neighboring Arab countries. He also urged Israeli businessmen, industrialists, and politicians to be less American-minded: Europe is not less important than the United States, he said, and it is much closer.

In December the mayors of Milan, Paolo Pillitteri, and Tel Aviv, Shlomo Lahat, signed an agreement for the twinning of the two cities, defined by Pillitteri as similar, "for they are both the pulsing heart of their own country's finance and trade: Milano and Tel Aviv are both dynamic, modern, and sophisticated."

Four Italians were honored this year as "Righteous Gentiles" by Israeli authorities. Giorgio Perlasca, an 80-year-old retired businessman, was called the "Italian Wallenberg" for the role he played in saving Jewish lives in Budapest in the years 1944–45. Himself trapped in Budapest in 1943 on business, he was interned but managed to escape. As a former soldier in the Italian contingent supporting Franco in the Spanish Civil War, he was entitled to Spanish citizenship, which he received from the Spanish legation in Budapest. In the guise of an official Spanish representative, he was able to rescue some 3,000 Jews, providing them with shelter, food, and false documents.

Pellegrino Riccardi, now a retired judge, was a magistrate in the northern town of Fornovo during the years 1943–45. He saved several Jewish families, providing them with documents under false names and organizing their flight to Switzerland. Riccardi also took care of a nine-month-old child until the child could be returned to his parents a few months later.

The brothers Oreste and Dante Soffici, who passed away some years ago, were Tuscany peasants who gave shelter for a year and a half to two Jewish children who managed to escape when their parents were arrested by the Fascist police in December 1943. The parents were subsequently killed in Auschwitz, whereas the children remained with the Soffici brothers up to the end of the war.

Anti-Semitism

In 1989 there were fewer anti-Semitic acts in Italy than in 1988, but still more than in previous years. At the annual meeting of the Commission on Anti-Semitism of the European Jewish Congress (EJC) held in London, March 9–10, Adriana Goldstaub of the Center for Contemporary Jewish Documentation (CDEC, a research institute based in Milan) reported that during 1988, the number of anti-Semitic incidents had increased in Italy by more than 30 percent (the count includes newspaper and magazine articles). From this point of view the Italian situation differed from the trend prevailing in the rest of the European continent, where the number of anti-Semitic acts was reported to be diminishing. According to Goldstaub, a new kind of anti-Semitism, based on anti-Zionism, was on the rise. Others at the meeting suggested that anti-Semitism might be increasing as part of the wave of xenophobia sweeping Europe. The growing presence of foreign workers from Third World countries, most of them of Muslim religion, who had come to Italy and other Western European countries in recent years, awakened latent racist attitudes, provoked acts of hostility against Asians and Africans, and led to the meteoric rise of right-wing groups on the political scene. Many worried that such a climate of opinion, though not directly hostile toward the Jews, fostered a general animosity toward all "foreigners," including the Jews.

In January, in Rome, the Associazione per l'Amicizia Ebraico-Cristiana (Association for Jewish-Christian Friendship), a group involved in interfaith dialogue, presented the results of a survey on anti-Semitic prejudice among adults and high-school students in Italy. The survey was based on a questionnaire of 44 items administered to 1,000 people in several towns and, though not scientifically conducted, showed interesting results: the lessening of old stereotypes rooted in Christian beliefs and the strengthening of anti-Zionist, sometimes even anti-Semitic, tendencies among the young. Only 2 percent of adults and 4 percent of students thought that Jews bore lasting responsibility for the death of Jesus, and 80 percent of both groups felt that Jews had the right to build their homeland in Palestine. On the subject of the Palestinians, 28 percent of the students and 6 percent of the adults said they had been forced out of their homes and land by the Israelis in 1948; 43 percent of the students and 23 percent of the adults assigned Israel heavy responsibility for the existence of Palestinian refugee camps; 12 percent of the students said that Israel was an imperialist state; 21 percent defined Israeli policy in the occupied territories as "genocide." Asked to express individual views about both the present situation in the Middle East and the Jews in Italy, some 40–45 percent of the students said that the "[Israeli] Jews were crushing others as others crushed them in the past," and that there were "too many Jews in Italy." Most of those interviewed, both adults and youngsters, estimated that the Italian Jewish community numbered more than 100,000, while in fact it included a third that number.

The most publicized episode of anti-Semitism occurred in the month of July. Ronnie Rosenthal, an Israeli soccer player, signed a contract with Udinese, an Italian A-League team based in the northern industrial town of Udine. Following his arrival in Udine in early July, Rosenthal and the managers of the team were targets of a strong anti-Semitic campaign aimed at preventing Rosenthal from playing. The campaign was based on anonymous threats and acts of intimidation, such as anti-Semitic graffiti bearing swastikas and coffins with the name of Rosenthal that appeared on the walls of Udine. The affair's climax came when Rosenthal underwent medical examinations required by his contract and the physicians found a congenital malformation in his spinal column. Udinese managers were advised to dismiss Rosenthal, which they did. Rosenthal and his agent maintained that the malformation was not serious and had not prevented the player from performing excellently in the recent past. They charged the managers of Udinese with hiding behind the malformation and actually seizing the opportunity to get rid of Rosenthal, who had become a cause of friction between the team and part of its supporters.

JEWISH COMMUNITY

Demography

An estimated 31,000 Jews were affiliated with one or other of the local Italian Jewish communities, with no significant change in number over the previous year.

Communal Affairs

The agreement ("*intese*") between the Unione delle Comunità Ebraiche Italiane (UCEI),[1] the roof organization of the Italian Jewish communities, and the Italian state, was finally approved by the Italian Chamber of Deputies and Senate at the beginning of the year and became an official law of the state on April 7. (On the agreement, its background, content, and significance, see AJYB 1989, pp. 328–30.)

The UCEI was active in the European Jewish forum and participated in several meetings organized by the European Jewish Congress (EJC). The activities of that body, a branch of the World Jewish Congress, gained momentum this year due to the process of political liberalization taking place in Eastern European countries, which enabled long-separated Jewish communities to establish closer contact. In addition, the growing economic, legislative, and political integration of European Community (EC) countries necessitated greater cooperation among the various national Jewish communities in Western as well as in Eastern Europe.

The annual meeting of the EJC, held in London, September 10–12, was attended by representatives from East Germany, Poland, Hungary, Czechoslovakia, Romania, Yugoslavia, and the USSR. The discussions, chaired by Israel Singer of the World Jewish Congress, dealt with the challenge facing "European Jewry under the new world order." Tullia Zevi, president of the UCEI and a member of the EJC's executive, chaired the session on relations with the Catholic Church in light of the controversy over the Carmelite convent at Auschwitz (see below).

The EJC executive meeting held in London in the same period was attended for the first time by a representative of Soviet Jewry, Michael Chlenov. UCEI representative Tullia Zevi raised strong objection to the congress rule limiting the presidency to French and English delegates, alternating in the position, and threatened to withdraw Italian participation in the EJC if it were not changed. The EJC executive held another important meeting in Paris on December 10, at which the situation in the countries of the collapsed Communist bloc was discussed at length with the representatives of Eastern European communities. It was decided to coordinate the struggle against anti-Semitism on a continental scale and to lay the groundwork for the establishment of a Jewish lobby in Brussels, the site of most of the EC's decision making as well as its representative bodies. More than 3,000 lobbies already operated in Brussels.

With the twin goals of reinforcing Jewish identity and producing new communal leadership, the board of governors of the European Council for Jewish Community Service (ECJCS), meeting in Frankfurt April 9–10, adopted a unified educational plan for all European Jewish communities. The governors, among whom was a representative of the UCEI, approved a common curriculum plan, courses for teachers in Jewish schools and Jewish social workers active in their communities, and other initiatives. The community of Rome was among those chosen for the

---

[1]Formerly UCII. One word was changed in 1987 from "Israelitiche" to "Ebraiche."

introduction of a new instructional approach in Jewish schools.

The Italian Zionist Federation, WIZO, and other Zionist organizations held a conference in Milan on "Italian Jewry and Israel," March 11–12, which was attended by representatives of all the Italian communities and by Israeli officials. Discussions focused on the stance taken by Italian Jewry toward the situation in Israel, in light of the general anti-Zionist atmosphere sweeping Italy. The Israelis expressed regret that the participants failed to declare Italian Diaspora support for Israel publicly when Israel was attacked. It was countered that Italian Jews did support Israel, but that the bilateral relations were more complex than could have been stated in a public document.

Representatives of Italian Jewry were invited by the Israeli embassy in Rome to participate in Prime Minister Shamir's international "Solidarity" conference held in Jerusalem, March 20–22. The Italians signed the final statement, which expressed support of Israel's desire for peace and affirmed the democratic nature and behavior of the Jewish state, but it was known that the statement was actually a modified version of an earlier statement that proved too controversial. Italians were instrumental in softening the original and drafting a text that was general enough to win wide support.

A group of Italian Jews who participated in the activities of the International Center for Peace in the Middle East organized an international forum in Milan, November 16–18, to discuss Israeli peace prospects. Among those who attended and participated in the discussions were Israeli Knesset members Lova Eliav (Labor party) and Shulamit Aloni (Civil Rights Movement); Yasir Abed Rabbu (PLO executive); and representatives of the Italian Communist party and the central committee of the USSR's Communist party. Abba Eban (former Israeli MK) and Richard Murphy (U.S. assistant secretary of state) sent videocassettes with prerecorded speeches. The forum attracted considerable media attention.

Community Relations

The long-lasting fight of the UCEI, the Protestant churches, and other groups for a complete secularization of the Italian public school (see AJYB 1988, p. 297) achieved a remarkable victory this year. In the spring the Corte Costituzionale (Italy's Supreme Court) ruled that students who chose not to attend the optional lessons in Catholic religion could not be compelled to attend a substitute class, that such a practice was inherently discriminatory. Problems arose, however, when it became clear that the minister of education, the Christian Democrat Giovanni Galloni, did not intend to implement the court's decision.

Since the early seventies, many Soviet Jews who were permitted to leave the USSR stopped in Italy on their way to the United States, most of them residing in Ladispoli, a small town on the seashore in the Rome metropolitan area. Over the years some 8,000 Soviet Jews arrived in the town, spending from a few months to two years there while waiting for permits to emigrate to the United States. Permits were granted to 85 percent of the Soviet Jews; 15 percent were refused and later decided either to move to Israel (10 percent of the whole) or to stay in Italy (5 percent). Financial aid and social assistance were provided to the immigrants by the American Jewish Joint Distribution Committee (AJDC), while the Roman community never became deeply involved in their situation. With the liberalization of Soviet emigration policy, the number of Soviet Jews in Ladispoli climbed in the course of 1989 to more than 10,000. In the meantime, the U.S. administration decided to adopt new, more restrictive criteria for granting refugee status, the only way in which these Soviet Jews could be permitted to enter the United States. This raised anxiety in the Soviet colony in Ladispoli, at a time when Jews were also becoming targets of hostile acts from the local population. AJDC president Sylvia Hassenfeld visited Rome in July in order to pursue ways to ease the tensions inside and outside the colony, meeting with Italian authorities, including Prime Minister Andreotti and leaders of the UCEI.

The second international meeting of Jews of Libyan origin was held in Rome, January 19–22. The gathering, which was mostly a social event, included discussions on the present situation of Libyan Jews, lectures on their history and culture, exhibitions and concerts, and dances. It concluded with a gala banquet attended by several leading Italian personalities, among them Foreign Minister Andreotti, who played a decisive role in the granting of Italian citizenship to Jews of Libyan origin who were forced to leave that Arab country following the Six Day War and chose Italy as their place of residence (see AJYB 1990, p. 350). Before 1948 there were about 40,000 Jews living in Libya. Some 33,000 left the country between 1948 and 1951, in the main emigrating to Israel. The rest of the community was expelled in 1967: most of its members settled in Italy, others preferred France, Spain, and the United States. In Italy there were about 3,000 Jews of Libyan origin, 2,000 in Rome, where they were very active in the local community and maintained a synagogue of their own.

Jewish-Catholic Relations

Overall, the relations of the Jewish world with the Catholic Church in 1989 could be described as complex and contradictory. The year started well, with signs of improvement and clarification in the relationship. In January the archbishop of Siena, Ismaele Castellano, paid a visit to the local Jewish community, in a meeting in the ancient synagogue of that town. He was welcomed by the *hazzan* and the rabbi of Siena, who read psalms and prayers in Hebrew and Italian. In his remarks, Archbishop Castellano said that all forms of anti-Semitism had to be eradicated, "for the Jewish people is the beloved brother of the Christian people" and "is still the covenanted people."

In February the Pontifical Commission "Iustitia et Pax" issued an interesting and important document on racism, a large part of which was devoted to anti-Semitism. The document praised the role of the Jewish people in the course of history as essential to the divine plan for salvation and redemption. The commission admitted that in the Middle Ages Christians had humiliated and often accused Jews of crimes that were never actually committed. The document declared modern anti-Semitism to be an ideology opposed to the teachings of the Church and strongly condemned Nazism as an aberration. Of particular interest, the document revealed that the encyclical *"Mit brennender Sorge"* ("With Burning Anxiety"), issued by Pope Pius XI in 1937, which strongly condemned Nazism and its myths of race and blood, was to have been followed by another, sharper and more specific, statement against Hitler's anti-Semitism, in an encyclical written by Pius XI but not completed before his death. According to the Iustitia et Pax document, his successor, Pius XII, "took in some elements" of his predecessor's fierce condemnation of Nazi anti-Semitism.

The document further affirmed that racism had not yet disappeared and that it was based on "the rejection of differences." From this point of view, anti-Semitism still represented the "most tragic form of racism." Anti-Zionism was defined as different from anti-Semitism, "since it consists of a protest against the State of Israel and its policy"; anti-Zionism, however, often is a way to "conceal anti-Semitism, which fuels and provokes it," the document stated. This last passage was regarded by several Italian Jewish figures—among them Chief Rabbi Elio Toaff and UCEI president Tullia Zevi—as an important turning point in the official position of the Church on this subject.

In September the Episcopal Conference of Italy (CEI; the decision-making body of the Italian Catholic Church formed by all the bishops of the country) decided to celebrate an annual day of "study and meditation to deepen the knowledge of Judaism and further advance the Catholic Church's relations with the Jewish people." This initiative was regarded as extemely positive by both Jews and Christians.

By contrast with all this, Pope John Paul II seemed still to express himself, at least in part, in the metaphors of an older Catholic theological tradition. In speeches delivered in August, he referred to the ancient Israelites as being "disloyal to the Covenant of Sinai." "Such a covenant," he said, "was established between the Lord and the people of Israel. The history of the Old Covenant shows us that this commitment [of the Jews] was often disregarded by them. The Prophets, in particular, rebuked Israel for its sins and lack of loyalty, and saw the grievances of its history as divine punishments. They [the Prophets] . . . announced a New Covenant to come." Such remarks, especially coming in the midst of the controversy over the Carmelite convent in Auschwitz, provoked a wave of sharp criticism from both Jews and Christians involved in interfaith dialogue.

The polemic over the Carmelite convent at Auschwitz—in which Italian Jews actively participated—largely dominated the second half of the year. Under the provisions of an agreement signed in Geneva in 1987 by the Catholic cardinals of Krakow, Paris, Lyons, and Brussels, and by European Jewish leaders, among them UCEI president Zevi, by the end of February 1989, an international center of "information, education, meeting and prayer" would be built by the European churches somewhere outside the Auschwitz camp. It was commonly understood—

though the written agreement was not actually specific on this point—that the Carmelite nuns, who had settled in a building at the edge of the Auschwitz death camp in 1984, would move to the new site by that deadline.

When it became clear that the terms of the agreement were not being implemented and that the deadline was approaching, international protest began. The tension between the Polish Catholic Church and the Jewish world reached its climax in mid-July, when a group of American Orthodox Jews, led by Rabbi Avraham (Avi) Weiss of New York, climbed over a fence into the convent and were attacked by some Polish workers. Cardinal Franciszek Macharski, head of the local diocese, later suspended the project, charging a "violent campaign of accusations and defamation" on the part of "certain Western Jewish circles."

UCEI leaders and other Jewish figures publicly protested and called for compliance with the Geneva agreement. The Italian press, though condemning the "intemperance of the extremists [among the Jews]," mostly sided with the Jewish position. Prominent Catholic figures in Italy, too, indicated that although they favored the idea of a Carmelite convent in Auschwitz, the feelings of the Jews, who had been the major victims of Nazism, should be taken into account and the convent moved elsewhere. According to a survey published by the Catholic weekly *Il Sabato,* most of the Italian bishops agreed with this position. The Protestant churches in Italy also expressed solidarity with the Jewish position and asked the Polish Catholic Church to honor and implement the Geneva agreement.

The president of the regional council of Valle d'Aosta, an alpine area on the Swiss and French borders, offered to host the nuns from Auschwitz in a Carmelite convent in that region. At the same time, Prime Minister Andreotti proposed to resettle the convent in the area of the Fosse Ardeatine, near Rome—the site chosen by the Nazis in 1944 for the execution of more than 340 Italians, many of them Jewish. The executions were in retaliation for a bombing carried out by partisans against German troops. Both Jewish and ex-partisan organizations rejected the prime minister's proposal, arguing that since the Nazis murdered Jews and Christians alike at the Fosse Ardeatine, the site should not be consecrated to any one religion, and should not be involved in parochial disputes.

At the beginning of September, in an interview with the Italian press, the primate of Poland, Cardinal Jozef Glemp, expressed his anger at the supposed anti-Polish attitude of the Jews. He said that Jewish lobbies around the world were attempting to discredit his country through the international media, which they controlled. His views were sharply condemned by the Italian press and public opinion, Catholic and secular alike.

Culture

Work continued in 1989 on the preservation of Italian Jewry's artistic and cultural treasures. Also this year, some of the cultural heritage of Italian Jews traveled overseas to be displayed to an appreciative American public, and Jewish and Israeli cultural programs again proved appealing to the Italian public.

The National Jewish Bibliographic Center in Rome continued its work of compiling a complete catalogue of Jewish bibliographic and archival materials in Italy. Librarians and experts of the Jewish National and University Library in Jerusalem visited Italy frequently in order to help the center's personnel with various problems, while Italian librarians attended special workshops in Jerusalem designed for them. The UCEI and the Hebrew University of Jerusalem drafted a cooperative program for increasing knowledge of Judaica sources in Italy and for their preservation.

Three important Jewish manuscripts, their existence previously unknown, were discovered this year in the National Library in Florence: a fragment of Ezekiel in "*masora magna et parva,*" possibly from the 10th century; a folio from a manuscript edition of the Babylonian Talmud (Ketubot 25), 14th century; and a codex with biblical fragments from approximately the same century. The last two items may have been written in Spain.

Two Italian local authorities announced that they would contribute financially to the preservation of the Jewish cultural heritage in the country: the Regione Lazio to activities of the National Jewish Bibliographic Center, and the Regione Veneto to the rich library and archive of the Jewish community of Venice.

Two interesting international conferences were organized under the terms of the cultural agreement signed in 1988 between Italy and Israel (see AJYB 1990, pp. 346–47). The fourth "Italia Judaica" conference was held in Siena, June 12–16. Scholars from different countries presented papers on "The Jews in United Italy, 1870–1945." A conference attended by Israeli, Italian, German, and American scholars on "Fascism-National Socialism-Antisemitism-Holocaust: Links, Interactions, Differences" was held at Bar Ilan University (Ramat Gan, Israel), December 11–14.

One of the most significant cultural events of the year took place in the United States: the exhibition "Gardens and Ghettos: The Art of Jewish Life in Italy," which was on view at the Jewish Museum of New York from September 17 to February 1, 1990. Organized with the help of Jewish institutions and individuals in the United States and Italy, the exhibition focused on four time periods (the Roman Empire; the Era of City States, 1300–1550; the Era of the Ghettos, 1550–1870; and From Risorgimento to the Present). Supplementing the exhibition were screenings of movies on Italian Jewish subjects, a concert of music written by the Mantuan Jewish composer Salomone Rossi (late 16th–early 17th centuries), and an international conference on the history and culture of the Italian Jews, with the participation of internationally renowned scholars (September 17–18). The American press showed considerable interest in the exhibition, which was praised by the critics and visited by huge crowds. An exhibition on Jewish art and culture in Emilia Romagna (an area in northern Italy) was on display in San Francisco, September 22–December 30. Organized and originally displayed in Ferrara (Italy) in 1988–89, this exhibition, too, drew many visitors.

The abbey of Praglia, near Padova, exhibited a series of oil paintings on wood on biblical subjects (September 11–December 3), possibly produced as part of a *sukkah*. The panels had been discovered in the abbey itself by a rabbi from Jerusalem, Marcel Goldstein, in 1986. The abbey also presented an exhibition on Jewish life and culture in Italy, "*Midor Ledor*" ("From Generation to Generation"), divided in three sections: books and manuscripts; the cycle of the holidays; the life cycle.

The Israeli film *Berlin Jerusalem* by Amos Gitai was screened at the Venice Festival in September, to acclaim from the Italian public and critics. The film is based on the confrontation of the German Jewish poet Elsa Lasker Schuller, who arrived in Palestine in the 1930s, and the Russian revolutionary Mania Shochat. Interest in Israeli cinema remained high when the Cinematheques of Bologna and Tel Aviv, in cooperation with Italian and Israeli institutions, organized a successful "Week of the Israeli Cinema" in Bologna, December 10–16.

The Israeli writer David Grossman, already popular in Italy, was awarded the Vallombrosa Literary Prize in June.

Publications

The proceedings of several important conferences were published this year. One was the third international "Italia Judaica" conference, held in Tel Aviv in June 1986 on "The Jews in Italy from the Period of Segregation to the First Emancipation." A second conference, "Ovadyah Yare da Bertinoro and the Jewish Presence in Romagna in the Fifteenth Century," took place in Bertinoro in 1988. A third conference, on recent developments in anti-Semitism and the so-called revisionist historiography, "Judaism and anti-Judaism," was held in Florence in 1988.

Two important studies in the history of Italian Jews were reissued this year: *Storia degli ebrei italiani durante il fascismo* ("History of the Italian Jews Under Fascism") by Renzo De Felice, a noted authority on the Mussolini regime; and *Storia del ghetto di Roma* ("History of the Ghetto of Rome") by Attilio Milano.

The findings of the preliminary investigation and trial of those who directed the only concentration camp established in Italy, San Sabba (near Trieste), were edited by Adolfo Scarpelli and published under the title *San Sabba—Istruttoria e processo per il Lager della Risiera*.

Il vino e la carne ("The Wine and the Flesh") by Ariel Toaff, professor at Bar Ilan University, a history of the Jewish presence in Perugia in the Middle Ages, was extremely well received.

The prestigious literary monthly *Nuovi Argomenti* dedicated its January issue to new Israeli poets and writers, publishing a selection of short novels, tales, poetry, and essays.

Personalia

The Gold Medal for civil bravery, Italy's highest decoration, was awarded posthumously to Nathan Cassuto, who perished in the Holocaust, by the Ministry of

Interior. Son of the famous Judaica scholar Moshe Umberto Cassuto, the younger Cassuto had been a physician and rabbi who served briefly as chief rabbi of Florence before being deported by the Nazis in 1944.

Cesare Musatti, one of the founders of modern psychoanalysis in Italy, died in Milan in March at the age of 92. He was born in Trieste to a Jewish father and a Catholic mother, but always considered himself fully Jewish. In the 1920s, after completing his medical studies in Padua, he became a pupil of the psychoanalyst Edoardo Weiss, who had trained earlier in Vienna under Sigmund Freud. Musatti played a crucial role in spreading Freud's theories and approaches in Italy and was among the founders of the Italian Society for Psychoanalysis. In 1938, following the promulgation of the racial laws, he was dismissed from the university. A prolific writer and a beloved professor at the universities of Padua and Milan in the postwar period, Musatti was very popular in Italy, appearing frequently on television programs.

Fausto Sabatello, an active Zionist and founder of the Jewish National Fund (KKL) in Italy, died in Jerusalem in April, aged 84. Sabatello, who directed the KKL in Italy for almost 50 years, took part in the activities of the Italian maquis against the German occupation in Rome in the years 1943–44.

Emilio Segrè, one of the most prominent physicists of the century, a Nobel Prize laureate, died in August, aged 84, in California. Born in Tivoli, near Rome, in 1905, upon completing his studies he became an assistant to Enrico Fermi. In 1938, after the racial laws were promulgated, Segrè emigrated to the United States, where he joined the physics department at the University of California and established his permanent home.

SIMONETTA DELLA SETA
MASSIMO TORREFRANCA

Federal Republic of Germany

National Affairs

IN THE ATMOSPHERE OF EAST-WEST détente that spread throughout Europe in 1989, the West German people showed growing impatience with the heavy burden of defense placed on them by membership in NATO. This was expressed, for example, in more open protest against the pervasive low-flying military aircraft of NATO, especially after several serious accidents. Moreover, a federal Parliament report on the state of the German army pointed to the declining acceptance of the Bundeswehr in German society and continuing problems with morale in the army itself. This shift in popular attitudes in turn forced changes in the defense policy of Chancellor Helmut Kohl's Christian Democratic (CDU)–Free Democratic (FDP) coalition. Due primarily to the dovish views of Foreign Minister Hans-Dietrich Genscher, Kohl was forced to resist U.S. pressure for modernization of short-range nuclear missiles and to press for U.S.-Soviet nuclear disarmament.

In early January, the *New York Times* revealed that a German firm, Imhausen-Chemie, had played a central role in the construction of a poison-gas factory at Rabta in Libya. The German Foreign Ministry at first denied the allegations, claiming insufficient evidence, and the government charged that a campaign against the Federal Republic was being mounted in the American media. Later on it became known that the German government had been informed by Washington in November 1988 about the involvement of German firms and even earlier by its own intelligence service (Bundesnachrichtendienst, BND). Indeed, the director of the BND, Bernhard Wieck, indicated that reports from his office to the government in August 1987 had not received proper attention. Subsequently, ever more evidence became available—on the falsification of freight papers by a firm in Antwerp, Belgium, the involvement of the firms Salzgitter and Siemens, and the fact that equipment was shipped to Libya via Hong Kong. Later in the year, a full-scale investigation was launched, and Imhausen-Chemie was brought to trial.

The Two Germanys

In West Germany, there was renewed debate this year on the German question, with the Christian Democrats (CDU) stressing the concept of one German nation and the Green party, in particular, opposing it. Despite dissatisfaction with the generally poor relations between the Federal Republic and the German Democratic Republic (GDR), lower-level contacts intensified. City partnerships were established, such as that between Bonn and Potsdam. The prime ministers of Baden

Württemberg (Lothar Späth), Hamburg (Henning Voscherau), and North Rhine-Westphalia (Johannes Rau) visited the GDR, aiming to ease travel restrictions and further economic ties and to have the order to shoot for border guards rescinded.

Foreign Minister Genscher in particular advocated a more rapid pace of international détente. At a meeting of the Council for European Cooperation (CEC) in April, he proposed that Western *Ostpolitik* be "modernized"; in June, at the Helsinki Conference in Paris, he appealed for a Europe without the Iron Curtain. He and other West German politicians urged the Eastern European countries to liberalize their systems (at an earlier CEC meeting, Genscher had urged the GDR and the USSR to show greater respect for human and civil rights). In retrospect, the state visit by Soviet leader Mikhail Gorbachev to the Federal Republic in June proved to be a decisive event: it improved the atmosphere between the FRG and the Soviet Union significantly, and it changed the mood in the GDR, whose government felt somewhat isolated due to the improved ties between Bonn and Moscow. Gorbachev was welcomed cordially by the German population; both countries agreed on the need to overcome the divisions in Europe and stressed Gorbachev's idea of "a common European house."

THE EAST GERMAN INFLUX

In response to increasing pressure from its citizens to leave the country, the GDR eased emigration rules in January and again later in the spring. However, growing unrest led thousands to flee to West German embassies in East Berlin and Budapest and later in Prague. The opening of the Hungarian border with Austria on September 10 led to a mass exodus that by early November 1989 brought 220,000 refugees to West Germany. Events surrounding the 40th anniversary of the GDR's founding, on October 7, created a setting for public protest. Swelling demonstrations peaked on October 9, when an estimated 100,000 marched in Leipzig, following which the East German state began to unravel quickly.

On November 8, as demonstrations continued in East Germany, West German chancellor Kohl delivered a state-of-the-nation speech in which he demanded free elections in the GDR and a multiparty system, offering increased aid as an inducement. The next day, East Berlin party secretary Günter Schabowski announced that citizens would be allowed to leave the country through any border crossing. Although he later claimed that such permission was not intended to be either unconditional or immediate, that very night, tens of thousands of East Germans climbed the wall and came to West Berlin and West Germany in what turned into a carnival type of atmosphere that continued into the 10th of November.

When West German politicians—including Social Democratic chief Hans-Jochen Vogel—proposed the opening of the Berlin wall as a new national holiday in Germany, the suggestion came in for strong criticism from Jewish representatives. Some, in fact, questioned whether the 9th of November had been intentionally chosen for the opening of the wall, as an attempt to overshadow the stigma of *Kristallnacht,* which occurred on the same date in 1938. On the basis of current knowledge, this appears unlikely, however. East German politicians were under continuous pressure from the street and had little room to maneuver. In addition, there was a complete lack of suggestions in this regard from the politicians involved, and the actual announcement of the open border was unspecific as to date. Nevertheless, in German history, the 9th of November has been a carnivalesque day of upheaval of the established order, enshrined as such in the public memory—from the revolution that produced the Weimar Republic in 1918 to Hitler's "beer-hall putsch" in 1923 to *Kristallnacht* in 1938. Some unconscious awareness of this may have helped trigger the late-evening move to the wall and its sudden breaching.

Relations with Israel

The Palestinian *intifada* had a definite impact on West Germany's relations with Middle Eastern states. In June the opposition Social Democratic party (SPD) invited a PLO delegation to talks in Bonn, SPD chief Hans-Jochen Vogel claiming that such contacts were important in the search for a peaceful solution in the Middle East. In early fall the federal government issued its own statement expressing interest in official dialogue with the PLO, and in October the first meetings were held between the PLO and the governing Christian Democrats. These contacts expressed a consensus in West German politics on the Middle East and indicated Israel's growing political isolation, a result of what was viewed as the inflexible attitude of the Israeli government in its dealings with the Palestinians. The only protests against this policy shift came from Israel and from the Central Council of Jews of Germany.

The changing climate in Germany also facilitated German arms shipments to the Middle East, which were criticized by Edgar Bronfman, president of the World Jewish Congress, on his visit to Bonn and Frankfurt in January, and by the German Coordinating Council of the Societies of Christian-Jewish Cooperation. The critical attitude toward Israeli policies was also evident in broader circles of German society. The German-Israeli Youth Exchange Program, for example, experienced a decline in its attractiveness after the beginning of the *intifada.* Even traditionally pro-Israel circles, such as groups in the Protestant Church active in Jewish and Israel-related issues, expressed more critical views. The head of the organized Jewish community, Heinz Galinski, gave hints of his own position on a number of occasions when he declared his strong support for Israel even though particular Israeli policies could be disputed.

Despite the definite cooling in German-Israeli relations, the underlying strong bonds between the two states were expressed in ongoing contacts of various sorts. Israeli foreign minister Moshe Arens came to Bonn in June, where he presented Israel's proposal for Israeli-Palestinian talks as outlined by Prime Minister Yitzhak Shamir, and where he met with the SPD leadership. Michael Pagels, chairman of the Berlin section of the DGB (German Labor Federation), visited Israeli Labor representatives in June, and an Israeli Labor delegation came to Bonn to talk with the DGB's committee on education and culture. Premier Björn Engholm of Schleswig-Holstein, current president of the Bundesrat (West German Upper House), who ranked second after the president of the Federal Republic, paid an official visit to Israel in July; other visitors included Frankfurt mayor Volker Hauff and Defense Minister Rupert Scholz. Haim Klugman, state secretary in the Israeli Ministry of Justice, and Foreign Minister Shimon Peres came to Bonn on the occasion of Willy Brandt's 75th birthday, in December.

Close contacts were also apparent in scholarly and cultural areas. In June, for example, at a colloquium held near Günzburg, German and Israeli scholars discussed joint projects relating to heart and circulatory diseases. In Freiburg/Baden, in May, German and Israeli writers held a joint meeting on the theme "Writers as Citizens and Critics of Their State."

Right-Wing Extremism and Anti-Semitism

There were a number of contradictory developments this year on the Right, involving Franz Schönhuber's Republican party (Die Republikaner) and a younger generation of neo-Nazis and other right-wing extremists. In January *Land* (state) elections in Berlin, the Republicans, running for the first time, managed to win 7.5 percent of the vote. It was apparent that their supporters, lower-middle-class and working-class voters, felt increasingly threatened by foreign workers, including Eastern Europeans declared to be ethnic Germans by the citizenship offices. In February the Republicans managed to gain 6.6 percent of the vote in local elections in Hesse, with some district tallies in the 20-percent range.

In the elections for the European Parliament, the Republicans gained 7.1 percent of the vote. The size of the vote was undoubtedly helped by support from some Christian Democratic leaders who, in the face of their own severe losses in all recent *Land* elections, advocated coalitions with the Republican party. Polls indicated, moreover, that one-third of CDU and one-half of CSU (Bavarian counterpart of the CDU) voters approved of political coalitions with the Republicans. Studies showed that the Republicans were not a party of old Nazis but rather of youthful protesters.

The Republican party's rise was abruptly halted in the fall, due to a number of new developments. First, the influx of East Germans and ethnic Germans from the USSR and Romania produced substantial hostility that deflected attention somewhat from ordinary racism against other immigrants. (Campaigns against both ethnic Germans from the Baltic and asylum seekers appeared in the *Deutsche National-Zeitung* of Gerhard Frey and other right-wing publications.) The Republicans were unable to turn this situation to their advantage. Chancellor Kohl's use of right-wing demagogy in his refusal to recognize the Oder-Neisse border and his probable role as chancellor in a possible unification with the GDR also managed to draw support away from the Republicans. These developments, in turn, brought

to the fore divisions within the Republican party, which weakened it considerably.
Cause for at least as much concern as the Republicans were some often violent groups on the fringe in the neo-Nazi spectrum. At the end of 1987, the Interior Ministry counted 25,200 right-wing extremists; the 1989 report showed an increase to 28,000 members of extremist groups. Some of these groups, including Michael Kühnen's Nationale Sammlung and similar successor organizations, were easily identifiable due to their stable organizational structure; others, however, were located in the volatile youth culture, often engaged in violent battles with left-wing rivals.

Among a number of particularly serious incidents that occurred during the year—and were attributed to right-wing groups—were the desecration, with pigs' heads, of the Putlitzbrücke, Plötzensee, and Rosa Luxemburg memorials in Berlin and an arson attack against the Gestapo headquarters memorial. There were also anti-Semitic excesses at soccer games, desecration of cemeteries such as that in Wetter (Hesse), and swastika daubings at Hamburg's city hall.

The rise of neo-Nazism gave rise to a rash of new publications such as *Der Adler, Erste Etappe,* and *Freiheit,* and revived others such as *Nation Europa,* with many of their articles directed specifically at young people. The neo-Nazi magazine *Leitheft* spread revisionist views and attempted to rehabilitate the Waffen-SS. It was published by the Waffen-SS Veterans' Association (Kameradenkreis der ehemaligen Waffen-SS). Moreover, as in other countries, neo-Nazi computer games were multiplying, and in some schools—evidenced by a report of the Berlin education ministry, for example—right-wing elements had made considerable inroads.

Various levels of government recognized the danger from extremist groups and their increasing proneness to violence. A New Year's Eve party of Wiking Jugend was broken up by police; 27 neo-Nazis were arrested. A few weeks later, a group of militant extremists, the Deutsch-Nationalen, were caught in East Frisia; they had planned terrorist actions. Members of the FAP of the National Front were arrested by police in Hildesheim; they were charged with arson directed at a dormitory for political refugees and at a youth center. In April police carried out a massive strike against the right-wing militia Stahlhelm-Bund; homes were searched and weapons seized. In February the Bonn Interior Ministry outlawed Michael Kühnen's Nationale Sammlung and carried out a search of members' homes.

A number of significant developments this year centered around Hitler's 100th birthday on April 20. To the extent that the press covered it at all, they dealt mostly with the Hitler "phenomenon" and welcomed the anti-Hitler memorial at his birthplace in Braunau; there was little commemoration of his victims. The right-wing extremists, on the other hand, managed to produce a great deal of publicity and exploited the date for their own purposes. Neo-Nazi leaflets on Hitler's birthday, for example, called for pogroms against Turkish immigrants. Other statements demanded the removal of the Dachau concentration-camp memorial. The connection between neo-Nazism and racism directed against the immigrants was generally not pointed out in the press.

On another anniversary, that of Rudolf Hess's death two years earlier, 200 neo-Nazis, including Michael Kühnen, held a demonstration in Hess's hometown of Wunsiedel; a counterdemonstration was held by a "Working Group Against Old and New Nazis"; arrests were made. There were many other instances of strong local reactions against right-wing manifestations.

Apart from Chancellor Kohl's own chauvinist remarks on various issues, problematic statements were made by other public figures. Hans Klein, a close aide to Kohl, spoke on a number of occasions expressing rightist views. His statements on the Waffen-SS were denounced by Central Council chairman Heinz Galinski as being intolerable for the victims of Nazism. He noted that the Waffen-SS units included concentration-camp guards and that the massacre of Oradour, for one, was the work of a Waffen-SS division. The SPD and the Greens asked the federal government to repudiate Klein's remarks regarding the Waffen-SS, and Hildegard Hamm-Brücher of the Liberals rejected his claim that the Waffen-SS had not been criminals. Klein defended his statements in an interview in June; he said he wanted the younger generation to identify with their "fatherland" and therefore with these phenomena as historical traditions. In the Bundestag, the Greens and SPD again demanded that the government repudiate Klein's statements, without success.

Nazi War Criminals

In January the Frankfurt prosecutor opened proceedings in 670 new cases of Nazi crimes, on the basis of documents that had been locked up in the United Nations archive until fall 1988. Gottfried Weise, an Auschwitz guard, was sentenced in May to life in prison. He then disappeared but was arrested and extradited from Switzerland in August. Other former concentration-camp guards sentenced to life were Horst Czerwinski in Sulze, for the murder of two Russians, and Wilhelm Wagner for the murder of three Jews in Poland. Two notorious gynecologists charged with euthanasia, Aquilin Ullrich of Stuttgart, and Heinrich Bunke of Celle, received three-year sentences following their Frankfurt trial. SS-Obersturmführer Karl-Friedrich Höcker was sentenced to four years in jail in Bielefeld. He was involved in mass murder at the Lublin-Maidanek concentration camp. Wolfgang Otto, accused as an accomplice in the murder of Communist leader Ernst Thälmann in 1944, was acquitted by the Supreme Court in a decision that was strongly criticized.

The Federal Republic requested the extradition of former SS guard Bruno Karl Blach from the United States. This was the second such request for extradition.

It was learned that the University of Tübingen Institute of Anatomy had preserved considerable quantities of tissue from corpses of Nazi victims. Most of the victims were believed to be members of the political resistance who had been executed by the regime. The Jewish community of Stuttgart was critical of the use of this human tissue for research, although a committee set up by the community did not find evidence that Jewish victims were involved. After discussion with university officials, it was agreed that all specimens would be removed from the institute and buried.

JEWISH COMMUNITY

Demography

As of January 1, 1990, overall Jewish community membership had risen to 27,711, a slight gain over the previous year's 27,552. The number of unaffiliated Jews was estimated to be an additional 20,000–30,000.

Some 695 Soviet Jews settled in West Germany in 1989, almost half of them in Berlin and the rest in larger Jewish centers such as Frankfurt, Hamburg, and Düsseldorf. Munich was excluded due to Bavaria's stubborn refusal to grant special permission for Soviet Jews to settle there.

Using the number of children 11 years old or younger as a measure of community vitality, of the communities with over 500 members, Cologne was first (1,358 members; 14.7 percent children); followed by Stuttgart/Württemberg (677; 12.4 percent), Hamburg (1,344; 11.9 percent); Frankfurt (4,842; 10.4 percent); Berlin (6,411; 9.7 percent); Munich (4,050; 8.5 percent); Düsseldorf (1,510; 7.7 percent); and Offenbach/Hesse (829; 7.35 percent). The figures suggest that Jewish families were moving into dynamic industrial areas that hitherto had not had a strong Jewish presence. Some smaller communities fitting that pattern were Karlsruhe, Mannheim, Nuremberg, Hannover, Aachen, and Dortmund. Smaller communities in more stagnant areas, on the other hand, continued to dwindle; significant drops were recorded this year in the Saarland, Westphalia, the Rhineland-Palatinate, and Lower Saxony.

Communal Affairs

After last year's turmoil in the wake of the Nachmann scandal, this year proved to be relatively calm. (See AJYB 1990, pp. 362–365. The scandal involved embezzlement of funds intended for Nazi victims by the late Werner Nachmann, when he was chairman of the Central Council of Jews in Germany.) The Nachmann case itself was put to rest by the prosecutors even though many questions remained unanswered and most of the missing funds were never located.

Elections were held this year in local Jewish community organizations (*Gemeinden*). In Berlin, in May, in a heavily financed campaign, although the opposition succeeded in doubling its share of votes to nearly one-third, Heinz Galinski was reelected chairman of the community. At a membership meeting of the North West German Jüdische Gemeindefonds, a new executive was elected, with Michael Fürst of Hannover as president. Elections also took place in the Hamburg community, after the death of its longtime president Günter Singer. Micha Guttmann, a journalist, was appointed new general secretary of the Central Council.

Heinz Galinski expressed displeasure publicly—on behalf of the Central Council—when he was not invited by Chancellor Kohl to a dinner for President George Bush in Bonn in May. In an interview, Galinski indicated that his predecessor had always received invitations to such events.

An academic forum arranged by the World Zionist Organization in June, in Frankfurt, entitled "Jewish Identity and Right-Wing Extremism in the Federal Republic," posed the question whether Jews should emigrate because of the electoral successes of the ultra Right. While participants generally agreed that the new rightist movements differed from the older National Democratic party—in that they consisted mostly of very young people who appeared openly in public—opinions were divided on the danger posed by these groups. There was clearly a great deal of fear on the part of Holocaust survivors, but many younger Jewish panelists felt that right-wing extremism had to be confronted openly and forcefully.

Much of the Israel-oriented activity in the community emanated from the energetic work of WIZO, the Women's International Zionist Organization. Successful WIZO bazaars were held this year in Düsseldorf, Frankfurt, Hamburg, Cologne, Stuttgart, Berlin, and Munich; the Frankfurt chapter of WIZO held a benefit concert on behalf of the Theodor Heuss Home for mothers in Herzliah. In Hannover, WIZO celebrated its 25th anniversary as part of the Israel Week celebrations of Lower Saxony. Some of the WIZO chapters, such as that of Berlin, had active non-Jewish members. The Israel embassy and the Central Council held a benefit concert for the reforestation of Mount Carmel. In individual philanthropy, the Prajs family of Berlin was a major benefactor of Keren Hayesod and dedicated a project in Tel Aviv. U.S. Jewish leader Seymour Reich, president of B'nai B'rith and chairman of the Conference of Presidents of Major American Jewish Organizations, visited the Federal Republic in March. He met with Chancellor Kohl and with Heinz Galinski in Berlin, seeking to strengthen American-Jewish ties with Germany.

The condition of postwar German Jewry and its relationship to the larger German society was discussed at the first international conference on the subject to be held outside of Germany. The conference, which convened in Toronto in November, was entitled "How Can Jews Live in Germany Today?" Papers dealt with the reestablishment of Jewish communities in Germany after the war, their pariah status vis-à-vis world Jewry, their symbolic importance for the West German state and its society, and the instrumentalization of Jewish officials there. Other contributions considered the significance of the increase in awareness of the Shoah among segments of the German public and the "myth of the émigré," especially in German cultural life. The latter paper suggested that whereas Jewish émigrés play an important symbolic role in Germany, the role of younger Jewish intellectuals living in German society is negligible.

In a resolution, the conference lamented the neglect and destruction of records relating to the history of the postwar German Jewish community and called for the establishment of proper archives; in a second resolution, a group of participants questioned the results of the inquiry into the Nachmann affair and called upon the Jewish leadership to hold a new and impartial investigation.

Holocaust-Related Matters

The Bonn coalition rejected the plan proposed by the Greens, in June, to set up a foundation to provide compensation to victims of Nazi forced labor. The government considered the existing compensation via the hardship funds sufficient. Occasionally, compensation of individual cases was hampered by officials; one such case was reported this year from North-Rhine Westphalia. An appointee of the state government, Dr. Halbekann-Esser, showed distinct prejudice against victims and put obstacles in the way of those seeking compensation.

In the continuing émigré visitor program (see AJYB 1990, p. 366), visits took place this year to Düsseldorf, Herford-Minden, Karlsruhe, Duisburg, Frankfurt/Main, Stuttgart, Freiburg, Weiden (Upper Palatinate; on the occasion of the 100th anniversary of the Weiden synagogue), Usingen, Emmendingen, Mönchen-Gladbach, Schleswig-Holstein, Minden, Wetzlar, Klever, Bad Nauheim, Ludwigshafen, Mannheim, and Berlin.

The eight-year battle over plans for an international youth center in Dachau showed no signs of resolution. The committee promoting the center encountered opposition from the Education Ministry in Munich, which disagreed with a pluralistic conception that would open the center to a variety of groups working with youth; it was also alleged that the ministry was not sufficiently sensitive to the victims of Nazism.

Memorials and Commemorative Events

A number of new memorial sites were dedicated this year, including a memorial to the "Victims of Nazi Justice," on the grounds of the German Judges' College, in Trier, which was dedicated by Justice Minister Hans Engelhardt. The memorial was of special significance because the German justice establishment had been particularly reluctant to accept its responsibility for Nazi crimes and had survived virtually unscathed into the Federal Republic.

Memorial plaques were dedicated this year to victims of the Kaufering concentration camp in Erpfing Forest near Landsberg, Bavaria, and in Kiel, where the synagogue was destroyed in November 1938. A memorial plaque was erected for Zionist leader Max Bodenheimer (1865–1940) in Cologne.

The synagogue in Straubing was rededicated in April after careful renovation; the former synagogue in Schweich/Moselle was restored and turned into a cultural center.

It was announced that the Wannsee Villa, site of the infamous conference at which Nazi leaders planned the "Final Solution," would become a center for documentation of Nazism. This followed the suggestion of the late historian Joseph Wulf, originally proposed 25 years ago.

As in previous years, there were again numerous commemorations of the November 1938 pogroms. The main event took place in Bonn with the participation of

Israeli ambassador Benjamin Navon. *Kristallnacht* was also observed in Frankfurt, Berlin, Bayreuth, Cologne, Wuppertal, Marburg, Neuss, Freiburg, Karlsruhe, Kassel, and Münster.

Jewish-Christian Relations

In February, Frankfurt celebrated the 18th anniversary of the founding of the Franz-Oppenheimer-Gesellschaft. The society, which promotes Jewish-Christian understanding, was established by Heinrich Guttmann, whose son came from Israel to attend the celebration. This year's annual Brotherhood Week, sponsored by the Coordinating Council of Associations for Christian-Jewish Cooperation, had as its theme "Law and Justice." Yehudi Menuhin was awarded the Buber-Rosenzweig Medal at the opening of Brotherhood Week early in March. The 40th anniversary of the 50 or so Associations for Christian-Jewish Cooperation was celebrated in October at a gathering in Bad Nauheim.

The German Protestant Church's convention in Berlin, in June, gave ample space to Jewish themes. However, the commentator in the *Allgemeine Jüdische Wochenzeitung* found that in the sessions relating to Jewish subjects, commonalities were emphasized to the point of being forced, without recognition of the fundamental differences between Judaism and Christianity. The Christian drive for harmony, which appeared to appropriate Judaism under a common Judeo-Christian umbrella, effectively paralyzed efforts at discussion. On the occasion of the convention, a memorial service took place on the grounds of former Gestapo headquarters, with Heinz Galinski as a speaker.

Culture

The Germania Judaica, an internationally recognized research library in Cologne, celebrated its 30th anniversary this year. The library was started as a private foundation at the initiative of a small group of writers and journalists, led by Nobel laureate Heinrich Böll. During its first 15 years it remained small and without much recognition; later it was given premises in Cologne's central library and began to receive state funding. The 40,000-volume library, which collaborates with the Leo Baeck Institute, specializes in the history and literature of German-speaking Jews since the Emancipation, and has holdings in anti-Semitica and the history of Zionism and of Palestine-Israel. Its present director, Monika Richarz, is an internationally respected historian of German Jewry.

A number of exhibits on Jewish history in Germany were presented this year, many of them focusing on the history of Jews in particular cities. Among several exhibits shown in Berlin were "*...als wär es nie gewesen—Menschen, die nicht mehr entkamen*" ("As if it had never happened—people who could not escape"), photographs from the last years of Jewish community life in Berlin; and "*Und lehrt sie: Gedächtnis*" ("And teach them not to forget"), organized by the East German government and the GDR Association of Jewish Communities, and shown the previous year in East Berlin. Another Berlin exhibit presented Weissensee cemetery as a mirror of Jewish history in Berlin, and another was on "Jewish Athletes in Berlin, 1898–1938." Exhibits portraying local Jewish environments and histories were presented in Düsseldorf ("Witnesses of Intolerance"), Cologne, Karlsruhe, Gütersloh (on Leo Baeck), in Bonn (on the Philippson family there), Munich, Hannover, and in small towns such as Gröbenzell. A Hannover exhibit on the history of Jews there, which was displayed in the Jewish cemetery's old funeral hall, was compiled, in part, by émigrés.

An exhibit honoring the writer and artist Arie Goral, on the occasion of his 80th birthday, was opened at the Institute for Social Research in Hamburg (November). The late Isaak Lachmann was honored with an exhibit, and his hand-written collection of music was donated to the European Center for Jewish Music in Augsburg.

Publications

The body of literature on local Jewish history continued to grow, much of it compiled by schoolteachers, usually focusing on the history up to and including the persecution in the particular town or city. Subjects of recent monographs and their authors included: Karlsruhe (Heinz Schmitt); Grossmannsdorf (Joachim Braun); Mainz Jewish cemetery (Bernd A. Vest); Hagen (Hermann Zabel); Bamberg (Karl Mistele); Osnabrück (Peter Jund and Martina Sellmeyer); Munich (Wolfram Selig); Darmstadt (Benno Szklanowski et al.); Lindau (Karl Schweitzer); Nienburg/Weser (Rainer Sabelleck); Dinslaken (Jürgen Grafen and Kurt Tohermes); Raesfeld (Adalbert Friedrich); Lichtenfels/Hesse (Josef Urban and Josef Motschmann); Baden-Württemberg (Joachim Hahn); Rheydt, Odenkirchen, Mönchen-Gladbach (Günter Erckens); Ahlen/Westphalia (Felix Fechenbach); Leverkusen (Rolf Müller).

Recently published books relating to the Nazi period included: Martin Broszat, *Nach Hitler, Schwierigkeiten im Umgang mit unserer Geschichte* ("After Hitler, the Difficulty of Coming to Terms with Our History"), edited by Hermann Graml and Klaus Dietmar Henke; Ursula Büttner, *Die Not der Juden teilen. Christlich-Jüdische Familien im Dritten Reich. Beispiel und Zeugnis des Schriftstellers Robert Brendel* (on the Nazi persecution of families of mixed origin); Ralph Giordano, *Wenn Hitler den Krieg gewonnen hätte* ("If Hitler Had Won the War"); Johannes Ludwig, *Boykott, Enteignung, Mord. Die Entjudung der deutschen Wirtschaft* (on the Aryanization of the German economy); Hartmut Müller, *Die Frauen von Obernheide. Jüdische Zwangsarbeiterinnen in Bremen 1944–45* (on Jewish female slave labor); Christian Pross, *Wiedergutmachung. Der Kleinkrieg gegen die Opfer* (on problems with reparations; 1988); Rudolf Schottlaender, *Verfolgte Berliner Wissenschaft* (on persecuted scholars); Yitzchak Schwersenz, *Die versteckte Gruppe* (on Jews in hiding in Berlin); Claude Spiero, *Und wir hielten sie für Menschen. Jüdisches Schicksal während der Emigration* (on Jewish fate during emigration); Wilhelm Treue, *Unternehmens-und Unternehmergeschichte aus fünf Jahrzehnten* (a history of Jewish firms); Jörg Wollenberg, *Keiner war dabei und niemand hat's gewusst. Die Deutsche*

Öffentlichkeit und die Judenverfolgung 1933–45 (on the amnesia of the German public on the Shoah); Renate Wall, *Verbrannt, verboten, vergessen. Kleines Lexikon deutschsprachiger Schriftstellerinnen 1933–1945* (a dictionary of persecuted female German writers; 1988).

New biographies, memoirs, and related works included Hartmut Binder and Jan Parik, *Kafka, Ein Leben in Prag;* Klaus Mann, *Tagebücher 1931–1933* (diaries of Thomas Mann's son); Karl Löwith, *Mein Leben in Deutschland vor und nach 1933. Ein Bericht* (autobiography of a leading German-Jewish philosopher); *Betty Scholem/Gershom Scholem: Mutter und Sohn im Briefwechsel 1917–1946,* edited by Itta Schedletzky and Thomas Sparr (the correspondence of Gershom Scholem and his mother); Resi Weglein, *Als Krankenschwester im KZ Theresienstadt Erinnerung einer Ulmer Jüdin,* edited by Silvester Lechner and Alfred Moos (memoirs of a Jewish nurse from Ulm in Theresienstadt); Erwin Blumenfeldt, *Durch tausendjährige Zeit* (memoirs of a well-known fashion photographer); Isaac Breuer, *Mein Weg* ("My Road"); Inge Deutschkron, *Milch ohne Honig. Leben in Israel* (reflections on the author's life in Israel); Joachim Kaiser, ed., *Leonard Bernsteins' Ruhm. Gedanken und Informationen über das Lebenswerk eines grossen Künstlers* (on Leonard Bernstein).

In the area of literature, new works included Meir M. Faerber, ed., *Auf dem Weg,* an anthology of German-language literature written in Israel, with an introduction by Siegfried Lenz; and Hans Otto Horch and Horst Denkler, eds., *Conditio Judaica, Judentum, Antisemitismus und deutschsprachige Literatur vom 18. Jahrhundert bis zum Ersten Weltkrieg,* part 1 (on Jews and German literature until 1914).

Among noteworthy new works of fiction were H.G. Adler, *Die unsichtbare Wand* ("The Invisible Wall"); Irene Dische, *Fromme Lügen. Ein Roman und sechs Erzählungen* ("Pious Lies: A Novel and Six Short Stories"), translated from the English by Otto Beyer and Monika Elwenspoek (based on the life of a Jewish woman in Washington Heights and Germany); Leo Sucharewicz, *Israelische Geschichten aus Deutschland. Kurzgeschichten zwischen Krieg und Frieden* ("Israeli Stories from Germany: Short Stories Between War and Peace"); and Esther Dischereit, *Joemis Tisch. Eine Jüdische Geschichte* (a young author dealing with the Jewish element in her background and past).

Works of Jewish history included Yehuda Eloni, *Zionismus in Deutschland von den Anfängen bis 1914* (a comprehensive history of the first 17 years of the German Zionist Federation, published by the Institute for German History, Tel Aviv University); and Arno Lustiger, *Schalom Libertad. Juden im Spanischen Bürgerkrieg* (Jews in the Spanish Civil War).

Other new works of interest were Israel Meir Levinger, ed., *Die Basler Hagada* (the Basle Haggadah); Peter N. Levinson, *Dem Andenken der Gerechten. Nachrufe* (eulogies by a leading German rabbi); Fritz Eschen, *Photographien Berlin, 1945–50* (photographs of postwar Berlin, by a photographer of Jewish origin); and Helge Grabitz and Wolfgang Scheffler, *Letzte Spuren* ("Last Traces," based on an exhibit about persecuted Jews from Berlin).

The new thematic issue of *Dachauer Hefte* dealt with medicine under Nazism.

Two books were published on the work of Jewish writer and playwright George Tabori, on the occasion of his 75th birthday. The books were by Gundula Ohngemach and by Jörg W. Gronius and Wend Kassens.

Personalia

Moshe G. Hess received the Federal Service Cross. He left Germany in 1935 for Palestine and later represented Israel in diplomatic missions abroad, including in Germany. In 1964, he returned to Germany, where he was a director of the Bank für Gemeinwirtschaft and cofounder of the Deutsch-Israelische Wirtschaftsvereinigung (economic association) in Frankfurt and Tel Aviv.

Schalom Ben-Chorin, a German-born writer living in Israel, received, jointly with Karl-Alfred Odin, a Protestant journalist, the prize of the Bible and Culture Foundation. Ben-Chorin also received the Golden Citizen's Medal of the City of Munich and was named an honorary member of the Jewish Community of Munich. Sociologist Leo Lowenthal, 89, last surviving member of the Frankfurt School for Social Research, later a faculty member at the University of California, Berkeley, was awarded the Theodor Adorno Prize in the Paulskirche Frankfurt, by the city. Rabbi Nathan Peter Levinson received an honorary professorship from the prime minister of Baden-Württemberg.

Sir Ernst Gombrich, the art historian, was honored on his 80th birthday with the Goethe Medal of the German Goethe Institute. Born in Vienna, he emigrated to England in 1936; he became famous with a popular art history published in 1950 and translated into 18 languages. For many years, he was director of the Warburg Institute in London.

Edgar Hilsenrath, a Jewish writer, was a corecipient of the Alfred Döblin Prize for his novel *Das Märchen vom letzten Gedanken* ("The Tale of the Last Thought"). The newly established Heinz Galinski Prize was awarded to writer Siegfried Lenz. The Leo Baeck Prize was awarded to Professors Gisbert zu Putlitz and Gerhard Rau. Putlitz was for a time the acting head of the College of Jewish Studies in Heidelberg.

The Rothschild banking houses (N.M. Rothschild & Sons, Limited, London; Rothschild & Cie Banque, Paris; and Rothschild AG, Zurich) returned to Frankfurt after an absence of almost 90 years. The Frankfurt branch was closed in 1901 because the last representative of the family there, Baron Wilhelm Carl von Rothschild, was left without male heirs.

Among prominent German Jews who died in 1989 were the following: Martha Markus de Vries, in Recklinghausen, aged 77, who with her husband helped to rebuild that Jewish community after the war (December 30, 1988); Ida Ehre, a nationally revered actress, in Hamburg, aged 88; publisher and writer Wieland Herzfelde, in East Berlin, aged 93; Dr. Ernst Katzenstein, who played a key role in achieving compensation for Nazi victims and served as director of the Claims Conference in Germany, near Frankfurt, aged 91; Otto Küster, who was instrumental in negotiating the Hague treaties in the early 1950s, in Stuttgart, in his late 80s; Max E. Levy, former director of ORT Germany, in Frankfurt; Günter Singer, for many years chairman of the Hamburg community, survivor of Theresienstadt, Auschwitz, and Birkenau, in Hamburg, aged 73; Hermann Zwi Wollach, Auschwitz survivor who emigrated to Palestine, was a candidate for mayor of Tel Aviv, returned to Germany, where he was active in the Stuttgart community, honorary citizen of Sarajevo, honored also by the Bonn government and the Hebrew University of Jerusalem, aged 82.

Lola Hahn-Warburg, who worked as a volunteer during the war with the Refugee Children's Movement in London and the Children and Youth Aliyah in London and Berlin, died in London at 88 years of age. Eric Lüth, a non-Jewish journalist, head of the Hamburg State Press Office and founder of "Peace with Israel," the first German program to come to grips with the past and confront Germany's relationship with Israel, died at the age of 87.

Y. MICHAL BODEMANN

German Democratic Republic

National Affairs

As IN THE OTHER COUNTRIES of Eastern Europe, the year 1989 saw dramatic political movement in the German Democratic Republic (GDR), culminating in the overthrow of the government of Erich Honecker in October and the opening of the border with West Germany in early November. The previous May, following local elections, the already frustrated and increasingly impatient East German population had been outraged by the government's announcement that 98.85 percent of the voters cast their ballots for the Socialist Unity party, when poll monitors in most districts observed that 20 percent of eligible voters had either boycotted the election or voted against the party.

The Honecker regime's support of the Tienanmen Square massacre in Peking a few weeks later heightened the already tense situation. The broadcasting of film footage of Tienanmen Square three times on GDR television was seen by many as an implicit threat. In late summer and early autumn tens of thousands of mostly young GDR citizens camped out in West German embassies in Prague and Warsaw and, after the border between Hungary and Austria opened in September, fled to West Germany. Over the course of 1989, 343,854 East Germans resettled in West Germany, disrupting the economy and the supply of goods and services in the GDR and creating a sense of panic. Those citizens who remained in the GDR took to the streets to demand political and economic reform.

Tension heightened as the Honecker government dug in and prepared to celebrate the 40th anniversary of the founding of the East German state on October 7. After bloody confrontations between police and demonstrators on October 7 and 8, on October 9, the government renounced the use of force and agreed to a peaceful dialogue with the people, many of whom were organizing in newly established opposition groups and revived non-Communist political parties. On October 18, Honecker resigned; many of his ministers were forced out of office shortly thereafter. On November 9, the border was opened, ending more than four decades of isolation of the East German population.

Jews and the GDR

The Jews of the GDR—a tiny but unusually visible and, given Germany's past, symbolically important group—participated in, and in turn were affected by, the social upheaval in many ways. Several Jews were among the officials close to Honecker who were forced to resign in October and November, among them Hermann Axen, Günther Schabowski, and Günter Mittag. The most notorious of these, Alexander Schalck-Golodkowski, disappeared after being accused of embezzling millions of marks which he deposited in Western banks. In December Gregor Gysi, a prominent lawyer of partly Jewish descent and a supporter of the Jewish community, was named the new head of the Socialist Unity party. Gysi had earned a reputation as a defender of dissidents and spokesperson for proreform forces within the party. Ibrahim Böhme, a dissident, emerged as leader of the new Social Democratic party. Böhme evaded reporters' queries about possible Jewish elements in his background, but he nonetheless received anti-Semitic hate mail.

Individual Jews were also among the intellectuals and leaders of the emerging opposition groups which articulated popular demands. These personalities included the writers Stefan Heym and Stefan Hermlin and former-spymaster-turned-reformer Mischa Wolf.

The Jewish community in the GDR remained close to the Socialist Unity party. It negotiated with the old and new administrations for diplomatic relations with the State of Israel, government protection against the attacks of the increasingly active right-wing elements of the population (see below), and for support for Jewish institutions and recognition of GDR Jews as active antifascists. The reluctance of the Jewish community to take a public position on the issues of national political and economic reform frustrated many members and supporters who stopped frequenting the Jewish community and began to work with the new reform groups. At the same time, many older Communists and young people attracted by the new youth programs (see below) began to appear at Jewish community events.

One casualty of the events of autumn 1989 was the observance of *Kristallnacht*: November 9, which had been previously observed by German Jews as a day of remembering the crimes of Germans against Jews, became a national celebration of the end of the division of Germany. And the weekly popular demonstrations in Leipzig, which started in early autumn and continued through the end of the year, became increasingly nationalistic with anti-Semitic overtones.

Anti-Semitism

Expressions of anti-Semitism increased and were more open after the Honecker government resigned in October, though often in conjunction with acts of hostility directed toward non-Jews: Russians, Communists, and homosexuals. For example, in October high school students attacked three blacks in a discotheque, shouting "Jewish Pigs!"

Jewish cemeteries in East Berlin and Erfurt were desecrated, neo-Nazi groups stepped up their activities, and, especially once Gregor Gysi became president of the Socialist Unity party, anti-Semitic slogans became increasingly visible at the weekly mass demonstrations in Leipzig. Particularly disturbing was the fact that those expressing positive feelings toward Jews tended to be older citizens and people from traditionally "antifascist" backgrounds, while the increasingly vocal anti-Semites were almost all young men 14 to 30 years old. The situation appeared even more complex in the fall when it became apparent that many "anti-Semitic" incidents were being instigated and/or misrepresented to the public by the Stasi (the state security service), which had come under pressure to shut down and wanted to prove that it was still needed.

Relations with Israel

Although the GDR remained the only Eastern Bloc state with no official ties to Israel, over the course of the year some contacts were initiated, creating the expectation that the realization of full diplomatic relations was only a matter of time.

In late January, Kurt Löffler, GDR minister for church-state affairs, visited Israel as a guest of the Holocaust institution Yad Vashem. This was the first visit to Israel of such a high-ranking East German official. Löffler, accompanied by two diplomats, met with Israeli minister of religion Zevulun Hammer. Although the Israelis were disappointed that Löffler continued to deny any responsibility of the GDR for the Holocaust, his visit was nonetheless considered the first step toward direct dialogue between the two states. One concrete result of Löffler's trip was an agreement between the GDR and Yad Vashem to exchange archival material and exhibits and to undertake cooperative research projects and academic exchanges. As a follow-up to Löffler's Israel trip, in March two representatives of Yad Vashem toured the GDR to meet with officers of the Jewish communities and to estimate the extent and location of the relevant GDR archival material.

Although the internal political crisis interrupted the development and implementation of foreign policy, in December the new prime minister, Hans Modrow, offered to establish diplomatic relations with Israel and to negotiate restitution payments to Holocaust survivors. Many observers close to the scene saw this move as part of an effort of the new government to broaden its legitimacy as a separate German state, and, at the same time, to win the sympathy of the international Jewish community and demonstrate its break with the Nazi as well as the Stalinist past. The Israeli government reacted to Modrow's verbal offer with a decided lack of enthusiasm, Foreign Minister Moshe Arens responding that Israel was awaiting a formal written application for diplomatic relations from the GDR.

In January conductor Kurt Masur toured Israel with the Leipzig Radio Choir. In June the Berliner Ensemble participated in a Jerusalem theater festival. Aktion Sühnezeichen-GDR (Operation Sign of Atonement), a Protestant group that had been rehabilitating Jewish cemeteries since the 1960s, was invited, for the first time, to undertake projects in Israel.

JEWISH COMMUNITY

Demography

For the first time in many years, precise statistics for Jewish communal membership were released by Jewish authorities. On December 31, 1989, 370 Jews belonged to the GDR's eight organized Jewish communities: 203 in East Berlin, 45 in Dresden, 37 in Leipzig, 35 in Magdeburg, 31 in Erfurt, 9 in Karl-Marx-Stadt, 5 in Halle, and 5 in Schwerin. The East Berlin figure—despite 8 deaths and considerable emigration to the West—actually showed an increase for the first time in decades. An additional 2,000–3,000 GDR citizens of Jewish ancestry did not belong to any of the Jewish communities, though approximately 400 of them frequented the Jewish communities' cultural programs. Thirty applications for membership were being processed, not only from individuals but also from entire families. Complaints were again heard that in several cases application procedures were being prolonged over years, though efforts were being made to alleviate this problem.

Communal Affairs

Through the months of national unrest, the Jewish communities of the GDR intensified their activities. Their strengthened ties to the international—and particularly to the West German—Jewish communities were evidenced in the many greetings sent to Heinz Galinski, president of the Central Council of Jews in West Germany and of the West Berlin Jewish community, on his birthday, and in the exchange visits of East and West German Jewish communities for Shavuot and Hanukkah celebrations. After the opening of the border, representatives of the Association of Jewish Communities of the GDR were invited to the Central Council's annual meeting to plan for future cooperation. The council, along with the Ronald Lauder Foundation in New York, donated equipment and financial support for various Jewish community activities.

The East Berlin Jewish community, which in previous years had sponsored four or five events per month, listed approximately ten events per month in 1989. Besides weekly Sabbath prayer services and the monthly Sunday-afternoon lecture series, meetings of the Friends of the Jewish Community, a children's program, youth group, and occasional special events, a monthly Friday community evening was instituted, and the Jewish women's group was revived. The women held open public discussions of topics considered too delicate for some of the other programs; they also organized programs for the Jewish elderly, and in December they held a bazaar that raised 2,105 marks for the planned Jewish cultural center, the Centrum Judaicum. In January a biweekly course in modern Hebrew was introduced. When it became oversubscribed and applicants were turned away, Pastor Johannes Hildebrandt arranged for a second course in Hebrew to be given at the nearby Sophienkirche. The East Berlin community also offered a course in Jewish customs taught by Prof. Shlomo Tischauer of West Berlin.

New Jewish activity outside East Berlin included the introduction of regular Sabbath prayer services in Erfurt and a weekend seminar in Dresden, in November, for Jews aged 12–47. (Other projects of Jewish interest organized outside the Jewish community are listed under "Culture" below.)

On May 10, the East Berlin Jewish community held a membership meeting where, for the first time, reference was made to Yom Ha'atzmaut, Israel Independence Day, and *Hatikvah* was sung. The Jewish communities in Dresden, Erfurt, and Leipzig, however, continued to observe the Tag der Befreiung (the day of liberation from the Nazis by the Soviet army) on May 8.

Over the year many GDR Jews made private visits to relatives living in Israel. Irene Runge of the East Berlin Jewish community spent the summer in Israel as a guest of the Jerusalem Foundation, and two members of East Berlin's Jewish youth group participated in the Israel Seminar for East European Youth. The Israelis who visited the GDR included Dahlia Itzik, Naphtali Eitan, and Mordechai Groner of Jerusalem's municipal government; Dr. Avi Becker of the Israel Office of the World Jewish Congress; Prof. Zeev Falk of the Hebrew University; Prof. Schalom Ben-Chorin, Dr. Jaacov Zur, and Izchak Schwersenz.

This year saw the introduction of a variety of programs for children and young people, a novelty in a Jewish community two-thirds of whose members were 60 years of age and older. The programs were made possible with considerable support from abroad, particularly from the West German and Western European Jewish communities and from the Lauder Foundation. In March, at a weekend seminar in Köpenick, organized by the East Berlin Jewish community, young Jews from East Berlin met with representatives of Western European Jewish youth organizations. Also in March, the East Berlin Jewish youth group organized an excursion of 20 young people to the restored former synagogue which now functioned as a Jewish museum in Gröbzig. In June a weekend seminar for young people was organized in Dresden.

Over the summer, 18 children aged 8–14 attended a three-week summer camp in Rügen, at which a trained Hebrew teacher (from West Germany) offered daily instruction in Hebrew and other Jewish subjects. Fourteen GDR children aged 12–16 attended another Jewish summer camp, sponsored by the Lauder Foundation, in Balatonfüreds, Hungary, where a teacher from Israel gave instruction in various Jewish subjects. Two members of the East Berlin youth group participated in a summer seminar in Israel (see above); eight young Jews attended the summer university of the European Union of Jewish Students in Montecampione, Italy; and in December four young people were guests at a Jewish ski camp in Switzerland.

The fall of the Honecker government intensified political conflict within the Jewish community and the larger circle of its supporters. On November 11, 150 people participated in a daylong colloquium in East Berlin for Jews within and outside the organized Jewish communities. For the first time since 1949, a large Israeli flag hung in the hall and was photographed by local camera teams. Participants in the colloquium debated the long-standing question of whether the GDR Jewish community should be a religious or a cultural organization and such new issues as the formation of a GDR-Israel Friendship Society and the future policy of the Jewish community with respect to the larger social changes taking place. Many of those present were disappointed that the Jewish community had not taken part in the October and November demonstrations—though many individual Jews had—and, unlike the Protestant Church, had not opened its doors to dissident Jewish and non-Jewish intellectuals.

After the border with West Germany opened, attendance at most Jewish community programs dropped significantly, as did attendance at cultural events generally in the GDR. It was assumed that most East Germans were engaged in reorganizing their lives, enjoying their new right to travel, and taking part in the intense political debates and struggles of those months.

NEW SYNAGOGUE BERLIN-CENTRUM JUDAICUM

The establishment of a foundation to create a cultural center and an archive on German Jewish history—to be housed in the once-grand synagogue on the Oranienburgerstrasse, slated for restoration—was announced in 1988 with great ceremony and publicity (see AJYB 1990, pp. 375–76). In 1989, however, the project moved slowly toward realization. Over the year several donations to the foundation—especially from the Protestant churches of the GDR—were announced, but the total sum raised was not made public.

The first regular meeting of the board of directors took place in June. In addition to GDR citizens, the board included Heinz Galinski, president of the Central Council of Jews in West Germany and of the West Berlin Jewish community; Rabbi Philip Hiat of New York; Rabbi Alfred Schöner of Budapest; Prof. Kurt Schubert of Vienna; and Sir Sigmund Sternberg of London. At the end of the year the foundation reported that the rebuilding of the synagogue was behind schedule due to a shortage of construction workers. Skilled workers were heavily represented among the GDR citizens who emigrated west in the second part of the year.

Holocaust-Related Matters

Internally there was no major event to compare with the massive observance of the 50th anniversary of *Kristallnacht* in 1988, but smaller commemorative projects were undertaken by various groups and institutions. In April the East Berlin Jewish community observed Holocaust Memorial Day (Yom Hashoah) for the first time. Avi Becker, director of the Israel office of the World Jewish Congress, was the speaker, and the GDR Ministry for Church-State Affairs sent a message. In July a local library in East Berlin was renamed for Anne Frank.

Throughout the year, Aktion Sühnezeichen-GDR continued to mobilize groups to work in Jewish cemeteries and to organize cultural events with Jewish content, as it had done since the 1960s. The city of East Berlin held a competition for the design of a monument to the achievements, the persecution, and the resistance of Berlin's Jews during the Nazi years. All 74 entries were exhibited at the Humboldt University in October. The winning design was by Karl Biedermann and Eva Butzmann.

In December the Central Committee of the Organization of Anti-Fascist Resistance Fighters invited two representatives of the Jewish community to discuss the long-standing Jewish complaint that while the East German state recognized Jews as victims of Fascism, it suppressed their active struggle against Hitler and denied them the privileges awarded to resistance fighters. It was agreed to pursue this grievance further at the local level. Also in December, Dr. Peter Kirchner, president of the Jewish community of East Berlin, called together a committee of Jews from different regions of the GDR to suggest changes and new concepts for teaching history and citizenship in GDR schools.

Jewish-Christian Relations

In May, at the first official meeting between representatives of the Association of Jewish Communities of the GDR and the board of directors of the GDR Federation of (Protestant) Churches, Bishop Werner Leich underlined the churches' guilt concerning the past. He stressed the need to inform members about Judaism and the Judeo-Christian tradition and to help older Germans confront and work through their wartime experiences. At the July conference of the (Protestant) Church of Saxony in Leipzig, the workshop on Christian-Jewish relations attracted at times 1,000 participants, of whom 300 signed a petition urging the GDR government to establish relations with Israel.

Culture

The intensification of Jewish life in the GDR in 1989 included an increased number of cultural events with Jewish content. However, because the GDR's Jewish population was small, and the antifascist theme played an important role generally in East German discourse, many producers of GDR "Jewish culture" were non-Jews.

In January the GDR exhibit on Jews in Berlin "*Und lehrt sie: Gedächtnis*" ("And Teach Them Not to Forget") was shown in West Berlin in exchange for the West Berlin exhibit "*Topographie des Terrors*" ("Topography of Terror"). An exhibit on Anne Frank was shown in East Berlin and Magdeburg, and Leipzig hosted an exhibit of the works of GDR Jewish artist Anatoli Kaplan. Works by the Viennese Jewish painter Heinrich Sussman (1904–1986) were shown in East Berlin. In Erfurt the Medical Academy held an exhibit of 600 art works collected by Alfred Hess, a local Jewish industrialist in the pre-Nazi decades.

The annual five-day Yiddish Cultural Festival, produced by Jalda Rebling in East Berlin, this year featured Yiddish culture in the USSR. The program included unusually straightforward presentations about the anti-Jewish measures that all but wiped out Jewish culture in the Soviet Union in the 1950s. In May the Deutsches Theater premiered *Schuldig Geboren* ("Born Guilty"), based on Peter Sichrovsky's book of interviews with children of Nazis. The play had been previously produced in West Berlin. DEFA, the GDR state film studio, released a short documentary, *Spuren* ("Traces"), an exploration of the remaining traces of prewar Jewish life in Berlin. The American klezmer clarinetist Giora Feidman gave concerts in East Berlin and Karl-Marx-Stadt, and the American folksinger Leonard Lehrman performed in East Berlin and Dresden. The musicians Daniel Barenboim, Itzhak Perlman, and Leonard Bernstein gave concerts in East Berlin. Important to the development of Jewish culture in the provinces were the formation of a Society of (largely non-Jewish) Friends of Jewish Culture in Halle and the establishment of a Working Group on the History of Jews in Leipzig, initiated by Erwin Märtin (also a non-Jew). This group organized a three-day Jewish cultural festival in Leipzig in November.

Publications

In 1989, 27 books of Jewish interest were published in the GDR. They included seven translations (one each from Hebrew, Polish, Hungarian, Dutch, Yiddish; two from English); nine works of fiction; six biographies of antifascists; two children's books; twelve books about the Nazi era; and one book about Palestine in the 1940s.

Among the most important new works were the following: *Kleine Kunst-Stücke* ("Small Feats"), a selection of short works by Walter Benjamin, written between 1928 and 1935, edited by and with an afterword by Klaus-Peter Noack; *Misstrauen lernen. Prosa, Lyrik. Essay* ("Learning to Distrust: Prose, Lyrics, and Essays") by Erich Fried, edited by Ingeborg Quaas, the posthumous first GDR publication of a major left-wing Jewish poet, an important influence on the West European student movement of the late 1960s, whose works had already been published in West Germany; *Curriculum Vitae. Erinnerungen eines Philologen. 1881–1918* ("Curriculum Vitae: Memoirs of a Philologist, 1881–1918") by Victor Klemperer, edited by Walter Nowojski, the remembrances of a major East German Jewish writer and his thoughts on Jewishness, Germanness, literature, and history; *Damit die Nacht nicht Wiederkehre* (English edition: *Beware Lest the Nightmare Recur*), prepared by Panorama (GDR State Office of Information), the programs and speeches given at the major events organized by the GDR government to commemorate the 50th anniversary of *Pogromnacht* (formerly called *Reichskristallnacht*), November 9, 1938; and *Berlin-Palästina und zurück. Erinnerungen* ("Berlin to Palestine and Back: Memories") by Günter Stillman, the experiences of a German Jewish Communist in Palestine in the 1940s.

ROBIN OSTOW

Austria

National Affairs

TWO MAJOR THEMES, ONE relating to Austria's historical past and the other to its political future, dominated Austrian politics in 1988 and 1989. In 1988 the country observed the 50th anniversary of its annexation by Nazi Germany. In numerous ceremonies and special events, Austria was forced to confront its largely unexamined role as part of the Third Reich. This process of self-examination and introspection took on a special significance as the country was still beset by the so-called Waldheim affair.

The other theme concerned Austria's future role in the 12-nation European Community (EC). The coalition government, made up of the Socialist party and its junior partner, the People's party, agreed to apply for full membership in the EC, even though the Socialists hesitated somewhat, out of concern for the possible effect on employment and agriculture. There was growing concern, too, about the impact of the move on the country's 33-year-old status of "permanent neutrality." The Soviet Union viewed with mistrust attempts to change this status but agreed not to try and block Austria's application to the European Community as long as it remained committed to permanent neutrality.

These developments, which cast a large question mark over the future direction of Austrian foreign policy, were further complicated by the completely unanticipated events in Eastern Europe, which brought about the end of the Communist-dominated governments in the region. With the demise of Communist rule in Eastern Europe and the winding down of the Cold War, Austria was faced with the prospect of losing its special position as a bridge between East and West. One not unlikely consequence of this change was that Vienna might prove less attractive as a venue for major political conferences. On the positive side of the ledger, Austria's stable economy would almost certainly attract more foreign companies to use Vienna as a springboard to the new markets of Central and Eastern Europe.

The Waldheim Affair

Contrary to public expectations, the controversy surrounding Kurt Waldheim's election as president of Austria in June 1986 did not quickly die down and disappear. Once in office, Waldheim was unable to discharge many of the largely ceremonial functions of his position. Because of the controversy surrounding his past, Western European countries declined to invite him for state visits; nor could he come to the United States, which had placed him on its "watch list" of undesirable persons.

Even more embarrassing was the practice of a number of foreign dignitaries of bypassing Vienna and meeting their Austrian counterparts in provincial cities in order to avoid being received by the president. Diplomatic snubs from the foreign ministers of Italy, Switzerland, and Yugoslavia were part of the continuing price Austria paid for the president's World War II record as a lieutenant in the German army and his attempted cover-up of that record. He was even shunned at home by many groups which refused to offer him the normal courtesy of invitations to their functions. He had become, as many observed, a virtual prisoner in the Hofburg, the presidential palace.

Beginning in 1988, the 50th anniversary of the *Anschluss,* the annexation of Austria by Nazi Germany in 1938, there were a number of demonstrations, staged mostly by young people, calling on Waldheim to resign. The protests only served to harden Waldheim's resolve to hang on to his office.

At the end of 1987 the government had appointed an international panel of six eminent historians to investigate Waldheim's record of wartime service and submit a report on its findings. President Waldheim approved the naming of the panel, implicitly agreeing, it could be argued, to be bound by its verdict. After an exhaustive investigation of wartime archives, the panel concluded (February 1988) that Waldheim had sought for decades to conceal his record as a staff lieutenant with a German army unit that waged a brutal campaign in the Balkans from 1942 to 1945, and then, once he could no longer hide it, tried to make it appear harmless. Although the panel found no evidence that he was personally guilty of war crimes, it was clear that while serving in that army unit, Waldheim had to have known about German atrocities yet did nothing to stop them. Waldheim had all along maintained that after being wounded on the Russian front in 1942, he was released from military service and spent the rest of the war in Vienna writing his doctoral thesis in law.

The report, and Waldheim's response to it, created a furor and prompted demands that he resign. In a brief televised address to the nation, on February 14, 1988, in which he showed no inkling of remorse or repentance, Waldheim rejected the findings of the panel and declared that he would not bow to "outside pressure" to resign. Instead of the detailed rebuttal to the findings that had been expected, Waldheim said only that "parts of the report do not correspond to the facts but are built on presumptions and hypotheses," and, "for that reason, the conclusions drawn cannot be upheld." The closest he came to acknowledging fault was in the admission that after the war he did not want to talk much about the "bitter period." That might have been a mistake, he conceded, ". . .but it was certainly not a strategy of covering up."

In political and intellectual circles, the findings were seen as formally endorsing charges that Waldheim had repeatedly lied about his past. Reaction in Socialist party circles stressed that Waldheim's continued presence in office would now become an even heavier burden for the nation to bear. A number of prominent figures, including former chancellor Bruno Kreisky and Simon Wiesenthal, called on Waldheim to resign. In rejecting these demands, Foreign Minister Alois Mock, head of the People's party and Waldheim's staunchest supporter, averred that the times called for unity and reconciliation.

These political differences reflected the deep division within the country. Following Waldheim's address, some 5,000 people demonstrated in front of the Cathedral of St. Stephen in Vienna to demand the president's resignation. The same demand appeared over the names of 1,500 prominent Austrian intellectuals, professionals, writers, and actors in a three-page advertisement in the magazine *Profil.* At the same time, letters from supporters of Waldheim filled the pages of the pro-Waldheim tabloid *Neue Kronen Zeitung,* some of them reflecting the sharp anti-Semitic tone of the debate surrounding the Waldheim affair. Former foreign minister Karl Gruber, a close associate of Waldheim, provoked a furor by asserting that the report was critical because the panel was composed of Socialists and Jews.

50th Anniversary of the Anschluss

The report came out as Austria was preparing to observe the 50th anniversary of the *Anschluss,* or annexation, by Nazi Germany. Waldheim's presence in office served to magnify the importance of the anniversary which, under more normal circumstances, would probably have attracted far less public attention. His enrollment in Nazi organizations, service in the German army, forgetfulness of this past, and refusal to show the least bit of remorse or contrition symbolized the past and mirrored the behavior and attitudes of a great many other Austrians.

Commemoration of the *Anschluss* on March 11, the day Austria lost its independence in 1938, was marked by a demonstration of an estimated 10,000 people outside the office of President Waldheim demanding that he resign. Some 2,000 Jews crowded into the Stadttempel for a service commemorating the sufferings inflicted on their families a half-century earlier. It was recalled in ceremonies taking place throughout the country that a great many Austrians enthusiastically joined the Nazis in persecuting Jews, forcing many to their hands and knees to wash gutters and toilets. Scores of thousands of Jews were jailed and their property confiscated; many thousands were forced to flee the country. Ultimately, 70,000 Austrian Jews were killed in German-occupied countries and in concentration camps, a great many of whose officers and guards were Austrians.

With President Waldheim barred from speaking before Parliament and other meetings dedicated to the occasion, Chancellor Franz Vranitzky played the leading role in urging citizens to ponder the past to ensure that the country did not fall "into an abyss as happened in 1938." Chancellor Vranitzky, while rejecting the notion that Austria bore a collective responsibility for Nazi crimes, told a special meeting of the cabinet, "one must face the fact of a historic guilt."

In an address before 15,000 people attending a memorial service at Mauthausen, on the 43rd anniversary of the liberation of the concentration camp by American troops, the chancellor stated that Austria bore no collective guilt for the crimes of the Nazis, which, he said, had to be laid at the doorstep of individuals. The Austrian state, Vranitzky averred, had gained its identify by resisting the Nazis and ". . . is the antithesis of the National Socialist regime of injustice. . . ."

A major theme of the anniversary, stressed by Socialists and Conservatives, was that Austria had lost its sovereignty in 1938 but that since 1945 it had rebuilt its democratic institutions in a way that would prevent a new dictatorship from arising. According to this view, the *Anschluss* was forced on an unwilling population, depicted in school textbooks as the victims of Hitler's aggression. Critics of this view argued that it glossed over the fact that a great many Austrians fervently wished for the *Anschluss* and fought for it. As if to underscore this point, many Austrians generally referred to the defeat in 1945 as the *Umbruch,* or "changeover," and not as the moment of liberation. Gustav Spann, a professor at the University of Vienna's Institute for Contemporary History and an expert on the teaching of history in Austrian schools, observed that hardly any mention was made in textbooks about Nazis in Austria. Spann left the People's party in 1987 because he disagreed with its position on the history of the Nazi period.

By and large, despite a nationwide agenda of speeches, ceremonies, historical exhibitions, and cultural events, the anniversary drew a limited popular response. Most of the demonstrations were attended largely by young people. Also, after this period of intense preoccupation, public interest in the Waldheim issue began to recede. People grew tired of it, particularly in view of the failure of the public protests to force Waldheim from office. Public-opinion polls taken in February 1988, after the historians' report, indicated that sentiment was evenly divided between those who wanted Waldheim to stay on and those who favored his resignation. This represented a decline in support for the president but did not signal the massive shift in public sentiment that analysts said would be needed to bring about his ouster.

There was other evidence that Austrians retained an ambiguous attitude toward the Nazi past. Historians estimated that fewer than 20 percent of Austrians were enthusiastic about Hitler before the annexation. However, many Austrians, while skeptical of the Nazis, had favored union with Germany since the breakup of the Austro-Hungarian empire at the end of World War I. Apparently these feelings persisted among a small segment of the population. A 1988 poll of 1,500 people, commissioned by Austrian television, found that 20 percent of Austrians believed that the *Anschluss* resulted in "the natural union of the German people." The same survey revealed that 47 percent of Austrians thought the annexation had good effects as well as bad ones. Only 15 percent said that it had an exclusively bad effect. The article reporting these results in the Vienna newspaper *Kurrier* carried the caption: "One-half believe: Hitler was not so bad."

Visit of Pope John Paul II

Although Pope John Paul II's pastoral visit to Austria in June 1988, the second in five years, was intended solely to provide religious encouragement to the overwhelmingly Catholic population and to celebrate the first East-West mass, in Eisenstadt, it received more than the usual amount of attention. The year before, in a meeting in the Vatican, the pope had become the first Western leader to receive President Waldheim, provoking much criticism from Jewish circles. Not only did John Paul II's visit to Austria revive memories of the Waldheim affair, but feelings worsened when the pope, during a visit to the Mauthausen concentration camp, failed to make specific reference to the Jewish victims who perished there. (At least 122,766 persons were murdered or died at Mauthausen and surrounding camps between 1939 and 1945, a great many of them Jews.) Chief Rabbi Chaim Eisenberg, echoing the sentiment of the Austrian Jewish community, deplored the omission, stating, "I profoundly miss the word 'Jews' in his speech. . . ."

At a meeting with Jewish leaders, the pope addressed this concern by stating: "The memory of the Shoah, the extermination of millions of Jews in the concentration camps, continues to burden you, and us as well." Paul Grosz, head of the Jewish community, expressed regret that the pontiff had not made a public statement concerning Austria's relationship to its past. The events of the past two years, Grosz observed, demonstrated that Austria had not come to terms with this past, and he urged the pope to stress the importance of this for all Austrians. He also requested the Catholic Church to examine why it had not more actively opposed the Nazis.

Anti-Semitism

The Waldheim affair set loose currents of anti-Semitism that rippled through Austrian society. Expressions of negative or hostile attitudes toward Jews that until then would have been suppressed or kept to a whisper were voiced openly in many social circles. No less disturbing were incidents involving the desecration of Jewish cemeteries and anti-Semitic graffiti scrawled in public places. Segments of the press and certain political leaders linked to conservative groups played no small role in fomenting this animus. With many Austrians convinced that the campaign against Waldheim was being orchestrated by international Jewish organizations, Jews became the special target of anger. Mindful of this, Chancellor Vranitzky, in a television interview in February 1988, called on the president and his supporters to stop blaming his problems on an "international Jewish conspiracy."

Segments of the Austrian press, notably the daily *Neue Kronen Zeitung,* did much to thicken the atmosphere of anti-Semitism. This sensationalist tabloid, which had the largest circulation of any newspaper in Austria, carried articles and letters from readers that many believed inflamed the already tense situation. Austrian state radio and television, and a number of newspapers, notably the *Salzburger Nachrichten,* by contrast, reported on the Waldheim affair in a restrained and balanced manner.

Sentiment toward Jews was further inflamed by a statement of World Jewish Congress president Edgar M. Bronfman in Brussels, early in 1988, urging the European Community not to accept Austria as a member as long as Waldheim remained president. These remarks drew a strong negative response from a wide spectrum of public opinion. They also created much uneasiness in the Jewish community, which felt that the statement was unfair and an attempt to interfere in a matter of great national importance to the government and people of Austria. In January 1989, in Luxembourg, the leader of the WJC reiterated his plea that the EC withhold approval of the Austrian application for membership, this time demanding that it accept responsibility to pay reparations to Holocaust survivors.

The Waldheim affair undoubtedly led to an increase in anti-Semitic feelings among Austrians. Results of a study done by the Institute for Conflict Research in 1988 showed a definite reversal of past trends of tolerance toward Jews. Racially inspired anti-Semitism, which had dropped from 18 percent in 1976 to a low of 7 percent, returned in 1987 to 18 percent. In 1973, roughly a fifth of Austrians were of the view that the country would be better off without Jews. This figure, which declined in the succeeding years to 8 percent, rose to 13 percent. According to the survey, 10 percent of the adult population described themselves as harboring strong feelings against Jews, and another 27 percent showed latent signs of anti-Semitism. Particularly disturbing was the increased number of educated people who revealed negative attitudes toward Jews.

Austrian Jews were shocked and angered by the upsurge in anti-Semitism, having come to believe that Austrian society had become more tolerant and open. There was the sinking feeling that much of the progress in promoting sound Christian-Jewish relations had been undone by the Waldheim affair. Not a few younger Jews wondered whether there could be a future for them in their own country when it revealed such an ugly face to them.

By 1989, much of the anti-Semitism that bubbled up in the aftermath of the Waldheim affair showed signs of returning to previous levels. In part, this could be attributed to the strong stand taken against it by government and church leaders. Also, other social concerns arose that absorbed public attention, notably a fear of the growing influx of refugees from Eastern Europe.

Relations with Israel

Despite the political fallout from the Waldheim affair, relations between Austria and Israel remained good. One exception to this was Israel's steadfast refusal to name a new ambassador to Vienna as long as President Waldheim remained in office. A new ambassador would have to present his credentials to the president of the Republic, a contact that Jerusalem had taken pains to avoid. As a result, Israel continued to be represented by a "chargé d'affaires ad interim," a title suggesting the temporary nature of the appointment. The Austrian Foreign Ministry, unwilling to exacerbate what was seen as a delicate issue, maintained ambassadorial-level representation in Tel Aviv. Once President Waldheim served out his term of office, Israeli officials had let it be known, Jerusalem would be quick to name a full-fledged ambassador.

Although a few political leaders expressed understanding of Israel's predicament in the matter, most, reflecting public sentiment, were critical of it. They did not understand why Israel refused to present credentials to the democratically elected president of the country. Indeed, the Vienna correspondent of the Israeli daily *Davar,* in an article on the subject, wrote that Israel lost more than it gained by being represented by a lower-level diplomat.

The issue of Jerusalem's representation in Vienna apart, relations between the two countries remained friendly. For example, Austria continued its liberal policy of providing transit facilities for Soviet and Iranian Jewish emigrants. (See more, below.)

In the more conventional areas of trade, tourism, and scientific and cultural exchanges, good to excellent ties were maintained. Trade in both directions amounted to about $100 million annually, a figure that had held fairly constant over the past years. Tourism between the two countries flourished, with an estimated 30,000 Austrians visiting Israel and approximately 50,000 Israelis traveling to Austria. The Jewish Welcome Center, a branch of the Austrian Tourist Office, assisted tourists from abroad to become acquainted with Jewish life in Vienna and arranged individual and group travel from Austria to Israel. Its director was Dr. Leon Zelman. The federal minister of science and research, Dr. Ewald Busek, visited Israel to sign contracts under which Austrian universities and the Weizmann Institute would engage in collaborative efforts in various scientific fields.

Cultural links between the two countries continued to develop in a strong manner. The Israel Philharmonic Orchestra had performed at the Salzburg Festival in 1987, and the Vienna Philharmonic, in turn, gave a series of five concerts in Israel under the direction of Leonard Bernstein. There were, in addition, a number of exchange visits of Austrian and Israeli artists. Austrian youth groups, under the sponsorship of the Austrian-Israeli Friendship Society, paid visits to Israel that were reciprocated by Israeli youth groups. An added dimension to these cultural ties was the signing in 1989 of a twin-city agreement between Bregenz, in western Austria, and Acco (Acre), the ancient Mediterranean port city.

Relations between the two countries were burdened by the Palestinian problem. The government's position was that Israel should recognize the Palestine Liberation Organization as a partner to negotiations under United Nations auspices. It did not, however, maintain a high profile on the Arab-Israeli conflict as it had done in the years when Bruno Kreisky was chancellor (1970 to 1983).

Holocaust-Related Matters

ANTIWAR MONUMENT

The Socialist-led government of the city of Vienna agreed to erect in the Albertinaplatz, a prominent part of the city, a stone and bronze monument against war and fascism. The monument was built by one of Austria's most famous architects, Alfred Hrdliczka. Hrdliczka, a former Communist and a controversial figure because of his espousal of left-wing causes, was an ardent opponent of Waldheim's presidential aspirations.

The focal point of the monument was a three-foot-high figure of a man, skullcap on its head, crouching on the paving stones, with a brush in its hand. Few Austrians could fail to recognize the image of an Austrian Jew forced to clean the gutters after the German annexation of Austria in 1938. The monument also included two large granite blocks set close together, symbolizing the violence of fascism; another figure seen disappearing into a block was symbolic of the victims buried beneath the rubble of an Allied bombing attack on the Albertinaplatz; another stone had an inscription of the Austrian declaration of separation from the Third Reich, proclaimed on April 27, 1945.

The monument stirred up much impassioned controversy, as much over where it should be sited as over its theme. Champions of the monument argued that it was a powerful reminder to Austrians of the fate that had befallen the Jews and the role they had played in this tragedy. At the unveiling of the monument on November 24, 1988, Chief Rabbi Chaim Eisenberg spoke of its powerful symbolism, saying: "If one stands shocked before this monument, then it can serve as atonement for those who complacently walked by the living street-washing Jew.... It should teach that one should not ignore injustice." While many if not most Jews expressed satisfaction with the monument, others took exception to it, notably to the kneeling figure as a flawed portrayal of the Jews and their fate.

A heated argument also broke out over where to place the monument. The mayor of Vienna, Helmut Silk, an ardent supporter of the monument, decided that it would be placed on the Albertinaplatz, right behind the State Opera, facing the historic Albertina museum, a spot traversed each day by thousands of tourists. The highly visible site was favored by the Socialist party but strongly opposed by the conservative People's party, which preferred to have the monument placed in Morzin Square, where the Gestapo headquarters were located between 1938 and 1945 and which was now dominated by a parking garage and gas station. The People's party was accused of opposing the memorial, but, lacking the courage to say so publicly, trying to have it shunted away from public view. Underlying these sentiments were the negative feelings of many conservative leaders toward Hrdliczka, whose strong opposition to Waldheim, they believed, should have disqualified him from being selected for the job. In protest, Foreign Minister Alois Mock, head of the party, and others of its leading members, stayed away from the unveiling ceremony.

REPARATIONS

Troubled by criticism that Austria had never paid reparations to Jews or to others who suffered at the hands of the Nazis, in March 1988 the Austrian Parliament voted $4.2 million to these victims. Sponsors of the legislation took pains to emphasize that the one-time payments of between $220 and $440 were a symbolic token, or *Ehrengabe* (gift of honor), as no amount of money could compensate the victims for the suffering they experienced. The fiercely debated measure had the approval of all parties represented in Parliament. In announcing her support for the bill, Freda Meissner-Blau, the leader of the Green opposition party, said she could only "blush with shame" at the niggardly sums offered.

Leaders of the Austrian Jewish community expressed deep misgivings about the measure, which they insisted provided no justice to the many victims of Nazism. Paul Grosz revealed that he had been repeatedly approached by members of the community who said they would not accept the money so as not to ease the conscience of the Austrians. Others said they would accept the money but would donate it to poor people. The New York-based Committee for Jewish Claims on Austria issued a statement declaring that the compensation offer "demeans the memory of those who perished and woefully ignores the needs of the aged Jewish Nazi victims from Austria."

KREISKY-WIESENTHAL CASE

A Vienna court rendered a judgment against former chancellor Bruno Kreisky for having made defamatory remarks about Simon Wiesenthal, the head of the Jewish Documentation Center in Vienna. The remarks were made in an interview given by Kreisky in 1986 in which he claimed that Wiesenthal managed to survive the war by collaborating with the Nazis. In ruling that Kreisky pay 270,000 shillings (about $20,000) to Wiesenthal, the judge suspended sentence on condition the offense not be repeated.

JEWISH COMMUNITY

Demography

The Jewish community of Austria was estimated to number about 12,000–15,000, of whom 6,400 were registered in the Israelitische Kultusgemeinde, the organized Jewish community. The great majority of the community lived in Vienna, with approximately 300–400 making their homes in the large provincial cities, notably Linz, Innsbruck, Baden, and Salzburg. The Jewish population had been augmented over the years by the arrival of Soviet Jews, mostly from Georgia and Bukhara, who had first gone to Israel and then returned to Austria, as well as others who arrived in Austria in transit to other countries but never left. The estimated number of this group was 2,000–3,000, about half of whom were members of the Kultusgemeinde. There was, in addition, a sizable population of assimilated Jews married to non-Jewish partners.

SOVIET AND IRANIAN JEWS

As noted above, Austria continued its traditional liberal policy of granting transit facilities for Jews emigrating from the Soviet Union and Iran. An estimated 55,000–60,000 Soviet Jews, with visas to Israel, came to Vienna in 1989, but fewer than 1,000 chose to go on to Israel. The rest were sent to transit camps in Italy where, after a wait of between six months to a year, they received visas to settle in the United States and Canada. Austrian Jewish leaders approached the government with a request that a number of these émigrés be allowed to stay in Austria. Although there was a government promise that 5,000 of the Soviet Jews would be granted permission to remain, nothing came of this.

Vienna also served as a transit point for a steady stream of Jews who came from Iran. After a waiting period ranging from one to six months, virtually all of these Jews went on to the United States.

A major change in U.S. immigration policy that went into effect on October 1, 1989, had the effect of sharply curtailing the Soviet traffic. Starting on that date, Soviet Jews could no longer process their papers to emigrate to the United States in a Western European country but had to do so in Moscow, where the waiting period was long and uncertain. As a result of the new administrative regulations, transit traffic to Vienna began drying up almost immediately. Soviet émigrés were now channeled to Bucharest, Budapest, and other points in Eastern Europe and from there were transported to Israel.

This dramatically changed pattern of emigration routes had both immediate and long-term consequences for Austria and its Jewish community. For Austrian officials, for whom Vienna's role as the major point of entry for Soviet Jews emigrating to Israel or to the West, which it had played for nearly two decades, posed diplomatic and security problems, the change was something of a relief. The loss of Vienna as a transit point also had serious demographic implications for the Jewish community. Over the years the small but important number of Soviet Jews who stayed on had nourished the modest growth of the country's Jewish life. Of the registered population, only about 1,400 were of Austrian origin, with the remainder having come from Hungary, Poland, Romania, Czechoslovakia, and the Soviet Union. During 1988–1989, the Jewish population grew by several hundred, partly as a result of the influx of Soviet Jews, mostly from Bessarabia, Georgia, Bukhara, and other regions of Soviet Central Asia.

Jewish-Christian Relations

Catholic Church leaders and a number of Christian groups were in the forefront of efforts to promote conciliation between Christians and Jews during the difficult period when the groundswell of anti-Semitism threatened to take on disturbing proportions. Rheinhold Stecher, archbishop of Innsbruck and Tyrol, was honored by the B'nai Brith for his work and for ordering the removal of an image of a ritual murder in Tyrol that had long been a tourist attraction. The archbishop was a strong supporter of Christian-Jewish dialogue.

An international seminar, sponsored by the Institute for the Study of Mankind, was convened in the Hofburg in November 1988, and was attended by a group of European and American intellectual and clerical leaders. A recurrent theme of the weeklong meeting was the need to deepen the dialogue between Christians and Jews. Had there been such dialogue, in the view of Cardinal Franz Koenig, former archbishop of Vienna, the Christian churches of Europe and North America might have been willing to take a forthright stand to protect the Jews against the Nazi onslaught and thus have prevented the Holocaust. Christians, Cardinal Koenig stated, were the "spiritual sons" of the "tribe of Abraham," and anti-Semitism had to be opposed, not alone for humanitarian reasons but for religious ones as well. At the closing session, Lord Coggan, former archbishop of York and Canterbury, announced the launching of an ecumenical foundation which would initially be based in London. The foundation, whose creation was mainly the handiwork of Lord Weidenfeld, the publisher, and Sir Sigmund Sternberg, chairman of the Council of Christians and Jews of England, would collect and disseminate information on interfaith matters.

Communal Affairs

Extensive renovations to Vienna's main synagogue, the Stadttempel, located on Seitenstettengasse, as well as to the offices of the Kultusgemeinde in the same complex, were completed in the fall of 1988. The estimated $3–4-million cost of the renovations was borne by the federal government and the city of Vienna. Chancellor Franz Vranitzky and Kultusgemeinde president Paul Grosz delivered addresses celebrating the event. The building project was intended, in part, to memorialize the 50th anniversary of *Kristallnacht* that took place on November 9–10, 1938. The Stadttempel was the only one of Vienna's many synagogues not destroyed in the November pogroms.

Culture and Education

Largely at the initiative of the city of Vienna, and with the approval of the Kultusgemeinde, a new Jewish museum was established in the city. The museum was assigned a section of the building that housed the Kultusgemeinde offices, on Seitenstettengasse, and would remain there until suitable permanent quarters were found. Most of the objects on display were part of the Max Berger Judaica collection, which was acquired from the family for the museum. The purchase price of the collection—28 million Austrian shillings, or approximately 2.2 million dollars—was shared by the federal government and the city of Vienna. The proceeds were given to the Jewish National Fund.

Considerable controversy within the Jewish community surrounded the establishment of the museum. Some were of the view that its location isolated it from the cultural and social mainstream of the city. Others contended that its contents were not representative of the contributions Jews had made to Austrian culture, the arts, science, and literature. Thus, there was a widely held view that both its location and its contents had the unintended effect of marginalizing Jewish culture.

A new play, *Heldenplatz,* by the Austrian playwright Thomas Bernhard, opened to great controversy at Vienna's Burg Theater in November 1988. The play consists of long monologues by relatives who have gathered after the death of a Jewish professor, a man who, having returned to Vienna after 50 years of self-imposed exile, was driven by despair to suicide. For most of the four-hour play, the professor's brother and daughters heap scorn on Austria. At the end, the professor's widow is driven to death by chants she alone can hear. It is the chanting of the crowds on the square outside—the Heldenplatz or Heroes' Square—shouting *"Sieg Heil"* as they had years before.

Hardly anyone or anything in contemporary Austria was spared Bernhard's caustic criticism. These included President Waldheim, Chancellor Vranitzky, the press, the Catholic Church, and the city of Vienna, which was described as a "cold, gray provincial city, where everything has been destroyed by Americanization." The opening-night audience cheered and jeered for 45 minutes after the curtain came down. The Austrian writer and playwright Peter Sichrovsky, a Jew, sharply criticized the play and attacked Bernhard for using "synthetic Jews" as a vehicle for personal grievances.

Two plays by Peter Sichrovsky opened in Vienna in 1988 to favorable reviews. One, *Born Guilty (Schuldig Geboren),* ran for three months at the Kreis Theater, and the other, *The Supper (Das Abendmahl),* had its premiere at the Akademie Theater. *Born Guilty* draws on a series of monologues by grown children who come from Nazi families in which they describe quite different reactions to their parents' past. In *The Supper,* the playwright starkly etches the trauma of a Christian woman and her Jewish husband when they are obliged to confront the Nazi past of her parents.

A new Jewish publication made its appearance in 1988. This was the *Judische Kulturzeitschrift,* a quarterly devoted to cultural and social issues related to Jewish life, edited by Ilan Berensin.

The Jewish Institute for Adult Education (Judisches Institut für Erwachenenbildung), located in Vienna's Second District, opened its doors to the public in 1989. The institute, which catered mainly to non-Jews, was financially and legally independent of the Kultusgemeinde but worked in close cooperation with it. It offered courses in Hebrew and Yiddish language, Jewish history, culture, and politics.

Dr. Jacob Allerhand's three-volume *History of the Jewish People* was published in 1989. Dr. Allerhand was a professor at the Institute of Jewish Studies, University of Vienna.

Personalia

Simon Wiesenthal, whose efforts in tracking down Nazi war criminals had brought him international renown, was given the Jabotinsky Award of the Anti-Defamation League in Los Angeles in 1988. He had been among the first to propose the creation of a panel of international historians to investigate President Waldheim's activities as an officer in the German army.

Hans Landesmann, a prominent lay figure in cultural and musical affairs, was named a member of the board of directors of the Salzburg Festival.

Stella Kadmon, well-known actress and singer, died in October 1989 in Vienna. She and her mother managed to flee Austria after the Nazis came to power and spent the war years in Palestine. She returned to Austria in 1947 where she later founded the Theater der Courage.

MURRAY GORDON

Eastern Europe

Soviet Union

National Affairs

THIS WAS A MOMENTOUS YEAR for the entire Communist world, as most of the East Europe states moved toward the abandonment of Communism, and the oldest Communist state, the USSR, underwent radical change. Mikhail Gorbachev's policy of *glasnost,* or openness, opened many past and present issues to public scrutiny and debate. Economic, cultural, political, and social issues were widely discussed and thoroughly debated. Jamming of foreign broadcasts virtually ceased, and foreign non-Communist newspapers became more widely available. Several constituent republics of the USSR made moves toward dissociation from the federation; spontaneous political activity spread across the country; the first meaningful elections since the revolution were held; a new legislative body convened and enthralled the public with the kind of open discussions almost never heard before; and the leadership continued its attempts to reform the economic system. Thus, joint ventures with foreign entrepreneurs and firms continued to grow in number, as did cooperatives. The legislature granted farmers the right to lease land for long terms.

On the other hand, the USSR suffered the consequences of a poor harvest in 1988, and there was no visible improvement in the standard of living. In the summer there were strikes of coal miners in Siberia and Ukraine, which forced government officials to negotiate with the strikers, something they had never done in the past. The government later passed a law permitting strikes, hitherto illegal, under certain circumstances.

A Congress of People's Deputies was established as a new legislative body to which there would be partially competitive elections, the Communist party retaining control of at least a third of the seats. In the March elections, many party functionaries were defeated, including the party secretaries of the Leningrad, Kiev, and Lvov regions. Boris Yeltsin, who emerged as Gorbachev's political rival, won 89 percent of the vote to an at-large seat in Moscow, after attempts to keep him off the ballot failed. In Lithuania, the Sajudis national movement captured 32 of the 42 seats allotted to that Baltic republic. In May, as the attention of the public was riveted on the proceedings of the legislature for the first time since the revolution, Mikhail Gorbachev was elected by the congress to the new office of president, winning 96 percent of the vote. However, conservatives managed to elect a much more conservative Supreme Soviet, the legislative body which ultimately shapes legislation.

In the elections to the Congress of People's Deputies, about 12 Jews were chosen. While none ran on a platform of representing Jewish concerns, some joined in an informal grouping after the elections with the aim of looking out for some basic Jewish interests. None of the eight Jews who had been elected to the Supreme Soviet in 1984 was reelected.

The second session of the Congress of People's Deputies met in December and voted an economic reform package which delayed price reforms, seen by many as crucial to any effective reform. The same session, acting on a report from a commission headed by Alexander Yakovlev, voted to condemn the Nazi-Soviet treaty of August 1939 which, in secret protocols, had divided Poland between the two nations and had assigned the Baltic republics to the Soviet sphere of influence. The media discussed the possibility that article six of the Soviet constitution, which grants the Communist party a monopoly of power, would be revised, paving the way for a multiparty system.

Some of the republics did not wait for such revision. In December the Baltic republics of Latvia and Lithuania legalized multiple parties. This was only one element in the growing separation of some republics from Soviet norms. Though the Supreme Soviet granted economic autonomy to the republics in July, this did not satisfy them, and they pushed for greater political autonomy.

The nationalities problem continued to be one of the most troublesome. Clashes between Armenians and Azerbaijanis forced the government to administer the disputed Nagorno-Karabakh region directly from Moscow, as of January, though later in the year it was assigned to Azerbaijan's jurisdiction, arousing the ire of Armenians. In Ukraine, the second most important republic, a national Ukrainian movement, Rukh, was founded. In Moldavia, the three Baltic republics, and Tajikstan, the languages of the respective indigenous majorities were declared the official languages of the republics. Russians in Estonia and Moldavia responded by demonstrating in protest, as did Gagauz in Moldavia. In Georgia, Soviet troops killed at least 20 peaceful nationalist demonstrators in April, using a poison gas and shovel handles.

Nationalist demands were couched in more political terms in the Baltic. In May the Lithuanian parliament unanimously passed a constitutional amendment granting Lithuania the right to veto Soviet laws and to control migration to Lithuania. After the Yakovlev commission reported on the secret protocols to the 1939 German-Soviet pact, a million people formed a human chain stretching through the Baltic republics as a symbolic protest against what they saw as the illegal annexation of their countries by the USSR. In December the Lithuanian Communist party congress voted to declare independence of the Communist party of the Soviet Union. This was unprecedented and broke the strict hierarchical party discipline that had always been a counterweight to the federal structure of the state. Lithuanian party leader Algirdas Brazauskas went further when he declared the Lithuanian party's intention to "establish an independent Lithuanian state."

Foreign Affairs

The Soviet Union continued to move toward understandings with rivals, with Gorbachev successfully projecting an image of a benign Soviet Union. He announced that the military budget would be cut by 14 percent and the armed forces reduced by half a million men and 10,000 tanks. When Poland elected a non-Communist government, the Soviet Union took no steps against that country. Gorbachev repeatedly assured East Europeans and the world that the USSR would not interfere in internal developments in the countries of the region and surprised many by keeping his word. Gorbachev visited Beijing in May in an attempt to improve relations with China. He tried to do the same with Japan. At the end of the year he met in Malta with President George Bush of the United States. Few concrete agreements were reached, but the atmosphere generated by the meeting set the stage for arms control and other agreements between the two countries; the meeting also seemed to establish a good personal relationship between the two leaders.

This was the most politically exciting year in memory. It ended with the Soviet population watching anxiously as the East European states pulled out of the Communist camp, and as their own political institutions and personalities were being revamped and reshuffled with unprecedented speed.

Relations with Israel

As part of its effort to improve relations with the West, the Soviet Union took steps toward a better relationship with Israel. In January an Israeli basketball team played in Moscow for the first time in 21 years, and 175 Israeli fans were permitted to attend. A large number of Soviet Jews cheered the Israelis on. In the following month, Soviet foreign minister Eduard Shevardnadze met with his Israeli counterpart, Moshe Arens, in Cairo, just after Shevardnadze had met with PLO chief Yasir Arafat. Israel received good publicity in the USSR for its assistance on the spot to the victims of the December 1988 earthquake in Armenia. Later, about 60 Armenians were brought to Israel for medical treatment in a project funded by the American Jewish Joint Distribution Committee. Armenians and Israelis spoke of establishing ties between the two peoples and their respective states.

In August a commercial agreement was signed between the Israeli Ministry of Agriculture and the Soviet Academy of Sciences. In the United Nations, for the first time, the Soviet Union did not vote with the Arab states to deny Israel a seat at the General Assembly session. This was seen as a symbol of the Soviet desire to normalize relations with Israel. In a development that was bound to influence immigration to Israel, about 25,000 Soviet citizens—most of them presumably Jews—traveled to Israel as tourists; they were provided with Russian-speaking guides and met with family and friends who had previously settled in the Jewish state.

In August a prominent Soviet journalist, Alexander Bovin, wrote an article in *Izvestia* which called on the USSR to extend full diplomatic recognition to Israel. Shortly thereafter, another Soviet writer, A. Smirnov, published an article in the same newspaper arguing against immediate recognition. This illustrated the pluralism that had come to Soviet public life and probably reflected debates within the policy-making elite.

Anti-Semitism

As political controls relaxed and ethnic tensions grew, there were increasingly visible signs of anti-Semitism at the grass-roots level. The government no longer seemed to churn out as much anti-Zionist and anti-Judaism propaganda as it had, but individuals and groups were openly expressing their hatred of Jews. Writers in Leningrad complained that Jews dominated the publishing houses and literary journals. Igor Shafarevich, a distinguished scientist, published an article entitled "Russophobia," in which he charged that the Jews, a "lesser people," live in their "own intellectual and spiritual world, detached from the people at large . . . an elitist group whose essential beliefs are *antithetical* to those of the people as a whole." He warned that if the " 'Lesser People' ideology were to succeed, it would spell the final destruction of the religious and national foundations of life." (*Nash Sovremennik,* no. 6, June 1989)

In the spring, rumors of pogroms spread in Ukraine and were discussed in the press. Such rumors were so widespread in Moscow, Kursk, and Odessa that in each case the authorities used the media to reassure the population that the rumors were unfounded. No pogroms materialized, but anxiety and even panic spread among Jews in several parts of the country.

Over 350 Jewish delegates to the Vaad congress in Moscow in December (see below) were surveyed on their perceptions of anti-Semitism. While 94 percent of those from Leningrad and 72 percent of those from Moscow thought an upsurge of anti-Semitism was possible, only 21 percent of those from the Caucasus and 29 percent of the delegates from Central Asia thought so. In areas in which, historically, anti-Semitism had been virulent—Ukraine, Lithuania, Moldavia—the national movements were at pains to reassure the Jews that they would be protected, and that in future independent or autonomous states they would enjoy complete equality. Indeed, the national movements supported efforts to revive Jewish culture. It was in Russia itself that the most anti-Semitic groups seemed to be operating.

JEWISH COMMUNITY

Demography

A national census was taken in January 1989, the first in ten years. Only preliminary results were released during the year. They showed the number of Jews who had reported themselves as such to the census taker as 1,449,167. This was a decline of nearly 20 percent from the 1979 census, compared with the previous intercensal period's decline of 16 percent. Only 11.1 percent of the Jews gave a Jewish language as their "mother tongue," down from 14 percent in the previous census. Thus, long-term tendencies of emigration, low fertility, high mortality, and assimilation seemed to be accelerating. For the first time, the Jewish population was divided into subethnic groups. Nearly 20,000 "Mountain Jews" ("Tats") were listed, as were 16,123 Georgian Jews, and 36,568 Central Asian ("Bukharan") Jews. The rest were Ashkenazim.

The republic with the most Jews was the Russian (550,422), followed by the Ukrainian (485,975). In Birobidzhan, designated as the "Jewish Autonomous Oblast," there were only 8,887 Jews; they constituted less than 10 percent of the oblast's population.

The new figures revealed the greatest intercensal decline in the number of Jews since 1959. During the year, the number declined still further as a result of massive emigration of Soviet Jews.

Emigration

The year 1989 saw the largest emigration of Soviet Jews since the 1920s. Whereas in 1988 about 20,000 had left, according to HIAS, 70,508 Jews left in 1989, of whom 17 percent went to Israel and the rest came mainly to the United States. However, owing to a change in U.S. policy, by December, 41 percent of the émigrés went to Israel. In September, Israeli prime minister Yitzhak Shamir predicted that a million Soviet Jews would emigrate and argued that they should come primarily to Israel. At the same time, organizations of Soviet immigrants in Israel and the Soviet Jewry Zionist Forum, headed by Natan (Anatoly) Sharansky, criticized the Israeli government as being unprepared to absorb large numbers of immigrants.

In October a prominent Lithuanian Jewish writer and deputy to the Congress of People's Deputies, Grigory Kanovich, published an article in the Lithuanian Communist youth organization newspaper which suggested that Jews were in imminent danger in the USSR, where anti-Semitism was highly visible, and that they had no future in the country.

In the same month, the U.S. government announced plans to limit the granting of refugee status to those who had first-degree relatives in the United States and to bring them directly to America. This would permit closing the transit stations in Vienna and the suburbs of Rome which, in fiscal year 1989, cost about $35 million to maintain. Israeli officials welcomed the announcement and said they were eager to receive the bulk of the émigrés. Until September 1988, Soviet Jews were almost automatically granted refugee status by the American Immigration and Naturalization Service, but at that point émigrés began to be interviewed more rigorously to determine whether they met the necessary criteria. Over the course of the next year, nearly 20 percent were denied refugee status. Under heavy criticism by American Jewish organizations, the American government admitted that its motivation was largely financial, claiming that it cost about $7,000 to transport and resettle each immigrant and that the budget could not stand such expenditures.

Early in the year, the Soviet refugee quota was raised by taking slots away from potential Asian immigrants. The organized American Jewish community was uncomfortable with that arrangement and successfully pressed for raising the Soviet quota without reducing others. By the end of 1989, the administration had raised the quota to 43,000, and an additional $75 million had been allocated to refugee resettlement. Some 14,000 Soviet Jews in Italy were to be the first admitted.

The National Conference on Soviet Jewry recommended in June that the Jackson-Vanik Amendment be waived for one year if President Bush were given certain Soviet assurances: that there would be sustained high levels of emigration; that long-term refuseniks would be allowed to leave; that access to state secrets would not be used widely as an excuse for preventing emigration; and that the problem of "poor relatives" (people prevented from leaving by relatives' claims) would be solved. In May, President Bush had said in a speech that he would consider a Jackson-Vanik waiver if the Soviets would codify new emigration laws and "faithfully implement" them.

The United Jewish Appeal launched a "Passage to Freedom" campaign to raise $75 million to facilitate immigration both to Israel and the United States. American philanthropist Joseph Gruss announced a contribution of $20 million to the Soviet Jewry Zionist Forum to provide housing mortgages to Soviet immigrants in Israel. Israel asked the American government to provide $400-million worth of loan guarantees to finance construction of housing, in the expectation that 100,000 immigrants would arrive in the following three years. Israel estimated the need as 30,000 housing units at an average cost of $65,000 per unit. Israel planned to pay $2 billion of the resettlement costs from its own resources and raise $600 million abroad.

Communal Affairs

The new atmosphere of political freedom and growing acceptance of ethnic assertiveness allowed Jews to begin to organize themselves. As a first step in creating needed communal structures for the third largest Jewish community in the world, a meeting was held in the spring of representatives of Jewish cultural organizations around the country. It was attended by 185 representatives of 48 cultural organizations in 27 towns and cities and by foreign observers, including Israelis. A decision was taken to form a national Jewish umbrella body.

That was accomplished in Moscow in December. In an atmosphere of great excitement and expectation, about 750 delegates representing 250 cultural associations or communities gathered in a large hall in central Moscow and established the "Vaad" (Committee) as a national coordinating body to carry out several functions: facilitate Jewish cultural and religious life, represent Soviet Jewry to world Jewry and to the Soviet government, assist in emigration to Israel, and defend against anti-Semitism. There was considerable debate on whether to focus on Soviet Jewish life or to assist in the emigration of Jews, primarily to Israel. If the former, the question was whether secular Yiddish culture, Hebrew-Zionist goals, or religion should be the top priority. It was as if the debates of a century ago were being rehearsed by the descendants of the Zionists, Bundists, the religious, and others who had established and represented the major Jewish movements of modern times. After much discussion, it was decided to assist *aliyah* as well as to nurture cultural and religious development within the USSR, much as an earlier generation of Russian Zionists had resolved in their meeting in Helsinki in 1906.

A presidium was elected, consisting of Dr. Mikhail Chlenov of Moscow, Iosif Zissels of Ukraine, and Samuil Zilberg of Latvia. Chlenov, an anthropologist, was a longtime Hebrew teacher in Moscow, a talented linguist, and a leader in the renaissance of Jewish scholarship. Zissels, active in the Ukrainian dissident movement, represented those who came to Jewish activity through involvement in the human-rights movement. Zilberg represented the Baltic perspective, more militant and nationalistic than that of most other delegates from the rest of the USSR.

The meetings encountered demonstrations outside the hall by Pamiat, the anti-Semitic organization, and pro-Arab, anti-Zionist demonstrators. Rukh, the Ukrainian national movement, provided security for the meetings, along with Soviet police, symbolizing a historic realignment of forces and alliances. The meetings were covered by the foreign press but were not mentioned in the Soviet media. Nor was Vaad registered by the Soviet authorities. Israeli officials regarded Vaad warily but were pleased by its commitment to assist *aliyah*.

Two months earlier, an All-Union Society of Soviet Jewish Culture had been established by Aron Vergelis, editor of *Sovetish Haimland,* and other "establishment Jews," but they were largely ignored by the Soviet and foreign publics.

The Politburo's special commission on Stalinist repressions published a decree ordering the release of materials belonging to the Jewish Anti-Fascist Committee. Though the committee had been "rehabilitated" in 1955, its files remained inaccessible. The same commission posthumously reinstated to Communist party membership Jewish cultural figures V.A. Shimiliovich and David N. Hofshtain, who had been murdered in Stalin's purges.

Culture and Religion

In the 1960s and 1970s, Soviet Jews actively involved in Jewish culture generally were of two types: those who followed the Communist party line and participated in the few officially approved publications and organizations, and those who were independent and, almost by definition, dissident. In 1989 a third type of cultural activist emerged into prominence: people who were neither politically conformist nor dissident but who took advantage of the new freedoms of expression and organization to establish Jewish cultural associations. Some of the latter were closer to the establishment and emphasized secular Yiddish culture, while others were more inclined toward Hebrew, Zionism, tradition, and Israel. In addition, foreign organizations were allowed for the first time to sponsor ongoing Jewish cultural activities in the USSR.

Jewish cultural associations were established in over 200 locales, including Donetsk, Kiev, Kherson, Kharkov, Lvov, and Zaporozhe in Ukraine; Minsk, Bobruisk, and Vitebsk in Belorussia; Kaunas, Klaipeda, and Vilnius in Lithuania; Riga and Daugavpils in Latvia; Kishinev in Moldavia; Penza, Ufa, and Leningrad in the RSFSR; and Tashkent in Uzbekistan. The "Jewish Cultural Society of the Moldavian SSR," in Kishinev, was typical. Founded under the aegis of the Moldavian division of the USSR Cultural Fund, it had sections for history, literature and linguistics, youth, and amateur arts. Cochairmen of the society were a composer and a Yiddish writer. The Aleph Society of Donetsk was reported to have historical, "philosophical-religious," and theatrical sections. Sections were planned for sports, youth, and war veterans. Aleph suffered from a lack of teachers, curricular materials, and a permanent meeting place.

Yiddish language courses were opened at the Moscow Steel Institute as well as in Vilnius, Vitebsk, Chernovtsy, Kishinev, and Kharkov, among others. Yiddish theater groups were formed or revived in Vilnius, Kiev, and Kishinev. Reports from Birobidzhan spoke of plans for a Jewish Sunday school and a bilingual (Yiddish and Russian) professional theater. Some of these groups encountered difficulties in obtaining official recognition, but most found ways to operate. For example, in Tashkent, when the municipal authorities refused to register the new Jewish cultural association, the group rented space from a cooperative and operated openly. All the associations were hampered by a lack of books and other materials and by a paucity of qualified teachers and lecturers.

Birobidzhaner Shtern, the Yiddish newspaper, announced in June that in the following academic year, Yiddish would be taught in three schools in Moscow. In addition, Yiddish circles would be established in youth organizations and institutions in the capital. Meanwhile, Bar-Ilan University in Israel brought 57 Soviet Yiddish teachers from 17 cities to its campus for an intensive three-week seminar.

Not surprisingly, it was in the Baltic states that cultural activity was most intense. In Vilnius, Lithuanian radio began monthly Yiddish broadcasts. In March, 500 delegates and several hundred guests attended the founding meeting of the Jewish Cultural Association of Lithuania. Thirty teachers began studying Yiddish pedagogy in preparation for the opening of a Yiddish school. The Vilnius city government restored two Jewish street names, Jews' Street and Ga'on Street, in the heart of the old ghetto. Jewish organizations, including the Maccabee sports club and the Tekumah Zionist movement, were founded. The first Jewish all-day school, encompassing ten grades, opened in Riga, Latvia. According to *Sovetish Haimland*, there were 404 applicants for 286 places. The school was headed by veteran Communist and Yiddishist Khone Bregman, and there were disputes about whether the curriculum should have a more Zionist and Hebrew orientation.

A professionally produced Jewish newspaper in Russian made its first appearance in April. It was sponsored by the Association of Activists of Soviet Jewish Culture, a group representing old-line party supporters. The *Herald of Jewish Soviet Culture* (VESK) was edited by Viktor Magidson, a member of the Anti-Zionist Committee of the Soviet Public. After the committee published a statement of its own in one issue, the editorial board dissociated itself from it as "totally unacceptable." Magidson was replaced by Tankred Golenpolsky, a journalist and businessman. Meanwhile, several of the cultural associations began publishing newspapers, mostly in Russian, with some in Yiddish or Ukrainian.

In January B'nai Brith International opened a 38-member lodge in Moscow. The Maccabee sports organization opened branches in several cities. The most publicized event of the year was the opening of the Solomon Mikhoels Cultural Center in Moscow. Named after the Yiddish actor and director who was killed on Stalin's orders in 1948, the center was hailed as the first officially recognized facility of its kind. Australian Isi Leibler, a vice-president of the World Jewish Congress (WJC), was the moving force behind the effort to open it. Edgar Bronfman, president of the WJC, writer Elie Wiesel, representatives of the Jewish Agency, and the ambassadors of several Western countries attended the opening in February, along with former refusenik Yuli Edelshtein—who returned to the USSR 19 months after his release from prison and immigration to Israel—and Soviet Jewish activists, including Yuli Kosharovsky.

Despite all the fanfare, for much of the time after its gala opening, the center was closed. Director Mikhail Gluz attributed this to "technical reasons" and complained privately that the Western sponsors were not coming through with funds. They, in turn, charged that the center was hewing too closely to official lines. For example, a visiting Israeli lecturer, Prof. Yaacov Ro'i, was initially denied permission to lecture, then finally allowed to speak, but in a small room in the building. Moscow Hebrew teachers boycotted the center, refusing to hold their classes in an institution they felt was hostile or indifferent to Israel and Zionism. By year's end, the publicity surrounding the center had faded, and its activities were eclipsed by those of the Vaad and the cultural and religious groups around the country.

Also in February, the first independent yeshivah since the revolution opened its doors in Moscow. In the late 1950s a yeshivah had been opened in the Moscow Choral Synagogue, but it operated only sporadically and was considered to be "official." The new yeshivah was under the aegis of the Academy of World Civilizations, a new institution backed by prominent Soviet scientists such as Evgenyi Velikhov and Roald Sagdeev. Plans called for the academy to have branches for Judaism, Islam, Christianity, and science and technology. The yeshivah was supervised by Israeli scholar Rabbi Adin Steinsaltz and staffed largely by teachers from Israel and the West. It opened with 35 students selected from over 150 applicants.

In March, Moscow's Taganka Theater and the Israeli Habimah Theater, which originated in the Soviet Union in 1917, signed an agreement to exchange performances.

Rabbi Adolf Shayevich of Moscow's Choral Synagogue attended a meeting of the Memorial Foundation for Jewish Culture in Stockholm, the first time a Soviet Jew participated as a full member rather than as an observer. The Memorial Foundation granted several fellowships for Jewish scholarship and training to Soviet Jews.

Several concerts featuring cantors from Israel and North America attracted large and enthusiastic audiences during the year. The Joint Distribution Committee sponsored a training seminar for ten Soviet cantors from six communities. The seminar was led by New York's Cantor Joseph Malovany and was designed to be a forerunner to an academy for synagogue professionals.

Some synagogues became more active as a result of the upsurge in cultural activity, especially in towns in which they were the only Jewish sites. Although the new cultural societies generally rented other types of premises, in some towns synagogues became the focal point of Jewish formal and informal meetings. In addition, local religious groups, often stimulated by foreign emissaries, began to invigorate local synagogues. In Lvov and Kharkov the Jewish communities asked local authorities for permission to return to synagogue buildings which had been seized and converted to other uses.

Personalia

American-born Abe Stolar, a refusenik for 14 years, finally left for Tel Aviv with his family in March. Stolar, 77, had been brought to the USSR by his parents in 1931.

Daniil Alexandrovich Granin, a well-known writer, received the honor of Hero of Socialist Labor with Order of Lenin and Hammer and Sickle Gold Medal "for great services in the development of Soviet literature and for valuable public service."

Yuli Daniel, son of a Yiddish writer and one of the early voices of dissent in the 1960s, died on December 30, 1988. His joint trial with fellow writer Andrei Sinyavsky, in 1966, set off a series of repressive measures. Yiddish writer Motl Gruvman, born in Nemirov in 1916, died on December 31, 1988. A lieutenant-colonel during World War II, he was a poet and worked in publishing. Yiddish prose writer Elie Gordon and literary critic and publicist Uran Guralnik passed away [n.d.].

ZVI GITELMAN

Eastern European Countries

THIS WAS THE MOST IMPORTANT year in East European history since the end of World War II. By the end of 1989, all the East European states except Albania had changed their governments, and almost all had left the Communist camp. This collapse of Communism in Eastern Europe generated enormous excitement the world over. Remarkably, it was accomplished with almost no violence—except in Romania—and with no Soviet intervention.

There were about 100,000–150,000 Jews in the region. Most looked upon the dramatic changes with a mixture of fear and hope. Fear was engendered by the possibility that anti-Semitism, traditional in some areas and espoused by some pre-World War II parties and movements, would reemerge as political and social restraints were removed and tensions heightened in societies seeking to redefine themselves and solve serious economic and social problems. Moreover, since Jews were associated in the minds of many East Europeans with the hated Communist regimes, it was feared that "revenge" would be taken on Jews for "having brought godless Communism to us." On the other hand, the reform or destruction of Communist regimes could portend new religious and cultural freedoms, better relations with Israel, and opportunities for emigration. In fact, Israel's trade with Eastern Europe rose 30 percent over 1988 and reached a volume of $250 million.

Poland

Poland and Hungary led the way from Communism. Strikes in Poland in the spring and summer of 1988 and the ongoing deterioration of the Polish economy forced the government to recognize the outlawed opposition Solidarity movement and begin discussions on a new form of government. The talks, held from February to April, resulted in the legalization of Solidarity and its participation in elections. In the spring elections, Solidarity won every seat for which it could compete in the lower house of the Sejm and all but one of the 100 seats in the newly reconstituted Senate. When the Communists failed to form a coalition government, Lech Walesa, longtime Solidarity leader, brokered the first non-Communist government since 1947, headed by Catholic journalist and Solidarity adviser, Tadeusz Mazowiecki. After the Mazowiecki government took office in September, the decline of the Communist party was hastened, though its former head, Gen. Wojciech Jaruzelski, retained the presidency of the country. Solidarity and the Catholic Church struggled to redefine their roles in public life.

In December Israeli vice premier and finance minister Shimon Peres spent four days in Poland, where he was assured that Poland would reestablish full diplomatic relations with Israel, severed since 1967. Peres discussed commercial relations between the two countries and the preservation of Jewish sites in Poland.

JEWISH COMMUNITY

Poland's Jewish population was generally assumed to number 5,000–10,000, only a minority of whom were actively identified with either the religious community or the secular Society for Jewish Culture.

In May the first rabbi to serve in Poland since the late 1950s took up his post in the only synagogue in Warsaw, a city once home to over 300,000 Jews. Rabbi Pinchas Menachem Yoskovich, 65 years old and a survivor of the Lodz ghetto and Auschwitz, came from Israel where he had been a businessman. He appeared on Polish television and radio and was treated as a leader of Polish Jewry.

The major public issue of the year was the convent of Carmelite nuns established at the site of the Auschwitz death camp. In 1987, Catholic leaders had agreed with Jewish groups to move the convent; the deadline had been set for February 22, 1989. Jewish groups had agreed to support the construction of an interfaith center of information, education, and prayer not far from the death camp. Though the Primate of France announced in January that the convent would be moved "soon," the February deadline was not met. Instead, a new 20-foot cross was put up at the convent. In July, when American rabbi Avraham Weiss and a small group of supporters demonstrated at the convent, they were physically attacked by Polish workers at the site. Later the same month, about 100 Jews representing four Jewish student organizations in Western Europe demonstrated at the site and demanded the removal of the convent. Local Poles were divided in their reactions to the demonstrations, some shouting "Go back to Palestine," while others tried to convince the demonstrators that the nuns were praying for all victims of the camp. The Communist media condemned the Jewish protests, while the Solidarity newspaper reported the incidents factually.

At a mass at the shrine in Czestochowa, in August, the Primate of Poland, Cardinal Jozef Glemp, warned Jews not to "talk to us from the position of people raised above all others and do not dictate conditions that are impossible to fill." He charged that Jews controlled the mass media "in many countries" and warned that "the feelings of all Poles" were under attack. A front-page editorial in the Solidarity newspaper denounced the cardinal, as did many Jewish groups. A month earlier, Cardinal Franciszek Macharski, Pope John Paul II's successor as archbishop of Krakow, had said that the Church would not honor the 1987 agreement in the face of "aggressive" Jewish demands. Cardinal Glemp called the agreement "offensive" and criticized Macharski for having signed it in the first place. However, three other non-Polish cardinals who had been signatories, along with Macharski, to the original agreement, affirmed the validity of the agreement. Pope John Paul II was reluctant to get involved in the issue and made no public statements about it.

Rabbi Yoskovich refused to participate in a prayer service marking the start of World War II that was to be held in Warsaw, as a way of protesting Cardinal Glemp's remarks. The Polish-born prime minister of Israel, Yitzhak Shamir, remarked that Poles "suck in anti-Semitism with their mother's blood"; Polish president Jaruzelski countered that Shamir's observation contradicted "the long tradition of Polish-Jewish co-existence in Poland." Cardinal Glemp canceled a visit to the United States, where demonstrations were threatened by Jewish groups. On the other hand, Lech Walesa did visit the United States in November and was greeted effusively by Jewish groups, though they were put off by his failure to condemn Cardinal Glemp's statement as anything more than badly formulated and unfortunate. Walesa also condemned the tendency to see all Poles as anti-Semitic. Finally, Cardinal Glemp wrote to a British Jewish leader in late September and affirmed the recommendation of a special Polish Church commission to move the convent. Prime Minister Mazowiecki and the Polish ambassador to London, Zbigniew Gertych, had urged Glemp to do so.

Hungary

Following the ouster of Communist party leader Janos Kadar in 1988, the Hungarian government was challenged by a deteriorating economy and the proliferation of anti-Communist political groups. The Communist party was split on the question of the pace of reform. It temporized by electing a four-man presidium in June, but by October the membership had voted to replace the party with a new entity calling itself the Hungarian Socialist party rather than the Hungarian Socialist Workers' party. The new party lost in a referendum on the timing of presidential elections, and national elections were scheduled for March 1990, to be followed by presidential elections. In foreign policy, Hungary moved away from its traditional support of Soviet positions. It established diplomatic relations with Israel and South Korea; liberalized travel and emigration policies; permitted Radio Free Europe to open an office in Budapest; and opened its border with Austria.

In January, Israel and Hungary signed an agricultural agreement involving trade, joint enterprises, and the exchange of technology and know-how. An Israeli-Hungarian Friendship Society was active, and there were regular flights between Israel and Budapest. By September, Hungary had become the first Communist country to restore full diplomatic relations with Israel, following the 1967 rupture. Hungary expected that Israel would help Hungary expand its economic ties to the West, though some Hungarian officials had already expressed disappointment in the failure of Israel to mobilize massive Jewish investments in Hungary. Foreign Minister Gyula Horn said, "The reestablishment of diplomatic ties with Israel . . . means that Hungary is getting rid of its past mistakes and is proof of its new way of thinking."

JEWISH COMMUNITY

The largest Jewish population in Eastern Europe, estimated at between 40,000 and 100,000, was in Hungary. In addition to the religious community, long recognized by Communist authorities, a Federation to Maintain Jewish Culture in Hungary was formed in 1989 by younger Jews, mostly of mixed Jewish and Gentile ancestry. Its aim was to broaden the concept of Jewishness to an ethnic one, thereby bringing in nonreligious Hungarian Jews to the community. Six months after its founding it claimed a membership of a thousand. A new Jewish journal, *Mult es Jovo* (Past and Future), began publication in 1989. It featured historical essays, poetry and prose, memoirs, interviews, translations, and photo essays. Within the first year that tourism to Israel was widely permitted, over 7,000 Hungarian citizens visited the Jewish state. Some 30,000 Israelis visited Hungary in 1988.

The emergence of new political groups raised some concerns among Hungarian Jews. The Democratic Forum, the largest opposition party, was suspected of embracing anti-Semitic elements and ideas, though spokesmen for the Forum denied that it was anti-Semitic, while admitting that individual anti-Semites might be found in its ranks.

Czechoslovakia

In Czechoslovakia, ruled by a conservative Communist party since the failure of reform attempts in 1968, the police brutally suppressed a student demonstration on November 17. The Communist party presidium and secretariat resigned a week later, and the party lost its constitutionally guaranteed leading role. In what came to be called "the velvet revolution," a new government was formed in December which, for the first time in 40 years, did not have a Communist majority. Alexander Dubcek, the reformist leader of 1968, was elected chairman of the legislature, and Vaclav Havel, a dissident playwright who had been imprisoned by the Communists several times, emerged as the leading candidate for the presidency, a post left vacant by Gustav Husak's resignation. Following the change in government in December, the new Czechoslovak foreign minister, Jiri Dienstbier, said in his first news conference that diplomatic relations with Israel would be considered soon. The Israeli representative in Warsaw, Mordechai Paltzur, visited Prague to discuss new forms of contact between Israel and Czechoslovakia.

Also, in the fall, the government made a few conciliatory gestures toward Israel and the Jewish community. Czechoslovak officials said they would welcome a visit by Edgar Bronfman, president of the World Jewish Congress. The State Jewish Museum in Prague was negotiating an exhibit of its rich collections at the Israel Museum in Jerusalem.

JEWISH COMMUNITY

Like the regime under which it operated, the Czechoslovak Jewish community was dominated by politically conservative leaders who sought to limit its contacts with Jews abroad and especially with the State of Israel. Twenty-five young activists of the Jewish community, said to number about 5,000, sent a letter to the community's leadership, asking them to discuss a loosening of restrictions on cultural life, but the signers were denounced by the people to whom the letter was addressed.

Following the change in government in December, the Jewish community began planning its reorganization, including a change in its leadership.

Romania

Romania, which under Nicolae Ceausescu had opposed Gorbachev's reforms consistently, became more isolated as reforms spread in Eastern Europe. It was also increasingly criticized in the West for human-rights violations. In March, six Communist party veterans wrote an open letter to Ceausescu protesting human-rights violations and mismanagement of the economy. But it was not until protests erupted against the harassment of a Hungarian clergyman, Laszlo Tokes, in Timisoara, that a spontaneous movement against the regime began. Ceausescu called a rally in Bucharest on December 21, which turned into a demonstration of solidarity with Timisoara and against Ceausescu. Following violent clashes in both Bucharest and Timisoara, Ceausescu was forced to flee but was caught and executed, together with his wife, Elena, on December 25. A "Front of National Salvation" headed by Ion Iliescu took power. Most of the leaders of the front were former Communist officials who had fallen from grace under Ceausescu.

In December, Israel sent six tons of medical supplies to Romania, praised the post-Ceausescu regime, and condemned what appeared to be violent attempts to overthrow the new government.

JEWISH COMMUNITY

Romania's Jewish community, which continued to shrink through emigration and attrition, numbered about 20,000. Following the fall of the Ceausescu regime, there was much speculation about the future of the Jewish community and Israeli relations with Romania, the only Communist country which did not break relations with Israel following the June 1967 war. Since the relatively privileged position of Romanian Jewry within the country and its ability to emigrate had seemed to depend largely on understandings reached between Ceausescu and Chief Rabbi Moses David Rosen, there was also speculation on the rabbi's future and that of the community as a whole.

In late December the Israeli newspaper *Yediot Aharonot* reported that Ceausescu had made between $50 and $60 million by extracting a ransom of $5,000 to $7,000 from Israel for every Romanian Jew who was permitted to emigrate. The money had actually come from American Jewish organizations. This report was in line with earlier allegations, some made by Romanian defectors who had served in the Securitate, the secret police.

Yugoslavia

Once in the forefront of reform, Yugoslavia appeared to lag behind her neighbors in 1989. Relations between Serbs and Albanians deteriorated further over the issue of Kossovo, inhabited largely by Albanians but of historic importance to Serbs. Political relations between Serbia and its demagogic and authoritarian leader, Slobodan Milosevic, and the more developed republic of Slovenia, headed by the liberal Milan Kucan, also worsened. Traditional tensions betweeen Serbs and Croats also escalated. An inflation rate of nearly 2,000 percent and many strikes plagued the economy and led Prime Minister Ante Markovic to announce a far-reaching economic reform program in December.

JEWISH COMMUNITY

The Belgrade city council voted $2 million for the restoration and repair of the only synagogue in the country's capital. Some Yugoslav Jews—who were said to number about 6,000—were fearful that heightened tensions among the nationalities would catch them in a variety of ethnic crossfires. The largest Jewish communities were in the Serbian city of Belgrade; the capital of Croatia, Zagreb; and the Bosnian capital, Sarajevo.

ZVI GITELMAN

Israel

O<small>N DECEMBER</small> 9, 1989, <small>THE</small> *intifada*—the Palestinian uprising in the West Bank and Gaza Strip—entered its third year. But well before that date, Israel's military, economic, and policy-making systems had effectively adjusted themselves to the idea that the revolt in the occupied territories was going to be a fixture of the Israeli reality for the foreseeable future, and that, in any case, the *status quo ante* was irretrievable. In particular, the authorities in the field—the Israel Defense Forces (IDF), in conjunction with the Shin Bet (General Security Service) and the Civil Administration—proved far more efficacious in dealing with both the uprising's violent overt aspect and its less visible, but probably more significant, internal civil-resistance dimension. The result was that in 1989 there was a big decline in large-scale riots, reflecting the sheer weariness of the Palestinians as they saw Israel standing its ground and no political progress being made. At the same time, Palestinian frustration found outlets in increased attacks on Israeli-driven vehicles in the territories, in terrorist outrages committed inside Israel, and in mounting internecine Palestinian violence.

A peace proposal initiated by Prime Minister Yitzhak Shamir generated considerable diplomatic activity during the second half of the year but accomplished virtually nothing. By year's end, too, the national unity government was wracked by internal dissension and in danger of coming apart at the seams.

The Intifada *and Responses to It*

The intensity of the violence in the early part of 1989, particularly in the West Bank, recalled the situation in the initial stage of the uprising a year earlier. In the first three months of 1989, 60 Palestinians were killed by Israeli troops and hundreds wounded, the security forces demolished 44 houses in the territories, arrests and curfews continued on a wide scale, and educational institutions that had been opened—except for universities—in December 1988, were closed down again in the following month.

The harsh measures taken by the military were largely ineffectual in the field; they also helped to dim Israel's already lackluster international standing. The year began with the deportation (January 1) to Lebanon of 13 Palestinians—seven from the West Bank and six from the Gaza Strip, for helping to "lead and direct the uprising." The fact that the original deportation orders had been issued the previous

August and that in the intervening period the uprising had continued without letup fueled the case of those who argued that deportations were an ineffective punishment (besides being prohibited under the Fourth Geneva Convention). The military retorted that the real problem was the loss of the element of immediacy: "candidates for expulsion," as the army called them, could set in motion protracted legal proceedings by appealing first to a military advisory committee and then to the High Court of Justice. Intermittent calls by Defense Minister Yitzhak Rabin to facilitate punitive measures were generally resisted by the Justice Ministry. In January Rabin did an about-face on the deportation issue, telling the Knesset's Defense and Foreign Affairs Committee that this "weapon" had been found ineffective. In fact, 13 more Palestinians were deported in 1989, eight in June and five in August, but in every case but one, the original order had been issued in August 1988. The United States and the international community continued to object to the expulsions.

Also unhappy with the situation were the Jewish settlers in the territories, who along with the security forces were the primary targets of the violence unleashed by the uprising. The major problem was the stoning, usually by children or teeenagers, of Israeli vehicles traveling in the territories. But attacks with firebombs and other lethal implements were also frequent. In early January, settlers retaliated by raiding Arab villages, blocking roads, and attacking cars bearing license plates from the territories. Nor did they balk at clashing with soldiers. On one occasion, scuffling broke out with troops sent in at the personal order of Defense Minister Rabin to disperse ceremonies held by settlers at improvised memorials for Jews killed in the territories (the body of a Petah Tikva taxi driver, Shimon Edri, was found near the Samaria village of Haris at the beginning of January). Leaders of the settlers held a two-month vigil in front of the Prime Minister's Office in Jerusalem to protest the government's inability to stamp out the uprising and to demand the removal of Defense Minister Rabin, whom they held responsible for the situation.

In late January, Deputy Chief of Staff Ehud Barak told a meeting of the Foreign Press Association that the IDF had "not run out of ideas" on how to put down the *intifada*. Barak may have been referring to recently introduced orders under which parents of children caught throwing stones at Israelis could be fined or have their homes sealed; and enabling some NCOs (in addition to officers) to fire plastic bullets at demonstrators. Barak denied reports that troops were now allowed to open fire at fleeing demonstrators, although conceding that soldiers who had undergone "special training" could shoot plastic bullets at the legs of those "whom [they] believe are leaders of a riot [and] are running to and fro." The trend within the military was to leave standing orders and regulations intact—in order to avoid hassles with army and civilian legal authorities—but to broaden definitions within those orders. Thus, in January, *Ma'ariv* quoted the chief of staff, Lt. Gen. Dan Shomron, as saying, "Fire may be opened at whoever brings about a concrete danger, and one such danger, for example, is the erection of [road] barriers."

In the same period, Defense Minister Rabin, who was under severe pressure from both Right and Left for his handling of the *intifada,* presented a plan for giving the residents of the territories increased autonomy in exchange for the cessation of violence (see below, "Diplomatic and Political Developments"). Rabin's next step was to order the release from prison of a leading Palestinian activist, Faisal al-Husseini. The 48-year-old Husseini had been incarcerated without trial under a series of administrative detention orders almost consecutively since April 1987. (In August 1989 a new directive allowed the military to hold persons in administrative detention for up to 12 months at a time, instead of the previous 6, renewable indefinitely. At any given time in 1989, some 1,500 Palestinians were held under this form of arrest. All told, more than 10,000 were in prison, at least half of them awaiting trial for offenses ranging from stone throwing to murder. In the first two years of the uprising, some 50,000 Palestinians were arrested.) When Husseini launched a series of meetings with dovish Knesset members, including some from Labor, the Prime Minister's Office decried these contacts as "pointless and unauthorized" and warned that such encounters "abet PLO terrorism."

In the territories, the violence continued to take its toll on both sides. On February 24, Sgt. Binyamin Meisner, 25, became the fifth Israeli soldier killed there since the start of the uprising, when an IDF patrol walked into a well-executed ambush in Nablus's labyrinthine old city. A ten-day curfew was imposed on the city's 100,000 inhabitants as security forces hunted the perpetrators of the ambush. In early March, two suspected perpetrators, aged 19 and 22, were arrested—they were reportedly members of the "shock squads" of the outlawed Fatah-affiliated Shabiba youth movement (see AJYB 1990, pp. 414–15, 425)—and their homes were demolished. (In July they were sentenced to life imprisonment; four other youths, who lured the patrol into the ambush, each received 15 years in prison.)

Demolition of suspects' homes, permitted under Article 119 of the Defense (Emergency) Regulations promulgated in 1945 by the British Mandate authorities and never repealed by Jordan (regarding the West Bank), Egypt (regarding the Gaza Strip), or Israel, was one of the issues addressed in the section on Israel in the U.S. State Department's annual report on the status of human rights, issued in February. The report cited a figure of 101 houses "totally demolished" and seven "partially demolished," and 46 houses sealed in 1988. In 1989, according to B'Tselem, the Israeli Information Center for Human Rights in the Occupied Territories—established in March by a group of activists and partly financed by the New Israel Fund—this form of punishment was expanded: 138 houses were demolished, 84 sealed, and more than 60 were partially demolished or partially sealed. Assistant Secretary of State for Human Rights Richard Schifter stated that "house demolition as punishment of families . . . contravenes the Fourth Geneva Convention in the view of the U.S." The Israeli Supreme Court consistently upheld the legality of house demolitions, rejecting the argument that such actions constituted collective punishment—prohibited under the Geneva Convention—because they harmed innocent people living in the same house as the suspect. (On July 30, 1989, the High Court for the first time partially curtailed the army's power to demolish houses as a punitive measure, ruling—in response to a petition submitted by the Association for Civil Rights in Israel—that unless "operational military needs" existed, persons whose homes were targeted for destruction must be allowed to appeal first to the military commander and then to the High Court of Justice.)

The Schifter report "[did] not improve the health of Israel's image," Prime Minister Shamir told Army Radio on February 9, maintaining that the document was one-sided and unbalanced. The Foreign Ministry said that the report "did not, unfortunately, give full consideration to the actions of local extremist elements and the major dilemmas which these cause for Israel. . . ."

In the meantime, the military was starting to take more aggressive steps to break the leadership of the uprising. In mid-March the security forces completed a month-long operation in which some 800 "field commanders" in the territories were arrested. Around the same time, tough paramilitary Border Police units were deployed on a semipermanent basis in the Gaza Strip. The uncovering of an 11-member Fatah-affiliated underground cell in the Gaza Strip highlighted what was to become one of the ugliest aspects of the *intifada*: the murder, often in the most brutal and barbarous manner, by Palestinians of fellow Palestinians who were suspected of "collaborating" with the Israelis. The Gaza group was said to have liquidated a cleaning woman in a local hospital for this reason. However, according to B'Tselem, some were murdered for committing "moral offenses," such as prostitution and drug dealing, and there were also killings stemming from "political rivalries and family feuds." Sporadic attempts by members of the PLO leadership in Tunis to put an end to this phenomenon were unavailing, and none of those considered moderates in the territories were willing to speak out against the killings—indeed, some of them condoned the murders implicitly or explicitly.

Violence escalated sharply in April. One of the year's most serious incidents took place on the 13th, in the West Bank village of Nahalin (pop. 2,800), near Bethlehem. A Border Police unit that entered the village in what was meant to be a surprise search-and-arrest operation encountered forcible resistance. In the ensuing clash, 5 villagers were killed and 13 wounded; 4 border policemen were hurt. An investigative committee appointed by the regional commander, Maj. Gen. Amram Mitzna—its report was released on May 4—found that the unit's operational planning had been "deficient," that it had "failed to exhaust all non-lethal means before resorting to live fire," and that most of the unit's personnel engaged in "excessive" live fire which "violated standard operating procedures." As a result, the military commander of the Bethlehem District and two Border Police officers were transferred from their posts, the commander of the Judea-Samaria Brigade was reprimanded, and a number of border policemen were suspended from duty.

Intercommunal violence reached a scale which not only played into the hands of demagogues but threatened to plunge the country into political chaos. In the south, after the battered body of a kidnapped soldier was found on May 7 (see "Terrorism, Antiterrorism, Extremism," below), Jews attacked passing Arab cars bearing license plates from the nearby Gaza Strip. A day earlier, three Gazans were shot dead and some 70 wounded by Israeli troops in fierce clashes. In the West Bank, after a prospective settler was stabbed by an Arab near the town of Ariel, in Samaria, hundreds of settlers raided Arab villages, doing large property damage. Militant settlers in Hebron and adjacent Kiryat Arba stepped up their vigilante patrols, aimed at least in part against the government's new peace proposal, as convoys of vehicles carrying gun-toting settlers terrorized local villages.

In one incident at the end of May, two weeks after the peace initiative was adopted, some 30 armed settlers, including students from the extremist "Joseph's Tomb" yeshivah in Nablus, carried out what a civilian judge would later describe as a "pogrom" in the village of Kifl Harith. In the course of the action, a 13-year-old village girl was shot to death, two villagers were seriously wounded, and extensive property damage was done, including the shattering of dozens of solar heaters and windows with gunfire and the torching of crops.

The attitudes underlying such behavior were given expression by two militant West Bank rabbis and by a very secular settlement. At a court hearing involving eight of his students who were suspected of involvement in the Kifl Harith incident, Rabbi Yitzhak Ginzburg, head of the Joseph's Tomb yeshivah, stated that Jews and Arabs should not be treated equally because Jewish blood was worth more than non-Jewish blood. (The students were subsequently released and no charges were laid.) Around the same time, Rabbi Moshe Levinger, the head of the Jewish community in Hebron, who was on trial for killing a Hebron man during an incident in September 1988, pleaded not guilty to a manslaughter charge but said he regretted "not having the privilege of killing the Arab." The secular Samaria town of Ariel came up with a plan to make Arabs working there wear identification tags stating that they were "foreign workers." Adverse public reaction, which included the evocation of what Jews underwent in 1930s Germany, forced the town to drop the plan.

More Palestinians were killed by Israeli forces in May—a total of 33, 18 of them in the Gaza Strip—than in any other month of 1989. In the Gaza Strip, the night curfew (9 P.M.–4 A.M.) in force since the start of the *intifada* was retained even after the blanket curfew imposed on the territories on May 9–10, in conjunction with Israel's Independence Day, was lifted. As the scale and intensity of the violence surged dramatically, at 7:30 P.M. on May 16, the Israeli military authorities abruptly declared a total curfew throughout the Gaza Strip; in an unprecedented step, all Gazans inside Israel were given 24 hours to return home. (Standing regulations forbidding residents of the territories to remain in Israel overnight were rarely enforced. Thousands of Palestinians, primarily from the Gaza Strip, slept over in Israel during the week, usually in abominable conditions, returning home at the weekend.)

The curfew remained in force for four days, and the military announced that criteria were being worked out for allowing residents of the territories to enter Israel on an "individual" basis. A measure of the decline of Israeli deterrence in the territories—one reason for the sudden curfew was to help restore that deterrence—was evident in the events that took place in Rafah, at the southern tip of Gaza Strip.

On May 19, hundreds of residents defied the curfew—which in their case had been in force for 14 days following previous incidents—and took to the streets. Five local residents were shot dead in the ensuing clash with Israeli troops, including a 50-year-old mother of ten. Inhabitants said the disturbance was caused by a serious shortage of flour and sugar due to the prolonged curfew, and by mass arrests of activists in Rafah the previous night. On May 20, Leaflet No. 40 of the United National Command of the Uprising, issued in East Jerusalem, called on the Palestinians' "shock squads" "to liquidate one soldier or one settler for every martyr of our people." The leaflet also rejected the Israeli peace initiative: "Shamir's plot has become the enemy's official plot, but our people will throw it onto the trash heap of history, as it did with the Camp David plan and other conspiracies."

A different kind of conspiracy was cited by Labor and Social Affairs Minister Moshe Katsav (Likud) in a letter to all cabinet ministers urging that the territories be completely sealed off for three months. In this period the army would be deployed there "massively" and operate to end the unrest once and for all. Katsav charged that workers from the territories were perpetrating acts of sabotage in their places of employment. Examples of such alleged acts were: textile workers slashing suits prior to their export; Arabs employed in construction stuffing drainage and water pipes and deliberately using less steel and cement than required, causing hidden long-term damage; and hotel and restaurant kitchen workers spitting and even urinating into food or seasoning some items with bits of broken glass. The feasibility of Katsav's plan seemed dubious, however, as even the brief mid-May curfew caused severe slowdowns in various sectors, particularly in the construction, agriculture, and textile industries. More important than Katsav's shoot-from-the-hip ideas, though, was the atmosphere that produced them; the mounting hysteria among the public, it seemed, was engulfing the government as well. Both Chief of Staff Shomron and Defense Minister Rabin were under constant fire from the Right for failing to "eradicate" the uprising—on May 16, a leading columnist for *Ha'aretz,* Yoel Marcus, wrote that "this chief of staff has to go . . . because the army as a professional arm under his leadership has failed in its dealing with the *intifada.*"

Many settlers and right-wing politicians felt a sense of satisfaction, therefore, when it was announced, in early June, that the head of Central Command, which included the West Bank, Maj. Gen. Amram Mitzna, frequently targeted by these groups for being too "soft" in dealing with the uprising, would, at his request, be leaving his post to go on a year's study leave. Named to replace Mitzna was the tough-talking head of Southern Command, Maj. Gen. Yitzhak Mordechai. (Mordechai took over on August 4, and in October he became the first regional commander to participate in the settlers' annual Sukkot hike in Samaria. Mordechai was replaced at Southern Command by Maj. Gen. Matan Vilnai, until then chief of the Manpower Branch. One of the final large-scale operations carried out under Mordechai's aegis in the Gaza Strip resulted in the arrest, in late May, of more than 200 members of Hamas, the Gaza-based Islamic Resistance Movement, including the organization's founder and leader, the wheelchair-bound Sheikh Ahmed Yassin, aged 52. Yassin was subsequently charged on 15 counts, including ordering the killing of three suspected "collaborators" with the Israeli authorities. Hamas, which was formed in the Gaza Strip after the eruption of the *intifada* and whose "Covenant" called for the liberation of all of Palestine through a *jihad,* or holy war, and the establishment of an Islamic state on Israel's ruins, was outlawed in the territories on September 28.)

The entire Gaza Strip was put under curfew for a week at the beginning of June, and when the curfew was lifted on June 11, Gazans wishing to enter Israel to work or for other purposes had to show a special entry permit. The idea was to furnish every resident of Gaza with a magnetic card as part of the effort to keep "undesirable elements" out of Israel, to prevent unauthorized labor, and generally to tighten Israeli control over the population.

Shamir got a personal taste of the atmosphere in the territories on June 20, while delivering a eulogy at Ariel for Frederick Rosenfeld, a resident of the West Bank town who had been murdered by Arab shepherds while hiking in the area. The prime minister was called "traitor" by some in the crowd and his car was jostled as he left. That the militants would not always be content with verbal protests was demonstrated later that day when two Arabs were shot and wounded as they waited at a bus stop near Tel Aviv. (In November a 23-year-old West Bank yeshivah student was convicted on an aggravated assault charge in the case, after a manslaughter charge was dropped in plea bargaining.) Rabin, seeking to mollify right-wingers and ease the pressure on Shamir, once more asked the Justice Ministry to broaden the military's punitive powers in the territories. Justice Minister Dan Meridor (Likud), while disinclined to accede to Rabin's request, told the Knesset that the use of undemocratic means by a democracy "fighting for its right to exist" was no vice.

On June 29, eight Palestinians, four each from the West Bank and Gaza, were deported to Lebanon. On July 4, the IDF announced that the previous night a "widespread operation" had been carried out in the West Bank during which some 200 activists of the outlawed "popular committees" and "shock squads" were arrested. The army communiqué stressed that this was a *pe'ulah yezumah*—an "initiated action" by the army. This phrase, borrowed from the Lebanese theater of operations and increasingly used during 1989, signaled a change of emphasis and of tactics in the military's handling of the uprising. The aim was to strike at the organizers behind the attempts to forge an autonomous socioeconomic infrastructure which would enable the Palestinians to disengage from the Israeli authorities. At the same time, the chief of staff informed the Knesset's Defense and Foreign Affairs Committee that the "rules of engagement" in the territories had been further relaxed to enable troops to open fire more readily at "masked individuals."

Around the same time, U.S. assistant secretary of state John Kelly, in Israel for an "orientation" visit, was told by Shamir that his country's dialogue with the PLO was hindering progress on the peace plan because it inhibited Palestinians in the territories from taking part in talks. Foreign Minister Moshe Arens told the American official that local Palestinians were inhibited by radicals' threats against their lives. Yet, in the territories themselves, growing numbers of Palestinians were ignoring calls regarding general strikes and other instructions contained in leaflets issued by the United National Command of the Uprising. This new attitude, reflecting what the *Jerusalem Post* described as "the erosion of the discipline and unanimity" that had characterized the *intifada,* was most strikingly displayed in two realms: commerce, where growing economic hardship was leading some merchants to evade the strictures of the uprising leadership concerning hours of business for shops and full observance of general strikes, and education. Beginning July 22, the Israeli military authorities permitted elementary schools (grades 1–6) and 12th-grade classes in the West Bank to reopen, followed by junior-high schools and—a month later—the rest of the high-school system. With the education system finally restored, after the loss of nearly two full school years, many parents were unwilling to heed the activists' calls to include the schools in the frequent general-strike days. (The schools were closed down again on November 13, just before the first anniversary of the PLO's declaration of the "State of Palestine," and had not reopened by year's end.)

JERUSALEM

Jerusalem remained a divided city in 1989, with few Jews venturing into the eastern section. Curfew, which generated shock waves when first imposed in a Jerusalem neighborhood in 1988—for the first time since 1967—was more frequent in 1989 and, as in the West Bank and Gaza, was sometimes declared largely to facilitate the collection of various levies: income tax, value-added tax, national insurance fees, and Broadcasting Authority fees.

No fewer than 220 cars were set ablaze in Jerusalem in 1989 by Palestinians for "nationalist" reasons, double the 1988 figure. The majority of the incidents took place in East Jerusalem, and two-thirds of the torched cars belonged to Jews. In addition, 118 firebombs were thrown in the city at civilian, police, and army vehicles, some 1,700 cases of stone throwing were recorded, and 2,100 Palestinians, the majority minors, were detained for "hostile activity." Charges were eventually brought against only 950 of those arrested.

In July the Arab areas of the mixed Jewish-Arab neighborhood of Abu Tor on the "seam" dividing East and West Jerusalem were placed under a three-day curfew after Molotov cocktails were thrown at police vans. Nearly 30 people were arrested for security offenses (many of the car torchings occurred in Abu Tor) in a house-to-house operation, and at the same time the tax authorities sent in their personnel to collect unpaid debts from the captive audience, while the Broadcasting Authority impounded television sets from households which had not paid the yearly license fee. Mayor Teddy Kollek complained about this utilization of the curfew.

Kollek was also a moderating influence in one of the year's most serious incidents, which occurred in late August in Beit Safafa, once a village whose main street constituted the border between Israel and Jordan, but since 1967 wholly incorporated into Jerusalem. According to the official account, police in an unmarked car were attacked as they drove along Unification of the Village Street by tens of masked villagers wielding knives and other implements. Fearing for their lives, the security men opened fire, killing one villager; the village was placed under curfew. A memorial ceremony for the slain man held a few days later also turned violent, and police fired tear gas and then rubber bullets to break up the crowd. Kollek afterward went to the village to pay his condolences to the bereaved family and to speak with community leaders, urging them to work to prevent hotheaded youths from stoning Israeli vehicles that drove through the village.

Kollek, however, continued to be outflanked by militant Palestinians on the one side and by the tactics of the Israeli military on the other. On October 2, the new head of Central Command, Maj. Gen. Yitzhak Mordechai, ordered the cordoning off of a section of East Jerusalem to prevent journalists from attending a press conference called by Palestinian activists at the National Palace Hotel. Kollek told the *Jerusalem Post* that this was the first time since 1967 that a "central area" in Jerusalem (as opposed to peripheral neighborhoods) had been subjected to a military closure. The move had been taken without notifying the mayor's office and worse, "What the authorities did was to ensure that the issue got greater publicity than it deserved."

BEIT SAHOUR

Indeed, the army's move backfired by focusing strong international media attention on the "issue." The press conference, at which prominent Palestinian nationalist Faisal al-Husseini was scheduled to speak—he did afterward speak informally with journalists on the street—had been intended to publicize a major battle which was being fought between the Israeli military authorities and the 9,000 Christian Arabs in the affluent town of Beit Sahour, near Bethlehem. No arms were involved in this campaign, which was to last some six weeks, but it was one of the landmark confrontations in the first two years of the *intifada*. Beginning on September 20, the Israeli authorities launched an operation in Beit Sahour with the aim of breaking a spreading tax revolt in the town. In the course of the operation, the town was declared a "closed military area"—thus barred to nonresidents—and had its phone links and finally even its water supply cut off by the military. When Defense Minister Rabin told the Knesset's Defense and Foreign Affairs Committee in mid-October that he intended "to teach [Beit Sahour] a lesson," he meant that "lesson" to be absorbed by the entire West Bank. Since the start of the uprising, tax collection—the source of the salaries of the hundreds of Israeli civilians employed by the Civil Administration and of the hundreds of soldiers serving within its framework—had declined by some 30 percent. (At one point, the residents of Beit Sahour seized on the anomaly of their tax money being used to pay their occupiers and floated a slogan calculated to appeal to the American press: "No taxation without representation.") But beyond the budgetary shortfall, the Military Government was determined to break the tax revolt because it symbolized the nonviolent civil disobedience which was considered more insidious, and ultimately more dangerous to continued Israeli rule, than the violent aspects of the uprising. In 1988 Beit Sahour had already been targeted by the army in its efforts to combat manifestations of "alternative government" and in its bureaucratic war to prevent the creation of a power vacuum that would eventuate in the establishment of a Palestinian state. (See AJYB 1990, pp. 414–16, 421–25.) A year later, the situation had become more complex and more pressing.

The growing frustration in the territories, aggravated by the tortuous course of the talks on a peace initiative, the intensifying internal terror within the Palestinian community, and a sharp IDF crackdown on what military sources described as the uprising's "hard-core activists," led the United National Leadership of the Uprising to issue a special leaflet in early October declaring a five-day general strike in which a "new state of rebellion" would be fomented by various nonviolent means. It was in this context that the Israeli authorities viewed the Beit Sahour events and apparently decided to make it a test case, especially after the Palestinians themselves cast a powerful spotlight on the town. In the Gaza Strip, the battle revolved around the recent introduction of magnetic ID cards which any Gazans wishing to enter Israel had to apply for. Even though the special leaflet asserted that "[v]ictory in this battle is inevitable," efforts by uprising agitators to convince residents who worked in Israel to forgo the cards were only partially successful; sheer economic necessity won the day.

Beit Sahour was a harder nut to crack. It took repeated "tax raids" in the course of 40 days on homes and businesses in the town, in which many of the premises were left a shambles by the troops and virtually everything of value, from furniture to fruit juice, was confiscated and taken to the unclaimed goods section of the Customs Authority warehouses at Ben-Gurion Airport, eventually to be sold in public auction, to induce residents to pay their assessments—which they claimed were completely arbitrary. On October 31, Brig. Gen. Shaike Erez, the head of the Civil Administration in Judea-Samaria, declared victory. "The tax revolt in Beit Sahour has been liquidated," he told reporters after the army lifted its closure of the town, and "all the objectives" of the Israeli authorities had been attained. A communiqué issued by the Government Press Office in the name of "official military sources" quoted Erez as saying he was aware of the "negative media effect of the campaign," but explained: "It is not pleasant to seize [goods] in homes, but when people insist on rebellion and refuse to pay taxes, but nevertheless continue to demand all the vital services such as education, health, telephones and social welfare, we have no choice but to do what we did." Pointedly, Erez concluded: "I hope that other places will not try to follow suit, because we will not permit tax evasion."

In a second communiqué, the "official military sources" stated that 398 persons owing taxes "were dealt with" during the operation, property worth NIS 3 million ($1.5 million) was seized along with cash and money in bank accounts, and 33 vehicles were confiscated (townspeople said the number was actually 150). Forty people were arrested and 35 were formally charged. Four had already been tried, and sentenced to a fine of NIS 6,000 or six months in jail; all four opted for the latter. The communiqué noted drily that "in the course of the operation, there was an increase in the number of people paying taxes elsewhere in Judea and Samaria." In a communiqué of their own, issued on October 27, "the people of Beit Sahour" declared: "The tax resistance movement is but one response to the occupation. Palestinians want to pay taxes to their own state, not to an occupation authority. We, the people of Beit Sahour are prepared, if necessary, to lose all our property, but we will never pay taxes to the occupation. We will continue using nonviolent resistance as a means of awakening the Israeli people to their need, as well as ours, to live together in a just peace, two peoples in two free and secure states."

IDF GAINS CONTROL

Nineteen Palestinians died in the first two weeks of October, while five Israeli soldiers were wounded in Nablus by Molotov cocktails and an attack using a bottle of acid. Gangs of Palestinian youths ran wild in Nablus and elsewhere, brutalizing and murdering suspected "collaborators" and carrying out a "moral crusade" as well. In one incident, a 35-year-old Nablus woman was stabbed to death for "promiscuity." Nevertheless, by October the Israeli military had gained the upper hand. As the respected defense analyst Ze'ev Schiff noted in *Ha'aretz* (October 2), the turnabout came when the IDF, after long months, grasped that the *intifada* was not a passing phenomenon and was in fact a form of war with rules of its own. Having reached this conclusion, the army deployed elite units in the territories in order to apprehend violent hard-core activists, stationed regular units in specific areas on an extended basis so they could get to know the turf, and upgraded the quality of the command level. In addition, better hardware, such as night-vision equipment, was brought in, small outposts were set up along the roads and on rooftops in the West Bank, and coordination between the military and the Shin Bet was enhanced. The army's purpose, as the chief of staff stated on numerous occasions, was to reduce the level of violence so that the political process could be implemented in a relatively conducive atmosphere.

As the second anniversary of the uprising approached, the security forces intensified their operations, notably in Nablus, a hotbed of radical militancy. On November 9, the "Red Eagle" gang, affiliated with George Habash's Popular Front for the Liberation of Palestine, was captured, followed at the beginning of December by the elimination by elite forces of the "Black Panther" gang during the biggest crackdown in Nablus since the start of the uprising. With the city under curfew, the military called in helicopters and ventured deep into the maze of the casbah where the street activists hid out. The Israeli authorities decided to act following a CBS-TV report showing masked youths holding a military parade in the casbah in broad daylight, carrying handguns and IDF M-16 rifles, along with members of the Black Panthers standing over one of the 15 suspected "collaborators" and "promiscuous women" they had murdered. In the best gangland style, the six Black Panthers were trapped by a seven-man special unit—disguised as Arabs and in one case as a woman, according to local eyewitnesses—in a barber shop; three were killed and three wounded in the shootout. Troops arrested dozens of other wanted persons and impounded weapons such as clubs, hatchets, and knives and paraphenalia including Palestinian flags and uniforms.

There were also setbacks. One of the most serious incidents occurred on November 13—two days before the first anniversary of the PLO's declaration of the Palestinian "state"—when two reserve soldiers, in their early 40s, became the first IDF fatalities in the Gaza Strip since the start of the *intifada*. In a rare case of the use of firearms in the uprising, they were gunned down with a Kalachnikov assault rifle by three terrorists in an ambush. To facilitate the hunt for the attackers, the entire Gaza Strip was put under curfew and navy boats blockaded the coast. (In a development that many Israelis found gratifying but which outraged others, the heart of one of the two soldiers, who died of head wounds two days after the attack, was transplanted into the body of an East Jerusalem Arab.) Overall, though, the military was in a buoyant mood at the end of the year, backed up by statistics: military sources quoted in the Israeli press stated that hundreds of "wanted Palestinians" had been flushed out and caught since August, among them 100 of the "hard-core" activists, of whom 30–40 more were still being sought.

More tellingly, some 60 percent of the violence in the territories was, by year's end, being directed against other Palestinians. Some 130 Palestinians died at the hands of other Palestinians in 1989, about six times as many as in 1988. This "internal terrorism," Defense Minister Rabin told Israel TV on December 6, was the only way the activists were able to get the populace to take part in strikes and other mass activities of a nonviolent nature.

In addition, nearly 300 Palestinians were killed by the security forces—the same as in 1988—and another 14 by Israeli civilians (settlers). In both years, nearly 60 percent of the fatalities were in the 17–24 age group, but the proportion of children aged 16 and below who were killed rose sharply from about 17 percent in 1988 to 27 percent in 1989; nearly 10 percent of those killed in 1989 were under 12 years old. The number of wounded ran into the thousands. These casualty statistics seemed to accord with a report by Defense Minister Rabin that stone throwing constituted 85 percent of all violent activity in the territories—and that 60 percent of such incidents were perpetrated by children aged 13 or below.

In an address at a Tel Aviv University symposium summing up two years of the *intifada*, Rabin spoke of a "comprehensive" Israeli policy, combining the political level, in the form of the peace initiative, and the military-Civil Administration level, which consisted of a three-tiered approach: military action as such, punitive measures, and economic pressure.

Statistics, however, and neat military structures did not tell the whole story. On the first anniversary of the uprising, the then-head of Central Command, Maj. Gen. Amram Mitzna, had spoken of the *intifada* as a "state of mind." A year later, the Palestinians' national consciousness had undoubtedly deepened. The idea of peace, insofar as it involved some form of Israeli-Palestinian coexistence, and certainly if it entailed contacts with the PLO, seemed as remote as ever.

Military Trials

This year saw a number of trials of soldiers charged with committing abuses in the course of putting down the *intifada,* particularly in 1988, soon after the uprising began, when chaos reigned and the initiative seemed to be with the Palestinians. Apart from the charges faced by the defendants, the trials also focused attention on the degree of blame to be assigned to high officials. Both the prime minister and the defense minister, in particular, had been accused of trying to evade responsibility for orders issued in the uprising's early phase. The primary focus of these criticisms was the headline-making court-martial of four soldiers from the Givati infantry brigade, a trial which in the eyes of many symbolically encapsulated the dilemmas the IDF faced in being made to act as a police force against unarmed civilians. The four, a staff sergeant and three privates, were charged with manslaughter for beating to death a 42-year-old Gaza man; in addition, a reservist physician with the rank of captain was charged with negligence in the case.

The incident occurred in Gaza's Jabalya refugee camp on August 22, 1988. Following unrest in the camp, the four were ordered by their commanding officer, a lieutenant, to enter the home of Hani al-Shami and to "blow away" stone-throwers thought to be hiding there. Al-Shami, who was inside with his children, tried to block the soldiers, but they overcame him and then beat him mercilessly for 15 minutes with rifle butts and a broomstick, kicked him and jumped on him from a bed. The court subsequently found that al-Shami was still on his feet and not in "respiratory distress" when he was finally taken to the army base in the camp. There, like many other bound-and-blindfolded detainees, he endured further savage beatings by an unknown number of soldiers, including a vicious "karate kick" in the chest which hurtled him with brutal force against a wall. He died soon afterward.

The four soldiers did not deny the basic facts in the case (they did deny some of the details) but pleaded, in their defense, that they were obeying orders issued by senior command levels—reaching all the way to the chief of staff and the defense minister, and certainly to the brigade commander—to "break the bones" of rioters and stone-throwers in order to punish them and deter others. On March 1, in a rare occurrence, Lt. Gen. Shomron himself took the stand—he was called by the defense—and testified for nearly three hours on the IDF's policy regarding beatings. It was not his finest hour in an otherwise distinguished military career.

He quoted from his message of February 23, 1988, to IDF commanders in the territories (see AJYB 1990, p. 406) sanctioning the use of "reasonable force"—

referring to riot batons—to disperse a riot, to overcome resistance to arrest, or during "hot pursuit," but barring the use of force as a punitive measure or after a mission ended. But Shomron also spoke of a vague, momentary "gray area" at the very end of an incident during which a soldier's "subjective" discretion came into play, when beating could still be considered legitimate "deterrence" and before the use of force metamorphosed, imperceptibly, into prohibited "punishment." Shomron was no less equivocal on the crucial question of an officer's responsibility. If it turned out that an officer had issued a "manifestly illegal order," the case could be examined in court, "and possibly responsibility lies with the officers and not with the soldiers." Pressed to apply this doctrine to the specific case at hand, the chief of staff said: "I cannot say that I know exactly what the situation was. If one says that blows are intended to deter solely within the context of a disturbance, that is alright. . . . If the order was to beat as deterrence, it was illegal, but at the same time I say that the responsibility of commanders must be weighed."

The military court's 93-page verdict, delivered on May 25, was unsparing in its condemnation of the defendants' actions—but not only theirs. The brutal violence perpetrated against Hani al-Shami, the tribunal wrote, "must shock every civilized person in whom beats a sense of morality and justice, and who holds human life, as such, precious." The judges added:

> We were appalled to hear some of the witnesses express hatred and contempt for the value of the life of the population which is ruled by the [IDF]. We shuddered when witnesses who are soldiers in the army [related how they] watched the humiliating spectacle of the beating of bound and helpless prisoners in an army camp, indifferent to what they saw and shutting their ears to the ghastly outcries of those being beaten. . . . [H]ow did it happen that combat soldiers from an elite unit, who in our assessment received a good education . . . cast off all the principles that their parents instilled in them and underwent a mental metamorphosis which left them ready and willing to deliver what the pathologist called "murderous blows" to a person old enough to be their father. . . .

The court also found that the Military Police investigation had been incomplete and unprofessional. The judges determined that the commanding officer of the military base in the refugee camp, a captain, and his superior, a lieutenant colonel, were responsible for not putting a stop to the beating of detainees on the base, and also singled out the colonel who commanded the Givati Brigade for intimating to his troops that the use of violence against Palestinians was permissible "irrespective of whether resistance was shown." The specific order in question was "manifestly illegal," and hence should not have been obeyed: "Beating a disturber of the peace who does not act up after being caught and no longer displays resistance, merely to deter him from repeating such behavior in the future, is not a military need and is a purely punitive action."

Yet, the defendants were acquitted of the two main charges—manslaughter and causing bodily harm with aggravated intent, each of which carried a maximum 20-year prison term—and convicted of the far lesser offense of physical abuse, for which the maximum punishment was three years in prison. (The manslaughter charge was dismissed because it was impossible to determine who, precisely, had caused al-Shami's death, and the judges ruled that "intent" had not been proved in the case of causing bodily harm.) The physician was cleared of all charges. Three of the soldiers were sentenced to nine months in prison, the fourth to six months; the staff sergeant was demoted to the rank of private. Outraged at what they considered the harsh sentences, the soldiers' families and supporters went on the rampage in the courtroom, attacking journalists.

Just before the outburst, the presiding judge noted that the case "perhaps symbolizes a breakdown in values, which must be addressed before it continues and deepens, and endangers basic values that have been—and, hopefully, will continue to be—pillars of our cultural heritage." The court explained that, if judged by their behavior alone, the defendants deserved far lengthier prison terms. However, there was a major mitigating circumstance: "We must not forget that the ground for their failure was prepared by their commanders, who repeatedly gave them an order that they were to use violence as long as they were [in the process of] arresting a disturber of the peace, irrespective of whether he resisted. That order is manifestly illegal." The Judge-Advocate General's Office announced that the investigation of Hani al-Shami's death would be reopened, to try to determine who was actually responsible, and that legal steps would be taken against officers who issued "manifestly illegal" orders.

There was reason to believe, however, that the policy-setters in the defense establishment were reluctant to have high-ranking officers face trial on charges relating to orders they may have issued during the *intifada*'s early stages. On September 29, the eve of Rosh Hashanah, the head of Southern Command, Maj. Gen. Matan Vilnai, reduced the sentences of the three soldiers who had received nine-month terms by a third. With time off for good behavior also taken into account, they were released the same day, having served four months in prison. (The fourth soldier had been released a month earlier after his sentence was reduced by 20 days.) None of the four would be allowed to return to the Givati Brigade. Ze'ev Schiff, the defense analyst of the daily *Ha'aretz,* noted that the whole affair left a "bad taste" and that its point had been to preclude further legal proceedings in the case.

On October 3, four more Givati soldiers, this time including two officers, a major and a lieutenant, went on trial for severely beating two handcuffed Gaza men following a riot. Ayad Mahmud Akal died in hospital the following day, while the second man sustained serious injuries, including a broken elbow. On October 4, the trial opened of yet another Givati officer, 2nd Lt. Yuval Wilf, who was accused of causing the death by negligence of a Rafah man in December 1988. His was the first trial involving a death caused by the use of plastic bullets. Later that month, a sergeant in the reserves was sentenced to two years in prison for the unwarranted shooting to death of two Palestinians during a violent incident near Hebron in May 1988.

The most sensational case involved the then-commander of the Nablus District, Lt. Col. Yehuda Meir, aged 37. On January 21, 1988, according to an account in the daily *Yediot Aharonot,* Meir ordered troops under his command to round up 12 men from the West Bank village of Hawara, take them to an isolated spot, and beat them until their arms and legs were broken. (The "rationale": they would no longer be able to throw stones or run from soldiers.) They were duly arrested that night and taken in a military bus to an outlying field. After being divided into groups of three, the 12, all of them bound and some gagged and blindfolded as well, were hurled to the ground and set upon by club-wielding soldiers. An officer supervised each group to ensure that the order was carried out in full. The bus driver ran the engine to muffle screams. Some of the soldiers' riot batons broke under the force of the repeated blows. One of the 12 was left in a physical state enabling him to go for help after the troops left.

It took a complaint by the International Red Cross in May 1988 to set in motion what turned out to be a lengthy IDF investigation. In May 1989, Meir, by now promoted to full colonel and serving in a Civil Defense unit in the Tel Aviv area, was given a "severe reprimand" by the chief of staff in a disciplinary hearing for the orders he had given 16 months earlier. Under an agreement reached with the army—evidently to forestall a trial of so high-ranking an officer and one, moreover, who threatened to open a "can of worms" which would implicate the highest levels of the defense establishment in the anarchic events of the *intifada*'s initial stage— Meir was to conclude his military service and join the Shin Bet, the General Security Service. However, that deal fell through and other state agencies approached by the military also balked at the idea of employing Meir. Finally, in October 1989 the IDF allowed Meir to take leave without pay until November 1992, when he would turn 40 and be able to retire with a full pension.

The Israeli public was kept in the dark about the Meir case until MK Yossi Sarid (Citizens' Rights Movement) published an article in *Ha'aretz* on May 4 disclosing the details of the Hawara incident and the cover-up efforts under way in the IDF. This prompted the Association for Civil Rights in Israel (ACRI), along with a group called "Parents Against Erosion" (referring to the erosion—physical, mental, and spiritual—suffered by their sons in fighting the *intifada*) and four of the Hawara residents who had been brutalized to ask the High Court of Justice to intervene and order the IDF to court-martial Meir. (He had already been court-martialed as the commanding officer when eight Israeli soldiers were kidnapped in Lebanon in September 1982, and it was in his sector as commander of Nablus that two of the most publicized outrages by Israeli soldiers in the *intifada* occurred: the burial alive of four West Bankers and the savage beating of two others that was screened by CBS-TV. See AJYB 1990, p. 405.) Meir's defense—and the IDF's and the state's (the formal respondent to the ACRI petition was the State Attorney's Office)— rested on the "unique circumstances" and the shifting policy that characterized the IDF's response to the mass demonstrations and provocations of the uprising's early days. True, Meir's order had been "manifestly illegal," the defense conceded in an affidavit submitted to the court in July, but Meir was being sufficiently punished by being forced to leave the army. This argument was undercut when the State Attorney's Office itself submitted a revised affidavit, in October, stating that Meir would in fact remain in the IDF for three more years.

On December 24, a tribunal of three justices ordered the Military Advocate General to court-martial Col. Yehuda Meir on the charge of "causing grievous bodily harm with intent." Brig. Gen. Amnon Strashnow announced that an indictment would be drawn up; if convicted, Meir would face a maximum penalty of 20 years in prison. High Court Justice Moshe Beiski wrote in the verdict: "Actions of this kind are an affront to every civilized person. No vagueness or unclarity can be a cover for them, and certainly not when such an order is given by a senior officer, who is duty-bound to be aware that the IDF's moral level unequivocally forbids such behavior."

One week after the High Court's ruling in the Meir case, an indictment was submitted against Col. Yaakov Sadeh, the deputy commander of the Gaza Strip, for causing the death by negligence of a 15-year-old boy, Mahmud Frej, in an incident in the Bureij refugee camp on July 31, 1989. Meir's, though, was the first case in which the commanding officer who gave an illegal order would face trial—rather than the junior officers and soldiers who carried it out. Five majors and three captains had been tried by year's end, but officers with higher ranks were given disciplinary hearings. Strashnow held a press conference (in October) to rebut public criticism that the big fish were being let off the hook. All told, by the end of 1989 more than 50 indictments had been submitted against nearly 90 soldiers in the territories for offenses committed since the start of the *intifada*, ranging from manslaughter to looting. More than 500 others faced disciplinary hearings.

Diplomatic and Political Developments

The Israeli peace initiative of 1989 was born when the most senior figures in the political establishment came to the realization that action had to be taken to counter growing domestic discontent at the persistence of the *intifada* and—no less—to halt the erosion of support for Israel in the international community in general and in the United States in particular, due to Israel's handling of the uprising. Prime Minister Yitzhak Shamir and Defense Minister Yitzhak Rabin were especially perturbed at Washington's decision in December 1988 to enter into a dialogue with the Palestine Liberation Organization (PLO). Moreover, that decision, together with the declaration by the Palestine National Council, a month earlier, of the establishment of the "State of Palestine," seemed to re-inspirit the insurrection in the territories.

On January 18, Defense Minister Rabin, replying in the Knesset to no-confidence motions based on the government's handling of the *intifada,* was heckled and taunted so vociferously by MKs from the Left—for excessive brutality in putting down the uprising—and from the Right—for not being tough enough against the

Palestinians—that he stalked out of the chamber in the middle of his statement. The next day, though, at a previously scheduled briefing with reporters, Rabin unveiled a plan envisaging a period of "expanded autonomy" in the territories, with elections to be held in which delegates would be chosen to hold talks with Israel on steps toward a settlement; in return, the Palestinians would cease their violence for up to six months. Should the Palestinians reject the plan and persist in the uprising, the defense minister noted, Israel would at least have obtained moral justification for suppressing the *intifada* with force.

The Palestinians in fact rejected the proposal, citing its obvious attempt to drive a wedge between the PLO and the inhabitants of the territories by creating an "alternative Palestinian leadership." A more positive response came from the Prime Minister's Office, where similar ideas were being broached in back rooms.

Meanwhile, the PLO endeavored to change its image in the eyes of Israelis. On February 22, Yasir Arafat held his first-ever press conference for Israeli journalists, in Cairo. (Israel TV permitted its viewers to see only selected excerpts two days later, and then only after a fierce row within the Israel Broadcasting Authority.) "We are cousins," Arafat declared. "You have to treat me as an equal and a human being." A day earlier, Arafat's second-in-command in Fatah, Abu Iyad (Salah Khalaf), addressed, via a videocassette smuggled into Israel, a symposium sponsored by the International Center for Peace in the Middle East. Calling for Israeli-PLO talks, Abu Iyad asserted that after 40 years of war, the Palestinians had concluded that "we cannot destroy the Israelis." Shamir, however, was having none of it. Such PLO statements, he told reporters, were "pure [propaganda] tactics," part of an ongoing campaign to delude the Israeli public.

Following a familiar pattern, Shamir's case was bolstered by acts of terrorism in Israel, the territories, and from Lebanon, which government spokesmen attributed to the PLO (few Israelis distinguished between the PLO's different wings, and to most the organization was synonymous with terror). Thus, following attempted infiltrations by two PLO groups across the Lebanese border around the beginning of March, the Foreign Ministry spokesman said that it was "hard to understand how the PLO expects public opinion in Israel and the West to take statements about changes in policy seriously, while the [organization's December 1988] commitment to stop terror is being mocked by continuous acts of terror."

Shamir also took heart from a sweeping Likud victory in the countrywide municipal elections held on February 28. In his campaign appearances, Shamir had declared that the local vote would be of crucial significance at the national level: Likud gains would be interpreted both at home and abroad as an endorsement of the party's foreign and security policy. Labor leaders poured scorn on this approach, but the tremendous inroads made by the Likud—capturing many of the cities Labor had held since the establishment of the state and gaining control of the Union of Local Authorities for the first time—seemed to vindicate the confident prediction of Foreign Minister Arens that the elections would result in "the second political turnabout in Israel's history," the first having been the Likud's victory in the 1977

Knesset elections. The results were a personal setback for Labor leader Shimon Peres and thus upped the stock of his archrival Yitzhak Rabin, both within the party and nationally, and heightened support for Rabin's initiative on the territories. (Later in the year, Labor partially redeemed itself with a creditable showing in the elections for the leadership of the Histadrut Federation of Labor—the party's last bastion of power. In the November 13 vote, Labor retained its near-total dominance of local workers' councils and outpolled the Likud by 55 percent to 27 percent at the national level, returning MK Israel Kessar as Histadrut general secretary. Three left-wing groups split the remaining 18 percent: Mapam, 9 percent of the vote; the Civil Rights Movement and a Jewish-Arab list, 4 percent each. In 1985 a united Labor-Mapam list won 66 percent of the vote to the Likud's 22 percent.)

In March, Foreign Minister Arens, the first high Israeli official to meet with ranking members of the newly installed Bush administration, was told by Secretary of State James Baker that he and President George Bush were expecting Shamir to come to Washington in April with concrete proposals to start the peace process moving. Pointedly, in the course of Arens's stay, Baker told a congressional committee that if "meaningful negotiations" could not be held with a body other than the PLO, "we would then have to see negotiations between Israelis and representatives of the PLO." Nothing was more calculated to goad Shamir into coming up with new ideas.

Shamir's peace initiative was designed to counter the incalculable damage that Palestinian casualty statistics were visiting on Israel's international standing, particularly in the United States. Shamir was also well aware that without Washington's prior endorsement of the plan, there was little point in presenting it in Israel. The plan itself, as Shamir told reporters following his meeting with President Bush at the White House on April 6, involved "free democratic elections [in the territories], free from an atmosphere of PLO violence, terror and intimidation." Speaking on the same occasion, Bush stated: "The United States believes that elections in the territories can be designed to contribute to a political process of dialogue and negotiation."

Shamir returned home in a buoyant mood on April 14, announcing that the elections he had in mind could not be held until "total order and calm" had returned to the territories, suggesting that as long as the *intifada* continued, the Israeli initiative could not begin.

April, in fact, was one of the year's most violent months in the territories. Thirty-one Palestinians were killed by the security forces, Palestinian nationalists set forest fires, intra-Palestinian liquidations intensified, and settlers retaliated against stone-throwing incidents by raiding Arab villages and, in some cases, by opening fire: two Palestinians, aged 16 and 24, were shot dead in Hebron by Jewish civilians in April. Against this background, it came as no surprise to most observers when 80 leading Palestinians in the territories in late April signed a statement rejecting the mooted elections plan by making it conditional on a prior Israeli military withdrawal. Foreign Minister Arens attributed this development to a PLO-instigated "reign of terror" in the territories; anyone who did not toe the organization's line, he said, was liquidated. Support for the plan, however, came from Labor leader Peres, who described it as a "serious plan capable of producing results."

Undaunted by Palestinian rejection and by a wave of anti-Jewish violence in both the territories and Israel—for the second time in three months, a soldier was kidnapped near Ashkelon, and in downtown Jerusalem a Ramallah man went on a knifing rampage (see "Terrorism, Antiterrorism, Extremism," below)—Shamir and Rabin, joined by Arens and Peres, put the finishing touches on the elections initiative for the territories. With the broad principles already endorsed by Washington, it remained to find specific formulations that both Likud and Labor could live with. Fundamentally, this meant avoiding the issues likely to arise at the stage of a final settlement, particularly the "territories for peace" formula which was anathema to the Israeli Right. On May 6, Industry Minister Ariel Sharon termed the evolving plan a "calamity" and a "colossal national blunder" which, if implemented, would inevitably result in a Palestinian state. Sharon's broadside was the opening salvo in the organized resistance within the Likud to the Shamir-Rabin plan.

PEACE INITIATIVE APPROVED

On May 14, the cabinet approved the "Peace Initiative of the Government of Israel" by a wide margin, 20–6, following a seven-hour meeting. Voting against it were Labor's Ezer Weizman—who thought the plan was outdated and irrelevant—and Rafael Edri; the National Religious party's Avner Shaki (the party split, as Religious Affairs Minister Zevulun Hammer voted in favor); and three ranking Likud ministers—Ariel Sharon, David Levy, and Yitzhak Modai—who would soon lead a revolt against Shamir, motivated by a combination of ideology and personal ambition. A senior State Department official, Dennis Ross, in Israel at the head of a U.S. delegation, waited outside the cabinet room to get a copy of the plan and to express his—and Washington's—satisfaction to Shamir that the plan was now official government policy.

Ironically, Shamir and Arens, who as Knesset members had been less than thrilled with the Camp David accords in 1977—Shamir abstained and Arens voted against—had now helped resuscitate that agreement. Of the four "basic premises" underlying the peace initiative, the first stated that "Israel yearns for peace and the continuation of the political process by means of direct negotiations based on the principles of the Camp David accords." The other three premises were negative: no "additional Palestinian state" (the first, presumably, was Jordan); no negotiations with the PLO; and "no change in the status of Judea, Samaria and Gaza other than in accordance with the government's Basic Guidelines." The proposed elections in the territories—another step long opposed by the Likud and many in Labor, ever since the sweeping triumph of PLO-affiliated Palestinian nationalists in municipal elections held in the West Bank in the mid-1970s—were, it turned out, part of a far broader process involving four "steps," all of which were to be "dealt with simultaneously":

1. Israel views as important that the peace between Israel and Egypt, based on the Camp David accords, will serve as a cornerstone for enlarging the circle of peace in the region, and calls for a common endeavor for the strengthening of the peace and its extension, through continued consultation.
2. Israel calls for the establishment of peace relations between it and those Arab states which still maintain a state of war with it, for the purpose of promoting a comprehensive settlement for the Arab-Israel conflict, including recognition, direct negotiations, ending the boycott, diplomatic relations, cessation of hostile activity in international institutions or forums, and regional and bilateral cooperation.
3. Israel calls for an international endeavor to resolve the problem of the residents of the Arab refugee camps in Judea, Samaria and the Gaza District in order to improve their living conditions and to rehabilitate them. Israel is prepared to be a partner in this endeavor.
4. In order to advance the political negotiation process leading to peace, Israel proposes free and democratic elections among the Palestinian Arab inhabitants of Judea, Samaria and the Gaza District in an atmosphere devoid of violence, threats and terror. In these elections a representation will be chosen to conduct negotiations for a transitional period of self-rule. This period will constitute a test for coexistence and cooperation. At a later stage, negotiations will be conducted for a permanent solution, during which all the proposed options for an agreed settlement will be examined, and peace between Israel and Jordan will be achieved.

The document went on to set forth technical stages and conditions for the achievement of peace, consisting of two "interlocking" stages, a five-year "transitional period for an interim agreement," to be followed by a "permanent solution." Negotiations for achieving the permanent solution would get under way "[a]s soon as possible, but not later than the third year after the beginning of the transitional period." During that period, the Palestinians in the territories "will be accorded self-rule, by means of which they will, themselves, conduct their affairs of daily life." However, Israel would retain responsibility for security, foreign policy "and all matters [pertaining to] Israeli citizens" in the territories. The negotiating partners "for the first [transitional] stage" would be, as Israel envisaged it, "the elected representation of the Palestinian Arab inhabitants" of the territories, with Jordan and Egypt invited to take part "if they so desire." Participating in the negotiations on the permanent solution would be Israel, the Palestinians' "elected representation," and Jordan, with Egypt an optional partner. The purpose of these talks would be to conclude the peace treaty between Israel and Jordan, including the "arrangements for . . . borders." (Pointedly, the Palestinians were not mentioned explicitly in connection with the contours of the permanent solution; the plan did state, though, that the permanent solution should be "acceptable to the negotiating parties," one of which was to be the Palestinian "representation.")

Most of the problems, technical and substantive, arose in connection with the section of the plan headed "Details of the Process for the Implementation of the

Initiative." "First and foremost," the first clause under this rubric said, were to come "dialogue and basic agreement by the Palestinian Arab inhabitants of [the territories], as well as Egypt and Jordan if they wish to take part, as above-mentioned, in the negotiations on the principles constituting the initiative." Left unanswered were the questions of whom the "dialogue" was to be held with and who was to state the Palestinians' "basic agreement" to the process before the elections were held. At all events, "[i]mmediately afterwards" would come the preparations for "free, democratic and secret elections" in which the "representation" would be chosen. This group of people—its makeup and size, the proportion of delegates from the West Bank and from Gaza were all left unspecified—would play a crucial role in the years ahead. They would negotiate the details of the transitional period, "constitute the self-governing authority" during that period, and "be the central Palestinian component, subject to agreement after three years, in the negotiations for the permanent solution." In short, this "representation" from the territories would effectively supplant the PLO as the Palestinian people's official spokesman.

A key stipulation for holding the elections was a "calming of the violence" in the territories. Less clear-cut was the form the elections were to take—"it is recommended that a proposal of regional elections be adopted, the details [to] be determined in further discussions"—and, most vexatious of all, was the question of who would be eligible to stand for election and to vote. According to the plan: "Every Palestinian Arab residing in Judea, Samaria and the Gaza District, who shall be elected by the inhabitants to represent them—after having submitted his candidacy in accordance with the detailed document which shall be agreed upon regarding the issue of the elections—may be a legitimate partner in the conduct of negotiations with Israel."

In an Independence Day interview with the *Jerusalem Post,* Prime Minister Shamir offered his interpretation of the initiative. A key element was the interlock between the Palestinian issue and the broader Arab-Israeli conflict: "[W]e are insisting that the conflict with the Palestinians cannot be ended without ending the conflict with the Arab states." The two problems must be resolved "in conjunction." As for who could take part in the elections, Shamir said that while it was premature to discuss the question, he was "absolutely" opposed to the participation of East Jerusalem residents. The prime minister's stand, based on Israel's formal annexation of East Jerusalem shortly after the Six Day War in 1967, effectively excluded the many leading Palestinians living in East Jerusalem, such as Faisal al-Husseini, from the peace process.

Indeed, that Shamir had not changed his stance was well demonstrated when he told a meeting of the Likud's Knesset representatives: "We will not give the Arabs one inch of our land, even if we have to negotiate for ten years. We will give them nothing. . . . The veto is in our hands." However, such rhetoric left many in the party unconvinced. The three Likud ministers who had voted against the plan—Sharon, Levy, and Modai—launched an organized campaign within the party to ditch the initiative, and by implication, Shamir as well; Modai, the leader of the

Likud's Liberal party component, openly called on Shamir to resign. The Knesset endorsed the plan on May 17, by a vote of 43–15, with 11 abstentions. However, a large number of coalition MKs, particularly from the Likud, absented themselves from the chamber, or simply did not raise their hands when the vote was taken.

As it turned out, only 17 of the Likud's 40 MKs voted for the peace initiative, along with the majority of Labor and the ultra-Orthodox Degel Hatorah; the far Left (Communists) and the far Right, including part of Agudat Israel, banded together to vote against; while the abstainees were the three dovish parties—Shinui, Citizens' Rights, and Mapam—along with two Shas MKs and one from Agudat Israel. In Labor, the initiative got a mixed reception. The party's Leadership Bureau endorsed it without a vote at the behest of Shimon Peres and, particularly, of Yitzhak Rabin, its coauthor. The defense minister explained that Shamir's hard-line statements were irrelevant, since he was referring to the stage of the permanent settlement, which the plan did not address.

The government lost no time in launching a diplomatic blitz to win support for the plan. Shamir visited England and Spain, Rabin and Arens were off to America, and Arens addressed a gathering of European Community foreign ministers. Following his meeting with Secretary of State Baker, Arens asserted that Washington's backing for the plan was "unreserved" and "wholehearted." A few days later (May 22), while Defense Minister Rabin was in the United States, Baker delivered a speech which signaled to Jerusalem that, peace plan or not, Washington's basic stance about a final settlement remained unchanged. Israel, he said, "must lay aside, once and for all, the unrealistic vision of a Greater Israel." (See below, "International Relations—United States.")

It was unclear whether Shamir and Arens were engaged in some sort of Machiavellian ploy—as some, Baker perhaps among them, were suggesting: putting forward a plan they knew was unacceptable to the PLO, with the aim of driving a wedge between the organization and local Palestinians, but which would relieve international pressure on Israel and allow it time to break the *intifada* and consolidate the status quo. Evidence in support of this notion came from Shamir himself. In his counteroffensive against the recalcitrant Likud ministers, the prime minister would declare that the plan had "improved our international standing" without Israel having "to pay any price," while Arens termed the plan a "tactical" move intended to undercut PLO diplomatic gains and regain international support for Israel. Both denied that the initiative conflicted with Likud principles.

REBELLION IN LIKUD

Throughout the turbulent period following the government's adoption of the Shamir-Rabin initiative in mid-May, unrest in the Likud rose to a fever pitch. The three senior Likud ministers who led the revolt against the peace plan—Sharon, Levy, and Modai— cited ideological outrage as their motive, but each also harbored far-reaching and mutually contradictory political ambitions. For the moment, though, the "rejection front," as they were dubbed, was united in its immediate goal: to discredit the peace plan—which Sharon, in an article in *Yediot Aharonot* (June 30) blasted as "a surrender to the so-called *intifada* and acceptance of the PLO's program"—and posit themselves as the true power brokers in the Likud. This accomplished, they believed, the 74-year-old Shamir would either step down, be forced to call a new election—thus sparking a contest for the party leadership—or find himself ousted from power in the wake of the unity government's collapse, followed by the formation of a new coalition led by Labor. The result was six weeks of fierce infighting within the Likud, climaxed by the convening of its Central Committee on July 5.

In the event, the 2,400 members of that body (a near-unanimous turnout), who came for what had been billed as a dramatic showdown, functioned as little more than extras in a distinctly nondramatic production. Following some frantic discussions and hard bargaining, involving close aides and ministerial go-betweens, the four principals closeted themselves before the crucial vote and emerged with the announcement that they had reached agreement on a draft resolution. This endorsed the Camp David accords and the government's peace initiative of May 14, but also obligated Likud representatives to act in the government and the Knesset in accordance with the principles of the Likud's platform: East Jerusalem Arabs could not participate in the elections in the territories; the terrorism and violence of the Palestinians had to be eliminated before the start of negotiations with the Arabs; Jewish settlement in Judea, Samaria and Gaza would continue; there could be no foreign sovereignty in any part of Eretz-Israel; no Palestinian state would be established in Eretz-Israel; no negotiations would be held with the PLO. The Central Committee ratified the resolutions unanimously.

To many, these constraints seemed to be the death knell of the peace initiative. The three "constraints ministers," as they were now called, proclaimed that they had achieved an enormous victory "for the sake of Greater Israel." "It is not my personal victory," gloated Sharon. "It is the victory of the Likud and of the Jews." "Now," David Levy exulted, "everything is shut tight, binding." Shamir, though, told Israel TV that there was "nothing new" in the resolution: "We did not alter one iota of the peace initiative that we proposed to the U.S., to the Arabs of [the territories] and to the Arab countries." As for the key issue of the nonparticipation of the Arabs of East Jerusalem—formally annexed to Israel but the Palestinians' intellectual center and the mooted capital of any future Palestinian state—Shamir explained that this was grounded in a 1982 cabinet resolution, passed by the Begin government during the autonomy negotiations, stipulating that East Jerusalem Arabs would not vote in the elections for the autonomy regime's administrative council.

Labor said it wasn't buying Shamir's version of events. "The resolution of the Likud's Central Committee, which surrendered to Sharon's dictate, constitutes a substantive change that harms the prospects of the government's peace initiative and [affects] the Labor Alignment's ability to remain in the government," thundered a communiqué issued by Labor's ministers within hours of the Likud move. At Peres's behest, Labor's Leadership Bureau decided to recommend to the party's Central Committee that Labor leave the government. However, Defense Minister Rabin, although telling Israel Radio on July 6 that the Likud's decisions "severely harm the chance of implementing the peace initiative," urged a go-slow approach. Time was needed to see whether Palestinian partners could in fact be found, and in the meantime there was no point in leaving the government. Like all the other actors involved, Rabin was not guided strictly by ideology: he had no wish to see the government collapse and his archrival Peres put together a new coalition with the religious parties. (In a knee-jerk action, Peres's aides put out feelers to the religious parties immediately after the Likud resolution.) The result was that no specific date was set for Labor's Central Committee to convene.

At the cabinet meeting on July 16, Shamir, in reply to a question by Interior Minister Arye Deri, of Shas, who was known to hold dovish views, stated that the government's May 14 peace initiative was "firm and abiding, and no changes have been made in it." One week later, any pretext Peres might have had for leading Labor out of the government disappeared when the cabinet, "at the suggestion of the prime minister and the vice premier" (Peres), reaffirmed the May 14 initiative by a vote of 21–4 and one abstention. Voting against were the Likud's "gang of three" and, as he had in the original vote, Labor's dovish Ezer Weizman.

On the day after the Likud Central Committee episode, a *Jerusalem Post* editorial summed up the conventional wisdom about what had happened. Shamir, it said, had "effectively capitulated" to the conditions set by his party adversaries and had thereby "opted for keeping his position and party intact as his highest priority." It was "more than puzzling" why Shamir had engaged his challengers in a protracted controversy, "only to submit to them so ignominiously." Actually, Shamir was doing what he did best: nothing at all. He had raised the tactic of bending with the wind to a high strategic art. The "gang of three" huffed and puffed—on July 27 they met, railed at reports that Shamir and his aides were meeting with known PLO supporters from the territories (reportedly to sound them out on the peace plan)—and decided to launch an "information drive" within the Likud against Shamir, lest the prime minister divest himself of the "constraints" imposed upon him. Reinforcing their allegations were a leading West Bank lawyer, Jamal Tarifi, known to have close ties with the PLO, who admitted having met with Shamir in the latter's office, and Deputy Finance Minister Yossi Beilin (Labor), who stated that Israel had been holding indirect talks with the PLO. But Shamir told Israel TV that talks with the PLO were "out of the question," said Beilin was "twisting the truth," and told a group of rabbis that he would not give up so much as a "sliver" of land.

Shamir was also aware that Labor had no real option to leave the national unity government. The party's Central Committee finally met in early August—after the mini-crisis had been resolved—and decided that Labor would remain in the government on condition that the peace initiative continue to move forward. The meeting adopted several principles of its own to counterbalance the "constraints" of its partner in the government, notably that East Jerusalem Arabs be allowed to vote outside Jerusalem, that Jewish settlement activity be halted during the elections, and that Palestinians from outside the territories (i.e., persons deported by Israel) be allowed to take part in talks. Also affirmed was the notion of "territory in exchange for peace." Yet, the true measure of Labor's vitality lay in the fact that only about a quarter of the Central Committee members bothered to turn up for the gathering.

Although the government's initiative may not have advanced the peace process much, it played a role in weakening the *intifada* by sowing the seeds of a possible rift between the Palestinians in the "homeland" and those in the "diaspora," and by generating a procedural debate involving not only the Palestinians and Israel but also the United States and Egypt, diverting attention from substantive issues. The agendas of the Palestinians in the territories and of PLO leaders in Tunis were perceived to be not wholly compatible: the former, who were on the front line of the conflict with Israel, perhaps wanted to cash in on their gains during the uprising by agreeing to elections for a delegation to negotiate with Israel; whereas the latter, concerned to maintain their leadership, effectively spurned the Israeli initiative by making elections in the territories conditional on the IDF's prior withdrawal. This was one of the issues addressed in a ten-point Egyptian plan for holding elections in the territories.

CAIRO PLAN

In effect, Cairo's plan, which was designed as a compromise between the Israeli and PLO positions, and incidentally to display Egypt's diplomatic clout, sought to fill in the lacunae in the Israeli initiative with concrete proposals and to ensure that the elections would indeed be only the first stage in a process toward peace. Thus, the Egyptian proposal stipulated that the IDF would not have to withdraw but on election day it would move away from polling stations; that the elections would take place under international supervision; that Jewish settlement operations would cease during the election period; and that the Israeli government would undertake to accept the results of the elections and to consider them part of the process leading to a permanent solution on the basis of Security Council Resolutions 242 and 338, entailing the "land-for-peace" principle and recognition of the Palestinians' political rights.

In addition, the Palestinians would be able to state at the outset of the talks that they were negotiating on the basis of the Egyptians' ten points and not the Israelis' four points (a concept accepted by Washington). Above all, though, President Hosni Mubarak's concept of a preliminary Israeli-Palestinian meeting in Cairo under Egyptian and American auspices seemed intended to circumvent the built-in logical flaw in the Israeli plan, the "Catch-22 of the process by which Palestinian representatives will be chosen," as the *Jerusalem Post* described it: "One needs representatives to talk about the elections, which in turn, are needed in order to select representatives." Reportedly, the Egyptian plan had been conveyed to Jerusalem as early as July, but it was not formally presented to the government until September 15 by Egyptian ambassador to Israel Mohammed Bassiouny. President Mubarak was also prepared to host a round of preliminary talks between Israelis and Palestinians under U.S., Egyptian, and possibly Soviet aegis, Bassiouny said. The following day the "forum of four" met to discuss the Egyptian ideas. Composed of Shamir and Arens for the Likud and Rabin and Peres for Labor, this body had in many ways superseded the cabinet as the country's top policy-making body on national-security matters since the May 14 initiative. Although the Labor duo advocated acceptance of the Mubarak plan, if only to prevent a serious rift with Washington, which supported it, and the Likud's team favored rejection, claiming the plan would confront Israel with the need to talk to the PLO, a government crisis was averted by the expedient of a decision to clarify the matter further. But the lines were drawn more firmly following the cabinet meeting on September 17, when the Likud ministers met and decided to reject the Egyptian plan, while Labor's ministers accepted it.

On September 18, Defense Minister Rabin paid a one-day visit to Cairo, where he met for three hours with President Mubarak, and emerged to tell reporters that the two had reached broad agreement. Israel and a Palestinian delegation would meet in Cairo, at Egypt's invitation, with the participants from the Palestinian side to be announced by Egypt "following coordination with elements whose identity I do not wish to elaborate on"—clearly a reference to the PLO. The Palestinian delegation would include a number of Palestinians in exile. Reportedly, Mubarak had agreed to a summit meeting with Shamir after the Israeli-Palestinian talks, something Jerusalem had long been seeking. In an oral message conveyed to Shamir via Rabin, Mubarak said he was working in full coordination with Arafat—who had been in Cairo just before the Rabin visit—and stated that after the PLO had made "major concessions" in the form of accepting Resolutions 242 and 338, renouncing terrorism and accepting Israel's right to exist within secure boundaries, "it is now Israel's turn. Both sides must make concessions."

Rabin briefed Shamir on his talks the next morning (September 19) in what was described as a tense meeting. Later that day, in an address to the Israel Bar Association, Shamir left no doubt about where he stood. Since the elections were "part of a plan" geared to bringing about "peace and coexistence" between Israel and the Arabs in the territories, he said, it followed that there was "no room or justification" to allow Palestinians living abroad to take part in the process: "not only because the [Arabs'] demand is a cover for PLO representation, but especially because our initiative is totally irrelevant to residents abroad, and it is inconceivable that Israel will agree to their so-called 'right of return.'" Having thus ruled out the participation of persons deported by Israel and Palestinians voluntarily living abroad—both of them groups containing leading Palestinian activists and nationalists—Shamir again vetoed "the involvement of Jerusalem and its Arab inhabitants" in the plan.

"Jerusalem was not and will not be included in the initiative because it is Israel's capital, and any breach . . . will diminish its status." Finally, the prime minister rejected the idea of "land for peace," not only because it related to the permanent solution and hence was not acceptable in the initial stage, but primarily "because the practical significance of the 'land for peace' formula is the establishment of a Palestinian Arab state in Judea, Samaria and Gaza. We shall never agree to this."

UNITY GOVERNMENT UNDER STRESS

Aides of Prime Minister Shamir asserted that by supporting President Mubarak's ten points, Labor ministers were "undermining Israel's own peace initiative." Rabin, however, told a meeting of the Labor party's Central Committee that the Egyptian ideas in no way countered Israeli stands, as they said nothing about the PLO or a future Palestinian state. Nor was it of significance that "one or two" deported Palestinians would take part in the talks.

As the rift between the parties widened, there was growing talk of an early election. In Labor, Rabin was seen as the "great white hope" who could lead the party to an electoral victory for the first time since 1973, instead of the four-time loser Peres. Rabin's standing in the party rose to unprecedented heights as even the party's most dovish MKs, including Ezer Weizman and former general secretary Uzi Baram, who had been sharp critics of his policies in the *intifada* and had supported the "Peres camp," fell into line behind the defense minister in his efforts to advance the peace process. Nationwide, too, Rabin was by far the most popular member of the cabinet, as a Smith Institute poll showed in late September. The poll also found that the government as a whole had only a 24-percent competency rating from the public, and the prevailing perception that the national unity government had come to the end of its tether spurred mounting calls for its dissolution from all shades of the political spectrum.

Rabin, though, had other ideas. As the coauthor of the peace initiative, and perhaps apprehensive that in a showdown in Labor he would not have the backing to wrest the leadership from his 15-year archrival Peres, he behaved as though he were the glue capable of holding the government together. That plenty of glue was needed was apparent to the entire international community during September, when Foreign Minister Arens and Finance Minister Peres paid simultaneous visits to the United States. As the *Jerusalem Post* observed in the aftermath, the two presented a "spectacle of a two-headed government" in Israel by contradicting each other at every turn. Both ministers met (separately) with President Bush and Secretary of State Baker, and with Egyptian president Hosni Mubarak and Soviet foreign minister Eduard Shevardnadze, who were also in the United States. Although Baker stated that Egypt's ten points were not intended to supersede the Israeli plan but "simply a method of trying to get implementation of the Shamir proposal" and to enable Palestinians and Israelis to sit together, and although Mubarak declared that the Palestinians in question would not be a "PLO delegation," Shamir termed Mubarak's proposed Cairo meeting "talks of capitulation" for Israel at which the perpetrators of the *intifada* would claim victory. Shamir said the idea was to get Israel to "talk with the PLO about the quickest way to establish a Palestinian state," whereas the "entire purpose" of the Israeli initiative had been "to liberate the Arab population [in the territories] from the rule of the PLO."

Finally, the inner cabinet, the ranking formal policy-making body, comprising six Likud and six Labor ministers, met for five hours on October 5 to consider the Egyptian proposal. Unable to complete the discussion, the 12 convened again the following day—as it happened, the 16th anniversary of the Yom Kippur War—and to no one's surprise emerged after a further three hours of debate with a 6–6 stalemate on the ten points, following Labor's insistence that a vote be taken on its motion to accept Mubarak's invitation for a meeting in Cairo with Palestinians. Under cabinet rules, a tie vote meant rejection of the motion. Peres and Rabin said the result virtually consigned the peace initiative to oblivion, but Shamir said nothing had changed and intimated he was expecting James Baker to play the part of the *deus ex machina* by adducing a compromise U.S. plan that would enable the government to hang together. In the meantime, Faisal al-Husseini also rejected the Egyptian points because they did not address Palestinian political aspirations.

BAKER PLAN

Secretary of State Baker came up with a five-point formula in October that was intended to find a way to reconcile what had become, in the wake of Cairo's ten-point proposal to facilitate the implementation of Israel's four-point plan, the major stumbling block to progress: Israel's refusal to sit with the PLO or with any Palestinian it deemed was affiliated or associated with or sympathetic to that organization. In effect, Israel was saying that it wanted veto power over the members of the delegation it would negotiate with. The third of Baker's five points in the document's mid-October final version addressed this issue:

1. The U.S. understands that Egypt and Israel have been working hard and that there is now agreement that an Israeli delegation will conduct a dialogue with a Palestinian delegation in Cairo.
2. The U.S. understands that Egypt cannot substitute for the Palestinians in that dialogue and that Egypt will consult with the Palestinians on all aspects of that dialogue. Egypt will also consult with Israel and the U.S.
3. The U.S. understands that Israel will attend the dialogue [in Cairo] after a satisfactory list of Palestinians has been worked out. Israel will also consult with Egypt and the U.S. on the matter.
4. The U.S. understands that the government of Israel will come to the dialogue on the basis of the Israeli government's May 14 initiative.

The U.S. further understands that elections and negotiations will be in accordance with the Israeli initiative. The U.S. understands, therefore, that the Palestinians will be free to raise issues that relate to their opinion on how to make elections and negotiations succeed.

5. In order to facilitate the process, the U.S. proposes that the foreign ministers of Israel, Egypt and the U.S. meet in Washington within two weeks.

The PLO once again played into Shamir's hands by immediately rejecting the Baker "understandings," since they seemed to deprive the organization of the power to name the Palestinian delegation. But Shamir, too, was not satisfied. He wanted "guarantees" from Washington that Israel would not have to negotiate with the PLO and that the issue of a Palestinian state, or anything other than the details of the elections in the territories, would not be raised at the talks. (The Israeli plan carefully differentiated between the first, interim, stage of a peace process and a later stage when the "permanent solution" would be addressed—with the latter phase being absolutely dependent on the prior implementation of the former.) Transoceanic telephone conversations between Shamir and Bush, Shamir and Baker, and Baker and Arens, in which the Israeli side tried to induce the Americans to toughen the language of the five points in the direction sought by Israel, produced little more than growing tensions between the two governments.

Tension also continued within the national unity government. But Labor seemed to be in a state of leaderless paralysis. Its leadership, well aware that Labor did not have the necessary support in the Knesset to topple the government and form a new one, fearful of taking a severe drubbing in a general election, and under pressure by the party's Histadrut leaders not to trigger a government crisis on the eve of the elections for the labor federation (November 13), decided to vote with the government on October 24 in no-confidence motions submitted by the opposition regarding the failure to move forward on the peace issue. In the event, though, only seven of Labor's 39 MKs voted with the government as Peres and Rabin had requested, while others abstained, did not take part, or simply absented themselves from the Knesset. Ronni Milo, the minister of environmental affairs, replying on behalf of the government, declared that "all the blame" for the stymied peace process rested with the PLO, "which is preventing the residents of the territories who are interested in a political solution from sitting with us at the [negotiating] table."

On October 23, Arens sent a letter to Baker couched in what were described as "positive" tones but asking that the five points be formally amended— Shamir was unwilling to accept oral assurances from the Americans—to state that the Palestinian delegation be composed only of inhabitants of Judea, Samaria, and Gaza (thus ruling out residents of East Jerusalem and Palestinians residing abroad); that the Cairo venue be changed; that the makeup of the Palestinian delegation be determined by Egypt, Israel, and the United States; and that the Palestinians not be permitted to raise any topic other than the election modalities. Baker, who was also under pressure from the Egyptian-PLO side, flatly rejected the first two requests but agreed to omit one sentence from the five points—the second sentence in Point 3: "Israel will also consult with Egypt and the U.S. on the matter" of the Palestinian delegation—and to add one word to Point 5, which would then read: "In order to facilitate the negotiating process . . . ," this to enable Israel to claim that the talks were on election procedures and not on substance, and the Arabs to claim that "negotiating process" was tantamount to "peace process," so that subjects not directly related to election modalities could also be put forward. In letters to Cairo and Jerusalem on November 1, on the eve of a visit to Australia, Baker asked for a reply to his ideas—which would also include various guarantees to both sides in letters accompanying the five points—by the time of his return on November 8.

Shamir was under additional pressure. Despite strong hints put out by Israeli officials that the prime minister would like to meet with President Bush while he was in the United States to deliver a speech to a Jewish gathering in mid-November, the White House had not been forthcoming. Closer to home, on October 25, the ultra-Orthodox Agudat Israel party had given the Likud two weeks to implement all its pledges or it would leave the coalition. (Its deputy labor and social affairs minister, Rabbi Moshe Zeev Feldman, had resigned six weeks earlier for the same reason.)

The Shamir-Arens camp now feared that a decision by the government to reject the Baker proposals would be too much for even the dispirited Labor party to accept; Peres, this time probably with Rabin's support, would break up the national unity government and turn to the religious parties in an effort to form a "narrow" government. The main candidates: the Aguda, which was furious with the Likud; and Shas, whose spiritual mentor, former Sephardi chief rabbi Ovadia Yosef, and "strong man," Interior Minister Arye Deri, had in the past both professed distinctly dovish views. (In a July meeting in Cairo with President Mubarak, Rabbi Yosef—accompanied by Deri—had stated that in his view, if returning the territories could guarantee a true peace, while retaining them posed the danger of war, then, according to the halakhic precept of *pikuah nefesh,* the saving of lives, they should be returned.)

On top of this, *Ha'aretz* reported (November 7) that Tom Dine and Bob Asher, the two ranking officials in AIPAC, the American Israel Public Affairs Committee, the foremost Israeli lobby in Washington, had paid an unpublicized lightning visit to Jerusalem where they had warned Shamir that rejection of the Baker proposals would have the most serious consequences for Israeli-U.S. relations and within the American Jewish community. Similar messages were reportedly received from Seymour Reich, the chairman of the Conference of Presidents of Major Jewish Organizations, and others. On the other side, the three "constraints" ministers—Sharon, Levy, and Modai—were again accusing Shamir of holding indirect talks with the PLO, violating the July 5 resolutions of the Likud Central Committee and demanding that that body be convened again if the Baker plan, even in its amended form, were accepted. The three, indeed, cast the only negative votes when Shamir put the matter to a vote in the 12-member inner cabinet on November 5.

However, although the results of the vote enabled Shamir to achieve his immediate purpose—get an invitation to meet with Bush on November 15—rough waters still lay ahead. The Israeli acceptance was not unconditional, but was given on the assumption that, following this assent and in accordance with the secretary of state's accompanying letter to the five points, the United States, for its part, would see to it that the entire process was compatible with Israel's peace initiative of May 14, including the following points: (a) The dialogue would begin after a list had been drawn up of Palestinian Arabs residing in Judea-Samaria and Gaza which was acceptable to Israel. (b) Israel would not negotiate with the PLO. (c) The substantive topic for discussion would be the procedures for the elections in Judea-Samaria and Gaza, in a manner compatible with the peace initiative. (d) The United States would publicly support the above Israeli positions and would back it in the event that one party to the dialogue deviated from what was agreed. (e) The United States and Egypt would declare their support for the principles of Camp David which underlay Israel's peace initiative, including the stages and substance of the negotiations. (f) One meeting, the first, would be held in Cairo, and the continuation would be considered in the light of its outcome.

Although Egypt on December 6 declared its "willingness to proceed" on the basis of Baker's amended proposals—as usual subject to "consultations" with the Palestinians, meaning the PLO—the Israeli "forum of four" decided, two days later, to accede to Baker's request to hold "contacts" preparatory to the trilateral foreign ministers' meeting. The secretary of state had proposed, in a phone conversation with Arens two days earlier, that Israel send a joint Likud-Labor delegation of officials to Washington for the preliminary talks, but Peres and Rabin accepted Shamir's suggestion that cabinet secretary Elyakim Rubinstein go alone. Although Rubinstein reportedly made a bit of headway in Washington, at year's end the peace process was effectively tangled up in a labyrinthine complex of "points" and "assumptions" about those points. In any event, within days the problems of the Middle East were abruptly shunted to a low place on the administration's agenda as upheaval shook Romania and Eastern Europe.

The governing coalition in Israel also suffered a series of jolts as the year drew to a close. Despite Shamir's promises to the ultra-Orthodox parties that the Likud would not support a human-rights bill that had been drafted by the party's own justice minister, Dan Meridor, and approved (April 9) by the cabinet, when the identical bill came up for a preliminary vote in the Knesset in mid-November— while Shamir was abroad—after being presented by Shinui's Amnon Rubinstein, it passed by a margin of 53-9 and was sent to committee, with the backing of most of the Likud MKs. Agudat Israel had pulled out of the coalition for a two-month period on November 8, in order to give the Likud a chance to fulfill some of its promises, and Shas was enraged by the Likud's support for the human-rights bill. At this juncture, Shimon Peres, further encouraged by Labor's big win in the Histadrut election, began maneuvering behind the scenes to try and swing the ultra-Orthodox parties behind Labor and topple the government in order to create what he called a "coalition for peace." The human-rights legislation was in fact soon killed in the Likud-chaired Constitution, Law and Justice Committee by a one-vote margin, and the Likud declared that it was abandoning its previous advocacy of electoral reform as well. But pressures continued to mount in Labor for a break with the Likud over the peace issue, while in the Likud the "constraints" trio demanded a harder line and said they were setting up their own Knesset bloc.

Peace Movement

Advocacy for peace was increasingly identified with people like Abie Nathan, the perennial "peacenik," perceived as a well-meaning eccentric, who in October began serving a six-month prison term under the 1986 amendment to the Prevention of Terrorism Ordinance for having met abroad with PLO leaders, including Yasir Arafat. (Typically, he was cheered into prison by about a thousand supporters, including Labor doves and left-wing MKs who promised to work for the law's repeal but did nothing.) There were, as well, radical-left Israelis like Michael Warshawsky, head of the Alternative Information Center in Jerusalem, who in November was sentenced to 20 months in prison for providing printing services to the Popular Front for the Liberation of Palestine (see AJYB 1989, p. 376), and the Derekh Hanitzotz group (see AJYB 1990, pp. 413–14), whose four Israeli members were sentenced to relatively light sentences in a plea-bargaining deal which they regarded as an "achievement" as it put an end to the "witch hunt," in the words of Ya'akov Ben-Efrat, who received the longest prison term, 30 months. There were also groups such as "The 21st Year," "Stop the Occupation," "Women in Black" and "Yesh Gvul" (There's a Border/Limit)—tiny organizations, often consisting largely of academics.

Only Yesh Gvul, which called on reservists not to serve in the territories and provided support for those sent to jail for refusing to serve, seemed to bother the authorities. For a time the organization was investigated by the Shin Bet, as a result of which several of its activists were summoned for interrogation by the police, prompting MK Shulamit Aloni, leader of the Citizens' Rights and Peace Movement, to write to Police Minister Haim Bar-Lev that Yesh Gvul was an open and legitimate protest movement, and that the actions of the security authorities seemed to signal "the end of the era of democracy in Israel."

But the most significant point was that of 300,000 Israeli soldiers who had been sent to do service in the territories, fewer than 100 had refused. Indeed, most of the dovish MKs strenuously opposed refusal to serve, as did the largest of the peace organizations, Peace Now. Peace Now had organized a few demonstrations, carried out sporadic forays of support into the territories (these convoys were often turned back by soldiers), and staged a few symbolic happenings, such as an event in the West Bank in October at which the speakers included Yael Dayan, the daughter of Moshe Dayan, and Faisal al-Husseini (son of Palestinian leader Abd al-Kadr al-Husseini, who was killed in the fighting near Jerusalem in 1948). However, as long as its own activists implicitly supported the occupation by continuing to accept reserve duty in the territories, and as long as they failed to convince other Israelis of the necessity and viability of their cause, the movement was destined to remain ineffectual. At the very end of the year, though, Peace Now committed the biggest sin of all in the eyes of most Israelis: it linked hands with the *goyim,* figuratively and literally, in an "initiative" that was inspired by the dramatic events in Eastern Europe.

"1990: Time for Peace" consisted of three days of meetings, discussions, and visits to the territories sponsored by dozens of international peace groups—about 1,000 activists from Europe came—and Peace Now. What caught the public's attention, though, was a "human chain" in which these visitors, together with thousands of Israeli Jews and Palestinians, were to link hands and encircle the wall of the Old City of Jerusalem. In fact, nearly 30,000 Arabs and Jews showed up for the event on a balmy December 30, and a festive atmosphere was maintained until the very end. At that point, police charged into one section of the "human chain," outside the Damascus Gate, where, according to a police communiqué, "extremist Palestinian elements" violated the terms of the permit for the demonstration by chanting PLO slogans and waving Palestinian flags. About 60 persons, half of them visitors from abroad, were injured by police tear gas, plastic bullets, and riot batons (one Italian woman lost an eye due to broken glass).

Peace Now and its supporters alleged that the police action had been unwarranted and certainly brutal to an extreme, while right-wing spokesmen deplored the fact that the demonstration had been allowed to take place at all. Even before the events got under way, the Prime Minister's Office linked the gathering with the PLO, and Ehud Olmert, the minister responsible for Arab affairs, told the cabinet the following day, December 31, that he had actual "evidence" that the PLO was behind "Time for Peace." It was at that same cabinet meeting that the year's most dramatic attempt was made to discredit those perceived as "doves" and "leftists" by identifying them with the PLO—and, indeed, to discredit the entire Labor party. Out of the blue, Prime Minister Shamir informed the cabinet that he had decided to dismiss Minister of Science and Development Ezer Weizman—a former Air Force commander and, as defense minister in the first Begin government, a major architect of the peace with Egypt—because he had "maintained contacts with the PLO, directly and indirectly, over a period of time." Reading from a prepared text, Shamir said Weizman had met with "an official PLO representative" in Europe, "and recently he sent messages to the head of the PLO, Arafat, and received messages from him via a courier." Shamir said Weizman had violated both the law—the Prevention of Terrorism Ordinance—and the government's Basic Guidelines. The cabinet was further taken aback to hear that Shamir had informed Vice Premier Peres of his intention to fire Weizmann three days earlier, and had asked Peres to induce Weizman to resign voluntarily. Shamir gave Defense Minister Rabin the same information just before the December 31 cabinet meeting. Neither Peres nor Rabin had passed the information on to Weizman or asked him to resign; Peres had told Shamir he would oppose any move to dismiss Weizman. Under the coalition agreement, Shamir needed Peres's consent in order to fire a Labor minister—as Peres pointed out in a letter to Shamir later that day, in which he also objected to "judgment being passed" on anyone without giving that person the opportunity to explain himself.

Shamir preempted Israel TV's children's hour that evening to take his case directly to the public. "There is one great rule in the government's peace initiative," Shamir asserted: "There will be no negotiations with the PLO." But Weizman, he said, a member of the inner cabinet and hence privy to the country's deepest secrets, not only rejected the peace initiative, "he speaks against the government's policy behind the prime minister's back, in agreement with our most dangerous enemies. He maintains contacts with PLO members, instructs them how to deal with our arguments, how to conduct their relationship with the U.S. and how to foil our moves, the moves of his own government.... Will there be a crisis, the government's dissolution? I say this is not necessary. I still hope that most Labor party cabinet members dissociate themselves from minister Weizman's opinions and actions...."

Weizman himself expressed no regrets over his moves, which he said were all made in the pursuit of peace, and indeed told *Ha'aretz* that he welcomed Shamir's action as it would at last force both Likud and Labor to decide where they stood on the peace process and on the question of contacts with the PLO. Shamir, too, in meeting with Jamil Tarifi, Weizman said, had in effect been in contact with the PLO. Despite Shamir's admonitions, Labor spokesmen threatened to leave the government if Shamir did not retract his dismissal of Weizman; once more Peres's aides began feeling out the ultra-Orthodox parties to see whether a Labor-led government was feasible. A few days before dropping the Weizman bombshell, Shamir had told a Likud meeting that the possibility of an early election would not deter him. "There will be no talks with Arafat's gang of murderers, and there will be no Palestinian state." The May 14 peace initiative, he added, was not meant as a springboard for "far-reaching concessions." Anyone who thought that was deluding himself, the prime minister asserted. That initiative "is the limit of our concessions."

Terrorism, Antiterrorism, Extremism

The spillover of the *intifada* across the Green Line into Israel proper continued and intensified in 1989. The effect was to unleash new depths of anti-Arab violence among Jews—and violence by extremists against fellow Jews who were considered "leftists" or, synonymously, "PLO-supporters." On more than one occasion the country's leaders found themselves having to call on the public to exercise restraint.

Yet, the messages of the leadership, too, were not always unequivocal. In May, following an incident in downtown Jerusalem in which a Ramallah man went on a knifing frenzy, killing two and wounding three others, and then was almost lynched by passersby, Prime Minister Shamir stated that such murderers "should not be allowed to escape in one piece." The following month, when anti-Arab feelings were running high following a number of incidents, it was announced that President Herzog had reduced the terms of the last three members of the Jewish underground still in prison. The three, Menachem Livni, Uzi Sharabaf, and Shaul Nir, were serving life terms for the murder of three students at the Islamic College in Hebron and other offenses. Intense and relentless behind-the-scenes political pressure was brought to bear on Herzog (he had commuted the sentences of 14 of the other 28 members of the underground), and although he occasionally condemned their deeds, in 1987 he reduced their terms to 24 years, in 1988 to 15, and finally, in 1989, to 10 years. The three were then moved to a Prisons Service yeshivah which functioned as a halfway house for "special" prisoners who had 18 months or less still to serve. Jailed in 1984, with Herzog's commutations and time off for good behavior, the three would be eligible for parole in 1990, after spending seven years in prison.

Less subtle messages condoning anti-Arab violence after terror attacks came from ultranationalist parties in the Knesset and extremist extraparliamentary groups such as Meir Kahane's Kach movement; the Temple Mount Faithful (who during Sukkot—October 16—laid the "cornerstone for the Third Temple" near the Pool of Siloam in Jerusalem); and the Kach-affiliated "State of Judea" group, established as "a possible alternative to Israeli rule if and when Israel vacates the territories." (In July it was the subject of a police crackdown; no charges were pressed, although two months earlier the group's leadership had resolved "to create an infrastructure for an army.")

One far-right group that did more than talk in 1989 was the self-styled "Sicarii," named after the Jewish zealots who assassinated suspected collaborators during the Romans' siege of Jerusalem, 67–70 C.E. The modern-day Sicarii specialized in setting fire to the front doors of apartments of persons they believed had "crossed the line" into the enemy camp. Their targets included Mapam MK Yair Tsaban, who had met with PLO officials; journalist Dan Margalit, for a planned interview on his TV show with Faisal al-Husseini; and pollster Mina Zemach. Her Dahaf Agency found, in a widely quoted February poll whose results appeared in the mass-circulation *Yediot Aharonot*, that 53 percent of the Israeli public supported negotiations with the PLO, provided the organization fulfilled its various pledges of moderation, including recognition of Israel and cessation of terrorism.

This finding was perhaps related to PLO chief Yasir Arafat's statements toward the end of 1988; at all events, polls conducted later in 1989 revealed a distinctly hard-line approach among the Jewish public, evidently reflecting the grim atmosphere engendered by the surging nationalist violence. In July *Ha'aretz* reported that, according to a poll conducted by a Tel Aviv University policy-planning institute, nearly half the population (46 percent) thought Israel was "too democratic"—up a full 10 percent since the last poll on the subject in 1987. In November a poll of 1,200 Israeli Jews by the Smith Research Institute, also reported in *Ha'aretz*, found that a majority (52 percent) was "ready to consider the expulsion of Palestinians if a way to peace is not found." This was the largest proportion of supporters for the "transfer" idea (the euphemism preferred instead of "expulsion" by its proponents) ever recorded by the institute. Moreover, the rise in the number favoring this mode of dealing with the problem had risen by a dramatic 14 percent since the beginning of the year—the cumulative effect of the *intifada*-related violence and of the growing incidence of terror inside the Green Line, according to the polling institute's director.

Police statistics bore this out. Inside Israel, 839 terrorist attacks were perpetrated in 1989, double the 1988 figure; stone throwing jumped by 54 percent, to 2,267 cases, and there was a minor rise in the number of Molotov cocktails thrown at Jewish targets. Terrorist outrages were sufficiently frequent, arbitrary, and widespread geographically to inject a sense of fear into a large part of the country's Jewish population.

Fear kept Jerusalem off-limits to many, although the western (Jewish) part of the city was relatively safe in 1989. (Jerusalemites themselves felt unprotected, if the fact that gun purchases in the city were up by 350 percent since the start of the *intifada* is any indication.) Still, the city had more than its share of terrorist killings. On February 18, Sgt. Shlomo Cohen, aged 21, was attacked and stabbed to death by a group of young Arabs outside the Old City's Zion Gate while walking with a friend—who was wounded—to the Western Wall for Sabbath prayers. On May 3, two people, aged 91 and 76, were stabbed to death, and three others, one a woman aged 80, were wounded by a 25-year-old Ramallah man at a bus station opposite the city's main post office; in the aftermath, police forcibly prevented followers of Meir Kahane from storming the Old City and protected Arabs from attacks by Jews on the city's streets. Prof. Menahem Stern, 64, a world-renowned expert on the Second Temple period and an Israel Prize laureate, was stabbed to death on June 22 while walking from his home across the Valley of the Cross to the National Library at the Hebrew University (at year's end no one had been arrested in the case).

Yet it was outside Jerusalem that Arab terrorism left its greatest impact in 1989. On March 21, a 29-year-old resident of the Jabalya refugee camp in Gaza stabbed to death Dr. Kurt Moshe Shellinger, aged 73, as he was walking on a Tel Aviv street. He also wounded two other passersby before being shot in the leg by a policeman and captured. Following the attack, Tel Aviv mayor Shlomo Lahat, a Likud member who espoused dovish political views, called for the introduction of the death penalty for terrorists who murdered civilians. Lahat estimated that as many as 20,000 Arabs from the territories who worked in Tel Aviv slept over in the city, despite the regulation prohibiting this.

Residents in Israel's southern coastal area, just north of the Gaza Strip, were shocked by two "nationalist" kidnappings within three months. Sgt. Avi Sasportas, 21, was last seen on February 16 while hitchhiking near Ashkelon on his way home to Ashdod for a weekend leave. Thousands of troops and civilians took part in searches for him over a wide area; on May 7 his body was discovered not far from where he was last seen. He had been shot and his body buried under half a meter of earth.

Hundreds of Ashdod residents ran wild after the news was received, chanting

"Death to the Arabs!" and savagely beating at least eight Arabs. All the Arabs in Ashdod fled the city, some under the protection of the police, who used smoke bombs and tear gas to disperse the rioters. The situation was aggravated by the disappearance of another soldier, 18-year-old Private Ilan Sa'adon, from Ashkelon, who was last seen hitchhiking on May 3 (the day of the downtown Jerusalem knifings), not far from where Sasportas was abducted. For days afterward cars bearing license plates from the territories were stoned by Jews along the roads leading from the Gaza Strip into Israel. Many Arabs were wounded and vehicles sustained extensive damage in the "counter-*intifada.*"

On May 22, a 42-year-old resident of a village near Hebron, Abd al-Aziz Zabdi, was killed when a stone hit his car near Kiryat Gat. President Herzog warned of a deterioration into "chaos" if Jews continued "to take the law into their own hands" in reprisal for Arab terror. (Despite large-scale searches, Sa'adon's body was not found, and finally the army declared him officially dead. Accomplices of the soldiers' murderers went on trial in December, although the actual killers of the two had evidently managed to flee to Libya.)

By far the worst single terrorist outrage of the year—indeed, since the "coastal road" massacre in 1977—occurred on July 6. At about 11 A.M. that day, a resident of the Nuseirat refugee camp in Gaza, Abd el-Mahdi Ghanem, aged 23, took his seat with the other 39 passengers on the No. 405 bus from Tel Aviv to Jerusalem. Some 45 minutes later, shortly after the bus completed the steep climb from the coastal plain, and just before the passengers were able to get their first glimpse of Jerusalem across the Judean Hills, Ghanem charged to the front of the vehicle shouting *Allahu akbar*! (God is great), seized the steering wheel and pulled with all his strength to the right. The bus crashed through a low stone fence and hurtled down a precipice of more than 100 meters into the ravine below, landing on its roof and bursting into flames. Fourteen of the passengers died in the crash and inferno and 27 (including the driver) were injured. Two more passengers died later of their wounds. Among those killed were two Canadians and an American.

The terrorist, tall and bearded, who sustained moderate wounds but survived—he was eventually brought to court in a wheelchair—told his interrogators that he had acted alone and did not belong to any organization, although he supported the Islamic religious movements in the Gaza Strip. He had planned the operation meticulously, making the trip from Tel Aviv, where he worked in the Carmel open-air market, to Jerusalem a number of times in the month before the attack. His motive was reportedly at least in part revenge for the shooting of a friend in Nuseirat early in the *intifada,* who was since confined to a wheelchair with a spinal injury. He himself, in common with most of the camp's 28,000 residents, had frequently taken part in clashes with Israeli security forces—11 of the camp's inhabitants had been killed in such confrontations—once even taking a plastic bullet in the hand. His family had arrived in Nuseirat in 1948, after abandoning its village near Ashdod.

Ashdod residents were among those who went on an anti-Arab spree in the days following the bus incident. The worst incident occurred on the day of the incident itself, near Netivot, in the Negev, when Kamal Samih Nasser, aged 31, from Gaza, was struck on the head and killed instantly by a large stone that was thrown through the windshield of the car he was driving from a passing Israeli vehicle; the four passengers in the car were injured. Kach supporters ran wild through the streets of Jerusalem, calling for "death to the Arabs" and attacking passing Arab vehicles and workers. Kach activists were dispersed with tear gas and riot batons, and six of them arrested, when they attacked members of the "Women in Black" group who were holding a weekly silent Friday-noon vigil in the city's Paris Square, just around the corner from the prime minister's residence. Fifteen persons were arrested when a mob gathered in front of the Jerusalem home of MK Dedi Zucker (Citizens' Rights), chanted slogans and threw stones. When the car of Labor leader Shimon Peres arrived at the funeral of one of the bus victims, a Jerusalem woman, Miriam Zarafi, aged 40, on the day after the attack—Peres was to deliver the eulogy on behalf of the government—it was stoned, and hotheads tried to get at Peres. He was forced to turn tail without even leaving the car.

These and other incidents and the seething atmosphere of outrage and frustration in the country led the cabinet to condemn the "harmful" and "irresponsible actions" of some Jews, while also acknowledging that the cumulative effect of "provocations" was "leaving its mark" on the Jewish population. President Herzog seemed to imply that the reaction of the political leadership had not been sharp enough when he stated that it was "the duty of every leader to come forth and speak out firmly and clearly in an attempt to restore sanity and put a stop to the hatred and lunacy of cowards who attack innocent Arabs, political rivals and even our leaders." On July 9, the home of the bus terrorist in the Nuseirat camp, which had been under curfew since the incident, was blown up by the army. (On October 30, Abd el-Mahdi Ghanem was sentenced to 16 life terms in prison and 24 additional terms of 20 years each.)

On July 14, with the country just beginning to recover from the shock of the bus attack, Zalman Shlein, a 64-year-old Holocaust survivor from the village of Gan Yavneh, near Ashdod, was stabbed to death by two Gaza teenagers who were members of an outlawed "popular committee." The entire village turned out for a demonstration after the murder, carrying signs deploring government inaction ("Enough of the ostrich policy") and calling for the parents of the killers to be deported. The Arabs from the territories who were employed in menial tasks in the village did not turn up for work on the day of the funeral and demonstration, but within days all was back to "normal." The homes of the two suspects were demolished.

The police learned about what turned out to be the year's final terrorist slaying in Israel—"one of the goriest" in the country's history, the *Jerusalem Post* called it—by chance. On the night of September 9, a young Ramallah man tried to repeat the July bus attack, stabbing the driver and wrenching the steering wheel to the right, above the same gully. This, time, however, the driver brought the bus to a halt; enraged passengers pummeled the would-be murderer until a passing police car took him away (and took the driver to hospital). During his interrogation the man disclosed that two nights earlier he had murdered a Jewish guard at the Tel Aviv construction site where they both worked. No one had been reported missing, but a search turned up the mutilated body of Michael Astamkar, 38. Later in the month, a West Bank Arab who was detained after he had aroused the suspicion of a bus inspector in Tel Aviv's main bus station as he was waiting to board a bus for Jerusalem, was found to be carrying a large commando knife. He told the police that he, too, had intended to plunge the bus over the cliff on the same stretch of road in order to "avenge my brothers who are being killed every day."

The country's attention was riveted on September 19 and 20 by the fire that broke out in one of Israel's most treasured nature sites, the heart of the forest atop Mount Carmel outside Haifa, known as "Little Switzerland." At 11:30 A.M. flames were spotted simultaneously at five different locations in the woodland—an unmistakable sign of arson. Before it was brought under control, after a full 48 hours, the conflagration consumed 2,000 acres, or 10 percent, of the national park, killed about 20 of the 160 rare animals that were housed in a special sanctuary there, came close to spreading to a Haifa neighborhood and a kibbutz, and forced the evacuation of Haifa University. Although thanks to better coordination and heightened vigilance, far less damage was caused by fires in 1989 than in 1988—the number of fires decreased by some 7 percent, but the acreage of forests and pasture land destroyed was halved—the Carmel fire stood out in its ferocity. It sent a shudder through both the Jewish and Arab communities in the land, seeming to afford a vision of the scorched earth that would remain if the conflict were not soon checked. Nearly 30 percent of forest fires were thought to have been caused by Palestinians' "nationalist arson," but there were hardly any more such torchings after the Carmel was ravaged.

A development that caused consternation in 1989 was the rise in the number of Israeli Arabs who turned to anti-Jewish terrorism—whether in solidarity with their brethren in the territories or in frustration at their second-class status in the country, or a combination of the two. They, however, tended to operate in more traditional ways, organizing in underground cells and utilizing weapons and means other than knives. A number of these cells were uncovered by the security forces during the year: in February it was announced that a resident of Umm el-Fahm who had been recruited by Fatah while on the hajj to Mecca had confessed to committing, along with others, acts of arson and sabotage including the torching of a kibbutz plastics factory; in July a four-member Fatah cell was uncovered in Jaffa even before it had acted; and in November, 27 Israeli Arabs—10 from Nazareth and 17 from the "Jatt National Front," named after the Triangle village where they resided—were arrested for stoning buses, torching cars of suspected "collaborators," and raising Palestinian flags.

To combat acts of terror, the security forces—the IDF and the police working in close coordination with the Shin Bet—invested tremendous efforts. Dozens of organized hostile groups were arrested in the territories, many of which had carried out attacks inside Israel. Others had attacked suspected "collaborators" and Israeli soldiers; frequently the homes of those detained were demolished or sealed.

Two of the many trials held during the year evoked bitter memories. In March the 17-year-old murderer of Ofra Moses and her son, Tal, from the Samaria settlement of Alfei Menashe, who died of burns when a Molotov cocktail hit the car they were traveling in in April 1987, was sentenced to life imprisonment by the Nablus military court (two of those three judges asked for the death penalty, which must be a unanimous decision). In December the three perpetrators of the firebomb attack on a bus near Jericho on October 30, 1988, which killed a woman, her three small sons, and a soldier, were sentenced to life imprisonment.

National Security

The cost of the *intifada,* in terms of its short- and long-range effects on the IDF's combat ability, as well as in the expenditure of monetary and human resources, continued to concern national-security policymakers. Commenting on a *Newsweek* report (May 1) that the uprising had seriously reduced the army's combat effectiveness, Defense Minister Rabin told the *Jerusalem Post* that he was certain the IDF's deterrent capability was not only "very effective," it "might even be more effective than before." His rationale was that the air force, a key element in achieving deterrence, "has not been affected in any way by the uprising." More broadly, Rabin pointed out that the Arab states did not "measure Israel's strength by the way we operate in the territories." Rabin conceded, though, that there was "no doubt" the deployment of regular and reserve forces in the territories "might, for a while, hurt their training for war." Finally, he noted, in a refrain heard throughout the year from the defense establishment, that the army had not received budgetary compensation "for our expenses in dealing with the uprising," and the funds that the military had been compelled to divert to suppressing the insurrection could have been used for weapons research and development.

An elaboration of the defense minister's assessment was offered in July by Brig. Gen. Michael Navon, the economic adviser to the chief of staff. A few days before the cabinet was to consider Rabin's request for an extra NIS 400 million ($200 million) for expenses incurred in the territories, Navon told the IDF weekly *Bamahane* that by the end of the 1989–90 fiscal year (March 31, 1990), the direct cost of dealing with the uprising would stand at NIS 1 billion, which averaged out to more than a million shekels a day. Navon spoke of "long-term implications" and said "damage" had already been done in areas such as force-building and procurement and stockpiling of matériel. In the event, the cabinet on July 23 authorized a supplementary defense budget of only NIS 150 million.

A month later, the IDF submitted its multiyear plan to the cabinet for discussion and endorsement. Although drawn up a full year earlier, the plan had not been presented due to the protracted aftermath of the Knesset elections, arguments about budget cuts, and the ongoing (and still unresolved) debate about whether to implement the navy's hugely expensive plan to modernize its submarine fleet. Overall, the plan was designed to implement the conceptual motto enunciated by Chief of Staff Dan Shomron when he took over in 1987: a "smaller and smarter" army. This entailed the broad restructuring of the IDF and the procurement of "over-the-horizon" and "high-kill ratio" weapons that would enable the IDF to retain its technological edge over the huge manpower advantage of the Arab armed forces.

But the plan's implementation was threatened, according to a "senior military source" quoted in the press at year's end, by the fact that by the end of the fiscal year in March 1990, the IDF would face a budgetary shortfall of NIS 900 million. That sum, instead of being used for genuine defense enhancement, had gone into the territories for purchasing ammunition and equipment to quell the uprising (such as the "gravel-thrower" invented by Israeli ingenuity to fight Palestinian stone-throwers in the period of the mass demonstrations) and for the construction of new prisons to accommodate the tens of thousands of Palestinians arrested, and for the upkeep of the prisoners. If the *intifada* costs were not covered by the Treasury, and if reserve duty in the territories continued on the same scale (a total of 2.5 million days in 1989), the IDF's preparations for a possible future full-scale war would be adversely affected.

On October 11, a Syrian pilot, flying low to avoid radar detection, landed his MIG-23 at a small airfield near Megiddo in northern Israel. Delight at acquiring what was described as the "most advanced Soviet aircraft to have fallen into Western hands" was tempered by awareness that the plane had not been intercepted during the seven minutes it overflew the country. Speculation that this apparent failure of the anti-aircraft defenses was in fact a deliberate omission, the result of prearrangement, was denied by the pilot, Maj. Mohammed Bassem Adel, 33, at a press conference. He said he had acted on his own, without prior coordination, in order "to live in a democratic country in which I could express my opinions freely." At the recommendation of two senior air force officers appointed by the chief of staff to investigate the incident, a colonel and a lieutenant colonel were reprimanded for an "error of judgment" and "faulty reporting." Chief of Staff Shomron told a press conference that "100 percent security" did not exist and that Israel's situation forced it to take constant "calculated risks."

As for the risks relating to Iraq, Maj. Gen. Barak said in his April briefing to reporters that that country's battered economy in the aftermath of the eight-year war against Iran would preclude its taking part in a war against Israel before 1991 at the earliest. Asked about a *Washington Post* story quoting "well-placed Israeli sources" to the effect that Iraq was proceeding with its nuclear program and was developing a delivery capability jointly with Egypt and Argentina in the form of a surface-to-surface missile, Barak said there was "at least a grain of truth" in the reports. More immediately, Israel, in messages to Jordan via the United States, during the summer, expressed its concern about intensifying Jordanian–Iraqi military cooperation. Press reports said that Jordan had allowed Iraqi aircraft to fly reconnaissance missions along the Israeli border, and that Iraq was supplying the Christian forces in Lebanon with arms—to fight Baghdad's bitter foe, the Syrians— via the southern Jordanian port of Aqaba.

Near the end of the year, official Israeli sources confirmed reports that Iraq had launched a rocket able to carry satellites into space. In late December, Defense Minister Rabin stated in the Knesset that Israel was monitoring the "technological developments" currently under way in Iraq, particularly in the realms of missiles, both intermediate and long-range, the entry into space, and nonconventional weapons. Rabin said Baghdad, spurred by the war with Iran, was devoting "tremendous" resources to these spheres, making it the Arab world's most "technologically sophisticated" state. Rabin added that Israeli efforts to induce friendly countries to scale down their military and technological aid to Iraq had been largely futile.

One of those countries was Germany. In January Finance Minister Shimon Peres, visiting West Germany, told Chancellor Helmut Kohl of Israel's "deep concern" at the fact that German firms were helping the Libyans build a chemical factory. Foreign Minister Arens requested Germany to look into reports that German companies were also aiding Iraq and Syria in their nonconventional weapons programs. At the same time, Defense Minister Rabin warned that any Arab country that attacked Israel with chemical weapons "will be smashed a hundred times harder in return." Given these alarming assessments, it was perhaps surprising that a report made in June to the Knesset's Audit Committee about the country's bomb shelters aroused hardly any public outcry. The state of private and especially public bomb shelters was reprehensible, the committee was informed, and the budgets available to ameliorate the situation were totally inadequate.

While such threats were still in the future, the situation on Israel's borders continued to be volatile, although overall, according to the Government Press Office, the number of infiltration attempts across the Lebanese, Jordanian, and Egyptian borders decreased in 1989 to 33 from 50 the previous year. The majority of the raids (20) originated in Lebanon, but there were 11 from Jordan, as compared to just one in 1988.

LEBANON, JORDAN, EGYPT

On the Lebanese front, the IDF was again active on land, at sea, and in the air. The air force was sent in sporadically throughout the year to bomb terrorist targets, particularly staging bases for raids into Israel. On June 21, Israeli warplanes attacked a base of Ahmed Jibril's Popular Front for the Liberation of Palestine–General Command in the Syrian-controlled Beka'a Valley. It was the first Israeli air strike in that sector in two years, and apparently was meant as a warning to Damascus to desist from supporting terrorist operations against Israel. Navy missile boats upheld their impressive record of protecting Israel's shores from seaborne terrorism. On April 4, two Lebanese boats bound for Cyprus were stopped, and 14 passengers thought to be terrorists were removed and taken to Israel for interrogation. Four days later, a Super Dvora fast patrol boat, the newest addition to the navy's fleet, sank a rubber dinghy carrying terrorists en route to Israel from Lebanon.

As in past years, however, it was the infantry that did most of the work in Lebanon. Not a single terrorist squad was able to cross the border into Israel, thanks to the combined efforts of the IDF and the South Lebanon Army in the Israeli-declared security zone in southern Lebanon. Israeli forces also ventured north of the security zone on several occasions in search-and-destroy operations, sometimes combining infantry, armor, and artillery, and usually targeting the Iranian-backed radical Hezballah militia. Two Israeli soldiers were killed during the year in Lebanon. Although Yasir Arafat's Fatah branch of the PLO was apparently not involved in any of the attempted raids in 1989, Israel constantly pointed out that despite Arafat's renunciation of terrorism in 1988—one of Washington's conditions for the start of a U.S.–PLO dialogue—other PLO groups were very active indeed. A Foreign Ministry booklet listed 14 attacks in or from Lebanon—the latter via Katyusha rockets, one of which wounded an infant in Metullah on May 28—carried out by PLO groups in 1989. Washington, however, largely disregarded these Israeli reminders.

The United States did not disregard Israel's abduction of Sheikh Abdel Karim Obeid from his home in southern Lebanon on July 28—although President George Bush confined himself to what the *Jerusalem Post* called a "mild rebuke." Before the affair faded from the headlines, Foreign Minister Moshe Arens was able to tell Israel Radio that "complete coordination" with Washington existed on the matter. Israel kidnapped the 36-year-old ranking Hezballah operative with the aim of trading him for three Israeli soldiers Hezballah had been holding since 1986. (Four other Israeli soldiers had been missing since the initial phase of the Lebanon War in 1982.) Israeli spokesmen, notably Prime Minister Shamir's media adviser, Avi Pazner, rebuffed international criticism of the action's "illegality," asserting that it was an "anti-terror action" and as such "absolutely legitimate"; those now condemning it, he added, had been silent when Obeid "sent people to murder and kill." According to the IDF, Obeid was active in organizing and supporting sabotage, subversion, and terrorism, and had a hand in the 1988 kidnapping of an American colonel, William Higgins, serving with UN forces in Lebanon. (Hezballah threatened to "execute" Higgins in retaliation for the Obeid kidnapping, and then released a videotape purporting to show Higgins's body after he had been hanged, but it was generally accepted that Higgins had in fact been killed months before.)

On July 31, the Defense Ministry issued a communiqué stating that "Israel calls for the immediate release of the Israeli POWs and the Western hostages held by the various Shi'ite groups in Lebanon." In exchange, Israel would release all the Lebanese Shi'ites it was holding, including Sheikh Obeid. The exchange would be carried out through the International Red Cross. Rabin, though, told reporters that Israel would not enter into talks about a prisoner exchange until "definite signs of life" were received from the missing Israeli soldiers. But a sign of a different kind came: five Israeli soldiers were wounded, one seriously, when a man said to be a friend of Sheikh Obeid's blew up the car he was driving, and himself with it, as he passed next to an Israeli military vehicle in southern Lebanon. At year's end, no prisoner exchange had taken place and Sheikh Obeid remained in an Israeli prison.

The heating up of the Jordanian border gave cause for concern, although Israeli military and political spokesmen noted that King Hussein's regime was making every effort to prevent such incidents. On March 17, an Israeli soldier was killed when a patrol was ambushed in the Arava desert by terrorists purportedly from the Syrian-backed Abu Musa faction; and on September 2, two reservists were killed in a firefight with a lone terrorist who ambushed a foot patrol after crossing the Jordan River near Kfar Ruppin. Following a Katyusha rocket attack from Jordan on September 7—the missiles landed harmlessly in the Jordan Valley—Prime Minister Shamir stated, in an interview with Israel TV's Arabic language service, that it was the "responsibility of the Jordanian authorities" to prevent such incidents.

The infiltrations from Egypt were more successfully dealt with. On March 15, two gunmen attacked an IDF base at Rafah, just across the Egyptian border, throwing grenades. Both were captured. On December 5, five terrorists who crossed from Sinai into the Negev were killed after a pursuit by Israeli forces across forbidding terrain. This time, the five gunmen were from Arafat's Fatah organization.

OTHER SECURITY MATTERS

On May 3, the Supreme Court began hearing the appeal of Mordechai Vanunu, the former technician at the Dimona nuclear facility who was sentenced in 1988 to 18 years in prison for treason and espionage after he divulged information about the plant to a London paper. (See AJYB 1990, p. 482.)

In March Nahum Admoni, 60, head of the Mossad intelligence agency for the past six years, retired after a 35-year career. Admoni's name was made public only on his retirement, and the name of his successor, too, would not be revealed during his term of service. In January, in a historic ruling, the Supreme Court restricted the power of the military censor and allowed the Tel Aviv weekly *Ha'ir* to publish an article about the outgoing Mossad chief (without revealing his identity) which claimed he was being dismissed for incompetence. The court held that freedom of speech overrode security considerations unless there was a "near certainty" that such freedom would threaten national security.

International Relations

UNITED STATES

Relations between the newly installed Bush administration and the Israeli government went somewhat askew this year. President George Bush and Secretary of State James Baker entered office determined to advance the Middle East peace process and committed to the pursuit of human rights. In their perception, Israel was wanting on both counts: recalcitrant on the peace issue and guilty of ongoing human-rights violations in the occupied territories, particularly since the start of the *intifada*.

The release in February of the State Department's annual report on the observance of human rights worldwide, with a hefty, and largely damning, chapter devoted to the situation in the West Bank and Gaza during 1988, the first year of the uprising, drew a barrage of strong official responses (see above, "The *Intifada* and Responses to It"). During the year, the two countries continued to play out the ritual in which Israeli actions such as deportations of Palestinians and house demolitions in the territories were followed by U.S. condemnation of such measures as violating the Fourth Geneva Convention, in turn eliciting a reaction from Jersualem to the effect that Washington's stand was known, but Israel had to defend itself and was acting within the law as interpreted by its Supreme Court.

A more serious issue in 1989 related to the decision by the outgoing Reagan administration, at the end of 1988, to open a dialogue with the PLO, following declarations by its chairman, Yasir Arafat, recognizing Security Council Resolutions 242 and 338 and renouncing the use of terrorism. That decision, which was actively implemented by the Bush government, was anathema to the Likud, which effectively held the reins of power in the national unity government. Jerusalem missed no opportunity, especially following attempted terrorist infiltrations from Lebanon, to apprise Washington that it was being deceived by Yasir Arafat. The State Department skirted the issue by questioning Arafat's ability to control the more radical PLO groups. Going even further, an unnamed "senior official" on the plane carrying Secretary Baker home from a Vienna meeting with his Soviet counterpart, intimated that PLO operations in southern Lebanon did not constitute terrorism.

The disagreement became even more acute following Israel's adoption of its peace initiative on May 14, a plan which was deliberately designed to exclude the PLO from any part in the peace process. (See also "Diplomatic and Political Developments," above.) A month earlier, when Shamir had made a visit to Washington for talks with Bush, Baker, and others, he had presented the plan in outline form and had been encouraged to proceed by the administration. Yet, days after Foreign Minister Moshe Arens, having met with Baker in Washington for the second time in two months, stated that Washington "wholeheartedly" accepted the plan, the secretary of state delivered a speech that jolted the Prime Minister's Office in Jerusalem and played into the hands of Shamir's adversaries within his own Likud party.

Most of the speech, delivered on May 22 to the annual conference of AIPAC, the American Israel Public Affairs Committee—the main Israeli lobby in Washington—dealt with generalities concerning the advancement of the peace process, such as the need for a "comprehensive settlement" based on Security Council Resolutions 242 and 338, which entailed the principle of exchanging "territory for peace, security and recognition for Israel and all of the states of the region, and Palestinian political rights." The "more detailed version" of the Shamir proposals adopted by the Israeli government on May 14, said Baker, was "an important and a very positive start down the road toward constructing workable negotiations," even if the plan did not address "all of the issues which are involved."

Baker then went on to outline, in near-perfect symmetry, what each side should do in order to push the process ahead. "For Israel," he asserted, "now is the time to lay aside, once and for all, the unrealistic vision of a Greater Israel. Israeli interests in the West Bank and Gaza, security and otherwise, can be accommodated in a settlement based on Resolution 242. Forswear annexation; stop settlement activity; allow schools to reopen; reach out to the Palestinians as neighbors who deserve political rights." Baker also had some tough advice for the Palestinians (identical, in fact, with Israel's demands): "Renounce the 'policy of phases'. . . . Practice constructive diplomacy. . . . Amend the [Palestinian] Covenant. Translate the dialogue of violence in the *intifada* into a dialogue of politics and diplomacy."

His words went virtually unheeded in Jerusalem, which seemed to hear only the phrase about the "unrealistic vision of a Greater Israel." Shamir sidestepped the entire issue by pretending that by "Greater Israel" Baker meant something other than *Eretz Yisrael hashlemah,* the "Whole Land of Israel." With feigned puzzlement, the prime minister asked, in an Israel Radio interview (May 23), how it was possible to speak about a "Greater Israel" when "Israel is a very small country. . . . It sounds quite ironic to speak of a 'Greater Israel.' " He then went on to recite the well-known litany: "We obviously differ on the matter of settlements. This is not new. I do not see any connection between settlements and the peace process. I . . . made this completely clear during my visit to the U.S., and, as they say, we agreed to disagree."

Disagreement intensified, however, as Washington upgraded its talks with the PLO. In June, U.S. ambassador to Tunis Robert Pelletreau met with Abu Iyad (Salah Khalaf), Arafat's deputy in the PLO. In the Israeli view, such moves were "putting the peace process in reverse," as Deputy Foreign Minister Benjamin Netanyahu put it, by encouraging those who opposed peace and frightening off "the Arabs anxious to work for peace." By July, in the aftermath of the "constraints" placed on the peace initiative accepted by Shamir at the demand of three Likud ministers—a development that led the United States to have "some genuine concern," as Baker told a Paris press conference, "that perhaps as a result of the actions by the Likud party, [the Israelis] were in a sense re-evaluating their own initiative"—Shamir's top aide, Yossi Ben-Aharon, said in an Army Radio interview that relations with the United States "have reached the level of actual tension." This was followed by a report in the press quoting "security sources" as saying that at least 10 of the terrorist attacks inside Israel since Arafat's "renunciation of terrorism" in December 1988 had been perpetrated by cells affiliated with Arafat's Fatah wing of the PLO. Yet, Assistant Secretary of State John Kelly, when asked about this and other similar Israeli claims, said that the State Department had no information on such PLO involvement.

In October, Israeli leaders charged that the contents of a two-part NBC-TV series on Israeli–South African nuclear cooperation were deliberately leaked by administration officials, seeking to embarrass Israel and pressure it into accepting James Baker's five points to advance the peace process (see "Diplomatic and Political Developments"). Prime Minister Shamir, for one, took the conspiratorial view, telling Israel TV that the NBC report could be part of an effort by certain U.S. officials to "sabotage" Israel-U.S. relations, adding: "It would not be the first time."

The report itself spoke of a "full-blown partnership" between the two countries "to produce a nuclear-tipped missile for South Africa." A "CIA document" was quoted to the effect that "the first missile flight of the Jerusalem-Pretoria alliance was on July 5th," in the form of a rocket launched toward Antarctica. Israel, it was said, supplied the technology and received in return the use of test sites and "a continuous supply of enriched uranium for its nuclear warheads." Jerusalem vehemently denied the allegations. A communiqué issued following the weekly cabinet meeting on October 29 reiterated the time-hallowed formula that "the policy of the Israel government was and remains that Israel will not be the first to introduce nuclear weapons into the Middle East," stated that there was "no basis" to the report on "alleged links between Israel and South Africa in the nuclear realm," affirmed that the defense establishment "adheres scrupulously to the Inner Cabinet decision of March 18, 1987 that no new contracts will be signed between Israel and South Africa in the realm of security," and concluded: "The defense establishment did not transfer American technologies or systems containing American components from Israel to other countries without receiving permission from U.S. authorities. This applies to all foreign countries, including South Africa. The claims made in the NBC report . . . are groundless."

A few days later the *Jerusalem Post* reported that, according to a CIA closed-doors briefing to congressmen and senators, there had indeed been extensive Israeli–South African cooperation in the area of ballistic missiles, but there was no evidence of nuclear cooperation or of Israeli technology transfers to Pretoria in violation of U.S. regulations. The lid was put on this particular fracas when Secretary of State Baker stated that reports of Israeli–South African military cooperation had been "overblown." Baker added that this episode would not affect Israeli-U.S. relations.

It was difficult to know how to interpret Baker's assurance in the light of what followed. As the Israeli four-point peace initiative of May became mired in almost incomprehensible trilateral dithering about arcane procedural points, with Jerusalem insisting on getting Baker's written assurances about various "guarantees" concerning the secretary's five points (which followed Egypt's ten points and preceded Israel's six conditional points in its acceptance of Baker's five points), President Bush expressed his extreme displeasure at Shamir's posturing by refraining from inviting him to visit the White House during the prime minister's scheduled visit to the United States in mid-November to address a Jewish gathering. Not even some very unsubtle hints by Israeli officials, who all but begged for the meeting, were helpful. Only after Israel accepted Baker's five points (and despite the six conditions) did Bush extend an invitation, virtually on the eve of Shamir's departure.

Although once again Shamir succeeded in averting an open confrontation with the administration, and was able to declare on his return home (November 24) that Bush had reaffirmed the continuation and strengthening of the "special relationship" between the two countries, behind the scenes the picture was less rosy. According to the well-informed columnist Yoel Marcus of *Ha'aretz* (November 28), the Shamir visit was "embarrassing" and "humiliating" from start to finish, with the "insult" of Bush's last-minute invitation being compounded by what Bush told Shamir when the two did meet privately on November 15. In their "unpleasant" meeting, Bush "harangued" Shamir for an hour and 20 minutes: a half-hour on the settlements and human-rights violations in the territories, then on Israeli-South African military cooperation, and finally on the Sheikh Obeid affair (see "National Security"), with the president stating he would not negotiate on an exchange involving hostages.

But worse was yet to come. According to Marcus, Bush "surprised" Shamir by reciting the whole litany of charges once more at the working session between delegations from the two sides. Shamir also learned that Washington had no intention of providing Israel with secret guarantees or with any sort of veto power regarding the peace talks, and that the United States still wanted Palestinians deported by Israel and the residents of East Jerusalem to take part in the elections to be held in the territories. Marcus's conclusion: "Often in recent years [Israeli] prime ministers have gone to the United States trailing predictions of a crisis but have always returned in triumph, having proved all the doom-sayers wrong. This is the first time the predictions have come true. Shamir returned [home] with his relations with the administration in a crisis. . . . The situation will only worsen if Shamir entrenches himself behind a wall of immobility. No president likes to be duped, and certainly not a president who's not so hot on Israel to begin with."

Yet, as in past years, in the strategic domain, relations between the two countries continued to flourish. In February Chief of Staff Dan Shomron paid a three-day visit to the United States for talks on military-related regional and bilateral issues and a tour of military bases. A visit in May by Defense Minister Rabin was somewhat overshadowed by Secretary Baker's AIPAC speech, but Rabin said he had a "very good" meeting with President Bush. In a speech to senior U.S. military personnel and experts, at a meeting in Washington sponsored by the Jewish Institute for

National Security Affairs, Rabin disclosed that in April, "the first U.S. Marine battalion completed its exercise in Israel"—previous maneuvers had been limited to the company level—with the use of attack helicopters and artillery. Israeli and U.S. forces had conducted "at least 27 or 28 combined exercises" in the past few years, Rabin said. The defense minister, who also met with his American counterpart, Richard Cheney, said that Israel was "more than glad—happy and satisfied—[to accede] whenever there is a request by the [U.S.] Air Force, the Navy [or] the Army."

The year ended on an upbeat note. On December 26, the Government Press Office reported a phone call from Shamir to Bush that day, in which the prime minister congratulated the president "on his country's recent success in bringing democracy back to Panama." The two also discussed the changes under way in Eastern Europe. "In the course of the very friendly conversation," the communiqué concluded, "the prime minister wished the president a happy new year, and the president thanked the prime minister for calling."

WESTERN EUROPE

As with the United States, relations with Western Europe were affected by the Europeans' opposition to Israeli policies in the occupied territories and by their displeasure with Israel's perceived unforthcoming attitude on the peace process. Talk in January of a European Community (EC) peace initiative, which would almost certainly entail an international conference and PLO involvement—two Israeli bugaboos—led Foreign Minister Moshe Arens to blast the Europeans for supporting the PLO, which he implicitly associated with the Nazis by saying that it was "responsible for some of the worst atrocities that have been committed since World War II." In the event, no formal EC initiative materialized, but a series of ranking European visitors to Israel kept harping on the identical themes and getting the identical responses from their hosts in Jerusalem. European Parliament president Lord Plumb, heading an EP delegation to Israel for the annual dialogue with the Knesset (January 4–11), was told by Prime Minister Shamir that Europe's "consistent pro-Palestinian policies" impeded its efforts to play a useful Middle East role. Another problem, Shamir noted, was that "the Arabs have a completely different scale of values from us." The Europeans possibly had some thoughts of their own about divergent cultural values when Defense Minister Rabin told them bluntly, "Stop preaching to us," and went on, in what *Ma'ariv* called "undiplomatic language," to tell his guests that the Israeli Military Government had never behaved like "you Europeans" did toward other nations during the colonial period.

In his address to the Knesset, Lord Plumb said that the Arab-Israeli conflict could be resolved only within the framework of an international solution and that no durable peace could be achieved without a solution of the Palestinian problem, including recognition of the Palestinians' "legitimate rights." Later in the month, current EC chairman (and Spanish foreign minister) Francisco Fernandez Ordonez paid a visit, followed a few days later by French foreign minister Roland Dumas, a member of the EC's ruling troika. Both diplomats came to sound out Israeli leaders on ways to revive the peace process. (In July Deputy Finance Minister Yossi Beilin visited EC headquarters in Brussels for talks on the impact on Israel of a united EC market in 1992. Beilin castigated as "national negligence" Israel's failure to prepare its economy for 1992.)

In marked contrast to 1988, high-level diplomatic contacts took place with all the major Western European countries. In mid-February Foreign Minister Arens held what were described as "constructive and fruitful" talks in London, and in an Army Radio interview praised Prime Minister Margaret Thatcher's "profound understanding of the complexity of the problems in the Middle East" and of "the dangers facing Israel." When Prime Minister Shamir paid a two-day visit to England, in May—his first as prime minister—one week after the government adopted its peace initiative on the occupied territories, he met with Thatcher for three hours, following which she told reporters that their talk had been "full and friendly" and that she had "great understanding" for Shamir's ideas. The following day (May 23), however, Shamir heard Foreign Secretary Sir Geoffrey Howe say that the Israeli plan was still at a skeletal stage and was "fundamentally flawed" because it omitted the crucial territory-for-peace component.

A meeting between Arens and newly appointed British foreign secretary John Major, held at the UN on September 25, produced similar results. The issue in dispute was again the situation in the territories, and the atmosphere at the meeting was described as "cold and tense." In October, the British consul-general in East Jerusalem, Ivan Callan, infuriated the Israeli authorities when he ignored military curfews to enter the city of Nablus and the town of Beit Sahour, near Bethlehem, where the army was trying to break a tax revolt by the residents.

It was much the same story with France. Shamir, who was well acquainted with the country from his days as a Mossad agent in Paris, held talks with President François Mitterrand in February which were described as "very friendly and useful," but did little to bring the sides closer together on the crucial issues. In response to France's decision to upgrade the status of the PLO's mission in Paris, Shamir said France "should encourage moderates, not extremists." A meeting between Mitterrand and PLO chief Arafat in May drew sharp criticism of Arafat in Jerusalem. He was spouting the "same old lies," said Shamir's media adviser, Avi Pazner, in reaction to Arafat's apparent rejection of the Palestinian Covenant following the meeting. Shamir held another meeting, described as "very warm," with Mitterrand in November, on the way home from his U.S. visit, at which the French leader reiterated his skepticism about the Israeli peace plan because it disregarded Palestinian political aspirations. French Prime Minister Michel Rocard, in a 24-hour visit to Jerusalem (December 17–18), reassured his Israeli hosts that the soon-to-begin Paris-initiated European-Arab dialogue would not harm Israel. Shamir noted that Israel was not worried about such a dialogue, as long as it was not at Israel's expense.

Jerusalem was more concerned that West German firms' sales of nonconventional weapons and missile technology to Arab states such as Libya and Iraq would ultimately be at Israel's expense. This was one of the main themes in talks between Israeli and German leaders during the year. (See also "National Security.") Speaking to reporters at the end of a three-day visit to Israel (April 9–11), West German defense minister Rupert Scholz stated that if reports of such transactions were true ("and I emphasize the 'if' "), Bonn would "impose the necessary sanctions" on such companies. Germany did not change its mind about the need for an international conference on the Middle East even after the Israeli peace initiative was adopted, as Foreign Minister Arens was informed in Bonn by his counterpart, Hans-Dietrich Genscher, during a June visit.

Italy continued its active interest in the Arab-Israeli conflict. In a three-day visit to Israel (April 23–25), a high-powered Italian delegation headed by Prime Minister Ciriaco De Mita and Foreign Minister Giulio Andreotti sounded out the Israeli leadership about the peace plan, then in its final stages of discussion. De Mita endorsed the initiative, but qualified this (from the Israeli viewpoint) by noting that he had done so because the PLO had not rejected it. In November, Andreotti (now prime minister) told Shamir, who was in Rome on his way home from his U.S. visit, that although Italy was not against the idea of elections in the territories, autonomy could not be the "definitive status" of the Palestinians.

Relations with Spain were deepened during the year via a series of mutual ministerial visits. In March a five-day visit to Israel by Spain's minister of culture resulted in an announcement that the two countries had decided to set up cultural centers in their respective capitals. On May 23, Yitzhak Shamir became the first Israeli prime minister to visit Spain since the two countries established relations in 1986. Shamir's efforts to sell the just-adopted Israeli peace initiative encountered a cool reception from his counterpart and host, Philipe Gonzalez, who urged Israel to talk to the PLO within the framework of an international conference. Bilateral relations proceeded on a smoother keel, with a reciprocal treaty signed during a visit to Israel by Spain's justice minister in late May and a scientific cooperation agreement signed in October during a visit by the Spanish minister of science and technology. This was followed by the holding of an international conference in Madrid and Barcelona, sponsored by Tel Aviv University and the Universidad Complutense de Madrid and Spain's Higher Council for Scientific Research. On December 10, President Chaim Herzog and Mrs. Aura Herzog lunched with King Carlos and Queen Sofia during a one-day stopover in Madrid en route to a South American visit.

Other contacts with Western Europe included the first visit to Austria by an Israeli minister—Absorption Minister Yitzhak Peretz, in March—since relations were virtually frozen following the election of Kurt Waldheim as president in 1986; a visit to Israel in April by Norwegian foreign minister Thorvald Stoltenberg who, although expressing his country's "enduring friendship" for Israel, criticized its "repressive" policies in the occupied territories and raised the issue of what had become of some 20 tons of heavy water which Norway sold to Israel in 1959, and which some reports said was utilized to manufacture nuclear weapons; and a memorandum of understanding on energy resources signed during the visit to Israel of Portugal's minister of energy and industry in July.

EASTERN EUROPE

Although formal relations with the Soviet Union were not restored in 1989, informal ties continued at high levels. Following a January meeting, held in Paris, between Foreign Ministers Moshe Arens and Eduard Shevardnadze, the latter announced that the status of the Israeli consular delegation in Moscow would be upgraded and its physical working conditions improved—welcome news to delegation head Arie Levin. (In June the delegation was permitted to reoccupy the former Israeli embassy building.) Arens and Shevardnadze met again on February 22, this time in Cairo, at the Soviet official's invitation, in an effort to move the stalled peace process. Arens described their meeting as "frank, very frank"—diplomatese for problematic—noting drily: "We achieved as much progress as we had a right to expect." They did, though, decide to set up joint working committees on the peace process and on bilateral relations.

Relations in other spheres looked more promising. In the same week that the foreign ministers spoke in Paris, Israel's basketball champions, Maccabi Tel Aviv, beat the top Soviet team, CSKA Moscow, in the Soviet capital, within the framework of the European Basketball Champions' Cup tournament. It was the first time an Israeli team had played in Moscow since 1967 and the first-ever Israeli sporting victory in the USSR. Mid-February saw another first: the first Soviet ship in 22 years to dock at an Israeli port (Ashdod), in order to take aboard food and clothing collected by peace activist Abie Nathan for Armenian earthquake victims.

In other humanitarian gestures, an Israeli army medical team went to the USSR for nine days in June in order to treat burn victims from a train disaster in the Ural Mountains. The head of the Israeli delegation met with the Soviet deputy health minister, who recalled that just six months earlier, two IDF teams had gone to Armenia to aid in earthquake relief efforts. Indeed, later in the month, in the first-ever El Al flight from the Soviet Union, 61 of the earthquake victims arrived in Israel for six weeks of treatment within the framework of the American Joint Distribution Committee's "Operation Healing" program. At year's end, 50 children who were in Chernobyl during the nuclear disaster there in 1986 arrived in Israel via Aeroflot as guests of the United Kibbutz Movement, in order to undergo medical tests.

Yet, despite these events and some commercial-industrial testing of the waters between the two countries, Prime Minister Shamir told the *Jerusalem Post* in September that at the "basic level, the substantive level," the USSR's negative attitude toward Israel remained unchanged. True, there had been some "positive developments," but these were "incidental." In talks with the Soviet Foreign Ministry, "you cannot sense any change." Moreover, Shamir observed, "The Soviet Union maintains its intimate relations with the terrorist organizations"—along with "[a]ll the communist countries, to this day." Later in the month the highest-ranking Soviet official to visit Israel since 1967, Supreme Soviet member and writer Chingiz Aitmatov, met with Shamir and other Israeli leaders. The prime minister, interviewed by a reporter from the Soviet *New Times,* who was in Israel to cover the Aitmatov visit, called on Moscow to renew full diplomatic relations with Israel.

However, despite a third Arens–Shevardnadze meeting, in late September at the UN in New York, and despite Shamir's statement in a November meeting with congressmen in Washington that Israel had dropped its objections to the granting of most-favored-nation trade status to the USSR by the United States, Soviet president Mikhail Gorbachev in November turned down an Israeli request for the restoration of full relations. The request was conveyed by Italian prime minister Giulio Andreotti following Shamir's visit to Rome (see above). Explaining, Soviet spokesman Gennady Gerasimov told a press conference: "We are ready for this step on condition that the Israeli government takes steps forward in the dialogue with the [PLO]." To which Shamir's media adviser, Avi Pazner, retorted, in the *Jerusalem Post,* that Israel "cannot accept conditions for diplomatic ties." In the meantime, Agriculture Minister Avraham Katz-Oz in December became the first Israeli minister to visit Moscow since 1967, having been invited on a semi-official basis by the Soviet Academy of Sciences. Back in Israel, Katz-Oz said that he had reached an agreement for Israel to supply $30-million worth of agricultural produce to the Soviet Union.

The signing of an agricultural cooperation agreement with Hungary in January—climaxing a visit by Agriculture Minister Jenoe Vancsa, the first official visit to Israel by a Hungarian minister—signaled the start of a fruitful year in relations with that country. In February Religious Affairs Minister Zevulun Hammer became the first Israeli minister to visit Hungary. His four-day visit focused on intensifying relations with Hungary's 80,000-strong Jewish community. March and April saw visits to Israel by Hungary's transport minister and its deputy foreign minister, with the latter, Laszlo Kovacs, noting that the restoration of diplomatic ties was conditional on improved trade and economic relations.

On April 18, Israelis were stunned to learn that Prime Minister Shamir, accompanied by Justice Minister Dan Meridor, was in Hungary. Their one-day stay, in which they met with Prime Minister Miklos Nemeth and other top officials, remained largely shrouded in mystery, although Meridor was quoted as saying that the visit's aim was to acquaint "the Soviet bloc" with Israel's peace proposals. Rumors of Hungarian displeasure that Israel had reneged on pledges to organize Israeli and Jewish investment in Hungary were denied. Exactly five months later (September 18), Hungary became the first East European country (with the exception of Romania) to renew diplomatic relations with Israel since the 1967 Six Day War. In Budapest for the signing ceremony, Foreign Minister Arens said the Hungarians' decision was "courageous," while his counterpart, Gyula Horn, observed that the formal restoration of relations with Israel "means that Hungary is getting rid of its past mistakes." The Foreign Ministry's representative in Budapest, Shlomo Marom, was named Israel's ambassador-designate.

Following Hungary's example in 1988, Poland sent its religious affairs minister, Wladyslaw Loranc, to make the first official ministerial visit from that country to Israel since 1967. During his weeklong April visit, Loranc met with Israeli officials, visited the Yad Vashem Holocaust Memorial, and toured religious sites. Loranc's Israeli counterpart, Zevulun Hammer, in August became the first minister to visit Poland officially since 1967. One of the issues dealt with by Hammer was the Polish Catholic Church's delay in removing a Carmelite convent from the grounds of the Auschwitz death camp, despite a 1987 agreement obligating the convent's transfer. Polish religious and government officials told Hammer that the intervention of Jewish American activists had had a boomerang effect. Hammer complained to his hosts about manifestations of anti-Semitism connected with the convent issue.

A month later Prime Minister Shamir helped fuel the controversy when he said in a *Jerusalem Post* interview that Poles "suck in [anti-Semitism] with their mother's milk! This is something that is deeply imbued in their tradition, their mentality." Polish president Wojciech Jaruzelski's spokesman declared that Shamir's comment "contradict[ed] the long tradition of Polish-Jewish coexistence in Poland" and "added a political, social and economic aspect" to the convent dispute. Shamir's bureau chief, Yossi Ahimeir, responded that Shamir drew a clear distinction "between events of the past and what is relevant for relations with the Polish people in the present and future." Israel, he added, sought "warm ties and full diplomatic contacts" with Poland. But that such ties would unavoidably be tinged with past memories was indicated when Ahimeir added: "In the final analysis, you cannot expect someone who narrowly escaped being a victim and whose father escaped from the Nazis only to be murdered by his fellow Poles, to forget about Polish anti-Semitism." But the year ended on an upbeat note in the form of a four-day visit at the end of November by Finance Minister Peres, who declared—notwithstanding Tourism Minister Gideon Patt's statement, while Peres was in Poland, that Israel should not be in a hurry to help Poland—that he had come "to open a new chapter" in relations between the two countries.

The long-standing cooperation in various spheres between Israel and the Ceaucescu dictatorship in Romania was evidently one of the reasons for Israel's delay in encouraging those who were behind the uprising in that country at year's end. The Knesset presidium on December 20 refused to recognize the urgency of three motions deploring the massacres perpetrated by the Ceaucescu regime, while the Foreign Ministry, although expressing "deep regret" at the loss of life in Romania, also did not condemn the regime. On December 23, a spokesman for Prime Minister Shamir said blandly that Israel was closely following the situation in Romania. This silence was explained as deriving from concern for Romania's 20,000-strong Jewish community and from a desire to have Bucharest continue to serve as a transit point for Jews en route to Israel from the Soviet Union. On December 24, the Israeli government finally acknowledged the new government in Romania, sending a message of cordial greetings and best wishes to the government and people of Romania.

EGYPT

On February 26, exactly one month before the tenth anniversary of the signing of the Israel-Egypt peace treaty, representatives of the two countries signed an agreement bringing to an end the dispute over Taba. The tiny, nonstrategic strip of coastline just south of Eilat, on which stood an Israeli luxury hotel—built after the signing of the Camp David accords—and a holiday village, was the last unresolved territorial element in the implementation of the March 26, 1979, peace treaty. It had soured relations between the two countries throughout the 1980s. In September 1988 an international panel of arbitrators awarded Taba to Egypt, but a number of issues still required discussion: Israeli access to Taba, the price the Egyptians would pay for the tourist sites, and the exact angle of the line running from Pillar 91, one of the disputed border points—the arbitrators had accepted the Egyptian position regarding its location—down to the seashore. In conjunction with the final settlement, Israel also wanted Cairo to pay the compensation it had promised for the killing of seven Israelis by an Egyptian policeman at Ras Burka in Sinai in 1985.

Talks aimed at implementing the arbitrators' decision began on January 19 at Taba's Aviya Sonesta Hotel, but the two-day round ended acrimoniously when Egypt's negotiator, Nabil el-Arabi, revealing the depth of his country's mistrust of Israel on the Taba question, demanded that Israel submit a timetable for withdrawing from Taba even before agreement was reached on Israeli access to the area. Egyptian sovereignty was supposed to have been restored in Taba by January 29, but when this date passed with the situation stalemated, President Hosni Mubarak branded Israel's behavior "repulsive," although he subsequently conveyed a mollifying message to Foreign Minister Arens. In the event, the U.S. mediator, State Department legal adviser Abraham Sofaer, who had played a key role in the Taba affair, got the sides to sign an agreement extending the deadline to February 28. Arens's visit to Cairo a week before that date for talks with Mubarak and Foreign Minister Esmat Abdel Meguid (and with his Soviet counterpart) helped clear up the final obstacles.

On February 26, the agreement was signed by al-Arabi for Egypt, Foreign Ministry director-general Reuven Merhav for Israel, and Sofaer as witness. Egypt waived its demand about the line from Pillar 91, giving Israel an additional 300 meters of shoreline. The luxury hotel went for $40 million and the holiday village—amounting, as the *Jerusalem Post* noted, to "a few huts on a beach which harbors what are now only memories of heady, bohemian days"—for $1.15 million. The Egyptian authorities and the hotel's owners agreed on the facility's future management. Arrangements were worked out to ease procedures for Israelis wishing to cross into

Taba (where Egyptian law would prevail) and southern Sinai, a favorite Israeli holiday area since 1967. Speaking at the signing ceremony, the Israeli delegation head, Reuven Merhav, said that Taba, "despite its small size, has become a symbol of complex negotiations, but it must . . . be turned into a cornerstone for cooperation in the best spirit of our peace treaty, and a springboard for the strengthening of mutual confidence between us." On March 15, the Egyptian flag was raised at Taba.

Although the Arens visit to Cairo marked the end of Egypt's undeclared boycott of the Likud, Prime Minister Shamir's hope of a summit meeting with Mubarak was not fulfilled in 1989. (Mubarak did phone him in September, following a meeting with Arens in New York, stating that he was ready in principle to meet, provided concrete results could be assured in advance.) In a statement to the cabinet on March 26 marking the tenth anniversary of the signing of the peace treaty, Shamir observed "with satisfaction" that peace with Egypt was by now "an integral part of our international relations." He added, however, that the "quality of the peace is not precisely as we would wish it," pointing to areas such as tourism from Egypt, more trade, cultural ties and a "more positive attitude toward Israel" in the Egyptian media.

The disparity between the two countries in tourism was glaring enough: figures released on March 27 by the Central Bureau of Statistics showed that since 1980 only 40,000 Egyptians had visited Israel, whereas in the same period 343,000 visits by Israelis to Egypt (including stays of up to a week in Sinai) took place, two-thirds of them since 1986. And in mid-April, Israel's ambassador to Cairo, Prof. Shimon Shamir, protested, at Jerusalem's request, a new spate of attacks on the Israeli prime minister in the Egyptian press, including one reference to him as "Hitler number two" and a description of him by Mubarak as "an obstacle to peace."

In early June, Arens sent a congratulatory message to his Egyptian counterpart following an Arab summit conference at Casablanca in which Egypt regained full membership in the Arab League (from which it had been suspended for signing the peace treaty with Israel). At the same time, Arens noted that some of the Casablanca resolutions, such as recognition of the Palestinians' "right of return," which Egypt also supported, ran counter to the spirit of the Israeli-Egyptian peace. President Mubarak, in a letter to Prime Minister Shamir sent via a U.S. senator visiting in the region, stated that Israel need have no cause for concern about a shift in Egyptian policy. This was followed (June 11–12) by a visit to Israel by Minister of State for Foreign Affairs Butros Ghali, the highest-ranking Egyptian official to visit in two years. Ghali, too, brought a letter from Mubarak to Shamir, this one containing an offer to have Cairo help advance the peace process—the Ghali visit took place less than a month after Israel adopted its initiative on the territories. In his talks in Israel, however, Ghali made it clear that in Egypt's view, no progress was possible without the PLO. (See "Diplomatic and Political Developments.")

On the ground, the consolidation of the Israeli-Egyptian peace continued to inch forward. On June 28, the first two of nearly 500 expected families crossed from the so-called Canada refugee camp in the Egyptian part of the town of Rafah, which was split in two in 1982 when Israel vacated Sinai under the peace treaty, into Gaza, to be reunited with their families. Their return had been held up for seven years due to "political and budget" problems, according to an Israeli army spokesman, but the Palestinians charged that pressure by Jewish settlers in Gaza against their return was responsible for the delay. In the months that followed, another 17 families crossed into Gaza, having given up their right, under the treaty, to build new homes. But in December, when five families crossed into Gaza with the intention of building new homes, hundreds of angry settlers demonstrated, alleging that over the years the PLO had "systematically" trained the returning refugees, with the result that "6,000 more terrorists are going to join the *intifada.*"

AFRICA, ASIA, LATIN AMERICA, CANADA

Relations with black Africa were advanced on November 3, when Ethiopia announced that it had decided to restore diplomatic relations with Israel, severed since the 1973 Yom Kippur War. The move gave hope that the approximately 16,000 Ethiopian Jews who had been stranded in the country when "Operation Moses" became public in 1985 would soon be able to rejoin their families in Israel. Speculation about the reasons for Ethiopia's decision, which followed two years of behind-the-scenes talks, ranged from the Mengistu regime's desire for Israeli military aid in its fight against the Eritrean and Tigrean rebels, to a need for Israeli agricultural know-how, to the hope for better access to Washington via the Israeli lobby.

In August, Foreign Minister Arens visited Kenya, which had renewed ties with Israel in 1988, signing what a Kenyan official described as an "all-embracing" agreement, "more or less what we used to have before we broke relations in 1973." The accord focused on economic and technological cooperation. An aviation agreement was signed the following month when Kenya's transport and communications minister, Josef K. Mwosa, visited Israel. July saw a four-day visit to Israel by Central African Republic president Gen. Andre Kolingba. A visitor who was greeted with mixed feelings was South Africa's Anglican archbishop and Nobel Peace Laureate Desmond Tutu, who spent the Christmas season in Israel and the occupied territories. Tutu caused anger when he equated South Africa's apartheid policy and Israeli policy in the territories. He told the Palestinians he supported their "struggle for justice, for peace, for statehood and independence," and the Israelis that "Israel has the right to exist, to territorial integrity and to the security due to an independent state."

The Israeli presence in Asia got a boost when Foreign Minister Arens and his Chinese counterpart, Qian Qi Chen, meeting at the UN in October, agreed on the establishment of an Israeli academic center in China, following the opening of a Chinese tourism mission in Israel. Relations with Japan, long kept on a low burner by Tokyo, gathered momentum. In a gesture that drew considerable appreciation in Japan, President Chaim Herzog attended the funeral of Emperor Hirohito in February, paying a condolence visit to his successor, Akihito. In September Japan for the first time invited an Israeli Industry and Trade Ministry representative to pay an official visit. (Israeli-Japanese trade passed the $1-billion mark in 1989, some two-thirds of it accounted for by Israeli diamond exports, making Japan Israel's third largest individual trading partner after the United States and Britain.) The year was capped by the first-ever visit by an Israeli foreign minister to Japan. In November, Moshe Arens reached agreement with Japanese foreign minister Taro Nakayama on the creation of a joint commission to improve and regularize relations between the two countries. In his meeting with Arens (November 9), Japanese prime minister Toshiki Kaifu called on Israel to negotiate with the PLO (whose head, Yasir Arafat, had visited Tokyo a month earlier, causing the Foreign Ministry to express its "regret and disappointment").

The Middle East policy of Canada also caused consternation in Jerusalem. In March Israel protested Ottawa's decision to upgrade its relations with the PLO, and although President Herzog paid a ten-day state visit to Canada in late June, the first there by an Israeli head of state, eliciting a statement of "unswerving support" for Israel by Prime Minister Brian Mulroney, in November a visiting senior official from the Canadian Ministry of External Affairs heard concern about "a negative trend in relations" between the countries from his interlocutors in Jerusalem.

Relations with South America were boosted by a visit to Argentina and Uruguay by President Herzog in December. In Buenos Aires he was given what the *Jerusalem Post* described as "the warmest of receptions" by President Carlos Menem. Argentine defense minister Dr. Jose Horacio Juanarenas visited Israel in April at the head of a ranking military delegation and was reported to have expressed an interest in the Israeli-made Kfir jet fighter.

Despite its good relations with Panama, Israel in September complied with an American request to express its support for Washington's efforts to depose Gen. Manuel Noriega. (President Bush had asked the world's democracies to "reassess" their ties with Panama if Noriega did not resign by September 1.) In August Jerusalem found itself constrained to react following allegations by NBC-TV that a former colonel in the Israeli army, Yair Klein, 44, along with other Israelis in his employ, had given military training to the Colombia drug cartel. A Foreign Ministry communiqué noted that Israel was looking into the matter but was "strongly committed to the war on drugs."

Israel and World Jewry

The Prime Minister's Conference on Jewish Solidarity with Israel, held in Jerusalem March 20–22, was widely viewed as an attempt by Prime Minister Shamir to demonstrate that he had the support of world, and particularly American, Jewry, two weeks before a crucial visit to Washington for talks with the heads of the newly installed Bush administration who were pressing him to present a peace plan. As such, many Diaspora leaders were leery of associating themselves with what was perceived as the policy of the Likud wing of the national unity government. Much the same attitude was expressed in the Israeli Labor party, even though its Minister Without Portfolio Mordechai Gur worked closely with the conference chairman, the Likud's Ehud Olmert, also a minister without portfolio and a close associate of Shamir. (Gur's high-profile presence did indeed serve to make the event more palatable to those who did not wish to be perceived as backing a Likud show.) The prime minister himself reportedly believed the conference was necessary to rally Jewish support in the wake of the flaccid reaction of U.S. Jewry to Washington's decision to launch a dialogue with the PLO in December 1988. (According to the *Jerusalem Post,* Deputy Foreign Minister Benjamin Netanyahu berated American Jewish leaders, in a meeting he held with them in January during a U.S. visit, for their "weak and ineffective response" to the launching of the U.S.–PLO dialogue.)

In the event, some 1,500 prominent Diaspora figures turned up in Jerusalem for three days of speeches—mainly by cabinet ministers—working groups, and briefings on some of the problems facing Israel. The climax of the event was a ceremony at the Western Wall at which the Jerusalem Declaration of Jewish Solidarity with Israel was read out and affirmed. "Linked by our common history and shared destiny," it asserted, "we support the democratically elected government of national unity in its effort to achieve peace and security with its neighbors."

AMERICAN JEWRY

Shamir played his hand well among the American Jewish community during his U.S. visit in April, capitalizing on the credit he had accumulated at the solidarity conference. In a speech to the Conference of Presidents of Major Jewish Organizations, Shamir outlined his proposals for elections in the territories, adding that measures Israel had taken to quell the uprising there "will no longer be necessary" once "the riots and manifestations of violence" had ceased. Shamir also reassured an audience of rabbis from the three major movements in Judaism that the "Who is a Jew?" issue—the notion of rewording the Law of Return in conformity with Orthodox demands—"is not on our agenda, even though the problem has not been solved permanently." By November, however, when Shamir paid his second U.S. visit, the differences and divisions within the American Jewish community, heightened by the prime minister's apparently inflexible stance on the Israeli peace initiative which bore his name, resulted in a far less enthusiastic reception for the Israeli leader. During his visit Shamir received a letter from 41 leaders, from the heart of the American Jewish establishment, urging him not to rebuff Washington's efforts to set up an Israeli-Palestinian dialogue and to be more forthcoming on the land-for-peace question. Signatories included Hyman Bookbinder of the American Jewish Committee, Edward Sanders of AIPAC, and three former heads of key Jewish organizations: Theodore Mann (Conference of Presidents), Morton Mandel (Council of Federations), and Peggy Tishman (UJA-Federation of New York). However, the current head of the Conference of Presidents, Seymour Reich, declared that American Jewry was "solidly behind the prime minister," that there was "no break in organizational ranks," and that the letter's authors were "a few individuals who are out of sync with the Jewish mainstream."

In his speech to the General Assembly of the Council of Jewish Federations in Cincinnati (November 16), Shamir, who had been raked over the coals the previous day by President Bush (see "International Relations—United States"), omitted the moderate-sounding phrases which had characterized his April address. Israel, he inveighed, "will not be pressured into committing national suicide. . . . For Israel, every step toward that common objective [of peace] is fraught with risk. One blunder can be fatal." Returning to Israel, he dismissed the "dissenters" from his policies among American Jewry as no more than a "vocal minority," and in an appearance a few days later before the Knesset's Defense and Foreign Affairs Committee, he blasted the "libelous" efforts of certain (unnamed) MKs to incite American Jewish opinion against him.

DEMJANJUK POSTSCRIPT

On June 14, Israel Yehezkeli, 70, a Holocaust survivor who threw acid at attorney Yoram Sheftel, the defense lawyer for convicted Treblinka war criminal John (Ivan) Demjanjuk, was sentenced to five years in prison. He was also ordered to reimburse Sheftel for an operation on his eye by a Boston opthalmologist ($6,000) and to pay him another NIS 10,000 ($5,000) for his suffering. (See AJYB 1990, pp. 500–501.)

Soviet Jewry; Immigration

That the winds of change were truly blowing through the Soviet Union was well symbolized in February by two events in Moscow: the opening of the Judaic Studies Center established by famed Jerusalem Talmud scholar Rabbi Adin Steinsaltz; and the inauguration of the Mikhoels Jewish Cultural Center. The latter event was attended by Yuli Edelshtein, who became the first former prisoner of Zion representing Soviet Jews in Israel—he went on behalf of the Jerusalem-based Soviet Jewry Zionist Forum, headed by Natan Sharansky—to meet with Soviet officials. In Moscow, Edelshtein and Dr. Mikhail Chlenov, head of the Jewish Cultural Association, representing 29 groups throughout the USSR, signed a proclamation of cooperation between Soviet Jews and those now living in Israel. March saw another symbolic occasion: the arrival in Israel of Yuli Kosharovsky, 48, the last major refusenik in the Soviet Union, who had waited 18 years before getting his exit visa. He and his wife and three sons were met at the airport by Prime Minister Shamir. Effectively, then, by early 1989, the "Zionist" element of Soviet Jewry was wholly in Israel.

Nevertheless, in late March, the *Jerusalem Post* reported that a secret document, drawn up by "top government analysts on Soviet Jewry," was predicting that "hundreds of thousands" of Jews would leave the USSR in the coming few years and that, since the United States would not be able to accept such huge numbers, they would turn to Israel. Prime Minister Shamir, pointing out that the majority of these Jews were well-educated professionals, admitted that Israel lacked "the appropriate tools" to absorb them, and consequently "we will have to create" those tools. In practice, however, besides talk and interdepartmental wrangling, little if anything was done in 1989 to prepare for this anticipated flood of immigrants.

In April the argument between the advocates of "direct absorption" and those favoring the traditional absorption centers flared up again, while the coordinator of the international campaign for Soviet Jewry in the Liaison Bureau for Soviet Jewry of the Prime Minister's Office, Sara Frankel, charged that HIAS and other groups were still trying to get Jews to settle in the United States rather than in Israel. The cabinet discussed the issue a number of times in May and June. On May 21, Immigrant Absorption Minister Rabbi Yitzhak Peretz told the cabinet that the absorption system was "in a state of collapse," with thousands of immigrants, particularly from Ethiopia, condemned to remain in absorption centers for years because they lacked the financial means to leave. However, Housing Minister David Levy asserted that his ministry would not build new apartments until the immigrants actually arrived. On May 28, the cabinet, proclaiming absorption a "cardinal national objective," formed a ministerial committee—Peres (finance), Levy (housing), and Peretz (absorption)—to submit within three weeks, "in coordination with the Jewish Agency," its solutions to the "pressing needs" of immigrant absorption.

The mud-slinging intensified in June: the head of the World Labor Zionist Movement, Yehiel Leket, charged that the "clandestine methods" of the Liaison Bureau were "anachronistic" in the "era of *glasnost* and *perestroika.*" This drove Sara Frankel to engage in a bit of *glasnost* herself, disclosing to the *Jerusalem Post* that her unit had sent Israelis to teach Hebrew in the Soviet Union, had brought Soviet Jews to Israel to study Hebrew and other subjects for teaching in the USSR, and had sent voluminous "cultural materials" to the Soviet Union for dissemination. The Liaison Bureau, she said, was "the arm of the Israeli government on the issue of Soviet Jewry," and its aim was "to foster Jewish consciousness with a Zionist orientation among Soviet Jews."

In the meantime, the joint government–Jewish Agency coordinating committee on June 25 released a communiqué which described the "prospects for a major wave of immigration to Israel," particularly from the USSR and Argentina, as "a matter of first-rate priority for Israel and the Jewish people." Consequently, "a master plan shall be prepared, as soon as possible," by the government and the Jewish Agency, to cope with the absorption of "the hoped-for immigration wave, including housing and employment." Later in the same week the Jewish Agency Assembly, meeting in Jerusalem, decided to "renegotiate"—meaning, effectively, cancel—what then-absorption minister Yaakov Tzur had called its "historic" decision to drop its role in immigrant absorption (AJYB 1990, p. 501). A few days later, the Agency's board of governors pledged that every new immigrant in Israel would be guaranteed "a place of residence." Housing Minister Levy's plan to settle new immigrants in the occupied territories was savaged by his fellow-Likud member, Jewish Agency treasurer Meir Shetreet, who declared that the government had "no real plan" for immigrant absorption and that the Jewish Agency was barred from allocating funds for projects across the Green Line.

Funding the absorption of 100,000 Jews expected to arrive from the USSR within the coming three years—this was the figure cited by all, even when it became obvious that it was wildly low—was one of the main issues addressed by Finance Minister Shimon Peres during a U.S. visit in September. Peres sought $400 million in loan guarantees from the Bush administration and at least $1 billion from world Jewry, the bulk of it from the American Jewish community, to help offset the projected $3-billion cost of absorbing the wave of new arrivals. Deputy Finance Minister Yossi Beilin stated that two-thirds of the money would be needed for new housing (30,000 units), $400 million for vocational training (half of the new immigrants would have to be retrained at a cost of $7,500 per immigrant), and $110 million would be required to build 110 new schools at $1 million each for the 40,000 school-age children. Infrastructure costs (new roads, expanded utilities) would total $490 million.

These grandiose programs remained abstractions, however. The Absorption Ministry, in growing desperation, proposed housing new immigrants in army camps, hotels, and remote development towns, although an interdepartmental committee chaired by Beilin had recommended that the newcomers be channeled to the center of the country. In late October the Housing Ministry spokeswoman chimed in by reiterating the conception propounded by David Levy earlier in the year. Noting that in the 1970s newly constructed public housing had remained empty because the expected immigration did not materialize, she stated that there was no need to start building "until the immigrants start arriving in large numbers." To offset mounting criticism, the Housing and Absorption Ministries and the government's Employment Service on October 20 ran three-and-a-half pages of ads in the weekend *Yediot Aharonot,* declaring that they were ready to absorb the mass wave of immigration. Featured prominently were photos of David Levy and Yitzhak Peretz with new immigrants.

On October 30, the government and the Jewish Agency announced that they had reached agreement on the absorption of Soviet Jews and issued a 15-point communiqué to prove it. The program, which largely followed the lines of the Beilin plan, asserted that the government and Diaspora Jewry were aware that this was a "historic moment" and that "everything possible must be done to successfully absorb [the Soviet Jews] in Israel." But the reality on the ground was rapidly making such plans and proposals irrelevant. With the gates to the United States closed since October to all but about 40,000 Soviet Jews a year, in November some 45,000 Jews in the USSR requested "invitations" from Israel so that they could obtain exit visas. The small staff at the Israeli consulate in Moscow, which had been processing the applications and issuing the visas since reoccupying the old Israeli embassy building in June, staggered under the workload; but, as Prime Minister Shamir told the Knesset's Defense and Foreign Affairs Committee at the end of November, the Soviet government would not allow the staff to be enlarged. With Shamir and others now talking about half a million to a million Jews entering Israel within three years, MK Michael Kleiner (Likud), chairman of the Knesset's Immigration and Absorption Committee, asserted that he could not take cabinet ministers' statements on the subject seriously.

By year's end, with Soviet immigration beginning to surge, Finance Minister Peres was castigating Diaspora Jewry for not raising the $500 million it had been charged with under the government-Jewish Agency plan. This was blatant "evasion of responsibility," Peres fumed in the Knesset. "Instead of giving more money to Israel, they increase the share of the [local] federations." Jewish Agency chairman Simcha Dinitz, back from Moscow, said that 360,000 "invitations" were already in the pipeline and that the Israeli consulate was issuing 200 visas a day. On December 18, Prime Minister Shamir sent greetings to the first Congress of Jewish Communities and Organizations, which opened that day in Moscow (and was attended by Dinitz). "Every bit of reawakening Jewish life is like a fresh breeze to our suffering people," Shamir wrote, but according to many officials, a good deal of suffering would be incurred by the Soviet Jews when they arrived in an Israel that was unprepared, mentally or materially, to absorb them.

Distress was the lot of many of the Ethiopian Jews who had arrived in Israel in the second half of the 1980s. A major problem was that many families had been split apart when "Operation Moses" was halted in 1985 after a leak to the press. In February a number of Ethiopian groups in Israel formed the Committee for Family Reunification, to try to spur governments and human-rights agencies "to pressure Ethiopia to allow more than 15,000 Jews still stranded [there] to join their families abroad." Israel, too, they charged, was not doing enough in this regard. That same month, the Israeli branch of the Geneva-based Defense for Children International held a press conference at which a clinical psychologist, Gadi Ben-Ezra, who worked with Youth Aliya, related that about 1,800 Ethiopian children in Israel whose parents were still in Ethiopia (or Sudan) were undergoing "acute emotional distress," leading to attempts at suicide and self-starvation. The entire 17,000-member Ethiopian community in Israel, he said, was affected by the situation.

In October the Association of Ethiopian Immigrants launched a public campaign to pressure Israel to allocate greater resources to bringing the remaining Jews from Ethiopia. The community in Israel was heartened in November when it was announced that Israel and Ethiopia were restoring diplomatic relations. At a joint press conference in Jerusalem on November 6 with Deputy Foreign Minister Netanyahu, Ethiopian presidential aide Kessa Kebede stated that his government accepted the principle of family reunification. "Those wishing to leave, as per our constitution, should be allowed to do so," he said.

Immigration to Israel rose dramatically in 1989, by 84 percent as compared to 1988. Of the 24,660 new immigrants who arrived in 1989, half (12,923) were from the Soviet Union, and of those more than 8,300 came in the year's last four months, 3,631 of them in December. (The year's final week saw 1,556 Soviet Jewish arrivals, including 460 on December 27 alone.) Immigration from the rest of the world remained depressingly low—there were fewer arrivals from the United States than in 1988, for example, and although immigration from Argentina, at 1,850, was up by some 300, the anticipated major movement of Jews from that country failed to materialize. Overall, it was the best immigration performance in a decade.

The Economy

The year began with a devaluation of 8 percent (January 1), following a 5-percent devaluation a few days earlier. This, along with big subsidy cuts, was part of an economic plan proposed by Finance Minister Shimon Peres which the cabinet approved by a vote of 18-2 (Ariel Sharon and Yitzhak Navon) on January 5, following a special 14-hour session. The gist of the program was an attempt to reduce the government deficit by NIS 1.1 billion. The method was the traditional one: across-the-board budget and subsidies slashes whose consequences would be borne largely by the public, although the government sector was to be reduced by 3 percent. One of the most controversial measures was a registration fee for high school, with low-earning families and development towns exempt—a transparent attempt (which, like many other clauses in the plan, ultimately failed to get by the Knesset or was victimized by bureaucracy) to reintroduce payment for high-school education without saying so.

Peres continued to be a lightning rod for Likud attacks all year. In February he was branded a "cheat," a "liar," and a "thief" by Likud MKs for reaching agreement on a cost-of-living allowance with the Histadrut labor federation in which the latter would accept only partial compensation for price rises, but would get higher government funding for its ailing medical insurance program, an extension of price controls, and greater taxes for high wage-earners. The package was expected to cost the Treasury some NIS 200 million. Knesset approval of the budget for fiscal 1989-90 was held up because the Likud would not vote for aid to the economically battered kibbutz movements unless money was also earmarked for the settlements in the territories. The religious parties tried to play both ends against the middle in order to get extra funding for their institutions. Ultimately, none of the three sectors was included in the budget of NIS 59.2 billion ($32.5 billion) approved in late March, but all got their cuts later in the year.

Indeed, Peres's tenure as finance minister, a job he never wanted, but which the labor movement's hard-pressed affiliated institutions and organizations insisted that he take once the idea was broached, may be remembered primarily for the rescue of the kibbutzim. Peres was able to engineer an arrangement in which the banks and the Treasury either wrote off or rescheduled at convenient terms kibbutz-movement debts of NIS 4 billion, and agreed to underwrite the kibbutzim to the tune of NIS 650 million over the coming six years. In return, the kibbutzim were to raise NIS

500 million by realizing assets and reduce their standard of living and their investments by 5 percent.

Peres's penchant for the spectacular instant solution was well demonstrated in his endeavors to solve the country's rapidly worsening unemployment problem. With some 10 percent of the workforce jobless by midyear—in some remote towns, particularly in the Negev, unemployment was over 20 percent—and reports rife of imminent large-scale immigration from the USSR, Peres in August got the cabinet to pass (14–2 and 10 abstentions) a so-called "overlords" plan. This would cut red tape by setting up a three-man ministerial committee that would approve 100 major projects within seven months and implement them by sidestepping the bureaucracy. However, with the national unity government feeling the strains of the Labor-Likud discord over the May initiative on elections in the territories, there was little chance that projects on a scale such as this could be carried out.

Peres, for his part, took to traveling around the country with a busload of officials (and reporters), explaining the projects he had in mind for various locales, and making promises. The legislation, though, was stuck in committee, with the Likud again demanding NIS 30 million for settlements as a condition of support for "overlords." In the meantime, no less a personage than the Finance Ministry's director-general, Ya'akov Lifschitz, scored the entire idea, saying it would increase inflation and that all resources should be diverted to housing construction to meet the anticipated immigration wave. At the end of September, Deputy Finance Minister Beilin removed the anti-red-tape bill from the Knesset agenda, declaring that codicils inserted by the Likud had effectively destroyed it. Finally, six weeks later, Peres himself formally asked the cabinet to kill the bill, which it did, unanimously. The Likud finally forced Peres to release the NIS 30 million for the settlements in December by threatening to block crucial income-tax legislation in the Knesset's Finance Committee.

Overall, indeed, the economic year was one of stagnation, particularly in the light of Peres's statements and plans at its start. "At the end of 1989," he told business leaders early in the year, "I would like to see three figures: 6 percent growth, inflation of 8–9 percent and an increase of 9 percent in exports." The actual figures were rather different: industrial production was down by 2 percent, the gross domestic product climbed by a minuscule 1.3 percent, private and public consumption was down by 1 percent, exports rose by only 4.6 percent. Inflation was above 20 percent (20.7) for the first time since the economic stabilization program of July 1985. Private consumption of durables was down by a full 15 percent, with some areas particularly hard hit: car sales decreased by 37 percent, and purchases of clothing and personal items declined by 10 percent on top of an 8-percent fall in 1988. One bright spot was a large fall, of $2.4 billion, in Israel's foreign debt (from $18.8 billion at the end of 1988 to $16.4 billion a year later). At the same time, the trade deficit declined from $5.2 billion in 1988 to $3.7 billion in 1989.

The effects of the *intifada* were felt less severely in 1989, indicating that the economy had largely adjusted to the situation. Overall, the two years of the uprising were estimated to have cost the economy between $800 million and $1 billion, with the great bulk of the loss occurring in 1988. Thus, according to a Bank Hapoalim newsletter, in terms of Israel's total GNP of about $42 billion, the *intifada* represented a loss of 1.5 percent in 1988 and between 0.5 percent and 1 percent in 1989.

However, there were some who continued to believe in the underlying resilience of the Israeli economy. British press magnate Robert Maxwell bought into two of the country's most successful firms, Scitex, a high-tech computer company, and Teva Pharmaceuticals; Australian investor Jack Lieberman became the sole owner of the Paz Oil Co., acquiring the final 25 percent of the company's stock not in his possession; Bankers Trust of New York agreed to a recovery plan for Koor Industries and halted its liquidation suit against the Histadrut's giant conglomerate for failing to repay a $20 million loan; and Hollinger Inc., a huge Canadian-based newspaper chain, purchased the *Jerusalem Post*. This development ultimately forced longtime chief editors Ari Rath and Erwin Frenkel to resign over the issue of editorial independence after Hollinger president David Radler installed Yehuda Levy, a 53-year-old former Israeli army colonel with no newspaper experience, as the paper's president and publisher.

Other Domestic Issues

The year saw a rise of 22 percent in the number of serious crimes committed, including murder (105 cases, a 61-percent leap), attempted murder, armed robbery, extortion, sexual assault, and arson. All told, 265,498 criminal files were opened during the year—an average of one crime every two minutes.

RELIGION

Although a public-opinion survey commissioned by the American Jewish Committee found, in May, that 51 percent of Israeli Jews thought Reform and Conservative rabbis should be accorded the same status as their Orthodox counterparts in marriage, divorce, and conversion, the High Court of Justice thought differently. On July 24, it handed down two landmark decisions in the realm of religious freedom and pluralism in Israel. In one case, the court voted 5–0 to reject the petition of two Reform rabbis asking to be allowed to perform marriages. However, although affirming the exclusive prerogative of the Chief Rabbinate (meaning Orthodox Jewry) to appoint marriage and divorce registrars, four of the five justices expressed their regret that the law (the 1953 Rabbinical Courts Law) gave them no leeway on the issue.

The court did, however, rule by 4–1 that population registry clerks were not entitled to question the halakhic status of new immigrants who declared themselves to be Jews (although a clerk could ask to see documentary proof of an applicant's Jewishness). The petitioners in this case included two political parties, the ultra-

Orthodox Shas (which controlled the Interior Ministry) and the National Religious party, as well as the Reform movement, the Association for Civil Rights in Israel, and 14 converts from the three main Judaic streams. Presiding over the panel of justices in both decisions was Supreme Court president Meir Shamgar, who, in writing the majority opinion in the second case, cited the precedent of the Shoshana Miller case. (See also AJYB 1990, p. 499; 1989, pp. 417–18; 1988, pp. 400–01.)

However, the Interior Ministry immediately found a way to circumvent the ruling. "Bowing to political necessity," the *Jerusalem Post* editorialized on July 26, "and, no less importantly, to a ruling by Shas's Council of [Torah] Sages, [Interior Minister Rabbi Arye Deri] proceeded to make a mockery of the institution of identity cards." Beginning July 31, ID cards no longer carried the signature of either the interior minister or the registration clerk; instead, a fine-print statement was added stating: "According to Article 3 of the 1965 Population Registry Law, the details registered in this document—with the exception of the categories of 'nationality' [i.e., religion], 'personal status' and 'name of spouse'—shall be considered prima facie evidence of their accuracy." Deri's predecessor as interior minister, Rabbi Yitzhak Peretz, also from Shas, had resigned rather than register the Reform convert Shoshana Miller as a Jew; but Deri found a way to retain his seat while, as the *Post* noted, doing "all he could to uphold the ultra-Orthodox reading of *halakha* [Jewish religious law] against the civil law."

At year's end the High Court handed down another benchmark decision in a case involving a religious issue, ruling that "messianic Jews" were not entitled to immigrant status under the Law of Return. The three justices determined unanimously that Gary and Shirley Beresford, originally from South Africa, and both born to Jewish parents, had in effect undergone a voluntary conversion when they joined a "Jews for Jesus" group in their native country and were therefore "members of a different faith." As such, they could apply for Israeli citizenship under the Citizenship Law but not under the Law of Return. The Beresfords entered Israel as visitors in 1986 but were turned down by the Interior Ministry when they asked for immigrant status. In court, they insisted that they were still Jews and that, in any event, they had been born Jewish and had not converted.

The High Court was also kept busy trying to settle a variety of cases of lesser principle in the ongoing struggle of the Orthodox and ultra-Orthodox religious establishments to prevent encroachment on their turf. In January the court ordered Interior Minister Deri to add his signature on the plan to build a new soccer stadium in Jerusalem; Deri had held up the start of construction for more than 18 months after all the other bureaucratic hurdles had been successfully negotiated because some Israeli National Soccer League games were played on the Sabbath (although this was not one of the various reasons he cited for not signing the document). In July a Jewish belly dancer, Ilana Raskin, won an interim injunction against the Jerusalem Religious Council from the court, when she charged that the council was effectively preventing her from appearing at social functions by threatening to withdraw the *kashrut* certificate of any hall that hired her.

In a case that was marred by violence, the High Court in August ruled, on a temporary basis, that a group of Jewish feminists called "Women of the Wall," representative of all three denominations, must worship at the Western Wall "in accordance with the custom of the site." As that "custom" was determined by the Orthodox rabbi of the Wall, Yehuda Getz, this meant that the women would not be allowed to wear prayer shawls, read from the Torah, or sing while worshipping at the Wall. On at least four occasions during the year, ultra-Orthodox worshippers, outraged by the women's actions, had physically assaulted them. In March police had to use tear gas to disperse extremists who attacked the women, the first use of tear gas at the Western Wall since 1967. In late November, the Israeli women were joined for a prayer service at the Wall—adhering to the court's instructions—by members of the International Committee for the Women at the Kotel (Wall). In a ceremony held at a Jerusalem school (scheduled to be held at a hotel, it was moved when the Jerusalem Rabbinate threatened to withdraw the hotel's *kashrut* license) the international group presented the Women of the Wall with a Torah scroll.

More than 20 alleged ultra-Orthodox extremists aged 18–30 were arrested by Jerusalem police, assisted by members of the antiterror unit, in two February sweeps through the Me'ah She'arim quarter. The detainees were suspected of belonging to an underground organization called Keshet, an acronym for *"Kvutza Shelo Titpasher"* (a group that will not compromise). The group's main activity consisted of planting bombs at the shops or homes of vendors of "secular" newspapers in the city of B'nei B'rak.

Israel's drug problem drew heightened attention during the year. A newly established government-sponsored body, the War on Drugs Authority, urged the establishment of a series of drug treatment centers to bolster the five already in existence, but in the meantime a new law, passed in July, increased police powers in combating drug traffickers and sharply stiffened the fines the courts could impose on users and dealers. A Health Ministry survey released in August found that there were 18,000 hard-drug addicts in the country, with twice that number using drugs regularly. The report said that drug use had increased by 25 percent per year in each of the past three years. Other officials said the problem had reached "epidemic" proportions and that no fewer than 200,000 Israelis, nearly 5 percent of the total population, were hard-drug users of one degree or another. A police estimate said that 1.5 tons of heroin were smuggled into Israel annually, primarily from Lebanon.

A problem of daily concern to Israelis, the government bureaucracy, was the object of a report by a blue-ribbon commission headed by former Interior Ministry director-general Haim Kubersky. The team's three-year study found, to no one's surprise, that the civil service was "bloated" in size and "mediocre" in quality. The commission called for the restructuring and depoliticizing of the civil service and less government interference in society.

In July the Maccabiah Games, the "Jewish Olympics," celebrated its bar mitzvah in 10 days of events, with the participation of 4,500 athletes from 47 countries, including a contingent from Lithuania. The closing event included a march by the participants through the streets of Jerusalem and a torchlight ceremony at the Western Wall. Not far from there, in a ceremony held some six weeks earlier, the cornerstone was laid for the development of the Mamilla Quarter, opposite the Old City wall, following 16 years of wrangling over the plans for the hypersensitive site. The bulk of the $250-million project was to be completed within four years.

Israel's population stood at 4,560,000 at the end of 1989, with hopes running high for a major population boost in the form of the surging immigration from the Soviet Union. In 1989 the population grew by 1.8 percent, up slightly from 1988 but below the annual average of 2.4 percent for the decade. Jews accounted for 81.5 percent of the population (3.7 million, an increase of 1.6 percent over 1988); Muslims for 14.4 percent (655,000, an increase of 3.2 percent); Christians for 2.2 percent (107,-000, an increase of 2.2 percent); and Druze and others for 1.8 percent (80,000, an increase of 2.8 percent). The Jewish proportion of the population in Galilee continued its slow but steady fall, standing at 47.8 percent of the total in that district. In the occupied territories, however, the Jewish population increased by 9.8 percent, standing at 73,000 at year's end.

Personalia

Personalities who died during the year included Dvora Netzer, founder and longtime head of the Working Mothers Organization (afterward Na'amat) and a Mapai Knesset member for 20 years, on January 4, aged 92; Yitzhak Tunik, Israel's third state comptroller (1982–87) and a former president of the Israel Bar Association, January 9, aged 77; David Laskov, the Israeli army's oldest soldier and an Israel Prize laureate for the invention of weapons systems, February 4, aged 87; Moshe Kol, veteran political leader of the Independent Liberal party, former cabinet minister, and a signatory on the Declaration of Independence, July 7, aged 78; Shmuel Rodensky, best known for over 1,800 appearances as Tevye the Milkman in the Israeli production of *Fiddler on the Roof,* and an Israel Prize winner for his life's work on the stage, July 16, aged 84; Binyamin Tammuz, noted writer and artist and a leading figure in the "Canaanite" movement in the 1940s, July 19, aged 70; Aviva Uri, considered Israel's leading abstract-expressionist painter, September 2, aged 62; Arye Dulzin, former chairman of the WZO and the Jewish Agency, a leading member of the Liberal party, and a member of the national unity government in 1969–70, September 13, aged 76; Dov Sadan, Hebrew University professor emeritus of Yiddish and an Israel Prize winner in Judaica, October 13, aged 87; Dahn Ben-Amotz, bohemian author and archetypical *sabra,* who held a "wake" to part with his friends upon learning he had incurable cancer, October 20, aged 66; Dorothea Krook-Gilead, professor of English literature, who helped shape two generations of students in Jerusalem and Tel Aviv, and an Israel Prize laureate,

November 13, aged 69; and Elisheva Cohen, emeritus chief curator of the Israel Museum, an Israel Prize laureate for her contribution to the advancement of the arts, December 20, aged 78.

RALPH MANDEL

Israeli Culture

ISRAEL, AT THE END OF THE 1980s, was a society with an impressive and dynamic cultural life. In poetry and music, fiction, art, and philosophy, Israel maintained a pace of creative achievement and intensity unmatched by many older, larger, and wealthier countries.

An important measure of Israel's vitality is that its cultural life is nourished largely from within. Despite Israel's openness to the West and the admiration for European or American culture which many intellectuals and artists profess, Israeli culture is distinctive not only in its flavor and shadings but in its content and core concerns. This distinctiveness is evident in the basic questions which Israeli literature, art, and thought address, in the manner in which new trends in literature and art react and respond to previous movements so as to form a uniquely "Israeli" tradition, and in the continued importance and influence within Israeli culture of seminal writers and thinkers that Zionism and the reality of the Jewish state have produced over the last 70 years.

The breakdown of Zionist ideology and the unresolved questions concerning self-definition which marked Israel in the 1980s did not seem to stymie the flow of creativity in Israeli literature and art as the decade drew to a close. Instead, these crises of identity prodded artists and writers into a deeper engagement with the past and present, releasing new sources of enrichment and inspiration.

Literature: Fiction

As the 1980s drew to a close, literature in Israel, and especially the prose forms, benefited from a double blessing: Mature writers such as A.B. Yehoshua and Amos Oz, David Shitz, and Yehoshua Koren continued to produce major works, while a younger generation with an abundance of talent and a new perspective on Israeli life brought fresh vitality to an already vigorous literary scene.

What distinguishes the wave of new prose being published in Israel from earlier Israeli fiction? New Israeli fiction is both more pluralist and more populist than the fiction which dominated the Israeli literary scene until the latter part of the 1980s. Writers of "the Native Generation"—a term used to describe the first generation of writers (such as Oz, Yehoshua, and Yaakov Shabtai) to come of age after the creation of the state—sought to create heroes and narratives which would define the meaning and nature of Israeli identity. However critical or ironic was their treatment of Israeli life, these writers assumed that there was a representative Israeli, and a single, more or less coherent, center to Israeli society. Contemporary Israeli fiction shows, however, as *Ha'aretz* critic Ariel Hirschfeld has said, that "there is a feeling that the word 'Israeli' does not mean one thing anymore, but is a collection of many things, very different from one another." While the classic hero of Israeli fiction was likely to be an Ashkenazi, secular, and a Sabra (native-born Israeli), new Israeli fiction is just as likely to be by or about immigrants, women, oriental Jews, religious, or formerly religious, Jews. This kind of fiction is more concerned with illuminating one aspect of Israeli existence in depth than making a statement about Israeli society as a whole.

Although David Grossman did not publish new fiction in 1989, his second novel, *See Under: Love* (published in 1987), is worth mentioning as an influential example of the trend in Israeli fiction described above. Grossman's hero in *See Under: Love* is the child of poor immigrants—Holocaust survivors—living in a neighborhood on the outskirts of Jerusalem. It is the shadow of the Holocaust, and not the promise or the disappointments of Zionism, which constitutes the inner world of Grossman's hero. The Native Generation in Israeli fiction wrote about the existential dilemmas of a new kind of Jew—the Israeli—who was the product of a conscious break with the past, with the Diaspora and all that it represented. Grossman's novel is concerned, in contrast, with links between generations, with the penetration of the present by the past, with the power and authenticity of private universes of experience.

Bernhard, one of the important new novels published in 1989, is an attempt to reconstruct the innermost experience of a German Jewish immigrant living in the Rehavia neighborhood of Jerusalem during the years of World War II and just before them. Yoel Hoffman, who wrote *Bernhard,* is an academic expert on Zen Buddhism; his style in *Bernhard* is both concise and poetic, like a Zen text. *Bernhard* is a lyrical and meditative work, written as a series of stream-of-consciousness musings which touch upon the most basic of questions. There is hardly any plot to *Bernhard:* its hero is absorbed in mourning for his late wife; he hears distant reports of the fate of European Jewry but these are always partial and fragmented. Through his isolated hero and his attempt to represent a group of immigrants who arrived in Israel more than 40 years ago, Hoffman pierces deep into the ground of all human experience: human consciousness, in the broadest and most universal sense of the word, is the real hero of *Bernhard.*

Dan Benayahu Seri, whose second book of short stories, *Birds of the Shade,* was published in 1989, writes about yet another kind of Israel: the poor Bukharan and Yemenite neighborhoods of Jerusalem and Tel Aviv. Seri's language and his storytelling devices reflect the oriental milieu of his settings: places where tradition, superstition, and families that span several generations are, if not intact, still a formidable presence. Seri's work has a folkloristic flavor to it, but he is sharp and sometimes bitter, more grotesque than nostalgic in his portrayals. He combines the simplest street language with an exceptionally rich, expressionistic, literary Hebrew, to startling effect.

Gershon Shaked, a prominent critic and historian of Israeli literature, remarked that 1989 might properly be called "the year of the woman" in Israeli fiction. Shaked was referring in particular to three women—Orly Kestel Blum, Chana Bat Shachar, and Yehudit Katzir—who were at the beginning of their path as writers; each published a collection of short stories in 1989 that met with both critical acclaim and popular success.

Orly Kestel Blum's collection of short stories *Hostile Surroundings* was her second in three years. Kestel Blum writes about men and women who exist on the periphery of society: criminals, prostitutes, alienated teenagers. She mixes literary styles together in anarchic fashion, alternating between—and sometimes combining—flat realistic language which mimics ordinary speech and fantastical plot devices that emphasize the absurdity of her heroes' lives. Kestel Blum's writing provokes strong reactions among critics and readers. Her admirers argue that she is highly original and that her shock techniques are an effective weapon aimed at unsettling the complacent Israeli bourgeoisie. Her critics say that she is gimmicky and capricious, that her anarchism is nihilistic, and that her originality is devoid of content.

Chana Bat Shachar is a pseudonym taken by the daughter of a prominent Orthodox rabbinical figure, herself the mother of five children and living an Orthodox life-style. The stories in her collection *To Call the Bats* describe an inner world colored by the tension between repression and desire. The heroine in *To Call the Bats* is usually a young or middle-aged woman from an Orthodox background; the stories are particularly concerned with relationships between fathers and daughters. The various episodes in *To Call the Bats* take place along the fluid borderline where secular and religious society in Israel meet. As with Seri's stories and Hoffman's novel, Bat Shachar uses her literary gifts to bring a setting or sector neglected in modern Israeli fiction into the mainstream of cultural life. According to Gershon Shaked, *To Call the Bats* is "a deep, intense, complex, and extraordinary book."

Yehudit Katzir was the first writer of her generation to write about growing up in Israel. At 26 the youngest of the writers we have mentioned, Katzir writes "like a family photographer" about Israeli childhood in the 1960s and '70s. Childhood, for Katzir, is not a world lost and longed for, but a place where both life and death are foreshadowed suddenly, amidst the seemingly reassuring trappings of bubble gum and afternoons at the movies. Her narrative voice moves back and forth between a childlike quality, innocent and enthused, and an adult knowingness or irony.

In addition to such relative newcomers as Bat Shachar and Benayahu Seri, Hoffman, and Katzir, writers such as Amos Oz, Aharon Appelfeld, and David Shitz, who have been prominent for 20 years or longer, published novels and collections of short stories in 1989.

Amos Oz's work *To Know a Woman* tells the story of Yoel, a former Mossad agent who has retired, though still middle-aged, after the death of his wife. Yoel's erotic musings, the regrets that haunt him, and his efforts to find a modicum of peace of mind are the main concerns of *To Know a Woman*. Oz's novel disappointed most Israeli critics, who found it shallow and passionless. Some critics suggested that Oz's writing had reached a stage of decline; since Oz was perhaps the representative writer of the Native Generation, they saw in his decline further evidence that a changing of the guard in Israeli literature had fully begun.

Other mature Israeli writers, however, who had not achieved the prominence of Oz, published books which were well received and widely read this year. David Shitz's novel *Avishag* explores the mystery of erotic attraction, while the short stories in Yehoshua Koren's *Funeral in the Afternoon* take place in stark, dusty settings—a development town, an army base somewhere in the desert—which Koren crafts skillfully into symbols of evocative simplicity.

Aharon Appelfeld, in contrast to both Oz and Koren, has never been considered a "representative" Israeli writer, because of both his Diaspora origins (he was born in Romania and spent the war years in Soviet labor camps) and his subject matter (Jewish life in Europe on the eve of the Holocaust). Appelfeld's previous novels turned an often harshly critical eye toward Jewish communities in Eastern Europe that remained paralyzed and willfully unaware as disaster approached. Appelfeld's novella *Caterina* presents another view of the prewar period. It tells the story of a Gentile woman from a small village who comes to work in a Jewish home after having grown up in an environment where Jews were considered the embodiment of everything demonic and evil. Caterina falls in love with the Jews in general—as well as with a specific Jew. Through her eyes, Appelfeld creates a picture of Jewish life as an island of decency and compassion surrounded by a society whose brutality is an allusion to the murderousness which the war will soon release.

As the decade drew to a close, not everyone agreed that the new trends in Israeli fiction were for the better. During the '80s, more effort was spent by Israeli publishers to advertise new books; the release of a new novel becoming in Israel, as it had been for some time in America, a media event. Some critics lamented this change. They argued that the commercialization of Israeli literature had already affected the quality of writing—by putting pressure on writers to produce more quickly so as to keep their names in the public eye, and by shifting literature from a serious and even visionary pursuit toward the domain of entertainment. "The attempt to bring literature 'closer' to the readers," according to Amnon Nevat, an Israeli critic who disapproved of recent literary trends, "becomes a surrender to the desire of the readers to see their lives reflected in its pages in an easily recognizable way."

Most critics, however, and if book sales are any indication, many enthusiastic readers, believe that literature in Israel is in the midst of a renaissance, and that the new generation of Israeli writers is a tremendously creative and renewing force. What these writers have in common, according to Hirschfeld and other critics, is that almost all of them turned backward at a certain point to the memory of an elemental trauma. Said Hirschfeld: "Contemporary Israeli literature is a literature that is searching for its father and its mother, whereas previous generations of Israeli writers didn't want to speak about who gave birth to it and where. This literature is an expression of a deep and positive cultural process occurring within Israel itself."

Literature: Poetry

Israel has had a strong poetic tradition, with the works of several major poets in each generation becoming part of the cultural heritage of the entire nation: Tchernichovsky and Bialik in the '20s and '30s; Natan Alterman and Uri Zvi Greenberg in the '40s and early '50s; Natan Zach, Dalia Ravikovich, Yehuda Amichai, and Amir Gilboa in the late '50s and '60s; Yona Wallach, Yair Hurwitz, and Meir Weiseltier in the '70s. At least until the 1980s, poetry was central to Israel's cultural life, even more so than fiction.

During the 1980s, much poetry continued to be written in Israel, and a number of new and gifted poets established themselves. Among those who published in 1989, mention should be made of Leah Ayalon (*Daniel, Daniel*) and Mordechai Goldman (*Milano*), Admiel Kosman (*The Clothes of a Prince*) and Tzvi Atzmon (*Substitute*). In addition to these younger poets, two older writers—Aryeh Sivan and Aharon Shabtai—who had been publishing for several decades, became, in the last few years, important voices in Israeli poetry.

As was the case with fiction, a critical debate accompanied the end-of-the-decade assessments of the state of Israeli poetry. Both sides in the debate conceded that Israeli poetry was in a novel situation: for the first time since the modern revival of Hebrew poetry, there existed no solid and agreed-upon group of leading poets, no single dominant poetic school. Natan Zach and David Avidan, who were leading poets into the '70s, had become increasingly peripheral. Yair Hurwitz and Yona Wallach, outstanding poets of the '70s, had died (Hurwitz in 1989).

Of the poets who were influential in the '60s and '70s, only Yehuda Amichai maintains a consistent presence in Israeli poetry. Amichai, who has been one of Israel's best-loved poets since the late 1950s, published a new collection of poetry in 1989: *Even the Fist Was Once a Palm and Outstretched Fingers*. The quality of Amichai's poetry has remained constant over the years (one critic termed Amichai "our only evergreen poet"), a trait that some critics deride as repetitiveness.

Ariel Hirschfeld, in a three-part essay titled "Poetry's Betrayal," published in *Ha'aretz,* argued that Israeli poetry, despite its outstanding quality and an abundance of talented young poets, has sung itself into a corner. Poetry is no longer being read as it once was, Hirschfeld claimed, because, beginning with Hurwitz, Wallach, and Weiseltier, it became increasingly obscure and inwardly directed, demanding unfair and even impossible decoding efforts from its readers.

Hirschfeld's essay drew sharp responses. If poetry has spent some time hiding from the spotlight, critics defending contemporary Israeli poetry argue, this turn inward has yielded beneficial results. Israeli poetry has freed itself from the Zachian model of highly intellectual verse written in spare language and has reestablished a plurality of poetic modes drawn from all the various layers of Hebrew literary history. The language of contemporary Hebrew poetry is rich and metaphorical; poetry, these critics maintain, is still the cutting edge of Israeli culture.

Literature: Continuity

In writing about contemporary Israeli literature, the continuing importance to Israeli culture of such "canonical" modern Hebrew writers as Agnon, Bialik, Brenner, Shabtai, Alterman, and S. Yizhar must be mentioned. Books of criticism on Agnon and Bialik and biographies of the poets Zelda and Yonatan Ratosh appeared this year; when S. Yizhar's great novel about the War of Independence, *Yemay Ziklag*, was republished after 40 years, A.B. Yehoshua, Amos Oz, and Yehoshua Kenaz all published essays in *Ha'aretz* about its significance. This continuing conversation between generations of writers makes Israeli literature a particularly rich and fertile component of Israeli culture.

Philosophy, Jewish Thought, and the Academy

Spinoza and Other Heretics, a long (566 pages), dense, learned work of intellectual and cultural history by Prof. Yirmiyahu Yovel, was the nonfiction phenomenon of 1989 in Israel. Some 10,000 hardcover copies of the work were sold, making it a runaway best-seller in Israeli terms.

According to Yovel, Spinoza was the first modern, secular Jew, and also the original and central philosopher—one is tempted to say prophet—of modern secular consciousness itself. Yovel's book is divided into two sections. In the first part, he proposes a fascinating if questionable "prehistory" of Spinoza. Spinoza's secularism, Yovel says, grew out of the very special situation of his ancestors, who were Marranos in Spain and Portugal. The double life that Marranos were forced to live left them alienated from both Christianity, which they had been taught to conform to outwardly while despising it inwardly, and from Judaism, which they experienced as a source of anxiety but not as a living tradition. The Marrano experience was thus the crucible of Spinoza's secularism; the Marranos' simultaneous disconnection from both Judaism and Christianity created a new and empty space from which Spinoza's secular philosophy could spring.

The second part of Yovel's book traces the history of Spinoza's influence on the development of modern thought and on such seminal figures as Kant, Hegel, Goethe, Freud, and Nietzsche. Spinoza's enormous importance to Western culture, according to Yovel, lies in his attempt "to liberate man from any dependence on factors that transcend the horizon of this world . . . to make do with reality as it exists."

Spinoza struck a responsive chord in Israel, in large part because Yovel proposed Spinoza as a spiritual forefather and archetype for the modern secular Israeli: a great Jew who rejected his ancestral religion without hiding or denying his Jewishness and went on to make a massive contribution to humanity as a whole. Yovel's Spinoza Institute, which he founded four years ago, supports Spinoza research and sponsors conferences, well attended by the general public, on subjects such as pluralism and religious tolerance.

Of course not everyone agreed with Yovel's portrait of Spinoza. Prof. Yosef Ben Shlomo, in a review essay of *Spinoza* (*Nativ,* Spring 1989), argued against all of Yovel's assessments: Spinoza, according to Ben Shlomo, was neither secular (he was, rather, "drunk on God") nor modern, but the last of the great metaphysical philosophers. Perhaps even more significantly, Spinoza was not Jewish—except, ironically, according to the strictly halakhic definition. "In none of his writings," says Ben Shlomo, "does he mention even one word about belonging to the Jewish people." Spinoza, Ben Shlomo asserts, was not the first modern secular Jew, "unless you wish to identify the modern secular Jew as a person who is completely alienated from his own national culture, and who expresses his world view through the concepts of a culture hostile to the Jewish people and their culture."

A book about a more recent effort to create a new kind of Jew is Yehoshua Porat's exacting and definitive biography of the philosopher-poet Yonatan Ratosh: *Weapon with a Pen in His Hand. Weapon* was, like *Spinoza,* an outstanding critical and popular success in Israel in 1989. Ratosh was the pen name of Uriel (Halpern) Shelach (1908–1981), one of the outstanding leaders and ideologues of the "Hebrew," later called "Canaanite," movement. *Weapon* tells the story of Ratosh's childhood in Warsaw and Vilna, where he grew up in one of the first exclusively Hebrew-speaking homes in Eastern Europe. In Paris, in 1929, Ratosh began to encounter members of Jabotinsky's Revisionist party and was quickly attracted to the maximalist faction, who wished to establish a Jewish state on both banks of the Jordan River.

During this time, Ratosh's Canaanite ideas began to take form. Ratosh believed that the Jewish return to Palestine necessitated a "complete disconnection" from the Jewish past and a return to the premonotheistic culture of the ancient Hebrew tribes. The British, argued Ratosh, should be forced out of Palestine immediately so that a Hebrew state could be established extending from the Nile to the Euphrates. The "Hebrew" people that would inhabit this state would include not only Jews but Druze and Maronite Christians as well. Ratosh emigrated to Palestine and remained faithful to his Canaanite ideas, which he disseminated until the end of his life. Ratosh's poetry is gripping and hypnotic and ranks among the best Hebrew poetry of modern times. As a cultural-political ideologue, Ratosh-Shelach battled with Yair (Avraham Stern) for domination of the prestate Lechi group, fought against the Latinization of Hebrew, and vehemently opposed including Jewish studies in the public-school curriculum in Israel. Ratosh-Shelach was the most radical expositor of ideas that, in various forms and incarnations, remain very much part of the Israeli scene.

Eli Schweid's new book, *Jewish Thought in the Twentieth Century: From 1900 to 1945,* is also very much concerned with the question of Jewish identity. In it, Schweid analyzes a wide range of thinkers who have been written about elsewhere—from Abraham Isaac Kook and Jacob Reines to Franz Rosenzweig and Martin Buber, from Yehezkel Kaufman and Abraham Joshua Heschel to Ahad HaAm and A.D. Gordon. Schweid makes an original contribution to the study of these thinkers by moving questions that were usually part of the background of each thinker's position onto center stage. For Schweid, the significant questions to Jews posed by the 20th century are sociocultural before they are theological or even political. What is Jewishness? What kind of Jewish civilization do these thinkers envision as ideal? What is their underlying reason or method in deciding between—or attempting to harmonize—the oppositionary poles of Israel and Diaspora, religious and secular, individual and community? Schweid's ultimate message is that for Judaism to thrive, it must allow for various aspects of human identity—political, cultural, spiritual—to be integrated and entwined.

In the world of Jewish studies, 1989 was also marked by the heated dispute that followed the publication of Moshe Idel's *Kabbalah: New Perspectives*. In *Kabbalah,* Idel, a 42-year-old professor at the Hebrew University of Jerusalem, challenges many of the assumptions and conclusions of Gershom Scholem (1897–1982), the undisputed master of modern academic study of Jewish mysticism, a field which he founded almost single-handedly.

Without diminishing the enormousness of Scholem's contribution to the study of Jewish mysticism, Idel calls into question a number of Scholem's basic assertions. Whereas Scholem believed that Kabbalah originated through the penetration of non-Jewish Gnostic notions and myths into Rabbinic Judaism in the second century, Idel argues that Kabbalah developed, for the most part, from within Judaism itself, that basic kabbalistic motifs were already present in the Talmud and Midrash. And whereas Scholem argued that the Kabbalah of Rabbi Isaac Luria (the "Ari"), with its stress on the trauma of exile and the process of redemption, was a response to the expulsion of the Jews from Spain in 1492, Idel argues that the theme of exile and redemption originated well before the "Ari" and before the Jewish expulsion from Spain.

There are also differences in the two men's scholarly approaches to the study of Jewish mysticism, differences with important implications for Jewish studies as a whole. Scholem used mainly historical and philological tools in the study of Kabbalah; he treated Kabbalah as a history of mystical ideas, and the main focus of his work was on the analysis of kabbalistic texts. Idel's methodology is phenomenological, that is, his concern is with what Kabbalah meant to kabbalists and not as much with the historical context of their work. Idel argues, as well, that mystical union with God was the goal of at least some kabbalists, a possibility which Scholem vehemently denied. Idel's challenge to the dominant Scholemian approach to Kabbalah aroused much heated debate in the academic community, debate that spilled over into the daily newspapers. The most vehement attack on Idel's views was mounted by Prof. Isaiah Tishby, a student and colleague of Scholem's and himself a renowned authority on Kabbalah. The two issues of *Tarbiz*—a journal for the study of Jewish history published in Jerusalem—that were published in 1989 featured a sometimes rancorous 80-page exchange between Idel and Tishby. The Scholem-Idel controversy was of more than the usual interest because of Scholem's extraordinary standing, not just as a scholar but as one of the intellectual masters

of the 20th century, a moral authority, and an important Zionist thinker.
Increasing efforts were made in 1989 to bring together, into a single framework, different and even conflicting approaches to Jewish studies, in an effort to stimulate creativity and to foster a new kind of dialogue. The Shalom Hartman Institute founded a center—the Advanced Institute—dedicated to the interdisciplinary study of Jewish texts and contemporary moral, political, and theological issues. Many of Israel's leading scholars in Judaic studies, philosophy, and related fields, along with visiting scholars from the Diaspora, participated in the institute's initial year of ongoing seminars. Ma'aleh—the center for the renewal of religious Zionism, which was founded in fall 1988—opened a *bet midrash* that combined traditional yeshivah study of the Talmud with insights drawn from academic Talmud study. In the fall of 1989, Ma'aleh opened a school of film and television, in the conviction that an understanding of modern media is crucial if religious Zionism is to emerge as a vital force in contemporary Israel. In the same period, a group of religious and secular Israelis together founded Elul—a pluralistic *bet midrash* promoting cooperation and dialogue between religious and secular Israelis; their goal is to develop a shared language drawn from a deep encounter with Jewish sources and history.

Art

Since the founding of the Bezalel Art Academy in 1906 in Jerusalem, "there has been enough art produced here," as one Israeli art historian expressed it, "for 10 countries of this size." The visual arts are, in one important respect, the most uniquely Israeli of the forms of cultural expression that developed in the country in the last century. For while the Jews carried with them a densely packed and always growing library of books throughout the centuries of exile, there was no distinctive tradition of Jewish visual arts preserved or produced in the Diaspora. Israeli painting and sculpture have had to invent themselves—and as such they are true children of the Zionist revolution. At the same time, the lack of a peculiarly Jewish artistic tradition has made Israeli art more open to Western influence than other Israeli forms of expression. Thus, the question of identity—the heart of the Zionist dilemma—is a question with which Israeli art is constantly engaged.

Tel Aviv and Jerusalem are the two centers of the Israeli art world. Each has a prestigious art academy—Bezalel in Jerusalem and the Ramat Hasharon Art Teachers Academy near Tel Aviv—where many of Israel's important artists teach. Each has a major museum which mounts frequent exhibitions of contemporary Israeli art: the Israel Museum in Jerusalem and the Tel Aviv Museum in Tel Aviv. Tel Aviv has the edge over Jerusalem in the number and quality of her galleries, especially where avant-garde art is concerned.

In addition to the activity centered in Jerusalem and Tel Aviv, there are at least 13 smaller art academies located throughout the country and a number of museums that feature contemporary Israeli art, including museums in Haifa, Herzliyah, Arad, Tefen (in the western Galilee), and Bat Yam. But despite the large number of artists, art schools, and museums, Israel has one significant missing link in its art scene: there have been few collectors of contemporary Israeli art, and therefore no significant art industry. Thus even the most successful and influential Israeli artists have had to supplement their income by teaching or through some other pursuit. Many artists feel, as well, that the Israeli press does not give contemporary art the coverage it deserves. Artists were particularly incensed when *Ha'aretz* ceased publishing gallery listings in their daily paper "for lack of public interest." Artists do receive some support from the municipal governments in Jerusalem and Tel Aviv: these cities each recently set aside several buildings to serve as low-rent studios for deserving artists, and many of Israel's prominent younger artists are in fact working in these subsidized quarters.

The trend or style that dominated Israeli art for close to two decades received a name and a definition in an important exhibition presented by the Tel Aviv Museum in 1986, which was called "The Want of Matter." According to the catalogue of this exhibition, which was written by Sarah Braidburg, then curator of the museum's contemporary art division, modern Israeli art was characterized by the use of simple, inexpensive materials—including "found" objects and industrial paint—by a tendency not to paint with intense or sensuous colors, by the extensive use of pencil and charcoal drawing within paintings, by the juxtaposition of words and images within paintings, and by paintings whose various elements look as if they were placed together almost by accident. The total effect is a deemphasis of the material and the sensual, a demystification of art, and a distancing of art from the world of symbols and mythology which nourished it in Europe.

This Israeli aesthetic, according to Braidburg, was the result of an internalization of the Socialist-Zionist ethos, which devalued outer forms in favor of the torn clothes and meager personal possessions of the Zionist pioneers. These pioneers had broken their ties with both European, and to a great extent Jewish, culture; what they valued was what could be made from scratch, from the materials that were at hand. The relationship of Israeli artists to this ethos was, to be sure, not a simple one. As was the case with Israeli poetry in the '60s, the ironic, skeptical, antimythological language of Israeli art was both an expression of, and a rebellion against, the ideology and pathos of Zionism itself.

The "Want of Matter" style was also a reflection of artists' continuing love affair with the city of Tel Aviv: a city built with much vitality but little esthetic awareness, a city without great monuments or buildings, a city built in a hurry with cheap materials, with peeling stucco walls and colors fading into white under the brightness of the Mediterranean sun.

The exhibition "The Want of Matter" was a summing up and a turning point for Israeli art. In a conscious demonstration of independence from this trend, young artists began in the late '80s to paint and sculpt in an altogether different manner, using expensive materials with polished finishes and a stylized look. " 'The Want of Matter,' " according to Yitzhak Livneh, a prominent painter and instructor at Bezalel, "is not an appropriate form for the era of the Likud, an era marked by the bourgeoisification of Israeli society." Another important artist, Tamar Getter, who was featured in the "Want of Matter" exhibition, spoke in spiritual rather than political terms: "A culture cannot be built on irony," she said. " 'Want of Matter' can also indicate 'Want of Spirit.' Cultures must be built out of richness—richness of myth and symbol—not out of poverty."

Some Israeli artists have begun to paint in ways that reflect a search for some sort of sublime. Artists such as Livneh, Larry Abramson, and Gabi Klasmer paint with abundant brushstrokes, creating images of figurative magic which suggest longing for something infinite. At the same time, the central object of the painting, which might be a common household object in the case of Livneh, or a dark, expressionless face in Klasmer's paintings, undercuts the quest for the infinite, as if suggesting that such a search can only end in disappointment.

An important theme in recent Israeli art criticism, and to some extent in Israeli art as well, is a renewed interest in Judaism and Jewish sources. The modern period in Israeli art began in 1948 with a manifesto called "New Horizons," which was prepared by a group of Israel's most prominent artists. This manifesto declared that art must be universal in its themes and abstract in its form. The New Horizons group declared themselves independent of such Diaspora Jewish artists as Chagall, who worked with themes specific to Jewish life. To a great extent, mainstream Israeli art faithfully adhered to the dictates of the New Horizons group and declared Judaism out of bounds as a subject for Israeli art. Artists such as Avraham Ofek, an immensely gifted and powerful painter whose work was inspired by a deep interest in Judaism and Jewish mysticism, were systematically excluded from the center of the Israeli art scene.

This attitude began to change, at least partly, in the early '80s, with the growing prominence of Moshe Gershuni, an abstract expressionist painter and perhaps the most influential artist of the decade in Israel. Gershuni's paintings, whose thick, dark swirls speak directly to the subconscious, often contain Jewish symbols, such as the Star of David, and have passages from the Psalms scrawled through the heart of the painting. Other mainstream artists, such as Jack Jano, Micha Ulman, and Pinchas Cohen Gat began to present work that reflected a new involvement with Jewish themes. "Judaism," wrote art historian Gideon Efrat, "which was once merely an entertaining aspect of the work of naive Israeli artists, finally, in 1989, reached the doorstep of non-naive Israeli art."

Perhaps even more than the paintings and sculptures themselves, essays about Israeli art—written by art critics and artists alike—sought increasingly to define the relationship between the Jewish tradition and modern Israeli art. Critics like Efrat, along with artists like Tamar Getter, argue that Israeli art has to return to the basic task of finding a Jewish-Israeli visual tradition, even if only fragments of such a tradition exist.

In a three-part essay published in August-September 1988, *Ha'aretz* art critic Itamar Levi argued that modern Israeli art is deeply connected to the essence of the Jewish tradition, despite its seeming indifference to overtly Jewish symbols and images. In fact, even the abstract universalism advocated by the New Horizons artists, Levi suggested, was itself an attempt to express a spirituality whose center is the Jewish God who cannot be directly seen. The collages and mixed-media creations of artists such as Rafi Lavi and Michal Neeman, Levi continued, were the artistic analogues of "a page of Talmud," with its infinite digressions and commentaries circling the original text. The poet Aharon Shabtai and artist Pinchas Cohen Gat continued Levi's theme, devoting essays in 1989 to the "Jewishness" of Israeli art.

Gideon Efrat, the most outspoken advocate for the return of Israeli art to Jewish sources, believes that critics like Levi are premature in their judgment. The kind of Judaism which Israeli artists and critics were willing, at the end of the '80s, to celebrate, he says, is itself an abstraction: a Judaism which negates the importance of physical land and concrete place, a Judaism which is more the product of secular Israel's utopian and universalist fantasies about Judaism than the result of a real engagement with Jewish texts and symbols.

Whether or not Efrat is correct in his assessment, Israeli art's dialogue with Judaism, which emerged as a major concern of critics and artists alike, seems bound to continue and deepen in the decade ahead.

Theater

Two million theater tickets are sold every year in Israel—the highest per capita number in the world. There are six major repertory theater companies in Israel: Habimah, the Cameri, and Beit Lessin in Tel Aviv, the Khan in Jerusalem, and the Haifa and Beersheva Municipal Theaters. In addition, there are a number of smaller theater companies, and the three large schools of theater—Bet Zvi in Tel Aviv, and the departments of theater at Tel Aviv and Hebrew Universities—also produce numerous plays.

The Acco Festival for Alternative Theater takes place every year during the Sukkot holiday (usually October) and provides a platform for actors and playwrights working outside the mainstream of Israeli theater. Alternative or avantgarde theater is also represented in Israel by the School for Visual Theater and the Kron Puppet Theater in Jerusalem and by small theater companies such as the Jerusalem Drama Workshop, which specializes in adapting traditional Jewish texts to the stage.

The major Israeli theater companies receive subsidies from the Ministry of Education and Culture equal to 25-30 percent of their budgets (in England, by comparison, repertory companies receive subsidies equal to 70-75 percent of their budgets). For the rest, Israeli theaters must rely on their audiences, which is why they alternate serious dramatic productions with musicals and other forms of popular drama.

Among the new plays written in Hebrew and produced for the Israeli stage in 1989, *Shira,* an adaptation for the stage of S.Y. Agnon's final novel, directed by

Yoram Falk, won the highest critical accolades. Other significant plays of 1989 included *The Work of Life* by Hanoch Levine, whom many consider Israel's finest playwright; *Hevre* by Hanan Peled, a critical look at a group of middle-aged Israelis who grew up in Zionist youth movements but have not lived up to their youthful ideals; *Zahav* by Yosef bar Yosef, about the efforts of a Holocaust survivor to keep her family together in Israel; and *Trumpets in the Wadi*, an adaptation of a book by Sami Michael about a Christian Arab family living in a wadi near Haifa.

Critics, writers, and performers who attempt to answer the question "What is Israeli about Israeli theater?" point in several directions. The plurality of accents, mannerisms, and cultural codes which must be integrated on the stage to produce an authentic representation of Israeli society in all its diversity is one important characteristic of Israeli theater. Another is Israeli theater's almost obsessive tendency toward "relevance"—the idea that today's plays should deal with yesterday's headlines; that the audience to a play should leave with a deeper insight into the moral dilemmas of Israel's political situation than when they came.

The intimate relationship between audience and performers is perhaps the most important characteristic of Israeli theater. To a far greater extent than in Europe or America, the audience in Israel feels included in the magic circle of creativity from which the play has emerged. Theaters are small, audiences are dedicated, and the themes are likely to be drawn from events or conditions which at least part of the audience has experienced firsthand.

Music

Israel has a highly developed musical culture. Its major symphony orchestra, the Israel Philharmonic, is considered one of the finest in the world, and other excellent orchestras, chamber groups, and choirs are part of Israel's lush musical landscape. Several contemporary Israeli composers have achieved international recognition for their work, and dozens of younger Israeli composers are involved in attempts to create a modern musical idiom. There is a large and devoted audience for classical music in Israel, and, until recently, when ticket prices began to climb beyond the reach of many ordinary citizens, all Philharmonic seats and many concerts of the other orchestras were sold out each year.

The richness and high quality of Israel's contemporary music scene is in many ways a consequence of the immigration of German Jews to Palestine during the Nazi period. It was German Jewish composers, conductors, teachers, performers, and intellectuals who created the possibility of a generation of world-class Israeli-born musicians.

Stylistically, many of the German Jewish composers prominent in the 1930s, '40s, and '50s were interested in creating music that reflected their new environment, and drew upon their personal Jewish roots and the pathos of the Jewish return to Zion as a whole. These early experiments grew into what was eventually known as "the Mediterranean school"—an attempt, in the years following the War of Independence, to create a distinct Israeli musical style. Composers of the Mediterranean school—the dominant force in Israeli composition throughout the 1950s—built symphonies around Jewish liturgical and Eastern European and Jewish folk melodies, attempted to integrate Arabic and oriental Jewish musical traditions with classical Western forms, and even made use of Jewish and Arabic folk instruments. The Mediterranean school was eventually considered a self-conscious and heavy-handed attempt to infuse Israeli music with a distinctive style, and such techniques as the melodic quotation of phrases from Jewish folk songs were abandoned by Israeli composers in the '60s.

The subsequent use of classical Hebrew texts or Judaic themes as inspiration for new Israeli compositions was much more successful. Such works as Mordecai Seter's oratorio *Tikun Hatzot* (1960–61)—based on a medieval Jewish liturgical text that is recited by kabbalists at midnight, Ami Maayaani's *Milhemet Bnai HaOr* ("The Battle of the Children of Light"; 1971), and Josef Tal's *Massada* (1972) are all considered classics of modern Israeli composition.

The attempt to create a uniquely Israeli musical style was not abandoned by composers here after the Mediterranean school lost its influence but was pursued in a more subtle way. Composers began to draw inspiration from such elements of their Jewish and Israeli surroundings as the natural rhythm of spoken Hebrew, the tonal modulations of traditional biblical intonation, and the intricate, syncopated rhythms of oriental music.

The near obsession with defining Jewish or Israeli music declined noticeably during the second half of the 1970s and the 1980s, for two reasons: first, the desire of composers to be part of the international music scene, to influence and be influenced by styles and trends not limited by country borders; and second, the growing confidence of many composers and musicians that "Israeliness" would seep into their music unconsciously, without having to be forced into existence. As one young Israeli composer, Oded Zehavi, said: "[My] experiences . . . are of course tied to the complicated reality into which I was born and in which I live. . . . My service in the army, my struggles to remain sensitive after taking part in a war, and being a member of a society that relies on strength to survive and cannot afford to fail, in certain ways shaped my creative tools. Furthermore, the air of this city [Jerusalem] . . . is full of sounds for me: Oriental sounds, the sounds from the Sephardic synagogues, Eastern European music—these are not exotic, they are not to be cited and analyzed as 'sources,' they are part of my being."

Perhaps the most sought-after Israeli composer in 1989 was Mark Kopytman, who immigrated to Israel from the Soviet Union in 1972. An orchestral piece called *Memory,* which he wrote in 1982, with a vocal solo sung by a Yemenite folksinger, was performed in 1989 in Moscow, Leningrad, Portugal, Spain, and at the Kennedy Center in Washington, D.C. According to Kopytman, although the composition is abstract in form and not connected to any particular text, it is concerned with Jewish collective memory. Kopytman, who teaches at the Rubin Academy in Jerusalem and also serves as personal mentor to a number of talented young musicians, is involved in efforts to set up a certification center where musicians immigrating from the Soviet Union can be tested and certified.

Mass immigration from the Soviet Union is expected to change the music scene in Israel more drastically than any event since the arrival of the German immigrants in the 1930s. In 1989 the Ministry of Education and Culture announced that it would grant orchestras hiring new Soviet immigrants a monthly stipend for a limited period of time, and some orchestras, particularly the Beersheva Symfonietta, did indeed hire a number of new Soviet musicians. Many more Soviet musicians were expected to immigrate to Israel in 1990 and in the decade to come. An early assessment by Israel's musical establishment found the Soviet musicians to be technically excellent—perhaps even superior to their Israeli counterparts—but with less developed feeling and artistic sensitivity.

A new orchestra—the Rishon LeZion Symphony—was founded in 1989, under the direction of Noam Sheriff, a prominent Israeli composer and conductor. The orchestra received high marks from critics during its first season's performances.

The Arthur Rubinstein competition—an international piano competition held annually in Tel Aviv—was won in 1989 by contestants from England and Poland.

The Zimriya—a festival of Jewish choirs from around the world, which had been held in Jerusalem tri- or biennially since 1952, was held in 1989. Over a thousand choir members from all over the United States, Israel, and Europe participated.

Dance

Dance style in Israel has been influenced by both Eastern European and Yemenite folk traditions and by European and American modern dance forms. Gertrude Kraus, who immigrated to Israel from Vienna in the early 1920s, is considered the founder of Israeli modern dance. According to Hassia Levy-Agron, the founder and head of the School of Dance at the Rubin Academy of Music in Jerusalem, Kraus, "an expressionist dancer of great emotional power," was "one of the lionesses and revolutionaries of modern dance in Europe." After World War II, the center of dance shifted from Europe to America, and Martha Graham became "the standard-bearer of progressive dance." Graham exerted a strong influence on Israeli dance, especially after her visit to Israel in 1958.

In 1989 the major dance companies in Israel included the Batsheva (founded by the Baroness Batsheva de Rothschild, with Martha Graham serving as artistic advisor), the Bat Dor, Sound and Silence, the Kibbutz Dance Company, and Inbal. Sound and Silence (Kol veDemama in Hebrew), founded and directed by Moshe Efrati, is an ensemble of deaf and hearing dancers. This combination, says Levy-Agron, "creates spontaneous ties and tensions that radiate expressive force."

The Inbal Dance Theater was founded by Sarah Levi-Tanai, who spent many years researching the unique forms and gestures of Middle Eastern dance, especially the dance movements of Yemenite Jews. Levi-Tanai virtually revived dance traditions that were in danger of being completely forgotten. Inbal's dancers, who are also trained in modern-dance techniques, have a repertoire that emphasizes biblical stories and the traditions of the various communities of oriental Jews in Israel.

Film

Film is the least developed of Israel's art forms. Although movie-making activity in the State of Israel began soon after the 1948 War of Independence, Israeli films have rarely reached the level of excellence that would distinguish them on the international scene. Even in Israel, foreign films—especially American—are far more popular than Israeli ones. Only about 10 percent of the 12 million cinema tickets sold each year are for Israeli films.

There are a number of reasons for Israel's relative lack of achievement in this field. Perhaps the most important is that filmmaking is too expensive for Israel's economy to support. With high-quality foreign films readily available, Israeli investors and producers have no assurance that a film will be a financial success even if they manage to complete it. Authentically Israeli films must be made in Hebrew—a fact that seriously limits their marketability in other countries.

Despite these obstacles, there is a small but vibrant filmmaking community in Israel. A concise overview of the history of Israeli films adds an important dimension to the understanding of Israeli culture.

According to Renan Schorr, a film historian, Israeli film can be divided into four main periods. "Zionist realism," the dominant filmmaking mode from 1948 until 1961, presented an uncritical celebration of Zionist ideology; it was centered around a hero who represented the mythological Sabra, who was everything the Diaspora Jew was not: strong, confident, and disconnected to a great extent from the pre-Zionist Jewish past. Since filmmaking at that time was completely dependent on government and Jewish Agency support, it is not surprising that many critics dismiss early Israeli films as propaganda pieces.

In the early 1960s, a new kind of Israeli film began to be produced. "The Native Generation" of writers, who were more individualistic and critical than their predecessors, became the dominant force in literature in the 1960s, and a parallel phenomenon emerged in film. Such movies as Uri Zohar's *Hole in the Moon* (1965) and Ephraim Kishon's *Sallah Shabati* (1965) poke gentle fun at the Zionist establishment and focus on individuals who have little in common with the mythological Sabra.

The "Bureka films" of the early 1970s, named after a salty Sephardic pastry, focus even more pointedly on what was once considered the periphery of Israeli society: the masses of Sephardic Jews who immigrated to Israel from North Africa and other Arabic-speaking regions. These films contrast Sephardic loyalty and simple wisdom with the hypocrisy and dishonesty of European Jews. Predictably enough, it was a European Jewish producer, Menachem Golan, who led the way in creating this genre, which exploited the feeling of many Sephardi Jews that they had been discriminated against by the European-dominated Israeli establishment.

During the years after the Yom Kippur War, a group of Israeli filmmakers created a political lobby for the establishment of a foundation to encourage the production of quality films. The Ministry of Trade and Industry and the Ministry of Education and Culture eventually agreed to fund such a foundation jointly, and this gave a needed push forward to a new generation of Israeli filmmakers.

In the 1980s the politics of the Arab-Israeli conflict and the moral dilemmas of war were the dominant themes of quality Israeli films. Movies such as *Hamsin* (Daniel Wachsmann, 1982) and *Beyond the Walls* (Uri Barbash, 1984) portray Palestinian Arabs in a positive light and are sharply critical of their Israeli heroes.

In the late '80s, the most successful of Israel's major films centered around the traumas of war and ethnic conflict, but in a somewhat more subtle fashion. *Shell Shock* (Yoel Sharon, 1988) and *Burning Memory* (Yossi Somer, 1989) both examine war from the perspective of an Israeli hospitalized after a psychological breakdown on the battlefield. *One of Us* (Uri Barbash, 1989) explores the conflict between truth and loyalty when an army investigator is sent to uncover the facts about a soldier accused of abusing a Palestinian. *Marriage of Convenience* (Haim Bouzaglo, 1988) is a dramatic comedy about a middle-class Israeli who leaves his family and changes his identity. Posing as a Palestinian Arab during the day and an American tourist at night, he takes a job as a construction worker. The film uses a light touch in examining some of the daily tensions of modern Israeli society.

Both *The Summer of Avia* (Eli Cohen, 1988) and *Because of That War* (Orna Ben Dor Niv, 1988) are about the Holocaust and its effects on the children of survivors. T*he Summer of Avia,* which won a "Silver Bear" at the 1989 film festival in Berlin, is the story of a 10-year-old girl who is reunited with her mentally disturbed mother, a Holocaust survivor. The film takes place in the newly established State of Israel, in 1951. Although it is told as fiction, it is based on the autobiographical experiences of Gila Almagor, a well-known Israeli actress, who co-wrote the screenplay and also starred in the film.

Because of That War is a documentary about two popular young Israeli rock stars, Yaakov Gilad and Yehuda Poliker, and their parents—specifically, Gilad's mother and Poliker's father—who are both survivors of extermination camps. The film weaves between the extraordinary testimony of the parents about the Holocaust and the children's account of the effect their parents' suffering had on their family life, fantasy life, and music.

As of the end of 1989, Israel had 190 movie houses, 7 film archives, and 3 cinematheques—in Jerusalem, Tel Aviv, and Haifa—which showed classic and contemporary films throughout the year. There were two film schools, one in Tel Aviv and one in Jerusalem, and two yearly film festivals—the Jerusalem Film Festival in the first weeks of July and the International Jewish and Israeli Festival which took place for the first time in April 1989 in Tiberias, but was slated to become an annual event.

MICHA Z. ODENHEIMER

World Jewish Population, 1989

Updated Estimates

THIS ARTICLE PRESENTS UPDATES, for the end of 1989, of the Jewish population estimates for the various countries of the world.[1] The estimates reflect some of the results of a prolonged and ongoing effort to study scientifically the demography of contemporary world Jewry.[2] Data collection and comparative research have benefited from the collaboration of scholars and institutions in many countries, including replies to direct inquiries regarding current estimates. It should be emphasized, however, that the elaboration of a worldwide set of estimates for the Jewish populations of the various countries is beset with difficulties and uncertainties.

About 96 percent of world Jewry is concentrated in ten countries. The aggregate of these ten major Jewish population centers virtually determines the assessment of the size of total world Jewry, estimated at 12.8 million persons in 1989. The country figures for 1989 were updated from those for 1988 in accordance with the known or estimated changes in the interval—vital events (i.e., births and deaths), identificational changes (accessions and secessions), and migrations. In addition, corrections were introduced in the light of newly accrued information on Jewish populations. Corresponding corrections were also applied retrospectively to the 1988 figures, which appear below in revised summary (see table 1), so as to allow adequate comparison with the 1989 estimates.

During the year 1989 under review here, data-collection projects relevant to Jewish population estimates were in planning or already under way in several countries. Some of this ongoing research is part of a coordinated effort to update the sociodemographic profile of world Jewry that was undertaken at the outset of the 1990s.[3] Two important sources have already yielded results on major Jewish

---

[1] The previous estimates, as of 1988, were published in AJYB 1990, vol. 90, pp. 514–32.
[2] Many of these activities have been carried out by, or in coordination with, the Division of Jewish Demography and Statistics at the Institute of Contemporary Jewry, the Hebrew University of Jerusalem.
[3] Following an international conference in 1987 on Jewish population problems, sponsored by the major Jewish organizations worldwide, an International Scientific Advisory Committee

populations: the official population census of the Soviet Union held in 1989, and the National Jewish Population Survey (NJPS) in the United States, completed in 1990.[4] The respective results basically confirm both the estimates reported by us in previous AJYB volumes and, perhaps more importantly, our interpretation of the trends now prevailing in the demography of world Jewry. At the same time, these new data highlight the increasing complexity of the sociodemographic and identificational processes underlying the *definition* of Jewish populations—hence the estimates of their sizes. While we address below some of these conceptual problems, users of population estimates should be aware of these difficulties and of the consequent limitations of the estimates.

Concepts and Definitions

In many respects Jewish populations are subject to the general difficulties involved in trying to define, identify, and enumerate minority groups. These difficulties are augmented by the uniquely blended character of Jewry, with its religious, ethnic, cultural, historical, and other components as well as the wide geographical scatter and distinctive socioeconomic structure of Jewish groups.

In contemporary societies experiencing intense processes of secularization, acculturation, and social interaction, the ideational (and statistical) boundaries between different religious, ethnic, or cultural groups are no longer clearly and rigidly defined, as they may have been in the past. Multiple bases of identification between individual and community can coexist. Since group identity is not regulated by legal provisions, individuals may change their preferences during their lifetimes. Individuals of Jewish origin may feel varying degrees of personal attachment to Judaism or the Jewish community and may choose to cut the respective links, whether or not formally adopting another group identity. These identificational changes are reversible: persons who disclaim being Jews at some stage of life may change their minds later. Even at the same time, some may admit or deny their Jewishness under different circumstances. Another element in this general picture is the growing frequency of mixed marriages. Some of the partners in interfaith marriages prefer to unify the home, one of them adopting the group identity of the other; others do not. Children of these marriages are likely to be exposed to the different religious and cultural backgrounds of their parents, out of which their own eventual identities will be shaped.

(ISAC) was established. Cochaired by Dr. Roberto Bachi of the Hebrew University and Dr. Sidney Goldstein of Brown University, ISAC's function is to coordinate and monitor Jewish population data collection internationally.

[4]The 1989–1990 National Jewish Population Survey was conducted under the auspices of the Council of Jewish Federations with the supervision of a National Technical Advisory Committee chaired by Dr. Sidney Goldstein of Brown University. Dr. Barry Kosmin of the North American Jewish Data Bank and City University of New York Graduate School directed the study.

These fluid and voluntaristic patterns of group identification imply that the concept of Jewish population is no longer simple and uniform, but one that offers ground for alternative interpretations and even some confusion and misunderstanding—especially when large and heterogeneous amounts of data are handled and compared. In an attempt to clarify these matters, we briefly outline here one conceptual framework—applied throughout this article—that appears useful in the sociodemographic study of contemporary Jewries.

Core Jewish population. In contemporary social-scientific research on Jews, including demography, it is usual to consider as Jews all those who, when asked, identify themselves as such; or, if the respondent is a different person in the same household, are identified by him/her as Jews. We define this aggregate as the "core" Jewish population. It includes all those who converted to Judaism or joined the Jewish group informally. It excludes those of Jewish descent who formally adopted another religion, as well as other individuals who did not convert out but currently refuse to acknowledge their Jewishness. This categorization is intentionally comprehensive, reflecting subjective feelings rather than halakhic (Rabbinic) or other legal definitions.[5] Our definition of a person as a Jew does not depend on any measure of that person's Jewish commitment or behavior—in terms of religiosity, beliefs, knowledge, communal affiliation, or otherwise. The "core" Jewish population is the conceptual target of our population estimates. In estimating the size of a Jewish population, we include, in principle, all marginal individuals who have not ceased to consider themselves Jewish.

Extended Jewish population. We adopt the term "extended" for the sum of the "core" Jewish population and all other persons of Jewish parentage who are not Jews currently (or at the time of investigation). These non-Jews with Jewish background, as far as they can be ascertained, include: (a) persons who have themselves adopted another religion, even though they may claim still to be Jews ethnically; (b) other persons of Jewish parentage who disclaim to be Jews currently. In survey-taking it is usual, for both conceptual and practical reasons, to consider in this context parentage only and not any more distant ancestry.

Enlarged Jewish population. We designate by the term "enlarged" the sum of the "core" Jewish population, all other persons of Jewish parentage included in the "extended" Jewish population, as well as their non-Jewish household members (spouses, children, etc.). For both conceptual and practical reasons, this definition does not include any other non-Jewish relatives living elsewhere.

These various definitions point to the importance of the household as the pri-

---

[5]The definition of "Who is a Jew?" according to Halakhah constituted the cardinal criterion of Jewish identification across history. Normatively, it continues to bind all Orthodox and many other Jewish communities in contemporary times. The constraints typical of empirical research do not allow for ascertaining on a case-by-case basis the halakhic identity of each individual included in surveys. Therefore, it is usual in most social-scientific research to rely on the subjective criteria defined here.

mary—and in social terms truly significant—reference unit for the study of Jewish demography. For demographic research purposes, "eligible Jewish households" are all those including at least one individual who is either currently Jewish or of Jewish parentage.[6] Ideally, information should be collected on all the members of Jewish households, Jews and others, to enable researchers to apply the above—and perhaps additional—definitions and to estimate the respective sizes of the various groups and subgroups involved.

Clearly, while in the past "core," "extended," and "enlarged" Jewish populations tended to overlap, today the respective sizes and characteristics may be quite different. The time perspective employed in these definitions mainly relates to the two generations of the surveyed individuals and their parents. Other, more extended generational or time perspectives might be considered in the attempt to estimate the size of populations of Jewish origin, based on prolonged genealogical reconstructions. Such approaches, albeit of some interest for historical research, will not be considered here.

Another definitional framework stems from the special position of Israel as a country of destination for Jewish international migration, nowadays chiefly from the Soviet Union. Israel's most distinctive legal framework for the acceptance and absorption of new immigrants is provided by the Law of Return (*Hok Hashvut*), first passed in 1950 and amended in 1954 and 1970. That basic law awards Jewish new immigrants immediate citizenship and other civil rights in Israel. According to the current, amended version of the Law of Return, a Jew is any person born to a Jewish mother, or converted to Judaism (regardless of denomination—Orthodox, Conservative, or Reform). Conversion from Judaism, as in the case of some "ethnic" Jews who currently identify with another religion, entails loss of eligibility for Law of Return purposes. Significantly, the law extends its provisions to all current Jews and to their Jewish or non-Jewish spouses, children, and grandchildren, as well as to the spouses of such children and grandchildren. It can readily be seen, therefore, that due to its three-generational time perspective and lateral extension, the Law of Return applies to a wide population. This population is of wider scope not only than the "core" but even than the "enlarged" Jewish population, as defined above.

Finally, it should be noted that the actual contents and patterns of Jewish identity and behavior may vary widely within the "core" Jewish population itself, from strongly committed to very marginal. The respective differentials are associated with sociodemographic trends that may ultimately affect Jewish population size. These issues are, however, beyond the scope of the present article, which is mostly concerned with the bare attempt to estimate the size of "core" Jewish populations in the countries of the world.

---

[6]This approach was followed in the two U.S. National Jewish Population Studies of 1970–1971 and 1989–1990.

Jewish Population Trends

The world's Jews are highly dispersed. In most countries their number is now rather small, and they constitute no more than a minute fraction of the entire population. Consequently, though Diaspora Jews tend to cluster in large cities, they are greatly exposed to assimilation. While the major thrust of the assimilatory process tends to be associated with secessions from the Jewish population (whether formal or informal), there also are gains through accessions of non-Jewish-born persons. It is the net balance of these identificational changes that matters demographically. Outmarriages may involve demographic losses to the Jewish population if less than half of the children are themselves Jews. Moreover, in the longer run, the overall cohesion of a Jewish community may be affected, with consequences for its population size as well. What counts in the demographic balance of Diaspora Jewries is "effectively Jewish" fertility and birthrate, including only those newborn who are Jews.[7]

The Jews in most countries of the Diaspora are characterized by very low fertility, which is the major cause for great population aging. An increased proportion of elderly in the population actually implies not only many deceased and a higher death rate, but also a reduced proportion of persons of reproductive age and therefore a relatively lower birthrate. While there are differences in the levels of these demographic factors between the Jews in various regions and countries, in all major Diaspora populations the joint balance of the natural and identificational changes is now close to nil or outrightly negative, with Jewish deaths frequently outnumbering Jewish births. These negative tendencies have been taken into account in updating the estimates of the Jews in many countries.

A notable paradox of Diaspora Jewish demography is that growth of an "enlarged" Jewish population—following intense outmarriage and an increasing number of persons in households with both Jewish and non-Jewish members—may go hand in hand with stagnation or even diminution of the respective "core" Jewish population. A case in point is provided by the recent demographic transformations of the Jewish population in the United States (see below).

With regard to the balance of external migrations, there is no regularity among the various Diaspora populations or even in the same population over time. Where the migratory balance is positive—e.g., in North America—it counteracts or even outweighs any numerically negative influence of internal demographic developments. Where the migratory balance is negative, as in Eastern Europe, it may cause or aggravate the decrease of a Jewish population. In 1989, the overall volume of international migrations of Jews was higher than in previous years, though the outflow of Jewish emigration from the Soviet Union was still restricted.

---

[7]A fuller discussion of the subject can be found in U.O. Schmelz, "Jewish Survival: The Demographic Factors," AJYB 1981, vol. 81, pp. 61–117. See also *Aging of World Jewry* (Jerusalem, 1984), by the same author.

In contrast, in Israel the impact of outmarriage and secessions from Judaism is statistically negligible. The fact that Israeli society has a Jewish majority encourages accessions (formal or informal) of non-Jewish members in mixed immigrant households. A positive net balance of accessions and secessions results. Moreover, until the early 1980s and again in 1990 Israel had a positive migration balance.

Jewish fertility levels in Israel are comparatively high, and the Jewish age structure is significantly younger than among Diaspora Jews and the general populations of the other developed countries. The previously substantial fertility differentials between Jews ingathered in Israel from Asia-Africa and Europe-America are no longer in evidence. Remarkably, European Jews in Israel have not participated in the drastic fertility decline that has characterized the developed nations and particularly the Diaspora Jews during the last few decades, but have actually raised their fertility somewhat. In recent years, both major origin groups among Israel's Jews have displayed a fertility level surpassing not only the vast majority of Diaspora Jewry but also the general populations in other developed countries.

In the overall demographic balance of world Jewry, the natural increase of Israel has, so far, made up for the losses in the Diaspora. But such compensation will not be possible for much longer. As a consequence of the intensifying demographic deficit in the Diaspora, a trend toward some reduction in the total size of world Jewry is probably setting in. The relative share of Israel in that total is on the increase, regardless of *aliyah* and *yeridah* (immigration to, and emigration from, Israel), which obviously constitute only internal transfers within the global Jewish framework.

Sources of Data and Estimation Problems

Available demographic information on Jews is deficient in both quantity and quality. Besides the conceptual problems discussed above, difficulties involved in estimating the size of Jewish populations reflect the substantive complexity of Diaspora demography. Relevant aspects are the great geographical scattering of Jews—a factor that makes multiple data collection mandatory but also hinders its feasibility; and the Jews' unusually strong demographic dynamics in many respects—migrations, social mobility, family formation patterns (including outmarriage), etc.. More specific difficulties in estimating the up-to-date size of Jewish populations are due to measurement problems.

Particular difficulties exist with regard to the countries of Eastern Europe, whose Jewish populations were drastically reduced during and after World War II. Prolonged antireligious policies in these countries have had a negative effect on the identity of genealogically Jewish persons, many of whom may have severed, insofar as it depends on themselves, all links with Jewishness. The resulting uncertainties have led to wishful thinking in terms of exaggerated estimates, and account for the widely differing numbers of Jews that have been circulated for these countries.

Figures on Jews from population censuses are unavailable for most Diaspora communities, though they do exist for some important ones. In general, the practice of self-determination is followed in relevant censuses and surveys which inquire into religion or ethnicity, thus providing results close to our definition of a "core" Jewish population. Even where census statistics on Jews are forthcoming, they are usually scant, because the Jews are a small minority of the total population. There have been instances where detailed tabulations on Jews were undertaken, through Jewish initiative, from official census material; examples are Canada, Argentina, and South Africa. In some countries where Jewishness is associated with actual or feared discrimination, individuals may prefer not to describe themselves as Jews. Elsewhere, as has happened in some Latin American countries, non-Jews may be erroneously included as Jews. These problems require statistical evaluation whose feasibility and conclusiveness depend on the relevant information available. Reliable figures are currently forthcoming for the Jews of Israel from official statistics.

Surveys are the major way of obtaining comprehensive information on Jewish populations in the absence of official censuses. In the Diaspora, Jewish-sponsored surveys have the additional advantage of being able to inquire into matters of specifically Jewish interest, e.g., Jewish education, observances, and attitudes. However, since they address themselves to a small and scattered minority with identification problems, surveys are not easy to conduct competently and may encounter difficulties with regard to both coverage and response, especially from marginal Jews. Again, these aspects require evaluation. Over the last decades, countrywide Jewish population surveys were undertaken in the United States, South Africa, France, Italy, and the Netherlands. Local surveys have been carried out in many cities of the United States, the United Kingdom, Argentina, Brazil, Australia, and some smaller communities. However, these several initiatives have so far been uncoordinated with regard to content and method.

In certain countries or localities, Jewish community registers include the largest part of the Jewish population. Often the same communities keep records of Jewish vital events—especially marriages performed with a Jewish ceremony and Jewish burials. However, communal registers tend to cover mixed households insufficiently. In addition, although the amount and quality of updating varies from place to place, communal registers generally lag behind the actual situation of the respective Jewish populations.

Finally, many estimates of Jewish Diaspora populations for which no solid data from censuses or surveys exist are regrettably of unspecified or dubious source and methodology. This situation contrasts with the amount and quality of demographic information available for Jews in Israel. Israel took its latest census in 1983, but has constantly updated statistics of its Jewish population size and characteristics.

Besides the conceptual and measurement difficulties affecting baseline figures on Jewish population size, similar problems recur with regard to the updating information which should account for all the various types of changes in the time elapsed since that base date. Age-sex-specific models can be of use for vital events and identificational changes. They may be applied after studying the evolution of the respective or similar Jewish populations. With regard to the migratory balance in any updating interval, concrete information must be gathered, because of the abovementioned irregularity, over time, in the intensity of many migratory streams.

Not a few Jews have some residential status in more than one country. This may be due to business requirements, professional assignments in foreign countries, climatic differences between countries, periods of prolonged transit for migrants, etc. The danger of double-counting or omissions is inherent in such situations. This is particularly critical regarding some countries in Central and tropical South America, Africa, and East Asia, where the relatively few Jews living permanently may be outnumbered by a floating population of temporary Jewish residents or tourists. As far as possible, we have tried to account for such persons only once, giving precedence to the usual country of residence.

The problem is even more acute with regard to residential status in more than one locality of the same country. This may adversely affect—through omissions, or more likely, double-counting—the accuracy of national Jewish population estimates obtained by summing up reports for individual localities.

Presentation of Data

The detailed estimates of Jewish population distribution in each continent (tables 2–6 below) aim at the concept of "core" Jewish population as defined earlier in this article. The reader will recall that "extended" or "enlarged" Jewish populations, including Jews, non-Jews of Jewish parentage, and respective non-Jewish household members, may result in significantly higher estimates. Separate figures are provided for each country with at least 100 resident Jews. Residual estimates of "other" Jews living in smaller communities, or staying temporarily in transit accommodations, supplement some of the continental totals. For each of the reported countries, the four columns in the following tables provide the United Nations estimate of mid-year 1989 total population,[8] the estimated end-1989 Jewish population, the proportion of Jews per 1,000 of total population, and a rating of the accuracy of the Jewish population estimate.

There is wide variation in the quality of the Jewish population estimates for different countries. For many Diaspora countries it would be best to indicate a range (minimum-maximum) rather than a definite figure for the number of Jews. It would be confusing, however, for the reader to be confronted with a long list of ranges; this would also complicate the regional and world totals. Yet, the figures actually indicated for most of the Diaspora communities should be understood as being the central value of the plausible range of the respective core Jewish populations. The relative magnitude of this range varies inversely to the accuracy of the estimate.

---

[8]See United Nations, Department of International Economic and Social Affairs, Statistical Office, *World Population Prospects 1988*. Population Studies, no. 106 (New York, 1989). The figures are projections for 1989 based on latest estimates available in 1988.

ACCURACY RATING

The three main elements affecting the accuracy of each estimate are the nature and quality of the base data, the recency of the base data, and the method of updating. A simple code combining these elements is used to provide a general evaluation of the reliability of the Jewish population figures reported in the detailed tables below. The code indicates different quality levels of the reported estimates: (A) base figure derived from countrywide census or relatively reliable Jewish population surveys; updated on the basis of full or partial information on Jewish population movements in the respective country during the intervening period; (B) base figure derived from less accurate but recent countrywide Jewish population investigation; partial information on population movements in the intervening period; (C) base figure derived from less recent sources, and/or unsatisfactory or partial coverage of Jewish population in the particular country; updating according to demographic information illustrative of regional demographic trends; (D) base figure essentially conjectural; no reliable updating procedure. In categories (A), (B), and (C), the years in which the base figures or important partial updates were obtained are also stated.

For countries whose Jewish population estimate of 1989 was not only updated but also revised in the light of improved information, the sign "X" is appended to the accuracy rating.

Distribution of World Jewish Population by Major Regions

Table 1 gives an overall picture of Jewish population for 1989 as compared to 1988. For 1988 the originally published estimates are presented along with somewhat revised figures that take into account, retrospectively, the corrections made in 1989 in certain country estimates, in the light of improved information. These corrections resulted in a net decrease of world Jewry's estimated size by 166,500, primarily due to the new estimate for the United States. Some explanations are given below for the countries whose estimates were revised.

The size of world Jewry at the end of 1989 is assessed at 12,810,300. According to the revised figures, the change between 1988 and 1989 was almost negligible—an estimated loss of 8,200 people, or about −0.06 percent. Despite all the imperfections in the estimates, it is clear that world Jewry has reached "zero population growth," with the natural increase in Israel compensating for the demographic decline in the Diaspora.

The number of Jews in Israel rose from a figure of 3,659,500 in 1988 to 3,717,100 at the end of 1989—an increase of 57,600 people, or 1.6 percent. In contrast, the estimated Jewish population in the Diaspora declined from 9,159,500 (according to the revised figures) to 9,093,200—a decrease of 66,300 people, or 0.7 percent. These changes were almost entirely due to internal demographic evolution, since in 1989 the estimated net migratory balance between the Diaspora and Israel amounted to about 11,000 (Israel gained migrants on balance).

TABLE 1. ESTIMATED JEWISH POPULATION, BY CONTINENTS AND MAJOR GEOGRAPHICAL REGIONS, 1988 AND 1989

Region	1988 Original Abs. N.	1988 Revised Abs. N.	1988 Revised Percent	1989 Abs. N.	1989 Percent	% Change 1988–1989
World	12,979,000	12,818,500	100.0	12,810,300	100.0	−0.1
Diaspora	9,320,000	9,159,500	71.5	9,093,200	71.0	−0.7
Israel	3,659,000	3,659,000	28.5	3,717,100	29.0	+1.6
America, Total	6,447,600	6,263,600	48.9	6,261,700	48.9	−0.0
North[a]	6,010,000	5,825,000	45.4	5,825,000	45.5	—
Central	46,500	46,500	0.4	46,700	0.4	+0.4
South	392,100	392,100	3.1	390,000	3.0	−0.5
Europe, Total[b]	2,607,500	2,622,800	20.4	2,558,400	20.0	−2.5
EC[b]	1,010,400	1,010,900[c]	7.9	1,019,200[c]	8.0	+0.8
West, other[b]	43,200	43,200	0.3	52,300	0.4	+21.1
East and Balkans[d]	1,553,900	1,568,700	12.2	1,486,900	11.6	−5.2
Asia, Total	3,692,400	3,692,600	28.8	3,750,700	29.3	+1.6
Israel	3,659,000	3,659,000	28.5	3,717,100	29.0	+1.6
Rest[d]	33,400	33,600	0.3	33,600	0.3	—
Africa, Total	141,900	149,900	1.2	149,900	1.2	—
North	12,700	12,700	0.1	12,700	0.1	—
Central	14,100	22,100	0.2	22,100	0.2	—
South	115,100	115,100	0.9	115,100	0.9	—
Oceania	89,600	89,600	0.7	89,600	0.7	—

[a]U.S.A. and Canada.
[b]Including Jewish migrants in transit.
[c]Unified Germany included in the EC.
[d]The Asian regions of USSR and Turkey are included in "East Europe and Balkans."

About half of the world's Jews reside in the Americas, with 45 percent in North America. Twenty-nine percent live in Asia, excluding the Asian territories of the USSR and Turkey—nearly all of them in Israel. Europe, including the Asian territories of the USSR and Turkey, accounts for one-fifth of the total. The proportions of the world's Jews living in Africa and Oceania are very small.

Among the major geographical regions listed in table 1, the number of Jews in Israel—and, consequently, in total Asia—increased in 1989. By the end of 1989, Israel's Jews constituted 29 percent of total world Jewry. The (revised) total number of Jews estimated for North America was not changed. Most other regions remained stable or sustained decreases in Jewish population size.

World Jewry constitutes about 2.5 per 1,000 of the world's total population. One in about 406 people in the world is a Jew.

Individual Countries

THE AMERICAS

In 1989 the total number of Jews in the American continents was somewhat more than six and a quarter million. The overwhelming majority (93 percent) resided in the United States and Canada, less than 1 percent lived in Central America (including Mexico), and about 6 percent lived in South America—with Argentina and Brazil the largest Jewish communities (see table 2).

United States. The 1989–1990 National Jewish Population Survey (NJPS), sponsored by the Council of Jewish Federations and the North American Jewish Data Bank (NAJDB), provided the much awaited benchmark information about size and characteristics of U.S. Jewry and the basis for subsequent updates. According to first releases of the results of this important national sample study,[9] the "core" Jewish population in the United States comprised 5,515,000 persons in 1990. Of these, 185,000 were converts to Judaism. An estimated 210,000 persons not included in the previous figures were born or raised as Jews but converted to another religion. A further 1,115,000 people, thereof 415,000 adults and 700,000 children below 18, were of Jewish parentage but followed a religion other than Judaism at the time of the survey. All together, these various groups formed an "extended" Jewish population of 6,840,000. NJPS also included 1,350,000 non-Jewish-born members of eligible (Jewish) households. The study's "enlarged" Jewish population thus consisted of about 8,200,000 persons.

Comparison with the results of the previous National Jewish Population Study, conducted in 1970–1971, is complicated by the following: various versions of the

---

[9]Council of Jewish Federations, news release, New York, Nov. 9, 1990; Barry A. Kosmin and Jeffrey Scheckner, "Jewish Population in the United States, 1990," AJYB 1991, vol. 91, pp. 204–224.

TABLE 2. ESTIMATED JEWISH POPULATION DISTRIBUTION IN THE AMERICAS, 1989

Country	Total Population	Jewish Population	Jews per 1,000 Population	Accuracy Rating
Canada	26,310,000	310,000	11.8	B 1981–86
United States	247,341,000	5,515,000	22.3	A 1990 X
Total Northern America	273,770,000[a]	5,825,000	21.3	
Bahamas	257,000	300	1.2	C 1973
Costa Rica	2,941,000	2,000	0.7	C 1986
Cuba	10,237,000	700	0.1	D
Dominican Republic	7,018,000	100	0.0	D
Guatemala	8,935,000	800	0.1	B 1983
Jamaica	2,483,000	300	0.1	B 1988
Mexico	86,737,000	35,000	0.4	C 1980
Netherlands Antilles	191,000	400	2.1	D
Panama	2,370,000	5,000	2.1	C 1989 X
Puerto Rico	3,658,000	1,500	0.4	C 1986
Virgin Islands	111,000	300	2.7	C 1986
Other	23,234,000	300	0.0	D
Total Central America	148,172,000	46,700	0.3	
Argentina	31,930,000	218,000	6.8	C 1960–89
Bolivia	7,113,000	600	0.1	C 1986
Brazil	147,399,000	100,000	0.7	C 1980
Chile	12,960,000	15,000	1.2	C 1988
Colombia	31,192,000	6,500	0.2	C 1986
Ecuador	10,490,000	900	0.1	C 1985
Paraguay	4,157,000	900	0.2	C 1984
Peru	21,790,000	3,500	0.2	B 1985
Suriname	397,000	200	0.5	B 1986
Uruguay	3,104,000	24,400	7.9	D
Venezuela	19,245,000	20,000	1.0	D
Total Southern America	290,892,000[a]	390,000	1.3	
Total	712,834,000	6,261,700	8.8	

[a]Including countries not listed separately.

1970–71 results were published;[10] time and circumstances did not allow for detailed analysis of the 1990 results before these lines were written; there are margins of error when two sample studies are compared, especially if they were conducted under differing circumstances 20 years apart. Still, it is sufficiently clear—and very relevant to the assessment of trends—that the "core" Jewish population hardly grew, if at all, whereas the "extended," and especially the "enlarged" Jewish population in the United States increased significantly. This attests numerically to the strengthening of assimilatory trends and to intensifying sociodemographic integration of American Jews with the general population. The new data also reflect the use of more systematic random surveying methods, and the somewhat wider definition of eligible households in the 1989–1990 NJPS, in comparison to the 1970–1971 study.

Our previous estimate of the size of U.S. "core" Jewish population, relating to end 1988, was 5,700,000—a figure we had kept steady for several years, explicitly waiting for the results of the new survey. The new estimate essentially confirms the order of magnitude of U.S. Jewry, but is lower by 185,000 persons (−3.3 percent). By reporting for the end of 1989 the NJPS figure, which actually refers to mid-1990, we assume that the current balance of demographic changes in the U.S. "core" Jewish population is close to nil. It is actually possible that in the most recent past the influence of internal evolution on the size of U.S. Jewry may have been negative (though there is no consensus with regard to this assessment). Indeed, several local surveys taken in recent years provide evidence of low "effectively Jewish" birthrates, increasing outmarriage rates, declining rates of conversion to Judaism, and increasing aging among the Jewish population.[11]

Over the whole 1970–1990 period, several hundred thousand Jews migrated to the United States, especially from the USSR, Israel, Iran, and Latin America. In the earlier years, the international migration balance of U.S. Jewry must have generated an actual increase of Jewish population size. The volume of Jewish international migration during most of the mid-1980s was small, but toward the end of 1988 signs of increase began to appear. In 1989, about 40,000 immigrants from the Soviet Union were admitted to the United States.[12] The fact that the expected

---

[10]The 1970–1971 NJPS results were reported by the study director, Fred Massarik, in "National Jewish Population Study," AJYB 1974–75, vol. 75, pp. 296–97; and, by the same author, "The Boundary of Jewishness: Some Measures of Jewish Identity in the United States," in U.O. Schmelz, P. Glikson, S. DellaPergola, eds., *Papers in Jewish Demography 1973* (Jerusalem, 1977), pp. 117–39. A different set of estimates was prepared by the 1970–1971 NJPS chief statistician, Bernard Lazerwitz, in "An Estimate of a Rare Population Group: The U.S. Jewish Population," *Demography*, vol. 15, 1978, pp. 389–94. The matter was summarized in U.O. Schmelz, *World Jewish Population: Regional Estimates and Projections* (Jerusalem, 1981), pp. 32–36.

[11]U.O. Schmelz and Sergio DellaPergola, *Basic Trends in U.S. Jewish Demography*, Jewish Sociology Papers, American Jewish Committee (New York, 1988); and Sidney Goldstein, "American Jewish Demography: Inconsistencies That Challenge," in U.O. Schmelz and S. DellaPergola, eds., *Papers in Jewish Demography 1985* (Jerusalem, 1989), pp. 23–42.

[12]U.S. Department of Justice, Immigration and Naturalization Service, 1990, unpublished

influence of international migration did not show up in the size of U.S. "core" Jewish population according to NJPS indicates that the balance of other factors of "core" population change over that whole 20-year period must have been somewhat negative. Referring again to our conceptual and definitional framework, it is worth noting that in 1990 the "core" Jewish population comprised about two-thirds of the "enlarged" Jewish population; conversely, the latter exceeded the former by roughly one-half.

The research team of the NAJDB, which is responsible for the primary handling of NJPS data files, has also continued its yearly compilation of local Jewish population estimates. These are reported elsewhere in this volume.[13] NAJDB estimated the U.S. Jewish population in 1986 at 5,814,000, including "under 2 percent" non-Jewish household members. This was very close to our own previous estimate of 5,700,000. The NAJDB estimate was modified to 5,943,700 for 1987, to 5,935,000 for 1989, and to 5,981,000 for 1990. These changes do not reflect actual sudden growth or decline, but rather corrections and adaptations made in the figures for several local communities. It should be realized that compilations of local estimates, even if as painstaking as in the case of the NAJDB, are subject to a great many local biases and tend to fall behind the actual pace of national trends. This is especially true in a context of vigorous internal migration, as in the United States. The new NJPS figure, in spite of sample-survey biases, provides a more reliable national Jewish population baseline.

Canada. In Canada the 1981 census enumerated 296,425 Jews according to religion. By adding 9,950 persons who reported "Jewish" as their single reply to the census question on ethnic origin, while not reporting any non-Jewish religion (such as Catholic, Anglican, etc.), the figure rises to 306,375. There were additional persons who did not report a non-Jewish religion but mentioned "Jewish" as part of a multiple response to the question on ethnic origin. It is likely that some of them were merely thinking in terms of ancestry and did not actually consider themselves as Jews at the time of the census. Yet, after including a reasonable portion of the latter group, a total "core" Jewish population of 310,000 was suggested for 1981. A further 5,140 Canadians, who reported being Jewish by ethnic origin but identified with another religion, were not included in our estimate.

The population census held in Canada in 1986 provided new data on ethnic origins but not on religious groups. A total of 245,855 persons reported being Jewish as a single reply to the question on ethnic origin, as against 264,020 in the same category in 1981. A further 97,655 mentioned a Jewish origin as part of a multiple

---

(ISAC) was established. Cochaired by Dr. Roberto Bachi of the Hebrew University and Dr. Sidney Goldstein of Brown University, ISAC's function is to coordinate and monitor Jewish population data collection internationally.

[13]The first in a new series of yearly compilations of local U.S. Jewish population estimates appeared in Barry A. Kosmin, Paul Ritterband, and Jeffrey Scheckner, "Jewish Population in the United States, 1986," AJYB 1987, vol. 87, pp. 164–91. The 1990 update appears elsewhere in the present volume.

response to the 1986 question on ethnic origin, as compared to apparently 30,000–40,000 in 1981. Thus, a substantial increase in the number of Canadians reporting partially Jewish ancestry seemed to offset the decline in the number of those with a solely Jewish identification according to the ethnic criterion. Besides actual demographic and identificational trends, changes in the wording of the relevant questions in the two censuses may have influenced these variations in the size of the Canadian "ethnically" Jewish population.

The 1986 census data indicated that about 9,000 Jews migrated to Canada between 1981 and 1986; more immigration arrived in the following years. In the light of this admittedly partial evidence, and considering the increasingly aged Jewish population structure, it is suggested that a migratory surplus may have roughly offset the probably negative balance of internal evolution since the 1981 census. Consequently, the 1981 figure of 310,000 was kept unchanged throughout 1989. The next census, in 1991, is again expected to include questions on both religion and ethnic origin and will thus provide a new baseline for the estimate of Canada's Jewish population.

Central America. The estimate for Mexico was kept unchanged at 35,000. The official Mexican censuses have given widely varying figures—17,574 in 1950; 100,750 in 1960; 49,277 in 1970; 61,790 in 1980. It is generally admitted that the last three censuses mistakenly included among the Jews many thousands of non-Jews living outside the known regions of Jewish residence in that country. In 1990 a new census was undertaken, but the reported figure of Jews was not available at the time of this writing. A Jewish-sponsored population survey of Mexican Jewry was launched at the end of 1990, and results are expected in 1991. Panama's Jewish population—the second largest in Central America—is estimated to have grown to 5,000.

South America.[14] The Jewish population of Argentina, the largest in that geographical region, is marked by a negative balance of internal evolution. Since the 1960s, the balance of external migrations was strongly negative; after the restoration of a democratic regime in the early 1980s emigration diminished and there was some return migration. In 1989, emigration increased again. Accordingly, the estimate for Argentinian Jewry was reduced from 220,000 in 1988 to 218,000 in 1989.

The official population census of Brazil in 1980 showed a figure of 91,795 Jews. Since it is possible that some otherwise identifying Jews failed to declare themselves as such in the census, a corrected estimate of 100,000 was adopted for 1980 and has been kept unchanged through 1989, assuming that the overall balance of vital events and external migrations was close to zero. The 100,000 figure fits the admittedly

---

[14]For a more detailed discussion of the region's Jewish population trends, see U.O. Schmelz and Sergio DellaPergola, "The Demography of Latin American Jewry," AJYB 1985, vol. 85, pp. 51–102. See also Sergio DellaPergola, "Demographic Trends of Latin American Jewry," in J. Laikin Elkin and G.W. Merks, eds., *The Jewish Presence in Latin America* (Boston, 1987), pp. 85–133.

TABLE 3. ESTIMATED JEWISH POPULATION DISTRIBUTION IN EUROPE, 1989

Country	Total Population	Jewish Population	Jews per 1,000 Population	Accuracy Rating
Belgium	9,931,000	31,800	3.2	D
Denmark	5,120,000	6,500	1.3	C 1988
France	55,979,000	530,000	9.5	C 1972–88
Germany[a]	77,271,000	35,000	0.5	C 1987–89
Great Britain	56,861,000	320,000	5.6	B 1988
Greece	10,031,000	4,900	0.5	B 1986
Ireland	3,685,000	1,900	0.5	B 1988
Italy	57,290,000	31,400	0.5	B 1986
Luxembourg	367,000	700	1.9	C 1970
Netherlands	14,700,000	25,700	1.7	C 1988
Portugal	10,264,000	300	0.0	B 1986
Spain	39,193,000	12,000	0.3	D
In transit[b]		19,000		A 1989
Total European Community	340,692,000	1,019,200	3.0	
Austria	7,493,000	6,300	0.8	B 1986
Finland	4,963,000	1,300	0.3	A 1987
Gibraltar	30,000	600	20.0	B 1981
Norway	4,200,000	1,000	0.2	A 1987
Sweden	8,343,000	15,000	1.8	C 1986
Switzerland	6,514,000	19,000	2.9	B 1980
Other	976,000	100	0.1	D
In transit[c]		9,000		A 1989
Total other Western Europe	32,519,000	52,300	1.6	
Albania	3,190,000	300	0.1	D X
Bulgaria	9,003,000	3,100	0.3	D
Czechoslovakia	15,632,000	7,900	0.5	D
Hungary	10,569,000	58,000	5.5	D
Poland	38,210,000	4,100	0.1	D
Romania	23,161,000	19,000	0.8	B 1988
Turkey[d]	54,564,000	20,000	0.4	C 1988
USSR[d]	285,861,000	1,370,000	4.8	B 1989 X
Yugoslavia	23,711,000	4,500	0.2	C 1986
Total Eastern Europe and Balkans	463,900,000	1,486,900	3.2	
Total	837,111,000	2,558,400	3.1	

[a]Including the German Democratic Republic, formerly listed in Eastern Europe.
[b]In Italy.
[c]In Austria.
[d]Including Asian regions.

rough estimates that are available for the size of local Jewish communities in Brazil. On the strength of fragmentary information that is accumulating, the quite tentative estimate for Uruguay was slightly reduced, while those for Venezuela, Chile, Colombia, and Peru were not changed.

EUROPE

Of the estimated over two and a half million Jews in Europe, 42 percent lived in Western Europe and 58 percent in Eastern Europe and the Balkan countries—including the Asian territories of the USSR and Turkey (see table 3).

European Community. The 12 countries that form the European Community (EC) had a combined Jewish population of 1,019,200. Economic integration between these countries is expected to increase after the end of 1992, following the implementation of existing treaties. This will most likely stimulate some geographical mobility in response to occupational needs and opportunities, with possible effects on the distribution of Jews among the EC's different countries. France has the largest Jewish population in Western Europe, estimated at 530,000. Monitoring the plausible trends of both the internal evolution and external migrations of Jews in France—including a study conducted in 1988 at the initiative of the Fonds Social Juif Unifié—suggests that there has been little net change in Jewish population size since the major survey that was taken in the 1970s.[15]

Periodic reestimations of the size of British Jewry are carried out by the Community Research Unit (CRU) of the Board of Deputies. Based on an analysis of Jewish deaths during 1975–1979, a population baseline for 1977 was set at 336,000 with a margin of error of $+/-34,000$.[16] An excess of deaths over births is clearly shown by the vital statistical records regularly compiled by the Jewish community. Allowing for some assimilatory losses and emigration, the update for 1984, as elaborated by the CRU, came to 330,000. The update for 1986 was 326,000; continuation of the same trends suggests an estimate of 320,000 for 1989.

West Germany, Belgium, Italy, and the Netherlands each have Jewish populations ranging around 30,000. There is a tendency toward internal shrinkage of all these Jewries, but in some instances this is offset by immigration. In 1989 the momentous process of German political unification began. Although it was formally completed only in 1990, our 1989 estimate is for the reunited country. In the German Federal Republic, the 1987 population census reported 32,319 Jews. Jewish community records—which are among the most complete and up-to-date availa-

---

[15]Doris Bensimon and Sergio DellaPergola, *La population juive de France: socio-démographie et identité* (Jerusalem and Paris, 1984); Erik H. Cohen, *Le point de vue du grand public juif, Avril-Juillet 1988* (Paris-Jerusalem, 1989).

[16]Steven Haberman, Barry A. Kosmin, and Caren Levy, "Mortality Patterns of British Jews 1975–79: Insights and Applications for the Size and Structure of British Jewry," *Journal of the Royal Statistical Society*, ser. A, 146, pt. 3, 1983, pp. 294–310.

ble—pointed to over 27,500 affiliated Jews, with minimal changes between 1986 and 1989. From the scarce information that existed about the number of Jews in the former German Democratic Republic, we gave an estimate of 500 for 1988. Our 1989 estimate for unified Germany is 35,000, the increase over the sum of Jewish populations in the previous West and East Germanys reflecting assumed recent immigration.

In Belgium, the size of Jewish population is probably quite stable owing to the comparatively strong Orthodox element in that community. In Italy, until 1984, Jews were legally bound to affiliate with the local Jewish communities. Since then, membership in the communities has been voluntary. Although most Jews reconfirmed their membership, the looseness of the new legal framework may reduce both the completeness of the communal registers and, in the long run, the cohesion of Italian Jewry.

Other EC member countries have smaller and, overall, slowly declining Jewish populations. An exception may be Spain, whose Jewish population is very tentatively estimated at 12,000.

Other Western Europe. Countries which are not EC members together account for a Jewish population of 52,300, including migrants in transit in Austria. Switzerland's Jews are estimated at below 20,000. While there is evidence of a negative balance of births and deaths, connected with great aging and frequent outmarriage, immigration may have offset the internal losses. The Jewish populations in Scandinavian countries are, on the whole, numerically rather stable.

USSR. East European Jewry is characterized by very low levels of "effectively Jewish" fertility, connected with a frequent and prolonged practice of outmarriage, and by heavy aging. Therefore, the shrinking of the Jewish populations there must be comparatively rapid. By far the largest Jewish population in Eastern Europe is still concentrated in the USSR, including its Asian territory.

Data on "nationalities" (ethnic groups) from the Soviet Union's official population census, carried out in January 1989, were released in 1990.[17] The new figure for Jews, 1,450,000, confirmed the declining trend already apparent in the previous three population censuses: 2,267,800 in 1959; 2,150,700 in 1970; and 1,810,900 in 1979. Our own estimate for Soviet Jewry, relating to the end of 1988 and projected from the 1979 population census, was 1,435,000. It thus deviated by only 1 percent from the new official baseline figure.

Our reservation about Soviet Jewish population figures in previous AJYB volumes bears repeating: some underreporting is not impossible, but it cannot be quantified and should not be exaggerated. Indeed, the official census figures appear to be remarkably consistent with one another—in view of the known volume of

---

[17]No detailed publication of the 1989 census results by "nationalities" has yet been issued. First data appeared in "Po dannym goskomstata SSSR," *Gazeta Soyuz*, Mar. 11, 1990; Mark Kupovetzky, "Yidish-dos mame-loschen fun 150 toysent Sovetische yiden," *Sovetisch Heimland*, 1990, no. 3, p. 131.

emigration, on the one hand, and the internal demographic evolution of the Jewish population in recent decades, on the other. The latter was characterized by very low fertility and birthrates, high frequencies of outmarriage, a preference for identification with non-Jewish nationalities among the children of outmarriage, aging, and a clear surplus of Jewish deaths over Jewish births.[18] Viewed conceptually (see above), the census figures represent the "core" Jewish population in the USSR. They actually constitute a good example of a large, empirically measured "core" Jewish population in the Diaspora, consisting of the aggregate of self-identifying Jews.[19]

The respective figures for the "enlarged" Jewish population—including all current Jews, any other persons of Jewish parentage, and their non-Jewish household members—must be substantially higher in a societal context like that of the USSR, which has been characterized by high intermarriage rates for a considerable time. It is not possible to provide an actual estimate of this "enlarged" Jewish population in the USSR, for lack of appropriate data. It is obvious, though, that its size is exceeded even by the wider provisions of Israel's Law of Return (see above), which apply to virtually the maximum emigration pool. Any of the high numbers attributed recently to the size of Soviet Jewry, insofar as they are based on demographic reasoning, do not relate to the "core" but to the various components of the "enlarged" Jewish population.[20]

Just as the numbers of declared Jews in successive censuses remained consistent, the numbers of persons of Jewish descent who preferred not to be identified as Jews were also rather consistent, at least until 1989. However, recent developments, especially the emigration urge so impressively illustrated by the exodus of 1990, have probably led to cases of self-identification as Jews by persons who did not describe themselves as such in the returns to the 1989 census. In terms of demographic accounting, such persons constitute net increments to the numbers of Soviet as well as world Jewry.

With regard to updating the January 1989 census figure to the end of the same year, it must be noted that Jewish emigration from the USSR increased significantly during that year. An estimated 71,000 Jews left—including non-Jewish family mem-

---

[18]U.O. Schmelz, "New Evidence on Basic Issues in the Demography of Soviet Jews," *Jewish Journal of Sociology*, 16, no. 2, 1974, pp. 209–23. See also Mordechai Altshuler, *Soviet Jewry Since the Second World War: Population and Social Structure* (Westport, 1987). Indeed, the consistency between the censuses, i.e., the respective declarations of self-identification by Jews, was such that our estimate for 1975 fit neatly as a demographic interpolation between the results of the 1970 census and the subsequent one held in 1979. See Schmelz, *World Jewish Population: Regional Estimates and Projections*.

[19]Though one should cautiously keep in mind the possible effects on census declarations of the prolonged existence of a totalitarian regime as well as societal preferences for other than Jewish nationalities in the various parts of the Soviet Union.

[20]The statistics of immigrants to Israel offer no help in determining the ratio between Jews and non-Jews in an "enlarged" Soviet Jewish population. Due to the highly self-selective character of *aliyah*, non-Jews constitute a small minority of all new immigrants from the USSR.

bers—as against 19,300 in 1988; 8,100 in 1987; and only 7,000 during the whole 1982–1986 period. (The spectacular upsurge in 1990—over 225,000 migrants—is not dealt with here, since the present article covers 1989.) Assuming that not all of the migrants were themselves Jewish, we deducted a figure of only 60,000 from the "core" Jewish population remaining in the USSR at the end of 1989. In view of the intervening political developments, we also assumed a greater readiness to declare their ethnicity on the part of some Jews in the USSR who previously had preferred to conceal it. These "returnees" imply an actual growth in the "core" Jewish population in the USSR. At the same time, the heavy deficit of internal population dynamics must have continued and even intensified, due to the great aging which is known to have prevailed for many decades. Aging cannot but have been exacerbated by the significantly younger age composition of the emigrants.[21] On the strength of these considerations, our estimate of the "core" Jewish population in the USSR was reduced from the revised figure of 1,450,000 at the end of 1988/beginning of 1989 (according to the recent census) to 1,370,000 at the end of 1989.

In 1989 the choice of country of destination by Jews leaving the Soviet Union followed the same pattern as in the preceding few years. A minority went to Israel (13,000 or roughly one in each 5–6 emigrants), while a majority chose to settle in Western countries. However, because of the strong preference for settling in the United States and that country's selective immigration policies, there were more would-be immigrants than available immigration permits (40,000 in 1989). Consequently, the number of Soviet Jews in transit in temporary accommodations in Europe increased from 10,000 at the end of 1988 to about 28,000 at the end of 1989: of these, 19,000 were living in Italy and 9,000 in Austria. The relevant figures are shown separately in table 3. It was only in the large emigration wave of 1990 that the destination again changed dramatically, the great majority moving to Israel.

Other Eastern Europe and Balkans. The Jewish populations in Hungary and Romania and the small remnants in Poland, Czechoslovakia, Bulgaria, and Yugoslavia are all reputed to be very overaged and exhibiting frequent outmarriage. Their inevitable numerical decline is reflected in reduced estimates. The size of Hungarian Jewry—the largest in Eastern Europe outside the USSR—is quite insufficiently known. Our estimate only attempts to reflect the declining trend that prevails there too, according to the available indications. Comparatively large emigration of Jews continued to take place from Romania, which was reflected in the detailed community records available there. Romania's Jewish population declined to 19,000 in 1989.

The Jewish population of Turkey, where a surplus of deaths over births was reported, was estimated at about 20,000.

---

[21]Age structures of Jewish migrants from the USSR to the United States and to Israel in 1989 are available, respectively, from: HIAS, *Statistical Abstract*, vol. 30, no. 4 (New York, 1990); Israel Central Bureau of Statistics, unpublished data.

ASIA

Israel accounts for 99 percent of all the three and three-quarter million Jews in Asia, excluding the Asian territories of the USSR and Turkey (see table 4). Israel's Jewish population grew in 1989 by about 58,000. About 81 percent of this growth was due to natural increase; 19 percent was due to the net migration balance.[22] It is difficult to estimate the Jewish population of Iran for any given date, but it continues to dwindle. The estimate for 1989 was kept at 20,000. In other Asian countries with small long-standing communities—such as India and Syria—the Jewish populations tend to decline slowly. Very small communities, partially of a transient character, exist in several countries of Southeast Asia.

AFRICA

About 150,000 Jews are estimated to remain now in Africa. The Republic of South Africa accounts for 76 percent of total Jews in that continent (see table 5).

In 1980, according to the official census, there were about 118,000 Jews among South Africa's white population.[23] Substantial Jewish emigration since then has been compensated in good part by Jewish immigration. Considering a moderately negative migration balance and an incipient negative balance of internal changes, the Jewish population estimate for 1988 was reduced to 114,000. In 1989, the numbers of emigrants, on the one hand, and immigrants and returning residents, on the other, possibly balanced—suggesting no considerable changes in Jewish population size compared to the previous year. A Jewish-sponsored survey of South African Jewry was launched in 1990, and results will be forthcoming in 1991.

According to recent reports, the Jews remaining in Ethiopia at the end of 1989 were estimated very roughly at 20,000, instead of 12,000 as was previously assumed. The remnant of Moroccan and Tunisian Jewry continued to shrink slowly through emigration. It should be pointed out, though, that not a few Jews have a foothold both in Morocco or Tunisia and in France, and their geographical attribution is uncertain.

OCEANIA

The major country of Jewish residence in Oceania (Australasia) is Australia, where 95 percent of the estimated total of nearly 90,000 Jews live (see table 6).

The 1986 census of Australia, where the question on religion was optional,

---

[22]For a comprehensive review of sociodemographic changes in Israel, see U.O. Schmelz, Sergio DellaPergola, and Uri Avner, "Ethnic Differences Among Israeli Jews: A New Look," AJYB 1990, vol. 90, pp. 3–204.

[23]Sergio DellaPergola and Allie A. Dubb, "South African Jewry: A Sociodemographic Profile," AJYB 1988, vol. 88, pp. 59–140.

TABLE 4. ESTIMATED JEWISH POPULATION DISTRIBUTION IN ASIA, 1989

Country	Total Population	Jewish Population	Jews per 1,000 Population	Accuracy Rating
Hong Kong	5,768,000	1,000	0.2	D
India	835,812,000	4,900	0.0	C 1981
Iran	54,889,000	20,000	0.4	D
Iraq	18,279,000	200	0.0	D
Israel	4,561,000[a]	3,717,100	815.2	A 1989
Japan	122,933,000	1,000	0.0	C 1988
Korea, South	43,107,000	100	0.0	D
Philippines	60,927,000	100	0.0	D
Singapore	2,674,000	300	0.1	C 1984
Syria	12,062,000	4,000	0.3	D
Thailand	54,916,000	300	0.0	D
Yemen	7,770,000	1,400	0.2	D X
Other	1,773,347,000	300	0.0	D
Total	2,997,045,000	3,750,700	1.3	

[a]End 1989.

TABLE 5. ESTIMATED JEWISH POPULATION DISTRIBUTION IN AFRICA, 1989

Country	Total Population	Jewish Population	Jews per 1,000 Population	Accuracy Rating
Egypt	52,757,000	200	0.0	C 1988
Ethiopia	45,687,000	20,000	0.4	D X
Kenya	24,097,000	400	0.0	B 1988
Morocco	24,521,000	10,000	0.4	D
South Africa	34,492,000	114,000	3.3	C 1980
Tunisia	7,990,000	2,500	0.3	D
Zaire	34,853,000	400	0.0	D
Zambia	8,148,000	300	0.0	D
Zimbabwe	9,419,000	1,100	0.1	B 1988
Other	386,353,000	1,000	0.0	D
Total	628,317,000	149,900	0.2	

enumerated 69,065 declared Jews. However, it also indicated that about 25 percent of the country's whole population either did not specify their religion or stated explicitly that they had none. This large group must be assumed to contain persons who identify in other ways as Jews. In addition, Australian Jewry received migratory reinforcements during the last decade, especially from South Africa. At the same time, there are demographic patterns with negative effects on Jewish population size, such as strong aging, low or negative natural increase, and some assimilation. Therefore, for 1989 we repeated a provisional estimate of 85,000. The new census in 1991, as well as a Jewish survey now being planned, will hopefully provide firmer data on Jewish population trends since previous censuses. The Jewish community in New Zealand—now estimated at 4,500—attracted some immigrants but incurred a negative migration balance with Australia.

TABLE 6. ESTIMATED JEWISH POPULATION DISTRIBUTION IN OCEANIA, 1989

Country	Total Population	Jewish Population	Jews per 1,000 Population	Accuracy Rating
Australia	16,553,000	85,000	5.1	C 1986
New Zealand	3,353,000	4,500	1.3	C 1988
Other	6,203,000	100	0.0	D
Total	26,109,000	89,600	3.4	

Dispersion and Concentration

Table 7 demonstrates the magnitude of Jewish dispersion. The individual countries listed above as each having at least 100 Jews are scattered over all the continents. In 1989, more than half (42 out of 74 countries) had fewer than 5,000 Jews each.

In relative terms, too, the Jews are now thinly scattered nearly everywhere in the Diaspora. There is not a single Diaspora country where they amount even to 3 percent of the total population. In most countries they constitute a far smaller fraction. Only three Diaspora countries have more than 1 percent Jews in their total population; and only nine countries have more than 5 Jews per 1,000 of population. The respective nine countries are (in descending order of the proportion of their Jews, regardless of the absolute numbers): United States (22.3 per 1,000), Gibraltar (20.0), Canada (11.8), France (9.5), Uruguay (7.9), Argentina (6.8), Great Britain (5.6), Hungary (5.5), and Australia (5.1). The other major Diaspora Jewries having lower proportions of Jews per 1,000 of total population are the USSR (4.8), South Africa (3.3), and Brazil (0.7 per 1,000).

TABLE 7. DISTRIBUTION OF THE WORLD'S JEWS, BY NUMBER AND PROPORTION (PER 1,000 POPULATION) IN VARIOUS COUNTRIES, 1989

Number of Jews in Country	Jews per 1,000 Population					
	Total	Below 1	1–4.9	5–9.9	10–24.9	25+
			Number of Countries[a]			
Total	74	49	15	6	3	1
Below 1,000	24	19	4	—	1	—
1,000–4,900	18	17	1	—	—	—
5,000–9,900	5	3	2	—	—	—
10,000–49,900	16	9	6	1	—	—
50,000–99,900	2	—	—	2	—	—
100,000–999,900	6	1	1	3	1	—
1,000,000+	3	—	1	—	1	1
		Jewish Population Distribution (Absolute Numbers)				
Total	12,810,300[b]	374,200	1,628,200	1,235,400	5,825,600	3,717,100
Below 1,000	9,700	7,400	1,700	—	600	—
1,000–4,900	48,200	43,700	4,500	—	—	—
5,000–9,900	32,200	20,700	11,500	—	—	—
10,000–49,900	353,300	202,400	126,500	24,400	—	—
50,000–99,900	143,000	—	—	143,000	—	—
100,000–999,900	1,592,000	100,000	114,000	1,068,000	310,000	—
1,000,000+	10,602,100	—	1,370,000	—	5,515,000	3,717,100
		Jewish Population Distribution (Percent of World's Jews)				
Total	100.0[b]	3.0	12.7	9.6	45.5	29.0
Below 1,000	0.1	0.1	0.0	—	0.0	—
1,000–4,900	0.4	0.3	0.0	—	—	—
5,000–9,900	0.3	0.2	0.1	—	—	—
10,000–49,900	2.8	1.6	1.0	0.2	—	—
50,000–99,900	1.1	—	—	1.1	—	—
100,000–999,900	12.4	0.8	0.9	8.3	2.4	—
1,000,000+	82.8	—	10.7	—	43.1	29.0

[a]Excluding countries with fewer than 100 Jews and Jews in transit in Europe.
[b]Including countries with fewer than 100 Jews and Jews in transit in Europe.

TABLE 8. TEN COUNTRIES WITH LARGEST JEWISH POPULATIONS, 1989

			\% of Total Jewish Population			
		Jewish	In the Diaspora		In the World	
Rank	Country	Population	%	Cumulative %	%	Cumulative %
1	United States	5,515,000	60.6	60.6	43.1	43.1
2	Israel	3,717,100	—	—	29.0	72.1
3	Soviet Union	1,370,000	15.1	75.7	10.7	82.8
4	France	530,000	5.8	81.5	4.1	86.9
5	Great Britain	320,000	3.5	85.0	2.5	89.4
6	Canada	310,000	3.4	88.4	2.4	91.8
7	Argentina	218,000	2.4	90.8	1.7	93.5
8	South Africa	114,000	1.3	92.1	0.9	94.4
9	Brazil	100,000	1.1	93.2	0.8	95.2
10	Australia	85,000	1.0	94.2	0.7	95.9

In the State of Israel, by contrast, the Jewish majority amounted to 81.5 percent in 1989, compared to 81.7 percent in 1988—not including the Arab population of the administered areas.

While Jews are widely dispersed, they are also concentrated to some extent (see table 8). In 1989, nearly 96 percent of world Jewry lived in the ten countries with the largest Jewish populations; 83 percent lived in the three countries that have at least a million Jews each (United States, Israel, Soviet Union). Similarly, nine leading Diaspora countries together comprised over 94 percent of the Diaspora Jewish population; two countries (United States and Soviet Union) accounted for 76 percent, and the United States alone for over 61 percent of total Diaspora Jewry.

U.O. SCHMELZ
SERGIO DELLAPERGOLA

Directories
Lists
Obituaries

National Jewish Organizations[1]

UNITED STATES

Organizations are listed according to functions as follows:

Community Relations	469
Cultural	473
Israel-Related	479
Overseas Aid	489
Religious, Educational Organizations	491
Schools, Institutions	501
Social, Mutual Benefit	510
Social Welfare	512

Note also cross-references under these headings:

Professional Associations	516
Women's Organizations	517
Youth and Student Organizations	517

COMMUNITY RELATIONS

AMERICAN COUNCIL FOR JUDAISM (1943). PO Box 9009, Alexandria, VA 22304. (703)836-2546. Pres. Alan V. Stone; Exec. Dir. Allan C. Brownfeld. Seeks to advance the universal principles of a Judaism free of nationalism, and the national, civic, cultural, and social integration into American institutions of Americans of Jewish faith. *Issues of the American Council for Judaism; Special Interest Report.*

AMERICAN JEWISH ALTERNATIVES TO ZIONISM, INC. (1968). 347 Fifth Ave., Suite 900, NYC 10016. (212)557-5410. FAX: (212)867-5166. Pres. Elmer Berger; V.-Pres. Mrs. Arthur Gutman. Applies Jewish values of justice and humanity to the Arab-Israel conflict in the Middle East; rejects nationality attachment of Jews, particularly American Jews, to the State of Israel as self-segregating, inconsistent with American constitutional concepts of individual citizenship and separation of church and state, and as being a principal obstacle to Middle East peace. *Report.*

AMERICAN JEWISH COMMITTEE (1906). Institute of Human Relations, 165 E. 56 St., NYC 10022. (212)751-4000. FAX: (212)-319-0975. Pres. Sholom D. Comay; Exec. V.-Pres. David A. Harris. Seeks to prevent infraction of civil and religious rights of

---

[1]The information in this directory is based on replies to questionnaires circulated by the editors.

Jews in any part of the world; to advance the cause of human rights for people of all races, creeds, and nationalities; to interpret the position of Israel to the American public; and to help American Jews maintain and enrich their Jewish identity and, at the same time, achieve full integration in American life. Includes Jacob and Hilda Blaustein Center for Human Relations, William E. Wiener Oral History Library, William Petschek National Jewish Family Center, Jacob Blaustein Institute for the Advancement of Human Rights, Institute on American Jewish–Israeli Relations. AMERICAN JEWISH YEAR BOOK (with Jewish Publication Society); *Commentary; AJC Journal; Capital Update.* Published in Israel: *Alon Yedi'ot,* a monthly bulletin of the Institute on American Jewish-Israeli Relations.

AMERICAN JEWISH CONGRESS (1918). Stephen Wise Congress House, 15 E. 84 St., NYC 10028. (212)879-4500. FAX: (212)-249-3672. Pres. Robert K. Lifton; Exec. Dir. Henry Siegman. Works to foster the creative cultural survival of the Jewish people; to help Israel develop in peace, freedom, and security; to eliminate all forms of racial and religious bigotry; to advance civil rights, protect civil liberties, defend religious freedom, and safeguard the separation of church and state. *Congress Monthly; Judaism; Boycott Report.*

ANTI-DEFAMATION LEAGUE OF B'NAI B'RITH (1913). 823 United Nations Plaza, NYC 10017. (212)490-2525. Chmn. Melvin Salberg; Dir. Abraham H. Foxman. Seeks to combat anti-Semitism and to secure justice and fair treatment for all citizens through law, education, and community relations. *ADL Bulletin; Face to Face; Fact Finding Report; International Reports; Law Notes; Rights; Law; Research and Evaluation Report; Discriminations Report; Litigation Docket; Dimensions; Middle East Notebook; Nuestro Encuentro.*

ASSOCIATION OF JEWISH COMMUNITY RELATIONS WORKERS (1950). 1522 K St., NW, Suite 900, Washington, DC 20005. (202)347-4628. Pres. Marlene Gorin. Aims to stimulate higher standards of professional practice in Jewish community relations; encourages research and training toward that end; conducts educational programs and seminars; aims to encourage cooperation between community relations workers and those working in other areas of Jewish communal service.

CENTER FOR JEWISH COMMUNITY STUDIES (1970). 1017 Gladfelter Hall, Temple University, Philadelphia, PA 19122. (215)787-1459. FAX: (215)787-7784. Jerusalem office: Jerusalem Center for Public Affairs. Pres. Daniel J. Elazar. Worldwide policy-studies institute devoted to the study of Jewish community organization, political thought, and public affairs, past and present, in Israel and throughout the world. Publishes original articles, essays, and monographs; maintains library, archives, and reprint series. *Jerusalem Letter/Viewpoints; Survey of Arab Affairs; Jewish Political Studies Review.*

COMMISSION ON SOCIAL ACTION OF REFORM JUDAISM (1953, joint instrumentality of the Union of American Hebrew Congregations and the Central Conference of American Rabbis). 838 Fifth Ave., NYC 10021. (212)249-0100. 2027 Massachusetts Ave., NW, Washington, DC 20036. Chmn. Harris Gilbert; Dir. Albert Vorspan; Assoc. Dir. Rabbi David Saperstein. Policy-making body that relates ethical and spiritual principles of Judaism to social-justice issues: implements resolutions through the Religious Action Center in Washington, DC, via advocacy, development of educational materials, and congregational programs. *Briefings* (social action newsletter); *Chai Impact* (legislative update).

CONFERENCE OF PRESIDENTS OF MAJOR AMERICAN JEWISH ORGANIZATIONS (1955). 110 E. 59 St., NYC 10022. (212)-752-1616. Chmn. Shoshana S. Cardin; Exec. Dir. Malcolm Hoenlein. Seeks to strengthen the U.S.-Israel alliance and to protect and enhance the security and dignity of Jews abroad. Toward this end, the Conference of Presidents speaks and acts on the basis of consensus of its 46 member agencies on issues of national and international Jewish concern. *Annual report.*

CONSULTATIVE COUNCIL OF JEWISH ORGANIZATIONS-CCJO (1946). 420 Lexington Ave., Suite 1733, NYC 10170. (212)808-5437. Pres.'s Adolphe Steg, Clemens Nathan, Joseph Nuss; Sec.-Gen. Warren Green. A nongovernmental organization in consultative status with the UN, UNESCO, ILO,UNICEF, and the Council of Europe; cooperates and consults with, advises and renders assistance to the Economic and Social Council of the UN on all problems relating to human rights and economic, social, cultural, educational, and related matters pertaining to Jews.

COORDINATING BOARD OF JEWISH ORGANIZATIONS (1947). 1640 Rhode Island Ave., NW, Washington, DC 20036. (202)-857-6545. Pres. Kent E. Schiner; Exec. V.-Pres. Dr. Sidney Clearfield; Dir. Internatl. Council Warren Eisenberg. Coordinates the UN activities of B'nai B'rith and the British and South African Boards of Jewish Deputies.

COUNCIL OF JEWISH ORGANIZATIONS IN CIVIL SERVICE, INC. (1948). 45 E. 33 St., Rm. 604, NYC 10016. (212)689–2015. Pres. Louis Weiser. Supports merit system; encourages recruitment of Jewish youth to government service; member of Coalition to Free Soviet Jews, NY Jewish Community Relations Council, NY Metropolitan Coordinating Council on Jewish Poverty, Jewish Labor Committee, America-Israel Friendship League. *Council Digest.*

INSTITUTE FOR PUBLIC AFFAIRS (*see* Union of Orthodox Jewish Congregations of America)

INTERNATIONAL CONFERENCE OF JEWISH COMMUNAL SERVICE (*see* World Conference of Jewish Communal Service)

INTERNATIONAL LEAGUE FOR THE REPATRIATION OF RUSSIAN JEWS, INC. (1968). 2 Fountain Lane, Suite 2T, Scarsdale, NY 10583. (800)448–1866. Pres. Morris Brafman; Chmn. James H. Rapp. Helped to bring the situation of Soviet Jews to world attention; advocates in world forums for the right of Soviet Jews to repatriation.

JEWISH LABOR COMMITTEE (1934). Atran Center for Jewish Culture, 25 E. 21 St., NYC 10010. (212)477–0707. FAX: (212)-477–1918. Pres. Lenore Miller; Exec. Dir. Martin Lapan. Serves as liaison between the Jewish community and the trade-union movement; works with the AFL-CIO to combat anti-Semitism and engender support for the State of Israel and Soviet Jewry; strengthens support within the Jewish community for the social goals and programs of the labor movement; supports Yiddish cultural institutions. *Jewish Labor Committee Review; Alumni Newsletter.*

———, NATIONAL TRADE UNION COUNCIL FOR HUMAN RIGHTS (1956). Atran Center for Jewish Culture, 25 E. 21 St., NYC 10010. (212)477–0707. FAX: (212)477–1918. Chmn. Sol Hoffman; Exec. Sec. Michael Perry. Works with the American labor movement in advancing the struggle for social justice and equal opportunity and assists unions in every issue affecting human rights. Fights discrimination on all levels and helps to promote labor's broad social and economic goals.

JEWISH PEACE FELLOWSHIP (1941). Box 271, Nyack, NY 10960. (914)358–4601. FAX: (914)358–4924. Pres. Rabbi Philip Bentley; Sec. Naomi Goodman. Unites those who believe that Jewish ideals and experience provide inspiration for a nonviolent philosophy and way of life; offers draft counseling, especially for conscientious objection based on Jewish "religious training and belief"; encourages Jewish community to become more knowledgeable, concerned, and active in regard to the war/peace problem. *Shalom/Jewish Peace Letter.*

JEWISH WAR VETERANS OF THE UNITED STATES OF AMERICA (1896). 1811 R St., NW, Washington, DC 20009. (202)265–6280. FAX: (202)234–5662. Natl. Exec. Dir. Steve Shaw. Natl. Commander Alfred Schwartz. Seeks to foster true allegiance to the United States; to combat bigotry and prevent defamation of Jews; to encourage the doctrine of universal liberty, equal rights, and full justice for all; to cooperate with and support existing educational institutions and establish new ones; to foster the education of ex-servicemen, ex-servicewomen, and members in the ideals and principles of Americanism. *Jewish Veteran.*

———, NATIONAL MEMORIAL, INC. (1958). 1811 R St., NW, Washington, DC 20009. (202)265–6280. FAX: (202)462–3192. Pres. Florence G. Levine. Operates a museum and library archive dedicated to telling the story of the activities and service of American Jews in the armed forces of the U.S. *Quarterly newsletter, Routes to Roots.*

NATIONAL CONFERENCE ON SOVIET JEWRY (formerly AMERICAN JEWISH CONFERENCE ON SOVIET JEWRY) (1964; reorg. 1971). 10 E. 40 St., Suite 1010, NYC 10016. (212)679–6122. FAX: (212)686–1193. Chmn. Shoshana S. Cardin; Exec.

Dir. Martin A. Wenick. Coordinating agency for major national Jewish organizations and local community groups in the U.S., acting on behalf of Soviet Jewry through public education and social action; stimulates all segments of the community to maintain an interest in the problems of Soviet Jews by publishing reports and special pamphlets, sponsoring special programs and projects, organizing public meetings and forums. *Newsbreak; annual report; action and program kits; Wrap-Up Leadership Report.*

———, SOVIET JEWRY RESEARCH BUREAU. Chmn. Charlotte Jacobson. Organized by NCSJ to monitor emigration trends. Primary task is the accumulation, evaluation, and processing of information regarding Soviet Jews, especially those who apply for emigration.

NATIONAL JEWISH COALITION (1980). 415 2nd St., NE, Suite 100, Washington, DC 20002. (202)547-7701. FAX: (202)544-2434. Hon. Chmn. Max M. Fisher; Cochmn. Richard J. Fox, George Klein; Exec. Dir. Benjamin Waldman. Promotes Jewish involvement in Republican politics; sensitizes Republican leaders to the concerns of the American Jewish community; promotes principles of free enterprise, a strong national defense, and an internationalist foreign policy. *NJC Bulletin; NJC in Brief*

NATIONAL JEWISH COMMISSION ON LAW AND PUBLIC AFFAIRS (COLPA) (1965). 450 Seventh Ave., Suite 2203, NYC 10123. (212)563-0100. Pres. Allen L. Rothenberg; Exec. Dir. Dennis Rapps. Voluntary association of attorneys whose purpose is to represent the observant Jewish community on legal, legislative, and public-affairs matters.

NATIONAL JEWISH COMMUNITY RELATIONS ADVISORY COUNCIL (1944). 443 Park Ave. S., 11th fl., NYC 10016. (212)684-6950. FAX: (212)686-1353. Chmn. Arden E. Shenker; Sec. Barry Ungar; Exec. V.-Chmn. Lawrence Rubin. National coordinating body for the field of Jewish community relations, comprising 13 national and 117 local Jewish community relations agencies. Promotes understanding of Israel and the Middle East; freedom for Soviet Jews; equal status for Jews and other groups in American society. Through the NJCRAC's work, its constituent organizations seek agreement on policies, strategies, and programs for effective utilization of their resources for common ends. *Joint Program Plan for Jewish Community Relations.*

NEW JEWISH AGENDA (1980). 64 Fulton St., #1100, NYC 10038. (212)227-5885. FAX: (212)962-6211. Cochmn. Tom Rawson, Lois Levine. Founded as "a progressive voice in the Jewish community and a Jewish voice among progressives." Works for peace in Central America and the Middle East, feminism, gay and lesbian rights, and economic justice, and against anti-Semitism and racism. *Agenda In-Brief.*

SHALOM CENTER (1983). 7318 Germantown Ave., Philadelphia, PA 19119. (215)247-9700. Hon. Pres. Ira Silverman; Bd. Chmn. Viki List; Exec. Dir. Arthur Waskow. National resource and organizing center for Jewish perspectives on moving from the cold war toward "One Earth"—in dealing with nuclear and other environmental dangers. Trains community organizers, holds conferences, assists local Jewish committees and coalitions on nuclear weapons and environmental issues. Sponsors Sukkat Shalom. Provides school curricula, sermon materials, legislative reports, adult-education texts, and media for Jewish use. *Shalom Report.*

STUDENT STRUGGLE FOR SOVIET JEWRY, INC. (1964). 210 W. 91 St., NYC 10024. (212)799-8900. Natl. Dir. Jacob Birnbaum; Natl. Coord. Glenn Richter; Chmn. Rabbi Avraham Weiss. Provides information and action guidance to adult and student organizations, communities, and schools throughout the U.S. and Canada; assists Soviet Jews by publicity campaigns; helps Soviet Jews in the U.S.; maintains speakers bureau and research documents. *Soviet Jewry Action Newsletter.*

UNION OF COUNCILS FOR SOVIET JEWS (1970). 1819 H St., NW., Suite 230, Washington, DC 20006. (202)775-9770. Natl. Pres. Pamela B. Cohen; Natl. Dir. Micah H. Naftalin. Its 50 local councils and 100,000 members throughout the U.S. support and protect Soviet Jews by gathering and disseminating news on the condition and treatment of Soviet Jews; advocacy to the administration, Congress, and instrumental agencies and forums; publications; educational programs, including briefings and policy analyses; rallies, demonstrations, and vigils; and travel to the Soviet Union to meet with Soviet Jewish leaders and senior officials of the Soviet Foreign Ministry. *UCSJ Quarterly Report; Refusenik Update; Congressional Handbook for Soviet Jewry, Anti-Semitism in the USSR—Status Report.*

WORLD CONFERENCE OF JEWISH COMMUNAL SERVICE (1966). 3084 State Highway 27, Suite 9, Kendall Park, NJ 08824-1657. (908)821-0282. FAX: (908)821-0493. Pres. Arthur Rotman; Sec.-Gen. Joel Ollander. Established by worldwide Jewish communal workers to strengthen their understanding of each other's programs and to communicate with colleagues in order to enrich the quality of their work. Conducts quadrennial international conferences in Jerusalem and periodic regional meetings. *Proceedings of international conferences; newsletters.*

WORLD JEWISH CONGRESS (1936; org. in U.S. 1939). 501 Madison Ave., 17th fl., NYC 10022. (212) 755-5770. FAX: (212)-755-5883. Pres. Edgar M. Bronfman; Chmn. N. Amer. Branch Leo Kolber (Montreal); Chmn. Amer. Sect. Evelyn Sommer; Sec.-Gen. Israel Singer; Exec. Dir. Elan Steinberg. Seeks to intensify bonds of world Jewry with Israel as central force in Jewish life; to strengthen solidarity among Jews everywhere and secure their rights, status, and interests as individuals and communities; to encourage development of Jewish social, religious, and cultural life throughout the world and coordinate efforts by Jewish communities and organizations to cope with any Jewish problem; to work for human rights generally. Represents its affiliated organizations—most representative bodies of Jewish communities in more than 70 countries and 35 national organizations in Amer. section—at UN, OAS, UNESCO, Council of Europe, ILO, UNICEF, and other governmental, intergovernmental, and international authorities. Publications (including those by Institute of Jewish Affairs, London): *Christian Jewish Relations; Coloquio; News and Views; Boletín Informativo OJI; Batfutsot; Gesher; Patterns of Prejudice; Soviet Jewish Affairs.*

CULTURAL

AMERICAN ACADEMY FOR JEWISH RESEARCH (1920). 3080 Broadway, NYC 10027. (212)678-8864. FAX: (212)678-8947. Pres. David Weiss Halivni; V.-Pres. & Treas. Arthur Hyman. Encourages Jewish learning and research; holds annual or semiannual meeting; awards grants for the publication of scholarly works. *Proceedings of the American Academy for Jewish Research; Monograph Series; Texts and Studies.*

AMERICAN BIBLICAL ENCYCLOPEDIA SOCIETY (1930). 24 W. Maple Ave., Monsey, NY 10952. (914)352-4609. Exec. V.-Pres. Irving Fredman; Author-Ed. Rabbi M. M. Kasher. Fosters biblical-talmudical research; sponsors and publishes *Torah Shelemah* (Heb., 41 vols.), *Encyclopedia of Biblical Interpretation* (Eng., 9 vols.), *Divrei Menachem* (Heb., 4 vols.), and related publications. *Noam.*

AMERICAN JEWISH HISTORICAL SOCIETY (1892). 2 Thornton Rd., Waltham, MA 02154. (617)891-8110. FAX: (617)899-9208. Pres. Ronald C. Curhan; Dir. Special Projects Bernard Wax. Collects, catalogues, publishes, and displays material on the history of the Jews in America; serves as an information center for inquiries on American Jewish history; maintains archives of original source material on American Jewish history; sponsors lectures and exhibitions; makes available historic Yiddish films and audiovisual material. *American Jewish History; Heritage.*

AMERICAN JEWISH PRESS ASSOCIATION (1943). c/o Northern California Jewish Bulletin, 88 First St., San Francisco, CA 94105. (415)957-9340. FAX: (415)957-0266. Pres. Marc S. Klein. Natl. Admin. Off.: 11312 Old Club Rd., Rockville, MD 20852-4537. (301)881-4113. Exec. Dir. L. Malcolm Rodman. Seeks the advancement of Jewish journalism and the maintenance of a strong Jewish press in the U.S. and Canada; encourages the attainment of the highest editorial and business standards; sponsors workshops, services for members. *Membership bulletin newsletter; Roster of Members.*

AMERICAN SOCIETY FOR JEWISH MUSIC (1974). 129 W. 67 St., NYC 10023. (212)-362-8060 X307. Pres. Cantor David Lefkowitz; Sec. Hadassah B. Markson. Promotes the knowledge, appreciation, and development of Jewish music, past and present, for professional and lay audiences. *Musica Judaica Journal.*

ASSOCIATION FOR THE SOCIAL SCIENTIFIC STUDY OF JEWRY (1971). City University of New York, 33 W. 42 St., NYC 10036. (212)642-2180. Pres. Rela Geffen Monson; V.-Pres. Steven M. Cohen; Sec.-Treas. Esther Fleishman. Arranges academic sessions and facilitates communication among social scientists studying Jewry through meetings, newsletter, and related materials. *Contemporary Jewry; ASSSJ Newsletter.*

ASSOCIATION OF JEWISH BOOK PUBLISHERS (1962). 838 Fifth Ave., NYC 10021. (212)-249-0100. Pres. Rabbi Elliot L. Stevens. As a nonprofit group, provides a forum for discussion of mutual problems by publishers, authors, and other individuals and institutions concerned with books of Jewish interest. Provides national and international exhibit opportunities for Jewish books. *Combined Jewish Book Catalog.*

ASSOCIATION OF JEWISH GENEALOGICAL SOCIETIES (1988). 1485 Teaneck Rd., Teaneck, NJ 07666. (201)837-2700. FAX: (201)837-8506. Pres. Gary Mokotoff. Confederation of over 30 Jewish Genealogical Societies (JGS) in the U.S. and Canada. Encourages Jews to research their family history, promotes membership in the various JGS, acts as representative of organized Jewish genealogy, implements projects of interest to persons researching their Jewish family history. Annual conference where members learn and exchange ideas. Each local JGS publishes its own newsletter.

ASSOCIATION OF JEWISH LIBRARIES (1965). c/o National Foundation for Jewish Culture, 330 Seventh Ave., 21st fl., NYC 10001. (212)678-8092. FAX: (212)678-8998. Pres. Linda P. Lerman; V.-Pres. and Pres.-Elect Ralph R. Simon. Seeks to promote and improve services and professional standards in Jewish libraries; disseminates Jewish library information and guidance; promotes publication of literature in the field; encourages the establishment of Jewish libraries and collections of Judaica and the choice of Judaica librarianship as a profession; cocertifies Jewish libraries (with Jewish Book Council). *AJL Newsletter; Judaica Librarianship.*

B'NAI B'RITH KLUTZNICK MUSEUM (1956). 1640 Rhode Island Ave., NW, Washington, DC 20036. (202)857-6583. A center of Jewish art and history in nation's capital, maintains temporary and permanent exhibition galleries, permanent collection of Jewish ceremonial and folk art, B'nai B'rith International reference archive, outdoor sculpture garden, and museum shop. Provides exhibitions, tours, educational programs, research assistance, and tourist information. *Semiannual newsletter; permanent collection catalogue; exhibition brochures.*

CENTER FOR HOLOCAUST STUDIES, DOCUMENTATION & RESEARCH (1974). Merged into A Living Memorial to the Holocaust–Museum of Jewish Heritage, Jan. 1991.

CENTRAL YIDDISH CULTURE ORGANIZATION (CYCO), INC. (1943). 25 E. 21 St., 3rd fl., NYC 10010. (212)505-8305. Mgr. Jacob Schneidman. Promotes, publishes, and distributes Yiddish books; publishes catalogues.

CONFERENCE ON JEWISH SOCIAL STUDIES, INC. (formerly CONFERENCE ON JEWISH RELATIONS, INC.) (1939). 2112 Broadway, Rm. 206, NYC 10023. (212)724-5336. Publishes scientific studies on Jews in the modern world, dealing with such aspects as anti-Semitism, demography, economic stratification, history, philosophy, and political developments. *Jewish Social Studies.*

CONGREGATION BINA (1981). 600 W. End Ave., Suite 1-C, NYC 10024. (212)873-4261. Pres. Joseph Moses; Hon. Pres. Samuel M. Daniel; Sec. Gen. Elijah E. Jhirad. Serves the religious, cultural, charitable, and philanthropic needs of the Children of Israel who originated in India and now reside in the U.S. Works to foster and preserve the ancient traditions, customs, liturgy, music, and folklore of Indian Jewry and to maintain needed institutions. *Kol Bina.*

CONGRESS FOR JEWISH CULTURE (1948). 25 E. 21 St., NYC 10010. (212)505-8040. Copres. Prof. Yonia Fain, Dr. Barnett Zumoff; Exec. Dir. Michael Skakun. An umbrella group comprising 16 constituent organizations; perpetuates and enhances Jewish creative expression in the U.S. and abroad; fosters all aspects of Yiddish cultural life through the publication of the journal *Zukunft,* the conferring of literary awards, commemoration of the Holocaust and the martyrdom of the Soviet Jewish writers under Stalin, and a series of topical readings, scholarly conferences, symposiums, and concerts. *Zukunft.*

HEBREW ARTS CENTER (1952). 129 W. 67 St., NYC 10023. (212)362–8060. FAX: (212)874–7865. Chmn. Lewis Kruger; Pres. Alvin E. Friedman; Exec. Dir. Lydia Kontos. Offers instruction in music, dance, art, and theater to children and adults, combining Western culture with Jewish traditions. Presents frequent performances of Jewish and general music by leading artists and ensembles in its Merkin Concert Hall and Ann Goodman Recital Hall. The Birnbaum Library houses Jewish music scores and reference books. *High Notes Newsletter;* bimonthly concert calendars; catalogues and brochures.

HEBREW CULTURE FOUNDATION (1955). 110 E. 59 St., NYC 10022. (212)752–0600. Chmn. Milton R. Konvitz; Sec. Herman L. Sainer. Sponsors the introduction and strengthening of Hebrew language and literature courses in institutions of higher learning in the United States.

HISTADRUTH IVRITH OF AMERICA (1916; reorg. 1922). 47 W. 34 St., Rm. 609, NYC 10001. (212)629–9443. Pres. Dr. David Sidorsky; Exec. V.-Pres. Aviva Barzel. Emphasizes the primacy of Hebrew in Jewish life, culture, and education; aims to disseminate knowledge of written and spoken Hebrew in the Diaspora, thus building a cultural bridge between the State of Israel and Jewish communities throughout the world. *Hadoar; Lamishpaha; Tov Lichtov.*

HOLOCAUST CENTER OF THE UNITED JEWISH FEDERATION OF GREATER PITTSBURGH (1980). 242 McKee Pl., Pittsburgh, PA 15213. (412)682–7111. Pres. Holocaust Comm. Jack Gordon; Pres. UJF David Shapira; Dir. Linda F. Hurwitz. Develops programs and provides resources to further understanding of the Holocaust and its impact on civilization. Maintains a library, archive; provides speakers, educational materials; organizes community programs.

HOLOCAUST MEMORIAL RESOURCE & EDUCATION CENTER OF CENTRAL FLORIDA (1981). 851 N. Maitland Ave., Maitland, FL 32751. (407)628–0555. FAX: (407)-645–4128. Pres. Dr. Earl Scarbeary; Exec. V.-Pres. Tess Wise. An interfaith educational center devoted to teaching the lessons of the Holocaust. Houses permanent multimedia educational exhibit; maintains library of books, videotapes, films, and other visuals to serve the entire educational establishment; offers lectures, teacher training, and other activities. *Newsletter.*

INSTITUTE FOR RUSSIAN JEWRY, INC. (1989). PO Box 96, Flushing, NY 11367. (718)969–0911. Exec. Dir. Rosa Irgal. Disseminates knowledge of Judaism in Russian language, from historical and cultural perspectives; promotes knowledge of the religious and cultural heritage of Russian Jews through Russian folk and fine art exhibits, lecture series, music and dance workshops.

INTERNATIONAL JEWISH MEDIA ASSOCIATION (1987). U.S.: c/o St. Louis Jewish Light, 12 Millstone Campus Dr., St. Louis, MO 63146. (314)432–3353. FAX: (314)-432–0515. Israel: PO Box 92, Jerusalem (2–533–296). Pres. Robert A. Cohn; Exec. Sec. Asher Weill; Staff Consultant Malcolm Rodman. A worldwide network of Jewish journalists in the Jewish and general media, which seeks to provide a forum for the exchange of materials and ideas, and to enhance the stature of Jewish media and journalists. *Presidents Bulletin; proceedings of international conferences on Jewish media.*

JCC ASSOCIATION LECTURE BUREAU (1922; formerly JWB). 15 E. 26 St., NYC 10010–1579. (212)532–4949. FAX: (212)481–4174. Dir. Sesil Lissberger. A nonprofit program service of JCC Association of N. America providing lecturers and performers from a broad range of Jewish and public life; also offers photo exhibits to stimulate Jewish programming of communal organizations. *The Jewish Arts—A Listing of Performers; Learning for Jewish Living—A Listing of Lecturers; Available Lecturers from Israel; Lecturers on the Holocaust.*

JEWISH ACADEMY OF ARTS AND SCIENCES, INC. (1926). 888 Seventh Ave., Suite 403, NYC 10106. (212)757–1627. Act. Pres. Milton Handler; Hon. Pres. Abraham I. Katsh; Dir. Benjamin Saxe. An honor society of Jews who have attained distinction in the arts, sciences, professions, and communal endeavors. Encourages the advancement of knowledge; stimulates scholarship, with particular reference to Jewish life and thought; recognition by election to membership and/or fellowship; publishes papers delivered at annual convocations.

JEWISH BOOK COUNCIL (1943). 15 E. 26 St., NYC 10010. (212)532-4949. Pres. Leonard S. Gold; Dir. Paula Gribetz Gottlieb. Promotes knowledge of Jewish books through dissemination of booklists, program materials; sponsors Jewish Book Awards, Jewish Book Month; presents literary awards and library citations; cooperates with publishers of Jewish books. *Jewish Book Annual; Jewish Books in Review; Jewish Book World.*

JEWISH MUSEUM (1904, under auspices of Jewish Theological Seminary of America). Temporary quarters: Exhibitions, programs, and shop at the New York Historical Society, 170 Central Park W., NYC; offices c/o American Bible Society Bldg., 1865 Broadway, NYC 10023. (212)399-3430. Dir. Joan H. Rosenbaum; Bd. Chmn. H. Axel Schupf. Repository of the largest collection of Judaica—paintings, prints, photographs, sculpture, coins, medals, antiquities, textiles, and other decorative arts—in the Western Hemisphere. Includes the National Jewish Archive of Broadcasting. Tours of special exhibitions and permanent installations; lectures, film showings, and concerts; special programs for children. *Special exhibition catalogues; annual report.*

JEWISH MUSIC COUNCIL (1944). 15 E. 26 St., NYC 10010. (212)532-4949. Chmn. Joseph Hurwitz; Coord. Paula Gribetz Gottlieb. Promotes Jewish music activities nationally; annually sponsors and promotes the Jewish Music season; encourages participation on a community basis. *Jewish Music Notes* and numerous music resource publications for national distribution.

JEWISH PUBLICATION SOCIETY (1888). 1930 Chestnut St., Philadelphia, PA 19103. (215)564-5925. FAX: (215)564-6640. Pres. Martin D. Cohn; Exec. V.-Pres. Rabbi Michael A. Monson. Publishes and disseminates books of Jewish interest for adults and children; titles include contemporary literature, classics, art, religion, biographies, poetry, and history. AMERICAN JEWISH YEAR BOOK (with American Jewish Committee); *The Bookmark; JPS Catalogue.*

JUDAH L. MAGNES MUSEUM—JEWISH MUSEUM OF THE WEST (1962). 2911 Russell St., Berkeley, CA 94705. (415)849-2710. FAX: (415)849-3650. Pres. Gary J. Shapiro; Dir. Seymour Fromer. Collects, preserves, and makes available Jewish art, culture, history, and literature from throughout the world. Permanent collections of fine and ceremonial art, rare Judaica library, Western Jewish History Center (archives), changing exhibits, traveling exhibits, docent tours, lectures, numismatics series, poetry award, a museum shop. *Magnes News; special exhibition catalogues; scholarly books.*

JUDAICA CAPTIONED FILM CENTER, INC. (1983). PO Box 21439, Baltimore, MD 21208-0439. Voice (after 4 PM) TDD (301)655-6767. Pres. Lois Lilienfeld Weiner. Developing a comprehensive library of captioned and subtitled films and tapes on Jewish subjects; distributes them to organizations serving the hearing-impaired, including mainstream classes and senior adult groups, on a free-loan, handling/shipping-charge-only basis. *Quarterly newsletter.*

JWB JEWISH BOOK COUNCIL; JWB JEWISH MUSIC COUNCIL; JWB LECTURE BUREAU (see Jewish Book Council; Jewish Music Council; JCC Association Lecture Bureau)

LEAGUE FOR YIDDISH, INC. (1979). 200 W. 72 St., Suite 40, NYC 10023. (212)787-6675. Pres. Dr. Sadie Turak; Exec. Dir. Dr. Mordkhe Schaechter. Encourages the development and use of Yiddish as a living language; promotes its modernization and standardization; publishes linguistic resource materials. *Afn Shvel* (quarterly).

LEO BAECK INSTITUTE, INC. (1955). 129 E. 73 St., NYC 10021. (212)744-6400. FAX: (212)988-1305. Pres. Yosef Hayim Yerushalmi; Exec. Dir. Robert A. Jacobs. A library, archive, and research center for the history of German-speaking Jewry. Offers lectures, exhibits, faculty seminars; publishes a series of monographs, yearbooks, and journals. *LBI Bulletin; LBI News; LBI Yearbook; LBI Memorial Lecture; LBI Library & Archives News.*

A LIVING MEMORIAL TO THE HOLOCAUST—MUSEUM OF JEWISH HERITAGE (1984). 342 Madison Ave., Suite 706, NYC 10173. (212)687-9141. FAX: (212)573-9847. Cochmn. George Klein, Hon. Robert M. Morgenthau, Peter Cohen, Sen. Manfred Ohrenstein; Museum Dir. David Altshuler. The museum will be New York's principal public memorial to the six million Jews murdered during the Holocaust.

Scheduled to open in 1992, will include permanent and temporary exhibition galleries, a computerized interactive learning center, a Memorial Hall, and education facilities. *Brochures; bimonthly newsletter.*

MAALOT (1987). 1719 Wilmart St., Rockville, MD 20852. (301)231–9067. FAX: (301)984–9031. Pres./Exec. Off. David Shneyer. An educational program established to train individuals in Jewish music, the liturgical arts, and in the use, design, and application of Jewish customs and ceremonies. Offers classes, seminars, and an independent study program.

MARTYRS MEMORIAL & MUSEUM OF THE HOLOCAUST OF THE JEWISH FEDERATION COUNCIL OF GREATER LOS ANGELES (1963; reorg. 1978). 6505 Wilshire Blvd., 12th fl., Los Angeles, CA 90048. (213)651–3175. FAX: (213)892–1494. Chmn. Jack I. Salzberg; Dir. Michael Nutkiewicz. A photo-narrative museum and resource center dedicated to Holocaust history, issues of genocide and prejudice, and curriculum development. *Pages* (quarterly newsletter).

MEMORIAL FOUNDATION FOR JEWISH CULTURE, INC. (1964). 15 E. 26 St., NYC 10010. (212)679–4074. Pres. the Right Hon., the Lord Jakobovits; Exec. V.-Pres. Jerry Hochbaum. Through the grants that it awards, encourages Jewish scholarship and Jewish education, supports communities that are struggling to maintain their Jewish identity, makes possible the training of Jewish men and women for professional careers in communal service in Jewishly deprived communities, and stimulates the documentation, commemoration, and teaching of the Holocaust.

NATIONAL FOUNDATION FOR JEWISH CULTURE (1960). 330 Seventh Ave., 21st fl., NYC 10001. (212)629–0500. FAX: (212)-629–0508. Pres. Sandra Weiner; Exec. Dir. Richard A. Siegel. The leading Jewish organization devoted to promoting Jewish culture in the U.S. Administers the Council of American Jewish Museums, the Council of Archives and Research Libraries in Jewish Studies, and the Council of Jewish Theatres; supports Jewish scholarship through Doctoral Dissertation Fellowships; provides funding to major Jewish cultural institutions through the Joint Cultural Appeal; organizes conferences, symposia, and festivals in the arts and humanities. *Council of Jewish Theatres Newsletter.*

NATIONAL HEBREW CULTURE COUNCIL (1952). 14 E. 4th St, NYC 10012. (212)-674–8412. Cultivates the study of Hebrew as a modern language in American public high schools and colleges, providing guidance to community groups and public educational authorities; annually administers National Voluntary Examination in Hebrew Culture and Knowledge of Israel in the public high schools. *Hebrew in Colleges and Universities.*

NATIONAL YIDDISH BOOK CENTER (1980). Old East Street School, Amherst, MA 01002. (413)256–1241. FAX: (413)253–4261. Pres. Aaron Lansky; Exec. Dir. Stephen Hays. Collects and disseminates Yiddish books; conducts activities contributing to the revitalization of Yiddish culture in America. *Der Pakn-treger/ The Book Peddler*

RESEARCH FOUNDATION FOR JEWISH IMMIGRATION, INC. (1971). 570 Seventh Ave., NYC 10018. (212)921–3871. Pres. Curt C. Silberman; Sec. and Coord. of Research Herbert A. Strauss; Archivist Dennis E. Rohrbaugh. Studies and records the history of the migration and acculturation of central European German-speaking Jewish and non-Jewish Nazi persecutees in various resettlement countries worldwide, with special emphasis on the American experience. *International Biographical Dictionary of Central European Emigrés, 1933–1945; Jewish Immigrants of the Nazi Period in the USA.*

ST. LOUIS CENTER FOR HOLOCAUST STUDIES (1977). 12 Millstone Campus Dr., St. Louis, MO 63146. (314)432–0020. Chmn. Fred Katz; Dir. Rabbi Robert Sternberg. Develops programs and provides resources and educational materials to further an understanding of the Holocaust and its impact on civilization. *Audio Visual and Curriculum Resources Guides.*

SEPHARDIC HOUSE (1978). 8 W. 70 St., NYC 10023. (212)873–0300. Exec. Dir. Janice E. Ovadiah; Bd. Chmn. Rabbi Marc D. Angel. A cultural organization dedicated to fostering Sephardic history and culture; sponsors a wide variety of classes and public programs on different aspects of the Sephardic experience; publication program disseminates materials of Sephardic value;

outreach program to communities outside of the New York area. *Sephardic House Newsletter.*

SIMON WIESENTHAL CENTER, Los Angeles, CA (*see* Yeshiva University)

SKIRBALL MUSEUM, HEBREW UNION COLLEGE (1913; 1972 in Calif.). 3077 University Ave., Los Angeles, CA 90007. (213)-749-3424. FAX: (213)747-6128. Dir. Nancy Berman; Curator Barbara Gilbert. Collects, preserves, researches, and exhibits art and artifacts made by or for Jews, or otherwise associated with Jews and Judaism. Provides opportunity to faculty and students to do research in the field of Jewish art. *Catalogues of exhibits and collections.*

SOCIETY FOR THE HISTORY OF CZECHOSLOVAK JEWS, INC. (1961). 87-08 Santiago St., Holliswood, NY 11423. (718)468-6844. Pres. and Ed. Lewis Weiner; Sec. Joseph Abeles. Studies the history of Czechoslovak Jews; collects material and disseminates information through the publication of books and pamphlets. *The Jews of Czechoslovakia* (3 vols); *Review I; Review II; Review III.*

SOCIETY OF FRIENDS OF THE TOURO SYNAGOGUE, NATIONAL HISTORICAL SHRINE, INC. (1948). 85 Touro St., Newport, RI 02840. (401)848-4794. Pres. Bella G. Werner; Coord. Kirsten L. Mann. Helps maintain Touro Synagogue as a national historic site, opening and interpreting it for visitors; promotes public awareness of its preeminent role in the tradition of American religious liberty; annually commemorates George Washington's letter of 1790 to the Hebrew Congregation of Newport. *Society Update.*

SPERTUS MUSEUM, SPERTUS COLLEGE OF JUDAICA (1968). 618 S. Michigan Ave., Chicago, IL 60605. (312)922-9012. FAX: (312)922-6406. CEO Dr. Howard Sulkin; Museum Dir. Dr. Morris Fred. Housing nearly 3,000 works in its permanent collection, the museum comprises five major components: a permanent gallery of Judaica; Gallery of Contemporary Art; Holocaust Memorial; Main Exhibition Gallery; and a unique hands-on archaeology gallery, the Artifact Center. Taken together, these components fulfill the museum's mission to preserve and transmit the cultural, social and spiritual legacy of the Jewish people. *Newsletter; exhibition catalogues.*

TOURO NATIONAL HERITAGE TRUST (1984). 85 Touro St., Newport, RI 02840. (401)847-0810. Pres. Zalman D. Newman; Exec. Dir. Kirsten L. Mann. Works to establish national conference center within Touro compound; sponsors Touro Fellow through John Carter Brown Library; presents seminars and other educational programs; promotes knowledge of the early Jewish experience in this country within the climate of religions which brought it about.

UNITED STATES HOLOCAUST MEMORIAL COUNCIL (1980). 2000 L St., NW, Suite 588, Washington, DC 20036. (202)653-9220. Chmn. Harvey M. Meyerhoff; Exec. Dir. Sara J. Bloomfield. Established by Congress as an independent federal establishment, to plan, build and operate the United States Holocaust Memorial Museum in Washington, D.C., and to encourage and sponsor observances of an annual, national, civic commemoration of the victims of the Holocaust known as the Days of Remembrance. Also engages in Holocaust education and research programs. Composed of 55 members of all faiths and backgrounds appointed by the president, plus five U.S. senators and five members of the House of Representatives. *Newsletter* (monthly); *Directory of Holocaust Institutions in the U.S. and Canada.*

YESHIVA UNIVERSITY MUSEUM (1973). 2520 Amsterdam Ave., NYC 10033. (212)-960-5390. Chmn. Bd. of Govs. Erica Jesselson; Dir. Sylvia A. Herskowitz. Collects, preserves, and interprets Jewish life and culture through changing exhibitions of ceremonial objects, paintings, rare books and documents, synagogue architecture, textiles, decorative arts, and photographs. Oral history archive. Special events, holiday workshops, live performances, lectures, etc., for adults and children. Guided tours and workshops are offered. *Seasonal calendars; special exhibition catalogues.*

YIDDISHER KULTUR FARBAND—YKUF (1937). 1133 Broadway, Rm. 1023, NYC 10010. (212)691-0708. Pres. and Ed. Itche Goldberg. Publishes a monthly magazine and books by contemporary and classical Jewish writers; conducts cultural forums; exhibits works by contemporary Jewish artists and materials of Jewish historical value; organizes reading circles. *Yiddishe Kultur.*

YIVO INSTITUTE FOR JEWISH RESEARCH, INC. (1925). 1048 Fifth Ave., NYC 10028. (212)535–6700. FAX: (212)879–9763. Chmn. Bruce Slovin; Exec. Dir. Samuel Norich. Engages in social and cultural research pertaining to East European Jewish life; maintains library and archives which provide a major international, national, and New York resource used by institutions, individual scholars, and laymen; trains graduate students in Yiddish, East European, and American Jewish studies; offers exhibits, conferences, public programs; publishes books. *Yidishe Shprakh; YIVO Annual of Jewish Social Science; YIVO Bleter; Yedies.*

———, MAX WEINREICH CENTER FOR ADVANCED JEWISH STUDIES (1968). 1048 Fifth Ave., NYC 10028. (212)535–6700. FAX: (212)879–9763. Provides advanced-level training in Yiddish language and literature, ethnography, folklore, linguistics, and history; offers guidance on dissertation or independent research. *The YIVO Annual of Jewish Social Science; YIVO Bleter; Jewish Folklore & Ethnology Review.*

ISRAEL-RELATED

ALYN—AMERICAN SOCIETY FOR HANDICAPPED CHILDREN IN ISRAEL (1934). 19 W. 44 St., NYC 10036. (212)869–8085. FAX: (212)768–0979. Pres. Caroline W. Halpern; Chmn. Simone P. Blum; Exec. Dir. Joan R. Mendelson. Supports the work of ALYN Hospital, long-term rehabilitation center for severely orthopedically handicapped children, located in Jerusalem. It serves as home, school, and hospital for its patients, with a long-term goal for them of independent living.

AMERICA-ISRAEL CULTURAL FOUNDATION, INC. (1939). 41 E. 42 St., Suite 608, NYC 10017. (212)557–1600. FAX: (212)-557–1611. Bd. Chmn. Isaac Stern; Pres. Carl Glick. Supports and encourages the growth of cultural excellence in Israel through grants to cultural institutions; scholarships to gifted young artists and musicians. *Hadashot newsletter.*

AMERICA-ISRAEL FRIENDSHIP LEAGUE, INC. (1971). 134 E. 39 St., NYC 10016. (212)213–8630. FAX: (212)683–3475. Pres. Samuel M. Eisenstat; Exec. V.-Pres. Ilana Artman. A nonsectarian, nonpartisan organization which seeks to broaden the base of support for Israel among Americans of all faiths and backgrounds. Activities include educational exchanges, tours of Israel for American leadership groups, symposia and public education activities, and the dissemination of printed information. *Newsletter.*

AMERICAN ASSOCIATES, BEN-GURION UNIVERSITY OF THE NEGEV (1973). 342 Madison Ave., Suite 1924, NYC 10173. (212)-687–7721. FAX: (212)370–0686. Pres. Michael W. Sonnenfeldt; Bd. Chmn. Irwin H. Goldenberg; Chancellor Ambassador Yosef Tekoah. Serves as the university's publicity and fund-raising link to the U.S. AABGU is committed to programs for the absorption of Soviet émigrés in the Negev, publicizing university activities and curricula, securing student scholarships, transferring contributions, and encouraging American interest in the university. *AABGU Reporter; BGU Bulletin; Negev; Overseas Study Program Catalog.*

AMERICAN COMMITTEE FOR SHAARE ZEDEK HOSPITAL IN JERUSALEM, INC. (1949). 49 W. 45 St., Suite 1100, NYC 10036. (212)354–8801. Pres. Charles H. Bendheim; Bd. Chmn. Ludwig Jesselson; Sr. Exec. V.-Pres. Morris Talansky. Raises funds for the various needs of the Shaare Zedek Medical Center, Jerusalem, such as equipment and medical supplies, nurse training, and research; supports exchange program between Shaare Zedek Medical Center and Albert Einstein College of Medicine, NY. *Heartbeat Magazine.*

AMERICAN COMMITTEE FOR SHENKAR COLLEGE IN ISRAEL, INC. (1971). 855 Ave. of the Americas, NYC 10001. (212)-947–1597. FAX: (212)643–8275. Pres. David Pernick; Exec. Dir. Charlotte Fainblatt. Raises funds for capital improvement, research and development projects, laboratory equipment, scholarships, lectureships, fellowships, and library/archives of fashion and textile design at Shenkar College in Israel, Israel's only fashion and textile technology college. Accredited by the Council of Higher Education, the college is the chief source of personnel for Israel's fashion and apparel industry. *Shenkar News.*

AMERICAN COMMITTEE FOR THE WEIZMANN INSTITUTE OF SCIENCE (1944). 51 Madison Ave., NYC 10010. (212)779–2500. FAX: (212)779–3209. Chmn. Bram

Goldsmith; Pres. Alan A. Fischer; Exec. V.-Pres. Bernard N. Samers. Through 14 regional offices in the U.S. raises funds for the Weizmann Institute in Rehovot, Israel, and disseminates information about its 800 ongoing scientific research projects. *Rehovot; Interface; Research.*

AMERICAN FRIENDS OF BAR-ILAN UNIVERSITY (1955). 91 Fifth Ave., Suite 200, NYC 10003. (212)337–1270. FAX: (212)337–1274. Chancellor Rabbi Emanuel Rackman; Chmn. Global Bd. of Trustees Ludwig Jesselson; Pres. Amer. Bd. of Overseers Belda Lindenbaum; Exec. V.-Pres. Gen. Yehuda Halevy. Supports Bar-Ilan University, a traditionally oriented liberal arts and sciences institution, where all students must take Basic Jewish Studies courses as a requirement of graduation; located in Ramat-Gan, Israel, and chartered by the Board of Regents of the State of NY. *Update; Bar-Ilan News.*

AMERICAN FRIENDS OF BETH HATEFUTSOTH (1976). 110 E. 59 St., NYC 10022. (212)752–0600. FAX: (212)826–8959. Pres. Philip M. Klutznick; V.-Pres. Sam E. Bloch; Exec. Dir. Gloria Golan. Supports the maintenance and development of Beth Hatefutsoth, the Nahum Goldmann Museum of the Jewish Diaspora in Tel Aviv, and its cultural and educational programs for youth and adults. Circulates its traveling exhibitions and provides various cultural programs to local Jewish communities. Includes the Douglas E. Goldman Jewish Genealogy Center (DOROT); the Center for Jewish Music, and the Grunstein Shamir Photodocumentation Center. *Beth Hatefutsoth quarterly newsletter.*

AMERICAN FRIENDS OF EZRATH NASHIM HOSPITAL-JERUSALEM, INC. (1895). 10 E. 40 St., Suite 2701, NYC 10016. (212)725–8175. Pres. Burton G. Greenblatt; Exec. Dir. Mira Berman. Supports research, education, and patient care at Ezrath Nashim Hospital in Jerusalem, which includes a 290-bed hospital, comprehensive outpatient clinic, drug-abuse clinic, geriatric center, and the Jacob Herzog Psychiatric Research Center; Israel's only nonprofit, voluntary psychiatric hospital; used as a teaching facility by Israel's major medical schools. *Friend to Friend; To Open the Gates of Healing.*

AMERICAN FRIENDS OF HAIFA UNIVERSITY (1972). 347 Fifth Ave., Suite 610, NYC 10016. (212)725–8175. FAX: (212)725–8253. Pres. Burton J. Ahrens; Exec. V.-Pres. Michael Weisser. Promotes, encourages, and aids higher and secondary education, research, and training in all branches of knowledge in Israel and elsewhere; aids in the maintenance and development of Haifa University; raises and allocates funds for the above purposes; provides scholarships; promotes exchanges of teachers and students. *Newsletter.*

AMERICAN FRIENDS OF TEL AVIV UNIVERSITY, INC. (1955). 360 Lexington Ave., NYC 10017. (212)687–5651. FAX: (212)687–4085. Board Chmn. Stewart M. Colton; Pres. Saul B. Cohen; Exec. V.-Pres. Harriet Kendell Kessler. Promotes higher education at Tel Aviv University, Israel's largest and most comprehensive institution of higher learning. The university has a law school, medical school, and more than 50 research institutes, including the Moshe Dayan Center for Middle East & African Studies and the Jaffe Center for Strategic Studies. *Tel Aviv University News; Tau Fax Flash.*

AMERICAN FRIENDS OF THE HEBREW UNIVERSITY (1925; inc. 1931). 11 E. 69 St., NYC 10021. (212)472–9800. Pres. Herbert D. Katz; Exec. V.-Pres. Robert A. Pearlman; Bd. Chmn. Stanley M. Bogen. Fosters the growth, development, and maintenance of the Hebrew University of Jerusalem; collects funds and conducts programs of information throughout the U.S., highlighting the university's achievements and its significance; administers American student programs and arranges exchange professorships in the U.S. and Israel. *News from the Hebrew University of Jerusalem; Scopus magazine.*

AMERICAN FRIENDS OF THE ISRAEL MUSEUM (1972). 10 E. 40 St., Suite 1208, NYC 10016. (212)683–5190. FAX: (212)683–3187. Pres. Maureen Cogan; Exec. Dir. Michele Cohn Tocci. Raises funds for special projects of the Israel Museum in Jerusalem; solicits works of art for exhibition and educational purposes. *Newsletter.*

AMERICAN FRIENDS OF THE SHALOM HARTMAN INSTITUTE (1976). 1029 Teaneck Rd., Teaneck, NJ 07666. (201)837–0887. Pres. Robert P. Kogod; Dir. Rabbi Donniel Hartman; Admin. Dorothy Minchin. Supports the Shalom Hartman Institute, Jerusalem, an institute of higher education and research center, devoted to applying the teachings of classical Judaism to the issues of modern life. Founded in

1976 by David Hartman, the institute includes a Beit Midrash and centers for philosophy, theology, *Halakhah*, political thought, and medical science, an experimental school, and programs for lay leadership. *A Word from Jerusalem.*

AMERICAN FRIENDS OF THE TEL AVIV MUSEUM OF ART (1974). 133 E. 58 St., Suite 704, NYC 10022. (212)593–5771. Chmn. Milton J. Schubin; Exec. Dir. Ursula Kalish. Raises funds for the Tel Aviv Museum of Art in Tel Aviv, Israel; enables Americans to better understand and become involved in Israeli art and culture.

AMERICAN ISRAEL PUBLIC AFFAIRS COMMITTEE (AIPAC) (1954). 440 First St., NW, Washington, DC 20001. (202)639–5200. FAX: (202)347–4921. Pres. Mayer Mitchell; Exec. Dir. Thomas A. Dine. Registered to lobby on behalf of legislation affecting U.S.-Israel relations; represents Americans who believe support for a secure Israel is in U.S. interest. Works for a strong U.S.-Israel relationship. *Near East Report; AIPAC Papers on U.S.-Israel Relations.*

AMERICAN-ISRAELI LIGHTHOUSE, INC. (1928; reorg. 1955). 30 E. 60 St., NYC 10022. (212)838–5322. Pres. Mrs. Leonard F. Dank; Sec. Frances Lentz. Provides education and rehabilitation for the blind and physically handicapped in Israel to effect their social and vocational integration into the seeing community; built and maintains Rehabilitation Center for the Blind (Migdal Or) in Haifa. *Tower.*

AMERICAN JEWISH LEAGUE FOR ISRAEL (1957). 30 E. 60 St., NYC 10022. (212)-371–1583. Pres. Rabbi Reuben M. Katz; Bd. Chmn. Joseph Landow. Seeks to unite all those who, notwithstanding differing philosophies of Jewish life, are committed to the historical ideals of Zionism; works, independently of class, party, or religious affiliation, for the welfare of Israel as a whole. Not identified with any political parties in Israel. Member, World Confederation of United Zionists. *Bulletin of the American Jewish League for Israel.*

AMERICAN PHYSICIANS FELLOWSHIP, INC. FOR MEDICINE IN ISRAEL (1950). 2001 Beacon St., Brookline, MA 02146. (617)-232–5382. Pres. Leonard F. Gottlieb, MD. Exec. Dir. Daniel C. Goldfarb. Helps Israel become a major world medical center; secures fellowships for selected Israeli physicians and arranges lectureships in Israel by prominent American physicians; runs medical seminars in Israel and U.S.; coordinates U.S. and Canadian medical and paramedical emergency volunteers to Israel; supports research and health care projects in Israel. *APF News.*

AMERICAN RED MAGEN DAVID FOR ISRAEL, INC. (1940). 888 Seventh Ave., Suite 403, NYC 10106. (212)757–1627. FAX: (212)757–4662. Pres. Robert L. Sadoff, MD; Natl. Chmn. Louis Cantor; Exec. V.-Pres. Benjamin Saxe. An authorized tax-exempt organization; the sole support arm in the U.S. of Magen David Adom, Israel's Red Cross Service; raises funds for MDA's emergency medical services for Israel's military and civilian populations, supplies ambulances, bloodmobiles, and mobile cardiac rescue units serving all hospitals and communities throughout Israel; supports MDA's 73 emergency medical clinics and helps provide training and equipment for volunteer emergency paramedical corps. *Lifeline.*

AMERICAN SOCIETY FOR TECHNION-ISRAEL INSTITUTE OF TECHNOLOGY (1940). 810 Seventh Ave., 24th fl., NYC 10019. (212)-262–6200. FAX: (212) 262–6155. Pres. Lewis M. Wesson; Natl. Chmn. Leonard Sherman; Exec. V.-Pres. Melvyn H. Bloom. Supports the work of the Technion-Israel Institute of Technology, Haifa, which trains nearly 10,000 students in 20 departments and a medical school, and conducts research across a broad spectrum of science and technology. *Technion USA.*

AMERICAN SOCIETY FOR THE PROTECTION OF NATURE IN ISRAEL (1986). 330 Seventh Ave., NYC 10001. (212)947–2820. FAX: (212)629–0509. Hon. Pres. Samuel W. Lewis; Exec. Dir. Tamar C. Podell. Seeks to increase the American public's awareness of, and support for, the critical conservation efforts conducted in Israel by the Society for the Protection of Nature in Israel (SPNI). Conducts educational programs and outdoor activities in the U.S. *Israel Land and Nature* (published quarterly in Israel).

AMERICAN ZIONIST FEDERATION (1939; reorg. 1949 and 1970). 110 E. 59 St., NYC 10022. (212)371–7750. Pres. Simon Schwartz; Exec. Dir. Karen Rubinstein. Coordinates the work of the Zionist constituency in the areas of education, *aliyah,* youth and young leadership and public and communal affairs. Seeks to involve the Zionist and broader Jewish community in programs and events focused on Israel and Zionism (e.g., Zionist Shabbat, Scholars-in-Residence, Yom Yerushalayim) and through these programs to develop a greater appreciation for the Zionist idea among American Jewry. Composed of 16 national Zionist organizations, 10 Zionist youth movements, and affiliated organizations. Offices in Chicago, Los Angeles, New York. Groups in Baltimore, Detroit, Philadelphia, Pittsburgh, Rochester, Washington, DC. *HaMakor.*

AMERICAN ZIONIST YOUTH FOUNDATION, INC. (1963). 110 E. 59 St., NYC 10022. (212)751-6070. Pres. Leon Levy; Exec. Dir. Ruth Kastner. Heightens Zionist awareness among Jewish youth through programs and services geared to high-school and college-age youngsters. Sponsors educational tours to Israel, study in leading institutions; sponsors field workers on campus and in summer camps; prepares and provides specialists who present and interpret the Israel experience for community centers and federations throughout the country. *Activist Newsletter; Guide to Education and Programming Material; Programs in Israel.*

AMERICANS FOR A SAFE ISRAEL (1971). 147 E. 76 St., NYC 10021. (212)628-9400. FAX: (212)988-4065. Chmn. Herbert Zweibon. Seeks to educate Americans in Congress, the media, and the public in general about Israel's role as a strategic asset for the West; through meetings with legislators and the media, in press releases and publications, promotes the notion of Jewish rights to Judea and Samaria and the concept of "peace for peace" as an alternative to "territory for peace." *Outpost.*

AMERICANS FOR PEACE NOW (1984). 27 W. 20 St., 9th fl., NYC 10011. (212)645-6262. FAX: (212)929-3459. Pres. Jonathan Jacoby; Exec. Dir. Mark Rosenblum. Conducts educational programs and raises funds to support the Israeli peace movement, Shalom Achshav (Peace Now), and coordinates U.S. advocacy efforts through APN's Washington-based Center for Israeli Peace and Security. *National Newsletter; For the Record.*

AMERICANS FOR PROGRESSIVE ISRAEL (1952). 27 W. 20 ST., Suite 902, NYC 10011. (212)255-8760. Pres. Naftali Landesman. A socialist Zionist movement that calls for a just and durable peace between Israel and its Arab neighbors; works for the liberation of all Jews; seeks the democratization of Jewish communal and organizational life; promotes dignity of labor, social justice, and a deeper understanding of Jewish heritage. Affiliate of American Zionist Federation, World Union of Mapam, Hashomer Hatzair, and Kibbutz Artzi Fed. of Israel. *Israel Horizons; API Newsletter.*

AMIT WOMEN (formerly AMERICAN MIZRACHI WOMEN) (1925). 817 Broadway, NYC 10003. (212)477-4720. Pres. Daisy Berman; Exec. Dir. Marvin Leff. The State of Israel's official *reshet* (network) for religious secondary technological education; conducts innovative children's homes and youth villages in Israel in an environment of traditional Judaism; promotes cultural activities for the purpose of disseminating Zionist ideals and strengthening traditional Judaism in America. *AMIT Woman.*

AMPAL—AMERICAN ISRAEL CORPORATION (1942). 10 Rockefeller Plaza, NYC 10020-1956. (212)586-3232. FAX: (212)245-7340. Pres. Lawrence Lefkowitz; Bd. Chmn. Michael Arnon. Finances and invests in industrial, agricultural, real estate, hotel, and tourist enterprises in Israel. *Annual report; quarterly reports.*

ARZA—ASSOCIATION OF REFORM ZIONISTS OF AMERICA (1977). 838 Fifth Ave., NYC 10021. (212)249-0100. FAX: (212)-517-7968. Pres. Norman D. Schwartz; Exec. Dir. Rabbi Eric Yoffie. Individual Zionist membership organization devoted to achieving Jewish pluralism in Israel and strengthening the Israeli Reform movement. Chapter activities in the U.S. concentrate on these issues and on strengthening American public support for Israel. *ARZA Newsletter.*

BETAR ZIONIST YOUTH ORGANIZATION (1935). 218 E. 79 St., NYC 10021. (212)-353-8033. Central Shaliach Eli Cohen; Tagar Shaliach Arie Salman. Organizes youth groups across North America to teach Zionism, Jewish pride, and love of Israel; sponsors summer programs in Israel for Jewish youth ages 13-21; sponsors Tagar Zionist Student Activist Movement on college campuses. *Etgar.*

BOYS TOWN JERUSALEM FOUNDATION OF AMERICA INC. (1948). 91 Fifth Ave., Suite 601, NYC 10003. (212)242-1118. Pres. Michael J. Scharf; Chmn. Josh S. Weston; V.-Chmn. Alexander S. Linchner; Exec.

V.-Pres. Rabbi Ronald L. Gray. Raises funds for Boys Town Jerusalem, which was established in 1948 to offer a comprehensive academic, religious, and technical education to disadvantaged Israeli and immigrant boys from over 45 different countries, including Ethiopia, Russia, and Iran. Enrollment: over 1,500 students in jr. high school, academic and technical high school, and a college of applied engineering. *BTJ Newsbriefs; Your Town Magazine.*

COUNCIL FOR A BEAUTIFUL ISRAEL ENVIRONMENTAL EDUCATION FOUNDATION (1973). 350 Fifth Ave., 19th fl., NYC 10118. (212)947–5709. Pres. Anita Kaskel Roe; Admin. Dir. Donna Lindemann. A support group for the Israeli body, whose activities include education, town planning, lobbying for legislation to protect and enhance the environment, preservation of historical sites, the improvement and beautification of industrial and commercial areas, and renovating bomb shelters into parks and playgrounds. *Yearly newsletter.*

EMUNAH WOMEN OF AMERICA (formerly HAPOEL HAMIZRACHI WOMEN'S ORGANIZATION) (1948). 7 Penn Plaza, NYC 10001 (212)564–9045. Pres. Gladys Baruch; Exec. Dir. Shirley Singer. Maintains and supports 200 educational and social-welfare institutions in Israel within a religious framework, including nurseries, day-care centers, vocational and teacher-training schools for the underprivileged, a community college complex, and Holocaust study center. Also involved in absorption of Ethiopian immigrants. *The Emunah Woman; Lest We Forget; Emunah Connection.*

FEDERATED COUNCIL OF ISRAEL INSTITUTIONS—FCII (1940). 4702 15th Ave., Brooklyn, NY 11219. (718)972–5530. Bd. Chmn. Z. Shapiro; Exec. V.-Pres. Rabbi Julius Novack. Central fund-raising organization for over 100 affiliated institutions; handles and executes estates, wills, and bequests for the traditional institutions in Israel; clearinghouse for information on budget, size, functions, etc., of traditional educational, welfare, and philanthropic institutions in Israel, working cooperatively with the Israeli government and the overseas department of the Council of Jewish Federations. *Annual financial reports and statistics on affiliates.*

FRIENDS OF LABOR ISRAEL (1987). 28 Ramban St., Jerusalem, Israel 92268. (02)664–342. FAX: 630–830. Membership Services Office: PO Box 17305, Milwaukee, WI 53217–9986. Chmn. Rabbi Daniel Polish; Exec. Dir. Rabbi Stanley A. Ringler. American organization committed to a program of education in America and Israel on behalf of institutions, organizations, and projects in Israel designed to promote democracy, pluralism, social justice, and peace. FLI is an affinity group of the Israeli Labor party and represents the concerns of progressive American Jews in Labor party circles. *Labor Political Briefs; Folio newsletter.*

FRIENDS OF THE ISRAEL DEFENSE FORCES (1981). 21 W. 38 St., 5th fl., NYC 10018. (212)575–5030. FAX: (212)575–7815. Bd. Chmn. Henry Plitt. Sec. Stephen Rubin. Supports the *Agudah Lema'an Hahayal,* Israel's Assoc. for the Well-Being of Soldiers, founded in the early 1940s, which provides social, recreational, and educational programs for soldiers, special services for the sick and wounded, and much more.

FUND FOR HIGHER EDUCATION (1970). 1768 S. Wooster St., Los Angeles, CA 90035. (213)202–1879. Chmn. Amnon Barness; Chmn. Exec. Com. Max Candiotty. Raises funds and disseminates information in the interest of institutions of higher education in the U.S. & Israel. Over $18 million distributed to over 100 institutions of higher learning, including over $11 million in Israel and $6 million in the U.S. *In Response.*

GIVAT HAVIVA EDUCATIONAL FOUNDATION, INC. (1966). 27 W. 20 St., #902, NYC 10011. (212)255–2992. FAX: (212)-627–1287. Chmn. Bruno Aron. Supports programs in Israel to further Jewish-Arab rapprochement, narrow economic and educational gaps within Israeli society, and improve educational opportunities for various disadvantaged youth. Affiliated with the Givat Haviva Center of the Kibbutz Artzi Federation, the Menachem Bader Fund, and other projects. In the U.S., GHEF, Inc. sponsors educational seminars, public lectures and parlor meetings with Israeli speakers, as well as individual and group trips to Israel. *News from Givat Haviva; special reports.*

GOLDA MEIR ASSOCIATION (1984). 33 E. 67 St., NYC 10021. (212)570–1443. FAX: (212)737–4326. Chmn. Alfred H. Moses; Pres. Robert C. Klutznick; Exec. Dir. Avner Tavori. North American support group for the Israeli association, whose large-scale educational programs address the issues of democracy in Israel, Sephardi-Ashkenazi integration, religious pluralism, the peace process, and relations between Israeli Jews and Arabs. Its "Project Democracy" has been adapted to help new Soviet immigrants integrate into Israeli society by providing them with an education in democratic ideals and principles. *Newsletter.*

HABONIM-DROR NORTH AMERICA (1934). 27 W. 20 St., 9th fl., NYC 10011. (212)-255-1796. Sec.-Gen. Melody Robens-Paradise; Exec. Off. Aryeh Valdberg. Fosters identification with pioneering in Israel; stimulates study of Jewish life, history, and culture; sponsors community-action projects, seven summer camps in North America, programs in Israel, and *garinei aliyah. Batnua; Progressive Zionist Journal; Bimat Hamaapilim.*

HADASSAH, THE WOMEN'S ZIONIST ORGANIZATION OF AMERICA, INC. (1912). 50 W. 58 St., NYC 10019. (212)355-7900. FAX: (212)303-8282. Pres. Carmela E. Kalmanson; Exec. Dir. Beth Wohlgelernter. In America helps interpret Israel to the American people; provides basic Jewish education as a background for intelligent and creative Jewish living; sponsors Young Judaea/Hashachar, largest Zionist youth movement in U.S., which has four divisions: Young Judaea, Intermediate Judaea, Senior Judaea, and Hamagshimim; operates six Zionist youth camps in this country; supports summer and all-year courses in Israel. Maintains in Israel Hadassah-Hebrew University Medical Center for healing, teaching, and research; Hadassah College of Technology; and Hadassah Career Counseling Institute. Is largest organizational contributor to Youth Aliyah and to Jewish National Fund for land purchase and reclamation. *Update; Headlines; Hadassah Magazine; Textures; Bat Kol; The Catalyst; The American Scene.*

———, YOUNG JUDAEA/HASHACHAR (1909; reorg. 1967). 50 W. 58 St., NYC 10019. (212)355-7900. Natl. Dir. Glen Karonsky; Coord. Hamagshimim (college level) Michael Balaban; Pres. of Sr. Judaea (high-school level) Allison Halpern. Seeks to educate Jewish youth from the ages of 9-27 toward Jewish and Zionist values, active commitment to and participation in the American and Israeli Jewish communities; maintains summer camps and year programs in Israel. *Hamagshimim Journal; Kol Hat'nua; The Young Judaean.*

HASHOMER HATZAIR, SOCIALIST ZIONIST YOUTH MOVEMENT (1923). 150 Fifth Ave., Suite 911, NYC 10011. (212)929-4955. Sec. David Suskauer; Central Shaliach Chaim Broom. Seeks to educate Jewish youth to an understanding of Zionism as the national liberation movement of the Jewish people. Promotes *aliyah* to *kibbutzim*. Affiliated with AZYF and Kibbutz Artzi Federation. Espouses socialist-Zionist ideals of peace, justice, democracy, and brotherhood. *Young Guard.*

INTERNS FOR PEACE (1976). 270 W. 89 St., NYC 10024. (212)580-0540. FAX: (212)-580-0693. Dir. Rabbi Bruce M. Cohen. An independent, nonprofit, nonpolitical organization dedicated to fostering understanding and respect between Jewish and Arab citizens of Israel.

ISRAEL HISTADRUT FOUNDATION (1960). 276 Fifth Ave., Suite 901, NYC 10001. (212)683-5454. FAX: (212)213-9233. Pres. Herbert Rothman; Exec. V.-Pres. Alvin Smolin. Specializes in planned giving, which includes testamentary bequests, charitable trusts, and endowment funds that benefit over 85% of the people of Israel through Histadrut social-service agencies: 17 major hospitals; over 1,300 medical, dental, and pharmaceutical clinics; several schools of medicine and nursing; 158 vocational trade schools; 6 senior-citizen geriatric centers; 5 children's villages; and 4 colleges.

JEWISH COMMITTEE FOR ISRAELI-PALESTINIAN PEACE (1982). PO Box 4991, Washington, DC 20008. (301)963-5673. Seth Grimes, Ellen Siegel, representatives. Promotes a two-state solution to the Israeli-Palestinian conflict, to be achieved through negotiations with the PLO, in order to ensure Israeli security and Palestinian rights. Sponsors educational and dialogue programs, writes articles and editorials, assists the Israeli peace movement, and holds a yearly Jewish-Palestinian Friendship Dinner. *Israeli-Palestinian Digest.*

JEWISH INSTITUTE FOR NATIONAL SECURITY AFFAIRS (JINSA) (1976). 1100 17th St., NW, Washington, DC 20036. (202)-833-0020. FAX: (202)331-7702. Pres. Sen. Rudy Boschwitz; Exec. Dir. Shoshana

Bryen. A nonprofit, nonpartisan educational organization working within the American Jewish community to explain the link between American defense policy and the security of the State of Israel; and within the national security establishment to explain the key role Israel plays in bolstering American interests. *Security Affairs.*

JEWISH NATIONAL FUND OF AMERICA (1901). 42 E. 69 St., NYC 10021. (212)-879-9300. FAX: (212)517-3293. Pres. Ruth W. Popkin; Exec. V.-Pres. Dr. Samuel I. Cohen. Exclusive fund-raising agency of the world Zionist movement for the afforestation, reclamation, and development of the land of Israel, including construction of roads, parks, and recreational areas, preparation of land for new communities and industrial facilities; helps emphasize the importance of Israel in schools and synagogues throughout the U.S. *JNF Almanac; Land and Life.*

JEWISH PEACE LOBBY (1989). 4431 Lehigh Rd., Suite 141, College Park, MD 20740. (301)589-8764. Pres. Jerome M. Segal. A legally registered lobby promoting changes in U.S. policy vis-à-vis the Israeli-Palestinian conflict. Supports Israel's right to peace within secure borders; a political settlement based on mutual recognition of the right of self-determination of both peoples; a two-state solution as the most likely means to a stable peace.

KEREN OR, INC. (1956). 1133 Broadway, NYC 10010. (212)255-1180. Bd. Chmn. Dr. Edward L. Steinberg; Pres. Dr. Albert Hornblass; Exec. V.-Pres. Paul H. Goldenberg. Funds the Keren-Or-Center for Multihandicapped Blind Children, at 3 Abba Hillel Silver St., Ramot, Jerusalem, housing and caring for 70 children,1½ to 16 years of age. Provides long-term basic training, therapy, rehabilitative, and early childhood education to the optimum level of the individual; with major hospitals, involved in research into causes of multihandicapped blind birth.

LABOR ZIONIST ALLIANCE (formerly FARBAND LABOR ZIONIST ORDER; now uniting membership and branches of POALE ZION–UNITED LABOR ZIONIST ORGANIZATION OF AMERICA and AMERICAN HABONIM ASSOCIATION) (1913). 33 E. 67 St., NYC 10021. (212)628-0042. Pres. Menachem Z. Rosensaft; Exec. Dir. Sarrae G. Crane. Seeks to enhance Jewish life, culture, and education in U.S. and Canada; aids in building State of Israel as a cooperative commonwealth, and its Labor movement organized in the Histadrut; supports efforts toward a more democratic society throughout the world; furthers the democratization of the Jewish community in America and the welfare of Jews everywhere; works with labor and liberal forces in America. *Jewish Frontier; Yiddisher Kempfer.*

LEAGUE FOR LABOR ISRAEL (1938; reorg. 1961). 33 E. 67 St., NYC 10021. (212)628-0042. Pres. Menachem Z. Rosensaft; Exec. Dir. Sarrae G. Crane. Conducts Labor Zionist educational and cultural activities for youth and adults in the American Jewish community. Promotes educational travel to Israel.

LIKUD-HERUT ZIONISTS OF AMERICA, INC. (1925). 38 E. 23 St., NYC 10010. (212)-353-9552. Exec. Dir. Glenn Mones. Educates the Jewish community and the American public about the views of Israel's Likud party; encourages support for a strong, secure State of Israel in all of its territory. *The Likud Letter.*

MEDICAL DEVELOPMENT FOR ISRAEL (1982). 130 E. 59 St., NYC 10022. (212)-759-3370. FAX: (212)759-0120. Bd. Chmn. Samuel C. Klagsbrun, MD; Pres. David E. Langsam. Raises funds to help improve the quality of health care in Israel, its primary goal the construction of the Children's Medical Center of Israel, a 224-bed tertiary care facility for the entire region. *Brochures and newsletters.*

MERCAZ (1979). 155 Fifth Ave., NYC 10010. (212)533-7800. Pres. Goldie B. Kweller; Exec. Dir. Renah Rabinowitz. The U.S. Zionist organization for Conservative/Masorti Judaism; works for religious pluralism in Israel, defending and promoting Conservative/Masorti institutions and individuals; fosters Zionist education and *aliyah* and develops young leadership. *Mercaz News & Views.*

NA'AMAT USA, THE WOMEN'S LABOR ZIONIST ORGANIZATION OF AMERICA, INC. (formerly PIONEER WOMEN/NA'AMAT) (1925; reorg. 1985). 200 Madison Ave., Suite 1808, NYC 10016. (212)725-8010. FAX: (212)447-5187. Pres. Harriet Green. Part of a world movement of working women and volunteers, NA'AMAT USA helps provide social, educational, and legal services for women, teenagers, and children in Israel. It also advocates legislation for women's rights and child welfare in the U.S., furthers Jewish education, and supports Habonim-Dror, the Labor Zionist youth movement. *NA'AMAT Woman magazine.*

NATIONAL COMMITTEE FOR LABOR ISRAEL—HISTADRUT (1923). 33 E. 67 St., NYC 10021. (212)628-1000. FAX: (212)-517-7478. Pres. Jay Mazur; Exec. V.-Pres. Yehuda Ebstein; Chmn. Trade Union Council Morton Bahr. Raises funds for the educational, health, social and cultural institutions of the Israeli Federation of Labor-Histadrut. Promotes relations between American trade unions and the Histadrut and the American Jewish community. *Backdrop Histadrut; Amal Newsletter.*

NEW ISRAEL FUND (1979). 111 W. 40 St., Suite 2300, NYC 10018. (212)302-0066. FAX: (212)302-7629. Pres. Mary Ann Stein; Exec. Dir. Norman Rosenberg. Supports the citizens'-action efforts of Israelis working to achieve social justice and to protect and strengthen the democratic process in Israel. Also seeks to enrich the quality of the relationships between Israelis and North American Jews through deepened mutual understanding. Publishes background booklets on civil rights, women's status, Jewish-Arab coexistence, religious pluralism, and community action in Israel. *NIF Report (quarterly newsletter);* annual report.

PEC ISRAEL ECONOMIC CORPORATION (formerly PALESTINE ECONOMIC CORPORATION) (1926). 511 Fifth Ave., NYC 10017. (212)687-2400. Pres. Joseph Ciechanover; Exec. V.-Pres. Frank J. Klein; Sec.-Asst. Treas. William Gold. Primarily engaged in the business of organizing, financing, and administering business enterprises located in or affiliated with enterprises in the State of Israel, through holdings of equity securities and loans. *Annual report.*

PEF ISRAEL ENDOWMENT FUNDS, INC. (1922). 41 E. 42 St., Suite 607, NYC 10017. (212)599-1260. Chmn. Sidney Musher; Pres. Sydney L. Luria; Sec. Harvey Brecher. Uses funds for educational, research, religious, health, and other philanthropic institutions in Israel. *Annual report.*

PIONEER WOMEN/NA'AMAT (see NA'AMAT USA)

POALE AGUDATH ISRAEL OF AMERICA, INC. (1948). 4405 13th Ave.., Brooklyn, NY 11219. (718)435-5449. Pres. Rabbi Fabian Schonfeld; Exec. V.-Pres. Rabbi Moshe Malinowitz. Aims to educate American Jews to the values of Orthodoxy and *aliyah;* supports *kibbutzim,* trade schools, *yeshivot, moshavim, kollelim,* research centers, and children's homes in Israel. *PAI News; She'arim; Hamayan.*

———, WOMEN'S DIVISION OF (1948). Pres. Aliza Widawsky; Presidium: Sarah Ivanisky, Miriam Lubling, Bertl Rittenberg. Assists Poale Agudath Israel to build and support children's homes, kindergartens, and trade schools in Israel. *Yediot PAI.*

PROGRESSIVE ZIONIST CAUCUS (1982). 27 W. 20 St., NYC 10011. (212)675-1168. Shlihim Aryeh Zaldberg, David Koran; Dir. Beth Martin. A campus-based grass-roots organization committed to a progressive Zionist agenda. Students organize local and regional educational, cultural, and political activities, such as speakers, films, *Kabbalot Shabbat,* and Arab-Jewish dialogue groups. The PZC Kvutzat Aliyah is a support framework for individuals interested in *aliyah* to a city or town. *La'Inyan; Makor.*

PROJECT NISHMA (1988). 1225 15th St., NW, Washington, DC 20005. (202)462-4268. FAX: (202)462-3892. Cochmn. Theodore R. Mann, Earl Raab, Henry Rosovsky; Exec. Dir. Thomas R. Smerling. Conducts educational programs on Israeli security and the peace process; arranges military briefings for Jewish leaders; publishes articles by senior Israeli defense experts; analyzes U.S. Jewish opinion; and articulates pragmatic positions. Sponsored by over 100 nationally active Jewish leaders from across the country.

RELIGIOUS ZIONISTS OF AMERICA. 25 W. 26 St., NYC 10010. (212)689-1414.

———, BNEI AKIVA OF NORTH AMERICA (1934). 25 W. 26 St., NYC 10010. (212)-889-5260. Pres. Yitz Feigenbaum; V.-Pres. Admin. Jerry Yudkowsky. Seeks to interest youth in *aliyah* to Israel and social justice through pioneering *(haluziut)* as an integral part of their religious observance; sponsors five summer camps, a leadership training camp for eleventh graders, a work-study program on a religious kibbutz for high school graduates, summer tours to Israel; establishes nuclei of college students for kibbutz or other settlement. *Akivon; Hamvaser; Pinkas Lamadrich; Daf Rayonot; Ma'Ohalai Torah; Zraim.*

———, MIZRACHI-HAPOEL HAMIZRACHI (1909; merged 1957). 25 W. 26 St., NYC 10010. (212)689-1414. FAX: (212)779-3043. Pres. Rabbi Louis Bernstein; Exec. V.-Pres. Israel Friedman. Disseminates ideals of religious Zionism; conducts cultural work, educational program, public relations; raises funds for religious educational institutions in Israel, including *yeshivot hesder* and Bnei Akiva. *Newsletters; Kolenu.*

———, MIZRACHI PALESTINE FUND (1928). 25 W. 26 St., NYC 10010. Chmn. Joseph Wilon; Sec. Israel Friedman. Fundraising arm of Mizrachi movement.

———, NATIONAL COUNCIL FOR TORAH EDUCATION OF MIZRACHI-HAPOEL HAMIZRACHI (1939). 25 W. 26 St., NYC 10010. Pres. Rabbi Israel Schorr; Dir. Rabbi Meyer Golombek. Organizes and supervises *yeshivot* and Talmud Torahs; prepares and trains teachers; publishes textbooks and educational materials; organizes summer seminars for Hebrew educators in cooperation with Torah Department of Jewish Agency; conducts *ulpan. Hazarkor; Chemed.*

———, NOAM-MIZRACHI NEW LEADERSHIP COUNCIL (formerly NOAM-HAMISHMERET HATZEIRA) (1970). 25 W. 26 St., NYC 10010. (212)684-6091. Chmn. Rabbi Marc Schneier; V.-Chmn. Sheon Karol. Develops new religious Zionist leadership in the U.S. and Canada; presents young religious people with various alternatives for settling in Israel through *garinei aliyah* (core groups); meets the religious, educational, and social needs of Jewish young adults and young couples. *Forum.*

SOCIETY OF ISRAEL PHILATELISTS (1948). 27436 Aberdeen, Southfield, MI 48076. (313)557-0887. Pres. Dr. Emil Dickstein; Exec. Sec. Irvin Girer. Promotes interest in, and knowledge of, all phases of Israel philately through sponsorship of chapters and research groups, maintenance of a philatelic library, and support of public and private exhibitions. *Israel Philatelist; monographs; books.*

STATE OF ISRAEL BONDS (1951). 730 Broadway, NYC 10003. (212)677-9650. Internatl. Chmn. David B. Hermelin; Pres. Ambassador Meir Rosenne. Seeks to provide large-scale investment funds for the economic development of the State of Israel through the sale of State of Israel bonds in the U.S., Canada, Western Europe, and Latin America.

THEODOR HERZL FOUNDATION (1954). 110 E. 59 St., NYC 10022. (212)752-0600. FAX: (212)826-8959. Chmn. Kalman Sultanik; Sec. Isadore Hamlin. Cultural activities, lectures, conferences, courses in modern Hebrew and Jewish subjects, Israel, Zionism, and Jewish history. *Midstream.*

———, HERZL PRESS. Chmn. Kalman Sultanik. Serves as "the Zionist Press of record," publishing books that are important for the light they shed on Zionist philosophy, Israeli history, contemporary Israel and the Diaspora, and the relationship between them. They are important as contributions to Zionist letters and history. *Midstream.*

———, THEODOR HERZL INSTITUTE. Chmn. Jacques Torczyner; Dir. Philip S. Gutride. Program geared to review of contemporary problems on Jewish scene here and abroad, presentation of Jewish heritage values in light of Zionist experience of the ages, study of modern Israel, and Jewish social research with particular consideration of history and impact of Zionism. Lectures, forums, Encounter with Creativity; musicales, recitals, concerts; holiday celebrations; visual art programs, Nouveau Artist Introductions. *Annual Program Preview; Herzl Institute Bulletin.*

UNITED CHARITY INSTITUTIONS OF JERUSALEM, INC. (1903). 1141 Broadway, NYC 10001. (212)683-3221. Chmn. Rabbi Pollak. Raises funds for the maintenance of schools, kitchens, clinics, and dispensaries in Israel; free loan foundations in Israel.

UNITED ISRAEL APPEAL, INC. (1925). 110 E. 59 St., NYC 10022. (212)339-6900. FAX: (212)754-4293. Chmn. Norman Lipoff; Exec. V.-Chmn. Herman Markowitz. Provides funds raised by UJF/Federation campaigns in the U.S. to aid the people of Israel through the programs of the Jewish Agency for Israel, UIA's operating agent. Serves as link between American Jewish community and Jewish Agency for Israel;

assists in resettlement and absorption of refugees in Israel, and supervises flow and expenditure of funds for this purpose. *Annual report; newsletters; brochures.*

UNITED STATES COMMITTEE SPORTS FOR ISRAEL, INC. (1948). 1926 Arch St., Philadelphia, PA 19103. (215)561-6900. Pres. Robert E. Spivak; Exec. Dir. Barbara G. Lissy. Sponsors U.S. participation in, and fields and selects U.S. team for, World Maccabiah Games in Israel every four years; promotes education and sports programs in Israel; provides funds and technical and material assistance to Wingate Institute for Physical Education and Sport in Israel; sponsors coaching programs in Israel. *USCSFI Newsletter; commemorative Maccabiah Games journal; financial report.*

WOMEN'S LEAGUE FOR ISRAEL, INC. (1928). 160 E. 56 St., NYC 10022. (212)838-1997. Pres. Trudy Miner; Sr. V.-Pres. Annette Kay; Exec. Dir. Dorothy Leffler. Promotes the welfare of young people in Israel; built and maintains homes in Jerusalem, Haifa, Tel Aviv; Natanya Vocational Training and Rehabilitation Center; the Orah Workshop for the Blind and Handicapped, and the National Library of Social Work. Also many facilities and programs on the campuses of the Hebrew University. *WLI Bulletin.*

WORLD CONFEDERATION OF UNITED ZIONISTS (1946; reorg. 1958). 130 E. 59 St., NYC 10022. (212)371-1452. Copres. Bernice S. Tannenbaum, Kalman Sultanik, Melech Topiol. Promotes Zionist education, sponsors nonparty youth movements in the Diaspora, and strives for an Israel-oriented creative Jewish survival in the Diaspora. *Zionist Information Views.*

WORLD ZIONIST ORGANIZATION—AMERICAN SECTION (1971). 110 E. 59 St., NYC 10022. (212)752-0600. FAX: (212)826-8959. Chmn. Bernice S. Tannenbaum; Exec. V.-Chmn. Zelig Chinitz. As the American section of the overall Zionist body throughout the world, it operates primarily in the field of *aliyah* from the free countries, education in the Diaspora, youth and Hechalutz, organization and information, cultural institutions, publications; conducts a worldwide Hebrew cultural program including special seminars and pedagogic manuals; disperses information and assists in research projects concerning Israel; promotes, publishes, and distributes books, periodicals, and pamphlets concerning developments in Israel, Zionism, and Jewish history. *Midstream; The Zionist Voice.*

———, DEPARTMENT OF EDUCATION AND CULTURE (1948). 110 E. 59 St., NYC 10022. (212)752-0600. FAX: (212)826-8959. Exec. Dir. Asher Rivlin. Renders educational services to boards and schools: study programs, books, AV aids, instruction, teacher in-service training, Judaic and Hebrew subjects. Annual Bible and Israel contests; Israel summer and winter programs for teachers and students; Ulpan centers in Greater N.Y. area; preparation for Israeli matriculation examinations.

———, NORTH AMERICAN ALIYAH MOVEMENT (1968). 110 E. 59 St., NYC 10022. (212)752-0600. FAX: (212)826-8959. Exec. Dir. Nellie Neeman. Promotes and facilitates *aliyah* and *klitah* from the U.S. and Canada to Israel; serves as a social framework for North American immigrants to Israel. *Aliyon; NAAM Newsletter; Coming Home.*

———, ZIONIST ARCHIVES AND LIBRARY OF THE (1939). 110 E. 59 St., NYC 10022. Dir. and Librarian Esther Togman. A depository for books, pamphlets, newspapers, periodicals, ephemera, and archival material; a primary center in the U.S. for research and authentic information on Israel, Zionism, the Middle East, and Jewish life in the Diaspora.

ZIONIST ORGANIZATION OF AMERICA (1897). ZOA House, 4 E. 34 St., NYC 10016. (212)481-1500. FAX: (212)481-1515. Pres. Sidney Silverman; Exec. V.-Pres. Paul Flacks. Seeks to safeguard the integrity and independence of Israel, assist in its economic development, and foster the unity of the Jewish people and the centrality of Israel in Jewish life in the spirit of General Zionism. In Israel, owns and maintains both the ZOA House in Tel Aviv, a cultural center, and the Kfar Silver Agricultural and Technical High School in Ashkelon, with a full-time student enrollment of 700 students. Kfar Silver, under the supervision of the Israel Ministry of Education, focuses on academic studies, vocational training, and programs for foreign students. *American Zionist Magazine; Zionist Information Service Weekly News Bulletin (ZINS); Public Affairs Action Guidelines; Public Affairs Action Report for ZOA Leaders.*

OVERSEAS AID

AMERICAN ASSOCIATION FOR ETHIOPIAN JEWS (1969). 1836 Jefferson Place, NW, Washington, DC 20036. (202)223-6838. FAX: (202)223-2961. Pres. Nathan Shapiro; Exec. Dir. William Recant. Informs world Jewry about the plight of Ethiopian Jews; advocates reunification with family members in Israel as a major priority; provides aid in refugee areas and Ethiopia; and helps resettlement in Israel. *Release; Newsline.*

AMERICAN FRIENDS OF THE ALLIANCE ISRAÉLITE UNIVERSELLE, INC. (1946). 420 Lexington Ave., Suite 1733, NYC 10170. (212)808-5437. FAX: (212)983-0094. Pres. Henriette Beilis; Exec. Dir. Warren Green. Participates in educational and human-rights activities of the AIU and supports the Alliance System of Jewish schools, teachers' colleges, and remedial programs in Israel, North Africa, the Middle East, Europe, and Canada. *Alliance Review.*

AMERICAN JEWISH JOINT DISTRIBUTION COMMITTEE, INC.—JDC (1914). 711 Third Ave., NYC 10017. (212)687-6200. FAX: (212)370-5467. Pres. Sylvia Hassenfeld; Exec. V.-Pres. Michael Schneider. Provides assistance to Jewish communities in Europe, Asia, Africa, and the Mideast. Current concerns include absorption and social needs in Israel; *glasnost*-facilitated program expansions in Eastern Europe, particularly in the USSR and Hungary; nonsectarian development and disaster relief. *Annual report; JDC World; Historical Album.*

AMERICAN JEWISH PHILANTHROPIC FUND (1955). 386 Park Ave. S., 10th fl., NYC 10016. (212)OR9-0010. Pres. Charles J. Tanenbaum. Provides resettlement assistance to Jewish refugees primarily through programs administered by the International Rescue Committee at its offices in Western Europe and the U.S.

AMERICAN ORT FEDERATION, INC.—ORGANIZATION FOR REHABILITATION THROUGH TRAINING (1924). 817 Broadway, NYC 10003. (212)677-4400. FAX: (212)979-9545. Pres. Murray Koppelman; Exec. V.-Pres. Donald H. Klein. Provides vocational/technical education to more than 200,000 students in 35 countries throughout the world. The largest ORT operation is in Israel, where 96,000 students attend 120 ORT schools and training centers. ORT programs have expanded greatly to meet the needs of the huge emigration of Jews from the Soviet Union: in Israel, special vocational training and job placement programs; in the U.S., special programs in New York, Chicago, and Los Angeles, with courses in English as a Second Language, bookkeeping, computer operations, and business math. Annual cost of program is approximately $170 million. *American ORT Federation Bulletin; ORT Yearbook.*

———, AMERICAN AND EUROPEAN FRIENDS OF ORT (1941). 817 Broadway, NYC 10003. (212)677-4400. FAX: (212)-979-9545. Pres. Simon Jaglom; Hon. Chmn. Jacques Zwibak. Promotes the ORT idea among Americans of European extraction; supports the Litton ORT Auto-Mechanics School in Jerusalem and the ORT School of Engineering in Jerusalem. Promotes the work of the American ORT Federation.

———, AMERICAN LABOR ORT (1937). 817 Broadway, NYC 10003. (212)677-4400. FAX: (212)979-9545. Pres. Sam Fine. Promotes the vocational/technical training of more than 200,000 young people with the marketable skills they need to become productive members of society. Promotes the work of the American ORT Federation in 35 countries around the world.

———, BUSINESS AND PROFESSIONAL ORT (1937). 817 Broadway, NYC 10003. (212)-677-4400. FAX: (212)979-9545. Pres. Rose Seidel Kalich. Promotes work of American ORT Federation.

———, NATIONAL ORT LEAGUE (1914). 817 Broadway, NYC 10003. (212)677-4400. FAX: (212)979-9545. Pres. Judah Wattenberg; First V.-Pres. Tibor Waldman. Promotes ORT idea among Jewish fraternal *landsmanshaften* and individuals. Promotes the work of the American ORT Federation.

———, WOMEN'S AMERICAN ORT (1927). 315 Park Ave. S., NYC 10010. (212)505-7700. FAX: (212)674-3057. Pres. Reese Feldman; Exec. V.-Pres. Nathan Gould. Advances the programs and self-help ethos of ORT through membership, fund raising, and educational activities. Supports 120 vocational schools, junior colleges and technical training centers in Israel; helps meet the educational needs of Jewish communities in 30 countries; spearheads growing ORT-U.S. school operations in New York, Los Angeles, and Chicago, and associate programs in Miami and Atlanta. Maintains a wide-ranging domestic agenda which espouses quality public education, combats anti-Semitism, champions women's rights, and promotes a national literacy campaign. *Women's American ORT Reporter; Close-Ups; Direct Line; The Highest Step; Women's American ORT Yearbook.*

CONFERENCE ON JEWISH MATERIAL CLAIMS AGAINST GERMANY, INC. (1951). 15 E. 26 St., Rm. 1355, NYC 10010. (212)696-4944. FAX: (212)889-9080. Pres. Dr. Israel Miller; Sec. and Exec. Dir. Saul Kagan. Monitors the implementation of restitution and indemnification programs of the German Federal Republic (FRG) arising from its agreements with West Germany and most recently with the united Germany, especially with respect to the new restitution law for property lost by Jewish Nazi victims on the territory of the former German Democratic Republic. Administers Hardship Fund, which distributes funds appropriated by FRG for Jewish Nazi victims unable to file timely claims under original indemnification laws. Also assists needy non-Jews who risked their lives to help Jewish survivors.

HIAS, INC. (HEBREW IMMIGRANT AID SOCIETY) (1880; reorg. 1954). 200 Park Ave. S., NYC 10003. (212)674-6800. FAX: (212)460-9242. Pres. Ben Zion Leuchter; Exec. V.-Pres. Karl D. Zukerman. International Jewish migration agency with headquarters in the U.S. and offices, affiliates, and representatives in Europe, Latin America, Canada, Australia, New Zealand, and Israel. Assists Jewish migrants and refugees from Eastern Europe, the Middle East, North Africa, and Latin America. Via U.S. government-funded programs, assists in the resettlement of Indo-Chinese and other refugees. *HIAS Reporter;* annual report.

INTERNATIONAL COALITION FOR THE REVIVAL OF THE JEWS OF YEMEN–ICROJOY(1989). 150 Nassau St., Suite 1238, NYC 10038. (212)766-5556. Chmn. Dr. Hayim Tawil. Seeks to enrich and assist the Jewish community of the Republic of Yemen.

JEWISH RESTITUTION SUCCESSOR ORGANIZATION (1947). 15 E. 26 St., Rm. 1355, NYC 10010. (212)696-4944. FAX: (212)889-9080. Sec. and Exec. Dir. Saul Kagan. Acts to discover, claim, receive, and assist in the recovery of Jewish heirless or unclaimed property; to utilize such assets or to provide for their utilization for the relief, rehabilitation, and resettlement of surviving victims of Nazi persecution.

NORTH AMERICAN CONFERENCE ON ETHIOPIAN JEWRY (NACOEJ) (1982). 165 E. 56 St., NYC 10022. (212)752-6340. Founding Pres. Jonathan Giesberg; Exec. Dir. Barbara Ribakove Gordon. Provides assistance to Ethiopian Jews in Ethiopia and in Israel; informs American and other Jewish communities about their situation; works to increase involvement of world Jewish communities in assisting, visiting, and learning about Ethiopian Jews. *Lifeline* (membership newsletter).

RE'UTH WOMEN'S SOCIAL SERVICE, INC. (1937). 240 W. 98 St., NYC 10025. (212)666-7880. Pres. Rosa Strygler; Chmn. Ursula Merkin. Maintains in Israel subsidized housing for self-reliant elderly; old-age homes for more dependent elderly; Lichtenstadter Hospital for chronically ill and young accident victims not accepted by other hospitals; subsidized meals; Golden Age clubs. *Annual dinner journal.*

THANKS TO SCANDINAVIA, INC. (1963). 745 Fifth Ave., Rm. 603, NYC 10151. (212)486-8600. FAX: (212)486-5735. Natl. Chmn. Victor Borge; Pres. and Chief Exec. Off. Richard Netter. Provides scholarships and fellowships at American universities and medical centers to students and doctors from Denmark, Finland, Norway, and Sweden in appreciation of the rescue of Jews from the Holocaust. Informs current and future generations of Americans and Scandinavians of these singular examples of humanity and bravery; funds books about this chapter of history. *Annual report.*

UNITED JEWISH APPEAL, INC. (1939). 99 Park Ave., Suite 300, NYC 10016. (212)818-9100. FAX: (212)818-9509. Natl. Chmn. Marvin Lender; Chmn. Bd. of Trustees Morton A. Kornreich; Pres. Stanley B. Horowitz. The annual UJA/Federation Campaign is the primary instrument for the support of humanitarian programs and social services for Jews at home and abroad. In Israel, through the Jewish Agency, campaign funds help absorb, educate, and settle new immigrants, build villages and farms in rural areas, support innovative programs for troubled and disadvantaged youth, and promote the revitalization of distressed neighborhoods. The Operation Exodus Campaign provides funds for the settlement of Soviet Jews in Israel. UJA/Federation funds also provide for the well-being of Jews and Jewish communities in 33 other countries around the world through the American Jewish Joint Distribution Committee. Constituent departments of the UJA include the Rabbinic Cabinet, University Programs Department, Women's Division, Young Leadership Cabinet, the Women's Young Leadership Cabinet, and the Business and Professional Women's Council.

RELIGIOUS AND EDUCATIONAL ORGANIZATIONS

AGUDATH ISRAEL OF AMERICA (1922). 84 William St., NYC 10038. (212)797–9000. Pres. Rabbi Moshe Sherer; Exec. Dir. Rabbi Boruch B. Borchardt. Mobilizes Orthodox Jews to cope with Jewish problems in the spirit of the Torah; sponsors a broad range of projects aimed at enhancing religious living, education, children's welfare, protection of Jewish religious rights, outreach to the assimilated, and social services. *Jewish Observer; Dos Yiddishe Vort; Coalition.*

———, AGUDAH WOMEN OF AMERICA–N'SHEI AGUDATH ISRAEL (1940). 84 William St., NYC 10038. (212)363–8940. Presidium Esther Bohensky, Aliza Grund. Organizes Jewish women for philanthropic work in the U.S. and Israel and for intensive Torah education.

———, CHILDREN'S DIVISION—PIRCHEI AGUDATH ISRAEL (1925). 84 William St., NYC 10038 (212)797–9000. Natl. Dir. Rabbi Joshua Silbermintz; Natl. Coord. Rabbi Mordechai Mehlman. Educates Orthodox Jewish children in Torah; encourages sense of communal responsibility. Branches sponsor weekly youth groups and Jewish welfare projects. National Mishnah contests, rallies, and conventions foster unity on a national level. *Darkeinu; Leaders Guides.*

———, GIRLS' DIVISION—BNOS AGUDATH ISRAEL (1921). 84 William St., NYC 10038. (212)797–9000. Natl. Dirs. Devorah Streicher and Leah Zagelbaum. Sponsors regular weekly programs on the local level and unites girls from throughout the Torah world with extensive regional and national activities. *Newsletters.*

———, YOUNG MEN'S DIVISION—ZEIREI AGUDATH ISRAEL (1921). 84 William St., NYC 10038. (212)797–9000. Dir. Rabbi Labish Becker. Educates youth to see Torah as source of guidance for all issues facing Jews as individuals and as a people. Inculcates a spirit of activism through projects in religious, Torah-educational, and community-welfare fields. *Zeirei Forum; Am Hatorah; Daf Chizuk; Ohr Hakollel.*

AGUDATH ISRAEL WORLD ORGANIZATION (1912). 84 William St., NYC 10038. (212)-797–9000. Cochmn. Rabbi Moshe Sherer, Rabbi Yehudah Meir Abramowitz. Represents the interests of Orthodox Jewry on the national and international scenes. Sponsors projects to strengthen Torah life worldwide.

AMERICAN ASSOCIATION OF RABBIS (1978). 350 Fifth Ave., Suite 3308, NYC 10001. (212)244–3350. Pres. Rabbi Harold Lerner; Exec. Dir. Rabbi David L. Dunn. An organization of rabbis serving in pulpits, in areas of education, and in social work. *Bimonthly newsletter; semiannual journal.*

ASSOCIATION FOR JEWISH STUDIES (1969). Widener Library M., Harvard University, Cambridge, MA 02138. Pres. Robert Chazan; Exec. Sec. Charles Berlin. Seeks to promote, maintain, and improve the teaching of Jewish studies in American colleges and universities by sponsoring meetings and conferences, publishing a newsletter and other scholarly materials, setting standards for programs in Jewish studies, aiding in the placement of teachers, coordinating research, and cooperating with other scholarly organizations. *AJS Review; newsletter.*

ASSOCIATION OF HILLEL/JEWISH CAMPUS PROFESSIONALS (1949). c/o B'nai B'rith Hillel Foundation, Tufts University, Curtis Hall, 474 Boston Ave., Medford, MA 02155. Pres. Rabbi Jeffrey Summit. Seeks to promote professional relationships and exchanges of experience, develop personnel standards and qualifications, safeguard integrity of Hillel profession; represents and advocates before National Hillel Staff,

National Hillel Commission, B'nai B'rith International, Council of Jewish Federations. *Handbook for Hillel Professionals; Guide to Hillel Personnel Practices.*

ASSOCIATION OF ORTHODOX JEWISH SCIENTISTS (1948). 1364 Coney Island Ave., Brooklyn, NY 11230. (718)338-8592. Pres. Seymour Applebaum, MD; Bd. Chmn. Allen J. Bennett, MD. Seeks to contribute to the development of science within the framework of Orthodox Jewish tradition; to obtain and disseminate information relating to the interaction between the Jewish traditional way of life and scientific developments—on both an ideological and practical level; to assist in the solution of problems pertaining to Orthodox Jews engaged in scientific teaching or research. Two main conventions are held each year. *Intercom; Proceedings; Halacha Bulletin; newsletter.*

B'NAI B'RITH HILLEL FOUNDATIONS, INC. (1923). 1640 Rhode Island Ave., NW, Washington, DC 20036. (202)857-6560. FAX: (202)857-1099. Chmn. B'nai B'rith Hillel Comm. David L. Bittker; Internatl. Dir. Richard M. Joel. Provides cultural, social, community-service, educational, and religious activities for Jewish college students of all backgrounds. Maintains a presence on 400 campuses in the U.S., Canada, and overseas. Sponsors National Leaders Assembly, Charlotte and Jack J. Spitzer Forum on Public Policy, Jacob Burns Endowment Fund for Programming in Ethics and the Campus, Sarah and Irving Pitt Institute for Student Leadership, National Jewish Law Students Network. *Mekorot; Igeret; Jewish Life on Campus: A Directory of B'nai B'rith Hillel Foundations and Other Jewish Campus Agencies.*

B'NAI B'RITH YOUTH ORGANIZATION (1924). 1640 Rhode Island Ave., NW, Washington, DC 20036. (202)857-6633. Chmn. Youth Comm. Edward Yalowitz; Internatl. Dir. Sidney Clearfield. Helps Jewish teenagers achieve self-fulfillment and make a maximum contribution to the Jewish community and their country's culture; helps members acquire a greater knowledge and appreciation of Jewish religion and culture. *D'var; Monday Morning; Shofar; Hakol; Kesher.*

CANTORS ASSEMBLY (1947). 150 Fifth Ave., NYC 10011. (212)691-8020. Pres. Robert Kieval; Exec. V.-Pres. Samuel Rosenbaum. Seeks to unite all cantors who adhere to traditional Judaism and who serve as full-time cantors in bona fide congregations to conserve and promote the musical traditions of the Jews and to elevate the status of the cantorial profession. *Annual Proceedings; Journal of Synagogue Music.*

CENTRAL CONFERENCE OF AMERICAN RABBIS (1889). 192 Lexington Ave., NYC 10016. (212)684-4990. FAX: (212)689-1649. Pres. Rabbi Samuel E. Karff; Exec. V.-Pres. Rabbi Joseph B. Glaser. Seeks to conserve and promote Judaism and to disseminate its teachings in a liberal spirit. *Journal of Reform Judaism; CCAR Yearbook.*

CLAL—NATIONAL JEWISH CENTER FOR LEARNING AND LEADERSHIP (1974). 47 W. 34 St., 2nd fl., NYC 10001. (212)279-2525. FAX: (212)465-8425. Pres. Irving Greenberg; Exec. V.-Pres. Paul Jeser. Dedicated to preparing Jewish leaders to respond to the challenges of a new era in Jewish history; challenges which include the freedom to accept or reject one's Jewish heritage, the liberty to choose from an abundance of Jewish values and life-styles, and the exercise of Jewish power after the Holocaust and the rebirth of the State of Israel. *News & Perspectives.*

COALITION FOR THE ADVANCEMENT OF JEWISH EDUCATION (CAJE) (1976). 261 W. 35th St., #12A, NYC 10001. (212)-268-4210. FAX: (212)268-4214. Chmn. Rabbi Michael A. Weinberg; Exec. Dir. Dr. Eliot G. Spack. Brings together Jews from all ideologies who are involved in every facet of Jewish education and are committed to transmitting the Jewish heritage. Sponsors annual conference on Alternatives in Jewish Education and Curriculum Bank; publishes a wide variety of publications; organizes shared-interest networks; offers mini grants for special projects. *Bikurim; Mekasher (a human resources directory); The Jewish Education News.*

CONGRESS OF SECULAR JEWISH ORGANIZATIONS (1970). 1130 S. Michigan Ave., #2101, Chicago, IL 60605. (312)922-0386. Pres. Harold Gales; Exec. Dir. Gerry Revzin. An umbrella organization of schools and adult clubs; facilitates exchange curricula and educational programs for children and adults stressing our Jewish historical and cultural heritage and

NATIONAL JEWISH ORGANIZATIONS / 493

the continuity of the Jewish people. *Newsletter; Holiday Celebration Book.*

COUNCIL FOR JEWISH EDUCATION (1926). 426 W. 58 St., NYC 10019. (212)713-0290. FAX: (212)586-9579. Pres. Reuven Yalon; Consultant Philip Gorodetzer. Fellowship of Jewish education professionals—administrators and supervisors and teachers in Hebrew high schools and Jewish teachers colleges—of all ideological groupings; conducts annual national and regional conferences; represents the Jewish education profession before the Jewish community; cosponsors, with the Jewish Education Service of North America, a personnel committee and other projects; cooperates with Jewish Agency Department of Education and Culture in promoting Hebrew culture and studies; conducts lectureship at Hebrew University. *Jewish Education; Sheviley Hahinnukh.*

FEDERATION OF JEWISH MEN'S CLUBS, INC. (1929). 475 Riverside Dr., Rm. 244, NYC 10115. (212)749-8100. FAX: (212)316-4271. Pres. Lawrence Allen; Exec. Dir. Rabbi Charles Simon. Promotes principles of Conservative Judaism; develops family-education and leadership-training programs; offers the Art of Jewish Living series and Yom Hashoah Home Commemoration; sponsors Hebrew literacy adult education program; presents awards for service to American Jewry. *Torchlight.*

INSTITUTE FOR COMPUTERS IN JEWISH LIFE (1978). 7074 N. Western Ave., Chicago, IL 60645. (312)262-9200. FAX: (312)262-9298. Pres. Thomas Klutznick; Exec. V.-Pres. Irving J. Rosenbaum. Explores, develops, and disseminates applications of computer technology to appropriate areas of Jewish life, with special emphasis on Jewish education; provides access to the Bar-Ilan University Responsa Project; creates educational software for use in Jewish schools; provides consulting service and assistance for national Jewish organizations, seminaries, and synagogues. *Monitor.*

JEWISH CHAUTAUQUA SOCIETY, INC. (sponsored by NATIONAL FEDERATION OF TEMPLE BROTHERHOODS) (1898). 838 Fifth Ave., NYC 10021. (212)570-0707 or 1-800-765-6200. FAX: (212)570-0960. Pres. Alvin R. Corwin; lst V.-Pres./Chancellor Roger B. Jacobs; Exec. Dir. Lewis Eisenberg. The society's six-point interreligious educational program provides for visiting rabbi lecturers to colleges and schools, resident lectureships (endowed courses on Judaism taught by rabbis), book grant package programs for colleges and schools, film and tapes, Interfaith Institutes, and a secondary-school interfaith program. *Brotherhood.*

JEWISH EDUCATION IN MEDIA (1978). PO Box 180, Riverdale Sta., NYC 10471. (212)362-7633. Pres. Bernard Samers; Exec. Dir. Rabbi Mark S. Golub. Devoted to producing radio, television, film, video-cassette and audio-cassette programming for a popular Jewish audience, in order to inform, entertain, and inspire a greater sense of Jewish identity and Jewish commitment. "L'Chayim," JEM's weekly half-hour program, airs on WOR Radio in New York and in radio and television syndication; it features outstanding figures in the Jewish world addressing the issues and events of importance to the Jewish community.

JEWISH EDUCATION SERVICE OF NORTH AMERICA (JESNA) (1981). 730 Broadway, NYC 10003-9540. (212)529-2000. FAX: (212)529-2009. Pres. Neil Greenbaum; Exec. V.-Pres. Dr. Jonathan S. Woocher. Coordinating, planning, and service agency for Jewish education in bureaus and federations; maintains a national educational resource center; runs regional and continental conferences; conducts surveys on Jewish education; engages in statistical and other educational research; provides community consultations; coordinates networks of educators and institutions; sponsors the National Board of License; provides placement of upper-level bureau and communal school personnel and educators; maintains an Israel office. *Pedagogic Reporter; TRENDS; Media "Meida"; Information Research Bulletins; JESNA Update, annual report.*

JEWISH MINISTERS CANTORS ASSOCIATION OF AMERICA, INC. (1896). 3 W. 16 St., NYC 10011. (212)675-6601. Pres. Cantor Nathan H. Muchnick. Furthers and propagates traditional liturgy; places cantors in synagogues throughout the U.S. and Canada; develops the cantors of the future. *Kol Lakol.*

JEWISH RECONSTRUCTIONIST FOUNDATION (1940). Church Rd. and Greenwood Ave., Wyncote, PA 19095. (215)887-1988. Pres.

Rabbi Elliot Skiddell; Exec. Dir. Rabbi Mordechai Liebling. Dedicated to the advancement of Judaism as the evolving religious civilization of the Jewish people. Coordinates the Federation of Reconstructionist Congregations and Havurot, Reconstructionist Rabbinical Association, and Reconstructionist Rabbinical College.

——, FEDERATION OF RECONSTRUCTIONIST CONGREGATIONS AND HAVUROT (1954). Church Rd. and Greenwood Ave., Wyncote, PA 19095. (215)887-1988. FAX: (215)576-6143. Pres. Valerie Kaplan; Exec. Dir. Rabbi Mordechai Liebling. Services affiliated congregations and havurot educationally and administratively; fosters the establishment of new Reconstructionist congregations and fellowship groups. Runs the Reconstructionist Press and provides programmatic materials. Maintains regional offices in New York, Los Angeles, and Boston. *Reconstructionist magazine; newsletter.*

——, RECONSTRUCTIONIST RABBINICAL ASSOCIATION (1974). Church Rd. and Greenwood Ave., Wyncote, PA 19095. (215)576-0800. FAX: (215)576-6143. Pres. Rabbi Sandy Sasso; Exec. Dir. Rabbi Bob Gluck. Professional organization for graduates of the Reconstructionist Rabbinical College and other rabbis who identify with Reconstructionist Judaism; cooperates with Federation of Reconstructionist Congregations and Havurot in furthering Reconstructionism in N. America. *Raayanot; newsletter.*

——, RECONSTRUCTIONIST RABBINICAL COLLEGE (*see* p. 506)

JEWISH TEACHERS ASSOCIATION—MORIM (1931). 45 E. 33 St., Suite 604, NYC 10016. (212)684-0556. Pres. Phyllis L. Pullman; V.-Pres. Eli Nieman. Protects teachers from abuse of seniority rights; fights the encroachment of anti-Semitism in education; provides legal counsel to protect teachers from discrimination; offers scholarships to qualified students; encourages teachers to assume active roles in Jewish communal and religious affairs. *Morim JTA Newsletter.*

MACHNE ISRAEL, INC. (1940). 770 Eastern Pkwy., Brooklyn, NY 11213. (718)493-9250. Pres. Menachem M. Schneerson (Lubavitcher Rebbe); Dir., Treas. M.A. Hodakov; Sec. Nissan Mindel. The Lubavitcher movement's organ dedicated to the social, spiritual, and material welfare of Jews throughout the world.

MERKOS L'INYONEI CHINUCH, INC. (THE CENTRAL ORGANIZATION FOR JEWISH EDUCATION) (1940). 770 Eastern Pkwy., Brooklyn, NY 11213. (718)493-9250. Pres. Menachem M. Schneerson (Lubavitcher Rebbe); Dir., Treas. M.A. Hodakov; Sec. Nissan Mindel. The educational arm of the Lubavitcher movement. Seeks to promote Jewish education among Jews, regardless of their background, in the spirit of Torah-true Judaism; to establish contact with alienated Jewish youth; to stimulate concern and active interest in Jewish education on all levels; and to promote religious observance as a daily experience among all Jews. Maintains worldwide network of regional offices, schools, summer camps, and Chabad-Lubavitch Houses; publishes Jewish educational literature in numerous languages and monthly journal in five languages. *Conversaciones con la juventud; Conversations avec les jeunes; Schmuessen mit Kinder un Yugent; Sihot la-No-ar; Talks and Tales.*

NATIONAL COMMITTEE FOR FURTHERANCE OF JEWISH EDUCATION (1941). 824 Eastern Pkwy., Brooklyn, NY 11213. (718)735-0200. Pres. Joseph Fisch; Chmn. Exec. Com. Rabbi Sholem Ber Hecht. Seeks to disseminate the ideals of Torah-true education among the youth of America; provides education and compassionate care for the poor, sick, and needy in U.S. and Israel; provides aid to Iranian Jewish youth; sponsors camps; Operation Survival, War on Drugs; Hadar HaTorah, Machon Chana, and Ivy League Torah Study Program, seeking to win back college youth and others to Judaism; maintains schools and dormitory facilities, family and vocational counseling services. *Panorama; Passover Handbook; Seder Guide; Cultbusters; Intermarriage; Brimstone & Fire.*

NATIONAL COUNCIL OF YOUNG ISRAEL (1924). 3 W. 16 St., NYC 10011. (212)929-1525. Pres. Chaim Kaminetsky; Exec. V.-Pres. Rabbi Ephraim H. Sturm; Natl. Dir. Isaac Hagler. Maintains a program of spiritual, cultural, social, and communal activity aimed at the advancement and perpetuation of traditional, Torah-true Judaism; seeks to instill in American youth an understanding and appreciation of the ethical and spiritual values of Judaism. Sponsors kosher dining clubs and fraternity houses and an Israel program. *Viewpoint; Hashkafa series; Masorah newspaper.*

———, AMERICAN FRIENDS OF YOUNG ISRAEL IN ISRAEL—YISRAEL HATZA'IR (1926). 3 W. 16 St., NYC 10011. (212)929–1525. FAX: (212(727–9526. Pres. Alter Goldstein; Treas. Steve Mostofsky. Promotes Young Israel synagogues and youth work in Israel; works to help absorb Russian and Ethiopian immigrants.

———, ARMED FORCES BUREAU (1912). 3 W. 16 St., NYC 10011. (212)929–1525. Advises and guides the inductees into the armed forces with regard to Sabbath observance, *kashrut,* and Orthodox behavior. *Guide for the Orthodox Serviceman.*

———, EMPLOYMENT BUREAU (1929). 3 W. 16 St., NYC 10011. (212)929–1525. Project Dir. Fed. Program Rabbi Ephraim H. Sturm. Under federal contract in Cleveland and St. Louis and under contract to New York City, operates employment referral service for unemployed people, offering OJT (On-The-Job-Training; no classroom training). Counsels on job-search techniques. Low income limit. Serves all adults, including Sabbath observers. Reimbursement incentives available to employers.

———, INSTITUTE FOR JEWISH STUDIES (1947). 3 W. 16 St., NYC 10011. (212)929–1525. Pres. Chaim Kaminetsky; Exec. V.-Pres. Rabbi Ephraim H. Sturm. Introduces students to Jewish learning and knowledge; helps form adult branch schools; aids Young Israel synagogues in their adult education programs. *Bulletin.*

———, YOUNG ISRAEL COLLEGIATES AND YOUNG ADULTS (1951; reorg. 1982). 3 W. 16 St., NYC 10011. (212)929–1525. Chmn. Kenneth Block; Dir. Richard Stareshefsky. Organizes and operates kosher dining clubs on college and university campuses; provides information and counseling on *kashrut* observance at colleges; gives college-age youth understanding and appreciation of Judaism and information on issues important to Jewish community; arranges seminars and meetings, weekends and trips; operates Achva summer mission to Israel for ages 18–21 and 22–27.

———, YOUNG ISRAEL YOUTH (reorg. 1968). 3 W. 16 St., NYC 10011. (212)929–1525. Dir. Richard Stareshefsky. Fosters a program of spiritual, cultural, social, and communal activities for the advancement and perpetuation of traditional Torah-true Judaism; strives to instill an understanding and appreciation of the high ethical and spiritual values and to demonstrate compatibility of ancient faith of Israel with good Americanism. Operates Achva Summer Mission study program in Israel. *Monthly newsletter.*

NATIONAL JEWISH CENTER FOR LEARNING AND LEADERSHIP (*see* CLAL)

NATIONAL JEWISH HOSPITALITY COMMITTEE (1973). 201 S. 18 St., Rm. 1519, Philadelphia, PA 19103. (215)546–8293. Pres. Rabbi Allen S. Maller; Exec. Dir. Steven S. Jacobs. Assists persons interested in Judaism—for conversion, intermarriage, or to respond to missionaries. *Special reports.*

NATIONAL JEWISH INFORMATION SERVICE FOR THE PROPAGATION OF JUDAISM, INC. (1960). 3761 Decade St., Las Vegas, NV 89121. (702)454–5872. Pres. Rabbi Moshe M. Maggal; V.-Pres. Lawrence J. Epstein; Sec. and P.R. Dir. Rachel D. Maggal. Seeks to convert non-Jews to Judaism and return Jews to Judaism; maintains College for Jewish Ambassadors for the training of Jewish missionaries, and the Correspondence Academy of Judaism for instruction on Judaism through the mail. *Voice of Judaism.*

OZAR HATORAH, INC. (1946). 1 E. 33 St., NYC 10016. (212)689–3508. Pres. Joseph Shalom; Sec. Sam Sutton. An international educational network which provides religious and secular education for Jewish youth worldwide.

P'EYLIM—AMERICAN YESHIVA STUDENT UNION (1951). 805 Kings Highway, Brooklyn, NY 11223. (718)382–0113. Pres. Jacob Y. Weisberg; Exec. V.-Pres. Avraham Hirsch. Aids and sponsors pioneer work by American graduate teachers and rabbis in new villages and towns in Israel; does religious, organizational, and educational work and counseling among new immigrant youth; maintains summer camps for poor immigrant youth in Israel; belongs to worldwide P'eylim movement which has groups in Argentina, Brazil,

Canada, England, Belgium, the Netherlands, Switzerland, France, and Israel; engages in relief and educational work among North African immigrants in France and Canada, assisting them to relocate and reestablish a strong Jewish community life. *P'eylim Reporter; News from P'eylim; N'shei P'eylim News.*

RABBINICAL ALLIANCE OF AMERICA (IGUD HARABONIM) (1944). 3 W. 16 St., 4th fl., NYC 10011. (212)242-6420. Pres. Rabbi Abraham B. Hecht; Menahel Beth Din (Rabbinical Court) Rabbi Herschel Kurzrock. Seeks to promulgate the cause of Torah-true Judaism through an organized rabbinate that is consistently Orthodox; seeks to elevate the position of Orthodox rabbis nationally, and to defend the welfare of Jews the world over. Also has Beth Din Rabbinical Court for Jewish divorces, litigation, marriage counseling and family problems. *Perspective; Nahalim; Torah Message of the Week; Registry.*

RABBINICAL ASSEMBLY (1900). 3080 Broadway, NYC 10027. (212)678-8060. Pres. Rabbi Irwin Groner; Exec. Dir. Rabbi Joel H. Meyers. Seeks to promote Conservative Judaism and to foster the spirit of fellowship and cooperation among rabbis and other Jewish scholars; cooperates with the Jewish Theological Seminary of America and the United Synagogue of America. *Conservative Judaism; Proceedings of the Rabbinical Assembly; Rabbinical Assembly Newsletter.*

RABBINICAL COUNCIL OF AMERICA, INC. (1923; reorg. 1935). 275 Seventh Ave., NYC 10001. (212)807-7888. FAX: (212)-727-8452. Pres. Rabbi Marc D. Angel; Exec. V.-Pres. Rabbi Binyamin Walfish. Promotes Orthodox Judaism in the community; supports institutions for study of Torah; stimulates creation of new traditional agencies. *Hadorom; Record; Sermon Manual; Tradition.*

RESEARCH INSTITUTE OF RELIGIOUS JEWRY, INC. (1941; reorg. 1964). 471 W. End Ave., NYC 10024. (212)874-7979. Chmn. Rabbi Oswald Besser; Sec. Rabbi Marcus Levine. Engages in research and publishes studies concerning the situation of religious Jewry and its history in various countries.

SHOLEM ALEICHEM FOLK INSTITUTE, INC. (1918). 3301 Bainbridge Ave., Bronx, NY 10467. (212)881-6555. Pres. Burt Levey; Sec. Noah Zingman. Aims to imbue children with Jewish values through teaching Yiddish language and literature, Hebrew and the Bible, Jewish history, the significance of Jewish holidays, folk and choral singing, and facts about Jewish life in America and Israel. *Kinder Journal* (Yiddish).

SHOMREI ADAMAH, A JEWISH STEWARDSHIP CENTER (1988). Church Rd. & Greenwood Ave., Wyncote, PA 19095. (215)887-1988. Dir. Ellen Bernstein. A research, development, and education institute involved with nature and environmental issues from a Jewish perspective. Provides liturgical, educational, and other materials to members. Resources include ecologically-oriented services, sermons, and children's activities for school, camp, and home, as well as guides for study and action. Works with congregations and groups across North America on "greening" their communities.

SOCIETY FOR HUMANISTIC JUDAISM (1969). 28611 W. Twelve Mile Rd., Farmington Hills, MI 48334. (313)478-7610. Pres. Robert Sandler; Exec. Dir. Miriam Jerris; Asst. Dir. M. Bonnie Cousens. Serves as a voice for Jews who value their Jewish identity and who seek an alternative to conventional Judaism, who reject supernatural authority and affirm the right of individuals to be the masters of their own lives. Publishes educational and ceremonial materials; organizes congregations and groups. *Humanistic Judaism* (quarterly journal); *Humanorah* (quarterly newsletter).

SYNAGOGUE COUNCIL OF AMERICA (1926). 327 Lexington Ave., NYC 10016. (212)-686-8670. FAX: (212)686-8673. Pres. Rabbi Joel H. Zaiman; Bd. Chmn. Martin C. Barell; Exec. V.-Pres. Rabbi Henry D. Michelman. Represents congregational and rabbinic organizations of Conservative, Orthodox, and Reform Jewry; acts as "one voice" for religious Jewry. *SCA News; special reports.*

TORAH SCHOOLS FOR ISRAEL—CHINUCH ATZMAI (1953). 40 Exchange Pl., NYC 10005. (212)248-6200. FAX: (212)248-6202. Pres. Abraham Pam; Exec. Dir. Henach Cohen. Conducts information programs for the American Jewish community on activities of the independent Torah schools educational network in

Israel; coordinates role of American members of international board of governors; funds special programs of Mercaz Hachinuch Ha-Atzmai B'Eretz Yisroel. *Israel Education Reporter.*

TORAH UMESORAH—NATIONAL SOCIETY FOR HEBREW DAY SCHOOLS (1944). 160 Broadway, NYC 10038. (212)227–1000. Pres. Sheldon Beren; Bd. Chmn. David Singer; Exec. V.-Pres. Rabbi Joshua Fishman. Establishes Hebrew day schools in U.S. and Canada and provides the gamut of services, including placement and curriculum guidance; conducts teacher-training on campuses of major yeshivahs as well as seminars and workshops; publishes textbooks, workbooks, charts, and reading books. Runs Shabbatonim, extracurricular activities. National PTA groups; national and regional teacher conventions. *Olomeinu-Our World; Visions; Parshah Sheets.*

———, NATIONAL ASSOCIATION OF HEBREW DAY SCHOOL ADMINISTRATORS (1960). 1114 Ave. J, Brooklyn, NY 11230. (718)258–7767. Pres. David H. Schwartz. Coordinates the work of the fiscal directors of Hebrew day schools throughout the country. *NAHDSA Review.*

———, NATIONAL ASSOCIATION OF HEBREW DAY SCHOOL PARENT-TEACHER ASSOCIATIONS (1948). 160 Broadway, NYC 10038. (212)227–1000. Natl. PTA Coord. Bernice Brand. Acts as a clearinghouse and service agency to PTAs of Hebrew day schools; organizes parent education courses and sets up programs for individual PTAs. *Fundraising with a Flair; Monthly Sidrah Series Program; PTA with a Purpose for the Hebrew Day School.*

———, NATIONAL CONFERENCE OF YESHIVA PRINCIPALS (1956). 160 Broadway, NYC 10038. (212)227–1000. Pres. Rabbi Yitzchok Merkin; Bd. Chmn. Rabbi Baruch Hilsenrath; Exec. V.-Pres. Rabbi A. Moshe Possick. A professional organization of primary and secondary yeshivah/day-school principals providing yeshiva day schools with school visitations, teacher and principal conferences—including a Mid-Winter Conference and a National Convention. *Directory of High Schools.*

———, NATIONAL YESHIVA TEACHERS BOARD OF LICENSE (1953). 160 Broadway, NYC 10038. (212)227–1000. Dir. Rabbi Yitzchok Merkin. Issues licenses to qualified instructors for all grades of the Hebrew day school and the general field of Torah education.

UNION FOR TRADITIONAL JUDAISM (1984). 261 E. Lincoln Ave., Mt. Vernon, NY 10552. (914)667–1007. FAX: (914)667–1023. Pres. Miriam Klein Shapiro; Exec. V.-Pres. Rabbi Ronald D. Price. Through innovative outreach programs, seeks to bring the greatest possible number of Jews closer to an open-minded observant Jewish life-style. Activities include the Kashrut Initiative, Operation Pesah, the Panel of Halakhic Inquiry, a speaker's bureau, adult and youth conferences, and congregational services. *Hagahelet (quarterly newsletter); Cornerstone (journal).*

UNION OF AMERICAN HEBREW CONGREGATIONS (1873). 838 Fifth Ave., NYC 10021. (212)249–0100. Pres. Rabbi Alexander M. Schindler; Bd. Chmn. Allan B. Goldman. V.-Pres. Rabbi Albert Vorspan and Rabbi Daniel B. Syme. Serves as the central congregational body of Reform Judaism in the Western Hemisphere; serves its approximately 850 affiliated temples and membership with religious, educational, cultural, and administrative programs. *Reform Judaism.*

———, AMERICAN CONFERENCE OF CANTORS (1956). 1 Kalisa Way, Suite 104, Paramus, NJ 07652. (201)599–0910. FAX: (201)599–1085. Pres. Edward Fogel; Exec. V.-Pres. Raymond Smolover; Admin. Nancy Hausman. Members receive investiture and commissioning as cantors at ordination-investiture ceremonies at recognized seminaries, i.e., Hebrew Union College–Jewish Institute of Religion, Sacred School of Music, or Jewish Theological Seminary, as well as full certification through HUC-JIR-SSM. Through Joint Cantorial Placement Commission, serves Reform congregations seeking cantors and music directors. Dedicated to creative Judaism, preserving the best of the past, and encouraging new and vital approaches to religious ritual, music, and ceremonies. *Koleinu.*

———, COMMISSION ON JEWISH EDUCATION OF THE UNION OF AMERICAN HEBREW CONGREGATIONS, CENTRAL CONFERENCE OF AMERICAN RABBIS, AND NATIONAL ASSOCIATION OF TEMPLE EDUCATORS (1923). 838 Fifth Ave., NYC

10021. (212)249-0100. Chmn. Rabbi Jonathan A. Stein; Cochmn. Robert E. Tornberg; Dir. Rabbi Howard I. Bogot. Long-range planning and policy development for congregational programs of lifelong education; network projects with affiliates and associate groups including: special needs education, Reform Jewish outreach, and Reform Day Schools; activities administered by the UAHC Department for Religious Education.

———, COMMISSION ON SOCIAL ACTION OF REFORM JUDAISM (*see* p. 470)

———, COMMISSION ON SYNAGOGUE MANAGEMENT (UAHC-CCAR) (1962). 838 Fifth Ave., NYC 10021. (212)249-0100. FAX: (212)734-2857. Chmn. Paul Vanek; Dir. Joseph C. Bernstein. Assists congregations in management, finance, building maintenance, design, construction, and art aspects of synagogues; maintains the Synagogue Architectural Library.

———, NATIONAL ASSOCIATION OF TEMPLE ADMINISTRATORS (NATA) (1941). c/o Reform Congregation Keneseth Israel, York Rd. & Township Line, Elkins Park, PA 19117. (215)887-8700. Pres. William Ferstenfeld. Prepares and disseminates administrative information and procedures to member synagogues of UAHC; provides training of professional synagogue executives; formulates and establishes professional standards for the synagogue executive; provides placement services. *NATA Journal; Temple Management Manual.*

———, NATIONAL ASSOCIATION OF TEMPLE EDUCATORS (NATE) (1955). 707 Summerly Dr., Nashville, TN 37209-4244. (615)352-0322. FAX: (615)356-9285. Pres. Robin L. Eisenberg; Exec. V.-Pres. Richard M. Morin. Represents the temple educator within the general body of Reform Judaism; fosters the full-time profession of the temple educator; encourages the growth and development of Jewish religious education consistent with the aims of Reform Judaism; stimulates communal interest in and responsibility for Jewish religious education. *NATE News; Compass.*

———, NATIONAL FEDERATION OF TEMPLE BROTHERHOODS (1923). 838 Fifth Ave., NYC 10021. (212)570-0707. Pres. Richard D. Karfunkle; Exec. Dir. Lewis Eisenberg. Seeks to strengthen Judaism through family programming, by reaching out to college youth, and by promoting adult Jewish education. Through service programs, deals with current concerns of the changing Jewish family. Sponsors the Jewish Chatauqua Society, the brotherhoods' interfaith educational program. *Brotherhood.*

———, NATIONAL FEDERATION OF TEMPLE SISTERHOODS (1913). 838 Fifth Ave., NYC 10021. (212)249-0100. Pres. Judith Hertz; Exec. Dir. Eleanor R. Schwartz. Serves more than 640 sisterhoods of Reform Judaism; promotes interreligious understanding and social justice; awards scholarships and grants to rabbinic students; provides braille and large-type Judaic materials for Jewish blind; supports projects for Israel, Soviet Jewry, and the aging; is an affiliate of UAHC and is the women's agency of Reform Judaism; works in behalf of the Hebrew Union College-Jewish Institute of Religion; cooperates with World Union for Progressive Judaism. *Leaders Line; Notes for Now.*

———, YOUTH DIVISION AND NORTH AMERICAN FEDERATION OF TEMPLE YOUTH (1939). 838 Fifth Ave., NYC 10021. (212)249-0100. FAX: (212)517-7863. Dir. Rabbi Allan L. Smith; Pres. Deborah Sternberg. Seeks to train Reform Jewish youth in the values of the synagogue and their application to daily life through service to the community and congregation; runs department of summer camps and national leadership training institute; arranges overseas academic tours, work-study programs, international student exchange programs, and college student programs in the U.S. and Israel, including accredited study programs in Israel. *Ani V'Atah; The Jewish Connection.*

UNION OF ORTHODOX JEWISH CONGREGATIONS OF AMERICA (1898). 45 W. 36 St., Suite 900, NYC 10018. (212)563-4000. Pres. Sheldon Rudoff; Exec. V.-Pres. Rabbi Pinchas Stolper. Serves as the national central body of Orthodox synagogues; sponsors Institute for Public Affairs; National Conference of Synagogue Youth; LAVE—Learning and Values Experiences; Our Way program for the Jewish deaf; Yachad program for developmentally disabled youth; Israel Center in Jerusalem; *aliyah* department; national OU *kashrut* supervision and certification service; Marriage Commission, Taste of Torah radio program; provides educational, religious, and organizational programs, events, and guidance to synagogues and groups; represents the Orthodox Jewish community in relation to governmental and civic bodies and the general Jewish community. *Jewish Action magazine; OU Kosher Directory; OU Passover Directory; OU News Reporter; Synagogue Spotlight; Our Way magazine; Yachad magazine; Luach Limud Torah Diary Home Study Program.*

———, INSTITUTE FOR PUBLIC AFFAIRS (1989). 45 W. 36 St., Suite 900, NYC 10018. (212)563–4000. FAX: (212)564–9058. Pres. Sheldon Rudoff; Chmn. Mandell Ganchrow; Exec. Dir. William E. Rapfogel. Serves as the policy analysis, advocacy, mobilization, and programming department responsible for representing Orthodox/traditional American Jewry. *Orthodox Advocate (quarterly newsletter); Briefing (monthly updates).*

———, NATIONAL CONFERENCE OF SYNAGOGUE YOUTH (1954). 70 W. 36 St., NYC 10018. (212)244–2011. Pres. Alyson Maslansky; Dir. Rabbi Raphael Butler. Central body for youth groups of Orthodox congregations; provides educational guidance, Torah study groups, community service, programs consultation, Torah library, Torah fund scholarships, Ben Zakkai Honor Society, Friends of NCSY; conducts over 300 national and regional events including weeklong seminars, Travel America with NCSY, Israel Summer Seminar for teens and collegiates, and Camp NCSY East Teen Torah Center. Divisions include Senior NCSY in 18 regions and 465 chapters, Junior NCSY for preteens, Our Way for the Jewish deaf, Yachad for the developmentally disabled, Mesorah for Jewish collegiates, Israel Center in Jerusalem, and NCSY in Israel. *Keeping Posted with NCSY; Face the Nation—President's Newsletter; Oreich Yomeinu—Education Newsletter; Mitsvah of the Month.*

———, WOMEN'S BRANCH (1923). 156 Fifth Ave., NYC 10010. (212)929–8857. Pres. Gitti Needleman. Seeks to spread the understanding and practice of Orthodox Judaism and to unite all Orthodox women and their synagogue organizations; services affiliates with educational and programming materials, leadership, and organizational guidance, and has an NGO representative at the UN. Supplies candelabra for Jewish patients in hospitals and nursing homes; supports Stern and Touro Colleges' scholarship funds and Jewish braille publications. *Hachodesh; Hakol.*

UNION OF ORTHODOX RABBIS OF THE UNITED STATES AND CANADA (1902). 235 E. Broadway, NYC 10002. (212)964–6337. Dir. Rabbi Hersh M. Ginsberg. Seeks to foster and promote Torah-true Judaism in the U.S. and Canada; assists in the establishment and maintenance of *yeshivot* in the U.S.; maintains committee on marriage and divorce and aids individuals with marital difficulties; disseminates knowledge of traditional Jewish rites and practices and publishes regulations on synagogal structure; maintains rabbinical court for resolving individual and communal conflicts. *HaPardes.*

UNION OF SEPHARDIC CONGREGATIONS, INC. (1929). 8 W. 70 St., NYC 10023. (212)873–0300. Pres. Rev. Dr. Salomon Gaon; Bd. Chmn. Victor Tarry. Promotes the religious interests of Sephardic Jews; prints and distributes Sephardic prayer books; provides religious leaders for Sephardic congregations.

UNITED LUBAVITCHER YESHIVOTH (1940). 841–853 Ocean Pkwy., Brooklyn, NY 11230. (718)859–7600. Supports and organizes Jewish day schools and rabbinical seminaries in the U.S. and abroad.

UNITED SYNAGOGUE OF AMERICA (1913). 155 Fifth Ave., NYC 10010. (212)533–7800. FAX: (212)353–9439. Pres. Alan J. Tichnor; Exec. V.-Pres./CEO Rabbi Jerome M. Epstein. International organization of 850 Conservative congregations. Maintains 12 departments and 20 regional offices to assist its affiliates with religious, educational, youth, community, and administrative programming and guidance; aims to enhance the cause of Conservative Judaism, further religious observance, encourage establishment of Jewish religious schools, draw youth closer to Jewish tradition. Extensive Israel programs. *United Synagogue Review; Art/Engagement Calendar; Program Suggestions; Directory & Resource Guide; Book Service Catalogue of Publications.*

———, COMMISSION ON JEWISH EDUCATION (1930). 155 Fifth Ave., NYC 10010. (212)533–7800. FAX: (212)353–9439. Cochmn. Joshua Elkin, Miriam Klein Shapiro; Dir. Rabbi Robert Abramson. Develops educational policy for the United

Synagogue of America and sets the educational direction for Conservative congregations, their schools, and the Solomon Schechter Day Schools. Seeks to enhance the educational effectiveness of congregations through the publication of materials and in-service programs. *Tov L'Horot; Your Child; Dapim; Shiboley Schechter; Advisories.*

———, COMMITTEE ON SOCIAL ACTION AND PUBLIC POLICY (1958). 155 Fifth Ave., NYC 10010. (212)533-7800. FAX: (212)353-9439. Chmn. Scott Kaplan. Develops and implements positions and programs on issues of social action and public policy for the United Synagogue of America; represents these positions to other Jewish and civic organizations, the media, and government; and provides guidance, both informational and programmatic, to its affiliated congregations in these areas.

———, JEWISH EDUCATORS ASSEMBLY (1951). 15 E. 26 St., NYC 10010. (212)-532-4949. FAX: (212)481-4174. Pres. S. Hirsch Jacobson; Exec. Dir. Bernard Dov Troy. Advances the development of Jewish education on all levels in consonance with the philosophy of the Conservative movement. Promotes Jewish education as a basis for the creative continuity of the Jewish people; sponsors an annual convention. Serves as a forum for the exchange of ideas, programs, and educational media. *Bulletins; Aleh V'aleh Newsletter.*

———, KADIMA (formerly PRE-USY; reorg. 1968). 155 Fifth Ave., NYC 10010. (212)533-7800. FAX: (212)353-9439. Exec. Dir. Rabbi Paul Freedman. Involves Jewish preteens in a meaningful religious, educational, and social environment; fosters a sense of identity and commitment to the Jewish community and the Conservative movement; conducts synagogue-based chapter programs and regional Kadima days and weekends. *Mitzvah of the Month; Kadima Kesher; Chagim; Advisors Aid; Games;* quarterly *Kadima* magazine.

———, NATIONAL ASSOCIATION OF SYNAGOGUE ADMINISTRATORS (1948). 155 Fifth Ave., NYC 10010. (212)533-7800. Pres. Rhoda F. Myers. Aids congregations affiliated with the United Synagogue of America to further the aims of Conservative Judaism through more effective administration (Program for Assistance by Liaisons to Synagogues—PALS); advances professional standards and promotes new methods in administration; cooperates in United Synagogue placement services and administrative surveys. *NASA Connections Newsletter; NASA Journal.*

———, UNITED SYNAGOGUE YOUTH OF (1951). 155 Fifth Ave., NYC 10010. (212)-533-7800. FAX: (212)353-9439. Pres. Adam Kligfeld; Exec. Dir. Rabbi Paul Freedman. Seeks to strengthen identification with Conservative Judaism, based on the personality development, needs, and interests of the adolescent, in a Mitzvah framework. *Achshav; Tikun Olam;* A.J. Heschel Honor Society Newsletter; SATO Newsletter; USY Alumni Assn. Newsletter; USY Program Bank; Hamad'rich Newsletter for Advisors.*

VAAD MISHMERETH STAM (1976). 4902 16th Ave., Brooklyn, NY 11204. (718)438-4963. FAX: (718)435-0374. Pres. Rabbi David L. Greenfeld; Exec. Dir. Rabbi Yakov Basch. A nonprofit consumer-protection agency dedicated to preserving and protecting the halakhic integrity of Torah scrolls, phylacteries, and *mezuzot.* Makes presentations and conducts examination campaigns in schools and synagogues; created an optical software system to detect possible textual errors in *stam.* Offices in Israel and Strassbourg, France. Publishes *Guide to Mezuzah* and *Guide to the Letters of the Aleph Beth. The Jewish Quill.*

WOMEN'S LEAGUE FOR CONSERVATIVE JUDAISM (1918). 48 E. 74 St., NYC 10021. (212)628-1600. Pres. Audrey Citak; Exec. Dir. Bernice Balter. Parent body of Conservative (Masorti) women's groups in U.S., Canada, Puerto Rico, Mexico, and Israel; provides them with programs and resources in Jewish education, social action, Israel affairs, Canadian public affairs, leadership training, services to the disabled, community affairs, and publicity techniques; publishes books of Jewish interest; contributes to support of Jewish Theological Seminary of America and its residence halls. *Women's League Outlook; Ba'Olam.*

WORLD COUNCIL OF SYNAGOGUES (1957). 155 Fifth Ave., NYC 10010 (212)533-7693. Pres. Rabbi Zachary Heller; Exec. Dir. Bernard Barsky. International representative of Conservative organizations and congregations; promotes the growth and development of the Conservative movement in Israel and throughout the world; supports educational institutions overseas; holds biennial international conventions; represents the world Conservative movement on the Executive of the World Zionist Organization. *World Spectrum.*

WORLD UNION FOR PROGRESSIVE JUDAISM, LTD. (1926). 838 Fifth Ave., NYC 10021. (212)249-0100. FAX: (212)517-3940. Pres. Donald Day; Exec. Dir. Rabbi Richard G. Hirsch; N. Amer. Dir. Martin Strelzer; Dir. Internatl. Relations & Development Rabbi Clifford Kulwin. International umbrella organization of Liberal Judaism; promotes and coordinates efforts of Liberal congregations throughout the world; starts new congregations, recruits rabbis and rabbinical students for all countries; organizes international conferences of Liberal Jews. *Ammi; Rodnik; Newsupdates.*

SCHOOLS, INSTITUTIONS

ANNENBERG RESEARCH INSTITUTE (formerly DROPSIE COLLEGE FOR HEBREW AND COGNATE LEARNING) (1907; reorg. 1986). 420 Walnut St., Philadelphia, PA 19106. (215)238-1290. FAX: (215)238-1540. Acting Dir. David M. Goldenberg. A center for advanced research in Judaic and Near Eastern studies at the postdoctoral level. *Jewish Quarterly Review.*

BALTIMORE HEBREW UNIVERSITY (1919). 5800 Park Heights Ave., Baltimore, MD 21215. (301)578-6900. FAX: (301)578-6940. Pres. Leivy Smolar; Bd. Chmn. Irving F. Cohn. Offers PhD, MA, and BA programs in Jewish studies, biblical and Near Eastern archaeology, philosophy, literature, history, Hebrew language and literature; School of Continuing Education; Joseph Meyerhoff Library; community lectures, film series, seminars. *The Scribe (annual newsletter).*

———, BALTIMORE INSTITUTE FOR JEWISH COMMUNAL SERVICE. Coord. Judith Yalin; Dean Robert O. Freedman. Trains Jewish communal professionals; offers joint degree program: MA in Jewish studies from BHU; MSW from U. of Maryland.

———, BERNARD MANEKIN SCHOOL OF UNDERGRADUATE STUDIES. Baltimore Hebrew University, 5800 Park Heights Ave., Baltimore, MD 21215. (301)578-6900. FAX: (301)578-6940. Dean Judy Meltzer. BA program; the Isaac C. Rosenthal Center for Jewish Education; on-site courses in Maryland and Jerusalem; interdisciplinary concentrations: contemporary Middle East, American Jewish culture, and the humanities.

———, PEGGY MEYERHOFF PEARLSTONE SCHOOL OF GRADUATE STUDIES. Dean Robert O. Freedman. PhD and MA programs; MA and MSW with University of Maryland School of Social Work and Community Planning in federation, community organization, center, and family services; MA and MEd in Jewish education and double MA in journalism with Towson State University; MA program in the study of Christian-Jewish relations with St. Mary's Seminary and University; MA program in community relations with University of Maryland Graduate School.

BETH MEDROSH ELYON (ACADEMY OF HIGHER LEARNING AND RESEARCH) (1943). 73 Main St., Monsey, NY 10952. (914)356-7065. Bd. Chmn. Emanuel Weldler; Treas. Arnold Jacobs; Sec. Yerachmiel Censor. Provides postgraduate courses and research work in higher Jewish studies; offers scholarships and fellowships. *Annual journal.*

BRAMSON ORT TECHNICAL INSTITUTE (1977). 6930 Austin St., Forest Hills, NY 11375. (718)261-5800. Dir. Dr. Seymour B. Forman. A two-year Jewish technical college offering certificates and associate degrees in high technology and business fields, including computer programming, electronics technology, business management, word processing, and ophthalmic technology. Houses the Center for Computers in Jewish Education.

BRANDEIS-BARDIN INSTITUTE (1941). 1101 Peppertree Lane, Brandeis, CA 93064. (818)348-7201. Pres. Gary Brennglass; Exec. V.-Pres. Dr. Alvin Mars. A pluralistic, nondenominational Jewish institution providing programs for people of all ages: Brandeis Camp Institute (BCI), a leadership program for college-age adults; Camp Alonim, a positive Jewish experience for children 8–16; House of the Book *shabbat* weekends for adults 25+, at which scholars-in-residence discuss historical, cultural, religious, and spiritual aspects of Judaism. *Brandeis-Bardin Institute Newsletter; BCI Alumni News.*

BRANDEIS UNIVERSITY (1948). 415 South St.,Waltham, MA 02254. (617)736-2000. Bd. Chmn. Louis Perlmutter; Interim Pres. Stuart Altman. Founded under Jewish sponsorship as a nonsectarian institution offering to all the highest quality undergraduate and graduate education. The Lown School is the center for all programs of teaching and research in the areas of Judaic studies, Ancient Near Eastern studies, and Islamic and Modern Middle Eastern studies. The school includes the Department of Near Eastern Studies, the Hornstein Program for Jewish Communal Service, and the Cohen Center for Modern Jewish Studies. The Department of Near Eastern and Judaic Studies offers academic programs in the major areas of its concern. The Hornstein Program is a professional training program leading to the degree in Jewish communal service. The Cohen Center conducts research and teaching in contemporary Jewish studies, primarily in the field of American Jewish studies. *Various newsletters, scholarly publications.*

CLEVELAND COLLEGE OF JEWISH STUDIES (1964). 26500 Shaker Blvd., Beachwood, OH 44122. (216)464-4050. Pres. David S. Ariel; Bd. Chmn. Donna Yanowitz. Provides courses in all areas of Judaic and Hebrew studies to adults and college-age students; offers continuing education for Jewish educators and administrators; serves as a center for Jewish life and culture; expands the availability of courses in Judaic studies by exchanging faculty, students, and credits with neighboring academic institutions; grants bachelor's and master's degrees.

DROPSIE COLLEGE FOR HEBREW AND COGNATE LEARNING (*see* Annenberg Research Institute)

GRATZ COLLEGE (1895). Old York Rd. & Melrose Ave., Melrose Park, PA 19126. (215)635-7300. FAX: (215)635-7320. Bd. Chmn. Steven Fisher; Pres. Dr. Gary S. Schiff. Offers a wide variety of bachelor's, master's, teacher-training, continuing-education, and high-school-level programs in Judaic, Hebraic, and Middle Eastern studies. Grants BA and MA in Jewish studies, MA in Jewish education, MA in Jewish music, certificates in Israel studies, Jewish education, Judaica librarianship, Jewish communal studies, Jewish chaplaincy, and other credentials. Joint bachelor's programs with Temple University and Beaver College and joint graduate program in Jewish communal service with U. of Pennsylvania. *Various newsletters, annual academic bulletin, and scholarly publications.*

HEBREW COLLEGE (1921). 43 Hawes St., Brookline, MA 02146. (617)232-8710. Pres. Samuel Schafler; Bd. Chmn. Herbert L. Berman. Provides intensive programs of study in all areas of Jewish culture from high school through college and graduate-school levels, also at branch in Hartford; offers the degrees of MA in Jewish studies, Bachelor and Master of Jewish education, Bachelor of Hebrew letters, and teacher's diploma; degrees fully accredited by New England Assoc. of Schools and Colleges. Operates Hebrew-speaking Camp Yavneh in Northwood, NH; offers extensive Ulpan program and courses for community. *Hebrew College Today.*

HEBREW THEOLOGICAL COLLEGE (1922). 7135 N. Carpenter Rd., Skokie, IL 60077. (312)267-9800. Acting Pres. Rabbi Dr. Jerold Isenberg. An institution of higher Jewish learning which includes a graduate school; school of liberal arts and sciences; division of advanced Hebrew studies; Fasman Yeshiva High School; Anne M. Blitstein Teachers Institute for Women. *Or Shmuel; Torah Journal; Likutei P'shatim.*

HEBREW UNION COLLEGE-JEWISH INSTITUTE OF RELIGION (1875). 3101 Clifton Ave., Cincinnati, OH 45220. (513)221-1875. FAX: (513)221-2810. Pres. Alfred Gottschalk; Exec. V.-Pres. Uri D. Herscher; V.-Pres. Academic Affairs Samuel Greengus; V.-Pres. Paul M. Steinberg; Chmn. Bd. of Govs. Richard J. Scheuer. Academic centers: 3101 Clifton Ave., Cincinnati, OH 45220 (1875), Kenneth Ehrlich, Dean; 1 W. 4 St., NYC 10012 (1922), Norman J. Cohen, Dean; 3077 University Ave., Los Angeles, CA 90007 (1954), Lee Bycel, Dean; 13 King David St., Jerusalem, Israel 94101 (1963), Michael Klein, Dean. Prepares students for Reform rabbinate, cantorate, religious-school teaching and administration, community service, academic careers; promotes Jewish studies; maintains libraries and a museum; offers master's and doctoral degrees; engages in archaeological excavations; publishes scholarly works through Hebrew Union College Press. *American Jewish Archives; Bibliographica Judaica; HUC-JIR Catalogue; Hebrew Union College Annual; Studies in Bibliography and Booklore; The Chronicle.*

———, AMERICAN JEWISH ARCHIVES (1947). 3101 Clifton Ave., Cincinnati, OH 45220. (513)221-1875. FAX: (513)-221-7812. Dir. Jacob R. Marcus; Admin. Dir. Abraham Peck. Promotes the study and preservation of the Western Hemisphere Jewish experience through research, publications, collection of important source materials, and a vigorous public-outreach program. *American Jewish Archives; monographs, publications, and pamphlets.*

———, AMERICAN JEWISH PERIODICAL CENTER (1957). 3101 Clifton Ave., Cincinnati, OH 45220. (513)221-1875. Dir. Jacob R. Marcus; Codir. Herbert C. Zafren. Maintains microfilms of all American Jewish periodicals 1823-1925, selected periodicals since 1925. *Jewish Periodicals and Newspapers on Microfilm (1957); First Supplement (1960); Augmented Edition (1984).*

———, EDGAR F. MAGNIN SCHOOL OF GRADUATE STUDIES (1956). 3077 University Ave., Los Angeles, CA 90007. (213)-749-3424. FAX: (213)747-6128. Dir. Stanley Chyet. Supervises programs leading to PhD (Education), DHS, DHL, and MA degrees; participates in cooperative PhD programs with the University of Southern California.

———, JEROME H. LOUCHHEIM SCHOOL OF JUDAIC STUDIES (1969). FAX: (213)747-6128. 3077 University Ave. Los Angeles, CA 90007. (213)749-3424. Dir. David Ellenson. Offers programs leading to MA, BS, BA, and AA degrees; offers courses as part of the undergraduate program of the University of Southern California.

———, NELSON GLUECK SCHOOL OF BIBLICAL ARCHAEOLOGY (1963). 13 King David St., Jerusalem, Israel 94101. FAX: 2-251-478. Dir. Avraham Biran. Offers graduate-level research programs in Bible and archaeology. Summer excavations are carried out by scholars and students. University credit may be earned by participants in excavations. Consortium of colleges, universities, and seminaries is affiliated with the school.

———, RHEA HIRSCH SCHOOL OF EDUCATION (1967). 3077 University Ave., Los Angeles, CA 90007. (213)749-3424. FAX: (213)747-6128. Dir. Sara Lee. Offers PhD and MA programs in Jewish and Hebrew education; conducts joint degree programs with University of Southern California; offers courses for Jewish teachers, librarians, and early educators on a nonmatriculating basis; conducts summer institutes for professional Jewish educators.

———, SCHOOL OF EDUCATION (1947). 1 W. 4 St., NYC 10012. (212)674-5300. FAX: (212)533-0129. V.-Pres. and Dean of Faculty Paul M. Steinberg; Dean Norman J. Cohen; Dir. Kerry M. Olitzky. Trains teachers and principals for Reform religious schools; offers MA degree with specialization in religious education; offers extension programs in various suburban centers.

———, SCHOOL OF GRADUATE STUDIES (1949). 3101 Clifton Ave., Cincinnati, OH 45220 (513)221-1875. FAX: (513)221-0321. Dir. Alan Cooper. Offers programs leading to MA and PhD degrees; offers program leading to DHL degree for rabbinic graduates of the college.

———, SCHOOL OF JEWISH COMMUNAL SERVICE (1968). 3077 University Ave., Los Angeles, CA 90007. (213)749-3424. FAX: (213)747-6128. Dir. H. Jack Mayer. Offers certificate and master's degree to those employed in Jewish communal services, or preparing for such work; offers joint MA in Jewish education and communal service with Rhea Hirsch School; offers MA and MSW in conjunction with the University of Southern California School of Social Work, with the George Warren Brown School of Social Work of Washington University, and with the University of Pittsburgh School of Social Work; offers joint master's degrees in conjunction with USC in public administration or gerontology.

———, SCHOOL OF JEWISH STUDIES (1963). 13 King David St., Jerusalem, Israel, 94101. FAX: 2-251-478. Dean Michael Klein; Assoc. Dean Rabbi Shaul R. Feinberg. Offers first year of graduate rabbinic, cantorial, and Jewish education studies (required) for American students; program leading to ordination for Israeli rabbinic students; undergraduate semester in Jerusalem and one-year work/study program on a kibbutz in cooperation with Union of American Hebrew Congregations; public outreach programs (lectures, courses, concerts, exhibits).

———, SCHOOL OF SACRED MUSIC (1947). 1 W. 4 St., NYC 10012. (212)674-5300. FAX: (212)533-0129. Dir. Israel Goldstein. Trains cantors and music personnel for congregations; offers MSM degree. *Sacred Music Press.*

———, SKIRBALL MUSEUM (*see* p. 478)

HERZLIAH-JEWISH TEACHERS SEMINARY (1967). Division of Touro College. 844 Ave. of the Americas, NYC 10001. (212)-447-0700. Pres. Bernard Lander; Dir. Jacob Katzman.

———, GRADUATE SCHOOL OF JEWISH STUDIES (1981). 30 W. 44 St., NYC 10036. (212)447-0700. Pres. Bernard Lander; Dean Michael A. Shmidman. Offers courses leading to an MA in Jewish studies, with concentrations in Jewish history or Jewish education. Students may complete part of their program in Israel, through MA courses offered by Touro faculty at Touro's Jerusalem center.

———, JEWISH PEOPLE'S UNIVERSITY OF THE AIR. (212)447-0700. Dir./Producer Jacob Katzman. The educational outreach arm of Touro College, it produces and disseminates Jewish educational and cultural programming for radio broadcast and on audio-cassettes.

INSTITUTE OF TRADITIONAL JUDAISM (1990). 261 E. Lincoln Ave., Mt. Vernon, NY 10552. (914)667-1023. FAX: (914)-667-1023. Rector (*Reish Metivta*) Rabbi David Weiss Halivni; Dean Rabbi Ronald D. Price. A nondenominational rabbinical school dedicated to genuine faith combined with intellectual honesty and the love of Israel. Graduates receive "*yoreh yoreh*" *smikhah.*

JEWISH THEOLOGICAL SEMINARY OF AMERICA (1886; reorg. 1902). 3080 Broadway, NYC 10027-4649. (212)678-8000. Chancellor Dr. Ismar Schorsch; Bd. Chmn. Stephen M. Peck. Operates undergraduate and graduate programs in Judaic studies; professional schools for training Conservative rabbis and cantors; Melton Center for Jewish Education; the Jewish Museum; and such youth programs as the Ramah Camps and the Prozdor high-school division. Produces network television programs in cooperation with interfaith broadcasting commission. *Academic Bulletin; Seminary Progress; The Second Century.*

———, ALBERT A. LIST COLLEGE OF JEWISH STUDIES (formerly SEMINARY COLLEGE OF JEWISH STUDIES-TEACHERS INSTITUTE) (1909). 3080 Broadway, NYC 10027. (212)678-8826. Dean Dr. Anne Lapidus Lerner. Offers complete undergraduate program in Judaica leading to BA degree; conducts joint programs with Columbia University and Barnard College enabling students to receive two BA degrees.

———, CANTORS INSTITUTE AND SEMINARY COLLEGE OF JEWISH MUSIC (1952). 3080 Broadway, NYC 10027. (212)678-8038. Dean Rabbi Morton M. Leifman. Trains cantors, music teachers, and choral directors for congregations. Offers full-time programs in sacred music leading to degrees of MSM and DSM, and diploma of *Hazzan.*

———, DEPARTMENT OF RADIO AND TELEVISION (1944). 3080 Broadway, NYC 10027. (212)678-8020. Dir. Marjorie Wyler. Produces radio and TV programs expressing the Jewish tradition in its broadest sense, including hour-long documentaries on NBC and ABC. Distributes cassettes of programs at minimum charge.

———, GRADUATE SCHOOL (formerly INSTITUTE FOR ADVANCED STUDY IN THE HUMANITIES) (1968). 3080 Broadway, NYC 10027. (212)678-8024. Dean Dr. Shaye J. D. Cohen. Graduate programs leading to MA, DHL, and PhD degrees in Jewish studies, Bible, Jewish education, history, literature, ancient Judaism, philosophy, rabbinics, and medieval studies; dual degree with Columbia University School of Social Work.

———, JEWISH MUSEUM (*see* p. 476)

———, LIBRARY OF THE JEWISH THEOLOGICAL SEMINARY. 3080 Broadway, NYC 10027. (212)678-8075. FAX: (212)678-8998. Librarian Mayer E. Rabinowitz. Contains one of the largest collections of Hebraica and Judaica in the world, including manuscripts, incunabula, rare books, and Cairo *Geniza* material. The 260,000-

volume collection is housed in a state-of-the-art building and is open to the public. *New Acquisitions List; Friends of the Library Newsletter.*

———, LOUIS FINKELSTEIN INSTITUTE FOR RELIGIOUS AND SOCIAL STUDIES (1938). 3080 Broadway, NYC 10027. (212)678-8815. Dir. Irving Levine; Assoc. Dir. Carlotta Damanda. A scholarly and scientific fellowship of clergy and other religious teachers who desire authoritative information regarding some of the basic issues now confronting spiritually minded individuals.

———, MELTON RESEARCH CENTER FOR JEWISH EDUCATION (1960). 3080 Broadway, NYC 10027. (212)678-8031. Dirs. Eduardo Rauch, Barry W. Holtz. Develops new curricula and materials for Jewish education; recruits and prepares educators through seminars and in-service programs; maintains consultant and supervisory relationships with a limited number of pilot schools; sponsors "renewal" retreats for teachers and principals. *Melton Journal.*

———, NATIONAL RAMAH COMMISSION (1951). 3080 Broadway, NYC 10027. (212)678-8881. FAX: (212)749-8251. Pres. Dr. Saul Shapiro; Dir. Sheldon Dorph. Sponsors 7 overnight Conservative Jewish camps in U.S. and Canada; offers opportunities for qualified college students and older persons to serve as counselors, administrators, specialists, etc. Offers special programs in U.S. and Israel, including Weinstein National Ramah Staff Training Institute, Ramah Israel Seminar, Ulpan Ramah Plus, and Tichon Ramah Yerushalayim. Summer day camp in Israel for Americans.

———, PROZDOR (1951). 3080 Broadway, NYC 10027. (212)678-8824. Principal Dr. Michael Panitz. The high-school department of JTS, it provides a supplementary Jewish education for students who attend a secular (public or private) full-time high school. Classes in classical Jewish studies, with emphasis on Hebrew language, meet twice a week. *Prozdor Pages.*

———, RABBINICAL SCHOOL (1886). 3080 Broadway, NYC 10027. (212)678-8816. Dean Rabbi Gordon Tucker. Offers a program of graduate and professional studies leading to the degree of Master of Arts and ordination; includes one year of study in Jerusalem and an extensive field-work program.

———, SAUL LIEBERMAN INSTITUTE OF JEWISH RESEARCH (1985). PO Box 196, Jerusalem, Israel 92102. (02)631121. Dir. Shamma Friedman. Engaged in preparing for publication a series of scholarly editions of selected chapters of the Talmud. The following projects support and help disseminate the research: Talmud Text Database; Bibliography of Talmudic Literature; Catalogue of Geniza Fragments; Teachers Training and Curriculum Development in Oral Law for Secondary Schools.

———, SCHOCKEN INSTITUTE FOR JEWISH RESEARCH (1961). 6 Balfour St., Jerusalem, Israel 92102. (02)631288. Dir. Shmuel Glick; Coord. for Educ. Programs Simcha Goldsmith. Comprises the Schocken collection of rare books and manuscripts and a research institute dedicated to the exploration of Hebrew religious poetry (*piyyut*). *Schocken Institute Yearbook (P'raqim).*

———, UNIVERSITY OF JUDAISM (1947). 15600 Mulholland Dr., Los Angeles, CA 90077. (213)879-4114. FAX: (213)471-1278. Pres. Dr. David L. Lieber; Dean of Academic Affairs Dr. Hanan Alexander; Dean of Student Affairs Rabbi Daniel Gordis. The undergraduate school, Lee College of Arts and Sciences, is an accredited liberal arts college offering a core curriculum of Jewish and Western studies, with majors including psychology, business, literature, political science, and Jewish studies. Accredited graduate programs in nonprofit business management, Jewish education, and Jewish studies, plus a preparatory program for the Conservative rabbinate. Two institutes for research and program development, the Wilstein Institute for Jewish Policy Studies and the Whizin Center for the Jewish Future. A broad range of continuing education courses, cultural arts programs, and a variety of outreach services for West Coast Jewish communities. *Direction Magazine; Focus Newsletter; Bulletin of General Information.*

MESIVTA YESHIVA RABBI CHAIM BERLIN RABBINICAL ACADEMY (1905). 1593 Coney Island Ave., Brooklyn, NY 11230. (718)377-0777. Exec. Dir. Y. Mayer Lasker. Maintains fully accredited elementary and high schools; collegiate and postgraduate school for advanced Jewish studies, both in America and Israel; Camp Morris, a summer study retreat; Prof. Nathan Isaacs Memorial Library; Gur Aryeh Publications.

NER ISRAEL RABBINICAL COLLEGE (1933). 400 Mt. Wilson Lane, Baltimore, MD 21208. (301)484–7200. FAX: (301)484–3060. Rabbi Yaakov S. Weinberg, Rosh Hayeshiva; Rabbi Herman N. Neuberger, Menahel. Trains rabbis and educators for Jewish communities in America and worldwide. Offers bachelor's, master's, and doctoral degrees in talmudic law, as well as teacher's diploma. College has four divisions: Mechina High School, Rabbinical College, Teachers Training Institute, Graduate School. Maintains an active community-service division. Operates special program for Iranian Jewish students. *Ner Israel Update; Alumni Bulletin; Ohr Hanair Talmudic Journal; Iranian B'nei Torah Bulletin.*

RABBINICAL COLLEGE OF TELSHE, INC. (1941). 28400 Euclid Ave., Wickliffe, OH 44092. (216)943–5300. Pres. Rabbi Mordecai Gifter; V.-Pres. Rabbi Abba Zalka Gewirtz. College for higher Jewish learning specializing in Talmudic studies and rabbinics; maintains a preparatory academy including a secular high school, postgraduate department, teacher-training school, and teachers seminary for women. *Pri Etz Chaim; Peer Mordechai; Alumni Bulletin.*

RECONSTRUCTIONIST RABBINICAL COLLEGE (1968). Church Rd. and Greenwood Ave., Wyncote, PA 19095. (215)576–0800. FAX: (215)576–6143. Pres. Arthur Green; Bd. Chmn. Jacques G. Pomeranz; Genl. Chmn. Aaron Ziegelman. Coeducational. Trains rabbis for all areas of Jewish communal life: synagogues, academic and educational positions, Hillel centers, federation agencies; confers title of rabbi and grants degrees of Master and Doctor of Hebrew letters. *RRC Report.*

SPERTUS COLLEGE OF JUDAICA (1925). 618 S. Michigan Ave., Chicago, IL 60605. (312)922–9012. Pres. Howard A. Sulkin; Bd. Chmn. William Gofen; V.-Pres. for Academic Affairs Byron L. Sherwin; Dir. Spertus Museum, Morris A. Fred; Dir. Asher Library, Michael Terry. An accredited liberal arts institution of higher learning offering five master's degree programs in Jewish studies, Jewish education, Jewish communal services, and human services administration. Offers extension classes at several locations and sponsors extensive continuing education lectures and seminars. Houses the Asher Library, the largest circulating library of Judaica in the Midwest, with notable collections of rare books, Yiddish and Hebrew, Jewish art and Holocaust literature and the Targ Center for Jewish Music, as well as the Chicago Jewish Archives.

———, SPERTUS MUSEUM (*see* p. 478)

TOURO COLLEGE (1970). Executive Offices: Empire State Bldg., 350 Fifth Ave., Suite 5122, NYC 10018.(212)643–0700. Pres. Bernard Lander; V.-Pres. Academic Affairs Solomon Simonson; Bd. Chmn. Max Karl. Chartered by NY State Board of Regents as a nonprofit four-year college with business, Judaic studies, health sciences, and liberal arts programs leading to BA, BS, and MA degrees; emphasizes relevance of Jewish heritage to general culture of Western civilization. Also offers JD degree and a biomedical program leading to the MD degree from Technion-Israel Institute of Technology, Haifa.

———, BARRY Z. LEVINE SCHOOL OF HEALTH SCIENCES AND CENTER FOR BIOMEDICAL EDUCATION. (1970) 135 Common Rd., Bldg. #10, Dix Hills, NY 11746. (516)673–3200. Dean Dr. Joseph Weisberg. Along with the Manhattan campus, offers 5 programs: Five-year program leading to MA from Touro and MD from Faculty of Medicine of Technion-Israel Institute of Technology, Haifa; BS/MA—physical therapy and occupational therapy programs; BS—physician assistant and health-information management programs.

———, COLLEGE OF LIBERAL ARTS AND SCIENCES. 844 Sixth Ave., NYC 10001. (212)575–0196. Exec. Dean Stanley Boylan. Offers comprehensive Jewish studies along with studies in the arts, sciences, humanities, and preprofessional studies in health sciences, law, accounting, business, computer science, education, and finance, health sciences, and law.

———, GRADUATE SCHOOL OF JEWISH STUDIES (1981) 844 Sixth Ave., NYC 10001. (212)575–0190. Pres. Bernard Lander; Dean Michael A. Shmidman. Offers courses leading to an MA in Jewish studies, with concentrations in Jewish history or Jewish education. Students may complete part of their program in Israel, through MA courses offered by Touro faculty at Touro's Jerusalem center.

———, INSTITUTE OF JEWISH LAW. Based at Fuchsberg Law Center, serves as a center and clearinghouse for study and teaching of Jewish law. Coedits *Dinei Israel* (Jewish Law Journal) with Tel Aviv University Law School.

———, ISRAEL CENTER. Rechov Shivtei Yisrael 23, PO Box 31356, Jerusalem. 2-894-086.

———, JACOB D. FUCHSBERG LAW CENTER (1980). Long Island Campus, 300 Nassau Rd., Huntington, NY 11743. (516)421-2244. Dean Howard A. Glickstein. Offers studies leading to JD degree.

———, JEWISH PEOPLE'S UNIVERSITY OF THE AIR. (1979). 844 Sixth Ave., NYC 10001. (212)447-0700. Producer/Dir. Jacob Katzman. Produces and disseminates courses in Jewish subject matter for radio broadcasting and on audio-cassettes. Printed course outlines for all courses and discussion-leader's guides for some.

———, MOSCOW BRANCH. 5 Jablockkova St., 127254 Moscow, USSR. 210-86-69; 210-61-73.

———, SCHOOL OF GENERAL STUDIES. 240 E. 123 St., NYC 10021. (212)722-1575. Dean Stephen Adolphus. Offers educational opportunities to minority groups and older people; courses in the arts, sciences, humanities, and special programs of career studies.

———, SHULAMITH SCHOOL. (1929). 1277 E. 14 St., Brooklyn, NY 11230. (718)338-4000. Pres. Sy Knapel; Exec. Dir. Rabbi M. Zwick. Religious Hebrew preschool, elementary, and high school.

WEST COAST TALMUDICAL SEMINARY (Yeshiva Ohr Elchonon Chabad) (1953). 7215 Waring Ave., Los Angeles, CA 90046. (213)937-3763. Dean Rabbi Ezra Schochet. Provides facilities for intensive Torah education as well as Orthodox rabbinical training on the West Coast; conducts an accredited college preparatory high school combined with a full program of Torah-talmudic training and a graduate talmudical division on the college level. *Torah Quiz; Kobetz Migdal Ohr.*

YESHIVA UNIVERSITY (1886). Joel Jablonski Campus, 500 W. 185 St., NYC 10033. (212)960-5400. FAX:(212)960-0055. Pres. Dr. Norman Lamm; Chmn. Bd. of Trustees Ludwig Jesselson. The nation's oldest and largest independent university founded under Jewish auspices, with a broad range of undergraduate, graduate, and professional schools, a network of affiliates, a widespread program of research and community outreach, publications, and a museum. Curricula lead to bachelor's, master's, doctoral, and professional degrees. Undergraduate schools provide general studies curricula supplemented by courses in Jewish learning; graduate schools prepare for careers in medicine, law, social work, Jewish education, psychology, Jewish studies, Semitic languages, literatures, and cultures, and other fields. It has six undergraduate schools, seven graduate and professional schools, and three affiliates, with four centers located in Manhattan and the Bronx. *Alumni Review/ Inside YU.*

Undergraduate schools for men at Joel Jablonski Campus: Yeshiva College (Dean Dr. Norman S. Rosenfeld) provides liberal arts and sciences curricula; grants BA degree. Isaac Breuer College of Hebraic Studies (Assoc. Dean Dr. Don Well) awards Hebrew teacher's diploma, AA, BA, and BS. James Striar School of General Jewish Studies (Assoc. Dean Dr. Don Well) grants AA degree. Yeshiva Program/ Mazer School of Talmudic Studies (Dean Rabbi Zevulun Charlop) offers advanced course of study in talmudic texts and commentaries.

Undergraduate school for women at Midtown Center, 245 Lexington Ave., NYC 10016. (212)340-7700: Stern College for Women (Dean Dr. Karen Bacon); offers liberal arts and sciences curricula supplemented by Jewish studies courses; awards BA, AA, and Hebrew teacher's diploma.

Sy Syms School of Business at Joel Jablonski Campus (Dean Dr. Michael Schiff) offers undergraduate business curricula in conjunction with study at Yeshiva College or Stern College; grants BS degree.

Sponsors one high school for boys (Manhattan) and one for girls (Queens).

Universitywide programs serving the community and the nation include the Carl C. Icahn Institute for Child Protection; Irving and Hanni Rosenbaum Aliyah Incentive Fund; Jacob E. Safra Institute of Sephardic Studies; Ivan L. Tillem Program for Special Services for the Jewish Elderly; Holocaust Studies Program; Interdisciplinary Conference on Bereavement and Grief; Yeshiva University Museum; Yeshiva University Press.

———, ALBERT EINSTEIN COLLEGE OF MEDICINE (1955). Jack and Pearl Resnick Campus, Eastchester Rd. & Morris Pk. Ave., Bronx, NY 10461. (212)430–2000. Pres. Dr. Norman Lamm; Chmn. Bd. of Overseers Burton P. Resnick; Dean Dr. Dominick P. Purpura. Prepares physicians and conducts research in the health sciences; awards MD degree; includes Sue Golding Graduate Division of Medical Sciences (Dir. Dr. Barbara K. Birshtein), which grants PhD degree. Einstein College's clinical facilities, affiliates, and resources encompass Jack D. Weiler Hospital of Albert Einstein College of Medicine, Bronx Municipal Hospital Center, Montefiore Medical Center, and the Rose F. Kennedy Center for Research in Mental Retardation and Human Development. *Einstein; AECOM Today; Einstein Quarterly Journal of Biology and Medicine.*

———, ALUMNI OFFICE, 500 W. 185 Street, NYC 10033. (212)960–5373. Dir. Dr. E. Yechiel Simon. Seeks to foster a close allegiance of alumni to their alma mater by maintaining ties with all alumni and servicing the following associations: Yeshiva College Alumni (Pres. Emanuel J. Adler); Stern College for Women Alumnae (Pres. Jan Schechter); Albert Einstein College of Medicine Alumni (Pres. Dr. Arthur Schapiro); Ferkauf Graduate School of Psychology Alumni (Pres. Dr. Alvin I. Schiff); Wurzweiler School of Social Work Alumni (Pres. Ilene Stein Himber); Bernard Revel Graduate School—Harry Fischel School Alumni (Pres. Dr. Bernard Rosensweig); Rabbinic Alumni (Pres. Rabbi Bernard E. Rothman); Benjamin N. Cardozo School of Law Alumni (Chmn. Noah Gordon, Jay H. Ziffer). *Alumni Review/Inside; AECOM Alumni News; Jewish Social Work Forum.*

———, BELFER INSTITUTE FOR ADVANCED BIOMEDICAL STUDIES (1978). Eastchester Rd. & Morris Pk. Ave., Bronx, NY 10461. (212)430–2801. Dir. Dr. Ernst R. Jaffé. Integrates and coordinates the Medical College's postdoctoral research and training-grant programs in the basic and clinical biomedical sciences. Awards certificate as Research Fellow or Research Associate on completion of training.

———, BENJAMIN N. CARDOZO SCHOOL OF LAW (1976). Brookdale Center, 55 Fifth Ave., NYC 10003. (212)790–0200. Pres. Dr. Norman Lamm; Bd. Chmn. Jacob Burns; Dean Monroe E. Price. Provides innovative courses of study within a traditional legal framework; program includes judicial internships; grants Doctor of Law (JD) degree. Programs and services include Jacob Burns Institute for Advanced Legal Studies; Bet Tzedek Legal Services Clinic; Leonard and Bea Diener Institute of Jewish Law; Samuel and Ronnie Heyman Center on Corporate Governance; Howard M. Squadron Program in Communications Law; Center for Professional Development; International Law and Human Rights Program. *Cardozo Studies in Law and Literature; Cardozo Law Review; Arts and Entertainment Law Journal; Women's Annotated Legal Bibliography; Cardozo Law Forum.*

———, BERNARD REVEL GRADUATE SCHOOL (1937). 500 W. 185 St., NYC 10033. (212)960–5253. Dean Dr. Leo Landman. Offers graduate programs in Judaic studies and Semitic languages, literatures, and cultures; confers MS, MA, and PhD degrees.

———, DAVID J. AZRIELI GRADUATE INSTITUTE OF JEWISH EDUCATION AND ADMINISTRATION (1945). Midtown Center, 245 Lexington Ave., NYC 10016. (212)-340–7705. Dir. Dr. Yitzchak S. Handel. Offers MS degree in Jewish elementary and secondary education; specialist's certificate and EdD in administration and supervision of Jewish education. Block Education Program, initiated under a grant from the Jewish Agency's L.A. Pincus Fund for the Diaspora, provides summer course work to complement year-round field instruction in local communities; grants MS, specialist's certificate, and EdD degrees.

———, FERKAUF GRADUATE SCHOOL OF PSYCHOLOGY (1957). Eastchester Rd. & Morris Pk. Ave., Bronx, NY 10461. (212)-430–4201. Dean Dr. Barbara G. Melamed. Offers MA in general psychology; PsyD in clinical and school psychology; and PhD in clinical, school, developmental, experimental, and health psychology. Programs and services include Robert M. Beren Center for Psychological Intervention; Leonard and Murial Marcus Family Project for the Study of the Disturbed Adolescent; Center for Psychological and Psychoeducational Services.

———, HARRY FISCHEL SCHOOL FOR HIGHER JEWISH STUDIES (1945). 500 W. 185 St., NYC 10033. (212)960-5253. Dean Dr. Leo Landman. Offers summer graduate programs in Judaic studies and Semitic languages, literatures, and cultures; confers MS, MA, and PhD degrees.

———, (affiliate) RABBI ISAAC ELCHANAN THEOLOGICAL SEMINARY (1896). 2540 Amsterdam Ave., NYC 10033. (212)960-5344. Chmn. Bd. of Trustees Judah Feinerman; V.-Pres. for Administration & Professional Education Rabbi Robert S. Hirt; Dean Rabbi Zevulun Charlop. Grants *semikhah* (ordination) and the degrees of Master of Religious Education, Master of Hebrew Literature, Doctor of Religious Education, and Doctor of Hebrew Literature.

The seminary includes Rabbi Joseph B. Soloveitchik Center of Rabbinic Studies; Morris and Nellie L. Kawaler Rabbinic Training Program; Gindi Program for the Enhancement of Professional Rabbinics; Caroline and Joseph S. Gruss Institute in Jerusalem (Dir. Rabbi Aharon Lichtenstein); Caroline and Joseph S. Gruss Kollel Elyon (Post-Graduate Kollel Program) (Dir. Rabbi Aharon Kahn); Marcos and Adina Katz Kollel (Institute for Advanced Research in Rabbinics) (Dir. Rabbi Hershel Schachter); Kollel L'Horaah (Yadin Yadin) and External Yadin Yadin (Dir. Rabbi J. David Bleich); Chaver Program (Dir. Rabbi J. David Bleich). Brookdale Chaplaincy Internship Program trains prospective rabbis to work effectively with the elderly. Maybaum Sephardic Fellowship Program trains rabbis for service in Sephardic communities here and abroad. The service arm of the Seminary, Max Stern Division of Communal Services (Dir. Rabbi Robert S. Hirt), provides personal and professional service to the rabbinate and related fields, as well as educational, consultative, organizational, and placement services to congregations, schools, and communal organizations around the world.

Other seminary programs are the Sylvia Freyer Professional Training Program in Community Outreach; Rudin Continuing Rabbinic Education Program; Stone-Sapirstein Center for Jewish Education; National Commission on Torah Education, a lay group; Sephardic Community Activities Programs; Dr. Joseph and Rachel Ades Sephardic Community Outreach Program. Camp Morasha (Dir. Zvi Reich) offers Jewish studies program.

PHILIP AND SARAH BELZ SCHOOL OF JEWISH MUSIC (1954). 560 W. 185 St., NYC 10033. (212)960-5353. Dir. Cantor Bernard Beer. Provides professional training of cantors and courses for others with an interest in Jewish liturgical music; offers classes for students of all ages, maintains a specialized library, and conducts outreach; awards associate cantor's certificate and cantorial diploma.

———, WOMEN'S ORGANIZATION (1928). 500 W. 185 St., NYC 10033. (212)960-0855. Natl. Presidium: Judy Kirshenbaum, Inge Rennert, Alice Turobiner; Natl. Chmn. Dinah Pinczower. Supports Yeshiva University's national scholarship program for students training in education, community service, law, medicine, and other professions, and its development program. *YUWO News Briefs.*

———, WURZWEILER SCHOOL OF SOCIAL WORK (1957). 500 W. 185 St., NYC 10033. (212)960-0800. Pres. Norman Lamm; Chmn. Bd. of Govs. Herbert H. Schiff; Dean Sheldon R. Gelman. Offers graduate programs in social group work, social casework, community social work; grants MSW and DSW degrees; two-year, full-time Concurrent Plan combines classroom study and supervised field instruction; Extended Plan permits some MSW candidates up to five years to complete requirements; Accelerated Plan grants MSW in 14 months to qualified students; Plan for Employed Persons is designed for those working in social agencies; Block Education Plan (Dir. Frances A. Sosnoff) designed for students living outside New York, provides field instruction in agencies in the U.S., Canada, Israel, and Europe; Clergy Plan provides training in counseling for clergy of all denominations. Part-Time Professional Education Plan enables human services professionals and others to take up to 12 credits as nondegree students, with credits applied to the MSW if students later matriculate. *Jewish Social Work Forum.*

———, (affiliate) YESHIVA OF LOS ANGELES (1977). 9760 W. Pico Blvd., Los Angeles, CA 90035. (213)553–4478. Dean Rabbi Marvin Hier; Bd. Chmn. Samuel Belzberg; Dir. Academic Programs Rabbi Sholom Tendler. Grants BA degree in Jewish studies. Has university program and graduate studies department. Also provides Jewish studies program for beginners. Affiliates are high schools, Jewish Studies Institute for Adult Education, and Simon Wiesenthal Center.

SIMON WIESENTHAL CENTER (1977). 9760 W. Pico Blvd., Los Angeles, CA 90035. (213)553–9036. FAX: (213)553–8007. Dean Rabbi Marvin Hier; Assoc. Dean Rabbi Abraham Cooper; Dir. Dr. Gerald Margolis. Regional offices in New York, Chicago, Miami, Orange County, Jerusalem, Paris, Toronto, Vienna. Dedicated to preserving the memory of the Holocaust through education and awareness. Programs: museum; library; archives; "Testimony for the Truth" oral history; educational outreach; Beit Hashoah—Museum of Tolerance (opening 12/91); interactive exploration of social dynamics of bigotry and racism; computerized learning center. In cooperation with Yeshiva of Los Angeles: Jewish Studies Institute; international social action; "Page One" (syndicated weekly radio news magazine presenting contemporary Jewish issues). *Simon Wiesenthal Center Annual; Response Magazine; Commitment; Museum Update.*

YESHIVATH TORAH VODAATH AND MESIVTA RABBINICAL SEMINARY (1918). 425 E. 9 St., Brooklyn, NY 11218. (718)-941–8000. Bd. Chmn. Chaim Leshkowitz. Offers Hebrew and secular education from elementary level through rabbinical ordination and postgraduate work; maintains a teachers institute and community-service bureau; maintains a dormitory and a nonprofit camp program for boys. *Chronicle; Mesivta Vanguard; Thought of the Week; Torah Vodaath News.*

———, ALUMNI ASSOCIATION (1941). 425 E. 9 St., Brooklyn, NY 11218. (718)941–8000. Pres. Marcus Saffer; Bd. Chmn. Seymour Pluchenik. Promotes social and cultural ties between the alumni and the schools through fund raising; offers vocational guidance to students; operates Camp Torah Vodaath; sponsors research fellowship program for boys. *Annual Journal; Hamesivta Torah periodical.*

SOCIAL, MUTUAL BENEFIT

ALPHA EPSILON PI FRATERNITY (1913). 8815 Wesleyan Rd., Indianapolis, IN 46268–1171. (317)876–1913. Natl. Pres. Stanford Odesky; Exec. V.-Pres. Sidney N. Dunn. International Jewish fraternity active on over 100 campuses in the U.S. and Canada; encourages Jewish students to remain loyal to their heritage and to assume leadership roles in the community; active in behalf of Soviet Jewry, the State of Israel, and other Jewish causes. *The Lion of Alpha Epsilon Pi (quarterly magazine).*

AMERICAN ASSOCIATION OF RUSSIAN JEWS (1989). 257 Bayview Ave., Amityville, NY 11701. (516)598–3375. FAX: (516)826–7152/(301)951–6435. Pres. Isaac Tarasulo; Sec. Inna Arolovich. Helps Soviet Jewish immigrants to the U.S. in adjusting to all aspects of American society, including employment, Jewish acculturation, and participation in social and civic activities; informs the American people about the situation of Soviet Jews and the Russian-Jewish community in the U.S. *Anti-Semitism in the USSR; Chronicle of Anti-Semitic Incidents in the USSR.*

AMERICAN FEDERATION OF JEWS FROM CENTRAL EUROPE, INC. (1938). 570 Seventh Ave., NYC 10018. (212)921–3871. Pres. Robert L. Lehman; Bd. Chmn. Curt C. Silberman; Exec. Asst. Katherine Rosenthal. Seeks to safeguard the rights and interests of American Jews of German-speaking Central European descent, especially in reference to restitution and indemnification; through its affiliate Research Foundation for Jewish Immigration sponsors research and publications on the history, immigration, and acculturation of Central European émigrés in the U.S. and worldwide; through its affiliate Jewish Philanthropic Fund of 1933 supports social programs for needy Nazi victims in the U.S.; undertakes cultural activities, annual conferences, publications; member, Council of Jews from Germany, London.

AMERICAN SEPHARDI FEDERATION (1973). 133 E. 58 St., Suite 404, NYC 10022. (212)308–3455. FAX: (212)980–9354. Pres. Leon Levy; Exec. Dir. Suri Kasirer. Central umbrella organization for all Sephardic congregations, organizations, and agencies. Seeks to preserve and promote Sephardi culture, education, and traditions. Disseminates resource material on all aspects of Sephardic life. Strives to bring a Sephardic agenda and perspective to American Jewish life. *Sephardic Highlights Newsletter.*

AMERICAN VETERANS OF ISRAEL (1949).136 E. 39 St., NYC 10016. (516)-431-8316. Pres. Paul Kaye; Sec. Samuel E. Alexander. Maintains contact with American and Canadian volunteers who served in Aliyah Bet and/or Israel's War of Independence; promotes Israel's welfare; holds memorial services at grave of Col. David Marcus; is affiliated with World Mahal. *Newsletter.*

ASSOCIATION OF YUGOSLAV JEWS IN THE UNITED STATES, INC. (1941). 130 E. 59 St., Suite 1202, NYC 10022. (212)371-6891. Pres. Mary Levine; Exec. Off. Emanuel Salom; Treas./V.-Pres. Mirko Goldschmidt. Assists all Jews originally from Yugoslavia; raises funds for Israeli agencies and institutions. *Bulletin.*

BNAI ZION—THE AMERICAN FRATERNAL ZIONIST ORGANIZATION (1908). 136 E. 39 St., NYC 10016. (212)725-1211. Pres. Werner Buckold; Exec. V.-Pres. Mel Parness. Fosters principles of Americanism, fraternalism, and Zionism; offers life insurance and other benefits to its members. Sponsors various projects in Israel: settlements, youth centers, medical clinics, Bnai Zion Home for Retarded Children (in Rosh Ha'ayin), B'nai Zion Medical Center (in Haifa), and the Herman Z. Quittman Center in Ha'kfar Hashwedi in Jerusalem. Has Young Leadership Division. *Bnai Zion Voice; Bnai Zion Foundation Newsletter; The Challenge; Haifa Happenings.*

BRITH ABRAHAM (1859; reorg. 1887). 136 E. 39 St., NYC 10016. (212)725-1211. Grand Master Robert Freeman. Protects Jewish rights and combats anti-Semitism; supports Soviet and Ethiopian emigration and the safety and dignity of Jews worldwide; helps to support B'nai Zion Medical Center in Haifa and other Israeli institutions; aids and supports various programs and projects in the U.S.: Hebrew Excellence Program—Gold Medal presentation in high schools and colleges; Camp Loyaltown; Brith Abraham and Bnai Zion Foundations. *Voice.*

BRITH SHOLOM (1905). 3939 Conshohocken Ave., Philadelphia, PA 19131. (215)878-5696. Pres. Jay W. Malis; Exec. Dir. Mervin L. Krimins. Fraternal organization devoted to community welfare, protection of rights of Jewish people, and activities which foster Jewish identity and provide support for Israel; sponsors Brith Sholom House for senior citizens in Philadelphia and Brith Sholom Beit Halochem in Haifa, a rehabilitation center for Israel's permanently war-wounded. *Brith Sholom Presents; monthly news bulletin.*

CENTRAL SEPHARDIC JEWISH COMMUNITY OF AMERICA (1941). 8 W. 70 St., NYC 10023. (212)787-2850. Pres. Emilie Levy; Treas. Victor Tarry. Pres. Women's Div. Irma Cardozo; Treas. Laura Capelluto. Promotes Sephardic culture by awarding scholarships to qualified needy students in New York and Israel; raises funds for hospital and religious institutions in U.S. and Israel. *Annual journal.*

FREE SONS OF ISRAEL (1849). 180 Varick St., 14th fl., NYC 10014. (212)924-6566. Grand Master Herbert Silverstein; Grand Sec. Stanley Siflinger. The oldest Jewish fraternal order in the U.S.; supports the State of Israel; fights anti-Semitism; helps Soviet Jewry. Maintains scholarship fund for members and children of members, insurance fund, and credit union; social functions. *Free Sons Reporter.*

JEWISH LABOR BUND (Directed by WORLD COORDINATING COMMITTEE OF THE BUND) (1897; reorg. 1947). 25 E. 21 St., NYC 10010. (212)475-0059. Exec. Sec. Joel Litewka. Coordinates activities of Bund organizations throughout the world and represents them in the Socialist International; spreads the ideas of socialism as formulated by the Jewish Labor Bund; publishes books and periodicals on world problems, Jewish life, socialist theory and policy, and on the history, activities, and ideology of the Jewish Labor Bund. *Unser Tsait* (U.S.); *Lebns-Fragn* (Israel); *Unser Gedank* (Australia); *Unser Shtimme* (France).

SEPHARDIC JEWISH BROTHERHOOD OF AMERICA, INC. (1915). 97-29 64th Rd., Rego Park, NY 11374. (718)459-1600. Pres. Esther Toledo; Sec. Michael Cohen. A benevolent fraternal organization seeking to promote the industrial, social, educational, and religious welfare of its members. *Sephardic Brother.*

UNITED ORDER TRUE SISTERS, INC. (UOTS) (1846). 212 Fifth Ave., NYC 10010. (212)679–6790. Pres. Laurette Blumenkrantz; Exec. Admin. Dorothy B. Giuriceo. Charitable, community service, especially home supplies etc. for indigent cancer victims; supports camps for children with cancer. *Echo.*

WORKMEN'S CIRCLE (1900). 45 E. 33 St., NYC 10016. (212)889–6800. FAX: (212)-532–7518. Pres. Harold Ostroff; Exec. Dir. Robert A. Kaplan. Provides fraternal benefits and activities, Jewish educational programs, secularist Yiddish schools, and summer camps; promotes public-affairs activities in the U.S. on international and national issues. Underwrites "Folksbiene" theater; sponsors Yiddish cultural, music, and theatrical festivals in U.S. and Canada. *Workmen's Circle Call; Kultur un Leben.*

SOCIAL WELFARE

AMC CANCER RESEARCH CENTER (formerly JEWISH CONSUMPTIVES' RELIEF SOCIETY, 1904; incorporated as AMERICAN MEDICAL CENTER AT DENVER, 1954). 1600 Pierce St., Denver, CO 80214. (303)233–6501. Dir. Dr. Joseph Cullen; Pres./CEO Bob R. Baker. A nationally recognized leader in the fight against cancer; employs a three-pronged, interdisciplinary approach that combines laboratory, clinical, and community cancer-control research to advance the prevention, early detection, diagnosis, and treatment of the disease. *Quarterly bulletin; annual report.*

AMERICAN JEWISH CORRECTIONAL CHAPLAINS ASSOCIATION, INC. (formerly NATIONAL COUNCIL OF JEWISH PRISON CHAPLAINS) (1937). 10 E. 73 St., NYC 10021-4194. (212)879–8415. FAX: (212)-772–3977. (Cooperates with the New York Board of Rabbis.) Pres. Rabbi Irving Koslowe; Exec. Off. Rabbi Moses A. Birnbaum. Supports spiritual, moral, and social services for Jewish men and women in corrections; stimulates support of correctional chaplaincy; provides spiritual and professional fellowship for Jewish correctional chaplains; promotes sound standards for correctional chaplaincy; schedules workshops and research to aid chaplains in counseling and with religious services for Jewish inmates. Constituent, American Correctional Chaplains Association. *Chaplains Manual.*

AMERICAN JEWISH SOCIETY FOR SERVICE, INC. (1949). 15 E. 26 St., Rm. 1304, NYC 10010. (212)683–6178. Pres. Arthur Lifson; Exec. Dir. Elly Saltzman. Conducts voluntary work-service camps each summer to enable high school juniors and seniors to perform humanitarian service.

AMERICAN JEWISH WORLD SERVICE (1985). 1290 Ave. of the Americas, NYC 10104. (212)468–7380. FAX: (212)468–7387. Exec. Dir. Andrew Griffel. Provides a Jewish vehicle for responding to hunger and poverty on a global scale and on a nonsectarian basis; seeks to promote a decent life, in both economic and social terms, for those who are daily beset by hunger and poverty. *AJWS Report (quarterly newsletter).*

ASSOCIATION OF JEWISH CENTER PROFESSIONALS (1918). c/o JCC, 3505 Mayfield Rd., Cleveland Heights, OH 44118 (216)-382–4000. FAX: (216)382–5401. Pres. Leonard S. Freedman; Exec. Sec. Paulette Buchler. Seeks to enhance the standards, techniques, practices, scope, and public understanding of Jewish Community Center and kindred agency work. *Kesher.*

ASSOCIATION OF JEWISH COMMUNITY ORGANIZATION PERSONNEL (AJCOP) (1969). 1750 Euclid Ave., Cleveland, OH 44115. (216)566–9200. FAX: (216)861–1230. Pres. Alan H. Gill; Exec. Dir. Howard R. Berger. An organization of professionals engaged in areas of fund raising, endowments, budgeting, social planning, financing, administration and coordination of services. Objectives are to develop and enhance professional practices in Jewish communal work; to maintain and improve standards, practices, scope and public understanding of the field of community organization, as practiced through local federations, national agencies, other organizations, settings, and private practitioners. *ProLog newsletter.*

ASSOCIATION OF JEWISH FAMILY AND CHILDREN'S AGENCIES (1972). 3084 State Hwy. 27, Suite 1; PO Box 248, Kendall Park, NJ 08824-0248. (908)821–0909; (800)634–7346. FAX: (908)972–8705. Pres. Marc S. Salisch; Exec. Dir. Bert J. Goldberg. The national service organization for Jewish family and children's agencies in Canada and the U.S. Reinforces member agencies in their efforts to sustain and enhance the quality of Jewish family and communal life. Operates the Elder Support Network for the National Jewish Community. *Bulletin (bimonthly); Directory; Professional Opportunities Bulletin; Resettlement Bulletin (monthly).*

ASSOCIATION OF JEWISH FAMILY AND CHILDREN'S AGENCY PROFESSIONALS (1965). 730 Broadway, NYC 10003–9543. (212)473–8764. FAX: (212)673–7903. Pres. Stephanie Speigel. Brings together Jewish caseworkers and related professionals in Jewish family, children's, and health services. Seeks to improve personnel standards, further Jewish continuity and identity, and strengthen Jewish family life; provides forums for professional discussion at national conference of Jewish communal service and regional meetings; takes action on social-policy issues. *Newsletter.*

BARON DE HIRSCH FUND (1891). 130 E. 59 St., Rm. 644, NYC 10022. (212)836–1358. FAX: (212)888–7538. Pres. Francis F. Rosenbaum, Jr.; Mng. Dir. Lauren Katzowitz. Aids Jewish immigrants and their children in the U.S. and Israel by giving grants to agencies active in educational and vocational fields; has limited program for study tours in U.S. by Israeli agriculturists.

B'NAI B'RITH INTERNATIONAL (1843). 1640 Rhode Island Ave., NW, Washington, DC 20036. (202)857–6600. FAX: (202)857–1099. Pres. Kent E. Schiner; Exec. V.-Pres. Thomas Neumann. International Jewish organization, with affiliates in 46 countries. Offers programs designed to insure the preservation of Jewry and Judaism: Jewish education, community volunteer service, expansion of human rights, assistance to Israel, housing for the elderly, leadership training, rights of Soviet Jews and Jews of other countries to emigrate and study their heritage. *International Jewish Monthly; Insider.*

———, ANTI-DEFAMATION LEAGUE OF (see p. 470)

———, HILLEL FOUNDATIONS, INC. (see p. 492)

———, KLUTZNICK MUSEUM (see p. 474)

———, YOUTH ORGANIZATION (see p. 492)

B'NAI B'RITH WOMEN (1897). 1828 L St., NW, Suite 250, Washington, DC 20036. (202)857–1370. FAX:(202)857–1380. Pres. Harriet J. Horowitz; Exec. Dir. Elaine K. Binder. Supports Jewish women in their families, in their communities, and in society. Offers programs that contribute to preservation of Jewish life and values; supports treatment of emotionally disturbed children in BBW Residential Treatment Center in Israel; advocates for Israel and for family issues. *Women's World.*

CITY OF HOPE NATIONAL MEDICAL CENTER AND BECKMAN RESEARCH INSTITUTE (1913). 1500 E. Duarte Rd., Duarte, CA 91010. (818)359–8111. Pres. and Chief Exec. Off. Dr. Sanford M. Shapero; Bd. Chmn. Richard Fiman. Offers care to those with cancer and major diseases, medical consultation service for second opinions, and pilot research programs in genetics, immunology, and the basic life process. *From the Top, City of Hope Cancer Center Report.*

CONFERENCE OF JEWISH COMMUNAL SERVICE (1899). 3084 State Hwy. 27, Suite 9, Kendall Park, NJ 08824–1657. (201)821–1871. FAX: (908)821–0493. Pres. Ronald I. Coun; Exec. Dir. Joel Ollander. Serves as forum for all professional philosophies in community service, for testing new experiences, proposing new ideas, and questioning or reaffirming old concepts; umbrella organization for seven major Jewish communal service groups. Concerned with advancement of professional personnel practices and standards. *Concurrents; Journal of Jewish Communal Service.*

COUNCIL OF JEWISH FEDERATIONS, INC. (1932). 730 Broadway, NYC 10003. (212)-475–5000. Pres. Charles H. Goodman; Exec. V.-Pres. Martin Kraar. Provides national and regional services to more than 200 associated federations embracing 800 communities in the U.S. and Canada, aiding in fund raising, community organization, health and welfare planning, personnel recruitment, and public relations. *Directory of Jewish Federations, Welfare Funds and Community Councils; Directory of Jewish Health and Welfare Agencies (biennial); What's New in Federations; Newsbriefs; annual report.*

HOPE CENTER FOR THE DEVELOPMENTALLY DISABLED (1965). 3601 Martin L. King Blvd., Denver, CO 80205. (303)388–4801. Bd. Chmn. Albert Cohen; Exec. Dir. George E. Brantley; Sec. Helen Fonda. Provides services to developmentally disabled of community: preschool training, day training and work activities center, speech and language pathology, occupational arts and crafts, recreational therapy, and social services.

INTERNATIONAL ASSOCIATION OF JEWISH VOCATIONAL SERVICES (formerly JEWISH OCCUPATIONAL COUNCIL) (1939). 101 Gary Court, Staten Island, NY 10314. (718)370-0437. FAX: (718)370-1778. Pres. Burton H. Olin; Exec. Dir. Richard M. Africk. Coordinating body of vocational and family-service agencies whose purpose is to support affiliated members, volunteers, and professional leaders in their service to the Jewish and general community.

INTERNATIONAL COUNCIL ON JEWISH SOCIAL AND WELFARE SERVICES (1961). c/o American Jewish Joint Distribution Committee, 711 Third Ave., NYC 10017. (NY liaison office with UN headquarters.) (212)687-6200. Chmn. David Cope-Thompson; Exec. Sec. Cheryl Mariner. Provides for exchange of views and information among member agencies on problems of Jewish social and welfare services, including medical care, old age, welfare, child care, rehabilitation, technical assistance, vocational training, agricultural and other resettlement, economic assistance, refugees, migration, integration and related problems, representation of views to governments and international organizations. Members: six national and international organizations.

JEWISH BRAILLE INSTITUTE OF AMERICA, INC. (1931). 110 E. 30 St., NYC 10016. (212)889-2525. FAX:(212)689-3692. Pres. Dr. Jane Evans; Exec. V.-Pres. Gerald M. Kass. Provides Judaic materials in braille, talking books, and large print for blind, visually impaired, and reading-disabled; offers counseling for full integration into the life of the Jewish community. Comprehensive braille and talking-book library on Judaic topics; many titles in large print. *Jewish Braille Review; JBI Voice.*

JEWISH COMMUNITY CENTERS ASSOCIATION OF NORTH AMERICA (1917; formerly JWB). 15 E. 26 St., NYC 10010-1579. (212)532-4949. Pres. Lester Pollack; Exec. V.-Pres. Arthur Rotman. Central leadership agency for 275 Jewish community centers, YM-YWHAs, and camps in the U.S. and Canada, serving over one million Jews. Provides informal Jewish educational and cultural experiences through Jewish Book and Music Councils and JCC Association Lecture Bureau and many projects related to Israel. U.S. government-accredited agency for the religious, Jewish educational, and recreational needs of Jewish military personnel, their families and hospitalized VA patients through JWB Jewish Chaplains Council. *Circle; Briefing; Zarkor; Personnel Reporter.*

——, JEWISH BOOK COUNCIL (see p. 476)

——, JEWISH MUSIC COUNCIL (see p. 476)

——, JWB JEWISH CHAPLAINS COUNCIL (formerly COMMISSION ON JEWISH CHAPLAINCY) (1940). 15 E. 26 St., NYC 10010-1579. Chmn. Rabbi Abraham Avrech; Dir. Rabbi David Lapp. Recruits, endorses, and serves Jewish military and Veterans Administration chaplains on behalf of the American Jewish community and the major rabbinic bodies; trains and assists Jewish lay leaders where there are no chaplains, for service to Jewish military personnel, their families, and hospitalized veterans. *CHAPLINES newsletter.*

——, LECTURE BUREAU (see p. 475)

JEWISH CONCILIATION BOARD OF AMERICA, INC. (A Division of the Jewish Board of Family and Children's Services (1920). 235 Park Ave. S., NYC 10003. (212)460-0900. FAX: (212)245-2096. Cochmn. Milton J. Schubin and Ruth Daniel. Offers dispute-resolution services to families, individuals, and organizations. Social-work, rabbinic, and legal expertise are available for family and divorce mediation and arbitration. Fee—sliding scale.

JEWISH FUND FOR JUSTICE (1984). 920 Broadway, Suite 605, NYC 10010. (212)-677-7080. Bd. Chmn. Lawrence S. Levine; Exec. Dir. Marlene Provizer. A national grant-making foundation supporting efforts to combat the root causes of poverty in the U.S. Provides diverse opportunities to individual, family, and synagogue involvement through memorial, youth endowment, and synagogue challenge funds; works cooperatively with other denominational funders and philanthropies promoting social and economic justice. *Newsletter; Five-Year Report.*

JWB (see Jewish Community Centers Association of North America)

LEVI HOSPITAL (sponsored by B'nai B'rith) (1914). 300 Prospect Ave., Hot Springs, AR 71902. (501)624–1281. Pres. Steven Kirsch; Admin. Patrick G. McCabe. Offers arthritis treatment, stroke rehabilitation, orthopedic rehabilitation, a psychiatric unit, a hospice program, and a work capacity center.*Quarterly newsletter.*

MAZON: A JEWISH RESPONSE TO HUNGER (1985). 2940 Westwood Blvd., Suite 7, Los Angeles, CA 90064. (213)470–7769. FAX: (213)470–6736. Bd. Chmn. Lee H. Javitch; Exec. Dir. Irving Cramer. Raises funds by asking American Jews to contribute a suggested amount of 3% of the cost of life-cycle celebrations; funds are granted to nonprofit organizations in the U.S. and abroad that work to alleviate hunger, malnutrition, and poverty. 1990 grants totaled $1.1 million. *Mazon Newsletter.*

NATIONAL ASSOCIATION OF JEWISH FAMILY, CHILDREN'S AND HEALTH PROFESSIONALS (see Association of Jewish Family and Children's Agency Professionals)

NATIONAL ASSOCIATION OF JEWISH VOCATIONAL SERVICES (see International Association of Jewish Vocational Services)

NATIONAL CONGRESS OF JEWISH DEAF (1956; inc. 1961). c/o Dr. Barbara Boyd, Temple Beth Solomon of the Deaf, 13580 Osborne St., Arleta, CA 91331. Pres. Dr. Barbara Boyd. Congress of Jewish congregations, service organizations, and associations located throughout the U.S. and Canada, advocating religious spirit and cultural ideals and fellowship for the Jewish deaf. Affiliated with World Organization of Jewish Deaf. Publishes *Signs of Judaism,* a guide to sign language of Judaism. *NCJD Quarterly; Jewish Deaf Trivia.*

NATIONAL COUNCIL OF JEWISH PRISON CHAPLAINS, INC. (see American Jewish Correctional Chaplains Association, Inc.)

NATIONAL COUNCIL OF JEWISH WOMEN (1893). 53 W. 23 St., NYC 10010. (212)-645-4048. Pres. Joan Bronk; Exec. Dir. Iris Gross. Furthers human welfare through program of community service, education, advocacy for children and youth, aging, women's issues, constitutional rights, Jewish life and Israel. Promotes education for the disadvantaged in Israel through the NCJW Research Institute for Innovation in Education at Hebrew University, Jerusalem. Promotes welfare of children in U.S. through Center for the Child. *NCJW Journal; Washington Newsletter.*

NATIONAL INSTITUTE FOR JEWISH HOSPICE (1985). 8723 Alden Drive, ASB/1 Bldg., Suite 652, Los Angeles, CA 90048. (213) HOSPICE. Pres. Rabbi Maurice Lamm; Exec. Dir. LaWana Skaggs-McMaster. Serves as a national Jewish hospice resource center. Through conferences, research, publications, video training courses, referral, and counseling services offers guidance, training, and information to patients, family members, clergy of all faiths, professional caregivers, and volunteers who work with seriously ill Jews. *Jewish Hospice Times.*

NATIONAL JEWISH CENTER FOR IMMUNOLOGY AND RESPIRATORY MEDICINE (formerly NATIONAL JEWISH HOSPITAL/NATIONAL ASTHMA CENTER) (1899). 1400 Jackson St., Denver, CO 80206. (1-800)222-LUNG. Pres. Michael Schonbrun; Bd. Chmn. Joseph Davis. Seeks to discover and disseminate knowledge that will prevent the occurrence of respiratory, allergic, and immunologic disorders and to develop improved clinical programs for those already afflicted. *New Direction (quarterly); Lung Line Letter (quarterly); Medical Scientific Update.*

NATIONAL JEWISH COMMITTEE ON SCOUTING (Boy Scouts of America) (1926). 1325 Walnut Hill La., PO Box 152079, Irving, TX 75015-2079. (214)580-2059. FAX: (214)580-2502. Chmn. Robert G. Kurzman; Dir. Andrew Hoffman. Assists Jewish institutions in meeting their needs and concerns through use of the resources of scouting. Works through local Jewish committees on Scouting to establish Tiger Cub groups (1st grade), Cub Scout packs, Boy Scout troops, and coed Explorer posts in synagogues, Jewish community centers, day schools, and other Jewish organizations wishing to draw Jewish youth. Support materials and resources on request. *Hatsofe (quarterly); Expressions (annually).*

NATIONAL JEWISH GIRL SCOUT COMMITTEE (1972). Synagogue Council of America, 327 Lexington Ave., NYC 10016. (212)686-8670. FAX: (212)686-8673. Chmn. Rabbi Herbert W. Bomzer;

Field Chmn. Adele Wasko. Under the auspices of the Synagogue Council of America, serves to further Jewish education by promoting Jewish award programs, encouraging religious services, promoting cultural exchanges with the Israel Boy & Girl Scouts Federation, and extending membership in the Jewish community by assisting councils in organizing Girl Scout troops and local Jewish Girl Scout committees. *Newsletter.*

NORTH AMERICAN ASSOCIATION OF JEWISH HOMES AND HOUSING FOR THE AGING (1960). 2525 Centerville Rd., Dallas, TX 75228. (214)327-4503. FAX: (214)320-9066. Pres. David Glaser; Exec. V.-Pres. Dr. Herbert Shore. Represents a community of not-for-profit charitable homes and housing for the Jewish aging; promotes excellence in performance and quality of service through fostering communication and education and encouraging advocacy for the aging. *Perspectives (newsletter); Directory.*

WORLD CONFEDERATION OF JEWISH COMMUNITY CENTERS (1947; reorg. 1977). Litt. Bldg., 12 Hess St., Jerusalem, Israel 94185. 2-251-265. FAX: 2-247-767. Pres. Ralph Goldman; Exec. Dir. Menachem Revivi. Composed of national center movements in Europe, Israel, Latin America, and North America; seeks to strengthen cooperation among center associations and individual centers; provides programs to enhance Jewish educational opportunities for lay leaders of centers and professional staffs. *Bamerkaz.*

PROFESSIONAL ASSOCIATIONS*

AMERICAN ASSOCIATION OF RABBIS (Religious, Educational)

AMERICAN CONFERENCE OF CANTORS, UNION OF AMERICAN HEBREW CONGREGATIONS (Religious, Educational)

AMERICAN JEWISH CORRECTIONAL CHAPLAINS ASSOCIATION, INC. (Social Welfare)

AMERICAN JEWISH PRESS ASSOCIATION (Cultural)

AMERICAN JEWISH PUBLIC RELATIONS SOCIETY (1957). 234 Fifth Ave., NYC 10001. (212)697-5895. Pres. Henry R. Hecker;
Treas. Hyman Brickman. Advances professional status of workers in the public-relations field in Jewish communal service; upholds a professional code of ethics and standards; serves as a clearinghouse for employment opportunities; exchanges professional information and ideas; presents awards for excellence in professional attainments, including the "Maggid Award" for outstanding achievement which enhances Jewish life. *AJPRS Newsletter; AJPRS Directory.*

ASSOCIATION OF HILLEL/JEWISH CAMPUS PROFESSIONALS (Religious, Educational)

ASSOCIATION OF JEWISH CENTER PROFESSIONALS (Social Welfare)

ASSOCIATION OF JEWISH COMMUNITY ORGANIZATION PERSONNEL (Social Welfare)

ASSOCIATION OF JEWISH COMMUNITY RELATIONS WORKERS (Community Relations)

ASSOCIATION OF JEWISH FAMILY AND CHILDREN'S AGENCY PROFESSIONALS (Social Welfare)

CANTORS ASSEMBLY (Religious, Educational)

CENTRAL CONFERENCE OF AMERICAN RABBIS (Religious, Educational)

CONFERENCE OF JEWISH COMMUNAL SERVICE (Social Welfare)

COUNCIL OF JEWISH ORGANIZATIONS IN CIVIL SERVICE (Community Relations)

INTERNATIONAL JEWISH MEDIA ASSOCIATION (Cultural)

JEWISH CHAPLAINS COUNCIL, JWB (Social Welfare)

JEWISH EDUCATORS ASSEMBLY, UNITED SYNAGOGUE OF AMERICA (Religious, Educational)

JEWISH MINISTERS CANTORS ASSOCIATION OF AMERICA, INC. (Religious, Educational)

JEWISH TEACHERS ASSOCIATION—MORIM (Religious, Educational)

---

*For fuller listing see under categories in parentheses.

NATIONAL ASSOCIATION OF HEBREW DAY SCHOOL ADMINISTRATORS, TORAH UMESORAH (Religious, Educational)

NATIONAL ASSOCIATION OF SYNAGOGUE ADMINISTRATORS, UNITED SYNAGOGUE OF AMERICA (Religious, Educational)

NATIONAL ASSOCIATION OF TEMPLE ADMINISTRATORS, UNION OF AMERICAN HEBREW CONGREGATIONS (Religious, Educational)

NATIONAL ASSOCIATION OF TEMPLE EDUCATORS, UNION OF AMERICAN HEBREW CONGREGATIONS (Religious, Educational)

NATIONAL CONFERENCE OF YESHIVA PRINCIPALS, TORAH UMESORAH (Religious, Educational)

RABBINICAL ASSEMBLY (Religious, Educational)

RABBINICAL COUNCIL OF AMERICA (Religious, Educational)

RECONSTRUCTIONIST RABBINICAL ASSOCIATION, JEWISH RECONSTRUCTIONIST FOUNDATION (Religious, Educational)

UNION OF ORTHODOX RABBIS OF THE U.S. AND CANADA (Religious, Educational)

WORLD CONFERENCE OF JEWISH COMMUNAL SERVICE (Community Relations)

WOMEN'S ORGANIZATIONS*

AMIT WOMEN (Israel-Related)

B'NAI B'RITH WOMEN (Social Welfare)

BRANDEIS UNIVERSITY NATIONAL WOMEN'S COMMITTEE (1948). PO Box 9110, Waltham, MA 02254–9110. (617)-736–4160. FAX: (212)736–4183. Natl. Pres. Estelle W. Jacobs; Exec. Dir. Harriet J. Winer. Provides financial support for the Brandeis Libraries and works to enhance the image of Brandeis, a Jewish-sponsored, nonsectarian university. Offers its members opportunity for intellectual pursuit, continuing education, community service, social interaction, personal enrichment, and leadership development. *Imprint.*

HADASSAH, THE WOMEN'S ZIONIST ORGANIZATION OF AMERICA (Israel-Related)

NA'AMAT USA, THE WOMEN'S LABOR ZIONIST ORGANIZATION OF AMERICA (Israel-Related)

NATIONAL COUNCIL OF JEWISH WOMEN (Social Welfare)

NATIONAL FEDERATION OF TEMPLE SISTERHOODS, UNION OF AMERICAN HEBREW CONGREGATIONS (Religious, Educational)

UOTS (Social, Mutual Benefit)

WOMEN'S AMERICAN ORT, AMERICAN ORT FEDERATION (Overseas Aid)

WOMEN'S BRANCH OF THE UNION OF ORTHODOX JEWISH CONGREGATIONS OF AMERICA (Religious, Educational)

WOMEN'S DIVISION OF POALE AGUDATH ISRAEL OF AMERICA (Israel-Related)

WOMEN'S DIVISION OF THE JEWISH LABOR COMMITTEE (Community Relations)

WOMEN'S DIVISION OF THE UNITED JEWISH APPEAL (Overseas Aid)

WOMEN'S LEAGUE FOR CONSERVATIVE JUDAISM (Religious, Educational)

WOMEN'S LEAGUE FOR ISRAEL, INC. (Israel-Related)

WOMEN'S ORGANIZATION, YESHIVA UNIVERSITY (Religious, Educational)

YOUTH AND STUDENT ORGANIZATIONS*

AMERICAN ZIONIST YOUTH FOUNDATION (Israel-Related)

B'NAI B'RITH HILLEL FOUNDATIONS (Religious, Educational)

B'NAI B'RITH YOUTH ORGANIZATION (Religious, Educational)

BNEI AKIVA OF NORTH AMERICA, RELIGIOUS ZIONISTS OF AMERICA (Israel-Related)

BNOS AGUDATH ISRAEL, AGUDATH ISRAEL OF AMERICA, GIRLS' DIVISION (Religious, Educational)

HABONIM-DROR NORTH AMERICA (Israel-Related)

HASHOMER HATZAIR, SOCIALIST ZIONIST YOUTH MOVEMENT (Israel-Related)

KADIMA, UNITED SYNAGOGUE OF AMERICA (Religious, Educational)

---

*For fuller listing see under categories in parentheses.

NATIONAL CONFERENCE OF SYNAGOGUE YOUTH, UNION OF ORTHODOX JEWISH CONGREGATIONS OF AMERICA (Religious, Educational)

NOAM-MIZRACHI NEW LEADERSHIP COUNCIL, RELIGIOUS ZIONISTS OF AMERICA (Israel-Related)

NORTH AMERICAN FEDERATION OF TEMPLE YOUTH, UNION OF AMERICAN HEBREW CONGREGATIONS (Religious, Educational)

NORTH AMERICAN JEWISH STUDENTS APPEAL (1971). 165 Pidgeon Hill Rd., Huntington Station, NY 11746–9998. (516)385–8771. FAX: (516)385–8772. Pres. Bennett Graff; Chmn. Magda S. Leuchter; Exec. Dir. Brenda Gevertz. Serves as central fund-raising mechanism for six national, independent Jewish student organizations; insures accountability of public Jewish communal funds used by these agencies; assists Jewish students undertaking projects of concern to Jewish communities; advises and assists Jewish organizations in determining student project feasibility and impact; fosters development of Jewish student leadership in the Jewish community. Beneficiaries include local and regional Jewish student projects; current constituents include Jewish Student Press Service, Student Struggle for Soviet Jewry, *Response Magazine,* Yugntruf Youth for Yiddish, Progressive Zionist Caucus, and the newest constituent, Project Orchim for outreach on campus.

NORTH AMERICAN JEWISH STUDENTS' NETWORK (1969). 501 Madison Ave., 17th fl., NYC 10022. (212)888–3417. FAX: (212)755–5883. Pres. Jacob Krasner-Davidson; V.-Pres. Elie C. Wurtman. The independent national Jewish student union for the United States and Canada; student-based, student-run, and student-oriented. The only common forum for the entire political, religious, and geographical spectrum of Jewish students. Activities include student leadership-training seminars, missions to Israel, educational forums. North American affiliate of World Union of Jewish Students (WUJS). *National Jewish Student Forum.*

STUDENT STRUGGLE FOR SOVIET JEWRY (Community Relations)

YOUNG JUDAEA/HASHACHAR, HADASSAH (Israel-Related)

YUGNTRUF YOUTH FOR YIDDISH (1964). 200 W. 72 St., Suite 40, NYC 10023. (212)-787–6675. Chmn. Itzek Gottesman; Editor Paul Glasser. A worldwide, nonpolitical organization for high school and college students with a knowledge of, or interest in, Yiddish. Spreads the love and use of the Yiddish language; organizes artistic and social activities, including annual conference for young adults; sponsors Yiddish-speaking preschool for non-Orthodox children; disseminates new Yiddish teaching materials. *Yugntruf.*

ZEIREI AGUDATH ISRAEL, AGUDATH ISRAEL OF AMERICA, YOUNG MEN'S DIVISION (Religious, Educational)

CANADA

B'NAI BRITH CANADA (1875). 15 Hove St., Downsview, ONT M3H 4Y8. (416)633–6224. FAX: (416)630–2159. Pres. Marilyn Weinberg; Exec. V.-Pres. Frank Dimant. Canadian Jewry's senior organization; makes representations to all levels of government on matters of Jewish concern; promotes humanitarian causes and educational programs, community volunteer projects, adult Jewish education, and leadership development; dedicated to human rights; sponsors youth programs of B'nai Brith Youth Org. (serving youth ages 13–18) and B'nai Brith Hillel Foundations (serving college and university students). *Covenant; Communiqué.*

———, INSTITUTE FOR INTERNATIONAL AND GOVERNMENTAL AFFAIRS (1987). 15 Hove St., Downsview, Ont. M3H 4Y8. (416)633–6224. Natl. Chmn. Brian Morris; Natl. Dir. Paul Marcus. Identifies and protests the abuse of human rights throughout the world. Monitors the condition of Jewish communities worldwide and advocates on their behalf when they experience serious violations of their human rights. *Comment.*

———, LEAGUE FOR HUMAN RIGHTS (1970). 15 Hove St., Downsview, Ont. M3H 4Y8. (416)633–6227. Natl. Chmn. Mark Sandler; Natl. Dir. Karen Mock. Dedicated to monitoring human rights, combating racism and racial discrimination, and preventing bigotry and anti-Semitism through education and community relations. Sponsors Holocaust Education Programs, the R. Lou Ronson Research Institute on Anti-Semitism; distributor of

Anti-Defamation League materials in Canada. *Review of Anti-Semitism.*

CANADIAN ASSOCIATION FOR LABOR ISRAEL (HISTADRUT) (1944). 7005 Kildare Rd., Suite 14, Cote St. Luc, Que. H4W 1C1. (514)484-9430. FAX: (514)487-6727. Pres. Harry J. F. Bloomfield. Conducts fund-raising and educational activities on behalf of Histadrut, Kupat Holim, and Amal schools in Israel.

CANADIAN FOUNDATION FOR JEWISH CULTURE (1965). 4600 Bathurst St., Willowdale, ONT M2R 3V2. (416)635-2883. Pres. Mira Koschitzky; Exec. Sec. Edmond Y. Lipsitz. Promotes Jewish studies at university level and encourages original research and scholarship in Jewish subjects; awards annual scholarships and grants-in-aid to scholars in Canada.

CANADIAN FRIENDS OF THE ALLIANCE ISRAÉLITE UNIVERSELLE (1958). PO Box 578, Victoria Station, Montreal, PQ H3Z 2Y6. (514)481-3552. Pres. Joseph Nuss. Supports the educational work of the Alliance.

CANADIAN FRIENDS OF THE HEBREW UNIVERSITY (1944). 3080 Yonge St., Suite 5024, Toronto, ONT M4N 3P4. (416)485-8000. FAX: (416)485-8565. Pres. Edward J. Winant; Exec. V.-Pres. Shimon Arbel. Represents the Hebrew University of Jerusalem in Canada; serves as fund-raising arm for the university in Canada; accepts Canadians for study at the university; sponsors educational programs. *Dateline Jerusalem.*

CANADIAN JEWISH CONGRESS (1919; reorg. 1934). 1590 Dr. Penfield Ave., Montreal, PQ H3G 1C5. (514)931-7531. Pres. Les Scheininger; Exec. V.-Pres. Alan Rose. The official voice of Canadian Jewish communities at home and abroad; acts on all matters affecting the status, rights, concerns and welfare of Canadian Jewry; internationally active on behalf of Soviet Jewry, Jews in Arab lands, Holocaust remembrance and restitution; largest Jewish archives in Canada. *National Small Communities Newsletter; Intercom; Ottawa Digest; National Soviet Jewry Newsletter; National Archives Newsletter; Community Relations Newsletter;* regional newsletters.

CANADIAN ORT ORGANIZATION (Organization of Rehabilitation Through Training) (1942). 5165 Sherbrooke St. W., Suite 208, Montreal, PQ H4A 1T6. (514)481-2787. Pres. Bernard Gross; Exec. Dir. Mac Silver. Carries on fund-raising projects in support of the worldwide vocational-training-school network of ORT. *ORT Reporter.*

———, WOMEN'S CANADIAN ORT (1948). 3101 Bathurst St., Suite 604, Toronto, ONT M6A 2A6. (416)787-0339. Natl. Pres. Joann Smith; Natl. Exec. Dir. Diane Uslaner. Chapters in 11 Canadian cities raise funds for ORT's nonprofit global network of schools where Jewish students learn a wide range of marketable skills, including the most advanced high-tech professions. *Focus Magazine.*

CANADIAN SEPHARDI FEDERATION (1973). c/o Or Haemet School, 210 Wilson Ave., Toronto, ONT M5M 3B1. (416)483-8968. Pres. Maurice Benzacar; Sec. Laeticia Benabou. Preserves and promotes Sephardic identity, particularly among youth; works for the unity of the Jewish people; emphasizes relations between Sephardi communities all over the world; seeks better situation for Sephardim in Israel; supports Israel by all means. Participates in *La Voix Sépharade, Le Monde Sépharade,* and *Sephardi World.*

CANADIAN YOUNG JUDAEA (1917). 788 Marlee Ave., Suite 205, Toronto, ONT M6B 3K1. (416)787-5350. FAX: (416)787-3100. Natl. Program Dir. Rebecca Glass; Natl. Shaliach Shmuel Levkowitz. Strives to attract Jewish youth to Zionism, with goal of *aliyah;* educates youth about Jewish history and Zionism; prepares them to provide leadership in Young Judaea camps in Canada and Israel and to be concerned Jews. *The Judaean.*

CANADIAN ZIONIST FEDERATION (1967). 5250 Decarie Blvd., Suite 550, Montreal, PQ H3X 2H9. (514)486-9526. FAX: (514)483-6392. Pres. Kurt Rothschild. Umbrella organization of all Zionist and Israel-related groups in Canada; carries on major activities in all areas of Jewish life through its departments of education and culture, *aliyah,* youth and students, public affairs, and fund raising for the purpose of strengthening the State of Israel and the Canadian Jewish community. *Canadian Zionist.*

———, BUREAU OF EDUCATION AND CULTURE (1972). Pres. Kurt Rothschild. Provides counseling by pedagogic experts, in-service teacher-training courses and seminars in Canada and Israel; national pedagogic council and research center; distributes educational material and teaching aids; conducts annual Bible contest and Hebrew-language courses for adults. *Al Mitzpe Hachinuch.*

FRIENDS OF PIONEERING ISRAEL (1950s). 1111 Finch Ave. W., Suite 154, Downsview, ONT M3J 2E5 (416)736-1339. Pres. Joe Podemsky. Acts as a voice of Zionist progressive points of view within the Jewish community; affiliated in Israel with Mapam and Hashomer-Hatzair.

HADASSAH—WIZO ORGANIZATION OF CANADA (1917). 1310 Greene Ave., Suite 900, Montreal, PQ H3Z 2B8. (514)937-9431. FAX: (514)933-6483. Natl. Pres. Naomi Frankenburg; Exec. V.-Pres. Lily Frank. Extends material and moral support to the people of Israel requiring such assistance; strengthens and fosters Jewish ideals; encourages Hebrew culture in Canada and promotes Canadian ideals of democracy. *Orah Magazine.*

JEWISH IMMIGRANT AID SERVICES OF CANADA (JIAS) (1919). 5151 Cote Ste. Catherine Rd., Suite 220, Montreal, PQ H3W 1M6.(514)342-9351. (514)342-8452. Pres. Mark Lazar; Exec. Dir. Joel Moss. Serves as a national agency for immigration and immigrant welfare. *JIAS Bulletin.*

JEWISH NATIONAL FUND OF CANADA (KEREN KAYEMETH LE'ISRAEL, INC.) (1901). 1980 Sherbrooke St. W., Suite 500, Montreal, PQ H3H 1E8. (514)934-0313. Pres. Neri J. Bloomfield; Exec. V.-Pres. Morris Zilka. Fund-raising organization affiliated with the World Zionist Organization; involved in afforestation, soil reclamation, and development of the land of Israel, including the construction of roads and preparation of sites for new settlements; provides educational materials and programs to Jewish schools across Canada.

LABOR ZIONIST ALLIANCE OF CANADA (1909).7005 Kildare Rd., Suite 10, Cote St. Luc, PQ H3W 1C1. (514)484-1789. FAX: (514)487-6727. Pres. David Kofsky; Chmn. Toronto City Committee Harry Weinstock; Chmn. Montreal City Committee Harry Froimovitch. Associated with the World Labor Zionist movement and allied with the Israel Labor party. Provides recreational and cultural programs, mutual aid, and fraternal care to enhance the social welfare of its membership; actively promotes Zionist education, cultural projects, and forums on aspects of Jewish and Canadian concern.

MIZRACHI-HAPOEL HAMIZRACHI ORGANIZATION OF CANADA (1941). 159 Almore Ave., Downsview, ONT M3H 2H9. (416)630-7575. Natl. Pres. Kurt Rothschild; Natl. Exec. V.-Pres. Rabbi Menachem Gopin. Promotes religious Zionism, aimed at making Israel a state based on Torah; maintains Bnei Akiva, a summer camp, adult education program, and touring department; supports Mizrachi-Hapoel Hamizrachi and other religious Zionist institutions in Israel which strengthen traditional Judaism. *Mizrachi Newsletter; Or Hamizrach Torah Quarterly.*

NATIONAL COUNCIL OF JEWISH WOMEN OF CANADA (1897). 1110 Finch Ave. W., #518, Downsview, ONT M3J 2T2. (416)665-8251. Pres. Gloria Strom; Exec. Dir. Eleanor Appleby. Dedicated to furthering human welfare in Jewish and non-Jewish communities, locally, nationally, and internationally; provides essential services, and stimulates and educates the individual and the community through an integrated program of education, service, and social action. *New Edition.*

NATIONAL JOINT COMMUNITY RELATIONS COMMITTEE OF CANADIAN JEWISH CONGRESS (1936). 4600 Bathurst St., Willowdale, ONT M2R 3V2 (416)635-2883. FAX: (416)635-1408. Chmn. Joseph J. Wilder; Exec. Dir. Manuel Prutschi. Seeks to safeguard the status, rights, and welfare of Jews in Canada; to combat anti-Semitism and promote understanding and goodwill among all ethnic and religious groups. *Community Relations Report.*

STATE OF ISRAEL BONDS (CANADA-ISRAEL SECURITIES, LTD.) (1953). 1255 University St., Suite 200, Montreal, PQ H3B 3B2. (514)878-1871. FAX: (514)874-7693. Pres. Melvyn A. Dobrin. Mobilizes productive investment capital for the economic development of the State of Israel.

Jewish Federations, Welfare Funds, Community Councils

UNITED STATES

ALABAMA

BIRMINGHAM
BIRMINGHAM JEWISH FEDERATION (1936; reorg. 1971); PO Box 130219 (35213); (205)-879-0416. FAX: (205)879-0466. Pres. Steven Brickman; Exec. Dir. Richard Friedman.

MOBILE
MOBILE JEWISH WELFARE FUND, INC. (inc. 1966); One Office Park, Suite 219 (36609); (205)343-7197. Pres. Nancy Silverboard; Admin. Barbara V. Paper.

MONTGOMERY
JEWISH FEDERATION OF MONTGOMERY, INC. (1930); PO Box 20058 (36120); (205)-277-5820. Pres. Jake Mendel; Exec. Dir. Beverly Lipton.

ARIZONA

PHOENIX
JEWISH FEDERATION OF GREATER PHOENIX (1940); 32 W. Coolidge, Suite 200 (85013); (602)274-1800. FAX: (602)266-7875. Pres. Andi Minkoff; Exec. Dir. Harold Morgan.

TUCSON
JEWISH FEDERATION OF SOUTHERN ARIZONA (1942); 3822 East River Rd. (85718); (602)577-9393. FAX: (602)577-0734. Pres. Harold Greenberg; Exec. V. Pres. Richard Fruchter.

ARKANSAS

LITTLE ROCK
JEWISH FEDERATION OF ARKANSAS (1911); 4942 W. Markham, Suite 5 (72205); (501)-663-3571. Pres. Dr. George Wolff; Exec. Dir. Ariel Barak Imber.

CALIFORNIA

LONG BEACH
JEWISH FEDERATION OF GREATER LONG BEACH AND W. ORANGE COUNTY (1937; inc. 1946); 3801 E. Willow St. (90815); (213) 426-7601. FAX: (213)424-3915. Pres. Morton Stuhlbarg; Exec. Dir. Sandi Goldstein.

LOS ANGELES
JEWISH FEDERATION COUNCIL OF GREATER LOS ANGELES (1912; reorg. 1959); 6505 Wilshire Blvd. (90048); (213)852-1234. FAX: (213)655-4458. Pres. David Finegood; Exec. V. Pres. Wayne Feinstein.

OAKLAND
JEWISH FEDERATION OF THE GREATER EAST BAY (Alameda and Contra Costa Counties) (1918); 401 Grand Ave. (94610); (415)839-2900. FAX: (415)839-3996. Pres. Dr. Miles Adler; Exec. V. Pres. Ami Nahshon.

This directory is based on information supplied by the Council of Jewish Federations.

ORANGE COUNTY
JEWISH FEDERATION OF ORANGE COUNTY (1964; inc. 1965); 1385 Warner Ave., Suite. A, Tustin (92680–6442); (714)259–0655. FAX: (714)259–1635. Pres. William Shane; Exec. Dir. Edward Cushman.

PALM SPRINGS
JEWISH FEDERATION OF PALM SPRINGS (1971); 255 El Cielo N., Suite 430 (92262); (619)325–7281. Pres. Jim Horvitz; Exec. Dir. Irving Ginsberg.

SACRAMENTO
JEWISH FEDERATION OF SACRAMENTO (1948); PO Box 254589 (95865); (916)486–0906. FAX: (916)486–0816. Pres. Barbara Ansel; Exec. Dir. Arnold Feder.

SAN DIEGO
UNITED JEWISH FEDERATION OF SAN DIEGO COUNTY (1936); 4797 Mercury St. (92111–2102); (619)571–3444. FAX: (619)-571–0701. Pres. Murray L. Galinson; Exec. V. Pres. Stephen M. Abramson.

SAN FRANCISCO
JEWISH COMMUNITY FEDERATION OF SAN FRANCISCO, THE PENINSULA, MARIN, AND SONOMA COUNTIES (1910; reorg. 1955); 121 Steuart St. (94105); (415)777–0411. FAX: (415)495–6635. Pres. Donald Seiler; Exec. Dir. Rabbi Brian Lurie.

SAN JOSE
JEWISH FEDERATION OF GREATER SAN JOSE (incl. Santa Clara County except Palo Alto and Los Altos) (1930; reorg. 1950); 14855 Oka Rd., Los Gatos (95030); (408)-358–3033. FAX: (408)356–0733. Pres. Bernie Kotansky; Exec. Dir. Michael Papo.

SANTA BARBARA
SANTA BARBARA JEWISH FEDERATION (org. 1974); 104 W. Anapamu, Suite A. Mailing Address: PO Box 90110, Santa Barbara (93190); (805)963–0244. FAX: (805)569–5052. Pres. Steven A. Amerikaner; Exec. Dir. Barbara Zonen.

COLORADO

DENVER
ALLIED JEWISH FEDERATION OF DENVER (1936); 300 S. Dahlia St. (80222); (303)321–3399. FAX: (303)322–8328. Pres. Stanton D. Rosenbaum; Exec. Dir. Sheldon Steinhauser.

CONNECTICUT

BRIDGEPORT
JEWISH FEDERATION OF GREATER BRIDGEPORT, INC. (1936; reorg. 1981); 4200 Park Ave. (06604); (203)372–6504. FAX: (203)-374–0770. Pres. Selig Danzig; Exec. Dir. Gerald A. Kleinman.

DANBURY
JEWISH FEDERATION OF GREATER DANBURY (1945); 39 Mill Plain Rd., Suite 4 (06811); (203)792–6353. Pres. Jean Wellington; Exec. Dir. Sharon Garelick.

EASTERN CONNECTICUT
JEWISH FEDERATION OF EASTERN CONNECTICUT, INC. (1950; inc. 1970); 28 Channing St., PO Box 1468, New London (06320); (203)442–8062. FAX: (203)444–0759. Pres. Reuben Levin; Exec. Dir. Jerome E. Fischer.

GREENWICH
GREENWICH JEWISH FEDERATION (1956); 600 W. Putnam Ave. (06830); (203)622–1434. FAX: (203)622–1237. Pres. Paula Lustbader; Interim Exec. Dir. Sol Margulies.

HARTFORD
GREATER HARTFORD JEWISH FEDERATION (1945); 333 Bloomfield Ave., W. Hartford (06117); (203)232–4483. FAX: (203)232–5221. Pres. Robert Siskin; Exec. Dir. Don Cooper.

NEW HAVEN
NEW HAVEN JEWISH FEDERATION (1928); 419 Whalley Ave. (06511); (203)562–2137. FAX: (203)787–3241. Pres. Stephen Saltzman; Exec. Dir. Susan Shimelman.

NORWALK
(See Westport)

STAMFORD
UNITED JEWISH FEDERATION (inc. 1973); 1035 Newfield Ave., PO Box 3038 (06905); (203)322–6935. FAX: (203)322–3277. Pres. Benson Zinbarg; Exec. Dir. Sheila L. Romanowitz.

WATERBURY
JEWISH FEDERATION OF WATERBURY, INC. (1938); 359 Cooke St. (06710); (203)756–7234. FAX: (203)573–0368. Pres. Dr. Alan Stein; Exec. Dir. Eli J. Skora.

WESTPORT-WESTON-WILTON-NORWALK

UNITED JEWISH APPEAL/FEDERATION OF WESTPORT-WESTON-WILTON-NORWALK (inc. 1980); 49 Richmondville Ave. (06880); (203)266-8197. FAX: (203)226-5051. Pres. Michael Stashower; Exec. Dir. Robert Kessler.

DELAWARE

WILMINGTON

JEWISH FEDERATION OF DELAWARE, INC. (1934); 101 Garden of Eden Rd. (19803); (302)478-6200. FAX: (302)478-5374. Pres. William N. Topkis; Exec. V. Pres. Robert N. Kerbel.

DISTRICT OF COLUMBIA

WASHINGTON

UNITED JEWISH APPEAL-FEDERATION OF GREATER WASHINGTON, INC. (1935); 6101 Montrose Rd., Rockville, MD 20852. (301)-230-7200. FAX: (301)230-7272. Pres. Edward Kaplan; Exec. V. Pres. Ted B. Farber.

FLORIDA

DAYTONA BEACH

JEWISH FEDERATION OF VOLUSIA & FLAGLER COUNTIES, INC.; 533 Seabreeze Blvd., Suite 300 (32118-3977); (904)255-6260. Pres. Gary Greenfield; Exec. Dir. Bette Kozak.

FT. LAUDERDALE

JEWISH FEDERATION OF GREATER FT. LAUDERDALE (1968); 8358 W. Oakland Park Blvd. (33351); (305)748-8400. FAX: (305)748-6332. Pres. Barbara Wiener; Exec. Dir. Kenneth B. Bierman.

JACKSONVILLE

JACKSONVILLE JEWISH FEDERATION (1935); 8505 San Jose Blvd. (32217); (904)-448-5000. FAX: (904)448-5715. Pres. Joan Levin; Exec. V. Pres. Alan Margolies.

LEE COUNTY

JEWISH FEDERATION OF LEE COUNTY (1974); 6315 Presidential Court, Suite A, Ft. Myers (33919-3568); (813)481-4449. FAX: (813)275-9114. Pres. Dr. Harvey Tritel; Exec. Dir. Helene Kramer.

MIAMI

GREATER MIAMI JEWISH FEDERATION, INC. (1938); 4200 Biscayne Blvd. (33137); (305)576-4000. FAX: (305)573-2176. Pres. Howard R. Scharlin; Exec. V. Pres. Myron J. Brodie.

ORLANDO

JEWISH FEDERATION OF GREATER ORLANDO (1949); 851 N. Maitland Ave., PO Box 941508, Maitland (32794-1508); (407)-645-5933. FAX: (407)645-1172. Pres. Ina Porth; Exec. Dir. Jordan Harburger.

PALM BEACH COUNTY

JEWISH FEDERATION OF PALM BEACH COUNTY, INC. (1962); 501 S. Flagler Dr., Suite 305, W. Palm Beach (33401); (407)832-2120. FAX: (407)832-0562. Pres. Alec Engelstein; Exec. Dir. Jeffrey L. Klein.

PINELLAS COUNTY

JEWISH FEDERATION OF PINELLAS COUNTY, INC. (incl. Clearwater and St. Petersburg) (1950; reincorp. 1974); 301 S. Jupiter Ave., Clearwater (34615); (813) 446-1033. FAX: (813)461-0700. Pres. James Soble; Exec. Dir. Robert F. Tropp.

SARASOTA

SARASOTA-MANATEE JEWISH FEDERATION (1959); 580 S. McIntosh Rd. (34232); (813)-371-4546. FAX: (813)378-2947. Pres. Doris Loevner; Exec. Dir. Norman Olshansky.

SOUTH BROWARD

JEWISH FEDERATION OF SOUTH BROWARD, INC. (1943); 2719 Hollywood Blvd., Hollywood (33020); (305)921-8810. FAX: (305)-921-6491. Pres. Dr. Howard Barron; Exec. Dir. Sumner G. Kaye.

SOUTH PALM BEACH COUNTY

SOUTH PALM BEACH COUNTY JEWISH FEDERATION (inc. 1979); 336 NW Spanish River Blvd., Boca Raton (33431); (407) 368-2737. FAX: (407)368-5240. Pres. Marvin Zale; Exec. Dir. Rabbi Bruce S. Warshal.

TAMPA

TAMPA JEWISH FEDERATION (1941); 2808 Horatio (33609); (813)875-1618. FAX: (813)876-7746. Pres. F. Sanford Mahr; Exec. V. Pres. Gary S. Alter.

GEORGIA

ATLANTA

ATLANTA JEWISH FEDERATION, INC. (1905; reorg. 1967); 1753 Peachtree Rd. NE (30309); (404)873-1661. FAX: (404)874-7043. Pres. Dr. S. Perry Brickman; Exec. Dir. David I. Sarnat.

AUGUSTA
AUGUSTA JEWISH FEDERATION (1937); PO Box 15443 (30909); (404)737-8001. Pres. Matt Marks; Exec. Dir. Michael Pousman.

COLUMBUS
JEWISH WELFARE FEDERATION OF COLUMBUS, INC. (1941); PO Box 6313 (31907); (404)568-6668. Pres. Jack Hirsch; Sec. Irene Rainbow.

SAVANNAH
SAVANNAH JEWISH FEDERATION (1943); PO Box 23527 (31403); (912)355-8111. FAX: (912)355-8116. Pres. Ricky Eichholz; Exec. Dir. Stan Ramati.

HAWAII

HONOLULU
JEWISH FEDERATION OF HAWAII (1956); 677 Ala Moana, Suite 803 (96813); (808)531-4634. FAX: (808)531-4636. Pres. Michael Washofsky; Exec. Dir. Rabbi Melvin Libman.

ILLINOIS

CHAMPAIGN-URBANA
CHAMPAIGN-URBANA JEWISH FEDERATION (1929); 503 E. John St., Champaign (61820); (217)367-9872. Pres. Helen Levin; Exec. Dir. Janie Yairi.

CHICAGO
JEWISH FEDERATION OF METROPOLITAN CHICAGO (1900); 1 S. Franklin St. (60606-4694); (312)346-6700. FAX: (312)855-2474. Pres. John C. Colman; Exec. V. Pres. Steven B. Nasatir.

JEWISH UNITED FUND OF METROPOLITAN CHICAGO (1900); 1 S. Franklin St. (60606-4694); (312)346-6700. FAX: (312)444-2086. Pres. John C. Colman; Exec. Dir. Steven B. Nasatir.

ELGIN
ELGIN AREA JEWISH WELFARE CHEST (1938); 330 Division St. (60120); (312)741-5656. Pres. Dr. Albert Simon; Treas. Richard Cutts.

PEORIA
JEWISH FEDERATION OF PEORIA (1933; inc. 1947); 3100 N. Knoxville, Suite 19 (61603); (309)686-0611. Pres. Dr. Irving J. Weigensberg; Exec. Dir. Eunice Galsky.

QUAD CITIES
JEWISH FEDERATION OF QUAD CITIES (incl. Rock Island, Moline, Davenport, Bettendorf) (1938; comb. 1973); 224 18 St., Suite 303, Rock Island (61201); (309)793-1300. Pres. Gordon Ney; Exec. Dir. Ida Kramer.

ROCKFORD
JEWISH FEDERATION OF GREATER ROCKFORD (1937); 1500 Parkview Ave. (61107); (815)399-5497. Pres. Jay Kamin; Exec. Dir. Tony Toback.

SOUTHERN ILLINOIS
JEWISH FEDERATION OF SOUTHERN ILLINOIS, SOUTHEASTERN MISSOURI AND WESTERN KENTUCKY (1941); 6464 W. Main, Suite 7A, Belleville (62223); (618)398-6100. Pres. Ronald Rubin; Exec. Dir. Stan Anderman.

SPRINGFIELD
SPRINGFIELD JEWISH FEDERATION (1941); 730 E. Vine St. (62703); (217)528-3446. Pres. Robert Silverman; Exec. Dir. Gloria Schwartz.

INDIANA

EVANSVILLE
EVANSVILLE JEWISH COMMUNITY COUNCIL, INC. (1936; inc. 1964); PO Box 5026 (47715); (812)477-7050. Pres. Jon Goldman; Exec. Sec. Maxine P. Fink.

FORT WAYNE
FORT WAYNE JEWISH FEDERATION (1921); 227 E. Washington Blvd. (46802); (219)422-8566. Pres. Carol Sandler; Exec. Dir. Vivian Lansky.

INDIANAPOLIS
JEWISH FEDERATION OF GREATER INDIANAPOLIS, INC. (1905); 615 N. Alabama St., Suite 412 (46204-1430); (317)637-2473. FAX: (317)637-2477. Pres. Stanley Talesnick; Exec. V. Pres. Harry Nadler.

LAFAYETTE
FEDERATED JEWISH CHARITIES (1924); PO Box 708 (47902); (317)742-9081. FAX: (317)742-4379. Pres. Arnold Cohen; Finan. Sec. Louis Pearlman, Jr.

MICHIGAN CITY
MICHIGAN CITY UNITED JEWISH WELFARE FUND; 2800 S. Franklin St. (46360); (219)-874-4477. Pres. & Treas. Harold Leinwand.

JEWISH FEDERATIONS, FUNDS, COUNCILS / 525

NORTHWEST INDIANA
THE JEWISH FEDERATION, INC. (1941; reorg. 1959); 2939 Jewett St., Highland (46322); (219)972-2250. FAX: (219)972-4779. Pres. Jerome Gardberg; Exec. Dir. Marty Erann.

SOUTH BEND
JEWISH FEDERATION OF ST. JOSEPH VALLEY (1946); 105 Jefferson Centre, Suite 804 (46601); (219)233-1164. FAX: (219)288-4103. Pres. Dr. William Gitlin; Exec. V. Pres. Kimball Marsh.

IOWA

DES MOINES
JEWISH FEDERATION OF GREATER DES MOINES (1914); 910 Polk Blvd. (50312); (515)277-6321. FAX: (515)277-4069. Pres. Harry Bookey; Exec. Dir. Elaine Steinger.

SIOUX CITY
JEWISH FEDERATION (1921); 525 14th St. (51105); (712)258-0618. Pres. Michael Potash; Exec. Dir. Doris Rosenthal.

KANSAS

WICHITA
MID-KANSAS JEWISH FEDERATION, INC. (1935); 400 N. Woodlawn, Suite 8 (67208); (316)686-4741. Pres. Ivonne Goldstein; Exec. Dir. Beverly Jacobson.

KENTUCKY

LEXINGTON
CENTRAL KENTUCKY JEWISH FEDERATION (1976); 333 Waller, Suite 5 (40504); (606)-252-7622. Pres. Michael Ades; Exec. Dir. Linda Ravvin.

LOUISVILLE
JEWISH COMMUNITY FEDERATION OF LOUISVILLE, INC. (1934); 3630 Dutchman's Lane (40205); (502)451-8840. FAX: (502)-458-0702. Pres. Ronald W. Abrams; Exec. Dir. Dr. Alan S. Engel.

LOUISIANA

ALEXANDRIA
THE JEWISH WELFARE FEDERATION AND COMMUNITY COUNCIL OF CENTRAL LOUISIANA (1938); 1227 Southhampton (71303); (318)445-4785. Pres. Alvin Mykoff; Sec.-Treas. Roeve Weill.

BATON ROUGE
JEWISH FEDERATION OF GREATER BATON ROUGE (1971); 11744 Haymarket Ave., Suite B; PO Box 80827 (70898); (504) 291-5895. Pres. Dr. Steven Cavalier; Exec. Dir. Louis Goldman.

NEW ORLEANS
JEWISH FEDERATION OF GREATER NEW ORLEANS (1913; reorg. 1977); 1539 Jackson Ave. (70130); (504)525-0673. FAX: (504)-568-9290. Pres. Dr. Julius L. Levy, Jr.; Exec. Dir. Jane Buchsbaum.

SHREVEPORT
SHREVEPORT JEWISH FEDERATION (1941; inc. 1967); 2032 Line Ave. (71104); (318)-221-4129. Pres. William Braunig, Jr.; Exec. Dir. Monty Pomm.

MAINE

LEWISTON-AUBURN
LEWISTON-AUBURN JEWISH FEDERATION (1947); 74 Bradman St., Auburn (04210); (207)786-4201. Pres. Scott Nussinow.

PORTLAND
JEWISH FEDERATION COMMUNITY COUNCIL OF SOUTHERN MAINE (1942); 57 Ashmont St. (04103); (207)773-7254. Pres. Lisa Cohen; Exec. Dir. Meyer Bodoff.

MARYLAND

BALTIMORE
THE ASSOCIATED: JEWISH COMMUNITY FEDERATION OF BALTIMORE (1920; reorg. 1969); 101 W. Mt. Royal Ave. (21201); (301) 727-4828. FAX: (301)783-8991. Chmn. Suzanne F. Cohen; Pres. Darrell D. Friedman.

MASSACHUSETTS

BERKSHIRE COUNTY
JEWISH FEDERATION OF THE BERKSHIRES (1940); 235 East St., Pittsfield (01201); (413)-442-4360. FAX: (413)443-6070. Pres. Joel Greenberg; Exec. Dir. Richard Davis.

BOSTON
COMBINED JEWISH PHILANTHROPIES OF GREATER BOSTON, INC. (1895; inc. 1961); One Lincoln Plaza (02111); (617)330-9500. FAX: (617)330-5197. Chmn. Edwin N. Sidman; Exec. V. Pres. Barry Shrage.

CAPE COD
JEWISH FEDERATION OF CAPE COD 396 Main St., PO Box 2568, Hyannis (02601); (508)778-5588. Pres. Melvin Cohen.

FRAMINGHAM (Merged with Boston)

LEOMINSTER
LEOMINSTER JEWISH COMMUNITY COUNCIL, INC. (1939); 268 Washington St. (01453); (617)534-6121. Pres. Dr. Milton Kline; Sec.-Treas. Howard J. Rome.

MERRIMACK VALLEY
MERRIMACK VALLEY UNITED JEWISH COMMUNITIES (Serves Lowell, Lawrence, Andover, Haverhill, Newburyport, and 22 surrounding communities) (1988); 805 Turnpike St., N. Andover (01845); (508)688-0466. FAX: (508)682-3041. Pres. Larry Ansin; Exec. Dir. Howard Flagler.

NEW BEDFORD
JEWISH FEDERATION OF GREATER NEW BEDFORD, INC. (1938; inc. 1954); 467 Hawthorn St., N. Dartmouth (02747); (508)997-7471. FAX: (508)997-7730. Pres. Elliot Rosenfield; Exec. Dir. Jerry S. Neimand.

NORTH SHORE
JEWISH FEDERATION OF THE NORTH SHORE, INC. (1938); 4 Community Rd., Marblehead (01945); (617)598-1810. FAX: (617)639-1284. Pres. Lawrence Slater; Exec. Dir. Bruce Yudewitz.

SPRINGFIELD
JEWISH FEDERATION OF GREATER SPRINGFIELD, INC. (1925); 1160 Dickinson St. (01108); (413)737-4313. FAX: (413)737-4348. Pres. Diane Troderman; Exec. Dir. Joel Weiss.

WORCESTER
WORCESTER JEWISH FEDERATION, INC. (1947; inc. 1957); 633 Salisbury St. (01609); (508)756-1543. FAX: (508)798-0962. Pres. Michael Sleeper.

MICHIGAN

ANN ARBOR
JEWISH COMMUNITY ASSOCIATION/UNITED JEWISH APPEAL (1986); 2939 Birch Hollow Dr. (48108). (313)677-0100. Pres. Dr. Owen Z. Perlman; Interim Dir. Nancy N. Margolis.

DETROIT
JEWISH WELFARE FEDERATION OF DETROIT (1899); Fred M. Butzel Memorial Bldg., 163 Madison (48226); (313)965-3939. FAX:(313)965-5778(executive offices);(313)-965-8217 (all other departments). Pres. Mark E. Schlussel; Exec. V. Pres. Robert P. Aronson.

FLINT
FLINT JEWISH FEDERATION (1936); 619 Wallenberg St. (48502); (313)767-5922. FAX: (313)767-9024. Pres. Nancy Hanflik; Exec. Dir. David Nussbaum.

GRAND RAPIDS
JEWISH COMMUNITY FUND OF GRAND RAPIDS (1930); 2609 Berwyck SE (49506); (616)956-9365. Pres. Joseph N. Schwartz; Admin. Dir. Judy Joseph.

MINNESOTA

DULUTH-SUPERIOR
JEWISH FEDERATION & COMMUNITY COUNCIL (1937); 1602 E. Second St. (55812); (218)-724-8857. Pres. David Blustin; Sec. Admin. Gloria Vitullo.

MINNEAPOLIS
MINNEAPOLIS FEDERATION FOR JEWISH SERVICE (1929; inc. 1930); 7600 Wayzata Blvd. (55426); (612)593-2600. FAX: (612)-593-2544. Pres. Herbert Goldenberg; Exec. Dir. Max L. Kleinman.

ST. PAUL
UNITED JEWISH FUND AND COUNCIL (1935); 790 S. Cleveland, Suite 201 (55116); (612)690-1707. FAX: (612)690-0228. Pres. Allen Freeman; Exec. Dir. Sam Asher.

MISSISSIPPI

JACKSON
JACKSON JEWISH WELFARE FUND, INC. (1945); 5315 Old Canton Rd. (39211-4625); (601)956-6215. Pres. Ruth Friedman; V. Pres. Erik Hearon.

MISSOURI

KANSAS CITY
JEWISH FEDERATION OF GREATER KANSAS CITY (1933); 5801 W. 115th St., Overland Park, KS (66211-1824); (913)469-1340. FAX: (913)451-9358. Pres. Ann R. Jacobson; Exec. Dir. A. Robert Gast.

JEWISH FEDERATIONS, FUNDS, COUNCILS / 527

ST. JOSEPH
UNITED JEWISH FUND OF ST. JOSEPH (1915); 509 Woodcrest Dr. (64506); (816)-279-7154. Pres. Dorathea Polsky; Exec. Sec. Martha Rothstein.

ST. LOUIS
JEWISH FEDERATION OF ST. LOUIS (incl. St. Louis County) (1901); 12 Millstone Campus Dr. (63146); (314)432-0020. FAX: (314)-432-1277. Pres. Alyn V. Essman; Exec. V. Pres. Ira Steinmetz.

NEBRASKA

LINCOLN
LINCOLN JEWISH WELFARE FEDERATION, INC. (1931; inc. 1961); PO Box 80014 (68501); (402)423-5695. Copres. Ruth & Irwin Goldenberg; Exec. Dir. Robert Pitlor.

OMAHA
JEWISH FEDERATION OF OMAHA (1903); 333 S. 132nd St. (68154-2198); (402)334-8200. FAX: (402)334-1330. Pres. Jay R. Lerner; Exec. Dir. Howard Bloom.

NEVADA

LAS VEGAS
JEWISH FEDERATION OF LAS VEGAS (1973); 1030 E. Twain Ave. (89109); (702)732-0556. FAX: (702)732-3228. Pres. Dr. Marvin M. Perer; Exec. Dir. Norman Kaufman.

NEW HAMPSHIRE

MANCHESTER
JEWISH FEDERATION OF GREATER MANCHESTER (1974); 698 Beech St. (03104); (603)627-7679. Pres. Dr. David Stahl; Exec. Dir. Mark Silverberg.

NEW JERSEY

ATLANTIC COUNTY
FEDERATION OF JEWISH AGENCIES OF ATLANTIC COUNTY (1924); 505-507 Tilton Rd., Northfield (08225); (609)646-7077. FAX: (609)646-8053. Pres. Howard A. Goldberg; Exec. Dir. Bernard Cohen.

BERGEN COUNTY
UNITED JEWISH COMMUNITY OF BERGEN COUNTY (inc. 1978); 111 Kinderkamack Rd., PO Box 4176, N. Hackensack Station, River Edge (07661); (201)488-6800. FAX: (201)-488-1507. Pres. Irwin Marks; Exec. V. Pres. James Young.

CENTRAL NEW JERSEY
JEWISH FEDERATION OF CENTRAL NEW JERSEY (1940; merged 1973); Green Lane, Union (07083); (201)351-5060. FAX: (201)-351-7060. Pres. Murray Pantirer; Exec. V. Pres. Burton Lazarow.

CLIFTON-PASSAIC
JEWISH FEDERATION OF GREATER CLIFTON-PASSAIC (1933); 199 Scoles Ave., Clifton (07012). (201)777-7031. FAX: (201)777-6701. Pres. Jon Gurkoff; Exec. Dir. Yosef Muskin.

CUMBERLAND COUNTY
JEWISH FEDERATION OF CUMBERLAND COUNTY (inc. 1971); 629 Wood St., Suite 204, Vineland (08360); (609)696-4445. Pres. Stanley Orlinsky; Exec. Dir. Daniel Lepow.

ENGLEWOOD
(Merged with Bergen County)

MERCER COUNTY
JEWISH FEDERATION OF MERCER AND BUCKS COUNTIES NJ/PA (1929; reorg. 1982); 999 Lower Ferry Rd., Trenton (08628); (609)883-5000. FAX: (609)883-2563. Pres. Richard Dickson; Exec. Dir. Haim Morag. (Also see listing under Pennsylvania.)

METROWEST NEW JERSEY
UNITED JEWISH FEDERATION OF METROWEST (1923); 60 Glenwood Ave., E. Orange (07017); (201)673-6800; (212)943-0570. FAX: (201)673-4387. Pres. Jerome Waldor; Exec. V. Pres. Howard E. Charish.

MIDDLESEX COUNTY
JEWISH FEDERATION OF GREATER MIDDLESEX COUNTY (org. 1948; reorg. 1985); 100 Metroplex Dr., Suite 101, Edison (08817); (201)985-1234. FAX: (201)985-3295. Pres. James Stahl; Exec. V. Pres. Michael Shapiro.

MONMOUTH COUNTY
JEWISH FEDERATION OF GREATER MONMOUTH COUNTY (1971); 100 Grant Ave., PO Box 210, Deal (07723-0210); (201)531-6200-1. FAX: (201)531-9518. Pres. Arnold Gelfman; Exec. V. Pres. Marvin Relkin; Exec. Dir. Bonnie Komito.

MORRIS-SUSSEX COUNTY
(Merged with MetroWest NJ)

NORTH JERSEY
JEWISH FEDERATION OF NORTH JERSEY (1933); One Pike Dr., Wayne (07470); (201)-

595-0555. FAX: (201)595-1532. Pres. Joanne Sprechman; Exec. Dir. Barry Rosenberg.

NORTHERN MIDDLESEX COUNTY
(See Middlesex County)

OCEAN COUNTY
OCEAN COUNTY JEWISH FEDERATION (1977); 301 Madison Ave., Lakewood (08701); (201)363-0530. FAX: (201)363-2097. Pres. Zev Rosen; Exec. Dir. Michael Ruvel.

PRINCETON
PRINCETON AREA UJA-FEDERATION; 15 Roszel Rd., Princeton (08540); (609)243-9440. Pres. Dr. Eliot Freeman; Exec. Dir. Jerilyn Zimmerman.

RARITAN VALLEY
(See Middlesex County)

SOMERSET COUNTY
JEWISH FEDERATION OF SOMERSET, HUNTERDON, & WARREN COUNTIES (1960); 120 Finderne Ave., Bridgewater (08807); (201)-725-6994. Pres. George Blank; Exec. Dir. Alan J. Nydick.

SOUTHERN NEW JERSEY
JEWISH FEDERATION OF SOUTHERN NEW JERSEY (incl. Camden, Burlington, and Gloucester counties) (1922); 2393 W. Marlton Pike, Cherry Hill (08002); (609)665-6100. FAX: (609)665-0074. Pres. Dr. Robert Paul; Exec. V. Pres. Stuart Alperin.

NEW MEXICO

ALBUQUERQUE
JEWISH FEDERATION OF GREATER ALBUQUERQUE, INC. (1938); 8205 Spain, NE (97109); (505)821-3214. FAX: (505)821-3355. Pres. Brian Ivener; Exec. Dir. Joel Brooks.

NEW YORK

ALBANY
(Merged with Schenectady; see Northeastern New York)

BROOME COUNTY
JEWISH FEDERATION OF BROOME COUNTY (1937; inc. 1958); 500 Clubhouse Rd., Vestal (13850); (607)724-2332. Pres. Marcelene H. Yonaty; Exec. Dir. Victoria Rouff.

BUFFALO
JEWISH FEDERATION OF GREATER BUFFALO, INC. (1903); 787 Delaware Ave. (14209); (716)886-7750. FAX: (716)886-1367. Pres. Dr. Richard Ament; Exec. Dir. Harry Kosansky.

DUTCHESS COUNTY
JEWISH FEDERATION OF DUTCHESS COUNTY; 110 S. Grand Ave., Poughkeepsie (12603); (914)471-9811. Pres. Morris Krakinowski; Exec. Dir. Allan Greene.

ELMIRA
ELMIRA JEWISH WELFARE FUND, INC. (1942); Grandview Rd. Ext., PO Box 3087 (14905); (607)734-8122. Pres. Arnold Rosenberg; Exec. Dir. Cy Leveen.

KINGSTON
JEWISH FEDERATION OF GREATER KINGSTON, INC. (inc. 1951); 159 Green St. (12401); (914)338-8131. Pres. Dr. Howard Rothstein.

NEW YORK
UJA-FEDERATION OF JEWISH PHILANTHROPIES OF NEW YORK, INC. (incl. Greater NY; Westchester, Nassau, and Suffolk counties) (Fed. org. 1917; UJA 1939; merged 1986); 130 E. 59th St. (10022); (212)980-1000. FAX: (212)867-1074. Pres. David G. Sacks; Chmn. Joseph Gurwin; Exec. V. Pres. Stephen D. Solender.

NIAGARA FALLS
JEWISH FEDERATION OF NIAGARA FALLS, NY, INC. (1935); Temple Beth Israel, Rm. #5, College & Madison Ave. (14305); (716)-284-4575. Pres. Howard Rushner.

NORTHEASTERN NEW YORK
UNITED JEWISH FEDERATION OF NORTHEASTERN NEW YORK (1986); Latham Circle Mall, 800 New Loudon Rd., Latham (12110); (518)783-7800. FAX: (518)783-1557. Pres. Rabbi Martin Silverman; Exec. Dir. Norman J. Schimelman.

ORANGE COUNTY
JEWISH FEDERATION OF GREATER ORANGE COUNTY (1977); 360 Powell Ave., Newburgh (12550); (914)562-7860. Pres. Richard Levin; Exec. Dir. Nancy Goldman.

ROCHESTER
JEWISH COMMUNITY FEDERATION OF ROCHESTER, NY, INC. (1939); 441 East Ave. (14607); (716)461-0490. FAX: (716)461-0912. Pres. Linda Cornell Weinstein; Exec. Dir. Lawrence W. Fine.

ROCKLAND COUNTY
UNITED JEWISH COMMUNITY OF ROCKLAND COUNTY (1985); 240 W. Nyack Rd.,

W. Nyack (10994–1711). (914)627–3700.
FAX: (914)627–7881. Pres. Mark Karsch;
Exec. Dir. Michael A. Bierman.

SCHENECTADY
(Merged with Albany; see Northeastern New York)

SYRACUSE
SYRACUSE JEWISH FEDERATION, INC. (1918); 101 Smith St.; PO Box 510, DeWitt (13214–0510); (315)445–0161. FAX: (315)-445–1559. Pres. Philip Pinsky; Exec. V. Pres. Barry Silverberg.

TROY
(Merged with Albany-Schenectady; see Northeastern New York)

UTICA
JEWISH FEDERATION OF UTICA, NY, INC. (1933; inc. 1950); 2310 Oneida St. (13501); (315)733–2343. Pres. Marsha Basloe; Exec. Dir. Meyer L. Bodoff.

NORTH CAROLINA

ASHEVILLE
WESTERN NORTH CAROLINA JEWISH FEDERATION (1935); 236 Charlotte St. (28801); (704)253–0701. FAX: (704)251–9144. Pres. Robert J. Deutsch; Exec. Dir. David Seidenberg.

CHARLOTTE
CHARLOTTE JEWISH FEDERATION (1938); PO Box 13369 (28211); (704)366–5007. FAX: (704)365–4507. Pres. Emily Zimmern; Exec. Dir. Michael Minkin.

DURHAM–CHAPEL HILL
DURHAM–CHAPEL HILL JEWISH FEDERATION & COMMUNITY COUNCIL (1979); 1310 LeClair St., Chapel Hill (27514); (919)967–1945. FAX: (919)962–1277. Pres. Barry Nakell.

GREENSBORO
GREENSBORO JEWISH FEDERATION (1940); 713-A N. Greene St. (27401); (919)272–3189. FAX: (919)272–0214. Pres. Joslin LeBauer; Exec. Dir. Marilyn Chandler.

WAKE COUNTY
WAKE COUNTY JEWISH FEDERATION, INC. (1987); 3900 Merton Dr., Suite 108, Raleigh (27609); (919)787–0666. FAX: (919)878–1548. Pres. Joseph Woodland.

OHIO

AKRON
AKRON JEWISH COMMUNITY FEDERATION (1935); 750 White Pond Dr. (44320); (216)-867–7850. FAX: (216)867–8498. Pres. Dr. Steven Kutnick; Exec. Dir. Michael Wise.

CANTON
CANTON JEWISH COMMUNITY FEDERATION (1935; reorg. 1955); 2631 Harvard Ave., NW (44709); (216)452–6444. FAX: (216)-452–4487. Pres. Robert Narens; Exec. Dir. Jay Rubin.

CINCINNATI
JEWISH FEDERATION OF CINCINNATI (1896; reorg. 1967); 1811 Losantiville, Suite 320 (45237); (513) 351–3800. FAX: (513)351–3863. Pres. Stanley M. Chesley; Exec. V. Pres. Aubrey Herman.

CLEVELAND
JEWISH COMMUNITY FEDERATION OF CLEVELAND (1903); 1750 Euclid Ave. (44115); (216)566–9200. FAX: (216)861–1230. Pres. Max R. Friedman; Exec. Dir. Stephen H. Hoffman.

COLUMBUS
COLUMBUS JEWISH FEDERATION (1926); 1175 College Ave. (43209); (614)237–7686. FAX: (614)237–2221. Pres. Benjamin L. Zox; Exec. Dir. Alan H. Gill.

DAYTON
JEWISH FEDERATION OF GREATER DAYTON (1910); 4501 Denlinger Rd. (45426); (513)854–4150. FAX: (513)854–2850. Pres. Lawrence T. Burick; Exec. V. Pres. Peter H. Wells.

STEUBENVILLE
JEWISH COMMUNITY COUNCIL (1938); 300 Lovers Lane (43952); (614)264–5514. Pres. Morris Denmark; Exec. Sec. Jennie Bernstein.

TOLEDO
JEWISH FEDERATION OF GREATER TOLEDO (1907; reorg. 1960); 6505 Sylvania Ave., PO Box 587, Sylvania (43560); (419)885–4461. FAX: (419)885–3207. Pres. James J. Akers; Exec. Dir. Steven J. Edelstein.

YOUNGSTOWN
YOUNGSTOWN AREA JEWISH FEDERATION (1935); PO Box 449, 505 Gypsy Lane (44501); (216)746–3251. FAX: (216)746–7926. Pres. Esther L. Marks; Exec. V. Pres. Sam Kooperman.

OKLAHOMA

OKLAHOMA CITY
JEWISH FEDERATION OF GREATER OKLAHOMA CITY (1941); 2800 Quail Plaza Dr. (73120). (405)752-7307. FAX: (405)752-7309. Pres. Jerry Bendorf.

TULSA
JEWISH FEDERATION OF TULSA (1938); 2021 E. 71st St. (74136); (918)495-1100. FAX: (918)495-1220. Pres. Curtis S. Green; Exec. Dir. David Bernstein.

OREGON

PORTLAND
JEWISH FEDERATION OF PORTLAND (incl. state of Oregon and adjacent Washington communities) (1920; reorg. 1956); 6651 SW Capitol Highway (97219); (503)245-6219. FAX: (503)245-6603. Pres. Stanley D. Geffen; Exec. Dir. Charles Schiffman.

PENNSYLVANIA

ALLENTOWN
JEWISH FEDERATION OF ALLENTOWN (1948); 702 N. 22nd St. (18104); (215)821-5500. FAX: (215)821-8946. Pres. Leonard Abrams; Exec. Dir. Ivan C. Schonfeld.

ALTOONA
FEDERATION OF JEWISH PHILANTHROPIES (1920; reorg. 1940; inc. 1944); 1308 17th St. (16601); (814)944-4072. Pres. Morley Cohn.

BUCKS COUNTY
JEWISH FEDERATION OF MERCER AND BUCKS COUNTIES NJ/PA (1929; reorg. 1982); 999 Lower Ferry Rd., Trenton, NJ (08628); (609)883-5000. FAX: (609)883-2563. Pres. Richard Dickson; Exec. Dir. Haim Morag. (Also see listing under New Jersey.)

ERIE
JEWISH COMMUNITY COUNCIL OF ERIE (1946); 701 G. Daniel Baldwin Bldg., 1001 State St. (16501); (814)455-4474. Pres. Richard Levick.

HARRISBURG
UNITED JEWISH COMMUNITY OF GREATER HARRISBURG (1941); 100 Vaughn St. (17110); (717)236-9555. FAX: (717)236-8104. Pres. Morton Spector; Exec. Dir. Elliot Gershenson.

JOHNSTOWN
UNITED JEWISH FEDERATION OF JOHNSTOWN (1938); 601 Wayne St. (15905); (814)-539-9891 (home). Pres. Isadore Suchman.

PHILADELPHIA
JEWISH FEDERATION OF GREATER PHILADELPHIA (includes Bucks, Chester, Delaware, Montgomery, and Philadelphia counties) (1901; reorg. 1956); 226 S. 16th St. (19102); (215)893-5600. FAX: (215)735-7977. Pres. Theodore Seidenberg; Exec. V. Pres. Robert P. Forman.

PITTSBURGH
UNITED JEWISH FEDERATION OF GREATER PITTSBURGH (1912; reorg. 1955); 234 McKee Pl. (15213); (412)681-8000. FAX: (412)681-3980. Pres. David S. Shapira; Exec. V. Pres. Howard M. Rieger.

READING
JEWISH FEDERATION OF READING, PA., INC. (1935; reorg. 1972); 1700 City Line St. (19604); (215)921-2766. FAX: (215)929-0886. Pres. Alma Lakin; Exec. Dir. Daniel Tannenbaum.

SCRANTON
SCRANTON-LACKAWANNA JEWISH FEDERATION (incl. Lackawanna County) (1945); 601 Jefferson Ave. (18510); (717)961-2300. FAX: (717)346-6147. Pres. Irwin Schneider; Exec. Dir. Seymour Brotman.

WILKES-BARRE
JEWISH FEDERATION OF GREATER WILKES-BARRE (1935); 60 S. River St. (18702); (717)-822-4146. FAX: (717)824-5966. Pres. Stephen Alinikoff; Exec. Dir. Ted Magram.

RHODE ISLAND

PROVIDENCE
JEWISH FEDERATION OF RHODE ISLAND (1945); 130 Sessions St. (02906); (401)421-4111. FAX: (401)331-7961. Pres. David M. Hirsch; Exec. V. Pres. Elliot Cohan.

SOUTH CAROLINA

CHARLESTON
CHARLESTON JEWISH FEDERATION (1949); 1645 Raoul Wallenberg Blvd., PO Box 31298 (29407); (803)571-6565. FAX: (803)556-6206. Pres. Judge Hugo Spitz; Exec. Dir. Michael Abidor.

JEWISH FEDERATIONS, FUNDS, COUNCILS / 531

COLUMBIA
COLUMBIA JEWISH FEDERATION (1960); 4540 Trenholm Rd., PO Box 6968 (29260); (803)787–0580. FAX: (803)787–0475. Pres. Hyman Rubin, Jr.; Exec. Dir. Alexander Grossberg.

SOUTH DAKOTA

SIOUX FALLS
JEWISH WELFARE FUND (1938); National Reserve Bldg., 513 S. Main Ave. (57102); (605)336–2880. Pres. Laurence Bierman; Exec. Sec. Louis R. Hurwitz.

TENNESSEE

CHATTANOOGA
CHATTANOOGA JEWISH FEDERATION (1931); 5326 Lynnland Terrace, PO Box 8947 (37411); (615)894–1317. FAX: (615)894–1319. Pres. Charles B. Lebovitz; Exec. Dir. Louis B. Solomon.

KNOXVILLE
KNOXVILLE JEWISH FEDERATION (1939); 6800 Deane Hill Dr., PO Box 10882 (37939-0882); (615)693–5837. Pres. Barbara Bernstein; Exec. Dir. Conrad J. Koller.

MEMPHIS
MEMPHIS JEWISH FEDERATION (incl. Shelby County) (1935); 6560 Poplar Ave. (38138); (901)767–7100. FAX: (901)767–7128. Pres. Jerome Makowsky; Exec. Dir. Gary Siepser.

NASHVILLE
JEWISH FEDERATION OF NASHVILLE & MIDDLE TENNESSEE (1936); 801 Percy Warner Blvd. (37205); (615)356–3242. FAX: (615)352–0056. Pres. Carolyn Levine; Act. Exec. Dir. Ruth Tanner.

TEXAS

AUSTIN
JEWISH FEDERATION OF AUSTIN (1939; reorg. 1956); 11713 Jollyville Rd. (78759); (512)331–1144. FAX: (512)331–7059. Pres. Rafael Pelc; Exec. Dir. Wayne Silverman.

DALLAS
JEWISH FEDERATION OF GREATER DALLAS (1911); 7800 Northaven Rd., Suite A (75230); (214)369–3313. FAX: (214)369–8943. Pres. Sanford Fagadau; Exec. Dir. Avrum I. Cohen.

EL PASO
JEWISH FEDERATION OF EL PASO, INC. (incl. surrounding communities) (1937); 405 Wallenberg Dr., PO Box 12097 (79913-0097); (915)584–4437. FAX: (915)584–0243. Pres. Joan Johnson; Exec. Dir. David Brown.

FORT WORTH
JEWISH FEDERATION OF FORT WORTH AND TARRANT COUNTY (1936); 6801 Dan Danciger Rd. (76133); (817)292–3081. FAX: (817)292–3214. Pres. Rowena Kimmell; Exec. Dir. Bruce Schlosberg.

GALVESTON
GALVESTON COUNTY JEWISH WELFARE ASSOCIATION (1936); PO Box 146 (77553); (409)763–5241. Pres. Harold Levine; Treas. Joe Nussenblatt.

HOUSTON
JEWISH FEDERATION OF GREATER HOUSTON (1936); 5603 S. Braeswood Blvd. (77096–3999); (713)729–7000. FAX: (713)-721–6232. Pres. Buster Feldman; Exec. Dir. Hans Mayer.

SAN ANTONIO
JEWISH FEDERATION OF SAN ANTONIO (incl. Bexar County) (1922); 8434 Ahern Dr. (78216); (512)341–8234. FAX: (512)341–2842. Pres. Sterling Neuman; Exec. Dir. Robert Posner.

WACO
JEWISH FEDERATION OF WACO AND CENTRAL TEXAS (1949); PO Box 8031 (76714-8031); (817)776–3740. Pres. Mike Stupak; Exec. Sec. Martha Bauer.

UTAH

SALT LAKE CITY
UNITED JEWISH COUNCIL AND SALT LAKE JEWISH WELFARE FUND (1936); 2416 E. 1700 South (84108); (801)581–0098. Pres. Fred Tannenbaum; Exec. Dir. Roberta Grunauer.

VIRGINIA

NEWPORT NEWS–HAMPTON–WILLIAMSBURG
UNITED JEWISH COMMUNITY OF THE VIRGINIA PENINSULA, INC. (1942); 2700 Spring Rd., Newport News (23606); (804)930–1422. FAX: (804)872–9532. Pres. Joanne Roos; Exec. Dir. Barbara Rostov.

RICHMOND
JEWISH COMMUNITY FEDERATION OF RICHMOND (1935); 5403 Monument Ave., PO Box 17128 (23226); (804)288–0045. FAX: (804)282–7507. Pres. Helen P. Horwitz; Exec. Dir. Robert S. Hyman.

TIDEWATER
UNITED JEWISH FEDERATION OF TIDEWATER (incl. Norfolk, Portsmouth, and Virginia Beach) (1937); 7300 Newport Ave., PO Box 9776, Norfolk (23505); (804)489–8040. FAX: (804)489–8230. Pres. Dr. Charles J. Goldman; Exec. V. Pres. Gary N. Rubin.

WASHINGTON
SEATTLE
JEWISH FEDERATION OF GREATER SEATTLE (incl. King County, Everett, and Bremerton) (1926); 2031 Third Ave. (98121); (206)443–5400. FAX: (206)443–0303. Pres. Herbert Pruzan; Exec. Dir. Michael Novick.

WEST VIRGINIA
CHARLESTON
FEDERATED JEWISH CHARITIES OF CHARLESTON, INC. (1937); PO Box 1613 (25326); (304)346–7500. Pres. Carl Lehman; Exec. Sec. William H. Thalheimer.

WISCONSIN
KENOSHA
KENOSHA JEWISH WELFARE FUND (1938); 8041 48th Ave. (53142); (414)694–6695. Pres. Richard Selsberg; Sec.-Treas. Steven Barasch.

MADISON
MADISON JEWISH COMMUNITY COUNCIL, INC. (1940); 310 N. Midvale Blvd., Suite 325 (53705); (608)231–3426. Pres. Judith Schreiber; Exec. Dir. Steven H. Morrison.

MILWAUKEE
MILWAUKEE JEWISH FEDERATION, INC. (1902); 1360 N. Prospect Ave. (53202); (414)271–8338. Pres. Joseph M. Bernstein; Exec. Dir. Rick Meyer.

CANADA

ALBERTA
CALGARY
CALGARY JEWISH COMMUNITY COUNCIL (1962); 1607 90th Ave. SW (T2V 4V7); (403)-253–8600. FAX: (403)253–7915. Pres. Robert Kalef; Exec. Dir. Drew J. Staffenberg.

EDMONTON
JEWISH FEDERATION OF EDMONTON (1954; reorg. 1982); 7200 156th St. (T5R 1X3); (403)487–5120. FAX: (403)481–3463. Pres. Michael Goldstein; Exec. Dir. Sidney Indig.

BRITISH COLUMBIA
VANCOUVER
JEWISH FEDERATION OF GREATER VANCOUVER (1932; reorg. 1987); 950 W. 41st Ave. (V5Z 2N7); (604)266–7115. FAX: (604)266–8371. Pres. Ted Zacks; Exec. Dir. Steve Drysdale.

MANITOBA
WINNIPEG
WINNIPEG JEWISH COMMUNITY COUNCIL (1938; reorg. 1973); 370 Hargrave St. (R3B 2K1); (204)943–0406. FAX: (204)956–0609. Pres. Sidney Halpern; Exec. Dir. Robert Freedman.

ONTARIO
HAMILTON
JEWISH FEDERATION OF HAMILTON, WENTWORTH & AREA (1932; merged 1971); PO Box 7258, 1030 Lower Lion Club Rd., Ancaster (L9G 3N6); (416)648–0605. FAX: (416)648–8388. Pres. Gerald Swaye, Q.C.; Exec. Dir. Claire Mandel.

LONDON
LONDON JEWISH FEDERATION (1932); 536 Huron St. (N5Y 4J5); (519)673–3310. FAX: (519)673–1161. Pres. Robert Siskind; Exec. Dir. Gerald Enchin.

OTTAWA
JEWISH COMMUNITY COUNCIL OF OTTAWA (1934); 151 Chapel St. (K1N 7Y2); (613)232–7306. FAX: (613)563–4593. Pres. Dr. Eli Rabin; Exec. Dir. Gerry Koffman.

TORONTO
TORONTO JEWISH CONGRESS (1917); 4600 Bathurst St.; Willowdale (M2R 3V2); (416)-

635–2883. FAX: (416)635–1408. Pres. Charles S. Diamond; Exec. Dir. Steven Ain.

WINDSOR
JEWISH COMMUNITY COUNCIL (1938); 1641 Ouellette Ave. (N8X 1R9); (519)973–1772. FAX: (519)973–1774. Pres. Alan R. Orman; Exec. Dir. Allen Juris.

QUEBEC

MONTREAL
ALLIED JEWISH COMMUNITY SERVICES (1965); 5151 Cote St. Catherine Rd. (H3W 1M6); (514)735–3541. FAX: (514)735–8972. Pres. Maxine Sigman; Exec. Dir. John Fishel.

Jewish Periodicals[1]

UNITED STATES

ARIZONA

ARIZONA JEWISH POST (1946). 3812 East River Rd., Tucson, 85718. (602)529–1500. FAX: (602)577–0734. Sandra R. Heiman. Fortnightly. Jewish Federation of Southern Arizona.

GREATER PHOENIX JEWISH NEWS (1947). PO Box 26590, Phoenix, 85068. (602)870–9470. FAX: (602)870–0426. Flo Eckstein. Weekly.

CALIFORNIA

B'NAI B'RITH MESSENGER (1897). PO Box 35915, Los Angeles, 90035. (213)659–2952. Rabbi Yale Butler. Weekly.

HADSHOT L.A. (1988). 13535 Ventura Blvd., Suite 200, Sherman Oaks, 91423. (818)-783–3090. Meir Doron. Weekly. Hebrew.

HERITAGE-SOUTHWEST JEWISH PRESS (1914). 2130 S. Vermont Ave., Los Angeles, 90007. (213) 737–2122. Dan Brin. Weekly. (Also SAN DIEGO JEWISH HERITAGE [weekly]; ORANGE COUNTY JEWISH HERITAGE [weekly]; CENTRAL CALIFORNIA JEWISH HERITAGE [monthly].) Heritage Group.

JEWISH JOURNAL (1986). 3660 Wilshire Blvd., Suite 204, Los Angeles, 90010. (213)738–7778. Gene Lichtenstein. Weekly.

JEWISH NEWS & ISRAEL TODAY (1973). 11071 Ventura Blvd., Studio City, 91604. (818)786–4000. Phil Blazer. Monthly.

JEWISH SPECTATOR (1935). 4391 Park Milano, Calabasas, 91302. (818)883–5141. FAX: (818)883–5382. Robert Bleiweiss. Quarterly. American Friends of Center for Jewish Living and Values.

JEWISH STAR (1956). 109 Minna St., Suite 323, San Francisco, 94105–3728. (415)-243–9668. FAX: (415)243–0826. Nevon Stuckey. Bimonthly.

NORTHERN CALIFORNIA JEWISH BULLETIN (1946). 88 First St., Suite 300, San Francisco, 94105. (415)957–9340. FAX: (415)-957–0266. Marc S. Klein. Weekly. San Francisco Jewish Community Publications Inc.

SAN DIEGO JEWISH TIMES (1979). 2592 Fletcher Pkwy., El Cajon, 92020. (619)-463–5515. Carol Rosenberg. Biweekly.

TIKKUN (1986). 5100 Leona St., Oakland, 94619. (415)482–0805. FAX: (415)482–3379. Michael Lerner. Bimonthly. Institute for Labor & Mental Health.

WESTERN STATES JEWISH HISTORY (1968). 2429 23rd St., Santa Monica, 90405. (213)-450–2946. Norton B. Stern. Quarterly. Western States Jewish History Association.

COLORADO

INTERMOUNTAIN JEWISH NEWS (1913). 1275 Sherman St., Suite 214, Denver, 80203. (303)861–2234. FAX: (303)832–6942. Miriam H. Goldberg. Weekly.

CONNECTICUT

CONNECTICUT JEWISH LEDGER (1929). 2475 Albany Ave., West Hartford, 06117. (203)233–2148. FAX: (203)232–9756. Berthold Gaster. Weekly.

---

[1] The information in this directory is based on replies to questionnaires circulated by the editors. For organization bulletins, see the directory of Jewish organizations.

DISTRICT OF COLUMBIA

B'NAI B'RITH INTERNATIONAL JEWISH MONTHLY (1886 under the name MENORAH). 1640 Rhode Island Ave., NW, Washington, 20036. (202)857–6645. Jeff Rubin. Ten times a year. B'nai B'rith.

JEWISH VETERAN (1896). 1811 R St., NW, Washington, 20009. (202)265–6280. FAX: (202)234–5662. Albert Schlossberg. Five times a year. Jewish War Veterans of the U.S.A.

MOMENT (1975). 3000 Connecticut Ave., NW, Suite 300, Washington, 20008. (202)-387–8888. FAX: (202)483–3423. Hershel Shanks. Bimonthly. Jewish Educational Ventures, Inc.

NEAR EAST REPORT (1957). 440 First St., NW, Suite 607, Washington, 20001. (202)-639–5300. Mitchell G. Bard. Weekly. Near East Research, Inc.

SECURITY AFFAIRS (1978). 1100 17 St., NW, Washington, 20036. (202)833–0020. FAX: (202)331–7702. Eric Rozenman. Monthly. Jewish Institute for National Security Affairs.

UCSJ QUARTERLY REPORT. 1819 H Street, NW, Suite 230, Washington, 20006. (202)-775–9770. Stacy Burdett. Quarterly. Union of Councils for Soviet Jews.

WASHINGTON JEWISH WEEK. See under MARYLAND.

FLORIDA

BROWARD JEWISH WORLD (1986). 6635 W. Commercial Blvd., Tamarac, 33319. (305)-726–6888. FAX: (305)722–8881. Anne S. Faivus. Weekly. Jewish Media Group, Inc.

JEWISH JOURNAL (1977). 2000 E. Oakland Park Blvd., Ft. Lauderdale, 33306. (305)-563–3311. FAX: (305)429–1207. Robert Sandler. Weekly. South Florida Newspaper Network.

JEWISH PRESS OF PINELLAS COUNTY (Clearwater-St. Petersburg; 1985). 301 Jupiter Ave. S., Clearwater, 34615–6561. (813)441–4500. FAX: (813)461–0700. Karen Wolfson Dawkins. Biweekly. Jewish Press Group of Tampa Bay (FL), Inc.

JEWISH PRESS OF TAMPA (1987). 2808 Horatio St., Tampa, 33609. (813)871–2332. FAX: (813)461–0700. Karen Wolfson Dawkins. Biweekly. Jewish Press Group of Tampa Bay (FL), Inc.

JEWISH WORLD (1982). 2405 Mercer Ave., W. Palm Beach, 33401. (407)833–8331. FAX: (407)659–5428. Anne S. Faivus. Weekly.

MIAMI JEWISH TRIBUNE (1986). 3550 Biscayne Blvd., 3rd fl., Miami, 33137–3845. (305)576–9500. FAX: (305)573–9551. Andrew T. Polin. Weekly. Jewish Media Group, Inc.

SOUTHERN JEWISH WEEKLY (1924). 8351 E. Knotts Landing Dr., Jacksonville, 32244. (904)272–1479. Phillip B. Lyon. Weekly. Southern Independent Operators, Inc.

GEORGIA

ATLANTA JEWISH TIMES (1925) (formerly SOUTHERN ISRAELITE). 1575 Northside Dr., NW, Atlanta, 30318. (404)352–2400. FAX: (404)355–9388. Vida Goldgar. Weekly.

JEWISH CIVIC PRESS (1972). 3330 Peachtree Rd. NE, Suite 500, Atlanta, 30326. (404)-231–2194. Abner L. Tritt. Monthly.

ILLINOIS

CHICAGO JUF NEWS (1972). One S. Franklin St., Rm. 722, Chicago, 60606. (312)-444–2853. FAX: (312)855–2474. Joseph Aaron. Monthly. Jewish United Fund/Jewish Federation of Metropolitan Chicago.

JEWISH COMMUNITY NEWS (1941). 6464 W. Main, Suite 7A, Belleville, 62223. (618)-398–6100. Stanley J. Anderman. Irregularly. Jewish Federation of Southern Illinois.

THE SENTINEL (1911). 175 W. Jackson Blvd., Suite 1927, Chicago, 60604. (312)-663–1101. FAX: (312)663–5646. J. I. Fishbein. Weekly.

INDIANA

ILLIANA NEWS (1975). 2939 Jewett St., Highland, 46322. (219)972–2250. Sharon Blumberg. Ten times a year (not July/August). Jewish Federation, Inc./Northwest Indiana.

INDIANA JEWISH POST AND OPINION (1935). PO Box 449097; 2120 N. Meridian, Indianapolis, 46202. (317)927–7800. FAX: (317)927–7807. Neila Pomerantz. Weekly.

NATIONAL JEWISH POST AND OPINION (1932). 2120 N. Meridian St., Indianapolis, 46202. (317)927-7800. FAX: (317)927-7807. Gabriel Cohen. Weekly.

KANSAS

KANSAS CITY JEWISH CHRONICLE. *See under* MISSOURI.

KENTUCKY

KENTUCKY JEWISH POST AND OPINION (1931). 1551 Bardstown Rd., Louisville, 40205. (502)459-1914. Julie D. Segal. Weekly.

LOUISIANA

COMMUNITY (1989). 924 Valmont St., New Orleans, 70115. (504)895-8784. FAX: (504)895-8785. Michael Blackman. Semiweekly. Jewish Federation of Greater New Orleans.

JEWISH CIVIC PRESS (1965). PO Box 15500, 924 Valmont St., New Orleans, 70115. (504)895-8785. Abner Tritt. Monthly.

MARYLAND

BALTIMORE JEWISH TIMES (1919). 2104 N. Charles St., Baltimore, 21218. (301)752-3504. Gary Rosenblatt. Weekly.

WASHINGTON JEWISH WEEK (1930, as the NATIONAL JEWISH LEDGER). 12300 Twinbrook Pkwy., Suite 250, Rockville, 20852. (301)230-2222. FAX: (301)881-6362. Andrew Silow Carroll. Weekly.

MASSACHUSETTS

AMERICAN JEWISH HISTORY (1893). 2 Thornton Rd., Waltham, 02154. (617)891-8110. FAX: (617)899-9208. Marc Lee Raphael. Quarterly. American Jewish Historical Society.

BOSTON JEWISH TIMES (1945). 169 Norfolk Ave., Boston, 02119. (617)442-9680. Sten Lukin. Fortnightly.

GENESIS 2 (1970). 99 Bishop Allen Dr., Cambridge, 02139. (617)576-1801. Lawrence Bush. Quarterly.

JEWISH ADVOCATE (1902). 1168-70 Commonwealth Ave., Boston, 02134. (617)-277-8988. Dr. Ira Korff. Weekly.

JEWISH REPORTER (1970). 76 Salem End Rd., Framingham, 01701. (508)879-3300. FAX: (508)879-5856. Marcia T. Rivin. Monthly. Combined Jewish Philanthropies of Greater Boston.

JEWISH WEEKLY NEWS (1945). PO Box 1569, Springfield, 01101. (413)739-4771. Leslie B. Kahn. Weekly.

JOURNAL OF THE NORTH SHORE JEWISH COMMUNITY (1977). 324 B Essex St., Swampscott, 01907. (617)581-7110. FAX: (617)581-7630. Barbara Wolf. Biweekly (one issue in July). Jewish Federation of the North Shore.

MICHIGAN

DETROIT JEWISH NEWS (1942). 27676 Franklin Rd., Southfield, 48034. (313)354-6060. FAX: (313)354-6069. Gary Rosenblatt. Weekly.

HUMANISTIC JUDAISM (1968). 28611 W. Twelve Mile Rd., Farmington Hills, 48334. (313)478-7610. FAX: (313)647-8025. M. Bonnie Cousens, Ruth D. Feldman. Quarterly. Society for Humanistic Judaism.

MINNESOTA

AMERICAN JEWISH WORLD (1912). 4509 Minnetonka Blvd., Minneapolis, 55416. (612)920-7000. FAX: (612)920-6205. Marshall Hoffman. Weekly.

MISSOURI

KANSAS CITY JEWISH CHRONICLE (1920). 7373 W. 107 St., Suite 250, Overland Park, KS 66209. (913)648-4620. FAX: (913)-381-9889. Ruth Baum Bigus. Weekly. Sun Publications.

MISSOURI JEWISH POST (1948). 9531 Lackland, Suite 207, St. Louis, 63114. (314)-423-3088. Kathie Sutin. Weekly.

ST. LOUIS JEWISH LIGHT (1947). 12 Millstone Campus Dr., St. Louis, 63146. (314)-432-3353. FAX: (314)432-0515. Robert A. Cohn. Weekly. Jewish Federation of St. Louis.

NEBRASKA

JEWISH PRESS (1920). 333 S. 132 St., Omaha, 68154. (402)334-8200. FAX: (402)333-5497. Morris Maline. Weekly. Jewish Federation of Omaha.

NEVADA

JEWISH REPORTER (1976). 1030 E. Twain Ave., Las Vegas, 89109. (702)732-0556.

Marla Gerecht. Monthly (except July and Aug.). Jewish Federation of Las Vegas.

LAS VEGAS ISRAELITE (1965). PO Box 14096, Las Vegas, 89114. (702)876-1255. Michael Tell. Biweekly.

NEW JERSEY

AVOTAYNU (1985). 1485 Teaneck Rd., Teaneck, 07666. (201)837-2701. FAX: (201)-837-8506. Sallyann Amdur Sack. Quarterly.

JEWISH COMMUNITY VOICE (1941). 2393 W. Marlton Pike, Cherry Hill, 08002. (609)-665-6100. FAX: (609)665-0074. Harriet Kessler. Fortnightly. Jewish Federation of Southern NJ.

JEWISH HORIZON (1981). 1391 Martine Ave., Scotch Plains, 07076. (908)889-9200. FAX: (908)889-9205. Fran Gold. Weekly.

JEWISH RECORD (1939). 1525 S. Main St., Pleasantville, 08232. (609)383-0999. Martin Korik. Weekly.

JEWISH STANDARD (1931). 385 Prospect Ave. Hackensack, 07601. (201)342-1115. FAX: (201)342-5746. Rebecca Kaplan Boroson. Weekly.

JEWISH STAR (1975). 100 Metroplex Dr., Edison, 08817. (201)985-1234. FAX: (201)985-3295. Mindy L. Belfer. Bimonthly. Jewish Federation of Greater Middlesex County.

JOURNAL OF JEWISH COMMUNAL SERVICE (1899). 3084 State Hwy. 27, Suite 9, Kendall Pk., 08824-1657. (908)821-1871. Gail Naron Chalew. Quarterly. Conference of Jewish Communal Service.

METROWEST JEWISH NEWS (1947). 60 Glenwood Ave., E. Orange, 07017. (201)-678-3900. FAX: (201)678-0804. David Frank. Weekly. United Jewish Federation of MetroWest.

NEW YORK

AFN SHVEL (1941). 200 W. 72 St., Suite 40, NYC, 10023. (212)787-6675. Mordkhe Schaechter. Quarterly. Yiddish. League for Yiddish, Inc.

ALGEMEINER JOURNAL (1972). 211 63 St. Brooklyn, 11220. (718)492-6420. FAX: (718)492-6571. Gershon Jacobson. Weekly. Yiddish-English.

AMERICAN JEWISH YEAR BOOK (1899). 165 E. 56 St., NYC, 10022. (212)751-4000. FAX: (212)751-4017. David Singer, Ruth R. Seldin. Annually. American Jewish Committee and Jewish Publication Society.

AMERICAN ZIONIST (1910). 4 E. 34 St., NYC, 10016. (212)481-1500. FAX: (212)-481-1515. Paul Flacks. Quarterly. Zionist Organization of America.

AMIT WOMAN (1925). 817 Broadway, NYC, 10003. (212)477-4720. FAX: (212)353-2312. Micheline Ratzersdorfer. Five times a year. AMIT Women (formerly American Mizrachi Women).

AUFBAU (1934). 2121 Broadway, NYC, 10023. (212)873-7400. Henry Marx. Fortnightly. German. New World Club, Inc.

BITZARON (1939). PO Box 623, Cooper Station, NYC, 10003. (212)293-5977. Hayim Leaf. Bimonthly. Hebrew; English abstracts. Hebrew Literary Foundation and Jewish Culture Foundation of New York University.

BUFFALO JEWISH REVIEW (1918). 15 E. Mohawk St., Buffalo, 14203. (716)854-2192. FAX: (716)854-2198. Harlan C. Abbey. Weekly. Kahaal Nahalot Israel.

CIRCLE (1943). 15 E. 26 St., NYC, 10010-1579. (212)532-4949. FAX: (212)481-4174. Shirley Frank. Quarterly. Jewish Community Centers Association of North America (formerly JWB).

COMMENTARY (1945). 165 E. 56 St., NYC, 10022. (212)751-4000. FAX: (212)751-1174. Norman Podhoretz, Neal Kozodoy. Monthly. American Jewish Committee.

CONGRESS MONTHLY (1933). 15 E. 84 St., NYC, 10028. (212)879-4500. Maier Deshell. Seven times a year. American Jewish Congress.

CONSERVATIVE JUDAISM (1945). 3080 Broadway, NYC, 10027. (212)678-8049. Rabbi Shamai Kanter. Quarterly. Rabbinical Assembly.

CONTEMPORARY JEWRY (1974 under the name JEWISH SOCIOLOGY AND SOCIAL RESEARCH). Center for Jewish Studies, CUNY Graduate School and University Center, 33 W. 42 St., NYC, 10036. (212)-790-4404. Paul Ritterband. Semiannually.

Association for the Social Scientific Study of Jewry.

ECONOMIC HORIZONS (1953). 350 Fifth Ave., Suite 1919, NYC, 10118. (212)971-0310. Ronny Bassan. Annually. American-Israel Chamber of Commerce and Industry, Inc.

FORVERTS (YIDDISH FORWARD; 1897). 45 E. 33 St., NYC, 10016. (212)889-8200. FAX: (212)684-3949. Mordechai Strigler. Weekly. Yiddish-English. Forward Association, Inc.

FORWARD (1897). 45 E. 33 St., NYC 10016. (212)889-8200. FAX: (212)447-6406. Seth Lipsky. Weekly. Forward Publishing Company, Inc.

HADAROM (1957). 275 Seventh Ave., NYC, 10001. (212)807-7888. Rabbi Gedalia Dov Schwartz. Annually. Hebrew. Rabbinical Council of America.

HADASSAH MAGAZINE (1914). 50 W. 58 St., NYC, 10019. (212)303-8014. FAX: (212)-303-8282. Alan M. Tigay. Monthly (except for combined issues of June-July and Aug.-Sept.). Hadassah, the Women's Zionist Organization of America.

HADOAR (1921). 1841 Broadway, Rm. 510, NYC, 10023. (212)581-5151. Shlomo Shamir, Yael Feldman. Weekly. Hebrew. Hadoar Association, Inc.

HAMACHNE HACHAREIDI (1980). PO Box 216. Brooklyn, 11218. (718)438-1263. FAX: (718)438-1263. Rabbi Yisroel Eichler. Weekly. Khal Machzikei Hadas.

ISRAEL HORIZONS (1952). 27 W. 20 St., Suite 902, NYC, 10011. (212)255-8760. Ralph Seliger. Quarterly. Americans for Progressive Israel.

ISRAEL QUALITY (1976). 350 Fifth Ave., Suite 1919, NYC, 10118. (212)971-0310. Beth Belkin. Quarterly. Government of Israel Trade Center and American-Israel Chamber of Commerce and Industry.

JEWISH ACTION MAGAZINE (1950). 45 W. 36 St., 9th fl., NYC, 10018. (212)244-2011. Heidi Pekarsky. Quarterly. Union of Orthodox Jewish Congregations of America.

JEWISH BOOK ANNUAL (1942). 15 E. 26 St., NYC, 10010. (212)532-4949. Jacob Kabakoff. English-Hebrew-Yiddish. Jewish Book Council.

JEWISH BOOK WORLD (1945). 15 E. 26 St., NYC, 10010. (212)532-4949. William Wollheim. Quarterly. Jewish Book Council.

JEWISH BRAILLE INSTITUTE VOICE (1978). 110 E. 30 St., NYC, 10016. (212)889-2525. FAX: (212)689-3692. Dr. Jacob Freid. Monthly (except May/June, July/Aug.) (audio cassettes). Jewish Braille Institute of America, Inc.

JEWISH BRAILLE REVIEW (1931). 110 E. 30 St., NYC, 10016. (212)889-2525. Dr. Jacob Freid. Monthly, except May/June, July/Aug. English braille. Jewish Braille Institute of America, Inc.

JEWISH CURRENT EVENTS (1959). 430 Keller Ave., Elmont, 11003. Samuel Deutsch. Biweekly.

JEWISH CURRENTS (1946). 22 E. 17 St., Suite 601, NYC, 10003-3272. (212)924-5740. Morris U. Schappes. Monthly (July/Aug. combined). Association for Promotion of Jewish Secularism, Inc.

JEWISH EDUCATION (1929). 426 W. 58 St., NYC, 10019. (212)713-0290. Dr. Alvin I. Schiff. Quarterly. Council for Jewish Education.

JEWISH FRONTIER (1934). 33 East 67 St., NYC, 10021. (212)988-7339. Nahum Guttman. Bimonthly. Labor Zionist Letters, Inc.

JEWISH JOURNAL (1969). 8723 Third Ave., Brooklyn, 11209. (718)238-6600. FAX: (718)238-6657. Harold Singer. Weekly.

JEWISH LEDGER (1924). 2535 Brighton-Henrietta Town Line Rd., Rochester, 14623. (716)427-2434. Barbara Morgenstern. Weekly.

JEWISH MUSIC NOTES (1945). 15 E. 26 St., NYC, 10010. (212)532-4949. Debra Wachsberger, Norman Summers. Bi-annually. Jewish Music Council.

JEWISH OBSERVER (1963). 84 William St., NYC, 10038. (212)797-9000. Rabbi Nisson Wolpin. Monthly (except July and Aug.). Agudath Israel of America.

JEWISH OBSERVER (1978). PO Box 510, DeWitt, 13214. (315)445-0161. FAX: (315)-445-1559. Mollie Leitzes Collins. Biweekly. Syracuse Jewish Federation, Inc.

JEWISH POST AND RENAISSANCE (1977). 57 E. 11 St., NYC, 10003. (212)420-0042. Charles Roth. Bimonthly.

JEWISH PRESS (1950). 338 Third Ave., Brooklyn, 11215. (718)330-1100. FAX: (718)935-1215. Rabbi Sholom Klass. Weekly.

JEWISH SOCIAL STUDIES (1939). 2112 Broadway, Rm. 206, NYC, 10023. (212)-724-5336. Tobey B. Gitelle. Quarterly. Conference on Jewish Social Studies, Inc.

JEWISH TELEGRAPHIC AGENCY COMMUNITY NEWS REPORTER (1962). 330 Seventh Ave., 11th fl., NYC, 10001-5010. (212)643-1890. FAX: (212)643-8498. Mark Joffe, Elli Wohlgelernter, Mark A. Seal. Weekly.

JEWISH TELEGRAPHIC AGENCY DAILY NEWS BULLETIN (1917). 330 Seventh Ave., 11th fl., NYC, 10001-5010. (212)-643-1890. FAX: (212)643-8498. Mark Joffe, Elli Wohlgelernter, Mark A. Seal. Daily.

JEWISH TELEGRAPHIC AGENCY WEEKLY NEWS DIGEST (1933). 330 Seventh Ave., 11th fl., NYC, 10001-5010. (212)643-1890. FAX: (212)643-8498. Mark Joffe, Elli Wohlgelernter, Mark A. Seal. Weekly.

JEWISH WEEK (1876; reorg. 1970). 1457 Broadway, NYC, 10036. (212)921-7822. FAX: (212)921-8420. Philip Ritzenberg. Weekly.

JEWISH WORLD (1965). 1104 Central Ave., Albany, 12205. (518)459-8455. Laurie J. Clevenson. Weekly.

JOURNAL OF REFORM JUDAISM (1953). 192 Lexington Ave., NYC, 10016. (212)684-4990. FAX: (212)689-1649. Lawrence A. Englander. Quarterly. Central Conference of American Rabbis.

JUDAISM (1952). 15 E. 84 St., NYC, 10028. (212)879-4500. FAX: (212)249-3672. Dr. Ruth B. Waxman. Quarterly. American Jewish Congress.

KIBBUTZ JOURNAL (1984). 27 W. 20 St., 9th fl., NYC, 10011. (212)255-1338. FAX: (212)929-3459. Shimon Schwartz. Annually. English-Hebrew. Kibbutz Aliya Desk.

KOL HAT'NUA (VOICE OF THE MOVEMENT) (1975). 50 W. 58 St., NYC, 10019. (212)-303-8256. Brian Levine. Four times a year. Young Judaea-Hashachar.

KOSHER DIRECTORY AND CALORIE GUIDE (1925). 45 W. 36 St., NYC, 10018. (212)-563-4000. FAX: (212)564-9058. Tziporah Spear. Every two years. Union of Orthodox Jewish Congregations of America.

KOSHER DIRECTORY, PASSOVER EDITION (1923). 45 W. 36 St., NYC, 10018. (212)-563-4000. FAX: (212)564-9058. Tziporah Spear. Annually. Union of Orthodox Jewish Congregations of America.

KULTUR UN LEBN—CULTURE AND LIFE (1967). 45 E. 33 St., NYC, 10016. (212)-889-6800. Joseph Mlotek. Quarterly. Yiddish. Workmen's Circle.

LAMISHPAHA. (1963). 47 W. 34 St., Rm. 609, NYC, 10001. (212)629-9443. Hanita Brand. Monthly (except July and Aug.). Hebrew. Histadruth Ivrith of America.

LIKUTIM (1981). 110 E. 30 St., NYC, 10016. (212)889-2525. Joanne Jahr. Two to four times a year (audio cassettes). Hebrew. Jewish Braille Institute of America, Inc.

LILITH—THE JEWISH WOMEN'S MAGAZINE (1976). 250 W. 57 St., #2432, NYC, 10107. (212)757-0818. Susan Weidman Schneider. Quarterly.

LONG ISLAND JEWISH WORLD (1971). 115 Middle Neck Rd., Great Neck, 11021. (516)829-4000. FAX: (516)829-4776. Jerome W. Lippman. Weekly.

MARTYRDOM AND RESISTANCE (1974). 48 W. 37 St., 9th fl., NYC, 10018-4708. (212)-564-1865. Eli Zborowski. Bimonthly. International Society for Yad Vashem.

MELTON JOURNAL (1982). 3080 Broadway, NYC, 10027. (212)678-8031. Eduardo Rauch, Barry W. Holtz. Biannually. Melton Research Center for Jewish Education.

MIDSTREAM (1954). 110 E. 59 St., NYC, 10022. (212)752-0600. FAX: (212)826-8959. Joel Carmichael. Monthly. Theodor Herzl Foundation, Inc.

MODERN JEWISH STUDIES ANNUAL (1977). Queens College, Kiely 802, 65–30 Kissena Blvd., Flushing, 11367. (718)520-7067. Joseph C. Landis. Annually. American Association of Professors of Yiddish.

NA'AMAT WOMAN (1926). 200 Madison Ave., Suite 2120, NYC, 10016. (212)725-8010. Judith A. Sokoloff. Five times a year.

English-Yiddish-Hebrew. NA'AMAT USA, the Women's Labor Zionist Organization of America.

OLOMEINU—OUR WORLD (1945). 6101 16th Ave., Brooklyn, NY 11204. (718)259-1223. FAX: (718)259-1795. Rabbi Yaakov Fruchter, Rabbi Nosson Scherman. Monthly. English-Hebrew. Torah Umesorah-National Society for Hebrew Day Schools.

PEDAGOGIC REPORTER (1949). JESNA, 730 Broadway, NYC, 10003. (212)529-2000. FAX: (212)529-2009. Rabbi Arthur Vernon. Quarterly. English-Hebrew. Jewish Education Service of North America, Inc.

PROCEEDINGS OF THE AMERICAN ACADEMY FOR JEWISH RESEARCH (1920). 3080 Broadway, NYC, 10027. (212)678-8864. FAX: (212)678-8947. Dr. Nahum Sarna. Annually. English-Hebrew-French-Arabic-Persian-Greek. American Academy for Jewish Research.

RCA RECORD (1953). 275 Seventh Ave. NYC, 10001. (212)807-7888. FAX: (212)-727-8452. Rabbi Basil Herring. Quarterly. Rabbinical Council of America.

REFORM JUDAISM (1972; formerly DIMENSIONS IN AMERICAN JUDAISM). 838 Fifth Ave., NYC, 10021. (212)249-0100. Aron Hirt-Manheimer. Quarterly. Union of American Hebrew Congregations.

REPORTER (1972). 500 Clubhouse Rd., Binghamton, 13903. (607)724-2360. FAX: (607)724-2311. Marc S. Goldberg. Weekly. Jewish Federation of Broome County.

RESPONSE (1967). 27 W. 20 St., 9th fl., NYC, 10011. (212)675-1168. Bennett Graff. Quarterly.

SHEVILEY HA-HINNUKH (1939). 426 W. 58 St., NYC, 10019. (212)713-0290. Zvulun Ravid. Quarterly. Hebrew. Council for Jewish Education.

SH'MA (1970). Box 567, 23 Murray Ave., Port Washington, 11050. (516)944-9791. FAX: (516)767-9315. Eugene B. Borowitz. Biweekly (except June, July, Aug.).

SHMUESSEN MIT KINDER UN YUGENT (1942). 770 Eastern Pkwy., Brooklyn, 11213. (718)493-9250. Nissan Mindel. Monthly. Yiddish. Merkos L'Inyonei Chinuch, Inc.

SYNAGOGUE LIGHT (1933). 47 Beekman St., NYC, 10038. (212)227-7800. Rabbi Meyer Hager. Semiannually. Union of Chassidic Rabbis.

TALKS AND TALES (1942). 770 Eastern Pkwy., Brooklyn, 11213. (718)774-4000 or 6000. Nissan Mindel. Monthly (also Hebrew, French, and Spanish editions). Merkos L'Inyonei Chinuch, Inc.

TRADITION (1958). 275 Seventh Ave., NYC, 10001. (212)807-7888. Rabbi Emanuel Feldman. Quarterly. Rabbinical Council of America.

TRENDS (1982). JESNA, 730 Broadway, NYC, 10003. (212)529-2000. Leora W. Isaacs. Semiannually. Jewish Education Service of North America, Inc.

UNITED SYNAGOGUE REVIEW (1943). 155 Fifth Ave., NYC, 10010. (212)533-7800. Lois Goldrich. Biannually. United Synagogue of America.

UNSER TSAIT (1941). 25 E. 21 St., 3rd fl., NYC, 10010. (212)475-0055. Editorial committee. Monthly. Yiddish. Jewish Labor Bund.

VOICE OF THE DUTCHESS JEWISH COMMUNITY (1990). 110 S. Grand Ave., Poughkeepsie, 12603. (914)471-9811. Dena Hirsh. Monthly. Jewish Federation of Dutchess County.

WOMEN'S AMERICAN ORT REPORTER (1966). 315 Park Ave. S., NYC, 10010. (212)505-7700. FAX: (212)674-3057. Eve M. Jacobson. Quarterly. Women's American ORT, Inc.

WOMEN'S LEAGUE OUTLOOK (1930). 48 E. 74 St., NYC, 10021. (212)628-1600. FAX: (212)772-3507. Lynne Heller. Quarterly. Women's League for Conservative Judaism.

WORKMEN'S CIRCLE CALL (1933). 453 FDR Dr., NYC, 10002. (212)889-6800. FAX: (212)532-7518. Walter L. Kirschenbaum. Quarterly. Workmen's Circle.

YEARBOOK OF THE CENTRAL CONFERENCE OF AMERICAN RABBIS (1890). 192 Lexington Ave., NYC, 10016. (212)684-4990. FAX: (212)689-1649. Rabbi Elliot L. Stevens. Annually. Central Conference of American Rabbis.

YIDDISH (1973). Queens College, Kiely 802, 65-30 Kissena Blvd., Flushing, 11367.

(718)520–7067. Joseph C. Landis. Quarterly. Queens College Press.

DI YIDDISHE HEIM (1958). 770 Eastern Pkwy., Brooklyn, 11213. (718)493–9250. Rachel Altein. Quarterly. English-Yiddish. Neshei Ub'nos Chabad.

YIDDISHE KULTUR (1938). 1133 Broadway, Rm. 1023, NYC, 10010. (212)691–0708. Itche Goldberg. Bimonthly. Yiddish. Yiddisher Kultur Farband, Inc.—YKUF.

YIDDISHE SHPRAKH (1941). 1048 Fifth Ave., NYC, 10028. (212)231–7905. Dr. Mordkhe Schaechter. Irregularly. Yiddish. Yivo Institute for Jewish Research, Inc.

DOS YIDDISHE VORT (1953). 84 William St., NYC, 10038. (212)797–9000. Joseph Friedenson. Monthly. Yiddish. Agudath Israel of America.

YIDDISHER KEMFER (1900). 275 Seventh Ave., NYC, 10001. (212)675–7808. Mordechai Strigler. Weekly. Yiddish. Labor Zionist Alliance.

DER YIDDISHER VEG (1981). 1274 49 St., Suite 1974, Brooklyn, 11219. (718)435–9474. FAX: (718)438–1263. Meir Dov Grosz. Weekly. Yiddish. Archives of Chasidai Belz.

YIVO ANNUAL (1946). 1048 Fifth Ave., NYC, 10028. (212)535–6700. Deborah Dash Moore. Annually. Yivo Institute for Jewish Research, Inc.

YIVO BLETER (1931). 1048 Fifth Ave., NYC, 10028. (212)535–6700. David E. Fishman. Irregularly. Yiddish. Yivo Institute for Jewish Research, Inc.

YOUNG ISRAEL VIEWPOINT (1952). 3 W. 16 St., NYC, 10011. (212)929–1525. Peter L. Nuchims. Six times a year. National Council of Young Israel.

YOUNG JUDAEAN (1910). 50 W. 58 St., NYC, 10019. (212)303–8271. Joel Grishaver. 4 times a year between Sept. and June. Hadassah Zionist Youth Commission.

YUGNTRUF (1964). 200 W. 72 St., Suite 40, NYC 10023. Paul Glasser. Quarterly. Yiddish. Yugntruf Youth for Yiddish.

ZUKUNFT (THE FUTURE; 1892). 25 E. 21 St., NYC, 10010. (212)505–8040. Yonia Fain. Bimonthly. Yiddish. Congress for Jewish Culture.

NORTH CAROLINA

AMERICAN JEWISH TIMES OUTLOOK (1934; reorg. 1950). PO Box 33218, Charlotte, 28233. (704)372–3296. Ruth Goldberg. Monthly. The Blumenthal Foundation.

OHIO

THE AMERICAN ISRAELITE (1854). 906 Main St., Rm. 508, Cincinnati, 45202. (513)621–3145. FAX: (513)621–3744. Phyllis R. Singer. Weekly.

AMERICAN JEWISH ARCHIVES (1948). 3101 Clifton Ave., Cincinnati, 45220. (513)221–1875. Jacob R. Marcus, Abraham J. Peck. Semiannually. American Jewish Archives of Hebrew Union College–Jewish Institute of Religion.

CLEVELAND JEWISH NEWS (1964). 3645 Warrensville Center Rd., Cleveland, 44122. (216)991–8300. FAX: (216)991–9556. Cynthia Dettelbach. Weekly. Cleveland Jewish Publication Co.

DAYTON JEWISH CHRONICLE (1961). 118 Salem Ave., Dayton, 45406. (513)222–0783. Leslie Cohen Zukowsky. Weekly.

INDEX TO JEWISH PERIODICALS (1963). PO Box 18570, Cleveland Hts., 44118. (216)-321–7296. Miriam Leikind. Semiannually.

OHIO JEWISH CHRONICLE (1922). 2862 Johnstown Rd., Columbus, 43219. (614)-337–2055. FAX: (614)337–2059. Judith Franklin. Weekly.

STARK JEWISH NEWS (1920). 2631 Harvard Ave. NW, Canton, 44709. (216)452–6444. FAX: (216)452–4487. Adele Gelb. Monthly. Canton Jewish Community Federation.

STUDIES IN BIBLIOGRAPHY AND BOOKLORE (1953). 3101 Clifton Ave., Cincinnati, 45220. (513)221–1875. Herbert C. Zafren. Irregularly. English-Hebrew-German. Library of Hebrew Union College–Jewish Institute of Religion.

TOLEDO JEWISH NEWS (1987). 6505 Sylvania Ave., Sylvania, 43560. (419)885–4461. FAX: (419)885-3207. Fred Flox. Monthly. Jewish Federation of Greater Toledo.

OKLAHOMA

SOUTHWEST JEWISH CHRONICLE (1929). PO Box 54975, Oklahoma City, 73114.

(405)789–1723. Sandy McQuay. Quarterly.

TULSA JEWISH REVIEW (1930). 2021 E. 71 St., Tulsa, 74136. (918)495–1100. Ed Ulrich. Monthly. Jewish Federation of Tulsa.

PENNSYLVANIA

JEWISH CHRONICLE OF PITTSBURGH (1962). 5600 Baum Blvd., Pittsburgh, 15206. (412)687–1000. FAX: (412)687–5119. Joel Roteman. Weekly. Pittsburgh Jewish Publication and Education Foundation.

JEWISH EXPONENT (1887). 226 S. 16 St., Philadelphia, 19102. (215)893–5740. Albert Erlick. Weekly. Jewish Federation of Greater Philadelphia.

JEWISH QUARTERLY REVIEW (1910). 420 Walnut St., Philadelphia, 19106. (215)-238–1290. FAX: (215)238–1540. Leon Nemoy, David M. Goldenberg, Vera B. Moreen. Quarterly. Annenberg Research Institute.

JEWISH TIMES OF THE GREATER NORTHEAST (1925). 103A Tomlinson Rd., Huntingdon Valley, 19006. (215)938–1177. FAX: (215)938–0692. Matthew Schuman. Weekly. Federation of Jewish Agencies of Greater Philadelphia.

NEW MENORAH (1978). 7318 Germantown Ave., Philadelphia, 19119–1793. (215)-242–4074. Arthur Waskow, Rabbi Shana Margolin. Quarterly. P'nai Or Religious Fellowship.

RECONSTRUCTIONIST (1934). Church Rd. & Greenwood Ave., Wyncote, 19095. Editor: Box 1336, Roslyn Heights, NY 11577. (516)621–2067. Rabbi Joy Levitt. Quarterly. Federation of Reconstructionist Congregations and Havurot.

RHODE ISLAND

RHODE ISLAND JEWISH HISTORICAL NOTES (1954). 130 Sessions St., Providence, 02906. (401)331–1360. Judith Weiss Cohen. Annually. Rhode Island Jewish Historical Association.

TENNESSEE

THE HEBREW WATCHMAN (1925). 4646 Poplar Ave., Suite 232, Memphis, 38117. (901)763–2215. Herman I. Goldberger. Weekly.

THE OBSERVER (1934). 801 Percy Warner Blvd., Nashville, 37205. (615)356–3242. Judith A. Saks. Biweekly (except July). Jewish Federation of Nashville.

TEXAS

JEWISH HERALD-VOICE (1908). PO Box 153, Houston, 77001–0153. (713)630–0391. FAX: (713)630–0404. Jeanne Samuels. Weekly.

JEWISH JOURNAL OF SAN ANTONIO (1973). 8434 Ahern, San Antonio, 78216. (512)-341–8234. FAX: (512)341–2842. Marion H. Bernstein. Monthly (11 issues). Jewish Federation of San Antonio.

TEXAS JEWISH POST (1947). 3120 S. Expressway, Fort Worth, 76110. (817)927–2831. FAX: (817)429–0840. 11333 N. Central Expressway, Dallas, 75243. (214)692–7283. FAX: (214)692–7285. Jimmy Wisch. Weekly.

VIRGINIA

RENEWAL MAGAZINE (1984). 7300 Newport Ave., Norfolk, 23505. (804)489–8040. FAX: (804)489–8230. Reba Karp. Quarterly. United Jewish Federation of Tidewater.

UJF VIRGINIA NEWS (1959). 7300 Newport Ave., Norfolk, 23505. (804)489–8040. FAX: (804)489–8230. Reba Karp. 21 issues yearly. United Jewish Federation of Tidewater.

WASHINGTON

JEWISH TRANSCRIPT (1924). 2031 Third Ave., Suite 200, Seattle, 98121. (206)441–4553. FAX: (206)443–0303. Craig Degginger. Bimonthly. Jewish Federation of Greater Seattle.

WISCONSIN

WISCONSIN JEWISH CHRONICLE (1921). 1360 N. Prospect Ave., Milwaukee, 53202. (414)271–2992. FAX: (414)271–0487. Andrew Muchin. Weekly. Milwaukee Jewish Federation.

INDEXES

INDEX TO JEWISH PERIODICALS (1963). PO Box 18570, Cleveland Hts., 44118. (216)321-7296. Miriam Leikind. Semiannually.

NEWS SYNDICATES

JEWISH TELEGRAPHIC AGENCY, INC. (1917). 330 Seventh Ave., 11th fl., NYC., 10001-5010. (212)643-1890. FAX: (212)-643-8498. Mark Joffe, Elli Wohlgelernter, Mark A. Seal. Daily.

CANADA

CANADIAN JEWISH HERALD (1977). 17 Anselme Lavigne Blvd., Dollard des Ormeaux, PQ H9A 1N3. (514)684-7667. Dan Nimrod. FAX: (514)737-7636. Irregularly. Dawn Publishing Co., Ltd.

CANADIAN JEWISH NEWS (1971). 10 Gateway Blvd., #420, Don Mills, ONT M3C 3A1. (416)422-2331. Patricia Rucker. Weekly.

CANADIAN JEWISH OUTLOOK (1963). 6184 Ash St., #3, Vancouver, BC V5Z 3G9. (604)324-5101. Henry M. Rosenthal. Monthly. Canadian Jewish Outlook Society.

CANADIAN ZIONIST (1934). 5250 Decarie Blvd., Suite 550, Montreal, PQ H3X 2H9. (514)486-9526. FAX: (514)483-6392. Five times a year. English-Hebrew. Canadian Zionist Federation.

DIALOGUE (1988). 1590 Dr. Penfield Ave., Montreal, PQ H3G 1C5. (514)931-7531. FAX: (514)931-3281. Rebecca Rosenberg. Semiannually. French-English. Canadian Jewish Congress, Quebec Region.

JEWISH EAGLE (1907). 4180 De Courtrai, Rm. 218, Montreal, PQ H3S 1C3. (514)-735-6577. B. Hirshtal. Weekly. Yiddish-Hebrew-French.

JEWISH POST & NEWS (1987). 117 Hutchings St., Winnipeg, MAN R2X 2V4. (204)694-3332. Matt Bellan. Weekly.

THE JEWISH STANDARD (1930). 77 Mowat Ave., Suite 016, Toronto, ONT M6K 3E3. (416)537-2696. Julius Hayman. Fortnightly.

JEWISH WESTERN BULLETIN (1930). 3268 Heather St., Vancouver, BC V5Z 3K5. (604)879-6575. FAX: (604)879-6573. Samuel Kaplan. Weekly.

JOURNAL OF PSYCHOLOGY AND JUDAISM (1976). 1747 Featherston Dr., Ottawa, ONT K1H 6P4. (613)731-9119. Reuven P. Bulka. Quarterly. Center for the Study of Psychology and Judaism.

OTTAWA JEWISH BULLETIN & REVIEW (1954). 151 Chapel St., Ottawa, ONT K1N 7Y2. (613)232-7306. Cynthia Engel. Biweekly. Jewish Community Council of Ottawa.

UNDZER VEG (1932). 272 Codsell Ave., Downsview, ONT M3H 3X2. (416)636-4024. Joseph Kage. Irregularly. Yiddish-English. Achdut HaAvoda-Poale Zion of Canada.

WINDSOR JEWISH COMMUNITY BULLETIN (1942). 1641 Ouellette Ave., Windsor, ONT N9E 1T9. (519)973-1772. FAX: (519)973-1774. Dr. Allen Juris. Quarterly. Windsor Jewish Community Council.

Salo Wittmayer Baron (1895-1989)

THE DEATH OF SALO WITTMAYER BARON, historian of the Jewish people, on November 24, 1989, at the age of 94, ended a career almost without parallel in its length and accomplishment. Few can remember a time when he was not an outstanding figure in the field of Jewish history, beginning with his first scholarly article in 1917, his first book in 1920, and until his last in 1986. The largest of his many works, the revised and expanded edition of *A Social and Religious History of the Jews,* unfinished in 18 volumes (New York and Philadelphia, 1952–1984), is an indispensable guide which, together with his other books and articles, made his name omnipresent in bibliographies and practically synonymous with Jewish history in the English language. These prodigious achievements gained Baron worldwide recognition including awards, medals, and honorary degrees.

Childhood and Education

Salo (Shalom) Baron was born in Tarnow, western Galicia, within the Hapsburg Empire, on May 26, 1895. His father was a private banker and investor who stood at the head of the local Jewish community, which numbered 12,000 persons. The son referred frequently in lectures and writing to the trials and responsibilities of communal leadership. As an adolescent he once took charge of the bank while his father was gone for a few weeks, and on a similar occasion he became responsible for the maternity aid (*kimpetorin*) society, also headed by his parents. Baron was in fact one of very few Jewish historians whose social origins did not lie in the rabbinate and communal employment nor in the lower middle class, but in the bourgeois leadership of the Jewish community.

Baron showed ability from an early age, even to being a chess prodigy at age three. He also showed decisiveness, quitting the game when still a young child, out of the conviction that chess was consuming time which had to be better spent. He had a thorough private Jewish education and also took examinations regularly as an external gymnasium student. He studied for a year at the University of Krakow and then left Tarnow for Vienna in 1912, to attend its university and rabbinical school. Baron already knew Bible, Talmud, and rabbinic literature thoroughly and was sufficiently at home in modern Hebrew to contribute to the Hebrew press. He had practically memorized Heinrich Graetz's great history. Besides his native Polish and his acquired Hebrew, he had mastered Latin, Greek, German, and probably French. Italian, English, and other tongues came somewhat later. In other words, he was well advanced toward the enormous erudition which became one of his trademarks.

At the University of Vienna the young Baron earned three doctorates, in history, jurisprudence, and political science. He also received rabbinic ordination at the Jewish Theological Seminary in Vienna but never practiced as a rabbi. While in Vienna, during the last years of its glory as the Hapsburg capital, the student from Galicia also enjoyed the city's musical life. He attended some of Freud's lectures and would see him passing in the streets of the neighborhood where they both lived.

Early Career

We do not know when Baron decided on his career as a Jewish historian. The field was unrecognized at universities in Vienna and elsewhere, while in rabbinical seminaries it consisted largely of the bio-bibliographic study of the great Jewish cultural figures. Baron, as it appears, had no particular guide or teacher in the field, although Prof. Avigdor Aptowitzer, scholar of rabbinics at the seminary, apparently came the closest. What is clear is that from the earliest stage of his career, Baron conceived of Jewish history differently from what was then accepted. This had been mainly to study the persecutions endured by Jews and the lives and writings of Jewish cultural heroes. Jewish history, as seen by him, constituted part of general history, and what happened to the Jewish people had to be understood in the light of historical developments among the peoples in whose midst the Jews lived. The young Baron also acquired in Vienna his lifelong conviction of the importance of utilizing sociology, economics, demography, and other social sciences in studying Jewish history. Thus, one of his first studies dealt with "The Israelitic Population Under the Kings," which he wrote in Hebrew during the 1920s. It drew extensively on sociology and demography.

For several years Baron taught at the Hebrew Teachers Seminary in Vienna, founded by the brilliant and charismatic, short-lived chief rabbi Zvi Peretz Chajes (1876–1926), with whom Baron became personally close. During the same time he also worked as an Austrian Jewish jurist for a League of Nations Union commission which dealt with the enforcement of minority-rights treaties.

Baron came to the United States in 1926 as professor of history and librarian at the Jewish Institute of Religion in New York, which had been founded a year earlier by Rabbi Stephen S. Wise as a nondenominational rabbinical seminary. Shortly thereafter, the young professor was invited to occupy the chair in Jewish history once held by Graetz at the Breslau Rabbinical Seminary. Feeling committed to America, Baron declined; there was no later reason to regret this decision.

During these early years of his career, the young Baron showed broad learning and originality in a series of notable works. His first work, in German, on "The Jewish Question at the Congress of Vienna" (*Die Judenfrage auf dem Wiener Kongress*), was an early consideration of the Jewish situation in modern international affairs. In striking essays that appeared in the Jewish literary magazine *Menorah Journal,* Baron reconsidered some fundamentals of Jewish status before and after emancipation, arguing that their status before emancipation was superior to that of the majority of the neighboring population, that by the standards of the premodern centuries, the Jews enjoyed comparative peace and security, except for sporadic, notorious episodes of physical attack. Baron's views, which caused surprise in many quarters, stood in contradiction to the apologetic conception of endless Jewish suffering, or, in Baron's phrase that became famous, against "the lachrymose conception of Jewish history." Moreover, Baron found the roots of Jewish emancipation not in ideologies nor in a change of heart toward the Jews, but instead in the logic of the 18th- and 19th-century revolutions. When legal privilege and autonomous corporate groups were abolished in favor of equal rights, they had to apply to the Jews as well.

Another article, "Nationalism and Intolerance," also revised accepted views, now concerning the connection between various types of states and their degrees of tolerance toward minorities, including Jews. Some years later, in "Modern Capitalism and Jewish Fate," Baron discussed the impact of capitalism and other economic systems on the status of the Jews.

These early essays have aged somewhat. Still, they remain stimulating examples of a historian coming to grips with commanding historical realities such as capitalism, emancipation, nationalism, and ghetto, subjecting each to penetrating analysis. The ideas first expressed in essays later appear conspicuously in Baron's larger writings.

The Columbia Years

Baron's great step forward came in 1930, when he was appointed by Columbia University to the newly endowed chair in Jewish History, Literature, and Institutions—the latter term was used for "Religion." It was the first such appointment at an American university, and the beginnings were slow. There was some question about which academic department the new professor would be affiliated with, since the existence of Jewish history as a genuine field was gravely questioned. Academic habit and convenience suggested that the small department of Semitic languages, where Hebrew was taught and whose chairman, Richard J.H. Gottheil, was a Jew and a Zionist, was the suitable place; as a historian, however, Baron wanted to be in the department of history, of which he would, incidentally, become the first tenured Jewish member. The intervention of the powerful president of Columbia, Nicholas Murray Butler, was required to place Baron in that department. Students at first were few; the late professor Sidney I. Pomerantz, who long taught American history at the City College of New York, once mentioned to me, "I thought it was my duty as a Jew" to enroll in a Jewish history course as a Columbia graduate student. Perhaps a few others thought likewise. There were students who enrolled not only for the sake of advancing their education but also to clarify their identity as Jews; many non-Jews also enrolled to learn about Jews and Judaism, sometimes in preparation for ministerial careers.

With the publication of *A Social and Religious History of the Jews* (3 volumes, New York, 1937) in its first edition, and *The Jewish Community: Its History and*

Structure to the American Revolution (3 volumes, Philadelphia, 1942), Baron became famous, at least in the sense of being recognized as a mentor to everyone seriously interested in Jewish history. In time he was recognized as one of the most illustrious, if not the most illustrious, members of a department that contained numerous renowned historians. His influence in department and university affairs increased. In the words of a colleague, the celebrated art historian Meyer Schapiro, "By his teaching and his books he has made the study of Jewish history a recognized part of that comprehensive learning which is an essential goal of the University."

Baron was an exceptionally effective lecturer to both graduate and undergraduate students at Columbia University. Characteristically, he arrived a few minutes late, after walking slowly and thoughtfully across the campus. He seated himself at the lecturer's desk, from which he did not move, and began to speak in a very soft voice which gradually rose to substantial volume. Lectures were carefully and logically organized and were delivered without any notes, no matter how technical the subject. Baron kept a small envelope with him, periodically removing from it index cards which held quotations from sources. He would stop even in midsentence to answer any question in detail, and then return precisely to where he had stopped. When he was a man past 80, already a legendary personage at Columbia, on a few occasions when one of the Jewish historians was unable to meet a class, a notice was posted that Professor Baron would teach the class that day. A full house turned up.

His seminar for M.A. and Ph.D. students was often conducted at his house. Students could select any topic they liked in Jewish history; when one presented his report orally—no written paper was required—first the other students commented and then Baron spoke, moderately and concisely. He was never sharp or belittling in tone. He never provided a virtuoso exhibition of erudition at a student's expense. Students at work on dissertations would submit a chapter at a time, and two or three weeks later there would be a session of criticism and correction and, sometimes, commendation. When there was criticism and correction, one always felt the undertone of support and encouragement. He was quite accessible, either during office hours or by appointment.

The dozens of books on Jewish history that open with expressions of gratitude to Baron on the part of their authors, his former graduate students, attest to his influence. It can fairly be said that Jewish history as a profession in America was created by Baron's teaching.

Baron's fame is above all as a historian, however. At Columbia, during the spring semester of 1931, he offered a series of lectures entitled "Jewish Society and Religion in Their Historical Interrelation," in which he proposed to illustrate a theme of universal significance—the relations between society and religion—from the history of the Jews. Out of ideas expressed in these lectures germinated his *Social and Religious History of the Jews,* published in 1937. It was a fresh, original study, whose 12 large chapters combined concentrated erudition with breadth of scope, in addition to a massive apparatus containing abundant bibliographic references with helpful annotations and excursuses on technical and controversial points. The author opened and concluded the work with his credo as a historian of the Jewish people. He believed that the history of the Jews is shaped by the interplay (a favorite term of his) between Jewish society and the Jewish religion. There can be no adequate history of one without the other. To use terms which he did not use, there cannot be a Jewish history conceived in purely secular terms, nor can there be a history of Judaism without its people. People and religion shaped one another. In his writings, Jewish history is molded in one immense continuity, without abysses and absolute breaks between one age and its successor. The "emancipation" of Jewish religion from a specific geographic location allowed it to develop out of a people's history rather than from a material environment and its imperatives. Thus, Judaism and the Jewish people could survive and prosper in exile from its land.

This work and *The Jewish Community,* which appeared five years later, were followed by a series of long articles on the Jews and the European revolutions of 1848 and a lengthy study of the political interests of the fathers of modern Jewish scholarship, many of whom had emphatic revolutionary sympathies in 1848. Perhaps Baron meant to show that these great pioneers were not aloof and neutral on the great issues of their day, as they and their successors later became.

His Major Work

It was late in the 1940s, at the midpoint of his career, that Baron began to work on a new, enlarged edition of his *Social and Religious History of the Jews.* This project was to set the course of the rest of his life. He planned seven volumes: two on ancient times, two for the Middle Ages, and two on the modern age, with a final volume for bibliography and index. The first two duly appeared in 1952. However, in his introduction to volume 3, which appeared in 1957 together with volumes 4 and 5, he announced that the medieval section, covering the centuries from 500 to 1200, would be expanded to take account of the vast increase of published source material and specialized scholarly studies. These three volumes deal with Jewish political, social, and economic life; volumes 6–8, which appeared in 1958, take up the magnificent cultural accomplishments of this era when the Jewish people were living mainly under Muslim rulers. The period from 1200 to 1650 is covered in the final ten volumes that their author lived to produce. (There were to be three more for the cultural history of "Late Middle Ages and Era of European Expansion," as the series was entitled.) The total of the 18 published volumes is 5,189 pages of text and 2,419 pages of notes.

Hardly any scholar in our time composes works of such immense dimensions. For breadth of conception and elaborateness of treatment one harks back to such 19th-century historians as Ranke, Bancroft, Mommsen, and a very few others who combined daring, erudition, and perhaps most of all, unwavering industry and self-confidence. However, unlike such masters and differently from his two major predecessors as Jewish historians in the grand manner, Graetz and Dubnow, Baron does not provide his readers with a narrative history. Although he does permit himself a few stories, he prefers to discuss the many varied facets of a problem or an issue (often, it must be admitted, less directly than the reader might wish).

His volumes on the ancient period culminate in two superlative closing chapters, "World of the Talmud" and "Talmudic Law and Religion," setting the stage for the medieval centuries. These chapters, and one entitled "Reign of Law" in volume 6, which is no less than a history of Jewish law from the Saboraim to Maimonides, are among the finest chapters in the entire enterprise. No talmudist has yet attempted these fundamental topics—a social history of talmudic times and the analytic, unhomiletic study of the social teachings of talmudic Judaism.

In general, Baron has much to say of social relations and intellectual debits and credits between Jews and Christians and Muslims, but without any tone of triumph or apology. For the realization never leaves that the Jews were only a minority constantly pressured to give up its existence by accepting the dominant religion. The task of leaders was to array and defend their people effectively against the hostile environment and to foster an internal Jewish life free from external sanction or interference. The virtues of Jewish leadership were thus prudence and circumspection and readiness for sacrifice when required, rather than boldness or aggressiveness. From this perspective, apostates and rebels, of whatever sort, posed far greater dangers than came from almost any existing internal abuses. This was particularly so under the confined conditions and tenuous tolerance accorded to medieval Jewry, which Baron portrays in convincing and extensive detail. In contrast with the sympathy which most historians accord to rebels who seemed to be in advance of their time, or were just ground under by the powers that be, Baron prefers the self-sacrificing, conservative leaders who realistically appraised the Jewish situation and could sternly repress messianic fervor and sectarian movements. The historian also gives short shrift to attempts at interpreting Jewish history in Marxian terms of class struggle. The fate of rich and poor Jews was interdependent—indeed all but identical, and this common Jewishness outweighed class divisions within.

An imposing exception to most of what has been said is Spain. Uniquely among medieval Jewish communities under Christendom, Jews held positions near the summit of the political, economic, and cultural life of Castile and Aragon. During the three centuries that terminated with the onset of mass attacks in 1391, the Jewish courtier-financiers, diplomats, physicians, and tax collectors alternately neglected, protected, and exploited their fellow Jews. Their Jewish loyalties became so shaky that when finally compelled to choose between Judaism and their courtly careers and princely style of life, they apostatized en masse. The courtier leaders do not come off too well at Professor Baron's hands. (See volume 10, pp. 217–219).

In Baron's historical outlook, the Jews as a minority under Islam and Christianity were unable to change their condition in any fundamental way. Their condition was subject in fact to one-sided alteration, often by arbitrary and violent means, as the historian shows at length. These conditions are the practical meaning of *galut* (exile). Baron recognizes unchangeable Jewish "givens," and observes how the Jews accepted their subordination, however unhappily. Revolutionary change was an impossibility, and even talk about it held perils. The Jewish genius was that of adaptation and creative effort within the situation imposed from without. Thus, they made the most of the autonomy which they were granted, they made a living often by pioneering endeavors, and they sustained an independent and frequently brilliant cultural life, which influenced both Islam and Christianity. Baron does not accept the periodization of postexilic Jewish history into literary epochs (e.g., "First Rabbinic Period," "The Period of Maimonides"), with its implication that literature was the be-all of Jewish history. Instead, he orients it to the dynamics of general history. Characteristically, most of his volumes draw their titles from general history, such as "Heirs of Rome and Persia," "Renaissance, Reformation, Wars of Religion."

In Baron's periodization, approximately 1200 is the date for the decisive shift of Jewish history from the Muslim Orient to the Christian north and west, and in the much debated issue of when modern Jewish history begins, he chooses the year 1650. This was when Polish Jewry entered its time of troubles, Jews began to settle in the New World and to resettle in western Europe, and the tide of westward migration began. Jews began to be viewed in secular political, rather than theological, terms. The medieval existed alongside the nascent modern, but a far-ranging change in the Jews' historical situation had clearly begun.

It is Baron's vigorous interest in drawing on other disciplines, such as sociology and political theory, which marks him as a historian of our own day. Indeed, his attention to every facet of Jewish life, not only the intellectual, marks him as downright radical when compared with most Jewish historians of the past and even some of the present generation.

One of the first subjects he takes up when entering a new historic epoch or land is its Jewish population. The difficulties of medieval population study—in fact, population study anywhere before 1800—are notorious. The pages on that subject (volume 12, pp. 4–25) show the author at his most powerful. From scattered, recondite, vague sources he undertakes to draw up Jewish population estimates for the various lands of the medieval Christian west. To reach figures with any claim to reflect reality, he weighs the surviving household tax records; determines the proper multiple for household size; reckons with estimates by informed contemporaries, reconciling contradictions between such sources; discounts for wars, plagues (above all the Black Death), and loss by murder or apostasy; gives due weight to general economic and social developments.

Baron deals with a range of subjects of interest not only to Jews. The political theory of Jewish town citizenship, rival claims to lordship over medieval Jews, and the highly practical question of who could and could not impose taxes on them, are important topics not only to Jewish scholars but to medievalists as well. The intensely important matter of Jewish moneylending and its relation to taxation is taken up comprehensively, to my knowledge for the first time. So often denounced, apologized for, and deplored, here the money trade is dispassionately discussed within the framework of general economic history.

Baron's vast learning is reflected in the extensiveness and diversity of his materials. They appear conspicuously in the notes, in which students and scholars for many years now have browsed, often in wonderment. Notes in a work of learning may merely provide references to sources mentioned in the text, or mention and sometimes evaluate additional literature. The Baronial note is the fullest form: starting from references and bibliography it proceeds to an excursus on related matters including technical problems of historical sources and related or tangential issues. While comparatively few unpublished manuscripts are cited, the notes are unbelievably rich in printed sources and secondary works. The latter, far from being confined to Jewish journals, are drawn from the endless repertoire of learned journals over the last century and longer, in almost all the ancient and modern languages of the Western world.

Altogether, Baron's *History* is one of the most immense historical projects ever undertaken by one man alone. His wife provided his only research assistance, as he declared with a touch of indignation, in denying stories that he employed a research staff (see the preface to volume 13).

Alongside his unparalleled production of books (and there were still others), Baron published numerous articles in many fields. They include studies on Jewish historiography and historians, some of the medieval spiritual masters, the Jewish question in modern international relations, American Jewish history, the population of biblical Eretz Israel, and the impact of anti-Semitism and nationalism on Jewish history. The list could be much longer.

Communal Activity

As if all this were not enough, Salo W. Baron was an active figure in numerous organizations, devoting to them not only his intellectual capacities but also his administrative skill and considerable business acumen. In 1938 he and the philosopher Morris Raphael Cohen, actively encouraged by Albert Einstein, founded the Conference on Jewish Relations (after 1955, the Conference on Jewish Social Studies) as a response to the menacing trends of the 1930s. It sought to promote by scholarly studies "a better understanding of the position of the Jews in the modern world." The conference's principal activity became the publication, since 1939, of *Jewish Social Studies,* the scholarly journal of which Baron was an active editor throughout his life. His concern for Jewish demography made him a leader in the establishment of the short-lived Office of Jewish Population Research in the late 1930s, attached to the Council of Jewish Federations. Its encouragement of local Jewish population surveys bore fruit in the pioneering *Jewish Population Studies* (1942), and in time population study became an accepted function of local Jewish communal federations.

As chairman of the American Jewish Committee's Committee on Library, Research, and Publications during the late 1940s and the 1950s, Baron provided valuable counsel to the *American Jewish Year Book* and supervised research projects on the then little-known condition of the surviving Jews in Eastern Europe. Two excellent volumes appeared under this sponsorship: *The Jews in the Soviet Union* by Solomon M. Schwarz (1951) and the collective work *The Jews in the Soviet Satellites* (1953). In public lectures, essays, and in committees Baron was a strong advocate of communal responsibility for Jewish education. This has since become a general policy, but when he spoke of it during the 1930s and 1940s, communal responsibility was opposed by a leadership that believed Jewish education had to be financed by committed parents and the schools on their own. The historian was also chairman of the Survey Committee of the Jewish Welfare Board, whose "Janowsky Report" (1948) led to the adoption by the Jewish community centers of avowedly Jewish educational programs and purposes.

By contrast, Baron's editorship of a projected documentary history of the Jews in the United States, which was begun with a research staff on the occasion of the official tercentenary of American Jewry in 1954, ended dismally. The American Jewish Tercentenary Committee devoted its efforts largely to public relations and apologetic glorification and raised very little of the funds it had promised for the documentary history. Yet, Baron and his friend and fellow editor Joseph L. Blau persevered after the project broke up and managed to publish one substantial section, *The Jews of the United States 1790–1840: A Documentary History* (3 volumes, New York and Philadelphia, 1963). Such was Baron's tenacity that when he was close to 90, with the tercentenary long past, he sought to revive the project, but without success.

Baron was a fellow of the American Academy for Jewish Research from 1928 and its president in 1940–43, 1958–66, 1968–73, 1975–80, and honorary president thereafter. He maintained the academy's scholarly standards, saw to the induction of younger fellows, and substantially improved its financial position. Of historic importance was his presidency of Jewish Cultural Reconstruction, which was authorized by the occupying powers in Germany to administer the millions of Jewish books and other cultural treasures stolen by the Nazis and stored in Germany. Most of the rightful owners were individuals murdered in the Holocaust, or institutions which the Nazis destroyed. Quietly and efficiently, these treasures were redistributed to Jewish libraries, museums, schools, and *yeshivot* in many countries, according to objective criteria.

His appearance as a prosecution witness in the trial of Adolf Eichmann, in 1961, placed Baron in the international limelight. He had been invited by the State of Israel, prosecuting the Nazi arch-murderer, to present a survey of the condition of European Jewry before and after the Holocaust, and he accepted the invitation as a solemn duty. His testimony on April 24, 1961, which included effective rejoinders during cross-examination, was published as "From a Historian's Notebook: European Jewry Before and After Hitler" in volume 63 of the *American Jewish Year Book* (1962, pp. 3–51). On his return from Israel, he scornfully turned aside offers of lucrative lectures to relate his experiences at the Eichmann trial.

The Man

Baron was an active man whose working hours in his prime exceeded one hundred a week. He unfailingly took lengthy walks, often with a companion, wherever he was. I accompanied him on a long stroll in Baka, Jerusalem, when he was 86, and once, after his 90th birthday, he said to me while I visited, "I haven't walked today. Let's go out." We walked more than two miles along Riverside Drive.

Baron retired in 1963 and spent a long and fruitful retirement. His routine did not change much. Living near the Columbia campus, he occasionally looked in at his old department, where his advice was often solicited, and visited Butler Library constantly. He spent the warmer months of the year at his home in Canaan, Connecticut, where he had a large house and library and substantial acreage, which he had purchased during the 1930s and improved extensively. The land backed on the Housatonic River, and its owner worked in a boathouse at the river's edge from 7:30 A.M. to 3:00 P.M. daily. He rested, ate, and received visitors until 6:30 P.M., and worked on in his house until late in the evenings. In his last years, when he had to reduce his work week, he passed part of the winter at a daughter's home in the warm climate of Phoenix, Arizona.

There was about Salo Wittmayer Baron the quality of a gracious academic grand seigneur. He was an imperturbably relaxed and serene man. He did not become visibly angry, nor did he even raise his voice in irritation. During his working hours he concentrated totally on research and teaching. He was thoroughly organized and with the aid of capable secretaries disposed smoothly of business. Outside the time he set aside for professional work he was a gregarious man who enjoyed food, drink, and company. Baron had a large fund of stories and reminiscences which he liked to dispense; his memoirs, which are being prepared for publication, no doubt will add much. Intimacy was shared with few outside his immediate family. Foremost was Jeannette Meisel Baron, his bride of 1934 and helpmate in every sphere until her death in 1985. She not only possessed scholarly capacity but was a superlative cook and baker.

Much was granted to Salo Wittmayer Baron—long life with robust health nearly to the day he died, excellent education, family felicity, high academic position, and

---

Note: Many of Salo W. Baron's studies and essays have been collected in three volumes: *History and Jewish Historians,* compiled with a foreword by Leon A. Feldman and Arthur Hertzberg (Philadelphia, 1964); *Steeled by Adversity: Essays and Addresses on American Jewish Life,* edited by Jeannette Meisel Baron (Philadelphia, 1971); *Ancient and Medieval Jewish History: Essays,* edited by Leon A. Feldman (New Brunswick, N.J., 1972). In the summer of 1987, Baron was videotaped at great length by his student and friend Prof. Zvi Ankori, for Beth Hatefutsoth in Tel Aviv. I am grateful to Professor Ankori for valuable advice and information.

"A Bibliography of the Printed Writings of Salo Wittmayer Baron," by his wife, complete to 1973, will be found in *Salo Wittmayer Baron Jubilee Volume* (3 vols., Jerusalem, 1974), 1, pp. 5–37.

substantial means. Of so fortunate a man it has to be asked what he did with all he was given. None could have done more. It is hard even to believe he did so much. It is difficult to imagine ever encountering such a historian again.

LLOYD P. GARTNER

John Slawson (1896–1989)

THE PASSING IN 1989, AT THE AGE of 93, of Dr. John Slawson, who served as executive vice-president of the American Jewish Committee for 24 years, removed from the scene one of the most creative and influential Jewish communal leaders of the post-World War II generation.

Trained as a social psychologist at Columbia University, which awarded him a Ph.D. in 1927, Slawson came to the AJCommittee following a distinguished career in the social-welfare field. He had served as executive director of the Jewish Board of Guardians of New York, executive director of the Jewish Welfare Federation of Detroit, and assistant director of the Jewish Welfare Federation of Cleveland.

Slawson took over the reins of agency in 1943, a critical point in American Jewish life. The war against Nazism and Fascism was then under way in Europe, and anti-Semitism had risen to new heights in this country. He was determined to launch a major assault on prejudice and discrimination, but to do so by utilizing the social sciences, thus moving the agency in an entirely new direction.

While at the Board of Guardians, he had come to know a group of German-Jewish social scientists associated with the Frankfurt School who had fled Hitler, among them Eric Fromm, Max Horkheimer, and Theodor Adorno. He conceived the idea of putting these scholars to work on a scientific study of prejudice and how it could be combated. The result was the five-volume "Studies in Prejudice," the lead volume of which was *The Authoritarian Personality*. The team of scholars led by Adorno argued that prejudice was a form of social pathology that had its origins in the way children were raised. If a child grew up in a rigid home environment where he had little opportunity for self-expression, he would be affected for life, the scholars contended. Such individuals, they argued, tended to project their anxieties on their families or vulnerable groups such as Jews.

The theories of the members of the Frankfurt School found wide acceptance, especially among liberals and others seeking to understand and combat bigotry in the postwar years. By 1962, the Adorno work had stimulated some 300 similarly oriented studies, and its theories came to define how many now began to view bigotry. (When the young lieutenant in Rodgers and Hammerstein's *South Pacific* sang that "you have to be taught to hate . . . before you are six or seven or eight," he was echoing the ideas developed by Slawson's team.)

Slawson's tenure coincided with the period in American Jewish life when an older group of German-Jewish "*shtadlanim*" who had led the community voluntarily for so many years was giving way to a new element of professional leaders, individuals born in Eastern Europe or who were the first-generation children of that immigration. (Slawson himself was born in a small village in the Ukraine and came to this country at the age of seven.) Unlike their predecessors, who were usually political conservatives, the new leaders were adherents of the Left who saw Judaism primarily as a sanction for progressive social action. They were concerned not only about discrimination against Jews but about the plight of other excluded groups, like blacks. Slawson brought AJC into the budding civil-rights movement following the war, when few Jewish communal leaders had made the connection between the fate of Jews and the struggle of minorities. A critical moment came at a meeting of the executive committee of the agency in Chicago in the fall of 1945, when the first resolution that marked AJC's involvement was adopted after considerable debate and with some of its southern constituents in opposition.

In 1950 Slawson approached a young black psychologist, Kenneth Clark, and asked him to prepare a paper discussing the effects of segregation on black children for the White House Conference on Children and Youth. In the seminal case challenging segregated schools, *Brown v. Board of Education of Topeka* (1954), Chief Justice Earl Warren, speaking for a unanimous court in his decision striking down school segregation, made explicit reference to the ideas of Clark and other social psychologists. "To segregate Negro students from others of similar age . . . solely because of their race," he wrote, "generates a feeling of inferiority . . . that may affect their minds in a way to be unlikely to be undone." AJC filed an amicus brief in the case, subscribed to by five other organizations.

Although he was left of center in his political beliefs, Slawson had little patience with the formulas of the extreme Left and actively fought Communist incursions at home and abroad. In 1948, under his direction, the agency initiated a long-range research project on the situation of Jews in the Soviet Union and the European satellite countries. The first half of the study was finished in August 1951 with the publication of *The Jews in the Soviet Union* by Solomon M. Schwarz. Two years later came *The Jews in the Soviet Satellites* by Peter Meyer, Bernard D. Weinryb, Eugene Duschinsky, and Nicholas Sylvain. The documented evidence provided by these studies helped to launch the Soviet Jewry movement of the 1960s.

In the decade of the 1960s, with overt anti-Semitism showing signs of decline, Slawson led the agency in a major thrust directed against the "last barrier," the general absence of Jews from such "WASP" citadels of power as large corporations, commercial banks, law firms, and social clubs. Slawson mobilized the social sciences once again, organizing and publicizing the research of historian John Higham on the origins and nature of social discrimination, of Lewis B. Ward of the Harvard Business School on conscious and unconscious prejudice by industry recruiters, as well as the work of others. Vance Packard's best-selling *The Pyramid Builders* drew heavily on AJCommittee materials. The most comprehensive study initiated by Slawson was University of Pennsylvania sociologist E. Digby Baltzell's *The Protestant Establishment,* an eloquent appeal to the Protestant leadership class to recapture, through inclusion in its ranks of ethnic outsiders, the progressive leadership role it had once played in American life. By the 1970s, as a result of the successes achieved in this area, "executive suite" discrimination was no longer considered a pressing issue.

In a speech delivered shortly after he joined the agency, Slawson expressed a view that marked a sharp break with the traditional AJC philosophy of stewardship held by earlier AJC leaders. He posited the need for the committee to collaborate with the Jewish community, rather than to lead it from on high. "One cannot do things for the Jewish people; one must do it with the Jewish people," he declared.

As part of this effort, in 1944 Slawson launched the AJC chapter movement, which saw the development of chapters in most of the major cities in the United States. From having some 384 corporate members when he took over the agency, AJC grew to some 40,000 members in 40 chapters when he retired in 1967. He initiated the construction of the agency's New York headquarters—named the Institute on Human Relations to symbolize the agency's primary focus—and oversaw the opening of offices in Israel, Paris, Mexico City, and Argentina.

Although Slawson was a universalist—probably as a result of his own harsh personal experiences with anti-Semitism he had changed his name from Slafson to Slawson early in his career—he came to feel that in the free and open society he sought to build, the chain of religious and cultural commitment might be damaged or lost sight of. He insisted that AJC be concerned with identity as well as integration. The agency's early studies of Jewish identity became the basis for its subsequent activities in the areas of Jewish education, Jewish family life, and intermarriage.

Hoping to spark a dialogue between the two remaining centers of postwar Jewish life, as well as to bring American know-how in intergroup relations to Israel, Slawson opened an office in Israel in 1961, making AJC one of the first major Jewish agencies to do so.

As part of his effort to give AJC a "new look," as well as to make it more representative of the Jewish community and strengthen its cultural resources, he launched *Commentary* magazine in 1945, with Elliot Cohen as its first editor. (Cohen was succeeded by Norman Podhoretz in 1960.) Slawson encouraged the controversial magazine's editorial independence from critics inside and outside the agency. As a result of its high standards, it attracted writers who previously had little contact with Jewish life, providing them with a means of expression within the Jewish community.

Slawson attracted to the committee's ranks, also, a group of professionals and intellectuals whose impact came to be felt not only in Jewish life but in American life more generally. They included David Danzig and Marc Tanenbaum, who fostered Jewish rapprochement with Roman Catholics and evangelical Protestants, respectively; Lawrence Bloomgarden, creator with Slawson of the "executive suite" program; Irving M. Levine and Murray Friedman, who helped to stimulate the "new ethnicity" movement of the late 1960s; and scholar-researchers Lucy Dawidowicz, Marshall Sklare, and Milton Himmelfarb.

Slawson himself was the author early in his career of *The Delinquent Boy*, which became the standard work in the field, and a seminal essay on the importance of group identity, "Mutual Aid and the Negro," which appeared in *Commentary* in April 1966. Following his retirement, he summed up his thought in the field of intergroup relations in *Unequal Americans*.

Standing just a little over five feet tall, Slawson ruled AJC during his long tenure with an iron hand. At the same time, he permitted staff great leeway in venturing out onto the frontiers of intergroup relations and Jewish public policy. A figure who thought deeply and creatively about these issues and acted on them with great courage and perceptiveness, he set a model of Jewish professional leadership that others would do well to study and emulate.

MURRAY FRIEDMAN

Obituaries: United States[1]

BELTH, NATHAN C., public-relations executive, communal worker; b. Sierpce, Poland, Dec. 11, 1908; d. NYC, Mar. 3, 1989; in U.S. since 1916. Educ.: NYU. Sportswriter and ed., *Daily Mirror* and *Brooklyn Eagle*, early 1930s; independent p.r. consultant, 1935–40 and 1944–46, for ORT, Anti-Nazi League, Joint Distribution Com., Anti-Defamation League; p.r. dir.: Army and Navy Com., JWB, 1940–44; ADL, 1946–71; exec. dir., Hebrew Free Loan Soc., 1971–83. Chmn.: Mass Media Com., Conf. of Presidents of Major Amer. Jewish Orgs.; public relations com., ADL; pres., Amer. Jewish Public Relations Soc.; bd. mem., Hebrew Free Loan Soc.; treas. and bd. mem., N.Y. Soc. for the Deaf; mem., Overseas Press Club. Author: *Barriers—Patterns of Discrimination Against Jews* (1958); *A Promise to Keep: A Narrative of the American Encounter with Anti-Semitism* (1979); ed., *Fighting for America*. Recipient: Silver Anvil Award, Public Relations Soc. of Amer.

BEN-ISRAEL, SHELOMO, journalist; b. Brisk (Brest-Litovsk), Poland, July 27, 1908; d. Ellenville, N.Y., Sept. 14, 1989; in U.S. since 1939. Educ.: Gymnasium, Poland. Settled in Palestine, 1926; originator of mystery stories in Hebrew, 1932; in Yiddish, 1939; traveling correspondent, *Doar Hayom*, Jerusalem, 1933–36; *N.Y. Times* correspondent, Cairo, 1938; Middle East correspondent and analyst, *Boston Globe*, 1943–46; UN correspondent and later editorial writer, *Jewish Daily Forward*, 1946–80; Yiddish radio commentator, WEVD, N.Y., 1950–89. Vice-pres., Fed. of Polish Jews; sec., Yiddish Writers Union; mem., UN Correspondents Assn.; educ. consultant, New England Zionist Region (1944–46). Author: *The Strange Adventures of Danny Noor* (English, Hebrew); *Mark of Vengeance* (Hebrew, Yiddish); numerous short stories, children's stories, and articles, in English, Hebrew, and Yiddish, as well as pageants and plays.

BERGER, ABRAHAM, librarian, scholar; b. Grzymalow, Austria-Hungary, May 30, 1902; d. NYC, Mar. 14, 1989; in U.S. since 1920. Educ.: Albany Coll. of Pharmacy; Columbia U. (BS, grad. fellowship in Jewish history, MS in library service). First assistant, Jewish Division, N.Y. Public Library, 1926–56; chief, Jewish Division, NYPL, 1956–67. Pres.: Jewish Librarians' Assn.; Jewish Book Club. Mem.: Historians' Circle, YIVO Inst. for Jewish Research; Amer. Acad. for Jewish Research; exec. bd. mem., Jewish Book Council. Author: articles on Jewish mysticism and folklore, Hassidism, bibliographic studies, and reviews.

BERLIN, IRVING (ISRAEL BALINE), songwriter; b. Tyumen, Russia, May 11, 1888; d. NYC, Sept. 22, 1989; in U.S. since 1893. Educ.: less than two years of school. His father, a cantor, died when he was 8; although he never learned to read or write music, a natural gift for music took him

---

[1]Including Jewish residents of the United States who died between January 1 and December 31, 1989.

quickly from saloon singing for pennies to the pinnacle of American popular culture. Composed 1,500 popular songs (incl. "Always," "Cheek to Cheek," "Blue Skies," "Easter Parade"); the scores for 18 films (incl. *Top Hat, White Christmas*), and 19 Broadway musicals (incl. *Annie Get Your Gun, Call Me Madam*). Recipient: Congressional Gold Medal (for "God Bless America"); Academy Award (for "White Christmas," one of the most frequently played songs ever written).

BLANK, SHELDON HAAS, professor, rabbi; b. Mt. Carmel, Ill., Sept. 17, 1896; d. Cincinnati, Ohio, Feb. 14, 1989. Educ.: U. Cincinnati; Hebrew Union Coll. (ord.); U. Jena, Germany (PhD); Hebrew U. and Amer. Schools for Oriental Research, Jerusalem. Prof., Bible, Hebrew Union Coll., 1926–71; Nelson Glueck Prof. of Bible emer., 1977 on; ed., HUC Annual, for 60 years. Pres., Soc. for Bibl. Lit.; exec. bd. mem., CCAR. Author: *Prophetic Faith in Isaiah*; *Jeremiah, Man and Prophet*; *Understanding the Prophets*; *Prophetic Thought—Essays and Addresses*; articles in numerous journals.

BLOUSTEIN, EDWARD J., professor; university president; b. NYC, Jan. 20, 1925; d. Nassau, the Bahamas, Dec. 9, 1989. Educ.: NYU; Oxford U.; Cornell U. (PhD, JD). Lect., Brooklyn Coll., 1950–51; instr., Cornell U., 1954–55; political analyst, U.S. State Dept., 1951–52, 1955–56; law clerk, chief judge, N.Y. Court of Appeals, 1959–61; prof., NYU Law School, 1961–65; pres.: Bennington Coll., 1965–71; Rutgers U., 1971 on. Chmn., Natl. Assn. of State Universities and Land-Grant Colleges; v.-chmn., Middle States Assn. Colleges and Schools; trustee, Conference Bd.; bd. mem.: Natl. Council on Crime and Delinquency; Amer. Council for Educ.; mem.: exec. com., Labor-Higher Educ. Council; Governor's Comm. on Science and Technology; N.J. Comm. on Individual Liberty and Personal Privacy. Coauthor: *Dimensions of Academic Freedom*.

BLUMBERG, DAVID M., insurance executive, communal worker; b. Forrest City, Ark., July 6, 1911; d. Washington, DC, Nov. 1, 1989. Educ.: U. Tenn.; Washington U., St. Louis (LLB). Served U.S. Navy, WWII. Instr., Life Underwriting Training Council, 1951–55; genl. agent, Mass. Mutual Life Insurance Co., 1955–76 (ret.). Pres.: Knoxville Assn. of Life Underwriters, Tenn. Assn. of Life Underwriters, Natl. Assn. of Life Underwriters; mem.: Million Dollar Round Table, 1956–68; Knoxville City Council, 1966–72; mem. bd. of trustees: Knoxville Public Library, 1955–58; U. Tenn. School of Religion, 1958 on; Tenn. Comm. for Human Devel., 1972–76; del., White House Conf. on Youth and Children, 1959–60; Scottish Rite, 33 degree Mason; Tenn. and Knoxville Bar Assns.; Kiwanis; Knoxville Sales and Marketing Execs. Pres., B'nai B'rith Internatl., 1971–78; v.-chmn.: World Conf. of Jewish Orgs., Natl. Jewish Community Relations Advisory Council, Natl. Conf. on Soviet Jewry; trustee, Amer. Friends of Hebrew U.; treas., Memorial Found. for Jewish Culture. Recipient: Chamber of Commerce Man of the Year, Knoxville (1961); B'nai B'rith Humanitarian Award (1967); Natl. Brotherhood Award, Natl. Conf. of Christians and Jews (1973). Internatl. Churchmen's Sports Hall of Fame (1973), and many other honors.

BUTTENWIESER, HELEN LEHMAN, attorney, civic leader; b. NYC, Oct. 8, 1905; d. NYC, Nov. 22, 1989. Educ.: Connecticut Coll.; NYU Law School. Commissioner, Bd. of Child Welfare, NYC, 1930–35. One of the first women admitted to NYC Bar Assn. and the first woman lawyer at Cravath, Swaine & Moore, she left after a year to set up a private law practice in Manhattan— maintained for 50 years—enabling her to combine work, family, and community service. Trustee: Connecticut Coll. for Women, Dalton Schools, Columbia U. School for Social Work, N.Y. Civil Liberties Union; bd. mem.: NAACP Legal Defense Fund, Fortune Soc., Citizens Com. for Children; chmn., NYC Com. on Adoptions; active in the Legal Aid Soc. for 50 years: lawyer, dir., and bd. chmn. (1st woman). Active in behalf of Alger Hiss in the 1950s and an investor in *The Nation* magazine. Served on many committees of N.Y. Fed. of Jewish Philanthropies (social legislation, legal counsel, Jewish Child Care Assn., etc.) for over 30 years; mem., Cong. Emanu-El; Cong. Shearith Israel. Recipient: Servant of Justice Award, NYC Bar Assn. (1st woman recipient) and other honors.

EDISON, IRVING, businessman, communal worker; b. Adel, Ga., Dec. 22, 1899; d. St. Louis, Mo., May 16, 1989. Educ.: grammar school. Cofounder, Edison Brothers

Stores, Atlanta, Ga. (with 4 brothers), 1922; company moved to St. Louis, 1929; pres., 1957-68, and bd. mem. thereafter. (The firm owned chains of apparel and women's shoe stores, among them Chandler's, Baker's, Joan Bari.) Mem., bd. dirs.: Cardinal Glennon Hosp., Barnes Hosp., St. Louis Symphony Soc.; v.-pres.: Greater St. Louis United Fund; Natl. USO; bd. chmn., St. Louis Chamber of Commerce; founding mem., St. Louis County Police Comm. Pres.: Natl. Jewish Welfare Bd., 1950-54, and hon. pres. thereafter; Jewish Community Center of St. Louis; World Fed. of JCCAs; dir., St. Louis Jewish Hospital; mem., adv. com., *St. Louis Jewish Light*; v.-pres. and campaign chmn., St. Louis Jewish Fed. Recipient: Frank L. Weil Award, JWB; hon. doctorate, Washington U.; Gold Star, U.S. Treasury Dept.; *Globe-Democrat* Humanities Award.

ELYACHAR, JEHIEL R., businessman, communal worker; b. Jerusalem, Oct. 20, 1898; d. NYC, Mar. 29, 1989; in U.S. since 1928. Educ.: David Yellin Teachers Coll., Jerusalem; French U., Beirut; engineering school, Paris. Served U.S. Army Corps of Engineers, WWII, achieving rank of colonel. Pres., Straight Construction Co., NYC, real-estate developers, 1929 on. Founder and hon. pres., Amer. Technion Soc.; founder and bd. mem.: Amer. Friends of Hebrew U., Amer. Associates of Ben Gurion U. of the Negev, Friends of David Yellin Hebrew Teachers Coll., Yeshiva U., Sephardic Home for Aged; bd. mem., UJA. Led efforts to create chair of Sephardic studies at Yeshiva U., whose library houses family collection of Ladino and Sephardic lit.; mem., Cong. Shearith Israel. Recipient: hon. doctorate, Haifa Technion; State of Israel Aleh Medal; N.Y. State Conspicuous Service Medal; Legion of Merit; David Yellin Award.

FESTINGER, LEON, professor; b. NYC, May 8, 1919; d. NYC, Feb. 11, 1989. Educ.: CCNY, State U. Iowa (PhD). Research assoc., psychology, U. Iowa, 1941-43; sr. statistician, Com. on Selection and Training of Aircraft Pilots, U. Rochester, 1943-45; asst. prof., social psych., MIT, 1945-48; assoc. prof. and program dir., Research Center for Group Dynamics, U. Michigan, 1948-51; prof., psych.: U. Minnesota, 1951-55; Stanford U., 1955-68; Else and Hans Staudinger Chair, New School for Social Research, 1968-89. Author: *A Theory of Cognitive Dissonance* (1957); *Conflict, Decision and Dissonance* (1964); *The Human Legacy* (1983), and numerous articles and papers. Recipient: Mem., Natl. Acad. of Sciences; Fellow, Amer. Acad. of Arts and Sciences; Distinguished Scientist Award, Amer. Psych. Assn. (1959); Distinguished Sr. Scientist Award, Soc. of Experimental Social Psych. (1980); hon. doctorate, U. Mannheim; Einstein Visiting Fellow, Israel Acad. Sciences and Humanities (1980-81).

GILDESGAME, LEON L., businessman, communal worker; b. Sompolno, Poland, Jan. 27, 1895; d. Mt. Kisco, N.Y., Apr. 30, 1989; in U.S. since 1940. Educ.: Yeshivah, Poland; Gymnasium Herzliah, Tel Aviv; Guildhall Sch. of Music, London; London U. School of Econ. and Polit. Sci. Served with Zion Mule Corps, British Army, and RAF, WWI; decorated Gallipoli Star. Managing dir., Eastern and Russian Trading Co., London, 1920-29; founder and chmn.: Agree Co., Ltd., 1928-58; Gildesgame Bros. Ltd., Eng., 1931-48; Gildesgame Corp., N.Y., 1941-71. Chmn., Jewish Conciliation Bd. of Amer.; v.-pres., Friends of the David Yellin Teachers Coll.; hon. pres., Amer. Friends of the Tel Aviv Museum of Art; hon. fellow, Hebrew U. of Jerusalem; bd. mem., Amer. Friends of Hebrew U.; founder, Temple Beth-El, N. Westchester; chmn., UJA-Federation of N. Westchester; active in behalf of Israel Bonds, ZOA, Amer. Jewish Cong., Histadrut Ivrit, Amer. Jewish Com., and a wide range of Jewish orgs. Recipient: First hon. fellow, Tel Aviv Museum; King Solomon trophy, America-Israel Cultural Found., and many other honors.

GOLDBERGER, LEO, I., journalist; b. Memphis, Tenn., Dec. 1, 1902; d. Memphis, Tenn., Apr. 28, 1989. Worked in the printing business for 12 years with his 3 brothers; in 1925 founded the *Hebrew Watchman*; served as publisher and editor until 1970. Helped found Amer. Jewish Press Assn., 1943. Active locally in Baron Hirsch Syn., Memphis Zionist Dist., B'nai B'rith, Memphis Hebrew Acad., Jewish Fed., Yeshiva of the South; also Israel Bond org., Shaare Zedek Hosp., JNF. Recipient: Joseph Polakoff Award for Integrity in Journalism; Amer. Jewish Press Assn. Awards (1975 and 1985); JNF Keter Shem Tov Award, and other honors.

GOODMAN, PERCIVAL, architect; b. NYC, Jan. 13, 1904; d. NYC, Oct. 11, 1989. Educ.: Beaux Arts Inst. of Design, NYC; Ecole des Beaux-Arts and Amer. Sch. of Fine Arts, Paris. Lect.-critic, NYU Sch. of Architecture, 1930–36; private architecture practice, 1936–79; prof., Columbia U. Sch. of Architecture, 1946–71. Architect of 54 modern synagogues in the U.S., built 1948–86, incl. Fifth Ave. Syn., NYC; Shaarey Zedek, Detroit; Fairmount Temple, Cleveland; Cong. Adath Israel, Riverdale, NYC. Designed modern houses in eastern Long Island in the 1930s, several schools and public buildings in New York, and created plans for sections of New York. An urban theorist and social thinker, he believed architects should serve as advocates for social improvement. Author: *Communitas: Means of Livelihood and Ways of Life* (with Paul Goodman, his brother); *The Double E: Ecology and Economy*; numerous articles and book reviews. Recipient: Fellow, Amer. Inst. of Architects; many design awards.

GOODMAN SVERDLIN, HANNAH GRAD, writer; b. Cincinnati, Ohio, Apr. 29, 1910; d. NYC, Jan. 19, 1989. Educ.: U. Cincinnati; Cincinnati Coll. of Music. Dir., cultural activities and drama group, Bureau of Jewish Ed., Cincinnati; natl. educ. sec., B'nai B'rith Youth Org., Washington, DC, mid-1940s; exec. sec., Hebrew Arts Com., NYC, and producer of Pargod Hebrew Theater, late 1940s; scriptwriter for many radio and TV programs, 1950s, incl. Show of Shows, GE Theater, Kraft Theater, Ken Murray Show, Eternal Light; public-relations writer, Natl. Council of Jewish Women, 1959–63; free-lance writer and editor; arts columnist, *Hadassah* magazine, 1971–89. Founding mem., Writers Guild; theater director, Lakeside Summer Theater, Manhattan Repertory Co.; lifelong activist in Zionist and communal affairs. Author: *The Story of Prophecy*; coauthor (with Azriel Eisenberg): *Eyewitnesses to Jewish History*; *Eyewitnesses to American Jewish History*.

GOURARY, SAMARIOUS, rabbi; b. Kremenchug, Ukraine, Dec. 1897; d. NYC, Feb. 11, 1989; in U.S. since 1940. Dir., for 48 years, United Lubavitcher Yeshivoth, the worldwide educ. network founded in Russia by his father-in-law, Rabbi Joseph I. Schneerson. (He was a brother-in-law of the present Lubavitcher rebbe, Menachem Mendel Schneerson.)

HABER, WILLIAM, professor, communal worker; b. Harlau, Romania, Mar. 6, 1899; d. Ann Arbor, Mich., Dec. 30, 1988; in U.S. since 1909. Educ.: U. Wisconsin (BA, MA, PhD). Labor mgr., Hart, Schaffner & Marx, 1923; instr., economics, U. Wisconsin, 1926–27; assoc. prof., Michigan State U., 1927–36; prof., U. Michigan, 1936 on, and dean, Coll. of Lit., Science, and the Arts, 1963–68. Admin., state emergency welfare relief, 1933–36; state dir., Natl. Youth Admin., 1935–36; deputy dir., UPA, 1934–36; mem., Mich. Unemployment Compensation Comm., 1936–37; special asst., U.S. Bureau of the Budget, 1942; staff, War Manpower Comm., 1943–44; adviser, Office of War Mobilization and Reconversion, 1945–46; chmn., federal advisory council on employment security, 1948 on; mem., President's task force on depressed areas, 1961, and numerous other govt. assignments. Adviser on resettlement of Jewish refugees and DPs, U.S. forces in Germany and Austria, 1948–49; pres., Amer. ORT Fed., 1950–75, and pres., World ORT Union, 1955–1980; chmn., B'nai B'rith Natl. Hillel Comm., 1949–64; mem.: bd. govs., Hebrew U. of Jerusalem; bd. of trustees, Brandeis U.; Amer. Jewish Com. natl. exec. council; bd. dirs., United Service for New Americans; v.-pres., Amer. Friends of Hebrew U. Author: *Industrial Relations in the Building Industry*; *Unemployment Relief and Economic Security*; coauthor: *Postwar Economic Reconstruction*; *Unemployment Insurance in the American Economy*, and other works, as well as articles in professional journals. Recipient: hon. doctorates, Hebrew Union Coll.; Michigan State U.; Hebrew U.; Brandeis U.; UJA Humanitarian Award; John Dewey Award, League for Industrial Democracy; and other honors. The Haber Chair in Economics was created in his honor at Hebrew U.

HIRSCHBERG, GUNTER, rabbi; b. Berlin, Germany, Apr. 28, 1920; d. NYC, July 18, 1989; in U.S. since 1947. Educ.: U. of London; Jews Coll., London; private voice study with Alexander Kipnis; Columbia U.; HUC-JIR, N.Y. (ord. 1963). Cantor and rabbi, Temple Emanuel, Sydney, Australia, 1941–46; cantor, Shaare Zedek, Brooklyn, 1947–51; associated for 37 years with Temple Rodeph Sholom, NYC: cantor, 1952–63; assoc. rabbi, 1963–72; sr. rabbi, 1972 on. Pres.: N.Y. Bd. of Rabbis;

HUC-JIR Alumni Assn.; mem., bd. govs., World Union of Progressive Judaism. Founder, first Reform day school, at Rodeph Sholom, 1970; active in interfaith and community causes. Recipient: hon. doctorate, HUC.

HIRSCHMANN, IRA A., businessman, author; b. Baltimore, Md., July 7, 1906; d. NYC, Oct. 9, 1989. Retail exec.: L. Bamberger & Co.; Lord & Taylor; v.-pres.: Saks Fifth Ave., 1935–38; Bloomingdale's, 1938–46. Active in NYC politics and govt.: campaign adviser to Fiorello LaGuardia; mem., Bd. of Higher Educ.; special inspector, UN Relief and Rehabilitation Admin. Special rep., War Refugee Bd., 1944, in which capacity he was sent to Turkey, where he succeeded in expediting the escape of some 100,000 Romanian Jews from Transnistria concentration camp. Founder and pres., New Friends of Music; cofounder and chmn., U. in Exile; speaker for Israel Bonds; mem.: LaGuardia Memorial Assn.; Hebrew U. bd. of govs.; Amer. Friends of Hebrew U. council of trustees; JNF bd. of dirs. Author: *Lifeline to a Promised Land* (1946); *The Embers Still Burn* (1949); *Caution to the Winds* (1962); *Red Star over Bethlehem* (1972); articles in various publications.

HOOK, SIDNEY, professor; b. NYC, Dec. 20, 1902; d. Stanford, Calif., July 12, 1989. Educ.: CCNY; Columbia U. (PhD). Teacher, NYC public schools, 1923–28; instr., philosophy, NYU, 1927–32; asst. prof., 1932–34; assoc. prof., 1934–39; prof., 1939–69; dept. chmn. for 35 years; emer. 1969 on; sr. research fellow, Hoover Institution on War, Revolution and Peace, Stanford U., 1973 on. Visiting prof.: Harvard U., U. Calif-San Diego; regents prof., U. Calif.-Santa Barbara. Hon. chmn., Social Democrats, USA; v.-pres., League for Industrial Democracy; bd. mem., Freedom House; pres., treas., John Dewey Found.; mem.: Natl. Endowment for Humanities Council, 1972–78. A politically involved academic philosopher, best known for his vigorous opposition to Communism and defense of political and academic freedom. Labeled by some a neoconservative, he preferred to call himself a "social democrat" and a "cold war liberal." Helped organize Cong. for Cultural Freedom in 1950 to counter Communist-led intellectual fronts; founder, Univ. Centers for Rational Alternatives. Author: *Toward the Understanding of Karl Marx* (1933); *From Hegel to Marx* (1936); *The Hero in History* (1943); *Education for Modern Man* (2nd ed., 1963); *Pragmatism and the Tragic Sense of Life* (1974); *Out of Step: An Unquiet Life in the 20th Century* (autobiog., 1987); and many other works. Fellow: Amer. Acad. Arts and Sciences; Amer. Acad. for Education. Recipient: Presidential Medal of Freedom, 1985; hon. doctorates: U. Maine, U. Calif., U. Fla., Hebrew Union Coll., U. Utah, U. Vt., Rockford Coll.

HOROWITZ, VLADIMIR, pianist; b. Kiev, Russia, Oct. 1, 1903 (?); d. NYC, Nov. 5, 1989; in U.S. since 1940. Educ.: Kiev Conservatory and private teachers. Russian debut, 1922–23; Berlin debut, 1926; U.S. debut, with N.Y Philharmonic, Jan. 1928. One of the most popular concert artists of his time, often described as a romantic or classical pianist, he played in the grand manner, electrifying audiences with his virtuosity. High-strung and known for personal eccentricities, including several periods of retirement from the stage, the longest 1953–1965. Recipient: Presidential Medal of Freedom, 1986; numerous Grammy awards for recordings.

LASTER, ISRAEL, communal worker; b. Dickson City, Pa., June 29, 1916; d. Rockport, Mass., Apr. 1, 1989. Joined staff of Amer. Jewish Com. in 1946 as field worker; assoc. dir., N.Y. chapter, 1952–62; dir., 1962–68; mem., natl. affairs dept., 1968–79.

LEDERMAN, SARAH, social worker, communal worker; b. NYC, Aug. 22, 1913; d. NYC, Jan. 8, 1989. Educ.: Hunter Coll. Social worker, Bridgeport, Conn. JCC and NYC Jewish family-service agencies; dir., Queens dist., JASA (Jewish Assn. for Services for the Aged), 1969–83; adj. prof., Wurzweiler School of Social Work. Pres., Central Bureau for the Jewish Aged; bd. mem.: Conf. of Jewish Communal Service; World Conf. of Jewish Communal Service; Assn. of Jewish Family & Children's Agency Professionals. Long active in the Labor Zionist movement: chmn., admin. com., *Jewish Frontier*; mem., admin. com., Labor Zionist Alliance; youth comm. chmn. Author: articles in professional journals on care of the aged. Recipient: JNF project in her honor, sponsored by Labor Zionist movement; Woman of the Year, Hunter College Alumni Assn.

LEKACHMAN, ROBERT, professor; b. NYC, May 12, 1920; d. NYC, Jan. 14, 1989. Educ.: Columbia Coll., Columbia U. (PhD). Served U.S. Army, WWII. Teaching asst., economics, Columbia U. Business School, 1947–48; faculty mem., Barnard Coll., 1948–65; prof., State U. of N.Y.-Stony Brook, 1965–73, and chmn. economics dept., 1965–68; Distinguished Prof. of Economics, Lehman Coll. and Graduate Center, CUNY, 1973 on. Mem.: Amer. Econ. Assn., AAUP; NAACP; League for Industrial Democracy; founding mem., Riverside Democrats (NYC); mem. ed. bd.: *Dissent*, *Challenge*, *New Leader*, *Civil Liberties Review*, *Christianity and Crisis*. A popular public and media speaker who espoused a philosophy of promoting social justice along with economic growth. Author: *A History of Economic Ideas* (1959); *The Age of Keynes* (1966); *National Income and the Public Welfare* (1972); *Greed Is Not Enough* (1982); *Visions and Nightmares: America After Reagan* (1987); numerous articles and reviews in scholarly journals and in the general press. Recipient: Liberal Arts Fellow, Harvard Law School; Rockefeller Fellow; Guggenheim Fellow; hon. doctorate, New School; Phi Beta Kappa Visiting Scholar; named one of 50 campus leaders by *Change* magazine, Aug. 1986.

LEVIN, NORA, professor, b. Philadelphia, Pa., Sept. 20, 1916; d. Philadelphia, Pa., Oct. 26, 1989. Educ.: Drexel U.; NYU; U. of Pa. Instr., modern Jewish history, Gratz Coll., 1970–77; asst. prof., 1977–84; assoc. prof. 1984 on; dir., Holocaust Oral History Archive, Gratz Coll., 1979 on; visiting prof.: Haifa U., Purdue U. Exec. dir., Pioneer Women, Phila. Council, 1948–53; bd. mem.: JCRC of Phila., HIAS, Soviet Jewry Council. Author: *The Holocaust: The Destruction of European Jewry, 1933–45* (1968; a Book-of-the-Month Club selection); *While Messiah Tarried: Jewish Socialist Movements, 1871–1917* (1977); *Jews in the Soviet Union: A History from 1917 to the Present* (1987). Recipient: hon. doctorate, Gratz Coll. (posth.)

LEVINE, SEYMOUR R., attorney, communal worker; b. Bobruisk, Russia, May 28, 1906; d. Peekskill, N.Y., Nov. 22, 1989; in U.S. since 1910. Educ.: NYU Law School. Private law practice, 1930 on; Peekskill city court judge, 1946–56; dir.: Citadel Life Ins. Co.; Natl. Bank of Westchester; Rassco Israel Corp. Pres. and trustee, bd. of educ., Peekskill, 1940–50. Natl. pres.: Amer. Jewish League for Israel; Natl. Conf. of Christians and Jews; chmn., N. Westchester UJA; pres.: First Hebrew Cong.; Westchester Zionist Region; delegate, World Zionist Cong., 1978; mem., World Zionist Action Com., 1978–80; v.-pres.: Amer. Zionist Fed.; Jewish Natl. Fund; trustee, United Israel Appeal; natl. chmn., Youth Centers of Israel; bd. mem., B'nai Zion. Recipient: Man of the Year, 1970, Natl. Conf. of Christians and Jews.

LYONS, HELEN HADASSAH LEVINTHAL, educator; b. Philadelphia, Pa., Apr. 22, 1910; d. New Rochelle, N.Y., Aug. 13, 1989. Educ.: U. of Pa., Columbia U.; Jewish Inst. of Religion (now HUC-JIR). The first woman to complete the full rabbinic curriculum and to graduate (1939) from a recognized Jewish theological seminary, but denied ordination; she was awarded a special diploma. Faculty mem., Adult Inst. of Jewish Studies, Brooklyn Jewish Center, 1939–44; lecturer and teacher for many groups. Active in Hadassah, AMIT Women, ZOA, Women's League for Israel; hon. v. pres. and trustee, Beth El Syn., New Rochelle.

MORRIS, RICHARD B., professor; b. NYC, July 24, 1904; d. NYC, Mar. 3, 1989. Educ.: City Coll. of N.Y.; Columbia U. (PhD). Instr. to prof., Amer. history, CCNY, 1927–49; visiting prof., Columbia U., 1946–49; prof., 1949; Gouverneur Morris Professor, 1959; emer., 1973. Pres., Amer. Historical Assn.; chmn.: NYC Mayor's Task Force on Municipal Archives; N.Y. State Bicentennial Coordinating Council; mem., Amer. Revolution Bicentennial Comm. Author: *Studies in the History of American Law* (1930); *Government and Labor in Early America* (1946, 1965, 1983); *The Peacemakers: The Great Powers and American Independence* (1965); *The Forging of the Union, 1781–1789* (1987); *The American Revolution Reconsidered* (1967); *Great Presidential Decisions* (1960), and many other works. Ed.: *The Papers of John Jay* (4 vols.), *The Encyclopedia of American History* (successive editions), and seven children's books. Recipient: Bancroft Prize (for the *Peacemakers*); hon. doctorate: Hebrew Union Coll.; Guggenheim Fellowship; Bruce Colton Prize, Soc. of Amer. Historians, for lifetime achievement; Townsend Harris Medal, CCNY; Fellow, Royal Hist. Soc.

NEIMAN, MORRIS, educator; b. (?), Russia, 1910; d. NYC, May 25, 1989; in U.S. since 1924. Educ.: Brooklyn Coll.; Yeshivat Rabbi Isaac Elhanan; Columbia U. (PhD). Teacher, Hebrew and Torah ed., Ramaz Yeshiva, NYC, 28 years; instr., Hebrew, Brooklyn Coll., 22 years; lect., Yeshiva U. Author: *Modern Hebrew Literary Criticism: 1788–1888* and numerous articles and poems in Hebrew.

NOVICK, PAUL, journalist; b. Brest-Litovsk, Russia, Sept. 7, 1891; d. Peekskill, N.Y., Aug. 21, 1989; in U.S. since 1913. Writer for Yiddish newspapers in Russia, Vilna, and Warsaw during revolutionary period and 1920s; for the *N.Y. Forward*, 1920–22; co-founder and asst. ed., *Morning Freiheit*, a left-wing Yiddish daily, 1922–38; ed., 1938 until it ceased publication in Sept. 1988. Regarded as the last of the great immigrant Marxist intellectuals; a fervent advocate of democratic socialism and secular Yiddish culture; following 1956 revelations about Stalin, was critical of Soviet policy and supportive of Israel. Mem., ed. bd., *Yiddishe Kultur, Jewish Currents*. Author: *Tsvishn milchomeh un sholem*; numerous pamphlets on current political and cultural topics.

PESIN, MEYER, attorney, communal worker; b. (?), Russia, Feb. 12, 1901; d. Caracas, Venezuela, Nov. 28, 1989; in U.S. since 1904. Educ.: NYU Law School. Private law practice in New Jersey; mem., Hudson County Bd. of Tax Appeals, 1952–56; appointed corp. counsel, Jersey City, 1962; mem., N.J. Civil Rights Comm. Ed., *Jewish Standard* (N.J.), 1931–75; natl. pres., JNF, 1971–77; pres., N.J. region, ZOA, 1953–55; natl. bd. mem., ZOA; founding mem., bd. of trustees, Amer. Jewish Museum of Art and Culture. Recipient: Jewish War Veterans Civil Rights Award.

SCHIFF, DOROTHY, publisher; b. NYC, Mar. 11, 1903; d. NYC, Aug. 30, 1989. Socialite granddaughter of investment banker Jacob H. Schiff and daughter of Mortimer; a Republican in her early years, she joined the Roosevelt campaign in 1936 but backed Thomas E. Dewey in 1948; in 1939, with family money, purchased the *N.Y. Post*, a liberal, deficit-ridden daily; became publisher in 1942; kept paper's political slant but turned it into a tabloid, adding more human-interest, scandal, columns, and comics; kept the paper going during 1962–63 newspaper strike; became editor-in-chief as well as publisher, pres., and treas.; in 1976 sold it to Rupert Murdoch (who later sold it to Peter S. Kalikow).

SCHWARTZ, ABBA, attorney, public official; b. Baltimore, Md., Apr. 17, 1916; d. Brussels, Belgium, Sept. 12, 1989. Educ.: Georgetown U.; Harvard Law School. Served U.S. Merchant Marine, 1942–44, U.S. Navy, 1944–45. Official, Intergovernmental Com. on Refugees, London, Engl., 1946–47; reparations dir., UN Internatl. Refugee Org., Geneva, Switz., 1947–49; partner, Washington law firm, 1949–62; admin., asst. sec., U.S. State Dept., Bureau of Security and Consular Affairs, 1962–66; law practice, Washington, 1967 on. Specialist in immigration law and proponent of liberalized policies for admission of refugees and visitors to the U.S. U.S. del.: Intergovernmental Com. on European Migration, 1962–65; 20th Internatl. Red Cross Conf., 1965; chief, White House Mission to Vietnam, 1965; special asst. to sec. of defense on POWs in Vietnam, 1967 on. Author: *The Open Society* (1968); articles on immigration and refugees in various periodicals. Recipient: Order of Orange Nassau (Netherlands).

SCHWARZSCHILD, STEVEN S., professor, rabbi; b. Frankfurt am Main, Germany, Feb. 5, 1924; d. St. Louis, Mo., Dec. 2, 1989; in U.S. since 1939. Educ.: U. Cincinnati; Hebrew Union Coll. (ord.; DHL). Rabbi: Berlin, Germany, 1948–51; Fargo, N.D., 1951–57; Lynn, Mass., 1957–64. Prof., Jewish studies, Brown U., 1964–66; prof., philosophy and Judaic studies, Washington U., 1966–89; visiting prof.: Notre Dame; Hebrew U. of Jerusalem. Contributing ed., *Sh'ma*; exec. com. mem., Jewish Peace Fellowship. Author: *The Pursuit of the Ideal* (1990) and hundreds of scholarly articles. Recipient: hon. doctorate, Hebrew Union Coll.

SEGRÈ, EMILIO G., physicist; b. Tivoli, Italy, Feb. 1, 1905; d. Lafayette, Calif., Apr. 22, 1989; in U.S. since 1938. Educ.: U. Rome (PhD). Asst. prof., U. Rome, 1932–36 (working with Enrico Fermi on neutron physics); prof. and dir., physics lab., U. Palermo, 1936–38; research asst., U. Calif.-Berkeley, 1938–43; group leader, Los Alamos (N.M.) Scientific Lab., 1943–46, where he conducted experiments in spontaneous fission; prof., Berkeley, 1945–72; emer., 1972 on; prof., U. Rome, 1974–75. Fellow: Amer. Physical Soc.; mem.:

Natl. Acad. of Sciences, Amer. Philos. Soc., Amer. Acad. of Arts and Sciences; mem., advisory bd., Sackler Faculty of Exact Sciences, Tel Aviv U. Author: *Experimental Nuclear Physics* (1953); *Nuclei and Particles* (1964); *Enrico Fermi, Physicist* (1970); *From X-Rays to Quarks* (1980); *From Falling Bodies to Radio Waves* (1988). Recipient: Co-winner, Nobel Prize in physics (1959), for discovery of antiproton; hon. doctorates: U. Palermo, Tel Aviv U., and others; Hoffmann Medal, German Chem. Soc.; Great Cross of Merit, Republic of Italy; Rockefeller, Guggenheim, Fulbright fellowships, and many other honors.

SHAPIRO, BETTY K., communal worker; b. Washington, DC, (?), 1908: d. Washington, DC, Mar. 18, 1989. Educ.: Business H.S. (basketball team captain and citywide tennis champion). School sec., 1924–28; sec.-office manager, HIAS, Washington, 1929–43. Internatl. pres., B'nai B'rith Women, 1968–71; del., UN Women's Conf., 1977 (Houston), 1980 (Copenhagen), 1985 (Nairobi); helped found Jewish Women's Caucus after Houston conf.; as caucus chairwoman in subsequent years, she helped prevent the inclusion of an anti-Zionist declaration in the conference final statement. Bd. mem.: Natl. Woman's party; Washington Conf. of Christians and Jews; Internatl. Development Conf.; Capital Area Division of UN Assn.-USA; B'nai B'rith; ADL Natl. Comm.; Jewish Community Council of Greater Washington; Jewish Council for the Aging; State of Israel Bonds; chmn.: Washington area Community Chest, Red Cross, March of Dimes, Cancer Crusade. Recipient: Selected for District of Columbia Women's Hall of Fame.

SILVER, DANIEL JEREMY, rabbi; b. Cleveland, Ohio, Mar. 26, 1928; d. Cleveland, Ohio, Dec. 20, 1989. Educ.: Harvard Coll.; Hebrew Union Coll. (ord.); U. Chicago (PhD). Assoc. rabbi, The Temple, Cleveland, Ohio, 1956–63; sr. rabbi thereafter, succeeding his father, Abba Hillel Silver. Adj. prof., religion, Case Western Reserve U. and Cleveland State U.; fellow, Post Graduate Centre for Jewish Studies, Oxford (1979, 1986). Pres., Natl. Found. for Jewish Culture, 1966–74 and founding chmn. its acad. advisory com.; chmn.: Congregational Plenum of Greater Cleveland; Israel Task Force, Cleveland Jewish Fed.; pres., Cleveland Bd. of Rabbis; mem. exec. bd.: Jewish Community Fed.; AIPAC; Synagogue Council of Amer.; sr. ed., *Journal of the Central Conf. of Amer. Rabbis*; chmn., CCAR Task Force on Jewish Identity; ed., CCAR Centennial Volume; v.-pres., Cleveland Museum of Art; bd. mem., Greater Cleveland Round Table. Author: *Maimonidean Criticism and the Maimonidean Controversy*; *A History of Judaism* (vol. 1); *Images of Moses*; *The Story of Scripture*; ed.: *In the Time of Harvest: Essays in Honor of Abba Hillel Silver*; *Judaism and Ethics*.

SILVERMAN, SOL, attorney, communal worker; b. San Francisco, Calif., June 25, 1900; d. San Francisco, Calif., Sept. 30 (?), 1989. Educ.: U. Calif.-Berkeley (BA, JD; 1st Jew to captain varsity boxing team). Private law practice, 1926 on; admitted to U.S. Supreme Court, 1935; chmn.: Calif. Comm. for Boxing Safeguards 1963–66; Comm. on Uniform Laws; S.F. Bar Journal; Cal. State Bar Journal; mem., Calif. Constitutional Revision Comm. Published., *Emanu-El* (predecessor of the *Jewish Journal*), 1930–45; pres.: N. Calif. JNF; S.F. Lodge B'nai B'rith; S.F. dist. ZOA; Histadrut; bd. mem.: Jewish Welfare Fed.; ADL.

SOSKIS, PHILIP, social-work executive; communal worker; b. Ostilla, Russia, July 4, 1910; d. Philadelphia, Pa., June 25, 1989; in U.S. since 1920. Educ.: Brooklyn Coll.; Columbia U. School of Social Work. Case supervisor and admin., NYC Dept. of Welfare, 1934–37; dir., staff training and development, NYC Dept. of Welfare, 1945–47; admin., United Service for New Americans, 1947–49; asst. dir., N.Y. Assn. for New Americans, 1949–52; dir., 1952–76; exec. consultant thereafter. Pres., Natl. Conf. Jewish Communal Service; cofounder and 1st cochmn., NACHES— Natl. Assn. Jewish Family and Children's Agency Professionals; bd. mem.: Amer. Immigration and Citizenship Conf.; adv. bd. mem., Social Service Exchange of the Community Council of Greater N.Y.; Columbia U. School of Social Work Alumni Assn.; bd. mem. and v.-pres., NYC chap., Natl. Assn. of Social Workers; chmn., UJA social service div.; chmn., Fed. of Jewish Philanthropies health and welfare div.; mem. exec bd., Brooklyn Coll. Inst. for Retired Professionals and Executives.

SPIRA, ISRAEL, rabbi; b. Bluzhev, Galicia, (?), 1899; d. Brooklyn, N.Y., Oct. 30, 1989; in U.S. since 1946. The Bluzhever Rebbe, a fifth-generation direct descendant of the Hassidic dynasty founder. Received *semikhah* from Rabbi Meir Arik of Tarnow at age 16; served as rabbi of Prochnik, Galicia; in 1932, succeeded his father as Rebbe. Survived Bergen-Belsen and other concentration camps, but his first wife and other family members perished. A leader of Agudath Israel of Amer.; sr. member, Council of Torah Sages of Agudah at the time of his death.

STONE, I. F. (ISIDOR FEINSTEIN), journalist; b. Philadelphia, Pa., Dec. 24, 1907; d. Boston, Mass., June 18, 1989. (He adopted the name Stone, with his initials, at age 30.) Educ.: U. Pa. (dropped out in junior year but was awarded a BA degree in 1975). Reporter, various N.J. newspapers and *Philadelphia Inquirer*, 1923–33; editorial writer: *Philadelphia Record*, 1933; *N.Y. Post*, 1933–39; assoc. ed., *The Nation*, 1938–40, and Washington ed., 1940–46; reporter, columnist, editorial writer: *N.Y. Post*, *PM*, *N.Y. Star*, *N.Y. Daily Compass*, 1942–52. Following the successive failures of the last 3, in 1953 started his own one-man, Washington-based newsletter, *I.F. Stone's Weekly*; in 1969, following a heart attack, it became *I.F. Stone's Bi-Weekly*; when it ceased publication in 1971, it had 70,000 subscribers. Disting. Scholar in Residence, American U., 1975 on; contributing ed., *N.Y Review of Books*. A skillful user of documents to expose government disinformation and malfeasance, his pugnacious muckraking and advocacy of civil liberties and international peace angered people of all views at one time or another: e.g., the Left, when he denounced the Soviet system; Jews, when after 1967, he urged creation of a Palestinian state. Author: 12 books, incl. *Underground to Palestine* (1946); *This Is Israel* (1948); *The Truman Era* (1953); *The Hidden History of the Korean War* (1969); *The Killings at Kent State: How Murder Went Unpunished* (1970); *The Trial of Socrates* (1989). Recipient: George Polk Memorial Award; Columbia U. Journalism Award; hon. doctorates: Amherst, Reed, Brown; subject of film *I.F. Stone's Weekly*.

SYRKIN, MARIE, writer, communal worker; b. Bern, Switz., Mar. 22, 1899; d. Santa Monica, Calif., Feb. 1, 1989; in U.S. since 1907. Educ.: Cornell U. English teacher, NYC high schools, 1925–50; assoc. prof., dept. of humanities, Brandeis U., 1950–66, and prof. emer. 1966 on. A founder of the Labor Zionist journal *Jewish Frontier*, 1934, and its editor, 1948–71; ed., Herzl Press, 1971 on; ed. bd. mem.: *Midstream*, *Middle East Review*. Mem., World Zionist Exec., 1965–69; hon. pres., Labor Zionist Movement U.S., 1965–70; mem. exec. bd., Amer. Profs. for Peace in the Middle East. Daughter of Labor Zionist leader Nachman Syrkin and lifelong friend and confidante of Golda Meir, she was acclaimed as a brilliant polemicist and orator in the Zionist cause. Author: *Your School, Your Children* (1944); *Blessed Is the Match: The Story of Jewish Resistance* (1957); *Nachman Syrkin: A Memoir* (1960); *Golda Meir: Israel's Leader* (1969; and two earlier biographies); *Gleanings: A Diary in Verse* (1979); *The State of the Jews* (1980); and numerous articles and essays in various publications. Recipient: Woman of the Year Award: Jewish War Vets Womens Aux.; U. of Judaism; hon. doctorates: Jewish Teachers Sem.; Brandeis U.; Hadassah Myrtle Wreath Award, and other honors.

TENENBAUM, SHEA, writer; b. Lublin, Poland, Apr. 14, 1908; d. NYC, Nov. 24, 1989; in U.S. since 1934. Author of 28 books and hundreds of stories, articles, and memoirs, in Yiddish. Mem.: Jewish Natl. Workers Alliance; Yiddish PEN Club. Recipient: Award from Amer. Com. for Emigré Scholars, Writers and Artists; Zvi Kessel Prize, Mexico; Fernando Jeno Award for Jewish Lit., Mexico; JWB Jewish Book Council Award (1985) for Yiddish lit.

TILLEM, IVAN L., businessman, communal worker; b. NYC, Aug. 13, 1956; d. in a plane crash in Ethiopia, on a medical and relief mission, Aug. 7, 1989. Educ.: Queens Coll.; Cardozo Law School (Yeshiva U.). Assoc. genl. counsel, Natl. Jewish Comm. on Law and Public Affairs, 1980–83; ed. and pub., *Jewish Directory and Almanac*; chmn., Pacific Group, a diversified industrial holding co.; asst. prof., social science, Stern Coll. for Women (Yeshiva U.). Benefactor, Yeshiva U., mem. its bd. of trustees (the youngest ever appointed), mem., bd. of dirs. Cardozo Law School and Stern Coll.; bd. mem.: North Amer. Conf. on Ethiopian Jewry (NACOEJ); Amer. Zionist Youth Found. Benefactor: Ohel Children's Home and Family Services and other organizations and institutions.

TUCHMAN, BARBARA W., writer, historian; b. NYC, Jan. 30, 1912; d. Greenwich, Conn., Feb. 6, 1989. Educ.: Radcliffe Coll. Daughter of banker Maurice Wertheim; granddaughter of Henry Morgenthau, Sr. Research asst., Inst. of Pacific Relations, 1934–35; editorial asst., *The Nation*, 1936 (NYC), 1937 (Spain); staff writer, *War in Spain* (London), 1937–38; Amer. corresp., *New Statesman and Nation* (London), 1939; Far East news desk, OWI (NYC), 1944–45. Mem., Smithsonian Council; trustee, Radcliffe Coll.; trustee and v.-chmn., N.Y. Public Library; treas., Authors Guild; council mem., Authors League; pres., Soc. of Amer. Historians; pres., Amer. Acad. of Arts and Letters. Author: *The Lost British Policy* (1938); *Bible and Sword* (1956); *The Zimmermann Telegram* (1958); *The Guns of August* (1962); *The Proud Tower* (1966); *Stillwell and the American Experience in China, 1911–45* (1971); *Notes from China* (1972); *A Distant Mirror* (1978); *Practising History* (1981); *The March of Folly: From Troy to Vietnam* (1984); *The First Salute* (1988); numerous articles and essays. Recipient: 2 Pulitzer Prizes (*Guns of August*; *Stillwell*); hon. doctorates: Yale, Columbia, and others; Order of Leopold 1st class (Belgium); Fellow, Amer. Acad. of Arts and Letters and winner its Gold Medal for history.

UVEELER, MARK, social-work executive, communal worker; b. Warsaw, Poland, Dec. 7, 1904; d. Jerusalem, Israel, Aug. 2, 1989; in U.S. since 1941. Teacher, Yiddish schools, Warsaw, 1922–23; genl. sec., Leather Goods Workers Union and Jewish Printers Union, 1924–26; exec. dir., Jewish Actors Union, 1926–32, 1936–39; mem.: exec. bd., Friends of YIVO Soc., Warsaw, 1932–39; cent. bd., YIVO, Vilna, 1939–40. Escaped to U.S. early in WWII; helped to revive the YIVO Inst. in New York and served as exec. dir., 1944–54; dir., dept of cult. and educ. reconstruction, Conf. on Jewish Material Claims Against Germany, 1954–64; founding exec. dir., Memorial Found. for Jewish Culture, 1964–72. A resident of Israel after 1972, served in a variety of volunteer capacities, partic. on behalf of the Hebrew U., Yad Vashem, and Yad Ben-Zvi. Recipient: Solomon Bublick Prize, Hebrew U.; hon. mem., Centre de Droit Hébraïque, Paris.

VOSK, MARC, sociologist; b. Odessa, Russia, Sept. 27, 1907; d. Williamsport, Pa., Aug. 8, 1989; in U.S. since 1912. Served U.S. Army, WWII. Dir., research div., Amer. Jewish Com., 1947–55; co-author (with Marshall Sklare), "The Riverton Study: How Jews Look at Themselves and Their Neighbors" (1957); collaborator (with John Slawson), *Unequal Americans: Practices and Politics of Intergroup Relations* (1979). Also served as director of surveys for the Amer. Found. for the Blind and was associated with the Amtorg Trading Co., which did business with the USSR. Active in peace causes all his life.

WEISS-ROSMARIN, TRUDE, writer, lecturer; b. Frankfurt am Main, Germany, June 17, 1908; d. Santa Monica, Calif., June 26, 1989; in U.S. since 1931. Educ.: U.'s of Berlin, Leipzig, Wurtzburg (PhD). Founded *The Jewish Spectator* in 1936 (with her first husband); assoc. ed., 1939–42; sole ed. and pub., 1942 on. Known for her well-informed, scholarly, outspoken, often iconoclastic views on Jewish life. Dir., School of the Jewish Woman, NYC, 1933–40; lect., Jewish hist., NYU, and a perennial favorite on the lecture circuit. Authored a series of popular-priced books on Jewish topics as well as more scholarly works. Mem.: Amer. Acad. of Religion; Soc. for the Scientific Study of Religion. Author: *Arabic and Arabs in Babylonian and Assyrian Sources*; *Religion of Reason: The Religious Philosophy of Hermann Cohen*; *The Hebrew Moses: An Answer to Sigmund Freud*; *Judaism and Christianity: The Differences*; *Jewish Survival*; *Saadia*.

WISCHNITZER, RACHEL, professor; b. Minsk, Russia, Apr. 15, 1885 (?); d. NYC, Nov. 20, 1989; in U.S. since 1940. Educ.: U. Heidelberg; U. Munich; Académie Royale des Beaux Arts, Brussels; Ecole Spéciale d'Architecture, Paris (architect's cert.); NYU (MA in art hist.). In Europe: art ed., *Rimon* and *Milgroim* magazines, 1922–24, and *Encycl. Judaica*, 1928–34; curator, Jewish Museum, Berlin, 1933–38. Living in Paris, 1938–40, arranged exhibit of Jewish artists residing there at the time. In U.S.: art ed., *Universal Jewish Encycl.*, 1942–44; research fellow, Amer. Acad. for Jewish Research, 1940–43; in 1956 established fine arts dept. at Stern Coll. for Women (Yeshiva U.), where she taught until retirement in 1968; consultant, Yeshiva U. Museum. One of the first women to become an architect and a pioneer in the scholarly field of Jewish art. Author: *Gestalten and Symbole der jüdischen Kunst*; *The Messianic Theme in the Paintings of the Dura Synagogue*; *Synagogue Architecture in the United States*; *The Architecture of the European Synagogue*; and numerous articles. Recipient: hon. doctorate, Yeshiva U.; fellow, Amer. Acad. for Jewish Research.

WOLMAN, ABEL, professor, engineering consultant; b. Baltimore, Md., June 10, 1892; d. Baltimore, Md., Feb. 22, 1989. Educ.: Johns Hopkins U. (AB, BS, D-Eng). Engineer: U.S. Public Health Svc., 1913; Maryland Dept. of Health, 1914, becoming chief engineer in 1922; lect., sanitary engineering, Johns Hopkins U., 1921–36; prof. and dept chmn., 1937–1962. Adviser to many federal agencies (Atomic Energy Comm., TVA, U.S. Geological Survey, armed forces, etc.); chmn., National Water Resources Bd. of the U.S.; mem., Defense Dept. Task Force on Water Supply; adviser on water problems to more than 50 govts. and the World Health Org. Best known as a pioneer in the standardized chlorination of the public water supply, a practice adopted worldwide as a means of protection against waterborne diseases. Pres.: Amer. Public Health Assn.; Amer. Water Works Assn.; mem.: Natl. Acad. of Sciences; Natl. Acad. of Engineering. Author: 4 books and over 300 professional articles. Recipient: U.S. Natl. Medal of Science (1975); Tyler Ecology Award (1976); Milton Eisenhower Medal for Disting. Service, Johns Hopkins U. (1973); Albert Lasker Special Award, Amer. Public Health Assn. (1960); Proctor Prize, Research Soc. of Amer.; 1st recip., Lewis L. Dollinger Pure Environment Award, Franklin Inst. (1968). Chair named in his honor at Technion-Israel Inst. of Technology as well as a municipal bldg. in Baltimore.

YASEEN, LEONARD C., businessman; b. Chicago Heights, Ill., June 27, 1912; d. Providence, R.I., Oct. 8, 1989. Educ.: U. of Ill. Founder, the Fantus Co., consultants to business on location of plants and offices; consultant to NYC on retention of business in the city. V.-pres. and natl. chmn., interreligious affairs comm., Amer. Jewish Com.; trustee, Hirshhorn Museum, Washington, DC; chmn., bd. of friends, Neuberger Museum, Purchase, N.Y.; mem., SUNY-Purchase Found.; founder, Yaseen Lecture Series, Metropolitan Museum of Art and Neuberger Museum, SUNY-Purchase. Author: *Industrial Plant Location* (1949, 1956); *The Jesus Connection* (1986; a refutation of anti-Semitism).

Calendars

SUMMARY JEWISH CALENDAR, 5751–5755 (Sept. 1990–Aug. 1995)

HOLIDAY	5751 1990			5752 1991			5753 1992			5754 1993			5755 1994		
Rosh Ha-shanah, 1st day	Th	Sept.	20	M	Sept.	9	M	Sept.	28	Th	Sept.	16	T	Sept.	6
Rosh Ha-shanah, 2nd day	F	Sept.	21	T	Sept.	10	T	Sept.	29	F	Sept.	17	W	Sept.	7
Fast of Gedaliah	S	Sept.	23	W	Sept.	11	W.	Sept.	30	S	Sept.	19	Th	Sept.	8
Yom Kippur	Sa	Sept.	29	W	Sept.	18	W.	Oct.	7	Sa	Sept.	25	Th	Sept.	15
Sukkot, 1st day	Th	Oct.	4	M	Sept.	23	M	Oct.	12	Th	Sept.	30	T	Sept.	20
Sukkot, 2nd day	F	Oct.	5	T	Sept.	24	T	Oct.	13	F	Oct.	1	W	Sept.	21
Hosha'na' Rabbah	W	Oct.	10	S	Sept.	29	S	Oct.	18	W	Oct.	6	M	Sept.	26
Shemini 'Azeret	Th	Oct.	11	M	Sept.	30	M	Oct.	19	Th	Oct.	7	T	Sept.	27
Simhat Torah	F	Oct.	12	T	Oct.	1	T.	Oct.	20	F	Oct.	8	W	Sept.	28
New Moon, Heshwan, 1st day	F	Oct.	19	T	Oct.	8	T.	Oct.	27	F	Oct.	15	W	Oct.	5
New Moon, Heshwan, 2nd day	Sa	Oct.	20	W	Oct.	9	W.	Oct.	28	Sa	Oct.	16	Th	Oct.	6
New Moon, Kislew, 1st day	S	Nov.	18	Th	Nov.	7	Th.	Nov.	26	S	Nov.	14	F	Nov.	4
New Moon, Kislew, 2nd day				F	Nov.	8				M	Nov.	15			
Hanukkah, 1st day	W	Dec.	12	M	Dec.	2	S	Dec.	20	Th	Dec.	9	M	Nov.	28
New Moon, Tevet, 1st day	M	Dec.	17	Sa	Dec.	7	F	Dec.	25	T	Dec.	14	Sa	Dec.	3
New Moon, Tevet, 2nd day	T	Dec.	18	S	Dec.	8				W	Dec.	15	S	Dec.	4
Fast of 10th of Tevet	Th	Dec.	27	T	Dec.	17	S	1993 Jan.	3	F	Dec.	24	T	Dec.	13

	1991			1992			1993			1994			1995	
New Moon, Shevat	W	Jan.	16	M	Jan.	6	Sa	Jan.	23	Th	Jan.	13	M	Jan.	2
Hamishshah-'asar bi-Shevat	W	Jan.	30	M	Jan.	20	Sa	Feb.	6	Th	Jan.	27	M	Jan.	16
New Moon, Adar I, 1st day	Th	Feb.	14	T	Feb.	4	S	Feb.	21	F	Feb.	11	T	Jan.	31
New Moon, Adar I, 2nd day	F	Feb.	15	W	Feb.	5	M	Feb.	22	Sa	Feb.	12	W	Feb.	1
New Moon, Adar II, 1st day				Th	Mar.	5							Th	Mar.	2
New Moon, Adar II, 2nd day				F	Mar.	6							F	Mar.	3
Fast of Esther	W	Feb.	27	W	Mar.	18	Th	Mar.	4	Th	Feb.	24	W	Mar.	15
Purim	Th	Feb.	28	Th	Mar.	19	S	Mar.	7	F	Feb.	25	Th	Mar.	16
Shushan Purim	F	Mar.	1	F	Mar.	20	M	Mar.	8	Sa	Feb.	26	F	Mar.	17
New Moon, Nisan	Sa	Mar.	16	Sa	Apr.	4	T	Mar.	23	S	Mar.	13	Sa	Apr.	1
Passover, 1st day	Sa	Mar.	30	Sa	Apr.	18	T	Apr.	6	S	Mar.	27	Sa	Apr.	15
Passover, 2nd day	S	Mar.	31	S	Apr.	19	W	Apr.	7	M	Mar.	28	S	Apr.	16
Passover, 7th day	F	Apr.	5	F	Apr.	24	M	Apr.	12	Sa	Apr.	2	F	Apr.	21
Passover, 8th day	Sa	Apr.	6	Sa	Apr.	25	T	Apr.	13	S	Apr.	3	Sa	Apr.	22
Holocaust Memorial Day	Th	Apr.	11	Th	Apr.	30	S	Apr.	18	F	Apr.	8*	Th	Apr.	27
New Moon, Iyar, 1st day	S	Apr.	14	S	May	3	W	Apr.	21	M	Apr.	11	S	Apr.	30
New Moon, Iyar, 2nd day	M	Apr.	15	M	May	4	Th	Apr.	22	T	Apr.	12	M	May	1
Israel Independence Day	F	Apr.	19*	F	May	8*	M	Apr.	26	Sa	Apr.	16	F	May	5*
Lag Ba-'omer	Th	May	2	Th	May	21	S	May	9	F	Apr.	29	Th	May	18
Jerusalem Day	S	May	12	S	May	31	W	May	19	M	May	9	S	May	28
New Moon, Siwan	T	May	14	T	Jun	2	F	May	21	W	May	11	T	May	30
Shavu'ot, 1st day	S	May	19	S	Jun	7	W	May	26	M	May	16	S	June	4
Shavu'ot, 2nd day	M	May	20	M	Jun	8	Th	May	27	T	May	17	M	June	5
New Moon, Tammuz, 1st day	W	June	12	W	July	1	Sa	June	19	Th	June	9	W	June	28
New Moon, Tammuz, 2nd day	Th	June	13	Th	July	2	S	June	20	F	June	10	Th	June	29
Fast of 17th of Tammuz	S	June	30	S	July	19	T	July	6	S	June	26	S	July	16
New Moon, Av	F	July	12	F	July	31	M	July	19	Sa	July	9	F	July	28
Fast of 9th of Av	S	July	21	S	Aug.	9	T	July	27	S	July	17	S	Aug.	6
New Moon, Elul, 1st day	Sa	Aug.	10	Sa	Aug.	29	W	Aug.	17	S	Aug.	7	Sa	Aug.	26
New Moon, Elul, 2nd day	S	Aug.	11	S	Aug.	30	W	Aug.	18	M	Aug.	8	S	Aug.	27

*Observed Thursday, a day earlier, to avoid conflict with the Sabbath.

CONDENSED MONTHLY CALENDAR
(1990–1993)

1989, Dec. 29–Jan. 26, 1990] TEVET (29 DAYS) [5750

Civil Date	Day of the Week	Jewish Date	SABBATHS, FESTIVALS, FASTS	PENTATEUCHAL READING	PROPHETICAL READING
Dec. 29	F	Tevet 1	New Moon, second day; Hanukkah, seventh day	Num. 28:1–15 Num. 7:48–53	
30	Sa	2	Mi-kez; Hanukkah, eighth day	Gen. 41:1–44:17 Num. 7:54–8:4	I Kings 7:40–50
Jan. 6	Sa	9	Wa-yiggash	Gen. 44:18–47:27	Ezekiel 37:15–28
7	S	10	Fast of 10th of Tevet	Exod. 32:11–14 Exod. 34:1–10 (morning and afternoon)	Isaiah 55:6–56:8 (afternoon only)
13	Sa	16	Wa-yehi	Gen. 47:28–50:26	I Kings 2:1–12
20	Sa	23	Shemot	Exod. 1:1–6:1	Isaiah 27:6–28:13 29:22–23 *Jeremiah 1:1–2:3*

Italics are for Sephardi Minhag.

1990, Jan. 27–Feb. 25]   SHEVAṬ (30 DAYS)   [5750

Civil Date	Day of the Week	Jewish Date	SABBATHS, FESTIVALS, FASTS	PENTATEUCHAL READING	PROPHETICAL READING
Jan. 27	Sa	Shevaṭ 1	Wa-'era'; New Moon	Exod. 6:2–9:35 Num. 28:9–15	Isaiah 66:1–24
Feb. 3	Sa	8	Bo'	Exod. 10:1–13:16	Jeremiah 46:13–28
10	Sa	15	Be-shallaḥ (Shabbat Shirah); Hamishshah-'asar bi-Shevaṭ	Exod. 13:17–17:16	Judges 4:4–5:31 *Judges 5:1–31*
17	Sa	22	Yitro	Exod. 18:1–20:23	Isaiah 6:1–7:6 9:5–6 *Isaiah 6:1–13*
24	Sa	29	Mishpaṭim (Shabbat Shekalim)	Exod. 21:1–24:18 Exod. 30:11–16	II Kings 12:1–17 *II Kings 11:17–12:17* I Samuel 20:18,42
25	S	30	New Moon, first day	Num. 28:1–15	

Italics are for Sephardi Minhag.

1990, Feb. 26–Mar. 26]   ADAR (29 DAYS)   [5750

Civil Date	Day of the Week	Jewish Date	SABBATHS, FESTIVALS, FASTS	PENTATEUCHAL READING	PROPHETICAL READING
Feb. 26	M	Adar 1	New Moon, second day	Num. 28:1–15	
Mar. 3	Sa	6	Terumah	Exod. 25:1–27:19	I Kings 5:26–6:13
8	Th	11	Fast of Esther	Exod. 32:11–14 Exod. 34:1–10 (morning and afternoon)	Isaiah 55:6–56:8 (afternoon only)
10	Sa	13	Tezawweh (Shabbat Zakhor)	Exod. 27:20–30:10 Deut. 25:17–19	I Samuel 15:2–34 *I Samuel 15:1–34*
11	S	14	Purim	Exod. 17:8–16	Book of Esther (night before and in the morning)
12	M	15	Shushan Purim		
17	Sa	20	Ki tissa' (Shabbat Parah)	Exod. 30:11–34:35 Num. 19:1–22	Ezekiel 36:16–38 *Ezekiel 36:16–36*
24	Sa	27	Wa-yakhel, Pekude (Shabbat Ha-hodesh)	Exod. 35:1–40:38 Exod. 12:1–20	Ezekiel 45:16–46:18 *Ezekiel 45:18–46:15*

Italics are for Sephardi Minhag.

MONTHLY CALENDAR / 577

1990, Mar. 27–Apr. 25]   NISAN (30 DAYS)   [5750

Civil Date	Day of the Week	Jewish Date	SABBATHS, FESTIVALS, FASTS	PENTATEUCHAL READING	PROPHETICAL READING
Mar. 27	T	Nisan 1	New Moon	Num. 28:1–15	
31	Sa	5	Wa-yikra'	Levit. 1:1–5:26	Isaiah 43:21–44:24
Apr. 7	Sa	12	Zaw (Shabbat Ha-gadol)	Levit. 6:1–8:36	Malachi 3:4–24
9	M	14	Fast of Firstborn		
10	T	15	Passover, first day	Exod. 12:21–51 Num. 28:16–25	Joshua 5:2–6:1, 27
11	W	16	Passover, second day	Levit. 22:26–23:44 Num. 28:16–25	II Kings 23:1–9, 21–25
12	Th	17	Hol Ha-mo'ed, first day	Exod. 13:1–16 Num. 28:19–25	
13	F	18	Hol Ha-mo'ed, second day	Exod. 22:24–23:19 Num. 28:19–25	
14	Sa	19	Hol Ha-mo'ed, third day	Exod. 33:12–34:26 Num. 28:19–25	Ezekiel 37:1–14
15	S	20	Hol Ha-mo'ed, fourth day	Num. 9:1–14 Num. 28:19–25	
16	M	21	Passover, seventh day	Exod. 13:17–15:26 Num. 28:19–25	II Samuel 22:1–51
17	T	22	Passover, eighth day	Deut. 15:19–16:17 Num. 28:19–25	Isaiah 10:32–12:6
21	Sa	26	Shemini	Levit. 9:1–11:47	II Samuel 6:1–7:17 *II Samuel 6:1–19*
22	S	27	Holocaust Memorial Day		
25	W	30	New Moon, first day	Num. 28:1–15	

Italics are for Sephardi Minhag.

1990, Apr. 26–May 24]   IYAR (29 DAYS)   [5750

Civil Date	Day of the Week	Jewish Date	SABBATHS, FESTIVALS, FASTS	PENTATEUCHAL READING	PROPHETICAL READING
Apr. 26	Th	Iyar 1	New Moon, second day	Num. 28:1–15	
28	Sa	3	Tazria', Mezora'	Levit. 12:1–15:33	II Kings 7:3–20
30	M	5	Israel Independence Day		
May 5	Sa	10	Ahare mot, Kedoshim	Levit. 16:1–20:27	Amos 9:7–15 *Ezekiel 20:2–20*
12	Sa	17	Emor	Levit. 21:1–24:23	Ezekiel 44:15–31
13	S	18	Lag Ba-'omer		
19	Sa	24	Be-har, Be-hukkotai	Levit. 25:1–27:34	Jeremiah 16:19–17:14
23	W	28	Jerusalem Day		

1990, May 25–June 23]   SIWAN (30 DAYS)   [5750

Civil Date	Day of the Week	Jewish Date	SABBATHS, FESTIVALS, FASTS	PENTATEUCHAL READING	PROPHETICAL READING
May 25	F	Siwan 1	New Moon	Num. 28:1–15	
26	Sa	2	Be-midbar	Num. 1:1–4:20	Hosea 2:1–22
30	W	6	Shavu'ot, first day	Exod. 19:1–20:23 Num. 28:26–31	Ezekiel 1:1–28 3:12
31	Th	7	Shavu'ot, second day	Deut. 15:19–16:17 Num. 28:26–31	Habbakuk 3:1–19 *Habbakuk 2:20–3:19*
June 2	Sa	9	Naso'	Num. 4:21–7:89	Judges 13:2–25
9	Sa	16	Be-ha'alotekha	Num. 8:1–12:16	Zechariah 2:14–4:7
16	Sa	23	Shelah lekha	Num. 13:1–15:41	Joshua 2:1–24
23	Sa	30	Korah; New Moon, first day	Num. 16:1–18:32 Num. 28:9–15	Isaiah 66:1–24 *Isaiah 66:1–24 I Samuel 20:18, 42*

Italics are for Sephardi Minhag.

1990, June 24–July 22] TAMMUZ (29 DAYS) [5750

Civil Date	Day of the Week	Jewish Date	SABBATHS, FESTIVALS, FASTS	PENTATEUCHAL READING	PROPHETICAL READING
June 24	S	Tammuz 1	New Moon, second day	Num. 28:1–15	
30	Sa	7	Hukkat	Num. 19:1–22:1	Judges 11:1–33
July 7	Sa	14	Balak	Num. 22:2–25:9	Micah 5:6–6:8
10	T	17	Fast of 17th of Tammuz	Exod. 32:11–14 Exod. 34:1–10 (morning and afternoon)	Isaiah 55:6–56:8 (afternoon only)
14	Sa	21	Pinehas	Num. 25:10–30:1	Jeremiah 1:1–2:3
21	Sa	28	Mattot, Mas'e	Num. 30:2–36:13	Jeremiah 2:4–28 3:4 *Jeremiah 2:4–28 4:1–2*

Italics are for Sephardi Minhag.

1990, July 23–Aug. 21] AV (30 DAYS) [5750]

Civil Date	Day of the Week	Jewish Date	SABBATHS, FESTIVALS, FASTS	PENTATEUCHAL READING	PROPHETICAL READING
July 23	M	Av 1	New Moon	Num. 28:1–15	
28	Sa	6	Devarim (Shabbat Ḥazon)	Deut. 1:1–3:22	Isaiah 1:1–27
31	T	9	Fast of 9th of Av	Morning: Deut. 4:25–40 Afternoon: Exod. 32:11–14 Exod. 34:1–10	(Lamentations is read the night before.) Jeremiah 8:13–9:23 (morning) Isaiah 55:6–56:8 (afternoon)
Aug. 4	Sa	13	Wa-ethannan (Shabbat Naḥamu)	Deut. 3:23–7:11	Isaiah 40:1–26
11	Sa	20	ʻEḳev	Deut. 7:12–11:25	Isaiah 49:14–51:3
18	Sa	27	Re'eh	Deut. 11:26–16:17	Isaiah 54:11–55:5
21	T	30	New Moon, first day	Num. 28:1–15	

1990, Aug. 22–Sept. 19] ELUL (29 DAYS) [5750]

Civil Date	Day of the Week	Jewish Date	SABBATHS, FESTIVALS, FASTS	PENTATEUCHAL READING	PROPHETICAL READING
Aug. 22	W	Elul 1	New Moon, second day	Num. 28:1–15	
25	Sa	4	Shofeṭim	Deut. 16:18–21:9	Isaiah 51:12–52:12
Sept. 1	Sa	11	Ki teze'	Deut. 21:10–25:19	Isaiah 54:1–10
8	Sa	18	Ki tavo'	Deut. 26:1–29:8	Isaiah 60:1–22
15	Sa	25	Niẓẓavim, Wa-yelekh	Deut. 29:9–31:30	Isaiah 61:10–63:9

1990, Sept. 20–Oct. 19] TISHRI (30 DAYS) [5751

Civil Date	Day of the Week	Jewish Date	SABBATHS, FESTIVALS, FASTS	PENTATEUCHAL READING	PROPHETICAL READING
Sept. 20	Th	Tishri 1	Rosh Ha-shanah, first day	Gen. 21:1–34 Num. 29:1–6	I Samuel 1:1–2:10
21	F	2	Rosh Ha-shanah, second day	Gen. 22:1–24 Num. 29:1–6	Jeremiah 31:2–20
22	Sa	3	Ha'azinu (Shabbat Shuvah)	Deut. 32:1–52	Hosea 14:2–10 Micah 7:18–20 Joel 2:15–27 *Hosea 14:2–10* *Micah 7:18–20*
23	S	4	Fast of Gedaliah	Exod. 32:11–14 Exod. 34:1–10 (morning and afternoon)	Isaiah 55:6–56:8 (afternoon only)
29	Sa	10	Yom Kippur	Morning: Levit. 16:1–34 Num. 29:7–11 Afternoon: Levit. 18:1–30	Isaiah 57:14–58:14 Jonah 1:1–4:11 Micah 7:18–20
Oct. 4	Th	15	Sukkot, first day	Levit. 22:26–23:44 Num. 29:12–16	Zechariah 14:1–21
5	F	16	Sukkot, second day	Levit. 22:26–23:44 Num. 29:12–16	I Kings 8:2–21
Oct. 6	Sa	Tishri 17	Hol Ha-mo'ed, first day	Exod. 33:12–34:26 Num. 29:17–22	Ezekiel 38:18–39:16
7–9	S–T	18–20	Hol Ha-mo'ed, second to fourth days	S Num. 29:20–28 M Num. 29:23–31 T Num. 29:26–34	
10	W	21	Hosha'na' Rabbah	Num. 29:26–34	
11	Th	22	Shemini 'Azeret	Deut. 14:22–16:17 Num. 29:35–30:1	I Kings 8:54–66
12	F	23	Simhat Torah	Deut. 33:1–34:12 Gen. 1:1–2:3 Num. 29:35–30:1	Joshua 1:1–18 *Joshua 1:1–9*
13	Sa	24	Be-re'shit	Gen. 1:1–6:8	Isaiah 42:5–43:10 *Isaiah 42:5–21*
19	F	30	New Moon, first day	Num. 28:1–15	

Italics are for Sephardi Minhag.

1990, Oct. 20–Nov. 17] HESHWAN (29 DAYS) [5751

Civil Date	Day of the Week	Jewish Date	SABBATHS, FESTIVALS, FASTS	PENTATEUCHAL READING	PROPHETICAL READING
Oct. 20	Sa	Heshwan 1	Noah; New Moon, second day	Gen. 6:9–11:32 Num. 28:9–15	Isaiah 66:1–24
27	Sa	8	Lekh lekha	Gen. 12:1–17:27	Isaiah 40:27–41:16
Nov. 3	Sa	15	Wa-yera'	Gen. 18:1–22:24	II Kings 4:1–37 *II Kings 4:1–23*
10	Sa	22	Hayye Sarah	Gen. 23:1–25:18	I Kings 1:1–31
17	Sa	29	Toledot	Gen. 25:19–28:9	I Samuel 20:18–42

1990, Nov. 18–Dec. 17] KISLEW (30 DAYS) [5751

Civil Date	Day of the Week	Jewish Date	SABBATHS, FESTIVALS, FASTS	PENTATEUCHAL READING	PROPHETICAL READING
Nov. 18	S	Kislew 1	New Moon	Num. 28:1–15	
24	Sa	7	Wa-yeze'	Gen. 28:10–32:3	Hosea 12:13–14:10 *Hosea 11:7–12:12*
Dec. 1	Sa	14	Wa-yishlah	Gen. 32:4–36:43	Hosea 11:7–12:12 *Obadiah 1:1–21*
8	Sa	21	Wa-yeshev	Gen. 37:1–40:23	Amos 2:6–3:8
12–14	W–F	25–27	Hanukkah, first to third days	W Num. 7:1–17 Th Num. 7:18–29 F Num. 7:24–35	
15	Sa	28	Mi-kez; Hanukkah, fourth day	Gen. 41:1–44:17 Num. 7:30–35	Zechariah 2:14–4:7
16	S	29	Hanukkah, fifth day	Num. 7:36–47	
17	M	30	New Moon, first day; Hanukkah, sixth day	Num. 28:1–15 Num. 7:42–47	

Italics are for Sephardi Minhag

1990, Dec. 18–Jan. 15, 1991] TEVET (29 DAYS) [5751

Civil Date	Day of the Week	Jewish Date	SABBATHS, FESTIVALS, FASTS	PENTATEUCHAL READING	PROPHETICAL READING
Dec. 18	T	Tevet 1	New Moon, second day; Hanukkah, seventh day	Num. 28:1–15 Num. 7:48–53	
19	W	2	Hanukkah, eighth day	Num. 7:54–8:4	
22	Sa	5	Wa-yiggash	Gen. 44:18–47:27	Ezekiel 37:15–28
27	Th	10	Fast of 10th of Tevet	Exod. 32:11–14 43:1–10 (morning and afternoon)	Isaiah 55:6–56:8 (afternoon only)
29	Sa	12	Wa-yehi	Gen. 47:28–50:26	I Kings 2:1–12
Jan. 5	Sa	19	Shemot	Exod. 1:1–6:1	Isaiah 27:6–28:13 29:22–23 *Jeremiah 1:1–2:3*
12	Sa	26	Wa-'era'	Exod. 6:2–9:35	Ezekiel 28:25–29:21

Italics are for Sephardi Minhag.

1991, Jan. 16–Feb. 14]   SHEVAṬ (30 DAYS)   [5751

Civil Date	Day of the Week	Jewish Date	SABBATHS, FESTIVALS, FASTS	PENTATEUCHAL READING	PROPHETICAL READING
Jan. 16	W	Shevaṭ 1	New Moon	Num. 28:1–15	
19	Sa	4	Bo'	Exod. 10:1–13:16	Jeremiah 46:13–28
26	Sa	11	Be-shallaḥ (Shabbat Shirah)	Exod. 13:17–17:16	Judges 4:4–5:31 *Judges 5:1–31*
30	W	15	Ḥamishshah-'asar bi-Shevaṭ		
Feb. 2	Sa	18	Yitro	Exod. 18:1–20:23	Isaiah 6:1–7:6 9:5, 6 *Isaiah 6:1–13*
9	Sa	25	Mishpaṭim (Shabbat Shekalim)	Exod. 21:1–24:18 Exod. 30:11–16	II Kings 12:1–17 *II Kings 11:17–12:17*
14	Th	30	New Moon, first day	Num. 28:1–15	

Italics are for Sephardi Minhag.

1991, Feb. 15–Mar. 15] ADAR (29 DAYS) [5751

Civil Date	Day of the Week	Jewish Date	SABBATHS, FESTIVALS, FASTS	PENTATEUCHAL READING	PROPHETICAL READING
Feb. 15	F	Adar 1	New Moon, second day	Num. 28:1–15	
16	Sa	2	Terumah	Exod. 25:1–27:19	I Kings 5:26–6:13
23	Sa	9	Tezawweh (Shabbat Zakhor)	Exod. 27:20–30:10 Deut. 25:17–19	I Samuel 15:2–34 *I Samuel 15:1–34*
27	W	13	Fast of Esther	Exod. 32:11–14 Exod. 34:1–10 (morning and afternoon)	Isaiah 55:6–56:8 (afternoon only)
28	Th	14	Purim	Exod. 17:8–16	Book of Esther (night before and in the morning)
Mar. 1	F	15	Shushan Purim		
2	Sa	16	Ki tissa'	Exod. 30:11–34:35	I Kings 18:1–39 *I Kings 18:20–39*
9	Sa	23	Wa-yakhel, Pekude (Shabbat Parah)	Exod. 35:1–40:38 Num. 19:1–22	Ezekiel 36:16–38 *Ezekiel 36:16–36*

Italics are for Sephardi Minhag.

1991, Mar. 16–Apr. 14]   NISAN (30 DAYS)   [5751

Civil Date	Day of the Week	Jewish Date	SABBATHS, FESTIVALS, FASTS	PENTATEUCHAL READING	PROPHETICAL READING
Mar. 16	Sa	Nisan 1	Wa-yikra' (Shabbat Ha-hodesh); New Moon	Levit. 1:1–5:26 Exod. 12:1–20 Num. 28:9–15	Ezekiel 45:16–46:18 *Ezekiel 45:18–46:15*
23	Sa	8	Zaw (Shabbat Ha-gadol)	Levit. 6:1–8:36	Malachi 3:4–24
29	F	14	Fast of Firstborn		
30	Sa	15	Passover, first day	Exod. 12:21–51 Num. 28:16–25	Joshua 5:2–6:1, 27
31	S	16	Passover, second day	Levit. 22:26–23:44 Num. 28:16–25	II Kings 23:1–19, 21–25
Apr. 1	M	17	Hol Ha-mo'ed, first day	Exod. 13:1–16 Num. 28:19–25	
2	T	18	Hol Ha-mo'ed, second day	Exod. 22:24–23:19 Num. 28:19–25	
3	W	19	Hol Ha-mo'ed, third day	Exod. 34:1–26 Num. 28:19–25	
4	Th	20	Hol Ha-mo'ed, fourth day	Num. 9:1–14 Num. 28:19–25	
5	F	21	Passover, seventh day	Exod. 13:17–15:26 Num. 28:19–25	II Samuel 22:1–51
6	Sa	22	Passover, eighth day	Deut. 15:19–16:17 Num. 28:19–25	Isaiah 10:32–12:6
11	Th	27	Holocaust Memorial Day		
13	Sa	29	Shemini	Levit. 9:1–11:47	I Samuel 20:18–42
14	S	30	New Moon, first day	Num. 28:1–15	

Italics are for Sephardi Minhag.

1991, Apr. 15–May 13]   IYAR (29 DAYS)   [5751

Civil Date	Day of the Week	Jewish Date	SABBATHS, FESTIVALS, FASTS	PENTATEUCHAL READING	PROPHETICAL READING
Apr. 15	M	Iyar 1	New Moon, second day	Num. 28:1–15	
19	F*	5	Israel Independence Day		
20	Sa	6	Tazria', Mezora'	Levit. 12:1–15:33	II Kings 7:3–20
27	Sa	13	Aḥare mot, Ḳedoshim	Levit. 16:1–20:27	Amos 9:7–15 *Ezekiel 20:2–20*
May 2	Th	18	Lag Ba-'omer		
4	Sa	20	Emor	Levit. 21:1–24:23	Ezekiel 44:15–31
11	Sa	27	Be-har, Be-ḥuḳḳotai	Levit. 25:1–27:34	Jeremiah 16:19–17:14
12	S	28	Jerusalem Day		

*Observed Thursday, a day earlier, to avoid conflict with the Sabbath.

Italics are for Sephardi Minhag.

1991, May 14–June 12] SIWAN (30 DAYS) [5751

Civil Date	Day of the Week	Jewish Date	SABBATHS, FESTIVALS, FASTS	PENTATEUCHAL READING	PROPHETICAL READING
May 14	T	Siwan 1	New Moon	Num. 28:1–15	
18	Sa	5	Be-midbar	Num. 1:1–4:20	Hosea 2:1–22
19	S	6	Shavu'ot, first day	Exod. 19:1–20:23 Num. 28:26–31	Ezekiel 1:1–28 3:12
20	M	7	Shavu'ot, second day	Deut. 15:19–16:17 Num. 28:26–31	Habbakuk 3:1–19 *Habbakuk 2:20–3:19*
25	Sa	12	Naso'	Num. 4:21–7:89	Judges 13:2–25
June 1	Sa	19	Be-ha'alotekha	Num. 8:1–12:16	Zecharia 2:14–4:7
8	Sa	26	Shelah lekha	Num. 13:1–15:41	Joshua 2:1–24
12	W	30	New Moon, first day	Num. 28:1–15	

1991, June 13–July 11] TAMMUZ (29 DAYS) [5751

Civil Date	Day of the Week	Jewish Date	SABBATHS, FESTIVALS, FASTS	PENTATEUCHAL READING	PROPHETICAL READING
June 13	Th	Tammuz 1	New Moon, second day	Num. 28:1–15	
15	Sa	3	Korah	Num. 16:1–18:32	I Samuel 11:14–12:22
22	Sa	10	Hukkat	Num. 19:1–22:1	Judges 11:1–33
29	Sa	17	Balak	Num. 22:2–25:9	Micah 5:6–6:8
30	S	18	Fast of 17th of Tammuz	Exod. 32:11–14 Exod. 34:1–10 (morning and afternoon)	Isaiah 55:6–56:8 (afternoon only)
July 6	Sa	24	Pinehas	Num. 25:10–30:1	Jeremiah 1:1–2:3

Italics are for Sephardi Minhag.

1991, July 12–Aug. 10] AV (30 DAYS) [5751

Civil Date	Day of the Week	Jewish Date	SABBATHS, FESTIVALS, FASTS	PENTATEUCHAL READING	PROPHETICAL READING
July 12	F	Av 1	New Moon	Num. 28:1–15	
13	Sa	2	Maṭṭot, Mas'e	Num. 30:2–36:13	Jeremiah 2:4–28 3:4 *Jeremiah 2:4–28 4:1–2*
20	Sa	9	Devarim (Shabbat Ḥazon)	Deut. 1:1–3:22	Isaiah 1:1–27
21	S	10	Fast of 9th of Av	Morning: Deut. 4:25–40 Afternoon: Exod. 32:11–14 Exod. 34:1–10	(Lamentations is read night before.) Jeremiah 8:13–9:23 (morning) Isaiah 55:6–56:8 (afternoon)
27	Sa	16	Wa-ethannan (Shabbat Naḥamu)	Deut. 3:23–7:11	Isaiah 40:1–26
Aug. 3	Sa	23	'Eḳev	Deut. 7:12–11:25	Isaiah 49:14–51:3
10	Sa	30	Re'eh; New Moon, first day	Deut. 11:26–16:17 Num. 28:9–15	Isaiah 66:1–24 I Samuel 20:18, 42

1991, Aug. 11–Sept. 8] ELUL (29 DAYS) [5751

Civil Date	Day of the Week	Jewish Date	SABBATHS, FESTIVALS, FASTS	PENTATEUCHAL READING	PROPHETICAL READING
Aug. 11	S	Elul 1	New Moon, second day	Num. 28:1–15	
17	Sa	7	Shofeṭim	Deut. 16:18–21:9	Isaiah 51:12–52:12
24	Sa	14	Ki teze'	Deut. 21:10–25:19	Isaiah 54:1–10
31	Sa	21	Ki tavo'	Deut. 26:1–29:8	Isaiah 60:1–22
Sept. 7	Sa	28	Niẓẓavim	Deut. 29:9–30:20	Isaiah 61:10–63:9

Italics are for Sephardi Minhag.

1991, Sept. 9–Oct. 8] TISHRI (30 DAYS) [5752

Civil Date	Day of the Week	Jewish Date	SABBATHS, FESTIVALS, FASTS	PENTATEUCHAL READING	PROPHETICAL READING
Sept. 9	M	Tishri 1	Rosh Ha-shanah, first day	Gen. 21:1–34 Num. 29:1–6	I Samuel 1:1–2:10
10	T	2	Rosh Ha-shanah, second day	Gen. 22:1–24 Num. 29:1–6	Jeremiah 31:2–20
11	W	3	Fast of Gedaliah	Exod. 32:11–14 Exod. 34:1–10 (morning and afternoon)	Isaiah 55:6–56:8 (afternoon only)
14	Sa	6	Wa-yelekh (Shabbat Shuvah)	Deut. 31:1–30	Hosea 14:2–10 Micah 7:18–20 Joel 2:15–27 *Hosea 14:2–10* *Micah 7:18–20*
18	W	10	Yom Kippur	Morning: Levit. 16:1–34 Num. 29:7–11 Afternoon: Levit. 18:1–30	Isaiah 57:14–58:14 Jonah 1:1–4:11 Micah 7:18–20
21	Sa	13	Ha'azinu	Deut. 32:1–52	II Samuel 22:1–51
23	M	15	Sukkot, first day	Levit. 22:26–23:44 Num. 29:12–16	Zechariah 14:1–21
24	T	16	Sukkot, second day	Levit. 22:26–23:44 Num. 29:12–16	I Kings 8:2–21
25–27	W-F	17–19	Hol Ha-mo'ed, first to third days	W Num. 29:17–25 Th Num. 29:20–28 F Num. 29:23–31	
28	Sa	20	Hol Ha-mo'ed, fourth day	Exod. 33:12–34:26 Num. 29:26–31	Ezekiel 38:18–39:16
29	S	21	Hosha'na' Rabbah	Num. 29:26–34	
30	M	22	Shemini 'Azeret	Deut. 14:22–16:17 Num. 29:35–30:1	I Kings 8:54–66
Oct. 1	T	23	Simhat Torah	Deut. 33:1–34:12 Gen. 1:1–2:3 Num. 29:35–30:1	Joshua 1:1–18 *Joshua 1:1–9*
5	Sa	27	Be-re'shit	Gen. 1:1–6:8	Isaiah 42:5–43:10 *Isaiah 42:5–21*
8	T	30	New Moon, first day	Num. 28:1–15	

Italics are for Sephardi Minhag.

1991, Oct. 9–Nov. 7]   ḤESHWAN (30 DAYS)   [5752

Civil Date	Day of the Week	Jewish Date	SABBATHS, FESTIVALS, FASTS	PENTATEUCHAL READING	PROPHETICAL READING
Oct. 9	W	Ḥeshwan 1	New Moon, second day	Num. 28:1–15	
12	Sa	4	Noaḥ	Gen. 6:9–11:32	Isaiah 54:1–55:5 *Isaiah 54:1–10*
19	Sa	11	Lekh lekha	Gen. 12:1–17:27	Isaiah 40:27–41:16
26	Sa	18	Wa-yera'	Gen. 18:1–22:24	II Kings 4:1–37 *II Kings 4:1–23*
Nov. 2	Sa	25	Ḥayye Sarah	Gen. 23:1–25:18	I Kings 1:1–31
7	Th	30	New Moon, first day	Num. 28:1–15	

1991, Nov. 8–Dec. 7]   KISLEW (30 DAYS)   [5752

Civil Date	Day of the Week	Jewish Date	SABBATHS, FESTIVALS, FASTS	PENTATEUCHAL READING	PROPHETICAL READING
Nov. 8	F	Kislew 1	New Moon, second day	Num. 28:1–15	
9	Sa	2	Toledot	Gen. 25:19–28:9	Malachi 1:1–2:7
16	Sa	9	Wa-yeẓe'	Gen. 28:10–32:3	Hosea 12:13–14:10 *Hosea 11:7–12:12*
23	Sa	16	Wa-yishlaḥ	Gen. 32:4–36:43	Hosea 11:7–12:12 *Obadiah 1:1–21*
30	Sa	23	Wa-yeshev	Gen. 37:1–40:23	Amos 2:6–3:8
Dec. 2–6	M–F	25–29	Hanukkah, first to fifth days	M Num. 7:1–17 T Num. 7:18–29 W Num. 7:24–35 Th Num. 7:30–41 F Num. 7:36–47	
7	Sa	30	Mi-keẓ; New Moon, first day; Hanukkah, sixth day	Gen. 41:1–44:17 Num. 28:9–15 Num. 7:42–47	Zechariah 2:14–4:7

Italics are for Sephardi Minhag.

1991, Dec. 8–Jan. 5 1992]   TEVET (29 DAYS)   [5752

Civil Date	Day of the Week	Jewish Date	SABBATHS, FESTIVALS, FASTS	PENTATEUCHAL READING	PROPHETICAL READING
Dec. 8	S	Tevet 1	New Moon, second day; Hanukkah, seventh day	Num. 28:1–15 Num. 7:48–53	
9	M	2	Hanukkah, eighth day	Num. 7:54–8:4	
14	Sa	7	Wa-yiggash	Gen. 44:18–47:27	Ezekiel 37:15–28
17	T	10	Fast of 10th of Tevet	Exod. 32:11–14 Exod. 34:1–10 (morning and afternoon)	Isaiah 55:6–56:8 (afternoon only)
21	Sa	14	Wa-yehi	Gen. 47:28–50:26	I Kings 2:1–12
28	Sa	21	Shemot	Exod. 1:1–6:1	Isaiah 27:6–28:13 29:22–23 *Jeremiah 1:1–2:3*
Jan. 4	Sa	28	Wa-'era'	Exod. 6:2–9:35	Ezekiel 28:25–29:21

Italics are for Sephardi Minhag.

1992, Jan. 6–Feb. 4]   SHEVAṬ (30 DAYS)   [5752

Civil Date	Day of the Week	Jewish Date	SABBATHS, FESTIVALS, FASTS	PENTATEUCHAL READING	PROPHETICAL READING
Jan. 6	M	Shevaṭ 1	New Moon	Num. 28:1–15	
11	Sa	6	Bo'	Exod. 10:1–13:16	Jeremiah 46:13–28
18	Sa	13	Be-Shallaḥ (Shabbat Shirah)	Exod. 13:17–17:16	Judges 4:4–5:31 *Judges 5:1–31*
20	M	15	Ḥamishshah 'asar bi-Shevaṭ		
25	Sa	20	Yitro	Exod. 18:1–20:23	Isaiah 6:1–7:6 9:5, 6 *Isaiah 6:1–13*
Feb. 1	Sa	27	Mishpaṭim	Exod. 21:1–24:18	Jeremiah 34:8–22 33:25, 26
4	T	30	New Moon, first Day	Num. 28:1–15	

Italics are for Sephardi Minhag.

1992, Feb. 5–Mar. 5]   ADAR I (30 DAYS)   [5752

Civil Date	Day of the Week	Jewish Date	SABBATHS, FESTIVALS, FASTS	PENTATEUCHAL READING	PROPHETICAL READING
Feb. 5	W	Adar I 1	New Moon, 2nd day	Num. 28:1–15	
8	Sa	4	Terumah	Exod. 25:1–27:19	I Kings 5:26–6:13
15	Sa	11	Tezawweh	Exod. 27:20–30:10	Ezekiel 43:10–27
22	Sa	18	Ki tissa'	Exod. 30:11–34:35	I Kings 18:1–39 *I Kings 18:20–39*
29	Sa	25	Wa-yakhel (Shabbat Shekalim)	Exod. 35:1–38:20 Exod. 30:11–16	II Kings 12:1–17 *II Kings 11:17–12:17*
Mar. 5	Th	30	New Moon, first day	Num. 28:1–15	

Italics are for Sephardi Minhag.

1992, Mar. 6–Apr. 3] ADAR II (29 DAYS) [5752

Civil Date	Day of the Week	Jewish Date	SABBATHS, FESTIVALS, FASTS	PENTATEUCHAL READING	PROPHETICAL READING
Mar. 6	F	Adar II 1	New Moon, second day	Num. 28:1–15	
7	Sa	2	Peḳude	Exod. 38:21–40:38	I Kings 7:51–8:21 *I Kings 7:40–50*
14	Sa	9	Wa-yikra' (Shabbat Zakhor)	Levit. 1:1–5:26 Deut. 25:17–19	I Samuel 15:2–34 *I Samuel 15:1–34*
18	W	13	Fast of Esther	Exod. 32:11–14 Exod. 34:1–10 (morning and afternoon)	Isaiah 55:6–56:8 (afternoon only)
19	Th	14	Purim	Exod. 17:8–16	Book of Esther (night before and in the morning)
20	F	15	Shushan Purim		
21	Sa	16	Ẓaw	Levit. 6:1–8:36	Jeremiah 7:21–8:3 9:22–23
28	Sa	23	Shemini (Shabbat Parah)	Levit. 9:1–11:47 Num. 19:1–22	Ezekiel 36:16–38 *Ezekiel 36:16–36*

Italics are for Sephardi Minhag.

1992, Apr. 4–May 3] NISAN (30 DAYS) [5752

Civil Date	Day of the Week	Jewish Date	SABBATHS, FESTIVALS, FASTS	PENTATEUCHAL READING	PROPHETICAL READING
Apr. 4	Sa	Nisan 1	Tazria' (Shabbat Ha-hodesh); New Moon	Levit. 12:1–13:59 Exod. 12:1–20 Num. 28:9–15	Ezekiel 45:16–46:18 *Ezekiel 45:18–46:15*
11	Sa	8	Mezora' (Shabbat Ha-gadol)	Levit. 14:1–15:33	Malachi 3:4–24
17	F	14	Fast of Firstborn		
18	Sa	15	Passover, first day	Exod. 12:21–51 Num. 28:16–25	Joshua 5:2–6:1, 27
19	S	16	Passover second day	Levit. 22:26–23:44 Num. 28:16–25	II Kings 23:1–9, 21–25
20	M	17	Hol Ha-mo'ed, first day	Exod. 13:1–16 Num. 28:19–25	
21	T	18	Hol Ha-mo'ed, second day	Exod. 22:24–23:19 Num. 28:19–25	
22	W	19	Hol Ha-mo'ed, third day	Exod. 34:1–26 Num. 28:19–25	
23	Th	20	Hol Ha-mo'ed, fourth day	Num. 9:1–14 Num. 28:19–25	
24	F	21	Passover, seventh day	Exod. 13:17–15:26 Num. 28:19–25	II Samuel 22:1–51
25	Sa	22	Passover, eighth day	Deut. 15:19–16:17 Num. 28:19–25	Isaiah 10:32–12:6
30	Th	27	Holocaust Memorial Day		
May 2	Sa	29	Aḥare Mot	Levit. 16:1–18:30	I Samuel 20:18–42
3	S	30	New Moon, first day	Num. 28:1–15	

Italics are for Sephardi Minhag.

1992, May 4–June 1] IYAR (29 DAYS) [5752

Civil Date	Day of the Week	Jewish Date	SABBATHS, FESTIVALS, FASTS	PENTATEUCHAL READING	PROPHETICAL READING
May 4	M	Iyar 1	New Moon, second day	Num. 28:1–15	
8	F*	5	Israel Independence Day		
9	Sa	6	Ķedoshim	Levit. 19:1–20:27	Amos 9:7–15 *Ezekiel 20:2–20*
16	Sa	13	Emor	Levit. 21:1–24:23	Ezekiel 44:15–31
21	Th	18	Lag Ba-'omer		
23	Sa	20	Be-har	Levit. 25:1–26:2	Jeremiah 32:6–27
30	Sa	27	Be-ḥuķķotai	Levit. 26:3–27:34	Jeremiah 16:19–17:14
31	S	28	Jerusalem Day		

*Observed Thursday, a day earlier, to avoid conflict with the Sabbath.

Italics are for Sephardi Minhag.

1992, June 2–July 1] SIWAN (30 DAYS) [5752

Civil Date	Day of the Week	Jewish Date	SABBATHS, FESTIVALS, FASTS	PENTATEUCHAL READING	PROPHETICAL READING
June 2	T	Siwan 1	New Moon	Num. 28:1–15	
6	Sa	5	Be-midbar	Num. 1:1–4:20	Hosea 2:1–22
7	S	6	Shavu'ot, first day	Exod. 19:1–20:23 Num. 28:26–31	Ezekiel 1:1–28 3:12
8	M	7	Shavu'ot, second day	Deut. 15:19–16:17 Num. 28:26–31	Habbakuk 3:1–19 *Habbakuk 2:20–3:19*
13	Sa	12	Naso'	Num. 4:21–7:89	Judges 13:2–25
20	Sa	19	Be-ha'alotekha	Num. 8:1–12:16	Zechariah 2:14–4:7
27	Sa	26	Shelaḥ lekha	Num. 13:1–15:41	Joshua 2:1–24
July 1	W	30	New Moon, first day	Num. 28:1–15	

Italics are for Sephardi Minhag.

1992, July 2–July 30] TAMMUZ (29 DAYS) [5752

Civil Date	Day of the Week	Jewish Date	SABBATHS, FESTIVALS, FASTS	PENTATEUCHAL READING	PROPHETICAL READING
July 2	Th	Tammuz 1	New Moon, second day	Num. 28:1–15	
4	Sa	3	Korah	Num. 16:1–18:32	I Samuel 11:14–12:22
11	Sa	10	Hukkat	Num. 19:1–22:1	Judges 11:1–33
18	Sa	17	Balak	Num. 22:2–25:9	Micah 5:6–6:8
19	S	18	Fast of 17th of Tammuz	Exod. 32:11–14 34:1–10 (morning and afternoon)	Isaiah 55:6–56:8 (afternoon only)
25	Sa	24	Pinehas	Num. 25:10–30:1	Jeremiah 1:1–2:3

1992, July 31–Aug. 29]   AV (30 DAYS)   [5752

Civil Date	Day of the Week	Jewish Date	SABBATHS, FESTIVALS, FASTS	PENTATEUCHAL READING	PROPHETICAL READING
July 31	F	Av 1	New Moon, first day	Num. 28:1–15	
Aug. 1	Sa	2	Maṭṭot, Mas‘e	Num. 30:2–36:13	Jeremiah 2:4–28 3:4 *Jeremiah 2:4–28 4:1–2*
8	Sa	9	Devarim (Shabbat Ḥazon)	Deut. 1:1–3:22	Isaiah 1:1–27
9	S	10	Fast of 9th of Av	Morning: Deut. 4:25–40 Afternoon: Exod. 32:11–14 Exod. 34:1–10	(Lamentations is read the night before.) Jeremiah 8:13–9:23 (morning) Isaiah 55:6–56:8 (afternoon)
15	Sa	16	Wa-ethannan (Shabbat Naḥamu)	Deut. 3:23–7:11	Isaiah 40:1–26
22	Sa	23	‘Ekev	Deut. 7:12–11:25	Isaiah 49:14–51:3
29	Sa	30	Re'eh; New Moon, first day	Deut. 11:26–16:17 Num. 28:9–15	Isaiah 66:1–24 *Isaiah 66:1–24* I Samuel 20:18,42

Italics are for Sephardi Minhag.

1992, Aug. 30–Sept. 27] ELUL (29 DAYS) [5752

Civil Date	Day of the Week	Jewish Date	SABBATHS, FESTIVALS, FASTS	PENTATEUCHAL READING	PROPHETICAL READING
Aug. 30	S	Elul 1	New Moon, second day	Num. 28:1–15	
Sept. 5	Sa	7	Shofetim	Deut. 16:18–21:9	Isaiah 51:12–52:12
12	Sa	14	Ki teze'	Deut. 21:10–25:19	Isaiah 54:1–10
19	Sa	21	Ki tavo'	Deut. 26:1–29:8	Isaiah 60:1–22
26	Sa	28	Nizzavim	Deut. 29:9–30:20	Isaiah 61:10–63:9

1992, Sept. 28–Oct. 27] TISHRI (30 DAYS) [5753

Civil Date	Day of the Week	Jewish Date	SABBATHS, FESTIVALS, FASTS	PENTATEUCHAL READING	PROPHETICAL READING
Sept. 28	M	Tishri 1	Rosh Ha-shanah, first day	Gen. 21:1–34 Num. 29:1–6	I Samuel 1:1–2:10
29	T	2	Rosh Ha-shanah second day	Gen. 22:1–24 Num. 29:1–6	Jeremiah 31:2–20
30	W	3	Fast of Gedaliah	Exod. 32:11–14 Exod. 34:1–10 (morning and afternoon)	Isaiah 55:6–56:8 (afternoon only)
Oct. 3	Sa	6	Wa-yelekh (Shabbat Shuvah)	Deut. 31:1–30	Hosea 14:2–10 Micah 7:18–20 Joel 2:15–27 *Hosea 14:2–10* *Micah 7:18–20*
7	W	10	Yom Kippur	Morning: Levit. 16:1–34 Num. 29:7–11 Afternoon: Levit. 18:1–30	Isaiah 57:14–58:14 Jonah 1:1–4:11 Micah 7:18–20
10	Sa	13	Ha'azinu	Deut. 32:1–52	II Samuel 22:1–51
12	M	15	Sukkot, first day	Levit. 22:26–23:44 Num. 29:12–16	Zechariah 14:1–21
13	T	16	Sukkot, second day	Levit. 22:26–23:44 Num. 29:12–16	I Kings 8:2–21
14–16	W–F	17–19	Hol Ha-mo'ed, first to third days	W Num. 29:17–25 Th Num. 29:20–28 F Num. 29:23–31	
17	Sa	20	Hol Ha-mo'ed, fourth day	Exod. 33:12–34:26 Num. 29:26–31	Ezekiel 38:18–39:16
18	S	21	Hosha'na' Rabbah	Num. 29:26–34	
19	M	22	Shemini 'Azeret	Deut. 14:22–16:17 Num. 29:35–30:1	I Kings 8:54–66
20	T	23	Simḥat Torah	Deut. 33:1–34:12 Gen. 1:1–2:3 Num. 29:35–30:1	Joshua 1:1–18 *Joshua 1:1–9*
24	Sa	27	Be-re'shit	Gen. 1:1–6:8	Isaiah 42:5–43:10 *Isaiah 42:5–21*
27	T	30	New Moon, first day	Num. 28:1–15	

Italics are for Sephardi Minhag.

1992, Oct. 28–Nov. 25]   ḤESHWAN (29 DAYS)   [5753

Civil Date	Day of the Week	Jewish Date	SABBATHS, FESTIVALS, FASTS	PENTATEUCHAL READING	PROPHETICAL READING
Oct. 28	W	Heshwan 1	New Moon, second day	Num. 28:1–15	
31	Sa	4	Noah	Gen. 6:9–11:32	Isaiah 54:1–55:5 *Isaiah 54:1–10*
Nov. 7	Sa	11	Lekh Lekha	Gen. 12:1–17:27	Isaiah 40:27–41:16
14	Sa	18	Wa-Yera'	Gen. 18:1–22:24	II Kings 4:1–37 *II Kings 4:1–23*
21	Sa	25	Ḥayye Sarah	Gen. 23:1–25:18	I Kings 1:1–31

Italics are for Sephardi Minhag.

1992, Nov. 26–Dec. 24]   KISLEW (29 DAYS)   [5753

Civil Date	Day of the Week	Jewish Date	SABBATHS, FESTIVALS, FASTS	PENTATEUCHAL READING	PROPHETICAL READING
Nov. 26	Th	Kislew 1	New Moon	Num. 28:1–15	
28	Sa	3	Toledot	Gen. 25:19–28:9	Malachi 1:1–2:7
Dec. 5	Sa	10	Wa-yeze'	Gen. 28:10–32:3	Hosea 12:13–14:10 *Hosea 11:7–12:12*
12	Sa	17	Wa-yishlaḥ	Gen. 32:4–36:43	Hosea 11:7–12:12 *Obadiah 1:1–21*
19	Sa	24	Wa-yeshev	Gen. 37:1–40:23	Amos 2:6–3:8
20–24	S-Th	25–29	Hanukkah, first to fifth days	S Num. 7:1–17 M Num. 7:18–29 T Num. 7:24–35 W Num. 7:30–41 Th Num. 7:36–47	

Italics are for Sephardi Minhag.

1992, Dec. 25–Jan. 16, 1993] ṬEVET (29 DAYS) [5753

Civil Date	Day of the Week	Jewish Date	SABBATHS, FESTIVALS, FASTS	PENTATEUCHAL READING	PROPHETICAL READING
Dec. 25	F	Tevet 1	New Moon; Hanukkah, sixth day	Num. 28:1–15 Num. 7:42–47	
26	Sa	2	Mi-ḳeẓ; Hanukkah, seventh day	Gen. 41:1–44:17 Num. 7:48–53	Zechariah 2:14–4:7
27	S	3	Hanukkah, eighth day	Num. 7:54–8:4	
Jan. 2	Sa	9	Wa-yiggash	Gen. 44:18–47:27	Ezekiel 37:15–28
3	S	10	Fast of 10th of Ṭevet	Exod. 32:11–14 34:1–10 (morning and afternoon)	Isaiah 55:6–56:8 (afternoon only)
9	Sa	16	Wa-yeḥi	Gen. 47:28–50:26	I Kings 2:1–12
16	Sa	23	Shemot	Exod. 1:1–6:1	Isaiah 27:6–28:13 29:22–23 *Jeremiah 1:1–2:3*

Italics are for Sephardi Minhag.

SELECTED ARTICLES OF INTEREST IN RECENT VOLUMES OF THE AMERICAN JEWISH YEAR BOOK

The American Jewish Family Today	Steven Martin Cohen 82:136–154
Attitudes of American Jews Toward Israel: Trends Over Time	Eytan Gilboa 86:110–125
The Bitburg Controversy	Deborah E. Lipstadt 87:21–37
California Jews: Data from the Field Polls	Alan M. Fisher and Curtis K. Tanaka 86:196–218
A Century of Conservative Judaism in the United States	Abraham J. Karp 86:3–61
A Century of Jewish History, 1881–1981: The View from America	Lucy S. Dawidowicz 82:3–98
The "Civil Judaism" of Communal Leaders	Jonathan S. Woocher 81:149–169
Counting Jewish Populations: Methods and Problems	Paul Ritterband, Barry A. Kosmin, and Jeffrey Scheckner 88:204–221
The Demographic Consequences of U.S. Jewish Population Trends	U.O. Schmelz and Sergio DellaPergola 83:141–187
The Demography of Latin American Jewry	U.O. Schmelz and Sergio DellaPergola 85:51–102
Ethnic Differences Among Israeli Jews: A New Look	U.O. Schmelz, Sergio DellaPergola, and Uri Avner 90:3–204
The Impact of Feminism on American Jewish Life	Sylvia B. Fishman 89:3–62
Israelis in the United States: Motives, Attitudes, and Intentions	Dov Elizur 80:53–67
Jewish Education Today	Walter I. Ackerman 80:130–148

Jewish Survival: The Demographic Factors	U.O. Schmelz 81:61–117
Jews in the United States: Perspectives from Demography	Sidney Goldstein 81:3–59
The Labor Market Status of American Jews: Patterns and Determinants	Barry R. Chiswick 85:131–153
Latin American Jewry Today	Judith Laikin Elkin 85:3–49
Los Angeles Jewry: A Demographic Portrait	Bruce A. Phillips 86:126–195
The National Gallup Polls and American Jewish Demography	Alan M. Fisher 83:111–126
New Perspectives in American Jewish Sociology	Nathan Glazer 87:3–19
The 1981–1982 National Survey of American Jews	Steven Martin Cohen 83:89–110
The Population of Reunited Jerusalem, 1967–1985	U.O. Schmelz 87:39–113
Recent Jewish Community Population Studies: A Roundup	Gary A. Tobin and Alvin Chenkin 85:154–178
Recent Trends in American Judaism	Jack Wertheimer 89:63–162
Reform and Conservative Judaism in Israel: A Social and Religious Profile	Ephraim Tabory 83:41–61
Religiosity Patterns in Israel	Calvin Goldscheider and Dov Friedlander 83:3–39
The Social Characteristics of the New York Area Jewish Community, 1981	Paul Ritterband and Steven M. Cohen 84:128–161
South African Jewry: A Sociodemographic Profile	Sergio DellaPergola and Allie A. Dubb 88:59–140
South African Jews and the Apartheid Crisis	Gideon Shimoni 88:3–58
Trends in Jewish Philanthropy	Steven Martin Cohen 80:29–51

OBITUARIES

Leo Baeck	By Max Gruenewald 59:478–82
Jacob Blaustein	By John Slawson 72:547–57
Martin Buber	By Seymour Siegel 67:37–43
Abraham Cahan	By Mendel Osherowitch 53:527–29
Albert Einstein	By Jacob Bronowski 58:480–85
Felix Frankfurter	By Paul A. Freund 67:31–36
Louis Ginzberg	By Louis Finkelstein 56:573–79
Jacob Glatstein	By Shmuel Lapin 73:611–17
Sidney Goldmann	By Milton R. Konvitz 85:401–03
Hayim Greenberg	By Marie Syrkin 56:589–94
Abraham Joshua Heschel	By Fritz A. Rothschild 74:533–44
Horace Meyer Kallen	By Milton R. Konvitz 75:55–80
Mordecai Kaplan	By Ludwig Nadelmann 85:404–11
Herbert H. Lehman	By Louis Finkelstein 66:3–20
Judah L. Magnes	By James Marshall 51:512–15
Alexander Marx	By Abraham S. Halkin 56:580–88
Reinhold Niebuhr	By Seymour Siegel 73:605–10
Joseph Proskauer	By David Sher 73:618–28
Maurice Samuel	By Milton H. Hindus 74:545–53
Leo Strauss	By Ralph Lerner 76:91–97
Max Weinreich	By Lucy S. Dawidowicz 70:59–68
Chaim Weizmann	By Harry Sacher 55:462–69
Stephen S. Wise	By Philip S. Bernstein 51:515–18
Harry Austryn Wolfson	By Isadore Twersky 76:99–111

Index

Abdel-Meguid, Ahmad Esmat, 154–56, 246, 408
Abdul Rahman, Ahmed, 149
Abecassis, Raphael, 103
Abed Rabbo, Yasir, 152, 162, 295
Abella, Irving, 232, 242
Aber, Ita, 116
Abinum, Avram, 275
Abinum, Moise, 275
Abram, Ido, 286
Abse, Dannie, 258
Abu Iyad (Salah Khalaf), 163–65, 181, 370, 399
Abu Lughod, Ibrahim, 150
Abu Sharif, Bassam, 151, 246–47, 251, 281
Abzug, Bella, 202
Acco Festival for Alternative Theater, 435
Adel, Mohammed Bassem, 394
Adler, Cyrus, 93
Adler, H.G., 313
Admoni, Nahum, 397
Afn Shvel, 537
Africa, 410
Agam, Yaacov, 76, 97
Agnon, S.Y., 435–36
Agudath Israel of America, 135, 136, 191–93, 491
Agudath Israel World Organization, 491
Ahimeir, Yossi, 407
Ahlstrom, Sidney, 5n
AIPAC, *see* American Israel Public Affairs Committee
Aitmatov, Chingiz, 406
Akal, Ayad Mahmud, 367

Akihito (emperor, Japan), 411
Albert Einstein College of Medicine, 508
Algemeiner Journal, 537
Allason, Rupert, 249
Allerhand, Jacob, 335
Allouche-Benayoun, Joelle, 274
Almagor, Gila, 440
Aloni, Shulamit, 295, 385
Alpha Epsilon Pi Fraternity, 510
Altes, Frits Korthals, 278
Altman, Benjamin, 111
Altman, Sidney, 243
Altshuler, David, 76, 94n, 95–96, 115
Altshuler, Mordechai, 458n
ALYN — American Society for Handicapped Children in Israel, 479
AMC Cancer Research Center, 512
America-Israel Cultural Foundation, 479
America-Israel Friendship League, 479
American Academy for Jewish Research, 473
American-Arab Anti-Discrimination Committee, 127–28
American-Arab Anti-Discrimination League, 126
American Associates, Ben-Gurion University of the Negev, 479
American Association for Ethiopian Jews, 489
American Association of Rabbis, 491
American Association of Russian Jews, 510
American Biblical Encyclopedia Society, 473
American Civil Liberties Union (ACLU), 134

American Committee for Shaare Zedek Hospital in Jerusalem, 479
American Committee for Shenkar College in Israel, 479
American Committee for the Weizmann Institute of Science, 479–80
American Conference of Cantors, 497
American Council for Judaism, 469
American and European Friends of ORT, 489
American Federation of Jews from Central Europe, 510
American Friends of Bar-Ilan University, 480
American Friends of Beth Hatefutsoth, 480
American Friends of Ezrath Nashim Hospital-Jerusalem, 480
American Friends of Haifa University, 480
American Friends of Tel Aviv University, 480
American Friends of the Alliance Israelite Universelle, 489
American Friends of the Hebrew University, 480
American Friends of the Israel Museum, 480
American Friends of the Shalom Hartman Institute, 480–81
American Friends of the Tel Aviv Museum of Art, 481
American Friends of Young Israel, 495
American-Israeli Lighthouse, 481
American Israelite, The, 541
American Israel Public Affairs Committee (AIPAC), 127–28, 149, 181, 182, 383, 399, 481
American Jewish Alternatives to Zionism, 469
American Jewish Archives, 503
American Jewish Archives, 541
American Jewish Committee, 125, 126, 133–36, 139, 177, 178, 181, 190, 192, 201, 202, 419, 469–70
American Jewish Congress, 133–37, 178, 179, 181–83, 186, 192, 202, 203, 470

American Jewish Correctional Chaplains Association, 512
American Jewish Historical Society, 115, 473
American Jewish History, 536
American Jewish Joint Distribution Committee (JDC), 489
American Jewish League for Israel, 481
American Jewish Periodical Center, 503
American Jewish Philanthropic Fund, 489
American Jewish Press Association, 473
American Jewish Public Relations Society, 516
American Jewish Society for Service, 512
American Jewish Times Outlook, 541
American Jewish World, 536
American Jewish World Service, 512
American Jewish Year Book, 537
American Labor ORT, 489
American ORT Federation, 489
American Physicians Fellowship, Inc. for Medicine in Israel, 481
American Red Magen David for Israel, 481
American Sephardi Federation, 510–11
American Society for Jewish Music, 473
American Society for Technion-Israel Institute of Technology, 481
American Society for the Protection of Nature in Israel, 481
Americans for a Safe Israel, 482
Americans for Peace Now, 482
Americans for Progressive Israel, 180, 482
American Veterans of Israel, 511
American Zionist, 537
American Zionist Federation, 481–82
American Zionist Youth Foundation, 482
Amichai, Yehuda, 428
Amit Woman, 537
Amit Women, 482
AMPAL — American Israel Corporation, 482
Amson, Daniel, 274

Andreotti, Giulio, 289–91, 296, 298, 404, 406
Andrews, Donald, 232
Annenberg Research Institute, 501
Anti-Defamation League (ADL), 121, 122, 125–26, 130, 131, 133, 134, 136, 137, 178, 189, 470
Appelfeld, Aharon, 257, 258, 427
Appleman-Jurman, Alicia, 257
Aptowitzer, Avigdor, 545
el-Arabi, Nabil, 408
Arad, Moshe, 142, 163
Arafat, Yasir, 142, 143, 146, 147, 150–52, 159–65, 169, 177, 178, 183, 230, 246–48, 251, 260, 263, 267, 268, 280, 339, 370, 379, 385, 386, 388, 396, 398, 400, 403, 411
Arens, Moshe, 141, 143–45, 154, 155, 157, 160–62, 168, 171, 179, 181, 246, 290, 318, 339, 359–60, 370–72, 375, 379, 382, 395, 396, 398–99, 402, 403, 405–11
Argentina, 411, 454
Ariel, Harry, 259
Arikha, 76
Arizona Jewish Post, 534
Aron, Isa, 77*n*
Ash, Eric, 258–59
Asher, Bob, 383
Ashkenazy, Yehuda, 286
Association for Jewish Studies, 491
Association for the Social Scientific Study of Jewry, 474
Association of American Museums, 74
Association of Hillel/Jewish Campus Professionals, 491–92
Association of Jewish Book Publishers, 474
Association of Jewish Center Professionals, 512
Association of Jewish Community Organization Personnel (AJCOP), 512
Association of Jewish Community Relations Workers, 470
Association of Jewish Family and Children's Agencies, 512–13

Association of Jewish Family and Children's Agency Professionals, 513
Association of Jewish Genealogical Societies, 474
Association of Jewish Libraries, 474
Association of Orthodox Jewish Scientists, 492
Association of Reform Zionists of America (ARZA), 195, 482
Association of Yugoslav Jews in the United States, 511
Astamkar, Michael, 392
Atlanta Jewish Times, 535
Atwater, Lee, 137
Atzmon, Tzvi, 428
Aufbau, 537
Auschwitz, 8, 12, 17–18, 20–24, 51, 121, 129–31, 271, 284–85, 297–98, 348–49, 407
Aus der Funten, Ferdinand H., 278–79
Australia, 461–63
Austria, 324–36, 404
Autant-Lara, Claude, 261–62
Avidan, David, 428
Avineri, Shlomo, 257
Avner, Uri, 461*n*
Avotaynu, 537
Axen, Hermann, 317
Ayalon, Leah, 428

Bachelot, Francois, 261
Bachi, Roberto, 442*n*
Backer, Avi, 321
Badanes, Jerome, 44–45
Badinter, Robert, 274
Bagley, David, 242
Baker, James, 127, 140, 142–47, 149–51, 154–59, 161–63, 169, 172, 174, 177, 180, 181, 371, 375, 380–85, 398–401
Bakhtiar, Shapur, 262
Baldran, Jaqueline, 273
Ball, George, 127
Ballin, Ernst Hirsch, 277
Baltimore Hebrew University, 501
Baltimore Jewish Times, 536
Baltzell, E. Digby, 556
Band, Max, 103

Barak, Ehud, 354, 394
Baram, Uzi, 380
Barbash, Uri, 440
Barenboim, Daniel, 323
Barer, Robert, 259
Bar-Lev, Haim, 385
Barnaby, Frank, 258
Baron, Salo Wittmayer, 544–54
Baron de Hirsch Fund, 513
Barrett, Dave, 228
Basch, Victor, 264
Baskin, Bernard, 244
Bassiouny, Mohammed, 153–54, 379
Bastiaans, Johan, 279
Bat Shachar, Chana, 426
Bauer, Yehuda, 257
Baum, Leuba, 93
Baum, Phil, 181
Baum, Ralph, 93
Baumann, Anton, 132
Bayer, Linda, 42
Becker, Avi, 320
Beilin, Yossi, 377, 403, 415, 418
Beiski, Moshe, 369
Belfer Institute for Advanced Biomedical Studies, 508
Belgium, 457
Belkin, Samuel, 91
Bellah, Robert N., 5n
Beller, Steven, 257
Bellow, Saul, 44
Belth, Nathan C., 559
Ben-Aharon, Yosef (Yossi), 165, 400
Ben-Amotz, Dahn, 422
Benatar, Albert, 269
Ben-Chorin, Schalom, 314, 320
Ben-Efrat, Ya'akov, 385
Ben-Elissar, Eliahu, 230
Ben-Ezra, Gadi, 416
Benforado, Sally, 42
Benguiat, Ephraim, 93
Benguigui, Fortunee, 276
Ben-Israel, Shelomo, 559
Benjamin, Walter, 323
Benjamin & Dr. Edgar R. Cofeld Judaic Museum of Temple Beth Zion (Buffalo), 115

Benjamin N. Cardozo School of Law, 508
Benn (Bension Rabinovitch), 276
Ben Shlomo, Yosef, 430
Bensimon, Doris, 274–75, 455n
Berensin, Ilan, 335
Beresford, Gary, 420
Beresford, Shirley, 420
Berger, Abraham, 559
Berger, Eli Michael, 244
Berger, Gerald, 243
Berkley, George E., 257
Berkovits, Eliezer, 8n, 18
Berlin, Irving (Israel Baline), 559–60
Berlin, Sir Isaiah, 251
Berman, Joseph, 244
Berman, Nancy, 103n, 114
Bernard Revel Graduate School, 508
Bernhard, Thomas, 335
Bernstein, Leonard, 323, 330
Bernstein, Louis, 201
Betar Zionist Youth Organization, 482
Beth Medrosh Elyon (Academy of Higher Learning and Research), 501
Beth Tzedec Museum (Toronto), 93, 115
Bettman, Batia, 244
Beyer, Otto, 313
Biale, David, 185
Biedermann, Karl, 322
Bilik, Dorothy, 43–44n
Billig, Joseph, 271
Binder, Hartmut, 313
Biran, Yoav, 247
Bitzaron, 537
Blach, Bruno Karl, 132, 307
Black, Eugene C., 257
Blacker, Harry, 257
Blank, Sheldon Haas, 560
Blau, Joseph L., 552
Bloemendal, Hans, 288
Bloom, Margo, 114
Bloomgarden, Lawrence, 557
Bloustein, Edward J., 560
Blue, Lionel, 258
Blum, Kestel, 426
Blumberg, David M., 560

Blumenfeldt, Erwin, 313
Blumenkranz, Bernhard, 276
Bnai Akiva of North America, 486–87
B'nai Brith Canada, 235, 518–19
B'nai B'rith Hillel Foundations, 492
B'nai B'rith International, 180, 184, 192, 345, 513
B'nai B'rith International Jewish Monthly, 535
B'nai B'rith Klutznick Museum (Washington, D.C.), 88, 90, 92, 93, 101, 102, 109, 110, 114, 474
B'nai B'rith Messenger, 534
B'nai B'rith Women, 513
B'nai B'rith Youth Organization, 492
Bnai Zion — American Fraternal Zionist Organization, 511
Bochurberg, Claude, 273
Bodenheimer, Max, 310
Bohme, Ibrahim, 317
Boll, Heinrich, 311
Bomers, Herman, 284
Bookbinder, Hyman, 412
Boren, David, 167
Borovoy, A. Alan, 243
Borowitz, Eugene, 3, 4n, 10–11, 14, 16, 30, 32, 196
Boschwitz, Rudy, 150
Boston Jewish Times, 536
Bourassa, Robert, 228
Bousquet, Rene, 265
Bouzaglo, Haim, 440
Bovin, Alexander, 340
Boys Town Jerusalem Foundation of America, 482–83
Bradman, Neil, 252, 253
Braidburg, Sarah, 433
Bramson ORT Technical Institute, 501
Brandeis-Bardin Institute, 501–2
Brandeis University, 502
Brandeis University National Women's Committee, 517
Brandt, Willy, 305
Brazil, 454–55
Bregman, Khone, 345
Breines, Paul, 46
Brenson, Michael, 80n, 85
Breuer, Isaac, 313

Brinkman, Elco, 279
Brith Abraham, 511
Brith Sholom, 511
British Friends of Peace Now, 251
Brodkey, Harold, 42
Broner, E.M., 46
Bronfman, Edgar M., 304, 328–29, 345, 350
Bronfman family, 242
Brook, Stephen, 257
Brookner, Anita, 258
Broszat, Martin, 312
Broward Jewish World, 535
Brym, Robert, 234
Buber, Martin, 29
Buffalo Jewish Review, 537
Bulawko, Henry, 269, 272
Bulka, Reuven, 241, 243
Bunke, Heinrich, 307
Busek, Ewald, 330
Bush, Barbara, 277
Bush, George, 122, 124, 127, 128, 137, 140, 143–47, 150, 151, 154, 155, 158, 166, 167, 169, 175, 177, 183, 193, 277–78, 308, 339, 342, 371, 380, 382, 383, 396, 398, 401, 402, 411
Business and Professional ORT, 489
Buttenwieser, Helen Lehman, 560
Buttner, Ursula, 312
Butzmann, Eva, 322

CAJE, see Coalition for the Advancement of Jewish Education
Callan, Ivan, 403
Canada, 227–44, 411, 453–54
Canada-Israel Committee (CIC), 230, 231, 236
Canadian Association for Labor Israel (Histadrut), 519
Canadian Foundation for Jewish Culture, 519
Canadian Friends of the Alliance Israelite Universelle, 519
Canadian Friends of the Hebrew University, 519
Canadian Friends of Peace Now, 230, 232, 237

Canadian Jewish Congress (CJC), 230, 231, 235–36, 519
Canadian Jewish Herald, 543
Canadian Jewish News, 543
Canadian Jewish Outlook, 543
Canadian ORT Organization, 519
Canadian Sephardi Federation, 519
Canadian Young Judaea, 519
Canadian Zionist, 543
Canadian Zionist Federation (CZF), 236, 237, 519–20
Candib, Raizel Fishman, 244
Cantors Assembly, 198, 492
Caplan, Benny, 259
Cardozo, Judith, 115
Carlos (king, Spain), 404
Carr, Donald, 236
Cassuto, Nathan, 300–301
Castellano, Ismaele, 296
Cavazos, Lauro, 132
Ceausescu, Nicolae, 351–52, 407
Center for Holocaust Studies, Documentation & Research, 474
Center for Jewish Community Studies, 470
Central Conference of American Rabbis (CCAR), 194, 492
Central Sephardic Jewish Community, 511
Central Synagogue (New York), 89, 115
Central Yiddish Culture Organization, (CYCO), 474
Chabad-Lubavitch movement, 135
Chagall, Marc, 79, 242
Chajes, Zvi Peretz, 545
Charters, David A., 258
Cheney, Richard, 402
Chernin, Kim, 46
Chesler, Phyllis, 202
Chicago JUF News, 535
Chinn, Trevor, 256, 258
Chirac, Jacques, 260–62
Chiswick, Barry R., 453*n*
Chlenov, Mikhail (Michael), 294, 343, 413
Christie, Douglas, 232
Christopher, Robert C., 111*n*
Chumir, Sheldon, 228

Cicippio, Joseph James, 166–69
Circle, 537
City of Hope National Medical Center and Beckman Research Institute, 513
CLAL (National Jewish Center for Learning and Leadership), 492
Clare, George, 257
Clark, Joe, 229, 230, 240
Clark, Kenneth, 556
Cleveland College of Jewish Studies, 115, 502
Cleveland Jewish News, 541
Coalition for the Advancement of Jewish Education (CAJE), 492
Coalition to Free Soviet Jewry, 129
Coggan, Lord, 334
Cohen, Arnold, 254
Cohen, Arthur A., 17–18, 21–24, 31, 36, 47, 55–57, 83
Cohen, Benny, 269
Cohen, Elaine R.S., 244
Cohen, Eli, 440
Cohen, Elisheva, 423
Cohen, Elliot, 557
Cohen, Euninie, 243
Cohen, Morris Raphael, 551
Cohen, Pinchas, 435
Cohen, Ran, 251, 281
Cohen, Shlomo, 389
Cohen, Stephen, 237
Cohen, Steven M., 178
Cohn, Louis, 275
Cohn-Sherbok, Dan, 257
Cokely, Steve, 138
Comay, Sholom, 192
Commentary, 537, 557
Commission on Jewish Education, United Synagogue, 499–500
Commission on Jewish Education of the Union of American Hebrew Congregations, Central Conference of American Rabbis, and National Association of Temple Educators, 497–98
Commission on Social Action of Reform Judaism, 470

INDEX / 615

Commission on Synagogue Management (UAHC-CCAR), 498
Community, 536
Confederation of British Sephardim, 254
Conference of Jewish Communal Service, 513
Conference on Jewish Material Claims Against Germany, 490
Conference on Jewish Social Studies, 474
Conference of Presidents of Major American Jewish Organizations, 127, 177, 181, 183–85, 412, 470
Congregation Beth Ahabah Museum and Archives Trust (Richmond, Va.), 100, 115
Congregation Bina, 474
Congress for Jewish Culture, 474
Congress Monthly, 537
Congress of Secular Jewish Organizations, 492–93
Connecticut Jewish Ledger, 534
Conservative Judaism, 537
Consultative Council of Jewish Organizations (CCJO), 470–71
Contemporary Jewry, 537–38
Cook, Christopher, 122–23
Cook, Phyllis, 111
Coordinating Board of Jewish Organizations, 471
Cossiga, Francesco, 290
Cotler, Irwin, 233
Council of American Jewish Museums (CAJM), 71, 72, 86, 89, 90, 92, 96, 108–10, 114–17
Council for a Beautiful Israel Environmental Education Foundation, 483
Council for Jewish Education, 493
Council of Jewish Federations, 90, 128, 184, 187, 188, 190, 206, 513
Council of Jewish Organizations in Civil Service, 471
Council of Reform Hebrew Day Schools, 193
Courtois, Stephane, 274
Cowan, Paul, 47
Cremieux, Adolphe, 274

Crotowski, Waldemar, 134
Cuddihy, John Murray, 6*n*
Cymerman, Boruch Moshe, 259
Czechoslovakia, 350–51
Czerwinski, Horst, 307

Daley, Richard, 138
D'Amato, Alphonse, 167
D'Ancona, Hedy, 277
Daniel, Yuli, 346
Danneels, Godfried, 130
Danto, Louis, 242
Danzig, David, 557
D'Appollonia, Ariane Chebel, 274
Dart, Iris Rainer, 42
David, Renee, 275
David J. Azrieli Graduate Institute of Jewish Education and Administration, 508
Davids, Louis, 288
Davis, Moshe, 258
Dawidowicz, Lucy, 557
Dayan, Hubert, 268
Dayan, Yael, 385
Dayton Jewish Chronicle, 541
De Benedetti, Carlo, 291
Decourtray, Albert, 130, 273
De Felice, Renzo, 300
DellaPergola, Sergio, 452*n*, 454*n*, 455*n*, 461*n*
Dellums, Ron, 176
De Michelis, Gianni, 289, 290
De Mita, Ciriaco, 289–91, 404
Demjanjuk, John (Ivan), 132, 413
Denkler, Horst, 313
Denzinger, Jakob Frank, 132
Deri, Arye, 377, 383, 420
Dershowitz, Alan, 131
d'Estaing, Valery Giscard, 263
Detroit Jewish News, 536
Deutschkron, Inge, 313
Devins, Driscoll, 103
De Vries, Martha Markus, 314
Dialogue, 543
Dickinson, Pat, 116
Dienstbier, Jiri, 350
Dine, Tom, 383
Dinitz, Simcha, 187–89, 416

Dinkins, David, 138, 139
Dische, Irene, 313
Dischereit, Esther, 313
Doctorow, E.L., 47
Dole, Robert, 127, 167, 168, 182, 183
Domnitz, Myer, 259
Donato, James, 123
Dore, Jean, 241
Dorff, Elliot, 7n
Drabinsky, Garth, 244
Drache, Sharon, 243
Drai, Raphael, 275
Dreyfus, Alfred, 99
Drogoul, Christopher, 289
Dubb, Allie A., 461n
Dubcek, Alexander, 350
Dukakis, Michael, 190, 287
Duke, David, 124
Dulzin, Arye, 422
Dumas, Roland, 262, 263, 403
Durafour, Michel, 261
Duschinsky, Eugene, 556

Eagleburger, Lawrence, 128
East Germany, see German Democratic Republic
Eban, Abba, 281, 295
Economic Horizons, 538
Edelshtein, Yuli, 345, 413
Edison, Irving, 560–61
Edri, Rafael, 372
Edri, Shimon, 354
Efrat, Gideon, 434, 435
Efrati, Moshe, 438
Eggar, Tim, 247
Egypt, 373, 374, 378–84, 397, 408–10
Ehre, Ida, 314
Ehrentreu, Osher, 255
Eichmann, Adolf, 552
Einstein, Albert, 551
Eisen, Arnold, 4n, 6n, 7n, 11n
Eisenberg, Chaim, 328, 331
Eitan, Naphtali, 320
Eksteins, Modris, 243
Eliav, Lova, 295
Elizabeth S. Fine Museum of the Congregation Emanu-El (San Francisco), 115

Elkann, Jean-Paul, 267–68
Elkin, J. Laikin, 454n
Elkin, Stanley, 47
Ellenoff, Theodore, 177, 201
Ellis, Julie, 42
Eloni, Yehuda, 313
El Reedy, Abdel Raouf, 142
Elwenspoek, Monika, 313
Elyachar, Jehiel R., 561
Emunah Women of America, 483
Engelhardt, Hans, 310
Engelstad, Ralph, 133
Engholm, Bjorn, 305
Epstein, Leslie, 44
Epstein, Seymour, 44
Erez, Shaike, 362
Eschen, Fritz, 313
Essid, Hamadi, 275
Ethiopia, 410, 416
European Jewish Congress (EJC), 294
Euro-Ring, 249
Evans, Timothy, 138
Evers, Bloeme Emden, 283
Evers, Raphael, 282–83
Ezrahi, Sidra, 44n

Fabius, Laurent, 263
Fabricant, Isaac Nathan, 259
Fackenheim, Emil, 3, 8–9, 17–21, 32n
Faerber, Meir M., 313
Falk, Yoram, 436
Falk, Zeev, 320
Farrakhan, Louis, 122, 138
Fascell, Dante, 176
Fechter, Claudia, 114
Federated Council of Israel Institutions (FCII), 483
Federation of Jewish Men's Clubs, 493
Federation of Reconstructionist Congregations and Havurot, 177, 494
Fein, Leonard, 200–1
Feinstein, Elaine, 258
Feldman, Leonore, 192
Feldman, Moshe Zeev, 383
Fenner, John, 253
Fenster Museum of Jewish Art (Tulsa), 91, 92, 114

Ferkauf Graduate School of Psychology, 508–9
Fernandez Ordonex, Francisco, 403
Ferris, Helene, 202–3
Festinger, Leon, 561
Fetterman, Bonny, 36
Fidler, Michael, 248, 259
Findley, Paul, 127
Finkielkraut, Alain, 270, 273–74
Finkler, Arnold, 244
Finta, Imre, 233
Fischer, Franz, 278–79
Fish, Morris, 243
Fisher, David, 257
Fisher, Eugene, 133–34
Fishman, Bernard, 116
Fitzwater, Marlin, 164, 168, 169, 174
Forta, Ayre, 258
Fortier, Yves, 231
Forverts, 538
Forward, 538
Foxman, Abraham, 181
France, 260–76, 403, 455
Frank, Anne, 322
Frank, Jacob, 243
Frankel, Anne, 259
Frankel, Joseph, 259
Frankel, Ruth, 244
Frankel, Sara, 414, 414
Frankel, William, 257
Franklin, Karen S., 115
Frauberger, Heinrich, 78–79
Fred, Morris, 109, 114
Fred Wolf, Jr. Gallery (Philadelphia), 101, 115
Freeman, Cynthia, 42
Free Sons of Israel, 511
Freij, Elias, 160
Frej, Mahmud, 369
Frenkel, Erwin, 419
Freudenheim, Leslie M., 116
Freudenheim, Tom, 72, 75n, 85–87, 112–13
Frey, Gerhard, 305
Fried, Erich, 323
Friedberg, Benjamin, 241
Friedenberg, Samuel, 93
Friedman, Harry G., 93–94

Friedman, Murray, 557
Friedman, Thomas, 39n, 68–69n
Friends of Labor Israel, 483
Friends of Pioneering Israel, 520
Friends of the Israel Defense Forces, 483
Fromberg, Susan, 44
Fromer, Seymour, 114
Fromkin, David, 258
Frosh, Sidney, 253
Fuks, Rena Mansfeld, 286
Fund for Higher Education, 483
Furst, Michael, 308

Gaitskell, Baroness Dora, 259
Galinski, Heinz, 307–9, 319, 321
Galloni, Giovanni, 295
Gebhart, Richard, 137
Gecas, Antanas, 249
Gelfand, Morrie, 243
Genesis 2, 536
Genscher, Hans-Dietrich, 302, 303, 404
Gerasimov, Gennady, 406
German Democratic Republic (GDR; East Germany), 302–4, 316–23, 457
Germany, Federal Republic of (West Germany), 302–15, 404, 455–57
Gershuni, Moshe, 434
Gerson, Phyllis E., 115
Gertych, Zbigniew, 349
Getter, Tamar, 434
Getz, Yehuda, 421
Ghali, Butros, 150, 409
Ghan, Linda, 243
Ghanem, Abd el-Mahdi, 390, 391
Gilad, Yaakov, 440
Gilbert, Martin, 257
Gildesgame, Leon L., 561
Gillman, Neil, 3, 5n, 9, 31
Gilman, Benjamin, 163
Ginzburg, Yitzhak, 357
Giordano, Ralph, 312
Girard, Patrick, 274, 276
Gitai, Amos, 300
Giuliani, Rudolph, 138
Givat Haviva Educational Foundation, 483

Glaser, Joost, 288
Glemp, Jozef, 130, 131, 271, 298, 348, 349
Glicksman, William G., 271
Glikson, P., 452n
Glinert, Lewis, 258
Gluz, Mikhail, 345
Gnehm, Edward, 173
Golan, Menachem, 439
Golda Meir Association, 483–84
Goldberg, David H., 243
Goldberger, Leo I., 561
Goldbloom, Victor, 244
Goldenberg, Naomi, 242
Goldman, Lionel, 244
Goldman, Mordechai, 428
Goldman, Steve, 243
Goldmann, Alain, 264
Goldmann, Nicole, 269
Goldmuntz, Laurence, 177–78
Goldreich, Gloria, 42
Goldstaub, Adriana, 292
Goldstein, Marcel, 300
Goldstein, Rebecca, 46, 47, 65–67
Goldstein, Roushell, 242
Goldstein, Sidney, 442n, 452n
Goldy, Robert G., 4n
Golenpolsky, Tankred, 345
Gombrich, Sir Ernst, 314
Gonzalez, Philipe, 404
Goodman, Allegra, 39
Goodman, Lord, 251
Goodman, Percival, 562
Goodman, Sholem, 244
Goodman Sverdlin, Hannah Grad, 562
Goral, Arie, 312
Gorbachev, Mikhail, 128, 253, 303, 337–39, 406
Gordis, Robert, 5n
Gordon, Elie, 346
Gore-Booth, David, 247
Gornick, Vivian, 43, 46
Gottheil, Richard J.H., 546
Gottschalk, Alfred, 195, 196
Goudeket, Mauritis, 288
Goudsmit, David, 288
Gourary, Samarious, 562
Gourgey, Percy, 258

Grabitz, Helge, 313
Graham, Martha, 438
Graml, Hermann, 312
Granin, Daniil Alexandrovich, 346
Gratz College, 502
Gray, William, III (Bill), 137, 176
Great Britain, 245–59, 403, 455
Greater Phoenix Jewish News, 534
Green, Arthur, 25–27, 31, 197
Green, Geoffrey L., 257
Greenberg, Irving, 11–12, 17–18, 22, 32
Greenberg, Joanne, 43
Greenberg, Simon, 8n
Greenstein, Michael, 243
Greenwald, Alice M., 78n
Gregoire, Abbe, 274
Griff, "Professor," 122
Groner, Mordechai, 320
Gronius, Jorg W., 314
Gross, John, 99
Grossman, Cissy, 115
Grossman, David, 300, 425
Grosz, Paul, 328, 332, 334
Gruber, Karl, 326
Gruenberger, Peter, 247
Gruss, Joseph, 342
Gruvman, Motl, 346
Grynberg, Anne, 271
Guedj, Edgard, 275
Guggenheim, Solomon, 111
Gur, Mordechai, 412
Guralnik, Uran, 346
Gutman, Rene, 270
Gutmann, Joseph, 80n
Guttman, Frank, 237
Guttmann, Heinrich, 311
Guttmann, Micha, 308
Gysi, Gregor, 317

Habash, George, 363
Haber, William, 562
Haberman, Steven, 455n
Habonim-Dror North America, 484
Hadarom, 538
Hadassah Magazine, 538
Hadassah Medical Center (Israel), 137
Hadassah, The Women's Zionist Organization of America, 192, 484

Hadassah — WIZO Organization of Canada, 520
Hadoar, 538
Hadshot L.A., 534
Hahn-Warburg, Lola, 259, 315
Hainen, Marsha, 243
Hajdenberg, Henri, 268
Halbekann-Esser, Dr., 310
Halevi, Uri Phoebus, 285
Hallaunbrenner, Ita-Rosa, 275
Halpenny, Shelley, 231
Halter, Marek, 273, 275
Hamachne Hachareidi, 538
Hamilton, Lee, 136, 167, 176
Hamm-Brucher, Hildegard, 307
Hammer, Zevulun, 318, 372, 406, 407
Harap, Louis, 68
Harris, David, 129, 190
Harris, Fredda, 116
Harris, Milton, 237
Harry Fischel School for Higher Jewish Studies, 509
Hartman, David, 14–17
Hartog, Alexander, 257
Harvey, Van A., 8
Hashomer Hatzair, Socialist Zionist Youth Movement, 484
al-Hassan, Hani, 251
al-Hassan, Khalid, 152
Hassenfeld, Sylvia, 296
Hauff, Volker, 305
Havel, Vaclav, 350
Hawatmeh, Nayef, 165
Hebrew Arts Center, 475
Hebrew College, 502
Hebrew Culture Foundation, 475
Hebrew Home for the Aged at Riverdale (New York), 89, 93, 115
Hebrew Theological College, 502
Hebrew Union College (Jewish Institute of Religion), 93, 94, 196, 502–4
 Joseph Gallery, 115
 Skirball Museum, 79, 87–88, 90, 92, 95, 101–9, 114, 115, 478
Hebrew Watchman, The, 542
Heidegger, Johann Heinrich, 13
Heilman, Samuel, 87
Heller, Joseph, 46

Helms, Jesse, 137, 164, 182
Helper, Bonnie, 243
Helprin, Mark, 45–47
Henke, Klaus Dietmar, 312
Henriot, Philippe, 265
Heritage-Southwest Jewish Press, 534
Hermlin, Stefan, 317
Herscher, Uri, 87–88
Hershon, Goldie, 244
Herskowitz, Sylvia, 91, 114
Hertzberg, Arthur, 6*n*
Herzberg, J. Abel, 288
Herzberg, Judith, 288
Herzfelde, Wieland, 314
Herzliah-Jewish Teachers Seminary, 504
Herzl Press, 487
Herzog, Aura, 404
Herzog, Chaim, 229, 257, 263, 269, 290, 387–88, 390, 391, 404, 411
Heschel, Abraham Joshua, 10, 15, 25–26, 84, 86
Hess, Alfred, 322
Hess, Moshe G., 314
Hess, Rudolf, 306–7
Heym, Stefan, 317
HIAS, 490
Hiat, Philip, 321
Hier, Marvin, 179
Higgins, William R., 127, 166–68, 247, 396
Higham, John, 556
Hilberg, Raul, 274
Hildebrandt, Johannes, 319
Hillesum, Etty, 287
Hilsenrath, Edgar, 314
Himmelfarb, Milton, 557
Himmelweit, Hilde, 259
Hirohito (emperor, Japan), 143, 411
Hirsch, John, 244
Hirsch, Samuel J., 286
Hirschberg, Gunter, 563
Hirschfeld, Ariel, 424–25, 427, 428
Hirschmann, Ira A., 563
Hirsh, Annette, 116
Histadruth Ivrith of America, 475
Hitler, Adolf, 19, 20, 306
Hobson, William, 233–34

Hocker, Karl-Friedrich, 307
Hoffenberg, Sam, 276
Hoffman, Allen, 47, 61–62
Hoffman, Yoel, 425
Hofshtain, David N., 343
Holocaust Center of the United Jewish Federation of Greater Pittsburgh, 475
Holocaust Memorial Museum (Washington, D.C.), 71, 88–89, 108
Holocaust Memorial Resource & Education Center of Central Florida, 475
Honan, William H., 104*n*
Hondius, Dienke, 287
Honecker, Erich, 316
Hook, Sidney, 563
Hope Center for the Developmentally Disabled, 513–14
Horacio Juanarenas, Jose, 411
Horch, Hans Otto, 313
Horn, Gyula, 349, 407
Horn, Otto, 132
Horowitz, Joseph B., 93
Horowitz, Olyn, 93
Horowiz, Vladimir, 563
Howe, Sir Geoffrey, 246, 403
Hrdliczka, Alfred, 330–31
Hughes, Robert, 96
Humanistic Judaism, 536
Hungary, 349–50, 406–7
Hunter, Sam, 82
Hurd, Douglas, 248
Hurwitz, Yair, 428
Husak, Gustav, 350
Hussein (king, Jordan), 141, 143–44, 147–48, 397
al-Husseini, Abd al-Kadr, 385
al-Husseini, Faisal, 141, 251, 355, 361, 374, 381, 385, 388
Hyman, Ralph, 244

Iancu, Carol, 274
Idel, Moshe, 431
Iliescu, Ion, 351
Illiana News, 535
Index to Jewish Periodicals, 541, 542
Indiana Jewish Post and Opinion, 535

Indig, Sidney, 244
Institute for Computers in Jewish Life, 493
Institute for International and Governmental Affairs, 518
Institute for Public Affairs, 499
Institute for Russian Jewry, 475
Institute of Traditional Judaism, 504
Intermountain Jewish News, 534
International Association of Jewish Vocational Services, 514
International Coalition for the Revival of the Jews of Yemen (ICROJOY), 490
International Committee for Women at the Kotel, 203
International Council on Jewish Social and Welfare Services, 514
International Jewish Committee for Interreligious Consultations (IJCIC), 133
International Jewish Media Association, 475
International League for the Repatriation of Russian Jews, 471
Interns for Peace, 484
Iran, 333
Iraq, 394–95
Isenberg, Shirley Berry, 258
Israel, 353–423
 Culture, 424–40
Israel Arts and Sciences Academy, 137
Israel Histadrut Foundation, 484
Israel Horizons, 538
Israel Museum (Jerusalem), 94, 99, 432
Israel Quality, 538
Italy, 289–301, 404
Itzik, Dahlia, 320

Jackson, Jesse, 138, 139
Jacob, Louis, 259
Jacobs, June, 251
Jakobovits, Lord Immanuel, 249, 253–56
Janner, Greville, 251
Japan, 410–11
Jaruzelski, Wojciech, 347, 407
JCC Association Lecture Bureau, 475

Jeffares, A. Norman, 257
Jerusalem Post, 231–32, 419
Jesselson, Erica, 91
Jesselson, Ludwig, 91
Jewish Academy of Arts and Sciences, 475
Jewish Action Magazine, 538
Jewish Advocate, 536
Jewish Book Annual, 538
Jewish Book Council, 476
Jewish Book World, 538
Jewish Braille Institute of America, 514
Jewish Braille Institute Voice, 538
Jewish Braille Review, 538
Jewish Chautauqua Society, 493
Jewish Chronicle of Pittsburgh, 542
Jewish Civic Press, 535, 536
Jewish Committee for Israeli-Palestinian Peace, 484
Jewish Community Centers Association of North America, 514
Jewish Community Museum (San Francisco), 88, 96, 102, 110, 116
Jewish Community News, 535
Jewish Community Voice, 537
Jewish Conciliation Board of America, 514
Jewish Cultural Reconstruction (JCR), 94
Jewish Current Events, 538
Jewish Currents, 538
Jewish Eagle, 543
Jewish Education, 538
Jewish Education in Media, 493
Jewish Education Service of North America, 493
Jewish Educators Assembly, 500
Jewish Exponent, 542
Jewish Federation Council of Los Angeles, 184
Jewish Frontier, 538
Jewish Fund for Justice, 514
Jewish Herald-Voice, 542
Jewish Historical Museum (Amsterdam), 285
Jewish Historical Society of Maryland, 116
Jewish Horizon, 537

Jewish Immigrant Aid Services of Canada (JIAS), 520
Jewish Institute for National Security Affairs (JINSA), 484–85
Jewish Journal, 534, 535, 538
Jewish Journal of San Antonio, 542
Jewish Labor Bund, 511
Jewish Labor Committee, 471
Jewish Ledger, 538
Jewish Ministers Cantors Association of America, 493
Jewish Museum (New York), 79, 81–95, 98, 99, 101, 102, 105–11, 113, 114, 299, 476
Jewish Museum (Prague), 94, 350
Jewish Museum (Vienna), 334–35
Jewish Music Council, 476
Jewish Music Notes, 538
Jewish National Fund of America, 485
Jewish National Fund of Canada, 520
Jewish News & Israel Today, 534
Jewish Observer, 538
Jewish Peace Fellowship, 471
Jewish Peace Lobby, 182, 485
Jewish Post & News, 543
Jewish Post and Renaissance, 539
Jewish Press, 536, 539
Jewish Press of Pinellas County, 535
Jewish Press of Tampa, 535
Jewish Publication Society, 476
Jewish Quarterly Review, 542
Jewish Reconstructionist Foundation, 493–94
Jewish Record, 537
Jewish Reporter, 536, 536–37
Jewish Restitution Successor Organization, 490
Jewish Social Studies, 539
Jewish Spectator, 534
Jewish Standard, The, 537, 543
Jewish Star, 534, 537
Jewish Students' Network, 127
Jewish Teachers Association — Morim, 494
Jewish Telegraphic Agency, 543
Jewish Telegraphic Agency Community News Reporter, 539

Jewish Telegraphic Agency Daily News Bulletin, 539
Jewish Telegraphic Agency Weekly News Digest, 539
Jewish Theological Seminary of America, 79, 82–86, 92, 93, 110, 113, 192, 197–98, 476, 504–5
Jewish Times (San Diego), 121
Jewish Times of the Greater Northeast, 542
Jewish Transcript, 542
Jewish Veteran, 535
Jewish War Veterans of the United States of America, 471
National Museum, Archives and Library, 116
Jewish Week, 539
Jewish Weekly News, 536
Jewish Western Bulletin, 543
Jewish World, 535, 539
Jews for Jesus, 134
John Paul II, Pope, 133–34, 270, 297, 327–28, 348
Johnston, J. Bennett, 124
Jones, David, 259
Jordan, 373, 374, 397
Joseph, Norma Baumel, 242
Joseph Baron Museum (Milwaukee), 116
Jospin, Lionel, 264
Journal of Jewish Communal Service, 537
Journal of the North Shore Jewish Community (Mass.), 536
Journal of Psychology and Judaism, 543
Journal of Reform Judaism, 539
Judah L. Magnes Museum (Berkeley, Calif.), 88, 90, 92, 97–99, 101, 109, 110, 114, 476
Judaica Captioned Film Center, 476
Judaica Museum, Hebrew Home for the Aged at Riverdale (New York), 89, 93, 115
Judaism, 539

Kadar, Janos, 349
Kadima, 500
Kadmon, Stella, 336
Kagedan, Ian, 244
Kahn, Lord Ferdinand, 259
Kahn, Jean, 268–71
Kahn, Lothar, 68*n*
Kahn, Yoel, 196
Kaifu, Toshiki, 411
Kaiser, Joachim, 313
Kalechofsky, Roberta, 43
Kaletzky, Jakub, 259
Kalms, Stanley, 255
Kamm, Antony, 257
Kampf, Avram, 79*n*, 83, 85
Kanner Heritage Museum (New York, Ontario), 116
Kanovich, Grigory, 341
Kansas City Jewish Chronicle, 536, 536
Kaplan, Anatoli, 322
Kaplan, Johanna, 42
Kaplan, Mordecai, 26, 27, 29, 31, 197
Kaplan-Samuels, Leah, 115
Karff, Samuel, 194
Karuger, Arthur, 242
Kassens, Wend, 314
Katsav, Moshe, 358
Kattan, Naim, 243
Katz, Karl, 91
Katz, Samuel M., 258
Katzenstein, Ernst, 314
Katzir, Yehudit, 426
Katz-Oz, Avraham, 406
Kaufman, Gerald, 251
Kayser, Stephen S., 81–82, 92*n*
Kebede, Kessa, 416
Keegstra, James, 232
Kellerman, Faye, 41
Kelly, John, 359–60, 400
Kenaz, Yehoshua, 429
Kentucky Jewish Post and Opinion, 536
Kenya, 410
Keren Or, 485
Kertes, Joseph, 243
Kessar, Israel, 371
Kessler, Colette, 275
Kessler, Edward, 257
Khalaf, Salah, *see* Abu Iyad
Khomeini, Ayatollah Ruhollah, 256
Kibbutz Journal, 539
Kinnock, Neil, 245, 253

Kipp, Abraham, 280
Kirchner, Peter, 322
Kirschberg, Reva, 116
Kirschheimer, Gloria, 42
Kirschstein, Salli, 93
Klarsfeld, Serge, 265
Klein, Hans, 307
Klein, Theo, 267–68, 271, 275
Klein, Yair, 411
Kleiner, Michael, 416
Klempeter, Victor, 323
Klugman, Haim, 305
Knoll, Edouard, 268
Koch, Edward, 138
Koenig, Franz, 334
Kohl, Helmut, 302, 303, 305, 307–9, 395
Kok, Wim, 277
Kol, Moshe, 422
Kol Hat'nua, 539
Kolingba, Andre, 410
Kollek, Teddy, 360–61
Kopelowitz, Lionel, 251
Kopytman, Mark, 437–38
Koren, Yehoshua, 424, 427
Korn, Rachel, 244
Kosharovsky, Yuli, 345, 413
Kosher Directory, Passover Edition, 539
Kosher Directory and Calorie Guide, 539
Kosman, Admiel, 428
Kosmin, Barry A., 442*n*, 453*n*, 455*n*
Kotalla, Joseph, 279
Kovacs, Laszlo, 406
Kramer, Aaron, 258
Krantz, Frederick, 237
Kraus, Gertrude, 438
Kravitz, Leonard, 196
Kreisky, Bruno, 325, 330, 332
Kremer, S. Lillian, 43*n*
Kroloff, Charles, 195
Krook-Gilead, Dorothea, 422–23
Krumbein, Cynthia, 115
Kubersky, Haim, 421
Kucan, Milan, 352
Kuhnen, Michael, 306, 307
Kultur un Lebn — Culture and Life, 539
Kupfer, Jacques, 269
Kupovetzky, Mark, 457*n*

Kushner, Tony, 257
Kuster, Otto, 314–15

Labbe, Claude, 261
Labor Zionist Alliance, 177, 485
Labor Zionist Alliance of Canada, 520
Lafontant, Jewel, 128
Lages, Willy, 279
Lahat, Shlomo, 389
Lambert, Phyllis, 242
Lamishpaha, 539
Lamm, Norman, 199–200
Landesmann, Hans, 336
Landsberg, Michelle, 242, 243
LaRouche, Lyndon, Jr., 123
Laskov, David, 422
Laster, Israel, 563
Las Vegas Israelite, 537
Latham, Michael, 247–48
Lauder, Ronald S., 138
Lautenberg, Frank, 150
Law, Bernard, 131
Lawrence, Ivan, 251
Lawson, Nigel, 245
Layton, Julian, 259
Lazarus, Charles, 244
Lazarus, Paul, 275
Lazerwitz, Bernard, 452*n*
League for Human Rights, 518–19
League for Labor Israel, 485
League for Yiddish, 476
Leahy, Patrick J., 174
Lebanon, 395–97
Lederman, Morris, 254
Lederman, Sarah, 563
Lee, Sara, 77
Leguay, Jean, 265
Lehman, Irving L., 93
Lehman, Robert, 111
Lehner, Silvester, 313
Lehrman, Leonard, 323
Leibler, Isi, 345
Leibowitz, Wendy, 73*n*, 87*n*
Leibowitz, Yeshayahu, 15, 16
Leich, Werner, 322
Lekachman, Robert, 564
Leket, Yehiel, 414
Lenz, Siegfried, 313, 314

Leo Baeck Institute, 476
Le Pen, Jean-Marie, 260–62
Lerman, Antony, 258
Lerman, Rhoda, 41
Lerner, Arthur, 244
Lerner, Michael, 180, 185
Levi, Itamar, 434–35
Leviant, Curt, 39, 47
Levi Hospital, 515
Levin, Nora, 564
Levine, Hanoch, 436
Levine, Irving M., 557
Levine, Mel, 163, 176
Levine, Seymour R., 564
Levinger, Israel Meir, 313
Levinger, Moshe, 357
Levinson, Peter N., 313, 314
Levitan, Seymour, 244
Levi-Tanai, Sarah, 438–39
Levy, B. Barry, 39*n*
Levy, Caren, 455*n*
Levy, David, 147, 150–51, 157, 178–79, 372, 374–76, 383, 414, 415
Levy, JoAnne, 115
Levy, Max E., 315
Levy, Michael, 228
Levy, Yehuda, 419
Levy-Agron, Hassia, 438
Lew, Maurice, 259
Lewis, Ann, 192
Lewis, Frank, 283
Lewis, Stephen, 230
Libman, Robert, 227, 228
Lichtenstein, Dayan Yaacov, 254
Lieberman, Jack, 419
Lieberman, Zevulun, 199
Lifschitz, Ya'akov, 418
Likud-Herut Zionists of America, 485
Likutim, 539
Lilith — *The Jewish Women's Magazine*, 539
Lipman, Eugene, 194, 195
Lipset, Seymour Martin, 200
Lipsky, Hyla, 193
List, Albert A., 82, 111
List, Vera, 82
Lithwick, Harvey, 236
Livermore, Harry, 259

A Living Memorial to the Holocaust—Museum of Jewish Heritage (New York), 88, 91, 95, 104, 108, 114–15, 476–77
Livneh, Yitzhak, 433–34
Livni, Menachem, 388
Loffler, Kurt, 318
Long Island Jewish World, 539
Lookstein, Haskel, 129, 186
Loranc, Wladyslaw, 407
Louis, William Roger, 258
Lowenthal, Leo, 314
Lower East Side Tenement Museum (New York), 89
Lowin, Joseph, 39*n*, 68*n*
Lowith, Karl, 313
Lubavitcher
 of Iowa, 135
 Machne Israel, 494
 United Lubavitcher Yeshivoth, 499
Lubbers, Rudolf, 277, 278
Ludwig, Johannes, 312
Luitjens, Jacob, 233
Lunn, Kenneth, 257
Luria, Isaac, 431
Lustiger, Jean-Marie, 130
Luth, Eric, 315
Lyons, Helen Hadassah Levinthal, 564

Maalot, 477
Maayaani, Ami, 437
McCormack, Robert, 173
MacGregor, John, 254
Macharski, Franciszek, 130, 284, 298, 348
Machne Israel, 494
Machon Alte Institute (Israel), 137
Mack, Connie, 163
McLoughlin, William G., 5*n*
Magidson, Viktor, 345
Magnes Museum (Berkeley, Calif.), *see* Judah L. Magnes Museum
Mahoney, Roger, 131
Maimonides, 15, 64
Major, John, 403
Malamud, Bernard, 44, 59
Malovany, Joseph, 346
Mamone, Arrigo, 103

Mandel, Morton, 412-13
Mann, Klaus, 313
Mann, Theodore, 178, 184, 412
Mannekin Institute, 113
Mannu, Marisa, 291
Mansbridge, Francis, 243
Marcus, David, 258
Marcus, Yoel, 358, 401
Margalit, Dan, 388
Markovic, Ante, 352
Markson, Morley, 243
Marmur, Dow, 241, 243
Marom, Shlomo, 407
Marrus, Michael, 244, 257
Martin, Erwin, 323
Martin, Ralph G., 257
Marton, Pier, 97
Martyrdom and Resistance, 539
Martyrs Memorial and Museum of the Holocaust of the Jewish Federation Council of Greater Los Angeles, 89, 477
Marus, Michael, 243
Marx, Herbert, 243
Maslin, Judith B., 116
Massarik, Fred, 452n
Mastelloni, Carlo, 290
Masur, Kurt, 318
Max Weinreich Center for Advanced Jewish Studies, 479
Maxwell, Robert, 419
May Museum of Judaica (Lawrence, New York), 116
Mazon: A Jewish Response to Hunger, 515
Mazowiecki, Tadeusz, 347, 349
Medical Development for Israel, 485
Meir, Yehuda, 368-69
Meisner, Binyamin, 355
Meissner-Blau, Freda, 332
Melton Journal, 539
Memorial Foundation for Jewish Culture, 477
Mendelson, Solomon, 198
Mendes-France, Marie-Claire, 275
Menem, Carlos, 411
Menuhin, Yehudi, 311
Mercaz, 485

Merhav, Reuven, 408, 409
Meridor, Dan, 359, 384, 406
Merkin, Daphne, 39
Merkos L'inyonei Chinuch (Central Organization for Jewish Education), 494
Merks, G.W., 454n
Mesivta Yeshiva Rabbi Chaim Berlin Rabbinical Academy, 505-6
Metropolitan Museum of Art (New York), 111
MetroWest Jewish News, 537
Metzger, Tom, 124
Mexico, 454
Meyer, Sir Anthony, 245
Meyer, Peter, 556
Miami Jewish Tribune, 535
Michael, Sami, 436
Michel, Ernest, 180
Midstream, 539
Mikhail-Ashrawi, Hanan, 146
Mikveh Israel Congregation (Philadelphia), 91
Milano, Attilio, 300
Miller, Harvey, 257
Miller, Judith, 89n
Miller, Shoshana, 420
Milo, Ronni, 382
Mina, Jeffery N., 116
Missouri Jewish Post, 536
Mittag, Gunter, 317
Mitterrand, Francois, 161, 260, 263, 403
Mitzna, Amram, 356, 358, 365
Mizel Museum (Denver), 91, 99, 100, 105, 108, 110, 114
Mizrachi-Hapoel Hamizrachi, 487
Mizrachi-Hapoel Hamizrachi Organization of Canada, 520
Mizrachi Palestine Fund, 487
Mock, Alois, 325-26, 331
Mock, Karen, 244
Modai, Yitzhak, 147, 148, 150-51, 157, 372, 374-76, 383
Modern Jewish Studies Annual, 539
Modrow, Hans, 318
Moment, 535
Moos, Alfred, 313
Morag, Shelomo, 258

Mordechai, Yitzhak, 358, 361
Morin, Edgar, 275
Morris, David, 259
Morris, Richard B., 564
Mosco, Maisie, 258
Moses, Ofra, 393
Moses, Tal, 393
Moss, Susan, 103
Motzen, Yaacov, 242
Mubarak, Hosni, 142, 143, 145–46, 150, 152–55, 157, 159, 246, 378–81, 383, 408, 409
Mulder, Dirk C., 281
Muller, Hartmut, 312
Mulroney, Brian, 227, 229, 411
Murray, Venetia, 257
Musatti, Cesare, 301
Museum of the Diaspora-Beth Hatefutsoth (Tel Aviv), 104
Museum of Jewish History (Frankfurt, Germany), 74, 104
Museum of Tolerance (Simon Wiesenthal Center; Los Angeles), 71, 108
Mwosa, Josef K., 410
Myer, Henry, 259

Na'amat USA, The Women's Labor Zionist Organization of America, 485–86
Na'amat Woman, 539–40
Nabulsi, Karma, 249–50
Naccache, Anis, 262
Nachmann, Werner, 308
Nadel, Ira B., 258
Nakayama, Taro, 411
Nasser, Kamal Samih, 391
Nathan, Abie, 385, 405
National Association for the Advancement of White People (NAAWP), 124
National Association of Arab Americans, 127
National Association of Hebrew Day School Administrators, 497
National Association of Hebrew Day School Parent-Teacher Associations, 497
National Association of Synagogue Administrators, 500
National Association of Temple Administrators (NATA), 498
National Association of Temple Educators (NATE), 498
National Committee for Furtherance of Jewish Education, 494
National Committee for Labor Israel — Histadrut, 486
National Conference of Catholic Bishops, 133
National Conference of Synagogue Youth, 499
National Conference of Yeshiva Principals, 497
National Conference on Soviet Jewry, 186, 190, 342, 471–72
National Congress of Jewish Deaf, 515
National Council for Torah Education of Mizrachi-Hapoel Hamizrachi, 487
National Council of Jewish Women, 515
National Council of Jewish Women (Canada), 228–29, 520
National Council of Young Israel, 494–95
National Federation of Temple Brotherhoods, 498
National Federation of Temple Sisterhoods, 498
National Foundation for Jewish Culture, 90, 110, 477
National Hebrew Culture Council, 477
National Institute for Jewish Hospice, 515
National Jewish Center for Immunology and Respiratory Medicine, 515
National Jewish Coalition, 472
National Jewish Commission on Law and Public Affairs (COLPA), 472
National Jewish Committee on Scouting, 515
National Jewish Community Relations Advisory Council (NJCRAC), 134, 178, 190–91, 472
National Jewish Girl Scout Committee, 515–16

National Jewish Hospitality Committee, 495
National Jewish Information Service for the Propagation of Judaism, 495
National Jewish Post and Opinion, 536
National Joint Community Relations Committee of Canadian Jewish Congress, 520
National Museum of American Jewish History (Philadelphia), 87, 88, 91, 92, 95, 99–101, 109, 114
National ORT League, 489
National Trade Union Council for Human Rights, 471
National Yeshiva Teachers Board of License, 497
National Yiddish Book Center, 477
Navon, Michael, 393
Navon, Yitzhak, 417
Near East Report, 535
Nederlands Israelietisch Kerkgenootschap (NIK), 282, 283
Neher, Andre, 276
Neiditch, Michael, 114
Neiman, Morris, 565
Nemeth, Miklos, 406
Ner Israel Rabbinical College, 506
Nesi, Nerio, 289
Netanyahu, Benjamin, 170, 399, 412, 416
Netherlands, 277–88
Netzer, Dvora, 422
Neugeboren, Jay, 47, 48, 63–64
Neusner, Jacob, 7, 77
Nevat, Amnon, 427
New Israel Fund, 486
New Jewish Agenda, 472
New Menorah, 542
New York Association for New Americans (NYANA), 188
New-York Historical Society, 109
New York Jewish Community Relations Council, 134
Nir, Shaul, 388
Nissenbaum, Zygmunt, 131
Nissenson, Hugh, 47, 53–54
Niv, Orna Ben Dor, 440
Noack, Klaus-Peter, 323

Noam-Mizrachi New Leadership Council, 487
Noel, Clio A., Jr., 163
Noriega, Manuel, 411
North American Aliyah Movement, 488
North American Association of Jewish Homes and Housing for the Aging, 516
North American Conference on Ethiopian Jewry (NACOEJ), 490
North American Jewish Students Appeal, 518
North American Jewish Students' Network, 518
Northern California Jewish Bulletin, 534
Norway, 404–5
Notkin, Anne Lerner, 244
Novak, David, 8*n*
Novick, Paul, 565
Nowojski, Walter, 323
Nyiri, Janos, 258

Obeid, Sheikh Abdul Karim, 127, 139, 166–69, 182, 247, 248, 396–97, 401
Obey, David, 136
Observer, The, 542
O'Connor, John, 131
Odin, Karl-Alfred, 314
Ofek, Avraham, 434
Ohio Jewish Chronicle, 541
Ohngemach, Gundula, 314
Olender, Maurice, 274
Olij, Jan, 280
Oliner, Pearl M., 257
Oliner, Samuel P., 257
Olmert, Ehud, 179, 386
Olomeinu — Our World, 540
Olsen, Tillie, 46
Orenstein, Henry, 257
Orenstein, Louis, 244
Orfus, Jacques, 267–68
Ottawa Jewish Bulletin & Review, 543
Otto, Wolfgang, 307
Ouaknine, Serge, 242
Oweida, Faisal, 248, 251, 251
Owen, Roger, 258
Oz, Amos, 424, 426–27, 429

Ozar Hatorah, 495
Ozick, Cynthia, 35, 46, 47, 57–61, 69

Packard, Vance, 556
Pagels, Michael, 304–5
Pa'il, Me'ir, 281
Palestine Liberation Organization (PLO), 127, 140–45, 147–65, 169–72, 177, 179, 181–83, 230–32, 237, 246–48, 251, 263, 267, 280–81, 290, 304, 330, 369–72, 374, 375, 377–88, 396, 398–400, 402, 404, 412
Palestine National Council, 369
Paley, Grace, 43, 46
Palley, Diane, 116
Paltzur, Mordechai, 350
Panama, 411
Parik, Jan, 313
Paris, Erna, 243
Park Avenue Synagogue (New York), 89, 116
Pasqua, Charles, 261
Patinkin, Mandy, 122
Patt, Gideon, 407
Pavic, Milorad, 258
Pawlowski, Michael, 233
Pazner, Avi, 150, 169, 396, 403, 406
Peace Now (Israel), 385–86
PEC Israel Economic Corporation, 486
Pedagogic Reporter, 540
PEF Israel Endowment Funds, 486
Pelavin, Michael, 191
Peled, Hanan, 436
Pelletreau, Robert, 148, 152, 161–64, 399
Pelten, Samuel, 259
Pepper, Claude, 139
Pereira, Hans Rodriques, 283
Peres, Shimon, 141, 145, 147, 153–55, 174, 178, 290, 291, 305, 347–48, 371, 372, 375, 377, 379–84, 386–87, 391, 395, 407, 414–18
Peretz, Yitzhak, 404, 414, 415, 420
Perez de Cuellar, Javier, 166, 172
Perlasca, Giorgio, 291–92
Perlman, Itzhak, 323
Peschansky, Denis, 274

Pesin, Meyer, 565
P'eylim — American Yeshiva Student Union, 495–96
Philadelphia Museum of Judaica at Congregation Rodeph Shalom, 103, 116
Pickering, Thomas, 171
Piercy, Marge, 46
Pinto, Roger, 267–69
Pius XI, Pope, 297
Pius XII, Pope, 297
Plain, Belva, 42
Plaskow, Judith, 27–31
Plaut, W. Gunther, 243
Plotkin, Sylvia, 116
Plotkin Judaica Museum of Greater Phoenix, 91, 116
Plumb, Lord, 402
Poale Agudath Israel of America, 486
Podhoretz, Norman, 557
Poland, 129–31, 347–49, 407
Poliakov, Leon, 274, 275
Poliker, Yehuda, 440
Politzer, Heinz, 81
Pomerantz, Sidney I., 546
Pompidou, Georges, 264
Porat, Yehoshua, 430
Posner, Ellen, 74*n*
Potok, Chaim, 36, 47–51
Pougatch, Isaac, 275
Poulsen, Charles, 257
Prajs family, 309
Price, Roger, 196
Proceedings of the American Academy for Jewish Research, 540
Progressive Zionist Caucus, 486
Project Nishma, 486
Prose, Francine, 46
Pross, Christian, 312
Pryce-Jones, David, 258
Pulzer, Peter, 257
Pursey, Howard, 123
Putlitz, Gisberg zu, 314

Qian Qi Chen, 410
Quaas, Ingeborg, 323
Quayle, Dan, 137, 142

Rabbi Frank F. Rosentahl Memorial Museum-Temple Anshe Shalom (Olympia Fields, Ill.), 116
Rabbi Isaac Elchanan Theological Seminary, 509
Rabbinical Alliance of America, 496
Rabbinical Assembly, 192, 198, 496
Rabbinical Council of America (RCA), 199, 202, 496
Rabbinical College of Telshe, 506
Rabin, Eli, 244
Rabin, Yitzhak, 141, 142, 145, 147, 149, 153, 154, 159, 167, 168, 170, 354–55, 358, 359, 361, 364, 369–72, 375, 377, 379–84, 386, 393, 395–97, 401–2
Rabinove, Samuel, 134–35
Rabinowicz, Harry M., 258
Rabkin, Yakov, 240
Radler, F. David, 228, 232, 419
Rafsanjani, Hojatolislam, 168
Ragache, Gilles, 273
Ragache, Jean-Robert, 273
Ragen, Naomi, 41
Raisky, Adam, 274
Rangel, Charles, 176
Rapaport-Albert, Ada, 257
Rapoport, Nessa, 39
Raskin, Ilana, 420
Rath, Ari, 419
Ratosh, Yonatan (Uriel Halpern Shelach), 430
Rau, Gerhard, 314
Rau, Johannes, 303
Ravel, Aviva, 242
RCA Record, 540
Read, Anthony, 257
Reagan, Ronald, 124, 140
Rebling, Jalda, 322
Reconstructionist, 542
Reconstructionist Rabbinical Association, 494
Reconstructionist Rabbinical College, 506
Redman, Charles, 161
Rees, Merlyn, 249
Reform Judaism, 194–96
Reform Judaism (journal), 540

Regional Museum of the Southern Jewish Experience (Jackson, Miss.), 71, 88
Reich, Seymour, 139, 144, 151–52, 172, 177, 178, 180–85, 309, 383, 413
Reich, Tova, 40
Reichert, Marilyn F., 115
Reitman, Dorothy, 230
Reizin, Saul, 259
Religious Zionists of America, 486–87
Renewal Magazine, 542
Renglich, Szloma, 244
Reporter, 540
Representative Council of Jewish Organizations (CRIF; France), 264, 267–69, 271
Research Foundation for Jewish Immigration, 477
Research Institute of Religious Jewry, 496
Response, 540
RE'UTH Women's Social Service, Inc., 490
Rhode Island Jewish Historical Notes, 542
Rhodes James, Robert, 248
Riccardi, Pellegrino, 292
Richarz, Monika, 311
Richler, Mordecai, 243
Richman, Gerald, 139
Richter, Glenn, 130–31
Rickey, Elizabeth, 124
Rigal, Margaret, 252
Rishon LeZion Symphony, 438
Ritterband, Paul, 453n
Roberts, Barbara, 243
Robinson, Linda, 115
Rocard, Michel, 260, 403
Rockoff, Alan, 123
Rodel, Joseph, 244
Ro'i, Yaacov, 345
Roiphe, Anne, 40–41, 46
Rokach, Isachar Dov, 241
Romain, Jonathan, 257
Romania, 351–52, 407–8, 459
Rome, David, 242
Rome, Rudi, 259
Ronen, Moshe, 236

Rosen, Moses David, 351
Rosen, Norma, 44
Rosenbaum, Joan, 76, 84, 98, 114
Rosenberg, Harold, 80, 81
Rosenberg, Rosita, 253–54
Rosenfeld, Alvin, 44*n*
Rosenfeld, Frederick, 359
Rosensaft, Menachem, 178, 180, 182
Rosensky, Shmuel, 422
Rosenthal, Ammon, 126
Rosenthal, Ronnie, 293
Rosensweig, Phyvle, 244
Rosenzweig, Franz, 5*n*, 6, 18, 23
Rosett, Arthur, 7*n*
Roskies, David, 44*n*
Ros-Lehtinen, Ileana, 139
Ross, Dennis, 149, 372
Ross, Malcolm, 232
Rossi, Salomone, 299
Rotenberg, Mattie, 244
Roth, Cecil, 79*n*, 93
Roth, Henry, 49
Roth, Joel, 7–8*n*
Roth, Philip, 36–37, 39, 47
Rothschild, Baron de (Sir Nathan Meyer), 78
Rothschild, David de, 267–68
Rothschild, Evelyn de, 251
Rozan, Stella, 275
Rubenstein, Richard, 17*n*, 18–19, 21
Rubinstein, Amnon, 384
Rubinstein, Elyakim, 384
Rucker, Patricia, 244
Rudin, James, 133, 134
Runge, Irene, 320
Rushdie, Salman, 256
Russell, John, 99
Rutberg, Alan, 103
Rykiss, Fern, 231

Saada, David, 272
Sa'adon, Ilan, 390
Sabatello, Fausto, 301
Sabbath, Michael, 281
Sachs, Samuel, 244
Sacks, Andrew, 198
Sacks, Jonathan, 253
Sadan, Dov, 422

Sadeh, Yaakov, 369
Safdie, Moshe, 92
Safieh, Afif, 280, 281
Sagdeev, Roald, 345
al-Sahaf, Mohammed Said, 289
Said, Edward, 150
St. Louis Center for Holocaust Studies, 477
St. Louis Jewish Light, 536
Salamon, Julie, 42
Salkowitz, Selig, 196
Sall, Joan C., 116
Samkalden, Ivo, 279
Samuel, Rinna, 258
Sanders, Edward, 412
San Diego Jewish Times, 534
Sandrel, Carole, 273
Sankoff, Abbey, 244
Sapirstein, David, 135
Sarid, Yossi, 368
Sasportas, Avi, 389
Sasso, Sandy, 196
Sawyer, Eugene, 138
Schabowski, Gunter, 303, 317
Schalck-Golodkowski, Alexander, 317
Schapiro, Meyer, 82, 547
Scheckner, Jeffrey, 453*n*
Schedletzky, Itta, 313
Scheer, Lilly, 273
Scheffler, Wolfgang, 313
Scheininger, Les, 236
Schelling, Friedrich Wilhelm Joseph von, 23
Scheuer, James, 163
Schiff, Dorothy, 565
Schiff, Ze'ev, 363, 367
Schifter, Richard, 189, 355, 356
Schindler, Alexander, 179–80, 194–95
Schlafly, Phyllis, 132
Schmelz, U.O., 445*n*, 452*n*, 458*n*, 461*n*
Schnitzler, Sholom, 259
Schochet, Immanuel, 241
Schoenfeld, Stuart, 235
Scholem, Gershom, 431–32
Scholz, Rupert, 305, 404
Schoner, Alfred, 321
Schonhuber, Franz, 305
Schorr, Renan, 439

Schorsch, Ismar, 197, 199
Schottlaender, Rudolf, 312
Schrager, Adam, 126
Schreier, Max, 201
Schubert, Kurt, 321
Schuller, Elsa Lasker, 300
Schumer, Charles, 167
Schwartz, Abba, 565–66
Schwartzchild, Steven S., 565
Schwarz, Solomon M., 552, 556
Schweid, Eli, 430–31
Schwersenz, Yitzhak (Izchak), 312, 320
Scorsese, Martin, 270
Seattle Jewish Museum, 71
Security Affairs, 535
Segal, Jerome, 182
Segre, Emilio G., 301, 565
Semaan, Khalil, 126
Sentinel, The, 535
Sephardic House, 477–78
Sephardic Jewish Brotherhood of America, 511
Seri, Dan Benayahu, 425
Servan-Schreiber, Jean-Jacques, 275
Seter, Mordecai, 437
Setton, Ruth, 42
Shabtai, Aharon, 428, 435
Shabtai, Yaakov, 424
Shafarevich, Igor, 340
Shafner, Janet, 103
Shahar, Charles, 234–35
Shaked, Gershon, 425–26, 426
Shaki, Avner, 372
Shalom Center, 472
Shamgar, Meir, 420
al-Shami, Hani, 365–67
Shamir, Ilana, 258
Shamir, Shimon, 409
Shamir, Yitzhak, 140–42, 144–47, 149–59, 161–63, 168–71, 175, 176, 178–85, 201, 237, 246, 251, 263, 269, 290, 295, 304, 341, 349, 353, 356, 358, 359, 369, 371, 372, 374–77, 379, 382, 386–87, 397–407, 409, 411–14, 416
Shapiro, Betty K., 566
Shapiro, Shari, 136
Sharabaf, Uzi, 388

Sharansky, Natan, 413
Sharon, Ariel, 148, 150–51, 157, 181, 372, 374–76, 383, 417
Sharon, Yoel, 440
Sharp, Sir Eric, 258
Shasta, Isaac, 259
Shavit, Shlomo, 258
Shavit, Yaacov, 258
Shayevich, Adolf, 346
Sheftel, Yoram, 413
Sheinin, Rose, 243
Shelach, Uriel (Halpern; Yonatan Ratosh), 430
Shellinger, Kurt Moshe, 389
Sher, Neal, 132
Sheriff, Noam, 438
Sherwin, Byron, 73n, 86
Sherwood, Lydia, 259
Shetreet, Meir, 415
Shevardnadze, Eduard A., 143, 161, 339, 380, 405
Sheviley Ha-Hinnukh, 540
Shimiliovich, V.A., 343
Shipman, Mel, 237
Shitz, David, 424, 427
Shlein, Zalman, 391
Sh'ma, 540
Shmuessen Mit Kinder Un Yugent, 540
Shochat, Mania, 300
Sholem Aleichem Folk Institute, 496
Shomrei Adamah, A Jewish Stewardship Center, 496
Shomron, Dan, 354, 358, 365–66, 394, 401
Showstack, Gerald, 194
Shulman,, Alix Kates, 46
Shultz, George, 140, 165, 177
Shwartz, Lynn Sharon, 46
Sichrovsky, Peter, 323, 335
Siegel, Judith C., 105, 112n
Siegman, Henry, 181–83, 203
Silberman, Charles E., 75
Silberman, Lou H., 3, 4, 24
Silk, Helmut, 331
Silman, Roberta, 42
Silver, Daniel Jeremy, 566
Silverman, Ira, 181, 190
Silverman, Sol, 566–67

Simon, John, 122
Simonis, Adrian, 284
Simon Wiesenthal Center (Los Angeles), 510
   Museum of Tolerance, 71, 108
Sinclair, Clive, 258
Sinclair, Daniel B., 258
Singer, Gunter, 308, 315
Singer, Isaac Bashevis, 39
Singer, Israel, 294
Siniora, Hana, 146
Sinyavsky, Andrei, 346
Sirat, Rene Samuel, 275
Sitruk, Joseph, 267–68, 270
Sivan, Aryeh, 428
Skirball Museum (Los Angeles), 79, 87–88, 90, 92, 95, 101–9, 114, 115, 478
Sklare, Marshall, 11*n*, 557
Slater, Lydia Pasternak, 259
Slavens, Eric, 244
Slawson, John, 555–58
Sloves, Chaim, 275–76
Smirnov, A., 340
Smith, Joann, 244
Smith, Larry, 176
Smith, Robert, 232
Soares, Mario, 283
Society for the History of Czechoslovak Jews, 478
Society for Humanistic Judaism, 496
Society of Friends of the Touro Synagogue, National Historical Shrine, 478
Society of Israel Philatelists, 487
Sofaer, Abraham, 408
Soffer, Ovadia, 262–63
Soffici, Dante, 292
Soffici, Oreste, 292
Sofia (queen, Spain), 404
Solarz, Stephen, 136, 176
Solomon, Alan, 82
Solotaroff, Ted, 38, 45, 69*n*
Soloveitchik, Aaron, 200
Soloveitchik, Joseph, 6, 10, 12, 15, 31
Somer, Yossi, 440
Sorlin, Pierre, 273
Soskis, Philip, 566
South Africa, 175–76, 400, 461

Southern Jewish Weekly, 535
Southwest Jewish Chronicle, 541–42
Soviet Jewry Research Bureau, 472
Soviet Union, 128–29, 174–75, 185–90, 240, 252–53, 295–96, 332, 333, 337–46, 405–6, 413–17, 457–59
Spadolini, Giovanni, 290
Spain, 404
Spann, Gustav, 327
Sparr, Thomas, 313
Spath, Lothar, 303
Spatz, Norman, 239
Spertus, Maurice, 90
Spertus College of Judaica (Chicago), 90, 92, 110, 134, 478, 506
Spertus Museum of Judaica (Chicago), 88, 90, 92, 97, 103, 105, 107, 109, 110, 114, 478
Spiero, Claude, 312
Spiller, Mortimer, 115
Spinoza, Baruch, 429–30
Spira, Israel, 566
Spitzer, Alex, 259
Springer, Meir Raphael, 259
Stanton, Walter, 259
Stark Jewish News, 541
Starr, Patricia, 228–29
Starr Gallery (Newton Centre, Mass.), 103, 116
State of Israel Bonds, 487
   of Canada, 520
Stecher, Rheinhold, 333–34
Steg, Ady, 267–68
Steinberg, Linda, 116
Steinsaltz, Adin, 291, 346, 413
Stern, Menahem, 389
Stern, Steve, 39–40
Sternberg, Sir Sigmund, 131, 321, 334
Stevens, Amy, 88*n*
Stillman, Gunter, 323
Stolar, Abe, 346
Stoleru, Lionel, 261–62
Stoltenberg, Thorvald, 404–5
Stone, Lady Beryl, 259
Stone, I.F. (Isidor Feinstein), 567
Storm, Gloria, 229
Stoutenbeek, J., 287
Strashnow, Amnon, 369

Strauss, J., 78
Student Struggle for Soviet Jewry, 472
Studies in Bibliography and Booklore, 541
Suall, Irwin, 124
Sucharewicz, Leo, 313
Sununu, John, 183
Susskind, Walter, 287
Sussman, Heinrich, 322
Switzer, Phyllis, 244
Sylvain, Nicholas, 556
Synagogue Council of America, 133, 496
Syngague Light, 540
Syrkin, Marie, 567–68

Tabori, George, 314
Takeshita, Noburu, 161
Tal, Josef, 437
Talisman, Mark, 128
Talks and Tales, 540
Tammuz, Binyamin, 422
Tanenbaum, Marc, 557
Taras, David, 243
Tarifi, Jamal, 377, 387
Tax, Meredith, 43
Taylor, Elizabeth Russell, 258
Temple Emanu-El (New York), 89, 93, 116
Temple Judea Museum of Keneseth Israel (Elkins Park, Pa.), 116
Temple Museum of Religious Art (Cleveland), 92, 114
Tenenbaum, Shea, 567
Texas Jewish Post, 542
Thalmann, Ernst, 307
Thanks to Scandinavia, 490
Thatcher, Margaret, 245, 246, 249, 253, 403
Theodor Herzl Foundation, 487
Theodor Herzl Institute, 487
Theodorovich, George, 132
Thomas, Sid, 122, 126
Thornburgh, Richard, 125, 128
Thurm, Marian, 42, 46
Tikkun, 185, 534
Tillem, Ivan L., 567
Tischauer, Shlomo, 319

Tishby, Isaiah, 431
Tishman, Peggy, 413
Tittjung, Anton, 132
Toaff, Ariel, 300
Toaff, Elio, 297
Tokes, Laszlo, 351
Toledo Jewish News, 541
Torah Schools for Israel — Chinuch Atzmai, 496–97
Torah Umesorah — National Society for Hebrew Day Schools, 135, 497
Touati, Emile, 269
Touro College, 506–7
Touro National Heritage Trust, 478
Touvier, Paul, 264–65
Tradition, 540
Traficant, James, Jr., 132
Trends, 540
Treue, Wilhelm, 312
Trigano, Shmuel, 270, 272
Tsaban, Yair, 388
Tuchman, Barbara W., 568
Tulsa Jewish Review, 542
Tunik, Yitzhak, 422
Turgel, Gena, 257
Turner, John, 229
Tutu, Desmond, 410
Tutwiler, Margaret, 147, 156, 159, 166
Tzur, Yaakov, 414

UCSJ Quarterly Report, 535
UJF Virginia News, 542
Ullendorff, Edward, 257
Ullrich, Aquilin, 307
Undzer Veg, 543
Ungerleider, Joy, 84
Union for Traditional Judaism, 497
Union of American Hebrew Congregations, 135, 179, 182, 497–98
Union of Councils for Soviet Jews, 472–73
Union of Orthodox Jewish Congregations of America, 191, 498–99
Union of Orthodox Rabbis of the United States and Canada, 499
Union of Sephardic Congregations, 499
Union of Soviet Socialist Republics (USSR), *see* Soviet Union

United Charity Institutions of Jerusalem, 487
United Israel Appeal, 487–88
United Israel Appeal (Canada), 237
United Jewish Appeal (UJA), 187–90, 342, 490–91
United Kingdom, 245–59, 403, 455
United Lubavitcher Yeshivoth, 499
United Order True Sisters, 512
United States Committee Sports for Israel, 488
United States Holocaust Memorial Council, 89n, 478
United Synagogue of America, 499–500
United Synagogue Review, 540
United Synagogue Youth, 500
Unser Tsait, 540
Uri, Aviva, 422
Uris, Leon, 45
Uveeler, Mark, 568

Vaad Mishmereth Stam, 500
Van Agt, Andries, 279
Van Creveld, I.B., 287
Vancsa, Jenoe, 406
Van den Broek, Hans, 142, 277, 278, 280, 281
Vandepoll, Maurice, 287
Vandepoll, Netty, 287
Van der Heide, Albert, 285
Vander Zalm, William, 228
Van Praag, Siegfried E., 288
Van Thijn, Ed, 287
Vanunu, Mordechai, 397
Vatican Commission on Catholic-Jewish Relations, 130
Vatican Commission for Religious Relations with the Jews, 131
Vega, Louis Alvarez, 288
Veil, Simone, 261–63
Velikhov, Evgenyi, 345
Vergelis, Aron, 343
Vigeveno, P., 287
Vilnai, Matan, 358, 367
Vogel, Hans-Jochen, 303, 304
Voice of the Duchess Jewish Community, 540
Vorspan, Albert, 139

Vorst, Isaac, 283
Voscherau, Henning, 303
Vosk, Marc, 568
Vranitzky, Franz, 326–28, 334, 335

Wachsmann, Daniel, 440
Wagner, Mitchell, 243
Wagner, Stanley M., 114
Wagner, Wilhelm, 307
Waldegrave, William, 246, 251, 253
Waldheim, Kurt, 132, 249, 270, 324–29, 335, 336, 404
Waldman, Stanley, 259
Walesa, Lech, 347, 349
Walfish, Binyamin, 202
Wall, Renate, 313
Wallach, Yona, 428
Wallage, Jacques, 277
Walters, Sir Alan, 245
Ward, Lewis B., 556
Warren, Earl, 556
Warshawsky, Michael, 385
Washington, Harold, 138
Washington Jewish Week, 536
Wax, Bernard, 115
Waxman, Gary, 228
Weglein, Resi, 313
Weidenfeld, Lord, 334
Weil, Rene, 270
Weinberg, Henry, 237
Weiner, Gerry, 243
Weinryb, Bernard D., 556
Weinstein, Jay, 92n
Weinstein, Leon, 244
Weisberg, Ruth, 102
Weise, Gottfried, 307
Weiss, Avraham, 130, 131, 298, 348
Weiss, Frans, 288
Weiss, Ted, 132
Weiss-Rosmarin, Trude, 82–83, 568
Weizman, Ezer, 148, 372, 377, 380, 386–87
Werner, Alfred, 83
Wertheimer, Jack, 3–4n
West Coast Talmudical Seminary, 507
Western States Jewish History, 534
West Germany, *see* Germany, Federal Republic of

Weyel, Helene, 287
Wheat, Alan, 176
Whiteson, Leon, 258
Wieck, Bernhard, 302
Wiesel, Elie, 36, 43, 47–48, 51–53, 99, 271, 285, 345
Wiesenthal, Simon, 249, 257, 325, 332, 336
Wilder, L. Douglas, 139
Wilf, Yuval, 367
Willebrands, Johannes, 131
Willis, Norman, 253
Wilson, William, 74n
Winant, Alice, 244
Windsor Jewish Community Bulletin, 543
Wischnitzer, Rachel, 91, 568
Wisconsin Jewish Chronicle, 542
Wise, Stephen S., 545
Wisse, Ruth, 68n, 190, 244
Wistrich, Robert S., 257
Wolf, Mischa, 317
Wollach, Hermann Zwi, 315
Wollenberg, Jorg, 312–13
Wolman, Abel, 569
Wolpe, Howard, 176
Wolpert, Ludwig, 93
Women's American ORT, 177, 489–90
Women's American ORT Reporter, 540
Women's Canadian ORT, 519
Women's Division of Poale Agudath Israel of America, 486
Women's Israel Zionist Organization (WIZO), 309
Women's League for Conservative Judaism, 192, 500
Women's League for Israel, 488
Women's League Outlook, 540
Wood, Daniel Alvis, 123
Workmen's Circle, 512
Workmen's Circle Call, 540
World Confederation of Jewish Community Centers, 516
World Confederation of United Zionists, 488
World Conference of Jewish Communal Service, 473
World Council of Synagogues, 500–501
World Jewish Congress (WJC), 131–33, 185, 271, 473
World Union for Progressive Judaism, 501
World Zionist Congress, 195
World Zionist Organization, 283, 309, 488
Wouk, Herman, 41
Wulf, Joseph, 310
Wurzburger, Walter, 199
Wurzweiler School of Social Work, 509
Wyschogrod, Michael, 5n, 12–14, 30–31

Yakovlev, Alexander, 338
Yaseen, Leonard C., 569
Yassin, Sheikh Ahmed, 358–59
Yearbook of the Central Conference of American Rabbis, 540
Yehezkeli, Israel, 413
Yehoshua, A.B., 424, 429
Yeltsin, Boris, 337
Yeshiva of Los Angeles, 510
Yeshivath Torah Vodaath and Mesivta Rabbinical Seminary, 510
Yeshiva University, 94, 199–201, 507–10
Yeshiva University Museum (New York), 88, 91–92, 98, 100, 103, 108–10, 114, 478
Yiddish (journal), 540–41
Yiddishe Heim, Di, 541
Yiddishe Kultur, 541
Yiddisher Kemfer, 541
Yiddisher Kultur Farband (YKUF), 478–79
Yiddisher Veg, Der, 541
Yiddishe Shprakh, 541
Yiddishe Vort, Dos, 541
YIVO Annual, 541
YIVO Bleter, 541
Yivo Institute for Jewish Research, 479
Yizhar, S., 429
Yoffie, Eric, 195
Yosef, Ovadia, 383
Yosef, Yosef bar, 436
Yoskovich, Pinchas Menachem, 348, 349

Young Israel Viewpoint, 541
Young Judaea/Hashachar, 484
Young Judaean, 541
Yovel, Yirmiyahu, 429–30
Yugntruf, 541
Yugntruf Youth for Yiddish, 518
Yugoslavia, 352
Yuter, Alan, 202

Zabari, Moshe, 93
Zabdi, abd al-Aziz, 390
Zach, Natan, 428
Zajdel, Saulie, 241
Zaleski, Philip, 36
Zamir, Zvi, 290
Zarafi, Miriam, 391
Zeitlin, Irving, 243
Zeller, Frederic, 257
Zelman, Leon, 330
Zemach, Mina, 388
Zevi, Tullia, 294, 297
Zilberg, Samuil, 343
Zilka, Morris, 244
Zionist Organization of America, 180, 488
Zipperstein, Steven J., 257
Zissels, Iosif, 343
Zlotnick, Alice, 103
Zohar, Uri, 439
Zucker, Dedi, 391
Zuckerman, Francine, 242
Zukunft (The Future), 541
Zundel, Ernst, 232
Zunz, Jack, 258
Zur, Jaacov, 320
Zwarts, Jacques, 283

296.05 A512
1991
American Jewish year book.

DATE DUE

WITHDRAWN

**Trexler Library
Muhlenberg College**
Allentown, PA 18104

DEMCO